THE ORIGINS
of
MAYA STATES

Penn Museum International Research Conferences
Holly Pittman, Series Editor, Conference Publications

Volume 7: Proceedings of "The Origins of Maya States,"
Philadelphia, April 10–13, 2007

PMIRC volumes

THE ORIGINS

of

MAYA STATES

EDITED BY

Loa P. Traxler and Robert J. Sharer

University of Pennsylvania Museum of Archaeology and Anthropology
Philadelphia

Library of Congress Cataloging-in-Publication Data

Names: Traxler, Loa P., editor of compilation. | Sharer, Robert J., editor of
compilation.
Title: The origins of Maya states / edited by Loa P. Traxler and Robert J.
Sharer.
Description: Philadelphia : University of Pennsylvania Museum of Archaeology
and Anthropology, 2016. | Series: Penn Museum international research
conferences ; volume 7 | Proceedings of the conference "The Origins of
Maya States," held in Philadelphia, April 10-13, 2007. | Includes
bibliographical references.
Identifiers: LCCN 2016028171 | ISBN 9781934536865 (hardback : acid-free paper)
Subjects: LCSH: Mayas--Politics and government--Congresses. | Mayas--Economic
conditions--Congresses. | Mayas--Social conditions--Congresses. |
Regionalism--Mexico--History--To 1500--Congresses. | Regionalism--Central
America--History--To 1500--Congresses. | Mexico--Politics and
government--To 1519--Congresses. | Central America--Politics and
government--To 1821--Congresses. | Mexico--Antiquities--Congresses. |
Central America--Antiquities--Congresses.
Classification: LCC F1435.3.P7 O75 2016 | DDC 972/.6--dc23
LC record available at https://lccn.loc.gov/2016028171

Published for the University of Pennsylvania Museum of Archaeology and Anthropology
by the University of Pennsylvania Press.

Printed in the United States of America on acid-free paper.

Dedicated in memory

of

Robert J. Sharer

Contents

Figures

Tables

Contributors

Marcello A. Canuto is Associate Professor of Anthropology and Director of the Middle American Research Institute at Tulane University. He is currently co-Director of the La Corona Archaeological Project in Guatemala and co-Director of the Proyecto Arqueológico Regional El Paraíso in Honduras. His publications include the co-edited volumes, *The Archaeology of Communities: A New World Perspective* (Routledge, 2000) and *Understanding Early Classic Copan* (University of Pennsylvania Museum, 2004).

John E. Clark is Professor of Anthropology at Brigham Young University and Director of the New World Archaeological Foundation. Throughout his career, he has investigated the origins of hereditary inequality in Mesoamerica, as manifest in the Soconusco region of coastal Chiapas, Mexico. His publications include the co-edited books, *The Political Economy of Ancient Mesoamerica: Transformations During the Formative and Classic Periods* (University of New Mexico Press, 2007), *Archaeology, Art, and Ethnogenesis in Mesoamerican Prehistory: Papers in Honor of Gareth W. Lowe* (Papers of the New World Archaeological Foundation, No. 68, 2007), and *The Place of Stone Monuments in Mesoamerica's Preclassic Transition: Context, Use, and Meaning* (Dumbarton Oaks, 2009).

Ann Cyphers is Senior Research Scientist at the Universidad Nacional Autónoma de México and Director of the San Lorenzo Tenochtitlán Archaeological Project in Mexico. She specializes in Formative period archaeology of Mesoamerica, with particular interest in the central Mexican highlands and Gulf coast regions. She is the author of *Escultura Olmeca de San Lorenzo Tenochtitlán* (Instituto de Investigaciones Antropológicas, Universidad Nacional Autónoma de Mexico, 2004) and numerous articles resulting from her research at San Lorenzo.

Francisco Estrada-Belli is Research Assistant Professor of Archaeology at Boston University and Director of the Holmul Archaeological Project. His research focuses on the ritual practices, iconography, and political institution of rulership in the Maya lowlands. His recent publications include the book entitled, *The First Maya Civilization: Ritual and Power Before the Classic Period* (Routledge, 2011), and the co-authored work, "A Maya Palace at Holmul, Peten, Guatemala and the Teotihuacan 'Entrada': Evidence from Murals 7 and 9" (*Latin American Antiquity*, 2009).

David C. Grove is Professor Emeritus of Anthropology at the University of Illinois at Urbana-Champaign, and Courtesy Professor of Anthropology at the University of Florida. His archaeological research focuses on the Preclassic period of the central Mexican state of Morelos. His publications include *Chalcatzingo: Excavations on the Olmec Frontier* (Thames and Hudson, 1984), *San Pablo, Nexpa, and the Early Formative Archaeology of Morelos, Mexico* (Vanderbilt University Publications in Anthropology No. 12, 1974), and the edited volume *Ancient Chalcatzingo* (University of Texas Press, 1987).

Norman Hammond is Professor Emeritus of Archaeology at Boston University. He has directed numerous projects in Belize, including the regional survey of northern Belize and excavations at Lubaantun, Nohmul, Cuello, and La Milpa. His books include *Lubaantun: A Classic Maya Realm* (Peabody Museum of Archaeology and Ethnology, 1975), *Ancient Maya Civilization* (Rutgers University Press, 1982, 1994), *Nohmul: A Prehistoric Maya Community in Belize* (BAR 250, 1985), and *Cuello: An Early Maya Community in Belize* (Cambridge University Press, 1991). He is also editor of *Social Process in Maya Prehistory* (Academic Press, 1977) and *Maya Archaeology and Ethnohistory* (University of Texas Press, 1979, with G.R. Willey).

Richard D. Hansen is Adjunct Professor of Anthropology at the University of Utah. He is the founder and president of the Foundation for Anthropological Research and Environmental Studies (FARES), a non-profit scientific research institution based in Idaho. Hansen has conducted research in the remote rainforests of northern Guatemala since 1978 and is the director of the Mirador Basin Project—formerly the RAINPEG project—which carries out long-term, multi-disciplinary investigations of that vast area of the northern Peten.

Eleanor M. King is Associate Professor in the Department of Sociology and Anthropology at Howard University, Washington, DC. As co-Director of the Maax Na Archaeology Project in the Three Rivers Region of northwestern Belize, she has published numerous articles, including "A Heterarchical Approach to Site Variability" (with Leslie Shaw in *Heterarchy, Political Economy, and the Ancient Maya*, University of Arizona Press, 2003) and is currently working on the final report from the Maax Na project and other research in economics.

Michael Love is Professor of Anthropology at California State University, Northridge, and Director of the La Blanca Archaeological Project in Guatemala. His research focuses on the Pacific coast region of Guatemala, investigating the early complex societies found there during the Preclassic period. He is author of *Early Complex Society in Pacific Guatemala: Settlements and Chronology of the Río Naranjo, Guatemala* (Papers of the New World Archaeological Foundation, No. 66,

2002), and co-editor of *The Southern Maya in the Late Preclassic: The Rise and Fall of an Early Civilization* (University Press of Colorado, 2011).

Simon Martin specializes in Maya epigraphic and iconographic research. He is Associate Curator and Keeper of Collections in the American Section of the University of Pennsylvania Museum of Archaeology and Anthropology in Philadelphia and a former Fellow in Pre-Columbian Studies at Dumbarton Oaks in Washington DC. He is currently conducting field research at Calakmul, Mexico. He is co-author of the recent books, *Chronicle of the Maya Kings and Queens* (Thames and Hudson, 2000; 2nd edition, 2008) and *Courtly Art of the Ancient Maya* (Thames and Hudson, 2004).

Astrid Runggaldier is Assistant Director at The Mesoamerica Center and Lecturer in the Department of Art and Art History at the University of Texas, Austin. Her 2009 doctoral thesis for the Department of Archaeology at Boston University, *Memory and Materiality in Monumental Architecture: Construction and Reuse of a Late Preclassic Maya Palace at San Bartolo, Guatemala*, focused on the built environment of the San Bartolo site core over time and explored the topic of Maya palaces as architectural manifestations of state-organized societies. Her research interests include Preclassic Maya civilization, state formation and the development of kingship, the foundations of urbanized society, and the social functions of architecture.

Robert J. Sharer (1940–2012) was Emeritus Shoemaker Professor of Anthropology at the University of Pennsylvania, and Emeritus Curator of the American Section at the University of Pennsylvania Museum of Archaeology and Anthropology in Philadelphia. Throughout his career he investigated the origins and development of ancient Maya states in El Salvador, Guatemala, and Honduras, and published several monographs reporting the results of his archaeological research. Among his many publications, he co-edited *Understanding Early Classic Copan* (University of Pennsylvania Museum, 2004), and authored the 6th edition of *The Ancient Maya* (Stanford University Press, 2006, with L. P. Traxler).

Loa P. Traxler is Director of Museum Studies and Assistant Professor of Anthropology at the University of New Mexico. Her archaeological research focuses on the architectural evolution of Classic Maya centers and the nature of sociopolitical organization in these societies. Her publications include reports on the excavations and research within the Acropolis of the Classic site of Copan, Honduras, "Redesigning Copan: Architecture of the Polity Center at the Time of the Dynastic Founding" in *Understanding Early Classic Copan* (University of Pennsylvania Museum, 2004), and *The Ancient Maya*, 6th edition (Stanford University Press, 2006) with senior author Robert J. Sharer.

Penn Museum International
Research Conferences

Foreword

For more than a century, a core mission of the University of Pennsylvania Museum of Archaeology and Anthropology has been to foster research that leads to new understandings about human culture. For much of the 20th century, this research took the form of worldwide expeditions that brought back both raw data and artifacts whose analysis continues to shed light on early complex societies of the New and Old worlds. The civilizations of pharonic Egypt, Mesopotamia, Iran, Greece, Rome, Mexico, Peru, and Native Americans have been represented in galleries that display only the most remarkable of Penn Museum's vast holding of artifacts. These collections have long provided primary evidence of many distinct research programs engaging scholars from around the world.

As we moved into a new century, indeed a new millennium, Penn Museum sought to reinvigorate its commitment to research focused on questions of human societies. In 2005, working with then Williams Director Richard M. Leventhal, Michael J. Kowalski, Chairman of the Board of Overseers of Penn Museum, gave a generous gift to the Museum to seed a new program of high level conferences designed to engage themes central to the museum's core research mission. According to Leventhal's vision, generating new knowledge and frameworks for understanding requires more than raw data and collections. More than ever, it depends on collaboration among communities of scholars investigating problems using distinct lines of evidence and different modes of analysis. Recognizing the importance of collaborative and multidisciplinary endeavors in the social sciences, Penn Museum used the gift to launch a program of International Research Conferences that each brought together ten to fifteen scholars who had reached a critical point in the consideration of a shared problem.

During the three years until the spring of 2008, it was my privilege to identify, develop, run and now oversee the publication of eight such conferences. The dozen or so papers for each conference were submitted to all participants one month in advance of the meeting. The fact that the papers were circulated beforehand meant that no time was lost introducing new material to the group. Rather, after each paper was briefly summarized by its author, an intense and extended critique followed that allowed for sustained consideration of the contribution that both the data and the argument made to the larger questions. The discussions of individual papers were followed by a day discussing crosscutting issues and concluded with an overarching synthesis of ideas.

The Origins of Maya States is the edited proceedings of a conference of the same name held in the spring of 2007. It is the seventh and last of the conferences to see publication. As Series Editor, I am gratified that all but one of the conferences have been realized in print. The publication of the results of these conferences allows the new knowledge and understanding that they achieved to be shared broadly and to contribute to the uniquely human enterprise of self understanding.

HOLLY PITTMAN
Series Editor
Deputy Director for Academic Programs
Penn Museum 2005–2008
Curator, Near East Section
Professor, History of Art
Bok Family Professor in the Humanities,
University of Pennsylvania

Preface
and
Acknowledgments

This volume stems directly from an International Conference on the origins of Maya states held at the University of Pennsylvania Museum in 2007. An organizing committee composed of Richard Leventhal, Jeremy Sabloff, Robert Sharer, and Loa Traxler planned the conference. The organizing committee identified potential participants and then sent letters of invitation to 14 potential conferees in the fall of 2006. Each invitee was assigned a topic relevant to the issue of the origins of Maya states by the planning committee, and asked to prepare and distribute a pre-conference paper on that topic at least one month prior to the conference.

Thirteen colleagues accepted the invitation, prepared pre-conference working papers, and attended the conference: Marcello Canuto, John Clark, Ann Cyphers, Francisco Estrada-Belli, David Grove, Norman Hammond, Richard Hansen, Eleanor King, Michael Love, Simon Martin, William Saturno, Robert Sharer, and Loa Traxler. As members of the planning committee, Richard Leventhal was able to participate in all the conference sessions, while Jerry Sabloff was able to attend about half of the sessions, and we are certainly grateful to both for their contributions. The conference sessions were also open to graduate students and other members of the Penn Museum community, and many of these individuals participated in the informal discussions that followed the formal conference sessions.

The conference was held over a period of four days with four morning and three afternoon sessions that generally followed a format patterned after the Advanced Seminars that have been held over many years at the School of Advanced Research in Santa Fe, NM. Prior to the conference each conferee was asked to prepare a review of another pre-conference paper. The first two days of the conference were devoted to discussions of each pre-conference paper, led by the designated reviewer. These discussions focused on the major issues, problems, and implications raised by each paper and often highlighted points of agreement and disagreement.

The remaining two days of the conference included a series of topical discussions chosen by a consensus of the participants. These discussions were also aimed at major issues, problems, and points of agreement or disagreement. On the final day the participants discussed plans for the published volume based on the conference, including the scope and content of each of the projected volume's chapters. Based on these discussions, conferees prepared their papers for publication and responded to reviews and editorial suggestions. Astrid Runggaldier joined Norman Hammond as co-author, and, ultimately, 13 authors and co-authors completed their manuscripts with final revisions in 2012. Some additions to the bibliography were made during the final stage of the publication process.

In preparing the chapters for this volume, the authors were asked to focus on the evidence for increasing complexity and the centralization of authority seen in the archaeological, iconographic, or historical record, and then discuss the trajectories of increasing complexity leading to the emergence of Maya states revealed by this evidence. Each author was also asked to consider several specific issues, where and when these were appropriate to his or her chapter. The first of these issues was to identify the major attributes or manifestations of increasing complexity. The second was to identify the most likely causes and consequences of this increasing complexity. The third was to identify the key problems or issues involved in better understanding the process of increasing complexity. And the final issue was to comment on the adequacy or inadequacy of extant models for the emergence of Maya states.

In closing, we want to acknowledge the combined efforts and contributions of many individuals without whom both the International Conference and the resulting volume would not have been possible. We are very grateful to all the conference participants and especially to those who contributed chapters to this volume. We especially want to thank the people at the Penn Museum who made the logistical arrangements and worked hard behind the scenes to ensure that the conference was a success: Holly Pittman (then Deputy Director for Academic Programs) and her assistant, Linda Meiberg, Margaret Spencer (Executive Assistant to the Director), Tena Thomason (Museum Special Events Coordinator) and her staff. We also want to thank Sarah Kurnick, Joanne Baron, and David McCormick who were of essential assistance to us in a multitude of ways in preparing this volume.

LOA TRAXLER
ROBERT SHARER

A FINAL NOTE

This volume represents the efforts and patience of many colleagues who contributed their time, thoughtful comments, and insightful work distilled in the chapters appearing here. As mentioned in the Preface and Acknowledgments, the Penn Museum and its professional staff supported the conference and publication process at every step, and I thank those who were especially important in that effort. Most recently, James Mathieu, Director of Publications, and Jennifer Quick, Senior Editor, have provided crucial support for the completion of the process. I also would like to thank my assistant, Maren Svare, at the University of New Mexico for her assistance with countless tasks related to the manuscript and its bibliography.

At a crucial juncture in the preparation of the volume, my colleague, spouse, and friend, Robert J. Sharer, fell ill and passed away in September of 2012. His passion for the subject of this volume, and for the prehistory of Mesoamerica and Maya civilization, carried him through his final days. He was excited by field research at several Preclassic period sites, which continues to add to our understanding of this pivotal era. With each new report another aspect of the developmental history of the Maya region comes into better focus. One hopes this volume contributes to the ongoing dialogue and encourages the pursuit and synthesis of new information for years to come.

Loa Traxler
Albuquerque
May 1, 2015

The Origins of Maya States: Problems and Prospects

ROBERT J. SHARER AND LOA P. TRAXLER

In 1973 the Origins of Maya Civilization Advanced Seminar was held at the School of American Research (SAR), in Santa Fe. The basic goal of the SAR conference was to construct a model to explain the appearance of Maya civilization between ca. 1–250 CE (Adams and Culbert 1977:3). Much has transpired in the years since that Advanced Seminar, especially given the great increase in archaeological data bearing on the origins issue. The mammoth site of El Mirador was not even mentioned at the 1973 Advanced Seminar or in the subsequent publication of its results (Adams 1977). Back then it was held that Maya civilization coalesced during the Terminal Pre-classic or Protoclassic period. Now we look back at least a thousand years earlier to the Middle Preclassic for the origins of Maya states. In 1973 little was known of Maya political organization or polities. When discussion turned to evolutionary concepts, the prevailing view often held that the Classic Maya represented a chiefdom-like society. In his summary of the SAR Seminar, however, Gordon Willey (1977:420) suggested that Tikal might have ruled over a centralized state during the Early Classic period, after establishing prestige-enhancing relationships with Teotihuacan.

THE 2007 PENN MUSEUM CONFERENCE

This volume is the result of an International Conference on the origins of Maya states held in Philadelphia at the University of Pennsylvania Museum on April 10–13, 2007. Prior to the conference each participant was asked to prepare an advance paper addressing a topic assigned by the conference organizers, Richard Leventhal, Jeremy Sabloff, Robert Sharer, and Loa Traxler. The scholars who prepared preliminary papers and attended this conference were (in alphabetical order), Marcello Canuto, John Clark, Ann Cyphers, Francisco Estrada-Belli, David Grove, Norman Hammond, Richard Hansen, Eleanor King, Michael Love, Simon Martin, William Saturno, Robert Sharer, and Loa Traxler. Once the participants submitted their preliminary papers, each was asked to review and critique a colleague's paper and lead the discussion of that paper during the conference. The discussions of the preliminary papers took place during the first two days of the conference. The exchanges of views stimulated by the preliminary papers prepared the way for the topical discussions that took place during the final two days of the conference.

By the end of the conference further discussions led to specific suggestions that guided the preparation of the chapters included in the present volume. All conference papers were revised to some extent in response to these suggestions, and one was substantially expanded. John Clark (Chapter 5) was asked to double his paper's length by adding synopses of archaeological data from early sites in the region west of the Maya area to provide a comparative perspective for understanding early Maya states and their external relationships. One non-conferee, Astrid Runggaldier, became Norman Hammond's co-author for Chapter 2 in this volume. On the other hand, one conferee, William Saturno, was unable to contribute a chapter to the published volume. To replace this chapter, envisioned to focus on early lowland Maya political organization, the authors of several chapters concerned with the development of complexity in the Maya lowlands were asked to include perspectives on political organization where appropriate to their topics. Richard Leventhal was also unable to contribute what had been planned as a summary chapter for this volume. In lieu of this chapter, we have expanded this introductory chapter to include a closing overview of current issues and a provisional model for the development of Preclassic Maya states.

THE SCOPE OF THE PRESENT VOLUME

The authors of this volume were asked to consider three themes in preparing their chapters. The first of these was the definition of the chronology and material signatures for the emergence of Maya states in the archaeological record. The second was to evaluate extant models for the emergence of Maya states, while the third was to consider refining these extant models, or replacing them with models that incorporate new archaeological data gathered over recent years.

In keeping with these themes, the present volume follows a chronology based on the generalized time periods used by most archaeologists working in the Maya area (Table 1.1). The conferees agreed that Maya states first developed during the Preclassic era as the predecessors of the political system that characterized lowland Maya society during the Classic period, ca. 250–850 CE. The chapters in the present volume deal in multiple ways with the material signatures in the Preclassic archaeological record for the emergence of Maya states. This initial chapter surveys the major research issues raised by current theoretical debates on the origins of Mesoamerican civilization and the organization of Maya states. We also provide a summary of the chapters in the present volume, an overview of the Preclassic origins of Maya states, and a provisional model to describe the developmental trajectory of Preclassic Maya states, which links them to the system of states that governed much of the Maya lowlands during the Classic period. In the next chapter Runggaldier and Hammond review the development of theoretical models of Maya states. To various degrees the chapters that follow also evaluate extant models for the emergence of Maya states, and most of these refine current frameworks, or in some cases, propose alternatives based on more recent archaeological data.

While the focus of the 1973 SAR Advanced Seminar was the origin of Maya civilization, the 2007 Penn Museum Conference and the present volume are concerned with the origins of Maya states. The plural is important, since the Pre-Columbian Maya were never unified into a single state, but rather were organized into a series of more or less autonomous *kingdoms* or *polities* (these two terms will be discussed further below). Maya states are often seen as exemplars of the pre-industrial or archaic state (Feinman and Marcus 1998), but it is important to note that this volume does not seek to define or explain *the state* as a specific political organization or system. Rather, both the conference and this volume are aimed at assessing the developments that led to the formation of multiple lowland Maya states.

A recent study of the evolution of 72 Maya polities concluded that Maya states originated in the Middle Preclassic characterized by punctuated phases of development, multiple cycles of expansion and collapse,

Table 1.1. Chronology: The Maya Preclassic and Early Classic Periods

EARLY PRECLASSIC (2000–1000 BCE): Origins of Complex Societies

MIDDLE PRECLASSIC (1000–400 BCE): Origins of States

900–600 BCE	La Blanca Mound 1, largest structure in Maya area
900–600 BCE	Earliest paired stelae and altars at Naranjo (Kaminaljuyu)
800–600 BCE	Earliest masonry architecture at Nakbe
500–400 BCE	Earliest irrigation canal at Kaminaljuyu

LATE PRECLASSIC (400 BCE–150 CE): Expansive States

400–200 BCE	Earliest carved monuments with texts (southern Maya and lowland areas)
400–100 BCE	Earliest preserved painted Maya texts (lowlands)
300 BCE–100 CE	Initial expansive states: apogee of Kaminaljuyu (highlands) and El Mirador (lowlands)
300 BCE–100 CE	El Mirador Tigre and Danta complexes, largest structures in Maya area
1–200 CE	Earliest monuments with Long Count dates in southern Maya area
ca. 100 CE	Founding of Tikal dynasty

TERMINAL PRECLASSIC (150–250 CE): Decline of Preclassic States

200–250 CE	Decline of Kaminaljuyu and southern Maya states
200–250 CE	Decline of El Mirador and other Late Preclassic centers in lowlands

EARLY CLASSIC (250–600 CE): Expansion of later Lowland States

292 CE	Tikal Stela 29, earliest Long Count date in lowlands
359 CE	Founding of Yaxchilan dynasty
378 CE	Arrival of new ruling faction at Tikal led by Siyaj K'ak'
426 CE	Founding of Copan dynasty

and weaker political stability as they became more complex through time (Cioffi-Revilla and Landman 1999). Perhaps the most important characteristic shared by all Maya states was their variability. Although the evidence indicates that the first Maya states appeared during the Middle Preclassic period, not all Maya states developed at the same time; in fact new Maya states continued to emerge throughout the Pre-Columbian era. The life spans of Maya states varied as well, some lasting only a few centuries, others enduring for over a millennium. Not all Maya states were equal; some were far larger and more powerful than others. Not all Maya states were organized in the same ways.

The explanations for the origin of Maya civilization available to the participants at the 1973 Advanced Seminar were labeled a "theoretical embarrassment" in the 1977 volume, since "no single explanation for the rise of Maya civilization has gained consensus approval" (Adams and Culbert 1977:17). Certainly, there are more theoretical frameworks to consult today than there were in 1973, yet a consensus among today's scholars remains elusive. While past scholars were often concerned with single explanations, today most Maya scholars would agree that explanations lie in identifying multiple interacting factors. In his summary chapter in the 1977 volume, Gordon Willey defined several such factors. His model was keyed to the chronological subdivisions of the Pre-Columbian era in which population growth in the Maya lowlands laid the foundation for the development of elite culture through competition and rivalry, stimulated by external contacts and trade that produced further competition and growth, which continued until the so-called collapse at the end of the Classic period (Willey 1977:418–21).

An examination of the spatial and temporal contexts for the Preclassic origins of Maya states confronts two fundamental issues that Mesoamerican and Maya scholars continue to debate. The first of these arises from the fact that the developments in the Maya area during the Preclassic era were inextricably involved with other societies in Mesoamerica. This implies that any study of the origins of Maya states must consider the larger picture of the developmental processes within Mesoamerica during this same time frame. This wider focus on developments across Preclassic Mesoamerica also means we must confront a familiar and sometimes contentious debate involving two opposing views on the origins of Mesoamerican civilization and states. The second major issue involves a debate over how to best comprehend the structure and functions of Maya states. We will discuss both issues in the following section of this chapter.

MODELS FOR THE ORIGINS OF MESOAMERICAN CIVILIZATION

Scholars continue to vigorously debate the merits of two competing models that seek to explain the origins of sociopolitical complexity and the other attributes of "civilization" within Mesoamerica. In this context, state systems are one of the consequences of this developmental process, and these models inevitably frame any consideration of the origins of Maya states. One model holds that Maya states, along with other Mesoamerican states, were descended from earlier Olmec prototypes. This so-called *cultura madre* (Mother Culture) model is based on a unilinear evolutionary pathway and assumes all Mesoamerican civilization derives from a single origin. The competing co-evolutionary model implies that Maya states developed as part of a mosaic of interacting and evolving social systems based on multiple evolutionary trajectories. In other words, that all Mesoamerican states had variable and multiple origins.

We feel it is important to consider the archaeological foundations that underlie both models in the hope that these can be of value in assessing the evidence for the origins of Maya states. It is equally important to clearly reiterate that scientifically documented archaeological data are crucial to any consideration of these issues, given their ability to provide far more reliable information than undocumented artifacts. A number of chapters in this volume highlight well-documented archaeological data that provide the essential baselines for establishing chronological and developmental sequences, and discerning relationships between sites and regions, all of which are essential for inferring the processes responsible for the origins and development of Maya states.

The Importance of Context

The problems with using objects from looted or other undocumented sources as evidence for understanding the past obviously result from their lack of archaeological context. Such objects are devoid of documentation about their provenience (where they were found) and their associations (what they were found with). Without knowing the provenience and associations of an artifact, it is difficult or impossible to understand its meaning, purpose, and uses within its original cultural setting. In addition, such objects often cannot be dated with the same degree of accuracy as most scientifically recovered and documented artifacts. A further difficulty arises when unprovenienced objects are in great demand on the art market, since their high value promotes the production of modern fakes. As a result undetected forgeries become "evidence" for reconstructions of the past.

Of course in many cases some information can be salvaged from unprovenienced materials, as long as they are not fakes. Stylistic dating is possible for some of these objects, even though such determinations are often educated guesses at best. Pottery can be tested by thermoluminescence to determine when it was fired or last heated to the Curie point, which usually distinguishes ancient from modern production. Instrumental Neutron Activation Analysis (INAA) can often identify where pottery was manufactured. Yet the original provenience, associations, and overall cultural context always remain unknown. While most objects inscribed with texts date to the Classic period, there are some Preclassic artifacts with inscriptions. In such cases decipherment of texts found on unprovenienced artifacts may provide information about their functions, perhaps even an owner's name or title, but again not their original provenience, associations, or context.

Obviously, therefore, the distinction between provenienced and unprovenienced materials translates into important differences in the reliability of information about the past. Since the present volume is primarily concerned with the Preclassic period, the contrast between provenienced and unprovenienced material is especially critical, given that our knowledge of this era is almost totally reliant on archaeological data (in contrast to the far richer sources of historical data available for the Maya Classic period). Because of these factors the participants in the Penn Museum Conference and this volume were asked to rely as much as possible upon provenienced archaeological data and to identify any evidence used in their discussions that was derived from unprovenienced sources.

It is also important to keep in mind that inferences about developmental relationships are usually based on similarities observed in the archaeological record. These similarities may involve artifacts, motifs, architecture, settlement patterns, and other forms of archaeological data. Similarity between two forms from separate archaeological contexts can either signify a relationship, or be the result of coincidence. The potential relationship represented by two similar forms cannot be directly observed; this information must be inferred. Two inferred relationships are possible—two similar forms may be descended from a single ancestral prototype, or one similar form gave rise to the other. Distinguishing between these alternatives depends on the relative age of the forms being assessed—whether two similar forms date to the same or different periods. Yet, given the time spans produced by most archaeological dating methods, it is often difficult to conclusively demonstrate the contemporaneity or non-contemporaneity of two similar forms. This means that the inferred temporal relationship between two similar forms is often based on supplemental evidence or, in many cases, pure supposition.

Both the cultura madre and co-evolutionary models rely on posited relationships signified by similarities observed in the archaeological record. In the case of the cultura madre model, similarities are understood to reflect the outward flow of forms and ideas from the Gulf coast Olmec heartland that transformed the Maya and other Mesoamerican societies. Support for this model comes from observed similarities of form used to posit connections between Olmec and non-Olmec sites or regions. These similarities lead to assumptions that certain forms arose earlier in the Olmec heartland, and that similar forms in external regions were later in time and derived from Olmec prototypes. In other words, similarities between forms found in different regions are assumed to be evidence for the diffusion of Olmec civilization throughout Mesoamerica. Yet it is clear that the expectations of the cultura madre model often influence or determine the identity of the originator and the recipient in the relationship. For example, even though similar forms may not be accurately dated, or come from unprovenienced sources, it is usually assumed that the example from an Olmec site is older and thus is the prototype for similar forms found outside the Olmec heartland. Less specific connections are also used to support the cultura madre model. Gulf coast origins for unprovenienced objects are often assumed if an object is rendered in "Olmec style" or decorated by an "Olmec motif." Thus such assumptions become "evidence" even without support from documented archaeological contexts.

Seeking Truth in Labeling

Suppositions of this sort are a consequence of the history of archaeological discovery in Mesoamerica, as John Clark points out in this volume

(Chapter 5). As in many areas of the world, distinctive artifacts and styles often carry labels given at the time of their discovery. In the early days of archaeology scholars were often more concerned with the origins than the meaning of artifacts (Sabloff and Lamberg-Karlovsky 1975). In Mesoamerica the term "Olmec" was initially applied to a variety of unprovenienced artifacts that exhibited an art style distinct from the previously known styles of central Mexico and the Maya area. Later, in the mid 20th century, archaeologists began working at sites in Mexico's Gulf coast lowlands, where monumental sculptures exhibiting attributes of this distinct style were discovered. As a result, the Gulf coast region was identified as the "homeland" of Olmec civilization. Thereafter, finds of sculpture, pottery, figurines, or other examples exhibiting this style from anywhere beyond the Gulf coast have been assumed to represent "Olmec" influence (Grove 1989a). Although dating is often problematic, "Olmec style" objects from outside the "homeland" are often judged to be either contemporary with Olmec civilization or "derived" from the Olmec. Therefore, some objects are assumed to reflect Olmec origins for developments in areas outside the Gulf coast or seen as evidence for Olmec "presence" in these external regions (Sharer 1982).

The consequences of such assumptions are far-reaching, for they often result in Olmec origins and influences being privileged in interpretations over possible influence from other areas of Mesoamerica simply because of the arbitrary labeling of certain objects as "Olmec." Objects found outside of the Gulf coast region but labeled Olmec because of their style, even when well documented by archaeological research (Grove 1974a, 1989a), are frequently assumed to have their origins on the Gulf coast. In an attempt to avoid these implications of the "Olmec style" label, scholars have proposed adopting a neutral label, such as "Middle Formative (Preclassic) Style" (Grove 1997). Yet as is often the case, custom and precedent have prevailed, and the "Olmec style" label appears to be here to stay.

In this volume Clark mentions this problem in conjunction with similar labels associated with two important Preclassic sites, La Venta and Izapa. In the case of "La Venta style," Clark states that referring to monuments by this label "colors their interpretation in favor of La Venta's presumed dominance" (Chapter 5). The same could be said of labeling any artifact as "Olmec style," including carved monuments, jade celts, and murals, since the Olmec label also colors their interpretation. As for the use of the "Izapa style" label, Clark concludes that "it is not certain that the Izapa style began at Izapa, was developed at Izapa, or that the promulgation of the Izapa style throughout eastern Mesoamerica had anything to do with elites living at Izapa" (Chapter 5), and thereby provides us with a succinct statement of the significance of the labeling problem.

The evidence for the spatial and temporal distribution of so-called Olmec style objects from documented archaeological excavations makes it clear that the problem with the Olmec style label is comparable to the dilemma created by the Izapa style label. Findings from well-documented archaeological contexts often contradict the untested assumptions based on the application of the traditional "Olmec" label to unprovenienced artifacts. These findings show that entire categories of so-called Olmec objects are rare or even absent in the Gulf coast region and suggest that the distribution of "Olmec style" artifacts across much of Mesoamerica represents a basic ideological system shared by most Mesoamerican societies without evidence for a single origin (Flannery and Marcus 2000; Grove 1989a, 1989b; Lesure 2004; Marcus 1989). Furthermore, a number of archaeological studies have indicated that so-called Olmec motifs functioned in different ways within different Mesoamerican societies (Demarest 1989; Flannery and Marcus 1976a; Grove 1989a; Hirth 1978; Pyne 1976; Sharer 1989a; Tolstoy et al. 1977), rather than signifying Olmec presence or influences emanating from the Gulf coast.

Did Maya States Originate with the Olmec?

The followers of the cultura madre model often conclude that the Olmec developed the first states in Mesoamerica, which in turn gave rise to Maya states. One common scenario holds that during the Early Preclassic period the Gulf coast site of San Lorenzo developed into Mesoamerica's first state, and that during the Middle Preclassic its successor, La Venta, developed into a more powerful state, which in turn spurred the development of the first Maya states. This volume provides critical archaeological information about these sites in Chapter 4 (San Lorenzo) and Chapter 5 (La Venta); Chapter 5 also presents important summaries of Preclassic sites in the intermediate region between the Olmec and Maya areas.

In contrast, the followers of the co-evolutionary model conclude that Maya states were the result of a long and complex process that involved interaction with a variety of people and places within the Maya area and the wider arena of Mesoamerica—including but not restricted to the Olmec.

The co-evolutionary advocates also raise questions about the validity of the proposed unilinear descent of statehood from San Lorenzo to La Venta and then to the first Maya states. These questions are based in the evidence documented by archaeology and its interpretation, excluding assumptions based on unprovenienced artifacts, so we will highlight a few of these questions here.

There is no doubt that archaeology reveals some intriguing similarities in key attributes of early states found at both Olmec and Maya sites, especially during the crucial Middle Preclassic era. But early Maya sites manifest similarities in these key attributes with many sites throughout Mesoamerica, not just to those in the Olmec area. At a minimum, this observation raises the possibility that San Lorenzo and La Venta were not the only potential ancestors of Maya states. Prime examples of such similarities come from archaeological research at a number of Middle Preclassic sites, including sites in highland Mexico such as Chalcatzingo and San Jose Mogote, and Maya area sites such as La Blanca, Kaminaljuyu, Chalchuapa, and Nakbe. (These potential connections will be discussed later in this chapter and in Chapters 3, 7, and 8.)

Of course the similarities among these key attributes must be assessed based on their relative age and the kind of relationship each represents. But above all, the significance of these attributes lies in what each of these attributes represents—as surviving material reflections of the increasingly centralized sociopolitical organizations within Maya states, or what Clark refers to as the "institutions and accouterments of power" (Chapter 5).

Specific questions are often raised about the archaeological evidence for concluding that San Lorenzo represents Mesoamerica's first state (Clark 2007a). These questions involve whether or not San Lorenzo possesses sufficient archaeological evidence supporting its development as a state and, perhaps more significantly, whether or not this evidence appears at San Lorenzo significantly earlier than anywhere else in Mesoamerica. As result, the potential influence from San Lorenzo on the development of Maya states remains an open question.

A similar situation exists in regard to La Venta, although the question as to whether or not La Venta represents a state is not the central issue. There is little doubt that La Venta was one of the largest and most impressive Middle Preclassic sites in Mesoamerica. In this case the questions focus on La Venta's posited role as the pivotal intermediary for the transmission of concepts of state organization to the Maya. The Chiapas region represents a crucial arena of interaction between La Venta and the Maya area (see Chapter 5). Yet to demonstrate that La Venta was the transmitter of concepts and symbols of state power to Maya societies located to the east, the archaeological evidence ought to show that La Venta's development as a state preceded the earliest Maya states. Firm evidence is also sought that demonstrates La Venta possessed earlier examples of the key attributes of Maya states and, ideally, how these developments were transmitted and responsible for generating the first Maya states.

As an alternative interpretation of the extant archaeological evidence, there is considerable support for a series of complex and varied pathways for the origins of specific key attributes of Maya states, suggesting that the first Maya states arose in concert with similar developments elsewhere in Mesoamerica. In this scenario it seems very likely that some attributes of Maya states had their origins at La Venta. But at the same time, connections having nothing to do with the Olmec, such as those between central and western Mexico (Grove, Chapter 3), or between the Maya lowlands and highlands (Estrada-Belli, Chapter 6) also contributed significantly to the development of Maya states. Thus it seems that the issue of origins remains too complex to support a single genesis for Maya states, especially given the considerable variability seen in their characteristics across time and space.

The developmental pathways for the origins of Maya states are too complex to be summarized here, but the known temporal and spatial distributions of several key attributes provide clues pointing to their multiple origins. For example, crucial evidence for centralized political authority in Preclassic and Classic Maya states comes from large stone monuments used to commemorate both calendrical cycles and the careers of individual rulers, consistent with the ideological links between rulers and the infinite cycles of time. In fact, there is evidence to suggest that monumental time markers originated in the Maya area. Archaeological excavations at Naranjo, Guatemala, near Kaminaljuyu, reveal that at the beginning of the Middle Preclassic era (ca. 900–700 BCE) upright stone stelae were set in rows paired with flat stone altars in a pattern identical to later Maya monuments used as K'atun (20 year) markers (Arroyo 2010). Interestingly, there is a similar Middle Preclassic stela-altar pairing in central Mexico at Chalcatzingo (Grove, Chapter 3).

On the other hand monuments commemorating rulers usually take two forms, and both apparently originated outside of the Maya area. Carvings in the round are represented by colossal portrait heads and tabletop altars found at Olmec sites on the Gulf coast, including both San Lorenzo and La Venta. In contrast, bas-relief portraits may have their origins in central Mexico, as at Chalcatzingo, and are also found at La Venta where they date to the later Middle Preclassic. But while bas-relief carved monuments became a hallmark of Maya states as early as the Middle Preclassic, colossal portrait heads and tabletop altars were never adopted in the Maya lowlands.

Another key attribute reflecting increasing centralized authority within the earliest Mesoamerican states, monumental architecture, clearly has diverse origins. The earliest examples include large conical earthen "pyramids," which apparently originated in the southern Maya area at sites along the Pacific coastal plain. The earliest known example is at La Blanca, Guatemala (Love, Chapter 7), and another Middle Preclassic example was constructed farther to the southeast at Chalchuapa, El Salvador (Sharer 1978). The most famous example is found at La Venta, Mexico, where it remains the site's most prominent construction. Other examples of Middle Preclassic monumental architecture with varied origins include ball courts and so-called E-Groups, both of which are discussed in this volume by Clark (Chapter 5).

The essential conclusion drawn from these few examples revealed by archaeological evidence is that the key attributes of early states followed complex developmental patterns. The evidence points to multiple origins, rather than a single genesis, for the institutions and accouterments of centralized power manifested by Mesoamerican states, including those of the Maya.

The Past as Supposition

Despite lack of agreement on the Olmec origins issue, all the contributors to this volume appear to agree that connections between sites or regions discussed herein should be treated as suppositions, not established fact, until there is more secure evidence for the origins of specific features, objects, or motifs. This need for caution is underscored by evidence already mentioned that suggests a number of so-called Olmec style motifs and objects actually originated outside the Olmec heartland (Flannery and Marcus 2000).

Beyond this issue of primacy, it remains extremely difficult to demonstrate that a connection based on similarity of form actually involved the transmission of ideas or innovations, which caused changes within recipient societies. In other words, *evidence for the spread of a distinctive form or motif is not evidence for the spread of an idea.* Yet this one-to-one correlation between form and meaning remains a basic tenet of the cultura madre model. For example, a study based on INAA data from a small sample of Mesoamerican sites appears to show that the Olmec center of San Lorenzo traded pottery to several Mesoamerican sites without receiving pottery from these sites in return (Blomster et al. 2005). Among the analyzed sample were a very small number of sherds decorated with what were labeled "Olmec motifs." This evidence that San Lorenzo exported pottery to other Mesoamerican sites has been used to support the cultura madre model (Neff 2006), although no evidence has been presented to show that these vessels (with or without "Olmec motifs") in any way transmitted Olmec ideas to the recipient sites (Sharer 2007).

As we learn more about temporal and spatial patterns in the archaeological evidence, these data increasingly contradict the assumption of a single origin for a process as complex as the development of states in Mesoamerica (Demarest 1989; Flannery and Marcus 2000). For many scholars, these considerations create severe doubts about the utility of unilinear evolutionary scenarios like the cultura madre model. The more complex co-evolutionary model appears far more compatible with the pattern of multiple origins of the key attributes of states revealed by current archaeological evidence, and therefore provides a better theoretical basis for unraveling the origins of Maya states. Support for the co-evolutionary model also derives from the evermore varied pattern of manifestations of sociopolitical complexity revealed by new research and the constantly expanding corpus of archaeological data.

It must be remembered that the co-evolutionary model is likewise based on observed similarities in the archaeological record, which in turn lead to a series of suppositions about the past. And while the Preclassic archaeological record in Mesoamerica continues to be enriched by unprecedented new discoveries, much more work needs to be done. Nonetheless, one of the strengths of the co-evolutionary model is that it places greater emphasis on well-provenienced data to document both the age and origins of specific attributes of states in the archaeological record, and relies less on cultural affiliations based on arbitrary stylistic labels and assumed temporal priorities attached to unprovenienced artifacts.

MODELS FOR MAYA STATES

The second major issue examined in this chapter involves the models used to describe and understand ancient Maya states. In the second chapter of this volume Runggaldier and Hammond review the development of some of these models. Here we simply note that in the decades since the 1973 SAR Advanced Seminar scholars have proposed a variety of political organizational models in attempts to characterize the governing systems of the ancient Maya (see Chase and Chase 1996; Fox et al. 1996; Sharer and Golden 2004). Most of these proposals have been based on models derived from sources outside of the Maya area, ranging from Medieval Europe to Africa or Southeast Asia (Adams and Smith 1981; Demarest 1992a; Sanders 1981a). Alternatively, some scholars have advanced models based on Maya archaeological and historical data (Marcus 1995; Sharer 1993). While external models may facilitate cross-cultural comparisons, it is both possible and desirable to create Maya-based models that also allow this comparative perspective (Sharer and Golden 2004).

Externally based models were especially popular before most Maya historical inscriptions could be read in any detail, at a time when our understanding of Classic Maya political systems was grounded in archaeological and ethnohistorical data. With the decipherment of Classic Maya texts our knowledge of Classic Maya political organizations has greatly expanded. Information about the careers of individual Maya kings, royal dynasties, hierarchies of governing officials, alliances, and warfare has transformed our understanding of Classic Maya states (Houston and Stuart 1996; Martin and Grube 2008), especially when combined with well-documented archaeological data (Fash and Sharer 1991). Although based on diverse analogies (e.g., Demarest 1992a, 2004; Sanders 1981a; Webster et al. 2000), the application of external models tended to support a view of Classic Maya states as decentralized polities—weakly integrated organizations without stratified and hierarchical political structures led by rulers lacking coercive power. Models based on combining Maya historical and archaeological data tend to view Classic Maya polities as more centralized states—strongly integrated organizations with stratified and hierarchical political structures led by rulers wielding coercive power (Chase and Chase 1996; Sharer and Traxler 2006). These models allow cross-cultural comparisons while providing more accurate and detailed portrayals of the organization

Robert J. Sharer and Loa P. Traxler

and workings of Classic Maya states, since they are directly derived from Maya sources (Sharer and Golden 2004).

Maya states during the Classic period formed a mosaic of independent polities spread across much of the lowland area. The distribution of these Classic polities continues to be defined by combining archaeological and historical research. Yet, as these data indicate, there was no single template that defined all Maya states. Classic Maya states were diverse in their organizational structure, scale, and duration. In recognition of this diversity, the 2007 Penn Museum Conference defined the general characteristics of Maya states to guide discussions of this issue (Table 1.2).

The current portrayal of Classic Maya states established the reference point for the 2007 Penn Museum Conference and the present volume. While our understanding of Classic Maya states is greatly enriched by information generated by combining archaeological and historical data, there is far less information available for understanding Preclassic Maya states and their origins. In reality there are very few historical data from the Preclassic period, and as a result some aspects of Maya states, like the prominent role of individual rulers and dynasties, are less visible before the Classic era. The data available for attempting to delineate the origins of Maya states is

**Table 1.2. General Characteristics of Classic Maya States
(as defined by the 2007 Penn Museum Conference)**

CAPITALS AND POLITIES

  Capitals were the controlling nexus of power domains within states

  Capitals and their territories typified by asymmetrical relationships, hierarchies, diverse roles and statuses,

  diverse ideologies, and integrative mechanisms

GOVERNING INSTITUTIONS

  Specialized governmental functions

  Nonkin-based institutional organizations

  Threat of coercive power

OTHER CHARACTERISTICS

  Membership defined by place or territory

  Promotion of institutionalized ideology

almost exclusively derived from the archaeological record. Historical data from the Classic period can provide templates for outlining the origins and evolution of Maya states, which can be evaluated against the expanding corpus of archaeological evidence from Preclassic contexts. Of course the archaeological record will always remain frustratingly incomplete, especially in the Maya lowlands, where the combination of a humid tropical environment and overwhelming disturbances from subsequent Classic period activity often obscures the remains of Preclassic occupation.

By virtue of its dependence on the material remains of past societies, archaeology cannot identify most sudden changes instigated by individuals or events, or define watershed moments when particular sites or regions crossed the nebulous threshold into statehood. In addition, there is no single agreed-upon definition of the state, or more appropriately in the Maya case, the pre-industrial or archaic state (Feinman and Marcus 1998), especially as reflected in the archaeological record (see the introduction in Love, Chapter 7). Given these realities, the conference participants agreed that instead of dwelling on questions of whether or not a given site represents a state by a particular time period, this volume would focus on the archaeological evidence for key attributes of statehood, namely increasing complexity and the centralization of authority over time. Discussions during the conference reiterated the hallmarks of complexity long recognized by archaeologists (Table 1.2), and their potential archaeological signatures, which often reflect increasing complexity through time (Table 1.3). The conferees discussed these archaeological correlates of Maya states from various perspectives. Tracing these archaeological manifestations over the course of the Preclassic era may point to the likely origins of these phenomena, recognizing that some manifestations of increasing complexity and centralization may be more relevant to the development of Classic Maya states than others. Following from this, the participants agreed it was important to define complexity in a way that was compatible with the theoretical and methodological issues highlighted by on-going debates concerning the origins and definitions of Maya states. Accordingly, the conference defined complexity in this context as,

> The increasing presence of nonkin-based organizations that integrated society under a centralized authority possessing coercive power.

Table 1.3. Potential Archaeological Correlates for Origins of Maya States
Likely indicators of increasing complexity and centralization of authority
during the Preclassic era.

POPULATION GROWTH

> Sites: increase in size, esp. residential remains

> Regions: increase in number of sites

SOCIAL STRATIFICATION

> Prestige goods

> Burials (as reflections of inherited vs. achieved status)

> Residences (as reflections of status differences)

APPEARANCE OF LARGE REGIONAL CENTERS

> Monumental architecture (temples, administrative buildings, palaces, plazas, ball courts)

> Extensive settlement remains (houses and middens)

> Monuments

SITE HIERARCHIES

> Number of tiers

> Definition of hierarchies

> Connections to centers (causeways)

LABOR MOBILIZATION (distinguish communal from corvée labor)

> Functional evidence

> Temples and monuments dedicated to deities as indicators of communal labor

> Temples, monuments, residences, and tombs dedicated to rulers as indicators of corvée labor

EXCHANGE (acquisition, manufacture, exchange, and distribution of commodities)

> Prestige goods

> Utilitarian goods

INTERACTION (evidence for movement of goods, people, and ideas)

> Alliances and diplomacy

> Colonization

> Trade and gifting

WARFARE (evidence of weapons, captives, garrisons, fortifications)

> Intervention

> Conquest

In sum, the difficulty in delineating the origins of Maya states is inherent given the limitations of archaeological data, compounded by the theoretical issues discussed previously, including the lack of consensus on the definition of states and the degree of centralization of power and organization within Classic Maya states. As a corollary to this, a further complication enters from the variability manifested by Maya states across time and space. A final hurdle derives from the difficulty of recognizing the diverse interplay between internal developments and external stimulation in any evolutionary process.

THE PRESENT VOLUME

In examining the origins of Maya states, we contend that combining an examination of topical issues with a regional perspective to examine the developmental trajectories of emerging complexity can partially mitigate these and other complicating factors. This allows differences measured on a centralized-noncentralized organizational continuum, and other dimensions of variability, to be defined and discussed from both topical and regional perspectives. Accordingly, this volume will highlight the role of interregional interaction and include discussions of two major Mesoamerican regions outside the Maya area—namely highland Mexico and the Gulf coast lowlands. Then, at the core of the study, we will examine the development of complexity during the Preclassic era within the major regions of the Maya area—the Pacific coast, highlands, and lowlands. Finally, the volume will consider the developmental context for the origins of Maya states with discussions of Preclassic economic, social, political, and ideological systems.

To provide an introduction to the volume, the present chapter is followed by a historical overview of Maya state models by Astrid Runggaldier and Norman Hammond. Their chapter reviews the complexities involved in defining Maya states, including the utility of cross-cultural comparisons, the use of settlement pattern studies, concepts of cities and urbanism, contributions of epigraphic data, and the importance of ideology. It concludes with perspectives on the Preclassic period as the era and setting for the origin of Maya states.

Part I of the volume samples the wider Mesoamerican context for the origins of Maya states. Chapter 3 by David Grove, "Preclassic Central

Mexico: The Uncertain Pathway from Tlatilco to Teotihuacan," along with the chapter by John Clark that follows, plays a central role in assessing the developmental trajectories that led to the origins of states in the non-Maya regions of Mesoamerica during the Preclassic period. At the core of his discussion, Grove asks, "Did the central Mexican region's interactions with the Gulf coast Olmec introduce 'social, political, and religious institutions' that persisted over time and were somehow relevant to regional highland developments that led ultimately to the Teotihuacan state?" To answer this crucial question, Grove examines the archaeological evidence to gain a broad overview by carefully drawing out meaningful patterns of developing complexity and their implications from the uneven data gleaned from the central Mexican highlands.

In the next chapter, "The Early Preclassic Olmec," Ann Cyphers applies her San Lorenzo excavation data to examine theories for the origins and development of Olmec civilization, concentrating on the role of San Lorenzo within the developmental course of Olmec civilization. She concludes that the extant data do not support proposals for San Lorenzo's origins via migrations from outside the Gulf coast, or the development of increasing complexity according to the river levee model proposed by Coe and Diehl (1980). Instead Cyphers relies on a model based on *in situ* development given the site's locational advantages for riverine transport, communication, subsistence, and protection. Regional settlement differentiation and specialization, and the proposed founding of subordinate polities including those represented by Laguna de los Cerros and possibly La Venta, point to San Lorenzo's growth in size and complexity as a polity capital. This issue has critical significance for assessing the degree to which San Lorenzo can be considered a progenitor of later states in Mesoamerica, including those of central Mexico and the Maya, as discussed by several other authors in this volume (see Grove, Chapter 3; Clark, Chapter 5; and Hansen, Chapter 8).

Readers will note that John Clark, author of Chapter 5, "Western Kingdoms of the Middle Preclassic," uses the terms *kingdom* and *kings* to refer to Preclassic polities and their leaders. Clark's usage follows that of investigators who infer the rule of "kings" at Olmec sites, based on individualized portraits on carved table-top altars, colossal heads, and stelae. Nonetheless, most conference participants preferred the comparable terms *polity* and *ruler* in their discussions of the Preclassic era since these terms carry fewer culture-specific connotations. *Polity* is used in this volume to refer to a complex hierarchical and territorially based political system, rather than the definition used in Political Science to refer to a system of governance (Cioffi-Revilla and Landman 1999).

Clark's presentation of data from several Middle Preclassic sites in Chiapas is an especially important contribution. The discussions of many of these sites are published here in Chapter 5 for the first time. In Clark's scenario these sites were part of a developmental link between the Olmec and the first Maya states, based on his proposal that "institutions and accoutrements of power" found at San Lorenzo and La Venta continued in later polities, including those of the lowland Maya. Clark concludes, however, that the extant data are not yet sufficient to fully evaluate or demonstrate beyond a reasonable doubt that La Venta was the critical unilineal developmental link between San Lorenzo and the origins of Maya states.

Part II of the volume examines our current understanding of the origins of Maya states from the perspective of interregional interaction and developments in both the southern Maya area (Pacific coast and highlands) and in the lowlands. In Chapter 6, "Regional and Interregional Interactions and the Preclassic Maya," Francisco Estrada-Belli points out that while diffusion and migration dominated previous theories for the origin and development of Maya civilization, current explanations rely on regional and interregional interaction based on far more data. In this volume, and in a more extensive discussion elsewhere (Estrada-Belli 2011), Estrada-Belli explores these interactions as the agents of both change and coherency in the development of increased complexity that led to Maya states, especially in the context of a common Mesoamerican ideology. This process is visible in the Middle and Late Preclassic Maya lowlands, expressed in the greater size and complexity of sites, along with continuities in ritual practice and the associated concept of kingship. Rather than seeing the Preclassic/Classic transition as a critical juncture in the development of Maya states, Estrada-Belli proposes their origins lie far earlier, traceable to the beginning of the Middle Preclassic (ca. 800 BCE) with the founding of initial ritual centers on hilltops by rulers who usurped the ideology of the Maize god as life-giver and symbol of central authority.

In Chapter 7, "Early States in the Southern Maya Region," Michael Love focuses on indications of social change to identify the emergence of two Preclassic states, Kaminaljuyu (Maya highlands) and El Ujuxte (Pacific coastal plain). These are very different examples and demonstrate the diversity of origins and development of Mesoamerican states. El Ujuxte's success was built upon the collapse of La Blanca, the capital of a large early Middle Preclassic polity with centralized authority, monumental constructions, and a pan-Mesoamerican ideology of rulership, although Love concludes that its political infrastructure was not large or complex enough to qualify as a state. El Ujuxte, however, certainly qualifies with a centrally planned capital, four secondary administrative centers, and smaller tertiary centers that administered a polity covering at least 600 km2. Kaminaljuyu's development was more gradual, but was marked by a growth spurt in the Late Preclassic. Both polity capitals show centralization and expansion of elite power, concentration of wealth, increased expenditures for public works, intensified subsistence, and an ideology of rulership. Kaminaljuyu differed from El Ujuxte in its huge irrigation canals and carved monuments with texts. Household data at El Ujuxte shows increased control of the economy by elites, while household and economic data is lacking at Kaminaljuyu. Both states collapsed at the end of the Preclassic, although new elite masters revived Kaminaljuyu in the Classic period.

The position taken by Richard Hansen in Chapter 8, "Cultural and Environmental Components of the First Maya States: A Perspective from the Central and Southern Maya Lowlands," favors an autochthonous development of lowland Maya states in the Preclassic period, spurred by competitive ideologies and interactions. He sees this as a part of an overall process that led to the origins of the first Mesoamerican states in the Middle Preclassic, and development of expansive states in the Late Preclassic. Hansen bases his scenario on the archaeological evidence from what may have been the core of this development in the Maya lowlands, the Mirador region (or Basin), where Nakbe appears to have emerged as a state in the Middle Preclassic, followed by the far larger El Mirador state in the Late Preclassic. These and other Preclassic states in the Maya lowlands were based on high levels of agricultural productivity, specialized production systems, mobilization of labor for public works (including investments in causeway networks that linked major polities into a cohesive unit in the Mirador region), and the manipulation of architectural art and religious ideology. Even though El Mirador and a number of other, smaller lowland states collapsed at the end of the Preclassic period, Hansen concludes that these developments were direct antecedents for the Maya lowland states of the subsequent Classic period.

Part III focuses on the Maya lowlands to discuss the theoretical contexts for understanding the origins of Maya states examined from economic, social, political, and ideological perspectives. Eleanor King's contribution, Chapter 9, "Rethinking the Role of Early Economies in the Rise of Maya States: A View from the Lowlands," goes beyond the traditional model of elite control of the economy to examine archaeological data from a non-hierarchical and emic perspective by identifying the resources utilized, how they were used, and how they were valued. Her analysis reveals how diverse economic conditions contributed to sociopolitical differences during the Middle and Late Preclassic eras. Thus across different places and times control over land, water, scarce resources, and trade likely supported growth in complexity. King concludes that the economic basis of authority rested on Maya concepts of value, for these determined economic choices made by rulers, elites, and nonelites. From a Maya viewpoint value was proportional to the amount of labor investment, and her model links value placed on labor with a heterarchical organizational structure. At the head of that structure, the ruler's wealth and power were dependent on labor investments, measured by the amount of labor he controlled and his obligations to both his subjects and the gods.

In Chapter 10, "Middle Preclassic Maya Society: Tilting at Windmills or Giants of Civilization?," Marcello Canuto takes on the difficult task of reconstructing the development of social complexity in the Maya lowlands during the Middle Preclassic period. His data are drawn from both the central lowlands of Belize and Guatemala, and the southeast region of Honduras, and his perspective is informed by both archaeology and ethnography. Canuto brings these threads together to outline an emergent lineage-community model that sees the beginnings of social inequality as an internal process within Middle Preclassic lowland society based on family, kinship, and descent group relationships. His discussion of the first steps toward the development of complexity, with specific applications for the mobilization of labor, trace a plausible pathway that could well have led to the organizational foundations of Maya states. The social changes outlined by Canuto also mesh well with Eleanor King's discussions of the economic basis for power in the preceding chapter.

Simon Martin in Chapter 11, "Ideology and the Early Maya Polity," is concerned with the ideological bases of political power. The central conclusion he draws from epigraphic and iconographic evidence is that the

ideology of Maya kingship was in place by the Late Preclassic period. As
he points out, "The regalia and rituals of lordship were consistent from at
least 100 BCE onwards....The term *ajaw* itself was in use from at least the
first part of the Late Preclassic onwards (ca. 400–200 BCE)." While the developmental course of Maya kingship is not fully documented given temporal and spatial gaps in the record, the implications of Martin's study are
that the institution of Maya kingship and its ideological bases, along with
rule by royal dynasties, as central components of Maya states as known
from the Classic period, were in place by the Late Preclassic in the Maya
lowlands. Although he is properly cautious about the existence of "holy"
kings before the Classic period, given the absence of historical evidence
for the *k'uhul* title in Preclassic contexts, Martin points to the continuities
between the Preclassic and Classic institution of kingship as presently understood: "Classic kings remade themselves in the image of their forefathers, wore their crowns, underwent their rituals, and thought themselves
imbued by the same procreative powers."

THE IMPORTANCE OF THE NORTHERN
MAYA LOWLANDS

The original plan for The Origins of Maya States Conference called for a
contribution focused on Preclassic developments in the northern Maya lowlands of Yucatan that would round out coverage of this topic for the entire
Maya area. Unfortunately, this contribution could not be realized within the
time frame of the conference schedule. Nonetheless the participants recognized the need for a chapter on the northern lowlands in the published
conference volume, and as a result, renewed discussions were held with
several colleagues currently working in Yucatan to secure such a chapter
for this publication. Ultimately, however, time constraints and conflicting
commitments again defeated our efforts to secure this northern lowland
chapter, and we had no choice but to go forward without being able to fill
this major lacunae in our coverage of the origins of Maya states.

So that the reader can gain some appreciation of the importance of
the northern Maya lowlands to any discussion of the origins of Maya
states, we offer the following brief commentary. We do so while acknowledging that until fairly recently the northern lowlands has been often
characterized as an area with sparse occupation during the Middle and

Late Preclassic eras. As a result, it was often assumed that the northern area was relatively peripheral to the early development of Maya states. This picture has been completely changed by the results of recent archaeological research. For example, in the region of northwest Yucatan, where only eight Preclassic sites had been reported previously, a recent archaeological survey documented 140 Preclassic sites, including 116 with Middle Preclassic and 92 with Late Preclassic occupation (Andrews and Robles Castellanos 2004; Anderson 2011). An unprecedented total of 23 Preclassic ball courts were discovered in this same region, and at least one of these Preclassic sites was also found to possesses a triadic structure (Anderson 2011), recalling a distinctive Preclassic architectural hallmark found at El Mirador, Nakbe, and other Preclassic sites farther south in the central Maya lowlands.

These recent findings, combined with further discoveries of Preclassic sites in other areas of Yucatan, have fundamentally changed the perception of early developments in the northern Maya lowlands. Rather than being a sparsely settled region in the Preclassic, we now know that relatively high population levels were in place in Yucatan throughout the Middle and Late Preclassic periods. As a result, it is clear that instead of being a peripheral region during the Preclassic, the northern lowland area was very much involved in the developmental processes that led to the formation of Maya states. This realization becomes even more important given the apparent unique status of Preclassic Yucatan in regard to interaction with other regions of Mesoamerica. The evidence from Preclassic architecture and artifacts in Yucatan demonstrates considerable trade and interaction with other areas of Mesoamerica, along with one notable distinction. There is almost no evidence that the northern lowlands shared the widespread and much-discussed inventory of symbols traditionally associated with the so-called Olmec style found associated with Middle Preclassic monuments and artifacts in other Mesoamerican regions. This absence has yet to be fully explained, but could reflect the presence of an alternative Preclassic ideological system in Yucatan (Anderson 2011). Further research is obviously needed to determine to what degree a distinct Preclassic ideological system may have operated in this northern region, as well as to provide a more complete understanding of the important role played by the northern Maya lowlands in the overall development of Maya states.

ORIGINS OF MAYA STATES: A SYNTHESIS

The authors of this volume present good cases for the origins of states in the Middle Preclassic period (ca. 1000–400 BCE) both in the Maya area and in several non-Maya areas of Mexico. The archaeological evidence from this era suggests the appearance of non kin-based organizations possessing coercive power that integrated society under centralized authority, consistent with the already mentioned conference definition of states. The beginnings of Maya states might be traced back to the founders of ritual centers that successfully formulated the basic ideology of rulership (Estrada-Belli, Chapter 6; Martin, Chapter 11). Well-documented examples of Middle Preclassic states include La Venta and several polities in central Chiapas (Clark, Chapter 5), the beginnings of El Ujuxte on the Pacific coastal plain and Kaminaljuyu in the Maya Highlands (Love, Chapter 7), and Nakbe in the Mirador region of the Maya lowlands (Hansen, Chapter 8). The following Late Preclassic period (ca. 400 BCE–200 CE) saw the growth of more powerful expansive states. Both El Ujuxte and Kaminaljuyu went on to become far larger states in the Late Preclassic, while Nakbe was succeeded by the immense Late Preclassic city of El Mirador.

Several examples of large and complex early Maya sites can be proposed as the capitals of these initial states. Both Kaminaljuyu and Nakbe are notable for evidence of the beginnings of intensified agricultural production in the Middle Preclassic—with implications for accelerated population growth, increases in social complexity, and centralization of authority. In addition to monumental architecture at both sites, at Kaminaljuyu this trajectory was reinforced by investments in excavating large irrigation canals, while Nakbe's developmental course was boosted by the construction of garden plots composed of transported fertile bajo soils (Chapters 7 and 8). Developments in the Mirador region included one unique feature that was probably decisive for the origins of the initial states in the Maya lowlands—the first known network of causeways in Mesoamerica. This network interconnected the major centers of the region from the Middle Preclassic period onward, and greatly facilitated communication and commerce within the region. Causeway construction and maintenance certainly required the mobilization of a labor force of unprecedented size, with clear implications for efficient centralized control.

This Middle Preclassic causeway system also indicates that the early rulers in the Mirador region operated in concert, given the need for cooperative efforts to build and maintain the network. Taking this implication a step further, the efficiency of such a coherent political system would have been increased if one of the Mirador region's leaders, perhaps the ruler of Nakbe, possessed a measure of authority over his companions. Such a proposal for the existence of a hierarchy among the rulers of the Middle Preclassic Mirador region is clearly conjectural at this point. However, an analogy lies in the later Classic system in which some Maya kings, like those ruling at Calakmul, Copan, and Tikal, had the power to "oversee" alliances and events such as inaugurations and heir designations in the capitals of subordinate rulers (Martin and Grube 2008). Thus, we feel it is reasonable to propose that the origins of such political hierarchies among Maya kings may hark back to the time of the emergence of the first rulers in the Maya lowlands—a proposition that could be tested by future research.

The timing and patterns in the development of Maya states are consistent in both the southern area and the lowlands to the north. The same can be said for the remainder of Mesoamerica, although one contributor to this volume advocates developmental primacy for the Gulf coast Olmec (Clark, Chapter 5). Yet, as we have discussed earlier, there is evidence for innovations and unique elements in this process within all regions of Mesoamerica, along with evidence of complex patterns of interaction that belie any assumption that all Mesoamerican states followed the same pathway. For example, trade connections between the Maya area and Highland Mexico apparently predate the process of emerging complexity (Grove, Chapter 3). These links were maintained into the Middle Preclassic when we can see continued connections between these two distant regions in ceramics and the use of stelae paired with flat stone "altars." Similarities in pottery may demonstrate long-distance trade or even social relationships, but probably had few if any developmental consequences. On the other hand, the presence of Middle Preclassic stela-altar pairs at both Chalcatzingo in Morelos and Naranjo in the Valley of Guatemala may be a direct reflection of the commemoration of calendrical cycles and the link between the passage of time and perpetuation of centralized authority, with clear sociopolitical developmental implications.

The lack of a single path towards statehood is also apparent from the unique aspects in the developmental process as it played out within each region of the Maya area, and indeed within all of Mesoamerica. These regional trajectories reflect varied environmental, social, and cultural circumstances, as well as unique historical events and choices made by individuals and factions within each society. The array of different or even unique factors was matched by general similarities discernable in all regions, including economic surpluses, population growth, occupational specializations, and the crucial role played by ideology to mobilize labor and justify distinctions in wealth and power. In Yucatan the evidence suggests an intense investment in the construction of ball courts, suggesting a distinct pathway for the reinforcement of authority.

Investments in irrigation agriculture and resultant increased food surpluses undoubtedly contributed to the development of Preclassic Kaminaljuyu, spurring population growth and greater prosperity. In the lowland Mirador region, increased agricultural yields made possible by rich bajo soils at Nakbe had similar consequences for surpluses and population growth. Equivalent growth likely occurred at several other Middle Preclassic sites in the Mirador region. At the same time, the choice to invest surpluses of labor and resources in a unique system of causeways paid off in increased efficiency of communication and movements of people and goods. This undoubtedly contributed to the Middle Preclassic development of the region. Later on an expanded causeway system was probably crucial to El Mirador's success in creating a more highly centralized economic and political organization that consolidated the Mirador region and gave rise to the largest and most powerful Late Preclassic state in the entire lowlands, if not all of Mesoamerica. The developmental pattern was somewhat different in the southern Maya area, but by the Late Preclassic the highland Kaminaljuyu state had become far larger than its regional contemporaries, and it must have dominated the central highlands and perhaps more distant areas beyond.

What is far less clear is the degree to which these Preclassic states were comparable in scale and organization to Classic period Maya states, as there is almost no historical evidence from the Preclassic era. We know far more about these later Maya states due to the greater availability of both archaeological and historical data. We can say that Middle Preclassic polities tended to be smaller in scale and less centralized than the larger "expansive" states of the Late Preclassic, acknowledging that considerable variation existed in Preclassic times as it did in the later Classic period. As suggested previously, given the documented continuities between the Preclassic and

Classic eras, we can use attributes of Classic Maya states to model some features of Preclassic states, subject to refinement and testing by further archaeological research.

Measured by the scale of public works, the archaeological evidence demonstrates that the Late Preclassic Maya capital of El Mirador was larger than its contemporaries; indeed its constructions outstripped those of any Classic era Maya capital. Yet the degree of organizational complexity and centralization at El Mirador remains unknown in comparison with what we know about Classic Maya states. One core feature of Classic Maya states was clearly present in the Preclassic, centralized power as manifested in the institution of kingship. It is likely that early versions of Maya kings were in place and ruling at the larger Middle Preclassic centers, based on the ar-chaeological evidence for increasing centralization of authority in various regions of the Maya area. The monumentality of El Mirador's temples and its causeway system testify to the power of its rulers. Carved portraits of Preclassic kings, best seen at Kaminaljuyu and other southern area capitals, share the paraphernalia and ideological associations of their Classic coun-terparts. In the Maya lowlands the San Bartolo murals provide the clearest evidence for Preclassic versions of the same royal ideology of world cre-ation and Maize god rebirth that reinforced the authority of Classic period Maya kings (Martin, Chapter 11; Saturno 2007a).

Aside from clear indications of trade and warfare, another unresolved issue concerns the kinds of interaction that took place between Preclassic Maya states, especially those associated with the largest Preclassic capi-tals, Kaminaljuyu in the highlands and El Mirador in the lowlands. As Michael Love points out (Chapter 7), we know very little about Kaminal-juyu's relations with its surrounding region. The same uncertainty exists for the lowlands regarding El Mirador's relationship with other Preclas-sic sites and regions. The nature of the Preclassic political landscape is especially murky. Were the Preclassic lowland Maya states autonomous polities, and if so, was El Mirador simply a far larger member of a system of independent states? Or did El Mirador exercise a degree of author-ity over its smaller lowland neighbors. If so, what kinds of authority did it command, and how far did its reach extend across the lowlands? One obvious model for defining the extent of El Mirador's power has already been mentioned, namely the Classic system of royal oversight recorded in a number of texts. If this system existed in the Preclassic, it is all but certain that the rulers of El Mirador possessed the authority to oversee events and even receive tribute from other kings who would have been placed in a subordinate position.

FROM PRECLASSIC TO CLASSIC MAYA STATES: A PROVISIONAL MODEL

In keeping with the conference goal of generating new models for the origins of Maya states, we will close with a provisional model that outlines a developmental trajectory for the emergence and demise of Preclassic Maya states. This follows the picture just presented, calling for the origins of centralized states in the Middle Preclassic, and the emergence of larger and more complex states in the Late Preclassic, led by Kaminaljuyu in the highlands and El Mirador in the lowlands. The model also includes the collapse of these paramount states in the Terminal Preclassic, setting the stage for the Classic period revival of a lowland system of states.

Middle Preclassic

1. Rise of small incipient states that coalesced around growing centers with successful rulers having authority rooted in control over labor, essential resources, prestige items, ideology, warfare and security (Pacific coast, highlands, and lowlands)
2. Royal authority reinforced by symbols and institutions adapted from multiple sources within the Maya area and Mesoamerica
3. Further growth in population, wealth, and centralized authority promoted by intensification of agriculture (documented by irrigation canals at Kaminaljuyu, bajo soil plots at Nakbe)
4. Further centralization and cohesion of authority associated with causeway construction in the Mirador region and ball court construction in Yucatan
5. Possible further cohesion and increased administrative efficiency by postulated hierarchy of Mirador region rulers headed by a paramount ruler at Nakbe.

Late Preclassic

1. Rise of larger expansionist states ruled by dynasties of kings, evident from carved monuments at Kaminaljuyu and likely at El Mirador

2. At Kaminaljuyu, further growth in population, wealth, and centralized authority promoted by expansion of irrigation system

3. Possible emergence of paramount ruler at Kaminaljuyu with limited authority over smaller states in highlands, southeast region, and portions of coastal plain

4. At El Mirador, further growth in population, wealth, and centralized authority promoted by expansion of agricultural and causeway systems

5. Possible emergence of paramount ruler at El Mirador, and consolidation of the Mirador region under a unified El Mirador state (possible ancestors of the Classic period *"Kan* State")

6. Postulated extension of paramount El Mirador ruler's authority over unknown number of smaller lowland states (hierarchy of Late Preclassic lowland kings headed by ruler of El Mirador).

Terminal Preclassic

1. Decline or collapse of Kaminaljuyu and other closely allied states in highlands, southeast region, and portions of coastal plain (possible incursions at Kaminaljuyu from central Maya highlands)

2. Collapse of El Mirador and allied lowland states (resource depletion, overpopulation, and related problems in the Mirador region and perhaps elsewhere)

3. Revival of states at surviving lowland capitals (Tikal re-founded ca. 100 CE by Yax Ehb Xook, possible ties to Kaminaljuyu) and founding of new capitals by remnants of Kan and other Preclassic dynasties; stage set for expansion of system of states in the Classic period.

2

Maya States: The Theoretical Background in Historical Overview

ASTRID RUNGGALDIER AND NORMAN HAMMOND

For most of the 150-year history of Maya archaeology, the conception of the "Maya state" used that term, if at all, to mean simply a polity. The state (versus the individual, as an anonymous mechanism of government) and the state (as the upper end of the band-tribe-chiefdom-state continuum envisaged by Service [1962, 1975]) only manifested themselves in Mayanists' thoughts in the past half-century. Also, for the first century or so the state and the city were synonymous: little was known of Maya culture outside the ceremonial centers or civic cores until rural and suburban settlement patterns were investigated in the 1950s. In this regard, Willey's Belize Valley project of 1953–56 and the University of Pennsylvania's Tikal Project, beginning in 1958, sparked a basic shift in perspective as to what constituted a Maya polity.

The present volume is primarily concerned with the origins of Maya states before the Classic period, known from both archaeology and epigraphy in the Maya lowlands as a diverse set of separate yet interdependent polities. The following overview is meant to highlight some of the literature that has contributed to the extant models of Maya states over the last half-century, as available at the time of the 2007 symposium. The two developments that underpin Maya state models are the study of settlement patterns and the decipherment of Maya hieroglyphic texts. Both of these lines of inquiry address common issues, combining archaeology and epigraphy, in particular in terms of scale—identifying the extent of Maya polities—and in terms of urbanism—distinguishing density and function in cities.

Overall, Maya state models were developed on the basis of evidence from the Classic period and sought to describe and characterize the nature of statehood, rather than offer an explanatory mechanism of formation. In other words, Maya state models are not about state formation, but rather about state characterization. As such they are not concerned with factors that can be considered movers of state development, but rather with understanding the nature of Maya states in their most unequivocal form, that of the Late Classic period. These descriptive rather than explanatory models are in part attributable to two factors related to chronology: the substantial role in envisioning Maya states played by hieroglyphic texts, which elucidate the political arena of the dynastic Classic period but not of earlier forms of kingship; and the fact that the Preclassic period was largely unknown until the 1970s. Thus, the pursuit of epigraphy and the study of the rise of Maya civilization followed parallel trajectories over the last thirty years. The resulting knowledge about the nature of relationships among Maya polities, and the accumulated evidence for sophisticated sociopolitical developments in the Preclassic period are creating the opportunity for discussion of Maya statehood in the context of Preclassic times.

Initially, two kinds of evidence were obvious as indicating ancient Maya governance: the ruins themselves, exhibiting the results of collective action under a central will, and the carved and inscribed monuments, which even before decipherment were understood to portray elite hierophants. The relative ranking of cities was predicated by Morley (1946) on the bulk and the beauty of the known remains, so Tikal and Copan, Uxmal and Chichén Itzá were seen as co-equal "metropolises" in the highest rank. Calakmul was a tier below and equal with Quirigua as "cities," while Izamal, Seibal, and La Milpa were all "large towns" on the third level. Dzibilchaltun, a "small town," was at the lowest level, and Caracol, although first explored in 1938, was not mentioned at all (Morley 1946: Plate 19). The cities of the south were in the "Old Empire," those of Yucatan in the "New Empire," but Morley envisaged neither emperor nor really, therefore, an imperium: Caldwell's later term "interaction sphere" was much closer to what Morley meant. Morley was aware of hierarchical relationships and variable histories, making this explicit in his discussion (1946:340) of the Cobá-Yaxuna sacbe. He used the number of stelae as a secondary indicator of hierarchy—Calakmul's rank was based on its 104 known monuments, not the size of its architecture: it was only after 1960, when the combination of known historical content in the texts (Proskouriakoff 1960) and the political geography adumbrated by the distribution of Emblem Glyphs (Berlin 1958a) made it possible that emic rather than etic hierarchies could be proposed.

THE MAYA CASE IN MESOAMERICA:
ISSUES OF SCALE AND DIVERSITY

State formation models have often been dependent on definitions of state size. The 'size' variable has great implications for the type of state model it engenders, along with correlate political and economic organization. The implications are not just in the broad schema of territorial states as opposed to city-states, but also in the subtler differences between regional and segmentary states, both of which in the Maya case represent formulations of city-state models, varying in the individual polities' degree of control over territory and over other polities.

Consequently, the definition of state size as a unit of analysis for the formulation of models of state formation is itself dependent on the definition of state, whether a city-state or a regional state, with all the permutations in between the two ends of the spectrum. Some of the terms that have been used over the years by scholars describing Mesoamerican states have included: empire, regional state, segmentary state, city-state, polity, kingdom, realm, and regal-ritual center.

The first term, while applicable in the case of the Aztec (and perhaps the Zapotec?), is the only one in the previous list that Mayanists agree is not applicable to Maya states at any point in time. An exception can be made for the use of the term "empire" in the early history of Maya archaeology (Morley 1946), when discussion of state formation had yet to become a matter of investigation. All other terms have been deemed appropriate at one point or another; in some cases, the same terms appealed to different Mayanists over a span of time, and in other cases different terms appealed to the same scholars at different points in time.

The range of options is a reflection of the range of diversity within Mesoamerican civilizations, which has contributed to the difficulty in finding agreement between Mesoamericanists on the nature, the timing, and the mechanism of the rise of states. While the differences between Mesoamerican cultures are highlighted by the unique trajectories resulting from the combination of individual culture histories and different environments, scholars, especially those with experience in more than one Mesoamerican culture area, have attempted to generate or apply models that explain the occurrence of state-level complexity in broad terms applicable to Mesoamerica as a whole. Typically, however, the Maya area is singled out as an exception in the schemata of state models, and in some cases even Mayanists' egos are themselves accused of being the reason that the Maya area is the example that does not quite fit the rule:

> Four-tiered settlement hierarchies are extremely widespread among archaic states, a pattern that has escaped many Mayanists. There may be several reasons for their failure to recognize hierarchies. For instance, some Maya archaeologists are reluctant to see 'their' Tier 2 or Tier 3 site as subordinate to any other center, apparently resenting it if their site is considered anything less than a capital. Some Maya epigraphers, in addition, assume that if a site possessed its own emblem glyph it could not be hierarchically below any other site. Some have, as a result, proposed that the Maya area had as many as 80 (!) autonomous "capitals," each ruling a miniscule territory (Mathews 1985). I know of no archaic state that had such a nonhierarchical structure. (Flannery 1998:18)

In the wider Mesoamerican context, the discussion ranging from chiefdoms to empires is not limited to the variable of size and degree of urbanization, but comes with evolutionary implications. If we agree that the topic of state formation is one deeply entrenched in evolutionary theory (Trigger 2004), and we accept that Maya states rose out of earlier chiefdoms (whether or not we currently have broad archaeological evidence for those), then we have to consider the value of looking at Maya states not only in their initial developmental trajectory but also in later political manifestations towards the end of the Classic period.

A broad chronological approach to the topic of Maya states in terms of their rise as well as their dissolution suggests some considerations related to cross-cultural evolution: had a system of Maya states not collapsed, could it ever have approximated other Mesoamerican state models, or are we talking about intrinsically different systems within the same broad cultural interaction sphere? And if there is interaction between different culture areas, why are these not adopting similar state forms? What constitutes the underlying substrate of Maya civilization that makes states develop differently in the Maya region than in other Mesoamerican culture areas?

At the core of the problem of defining Maya states in the context of Mesoamerican political complexity is the fact that Mesoamerica represents an area of extreme variability and diversity (Sanders and Webster 1988; Demarest 1996; Sinopoli 2001; Sharer and Golden 2004). In addition to diversity of political forms, certain basic tenets that are taken for granted in the context of Old World state formation need discussion, such as the presence and degree of urbanism as an inalienable component of the state (Smith 1989; Stein 2001), or the now-dated argument deriving from Childe's criteria (1950) over whether primary state formation is necessarily accompanied by writing.

The study of state formation, characterized by investigating the development of large-size units as opposed to site-centered archaeology, is the direct outcome of settlement pattern studies, and thus a contribution from New World archaeology to a worldwide discussion (Willey 1953). At the same time, it is within New World archaeology that models of state formation are complicated by the lack of uniform traits among different civilizations, such as the adoption and use of writing, and degrees of urbanization.

CROSS-CULTURAL COMPARISONS, UNIVERSAL MODELS, AND POSTMODERN CAVEATS

In order to summarize the theoretical framework and to identify the pertinent boundaries of discussion for the rise of Maya states, an "intellectual history" of the models themselves can be useful for understanding the developmental trajectory and scope of the topic of complexity and state formation in the Mesoamerican context. Before attempting this historical journey, it might be worth noting that contemporary postmodern archaeological theory views state formation itself as a topic with its own history of debated value and relevance. According to Jansen, for example, when assessing the aims and attitudes of archaeology in relation to indigenous peoples—pertinent especially in the case of the Americas—the biases and agendas of the topic of "the state" become apparent. In this light the last half-century of the history of Mesoamerican archaeology has been a "biography of the state" as the "hallmark of civilization and progress" (Jansen 2004:240), often blind to the implications for nationalist ideologies. To

indigenous peoples, who now have more direct involvement and participation in issues and theories concerning their past than ever before, the
study of state formation may seem like a "hollow topic, of limited interest"
(Jansen 2004:241).

With this in mind, it is worth appraising the current goals and purposes
of addressing the nature and development of the Maya state, and whether
they have changed over time. The concept today remains of considerable
interest, because the variety of views on the issue indicates that the topic
is far from being exhausted (Manzanilla 2001; Flannery 2006), but also because an updated view of Maya states will doubtless contribute to a broader
discussion on the development of complexity by those interested in cross-
cultural comparisons between early civilizations.

Only by considering Maya states through their long-term chronology,
encompassing both the Preclassic and Classic periods, not as equivalent to
two discrete stages of chiefdom and state but as two phases of a historical
continuum, can we do justice to the culturally specific case of the Maya and
transcend the danger of discussing states as empty abstract notions. Emphasizing the culturally specific could be the antidote to the taxonomic tendencies of neo-evolutionary theory, which measures the progression of societies through typological categories in a great chain from band to state, and in
so doing creates a useless argument devoid of context and information on
what people did and how they constructed their lives (Yoffee 2005). Specifically in the Maya case, Sharer and Golden (2004) argue for the necessity to
recognize the considerable variability in the data pertaining to Maya polities
in time and space, and against wholesale comparative models for political
organizations that create grossly generalized cross-cultural parallels.

While drawing attention to the limitations of discussing states according
to neo-evolutionism might appear to advocate a return to culture history,
criticism of the study of the state is in fact meant to facilitate, not discourage, cross-cultural discussion, albeit with awareness of its potential dangers.
While "holistic models derived from a culturally specific context should not
be applied cross-culturally" because they establish false equivalencies, we
should instead "apply specific attributes derived from culturally specific
contexts" (Sharer and Golden 2004:42). This suggestion requires that we
understand the historical particulars of the situations we wish to compare,
and although our knowledge of Classic Maya political organization benefits
from extensive archaeological and epigraphic evidence, we cannot discuss

Maya states without a broad perspective and the pertinent evidence both on their origins before the Classic period, and on their demise.

THE BACKGROUND: SETTLEMENT PATTERN STUDIES AND THE DISCOVERY OF PRECLASSIC MAYA CIVILIZATION

Among the far-reaching effects of the concept of settlement pattern studies (Willey 1953) is the notion that sites do not exist on their own as discrete units of analysis. The study of state formation thus arose from conceptualizing these patterns as systems of interrelated entities that can be characterized according to different forms of political organization, including those associated with state systems.

Also in the 1950s, Michael D. Coe (1957) published one of the first ethnographic comparisons between the Maya and tropical forest civilizations elsewhere, suggesting that they might be similarly organized into sacred cities supported by a rural hinterland. While this was a short publication, it contributed to the contemporaneously held notion that Maya cities were vacant ceremonial centers (Becker 1979), popular until the proof of historicity in Maya texts and the advent of fine-grained settlement mapping (Proskouriakoff 1960; Carr and Hazard 1961). It also foreshadowed a slightly different approach to the Maya city as ceremonial center, which became known as the regal-ritual model of the late 1980s (Sanders and Webster 1988). Most importantly, it provided a template for advancing Maya state formation models on the basis of analogical reasoning that became a standard feature of Mayanists' theories for the following half century.

While much has been written about the nature of the Maya political system and its permutations both through time and in kind, not many models *per se* have been proposed, and these generally cluster into conceptions of decentralized city-states or centralized regional states, with some combining the two.

In addition, in the Maya context these are generally models that describe the nature of the state and explain the ways in which it functioned in the Classic, or even the Postclassic period, but do not explain the process of state development. The reason for this apparent gap lies in the fact that in the 1960s, with the New Archaeology seeking to explain the mechanisms behind the transformations of chiefdoms into states and the material and ecological underpinnings of social change in central Mexico and Oaxaca (Sanders and Price 1968; Flannery 1972; Flannery and Marcus 1976a), Mayanists were just beginning to turn their interests towards the Preclassic period. In the Maya area the exploration of the rise of Maya civilization in the Preclassic became a focus of research in the early 1970s, but it was not then known that this equated with the rise of Maya states.

Willey's Belize Valley research (Willey et al. 1965) resulted in numerous other settlement pattern studies, as well as work in site centersar, and in the realization that long Preclassic occupations underlay many Classic sites. The SAR Advanced Seminar of 1974 on The Origins of Maya Civilization (Adams 1977) summarized evidence to date on the subject, and yet underscored the "yawning chasms in our knowledge of the Maya" (Pendergast 1984:232). At the time, however, Adams's volume was the first attempt to go beyond a description of the historical framework and to offer an explanation for "the appearance of Maya civilization" with a section on "Processes and Models" that took into consideration potential movers such as ecology, demography, warfare, and trade, not discounting external contact as the means of development of the Maya lowlands, but at the same time cautioning against the failure of models that rely on "outright diffusion or in influences thrust upon the Maya by contact with highly organized systems from more salubrious environments" (Adams and Culbert 1977:18).

The SAR volume was an exploration into the rise of Maya civilization, not the rise of Maya states, but it did suggest that some of the mechanisms considered could be "potentially applicable for anyone who feels that the Maya did reach statehood" (Adams and Culbert 1977:19). Such statements suggest a shared incredulity at the time for the eventual existence of Maya states, and in fact the final summary view by Willey (1977) characterized different periods in socio-cultural terms but never discussed statehood: Maya civilization through time evolved from Middle Preclassic egalitarian communities, putatively organized into what Ball suggested in that same volume to be a "segmentary tribal level of social organization" (Ball 1977:107), to a ranked society with the appearance of an elite class in "the Protoclassic Period," and ultimately to a "ruling aristocracy" (Willey 1977:387–94). Willey's "Overarching Model" was well aware of the limitations that the evidence then available imposed on explanatory models, admitting that his was "obviously a very 'historical' one" and that the overview of forces and factors still amounted to a "historical explanation—something that is decried by some as no explanation at all" (Willey 1977:421, 422). While today the evidence is less sparse, we still have not identified the causation factors of Maya state formation, although we have come to agree that Maya state-hood did exist, and that "one needs to distinguish between Maya civiliza-tion (or Mesopotamian civilization) and Maya (or Mesopotamian) states" (Yoffee 2005:44).

While data were being carefully collected over the last 40 years on the early Maya, other publications of the 1970s were beginning to character-ize Classic Maya sites through Central-Place Theory and other locational models in terms of their extent, their organization, and their political and economic strategies in relation to their resources (Hammond 1972a, 1974, 1975; Marcus 1973, 1976a; see also Flannery 1972). Unlike Hammond's, Marcus's approach involved epigraphy and cosmography in identifying Maya sites as ceremonial-civic centers in which one could observe that, "like other Mesoamerican states, the Maya state had a professional ruling class that had almost no bonds of kinship with the common people" (Marcus 1973:914).

Instead of the vague ceremonial-civic terminology, Hammond used the term "realm" with the intention of describing a polity with clear internal hierarchy (1975:134). Regardless of choice, with neither "city-state" nor "realm" was it necessary to define political power in terms of a specifically delimited territorial size and, as evidence continued to accumulate and fill out the picture of what Maya cities were like and how they operated, it became clear that supporters of different models of Maya states inevitably argued about size, and whether Maya states were represented by one city and its hinterland, or by several hierarchically organized cities and the land between them.

The term "realm" used by Hammond (1975) derives from the Latin *regere* "to rule" and *regimen* "government," and does not require a commit-ment to defining who ruled in what type of government, while at the same time implying the existence of a state; but it has not caught on as a descrip-tive term for Maya states, perhaps because of its other, more vague, mean-ing of "domain" or "region."

While the examples highlighted so far constitute the general backdrop for the theories on Maya states up through the 1970s, they are neither ex-planatory nor descriptive models. Starting in the 1980s and throughout the 1990s ideas on state formation, influenced by concurrent publications on the topic about other complex societies in the world (Price 1977; Renfrew 1982; Renfrew and Cherry 1986; Wright 1986), resulted in a vast range of literature, much of which had direct relevance for Maya states.

In general, two parallel lines of inquiry continued to develop out of the previous decades—the political institution of the state and the Preclassic period—and they have become fused together in recent years, now that the two subjects are more widely held by Mayanists to be the same field of inquiry.

SITES, CITIES, AND URBANISM

For the purposes of highlighting developments directly relevant here, we have selected for mention some of the contributions to the first subject, that of the nature of the state confined mostly to the Classic period, and a few to the subject of Preclassic societies and their development.

Despite the general agreement that the development of complex societies in Mesoamerica took place in the Middle and Late Preclassic (Grove 1981a; Kowalewski 1990; Fowler 1991), complexity is not synonymous with state-level society. Until the Late Preclassic period throughout Mesoamerica there were chiefdoms at varying levels of complexity, but no real states, according to Spencer and Redmond (2004). While the differences between complex chiefdoms and archaic states are a matter of lively debate (Blake 1991; Grove and Gillespie 1992; Clark and Blake 1994; Clark 1997; Feinman and Marcus 1998), it is in the arena of characterizing the nature of Classic Maya centers that state models are best observed.

During the 1980s and 1990s Mesoamericanists diversified their research into several lines of inquiry, asking questions about society and economy that could be addressed by, among other approaches, locational analysis, spatial patterns, settlement size and density, population demographics, and resource procurement and distribution, which in turn informed discussions on the nature of Maya sites.

Identifying and defining sites questioned the very nature of urbanism in Mesoamerica, and several studies established that Maya centers were large, complex, populated, dense, and heterogeneous enough to warrant calling them "cities." Among the innovative and influential publications in this group are Adams and Jones's "Spatial Patterns and Regional Growth Among Classic Maya Cities" (Adams and Jones 1981), Marcus's "On the

Nature of the Mesoamerican City" (Marcus 1983a), and Sanders and Webster's "The Mesoamerican Urban Tradition" (Sanders and Webster 1988).

In the first article, Adams and Jones decried the problem of scholars making generalizing statements about Maya centers without solid means of establishing the size and interrelationships between them. They offered as a solution the "systematic description and assessment of Maya cities" (Adams and Jones 1981:302; see also Turner, Turner, and Adams 1981) through courtyard group counts that allowed quantification and hierarchical ordering of sites in a dispersed pattern throughout the Maya area.

The solution seems relatively simple, but over thirty years have passed, and many of the disagreements among supporters of different Maya state models are still generated by the same problem: we cannot generalize what we do not know. Therefore, while our goal is to strive for a theoretical synthesis, we cannot skip ahead of the task of compiling a database of systematically collected evidence and description, accounting for such aspects as territorial extent, density, and hierarchical relationships. One of the problems with Maya state formation models thus far has been that scholars describe Maya states differently, and they do so because they view Maya cities differently.

The heated debates between opposing camps in identifying the nature of Maya statehood resulted by the late 1990s in a dichotomy between "centralists" and "decentralists" (Fox et al. 1996). At one end, the centralists may be described as those scholars who see Maya states as regional, unitary, bureaucratic entities held together by relationships of hierarchical administration as opposed to kinship. The decentralist camp clusters at the opposite end of the spectrum, preferring small entities equated with city-states or segmentary states, whose nuclei are formed by the palace-and-temple unit and whose political power is negotiated by lineage connections.

With the exception of Joyce Marcus's work suggesting a few large territorial units controlling all of the Maya lowlands (1976a) and Adams's (1986:437) reduction of the entire Maya lowlands to eight "regional states"—based on Copan, Tikal, Palenque, Yaxchilan, Calakmul, Rio Bec, Cobá, and the "Puuc-Chenes" region centered on Uxmal—the concept of the unitary regional state did not develop as a model proposed by Mayanists; rather, it formed as a response to disagreements with supporters of the varied manifestations of the segmentary model. The success of the latter can be linked directly to the two aforementioned publications of the 1980s on Mesoamerican urbanism (Marcus 1983a; Sanders and Webster 1988).

In her contribution, Marcus suggested that Richard Fox's Old World model (1977), including among others regal-ritual cities, could be applicable to cities such as Mitla (Marcus 1983a:208–9), and that religion could account for one of three aspects of city functions in various proportions, the other two being administration and craft production.

For Sanders and Webster, the aspect of craft production was not a driving force in their model, which saw Mesoamerican urban centers as part of "low-energy societies," geared towards consumption rather than production. On the other hand, Fox's (1977) functional typology that included five categories—regal-ritual, administrative, mercantile, colonial, and industrial—gave rise to what became the "regal-ritual model" of Maya cities (Sanders and Webster 1988:523–25). While this model is not a model of the Maya state *per se*, it is the basis of both segmentary state and galactic-polity models and all their permutations.

In their characterization of the Maya city, represented *pars pro toto* by Copan, Sanders and Webster were concerned with accounting for the dramatically diverse sizes of Mesoamerican cities through function, and did not further develop the concept of segmentary states proposed by Fox. Nevertheless, they did report that "Fox links the regal-ritual city to the political form he calls the segmentary state," and while admitting that Fox lumped Service's chiefdoms, Fried's ranked societies, and their own conception of the state into one category, they preferred to "restrict the definition of the segmentary state to those centralized political systems in which kinship still plays the dominant role in overall social and economic organization" (1988:528).

At the same time that Sanders and Webster formulated their view of Maya cities based on Richard Fox's model, John Fox (1987, 1988, 1989) was applying Southall's (1956) characterization of the African Alur segmentary lineage organization to the Maya area, in a return to using ethnography from outside Mesoamerica for comparative models, much as Coe (1957) had done with Khmer settlement patterns thirty years earlier.

While John Fox found application for Southall's study in explaining competition and unification among the Postclassic Maya, in particular the Quiché, Peter Dunham (1990) went on to apply the concept to lowland Maya political organization as a whole and to organize a conference on the topic at Cleveland State University in 1992 titled "The Segmentary State and the Classic Lowland Maya: A 'New' Model for Ancient Political Organization."

The latter, sadly, never resulted in a publication of the contributors' papers, but most of the participants had already been drawn to this model from a variety of perspectives, and they continued to conceive of and write about Maya political entities in terms of segmentary states, i.e., polities of small territory ruled by elites connected through kin relations that were too volatile and unstable to ever become large and centralized (Ball 1993; de Montmollin 1992; Demarest 1992a, 1996; Houston 1993, 1997; Ringle 1999). What is not clear is whether any of them regarded Maya sites as urban—preindustrial cities in function and in most aspects of form except population density—or whether they followed the Alur model (and the views of highland-based Mesoamericanists) and regarded Maya "cities" as low-density, low-diversity, civic nuclei amidst a populace lacking significant social layering.

THE STATE: KINGDOMS AND KINGSHIP IN HIEROGLYPHIC DECIPHERMENTS

Before continuing with the historical trajectory of theories on the Maya state in the 1990s, it is worth pointing out that several other contributions of the 1980s had a significant impact on the topic. By the time publications on the Maya multiply in the 1980s, it is clear that Maya scholarship had resulted in vibrant and prolific discussions on such a variety of approaches that it is increasingly difficult to separate strands and reconstruct how themes influenced each other in a unilineal fashion.

Among the most significant forward leaps in Maya scholarship, the achievements of epigraphic decipherments in the 1980s contributed a more humanistic approach to our view of the Maya, in contrast with the socio-economic aims of processual studies, resulting in complementary conceptions for modeling Classic Maya state society. Epigraphy demonstrated that we could track the achievements of individual rulers and their relationships with each other, and that political events could not be disassociated from ritual practice. This realization had a profound effect on reintegrating cosmology and religion with views of the state and important factors in its formation. Among those to treat this topic explicitly were Michael Coe (1981a) and David Freidel (1981), who looked at state and ritual among the Maya, the Olmec, and Teotihuacan.

Inspired by the new views of Maya society that the Maya texts could bring about, archaeologists, art historians, and epigraphers produced an extensive literature, much of which was concerned with the state by way of analyzing kingship, royal ritual and sacrifice, the royal person, and the material symbols of prestige (Stuart 1984; Freidel 1986a; Schele and Miller 1986; Freidel and Schele 1988a; Schele and Freidel 1990).

In addition to the art-historical and epigraphic analysis of kingship, epigraphy played an instrumental role in the utilization of "emblem glyphs," first identified by Berlin (1958a) and then used by Barthel (1968), to suggest a hierarchical structure based on the notion that Copan Stela A and Seibal Stela 10 each named four (partly different) regional "capitals." Marcus (1973, 1976a) adopted the idea, and surmised correctly that Barthel's unnamed fourth capital alongside Copan, Tikal, and Palenque on Copan St. A was Calakmul. She then suggested a 'hierarchy of mentions' (our term) in which lower-order centers would mention the Emblem Glyphs of their superiors, but not vice-versa. Marcus applied Central-Place Theory (a technique designed for use in modern urbanized landscapes with developed communications) to construct hypothetical models, notably for Calakmul, in which many of the lower-order sites had to be assumed for lack of adequate surveys.

At the same time Hammond (1972a, 1974) took a different tack, using Thiessen polygons, which simply defined the territory closest to each assumed Late Classic polity center (using 83 centers claimed in the literature as "major ceremonial centers" on the basis of substantial and/or special-purpose architecture and/or inscribed monuments). The approach would define the likely core area under the polity's rule, "suggesting where evidence for natural or artificial frontiers may be sought" (1974:322), and attempted a best-fit with topographic data to sketch possible polity boundaries on a pragmatic basis. Hammond also took the view that in the absence of explicit evidence of hierarchy all centers should be treated as of equal political status, knowing that "this may not be so, indeed probably is not so" (1974:318) but that both the nature of the inequality and its permanence could not be established on then-available data.

A decade later, Mathews (1985: figs. 8–14) again used Thiessen polygons, now in combination with the distribution of Emblem Glyphs for Early Classic sites in the southern lowlands and the known periods of monument dedication, to produce successive period maps that showed the origins of monument dedication in the Tikal region and the rapid adoption of the practice southwestwards into the Usumacinta basin, then southeast into

Belize. Mathews, like Hammond, made the explicit assumption of co-equality of centers possessing the entry criterion, in this case an Emblem Glyph (EG), and the size and patterning of the polities he defined were remarkably similar to those Hammond had obtained using different criteria. Mathews's caveats on the likelihood of co-equality (1985:53–54) were less pessimistic than Hammond's, being based on more explicit dating evidence of contemporaneity or otherwise.

In both cases, a small-polity, if not quite "city-state" model emerged: Hammond's largest territories were around 1500 km^2, the smallest around 100 km^2, the mean (n=45) around 500 km^2 (Mathews did not use closed polygons nor calculate territory sizes). This in essence bore out Morley's and Thompson's long-held assumption that parallels with the city-states of the ancient Near East and Mediterranean were valid, while the likely population sizes within such states were similar to those proposed by Bray (1972) for central Mexican polities. Both studies produced an unrealistic landscape of independent polities, with the smallest territories clustered in the areas most densely populated with EG-using sites, notably in the northeastern Petén region where the earliest (and latest) uses of EGs were found.

While this approach continues to be criticized by Mesoamericanists focusing outside the Maya area, as well as by Mayanists who disagree with the decentralized states model, Mathews nevertheless had very clearly stated that Emblem Glyphs could not be the only line of evidence for reconstructing political boundaries (1985:33). Contrary to Berlin's view that they were place names, Mathews believed correctly that they represented the title for "lord," and suggested that the political office of ruling lords at different sites being equal, Maya polities reflected a network of independent states by the Early Classic period.

Today, identifying what Emblem Glyphs represent has become further complicated by the subtleties afforded by epigraphic research, which indicate that Emblem Glyphs were indeed titles: "Holy Lord of X," where "X" designated the polity. But there is now evidence of toponymic glyphs referring to a range of meanings for "place," from city-center names to polities with large hinterlands, specific places within sites, alternate names for polities, or even mythological place-names (Stuart and Houston 1994). What is clear from this more complex interpretation of location glyphs, including Emblem Glyphs, is that while they can inform us of Maya conceptions of place, they have become less instrumental for understanding state models.

Beyond the study of Emblem Glyphs, the advances brought forth in Maya polity analysis by integrating art history and epigraphy with archaeological questions became the subject of an SAR Advanced Seminar in 1986 on "Classic Maya Political History" (Culbert 1991a), with contributions on the extent of the Tikal state, the size and internal organization of Maya polities, and the dynamics of maintaining power relations between elites across the Maya area (Culbert 1991b; Hammond 1991a; Mathews 1991; Mathews and Willey 1991; Schele and Mathews 1991; Sharer 1991). In this volume, both cosmology and territory were recognized as significant aspects of the political panorama of the Classic period, a pairing that later constituted the basis of Marcus's (1992a, 1998a) "dynamic" model and its extensions, and also in Mathews and Willey's adumbration of the balloon-like expansion and deflation of Dos Pilas, the first inkling of a (temporary and rather small) "Maya superstate."

Hammond's (1991a: fig. 11.3) rather static typology of contrasting trajectories of polity-center (and arguably polity) florescence was less successful than Sharer's (1991: fig. 8.1, bottom) "spaghetti" (his *ad hoc* term) model of the non-coincident and overlapping rise and fall of different Maya polities. Marcus's similar 1992 model, based on territorial expansion through militarism, best describes the situation in Oaxaca and the rise of the Zapotec state of Monte Alban in the Late Preclassic, and, being essentially evolutionary in character, it sought pan-Mesoamerican regularities.

The idea combined the scenario of small city-states with that of large regional ones at different points in time in the same regions, suggesting that the overall trajectory could oscillate back and forth, with small states forming from the breakdown of the large unitary ones. This view implied that the existence of city-states, as in the Maya area, at any given time was the result of the dissolution of a previously centralized regional state. These contrasting models only made it more apparent that there was no single template for describing or understanding Maya states. Maya states were diverse in size and organization, in addition to representing individual historical trajectories (Marcus 1993; Sharer 1991).

While the agreement over Maya regional states is not widespread, Marcus's model incorporated dynamic processes that create an intellectually more complex and realistic view than static models can describe. However, despite suggesting a mechanism of change that accounted for opposing types of states, the dynamic model did not address the reasons for the transitions between centralizing and fragmenting forces. The model has found

most acceptance among those whose work has focused on the largest of
Maya sites, like Tikal, Calakmul, and Caracol.

The latter, investigated through the work of Arlen and Diane Chase,
exemplifies the kind of Maya state that in the Chases' view extended regional control over other polities in the lowlands by means of territorial
and political power independent of lineage relations, with the development
of a "middle class" (Chase and Chase 1996). The disagreement over the
role of kinship in Maya state formation developed in reaction to the regal-
ritual urbanism model, which had generated divergent opinions both in the
context of central Mexico and of the Maya (Smith 1989; Chase, Chase, and
Haviland 1990). The debate ensued primarily because Sanders and Webster's view of ideology and ritual as manifestations of political power (Sanders and Webster 1988:528) was taken as an explanatory model for the rise of
states that denied the economic powers of cities.

By extension, while economic gain was emphasized as a driving force
in the rise of the state, the role of lineages was called into question in the
context of sites like Tikal and Caracol where, by Classic times, populations
were dense and socially stratified, organized into economically diverse specialization classes, and connected by bureaucratic rather than kinship-based
ties. Lineages were described as such a fundamental aspect of segmentary
states, in spite of Dunham's and Mathews's warning that they need not be
(1992:1), that scholars who did not agree with such a view of Maya society felt it necessary to reject the entire segmentary state model (Chase and
Chase 1996:803–4; Haviland 1997:444). Consequently, a "centralist" camp
was created for those who disagreed with the segmentary state model (Fox
et al. 1996:797–98), giving the impression that Mayanists had developed opposite competing models of the state, while instead an explicit model of the
unitary, bureaucratic, and centralized Maya state has yet to be formulated.

The incorporation of evidence resulting from the decipherments of the
1980s into discussions of Maya state models produced a general tendency
to polarize the argument into two groups: those who focused on epigraphy
and viewed Maya states as weak kingdoms rendered unstable by ritual warfare and dynastic concerns, and those who focused on massive public works
and monumental architecture and saw these as evidence for far-reaching
centralized control. Martin and Grube (1995:42) and Iannone (2002:69) noticed the pattern; the latter further suggested that "decentralized" models
derive from ethnographic data and are essentially deductive, while "cen-

tralized" constructs, in relying on archaeological data, allow for inductive model building.

Martin and Grube, however, had not seen a need for such opposing views, and suggested that a closer reading of the titles of lords and of accession texts provided evidence for a hierarchy between states. This in turn pointed to the occurrence of some polities controlling a number of other ones, with some, such as Calakmul and Tikal, consistently dominant over time—the "superstates." These dominant polities indicate a pattern of regional powers not unlike the organization of the Aztec empire into loose confederations (Martin and Grube 1995:46), but rather different from Marcus's dynamic model of regional states as territories headed by a capital polity and organized into ranked units administered by the center.

The superstate approach attempted to bridge the two scenarios of multiple independent polities and of regional states, and clearly rejected the notion of two polarized views: "The picture that is emerging is neither one of a centralized administration of regional states nor one of a political vacuum populated by weak ones" (Martin and Grube 1995:46). Indeed, in bridging the peer polity and unitary state models, perhaps at the time it would have been clearer to have retained the pre-publication terminological choice of "superpower," as the authors intended (Martin 2007, pers. comm.), so as not to confuse the superstates with large territorial states. The authors did not believe these existed in the case of the Maya, which "were never politically unified" and struggled for dominance in a "turbulent landscape [where] no kingdom achieved a permanent hold on power" (Martin and Grube 2000:7).

In addition to decrying these needlessly polarized scenarios, Martin and Grube (1995) also blamed epigraphers for relying too heavily on the contents and themes of inscriptions when reconstructing the nature of Maya states, thus producing an overly decentralized picture of kingdoms concerned with ritual and cosmology, but not with pragmatic ambitions.

EPIGRAPHY AND ETHNOGRAPHY:
THE INCORPORATION OF IDEOLOGY

Beyond investigating the role of kings and the size of their polities, the epigraphic advances of the 1980s are to be credited with allowing ideology, often expressed in ritually charged texts and monuments to individuals and political events, to be recognized as a significant component of Maya political discourse by more than just epigraphers.

Combining some of the approaches of epigraphy with the comparative framework of ethnological studies in Southeast Asia (Geertz 1973, 1980; Tambiah 1977; Fritz 1986), Demarest proposed a model of "pulsating galactic polities" that was meant as a response to archaeologists' views that were too evolutionary and dictated solely by ecology and economics (1992a). The model was the result of a 1987 seminar (Demarest and Conrad 1992) dedicated to addressing the power of ideology in state affairs beyond the context of Maya states alone, so that ideology could be the basis of explanatory models for a variety of state forms across all of Mesoamerica (Cowgill 1992; Freidel 1992; Grove and Gillespie 1992).

In the case of the Maya, states were independent political entities, dependent on shared ideological sources of power. The latter are exemplified by archaeological as well as epigraphic evidence: non-subsistence exchange systems of prestige goods, and inter-dynastic elite interaction that includes warfare for purposes other than territorial gain, such as marriage alliances and sacrificial victims. The resulting polities clustered into "galaxies" loosely headed by capitals that could effect strong control over allegiance and labor for public display of the rulers' powers, but were not concerned with local economies. Because their sources of power could not allow that kind of economic control, hegemonies fluctuated, or "pulsated," with regionalized histories, and could never grow stable enough to form a centralized state.

The emphasis on instability has been used to categorize the galactic polity as a variation of the segmentary state model, but one important difference exists: the galactic polity theory, while relying on shared ideology, did not require shared kin-relations (Demarest 1996:822), and thus freed the model from a dependence on lineage as a structuring aspect of the state. In addition, Demarest's construct effectively focused attention on the variability of the Maya data. In his argument, Demarest discussed variability in the form of heterogeneity through time and across space, but warned that variability alone should not be construed by Mayanists as evidence of discordant models. Rather, the range of political forms indicated periods of experimentation at particular times, such as the "transition to statehood and shift in political ideology at the end of the Preclassic" (1996:821–22).

This view of the rise of states emphasizing ideology as political legitimation of power also denies warfare as the mechanism behind the rise of states in the Maya area. In particular, conflict is seen as an unlikely mover of state formation for Maya civilization because epigraphic and archaeological evidence date warfare to the Classic period, which is much too late to account for events of the Preclassic period. This argument, of course, treats absence of evidence—the lack of Preclassic texts about conflict—as evidence of absence, and ignores such contrary archaeological evidence as the massive and apparently Terminal Preclassic moat around Becan (Webster 1974). In Demarest's opinion the focus of the 1960s and 1970s on materialist explanations had missed the point and had characterized the development of the Maya state as an argument restricted to demographic pressures: "the Maya lowlanders were believed to have bred themselves into an ecological crisis leading to state formation" (1992a:281).

THE DAWN OF PRECLASSIC MAYA STATE FORMATION

While archaeologists, starting in the 1970s and throughout the 1980s, were busy creating a corpus of information on the identification, settlement patterns, chronology, subsistence, religious beliefs, mortuary practices, households, and public works of Preclassic Maya sites, some indications existed of just how large a scale and complexity certain sites achieved before the Classic period. As far back as the early 1960s, William R. Coe had drawn attention to the long Preclassic occupations of Tikal and Uaxactun, and suggested that the massive construction efforts of Preclassic times made the site center of Tikal in this time period just as extensive as its Classic period counterpart (W. Coe 1962a, 1962b, 1965a).

When information about the site of El Mirador began to circulate it became clear that the achievements of Tikal in the Preclassic period were not an isolated occurrence, and that enormous construction and elaborate hydraulic systems such as those of El Mirador and Edzna might warrant calling them Preclassic states (Matheny, Hansen, and Gurr 1980; Dahlin 1984; Matheny 1986a). Today the notion that the Late Preclassic was the time of state formation in the Maya area as well as in other cultural zones of Mesoamerica is not a contested issue (Demarest 1992a; Feinman and Marcus 1998; Schele 2000; Marcus 2003; Spencer and Redmond 2004; Guderjan 2004).

Still, the bulk of publications to date pertaining to Maya states have concentrated on the Classic period. While archaeological and ethnohistorical data, as well as anthropological analogies, have informed the models proposed thus far—the segmentary state and its variants, the dynamic model, and the less explicit unitary state model—the impetus for these discussions owes much to advances in deciphering the political records of the Maya, highlighted by the close correspondence in publication dates between new epigraphic readings and inferences on the nature of polity interactions. In fact, Grube considers hieroglyphic writing "our principal source for the investigation of the Maya states," and, citing scarcity of written records for both the Preclassic and Postclassic periods, suggests that while "the institution of statehood was in no way limited to the Classic period," scholarly discussion is limited to this period by the nature and availability of sources (Grube 2000:547).

Also, the bulk of publications on comparative state formation have often bypassed the case of the Maya in favor of other examples from Mesoamerica: a case in point was the publication of the volume *Archaic States* (Feinman and Marcus 1998). Dominated by examples from Mesoamerica, city-states such as those of the Maya were not considered true examples of long-lasting early state forms; rather these were to be understood as transitional positions in the formation and dissolution of the unitary state, which apparently was to be understood as the initial form of all archaic, or preindustrial, states (Feinman and Marcus 1998). The state formation model most forcefully presented in that volume was an elaboration of Marcus's dynamic model (1992a), which described not only the oscillations between unitary states and city-states over time, but the initial state consolidation in the form of a large territorial unit, evolved out of competing chiefdoms and different from them essentially only in terms of scale, identifiable in a change from a 3-tier to 4-tier hierarchy (Marcus and Feinman 1998; Flannery 1998). Warfare, or any form of endemic conflict, represents the prime mover in the development of simple chiefdoms as in the "chiefly cycling" of complex chiefdoms into states (Flannery 1999). It is interesting then to wonder whether the inclusion of the only example from the Maya area— the last chapter in *Archaic States* on the comparison between Maya and Polynesian warfare by David Webster (1998)—was meant to underscore the military component of early states, and at the same time justify their city-state form as a transitory consequence of rivalry and conflict.

There are many aspects of that volume that make it an important publication for cross-cultural studies of early states, not least the fact that it created a common realm of discussion for the definitions and terms used by scholars of different areas; yet, it has remained outside the realm of Mayanists' discussion of state formation, most likely because it treated Maya city-states as epiphenomenal. That the first archaic states were large unitary entities with an administrative hierarchy almost makes the concept of city-states a misnomer. They have to be explained away in one of two ways: either as the breakdown of the larger unitary state, or as a landscape of long-term autonomous political units, which in turn makes them chiefdoms. This characterization of Maya political organization is an inadequate evaluation of the extant data, especially when it is presented in a cross-cultural forum. In fact, it has not gone unnoticed that the editors' presentation of the concept of city-state is too vague and generalized to account for other city-state scenarios such as that of Mesopotamia, and that the envisioning of the first states as unitary has to be evaluated with skepticism (Adams 2000:188–89).

Perhaps the time has come to question whether the extant models for the Maya state can be updated with the wealth of information that has accumulated about the Late Preclassic in recent years. It is no simple task, and plenty of questions immediately arise from considering the debates over Classic states in the context of the Preclassic period. Some of the questions that could generate new thoughts on Maya states follow.

Did Maya states begin as small city-states vying for territorial gain or for political power through the establishment of shared ideologies? Or did they begin as regional states when a dominant chiefdom-level power gained control over their neighbors?

Are Late Classic city-states the result of the breakdown of Late Preclassic unitary centralized states? Do the Late Classic states reflect a segmentary nature because of the proliferation of elites with claims to power resulting in a "balkanization" of the lowlands, leading, together with other factors, to the collapse? Or were Maya states always intrinsically segmentary as far back as their Preclassic origins because of the particular sources of power of Maya kingship?

Was the institution of a shared Maya concept of divine kingship the initial development in the rise of states? What role, if any, do lineage and kinship play in the development of such an institution?

How much of the nature of Maya states that warrants claims to differences from other Mesoamerican states is the result of differences in the socioeconomic underpinnings of Maya culture? Or is the wide variety of state forms in Mesoamerica to be explained by ideological differences that were present from the initial development of the separate cultures?

A definite advantage to discovering the deep history of Maya civilization in the Preclassic period is the realization that while the above questions will be the source of renewed debates, the period of Maya state formation coincides with that of state formation across Mesoamerica, in the Valley of Mexico, Oaxaca, and perhaps the Olmec heartland, if states there are of "La Venta" rather than "San Lorenzo" age (Clark 2007a). A broader alignment of theories on the Maya state will also broaden the argument beyond the scope of the Classic period and into the realm of cross-cultural discussions on state formation, where the case of the Maya is still limited and underrepresented (see Trigger 2004; Yoffee 2005). Comparisons between early states rarely omit to mention Mesoamerica, yet at the same time discussion is limited to a few and generalized considerations that vary broadly across time, space, or civilization, often employing *ad hoc* examples (Teotihuacan for urbanization, the Olmec for early complexity, the Maya for city-state networks, the Late Classic Maya for collapse, etc.) while conveying the sense that Mesoamericanists are in agreement on the characterization of such examples, and that Mayanists might uniformly describe Maya polities as "our clearest examples" (Yoffee 2005:49) of the earliest city-states. More interesting would be to recognize the variability, not only in the evidence from Mesoamerica, but also in the socio-cultural characterizations employed by Mesoamericanists. This would ground cross-cultural comparisons in the realities perceived by the specialists in each culture area, rather than establish universal trajectories as based on homogenized packages of notions from each of those areas.

In the context of urbanism models and political structure, Webster and Sanders (2001) reconsidered their regal-ritual model as the precursor of the current views on palaces and royal courts embodying the physical and symbolic capitals of Maya states (Grube 2000; Inomata and Houston 2001a, 2001b). The most recent research in the Maya area related to statehood is fruitfully incorporating revised versions of Geertz's (1980) theater-states concept into a better understanding of how Maya states operated as political theaters using ritual, performance, and the design of public space as tools of integration between political control and the maintenance of shared ideologies (Inomata 2001, 2006a, 2006b). Rather than a direct equivalence between

Bali and the Maya, this comparison of components of the Balinese theater state is an example of what Sharer and Golden (2004) advocated as fruitful cross-cultural discussion of state models based on their attributes. This type of selection based on the knowledge of culturally specific contexts leads to cultures understood on their own terms and not as ideal types classified into discrete stages. Such models allow the integration of Maya data into theoretical discussions about the origins and nature of political systems and, more generally, socio-cultural complexity without obscuring either the diversity or unique characteristics of Maya states (Marcus 1993; Sharer 1991).

Historical context also allows Mayanists to overcome the polarization that has resulted in the two apparently separate camps, precisely because of the application of cross-cultural models together with all of their components. Supporters of the scenario of "weak states" are often associated with the notion of segmentary states and therefore with power inalienable from kinship ties, or with the notion of galactic and theater states that rely on the control of people and labor rather than territory; in contrast, "centralists," who argue for states that are concerned with territorial control, must therefore support the notion that unified, strong states are represented by bureaucratic institutions that transcend lineage. Neither of these two characterizations is accurate when applied to the Maya; perhaps the simple consideration of culturally and historically specific situations—that, for example, Maya warfare between polities was not just about ideology but also about territory (Sharer and Golden 2004:29)—characterizes Classic Maya states as somewhere between galactic/theater states with authority over people, and unitary states controlling territory: decentralized city-states whose power source lay beyond lineage, relied on control of people and labor, and placed importance on territoriality, *inter alia* as a means of extracting tribute in both labor and material resources.

Recent research also broadens our understanding of the anthropological underpinnings of Maya kinship ties in relation to the centralizing powers of the institution of kingship (McAnany 1995:131–56), and suggests that these very tensions lie at the base of Maya state formation (Iannone 2002). Iannone's study is also interesting as the first Maya application of the *Annales* approach long used in European archaeology by John Bintliff and Bernard Knapp, itself a kind of "dynamic model" based on long-term historical trends. We could do worse than utilize the concepts of *évenements*, *conjunctures*, and *longue durée* in thinking about the rise of Maya states.

Concepts that acknowledge the ideological power of Maya ritual display and practices as political tools are applicable to the context of Preclassic Maya polities. The evidence from this period provides the basis for new theories incorporating aspects of the existing models, whether centralized or decentralized, bureaucratic and economically based, or related to lineage and ideologically based. It also provides an opportunity to approach the Maya state without static paradigms and polarized dichotomies, in favor of a more comprehensive view that accounts for the uniqueness of Maya state-hood as well as its connections with other Mesoamerican Preclassic states.

3

Preclassic Central Mexico: The Uncertain Pathway from Tlatilco to Teotihuacan

DAVID C. GROVE

The Basin of Mexico, in Mexico's central highlands, was the location of one of Mesoamerica's greatest Classic period cities, Teotihuacan. Teotihuacan was also one of Mesoamerica's earliest state-level societies, and until recently many scholars assumed that Teotihuacan-Maya interactions played a significant role in the origin of Maya states (see Braswell 2003a). In spite of the importance of Teotihuacan—one of the largest cities in the world for its time—its origins nevertheless remain little understood, thus raising numerous questions. For example, how much of Teotihuacan's origins were linked to previous Preclassic developments in the Basin and adjacent areas? Did the region's contacts with distant societies such as the Olmec play any role? In this chapter I review and evaluate the evidence in the central Mexican archaeological record for the Early, Middle, and Late Preclassic periods in a search for answers. The paucity of data is frustrating; nevertheless, the results reveal early local precocity, intraregional social diversity, and both important continuities over time as well as significant disjunctions and shifting interregional interaction networks that have not been fully appreciated.

Archaeologists dealing with the question of the origins of Maya states and accustomed to working in the context of sites hidden beneath dense tropical vegetation might assume that archaeological knowledge of state origins in the Basin of Mexico, with its more open and accessible landscape, is better understood. They would be mistaken. Rather than dense vegetation, the floor of the Basin is instead obscured by a built environment of paved streets, apartment complexes, and office towers. The Basin is the location of Mexico City, and the rapid expansion of urbanization across that area over the past seven decades has always greatly outpaced and overwhelmed any attempts at doing archaeology there. As a result, scholars studying the Preclassic today are forced to rely heavily on limited data that in many instances were obtained in excavations carried out over seventy-five years ago (e.g., Vaillant 1930, 1931, 1935). Consequently quite significant gaps exist in the archaeological knowledge of the region.

In addition, until the commonly accepted and widely used Preclassic chronology of the Basin of Mexico/central Mexico was corrected by Tolstoy and Paradis (1970) and further refined by Niederberger (1987), the sequence was seriously flawed (e.g., Niederberger 2000:171–73), leading to the erroneous dating of sites and faulty interpretations. Although the sequence has now been nicely rectified, there are nevertheless occasions when ghosts of the obsolete chronology and interpretations seem to still haunt some perceptions about the central Mexican Preclassic.

The primary geographic focus of this chapter is the Basin of Mexico (the present-day Federal District and some portions of the state of Mexico), together with the state of Morelos to the south of the Basin (Fig. 3.1). The Preclassic period of these two areas of the central highlands has received more archaeological attention and therefore presents the best current picture of highland Preclassic cultural developments. Because of the lack of sufficient data, the states of Guerrero, Puebla, and Tlaxcala (Fig. 3.2) are only briefly discussed. In addition, because the rise of the Monte Alban state in the Valley of Oaxaca, 300 km to the south, presents a valuable comparative data set, the organizers of this volume have asked that Oaxaca also be briefly discussed in the summary portion of this chapter. Finally, no effort is made in the pages that follow to explain the rise of Teotihuacan. Instead this chapter focuses on the major Preclassic sites in the central highlands and any developments there that may have been relevant to the origins of Teotihuacan. It also points out some developments that might seem potentially significant, but ultimately were not.

THE CENTRAL MEXICAN LANDSCAPE

The central Mexican states of Morelos, Puebla, Tlaxcala, and Guerrero (Figs. 3.1, 3.2) are blessed with temperate to subtropical climates and fertile river valleys that provided excellent conditions for Preclassic farmers. Today their

3.1. Map of Central Mexican Preclassic period archaeological sites mentioned in this chapter.

village sites are abundant in those areas, although few have been seriously investigated. Preclassic villages likewise occurred in the Basin of Mexico, although its 2200 m elevation (7200 ft.) and colder climate presented somewhat greater risks for those early agriculturists. However, the risks of farming were perhaps off-set by the rich lacustrine resources provided by the lake system that dominated the Basin's floor. Interestingly, the Teotihuacan state developed in a more arid and marginal area of the northern Basin, approximately 20 km to the east of the lake.

Central Mexico is characterized by a great ecological diversity and geological complexity that produced an abundant and varied set of natural

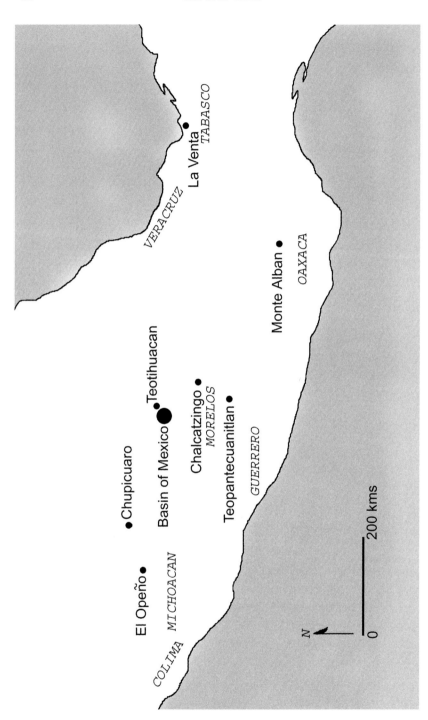

3.2. Map of some of the major Preclassic period sites and states (in italics) mentioned in the chapter.

resources and materials which were exploited by its prehispanic populations, including those of the Preclassic. The uneven distribution of those resources, even within the same valley system, meant that individual villages frequently had access to very different resources and commodities than did their neighbors. Such differences underlay the exchange networks that developed to circulate commodities desired locally, regionally, and interregionally (e.g., Niederberger 2000:186–87; Sanders and Price 1968:188–94). Importantly, as will be mentioned several times in this chapter, those interregional interaction networks underwent reorganizations and major shifts in regional emphases over the span of the Preclassic.

THE EARLY PRECLASSIC (CA. 1400–900 BCE)

In the Basin of Mexico the Early Preclassic is known primarily from excavations at two sites, Tlatilco and Tlapacoya. Tlatilco, in the western Basin, is the most extensively excavated Early Preclassic site in central Mexico, and the site dominates discussions in the literature of the Preclassic in the Basin of Mexico. Tlatilco is often believed to have been a special settlement, unusually large for its time, and to have been a major center (e.g., Niederberger 1996:173–74). Tlapacoya, across the Basin on the southeastern lakeshore, lags far behind its western neighbor in fame. While the two sites provide the majority of the Early Preclassic period archaeological data for the Basin, their data sets are unfortunately difficult to compare. Furthermore, today the Tlatilco area lies beneath the high-rise office buildings and apartment complexes of western Mexico City; the archaeological site no longer exists. Most of the Tlapacoya area has suffered a similar fate.

Tlatilco came to light in the late 1930s when collectors, such as artists Diego Rivera and Miguel Covarrubias, began visiting brickyards in the vicinity of the village of San Luis Tlatilco to purchase ceramic vessels and figurines that were being found by brickyard workers during their clay mining operations. Those ceramic objects had been burial furniture associated with human skeletal remains. Covarrubias recognized the importance and antiquity of the graves being unearthed at Tlatilco, and he was largely responsible for initiating the first archaeological excavations there in 1942 (Covarrubias 1943). Additional excavations were occasionally carried out at Tlatilco until 1969 (García Moll et al. 1991:10–12; Ochoa Castillo 2003:17–22; Porter 1953:18). Those projects were dedicated to uncovering burials and were carried out on the remaining patches of land not yet destroyed by the expanding mining activities of the various brick yards. In addition, except for the publication by García Moll et alia (1991), most excavations there were poorly reported. It is therefore difficult to estimate the quantity of burials uncovered by official excavations and, of course, the brickyard workers' finds, but the number may exceed one thousand. No architecture, either domestic or public, was ever detected at Tlatilco, although Porter (1953:34) mentions that "steps and terraces can be seen in the profiles of fresh cuts," and Tolstoy (1989a:102, fig. 6.7) makes a strong case that the graves had been sub-floor interments in domestic structures.

In contrast, the Tlapacoya data base was obtained by research that was primarily aimed at refining the Preclassic stratigraphic sequence for the site and the Basin. The excavations at Tlapacoya (also known as Zo-hapilco) were quite successful in that goal and today provide much of the basic Early and Middle Preclassic chronological sequence for the Basin of Mexico (Niederberger 1976, 1987; see also Gámez Eternod 1993). However, no burial assemblages or architecture were recovered there. Furthermore, in my opinion, the ceramic assemblage of Tlapacoya (e.g., Niederberger 1976:109–232; 1987, 1996) appears to have some significant differences with the assemblage at Tlatilco in the western Basin. Thus, if Tlapacoya and Tlatilco are taken as representative of their respective areas of the Basin, the Early Preclassic "cultures" of the eastern and western Basin were some-what different (e.g., Grove 2000b:133–34), and therefore their Preclassic developmental trajectories may have been different as well. However, we may never know because the Early and Middle Preclassic of the eastern Basin remains virtually unknown and the region is being rapidly engulfed by urban expansion.

There is another problem. Tlatilco has been privileged in the literature to the extent that developments elsewhere in the central highlands go un-recognized by many scholars. The state of Morelos, immediately to the south of the Basin of Mexico, is one of those areas often overlooked. For thirty years I have pointed out that the ceramic assemblage at Early Preclas-sic sites across all of Morelos is essentially identical to what was found at Tlatilco (Grove 1974b:3–4; 1981a:383; 2006, 2007b), and I continue to use the term "Tlatilco culture" to refer to that closely shared assemblage. Only a few Tlatilco culture sites are known in the western Basin, and I would not include the eastern Basin site of Tlapacoya as within the Tlatilco culture sphere. However, Tlatilco culture sites are abundant along the subtropical river valleys of Morelos.

The characteristics of Tlatilco culture ceramics in Morelos and the Basin include specular-red-on-brown vessels (usually bottles) that are frequently decorated in a smudge resist technique and a variety of exotic vessel forms in both specular-red-on-brown and brown wares, including tubular-spouted and stirrup-spouted bottles. A very minor part of the Tlatilco culture assemblage (<3–5%) consists of vessels decorated with "Olmec motifs." However, that minor percentage receives virtually 100 percent of the attention in publications and in interpretations concerning Early Preclassic central Mexico, its development, and its interactions. This is because of a sixty-year-old assumption that those motifs are somehow directly Olmec-related. In addition, some scholars still assert that the presence of the Olmec-like pottery in the highlands is "linked with the dissemination of the social, political, and religious institutions of the Olmec" (Blomster et al. 2005:1068). However, that hypothesis has never been adequately modeled for testing, and many scholars strongly disagree with it (e.g., Flannery et al. 2005). Nonetheless, the hypothesis is relevant to a question posed in the introduction to this chapter and paraphrased here: Did the central Mexican region's interactions with the Gulf coast Olmec introduce "social, political, and religious institutions" that persisted over time and were somehow relevant to regional highland developments that led ultimately to the Teotihuacan state? As is discussed below, Early, Middle, and Late Preclassic archaeological data offer no support for this suggestion.

Significantly, a few of the Tlatilco culture sites in Morelos contain public architecture, the earliest known in central Mexico. Public architecture is rare in Early Preclassic Mesoamerica, and therefore it is usually taken as an archaeological signature of complexity. Thus it is a trait I will follow in this chapter as I review Preclassic developments in Mexico's central highlands. One site with public architecture is Chalcatzingo, in the Amatzinac Valley of eastern Morelos. Although best known for its Middle Preclassic period bas-relief rock art, Chalcatzingo was also an important center during the Early Preclassic. At that time it manifested the standard Tlatilco culture ceramic assemblage, although the Olmec-like sherds made up less than one percent of the assemblage there.

Two examples of Early Preclassic platform mounds, one of which is stone-faced, were identified in excavations at the site (Avíles 2000; Prindi-

ville and Grove 1987:63–65). Was that Early Preclassic architecture autochthonous, or could it somehow have been Olmec inspired? The latter
hypothesis seems highly unlikely because nothing remotely comparable
in the way of Early Preclassic stone-faced architecture has been found at
Olmec sites (it does occur later at Middle Preclassic La Venta). Nor, in fact,
has anything similar been published for Early Preclassic sites elsewhere in
the central highlands of Mexico. Chalcatzingo's architecture is precocious
and seems to have been a local innovation. The nearest similar architecture
occurs at San José Mogote, Oaxaca (Structures 1 and 2; Marcus and Flannery 1996:109, fig. 113), but there is nothing in Chalcatzingo's Early Preclassic artifact record to link the site to Oaxaca.

     With the above in mind, I question whether interregional interac-
tions between the Morelos-Basin of Mexico region and other areas have
been properly understood. Nobody doubts that there were two-way interregional interactions with the Gulf coast region (i.e., the Olmec) during
the Early Preclassic. At a minimum, those interactions involved trade in
obsidian, ceramics, and even bitumen (*chapapote*; Wendt and Lu 2006:92).
However, central Mexico was involved in interactions with other regions
as well, but those have frequently been overlooked by archaeologists with
their gaze turned solely to the southeast. The vast majority of the decorated and exotic ceramics of the Tlatilco culture sphere suggest a much
more significant and closer relationship with a very different area of Mesoamerica—West Mexico. The exotic bottle forms and specular red-on-brown
ceramics of Tlatilco culture have strong similarities to the precocious Early
Preclassic period ceramics and figurines of the Capacha complex of Colima,
Michoacán, and Jalisco (Greengo and Meighan 1976; Kelly 1980), and more
particularly with the ceramics of El Opeño, Michoacán (Oliveros 1974,
2004:76–111). Furthermore, 10% of the obsidian tested from Early Preclassic settlements in the Basin of Mexico was found to come from sources in
Michoacán (Boksenbaum et al. 1987: table 3; Healan 1997: table 1). Those
interactions with western Mexico cannot be disregarded in any serious
consideration of the developments and interrelationships that took place
in Early Preclassic central Mexico (see also Baus and Ochoa 1989; Grove
1974b:60; 2006:110–11; 2007b:219–20; Tolstoy 1971:26).

     To summarize this section, I suggest that interpretations of the Early
Preclassic of the Basin and Morelos have privileged Tlatilco as a site and
have concurrently privileged the "Olmec-like" ceramics in the Tlatilco cul-

ture assemblage, thereby creating a distorted view of Early Preclassic developments in the highlands. Instead, the available data suggest to me that the major developments of the Early Preclassic in that region probably took place in the warmer subtropical landscape of Morelos rather than in the Basin of Mexico. Early Preclassic sites in Morelos seem to surpass those of the Basin in quantity and in architectural complexity as well. Furthermore, the overall interregional interaction patterns appear to have been focused westward toward Michoacán rather than in a southeastwardly (Gulf coast Olmec) direction. However, it is regrettable that data on the true nature of Tlatilco as a settlement are lacking. We will never know if it had been an unusually large mega-site, as often represented, or if instead the brickyard workers and archaeological projects there had actually uncovered the remains of perhaps three smaller, separate villages (Grove 1981a:382; 2006, 2007b:218–19). Those smaller settlements would be more in line with the size of Tlatilco culture sites in Morelos. However, due to the incomplete archaeological record in the Basin, there will always be uncertainty.

THE MIDDLE PRECLASSIC (CA. 900–500 BCE)

The Middle Preclassic across Mesoamerica can be described as a period of emerging elites and evolving complexity (e.g., Grove 2000b:137–39; Grove and Gillespie 1992:29–30). In central Mexico it is marked in the archaeological record by different pottery styles, a substantial increase in greenstone objects, and in a few areas, an increase in public architecture. In the Basin of Mexico and Morelos, the red-on-brown and exotic Tlatilco culture ceramics (including the <3–5% "Olmec-motif" vessels) gave way to a much plainer ceramic complex that includes white ware bowls with rims decorated with linear motifs (often lumped together under the rubric "double-line-break"). Figurine types also changed. Stratigraphic data from Tlapacoya (Niederberger 1976, 1987) inform us that the changes from Early to Middle Preclassic assemblages there occurred as a gradual transition. The same is probably true of the central highlands in general.

An important component in the material culture of the Middle Preclassic period is greenstone and jadeite jewelry and implements. Those objects include items of personal adornment, celts, and perforators. Such greenstone is found only rarely in Early Preclassic contexts, but it became more abundant in the Middle Preclassic as an "exotic" that generally seems to have been restricted to people of elite rank. The occurrence of greenstone and other exotics at central Mexican sites indicates the presence of new or restructured interregional exchange networks. The nearest good sources of quality greenstone occur in Guerrero (e.g., Mastache 1988:197), but it seems probable that some of the high quality greenstone found at central Mexican sites such as Chalcatzingo (Thomson 1987) may well have originated at sources in southern Mesoamerica.

Unfortunately, most of the areas in the western Basin of Mexico that would have been preferred by Preclassic agriculturalists have been covered by Mexico City and its suburbs, while the eastern Basin is underexplored yet rapidly urbanizing. Consequently, archaeological knowledge of the Middle Preclassic in the Basin still relies heavily on the data recovered by Vaillant's excavations at El Arbolillo and Zacatenco (Vaillant 1930, 1935) eight decades ago. Those data are somewhat supplemented by research in the southern Basin (Serra Puche 1988, 1989; Ramírez et al. 2000) and salvage archaeology (Castillo Mangas et al. 1993; Pulido Méndez et al. 1993; Sánchez Vásquez et al. 1993). Important supplementary data are provided by the surface survey projects conducted by Sanders, Parsons, and others (e.g., Sanders et al. 1979). However, many of those surveys were carried out before the Basin's Preclassic ceramic chronology was refined by Tolstoy and Paradis (1970) and by Niederberger (1987). The Basin surveys identified 8 large Middle Preclassic villages, 11 small villages, and 49 hamlets (Sanders et al. 1979:96). However, we will never know the quantity or complexity of the sites that had been destroyed by urbanization prior to those surveys. Nevertheless, with that caveat in mind, what are lacking in the available data from both survey and excavation are any clear markers of developing complexity, such as public architecture, one or more large central place settlements, or any other evidence of significant site hierarchies. Once again, those markers do occur in Morelos, as well as in the states of Guerrero and Tlaxcala.

While most known Middle Preclassic sites in Morelos and Guerrero are as undistinctive as their Basin counterparts, three stand out as extraordinary: Chalcatzingo; the newly discovered site of Zazacatla, Morelos; and Teopantecuanitlan, Guerrero. All three are atypical in two ways: they have abundant public (mound) architecture and sophisticated carved stone art. Their stone art clearly has some Olmec antecedents, but their architecture has no similarities to anything known on the Gulf coast and may represent indigenous central Mexican innovations. Be that as it may, once again the signs of complexity in the central Mexican highlands are found outside of the Basin rather than in the Basin itself. However, as will be discussed below, the possibility exists that such complexity may have been present at the problematic site of Cuicuilco in the southern Basin.

Chalcatzingo, in the Amatzinac Valley of eastern Morelos, was the valley's major Middle Preclassic center, at the top of a three-tiered site hierarchy (Hirth 1987a, 1987b). Chalcatzingo and at least three other Middle Preclassic Amatzinac Valley sites—Telixtac, Las Pilas, and Campana de Oro—are notable for having public architecture (Hirth 1987a:356; 1987b:510–11, 519; Majewski 1987).

Middle Preclassic Chalcatzingo was a dispersed settlement that spread across a wide terraced landscape (Grove 1984; Grove [ed.] 1987b). Dominating the village was a massive earthen platform mound, ca. 70 m long and over 7 m in height, the largest example of public architecture known in Middle Preclassic central Mexico. Significantly, the Middle Preclassic mound represents a series of rebuildings and enlargements of one of the site's Early Preclassic mounds, demonstrating a continuum of increasing complexity at Chalcatzingo. Three stone-faced Middle Preclassic platform mounds, with associated stone monuments, occur on separate terraces nearby, as does a large, stone-faced sunken patio containing an Olmec-style tabletop altar-throne (e.g., Fash 1987; Grove 1984:49–68; 2005; Prindiville and Grove 1987a:63–66). The altar-throne is just one example of the wide variety of stone monuments that occur at the site. Over 35 carvings have been found at Chalcatzingo (Grove 2005, 2007a:34; Grove and Angulo 1987; Córdova Tello and Meza Rodríguez 2007), a number exceeded in Middle Preclassic Mesoamerica only at La Venta. A few carvings at Chalcatzingo and La Venta share certain iconographic motifs (such as paired quetzal birds) that indicate a special relationship of some sort existed between the two centers (Grove 1989b:133–36). At the same time, however, other iconography in the monuments seems to be local, unique to Chalcatzingo.

Among the monuments at Chalcatzingo are a dozen stelae (both broken and complete; Grove 2005; Grove and Angulo 1987). This is the largest quantity of carved stelae known at any Middle Preclassic Mesoamerican site. One of those stelae (Monument 26) was found in association with a round altar (Monument 25) (Grove and Angulo 1987:128–29, figs. 9.23, 9.24), a pairing more common at Late Preclassic Izapa and Classic period lowland Maya sites. Although a series of plain stela–round altar pairs have been discovered at the Middle Preclassic (Las Charcas phase) site of Naranjo in the Maya highlands (see Love, this volume), the two Chalcatzingo monuments are the oldest carved stela–round altar combination presently known in Mesoamerica. They are examples of what I have called Chalcatzingo's "southern connection" (Grove 1989b:141–42), that is, objects and traits with similarities to those of southern Mesoamerica. A second example is the Maya-like scroll-and-mat design on Monument 34, a stela excavated in 1998 (Gillespie n.d.; Grove 2005:29–30). A third and different example is the Peralta Orange pottery type at Chalcatzingo. Peralta Orange is not a highland central Mexican ceramic type, and although locally manufactured at Chalcatzingo, its closest similarities seem to be with Mamom phase orange wares of the Maya lowlands and certain ceramic types of Chiapas and the Gulf coast (Cyphers 1987:231–34). These traits at Chalcatzingo suggest interactions with the south, but perhaps via networks that bypassed the Gulf coast Olmec (see also Pye and Gutiérrez 2007).

Guerrero's analogue to Chalcatzingo is the site of Teopantecuanitlan. Located approximately 80 mountainous kilometers south of Chalcatzingo, Teopantecuanitlan is situated at the junction of two of the major rivers that drain the central highlands, the Río Amacuzac and the Río Balsas. Teopantecuanitlan's Middle Preclassic architecture includes platform mounds with unusual stone-facing (Martínez Donjuán 1994: figs. 9.18, 9.19) and a large stone-faced sunken patio decorated with four monolithic Olmec-like faces carved in bas-relief (ibid., figs. 9.12–9.14). The site's location at the junction of two major riverine arteries is certainly not coincidental, and the center must have played a major role in regional and interregional exchange networks. Not only does Teopantecuanitlan provide evidence of interactions with Chalcatzingo via a limited set of architectural and iconographic motifs (Grove 1987a:429; 1989b:142–45), but two of Teopantecuanitlan's stone monuments—an Izapa-like frog "altar" and a large non-Olmec stone head similar to those from the Pacific piedmont of Guatemala (Martínez Donjuán 1994: figs. 9.16, 9.17)—suggest that a "southern connection" occurred there as well (see also Pye and Gutiérrez 2007).

The third site with public architecture and Olmec-like stone carvings is Zazacatla, in western Morelos about 15 km south of the city of Cuernavaca and 50 km to the west of Chalcatzingo. It is a recent discovery and was brought to light by salvage operations carried out prior to the construction of a large warehouse. Middle Preclassic platform mounds with Teopantecuanitlan-like stone facings were uncovered, but the biggest surprise was the discovery of two stone statues, each ca. 60 cm tall, and both strongly in the La Venta Olmec style (Canto Aguilar and Castro Mendoza 2007). The statues are quite different from those known at Chalcatzingo, and Zazacatla's ceramics are apparently somewhat different as well (Canto Aguilar, pers. comm., 2007).

In contrast to Morelos and northern Guerrero, the majority of the Basin of Mexico seems to lack any clear archaeological evidence of complexity during the Middle Preclassic. However, a major unresolved question concerns the nature of the Basin site of Cuicuilco. Cuicuilco is situated on what once was the largest expanse of good agricultural land in the southern Basin, and by 200 BCE it may have been the largest Late Preclassic center in the Basin / Morelos region of the highlands. The site, with an immense circular pyramid ca. 80 m in diameter and over 20 m in height, covered perhaps 400 ha and could have had a population of 20,000 (Sanders et al. 1979:99).

Late Preclassic Cuicuilco is thought by many to have been central Mexico's first major urban center. However, while seemingly at its prime, Cuicuilco was devastated by a massive lava flow emanating from the Xitle volcano, a mere 7 km to the south. A thick mantle of lava covered most of the site, leaving only the top of the circular pyramid exposed. Today that cap of lava thwarts any serious attempts at archaeological research to understand the size, nature, and time depth of the site, thus rendering Cuicuilco enigmatic in many ways.

Was there a significant settlement at Cuicuilco also during the Middle Preclassic? That question is highly pertinent to any consideration of developing complexity in the Basin, and the answer has been elusive. In 1957 Robert Heizer and James Bennyhoff worked for about a month at a modern lava quarry at Cuicuilco (Heizer and Bennyhoff 1958, 1972). Their investigations recovered some Middle Preclassic ceramics and noted evidence of buried structures, including clay-surfaced earthen platforms which they believed dated to the Middle Preclassic. From their investigations they proposed that Cuicuilco had been a "major ceremonial center" at that time and that the "basal platform" of the circular pyramid dated to that period (Heizer and Bennyhoff 1972:98). That is an intriguing possibility, but no supporting data were ever published and for three decades the Heizer and Bennyhoff proposition remained unverified.

However, a recent general article on the site by archaeologist Mario Pérez Campa (2007), who has been investigating Cuicuilco and its massive circular pyramid, seems to confirm that the pyramid's initial stages do indeed date to the Middle Preclassic (Pérez Campa 2007:42; see also Pastrana 1997). Therefore, although the supporting data remain to be published, it may be the case that Cuicuilco, in the southern Basin, had attained a level of complexity during the Middle Preclassic that is not presently evident in the archaeological record elsewhere in the Basin. Of course, that raises new questions. If Cuicuilco had indeed been a significant center during the Middle Preclassic, what relationship and interactions, if any, did it have with the important sites of Chalcatzingo, Zazacatla, or Teopantecuanitlan? Only excavations at Cuicuilco can begin to provide answers.

In summarizing the Middle Preclassic it should be noted that one of the most significant aspects of the Middle Preclassic archaeological record of the Basin of Mexico and Morelos is the disappearance of the strong interactions with western Mexico that characterized the Early Preclassic. With the Middle Preclassic there seems to have been a marked shift to a pattern that strongly emphasized interactions with southern Mesoamerica and the Gulf coast. However, that southern emphasis seems to end ca. 500 BCE, as Chalcatzingo and Teopantecuanitlan (and presumably Zazacatla) faded away and were replaced by other sites in their regions that rose to the status of centers. Was their demise somehow related to the decline of La Venta (also poorly understood) and its interaction networks, or merely reflective of the general changes that were sweeping non-Maya Mesoamerica; or were all those changes somehow related?

Whatever the cause, the outcome was significant, for with the end of Chalcatzingo and Teopantecuanitlan, the creation of stone monuments and the use of Olmec-like iconography and the various traits related to a "southern connection" likewise disappeared in central Mexico. Unlike the situation on Mesoamerica's southern Pacific coast (e.g., Izapa, Takalik Abaj), no Late Preclassic heritage of monumental art continued in central Mexico. In other words, it appears that Chalcatzingo, Teopantecuanitlan, and Zazacatla left no "Olmec legacy" for central Mexico's Late Preclassic societies. Their Gulf coast and southern connections were ultimately quite ephemeral.

Significantly, Cuicuilco, in the southern Basin of Mexico, did not decline but continued as a settlement and flourished. That fact suggests that perhaps Middle Preclassic Cuicuilco had not participated significantly in the interaction networks that had linked Morelos and Guerrero with southern Mesoamerica and the Olmec domain.

THE LATE PRECLASSIC (CA. 500 BCE–100 CE)

The Late Preclassic is probably the least understood period in central Mexico, and yet it is obviously also the most crucial in terms of understanding the origins of states there. In central Mexico, and Mesoamerica in general, the Late Preclassic begins ca. 500 BCE and is characterized by a substantial restructuring of regional political organizations, site hierarchies, and interaction networks. New centers rose to prominence, and there was a significant nucleation of population around those centers. Pyramid architecture became abundant, and new pottery and figurine types appeared. In the Basin of Mexico and Morelos the ceramics once again show strong similarities to ceramic complexes to the northwest, and in particular with the Chupicuaro phenomenon of eastern Michoacán and western Guanajuato. In addition, whereas for the Early and Middle Preclassic the best evidence of the trajectory of increasing complexity is found outside of the Basin, the opposite is true of the Late Preclassic. At that time the Basin became a major focal point for developing complexity, as seen at Cuicuilco and somewhat later at Teotihuacan.

Although the site of Cuicuilco is covered by a thick cap of lava, enough is known about its Late Preclassic manifestation to confirm that early in that period Cuicuilco was already a proto-urban settlement and probably the largest center in the Basin. In addition to the site's huge circular pyramid, several other large Late Preclassic rectangular pyramid structures were exposed in 1968 when a large area of lava was removed to permit the construction of apartment complexes (the Villa Olímpica). In addition, there is archaeological evidence for Late Preclassic irrigation canals near the site (Palerm 1972).

In the initial centuries of the Late Preclassic the Basin's population growth seems to have taken place primarily in the southern area (e.g., Cuicuilco, Tlapacoya [Barba de Piña Chan 1956]). The northern Basin and Teotihuacan Valley did not match the southern developments, and a variety of environmental and climatic factors may account for that. Whatever the reasons, until ca. 300 BCE "the far northern Basin remained almost uninhabited" (Sanders et al. 1979:97). However, between 300 and 100 BCE, significant changes were also under way in the northern Basin. By 100 BCE, in the Patlachique phase of Teotihuacan, two separate settlements near large springs in the Teotihuacan Valley had begun growing, and they ultimately coalesced into what Sanders and colleagues (1979:101) identify as a "regional center, covering 6–8 square kilometers, with an estimated population of 20,000–40,000 and containing elaborate public architecture" (see also Cowgill 1974:381–82; Millon 1973:51–52 for similar estimates).

It has been commonly accepted that until the destruction of Cuicuilco by lava, Cuicuilco and the nascent Teotihuacan may have briefly been "balanced powers" at opposite ends of the Basin (e.g., Evans and Berlo 1992:6). Of course, the devastation of Cuicuilco by the Xitle lava would have ended the balance of power, with Teotihuacan continuing to develop to become the single most important urban center in the highlands. However, because Cuicuilco is obscured by lava, even understanding the destruction of that site has proven difficult. When did the Xitle eruption take place?

Based upon several early radiocarbon assays, for several decades it was commonly assumed that the Xitle eruption occurred ca.100 BCE. In addition, some scholars suggested that there had been two eruptions of Xitle, with the first only partly damaging Cuicuilco, thus allowing the site to continue for several hundred years into the Classic period until a second eruption brought total devastation to the center (e.g., Blanton et al. 1981; Heizer and Bennyhoff 1972:101–2). Others believe that the destruction was a one time and complete event. For discussions of the various radiocarbon dates and theories see Gonzalez et alia (2000:217) and Siebe (2000:57–59).

Recent investigations have clarified the situation somewhat. Geologic research has shown that Xitle was a monogenetic volcano, a type of volcano that erupts only one time. Thus Xitle could not have sent lava over Cuicuilco in two different eruptions separated by centuries. It is nevertheless possible that other volcanic activity in the region, such as the major eruption of the volcano Popocatepetl at ca. 200–100 BCE (Gonzalez et al. 2000:223; Siebe 2000:61) and/or other regional volcanic activity (e.g., Cordova et al. 1994:594–95; Sanders et al. 1979:106), could have impacted regional geomorphology and affected sites across the southern Basin, including Cuicuilco.

Of equal significance is the fact that two recent independent sets of research at Cuicuilco have provided data indicating that the site's destruction took place several centuries more recently than previously imagined. Radiocarbon dates discussed by Cordova et alia (1994) suggest the Xitle eruption occurred ca. 400 CE. Those researchers also believe that Cuicuilco had already been in decline by 150 CE (Cordova et al. 1994:593–94). In contrast, radiocarbon assays by Gonzalez et alia (2000) suggest the flow covering

Cuicuilco dates to ca. 280 CE. Those investigators also believe that "the abandonment of Cuicuilco was the direct result of the birth and activity of Xitle" (Gonzalez et al. 2000:208; see also Pastrana 1997 and Seibe 2000). Although not in complete agreement, the implications of both sets of dates are nevertheless significant. Teotihuacan was not a fledgling settlement at the time Cuicuilco was devastated by Xitle's lavas; it was already a huge city.

THE ORIGINS OF THE STATE IN OAXACA: ARE THERE PARALLELS?

In contrast to what we know of the Basin/Morelos region, the Preclassic period archaeological record of the Valley of Oaxaca is richly documented. The regional surveys by Blanton et alia (1981:43–75; 1982) and excavations carried out at San José Mogote and other valley sites by Flannery, Marcus, and their collaborators (e.g., Flannery and Marcus [eds.] 1983, 1994; Marcus and Flannery 1996:71–171) present a much more complete and coherent picture of developments there.

The earliest archaeological evidence for a Preclassic period agricultural settlement in the Valley of Oaxaca is the Espiridión Complex (1900?–1400 BCE) at San José Mogote. Although only a small sample of sherds and a few postholes were uncovered (Flannery and Marcus 1994:45–54; Marcus and Flannery 1996:75), they nonetheless mark the beginnings of village life in the valley. From then on the growth and development in the Valley of Oaxaca are nicely documented by archaeological research, which presents a picture of continuity throughout the Early and Middle Preclassic period. However, a major disjunction at the Middle Preclassic/Late Preclassic interface in the Valley of Oaxaca once again raises more questions than answers about the origins of the state in that region.

The Espiridión Complex is followed by the Tierras Largas phase (1400–1150 BCE), documented at nearly twenty sites including San José Mogote. At that time San José Mogote had a population of perhaps 200–300 people (Flannery and Marcus:1994:55–133; Marcus and Flannery 1996:78–79). In addition to domestic structures, the Tierras Largas phase village at San José Mogote was beginning to differ in complexity from its contemporaries, as evidenced by the settlement's size and the presence of public architecture there—rectangular buildings with lime-plastered floors (Flannery and Marcus 1976b:209–11; Marcus and Flannery 1996:87–88). Social differentiation continued and grew in the following San José phase (1150–850 BCE), when it is clear that San José Mogote was a chiefly center (e.g., Blanton et al. 1981:50–63) with a population of perhaps 1000 individuals (Marcus and Flannery 1996:106). New forms of public architecture appeared, including platforms faced with stone or adobes (Flannery and Marcus 1976b:211–12; Marcus and Flannery 1996:109–110). Greenstone jewelry was found with some burials of this phase. Craft production at the site included iron ore mirrors that were traded locally and interregionally. Pottery includes a small percentage of "Olmec" designs, which seem to be differentially distributed in different areas (*barrios*) of the settlement (Flannery and Marcus 1994:135–286; Marcus and Flannery 1996:93–106; Pyne 1976).

In the subsequent Middle Preclassic Guadalupe (850–700 BCE) and Rosario (700–500 BCE) phases at San José Mogote, the settlement increased in complexity and maintained its role as a major chiefly center (Blanton et al. 1981:63–65; Flannery and Marcus 1976b:13–15; Marcus and Flannery 1996:111–35). What happened next, however, at ca. 500 BCE, is perhaps best summed up in the words of Marcus and Flannery (1996:139): "At the end of the Rosario phase…San José Mogote, the largest community in the valley for more than 800 years, suddenly lost most of its population." And apparently simultaneously, a new center arose in the Valley of Oaxaca, the hilltop site of Monte Alban (Blanton et al. 1999:62–67; Marcus and Flannery 1996:139–46).

The disjunctive transition from Middle to Late Preclassic in the Valley of Oaxaca seemingly parallels events occurring elsewhere in Mesoamerica at that same time: the major reorganization that characterizes the beginning of the Late Preclassic. What seems different in the case of Monte Alban is that within about a century it had unified the Valley of Oaxaca and had perhaps become Mesoamerica's first state (Blanton et al. 1981:65–75; Marcus and Flannery 1996:139–94). An interesting aspect of the rise of the Monte Alban state is the possibility that it was linked to conquest warfare (Spencer 2003; Spencer and Redmond 2004:175–84).

Do the data on Preclassic developments in the Valley of Oaxaca compare at all to those from central Mexico? The answers depend upon the areas of central Mexico being considered. Although Chalcatzingo and San José Mogote were very different types of settlements and regional centers, their temporal spans correspond well. Both have Early Preclassic beginnings and both declined at ca. 500 BCE and were replaced by new regional centers. But there the parallels stop. The significant developments of the Late Preclassic did not take place at another center in Morelos, but rather at two sites in the Basin of Mexico, Cuicuilco and (later) Teotihuacan. Unfortunately, the lava capping the settlement at Cuicuilco masks any good evidence of the site's early development. There may have been continuity from the Middle to Late Preclassic there, and if so, then the Cuicuilco situation differs from that at Chalcatzingo or San José Mogote. Rather than declining or disappearing at ca. 500 BCE, Cuicuilco continued and flourished, and it was probably the Basin's most important center in the early centuries of the Late Preclassic.

Comparisons with the Valley of Oaxaca data are more difficult for the Teotihuacan area of the northern Basin of Mexico. We cannot speak of settlement continuity or of a local evolution of complexity there because no evidence exists of any Early or Middle Preclassic settlements at Teotihuacan. It is in that sense, however, that Teotihuacan is comparable to Monte Alban, for both arose on previously unsettled lands. With the emergence of Teotihuacan at ca. 300 BCE, Cuicuilco had a potential competitor, although the centers were on the far distant extremes of a large lake and 70 km apart by land. The question is, what was the relationship between the two centers? Were there serious conflicts between them (e.g., Diehl 1976:279)? Did both centers seek to expand their spheres of influence (Sanders et al. 1979:103)? The same questions can be asked regarding Teotihuacan and contemporary centers in Tlaxcala and Puebla. Nevertheless, at the moment any evidence of warfare or conflict is circumstantial and tenuous (see Spencer and Redmond 2004:191–92). While warfare may have had a role in the development of the Monte Alban state, there presently are no good data suggesting that it also had a similar role at Teotihuacan.

THE UNCERTAIN PATHWAY TO TEOTIHUACAN

What traits truly provide evidence of complexity during the Early Preclassic period in central Mexico? For decades Tlatilco was seen as more complex and a central place because it had "Olmec" pottery, and its neighbors (Zacatenco, El Arbolillo) did not. However, when the Basin chronology was clarified by Tolstoy and Paradis (1970), the differences between those sites were seen instead to be chronological, not hierarchical (e.g., Grove 1974b:1–2; Niederberger 2000:171–93). This chapter has used public architecture, instead of "Olmec" motifs on pottery, as a more unequivocal attribute of developing complexity. With regard to that trait, Early Preclassic Morelos presently appears to have had an edge over the Basin of Mexico, because we do not have good archaeological evidence of what really existed at Tlatilco, Tlapacoya, or elsewhere in the Basin at that time. Nevertheless, even if Tlatilco had been one unusually large settlement and/or did contain public architecture that was undetected by archaeological research, then following its decline ca. 900 BCE nothing comparable in site size or complexity (i.e., with public architecture) seems to have replaced it locally or elsewhere in the Basin. In other words, we do not have evidence of a direct pathway from Tlatilco to Teotihuacan. Or, does a Middle Preclassic successor to Tlatilco lie hidden beneath the lava at Cuicuilco?

The rich agricultural, lacustrine, and natural resource potential of both the Basin of Mexico and Morelos were attractive to early agriculturalists, but do not in and of themselves explain the evolution of complexity in that region. However, beyond this subsistence model, there are presently also two popular viewpoints to explain the origins of central Mexico's complexity. One interprets the presence of pottery with "Olmec" motifs as indicative of Gulf coast influences that stimulated sociopolitical complexity there (and elsewhere; e.g., Blomster et al. 2005; Tolstoy 1989b). The opposing view (e.g., Demarest 1989; Flannery and Marcus 2000; Flannery et al. 2005; Grove 1989a) interprets local and regional highland developments as autochthonous until demonstrated otherwise. I believe that the complexity at Chalcatzingo during the Early Preclassic can best be explained by the latter approach, particularly because the Early Preclassic ceramic vessels and figurines of Morelos and the Basin of Mexico show their strongest similarities to those of West Mexico, not the Gulf coast.

The Middle Preclassic saw expanding populations and a transformation to much more southward-oriented interaction networks. Because so much of my research has been dedicated to Chalcatzingo, the changes there are quite striking to me. The greatest change was, of course, the adoption and creation of Olmec-like stone monumental art at the site. But take away those monuments, and in its material culture Chalcatzingo becomes very little different from the Basin sites of Zacatenco and El Arbolillo. In sum, Chalcatzingo had some form of significant two-way interaction with the Gulf coast Olmec and most probably the site of La Venta. I certainly attribute the adoption of stone monuments by Middle Preclassic Chalcatzingo to its Gulf coast interactions. However, Chalcatzingo was inhabited by central Mexican peoples who seem to have had a strong sense of independence, for they manipulated monumental art in their own way (e.g., Grove 1999:287–88; 2000a; 2007b:220). They were not merely emulating La Venta Olmecs. Furthermore, the site's massive Middle Preclassic earthen platform mound has its beginning stages in the Early Preclassic and represents local continuity rather than a new external "influence." Likewise, the smaller Middle Preclassic stone-faced platform mounds share nothing with La Venta and are likewise highland innovations. As always, the major problem is a lack of comparable data elsewhere in Morelos, the Basin of Mexico, Puebla, Tlaxcala, or Guerrero (aside from Teopantecuanitlan).

Although I have not argued the case in this chapter, I believe that in the Middle Preclassic a special relationship developed between La Venta and the highland centers of Chalcatzingo and Teopantecuanitlan. I believe that it was a relationship based on the exploitation and movement of greenstone and other exotic items from Guerrero and other central Mexican regions, through Morelos and onward to the Gulf coast (e.g., Grove 1987a:438–40; 1989b:145–47). Thus I believe that Hirth's (1978) Gateway City model is still highly relevant in terms of explaining the importance of both Chalcatzingo and Teopantecuanitlan. Furthermore, it is probably not coincidental that all three centers declined and faded away at about the same time, ca. 500 BCE. Cuicuilco, in the Basin, did not decline, however, but continued into the Late Preclassic and thrived, a fact that suggests it had not been part of the Middle Preclassic Guerrero-Morelos-Gulf coast interaction network, and that it perhaps also somehow benefited from Chalcatzingo's decline.

There is, however, another element of that equation that should be taken into consideration—the poorly understood Middle Preclassic "southern connection," expressed by the presence of several different "southern" traits at the central Mexican centers of Teopantecuanitlan and Chalcatzingo. Southern interactions with central Mexico in the Middle Preclassic have not been considered in previous discussions of long-distance exchange networks vis-à-vis the origins of Maya states. Although the nature of the connection remains unclear, these contacts are nonetheless relevant to such discussions. Significantly, there are also data suggesting that a southern connection was already operative in the Early Preclassic. Greenstone beads from Early Preclassic tombs at the West Mexican site of El Opeño, Michoacán (ca. 250 miles northwest of both Chalcatzingo and Teopantecuanitlan), have been identified by the Smithsonian Institution as Motagua Valley jadeite (Arturo Oliveros, pers. comm.). If the ca. 1300 BC radiocarbon dates for El Opeño (Oliveros and Paredes 1993) are correct, then Motagua jadeite occurs earlier at that West Mexican site than at Gulf coast Olmec or central Mexican sites! This implies that the Motagua jadeite had reached El Opeño via an Early Preclassic interaction network that bypassed those other areas, perhaps via a sea route along the Pacific coast. Motagua jadeite may likewise have played a role in the Middle Preclassic southern connection, together with archaeologically less visible southern items such as cacao and quetzal feathers.

A completely new set of interactions characterize the Late Preclassic of the Basin and Morelos. Throughout that period and during the initial stages of Teotihuacan's developments, the ceramics and figurines of the Basin and Morelos once again show very strong similarities to complexes in the west, and particularly to the Chupicuaro phenomenon of eastern Michoacán and western Guanajuato. That northwest connection is strongly reflected in the pottery throughout the Basin, including at Cuicuilco, Ticoman, and the Cuanalan and Patlachique phases at Teotihuacan (e.g., Bennyhoff 1966:20–24; Heizer and Bennyhoff 1972:100–101). In fact, the figurines recovered from the 1959 investigations in the interior of the Pyramid of the Sun (Millon et al. 1965) are primarily H-type "Chupicuaro" figurines. While it is likely that the strong Chupicuaro-like roots to the Basin's Late Preclassic ceramics had little to do with the architectural foundations of Teotihuacan, their potential contributions in that or other realms (e.g., ideology) have never been seriously explored, and they serve as a reminder that the beginnings of Teotihuacan were multifaceted.

In addition to the strong Chupicuaro flavor of early Teotihuacan ceramics, Bennyhoff (1966:24) also noted several traits that might have Puebla-Tlaxcala roots. René Millon (1981:221) has likewise suggested that Late Preclassic Teotihuacan may have been strongly "influenced by peoples from the Puebla-Tlaxcala region." Unfortunately, the Early and Middle Preclassic manifestations in that region are poorly known, and thus have not been discussed in this chapter. Some Puebla-Tlaxcala Middle Preclassic sites may have public architecture (e.g., García Cook 1981:245–56), and the Late Preclassic there saw a burst of complexity that included impressively large pyramidal architecture at sites such as Cholula (Uruñuela et al. 2006), Xochitécatl (Serra Puche and Beutelspacher 1994), and Totimehuacan (Spranz 1970). Any Late

Preclassic interactions of that region with the northeastern Basin of Mexico and Teotihuacan would probably have taken place via the so-called Teotihuacan corridor that geographically links the two areas (e.g., García Cook 1981:267; Millon 1981:221). Evidence that significant interactions did occur can be seen in the fact that *talud-tablero* architecture, a trait considered a diagnostic of Classic period Teotihuacan, is present several centuries earlier in the Puebla-Tlaxcala region. Late Preclassic *talud-tablero* facades are known at Tlalancaleca (García Cook 1981:252) and decorate residential house platforms at Tetimpa, near Cholula (Plunket and Uruñuela 1998).

Was there also an "Olmec legacy" that established itself in central Mexico in the Early or Middle Preclassic periods, and then centuries later served as an underpinning of the Teotihuacan state? The disappearance in central Mexico of Olmec-like stone monumental art and iconography and "southern connection" traits with the decline of Chalcatzingo and Teopantecuanitlan at ca. 500 BCE, together with the strong Chupicuaro (northwestern Mexico) flavor of the Late Preclassic Basin and Morelos, suggest that there was no such legacy (see also Diehl 1976:256; Tolstoy 1989b:299). As Sanders and his colleagues (1979:392) note, Teotihuacan's emergence "represents a revolutionary break with the past, and a complete redesign of the ecosystem of the Basin."

The Basin of Mexico surveys indicate significant growth in sites and population in the initial centuries of the Late Preclassic (Sanders 1981b:165–75; Sanders et al. 1979:97–106). Therefore, just as in the case of the Valley of Oaxaca and Monte Alban, Teotihuacan's beginning was not a matter of resource potential nor of human numbers, for those were already in place. The basic ecological model proposed by Sanders et alia (1979:392–95) nearly three decades ago remains viable today. It sees the rise of Teotihuacan as closely related to hydraulic agriculture tied to two major springs in the large expanse of the middle and lower alluvial plain of the Teotihuacan Valley, and assumes the growth in the emerging city was also related to craft production and trade, including the exploitation of the nearby Otumba obsidian source. But there remain significant archaeological unknowns that impede our understanding of just how and why everything came together as it did in the northeast area of the Basin of Mexico. For example, we need much more data on Puebla-Tlaxcala, but at the same time there also needs to be a serious consideration of the Late Preclassic ties in the Basin and Morelos to the northwest, and how or what those ties may have contributed to both Cuicuilco and Teotihuacan. Of course, we need to know much more about Cuicuilco, but it is likewise crucial to learn more archaeologically about the Cuanalan and Patlachique phase settlements that grew to become Teotihuacan and thus were its true physical foundation. What intraregional and interregional ties did they have? And there is the question of what role, if any, volcanic activity in the mountains just beyond the southern Basin may have played in the equation. Did it nudge southern Basin populations northward?

Every day that passes sees urban development persistently spreading outward over the Basin of Mexico, making the answers to all those questions ever more difficult to obtain.

ACKNOWLEDGMENTS

Susan Gillespie's many thoughtful critiques, insights, and comments improved this chapter significantly.

4

The Early Preclassic Olmec: An Overview

ANN CYPHERS

Basic questions about the Olmec concern their identity, origins, development, and role in Mesoamerican prehistory. Years ago, there was no quibble in calling them the *cultura madre* or Mesoamerica's first civilization (Caso 1965; Covarrubias 1957; M. Coe 1965a, 1968), but now this label is questioned (Demarest 1989; Flannery and Marcus 2000; Grove 1989a; Marcus 1989; Sharer 1989b). The Olmec, here considered Early and Middle Preclassic inhabitants of the southern Gulf coast (following Coe 1968:6–7; Diehl 1989:18; 2004:13; Grove 1989a; Lowe 1989b), have been characterized as having a "complex hierarchical society" (Diehl and Coe 1995:11), a portrayal warranting close examination.

The question of the nature and relative scale of their Early Preclassic complexity is a major issue in extant debates about the impact or influence of the Olmec on their contemporaries, particularly in light of the often disputed evidence for widespread contacts among these societies (see Blomster et al. 2005; Coe 1968:98, 110; Earle 1991b; Flannery 1968; Flannery and Marcus 2000; Flannery et al. 2005; Grove 1968; Neff et al. 2006a; Neff et al. 2006b; Price 1977; Sharer and Grove 1989; Sharer et al. 2006; Stoltman et al. 2005). The issue of primary state formation for the Olmec is rather a "to be or not to be" question, due to the absence of historic cases for comparison (Trigger 1974:96–97) and their limitrophe position in many evolutionary schemes. Since the present volume is not aimed at the state as an evolutionary stage, but rather with the origins of Maya polities, this chapter will discuss the archaeological evidence for viewing San Lorenzo as the capital of an early Olmec polity. The question that follows from this is the degree to which this development was ancestral to Maya and other Mesoamerican polities. While other contributors to this volume will also consider this issue (see chapters by Grove, Clark, and Hansen), this chapter will consider whether San Lorenzo spawned daughter polities, such as Laguna de los Cerros and possibly La Venta.

The emphasis taken in the present chapter, to paraphrase Michael Smith (2004:77), will be on empirical research rather than on theory-driven speculation, even though I will make reference to theories that embrace the Early Preclassic Olmec as an early state and the contrary view. The evidence and interpretations of the nature and scale of Olmec heartland organization are covered in this review, which examines topics such as territory, origins, society, regional organization, and exchange networks.

THE OLMEC HEARTLAND

What has traditionally been called the Olmec heartland of Veracruz and Tabasco's Gulf coast is limited by the Papaloapan and Tonalá rivers, a geographic definition maintained by Barbara Stark and Philip Arnold (1997), who call it the "southern Gulf lowlands." The term "heartland" (Fig. 4.1) has been used to identify the place of origin of this culture in accord with the culture-area concept (Bernal 1969:13, 15; Caso 1965; Coe 1968:6–7; Grove 1997:53; Lowe 1989b). At the same time, the inherent meaning of "heartland" refers to a political territory defined by the spatial extent of stone political and religious symbols (Bernal 1969:52–54; Drucker 1981:29).

The heartland's lowland and upland landscape, characterized by great environmental diversity and numerous resources, ranges from the coast and littoral to the riverine lowlands of the Papaloapan, Coatzacoalcos, and Tonalá river systems, and the Tuxtlas volcanic massifs. The significant matter of its southern limits has attracted little attention. Internal distinctions in David Grove's model of "zonal complementarity" (1994:151–54; 1997:76) correspond to the locations of major Olmec sites: coastal lagoon (La Venta), riverine (San Lorenzo), and uplands (Laguna de los Cerros). The region is heterogeneous and dynamic even though the vision of a low, flat undifferentiated landscape (e.g., Bernal 1969:17; Blanton et al. 1996:8; Earle 1976:213; Sanders and Webster 1978:288–91) promotes the now discredited idea that this humid tropical environment was not apt for the rise of civilization.

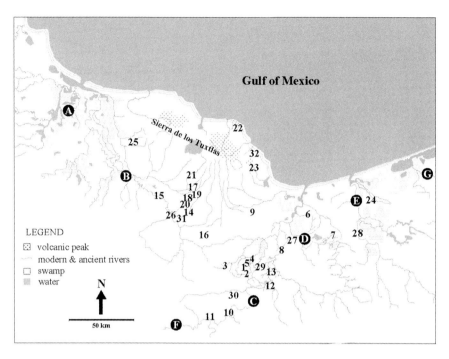

Gulf of Mexico

LEGEND
- ⊡ volcanic peak
- modern & ancient rivers
- ☐ swamp
- water

N

50 km

ARCHAEOLOGICAL SITES

1. San Lorenzo	12. El Manatí	23. Pajapan
2. Loma del Zapote	13. La Merced	24. La Venta
3. Estero Rabón	14. Laguna de los Cerros	25. Tres Zapotes
4. El Remolino	15. Cuatotolapan	26. El Marquesillo
5. Tenochtitlán	16. Cruz del Milagro	27. Sta. Ma. Uxpanapa
6. Ixhuatlán	17. La Isla	28. Los Soldados
7. Arroyo Sonso	18. El Cardonal	29. Ahuatepec
8. Emilio Carranza	19. Loma de la Piedra	30. Ojo de Agua
9. Chiquipixta	20. Llano del Jícaro	31. El Nuevo Órgano
10. La Oaxaqueña	21. Los Mangos	32. Piedra Labrada
11. Las Limas	22. Zapotitlán	

WATERWAYS
- A. Papaloapan system
- B. San Juan River
- C. Coatzacoalcos River
- D. Uxpanapa River
- E. Tonalá River
- F. Jaltepec River
- G. Pajonal channel

4.1. Map showing the Olmec heartland with the location of notable archaeological sites, many with stone monuments.

The Gulf coast environment has figured prominently in materialist models for the emergence of social complexity in which variables such as population pressure, competition, circumscription, agricultural risk, productivity and intensification, and environmental diversity are considered (e.g., Coe and Diehl 1980; Price 1971; Sanders and Price 1968). It is also a prominent feature of Alfonso Caso's (1965), Ignacio Bernal's (1969), and Michael Coe's (1965b) proposals of an Olmec empire based in the heartland.

ORIGINS

The Olmec have been subject to diverse debates concerning their temporal and spatial placement. Following the appearance of the new artistic style, scholars concentrated on unraveling Olmec origins and geographic extent while endeavoring to define their placement in then existing chronological sequences (e.g., Boas 1921; Caso 1942; Covarrubias 1942; Gamio 1942; Vaillant 1930, 1931, 1935; Stirling 1940a, 1943a, 1947; Covarrubias 1946a, 1950, 1957; see also M. Coe 1965a, 1965b, 1965c). After numerous attempts to find a correlation with historic cultures, the art style was named, or rather misnamed, as the "Olmec," a term that has found more favor than others. The most well known debate revolved around their chronological relationship to the Classic Maya, which was settled with the La Venta radiocarbon dates (Drucker et al. 1959; Morley 1946; Thompson 1941). Once basic temporal hurdles were surpassed, issues involved Olmec origins and their impact on other cultures, often characterized as the Highland-Lowland debate (see Sharer 1982), but this discussion was complicated by the lack of refined chronological sequences.

The vision of external origins and migrations, brought into play numerous times for the Olmec, gained momentum with the acquisition of more archaeological knowledge. The highland school of thought favored origins outside the Gulf coast, with beginnings proposed for Guerrero (Covarrubias 1957), Morelos (Piña Chan 1955), Oaxaca (Wicke 1971), and the Pacific coast (Graham 1982). Chronological problems plagued the early studies because excavations, such as at El Arbolillo, Zacatenco, and Tlatilco, were not rigorously stratigraphic; this led to the proposal of a local peasant culture residing alongside an elite culture of Olmec origin (Covarrubias 1946a). Despite eventual refinements (see Tolstoy and Paradis 1970; Grove 1974a; Niederberger 1976), scholars continue to debate the matter of Olmec influence in the highlands (see Sharer and Grove 1989).

Even with the research conducted by the Río Chiquito Project at San Lorenzo in the late 1960s (Coe and Diehl 1980), the questions of origins and migration were not laid to rest despite the sound chronological sequence founded on stratigraphic excavations and 14 radiocarbon dates. Some scholars believed the long uninterrupted sequence at San Lorenzo to be indicative of an *in situ* development (Grove 1974a; Sharer 1982), and others sought origins in the Tuxtlas Mountains (Heizer 1968:24). Michael Coe and Richard Diehl (Coe 1968:75; Coe and Diehl 1980:I:143) maintained that the earliest pottery was most similar to Pacific coast ceramics, which in turn show similarities to early South American ones (see Coe 1961, 1981b; Lowe 1975). Added to their view that the San Lorenzo ceramic sequence shows abrupt changes, a scenario of migration from the Pacific coast was born (see also Lowe 1989b; for a different viewpoint, see Diehl 2004:28).

Further elaboration of the Pacific coast migration theory is formulated by researchers working on the Pacific coast (e.g., Clark 1990, 1997; Clark and Blake 1989) and involves the early establishment of the Mokaya culture, which developed alongside the early cultures of the northern Isthmus of Tehuantepec but achieved a higher degree of complexity. Rank and simple chiefdoms of the Mazatán region were proposed to be in contact with the Olmec and may have stimulated their complexity (Clark 1997:228); and later, Olmec expansion in the form of colonies materialized in Chiapas (Agrinier 1989; Cheetham 2006, 2007, 2010; Clark 1993:166–67; 1997:229; Lowe 1998c).[1] The theory regarding the emergence of rank society in the Soconusco hinges on sequentially contingent, unbalanced reciprocal exchanges—in the course of competitive feasting sponsored by aggrandizing individuals—that led to prestige and power inequalities (Clark and Blake 1994). The supporting data center largely on the celebrated quality of the Barra phase ceramics; these primitive valuables (Clark and Gosser 1995) were displayed and used for serving beverages in feasts. Insofar as John Clark has proposed that "[t]he Olmecs may have received their initial stimulus to develop complex society from the coastal dwellers of the Soconusco region" (1997:228), this stimulus is understood to be the adoption of the feasting complex, whose alleged presence in the Gulf coast is based on some pottery similarities.

However, this proposal as yet finds little support. Recent studies show that Ojochi and Bajío phase pottery has a few similarities to coeval types from the Pacific coast, but the assemblages are not identical (Arnold 2003; Cyphers n.d.-a; Rodríguez and Ortíz 1997; Symonds et al. 2002) and, importantly, that there is continuity in the cosmological meaning of certain decorated vessels from the Bajío phase through the apogee at San Lorenzo (Di Castro and Cyphers 2006). My analysis of San Lorenzo pottery indicates that less than 15% of Ojochi, Bajío, and Chicharras pottery vessels are large serving containers which could be used in feasting (Cyphers n.d.-a); this stands in sharp contrast to the Soconusco materials. Philip Arnold's (2003) well-documented ceramic evidence from the La Joya site, located in the central Tuxtlas, shows no sharp transition from the Tulipan to Coyame phases that would indicate possible migrations. In the same vein, Barbara Stark believes that the degree of forest disturbance exhibited in the Tuxtlas pollen cores indicates a greater maize production than would have been necessary for brewing maize for feasting (2000:32).

In sum, the pre-San Lorenzo phase ceramics on the Gulf coast do not provide unequivocal evidence that migrations from the Pacific coast (or from anywhere else, for that matter) stimulated complexity in the Olmec heartland. Rather, the Ojochi and Bajío assemblages that show participation in a southern ceramic sphere(s) or tradition(s) (Clark 1991; Winter 1994:130–34; Zeitlin 1994) may be a local development. Formal similarities to some highland pottery seem best viewed as the result of early interregional interactions, including exchange relationships. Stark suggests that it was the Gulf coast agricultural potential that was a major factor in attracting population rather than aggrandizing leaders (2000).

OLMEC SOCIETY

Much of what is inferred about the Early Preclassic florescent period comes from the study of monumental sculpture complemented by analogies to later Mesoamerican cultures. But not everyone agrees that stone art should occupy an important place in interpretation or that it indicates greater sociopolitical complexity than in other societies (e.g., Flannery and Marcus 2000; Grove 2007b; Sanders and Price 1968:127; for a different viewpoint, see Clark 1997; Cyphers 2004a; Diehl and Coe 1995; Drucker 1981:29; Haas 1982:186; Stark 2000). What remains glaringly clear is that only the Olmec designed, created, transported, and utilized monumental sculpture at this time, which not only constitutes an important defining characteristic of their society but also reflects their unique inclination towards intense labor mobilizations. For this reason alone, it should and does figure prominently in Olmec studies, just as the scale, frequency, and design of monumental architecture is widely used as a diachronic material measure of sociopolitical development throughout Mesoamerica (e.g., Balkansky 1999; Feinman and Nicholas 1999; Sanders et al. 1979).

Olmec art studies have provided us with a view of that society as composed of ruling and commoner classes (Fig. 4.2). Michael Coe's influential

4.2. Images of Olmec stone monuments. From left to right, transformation figure, Monumento 10 from San Lorenzo; colossal head, Monument 89 from San Lorenzo; throne, Monument 14 from San Lorenzo; and anthropomorphic figure from Cruz del Milagro.

views of elite social order, based largely on stone monuments and iconography with liberal analogies to the Maya and other later cultures, center on a state organization, a royal cult ruled by powerful dynasties in which the rulers and their dynasties calculated their descent from a jaguar deity, analogous to the later god Tezcatlipoca (Coe 1968, 1972, 1989a; see also Carneiro 1977; for a different viewpoint, see Demarest 1989; Diehl, in Coe and Diehl 1980; Marcus and Flannery 2000). He also proposed that San Lorenzo attained statehood (in Coe and Diehl 1980:II:147). Findings in the field helped him realize that the manpower necessary for many activities, such as monument transport and plateau construction, must have been obtained from the near and more distant hinterlands of the capital. His analysis of political organization led him to reject the proposal of an Olmec theocracy (Heizer 1960) and, based on analogies to inscriptions from the Maya area, apply the concept of secular leadership by a hereditary lineage or dynasty. He proposed the identification of the rulers in the colossal heads (which includes their role as warriors and ballplayers) and the recognition of lineage or descent emblems in the seated figures found in altars, a proposal that continues to be endorsed (Cyphers 2004a, 2004b, 2008; Gillespie 1999; Grove 1970, 1973). Based on the variety and sources of trade materials, he suggested that Olmec society contained a group of merchants, analogous to the armed Aztec *pochteca*, who operated a far-flung trading network and participated in conquests (M. Coe 1965c; see also Soustelle 1984; for a different viewpoint, see Drennan 1984:35; Price 1970). And finally, with regard to religion, the presence of standardized deity representations that were identified in Olmec art points to a state religion (Coe 1968:65, 110–11; 1989a; Diehl 2004:105; Joralemon 1971; for a different viewpoint, see Flannery 1968; Marcus 1989; Price 1977). Coe touched upon several points that are shared in one form or another among proponents of a similar view (e.g., Drucker 1981; Haas 1982): (1) the social and economic costs of monument transport imply high population levels and high manpower requirements necessitating labor tribute and surplus subsistence production; (2) social stratification is manifested by and in stone sculpture with an emphasis on divine kingship to the detriment of lesser social categories; (3) distant trading contacts were managed by the elite; and (4) the state controlled religion.

Because these views are controversial, a look at the data and specific interpretations may be instructive. Although it has not always been stressed in Olmec studies, archaeological context is an indispensable instrument for understanding synchronic and diachronic uses, meanings, and discard of sculpture and other cultural materials (Cyphers 1999). Interpretations of the intrinsic meaning of stone monuments and other ritual objects, based on formal and iconographic studies, require backup from studies of other kinds of artifacts, which are equally as important as aesthetically attractive monuments. Therefore, archaeological data obtained from excavations and surveys are indispensable in verifying or rejecting the views inscribed in stone at the behest of ancient elites (see Joyce and Winter 1996; Marcus 1974)—with the qualifier that the intensive energetic investment in stone monuments and architecture corresponds to quantifiable per capita labor measures (Haas 1982) that may be evaluated in environmental and demographic contexts in order to appraise the role of tribute, surplus, and coercion in their creation (see Heizer 1966).

Little is known about early Olmec society prior to 1400 cal BCE because of the thick overburden that obscures these deposits. Unfortunately, we have little information about the dwellings and burials of this time period (Fig. 4.3); nonetheless, various peeks into the bowels of San Lorenzo give provocative hints about what was happening at this early time. Even though its full dimensions are unknown, a 2 m high stepped earthen platform (Coe and Diehl 1980:I:104–106) suggests early monumental constructions. Likewise, a 400 m² sunken quadrangle is another indicator of large-scale construction (Cyphers n.d.-b), and its blueprint and uses imply that very early cosmological concepts were involved in its creation and design. Both examples constitute the first of many construction stages that would appear on a valuable and limited resource, the highest terrain of the Island, and, along with the earliest offerings placed at El Manatí (Ortiz and Rodríguez 2000), illustrate that Olmec beliefs and ritual did not appear suddenly in the Chicharras phase but were already in place centuries earlier. These edifices and the open-air sacred theater at the base of El Manatí hill likely served as private and public ritual spaces for many groups from the region, including the emerging elite of San Lorenzo. At the same time, the appearance of pottery vessels with divine symbols of Earth and Sky (Di Castro and Cyphers 2006) may be associated with activities intended to emphasize social differences. The view that the Bajío phase was a time of egalitarianism with no evidence for interest in the monopolization of the cosmology (Coe and Diehl 1980:I:149) is now outdated.

radiocarbon years B.C.	San Lorenzo	Tabasco	Central Tuxtlas	Soconusco	PERIODS	calibrated date B.C. (OxCal 4.0)
700						800
800	Nacaste	Early Puente	Gordita	Duende	Middle Preclassic	900
				Conchas		
900	San Lorenzo B	Palacios	Coyame	Jocotal	Early Preclassic	1000
1000						1200
1100	San Lorenzo A	Molina		Cuadros		1300
1200	Chicharras		Tulipán	Cherla		1425
1300	Bajío			Ocós	Initial Early Preclassic	1500
1400	Ojochi	Pellicer		Locona		1680
1500				Barra		1780
1600						1900

4.3. Chronological chart that correlates sequences from San Lorenzo, Tabasco, the central Tuxtlas and the Soconusco.

The name Olmec invariably summons the mental image of colossal heads (Fig. 4.2), which could be considered the beginning point for interpretations about Olmec society since they have been subject to numerous and wide-ranging interpretations since José María Melgar y Serrano (1869) reported the first one from Tres Zapotes and suggested Olmec origins in Ethiopia. From the time when Matthew Stirling recognized that the size and individuality of the colossal heads must indicate portraits of prominent individuals (Stirling 1955:20; see also Gillespie 1999), this idea then blossomed into the widespread notion that they represent portraits of hereditary rulers, the maximum representatives of powerful dynasties (Coe 1968, 1977, 1989a; De la Fuente 1992; Grove 1981b; for a different view, see Flannery and Marcus 2000:7). The heads from each site may represent a single dynasty or related lineages (De la Fuente 1992:102; Grove 1981b:67). De la Fuente adds that they also reflect profound ideas and beliefs related to cosmic order (1992:15). Other related interpretations include the heads as dead or ancestral rulers (Cyphers 2004b; Wicke 1971), idealized portraits

(Kubler 1961), ballplayers, warriors, or shamans (Bernal 1969:56; M. Coe 1965c:763–64; Piña Chan and Covarrubias 1964:36; Coe 1977), and rivals for the throne (Clark 1997:222).

The fact that most colossal heads were not excavated *in situ*—added to the possibility of resetting in ancient times (see Graham 1989:229)—contributes to discussions regarding their antiquity, although the contexts of a head (Cyphers n.d.-b) and a throne (Coe and Diehl 1980:I:94–99) in process of being recycled at San Lorenzo suggests their creation near the end of the San Lorenzo phase. William Clewlow (Clewlow et al. 1967) proposed that the then known 12 colossal heads, corresponding to three groups defined by site of origin (San Lorenzo, La Venta, and Tres Zapotes), share enough similarities to postulate contemporaneity within one or two centuries, which implies overlapping occupation of the three sites. In contrast, Charles Wicke showed a temporal sequence of heads beginning with San Lorenzo and followed by La Venta and Tres Zapotes, suggesting a sequential rise and fall of the three sites (1971). Although the question of temporal overlap in the centers' occupations has received some clarification from field data, the heads stand as monuments to our uncertain knowledge about the kinds and duration of the relationships between these sites.

At the site level, some interpretations of colossal head locations and layouts include assumptions that all were relatively contemporaneous (Beverido 1970; Grove 1999), such that their position in relation to each other, as well as cardinal orientation, has cosmological significance. Francisco Beverido's observation that the San Lorenzo heads were laid out in two north-south lines receives some support from recent work, although the close examination of original context does not fully bear out the lines as he defined them; rather, two parallel lines crossing the southern plateau are thought to form an unfinished commemorative scene composed of ancestral rulers, perhaps designed to revitalize the sacred underpinnings of dynastic legitimization during difficult times at the end of the apogee phase, ca. 900–850 BCE (Cyphers 2004b; see also Grove 1999; for a different viewpoint, see Clark 1997:222). Lines of ancestor portraits survive into the Middle Preclassic at La Venta.

Even as colossal heads are a hallmark of Olmec culture and its rulers, they conceivably should be considered secondary in political importance to monolithic stone thrones (Cyphers 2004a, 2004b, 2008; Grove 1981b). The recycling of heads from thrones provides important evidence on the sequence of monument manufacture and suggests that such recycling was involved in ruler commemoration (Porter 1989). Once called "altars" until David Grove identified their functions and meanings (1970, 1973), they can be viewed as the seats of rulers that contain genealogical and cosmological testimony related to the rulers' legitimation (and of their corporate descent group or "house"; see Gillespie 1999) and their right/ascent to office (Cyphers 2008). As well, because the thrones (Fig. 4.2) are consistent with first phase monuments, as opposed to recycled ones, there was a heavy labor investment in their transport from the source, unlike colossal heads shaped on-site through recycling (Cyphers 2004b).

While attention focuses on the powerful rulers and elite because of the impressive size, form, and elaborateness of statuary, stone art also provides clues to identifying other social groups based on dress, ornament, and physical appearance, which are interpreted in terms of significant social differences and ascribed status (Drucker 1981:33; Grove 1997:76). Transformation figures (Fig. 4.2) showing a mixture of anthropomorphic, zoomorphic, and/or fantastic features may be shamans participating in ecstatic experience in which communication with the supernatural world was possible, rain deities, or impersonators of such deities or shaman kings (Furst 1968; Grove 1981b; Kappelman 1997; Reilly 1989; Taube 1996b). Kent Reilly's argument for state shamanism as a charter for rulership includes the postulation of a political hierarchy of such specialists (1995a).

All in all, interpretations of art provide insights into what is frequently construed as the Olmec ideology of stratification in which founder/origin principles are the basis for social exclusion and lineage ranking, placing rulers at the apex of society and commoners as non divine with separate descent. Divine kingship is but one aspect of social stratification, and there is a need to understand its economic bases, such as in the restricted access to assets, labor, utilitarian and sumptuary items, in order to materially verify such ideology.

Burials are usually assumed to be excellent indicators of social differentiation, with regard to their placement, offerings, and the evidence obtainable from bones that relates to diet (see Hendon 1991; Paynter 1989; Whalen 1983). To date, a few Middle Preclassic interments at La Venta include likely burials of rulers (Grove 1997:77), but at San Lorenzo and lesser centers no such burials have been found, and unfortunately, the ones excavated do not constitute a large enough sample for generating status inferences. Two San

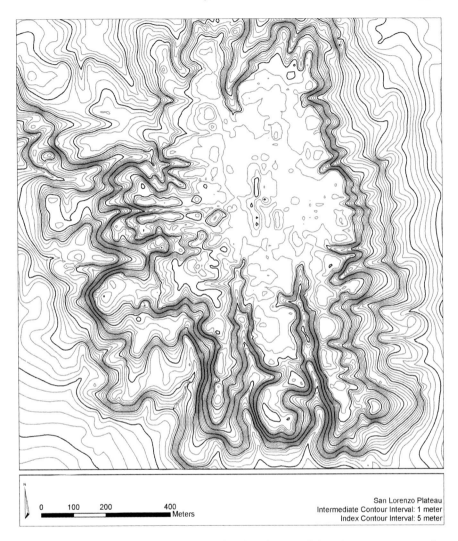

4.4. Topographic map of San Lorenzo showing the top of the plateau, terraces and part of the periphery. Courtesy Timothy Murtha.

Lorenzo phase contexts provide information from human burials likely related to human sacrifice (Villamar 2002). The first context from the Loma del Zapote site provides evidence of a large ceremonial structure associated with a mutilated human sculpture and possible ritual bath in which the reburied remains of one individual were found interred between floors. The second context from San Lorenzo consists of an ossuary with remains of at least six individuals, including one complete individual and many assorted long bones that had been dismembered from corpses upon their deterioration. Remains of infants found at El Manatí may be vestiges of sacrificial rituals (Ortiz et al. 1997:57, 135–36) and re-interment.

Architecture provides another set of material indicators of social differentiation, particularly ancient residences and monumental constructions that require forethought, finance, planning, organization, and maintenance. Settlement organization during the San Lorenzo phases on the sacred San Lorenzo plateau and its periphery relates to social and political differentiation, which is echoed in the site's topography and placement of residential areas, i.e., the political elites located atop the plateau, with diminishing status generally paralleling lower altitude, terrace, and periphery position. This layout seems to reproduce the cosmic map of a sacred mountain (see also Bernal-García 1994). The apex of the site, the plateau, was reserved for the most important people and their activities, followed by terrace locations, where the nobles lived, and lastly the periphery for the commoners (Fig. 4.4). The shape of the social system, reiterated in the form of the built environment, is a message reinforcing principles of social differentiation.

Dwellings excavated at San Lorenzo provide evidence of social position, as manifested by size, design, and construction materials and techniques, a tendency also observed in hinterland sites (Cyphers 1997a, 1997b, n.d.-b; O'Rourke 2002; Wendt 2003a) during the San Lorenzo phase. Dwellings range from the most grandiose that contain imported stone architectural elements (such as columns and step/bench coverings), colored floors, and stone pavements, to the poorest houses with packed dirt floors. Structure size, as well as their stratigraphic depth, often inhibits complete excavation. It is worth mentioning that one of the most extensive terrace excavations at San Lorenzo revealed a multi-room domestic structure with masonry walls, paved floor, and sub-floor aqueduct or drain that has a minimum spatial extent of 224 m^2 (Fig. 4.5) and, as well, forms part of a domestic cluster covering 800 m^2 (Arieta 2009). Whereas the low surface mounds at San Lorenzo (Coe and Diehl 1980:I:29–30) have been rejected as Olmec house platforms (Cyphers 1997b), floors found at deeper levels through the site reveal that greater size and functionally discrete room divisions correspond to higher status, which in turn correspond to higher elevation on the site, such that the concept of a "sacred hill" may have been an early template for internal spatial social arrangement. Pool's recent characterization of the typical

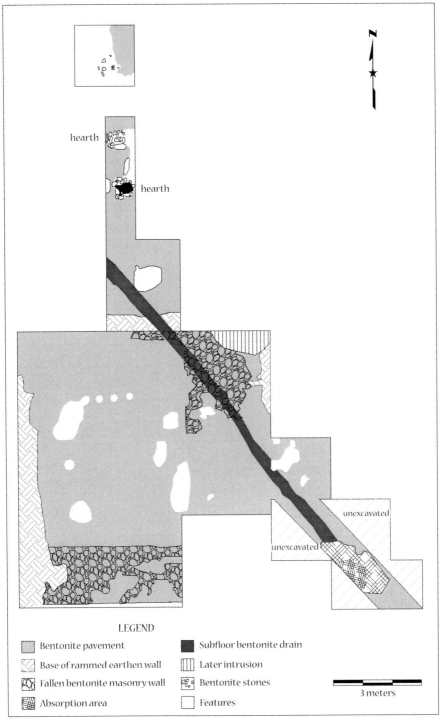

LEGEND

Bentonite pavement		Subfloor bentonite drain	
Base of rammed earthen wall		Later intrusion	
Fallen bentonite masonry wall		Bentonite stones	
Absorption area		Features	

3 meters

4.5. Plan map of principal construction features of a San Lorenzo phase dwelling which illustrates room differentiation, paved floors, subfloor aqueduct and mud and stone walls.

Early Preclassic Olmec dwelling as a 3 by 5 m structure is not supported by the archaeological data from San Lorenzo and its hinterland (2009:246).

The discovery of a remarkable construction, the Group E architectural precinct (Cyphers et al. 2006; Cyphers and Di Castro 2009), makes it necessary to revise previous assessments that no notable Early Preclassic mounded architecture was present at San Lorenzo (Cyphers 1997a, 1997b, 1999). Nearly 300 m² of excavation and more than 100 auger cores reveal that this buried precinct, composed of northern, eastern, western, and southern platforms surrounding a central sunken patio, covers about 10,000 m² (Fig. 4.6).[2] With a multi-stage construction and continuous occupation sequence through the San Lorenzo phase, the complex stood several meters above the ancient exterior ground surface in its final building phase, conspicuous for its large size, unusual construction style, and central position. Four associated stone sculptures (a large throne, SL-14; a 181 m long stone aqueduct; a colossal head, SL-61; and an anthropomorphic stone standard bearer, SL-52) help in appreciating its special qualities and interlinked cosmological connotations, which highlight rulership, ancestor veneration, water, and the underworld. Private ritual was conducted in its interior, with public ritual staged outside. Both construction phases show ritual destruction and the placement of offerings on the patio floors. Group E's layout is evocative of later period architectural complexes, such as platforms bearing sunken plazas and temple groups. The themes shared by the stone monuments impart additional reinforcement for interpretations of sunken patios as the symbolic access to a watery underworld in the Olmec belief system (Reilly 1999), as well as in other Mesoamerican cultures. Concepts of sovereignty, ancestry, water, and the underworld are imbedded in its blueprint and non-domestic artifacts. Specialized public and private functions varied spatially in and around the complex, as exemplified by the northern platform's link to maximum regional leadership, the eastern platform's burial and veneration of an ancestral ruler, and the southern platform's connection to water. Its symbolism seems to parallel Reilly's symbolic model of the Olmec universe as applied to La Venta's Complex A, in which the enclosed court is conceived as an otherworld and ancestral location. In sum, the Group E complex is an extraordinary example of the early architectural and conceptual sophistication of the San Lorenzo Olmec and appears to be tangible evidence for the development of complex sociopolitical institutions.

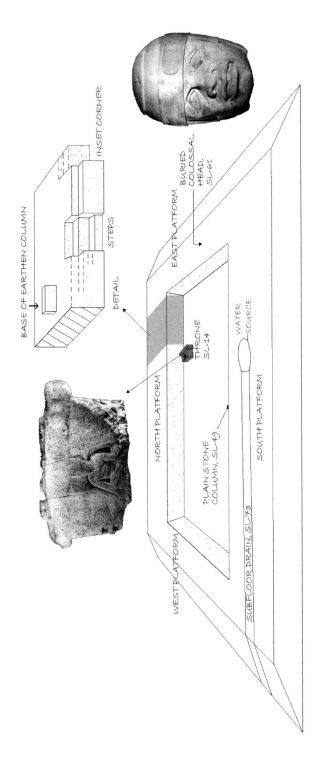

4.6. Hypothetical reconstruction of the Group E architectural precinct based on excavations and coring. Its approximate size is 10,000 m². Several important stone monuments are shown in their original position. The inset shows architectural details discovered in excavation.

The relative proximity of the Group E precinct to Group D structures suggests to Richard Diehl (2004:36–40) that such constructions, and others nearby, form the rulers' home, a royal compound. However, the nature of structures and activities located across the highest part of the site may be a sign that the whole central plateau's upper surface was an area of privileged pursuits linked to political authority. For example, suggestive spatially restricted elements include the recycling of extremely large monuments—in one case associated with a known sunken patio. A second example consists of a structure with connotations of warfare: a bas-relief representation of what appears to be a scantily clad fallen enemy warrior was placed beneath the floor (Zurita and Cyphers 2008) so that occupants would tread on him, a symbolic act similar to that reported for the Maya (Marcus 1974). In the third case, recent auger coring indicates very clearly that, despite construction obscuring it from view, the Olmec planned and located privileged buildings and activities precisely on the highest part of the natural landform that underlies the artificial plateau, thus reserving at all times the sacred heights for the noble sector.

San Lorenzo's plateau (Fig. 4.4) was surmised to be major monumental architecture by Coe and Diehl (Coe 1989a:80; Coe and Diehl 1980; Diehl 1981), but the proposal that it represents a huge bird effigy has not been popular (e.g., Flannery 1982; Diehl 1981; for a different viewpoint, see Diehl 2004:36) insofar as millennia of erosion have affected its original terraced appearance (Cyphers 1997a:102). The tendencies to ignore labor calculations done in the past (e.g., Heizer 1960, 1966; Velson and Clark 1975), which derive largely from gaps in our knowledge about ancient technology, feasibility, and labor organization, should be reversed, with new attention paid to the constraints and possibilities available to the Olmec. Recent auger coring at the site during 2005, 2006, and 2007, stratigraphic analyses, and digital modeling provide preliminary calculations of the volume of earthen fill that was placed during the San Lorenzo phases; that volume falls in the range of six to eight million cubic meters of construction fill (Cyphers et al. 2008–2007; Cyphers et al. 2014). If Robert Heizer's rough calculations (1960) for dry season labor are used as a basis for general comparison, then San Lorenzo's plateau construction would have involved more than 50 times the manpower that was used in building La Venta's great pyramid. It has about seven times the volume of the Pyramid of the Sun at Teotihuacan and is roughly equivalent to 50 Temple I's at Tikal.[3] An approximation (based on Heizer 1960) suggests a massive and intensive labor investment in plateau building that would have required approximately 1400 able-bodied men working during yearly episodes of 100 dry season days (Heizer 1960; Velson and Clark 1975) over a period of 300 years. If compared to population estimates based on survey, this strongly suggests the compulsory participation of the bulk of able-bodied men from San Lorenzo and its near hinterland in these building activities. The moving of stone monuments and the construction of other buildings likely were additional obligatory enterprises. As the largest Early Preclassic monumental work thus far known in Mesoamerica, the effort and organization involved in plateau construction far surpass that of any other contemporary edifice and of many later ones.

REGIONAL ORGANIZATION

Regional settlement studies began with Philip Drucker and Eduardo Contreras' (1953) unsystematic survey, followed by Edward Sisson's (1970, 1976) milestone work in the Chontalpa. Beverido (1987) defined centers based on the architectural pattern of parallel long mounds and conical mounds defining plazas, similar to La Venta's visible architecture, once considered an architectural hallmark of the Olmec (Coe 1981b). Hernando Gomez's survey of principal sites in the Coatzacoalcos and Papaloapan drainages, the first to effectively distinguish between Classic and the Olmec occupations (1996a), clearly assigns this architectural arrangement to the Late and Terminal Classic periods (see also Borstein 2005).

The combined efforts of all recent survey projects (e.g., Borstein 2001, 2008; Kruger 1996; Lunagómez 2010; Jiménez 2008; Sisson 1976; von Nagy 1997, 2003; Killion and Urcid 2001; Santley et al. 1997; Rust and Sharer 1988; Symonds et al. 2002) have covered only about 10% of the Olmec heartland. Difficulties in comparing even these limited survey results include the use of dissimilar chronological frameworks, survey methodologies, and site definitions, all complicated further by visibility problems associated with dense land cover and alluvial deposition.[4] The recognition of environmental changes is important for surveys in this region since geomorphological studies conducted around La Venta and San Lorenzo, respectively, show that the coastal and riverine environment has varied since Olmec times due to lateral shifts in river courses and tectonic uplift (Jiménez 1990; Cyphers and Ortiz 2000; Ortiz and Cyphers 1997; von Nagy 2003; West et al. 1969).

Prior to 1800 cal BCE there is no clear evidence for human occupation in the San Lorenzo region, which is most likely a result of poor surface visibility. The Tuxtlas pollen evidence suggests limited forest clearance and some cultivation (Goman and Byrne 1998) but such occupation has yet to be recorded archaeologically (Santley et al. 1997).

For the Initial Early Preclassic period, there is considerable settlement evidence from the San Lorenzo region but less is known about other portions of the heartland. In Tabasco, a handful of sites are reported along the Barí and Blasillo rivers, including Isla Alor, San Andrés, Isla Chicozapote, Isla Yucateca, and three sites within La Venta proper (Rust and Sharer 2006). Barí pottery at San Andrés (Rust and Sharer 1988; Rust and Leyden 1994) has been identified as the earliest evidence of occupation in the La Venta region, while the Pellicer complex (Sisson 1976; von Nagy 2003) may be the earliest in the Chontalpa region to the east.

In the central Tuxtlas, an evaluation of this time period is impossible due to the chronological phase that subsumes these phases with the later San Lorenzo phase (see Santley et al. 1997:179). In the Tuxtlas foothills (Borstein 2008) no dominant site was found and contemporary occupation appears as a dispersed population moving into preferred wetland environments, constituting initial colonization from unspecified origin(s).

The largest population concentration (262–625 people) during the Initial Early Preclassic on the Gulf coast appears around San Lorenzo (Fig. 4.7), which is located in a privileged geographical setting involving a river island surrounded by ample floodplains and river channels and lagoons (Cyphers and Ortiz 2000; Symonds et al. 2002; Ortiz and Cyphers 1997). Population density on the San Lorenzo Island was around 22 people per km² on permanently inhabitable terrain. Subsistence activities concentrated on wetland aquatic resource procurement, hunting, collecting, and some agriculture (Symonds et al. 2002). Settlement preference for elevated terrain close to permanent water sources was integral to their way of life and also an important part of their world-view (Symonds et al. 2002; Stark 2000).

San Lorenzo, a 20 ha village, was surrounded by several clusters of smaller villages that in turn were encircled by hamlets of varying sizes. Sixty-two percent of the regional population resided on the San Lorenzo Island, with another smaller concentration to the west around Estero Rabón, which appears to have been an aspiring equal and a competitor of the larger village of San Lorenzo. Competition between the two villages would not

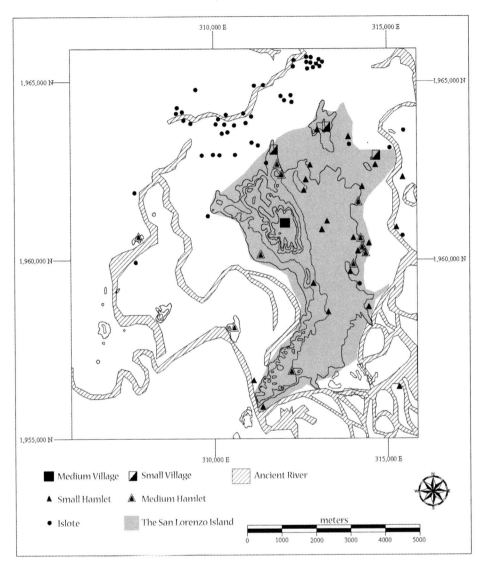

4.7. Settlement distribution during the Initial Early Preclassic (Ojochi-Bajío phases) in the inner hinterland of San Lorenzo, which is the medium village located in the center of the map.

appear to be related to a struggle for subsistence resources in light of the generally low regional population levels, but perhaps it was for human resources. This time period, although lacking in monumental stone art, shows evidence for early architecture that appears in the interfluvial wetlands of the San Lorenzo Island, whose great productive potential was recognized by the Olmec. Distinctive archaeological indicators of intensive exploitation date from 1800–1400 cal BCE and take the form of 47 artificial earthen platforms, called *islotes*, built near or upon the ancient river levees, which are possible evidence for subsistence specialization and usufruct rights.[5]

In the Tuxtlas foothills the pre-San Lorenzo phases show little occupation, only a few hamlets and other small sites, possibly campsites, located on the floodplains of the San Juan and Tizapa rivers, and there is no evidence for a significant exploitation of basalt boulders at nearby Llano del Jícaro (Borstein 2001, 2008). In general, although differentiation among permanent settlements seems minimal, this may be a consequence of poor surface visibility, especially in light of the presence of the ritual site of El Manatí (Ortiz and Rodríguez 2000; Ortiz et al. 1997; see also Diehl 2004:27) that shows that the Olmec landscape held an array of meanings and functions with early cosmological concepts well established in the Initial Early Preclassic.

In sum, the Ojochi-Bajío phases show the highest heartland population concentration on the San Lorenzo Island, with some settlement differentiation across the lowland landscape and with the largest villages in competition for certain resources. The initial colonization of upland areas followed the river systems. A greater reliance on aquatic resources, hunting, collecting, and probable manioc cultivation dominated subsistence, with a lesser interest in maize indicated around San Lorenzo.

The San Lorenzo phase, one of the most densely occupied phases in the history of the region, was a time of major sociopolitical changes (Fig. 4.8). Population exploded, with an 18-fold increase over the previous phase, to 8554–18,735 inhabitants. The concentration of 226 sites in the 400 km^2 survey area around San Lorenzo, with 97 of these sites falling on the 75 km^2 of the San Lorenzo Island (Symonds et al. 2002), constitutes a population agglomeration with no known parallels in Early Preclassic Mesoamerica. Island population density on permanently inhabitable terrain reached 600 people per km^2. At this time San Lorenzo's central core or plateau is notable for its size and complexity of occupation, and the capital attained its maximum size of 690 ha, with a resident population ranging between 5000 and 10,000 inhabitants. Although some scholars have manifested skepticism about this size assessment (e.g., Flannery and Marcus 2000:4; Spencer and Redmond 2004:185), recent 20 m interval cores across the site confirm this calculation (Cyphers et al. 2008–2007).

In the 400 km² study region, San Lorenzo dominated a population of about 13,000 people distributed in at least five other types of permanent sites. San Lorenzo occupied a nodal position on the Island and was surrounded by four lesser centers. Increasing settlement differentiation is illustrated by the specialized sites, such as the 59 *islotes*, bitumen-processing

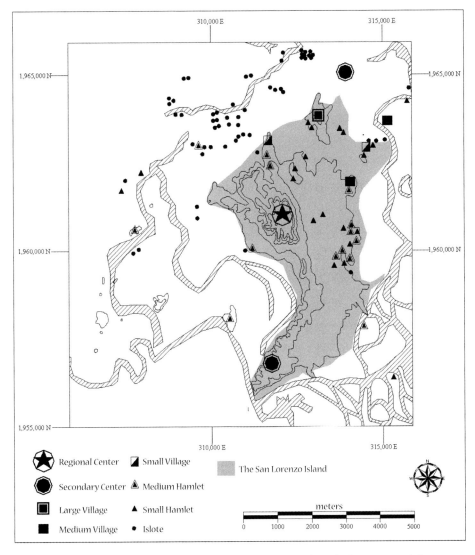

4.8. Settlement distribution during the San Lorenzo phase in San Lorenzo's inner hinterland.

sites (Wendt 2003a), causeways (Cyphers and Ortiz 2000; Ortiz and Cyphers 1997), and the ritual site of El Manatí (Ortiz and Rodríguez 2000; Ortíz et al. 1997), which also is one of several locations where red hematite may have been extracted.

Settlement distribution points to the existence of transportation networks designed according to natural fluvial and terrestrial pathways (Symonds et al. 2002). Often, the nature of the region's topography—in other words, strands of high ground set in vast floodplains—leaves little alternative for the location of communication routes. The selective layout of planned routes is suggested by the patterning of key site locations at fluvial intersections and the causeways in the San Lorenzo hinterland (see Ortiz and Cyphers 1997). For example, San Lorenzo's location could facilitate the fluvial and terrestrial transportation and communication management via the secondary and tertiary centers (i.e., Loma del Zapote, El Remolino, Tenochtitlán, Estero Rabón), each strategically situated in the semi-radial fluvial system centered on the Island. Within the Island, San Lorenzo and Tenochtitlán may have once been rivals but the latter site appears to have eventually been integrated into the emerging power sphere of the former. The principal western competitor of San Lorenzo, Estero Rabón, occupied a favorable position to intercept upriver groups moving along the fluvial courses and to access local hematite sources.

The founding of Laguna de los Cerros as a 50 ha village in the San Lorenzo-A phase is not accompanied by a significant regional settlement development in the Tuxtlas foothills (Borstein 2001, 2008). Small and large villages, hamlets, and floodplain sites form the settlement panorama at this time in the foothills, showing only a minor degree of site differentiation. It perhaps was founded in this phase by San Lorenzo in order to have a permanent base close to the nearby basalt flow at Llano del Jícaro (Medellín 1960; Gillespie 1994) and other workshop sites. The often mentioned singular sculptural style of some monuments from Laguna de los Cerros may have been the innovative products of pioneering sculptural endeavors.

The first half of the San Lorenzo phase shows two different trends—significant population growth and expansion into the Tuxtlas foothills, and the growth of Estero Rabón as a secondary center in San Lorenzo's immediate hinterland. Overall, the heartland settlement picture is one of colonization moving along the lowland and upland rivers and the establishment of key sites in strategic places. The abrupt appearance of Laguna de los Cerros in the San Lorenzo-A phase may point to San Lorenzo's early involvement in the founding and management of regional populations, which may have included conquest. It seems that the expansion and development of rural populations were not encouraged, and certain population rearrangements would have facilitated access to human labor.

The great population growth and nucleation during the second half of the San Lorenzo phase on the San Lorenzo Island, which is paralleled by trends around Laguna de los Cerros, suggests regional population movements as centers attracted more and more people. The growth of Laguna de los Cerros accelerates in the San Lorenzo-B phase as it became a regional power dominating the Tuxtlas foothills and perhaps beyond, conceivably changing the nature of its relationship to San Lorenzo. Mutual antagonism reflected by the regular spacing of major Gulf coast centers (Bove 1978; Earle 1976) may be due to competition or warfare. Interestingly, both Laguna de los Cerros and the San Lorenzo Island have sculptures representing possible conquest or domination, as well as monuments showing weapons. The increasing political role of sites such as Cruz del Milagro, Cuatotolapan, La Isla, Tres Zapotes, Loma de la Piedra, Zapotitlán, Piedra Labrada, Chiquipixta, and Emilio Carranza is illustrated by their possession of stone sculptures (Fig. 4.1).

Despite Laguna de los Cerros' 300 ha size and importance, settlement development is poor; it is surrounded only by five large and small villages and a crowd of small hamlets, corresponding to four settlement tiers. Laguna de los Cerros seems to have had multiple roles, first, as a major center in its immediate region, and second, as a subordinate center or estate whose principal services for the riverine capital of San Lorenzo included the procurement and manufacture of small and large stone items. Transport of large sculptures or preforms to San Lorenzo from the Llano del Jícaro workshop at this time or earlier would have necessarily entailed the participation of a greater population of able-bodied men than was available in the immediate hinterland of Laguna de los Cerros, suggesting close ties between the centers that enabled the mobilization of manpower. Increased monument recycling tendencies at San Lorenzo may be a sign that these services suffered a reduction during the latter part of the San Lorenzo-B phase, with the reduced availability of large basalt boulders at Llano del Jícaro, competition between the rulers of Laguna de los Cerros and San Lorenzo, and La Venta intervention as possible causes.

In the central Tuxtlas, occupation at 1200 cal BCE shows a relatively egalitarian setting manifested as a cluster of small villages near the bifurcation
of the Catemaco River (Santley et al. 1997:181). This has been interpreted in
various ways: (1) as physical conquest by major lowland centers in order to
obtain basalt and other resources; (2) as an initial colonization of the central
Tuxtlas; or (3) that Tuxtlas egalitarian societies (pertaining to separate political entities and unrelated to Tres Zapotes) participated in regional networks
between 1400 and 1000 cal BCE as a consequence of economic crises consequent to volcanic eruptions (Santley et al. 1997:185–86, 200–201). In general
local events are viewed as somehow different from the riverine Olmec lifeways due to the absence of monumental art, a complex sociopolitical hierarchy, and diagnostic pottery motifs which are offered as evidence of socio-
cultural variability and processes of ethnic differentiation within the Olmec
heartland (Arnold 1995; Pool 2006a; see also Diehl 2004:13) and a lack of incorporation in the Olmec political realms (Pool 2007:132; 2010; Santley et al.
1997:210). The possible relationships of the central Tuxtlas to adjacent areas
requires taking into account the center of Laguna de los Cerros as a possible factor influencing the notable site clustering in the southern portion
of the surveyed area and, as well, nearby sites known to have Olmec elite
status materials, such as Piedra Parada and Zapotitlán. Due to chronological
divisions that are incompatible with the San Lorenzo sequence, settlement
patterns coeval with the apogee phases of San Lorenzo and Laguna de los
Cerros are not discernable, but the subsequent phase in the central Tuxtlas,
1200–400 cal BCE, which lumps the peak periods of San Lorenzo and La
Venta, shows three settlement tiers, a salt extraction site (Santley 2004), and
an 88% population increase (Santley et al. 1997:187).

Given the pre-1400 cal BCE low population density and the purposeful
establishment of Laguna de los Cerros in the early San Lorenzo phase, the
question of a possible "frontier" or cultural interface in the Tuxtlas is raised,
which cannot be adequately evaluated on the basis of presently available
data. Even if the central Tuxtlas once had an independent political organization, the existing sparse data hint that it eventually became somehow linked
to the great riverine capitals.

What is occurring around La Venta during the Early Preclassic period
is not totally clear since few sites have been registered (Sisson 1976; von
Nagy 1997:267; Raab et al. 2000; Rust and Sharer 1988, 2006). A central
issue has always been whether or not La Venta was a major competitor of

San Lorenzo's during the latter's apogee due to shared sculptural similarities.[6] There may be some temporal overlap in their occupations (Gonzalez 1990, 1996; Grove 1981b; Lowe 1989b), but the early size and complexity of La Venta is as yet unknown. Current research provides the initial outline of La Venta's development from the Early Preclassic onwards (Rust and Sharer 1988, 2006). William Rust and Robert Sharer (2006) attribute the emergence of social stratification to a shift from local village access to preferential trade and food production locations by a more centralized group at La Venta itself.

Overall, settlement growth in the known sections of the Gulf coast lowlands shows the emergence of an unusually dense population concentration on and near the San Lorenzo Island during the San Lorenzo phases, perhaps akin to what Stark calls a "capital zone" (1999). In light of lighter population densities further away, such an agglomeration raises the question of population rearrangement such as local or regional migrations and resettlement. As labor-expensive projects increased in size and frequency, population aggregation would facilitate the command of human labor resources. The establishment of new sites near specific resources and the creation of ties with possible competitors and allies formed part of a regional integration strategy.

Monumental art may provide elements that are useful in the analysis of political organization, as in the case of the Maya (e.g., Flannery 1972; Marcus 1973, 1974, 1976a). Although lacking in inscriptions, Olmec monuments provide indirect evidence of political organization based on the size, meaning, and distribution of monumental stone sculpture—an approach that has been both embraced (Diehl and Coe 1995) and decried (Flannery and Marcus 2000:5–6). Perhaps a chiefdom organization may be capable of the labor expenditure represented by San Lorenzo's 450 tons of stone sculpture, however, the opposite view is perhaps best represented by Stark's statement that "[i]nterestingly, no historic chiefdom matches the degree of mobilization of public labor and specialist skill that are indicated by the Gulf Olmec 'art' and architecture" (2000:35). This impasse likely has no resolution in the near future, but the comparison of monument distributions and regional settlement patterns may shed some light on this question.

Aside from the general rule of thumb correlating site importance to the number of stone monuments (see Gillespie 2000a; Grove et al. 1993), there is a pattern of large sculptures explicitly associated with rulership that occur in the most important sites. Of the two notable forms with this theme, thrones and colossal heads, only the former are not recycled pieces, hence their variable sizes are directly related to the degree of control over stone and labor resources. Interpretations of throne form and iconography suggest that these seats of power contain messages regarding the identity of the ruler and his right to rule based on his hereditary distance to the apical ancestor of his corporate descent group (Grove 1970, 1973). As symbols of rulers, their "houses," and houses' history, thrones served to endorse and differentiate property rights through supernatural connections (Gillespie 1999), to mark the succession to office, and to distinguish the regional chain of command (Cyphers 2004a, 2008; see also Porter 1989:27).

Types of thrones appear to represent a well-defined chain of regional command composed of at least three levels, while the Early Preclassic spatial distribution of all stone monuments in the Olmec heartland suggests at least four levels in the regional political system. Throne size and iconography correlate well with site size and importance in regional settlement studies, which strongly suggests that thrones served as emblems for sites and political entities as well as for rulers and "houses." In the San Lorenzo region, the capital is the only place with large thrones with explicit ancestor iconography, while smaller thrones identical in size and symbolism are found at the secondary centers of Loma del Zapote and Estero Rabón (Fig. 4.9). Even as these latter pieces indicate their rulers occupied similar political levels in the system, the absence of iconography manifesting the divine genealogical charter may suggest that principles other than kinship were implicated in their taking office. Large and small thrones with nearly identical ancestor imagery also may indicate a chain of command with a different twist—the placement of the San Lorenzo ruler's close kin, possible heirs, as rulers of lesser centers or estates such as La Venta and Laguna de los Cerros (Cyphers 2008; see also Clark 1997).

The isolated occurrence of small- to medium-sized anthropomorphic and transformation sculptures at lower level sites (Fig. 4.1) may indicate an additional level of command in the regional system (Symonds et al. 2002; Cyphers and Zurita 2006a; Clark 1997). The seemingly dispersed distribution of nodal communities, each with at least one monument, seems to obey principles similar to those observed around San Lorenzo where the judicious location of secondary and tertiary sites at river confluences and other nodal sites points to the integration of a fluvial and terrestrial com-

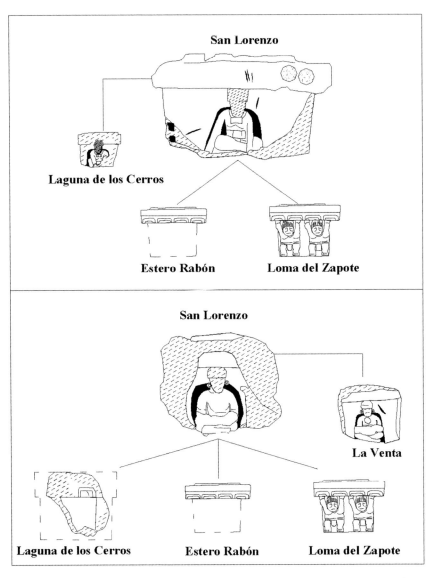

4.9. Hypothetical reconstructions of the relationship of San Lorenzo to other centers during two different moments. Throne size and iconography illustrate the reconstructed chain of command which is supported by regional settlement patterns in the case of San Lorenzo, Laguna de los Cerros, Estero Rabón and Loma del Zapote.

munication web (Symonds et al. 2002; Cyphers and Zurita 2006b). Rural sites may have participated in periodic activities by including their monuments in centrally sponsored rituals (Cyphers 1993a, 1994, 1999). Such ritual participation could create and maintain certain identities and increase social and religious integration by promoting the lateral unification of a poorly developed distant hinterland in the belief system. Also, organized activities of this nature could forge pathways for dependency relationships, trade, and social interaction. In this way, difficulties in sociopolitical integration and in the movement of people and goods could be offset in the vast deltaic plains and uplands.

RESOURCE EXPLOITATION, CRAFT PRODUCTION, AND EXCHANGE NETWORKS

Fundamental issues involve the relative order of appearance of exchange networks and social stratification and the possible role of the former in stimulating the latter. The Ojochi-Bajío time frame would seem particularly important in this respect due to its antiquity. Pertinent materials consist primarily of obsidian, bitumen, and basalt artifacts, with the latter two available in the heartland. The relatively low population densities near the basalt and bitumen resources suggest that competition likely was not involved in their procurement.

During the San Lorenzo A and B phases, internal heartland trade (and/ or procurement; see above) concentrated on the following locally available materials: (1) basalt for utilitarian grinding tools and sculpture (Williams and Heizer 1965; Coe and Fernández 1980); (2) sandstone for sculpture and as abrasives; (3) bitumen (Wendt 2009; Wendt and Lu 2006; Wendt and Cyphers 2008) for sealing, lighting, and waterproofing; (4) pigments (Coe and Diehl 1980:I:16–18); (5) rubber[7] (Hosler et al. 1999); (6) crocodile teeth; (7) salt; (8) foodstuffs (Symonds et al. 2002); (9) limestone; and (10) ceramic vessels. There perhaps was interest in perishable goods such as cacao (Stark 1974:218; Powis et al. 2011), cotton (Stark 1974; Stark et al. 1997), tobacco (Furst 1968, 1995), precious woods, shells, basketry, feathers, animal hides, gourds, turtle shells, and stingray spines. In the case of most items, we have no idea how or who produced or procured them; however, in the case of basalt and bitumen, material analyses point to the exploitation of various sources, which probably is also the case for pigments.

Bitumen procured from a variety of open seeps was processed or prepared in domestic contexts at specific sites for local consumption and export (Wendt 2003a, 2009; Wendt and Lu 2006). Initial source analyses are not conclusive because further temporal refinements are necessary in order to evaluate the questions of independent exploitation by individuals and communities or the existence of different procurement networks (Wendt and Lu 2006). Surface survey included an area with bitumen deposits in the San Lorenzo region (Symonds et al. 2002), but due to overlying modern occupation, it is unclear if there was a community there that was dedicated to its extraction.

Without a doubt, basalt was the principal non-perishable inorganic resource moved within the Olmec heartland and it shows an ample spatial distribution in the form of sacred symbols and utilitarian products. Its use in monumental sculpture began sometime in the San Lorenzo-A phase. Basalt was by no means scarce, although appropriate locales for stone-working and subsequent transport of sculpture may have been limited since the Olmec sought locations with large surface boulders and a terrain propitious for monument conveyance. Knowledge of sculpture production was not shared but was restricted to specific locations. Some workshops, such as Llano del Jícaro (Gillespie 1994; Medellín 1960), could not produce sculpture year-round due to the seasonal presence of standing water (whose subsurface percolation is inhibited by the underlying basalt stratum), but smaller surface stones for making grinding implements could be easily moved to other places for rainy season tool production. Another workshop located less than 10 km from Llano del Jícaro has been discovered (Killion and Urcid 2001). In general, it seems that sculpture and preform production *per se* was not an economically significant activity since it required relatively few skilled craftsmen. It was the labor involved in the movement of these products to their final destination that represented the greatest cost.

The abrupt founding of the large village at Laguna de los Cerros in the San Lorenzo-A phase appears to be related to initial interest in this resource and the early production of stone items, and since this site had insufficient human resources to physically command the basalt workshop and export the sculpture, there is the distinct possibility that San Lorenzo was directly implicated in its production, but the exact mechanisms are unknown. The situation appears to have changed in the San Lorenzo-B phase when Laguna de los Cerros became more important, attained greater autonomy, and headed a complex three-tier settlement organization. It may have become more directly involved, perhaps usurping production management and expanding it to at least seven separate places on the basalt flow to meet increasing demand.

Among the various workshops at San Lorenzo, the Group D monument storage and recycling area, which is located within an ostentatious dwelling, stands out as a case of attached production (Cyphers 1999). Another workshop at San Lorenzo contains many tons of multi-drilled ilmenite blocks.[8] Not only are such artifacts carefully accommodated in three subterranean pits, but others are also present on an occupational surface containing greenstone polishing tools, drill bits, drilled and shaped greenstone artifacts, flakes and chunks, drilled basalt beads, and worked iron-ore ornaments, which are suggestive of multi-crafting activities (see Hirth 2009) that include polishing and drilling. Because their sequential perforations appear to be the product of their use as a bearing in a drilling apparatus, the discarded artifacts may be wasted tools (Cyphers and Di Castro 1996; Di Castro 1997).[9] The motivation for stockpiling them in subterranean pits perhaps was to reserve this imported ore with marked crystalline veins for later production of low-quality reflective status paraphernalia, and/or simply to keep it out of circulation, which was imperfectly achieved since tiny amounts are found in domestic contexts at several locales.

Some of the above heartland resources and products were traded throughout Mesoamerica during the San Lorenzo phase, for example, bitumen (Wendt and Lu 2006), ceramic vessels (Blomster et al. 2005; Herrera et al. 1999), and probably so far undetected perishable items. Incoming materials included obsidian (Cobean et al. 1971; Cobean et al. 1991), iron ore objects including solid mirrors, ilmenite blocks (Di Castro et al. 2008; Pires-Ferreira 1975, 1976; Pires-Ferreira and Evans 1978) and mosaics, mica, quartz crystals, and diverse greenstones and other metamorphic stones. Sculptures are not known to have been moved outside the heartland area. It is clear that widely distant peoples were in contact at this time, but their specific social relations and the means of exchange remain uncertain. It is mostly assumed that long-distance trade in exotics occurred between and among elites rather than via professional merchants. Although the use of exotic items in heartland rituals and exchanges may have enhanced elite status and served the purpose of keeping followers contented, it is hard to imagine that relatively minor-scale, intermittent exchange and the distribution of ritual "perks" such as obsidian tools, mirrors, and the like had any major impact on the heartland economy or significantly contributed to the social and political backing and power that Olmec leaders required.

THE EMPIRE STRIKES BACK?

John Clark's proposal on the subject of Olmec government further focuses on certain material expressions—particularly monumental and portable art and public works—that figured actively in political rituals designed to manipulate belief systems (1997). His perspective places government within the religious and political realms, and it seemingly attempts to divert focus from the state and concentrate on political motivation and related technologies. Carefully threaded through the article are the main components of a developmental model for a supreme Olmec ideology in the Early and Middle Preclassic periods, a rather familiar thought since it also appears in Caso's, Bernal's, and Coe's discussions of an Olmec empire.

Clark contends that images of Olmec kings appear chronologically later than the Chiapas figurines that he interprets as village shaman chiefs. This linear evolution indirectly supports his familiar argument that the more complex Mokaya of the Soconusco influenced the rise of Olmec civilization. Chronologically the early kings precede the Middle Preclassic divine kings with shamanic powers. This chronological framework, the purported shift in power paradigms, and the artifact interpretations may seem questionable, but they are vital to the argument.

According to Clark, early Olmec ideology was composed of two facets, one related to origin myths and the other to the supernatural. In the heartland region, the rulers were most concerned with creation myths and social superiority and not with access to the supernatural. Rulers *cum* ballplayers, as represented in San Lorenzo figurines, were the embodiment of the association of rulers with creation myths and the importance accorded the physical prowess of these leaders. The second facet, the supernatural, is represented by pottery vessels decorated with cosmological concepts ("dragon pots"), which are inferred to have been used in heartland rituals to invoke sacred beings, but when found in distant regions are considered evidence of the hinterland's alliances with the heartland and of the search for exterior status trappings. As these material expressions facilitating access to the supernatural conform to an expansionist strategy, a further implication is that, as other regions developed greater social differentiation and adopted or imitated Olmec forms of political organization, the Middle Preclassic Olmec rulers then withdrew "dragon pots" from circulation in order to monopolize access to the supernatural realm as their basis for power. Consequently, it would appear that the ever flexible Olmec leaders would have re-established, rediscovered, and again put into practice the ideological bases of their supreme religion for the next wave of expansion.

Despite Clark's gripping argument which follows closely on the heels of his predecessors, the issue of the extent of the Olmec's political sovereignty remains a tenuous matter. Previous sections of the present chapter have shown that their political influence in the heartland was variable over time and space, although it is possible that by the end of the Early Preclassic they were able to achieve extensive regional integration. To date there is no clear-cut evidence for their military expansion out of the heartland or for their sovereignty over far-flung places in this time period, so the "empire" concept seems to have little applicability.

FINAL OBSERVATIONS

The critical time period for understanding the emergence of complexity and centralization in the Olmec heartland is the initial Early Preclassic. The proposals regarding pre-1400 cal BCE migrations are not upheld by the present data, so it is preferable to think in terms of a fundamentally local development (however, not without external contacts). As noted above, the model proposed for the emergence of rank society in the Soconusco which involves competitive feasting sponsored by aggrandizers is not compatible with the available evidence from the Olmec heartland, either as a consequence of Isthmian migrations or as in local development.

A major theory by Coe and Diehl (1980) regarding the emergence of social stratification centers on competition for scarce river levee lands. Given conditions of normal demographic growth and sufficient food production, this competition led to inter-group conflict and the eventual domination of the levee owners over others. Their proposal is based largely on ethnographic analogy and ecological studies but lacks empirical support regarding population growth, competition, and conflict arising over these lands, their use for maize cultivation, and crop productivity. As Kent Flannery wrote, "It would be difficult to find a single aspect of the model that depends heavily on the archaeological discoveries made at San Lorenzo between 1966 and 1968" (1982:446). Recent research does not support their model insofar as several lines of evidence suggest that levee cultivation was of less interest than recessional floodplain agriculture and the exploitation of aquatic resources (Cyphers 2009; Cyphers and Zurita 2012; Symonds et al. 2002; see also Stark 2000). As well, Lane-Rodríguez and collaborators (Lane 1998; Rodríguez et al. 1997) compare the production of maize on levees and uplands around San Lorenzo over a two-year period in 1991 and 1992 for winter (*tapachol*) and rainy season (*temporal*) plantings, concluding that, despite the greater fertility of levee soils, when winter rainfall is insufficient, productivity tends to be less than on upland soils.[10] It is important to note that later studies indicate climatic fluctuations (Haug et al. 2001; Goman and Byrne 1998) that created winter droughts detrimental to levee agriculture (see also Coe and Diehl 1980:II:140, who recognized this as a potential flaw in their model), thus supporting the observation of increased risk in levee cropping.

Another model involving the appropriation of scarce resources and cosmological principles intertwines the development of economic infrastructure and sociopolitical leadership (Cyphers and Zurita 2012). In this view, founding groups arrived at the San Lorenzo Island, which was composed of a natural hilly terrain circumscribed by a wet riverine wilderness. Attracted there by the subsistence opportunities and the natural geographical conditions favorable for defense, protection against flood disaster, and the organization of communication and transport, they did not delay in recognizing the economic advantages afforded by specific portions of the natural environment. In this period of climatic drying, the wetlands in the northern part of the Island may have been particularly attractive due to their superior water capture over upriver and downriver areas, high fertility, and subsistence resource concentration. Under conditions of little trade and minimal storage possibilities in the tropical ambiance, this area afforded the possibility of surplus food production for offsetting risk and disaster via recession agriculture and the procurement of aquatic resources. The *islotes* required a labor investment beyond what could be met by nuclear families and were a vehicle for establishing corporate usufruct rights to highly productive resources in these wetlands. They may be conceptually linked to related notions of origins and the place of humans in the universe insofar as they take the form of a miniature hill surrounded by water, a key cosmological notion in Mesoamerica. Each *islote*, a symbol of the primeval monster and the sacred mountain emerging from the watery underworld, stood for the appropriation of cosmological principles by specific groups in order to establish exclusionary rights based on principles of ancestry and first occupation. These early architectural vestiges and associated cosmological concepts may be implicated in nascent sociopolitical asymmetry via the formation of corporate descent groups with hereditary rights in the wetlands, the establishment of exclusive and inherited rights to property and resources based on ancestry, and the appropriation of a cosmological charter, a process that set the stage for later apogee phase political development (Cyphers and Zurita 2012).

The study of the potential role of conflict in the initial Early Preclassic is laden with problems such as the heavy overburden that obscures these occupations and makes excavation extremely difficult and alluvial sedimentation that affects site visibility in regional survey. As well, limited regional survey coverage hinders fuller attempts to understand the early landscape, which likely has more settlement differentiation than is actually perceived, as is illustrated by the site of El Manatí. Despite the generally low population densities, inter-village conflict seems likely, and San Lorenzo may have had clashes with smaller villages located on the Island and nearby promontories.

Proposals involving the Early Preclassic fluvial and terrestrial movement of goods within the heartland are those mentioned by Stark (2000) and Symonds et al. (2002), in which responses to subsistence risk, environmental problems, and the provisioning of an environmentally circumscribed, growing population made central leadership necessary for arbitrating land disputes, amassing and distributing foodstuffs, and providing basic services in times of need. Although Stark points out that the lack of periodicity of environmental problems and risks may work against this association (2000:39), paleoclimate studies (Haug et al. 2001) suggest that increasing tendencies toward climatic extremes make this a viable scenario.

In the San Lorenzo-A and B phases, political development involved different strategies across the heartland. The greatest degree of centralization was found on the San Lorenzo Island and immediate environs and was driven by multiple factors such as population increase, subsistence/resource competition, and rivalry in trade and for control of communication along fluvial and terrestrial pathways. By this time, the well-embedded exclusivity of the cosmological charter of royalty and nobles became an instrument of political inequality. The increasing integration of this rapidly growing population over a period of four centuries resulted in regional settlement differentiation consistent with major and minor centers, resource extraction sites, production sites, ceremonial places, transportation architecture, and fluvial and terrestrial traffic control nodes. After drawing to it a significant population early in this period, San Lorenzo then may have directed the colonization of more distant but economically important zones.

With the march of time, the forms and degree of political integration changed across the heartland but at disparate rates and via multiple experimental strategies. Some largely undifferentiated settlements of the heartland were slowly incorporated into the social and political spheres of San Lorenzo, its dependent centers, and smaller allies, while others may have maintained some autonomy while participating in heartland exchange networks. New sites were founded in strategic points to manage resource exploitation. Regional integration was fomented by diverse alliances and the inclusion of leaders of local groups in politico-religious ritual. Monumental construction at the capital was incessant during the apogee as well as the use of monumental sculpture by the rulers and nobles in public rituals. Set in the context of regional demography, the scale of stone and architectural monument building and transport undoubtedly required labor tribute and coercion. Osteological, iconographic, and settlement evidence provide tantalizing signs of warfare.

Social stratification, as evidenced by monumental sculpture themes and dwelling size, design, and position, became a way of life in the San Lorenzo Island and perhaps beyond. The production of high-status goods was directed by the rulers and nobility, who also employed the imported status trappings for their own purposes. The appearance of the institution of divine kingship between 1400 and 1000 cal BCE was extended to some subordinate centers which were ruled by nobles or potential heirs to the capital's throne. The rulers' right to office was defined by genealogy, as were other positions of leadership held by noble subordinates such that a hierarchical array of formal political offices was occupied by members of the upper class. However, kinship bonds were surpassed in that not all members of the upper class held positions and the leadership of some dependent centers and villages was given to non-kin.

San Lorenzo appears to have had an impact on the development of La Venta given the continuation of similar customs related to divine rulership, ancestor worship, origin myths, cosmological concepts, portraiture in colossal heads and bas-relief forms, sponsored craft production, social stratification, wetland subsistence strategies, shamanism, and so on. The persistence of these customs must be related to two principal factors: Early Preclassic contacts between the two sites, and local migration from San Lorenzo to La Venta beginning at the end of the former's apogee.

In conclusion, the present review has attempted to define principal features and forces of change in Olmec society throughout the initial and Early Preclassic and contribute evidence pertinent to the conference theme. Emphasis has been placed on the data that are relevant to understanding the dynamic nature of cultural development in the heartland rather than on typological categories and speculation based on theoretical expectations. Be that as it may, the Olmec case has and probably always will be controversial, as was indicated by Barbara Price nearly four decades ago: "the most striking characteristic of the entire Olmec phenomenon would seem to be its almost unparalleled power to excite controversy" (1970:393). It is this controversy that makes Olmec archaeology a challenging and exciting field of study.

ACKNOWLEDGMENTS

I would like to thank Dave Grove, Ken Hirth, Marci Lane Rodríguez, Bob Sharer, Saburo Sugiyama, and Tim Murtha for helpful remarks and information, Marisol Varela for editorial assistance, and Kent Reilly for the gift of a very special book. This paper was submitted in November 2007.

NOTES

4.1. This scenario for the development of Isthmian cultures bears a noteworthy similarity to some interpretations of Mormon sacred history and geography. The Book of Mormon is considered by some to be a reliable historic testimony, although this position finds considerable opposition outside the Church of Latter Day Saints (e.g., Coe 1973a; Green 1969; Brodie 1992). Just as in Biblical studies, the Mormons have spent considerable effort in identifying the places mentioned in their sacred scripture, and some studies correlate them to Mesoamerican archaeological sites and cultures (e.g., Sorenson 2000; Clark 2005a). Without delving into Mormon debates about specifics, suffice it to say that the concern with a specific geographical location, the "narrow neck of land" mentioned in the Book of Mormon, has motivated intense sponsorship of archaeological work in and near the Isthmus of Tehuantepec. Simply put, early

Mormon groups (lost tribes) were thought to have colonized the southern portion of the narrow neck of land and then moved across it to create a great civilization which then returned to exert influence on the southern portion of the narrow neck of land.

4.2. Due to the large size of the Group E precinct, excavations and coring have not been able to define the exact shape of the platforms. It is as yet unknown if they were free-standing or joined, as represented in Figure 4.6.

4.3. The volume of the Pyramid of the Sun is based on Millon (1960), and Timothy Murtha kindly provided the volume of Temple 1 at Tikal.

4.4. Some methodologies involve sherd densities and the size of architecture borrowed from highland areas (e.g., Santley et al. 1997:177), while others attempt to appraise site types on a regional basis (e.g., von Nagy 1997; Symonds et al. 2002) and estimate populations from house densities as interpreted from visible surface remains (e.g., von Nagy 1997) or from house excavations (e.g., Symonds et al. 2002). Correspondingly, the methods used in generating population estimates are quite variable, generally varying from high (Santley et al. 1997) to low (Symonds et al. 2002). Another problem is the use of contrasting chronologies, a situation partly related to the generally low frequency of surface diagnostics.

4.5. By definition, *islotes* are low platforms constructed only in the wetlands that served to elevate the structures built atop them from rising floodwaters. They were not built as surfaces for planting, nor do they form clusters that could be compared to mound-and-plaza architecture, although one set of four *islotes* seems to form a group. Excavations by the San Lorenzo Tenochtitlán Archaeological Project in numerous *islotes* discovered occupational surfaces and structural elements as well as typical rectangular hearths that may have been used for smoking foodstuffs procured via aquatic subsistence strategies and recession agriculture conducted in areas with the least vegetation cover such as the low floodplain (Symonds et al. 2002).

4.6. Proposals of a temporal/power hiatus between the apogees of San Lorenzo and La Venta (e.g., Clark and Pye 2000b; Lowe 1989b; von Nagy 2003) are at present speculative.

4.7. *Castilla elastic* Cerv. is reported from the upper Miocene Coatzacoalcos Paraje Sola Formation, corresponding to the *Selva Alta Subperrenifolia* (Graham 1976:797). Even as late as the early 20th century, capes were dipped in rubber in the Oteapan, Veracruz, area, just as reported for the 16th century (Whaley 1946:21). In addition to its use for making balls, rubber was also a medicine and aphrodisiac in prehispanic times (Elferink 2000:28).

4.8. Pierre Agrinier suggests there are ilmenite sources in central Chiapas (1984:75–76) that were exploited for making these blocks; however, geologists have not found evidence there for a pre-Cambrian formation appropriate for such deposits (F. Ortega, pers. comm.). Apparently the nearest such terrain is located in neighboring Oaxaca (see Schulze et al. 2004; Solari et al. 2004).

4.9. Clark (1996:193) and Pool (2007:105) presume that the ilmenite blocks arrived in San Lorenzo already in drilled form,which is possible but not demonstrable on the basis of current data.

4.10. Pool misrepresents this landmark study in agronomy, alleging that the authors did not take into account the fallow cycle (2006a:202); however, cultivated land that is allowed to lie idle during the growing season, which is called *barbecho* in Spanish, is without a doubt taken into consideration (see Rodríguez et al. 1997: 55–56, 63). They show that levee productivity over the long haul cannot be considered constant due to its dependence on variable and unpredictable climate and flood patterns.

5

Western Kingdoms of the Middle Preclassic

JOHN E. CLARK

The Middle Preclassic was the critical era in the development of Meso-american civilizations. The period began about 1000 BCE with the collapse of San Lorenzo and ended with the abandonment of its successor city, La Venta, about 400 BCE (dates are calibrated). Just a century later there were kingdoms and states in most regions of Mesoamerica, including the Maya lowlands and highlands. Olmec kings ruled at San Lorenzo for about three centuries and at La Venta for about five. It is still not known how either kingdom came into being or why either ceased. Nonetheless, two conjectures appear warranted. First, many institutions and accouterments of power evident at San Lorenzo and La Venta show up in later regional polities, especially those in the Maya lowlands, so some historic connection is indicated. Second, La Venta appears to have been the principal historic bridge between the earliest Olmec kingdom at San Lorenzo and the numerous Mesoamerican kingdoms of the Late Preclassic period. Data are currently insufficient to evaluate fully or to establish beyond reasonable doubt either conjecture. In this chapter I attempt to fill the gap between the fall of the Early Preclassic polity at San Lorenzo and the rise of Late Preclassic states.

The analytic objective of this book is the origin of early Maya states during the Preclassic period, so it is appropriate to view developments on the western edge of the Maya world from this point of view without prejudging matters of ancient foreign policy and relations, or their possible effects on different peoples. Much of the controversy in the literature concerning Olmec-Maya relations in Preclassic times might have been avoided if these ethnonyms had been taken to represent specific kingdoms or regional polities rather than monolithic entities for macro-language groups. By Middle Preclassic times Olmecs populated many different polities, as did the lowland Maya and other peoples of Mesoamerica, so it makes no analytic sense to extol the actions of Olmecs or Mayas in collective aggregate. Decision-making, actions, and their consequences did not occur at the global level of all peoples but at regional and local levels of polities directed by kings or councils. Each polity had its own history. To work out the connections between polities and their causal effects on each other, one must reconstruct histories of contact, the nature of the contact, and the responsible agents involved. This chapter is meant as a step towards historic specificity and concreteness.

The units of analysis I rely on to address the evolution of political complexity during the Middle Preclassic are *kingdoms*, meaning regional polities based on social stratification and directed by kings, regents, or royal councils. "Kingdom" is a more ample and generous category than "state" and includes complex chiefdoms as well as states (Clark 1997). This category allows one to investigate the origins of states *sans* the analytical trauma of having to decide beforehand the precise status of all polities involved. Space limitations preclude discussion here of all Mesoamerican kingdoms outside the Maya region. I describe the most proximate for which some useful information is available (see Fig. 5.1), beginning with La Venta and then moving south along the western edge of the Maya world and then farther west to Tres Zapotes and Laguna Zope. These were political and social entities probably created and managed by speakers of Mixe-Zoque and Otomanguean languages (Campbell and Kaufman 1976; Hopkins 1984; Lowe 1977, 1998a; Lowe et al. 1982; Warren 1978; Winter 1989, 2004). In the final section I consider briefly the general pattern of the histories of these occidental polities. The societies represented all became kingdoms during the Middle Preclassic. The regional chronologies involved and their correspondences as I understand and describe them are shown in Figure 5.2.

LA VENTA, TABASCO

La Venta is the best known Olmec city in Mesoamerica. By "city" I simply mean a semi-urban center of at least 4,000–5,000 people (see Flannery 1994). Most information for La Venta comes from excavations carried out in the 1940s and 1950s of its northern sector (Drucker 1952; Drucker et al. 1959). Early speculations on Olmec-Maya relations were based on evidence from La Venta and understandable misconceptions of its antiquity and form. The archaeological indicators that La Venta was the seat of an ancient kingdom include the size of the site, the arrangement of its plazas and large earthen platforms, the number, size, and themes of its stone monuments, the size and contents of buried offerings, evidence of elite burials, and its central place in a regional settlement system (Drucker 1981). Although earlier peoples lived in the area, the city of La Venta was founded about 900–850 BCE and lasted until about 400 BCE; this interval represents its history as one of Mesoamerica's preeminent kingdoms. Issues of continuing controversy are the construction date of La Venta's buildings and sculptures, the origins of its planned space and its significance for rulership and power, the type of government practiced there, and the influence on neighbors or received from them (see Gillespie 2008, 2011). General summaries of La Venta are readily available (Diehl 2004; Pool 2007), so I focus on controversial points germane to the larger issues of Middle Preclassic kingdoms and Maya states.

Site and Kingdom History

Although earlier peoples lived in the immediate zone as early as 1750 BCE and probably earlier (González Lauck 1996, 2001; Pope et al. 2001; Rust 1992; Rust and Leyden 1994; Rabb et al. 2000; Rust and Sharer 1988; see Pool 2007:127, 305 for best summary), the architectural core of the city of La Venta appears to have been built from scratch about 900 BCE on an elongated, 20 m high island in a vast swamp in western Tabasco, just 15 km south of the Gulf coastline. The map of the site presented in Figure 5.3 indicates the conjectured starting and final forms of this city. The basis of my conjectures are comparisons with Chiapas sites rather than excavation data from La Venta. Little is clear about La Venta's construction history, for a host of lamentable reasons, and the intensively excavated northern sector (Complex A) is a mess to straighten out (see Gillespie 2008). My model for La Venta's history reads planning and organization from the site's precisely partitioned space (Clark 2001; Clark and Hansen 2001). Susan Gillespie (2008, 2011) argues that the construction history of Complex A, the best known part of the site, should not be read in this way and that the site's bilateral symmetry developed through time rather than being present at the site's founding, as I argue. Her evidence undercuts her own ar-

John E. Clark

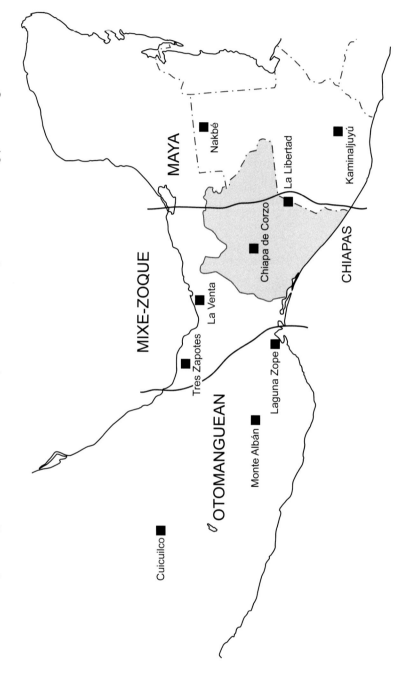

5.1. General map showing Middle Preclassic sites in Chiapas and Mesoamerica, with lines delimiting possible linguistic territories.

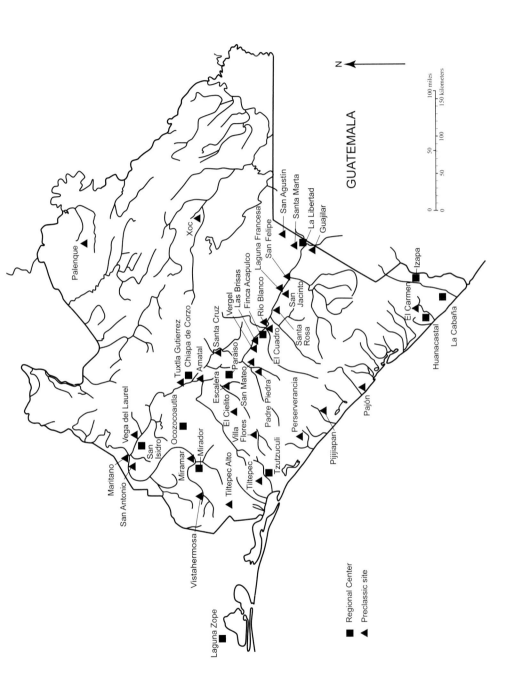

Time (AD/BC)	Period	Valley of Oaxaca	Laguna Zope	San Lorenzo	Tres Zapotes	Greater La Venta	Chiapas
100 AD – 0 BC	Late Formative	NISA	NITI	(gap)	NEXTEPETL		VI
100 – 200	Late Formative	PE	KUAK	REMPLÁS	HUEYAPAN		V
300 – 400	Middle Formative	DANIBAAN	GOMA			LATE FRANCO	IV
500 – 600	Middle Formative	ROSARIO	RÍOS	PALANGANA	TRES ZAPOTES	EARLY FRANCO	III
700	Middle Formative					LATE PUENTE	
800	Middle Formative	GUADALUPE					II-B
900	Middle Formative			NACASTE		EARLY PUENTE	II-A
1000 – 1100	Early Formative	SAN JOSÉ	GOLFO	B / SAN LORENZO	ARROYO	PALACIOS	I-B
1200	Early Formative			A			I-A
1300 – 1400	Early Formative			CHICHARRAS		MOLINA	0
1500	Early Formative	TIERRAS LARGAS	LAGUNITA	BAJIO			
1600 – 1700	Early Formative			OJOCHI	"OCOS"	PELLICER	
1800 – 1900	Early Formative	ESPIRIDÓN					
2000							

5.2. Comparative chronology of the Middle Preclassic. (Sources for regional chronologies discussed in the text.)

	Tzutzuculi	San Isidro	Chiapa de Corzo	La Libertad	Izapa	Kaminalijuyu	Maya Lowlands
Late Formative		IPSAN	HORCONES	HUN	HATO	ARENAL	CHICANEL
		GUAÑOMA	GUANACASTE	GUAJIL	GUILLÉN		
Middle Formative	TUSANTECO	FELISA	FRANCESCA	FOKO	FRONTERA	PROVIDENCIA	LATE MAMOM
	ARISTA	EQUIPAC	ESCALERA	ENUB	ESCALÓN	LAS CHARCAS	EARLY MAMOM
	LATE TRES PICOS	DZEWA	DZEMBA	DYOSAN	DUENDE		
	EARLY	DOMBI	DILI	CHACTE	CONCHAS	AREVALO	EB
Early Formative	ZANATENCO	CACAHUANÓ	JOBO	JOCOTE	JOCOTAL		
			COTORRA	CHACAJ	CUADROS		
			OCOTE	OJALÁ	CHERLA		
					OCOS		
				LATO	LOCONA		
					BARRA		

gument, and her interpretation of site structure exhibits the *pars pro toto* problem she tries to correct. Like the hosts she criticizes, Gillespie lets the construction history of Complex A stand in for that of the whole site. My arguments ignore Complex A and focus instead on the main body of the site and its aboveground monumental architecture. My model is based on conjectured parallel histories with Middle Preclassic Chiapas capital centers. In this model, La Venta at its founding was staked out along the eastern edge of the island. This north-south tending eastern escarpment was cut and terraced to bring it into alignment with the principal site axis of this cross-shaped city (Clark 2008). The dominant construction was a 32 m tall clay pyramid (Mound C-1) built on a large platform at the northern edge of a long, central plaza. The pyramid was counterbalanced in the northern sector with several large offerings (buried mounds of serpentine) placed in pits over 7 m deep (Drucker et al. 1959:97).

La Venta was constructed along a centerline oriented 8 degrees west of north (Drucker et al. 1959: fig. 4). My hypothesis is that the original city center was segmented into intervals 86.6 m in length, or simple fractions and multiples of this length. La Venta was 10 of these intervals long and 8 wide (Clark 2001, 2008). Subsequent platform additions to the city center respected the original orientation and measurement interval. Later mounds encroached on early mounds in the north. The city center eventually extended 1,482 m north-south. Towards the end of La Venta's history, large stone monuments were set up as boundary markers. Three colossal basalt heads were placed at the northern edge of the city, and they faced the sea to the north. Three even larger sandstone heads were placed near the southern end; two faced south and one faced north (González Lauck 1995:39; 1996: fig. 1; 2004: fig. 1; Grove 1999: fig. 6; Stirling 1968). These northern and southern lines of monuments were 1,300 m apart (Fig. 5.3).

La Venta appears to have been partitioned and arranged according to function. The original layout shows a 346 m long, 6 ha plaza with special architecture flanking it in each cardinal direction. This plaza was probably for public ceremonies and for viewing rituals performed on the platforms surrounding it. The plaza could have accommodated comfortably well over 100,000 standing spectators but may never have been that crowded. Looking north, a spectator during the city's heyday would have seen the 32 m high, stepped pyramid made of about 90,000 cubic meters of dirt and clay (Heizer 1968:17). A temple of perishable materials probably graced

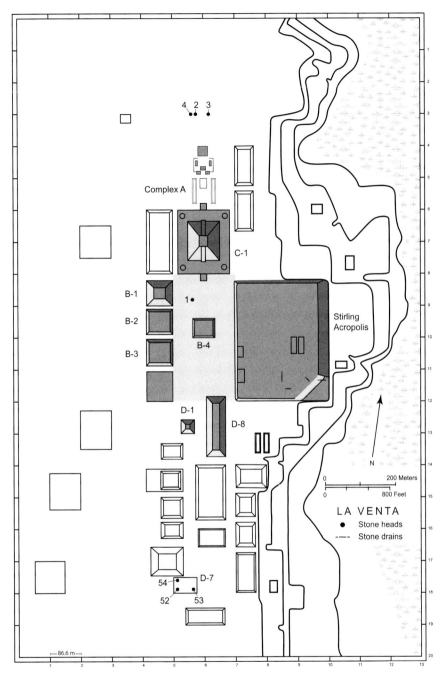

5.3. Map of La Venta, Tabasco, Mexico. The gray areas indicate the hypothesized earlier complex of the city. Contour data and monument locations were taken from González Lauck (1988:fig.1, 1996:fig.1).

the summit of this artificial mountain. The temple could be accessed from stairs on the south and north faces and maybe on the other two sides as well (González Lauck 1997, 2006). The pyramid is the only promontory of this size for over 100 km on this coastal plain and can be seen from 10 km away. It would have been very impressive close up in its final form. The pyramid was given a new clay skin several times during the city's history, each time making it bigger and taller. The final clay cap dates to before 400 BCE (González Lauck 1996:75; 1997:93). The height of the original pyramid and its construction history have not been determined.

East of the plaza lies a broad 8 ha low platform (Stirling Acropolis) that required nearly twice as much earth and clay to build as the main pyramid. This platform probably supported the residence of the king, his courtiers, and servants (Clark and Hansen 2001; Reilly 1990). A small ballcourt and an elaborate system of subterranean stone drains have been identified there (Heizer et al. 1968). The eastern edge of the platform shows evidence of deliberate sculpting and terracing (Fig. 5.3), cultural practices known for the earlier Olmecs at San Lorenzo (Clark 2007b; Coe and Diehl 1980; Cyphers 1997a-c). The evidence suggests that many buildings rested atop this acropolis (Clark and Hansen 2001:5) and were occupied for the full duration of the site, 900–400 BCE (Heizer et al. 1968:152).

Just south of the main plaza lies a long mound (D-8) flanked on the west by a short pyramid (Mound D-1). Such building pairs are known in the Maya region as E-Groups because they were first identified at Uaxactun in Group E (Ricketson 1937). Together, the centered pyramid and the long eastern mound may have constituted an observatory for monitoring the movements of the rising sun throughout the year, perhaps to coordinate the agricultural cycle and rituals (Lowe 1989b). To the west of the main plaza at La Venta was a row of low platforms (Mounds B-1, B-2, and B-3), probably special residences or temples. Axial asymmetry is evident in the placement of platforms. Buildings around the plaza were complementary sets: the central pyramid and observatory formed a N-S pair, and the eastern acropolis and western platforms an E-W pair.

Complex A, north of the tallest pyramid, was built at 1/4 the scale of the original plaza arrangement (Clark 2001; Drucker et al. 1959). The northern half of Complex A included five low mounds surrounded by a 2 m high rectangular palisade of upright, natural basalt pillars. This compound arrangement appears to have been a novel architectural feature first seen at La Venta. The small court at Teopantecuanitlan (Martínez 1986, 1994, 2010) may have been patterned after the court at La Venta, and Group E at Uaxactun probably was in some way. The compound at Uaxactun is a scale model of the court in Complex A at La Venta. Spectacular jade and serpentine offerings, and royal tombs, were found in La Venta's Complex A court, along the principal axis and in mirror symmetry on both sides of it. At least one of these offerings had more than 1000 tons of serpentine (Drucker et al. 1959:97). Its little-explored companion offering probably had as much (Wedel 1952: fig. 20; see Clark and Colman 2012). Another addition was the importation of tons of basalt for stone monuments and architectural enhancements. These were brought in from over 100 km away (Williams and Heizer 1965:17; Pool 2007:148), probably on canoes or rafts.

To date, 73 carved stone monuments and over 200 one-ton columnar basalt pillars have been discovered in the city (González Lauck 2004, 2010b). Sculptures include colossal stone heads, tabletop thrones, full-figure images of seated kings, and low-relief carvings on stelae. At the base of the south side of the great pyramid stood 7 stelae facing the main plaza and flanking the staircase. Of the stelae on each side, 2 were representations of supernaturals (González Lauck 1996:76; 1997), perhaps anticipating a later Maya practice of modeled-stucco supernatural masks flanking the stairs of pyramids, or copying earlier Maya practices, first evident at El Cival (see Francisco Estrada-Belli, Chapter 6, this volume). The paired stelae on each side of the stairs were matched sets (the width of the stairs is hypothesized here), as evident in the diagonal markings of their ropes in the lower register of each axe-shaped monument of a supernatural.

With the exception of the six colossal stone heads used as boundary markers, stone sculptures were confined to the northern part of the city, the domain of La Venta's lords and priests. The oldest platforms in the north were rebuilt or refurbished many times during their four to five centuries of use (Drucker et al. 1959; Gillespie 2008). I think platforms were added to the southern end of La Venta after the initial construction of the northern buildings because the southern platforms are not as logically arranged as those of the early city, and they have no counterparts in coeval centers in Chiapas (see below). The southern part of La Venta dates to at least 500 BCE. Presumably, these southernmost platforms were for privileged personnel and state functionaries—a class of people that probably increased through time.

Some features of La Venta's layout appear to have been copied from San Lorenzo and modified (Cyphers, Chapter 4, this volume), other features were borrowed from other societies, and still others were instigated at La Venta (Clark 2008). These features came together in a pyramid city that established a new architectural ideal in Mesoamerica (see Clark and Colman 2012; Clark and Hansen 2001:3). The most obvious prototype for La Venta's main pyramid was built at least a century earlier at La Blanca on the south coast of Guatemala (Love 1991, 1993, 2002c, Chapter 7, this volume). I suspect that the idea of the La Venta plaza came from San Lorenzo, but the earliest plaza currently known was constructed at Paso de la Amada in the Mazatan region of the Soconusco about 1650 BCE. It was about half the size of the plaza at La Venta and of different orientation (Clark 2004a: fig. 2.6). The earliest known ballcourt is also from Paso de la Amada and is slightly earlier than its plaza (Hill et al. 1998; Hill and Clark 2001). The oldest securely dated E-Group of which I am aware is at Chiapa de Corzo. It dates to the Chiapa II-A phase (1000–850 BCE); the E-Group at Tzutzuculi dates to Chiapa II-B times (850–750 BCE). I think E-Groups were a local invention at La Venta about 900–800 BCE and that the idea spread from La Venta to contemporaneous centers in Chiapas and even later to centers in the Maya lowlands (Clark and Hansen 2001; see Estrada-Belli, Chapter 6, this volume, for a counter opinion). Because most buildings at La Venta have not yet been dated with radiocarbon or with associated ceramics, my argument remains inferential and unsubstantiated.

In its final form the central and monumental part of La Venta was about 58 ha in extent. With its residential neighborhoods, the city covered at least 200 ha (González Lauck 1996:75; 2001) and could have accommodated several thousand people, thus my preference for the term "city" instead of "town" or "village." Many more people lived on small islands and river levees within 10 km of the city (Pohl et al. 2002; Rust and Leyden 1994). The size of La Venta, the number of its stone sculptures and their royal themes, the number, size, and contents of its special offerings, and the presence of burials of high-status individuals demonstrate it was a special place and a regional polity or capital (Drucker 1952, 1981; Drucker et al. 1959). The extent of the La Venta polity has not been determined and remains a matter of speculation. A survey around the site by William Rust (Rust 1987, 1988; Rust and Leyden 1994) shows that the La Venta settlement hierarchy may have extended 40 km from the city center. It may have been greater than this. Christopher Pool (2007:154) argues that La Venta's control did not extend to the rival center of Tres Zapotes (see below) but likely included the famous sites of Arroyo Pesquero, 20 km south of La Venta, and Arroyo Sonso, 35 km to the southwest. Antonio Plaza, located a few kilometers farther west from this last site may have been another secondary center; the famous "wrestler" statue is from there (Cyphers and López Cisneros 2007). If Antonio Plaza was a secondary center, then the effective boundaries of the La Venta polity would have extended beyond the 40 km radius mentioned, at least in that direction. Final assessments of La Venta's influence depend on reconstructions of its foreign relations and historic connections to its predecessor at San Lorenzo.

It is presumed that La Venta was ruled by kings (for summaries, Clark 1997, 2004b), but the evidence comes from representations on stone monuments. No one has yet produced a body. The mortal remains of La Venta's rulers, and of all its other denizens, have not been recovered because bones and teeth do not preserve in the tropical conditions of the locale. Interpretations of royal history thus require a series of guesses about ancient burials and/or conjectures concerning the meaning of art and its chronological sequence. The preservation problem dictates that only graves with durable objects will be recovered. Thus, the bias is towards recovering the mortuary offerings of elite individuals, but this suits my current purpose. Many elite graves have been reported for La Venta, but most have been classified as "offerings" because no human remains were found in association with the jade jewelry and stone axes (see Drucker and Heizer 1965:56–58; *contra* W. Coe and Stuckenrath 1965). At least 10 graves are known for the site and they span its history (Colman 2010). All but one are from Complex A, north of the pyramid.

Burials are ordered by construction phases of Complex A (Drucker et al. 1959; the following summary based on Colman 2010). Only one burial each is known for Phase I (Offering No. 7: Drucker et al. 1959:171–74; Drucker and Heizer 1965:59) and for Phase II (Offering No. 3: Drucker et al. 1959:146–52). Two burials have been assigned to Phase III (Offerings No. 5 and 6: Drucker et al. 1959:162–71) and seven to Phase IV (Offerings 1940A, 1942A, 1942B, 1942D, 1943F, 1943G, and 1943L: Drucker 1952; Drucker et al. 1959:272–74). These "offerings" were elite burials, most of them primary but some secondary. Jade jewelry, figurines, and axes were the mortuary offerings of choice from the very beginning. Pots are rare in these graves, so these burials have been dated by gross architectural association rather than through pottery styles. It is not certain that any of these burials were of kings, but they were certainly of persons of privilege. The most common elements were jade earspools, necklaces, bracelets, and sometimes a jade bead belt and simple headdress with a jade maskette with other jade spangles, all indicating use as mortuary offerings that accompanied elite burials for which no osteological remains have survived (see Clark and Colman 2013). The few clues available indicate that children as well as adults were buried with these symbols of high status (Drucker 1952:23–26; Stirling and Stirling 1942:640–43). Bodies were positioned to the cardinal directions (as determined by the disposition of head and body ornaments), with no preference apparent for a particular direction in the small burial sample. Most burial facilities were simple graves, but three special tombs are known. These tombs (Offerings 1942A, 1952B, 1943G) were all on La Venta's central axis in Complex A, and they all date to the last construction phase (Drucker 1952; Drucker et al. 1959; Gillespie 2011; Stirling 1943a, b; Stirling and Stirling 1942). Another interesting feature is that the primary burials in these tombs were all accompanied by jade bloodletters; no bloodletters were found in the other elite graves. Bloodletters may thus have been symbols of royal status (Drucker 1952: Plate 53; Stirling 1943a; Stirling and Stirling 1942:640–43). Among the elite burials excavated at Chiapa de Corzo in 2010 were a male-female pair; a stingray spine was found with the woman but not the man (Bachand and Lowe 2011).

The famous basalt pillar tomb had two bundle burials of children (Offering 1942A), as well as numerous offerings (Drucker 1952:23–26; Stirling 1943b; Stirling and Stirling 1942), including two jade bloodletters and six stingray spines. The burial bundles are evidence of elaborate mortuary treatments for some individuals and curation of some human remains for later burial. The sandstone sarcophagus, Monument 6, just to the south of the pillar tomb contained a primary burial, perhaps of a king (Offering 1942B), with his head oriented to the south as indicated by the positions of the jade jewelry and bloodletter (Drucker 1952:26–27, 178; figs. 9, 58, 60, Plate 2; Stirling 1943a, b; Stirling and Stirling 1942). Both the basalt pillar tomb and stone sarcophagus were placed on top of a low platform (Mound A-2), and another construction layer was added to the mound to cover both tombs. In contrast, the burial in between these tombs (Offering 1942F) was intruded into the earlier mound and then covered with a roof of basalt pillars (Drucker 1952:27, 64, 161, 165, 167; Stirling 1943a: Plate 1). The bodies interred in these burial chambers were covered with thick layers of cinnabar.

The novelty of the basalt tomb has detracted from a far more spectacular tomb (the best candidate for a ruler) in Mound A-3. The so-called cist tomb or "Tomb C" (Offering 1943G) was much larger than the rest and perpendicular to the site's axis, but straddling the axis perfectly. This tomb measured 5.2 m from east to west and 1.8 m from north to south (Wedel 1952:68). Mound A-3 was built over this tomb. First an elaborate floor of carefully shaped and fitted flagstones was created, and stone slabs and wooden planks (my conjecture) were set upright around this pavement to create the crypt. Five large stone slabs were also used for the roof (Drucker 1952: figs. 21, 22, Plates 14 and 52). This crypt "was completely surrounded, underlain, and covered by the massive red clay and clay rubble of which the mound core had been constructed. Directly over the cist, the upper surface of the red clay reached its highest point, suggesting that when the tumulus was raised, its primary purpose was to cover this boxlike structure" (Drucker 1952:67–68). The arrangement of jade jewelry in this tomb indicates a primary individual with his or her head to the east. This person was buried with jade earspools, ear pendants, a hairpiece with a jade tube, clothing with approximately 110 small jade spangles or beads sewn on, a belt or girdle of fancy jade beads, a serpentine figurine on the stomach, and a jade bloodletter and an incised obsidian core at the waist (Drucker 1952:69, fig. 22; Stirling 1943a:322). This individual also had an obsidian blade and fragment of an iron-ore mirror (Colman 2010:219). Around the edges of the crypt were 29 jade and 9 serpentine axes and 3 ceramic vessels.

> Scattered through the heavy masses of cinnabar surrounding these objects were scores of tiny jade beads, pendants, spangles, and other objects. Many of these pieces were less than 1 cm or so long and not more than 1 or 2 cm in transverse diameter, but all had been polished and perforated for attachment to some material, presumably a textile. Several small tubular beads, 2 cm or so long, had been carved into faithful representations of duck heads. Along with these objects were several small bits of worked and bored rock crystal (Drucker 1952:70). In an irregular curving line 90 cm long and centering at the jade punch [bloodletter] was a row of 64 globular jade beads, several of them with fluted sides.

At each end of this bead row was a small flattened elliptical jade object apparently representing a turtle carapace. (Drucker 1952:71)

There was enough space in this tomb to have accommodated four or six sacrificed attendants (indicated by the axe offerings) placed around the primary body in a manner analogous to coeval royal burials at Chiapa de Corzo and La Libertad in Chiapas (see below).

La Venta burials provide a minimal view of revered rulers for this polity. The most obvious places to recover royal tombs have not yet been excavated, so future excavations could add to the list. The perishable items of royal dress tantalizingly suggested by the distribution of small jade beads in the cist tomb are better evident in depictions of rulers and elite individuals on stone monuments (Clark and Colman 2013). Representations of rulers at La Venta differ significantly from those at the earlier city of San Lorenzo (Clark 1997, 2004b), but there are also clear continuities in the sculptural programs of these two Olmec kingdoms. Celebrated continuities include colossal stone heads, tabletop thrones, sculptures of seated figures in the round, and U-shaped trough stones and covers used in drain systems (Cyphers 1999, 2004a; Diehl 1981; Heizer et al. 1968; Lowe 1989b). Innovations at La Venta include massive stelae and an emphasis on low-relief depictions, including possible narrative scenes on stelae (these are rare at La Venta), and the incorporation of standing stone monuments in the monumental architecture (Clark 2004b). The evolution and precise chronology of early sculpture in Mesoamerica is up for grabs (see Clark et al. 2010; Clark and Hodgson 2008; Clark and Pye 2000a; Clark 2004b) and continues to be a point of contention for those questioning the relative merits of early Olmec and Maya civilizations. Ann Cyphers (Cyphers et al. 2006; Cyphers and Zurita-Noguera 2006a) reports a colossal head and a tabletop throne at San Lorenzo in an early architectural context, and there is other supporting evidence that the carving of massive stone monuments began before 1300 BCE at San Lorenzo (Coe and Diehl 1980:246; Pool 2007:134). Olmec sculpture in the Soconusco of Chiapas dates to at least 1100 BCE and most likely to 1250 BCE (Clark and Hodgson 2008; Clark and Pye 2000b; Pinkowski 2006), so those at San Lorenzo that were being copied must be at least this early. Given the site histories, arguments for a late chronology for San Lorenzo sculpture (Graham 1989; Hammond 1988) and of the contemporaneity of San Lorenzo and La Venta monuments are not credible.

Many, but not all, Middle Preclassic stone monuments across Mesoamerica outside the Maya area appear to be in the La Venta style (Fig. 5.4; see also Grove, Chapter 3, this volume), but such labeling of styles colors their interpretation in favor of La Venta's presumed dominance. Sculptures are low-relief carvings on boulders or rock faces, generally of standing figures shown in profile. Mural art in the same regions relates to the stone carvings in theme and presentation. I think most of these monuments and paintings date to 900–750 BCE, soon after the founding and establishment of La Venta as a city and its rise to prominence, but secure evidence for dating these monuments is lacking (Clark et al. 2010). Some carvings could be earlier, and those along the Usumacinta River on the edge of the Maya lowlands are clearly later (ca. 600–500 BCE, see below). Stone sculptures found at La Venta suggest a developmental sequence from large boulder stelae to smaller stelae shaped on all sides. Four of the seven stelae found at the base of the great pyramid are carved as giant incised celts (Porter 1992), and one is a giant scepter (González Lauck 2010b). The upper registers of the giant celts display the frontal images of a bundled earth or corn god, as on some jadeite celts (Fig. 5.5).

The idea of erecting stelae at La Venta probably derives from the earlier practice of placing jade and greenstone axe offerings, as seen at El Manatí and La Merced (Jaime Riverón 2003; Ortíz and Rodríguez 1994, 1999, 2000, 2008; Ortíz et al. 1997). At La Merced, plain and carved axes were planted on their poll ends, with the broader bit or blade ends in the upright position (Rodríguez and Ortíz 2000), as most obviously seen with Offering 4 at La Venta, the famous scene of jade and serpentine figurines standing in front of upright celts (Drucker et al. 1959:152, fig. 38). Some axe-like stelae at La Venta were carved from green rock and positioned in this same manner, with their carved images facing the plaza. The final architectural setting of these monuments dates before 400 BCE, providing a terminal date for these sculptures (González Lauck 1996:75; 1997:93). The massive Stela 2 depicting a king in frontal view probably dates to about 700 BCE, given its similarities to boulder sculptures and its high relief. I think Stela 3 dates to about 600 BCE. It is similar in style and theme to both Stela 2 and Stela 5 (González Lauck 1988: fig. 2; 1994: figs. 6.9–6.11; 1997:87) (see Fig. 5.5).

Foreign Relations

Stela 3 is 4.27 m tall and weighs 26 metric tons (Heizer 1967:28). It has a well-known scene of two life-size standing men in elaborate garb facing

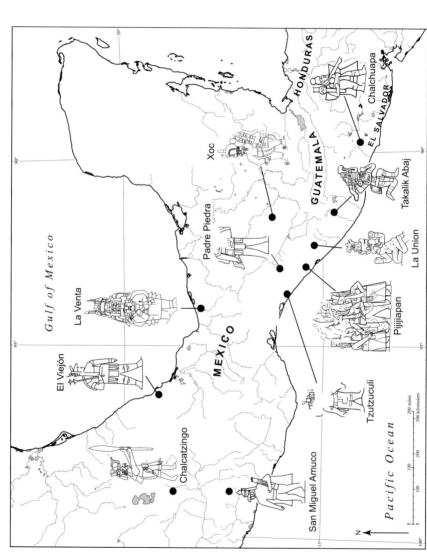

5.4. Distribution of early Middle Preclassic bas-relief monuments in Mesoamerica.

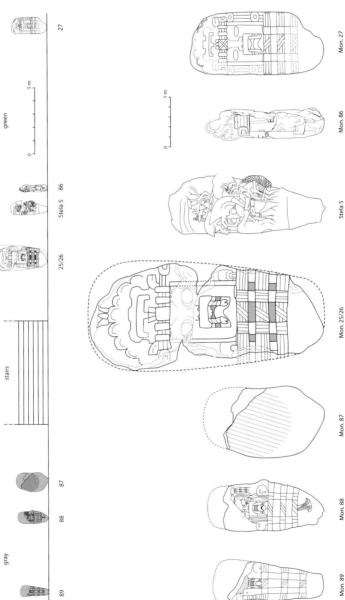

5.5. Reconstruction of the stelae on the south side of the Mound C-1 at La Venta. Redrawn from photographs and drawings (González Lauck 1988, 1994, 1997; Porter 1992), with additions from personal examination of the monuments.

green

5 m

0

gray

stairs

89 88 87 25/26 Stela 5 86 27

3 m

0

Mon. 27

Mon. 86

Stela 5

Mon. 25/26

Mon. 87

Mon. 88

Mon. 89

each other (Fig. 5.6). One, the famous "Uncle Sam" bearded figure standing on the right, is a personage unique in Olmec art; he looks rather Mayan. Standard interpretation of this scene as a narrative of an event involving a foreign dignitary or "outlander" (Covarrubias 1957:67; Heizer 1967:30; Pool 2007:167) strikes me as probable. Uncle Sam, with his false beard and unusual nose (incorrectly rendered in most drawings), does not look Olmec. Both figures are shown with elaborate headdresses, jade jewelry, and clothing. One does not have to know the specific polity that this individual represented, however, to realize he was accorded equal billing on this stone marquee of foreign diplomacy. Late kings of La Venta apparently publically acknowledged and recognized in a permanent medium the existence of political and social equals among their neighbors or friends. It is interesting that the face of the presumed Olmec dignitary on Stela 3 has been obliterated and that the face of Uncle Sam was left intact—perhaps an indicator of changing political fortunes, near the end of La Venta's history, of the individuals involved and the polities they represented.

Different classes of artifacts found at La Venta demonstrate that the city started strong and declined through time. Most of the spectacular offerings, monuments, and constructions at the site date to the first centuries of its history (Drucker et al. 1959; González Lauck 2007). Through time, the site saw the incorporation of new elements from different places. The final centuries of occupation at La Venta witnessed unincorporated foreign elements indicative of relations between peers, most evident in the confrontation represented on Stela 3. The burial record at the present time appears to counter the evidence of the massive offerings. The only known tombs date to the last construction phase of Complex A. They were the easiest to find. The construction of the basalt column tomb, I think, demonstrates the declining power and reach of the La Venta kingdom. The natural columns for this sepulcher were clearly taken from the palisade built several centuries earlier (see Wedel 1952:65), so some of the expensive materials for this burial facility were recycled from the site itself.

Obsidian source analyses indicate access to obsidian from both the major source areas of western and eastern Mesoamerica. The majority of the obsidian found at the site came from Guatemalan sources (Rebecca González Lauck, pers. comm. 2008). Obsidian that arrived at the small dependency of San Andrés just north of La Venta is the most abused I have seen in 30 years of analyzing collections (Doering 2002; Pohl et al. 2002).

5.6. Stela 3 from La Venta showing the possible meeting of Olmec and foreign dignitaries. Drawn from a photograph (Heizer 1967:plate 1).

Obsidian appears to have been in short supply at this dependent site, and it was used and broken up until there were just slivers of shattered blades left. Obsidian flakes and blades were more common at La Venta itself and at other dependencies such as Isla Alor (Rabb et al. 2000, 2001; Stokes 1999; William Rust, pers. comm. 2007).

Imported pots from the Maya area show up at La Venta by 800 BCE and become more frequent through time (Andrews 1990; von Nagy 2003:822, 834, 843; von Nagy et al. 2002; von Nagy et al. 2000). These Maya imports (mostly Joventud Red) date to the Mamom phase. Some pots were also imported from central Chiapas (von Nagy 2003:843). Not all red pottery at La Venta was imported; some was made locally to imitate the imports (Rust's Uxpanapa ceramic group, pers. comm. 2007). I am not aware of any La Venta pottery at lowland Maya sites, but white-and-black bowls (from the Franco complex at San Andrés) show up in Chiapa III times at San Isidro (Lowe 1999), Chiapa de Corzo (Warren 1959:101), Mirador (Agrinier 2000), Ocozocoautla (personal observation), La Libertad (Miller et al. 2005), Izapa (Lowe et al. 2013), and possibly at Tres Zapotes and Estero Rabón in Veracruz (King 2002; Pool 2007:146; von Nagy 2003:199). There are also two low-relief monuments in the epi-Olmec style from the Ocozocoautla and Villa Flores region, the only such carvings currently known for central Chiapas (see below). The possible imported red serving bowls at La Venta need to be analyzed to determine their loci of manufacture. Some could have come from Chiapas, but I suspect most are from the Maya lowlands.

The blue-green jade at La Venta came from sources in highland Guatemala (Seitz et al. 2001; Taube 2004), and the many tons of serpentine came from Oaxaca (Jaime Riverón 2003). I once thought that San Martín Jilotepeque obsidian and Guatemala jade arrived at La Venta via the string of centers along the Grijalva River (Clark and Hansen 2001:11; Clark and Lee 1984, 2007), starting at La Libertad up river, coming through Chiapa de Corzo, Ocozocoautla, and San Isidro to arrive at La Venta (Fig. 5.1). This is a natural travel route. However, the artifacts I have recently seen from La Venta and nearby San Andrés convince me I was wrong about this trade route, at least for late La Venta times. Residents at La Venta had different supply lines and obtained different products than I supposed. For its final phase, most of the obsidian came from highland Mexico sources instead of from Guatemala, counter to my speculation based on the pioneering obsidian source studies at La Venta in the 1970s (Jack et al. 1972; Jack and Heizer

1968; Sisson 1976). As for jade, the distribution of late Olmec sculptures and carved axes along the edge of the Maya lowlands (García Moll 1979; Ochoa 1983; Ochoa and Hernández 1977; Rivero Torres 1992:10) suggests the principal trade route to the Guatemalan jade mines was up the Usumacinta and overland through the Northern Maya Highlands (Fig. 5.4). Kaminaljuyu and centers in the Chiapas interior were off the main route.

SAN ISIDRO, CHIAPAS

San Isidro is located about 135 km southwest of La Venta near the northern edge of the rugged northern highlands of Chiapas in the Middle Grijalva Region (Lowe 1998a, 1999). This is an area of high rainfall and evergreen tropical forest. San Isidro is the northernmost Preclassic center in Chiapas and one of the closest regional centers to La Venta. San Isidro extends over 100 ha and was a regional center in early Olmec times, closely related to San Lorenzo (Lowe 1998a, b). The site was nearly continuously occupied until Late Classic times and was a locus of occasional pilgrimage and offerings into Early Postclassic times (Lee 1974a; Lowe 1999). San Isidro was advantageously situated on a broad terrace on the left bank of the Grijalva River and about 30 km upstream from the Grijalva's confluence with the La Venta River and the dry-season rapids or *"mal paso"* (bad passage) there (Lee 1974a, b; Lowe 1981, 1998a, 1999). Limited excavations were undertaken at the site from March to June in 1966 as part of salvage operations for the Mal Paso reservoir, with many of the numerous features at the site recorded as dammed water began to cover the site (Lee 1974b; Lowe 1967, 1981). Evidence that San Isidro was the seat of an ancient kingdom is its size, the number, size, and arrangement of its earthen platforms and offerings, and its regional settlement pattern. Some axe offerings are similar to those known for La Venta (Drucker 1952; Drucker et al. 1959) and La Merced (Rodríguez and Ortíz 2000; Ortiz and Rodríguez 2008).

Site and Kingdom History

The main mounds at San Isidro were constructed mostly during the Middle Preclassic. Some were erected over low clay platforms built about 1200 BCE (Fig. 5.7). Of the numerous large mounds at the site, only six were somewhat adequately tested in the few months available for exploration. Test excavations were carried out at Mound 20 (Lowe 1981, 1998a, 1999),

Mound 4 (Lee 1974a, b), Mounds 1, 2, 3, and 29 (Lowe 1998a), and near other mounds (Lowe 1999). Rising water prevented excavation to sterile layers in the tallest mounds, so information is only available for the latest stages of construction. Thus, many of these mounds are presumed to be older than the periods verified with the partial excavations. Lowe (1967:136) reports that traces of early Olmec occupations (coeval with the San Lorenzo phase at that site) were recovered from all areas of San Isidro where excavations penetrated to sterile layers. At 1200 BCE, San Isidro was at least 7.5 ha (Lowe 1998a:37) and probably three to four times that size. A decapitated sculpture in the round of a seated jaguar was found at this site (Lowe 1998a:48; Navarrete et al. 1993: fig. 3), similar to those known for Loma del Zapote near San Lorenzo (Cyphers 2004a:246–48). Along with four sculptures and several fragments found in the Soconusco region (Clark and Hodgson 2008; Clark and Pye 2000b), this headless jaguar is one of the few early Olmec sculptures known outside the Gulf lowlands. San Isidro is also one of the few sites outside of Olman for which early platforms are reported (Lowe 1981, 1989b, 1998a, 2007; Navarrete et al. 1992; see Clark 1997 for others). The fate of San Isidro appears to have been tied up with the fortunes of San Lorenzo. Both experienced the same episode of abandonment at the end of the Early Preclassic period. San Isidro was again reoccupied beginning about 900 BCE, and pyramid-building began soon after (Lowe 1999).

The major building efforts at San Isidro were contemporaneous with those at La Venta, but with different results. As described in following sections for other kingdoms, many new regional centers built in central Chiapas during the Middle Preclassic were based on the designed layout of La Venta. San Isidro, La Venta's closest neighbor in Chiapas, is an ironic exception. San Isidro "includes four pyramidal mounds, two rectangular courts, and eight platform complexes ranging from simple to complex substructures of huge dimensions" (Lowe 1967:136). Based on Lowe's (1981, 1998a) observations of early clay platforms under Middle Preclassic mounds, I suggest a possible reason for the differences in layout of these two centers may be that the Middle Preclassic occupants at San Isidro deliberately erected their pyramids over earlier platforms to conserve or capture their essence. Among the centers described here, San Isidro is one of two that had relic mounds on its future cityscape by the Middle Preclassic. San Isidro exhibits evidence of planning along major and minor axes and of large platforms clustered around north-south trending plazas (see, Lowe 1999:30–33).

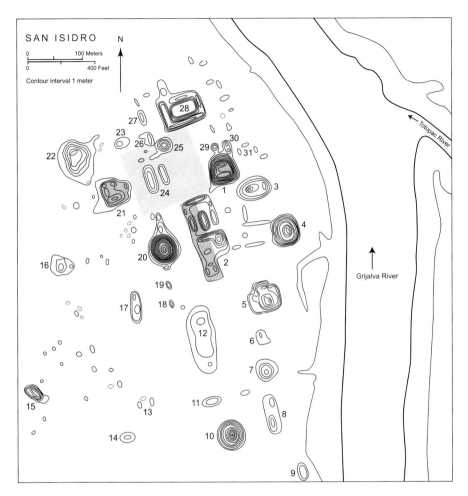

5.7. Site map of San Isidro.

In an earlier study, Richard Hansen and I described a Middle Formative Chiapas pattern, or MFC complex (Clark and Hansen 2001). This consists of a long north-south plaza (sometimes a double square) with a pyramid at the northern end of this plaza, a long mound with an offset eastern pyramid (an E-Group) on the southern end, a large acropolis or broad mound on the eastern margin of the plaza, and a row of smaller platforms to the west of the plaza—basically the hypothesized central and early part of La Venta (Fig. 5.3). These observations of site layout build on those made by Andrew McDonald (1974, 1999) and Lowe (1977) for the patterning of

Middle Preclassic centers in Chiapas. Both these scholars include San Isidro among the Middle Preclassic centers in Chiapas that conform to their pattern. I do not see sufficient evidence that San Isidro conforms to the full MFC pattern. Lowe (1998a:85; 1999:31) argues that Mounds 20 and 2 at San Isidro constitute a solstice observatory or astronomic complex (an E-Group). This is only half of the MFC pattern. Future research may reveal that another critical component of the MFC complex is architecture techniques. Lowe (1967:136) observes that at San Isidro "Platform floors and walls were of clay, frequently highly polished and fired and having inset stairways." The practice of firing the clay veneer of a mound to give it a red color has also been described for Chiapa de Corzo, Finca Acapulco, La Libertad, and Tzutzuculi.

The survey results of the Mal Paso project show that one peak period of occupation was the Middle to Late Preclassic (Lee et al. 2013; Martínez Muriel 1988:103; Martínez Muriel and Navarrete 1978:233). Besides San Isidro, at least two Middle Preclassic sites in the region, La Vega del Laurel and El Maritano, had small pyramids by this time (Lee 1974a:6; Lee and Clark 2015; Lowe 1991:114, fig. 10; 1998a:50; 2007:99; L. Lowe 1998:35). La Vega del Laurel, erroneously published as "El Laurel" (Lowe 1991, 2007), is located across the river and about a kilometer east of San Isidro. It had a small pyramid by 800 BCE (Lee and Clark 2015) and likely was a secondary center to San Isidro by Chiapa II-B times. Excavations have verified Middle Preclassic features for three other sites in the region: El Achiote, Banco Nieves, and San Antonio (L. Lowe 1998). An early elite burial dating to Chiapa III times was excavated at El Achiote. This individual had, among other things, a necklace of 460 jade beads, a small jade earspool, and several ceramic offering vessels. El Achiote is located about 40 km from San Isidro by river (Lee et al. 2015). It may have been an independent center or a secondary center. More sites had been occupied, of course. The limited information from salvage excavations suffices to indicate a three-tier settlement hierarchy by 750 BCE in the Middle Grijalva region. This settlement pattern continued at least until 400 BCE (Lee 1974a, b). In a final synthesis on San Isidro, Lowe provides the following summary observations.

> At the close of the Dzewa phase [Chiapa II-B], surely before 600 BCE, the proto-Zoque Olmecs of the Middle Grijalva had established their regional center and community, the most important in the San Isidro

region. During this time, in Mound 20, we find a pyramidal platform 7–8 m tall. This same architectural development is also evident in the large acropolis-like platforms at Mounds 1 and 4 during the Felisa phase [IV], both constructed on top of occupations of the Cacahuanó [I] and Dombi [II-A] phases. Other platforms at the site that were not explored probably have similar sequences of growth. The locations of structures along axial lines, leaving open places for plazas, suggests planning and probably a division of tasks and ranks among the population. It is important to note that Mound 20 at San Isidro, along with the elongated platform at Mound 2, would form part of an astronomical commemoration complex, emphasized in the Equipac [III] or Felisa [IV] phase, if not before (Lowe 1989b:365). (Lowe 1998a:85, my translation)

The second half of the Middle Preclassic is well represented in Mounds 1, 4, and 29. Mounds 1 and 4 would cover acropolis-like platforms and become 8 and 10 m high, respectively, dating to the Felisa phase. Surely their centers or cores consisted of lower platforms of the Equipac and Dzewa phases, as was the case in Mound 20. Pyramids 5 and 10, also over 10 m tall, were not explored but they probably had their own sequence of development starting in the Middle Preclassic. (Lowe 1998a:50, my translation)

Foreign Relations

Evidence of interregional contacts for Middle Preclassic San Isidro are most apparent in ceramic similarities and in cultural practices of axial offerings. Obsidian artifacts for this site have not been reported, and I have not examined any. Jade beads, earspools, and other objects have been found at Chiapa II-B, III, and IV sites (Lowe 1998a, 1999; L. Lowe 1998). The pottery for these eras shows the closest connections to that from Middle Preclassic centers in the Chiapas interior, and the phase sequence is set up to parallel those from Mirador and Chiapa de Corzo (Lee 1974b). I can do no better than present Lowe's final assessment of ceramic ties to other regions. He saw significant connections between the inhabitants of San Isidro and Gulf coast Olmec peoples from 1300 to 500 BCE (Chiapa I–III), with a turn towards the Maya lowlands from 500–300 BCE (Chiapa IV), and then renewed ties with Gulf societies from 300 BCE onward (Chiapa V–VII).

The presence of smudged black and white ceramics in the Equipac phase, although scarce, is significant because it indicates a continual interaction with Olmec centers in the Gulf. This interaction was typical of the other Chiapa III centers, and it greatly contrasts with the situation in Chiapa IV times when this [black-and-white] tradition practically disappeared. During Chiapa IV times, slipped black, red, and orange monochromes were in vogue, indicative of constant interaction with the lowland Maya. In western Chiapas during Chiapa V times there was a reintroduction of white-rim black pottery, and this renewed tradition suggests that the Zoques rejected part of the Maya influence and returned to the older system of interaction. In the Equipac phase, the population maintained their roots and relationships with the Gulf, even though they were interacting more frequently with other neighbors. (Lowe 1999:108–9, my translation)

We can consider the absence of typical white-rim black Olmec pottery at Chiapa IV sites—and its wide distribution during Chiapa V times in western Chiapas—as evidence of a special readjustment that occurred at the end of the Middle Preclassic. At first glance, this phenomenon could have two simple explanations: (A) a new and dominant stylistic influence arrived in Chiapas from the Maya lowlands during the Mamom phase, or (B) the rise of a brief development of Zoque local independence during Chiapa IV times. Whichever may prove to be the case, we must conclude that the Zoques of Chiapas and the lowland Maya of the Middle Preclassic rejected the ancient [La Venta] Olmec tradition of making differentially fired [white-rim black] vessels, for technical or aesthetic reasons, favoring instead colored, slipped monochromes. Thus, a type of "Zoque development towards greater independence" postulated as a possibility for Chiapas during Chiapa IV [500–300 BCE] could still closely share the local style of the Maya lowlands (we note that the developed style of Usulutan negative-resist, typical of Central America, did not reach Chiapas in this period, and neither was the predominant gray pottery of Oaxaca influential). The situation suggests that the Zoques of Chiapas during Chiapa IV times abandoned the cultural mores of the Gulf Olmec, as we understand them (or they limited their reciprocal exchange; much of the early black-and-white pottery in Chiapas was imported from the Gulf). (Lowe 1999:118–19, my translation)

It is worth noting that pottery was imported into San Isidro, Chiapa de Corzo, and other Chiapas centers from the Maya lowlands in Chiapa V times, as were pots from the Valley of Oaxaca (Lowe 1999, 2007; L. Lowe 1998:35; Miller et al. 2005; Warren 1959). Christopher von Nagy (2003:199) identified some sherds from imported pottery vessels from La Venta at San Isidro.

San Isidro is best known for a series of jade axe and pseudo-axe offerings found extending east of Mound 20 on the short axis of the site (Fig. 5.8; see Lowe 1981: figs. 4–7). In his early report, Lowe (1981) assigned these to the Chiapa III or Equipac phase. In his final revision of Chiapas Preclassic chronology (Lowe 1998a:59; 2007), he reassigned them to the Chiapa II-B or Dzewa phase (850–750 BCE). These "stone chisel or axe offerings [were] laid out much in the La Venta Olmec manner, both with and without associated human interments. These offerings...followed an axis extending westward beneath one of the major pyramids and an unknown distance beyond the center of the plaza 25 m to the east" (Lowe 1967:136). Given the limited excavation possible at San Isidro, we have no basis for extrapolating the pattern because other alignments were not tested. The earliest axe offering in the San Isidro or Mal Paso region dates to the Cacahuanó phase (1300–1100 BCE) in Mound 3 at El Maritano (Lowe 2007:100; Navarrete 1992:122, 157, fig. 15b).

Lowe (1981, 1998a) demonstrated that axe offerings date to Chiapa II-B and III times, that they were on a west-east alignment east of Mound 20, and that the number of axes of high-quality and low-quality stone varied with each offering, as did the number of axes, ceramic vessels, and other items. The most famous is Offering 11 of Excavation 5 (Fig. 5.8). It is a quincunx of jade axes and giant earspools arranged around a ceramic bowl. It is reminiscent of early cruciform offerings at La Venta (Drucker et al. 1959: fig. 51), as well as Cache 7 at Seibal [Ceibal] (Sabloff 1975:230; Smith 1982:115–19, 243–45; Willey 1978:88–89, 97; Willey et al. 1975:44) and Caches 109 and 118 at the same site (Inomata 2012; Inomata et al. 2010), and the El Cival cache (Estrada-Belli 2004a, 2006a: fig. 3, Chapter 6, this volume; Estrada Belli, Bauer et al. 2003) in the Maya lowlands. Offering 11 at San Isidro is unusual because two of the axes were set upright—an attribute also seen at La Venta (Offerings Nos. 1, 4, 13, 1943-D; Drucker et al. 1959), at El Cival in northern Guatemala, in earlier offerings at La Merced (Jaime Riverón 2003; Rodríguez and Ortíz 2000), and in recent offerings found at Chiapa de Corzo (Bachand and Lowe 2011). Celts and axes in all

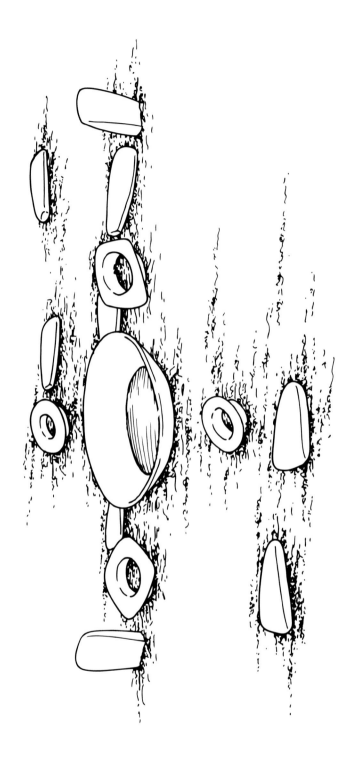

5.8. Cruciform Offering 11 from San Isidro showing the jade earspools and standing jade celts around a ceramic bowl.

the other caches at San Isidro were placed horizontally, with their long axes arranged east-west.

The axe offerings at San Isidro are presumed to be Olmec because similar offerings were first reported from La Venta (Drucker 1952; Drucker et al. 1959). Axe offerings at La Venta were placed along the principal north-south axis rather than east-west, as at San Isidro. It is worth pointing out that the alternative axial lines at both these sites were not investigated, so we still do not know whether these differences represent real differences rather than accidents of excavation strategy. The axe caches found at Chiapa de Corzo (Bachand and Lowe 2011) were on the interior east-west axis of the E-Group as at Ceibal (Inomata 2012) and in a large offering pit, as at La Venta. A cruciform axe offering was found at the foot of the E-Group pyramid at Chiapa de Corzo, similar to axe arrangements at La Venta. In Lowe's interpretation, the San Isidro axe caches are on the interior axis of the E-Group there, constituted by Mounds 20 and 2 (see Fig. 5.7). There is some evidence of caches at La Venta on the east-west axis that passed through its E-Group. Offering 1940A (Stirling 1940a:325; 1943b:55) was placed just east of Altar 4, one of two altars placed on Mound D-8 marking its short axis (Drucker 1952:166; Lowe 1989b: fig. 4.10a; Stirling 1940a:325; 1943b:55). It is important to emphasize that none of the celts found at San Isidro was incised (Lowe 1977:224), so there is nothing explicitly Olmec about them. The same can be said of axe offerings in the Maya lowlands (Inomata 2012; Inomata et al. 2010). I think these offerings derived from lowland Olmec practices going back to at least 1400 BCE, as is most evident in the sequence of axe offerings at El Manatí (Ortíz and Rodríguez 1989, 1994, 1999, 2000). By 700 BCE the practice of offering axes was widely distributed across cultures, but the cruciform arrangement was not. The only other Middle Preclassic site in Chiapas known to have axe offerings in cruciform arrangements is Chiapa de Corzo.

In Chiapa IV times the types of offerings at San Isidro shifted from celts and axes to urn burials, some of them child sacrifices (Lee 1974a:75).

Overlying the zone of axe offerings at San Isidro was a series of later Preclassic caches and burials, outstandingly exemplified by urn burials of infants or children, a trait noted within or surrounding all major pyramidal structures, with over a score being recovered by the limited excavations. Additionally, sub-floor platform offerings dating to about the beginning of our era appear to have originally contained hundreds of vessels, many of them of the coarse bowl type intended exclusively for offertories; there was never sufficient time to follow these giant offerings to their extremities. (Lowe 1967:136)

One obvious difference between San Isidro and La Venta is the absence of stone sculpture at San Isidro—an absence characteristic of almost all Middle Preclassic sites in Chiapas. Thomas Lee (1982, 1989: fig. 9.7c) reports a low-relief carving from Rancho Acapulco, a site a few kilometers south of San Isidro. He argues that this sculpture is a frontal image of an Olmec face similar to those reported for Tzutzuculi on the Pacific coast of Chiapas (see below; also, Fig. 5.11). The Rancho Acapulco monument is crudely executed and fragmentary (see Navarrete et al. 1993:56, fig. 22).

OCOZOCOAUTLA, CHIAPAS

This 1 km² site is located in the central valley of Chiapas 40 km south of San Isidro and 40 km west of Chiapa de Corzo. The site is aligned 50 degrees east of north (McDonald 1999:62). It is near the southern edge of the northern Chiapas highlands on the overland route to San Isidro. As with this latter site, Ocozocoautla had a long history that spanned the early Middle Preclassic to Classic periods, with peak periods of development in the Middle Preclassic and Early Classic. Ocozocoautla appears to have been first occupied in Chiapa II-A times (McDonald 1999:61). Many large earthen mounds at the site were built in the Chiapa III phase and exhibit formal features also seen at La Venta and Chiapa de Corzo (Fig. 5.9). At early Ocozocoautla "wall and floor surfaces of rough stones and fired clay were in keeping with building practices at the time elsewhere in Chiapas" (McDonald 1999:62). During the following phase, cut stone masonry is evident. This shift in construction techniques parallels a similar change seen at nearby San Agustin (Navarrete 1959b) and at the distant center of La Libertad (see below).

The important datum about Ocozocoautla is that it has a MFC complex comprising Mounds 10, 11, 5, 6, and 7a (Fig. 5.9). Mound 18 dates to the Chiapa III phase but is not part of the MFC complex as defined here. It is evidence, however, of a significant population and architectural elaboration at the site in this early period. An unusual feature is the cruciform

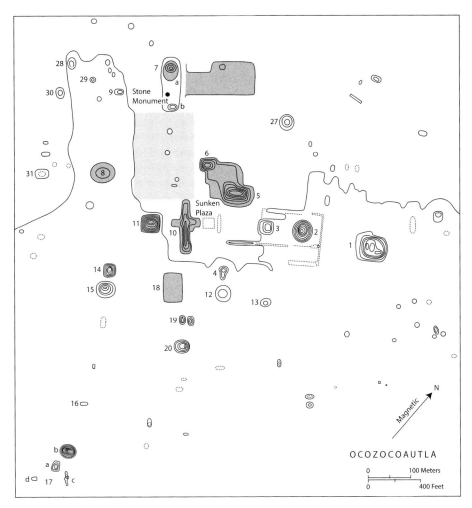

5.9. Map of Ocozocoautla. The mounds shown in gray indicate the MFC complex as well as known Middle Preclassic mounds.

shape of the long mound in the E-Group. Its MFC complex, the size of the site, and its location within the greater region are the principal evidence that Ocozocoautla was one of a string of regional centers and kingdoms along the Central Depression of Chiapas (Lowe 1977). Excavations were undertaken at this site by New World Archaeological Foundation (NWAF) personnel in 1972–1974. No Preclassic-era elite burials are known for Ocozocoautla, but three carved jade Olmec figurines have been found in the general region (Lee 1989; Navarrete 1974), and a low-relief sculpture in late Olmec style was discovered at the site several years after excavations had been completed there (Fig. 5.10). This monument was found just south of the northern mound (see Fig. 5.9) and probably dates to the late Middle Preclassic period (Tejada and R. Lowe 1993). The monument is carved on a thick slab of limestone and has a typical stela form, but the disposition of the carving shows the monument would have been seated with the long dimension horizontal rather than vertical. The image of the seated person encircled by a large, plumed serpent recalls the much smaller image of Monument 19 at La Venta (Drucker et al. 1959:197–200, fig. 55, Plates 49a, b). Details of the principal personage on the Ocozocoautla monument were defaced in prehistory. These sculptures appear stylistically to date to the end of the Middle Preclassic period. Most related sculptures in Meso-america appear to have been rather small, and with an emphasized theme of contortionists (Fig. 5.11).

Excavations were undertaken in various mounds. Mound 1 is a palace structure that dates to the Early Classic; a low platform with a Chiapa V burial was found beneath this mound (Agrinier 2013). Mound 2 also dates to the Early Classic but was built over a Protoclassic platform dating to Chiapa VI times (Gareth W. Lowe, NWAF report, May 20, 1972). A zone of Chiapa III refuse was found under this platform. Excavations showed that Mound 17 also dates to the Chiapa VI phase. Mound 15 dates to this time, too, and was systematically ravaged at the end of the period. Numerous ceramic trade wares from the Maya lowlands were found at this structure. (Maya influence in the Central Depression is discussed below in relation to Chiapa de Corzo, a site for which there is much more information.) The destruction of Mound 15 at Ocozocoautla may correspond to the burning of the Chiapa VI palace at Mound 5 at Chiapa de Corzo. The defacement and breaking of stone monuments at both sites was probably related to the destruction of these buildings (see below).

> Test pits in the long Mound 10 show it to be entirely a Chiapa III... construction. As such it joins Ocozocoautla with the ranks of a great number of similar sites, from Tres Zapotes and La Venta south across Chiapas, all of which I label as part of the Modified Olmec horizon. At Ocozocoautla there are other mounds and almost surely a pyramid of this date also. Underlying Mound 10 was a deposit of Chiapa II or con-

a

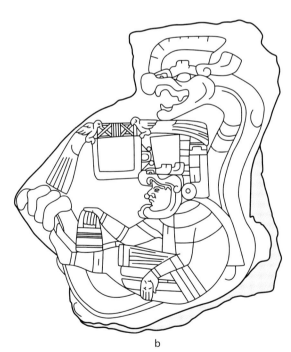

b

5.10. Middle Preclassic monuments depicting seated individuals encircled by serpents. A. Monument 1 from Ocozocoautla. B. Monument 19 from La Venta.

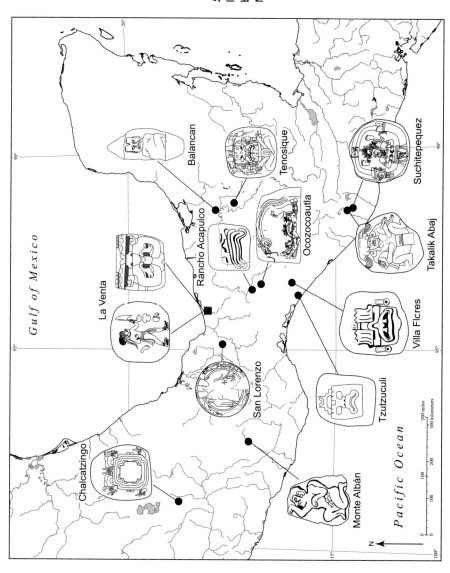

5.11. Distribution of late Middle Preclassic bas-relief monuments in Mesoamerica.

temporary Late Olmec sherds. Mound 18 is a great squarish platform forming part of an even greater terrace extension crossing the center of the site. Pits in Mound 18 show it also to be almost entirely a Middle Preclassic construction. An old abandoned and deeply eroding road cut through the 8 foot high terrace edge between Mounds 10 and 18 shows some eighty feet of deliberate platform construction. Sherds from this fill show a Late Preclassic upper limit, with some connections to the great enigmatic ruin of Perserverancia on the Pacific Coast. (Lowe, NWAF report, May 20, 1972)

Only one of the buildings of the MFC complex was excavated, Mound 10, and it was found to date to Chiapa III times, beginning about 750 BCE. Test pits around this structure encountered deposits of the same age. Mc-Donald found a specially constructed stone-lined pool just to the east of Mound 10 on the axis of this E-Group. This pool was filled in at the end of the Chiapa III phase. We can be reasonably certain that Mound 11, the companion mound of the E-Group, dates at least to Chiapa III times. The other remaining mounds of the MFC complex, Mounds 5, 6, and 7, have not been verified as early. I visited these mounds in February of 2008 and found Middle Preclassic sherds on Mounds 5 and 6, and on the large platform just east of Mound 7. Most of the sherds on this last platform date to the Chiapa II phase. The sherds directly on Mound 7 date to the Protoclassic period, but I would not be surprised if this mound covers an earlier construction.

Some white-rim black bowl fragments found in Chiapa III deposits were from vessels imported from the Gulf coast. The overall ceramic history at Ocozocoautla follows that described for San Isidro of a shift from trade with Gulf coast peoples in Chiapa III times to trade with lowland Maya by Chiapa V times, with a rejection of this Maya influence at the end of the Chiapa VI phase, or 100 CE. This is also the pattern at Chiapa de Corzo and Mirador. Clearly the histories of these kingdoms were linked.

MIRADOR, CHIAPAS

Mirador is the largest site located in the western end of the Central Depression, the narrow valley that runs through the middle of Chiapas. As with Ocozocoautla, Mirador was advantageously located to control travel along a natural route that ran north-south through Chiapas and connected the Pacific coast with the Gulf coast. It was also on the principal east-west route to the Isthmus of Tehuantepec and Laguna Zope (Agrinier 1984). Site history parallels those of its sister centers at San Isidro and Ocozocoautla. The Mirador locale was first occupied in the Early Preclassic about 1600 BCE (Agrinier et al. 2000) and was abandoned in the Late Classic period. No sculptures or elite burials are known for the Preclassic era of the site. A small greenstone carved Olmec axe was found at the site (Agrinier 1975: fig. 20), and two small jade Olmec figurines have been reported nearby in Miramar and Vistahermosa (Lee 1989: fig. 9.8b). These artifacts show connections to the coastal Olmecs and likely date to Chiapa II-B or III times.

The scant information on regional settlement indicates that both sides of the La Venta River that flows by Mirador were heavily populated for a distance of 15 km and about 2 km on each side during the Late Classic period (Peterson 1961, 1963:2). Several of these sites also had some Middle and Late Preclassic occupation (Clark 2014; Peterson 2014). Other Middle Preclassic pyramid sites in the greater Cintalapa-Jiquipilas Valley are Tiltepec Alto and Vistahermosa (López Jiménez and Esponda 1998, 1999; Treat 1969, 1986). Given their distances from Mirador, these two sites are assumed to have been independent, smaller centers (Lowe 1969:357; 2007). The Mirador locale was the heart of Middle Preclassic occupation, with 11 sites within an 8 km radius having Chiapa III and IV occupation (Clark 2014). None of these sites has been excavated so their pyramids have not been dated. Mirador was clearly a capital center; secondary centers have yet to be identified. As at Ocozocoautla and Chiapa de Corzo, the evidence that Mirador was the seat of an ancient kingdom is largely internal to the site itself, coupled with the overall distribution of large pyramid centers in central Chiapas (Lowe 1977). During the Middle Preclassic, Mirador, Ocozocoautla, and Chiapa de Corzo were participants in the same ceramic sphere, with the same ceramic types (Agrinier 1975, 1984, 2000; Agrinier et al. 2000; Clark and Cheetham 2005; Lowe 1999, 2007).

Mirador was probably home to Zoque speakers throughout its history. It was first occupied in the Early Preclassic (Agrinier et al. 2000; Lowe 2007), but the large pyramids and plazas at the site were not built until about 750 BCE (Agrinier 1970, 1975, 2000; Lowe 1999). This ceremonial center of 32 earthen mounds covers 1.5 km² and shares basic similarities in layout to Ocozocoautla, Chiapa de Corzo, Finca Acapulco, La Libertad, and La Venta, and its mounds were coeval with those at these other centers. The MFC complex at Mirador includes Mounds 10, 12, 20, 25, 27, and 33 (Fig. 5.12). All but Mound 33 have been tested and found to have been constructed by 750–700 BCE. The main axis of the site is 8 degrees west of magnetic north, similar to that at La Venta (Agrinier 2000:3).

The E-Group at Mirador consists of Mound 25 flanked on the west by Mound 20, a mound 15 m tall. During its first stage of construction, Mound 20 was a 5 m high clay platform with a wattle-and-daub superstructure, with stairs on its eastern side facing Mound 25 (Agrinier 1970:9). During the Chiapa IV phase, this mound was elevated to 12 m in height. The flanking 100 m long Mound 25 to the east was tested with one excavation through its center. This platform was 20 m wide and 4 m high and constructed at the same time as Mound 20. "The contour of the mound [25] suggests two buried stairways: a main one to the east side and a rear one on the west side facing Mound 20" (Agrinier 2000:4).

The northern mound on the main axis is Mound 10. During Chiapa III times, this was only a 70 cm high platform (Agrinier 1975:6). Eventually it became the second tallest mound at Mirador, but it was not a significant mound in terms of size or labor investment when the center was first built. Mound 12 or 33 may have been the original small platform associated with the MFC pattern at Mirador. These are nearly equally spaced from the axial line that bisects the E-Group. Mound 33 has not been tested. Mound 12 is 2 m high and 28 m in diameter. Investigations there revealed nine superimposed floors dating to 700–650 BCE (Agrinier 2000:31).

Mound 27 was built on the east side of the plaza. Extensive trench explorations of this acropolis revealed a complex construction history, with platform building being limited to Chiapa III times. Pierre Agrinier (2000) describes six construction episodes for buildings discovered inside this platform. The acropolis covers earlier stages of what I presume was the same functional complex, but the earliest buildings were separate and only later elevated on the same platform. The original separate small platforms coalesced with later expansions. All the sub-platform structures were associated with trash pits, hearths, caches, and subfloor burials, an indicator of domestic activities and overall function. What began as multiple platforms became a large elevated platform, presumably with multiple perishable buildings on top. Of particular interest is a stone drain 57.5 m long associated with this complex. It is oriented 15 degrees east of magnetic north (Agrinier 2000:24). Portions of another, parallel drain were also recovered. Agrinier suggests that water drained from the Mound 27 complex ran off to the north to a prepared reservoir. Another reservoir was located 200 m east of Mound 27 (Agrinicr 2000:3). Reflecting pools or reservoirs have been reported for Ocozocoautla and Izapa (Gómez Rueda 1995, 1996b; Lowe et al. 1982).

The best indicator of external relations at Mirador comes from pottery. No obsidian for the Middle Preclassic has been analyzed or is available for analysis. A fragment of a large, stemmed macroblade of Colha (Belize) chert was found at this site (Clark and Lee 2007:115), probably dating to Chiapa V times. Two whole stemmed macroblades of Colha chert were found in Tomb 7 at Chiapa de Corzo (Lowe and Agrinier 1960:40, 42), and two fragments were recovered from La Libertad (Clark 1988:63). Tomb 7 dates to the Guanacaste or Chiapa V phase (see below). All these chert artifacts came ready-made from Belize and indicate trade in valuable goods with the lowland Maya, starting before 300 BCE. Shifts in pottery styles reveal the same connections.

Similar to the history of San Isidro, the earliest pottery at Mirador was part of the San Lorenzo horizon and exhibits close connections to the Gulf coast (Agrinier 1984; Clark and Cheetham 2005). These connections continued until the Chiapa IV phase, at which time there was more influence coming from the Maya lowlands. The most outstanding differences between phases was the lack of differentially fired black-and-white pottery (Lowe 1999:65) and the presence of Chicanel phase, Sierra Red pottery (Lowe 1999:81). The Late Preclassic (Chiapa V) was a time of great change as Mirador developed its own special style of ceramic vessels, incense burners, and figurines (Lowe 1999:91–92). The "designs of early Chicanel ceramics of the Late Preclassic lowland Maya were incorporated into the local Zoque tradition, notably in the production of vessels of the Mirador Group, Vitrified Orange (Peterson 1963:16–19, figs. 14–15, 37–49, *passim*, 75); Vitrified Orange ceramics have been confused for 'Mars Orange' of the Maya area" (Lowe 1999:92, my translation). As at San Isidro, another marker of the Chiapa V phase at Mirador was the resumption of differential firing, presumably reflecting renewed ties to Gulf coast peoples.

CHIAPA DE CORZO, CHIAPAS

Chiapa de Corzo is arguably the most important site in central Chiapas, not because of its size or ancient splendor—neither of which was spectacu-

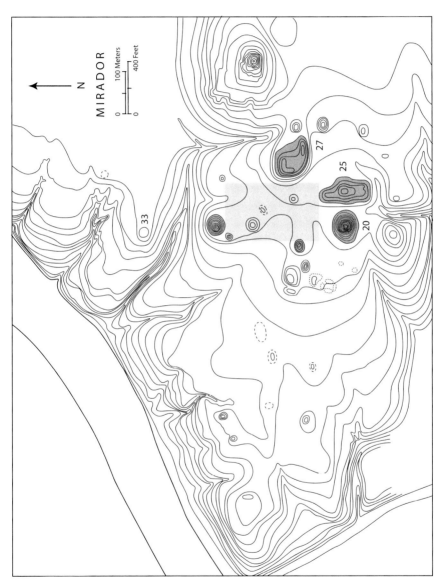

5.12. Site map of Mirador, with gray coding to indicate the early mounds and plaza at the site.

lar compared to Palenque or other Classic Maya cities—but because of its unique evolutionary history and its shifting ethnic or cultural identity, by which I mean how its inhabitants chose to represent themselves socially and culturally, not their biological pedigree or bloodlines. Chiapa de Corzo is situated on the right bank of the Grijalva River just before this river enters the impassable Sumidero Canyon where steep rapids and falls render the river unnavigable. The location of Chiapa de Corzo corresponds to the broadest and most fertile levee lands along the whole course of this large river (Lowe and Agrinier 1960:1), an ideal place for agriculture as well as for benefitting from trade along the river. Chiapa de Corzo would have been a break-of-bulk or portage point for trade goods coming downriver from Finca Acapulco and La Libertad (described below). Trade goods would have been carried around the Sumidero Canyon overland to Ocozocoautla and then across the northern highlands down to San Isidro where river transport to La Venta and the Gulf of Mexico could be resumed (Fig. 5.1).

Chiapa de Corzo was first excavated in 1941 (Berlin 1946), and major excavations were undertaken there by the New World Archaeological Foundation from 1955–63 (Lowe and Mason 1965), with some later salvage operations (González Cruz and Cuevas García 1998; Lee 1969b; Lowe 1995; Warren 1978). It was most recently excavated by the NWAF in 2008 and 2010. These excavations reveal that Chiapa de Corzo was one of the earliest cities in the Chiapas interior, and it has been continuously occupied until the present day. The Chiapas Preclassic chronology and phase sequence was first established at this site (Lowe and Mason 1965; Warren 1959, 1961b, 1978), and this chronology has been used ever since to correlate all other developments in the state. During the Middle Preclassic, Chiapa de Corzo was one of the principal kingdoms in Chiapas (Finca Acapulco, located upriver, was larger in Chiapa II and III times). Chiapa de Corzo may have become a small state by 100 BCE, owing principally to meddling from kingdoms in the Maya lowlands (Clark et al. 2000). The Middle Classic period witnessed a severe decline in population and the near abandonment of the site (Lowe 1962a; Lowe and Mason 1965:226; Sullivan 2009; Warren 1978:85), with a resurgence in the Late Classic and Postclassic periods. Mound construction ceased by Classic times, but the site continued to be occupied (Lowe and Agrinier 1960:3).

Chiapa de Corzo takes it name from the Chiapanec peoples who occupied it during the Late Classic and Postclassic periods. Renowned as fierce warriors, the Chiapanecs took the city from its traditional Zoque residents, later protected it from an attempted Aztec takeover, but were unable to safeguard it from the Spanish (Berlin 1958b; Lowe 1995; Navarrete 1966). Archaeologically, Chiapa de Corzo shows evidence of Olmec occupation during the Early and Middle Preclassic periods and Maya occupation during the Late Preclassic and Protoclassic. For the Middle Preclassic period of central Chiapas, the loose archaeological label "Olmec" is another word for the ethnic and linguistic label "Zoque." Over the first 3600 years of its existence, the city has been sequentially occupied by Mixe-Zoques (pre-Olmecs), Zoques (Olmecs), Mayas and Zoques together, Zoques, Chiapanecs, Spanish, and Mexicans. The Olmecs at Chiapa de Corzo were Mixe-Zoque or Zoque speakers, depending on the time period in question and the tempo of dialectic divergence of the proto-Mixe-Zoque language during the Middle Preclassic. The rift between Mixe and Zoque speech probably began about 1000 BCE (Clark 2000a; Kaufman 1974, 1976; Lowe 1991:114; Warren 1978). Granting this plausible correspondence between archaeological labels and linguistic groups, the cultural sequence at Chiapa de Corzo can be simplified as follows: Zoques as principal occupants, an interlude of Maya elites and kings lording it over the locals, a return to Zoque self-rule, conquest by Chiapanecs, and much later by Spaniards.

Evidence that Chiapa de Corzo was the capital of an ancient kingdom includes the size and complexity of the site (Fig. 5.13), the building histories of its principal mounds, the placement and contents of burials and offerings, and to a lesser extent, its regional settlement pattern (Bachand and Lowe 2011; Clark and Lee 1984; Sullivan 2009). Middle Preclassic stone sculptures are not known for the site, but there are some for the Late Preclassic, including Stela 2, a monument with a long-count date of December 7, 36 BCE, the oldest attested in Mesoamerica (Coe 2005:64; Lee 1969c:105). An Olmec jade figurine head was found in the northern sector of Chiapa de Corzo, but it was stolen before it could be carefully studied (Lee 1989: fig. 9.8c, 1993; Lowe 1994: fig. 7.1; Martínez 1982[1971]; Paillés 1980: fig. 14). A small serpentine axe with an incised Olmec frontal face was found in 2008 above a large offering pit with over 100 pseudo-axes made of limestone and andesite (Bachand and Lowe 2011); these were laid out in patterns at different levels of the offering pit dug into soft bedrock. A cruciform axe cache was found at the eastern edge of Mound 11 on its east-west axis, also in a pit dug into bedrock. These La Venta-like axe offerings date at least to late Chiapa II-B times, or about 800 BCE.

Site and Kingdom History

Chiapa de Corzo was a sister city to La Venta and constructed to the same MFC plan; it expanded through time in ways similar to La Venta's growth (Clark 2001). The earliest documented mound at Chiapa de Corzo is a low, broad platform beneath Mound 36, the northernmost mound (Lowe 1962b:57–59). The pyramid erected on this basal platform reached its final 9 m height by 450 BCE and was built over an earlier pyramid dating to 700 BCE. This platform was oriented 28 degrees east of true north, an orientation followed by later buildings at the site (Sullivan 2009). Excavations did not reach sterile layers, so it was not determined whether or not there is an even earlier pyramid in Mound 36 (Lowe 1962b:58). In the MFC pattern this mound is in the same structural position as the great pyramid at La Venta, so it is interesting that Mound 36 attained most of its height 200 years after its initial construction (an observation also true of Mirador). The largest mounds at Chiapa de Corzo achieved their final size in the Francesa phase. The platform under Mound 36 dates to the Dili phase (1000–850 BCE), probably near the end, and shares the middle Olmec style of decorative stone work described for Chalcatzingo and Teopantecuanitlan in the Mexican Highlands (see Grove 1984, 1989b:143; Martínez Donjuán 1994). At Chiapa de Corzo, horizontal sandstone slabs set in black clay mortar bracket a double row of river cobbles (Lowe 1962b:57–59, fig. 37, Plate 29h); see Figure 5.14. On the south side of Mound 36, "immediately below the surface there are constructed walls made with large stone slabs up to a meter long, with other rows of horizontal slabs. Below the northern side of Mound 36 there are large terraces made of enormous stones, where we find Cotorra-phase sherds [Chiapa I-B] in the fill" (Lowe 1991:115, my translation). David Grove (1989b:144) argues that a similar architectural style is a highland Olmec characteristic that distinguishes these sites from La Venta. Had the Mound 36 wall been noticed, this argument could not have been made. The practice of making designs in walls by alternating horizontal and vertical stone slabs with cobble insets mimics the more elaborate stone facings known from early La Venta in which squared serpentine and basalt slabs were placed in alternating horizontal and vertical patterns, which also alternated with layers of clay and adobes to produce a mosaic effect (see Drucker et al. 1959: Plates 7, 10–13), a pattern that may have begun during construction phase I of Complex A, the earliest occupation of the city (see Drucker et al. 1959:31).

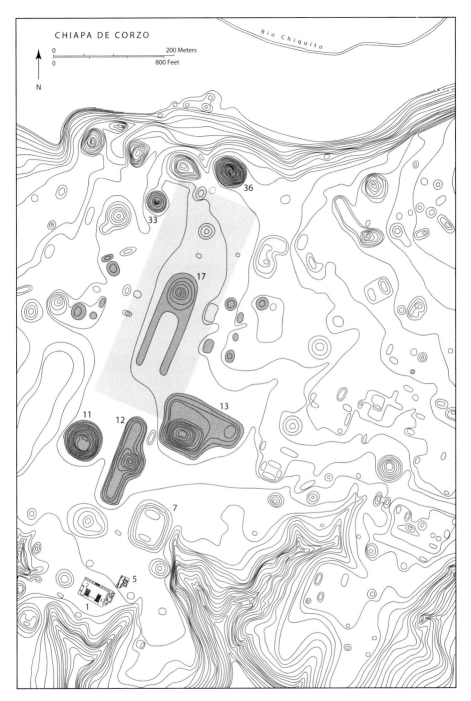

5.13. Map of Chiapa de Corzo, with gray coding to indicate the early mounds at the site.

a

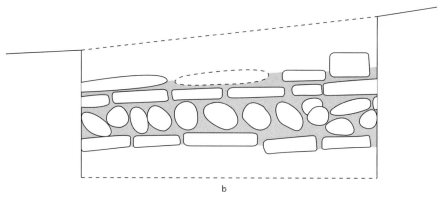

b

5.14. Chiapa II phase stone wall at Chiapa de Corzo. A. Photograph from Lowe (1962b:Plate 29h). B. Drawing of the wall from the photograph and field description. The gray shading indicates a black clay matrix.

The MFC complex at Chiapa de Corzo comprises Mounds 11, 12, 13, 22, 36, and probably 17. Mound 36, the northern pyramid of the MFC pattern, dates to Chiapa II through IV times. On the southern end, Mounds 11 and 12 constitute an E-Group. At the time Chiapa de Corzo was excavated in the 1960s, Mound 11 supported a municipal water tank and could not be excavated, but investigations in its flanking, complementary structure, Mound 12, uncovered a 3.5 m high platform that dates to Chiapa III times (Mason 1960a:2–3). The length of this early structure has not been determined. Recent explorations of Mound 11 excavated from the summit all the way through the mound down to bedrock and found 20 construction episodes. The earliest platform was 4 m high and was built during the Dili or Chiapa II-A phase (Lynncth Lowe, pers. comm. 2012). The large offering pit found on the eastern edge of Mound 11 dates to about 750 BCE (Bachand and Lowe 2011:81) and represents a clear link to La Venta patterns of axe caches. The cruciform offering of jade axes just in front of Mound 11 must date at least to Chiapa II-B times around 800 BCE. These excavations securely date the construction of the E-Group at Chiapa de Corzo to before 850 BCE based on ceramic associations. Radiocarbon samples have not been processed.

Mound 17 to the north was constructed in the middle of the plaza as a broad low platform in Escalera times (Lee 1969b), as were the two 100 m long, parallel low platforms extending southward from it (Lowe 1962b:56). These 1.25 m high wings of Mound 17 may have been an early ballcourt. These structures were just north and west of the broad platform at Mound 13. This latter structure has not been extensively explored so its beginning construction date has not been ascertained. One of the earlier buildings in Mound 13, dating to 700 BCE, was a stepped earthen platform 6.2 m high (Lowe and Mason 1965:212). An even earlier platform was discovered inside (Hicks and Rozaire 1960:5).

Mound 7 was built as part of the same plaza complex. In Chiapa III times this clay mound was about 1.3 m high and had steps on its western and northern sides, and perhaps on the other two sides as well. It measured at least 15 by 15 m at the base and was resurfaced four times during the Escalera phase. In the following Francesa phase, this platform was expanded and elevated to a height of 3.4 m. All these data indicate that the MFC complex was completed at Chiapa de Corzo by 700 BCE. Characteristics of site layout are compelling evidence that Chiapa de Corzo was planned, measured, and marked out by 750 BCE by engineers and builders who had precise knowledge of La Venta as it appeared at that time (Clark 2001).

The early pyramid at Mound 13, Chiapa de Corzo, lacks an obvious counterpart at La Venta. The primary, early construction of Mound 13 appears to have been a broad platform which supported at least one low mound (Mason 1960b). This platform may have been a royal compound, a function subsequently superceded by the placement of a temple mound over the early platform (Clark and Hansen 2001). At this time the royal compound may have been relocated south to Mound 7. At the start of the

Chiapa VI phase, the royal compound was moved to the palace at Mound 5 in the southern sector of the site.

Early investigations at Chiapa de Corzo emphasized site chronology and history to the detriment of its local context, an oversight rectified by Timothy Sullivan (2009). He surveyed 107 km² around the site and recovered information of changing settlement patterns. Given the proximity of Chiapa de Corzo to Tuxtla Gutiérrez, the modern capital and urban center of Chiapas, it is unlikely that the full settlement pattern will ever be known. I once thought the small Chiapa IV temple site at San Agustin (Navarrete 1959b), 25 km to the west, was a secondary capital to Chiapa de Corzo, but this small center is located midway between Ocozocoautla and Chiapa de Corzo and may have been independent of both of them. One high-status burial dating to Chiapa IV times was found in a special tomb at this site, so it was a first- or second-order community (Navarrete 1959b:4–5; Warren 1961b).

Sullivan estimates the population of Chiapa de Corzo and its surrounding region per phase based on the distribution of diagnostic sherds and their relative densities. Mound sites are rare in the survey region, but the variable sizes and densities of ancient occupation indicate that Chiapa de Corzo functioned as a regional center by Chiapa II times. Sullivan (2009:83) estimates the site at 71 ha with a population of about 1100 persons. The next largest site in the region had an estimated population of 270 people. The 107 km² survey region had an estimated 5000–5400 people; this represented a 37 percent increase from Chiapa I-B times. The earliest public architecture at Chiapa de Corzo dates to Chiapa II times. This community represented a departure from the previous period in demographic distribution, with 21 percent of the estimated population of the small survey region being at Chiapa de Corzo itself. These data indicate a large population in central Chiapas by 850 BCE, a finding in accord with more general assessments of regional population patterns described by Lowe and J. Alden Mason (1965:210) and Bruce Warren (1978:41, 198).

The Escalera phase (750–500 BCE) continued this trend. Most of the large mounds at Chiapa de Corzo were built by this time, and the center had achieved most of its present formality. The spatial arrangement of platforms around a long plaza was copied from La Venta, but with a different alignment. The main axis at Chiapa de Corzo is 28 degrees east of true north, and that at La Venta is 8 degrees west of north. Sullivan (2009:143) estimates a resident population at Chiapa de Corzo of 1450 persons and an overall size of 68 ha. This represented a 33 percent population increase. The population of the region in Chiapa III times decreased slightly to 4590 people. Probable secondary centers in the region were at Ribera Amatal and Bulmaro Abadilla. Small mounds possibly dating to Chiapa III times were found at Ribera Amatal, Rancho San Isidro, and Cupía. These observations indicate that Chiapa de Corzo was the center of at least a three-tier settlement system (Sullivan 2009:144). It remained the primary capital of its region until the Classic period.

In the Francesa phase, Chiapa de Corzo increased in size 20 percent, and the population in the region increased 8 percent (Sullivan 2009:195). It is important to point out that Sullivan's survey represents a sample of the full settlement system. The western sector is now covered over by the urban sprawl of Tuxtla Gutiérrez, but several Middle Preclassic sites are known to have existed there (Lowe 1959; Navarrete and Martínez 1961; Sorenson 1956; Warren 1978). The full regional system may have been 25 percent or more larger than Sullivan estimates. The limited data available indicate general trends through the Middle Preclassic, patterns corroborated by burial data. The southern plaza appears to have been a community cemetery in Chiapa IV times.

A larger sample of human burials is available for Chiapa de Corzo than for any of its neighbors, and these are a rich source of information for inferring social organization and history. Differences in mortuary treatments and offerings indicate the presence of hereditary chiefs or kings at Chiapa de Corzo by the beginning of Escalera times (Clark and Lee 1984). Space does not permit review of the more than 100 Preclassic burials at this site (see Agrinier 1964). Consideration of six royal burials from a longer dynasty will highlight key moments in the history of Chiapa de Corzo. The earliest elite burial from Chiapa de Corzo comes from Lee's (1969b, n.d.) two-week salvage of Mound 17, the pyramid located in the exact center of the main plaza (Fig. 5.13). Given the harried conditions under which this mound was excavated, the information available is remarkable. Mound 17 was built about 750 BCE and was expanded up until Chiapa VI times (100 BCE–100 CE).

Only one formal crypt was found in Mound 17, and it was for Burial 11, the earliest special burial at Chiapa de Corzo currently known. The crypt was lined with unworked river cobbles laid two courses high (Lee, pers.

comm. 2007), oriented roughly north-south on the site's axis, just slightly east of the axial line through the center of Mound 17. The occupant of this crypt was an adult female. Burial goods included jade jewelry, carved alabaster vessels, and ceramic vessels (Cheetham and Lee 2005: figs. 22–24; Lee 1969a: foto 9). The crypt and its stone lining and alignment remind one of burials and tombs at La Venta, especially Offering No. 5 (see Drucker et al. 1959: fig. 41). The goods found with Burial 11 reinforce this impression.

> Burial 11 was located approximately 2 m below the floor of an Escalera phase platform. This tomb, formally prepared—the only one known for this phase at the site—contained the remains of a woman at least 40 years old. This member of the elite class was placed in an extended position, head to the north…with a rich offering that included 62 jade beads and three alabaster vessels. More important for present discussion are the 10 accompanying ceramic vessels, three of which are identical to types imported from the Gulf Coast, particularly the fine graywares. Also, another four fine-paste vessels were probably imported; these seven vessels have precise counterparts at La Venta. (Cheetham and Lee 2005:291, my translation)

A large jar with wide everted rim found in the tomb is also a precise copy of La Venta vessels, or an import (Lee 1969b: foto 9; n.d.; compare to von Nagy 2003:840, fig. 6.9c). A similar pot was found in Tomb 1 of Mound 11. David Cheetham and Lee's (2005) study of Escalera phase ceramics from Chiapa de Corzo identified 90 sherds in the NWAF type collections that represent imports. Of these, one was from the Maya lowlands and the rest from the Gulf region. Most of these sherds came from the fill of Mound 17.

I have proposed in previous publications that the woman of Burial 11 was from La Venta and represented a marriage alliance between the leaders at Chiapa de Corzo with La Venta kings and the founding of a La Venta cadet royal line at Chiapa de Corzo (Clark and Pérez 1994:271; Clark and Pye 2000b:243–45). Cheetham and Lee (2005:291) concur and, based on their more thorough study of the artifacts, find more connections to La Venta. They suggest that a group of retainers accompanied this La Venta noblewoman to Chiapa de Corzo and that she and they lived on or around Mound 17. If so, she was buried beneath the floor of her own dwelling. The creation of one cadet line would not have been an isolated event in La Venta foreign policy. The Middle Preclassic sculptures at Pijijiapan on the Chiapas coast (Fig. 5.4) and Monument 21 at Chalcatzingo (Cyphers 1984: fig. 5.2), which depict elite women in elaborate dress, may indicate bride exchange and marriage alliances with La Venta's kings (Clark and Pye 2000b:245). These speculations can be tested through DNA analysis.

Another 14 burials (for the Chiapa III-V phases) were recovered from Mound 17, most of them of elite adult males and children (Lee n.d.). The second special burial interred in Mound 17 is of particular interest. It was a multiple interment with a primary adult male, about 25 years of age, and two sacrificed adults as burial offerings. These are known as Burials 6, 7, and 8 (see Fig. 5.15). The principal individual, Burial 6, was placed on his back in an extended position, with his head to the southeast. Several of his teeth had been filed, a mark of high status. His head "rested on the small of the back of Burial 8 while his legs were stretched out with the knees over the waist and chest of Burial 7" (Lee n.d.). As identified by Phillip Walker, Burial 8 is an adult male. He appears to have been thrown face down into the burial pit. Burial 7 is an adult female. These individuals were sacrificed and buried in opposite cardinal orientations. One served as a headrest and the other as a footrest for Burial 6. A similar multiple burial is known for La Libertad for the same period (see below). Both burials date to the Francesa or Chiapa IV phase. In terms of mortuary offerings, Burial 6 was the "richest" recovered at Chiapa de Corzo until 2010 (see Clark 2000a:50; Clark et al. 2000: fig. 19).

[Burial 6] was adorned with bracelets on his wrists, biceps, knees, and ankles, all made of jade and shell disks. A small necklace of [57] pearls was around his neck while a [shell inlaid] clam shell covered his mouth. Mosaic jade earspools were on both sides of the head. A personal adornment of greater importance was a wide jade belt consisting of more than 250 tubular jade beads, with a central part of 36 long, spiral carved beads and rings...[and a sash made of 341 jade and shell beads]...Nine ceramic vessels completed the mortuary offering. (Lee 1969b:19, 21, my translation; other details from Lee 1969a)

The principal individual also had two jade and pearl bracelets and three fresh water clam shells (Lee, pers. comm.). One remarkable thing about this burial is that it was not placed in a special crypt—at least not one that was recognized in the hurried salvage operation. This burial shares elements

with the cist tomb burial at La Venta. The jade bead belt-and-sash is especially significant. Later burials in Mound 17 were of individuals with jade
jewelry and with shells over their mouths (Lee 1969a). Burials 11 and 6 provide a picture of the early rulers at Chiapa de Corzo.

Ceramic vessels similar to those found in the cist tomb at La Venta were
found in the capping levels of the massive axe offering pit at Chiapa de Corzo
at the eastern foot of Mound 11 (Bachand and Lowe 2011:77). Royal burials
in the mound itself appear to date to the period between the two burials (11
and 6) just described for Mound 17. Two Chiapa III phase tombs, one of a
man and the other of a woman, were found side-by-side in the heart of the
Mound 11 pyramid. Tomb contents are still being analyzed. They include
large, square pyrite mirrors in both burials, spondylus shells over the faces
that appear to have been mosaic masks, and jade bead necklaces, bracelets,
anklets, kneebands, and armbands. The male in Tomb 1 was supine, with
his head to the north. He had a shell bead belt and was accompanied by
16 ceramic vessels and two human sacrifices: a two-month-old baby and a
young adult (Bachand and Lowe 2011:81–82). The beaded belt and paired
human sacrifices were features described for Burial 6 in Mound 17 dating to
the following phase. The early king in Mound 11 had multiple dental inlays
of jade and pyrite. His queen, buried just outside his crypt, lacked the bead
belt but, as mentioned above, had a stingray spine. No analogous item was
found with the king.

Burial 4 was interred in Mound 11 in Chiapa IV times nearer to the top
of the pyramid. This individual has not been exhumed, but some of his/
her burial goods have. This burial is of interest for exemplifying a later elite
interment in the same mound and also because of a pendant that depicts an
Olmec face carved in profile (Bachand and Lowe 2011:81), thereby indicating continued ties to the Gulf coast Olmec in this phase. During the Late
Preclassic and Protoclassic, the kings at Chiapa de Corzo were interred in
tombs below the floor of the main temple at Mound 1 (Agrinier 1964; Lowe
1960, 1962b; Lowe and Agrinier 1960). Most were "looted" in antiquity, so
only limited information is available on their occupants and offerings. The
earliest of these is Tomb 7, the only one not disturbed in prehistory.

Tomb 7 was discovered in early investigations at Chiapa de Corzo and
has only been described but not analyzed in any detail. The tomb was
originally thought to date to the early Horcones phase (Agrinier and Lowe
1960:47), but this assessment was later pushed back to the end of the Gua-

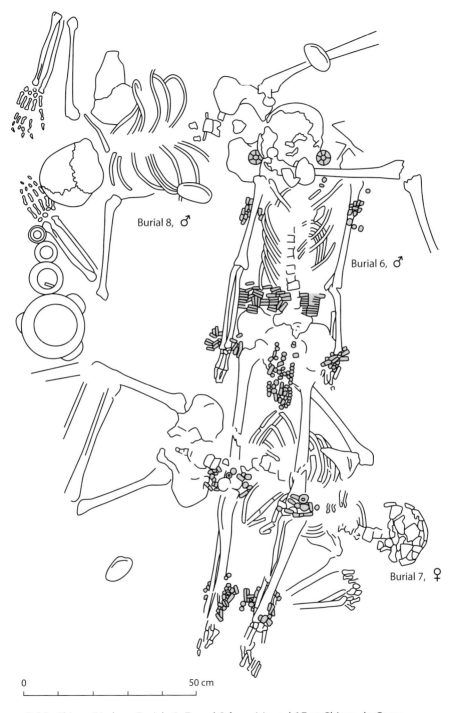

5.15. Chiapa IV phase Burials 6, 7, and 8 from Mound 17 at Chiapa de Corzo.

nacaste phase (Agrinier 1964:33), or about 150 BCE. At this time a low platform existed in the Mound 1 location. Tomb 7 was cut through this platform and into the soft limestone bedrock beneath it (following information
from Agrinier and Lowe 1960:47–50, figs. 47–53, Plates 24–28). The crypt
for Tomb 7 was 3.25 by 1.45 m and aligned roughly north-south parallel
to the site's axis but west of it. Above the bedrock, the east and west walls
of the burial pit were shored up with four courses of large adobes, and the
north and south ends were closed off with stone slabs. Large sandstone
slabs covered the burial chamber. Some of these were carefully squared.
Apparently, these sandstone slabs rested on wooden timbers for structural
support. Wooden planks were also placed on the floor of the tomb perpendicular to its long axis, a practice evident in Tomb 1 of Mound 11 (Bachand
and Lowe 2011:82).

The bones in Tomb 7 were poorly preserved, but the teeth indicate a
young adult about 25 years old, about 1.70–1.80 m tall (Agrinier and Lowe
1960:50), and given this stature, presumably male. He was placed in the
burial chamber on his back, with his head to the south, and with his hands
over his pelvis (Agrinier and Lowe 1960: fig. 48). The body was surrounded
by vessels on all four sides. These included 34 ceramic vessels, 1 painted
gourd or wooden bowl, and 8 or more small vessels of perishable material
on the south end by his head. Vessels were placed carefully in the tomb according to shape, color, and size. What the excavators found remarkable is
that all 35 ceramic vessels had been imported, with most coming from the
Gulf lowlands and the lowland Maya area, but also 3 bridge-spout grayware
jars from the Valley of Oaxaca and 5 painted Usulutan vessels from El Salvador (see below). Almost everything in this tomb had been imported.

Most of the burial goods were vessels or items of personal adornment.
The few exceptions are particularly interesting. In the northwest corner of
the crypt at the feet of the burial were found two stemmed chert macroblade spearpoints from Colha, Belize, and an equally long obsidian macroblade from El Chayal, Guatemala. These were placed in a large pot. Just to
the east of these was a large sheet of mica as well as two clam shells filled
with mica fragments. In a small black jar in the northeast corner of the
tomb were two worked ulnas of a small mammal, and possibly an obsidian
pressure blade (its location is not specified, but objects were placed in contrasting triads). These may have been bloodletters. A small rod of limestone
was also found nearby.

This tomb was ignited after it was closed, so many items, such as the planks, were carbonized. Traces of leather straps were seen on the forehead of the skull, probably straps of a headdress of perishable materials. A single strand of jade beads encircled the neck, and a pair of elaborate composite earspools flanked the head. These consisted of jade earspools, amber cylinders (cautiously called "resin" in the descriptions), and a large cross-shaped piece of shell. Four small tear-shaped pieces of mother-of-pearl were found by the face, as were 10 small smooth pebbles. I think these pebbles may have been part of a rattle. To complete the assembly, a large sea shell was placed over the mouth of the buried individual, a practice seen for Burial 6 of Mound 17 and in Tomb 1 of Mound 11. All burials were supine and oriented north-south. The burial in Tomb 7 had many fewer jade ornaments than were placed in Tomb 1 or with Burial 6, and there were no sacrificial victims included in his tomb, but an infant (Burial 24) may have been placed above the tomb (Agrinier 1964:72). "This may represent a dedicatory sacrifice connected with Tomb 7" (Agrinier and Lowe 1960:17).

On the basis of the foreign pottery, it might be conjectured that the offerings were sent to a famous personage, priest or ruler, from the widely separated source areas in Oaxaca, Veracruz, El Salvador and Guatemala (Lowe and Agrinier 1960:49). But since there was no clustering of the objects in the tomb according to their source area, it seems much more likely that purely luxury goods already imported were placed with a highly honored personage as tribute or for his use in an afterlife. As with burial vessels, these probably contained food and drink, a postulate supported by the apparent presence of a zapote-like fruit in the offerings. The three chalcedony [chert] and obsidian spearheads were offered inside vessels and without shafts, suggesting their inclusion as wealth symbols rather than for their utility.

The construction of Tomb 7, the placement of its occupant and offerings, and the apparently immediate construction of a stone-walled platform over it afford the first sure indication that we have of an elaborate architecturally related ceremonial funeral at Chiapa de Corzo. (Lowe 1964:72)

Of special interest is the compelling evidence that the exact placement of Tomb 7 was remembered and commemorated through different remodeling of the structures in Mound 1 during the Horcones phase. Lowe and Agrinier (1960) described a possible offering placed above the tomb and subsequent removal of the offering, and construction of a small stone and plaster platform or altar above this spot. All that remained of these activities in the two intrusive pits was the scapula of a giant tortoise (Lowe and Agrinier 1960: Plate 24c). Four royal tombs were placed in the top of Mound 1 during the Chiapa VI phase. None was on the axial line, and each was "looted" one or more times in prehistory. I think some of these tomb reopenings could have been by descendants of the deceased who removed valuable heirlooms and other memorabilia, including human bone (Clark and Colman 2013). The six burials discussed here reveal the continuity of elite interments at Chiapa de Corzo from 750 BCE to 100 CE. For the main plot of the Chiapa de Corzo story, it is of interest that the earliest elite burial known for the site was a female—the likely founder of the Chiapa de Corzo dynasty. Burial practices and mortuary offerings associate her with La Venta.

Foreign Relations

Whether or not my speculations about Chiapa de Corzo's queen mother and subsequent kings prove correct, the Chiapa de Corzo data for the early Middle Preclassic show exceptionally strong ties to the La Venta kingdom in terms of ceramic vessel types and forms, hand-modeled figurines, site layouts, massive offerings of pseudo-axes, and incised iconography on cached objects. The absence of carved stone monuments at Chiapa de Corzo is a remarkable difference that must have been intentional, meaningful, and significant. This absence may signal Chiapa de Corzo's secondary status and dependency on La Venta. The few busted stelae fragments found at Chiapa de Corzo (Lee 1969c:105–9) date to the Chiapa V or VI phases and postdate La Venta's demise. This was the period of the strongest Maya influence in central Chiapas, as also recognized for San Isidro, Ocozocoautla, and Mirador (Lowe and Mason 1965:217).

The best evidence for shifting foreign relations comes from obsidian, pottery, burial practices, and architecture. Not much obsidian is available from dated contexts at Chiapa de Corzo. Most of it came from two sources in highland Guatemala. During the Middle Preclassic, obsidian arrived as preformed blade cores from San Martin Jilotepeque, a source located near

Chimaltenango (Clark 1988; Clark and Lee 2007; Nelson and Clark 1998). These cores were broken down into fine blades locally (Clark 1987). During the Late Preclassic and Protoclassic periods (Chiapa V-VI), most obsidian came from El Chayal, a source located 30 km east of Kaminaljuyu and presumably under the loose control of the state society there (Clark and Lee 2007). Obsidian was imported into central Chiapas as ready-made fine blades. The increased importance of El Chayal blades in Chiapas beginning about 300 BCE corresponds to a lowland Maya intrusion and occupation in the Upper Grijalva River valley (Bryant and Clark 1983, 2005b; Clark and Lee 2007; Clark et al. 2005), as well as the mayanization of Chiapa de Corzo (Lowe 1995).

Changes in pottery styles corroborate the noted shifts in obsidian trade. Ceramic wares during the Chiapa II phase were a clear continuation from the tecomate and gray plate tradition of the preceding phase. The Chiapa III phase witnessed abrupt changes all across Chiapas (Brockington 1967:67; Warren 1978). This era of city building in Chiapas is marked by different ceramic wares and forms that appear inspired by earlier ceramic vessels from the Maya lowlands. The diagnostic ceramics of Chiapas in Chiapa III times were slipped, waxy orange-resist wares, black and brown burnished monochromes, and a shift to plain, necked jars instead of tecomates. There was also a change in figurine styles and other new vessel forms, such as double-chamber whistling pots, chamferred cylinders, and cuspidor-shaped bowls. This era also saw the first ballcourts constructed in central Chiapas (at Finca Acapulco, San Mateo, and Vergel upriver from Chiapa de Corzo in the Acala region). These changes were so extensive and pervasive that Warren (1978:45) argues they represent a new group of people, perhaps from the Gulf coast. Most imported pottery found at Chiapa de Corzo for this era is fine-paste black and white pottery from either Tres Zapotes or La Venta, an observation made by Anna Shepherd to Warren in 1958 (1978:60) and more recently corroborated by Cheetham and Lee (2005). These differences in pottery usage indicate important changes beginning about 750 BCE, but wholesale migration cannot account for them. Central Chiapas had more population in Chiapa II times than is known for any other region of Mesoamerica (see Sullivan 2009). These people did not leave, so the dramatic changes in cooking and serving pots are probably due to other processes by which the local Chiapas population adopted foreign styles and made them their own.

Lowe (1977, 1978, 2007) interprets the changes in ceramic inventories at the beginning of the Chiapa III phase as evidence of a stable local population of Mixe-Zoques that adopted new forms and styles of vessels—both utilitarian and service wares. The distribution of orange, cloudy-resist pottery across Chiapas and into the Isthmus of Tehuantepec and Tres Zapotes was the key marker of Mixe-Zoque identity (Lowe 1977). The irony of Lowe's proposal—and one that continues to this day—is that this marker of Mixe-Zoque identity was adopted and adapted from eastern Maya neighbors.

Ceramic complexes in Chiapa IV times were a clear continuation of the monochromes adopted earlier, and also clearly similar to Mamom pottery in the Maya lowlands. The Chiapa IV ceramic sphere represented an era of great uniformity in ceramics in Chiapas (Miller et al. 2005:263; Warren 1978:54). The main diagnostics were slipped, highly burnished red monochromes and the popularity of flat-bottomed plates with wide everted rims. This distribution "represents the zenith of Zoquean cultural developments (Lowe 1977:226–27). This cultural florescence, in a period of pre-Maya dominance, was perhaps also the time when Zoquean influence was felt the most strongly in adjacent areas" (Miller et al. 2005:263). "The little evidence for trade from Francesa phase areas indicates a changing pattern of external contacts. The earlier Escalera phase had pottery traded in from the Olmec area of southern Veracruz and Western Tabasco, but the only identified trade items in the Francesa phase seem to be from the Oaxaca Valley" (Warren 1978:54).

The story of the following Guanacaste phase (300–100 BCE) in Chiapa de Corzo is of particular interest because it represents the post–La Venta era in Mesoamerica. Sullivan (2009:197) estimates a reduction in the size of Chiapa de Corzo to 61 ha. To judge from the mortuary offerings in Tomb 7 at Chiapa de Corzo, it was a time of heightened international trade and commerce. One of the remarkable changes was the cessation of the manufacture and use of human figurines, a pattern shared with lowland Maya societies at that time.

Tomb 7 in Mound 1...had 34 ceramic offerings. Several of the tomb's bridged-spout face-necked jars (Cuilapa Slipped group) were brought in from the Oaxaca area. Other large red slipped florero-shaped vessels (Sierra Slipped group) were from somewhere in the Highlands [sic] of Guatemala or adjacent areas, some Usulutan (Sartenejo Slipped group) from El Salvador and still other vessels were from southern Veracruz (Cueva Grande Slipped group). All of these vessels were traded in from distant regions and none were of the local ceramic tradition at Chiapa de Corzo. In the case of the Tomb 7 burial we have evidence of a very important person being honored at his death with elaborate sophisticated pottery transported from a radius of some 600 miles. (Warren 1978:59)

Ceramic modes and styles paralleled those of Chicanel pottery in the Maya lowlands, and some trade wares are apparent—including those in Tomb 7 (see Lowe 1995) that Warren misattributed to the highlands.

The importation of pottery from many distant neighboring regions continued at Chiapa de Corzo through the Horcones or Chiapa VI phase. There was also pervasive experimentation locally in forms and decorations. Warren (1978:65) sees this phase as the climax of Chiapa de Corzo, and he estimates that the site covered over 3 km² and had 7000 inhabitants (1978:199). Sullivan (2009:199) infers the opposite pattern. He estimates the site was 56 ha in extent and housed 1450 people, as people left the center for the countryside. The demographic trend thus represented a further reduction in the size of this center. Chiapa de Corzo lost population at the same time as the number of inhabitants in its hinterland increased. This era ended in the general destruction of major buildings at Chiapa de Corzo and a pervasive shift in cultural practices. The palace at Mound 5, erected at the beginning of this phase, was burned. Architectural styles, pottery traditions, and burial practices were terminated (Warren 1978:66). I suspect the carved stelae at Chiapa de Corzo were also broken at this time and the royal tombs in Mound 1 looted. Agrinier and Lowe (1960:39) place the looting of Tomb 1 at the beginning of the Chiapa VII phase. During this Istmo phase, those who remained at Chiapa de Corzo went back to making and using white-rimmed black pottery and became closely and permanently affiliated with the Zoques of western Chiapas. They distanced themselves from any Maya connections. These changes in the Protoclassic period are important because they shed light on the earlier changes at the beginning of the Late Preclassic.

During Guanacaste times (300–100 BCE), Chiapa de Corzo underwent mayanization, as best seen in the distribution of imported Maya pottery. These special wares were mostly for elite usage (Lowe 1977:230; 1995), perhaps overt symbols of paraded identity. There was clear continuity in the local population, however, and utilitarian wares remained those of long tradition. Only traditional Zoque pottery was interred with commoners as mortuary offerings (Lowe 1977:230; 1995:329). The kings buried in the newly constructed Mound 1 were accompanied by elaborate imported pottery (Lowe 1995:324). Lowe (1977:230; 1995:329) argues that the use of imported lowland Maya pots ceased at the beginning of the Horcones phase. During Chiapa VI times,

> the previously abundant Chicanel-like types are notably absent. This pattern is characteristic for the length of the Chiapa VI occupation during which the rudimentary Maya modes are mostly lacking in the five tomb offerings and many dedicatory caches and ceremonial dumps of the period found at Chiapa de Corzo. Chiapa VI seems to have had its closest affiliations with the Arenal phase of sites such as Kaminaljuyu in the highlands of Guatemala, but both its architecture and its ceramics show local development or manufacture with the exception of certain finer vessels which appear to be imports from southern Veracruz, Oaxaca, and El Salvador. (Lowe and Mason 1965:218)

Chiapa de Corzo experienced a renaissance of sorts in Chiapa VI times as old clay and adobe brick platforms were covered over with veneers of cut limestone blocks and then with red-painted stucco (Lowe 1960:6; Warren 1978). A new palace was constructed at Mound 5 in the south plaza of Chiapa de Corzo at this time to accompany the temple at Mound 1; both appear inspired by lowland Maya prototypes. This Maya influence was rather short-lived and ended about 100 CE.

> When we look at the ceramic vessels with Guanacaste phase [Chiapa V] burials of commoners at Chiapa de Corzo (Agrinier 1964: figs. 57–66), we see the general absence of Chicanel ceramics. And, if we examine the vessels of the Istmo phase [Chiapa VII] burials of the same site (Agrinier 1964: figs. 68–117) we see that the differences in ceramics are even more marked...The contents of two Guanacaste phase tombs...included a good percentage of vessel forms and slips typical of Chicanel ceramics (Lowe and Agrinier 1960: fig. 53, plates 27b-h, q, s, 28a-c, I; Lowe 1962b: fig. 22a-g). And in a similar manner, we see three Sierra Red floreros...in the great tomb of Burial 11 of the Guañoma phase at

San Isidro...Definitely, imported Maya ceramics were luxury wares in western Chiapas and were not used—or accessible—for everyday uses. (Lowe 1999:124, my translation)

I, along with Richard Hansen and Tomás Pérez, have suggested (Clark et al. 2000; also, Clark and Hansen 2001) that Late Preclassic kings at Chiapa de Corzo (beginning in Chiapa V times) were Maya regents affiliated and subject to those at El Mirador. Gareth Lowe (pers. comm., 1989) believed there was a lowland Maya enclave at Chiapa de Corzo residing at Mound 3 just west of the temple at Mound 1 (see Lowe 1989a; 1995). Chiapa de Corzo's Maya interlude came to an end by 100 CE when the palace at Mound 5 was burned and torn down and its inhabitants presumably killed or run out of town. These are interpretations that will benefit from DNA and isotopic analyses of human remains to determine genetic relationships and possible movements of nobles between kingdoms. The larger point is that Chiapa de Corzo during the Late Preclassic cast off its Olmec ways and adopted Maya ones. If nothing else, these shifts in vogue practices and symbols indicate changes in the balance of power and global politics. Burial practices evident at Chiapa de Corzo for this era clearly show that the resident population at Chiapa de Corzo remained the same, with the major changes being confined to the governing elites.

This era of Chiapa de Corzo's history carries us beyond the Late Preclassic transformation of principal concern, but this longer trajectory indicates that the residents of Chiapa de Corzo adopted trappings of Maya identity, both lowland and highland in turn, at the beginning of the Late Preclassic (300–200 BCE) only to discard them three or four centuries later. There is much to do here. Lowe discusses the different uses of pottery in mortuary ritual rather than that in everyday use, with the implication being that elites had exclusive assess to these symbols. Consideration of everyday practices suggests that commoners as well as elites were using Maya pottery, so a critical distinction may have been between imported pots and local copies of foreign wares. Sullivan's (2009) reconnaissance indicates the wide-spread use of Maya-like ceramics at Chiapa de Corzo and in the hinterland, so Maya-style pottery was in common use in domestic settings—but not as mortuary offerings. This pattern of selective use of imported Maya pots and locally made Maya-style vessels suggests its use in signaling identity and cultural practices and, most importantly, some long-lived tensions in the identities of commoners and elites at Chiapa de Corzo that led to a return to traditional Zoque values and material symbols about 100 CE. This coincided with the collapse of the El Mirador state in the Peten and Kaminaljuyu in the highlands (Clark et al. 2000) and presumably with the loss of foreign muscle to support the kings at Chiapa de Corzo. The rapidity of this change, and the signal reversals in domestic symbolism that accompanied it, indicate that the base population at Chiapa de Corzo during the Late Preclassic and Protoclassic had maintained its Zoque identity all along. If so, the major changes at the end of the Middle Preclassic concerned more the trappings of rulership and its overt identity rather than changes in the base population. The destruction of the few stone monuments at Chiapa de Corzo may have been part of the repudiation of foreign kings.

FINCA ACAPULCO, CHIAPAS

Finca Acapulco is located about 100 km from Chiapa de Corzo following the twists and turns of the Grijalva upriver. In Lowe's (1959:42) original survey, this site was designated as Buenos Aires of the Acala subregion. As with San Isidro, Finca Acapulco is now buried beneath the waters of the Grijalva River. Limited information was obtained during a three-month salvage operation there in 1971 as part of the Angostura Project, 1970–74 (Gussinyer 1972; Martínez Muriel and Navarrete 1978).

> [Finca Acapulco was] very near the Grijalva River but high enough above it to be free of flooding. The zone consisted of horizontal layers of almost level limestone bedrock, with a submerged layer of unembedded old river stones eroding out below the riverbed itself, accessible at low water. There is little doubt that this locality was chosen for its ability to sustain a community of high strategic value rather than a center for agricultural pursuits (recent cultivation was largely limited to the Prehispanic mounds themselves or to pockets of soil forming around their bases). (Lowe 2007:89)

Finca Acapulco is located about midway between the large centers of Chiapa de Corzo and La Libertad. This latter site lies near the headwaters of the Grijalva at the base of the Cuchumatan Mountains of Guatemala

(Fig. 5.1). Finca Acapulco was built as a pyramid center before either of its neighbors. It was the largest Preclassic site in its region and the earliest city in central Chiapas. It was also the first city to be abandoned, an event that occurred by 500 BCE (Lowe 2007:89). "The site is an extensive one consisting principally of many stone-bordered platform mounds, some long and rectangular, others smaller and squarish, with several taller pyramidal mounds with complex adjoining platform features" (Lowe 1959:42). Finca Acapulco appears to have been the primary capital of three closely spaced centers and other sites in the center of the Upper Grijalva River valley (Fig. 5.16). Each had broad platforms and an earthen ballcourt that date to Chiapa III times (Con Uribe 1976:176; Gussinyer 1972:10; Lowe 1977:226; Martínez Muriel and Navarrete 1978:234). The mounds of the E-Group were also tested (see Lowe 1977:225, fig. 9.4 for the location of excavations) and dated to Chiapa II-III times. Based on size and architectural elaboration, Finca Acapulco with its more than 50 mounds was the primary center and San Mateo and Vergel were secondary centers. These latter two sites had ballcourts but not the full MFC complex. The ballcourt at Vergel was of the same proportions, size, and construction as that at Finca Acapulco (Gussinyer 1972:10). The San Mateo ballcourt was smaller. The long mounds at Chiapa de Corzo south of Mound 17 may have been a ballcourt. San Isidro probably also had a ballcourt in Chiapa III times (Lowe 1999:113), and La Libertad definitely did (Lowe 1977). These ballcourts were placed in different locations at all these sites and were not part of the same MFC standard arrangement.

The limited salvage work at Finca Acapulco has never been reported. Lowe was unable to finish his planned synthesis of the Chiapas Middle Preclassic, but he drew attention to Finca Acapulco in all his later works. In his fullest assessment, he described the site as follows:

> Finca Acapulco was without doubt the best example known of a Middle Preclassic city of the Escalera horizon [Chiapa III]. It is clear that it has the basic pattern of a large mound, pyramid, and large and wide platforms in perfect order. It also had a ballcourt. A burial with an offering of a polished orange plate and a jade axe were found ["at the foot of a pyramid"; Lowe 1991:115; illustrated in Gussinyer 1972:13]. Much could be said of the planning of this regional center of first order and the possible reasons for its early abandonment [by 500 BCE]. The

mounds were constructed with large quantities of fill that contained
Early Preclassic and early Middle Preclassic ceramics, but polished
orange ceramics [Chiapa III] constitute between 10 to 20 percent of all
sherds. Salvage of the site was undertaken by the New World Archaeological Foundation and the National Institute of Anthropology and History, but there was not time to do more than trench a few platforms.
(Lowe 1989a:366, my translation)

The platforms were made of earth, or earth and rubble fill, with carefully laid stone veneers of natural stone covered with a thick layer of clay
(Gussinyer 1972:8–10).

The above translation preserves a grammatical ambiguity that becomes
apparent only in reading the fieldnotes. Lowe appears to claim, and actually
may have done so, that a burial at Acapulco had a polished orange offering
plate and an axe. These were two different deposits and events. Both were
buried on the axial line of the E-Group constituted by Mounds 1 and 2 (the
following observations from a report by Raziel Mora López, June 1971).
Mound 1 at Acapulco, the long eastern mound of the E-Group, was about
90 m long, 15 m wide, and 2 m tall. The axial pyramid to the west across the
plaza was 5.5 m high and about 20 m² at the base (smaller than the map in
Fig. 16 implies).

Two elite burials dating to early Chiapa III times were found on the
E-Group axis in front of Mound 1 (western face). Burial 1 was in very
poor condition but appears to have been an extended burial, supine, oriented north-south, with the head to the south. This individual was buried
with a small orange dish and a necklace of 59 mostly small jade beads of
various shapes. Burial 2 was also extended north-south in a supine position, with head to the north. The trench placed along the axis of the
E-Group bisected this burial, so extensions to the trench had to be made
north and south to expose the head and feet. Like Burial 1, Burial 2 also
had jade beads and a polished orange dish. No evidence of earspools was
found with either interment. Burial 2 had a belt and bracelets of spherical
green or white stone beads (information on artifacts from notes by Lynneth Lowe, March 1986). The belt had 39 beads, 26 green and 13 white.
The right bracelet had 16 beads, 10 green and 6 white. The left bracelet
consisted of 10 stone beads (5 green and 5 white) and a perforated shell.
Two other burials with jade pendants and beads were found in Mound

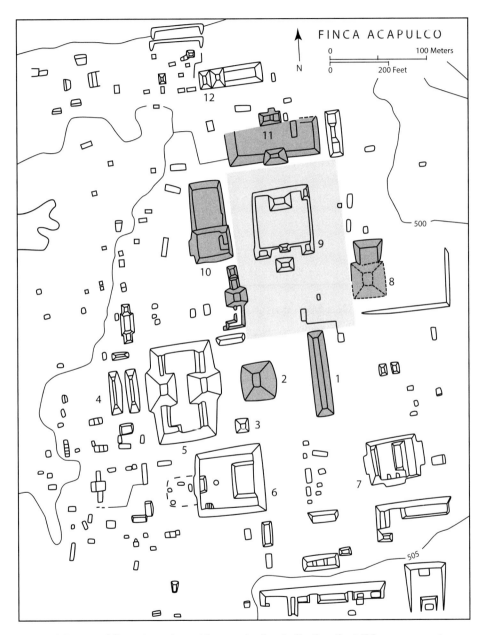

5.16. Map of Finca Acapulco, with gray shading indicating the MFC arrangement.

3, just south of the E-Group. Burial 3 had a jade spoon pendant with an incised cross design.

A large greenstone axe was found at the opposite side of the plaza at the foot of Mound 2, and on the centerline. The axe measures 26.9 cm long and 9.0 cm wide and has a rounded poll like early axes. It also had an incised line, but no incised design. Perhaps an earlier incised design was erased, as was the case for a jade axe found in the massive axe offering pit at Chiapa de Corzo (see Bachand and Lowe 2011). In the same general area at the foot of Acapulco Mound 2 was found a large spherical jade bead, perhaps a separate offering. The axe likely dates to Chiapa II times, since it was found in the earlier stratum. The burials date to early Chiapa III times by logical necessity, since Acapulco was abandoned by 500 BCE. Another offering of similar date was found on top of Mound 6. It consisted of 10 jade beads, 3 tri-pointed jade spangles with multiple perforations for sewing on clothing, and 11 cut human teeth, 3 of which show evidence of dental filing. The jade spangles are similar to some from the Cist Tomb at La Venta.

A filed and inlaid human tooth was also found on the surface of Mound 1 at San Mateo (Gussinyer 1972:10), and several burials with jade beads were found in this mound, the northernmost mound at the site (information from Gareth Lowe fieldnotes, June 1971). Mound 1 was 2 m high and about 20 m^2 at the base. Burial 2 in this mound was oriented north-south, in a supine position, and with head to the north. This individual was accompanied by an impressive collection of material, including two black and one orange ceramic vessels, the long pedestal base of an incense burner (see Lowe 1989a:381, fig. 14), a small axe, a pair of earspools, and a necklace of three jade beads. Some small jade pieces were also found that may have been part of a mosaic. Most other burials at the site lacked offerings. San Mateo Burial 2 is clear evidence of an elite individual at one of Acapulco's secondary centers.

Many Chiapa III burials and offerings were also recovered in salvage operations at the companion site of El Vergel, but not a single piece of jade or greenstone was reported. An offering found at the center of the San Mateo ballcourt consisted of a small jar with a jade bead and some unidentified organic remains (Jesús Mora Echevarría, pers. comm. 2007). No offering was found in the El Vergel ballcourt excavations. Two jade Olmec figurines are known for the Acala region (Clark and Pye 2000b: fig. 1e; Lee 1989: fig. 9.8a, I).

Obsidian artifacts from the surface and from excavations reveal an interesting contrast between sites. Nearly all the obsidian found at San Mateo came from the San Martin Jilotepeque source in Guatemala, with trace amounts from El Chayal and Tajumulco (Clark, unpublished notes on the Angostura obsidian artifacts, 1987). At Finca Acapulco nearly equal amounts came from San Martin Jilotepeque (46.8%) and El Chayal (42.6%), with the rest from Tajumulco (12.6%). This is more like the pattern characteristic of the southern Soconusco (Clark et al. 1989). The distribution of obsidian at San Mateo is very much like that at La Libertad (see below). I suspect that some of the differences in sites is chronological, with Finca Acapulco having more early deposits than San Mateo. Of particular interest at both sites is the low frequency of pressure or percussion blades. Most of the obsidian artifacts are flakes. This suggests that obsidian blades did not become popular in central Chiapas until late Chiapa III times. Alternatively, people in these centers in the middle stretch of the upper Grijalva River may not have had access to obsidian blades. As discussed below, blades occur in high frequencies at La Libertad.

Part of the trouble with understanding Finca Acapulco is that it has always been seen as part of a sweeping pattern that began elsewhere rather than as a community or seat of a kingdom in its own right. Thus, it has been a footnote to the more extensive work done at Chiapa de Corzo, La Libertad, and Santa Rosa (Brockington 1967; Delgado 1965b) along the Grijalva River. The few facts available for Finca Acapulco are impressive and suggest that the standard interpretations of the Middle Preclassic horizon in Chiapas should be revised. The following observations can be reasonably established.

1.   Finca Acapulco had an extensive occupation in Early Preclassic times, 1500 BCE (Lowe 2007:89).

2.   This site also had a major occupation in Chiapa II times (1000–750 BCE), and many of its platforms were probably begun at this time, as known for coeval centers on the Pacific coast (Lowe 1977, 1989a, 2007).

3.   Finca Acapulco achieved its final form by Chiapa III times and was abandoned during the same era, before 500 BCE (Lowe 1977:226; 1989a:366). The number of sites in the Acala region declined from the early Middle Preclassic to the Late Preclassic (Martínez Muriel 1976), perhaps reflecting population nucleation in Chiapa III times as well as site abandonment later in the same phase.

4. Finca Acapulco was the earliest and largest Middle Preclassic city in Chiapas and the premier Chiapas kingdom in its day (Fig. 5.16).

5. Finca Acapulco is the only Chiapa III center in Chiapas known to have had monumental secondary centers close to it. The secondary status of San Mateo and Vergel (usually accorded equal status to Finca Acapulco in Lowe's summaries of these sites) is signaled by their smaller size and the simplification of the MFC pattern. Instead of the full complement of buildings, these sites have plazas, E-Groups, and ballcourts. The same simplification of the MFC pattern seen at San Mateo may characterize Santa Rosa (upriver from Finca Acapulco; Brockington 1967) during the earliest part of the Chiapa III phase.

6. The affiliation of Finca Acapulco, Vergel, and San Mateo is evident in their similar ceramic inventories and by the presence of ballcourts with central stone markers and offerings (see Gussiyer 1972:10; Warren 1978:42).

7. Chiapa de Corzo and Finca Acapulco witnessed the construction of public architecture during the same period (Chiapa II-B, 850–750 BCE), but Finca Acapulco was much larger and more complex.

8. Finca Acapulco was older than the centers founded upriver. La Libertad (see below) was clearly a planned settlement, perhaps with some population from Finca Acapulco and/or Chiapa de Corzo.

9. The oldest pyramids and platforms in Chiapas are on the Pacific coast (see following sections) and in the Acala region of the Grijalva River dominated by Finca Acapulco. The mound building tradition in Chiapas spread from the coast to the Acala region, and then from there up and down the Grijalva River valley and Central Depression. This is supported by the evidence of obsidian trade. San Isidro was an exception to this historic progression.

10. Warren (1978:49) suggests that Finca Acapulco was settled by people from the Pacific coast who "may have entered the Central Depression by the same route as the later Chiapanec Indians from the Pacific coast of Chiapas crossing through the mountains near Tonala [by Tzutzuculi] to Parian and traveling down past Villa Corzo in the Frailesca." It is of interest that the few early Olmec monuments in Chiapas appear to mark these mountain passes from the coast into the interior (Figs. 5.4 and 5.11; see Clark and Pye 2000b: fig. 1). The carved Olmec monument at Padre Piedra marks the inland side of a major pass connecting the Finca Acapulco region to the Pacific coast (Green and Lowe 1967; Navarrete 1974).

11. The distribution of early stone monuments and mounds supports the idea that the Finca Acapulco kingdom was the primary development in the Chiapas interior during Chiapa II and early III times and that the others were secondary.

12. The Finca Acapulco kingdom was the first to rise and the first to fall. Its demise does not correspond to any geopolitical events known for eastern Mesoamerica at the time. (It does coincide with the founding of Monte Albán, but I do not suppose there was any direct connection.)

These observations provide a basis for better understanding events in southern Mesoamerica. Consideration of the history of Finca Acapulco within its own macro-region suggests that this kingdom may have been undone by its own local success. The leaders at Finca Acapulco either founded daughter colonies up and down the Grijalva River or supported/tolerated those who did. During the Chiapa III phase, Finca Acapulco became boxed in by kingdoms upstream and downstream; these grew and, within two centuries, choked off the original kingdom in between (a phenomenon that could also account for the fall of La Venta in its marginal geographical location). I suggest the Finca Acapulco kingdom fell victim to regional competition it helped generate, and among peoples of the same culture and language.

I have made much of the MFC complex, and given the preceding list of facts and conjectures, the configuration of this complex requires additional comment. The MFC pattern is not very clear at Finca Acapulco (Fig. 5.16); it becomes lost in the proliferation of platforms at this urban center. Chiapa de Corzo (Fig. 5.13) and La Venta (Fig. 5.3) share more features of site layout with each other than either does with Finca Acapulco. It is possible that Finca Acapulco was established as a regional center with monumental buildings before either of these other centers. It certainly had a deeper and more continuous history. Lowe (2007:89) argues that Finca Acapulco was established to control trade and was thus built in a place with relatively poor agricultural potential. If superior control points were subsequently established up- and downriver, this new distribution of population could have led to instability in the Finca Acapulco kingdom.

The early history of Chiapa de Corzo could relate to its own marginal position in central Chiapas during Chiapa II times (Warren 1978). Both geographically and geopolitically, the Finca Acapulco kingdom was more central, developed, complex, and powerful than the kingdoms at Chiapa de

Corzo. This uneven development may have stimulated some of the events listed above for the leaders of Chiapa de Corzo during Chiapa II times. Consummating an alliance with the royal house of La Venta, and building a version of this coastal sacred center at Chiapa de Corzo to seal the deal, could have been an easy ticket to change the balance of power along the Grijalva River. I think this is what happened and that the Finca Acapulco kingdom lost its cachet within the region and was deliberately marginalized. Part of this involved founding and building a center upriver from the Finca Acapulco kingdom, and this was done with the founding of La Libertad about 700–650 BCE. The layout of La Libertad appears to have been patterned more after Chiapa de Corzo/La Venta than after Finca Acapulco.

These are interregional connections for future investigation. As pointed out, San Isidro is a surprising exception to the MFC pattern. I proposed one reason for the differences of configuration between San Isidro and La Venta, but a more obvious one may be that San Isidro was older than La Venta and already established. The similarities in site layouts seen among Chiapas centers must have been time sensitive. The spread of the MFC complex depended on two conditions that need not have applied in all cases. First, there had to be a pattern to copy—the La Venta pattern had to be available for emulation. If the La Venta plan developed through time before coalescing (cf. Gillespie 2008), early emulation could show up as a partial MFC complex. The second condition would have been the desire to emulate features of a foreign kingdom. The people of San Isidro clearly adopted cultural practices seen at La Venta and early Olmec centers in Olman, but they did not build their center to mimic that at La Venta. Perhaps this is because they were building San Isidro before La Venta was completed. Finca Acapulco could have been another case of an older site being different. In contrast, the center at Tres Zapotes (see below) shows a total disregard for the MFC pattern. The Tres Zapotes case cannot be attributed to temporal priority. I suspect the Olmecs at Tres Zapotes were not interested in imitating their cousins at La Venta.

LA LIBERTAD, CHIAPAS

La Libertad was a kingdom on the edge—purposely planted in liminal space to stretch the domain of Chiapas kingdoms, most likely that of Chiapa de Corzo. La Libertad is the easternmost early pyramid center on the Grijalva

River, and it was advantageously located at the headwaters of the Grijalva River, perhaps so its rulers could regulate trade coming from the Guatemala highlands and down river (Clark 1988). La Libertad lies at the edge of the Cuchumatan Mountains and occupies a flat peninsula between four rivers. Evidence of its kingdom status comes from 56 excavations undertaken at the site in 1975–76. Its large earthen mounds were built about 700 BCE and enlarged several times in the following centuries (Fig. 5.17). The site was founded in a region sparsely populated at the time, and it was abandoned about 400–300 BCE (Clark 1988; Lowe 1977; Miller et al. 2005).

La Libertad's massive architecture spreads over 45 ha and conforms to the MFC pattern. "The site center is dominated by a long cruciform platform mound flanked by 12 m high pyramids on both the east and west sides. A multi-plaza group is located just north of the line of three mounds. The entire plaza group—divided into four or five plazas surrounded by 1.5–2.5 m high mounds—is elevated 1–2 m above the surrounding surface. This area appears to have been an elite residential area or palace... All mounds and elevated plazas were constructed with earth fill" (Miller et al. 2005:141–42). The cruciform mound and its flanking pyramids constitute the E-Group at La Libertad. These mounds were tested and found to have been mostly constructed during the Enub or Chiapa III phase and enlarged very little in the following phase. The western pyramid of the E-Group (Mound 5) was 9.5 m high at the end of the Enub phase. As at Finca Acapulco, some of these earthen platforms had a veneer of unmodified stone cobbles or cut travertine (Miller 2014). The rest of the MFC pattern at La Libertad comprises the northern pyramid, Mound 12, and the eastern acropolis.

The acropolis at La Libertad was extensively tested by Donald Miller in 1975–76 and found to have been built at the same time as the large pyramids—with substantial enlargements in Chiapa IV times. This broad, 3 m high platform supported four large and two low mounds. Stairways to the plaza were found on three sides of the acropolis. The largest structure excavated was a stone-veneer base of a building that measured 15 by 21 m (Miller 1976a, 1979, 2014), perhaps an elite residence. Two elite house mounds were excavated by Gareth Lowe and Glenna Nielson at the southern edge of the site, and these measured 24 by 18 m and 15 by 18 m (Clark 1988; Miller 2014). Significant differences among elite domestic structures were their location and relative elevation on special platforms rather than their basal dimensions. The eastern raised compounds at Chiapa de Corzo

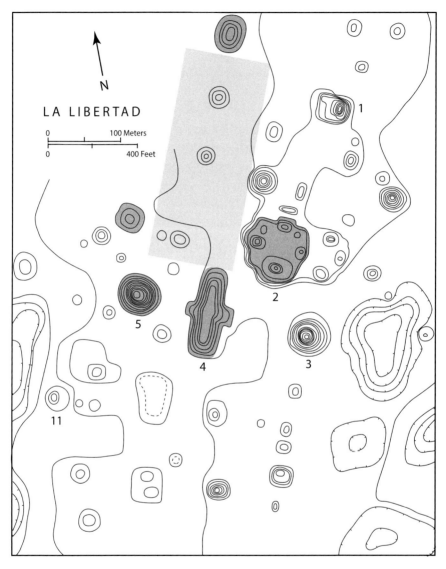

5.17. Map of La Libertad, with gray indicating the MFC arrangement.

and La Libertad both measure about 80 m² at their bases and are about 3 m high, an order of magnitude smaller than the Stirling Acropolis at La Venta, but probably the same idea and for similar purposes. The noteworthy features of the Chiapas compounds are the numerous individual buildings involved. I think these were palace complexes (Clark and Hansen 2001). The good state of preservation at La Libertad provides the best evidence of the arrangement of one of these compounds.

La Libertad was the primary regional center of the Upper Grijalva River Basin during the late Middle Preclassic. Secondary and tertiary pyramid centers to this site have been tentatively identified (Clark and Lee 1984). The pyramids at these satellite centers, however, date to Chiapa IV times, and none is known for Chiapa III times. A handful of Chiapa II-B sherds have been found at La Libertad and indicate a light population there before the site was established. The temporal pattern is a common one for Chiapas in which a primary center was set up in a sparsely populated region during Chiapa II or III times, with the later establishment of secondary centers and villages as a result of natural demographic growth. La Libertad looks like a classic colony.

> The Middle Preclassic was the peak period of city-building in the upper Grijalva region. Local Zoques followed lowland Olmec norms from La Venta, Tabasco, in laying out their cities and towns... Major sites were located along the banks of principal rivers, with smaller secondary and tertiary sites, each with at least one small pyramid, located within 5 to 10 km. Unlike the previous period, the strongest ties evident in shared ceramic conventions were with the Zoques at Chiapa de Corzo. Ties with the cultures of the Soconusco were less pronounced, and the ceramic influence appears to have gone in the opposite direction...This Zoque climax in the upper Grijalva region was soon followed by their demise and abandonment of the region. They relocated down river. We find evidence of Middle Preclassic occupation all up and down the major rivers, but evidence of the Late Preclassic is hard to come by... the Zoque occupation of the upper Grijalva region paralleled that of La Venta, with both regions being abandoned about 400 to 300 BCE.... (Clark 2005b:652–53)

Reconstruction of Middle Preclassic trade patterns suggests that the main route from the Guatemala highlands to La Venta followed the central valley of Chiapas (Clark and Lee 1984). The principal capitals and way stations along this route were Kaminaljuyu, La Libertad, Santa Rosa, Finca Acapulco, Chiapa de Corzo, Ocozocoautla, San Isidro, and La Venta, with smaller centers being strategically placed between the larger ones (Fig. 5.1). Early Kaminaljuyu does not share the MFC pattern and lacks an obvious E-Group (see Michels 1979a), although it has other complexes for taking astronomical observations. The earlier center in the Valley of Guatemala, Naranjo, may have had a simple E-Group that dates to 800–600 BCE, but Naranjo lacks the other features of the MFC pattern (Arroyo 2011). It is probable that the peoples of highland Guatemala were a different cultural group than those living in the Grijalva River Basin. The best evidence of connections between these groups is obsidian and ceramic artifacts. Obsidian is more abundant at La Libertad than at any other site I have seen outside the obsidian source areas. Almost all is from the San Martin Jilotepeque source (Nelson 1988). Half of the obsidian came in as large blade cores and the other half as small spalls for making flakes (Clark 1988:13–33). Obsidian from this source reached Finca Acapulco, San Mateo, and Chiapa de Corzo. Basalt manos and metates were also imported into La Libertad from the western highlands of Guatemala, but the bulk of the grinding stones were made from materials available in the region (Clark 1988:129–32).

Pottery and figurines at La Libertad are similar to those at Chiapa de Corzo during Chiapa III times and show some divergence by Chiapa IV times (Miller 2014). In this final period of occupation, La Libertad had some ceramic vessel types similar to those at Kaminaljuyu. The "specular red-and-white bichrome Nawa type was absent at Chiapa de Corzo…[and]…appears to have been a late Middle Preclassic copy of zoned bichromes from the highlands of Guatemala and/or inspired by purple-painted whitewares from Kaminaljuyú" (Miller et al. 2005:263). A figurine in the La Libertad style has been found at Takalik Abaj in coastal Guatemala (personal observation).

The big story of the upper Grijalva region is what happened after the collapse of La Libertad about 400–300 BCE. In the ensuing Chiapa V phase, sites in the Upper Grijalva River Basin were small, few, and in defensible positions. Chicanel sherds from imported pots are evident at sites of this period, but most of the local wares were a continuation of traditional pottery (Bryant and Clark 2005a). The Chiapa V and VI complexes show the presence of lowland Maya trade wares and local copying of Maya serving vessels, especially Sierra Red bowls. With others, I have interpreted the changes in ceramic assemblages and other cultural practices as an intrusion of lowland Maya peoples into central Chiapas and the mayanization of the local population (Bryant and Clark 1983, 2005b; Clark et al. 2000). The lowland

Maya occupied the upper Grijalva region by 200 BCE. I view this change as related to the expansionist policies of the Mirador state (Clark et al. 2000).

The burials at La Libertad demonstrate the presence of rank differences and also close connections to Chiapa de Corzo.

> Several burials were exhumed from beneath the floors of the two elite housemounds. Only one burial was found in Mound 11, but 6 were discovered in Mound 9. Miller (1979) notes that this difference may in part be due to chronological differences or to different excavation strategies. All burials were extended. Modest mortuary offerings, consisting of several pots or a few jade beads, were associated with several individuals; others lacked non-perishable offerings. In contrast, sumptuous tomb burials were recovered from several of the large mounds. Two sacrificial victims accompanied one jade-laden male on his final journey. The style of this burial closely replicates that of one discovered by Lee...at Chiapa de Corzo. (Clark 1988:9)

Burial 28a at La Libertad was found in Tomb 1, 1.7 m below the surface of Mound 3 at the summit of this mound (all information from Miller 2014). This adult male was accompanied by two other adults, probably sacrificial victims, one male and the other female; limestone slabs covered all three bodies. The principal individual was lying on top of the body of Burial 28b and also had his left hand over her face. Burial goods included a large alabaster bowl with a notched medial flange (imported from highland Guatemala, see Clark 1988: fig. 76), 6 ceramic vessels, and elaborate jade and shell jewelry. Burial 28a had 2 earspools and 3 or 4 jade bead necklaces, 3 large sea shells in his headdress, a large shell pendant, a shell mosaic mask, and a special belt and sash similar to that described for Burial 6, Mound 17, at Chiapa de Corzo. The belt arrangement with Burial 28a included 26 elongated jade beads, at least 602 tiny jade beads, 695 tiny cut shell beads, 80 mini-conch shells, and at least 1,100 olivella shell beads. The similarities between the burial treatments and accoutrements of the Chiapa IV phase kings at La Libertad and Chiapa de Corzo demonstrate a close relationship between the nobility of these kingdoms, connections going back to Chiapa III times. I think the elites of La Libertad were more closely connected to those at Chiapa de Corzo than to those of other kingdoms. Another characteristic of this period was burials of high-status individuals at smaller centers such as at San Augustin, located between Chiapa de Corzo and Ocozocoautla (Navarrete 1959a), and El Achiote, near San Isidro (L. Lowe 1998). In the upper Grijalva region, a triad of elite burials was found at Santa Marta Rosario, a site less than one fifth the size of La Libertad and located about 20 km east of it (Bathgate 1980; Clark and Lee 1984: fig. 11.8).

IZAPA, CHIAPAS

Izapa is the most famous Preclassic site in Chiapas, and the most anomalous. It differs in nearly every dimension from the Zoque capitals described thus far, so I consider it of different cultural affiliation. Whether or not Izapa qualifies as a non-Mayan kingdom on the western frontier of the Maya world or was, in fact, the westernmost Maya kingdom on that frontier is a pending question. Michael Coe (2005:67–69) has consistently argued on the basis of its numerous stone monuments and their themes that Izapa was Mayan. Based on a comparative study of ceramic complexes, I proposed that the Middle Preclassic builders and occupants of Izapa were Mixe, first cousins of the Zoques (Clark 2000a; Clark and Pye 2011). Determining the ethnic affiliation of the Preclassic inhabitants of Izapa will require a detailed historical and regional analysis.

Izapa lies nearly directly south of La Libertad, 110 km away and on the other side of the Sierra Madre mountains at their widest and highest point. Izapa is situated about 240 m above sea level in the piedmont zone of the southern Soconusco in an area of evergreen tropical forest, a locale ideal for growing cacao. It is thought that cacao and other tropical products, such as bird plumes and jaguar pelts, were major exports of this capital during its heyday (Lowe et al. 1982:47). Procurement of these products for exchange may have been the reason Izapa was established in the first place.

The apogee of Izapa was in the Late Preclassic period, but its history extended another millennium in both directions to the Postclassic and Early Preclassic. The earliest sherds found at Izapa relate to those found in the Mazatán coastal region just to the west. These artifacts date to 1800 BCE and are evidence of the first sedentary occupation of the Izapa piedmont zone (Clark and Lowe 2013). At its height in the Late Preclassic, Izapa extended over 4 km^2 and had at least eight plaza groups, each surrounded on three or four sides by small pyramids. Of particular interest are the numerous stelae and altars set up along the edges of some of the larger plaza groups. Evidence of the kingdom status of Izapa during the Middle Preclassic includes its mounds, site size, monuments, offerings, and burials. Most of the monuments postdate the era of concern here, but some were carved at the end of the Middle Preclassic (Clark et al. 2010; Clark and Hodgson 2008; Ekholm 1993).

During the Middle Preclassic, Izapa was remarkable for what it was not: It was not Gulf Olmec or Chiapas Zoque; it was not like La Blanca, and it did not have a MFC complex. The dominant kingdom in the Soconusco during the early Middle Preclassic was centered at La Blanca in the outer coast of western Guatemala (Love 1991, 2002a, b, c, Chapter 7, this volume). This site was the hub of a kingdom that held sway from 1000–850 BCE. The question is whether Izapa was coeval with La Blanca and a secondary center to it. The 25 m high pyramid at La Blanca was built by 900 BCE (Blake et al. 1995:163, 180; Love 2002c:57) during the Conchas phase (Chiapa II-A). The earliest pyramid at Izapa (Mound 30) dates to 850–750 BCE (the Chiapa II-B phase). In a preliminary synthesis of Soconusco chronology, various authors pooled their radiocarbon dates. In this article, we did away with the Duende phase at Izapa and subsumed it under the Conchas D phase at La Blanca, based on observations Love and Lowe made together of the Izapa ceramic collections (Blake et al. 1995:179, n. 8). This assessment proved ill-founded, so we restored the Duende phase for Izapa and its region (Clark and Cheetham 2005) and have confirmed its content and chronology at the neighboring center of Huanacastal and related sites (see below). The Duende ceramic complex is significantly different and later than the Conchas complex at La Blanca. I have seen no evidence of a Duende-phase occupation at La Blanca (there is one at Takalik Abaj), so I doubt the La Blanca kingdom persisted much past 850 BCE, the time of the emergence of rival and flanking kingdoms at Izapa and Takalik Abaj. There was virtually no Conchas phase occupation at Izapa, so it is unlikely to have been part of the La Blanca kingdom (Clark and Lowe 2013). That La Blanca had secondary and tertiary centers with monumental architecture has been well established (Love 1991, 2002c, 2007, Chapter 7, this volume), but Izapa was not one of them. The westernmost subsidiary center of the La Blanca kingdom appears to have been Cuauhtémoc in the southeast corner of the Chiapas Pacific coast (Rosenswig 2005, 2006, 2007, 2010; La Cabaña 10 km farther west is another possibility, see Fig. 5.1). During the Duende phase the centers of power moved from the far coast to the piedmont.

The first pyramid at Izapa was constructed in Chiapa II-B times. Mound 30 at the site (see Fig. 5.18) was built and enlarged half a dozen times in this phase until by 750 BCE it was 12 m high and 45 m wide at the base (Ekholm 1969; Lowe et al. 1982:123). Lowe and others (2013) argue that Izapa extended 25 ha at this time and that the early mound complex likely included Mounds 50, 47, and 25. The Duende settlement seems "to have been concentrated upon the restricted Group B terrace overlooking the Río Izapa" (Lowe et al. 1982:127). This arrangement would have been Izapa's earliest plaza (see Fig. 5.18). Izapa was a large center or town in Chiapa III times. Pottery of this phase is found all across the central zone of the site (Ekholm 1989:335; Lowe et al. 2013; Lowe et al. 1982:127). Ironically, very little construction has been detected at Izapa for Chiapa III times beyond a few thin layers added to the Duende mound in Group B (Lowe et al. 1982:127) and a small platform under Mound 60 (Lee and Clark 2013). By Chiapa IV times, Mound 30 was 16 m high, and there were also large platforms at Mounds 9, 25, and 56. The known early mounds do not conform to the MFC layout. Izapa does not appear to have subscribed to the same architectural system as at Chiapa de Corzo, La Libertad, and La Venta. Based on site histories and localities, I think MFC sites were inhabited by Zoque speakers and that Izapa was not part of this culture. I postulate they were Mixe speakers. A branch of this language family was present in the Izapa area at the time of the Conquest (Campbell 1988:305; Coe 2005:67; Lowe et al. 1982:11).

The numerous low-relief stone carvings and altars at Izapa further distinguish it from all other Preclassic sites in Chiapas. In terms of monuments, Izapa shows more affinities with Takalik Abaj and Kaminaljuyu than to sites in central Chiapas (Clark et al. 2010). The ceramic evidence is ambiguous on the matter. The Duende complex which dates the era of pyramid building is intrusive in the Soconusco from the central Pacific coast of Guatemala (Lowe et al. 1982:123, 127). Duende pottery shares many features with the burnished brown monochrome pottery from El Balsamo (Shook and Hatch 1978). In Chiapa III times, the ceramic assemblage of Izapa changed from this thick, soft pottery to harder, fine-paste orange negative-resist wares typical of all the sites in central Chiapas (Clark and Cheetham 2005; Lowe et al. 2013; Lowe et al. 1982: figs. 7.6 and 7.7). Ceramically, Izapa was very much a participant in the Chiapas Middle Preclassic era. Ceramic figurines at Izapa for Chiapa III and IV times are more similar to those in central Chiapas than to those in the Maya region (Ekholm 1989:336). Izapa's architecture does not

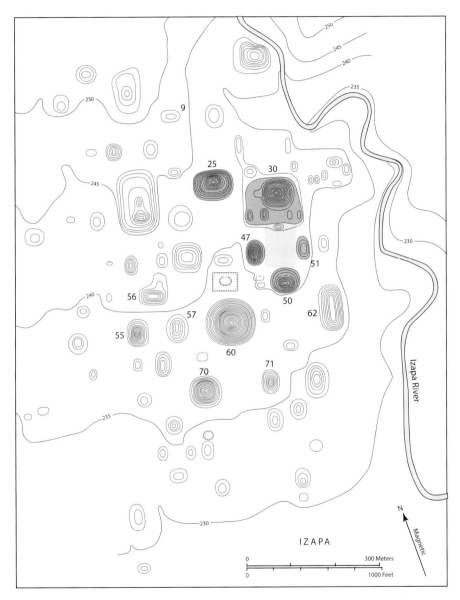

5.18. Map of Izapa, with gray shading indicating the distribution of Middle Preclassic (Chiapa III and IV) pottery and early mounds, and possible early mounds.

reflect these ties, but neither does the architecture at San Isidro. It should be remembered that La Blanca provided the people of Izapa a more proximal model of impressive architecture and city planning than did La Venta.

"At the end of the Frontera phase or very early in the Guillen phase, Burial 30e-1 was placed in the Mound 30 acropolis platform, with offering vessels that indicate an alignment with Guatemala or El Salvador...the earliest jade offering known at Izapa was also in this tomb" (Lowe et al. 1982:129). At this same time there was a pronounced regionalization in ceramic complexes. The ceramic complex at Izapa diverged from those in the interior and along the Pacific coast (Lowe et al. 2013). These changes in pottery are significant because this is the phase that Lowe claims as the apogee of mound building at Izapa. "All of the Izapa plaza groups except [Group] F appear to have achieved their present proportions during the Guillen phase [Chiapa V]. It is probable that almost all of the Izapa stone monuments were carved and erected during this phase" (Lowe et al. 1982:133). It turns out that the distribution of Guillen pottery is extremely limited in its region—virtually isolated by other complexes of greater geographic range. Guillen pottery does not show up in coastal Guatemala just across the river (the Ujuxte state was the dominant power there [Love 2002b, 2007, Chapter 7, this volume]) or in the Mazatán region to the west (Clark and Cheetham 2005). In terms of its pottery preferences, Izapa looks like an enclave population by Chiapa V times. The pottery distribution pattern is the main reason I proposed Izapa was an isolated Mixe community surrounded at the time by Maya communities (Clark 2000a:52).

The picture of foreign relations for Izapa during the Late Preclassic era is counterintuitive because the Izapa art style is so pervasive. The issues cannot be resolved at the present time, but it is appropriate to remember what really is known about this kingdom. First, the Izapa art style has a label problem that rivals the Olmec's. That an art style carries this brand label is an accident of the history of archaeological investigation. It is not certain that the Izapa style began at Izapa, was developed at Izapa, or that the promulgation of the Izapa style throughout eastern Mesoamerica had anything to do with elites living at Izapa. Second, the clearest antecedents to the carved stela–altar complex seen at Izapa are in the Mexican highlands at the early Middle Preclassic sites of Teopantecuanitlan, Guerrero (Martínez Donjuán 1986, 1994, 2010), and Chalcatzingo, Morelos (Grove 1987b, 1989b, 1997, 2000b, Chapter 3, this volume). These regions appear to have had special trade connections with the Soconusco from Early Preclassic times onward (Pye and Gutiérrez 2007, 2011), so the stela-altar complex could easily have been borrowed from highlanders living to the north. Third, the era of the sculpting of Izapa stone monuments has not been established, and the original logic for their chronological placement is not compelling. Lowe acknowledged that central Izapa was well developed by Chiapa III and IV times (Lowe et al. 2013), so an argument based on the presence of plaza groups could date the Izapa monuments five centuries earlier if need be. I think Izapa's stela-altar complex began in Chiapa IV times (550–300 BCE) and was a continuation of earlier practices of carving monuments in the round (Clark and Pye 2000b: fig. 16). The earliest monument at Izapa in a structure context is Miscellaneous Monument 2 (Norman 1973: fig. 64; 1976:256–58), known locally as El León (Fig. 5.19). This monument shares similarities with monuments from Tiltepec and Tres Zapotes. My earlier estimate of 600 BCE for this sculpture was based on an erroneous assessment of the age of Tiltepec and its Olmec-like monuments. It is more likely that El León dates to 400 BCE, near the end of the Middle Preclassic period (Clark and Hodgson 2008:89; cf. Norman 1976:257; Lowe et al. 1982:8, 133). The head of a "dancing jaguar" sculpture was found in a Middle Preclassic midden and dates to about 500 BCE (Ekholm 1993), so the sculpture tradition is older at the site than the El León monument. The sculptural program at Izapa distinguished this kingdom from its Middle Preclassic contemporaries in central Chiapas and made it more akin to La Venta, Tres Zapotes, and Chalcatzingo—with an emphasis on this last kingdom (Grove 1987b, 1989b, Chapter 3, this volume).

Other evidence of foreign relations is also equivocal. The ceramic history of Izapa shows growing regionalism during the Late Preclassic. Gulf coast trade wares date to Chiapa III times. During the Chiapa IV era there were fewer trade wares, and they appear to have come from the La Libertad region (Lowe et al. 2013). Figurine styles show the same trend (Ekholm 1989). Obsidian found at the site came from highland Guatemala sources, but we lack an adequate sample per phase. The data show that obsidian from the Tajumulco and San Martin Jilotepeque sources predominated in the Middle Preclassic and continued into the Protoclassic. Results from an analysis of a larger sample of Izapa obsidian negate my previous suggestion that most obsidian came from El Chayal in Protoclassic times (i.e., Clark et al. 1989: table 12.1). El Chayal obsidian is rare at Izapa (Lee and Clark 2013).

The limited burial evidence from Izapa, as noted, shows some relation to kingdoms in Guatemala and El Salvador. Because human bone does not preserve in the Izapa environment, the best traces of possible kings or leaders are the images on the numerous stelae and altars at the site. Izapa is well known for its narrative style and mythic themes. Many of the images may represent kings dressed as heros or as avian deities (Guernsey 2006). Kings dressed in bird costumes are known for La Venta (Clark 1997: fig. 2; 2004b: figs. 18.2a and 18.4a). Thus far, no evidence of burials or special tombs for kings has been found at Izapa for the Middle or Late Preclassic periods. Julia Guernsey (2006:105) makes a case for such a royal burial at Kaminaljuyu for the Late Preclassic period. The ideal of kingship and its stylistic representations were widespread, and certainly peoples of different cultures and languages participated in the same system.

HUANACASTAL, CHIAPAS

There is not much to describe about this site other than to record it for future consideration in the current lineup of Middle Preclassic kingdoms. Huanacastal is located 30 km west of Izapa on the coastal plain of the Mazatán region, on the west bank of the Coatan River and 5 km inland from the ocean (Fig. 5.1). Its peak occupation was in the Classic period, but the early stages of its largest pyramid were built in Chiapa II-B and III times. Evidence that Huanacastal was a kingdom comes from regional survey, the existence of constructed pyramids, and the presence of an early mound burial at this site. Only one test excavation has been undertaken, and this was in the footprint left by the largest pyramid which had been carted away as fill to make an elevated all-weather road to the beach. The principal mound is said to have been 20 m tall, a plausible height given the extent of its footprint. It was probably largely Protoclassic.

My excavation in the basal scar of this mound recovered evidence of its early construction sequence and also of an extended burial of an adolescent male with Olmec-style tabular-erect cranial deformation (Fig. 5.20). This burial is similar to the contemporaneous burial found at the ceremonial center of El Pajón 100 km up the coast (Lowe 1989a, 1994: fig. 7.4; Pailles 1980: figs. 54–60) and to Burial 7 of Santa Rosa along the upper Grijalva River (Brockington 1967:22; Delgado 1965b:25, 37–39). All three individuals were buried extended and face down, but there was no consistent orienta-

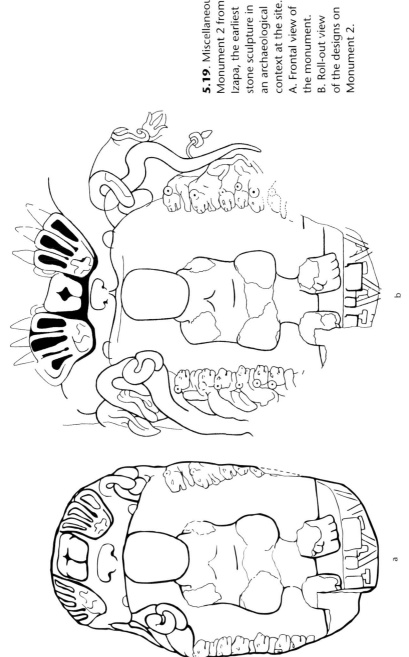

5.19. Miscellaneous Monument 2 from Izapa, the earliest stone sculpture in an archaeological context at the site. A. Frontal view of the monument. B. Roll-out view of the designs on Monument 2.

tion of these burials. The burial at Huanacastal lacked obvious mortuary goods but was buried in a low platform about 1.5 m high constructed about 900 BCE (Blake et al. 1995:13, sample B-22613). This platform was later elevated in Chiapa III times to 6 m high. It is not known how many of the other mounds at this site date to this period. Nothing approaching the MFC complex is apparent in the mounds at the site. Half a dozen other sites in the Mazatán zone have small pyramids dating to the Chiapa IV phase, and some of these would have been secondary centers. There is no evidence of E-Groups or Middle Preclassic ballcourts in this region. Surface collections of pottery indicate a strong Middle Preclassic occupation at Huanacastal, but none during the Late Preclassic. Termination at the beginning of the Late Preclassic was a fate shared by many Chiapas regional centers.

TZUTZUCULI, CHIAPAS

This 35 ha site is located on the other end of the Chiapas coast from Huanacastal and Izapa and 12 km in from the Pacific Ocean (Fig. 5.21). Andrew McDonald's 39 excavation units there in 1971 have been fully reported (McDonald 1977, 1983). Of particular interest, this is the only site in Chiapas with Middle Preclassic sculpture found in association with public architecture. Because of their setting, these monuments must date to 600–500 BCE (McDonald 1983:16). Two stone monuments flank each side of the 4 m wide southern stairway of Mound 4. The monuments adjacent to the river cobble steps of this stairway are carved in low relief; the outer flanking monuments are stones of similar shape and size but are uncarved (Fig. 5.22). The paired low-relief monuments bear a family resemblance to Olmec-style sculpture (Fig. 5.11). One represents a serpent in profile and the other a frontal view of a jaguar-like creature (McDonald 1977). The so-called jaguar face is the same as that on the celtiform stelae in front of the main pyramid at La Venta and carries a representation of the same foliated crown (cf. Fig. 5.5). The monuments at Tzutzuculi, however, are not stelae. They are freestanding boulder sculptures; the bases of these monuments rested on the plaza surface rather than needing a buried tenon for stability, as is characteristic of the stone slab stelae at La Venta. McDonald (1977) speculates that the principal idea conveyed with the placement of the stone images at Tzutzuculi on each side of the central stairway of Mound 4 is of an encircling serpent, such as seen on Olmec scepters and on some pyramids in the Classic period.

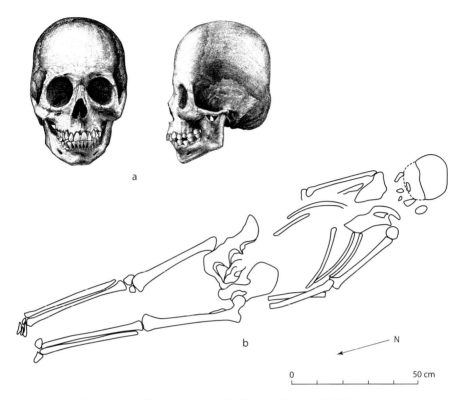

5.20. Burials from the Chiapas coast with Olmec-style cranial deformation. A. Drawing of skull from Pajón (redrawn from Pailles 1980:fig. B). Burial 1, Huanacastal, of a young male interred face down.

Evidence that Tzutzuculi was the seat of an ancient kingdom is its public architecture, the MFC complex, stone sculpture, and size and configuration of the site. No elite burials or offerings are known, but an empty stone crypt was found just west of Mound 4 that is reminiscent of the cist tomb in Complex A at La Venta (Guernsey 2006: fig. 2.25; McDonald 1977:561). The cist at Tzutzuculi was associated with Monuments 3 and 4; each of these stela shows a low-relief frontal image of an adult male with an elaborate headdress (McDonald 1983:23, 39). These two monuments were set upright on the west end of the cist, and they were placed with a plain stone altar between them (McDonald 1983:23). This cist dates to Chiapa IV times (Mc-Donald 1983:39), but the sculptures are probably earlier and in a secondary setting (Clark and Pye 2000b: fig. 15). McDonald (1983:25) speculates that this crypt once contained a burial whose bones and offerings were removed in antiquity. Only one earspool was found on the floor of the crypt.

The hierarchical position of Tzutzuculi remains to be determined because no contemporaneous Middle Preclassic sites are known for this coastal region. The large site of Tiltepec lies just 9 km northwest of Tzutzuculi, and it has a variety of sculptures in late Olmec style and stone architecture made from granite boulders from the adjacent river (Lowe 1967, 1977:231; Martínez Espinosa 1959; Milbrath 1979; Navarrete 1959a). These two centers appear to have been sequential. The 25 mounds at Tzutzuculi are arranged in the La Venta pattern, but at 1/4 scale. In contrast, the site plan at Tiltepec bears no resemblance to this plan (see Navarrete 1959a) and dates to the Late Preclassic, beginning about 400–300 BCE. Tiltepec would have been a contemporary of the Tres Zapotes kingdom rather than of La Venta.

Tzutzuculi was built on a broad terrace on the south margin of the Zanatenco River. Some of the site's tight configuration was dictated by local hills and topography. Even so, the main features of the MFC pattern are clear, especially when the dates of the different mounds are considered (Fig. 5.21). Basic components of the MFC pattern include Mounds 4, 5, 6, 7, Enclosure B, and possibly Mounds 8 and 10. Of these, Mounds 4, 5, 7, and 8 have been tested and shown to have been built in late Chiapa II-B times, about 850–750 BCE (McDonald 1983:10, 16, 32, 33). Mound 4 was enlarged until it was 8 m tall by 500 BCE. When first constructed, it was less than 4.5 m high (McDonald 1974). It rests upon a broad, low platform, just like its larger counterparts at La Venta and Chiapa de Corzo. The main plaza at the site is obscured by the presence of Enclosure A. Excavations there show that it was built in Chiapa IV times, long after the original site was built, so the plaza was originally open. Mound 6 and Enclosure B were not tested, but they conform to the MFC pattern known from other Chiapa III sites and probably date to that time period. The main axis of Tzutzuculi is 38 degrees east of magnetic north, an axis which aligns the site with Tres Picos, a prominent peak of the Sierra Madre range (McDonald 1977:561).

Figurines at Tzutzuculi are very rare, and the pottery is largely local, so there are few clues of distant cultural contacts other than the stone monuments, architecture, and site layout. The sculpture and architectural evidence points to strong ties to La Venta. These sites had parallel histories as well. Both were established about 900–850 BCE and abandoned about 400 BCE (Fig. 5.2). Tzutzuculi shows the greatest contrasts with its clos-

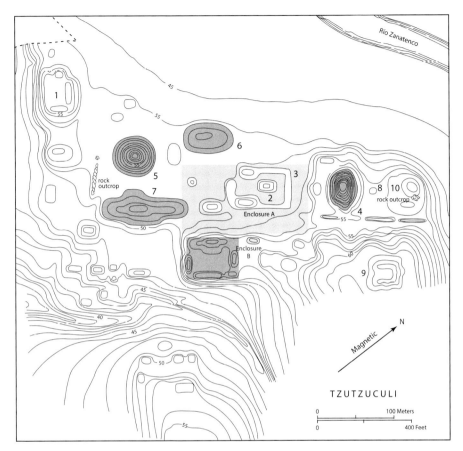

5.21. Site map of Tzutzuculi, with gray coding showing the location of the earliest mounds.

est coastal neighbor, Laguna Zope, located 130 km to the northwest in the Isthmus of Tehuantepec. The contrasts between these two sites in material culture, given their proximity, indicate that the differences were cultural and deliberately marked.

LAGUNA ZOPE, OAXACA

Laguna Zope was the largest site in the southern Isthmus of Tehuantepec from Early Preclassic to Classic times, 1750 BCE to 300 CE (my chronological adjustments to the phases). The site is located 1 km west of the Los Perros

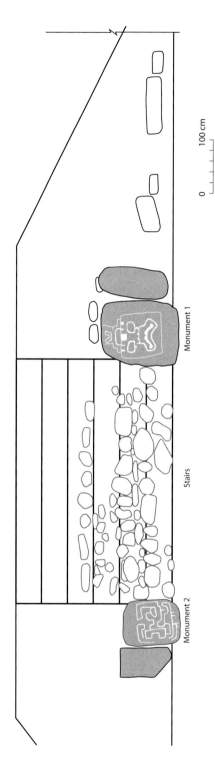

5.22. Reconstruction of the façade of Mound 4 at Tzutzuculi.

River and 10 km upriver from the Laguna Superior (Fig. 5.1). Robert Zeitlin (1978, 1979, 1982, 1993, 2001a; see Delgado 1965a) observes that the site was established in a favorable location at the nexus of several trade routes between lowland and highland regions that connected Oaxaca with the Soconusco, both with Olman, and all of these with central Chiapas. The inland estuary waterway reported by Carlos Navarrete (1978) that connected coastal Oaxaca to El Salvador ran through the Laguna Superior, just about two hours' walk from Laguna Zope, so the community was well positioned and connected. Even today, all the major roads and railways through the Isthmus pass near this site (Zeitlin 1978, 1993). The people at Laguna Zope specialized in making and trading items of marine shell (Zeitlin 1993). Evidence of ancient connections and trade are best seen in changes in imported obsidian goods through time and in changing ceramic complexes and their stylistic similarities to those in adjacent areas. There are enough shared modes in ceramic types and forms to correlate the ceramic chronology of Laguna Zope to those of Middle Preclassic centers of western Chiapas (Fig. 5.2) but sufficient dissimilarities to mark different cultural traditions. Kingdom building occurred all across Mesoamerica during the Middle Preclassic and involved many different linguistic and cultural groups. Marcus Winter (2007:200) speculates that the people of Laguna Zope were proto-Mixe speakers.

The three large earthen mounds that constitute the monumental center of Laguna Zope date to Middle and Late Preclassic times. These grew by accretion and are more akin to Near Eastern tells than to pyramids. Zeitlin (1993) argues that they were platforms for elite houses, and he reports several Late Preclassic domestic structures on top of Mound III, the tallest mound at the site at 9 m high. During the Middle Preclassic, this platform was less than 6 m high. As apparent in Figure 5.23, there is no obvious orientation to the disposition of the principal mounds at Laguna Zope. They do not appear to have been platforms for public or civic-religious buildings such as described above for other sites. Of the regional centers considered here, Laguna Zope is one of the smallest. Its three large platforms were in place by 600 BCE. The Ríos phase (900–500 BCE) community extended over 90 ha and probably had 1000 to 2000 people (Zeitlin 1993:86; 2001a:393; 2001b:541).

The ceramic and obsidian records at Laguna Zope are complicated and show swings of influence from west to east, then back again (Zeitlin 1979; 2001b). Middle Preclassic Ríos phase ceramics were typical of the widespread horizon style of white, flat-bottomed, out-leaning-wall bowls with double-line break designs incised on their interior rims—a design typical of the early Middle Preclassic all across Mesoamerica. The Goma phase (500–300 BCE) at Laguna Zope saw close ties to eastern kingdoms, with obsidian imported from highland Guatemala, and pottery including orange splotchy-resist vessels and waxy red wares typical of western Chiapas and even the Maya lowlands. Ceramic wares changed abruptly about 300 BCE to emulate the gray wares from the Valley of Oaxaca (Zeitlin 2001b) and the differential-fired black-and-white pots from Tres Zapotes (Zeitlin 1979). This was the time of the expansion of the Zapotec state at Monte Albán throughout the Oaxaca highlands (see below). Laguna Zope apparently came under the influence of the Monte Albán state, but not under its domination. Zeitlin (1993, 2001b; Zeitlin and Joyce 1999) claims that the pottery similarities between Laguna Zope and Monte Albán are better accounted for as consequences of trade with a powerful neighbor rather than from a Monte Albán conquest of Laguna Zope. As noted, some Oaxaca pots made it to San Isidro and Chiapa de Corzo.

Laguna Zope is located almost equidistantly between Tres Zapotes, Monte Albán, and Chiapa de Corzo (Fig. 5.1), so it is not surprising that its ceramic inventory reflects its medial position and was particularly sensitive to changes in the relative power of its neighbors. Zeitlin (1979:62) explains the situation during the Kuak phase (300 BCE to 1 CE).

> During the Late Preclassic a noteworthy overlap of horizons is articulated by the Isthmus of Tehuantepec. The northern and southern regions share both greyware traditions with the Oaxaca Valley to the west and differentially-fired white-rim blackware traditions with the Chiapas Central Depression to the east. At the same time, the Chiapas Central Depression had strengthened its connections with the Maya Chicanel–related waxy-slipped orange and other pottery types (Lowe and Mason 1965:217–18; Peterson 1963:12).

Shifts in obsidian exchange evince the same complexity. Differences in the frequencies of obsidian tools show changes in sources. During the Early Preclassic, the principal sources of obsidian were El Chayal, Guatemala, and Guadalupe Victoria in eastern Puebla, Mexico. Use of El Chayal obsidian continued through the Preclassic period, but during the Middle Preclassic Guadalupe Victoria obsidian dropped out and was replaced by that from

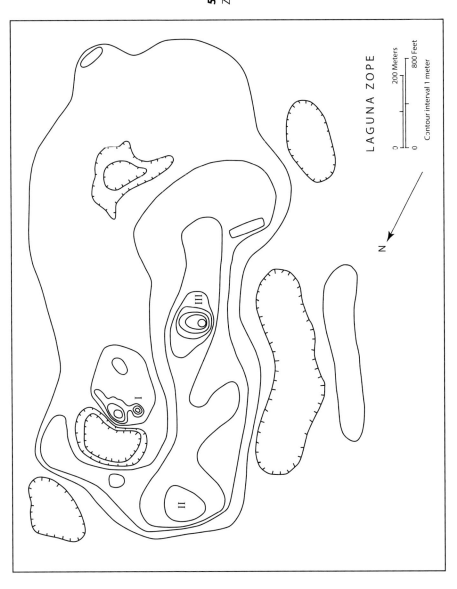

5.23. Map of Laguna Zope.

Altotongo in central Veracruz, Mexico, and another unidentified source (Zeitlin 1982:268). Zeitlin observes that this was the same obsidian used at La Venta (Hester et al. 1973:167). At about 400 BCE, with the collapse of La Venta, obsidian was once again imported from the Guadalupe Victoria source (Zeitlin 1982:268). These changes indicate power shifts in Mesoamerica during the Middle Preclassic period. The history of Laguna Zope's shifting alliances and economic connections is important for monitoring changes in the global economy in Middle Preclassic Mesoamerica and in identifying its major players. Just on the basis of ceramics alone, the eastern kingdoms in Chiapas and the Maya area appear to have been particularly influential beginning about 500 BCE, with the Monte Albán Zapotecs countering and pushing back this influence by 300 BCE. Tres Zapotes appears to have been nearly as influential, too. Laguna Zope was a primary center and had no close rivals or known secondary centers in its immediate region.

A Middle Preclassic hamlet has been reported 18 km upstream from Laguna Zope at Barrio Tepalcate (Winter 2007:198), formerly called Iglesia los Tepalcates (J. Zeitlin 1978:173). The earliest secondary centers date to the Late Preclassic period (Zeitlin 2001b:541). Similar to the situation at Tres Zapotes, the closest kingdom to the north, Laguna Zope lacked an E-Group or any semblance of deliberate planning and was not part of the MFC pattern described for La Venta, Tzutzuculi, and other Chiapas centers. These obvious differences in cultural practices and representations vis-à-vis the Chiapas kingdoms signal cultural differences and a likely cultural boundary between the Isthmian lowlands and highland Chiapas, as indicated in Figure 5.1. Tres Zapotes, located 240 km north of Laguna Zope, exhibits some of the same sorts of differences.

TRES ZAPOTES, VERACRUZ

Tres Zapotes was located on the western fringe of the Olmec heartland about 160 km west of La Venta. It was in an area of good farmland at the foot of the Tuxtlas Mountains and on the edge of the Papaloapan River floodplain and on a natural travel and trade route (Pool 2007:246–47; Pool and Ohnersorgen 2003:31). Tres Zapotes was contemporaneous with San Lorenzo and La Venta, both in their day, but does not appear to have been a serious rival to either kingdom. Rather, the apogee of Tres Zapotes came during the Late Preclassic and Protoclassic periods after the collapse of the La Venta kingdom. During its golden age, Tres Zapotes had over 160 mounds and spread over 5 km² (Pool 2003, 2007:19). Much of Tres Zapotes is deeply buried, but limited excavations and auger tests reveal the presence of an Early Preclassic occupation coeval with and stylistically similar to that of San Lorenzo (Ortíz 1975; Pool 2000:141–42; Pool and Ohnersorgen 2003:3; Wendt 2003b). Some ceramics and figurines also show stylistic similarities to those in highland Mexico (Pool 2006b). Tres Zapotes was occupied until Late Classic times, with some reoccupation in Postclassic times (Pool 2007:250).

The first Olmec colossal head was reported for Tres Zapotes in 1869 (Melgar 1869; see Bernal 1969: plate 5), and the earliest excavations were carried out in 1939 (Stirling 1940a). Thus, Tres Zapotes began as the type site for Olmec culture and sculpture, but in retrospect, its sculptures largely postdate Olmec times (Pool 2007). Some overlap with earlier Olmec centers is evident in ceramic and figurine inventories and the presence of two colossal heads found at the site (Fig. 5.24). These heads are thought to have been portraits of kings; if true, their presence at Tres Zapotes indicates that it was an ancient kingdom independent from that at La Venta. These two centers were probably the capitals of contemporaneous kingdoms during the early Middle Preclassic period, the likely time these basalt heads were brought in to both sites. El Marquesillo, a site where a 12 ton tabletop throne has been discovered (*Arqueología Mexicana* 54:15 [2001]), is located 60 km east-southeast of Tres Zapotes (Pool 2007: fig. 1.3). It may prove to have been another rival kingdom (Doering 2007). Numerous niched altars are known for La Venta, but none for Tres Zapotes.

Of particular interest for discussion here are the striking differences in site layouts between Tres Zapotes and La Venta (compare Figs. 5.24 and 5.3). Four low platforms are known for the Middle Preclassic period at Tres Zapotes.

> One of these structures formed the initial construction phase of Mound 5, at the east end of the plaza in Group 1, and consisted of a red clay platform, about 1.5 m tall (Weiant 1943:6). On the south edge of Group 2, an altar consisting of a small, carved serpentine column set upright in a hole carved through a basalt slab was set on a low platform and surrounded by upright basalt columns, reminiscent of Tomb A at La Venta (Millet 1979). Basalt columns also ringed a 2 m high earthen platform a short distance to the south. (Pool 2007:248)

The other low mound is about 80 cm high and located in Group 2, north of a long mound (Pool, pers. comm. 2008). Other than these modest mounds, all platforms and pyramids at Tres Zapotes appear to have been constructed in the Late Preclassic period (Pool 2007:247). If the colossal heads found at Tres Zapotes really were originally of rulers of that place, there apparently were no tall mounds to go along with them. Of course, the same correspondence holds for the colossal heads at the earlier site of San Lorenzo (Cyphers 1996:70, Chapter 4, this volume). Monumental construction at these sites was horizontal rather than vertical and manifest in broad terraces, house platforms, and causeways (Clark 1997; Cyphers 1996; Lowe 1989b). Monumental construction at early Tres Zapotes could have been in terraces, although there is not much evidence of it (Pool and Ohnersorgen 2003; Wendt 2003b). Alternatively, the colossal heads at Tres Zapotes could have been hauled in at a later date from a nearby Middle Preclassic center that has yet to be identified (I presume these colossal heads are stylistically later than those of San Lorenzo). If the colossal heads were carved for Tres Zapotes rulers—governing a town without towers—this pairing of low mounds and giant heads has interesting implications for the four colossal basalt heads found at La Venta. Matthew Stirling's (1943b:17) excavation of Monument A at Tres Zapotes, the colossal head in Group 1, "discovered that it had been placed upon a foundation consisting of a layer of unworked stones at the ancient plaza level...." This sounds like a primary and early context for Tres Zapotes Monument A.

The colossal basalt heads at La Venta appear associated with monumental architecture and the MFC complex. The arrangement of pyramids, plazas, and modest mounds at Tres Zapotes clearly differs. The principal mounds are spaced about 900 m apart (Pool 2000:140, 2007:250) and are clustered into four groups around plazas (Fig. 5.24). These vary in orientation and the size of the mounds (Pool 2007:248). The principal plaza groups conform to a different pattern than at La Venta but incorporate some of the same elements.

The basic Late Formative plan of these mound groups consists of a large plaza, oriented approximately east-west, with a tall, pyramidal, temple mound on the west end and a lower, longer mound on the north edge. The long mounds probably supported administrative buildings, but refuse deposits behind the long mounds in the Nestepe Group and

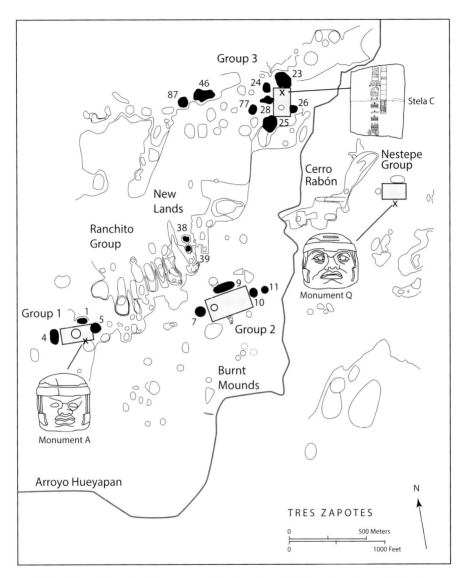

5.24. Map of Tres Zapotes showing the location of colossal heads and Stela C as well as plazas (shown as gray rectangles).

Groups 2 and 3 suggest they also were places of elite residence. In each group a low platform placed on the central axis of the plaza appears to have functioned as an altar. (Pool 2007:248)

What is particularly interesting at Tres Zapotes is the repetition of the elemental pattern within the same site rather than having one rationalized, overall layout such as seen at La Venta, with simplified copies throughout a region. The duplication of units is the classic signature of mechanical versus organic solidarity. The architectural redundancy at Tres Zapotes suggests a parallel duplication of functions at the site, and one not seen at La Venta or any of the other western kingdoms considered here. Pool (2007:248–50) attributes the dispersed pattern of platforms and plazas at Tres Zapotes to a different organizational principle of social and political life than seen at La Venta. He postulates Tres Zapotes was governed by a council or coalition of lineage leaders and that each cluster of pyramids around a plaza represented the seat of one of these ruling lineages. This becomes another argument for the images of kings on the colossal heads and two stelae from the site (Monuments A and F) being earlier in the sequence (see Pool 2010 for discussion of new monuments and their implications). The two colossal heads are associated with plaza groups at opposite ends of the site (Fig. 5.24), analogous to the north and south lines of heads at La Venta's boundaries (Fig. 5.3). If colossal heads portrayed single, strong leaders, then another expectation is that Tres Zapotes took a different path to political stability later in the Late Preclassic. It is not clear when this occurred, if indeed it did. But the main points of Pool's argument, that there were multiple kingdoms in Middle Preclassic Olman and of different organizational complexity and/or type, are confirmed.

The Middle Preclassic at Tres Zapotes is still poorly dated by one long phase (Fig. 5.2), so it is difficult to monitor changes. At this time, "Tres Zapotes emerged as a regional center covering some 80 ha (Pool and Ohnersorgen 2003). The two Olmec colossal heads from Tres Zapotes may date from early in the Middle Preclassic period" (Pool 2007:152). The broad regional settlement has not been dated with sufficient precision to determine the emergence of a regional polity at Tres Zapotes (Pool 2007:152), but the settlement just around the site has. "Several concentrations of Tres Zapotes phase pottery surrounding the center suggest the existence of rural homesteads and villages. The largest of these, revealed only by auger tests, covered about 15 ha on the opposite bank of the Arroyo Hueyapan. The remaining concentrations cover less than 5 ha" (Pool and Ohnersorgen 2003:24). On the basis of these clustered settlements, Pool (2007:154) posits that Tres Zapotes had at least a two-tier settlement hierarchy in the Middle

Preclassic period (Pool 2007:176). The presence of Middle Preclassic sculptures in the round of full-figure seated males (kings or princes) at other sites in the Tres Zapotes region (Loughlin and Pool 2006) indicates the existence of at least a three-tier settlement hierarchy for this period. These early sculptures are similar to those at La Venta, but this is not surprising because the basalt outcrops used for La Venta sculptures were near Tres Zapotes (Pool 2007). The use of columnar basalt is another feature shared between these centers.

Other indicators of foreign relations are evident in obsidian exchange and ceramic styles. As mentioned, some sherds from ceramic vessels imported from La Venta have been found at Tres Zapotes (King 2002; Pool 2007:146; von Nagy 2003:199). Most obsidian is from surface collections (Knight 2003), so it cannot be attributed precisely to phase. During the Middle Preclassic, the principal sources were Guadalupe Victoria and Pico de Orizaba obsidian, with minor amounts of obsidian coming from the more distant Zaragosa, Puebla, source (Knight 2003:87; Pool 2007:150). Obsidian from San Martin Jilotepeque, Guatemala, has been found in the Los Tuxtlas region but not at Tres Zapotes (Pool, pers. comm. 2008). Most of the obsidian came from western sources in the Mexican uplands, as observed for La Venta and Laguna Zope. The ceramics complicate this story.

> In general, and in contrast to obsidian exchange... ceramic affinities suggest less interaction of the southern and south-central Gulf lowlands with western Mesoamerica and greater interaction along the old corridor through Chiapas and southern Guatemala. That distribution coincides reasonably well with commonalities between epi-Olmec and "Izapan" writing and sculptures.... (Pool 2007:269)

Pool's diachronic, regional comparison between Tres Zapotes and La Venta (2007:154) nicely shows that the advent of the Late Preclassic was a time of radical demographic change. This was accompanied by changes in ceramic styles, a reduction in traded luxury goods such as jade (Pool 2007:245, 268), new sculptural styles, and the beginning of writing (Pool 2007:243). As discussed above, the Late Preclassic was a period that also witnessed the maximum influence from Tres Zapotes on sites in the Isthmus and western Chiapas, especially in the resurgence of white-rim blackware as a marker of identity. Tres Zapotes appears to have had less influence

on the more westward kingdoms in Oaxaca and those reported by David
Grove (Chapter 3, this volume) for the Mexican plateau.

SOME OBSERVATIONS

My purpose in this chapter has been to put basic facts and proposals on
record to provide broad historical context for developments in the Maya
area that led to state societies there about 300–200 BCE. Space precludes
drawing out very many of the implications of the preceding site biogra-
phies. I highlight five implications of particular significance that may help
in understanding the rise of early Maya states.

First, it is clear that developments in the Maya lowlands and highlands
during the Middle Preclassic period were part of a broader pattern of the
construction of cities and towns and the establishment of kingdoms all
across Mesoamerica. In each region, developments conform to a spatio-
temporal series, so it is clear that concepts about how to organize and run
a kingdom got around quickly after the emergence of early kingdoms at
San Lorenzo, La Blanca, and La Venta. It follows as patently obvious that all
Middle Preclassic kingdoms in Mesoamerica were secondary rather than primary developments (see Chapters 3, 6, 7, 8 for contrary views on the logical
necessity of this proposition). By 1000 BCE most sentient Mesoamericans
had heard of the wonders of San Lorenzo and the deeds of its rulers. Stories
and gossip of the San Lorenzo kingdom would have contained some basic
facts about how it was organized and governed. Consequently, later polities
could have been, and were, made to order along preconceived plans with
foreknowledge of how kingdoms elsewhere successfully operated. That
is, developments could have been teleological. Middle Preclassic peoples
could pursue kingdom-building as an overt and premeditated option, and
do it swiftly. Mesoamerica as a hyper-connected geographic area of shared
cultural practices and beliefs was in place by 1300 BCE, and developments
in one of its regions could have been quickly known in others. Explanations for the rise of Middle Preclassic kingdoms, or even of states, need to
take into account the knowledge of complex polities that was making the
rounds and not restrict critical causal factors of political evolution solely to
ecological processes or economics.

Second, one of the exciting features of the Middle Preclassic is that it
was Mesoamerica's era of kingdom and city building. At the beginning of

this period many cities were started from scratch as colonies, and they subsequently budded off in their own regions. The second half of the Middle Preclassic and the beginning of the Late Preclassic was an era of settling down and regionalization. Most Middle Preclassic Chiapas kingdoms, for example, started as towns or cities in the middle of nowhere, with no discernable support populations around them. These were top-down entities at the beginning. One curiosity of the Middle Preclassic data for central Chiapas is that there are more primary than secondary centers. The settlement hierarchy filled in as population grew, so secondary and tertiary centers were established later in most kingdoms. It follows that most of the regional centers in Chiapas did not develop locally from extant populations but were transplanted from elsewhere. This is most clearly seen in central Chiapas with the imposition of the MFC complex. Whether or not the historical conditions that led to the establishment of new centers in Chiapas apply to the Maya lowlands or any other area of Mesoamerica remains to be seen. Data in hand indicate the existence of multiple kingdoms in the Maya lowlands during the late Middle Preclassic. I expect that the situation in the Maya lowlands during this period was at least as complicated as that in central Chiapas.

Third, the preceding case histories indicate the need to analyze kingdoms at multiple spatial scales. Clearly some of the events in greater Mesoamerica impacted kingdoms in distant regions, but most critical events were probably closer to home. Given the facts of secondary development and colonization, issues of kingdom origins are sometimes less problematic than those of kingdom collapse. Origins questions require an interregional, historic perspective to trace Middle Preclassic colonies to original founder populations. Long-distance exchange of various kinds came and went during the Middle Preclassic, with influence from Olman being important early on. In Chiapas, Gulf Olmec influence was eclipsed near the end of the period with strong influence from the Maya region—both lowland and highland. Maya influence was even felt in the Valley of Oaxaca and at early Teotihuacan at the height of Maya state development in the lowlands, so something especially important happened in Mayaland at this time. The areal impact of Maya influence was significantly greater than Zapotec influence from Oaxaca.

Lowe argued for competition between Zoques and Mayas at the macroregion level to explain parallel developments in these adjacent groups. As is apparent in the preceding kingdom histories, this hypothesized ethnic competition is a scholarly construct, not a historic reality. Different Zoque kingdoms in central Chiapas competed with each other, and this was more critical than competition with more-distant kingdoms in the Maya lowlands, the Isthmus of Tehuantepec, or the Valley of Oaxaca. Once more information becomes available, it should become clear that independent Maya kingdoms competed with each other to the same degree. There are no grounds for generalizing to entire ethnic or language groups from histories of individual polities. The differences between the Zoque kingdoms at Finca Acapulco and Chiapa de Corzo, for example, are striking. These adjacent polities differed significantly from those at San Isidro, La Venta, Izapa, or Tres Zapotes. The divergent histories of Chiapa de Corzo and neighboring Finca Acapulco derive partly, I think, from alliances forged between the leaders at Chiapa de Corzo and La Venta that eventually undercut the power and authority of the leaders at Finca Acapulco. I suspect that leaders of Chiapa de Corzo cemented foreign alliances to compete better locally. A similar arrangement may have occurred later when Chiapa de Corzo regents shifted loyalties from La Venta to a lowland Maya polity or polities about 300 BCE, perhaps to save their skin. Zoque centers upriver from Chiapa de Corzo were disbanded just before this time, perhaps because they rejected Maya hegemony. Whether future data will support these specific speculations of inter-polity alliances is not the point. The larger issue is that one needs to identify archaeologically the polities that had regional decision-making capabilities at any given time and leave open the likelihood that leaders or rulers of these polities could and did pursue strategic partnerships involving different cultural groups. We should not assume that in prehistory blood was thicker than water or that peoples of different cultural and language groups did not cooperate with one another at the expense of peoples of their own cultures. One of the interesting things about the Late Preclassic was the manipulation of identity and ethnicity in the era of coalition and kingdom-building, as most clearly seen at Chiapa de Corzo.

Fourth, the polity histories presented here were the prelude to the development of regional states at the beginning of the Late Preclassic period. In contrast to the start of the Middle Preclassic, Late Preclassic kingdoms confronted populated landscapes—at least in the best spots of the most productive agricultural regions. The Middle Preclassic was an era of colonization, founding, building, and filling the landscape. At 1000 BCE, most of

Mesoamerica was still open, and people moved around. With subsequent population packing, the demographic resources littering the landscape changed the possibilities for political maneuvering and development, as most clearly seen in the Valley of Oaxaca (Grove, Chapter 3, this volume) and the Mirador Basin (Hansen, Chapter 8, this volume). One of the facts evident in the preceding census of western kingdoms is their variety. I have attributed much of this to cultural differences, but as Pool (2007) has argued for Tres Zapotes, some complex regional polities may have been organized in fundamentally different ways, and this would have affected the types of alliances and strategies pursued by the governing body of each polity, as well as their capacity for international influence. It follows that the term "kingdom" would be inappropriate for political entities with collective decision-making at the highest level and that a more appropriate descriptive label ought to be used that better approximates the structure of ancient decision-making of these polities.

Finally, the timing of the rise and fall of Middle Preclassic kingdoms is too close to be random or autonomous. Given the spread of regional polities in the Middle Preclassic, I find it remarkable that most of them fell apart just before the emergence of regional states in most areas of Mesoamerica. The spread of kingdoms and related polities established the conceptual and practical bases for their own obsolescence and the rise of regional states (Clark 2009). Some polities in the Late Preclassic were significantly larger than earlier kingdoms. Just in this sample of western kingdoms, one sees several examples of older kingdoms that were squeezed out by daughter communities established during the era of expansion. Territorial expansion was destabilizing in several ways, as is especially evident in the histories of La Blanca, Finca Acapulco, and La Venta. These kingdoms were outflanked and choked off by rivals they established or sponsored. The histories of Monte Albán and El Mirador appear to have been the reverse—polities growing up in the center of large populations that eclipsed or absorbed flanking kingdoms (see Hansen, Chapter 8, this volume). These patterns of kingdom emergence and collapse suggest that the most critical competition facing Middle Preclassic rulers was that nurtured within the boundaries and at the edges of their own domains. If so, the rise of regional states at the beginning of the Late Preclassic may have been largely a regional affair promoted by internal and factional competition among the elites of these selfsame kingdoms. The data for the Valley of Oaxaca certainly can be read in this way, and I suspect those for the Mirador Basin, given the number of large, early centers there and their tight packing, will prove to conform to this pattern also. This is to suggest that the catalyst for the rise of Maya states may have been internal, structural contradictions aided and abetted by strategic alliances to kings and nobles in neighboring polities.

ACKNOWLEDGMENTS

Many colleagues helped improve the accuracy and quality of this essay. Thomas A. Lee, John Hodgson, Timothy Sullivan, and Arlene Colman helped track down information for some Chiapas sites. For other cases, I received generous comments, drafts of unpublished articles, and uplifting criticism from Barbara Arroyo, Rebecca González Lauck, Arthur Joyce, Christopher Pool, William Rust, Robert Sharer, Loa Traxler, Javier Urcid, Marcus Winter, and Robert Zeitlin. I appreciate their research and current aid. I am particularly grateful to Kisslan Chan, Arlene Colman, Ryan Moore, and Meagan Wakefield for their artwork and to Arlene Colman for her fact-checking and editorial assistance.

6

Regional and Interregional Interactions and the Preclassic Maya

FRANCISCO ESTRADA–BELLI

For over a century, theories on the origins of civilization in Mesoamerica have favored influences from a single place of origin, usually attributed to diffusion of ideas or actual migrations. This is nowhere more apparent than in past explanations for the development of Classic civilization in the Maya lowlands. Recently, a growing body of archaeological evidence has pointed to interaction within and between regions as a major contributor to the development of complexity throughout Mesoamerica. The role of regional and interregional interaction in maintaining the coherency of various developmental trajectories while fostering innovation and change are certainly reflected in the Maya archaeological record during the Preclassic period, as it will be demonstrated below. But, among scholars there was almost always a preference for searching for cultural innovation outside of the Maya region, and that has caused many lacunae in our understanding of other, perhaps more significant, local processes.

Since the beginning of archaeological inquiry on the origins of Maya civilization almost a century ago, a postulated Highland-to-Lowland flow of people and ideas has dominated the discourse. This was partly because the lowland regions of modern Guatemala, Belize, and southeastern Mexico states have remained vastly inaccessible for much longer than the highland regions. At the same time, the pre-Hispanic achievements of the highland Maya people have been readily visible to archaeologists from very early in the history of our discipline. The predominance of Highland-to-Lowland theories to explain lowland Maya achievements may also be due to the direction taken by lowland Maya archaeology in the 20th century, favoring Late Classic period sites with inscriptions and effectively leaving the problem of the origins of civilization to be grappled with by a small number of specialists with an impossibly small sample. Each time significant amounts of new data were brought forward, our assumptions had to be necessarily adjusted (Adams and Culbert 1977; Grube 1995). Once again, today we have new data from archaeological excavations and survey projects and the time has come for us to re-evaluate Highland-to-Lowland models of interaction in light of this evidence.

THEORIES ON THE ORIGINS OF MAYA CIVILIZATION IN THE EARLY 20TH CENTURY (1910–1960)

When the Carnegie Institution of Washington began its excavations at Uaxactun in the 1930s there was little actual archaeological evidence for any period before the Classic. One of the most authoritative views on the antecedents to the Classic Maya was held by Herbert Spinden (1928). Based on scanty evidence from highland Mexico and Guatemala he concluded that complexity had emerged in those areas with the longest history of occupation. The few known sites in highland Guatemala with Paleoindian-period occupations, dating to about 11,000 years ago, were believed to belong to a culture of hunters directly ancestral to the first Maya farmers. The only known cultural manifestations of these people were so-called Archaic figurines found throughout the highlands, but which actually dated to much later. Spinden (1928) also believed that highland farmers had colonized the lowland region long after having established an agricultural way of life in the more fertile highland valleys. The existence of similar styles of "Archaic" figurines in both regions indicated to him the general ethnic identity of highland and lowland Maya populations and supported his Highland-to-Lowland migration theory.

Highland-to-Lowland migratory theories gained momentum in the post–World War II years after being adopted by authoritative figures in Maya archaeology such as Alfred Tozzer (1957). At the time, the field of archaeology was dominated by the culture-historical paradigm, and migration and diffusion were the explanatory theories of choice in New World and Old World prehistory (Willey and Sabloff 1980). In Central America, large-scale archaeological excavations at centers such as Kaminaljuyu and

Chalchuapa had shown a great antiquity of magnificent temples, tombs, and inscriptions there. Alfred Kidder reasoned that the highlanders had the advantage of more productive and easier to manage lands compared to the lowlanders who had to tame the insidious rainforest in order to survive. This, he wrote, "would have been an almost prohibitively difficult environment for pulling oneself up, so to speak, by the bootstraps" (Kidder 1950:6). Thus the highland Maya, who had had a longer history of sedentary life and agriculture in an "easier" environment, would have developed the skills to tame the hostile lowland environment and make a living in it.

Sylvanus G. Morley (1946) took a more lowland-centric position on this issue. He argued that the existence of the earliest inscriptions and dated monuments at Tikal and Uaxactun could not be explained by highland migrations alone but must have been the result of a long accumulation of knowledge in the same area. Kidder (1950) concurred on this point and added that this could only have been accomplished by a class of specialists who were long removed from the labors of subsistence and free from interruptions. The invention of the Maya hieroglyphic script and, by extension, of civilization was a purely lowland phenomenon. Morley (1946) also prudently noted that as archaeological investigation made progress in the lowlands, the developmental stages of lowland Maya culture would become apparent. This point had been increasingly evident from the extraordinary architecture of the only lowland Preclassic period pyramid known at the time, Temple E-VII-sub at Uaxactun, whose astronomical alignments and large-scale sculptural reliefs bespoke a highly developed culture.

The Carnegie Institution's excavations at Uaxactun (Smith 1950) brought to light not only that impressive Preclassic temple but also an extensive series of stratigraphic levels of occupation that predated it. The temple itself was assigned to the later part of the Late Preclassic Chicanel ceramic phase (400 BCE–200 CE) and its elaborate iconography closely presaged Classic Maya art. Below these levels were ceramics of the Mamom phase (800–400 BCE), which were interpreted as the remains of the first "Archaic" lowlanders. Their antiquity and highland origin were suggested by similarities in monochrome vessel styles in Formative Oaxaca, Veracruz, and highland Guatemala (Kidder 1950:7).

In his 1954 book *The Rise and Fall of Maya Civilization*, Sir J. Eric Thompson rejected his own earlier conviction that the Maya were the recipients of cultural innovations from their highland neighbors, having witnessed firsthand the impressive complexity of the stucco sculptures on Temple E-VII-sub. Instead, he believed the highland and lowland Maya cultures to be a case of parallel development of two closely related but distinct cultural traditions. In addition, he noted that the then newly discovered Olmec sculptures and architecture at La Venta, Tabasco, also had much in common with Maya art, and probably represented another case of parallel development.

In fact, at the time of its discovery, the site of La Venta was suspected to have been built by a Mayan-speaking people (Stirling 1957). This discovery followed earlier sculptural finds at Tres Zapotes with carved inscriptions (Stirling 1940b) and seemed to support a theory that proposed that the origins of Mesoamerican civilization had to be researched in the tropical lowlands of the Gulf coast of Mexico. Miguel Covarrubias (1946b) and George Vaillant (1930) were early proponents of this theory based on the observation of early sculpture, ceramics, and calendar inscriptions in that region (Pool 2007). Later, the monumentality of La Venta and its complex iconography became better known, and its chronological priority with respect to any known temple in the Maya region (mostly Late Preclassic) was accepted. Alfonso Caso (1947) and Michael Coe (1966a) were strong proponents of the theory that much, if not all, that was civilized in Mesoamerican cultures could be traced back to the Olmec. Other scholars joined this position and proposed that Olmec farmers had migrated from the Gulf coast to the Maya lowlands during Preclassic times (e.g., Borhcgyi 1965; Jiménez Moreno 1966). This view of the Olmec became known as the "Mother Culture" theory of the origins of Mesoamerican civilization and continues to be debated today (Blomster et al. 2005; Clark and Pye 2000b; Coe 1966a, 2005; Diehl 2004; Flannery and Marcus 2000; H. Neff et al. 2006b; Sharer 2007; Sharer et al. 2006).

Meanwhile, Maya archaeology of the mid-20th century largely focused on the highland and Pacific coast region partly because of accessibility and encroaching urban development. The bounty of data thus collected reinforced the notion that the highland Maya had produced great artistic and cultural sophistication before the onset of the Classic period and before the lowland Maya. Excavations at Kaminaljuyu by Edwin Shook and Alfred Kidder had uncovered richly furnished tombs and great temples that overshadowed anything else known in the lowlands (Kidder et al. 1946). Excavations at the site of Izapa, Chiapas, produced scores of stelae and altars, representing the largest corpus of carved stone monuments south of the Maya lowlands. While inscriptions were notably absent from Izapan monuments, the carving style and narrative content were clearly similar to that of Kaminaljuyu and appeared to be ancestral to that of the Classic lowland Maya (Coe 1966a; Norman 1973). The apex of the Izapan sculptural style was dated within the Late Preclassic period and thus represented a perfect chronological as well as geographical bridge between the Gulf coast Olmec and the Maya (Coe 1966a). Based on these approximations, the Highland-to-Lowland theory of decades before gained strength. Michael Coe and others proposed that the Izapans and Kaminaljuyu Maya, having reached their cultural pinnacle after the Olmec and before the Classic Maya, were largely responsible for transmitting the sculptural style, hieroglyphic writing, and iconogaphic motifs from the Olmec to the lowland Maya thus stimulating the emergence of Classic Maya civilization (Coe 1966a, Parsons 1986). In the mid-to-late 20th century, the literature became dominated by discussions of stylistic and linguistic relationships among Olmec, Izapans, and highland Maya to help explain the similarity and geographical distribution of archaeological traits (Campbell and Kaufman 1976; Lowe 1977).

Archaeological research and salvage operations at numerous Preclassic sites in Chiapas undertaken in the mid 20th century focused on the relationship of Chiapas cultures with the Gulf coast Olmec (see Chapter 5, this volume). In contrast to this state of affairs, archaeological research in the Maya lowlands was largely confined to documenting the complexity of the Classic Maya and much less was known about the Maya of the Preclassic period.

THEORIES ON THE ORIGINS OF MAYA CIVILIZATION IN THE LATE 20TH CENTURY (1960–2000)

Archaeological research in the latter half of the 20th century completely changed the perspective on the origins of lowland Maya civilization. Critical new data came from landmark research, including large-scale excavations carried out in the central lowlands at Tikal by the University of Pennsylvania and the Guatemalan Institute of Anthropology and History, followed by research in the previously little-known Mirador Basin, initially led by Brigham Young University. This period also saw a general increase in research on the Preclassic period across the northern and southern lowlands. The debate on the "origins" in the late 20th century centered on two main issues: *the timing of the arrival of the first farmers* in the lowlands and *the sudden emergence of civilization at the end of the Preclassic period.* El Mirador's spectacular temples and art were of such unprecedented scale and sophistication for the Preclassic period that they instantly challenged any prior assumptions and brought earlier theories under closer scrutiny (Sharer 1992; Hammond 1992). The debate that ensued continues well into the present and in the following sections is discussed with the aid of current data.

Until recently, the prevailing view has been that the first permanent occupants of the lowlands were farming colonizers of an empty area coming from the west, east, and south along the main river systems. These so-called pioneer farmers are known primarily from scanty ceramic remains which have been dated by C-14 to 900/1000 BCE. These ceramics and their associated architecture are significantly later than the earliest known farming villages on the Gulf coast and in the southern highlands (including Chiapas, Guatemala, and El Salvador), as well as in Central Mexico and Oaxaca. Because of the similarity of these ceramics with styles of neighboring highland regions, it was believed that the pioneer farmers had migrated into the lowlands from those regions.

By the 1970s, the theory that farmers had migrated into the Maya lowlands from the south or the west was treated as a corollary to other theories. These dealt with later developments in the lowlands and stressed ecological conditions, as well as processes of adaptation and competition. In a sense, while these theories sought to replace external influences and diffusion with social processes, change was essentially still seen as stimulated by causes or circumstances external to lowland society itself. In many cases, environmental factors were considered the strongest forces of cultural change.

Olga and Dennis Puleston (Puleston and Puleston 1971a) suggested a model by which colonizing farming communities spread into the interior along river routes by the process of village fissioning, thanks, at least initially, not to maize agriculture but to harvests of *ramon* tree nuts as the main staple. This model presupposed an egalitarian society, exponential population growth, and vast empty spaces away from rivers to be filled by newcomers.

Other models proposed in the 1970s contemplated the interplay of social processes such as population pressure and competition over increasingly scarce resources (land and water) internal to the Maya lowland region. After initial settlement it was proposed that resource scarcity may have led to settlement consolidation in areas of greater productivity (the Central Zone, including northern Peten region of Guatemala, southern Campeche, and Quintana Roo, Mexico), while areas of lesser productivity and lower population density remained in geographically marginal zones (the Belize, Pasion, and Northern zones). The Central Zone, where Tikal, Uaxactun, and some of the largest known sites were located, was viewed as the dynamic core in a pattern of lowland core-periphery interactions (Rathje 1971; Sanders 1977). In addition, warfare and trade were identified as the most significant mechanisms in the process that led to greater social complexity in the lowlands. Both mechanisms were stimulated by resource scarcity and population pressure as pre-conditions (Rathje 1971; Webster 1977).

The issue of the sudden appearance of civilization was logically related to the issue of the "arrival" of farming. Since the Maya were believed to have arrived relatively late in the lowlands, they also were delayed in the process of civilization when compared to their neighbors of the Gulf coast and southern highlands. The general lack of archaeological evidence for any sort of complexity prior to 300 BCE was largely responsible for the wide acceptance of this view. Basic components of civilization, such as monumental architecture, complex ceremonialism, and hierarchical organization were believed to have entered the lowlands from the highlands in a separate wave much after the arrival of the first farmers and along similar routes. The conditions could not be ripe for their adoption by lowland Maya until the Late Preclassic (ca. 300 BCE) or even the Protoclassic period (ca. 50–250 CE). Excavations in the Gulf coast region, on the other hand, had proposed the precocity and monumentality of sculpture at an even earlier Olmec site, San Lorenzo (Coe and Diehl 1980).

The impressive monuments from the Gulf coast and their great antiquity led a number of U.S. and Mexican scholars to embrace the Mother Culture Theory. Although waves of Olmecs fleeing from the collapse of La Venta were proposed as a stimulus to Maya florescence, few believed in direct contacts between the Gulf coast Olmec and the lowland Maya. Prior to the discoveries of large Late Preclassic centers in the lowlands, the non-contemporaneity of Olmec and Maya periods of florescence represented a major problem to any theory of direct contacts between the two cultures. As already mentioned, the solution to this problem was that the Gulf coast

Olmec and lowland Maya cultures were connected through cultures that flourished in intermediate regions. These were the Late Preclassic Izapan and highland Maya of southern Chiapas and Guatemala, who clearly shared many "cultural traits" with the earlier Gulf Olmec and later lowland Maya. The Late Preclassic period was viewed as a time of rapid growth in the lowlands and therefore the most likely period of cross-fertilization between highland and lowland cultures.

THE ELUSIVE PEASANT PIONEERS

The question of when the colonization of the Maya lowlands occurred is obviously central to the issue of the emergence of civilization in the same area. Direct archaeological evidence of the first colonizers includes little more than a few ceramic sherds from a handful of sparsely distributed sites, although pollen data from sediment cores is also crucial to this issue. The earliest ceramics in the lowlands are usually seen as evidence for the first appearance, i.e. "arrival" of groups of settlers during the pre-Mamom period, so named because these ceramics predate the first extensively distributed lowland ceramic complex. First defined during the Carnegie excavations at Uaxactun, Mamom ceramic types or their equivalent have been found at most lowland sites and date to the later part of the Middle Preclassic period from 800–400 BCE (R.E. Smith 1950). Pre-Mamom ceramics, on the other hand, are known from very few locations and are not firmly dated. They were first identified at Altar de Sacrificios and Seibal in the Pasion region, at Belize River valley sites, and at Tikal (Fig. 6.1). Since then, additional sets of pre-Mamom ceramics have been found in northern Belize, in the Central Zone, and most recently in the Holmul area.

The known samples of Pre-Mamom ceramics from individual sites are often too small to form distinct ceramic complexes and as a whole do not form a homogeneous group, as Mamom-style ceramics do (i.e., the Mamom interaction sphere, Gifford 1965). Instead, there is a relative degree of stylistic diversity among them from region to region (Cheetham 2005). Similarities are strongest among neighboring sites and areas. The pre-Mamom ceramics of Altar de Sacrificios (Xe) and those of Seibal (Real Xe) appear to be more similar to one another than samples farther afield and form a more or less distinct group. The pre-Mamom ceramics of the Holmul area share many similarities with the Belize River valley (Cunil)

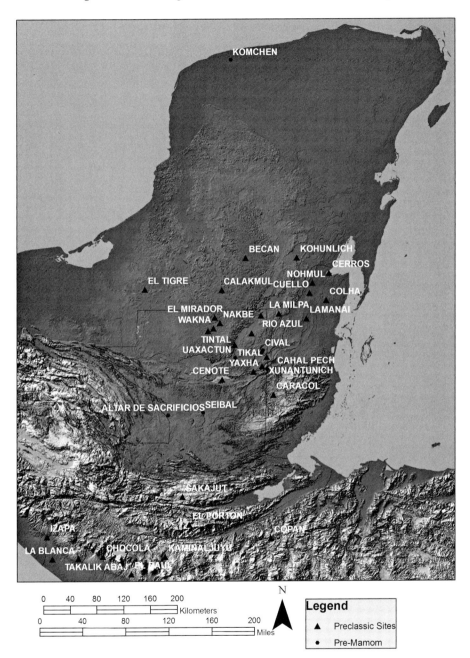

6.1. Map of Maya Region showing distribution of pre-Mamom and other early Middle Preclassic ceramic complexes.

and the Tikal (Eb) complexes, but are dissimilar enough to be placed in separate groups. The similarities across areas can be seen in forms and decorations of serving vessels, while utilitarian vessels denote greater local diversity. John Clark and David Cheetham (2002) have grouped these early ceramic complexes into four major stylistic regions of interaction, but these should be expanded to at least six in light of current data. These now include a western Pasion group represented by the Xe ceramic complex of Seibal and Altar de Sacrificios (Adams 1971; Sabloff 1975). The central Peten group is represented by the Eb ceramic complex of Tikal and Uaxactun (Culbert 1977; Laporte and Valdes 1993), the Ah Pam complex of the Yaxha-Sacnab lake area (Rice 1979), and the related early Ox complex of Nakbe (Hansen 2005). A third group comprises the Cunil ceramic complex of the Belize River valley. Holmul's pre-Mamom types seem to stand on their own as a stylistic group (Awe 1992; Healy, Cheetham, et al. 2004; Strelow and LeCount 2001; Callaghan 2006; Cheetham 2005; Estrada-Belli 2006b). A fifth group is represented by the Swasey complex of the northern Belize area (Hammond 1973; Pring 1979; Kosakowsky 1987; Kosakowsky and Pring 1991). This complex is stylistically much more distinct than any of the other pre-Mamom groups (Andrews 1990b; Cheetham 2005). Finally, a sixth group is represented by the Ek complex of Komchen in northern Yucatan (Andrews et al. 2008).

The few radiocarbon dates available for the Xe, Eb, and Cunil ceramic complexes cluster around 1100 to 850 BCE (Clark and Cheetham 2002). Based on a C-14 date from a Cival closed context (chultun), the Holmul complex certainly dates to before 800 BCE (Beta-234440, C-14 age: 2670+40 BP; 1-sigma range calibrated years: 840–800 BCE; 2-sigma calibrated years: 900–790 BCE). Similar dates were also obtained for the Ek complex at Komchen and Kiuic, Yucatan (Andrews et al. 2008). In sum, at present there are no ceramics that can be securely dated to before 1100 BCE in the Maya lowlands. In lack of other direct evidence, pre-Mamom ceramics have been seen as the earliest evidence of farming settlements in the lowlands. The relatively late dates for the earliest lowland ceramics, when compared to neighboring regions, led many to conclude that the influx of sedentary farmers and their spread into the interior must have occurred fairly rapidly. So strong was the belief in the validity of this model that many scholars failed to acknowledge other sets of data that suggested very different scenarios.

THE *ACTUAL* EARLIEST FARMERS

As early as 1966, pollen data from the Peten lakes revealed signs of wide-spread deforestation and maize agriculture early in the Preclassic period, beginning by at least 2000 BCE (Cowgill et al. 1966; Rice 1976a). Interestingly, charcoal from the lowest archaeological levels at Cuello, Belize, the lowland's earliest village site, were then also dated by C-14 to 2600 BCE (Hammond et al. 1976) but were dismissed as erroneous (Andrews and Hammond 1990). Cuello's early dates remained controversial for some time but in hindsight may have been correct in representing the first human activity in the area, as the Peten lake cores did, instead of the earliest architecture. Later, more sediment data from Belize and Peten began to show more conclusively that deforestation and maize agriculture pre-dated the advent of ceramics in the lowlands by some 1500 years. Some sediment cores showed the first signs of deforestation and maize agriculture in the lowlands beginning at 2500 BCE, while in others corn appeared slightly later but still centuries before ceramics (Estrada-Belli and Wahl 2010; Mueller et al. 2009; Neff et al. 2006c; Pohl et al. 1996; Wahl et al. 2006; Wahl, Schreiner et al. 2007; Wahl et al. 2013).

Although the number of core samples is still small, the sediment data are from geographically widespread lowland locations and form a discernible pattern. They are the only evidence we have of early or incipient agricultural societies throughout the Yucatan's interior long before the postulated ceramic-producing migrating pioneers. Who were these early farmers? Some suggest that they were the direct descendents of hunters and gatherers who roamed the lowlands in the Late Archaic period. These lowland hunters are known from small samples of stone tools from the Belize coastal lowlands (Clark and Cheetham 2002; Lohse et al. 2006). Two particular types of stone tools are known, the stemmed biface point (or Lowe point) and a type of heavy axe known as constricted unifaces. Both appear in Belize's pre-ceramic and early ceramic period levels between 3000 and 850 BCE.

The Belizean stone tool data, while limited, do provide an additional indication for the existence of elusive communities of pre-ceramic agriculturalists in the lowlands as early as 2500 BCE. The wide distribution of the pollen core data and the ephemeral nature of their archaeological remains suggest that these early inhabitants lived in small non-permanent communities and probably exploited different lowland resources on a seasonal basis. Any temporary dwellings would likely go undetected except in special archaeological conditions.

EARLY VILLAGERS AND SOCIAL RANKING

Today pre-Mamom ceramics constitute the best archaeological evidence for the earliest sedentary inhabitants of the lowlands circa 1000 BCE. They are mainly found in deeply buried contexts at the base of ritual plazas or directly on the modified natural rock surface. They are almost always found on the highest and most prominent locations of ceremonial centers (Fig. 6.2). These locations may have been selected by early farmers for the practical advantage of visually controlling nearby resources or for their symbolic value as hilltops. In later periods, these locations tend to remain the most sacred within the space of a ceremonial plaza or acropolis, and this may denote that they were originally chosen for ritual practices. Unfortunately, few structures of any kind have been reported in association with pre-Mamom ceramics. At Cahal Pech, a few simple house platforms with pre-Mamom (Cunil) ceramics have been found at the bottom of Plaza B. One was more elaborate than the others by containing a bench and red-painted plaster in the interior (Awe 1992; Cheetham 1998). A relatively high-quality structure (Structure B1-10th-13th) was found in association with pre-Mamom ceramics below a temple building at Blackman Eddy, a few miles downstream from Cahal Pech along the Belize River (Garber et al. 2004a).

Clear architectural remains have been found at no other sites for this period, nevertheless pre-Mamom ceramics are found in bedrock pits or construction fill deposits below temple buildings and plazas at a few locations. These include the North Acropolis and Mundo Perdido complexes at Tikal (Culbert 1977; Laporte and Fialko 1993a; Hermes 1993), the E-Group plaza at Cival (Fig. 6.3), and the Group II temple platform at Holmul (Estrada-Belli 2006b). In a few other cases, pre-Mamom ceramics have been found in actual ritual contexts, such as the *k'an*-cross cache with jade axes and a bloodletter of Seibal (Willey 1970a) and a jade cache at Uolantun (Puleston 1973). In addition, a shell cache at Pacbitun, Belize, which contained no ceramics, was dated to this period by radiocarbon (Healy, Hohmann, et al. 2004). These specific associations suggest that early ceramics were used also in elite or ritual contexts, or perhaps exclusively in those contexts at that

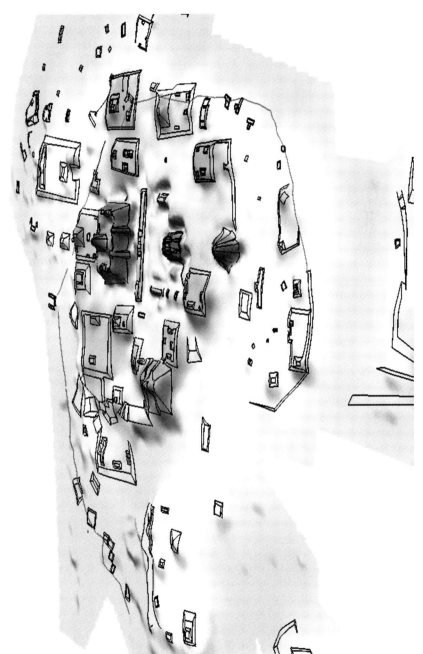

6.2. Map of Cival's ceremonial core in 3-D perspective from the southwest.

Northwest Group

Far North Plaza

North E-Group

West Transect
1km

Group XIII

Group XII

Group IX

North East Plaza

Group X

North Plaza

North Pyramid

Group VIII

Group XI

Group VII

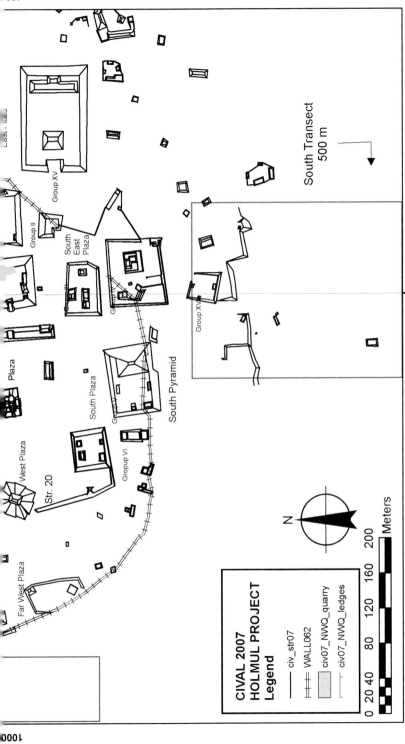

South Transect
500 m

Group XV

Group II

South
East
Plaza

Group XVI

Plaza

South Plaza

South Pyramid

West Plaza

Str. 20

Group VI

Far West Plaza

**CIVAL 2007
HOLMUL PROJECT
Legend**

——— civ_str07

╫╫ WALL062

▦ civ07_NWQ_quarry

╶┼╴ civ07_NWQ_ledges

N

0 20 40   80   120 160   200
Meters

1000

6.3. Map of Holmul's ceremonial core.

time. At Tikal, extensive excavations away from the main plazas have failed to locate additional clusters of early ceramics. Therefore, the isolation of pre-Mamom contexts is not due to lack of sampling but suggests a special-purpose function.

All known samples of pre-Mamom ceramics include a majority of serving vessels and jars. The most typical forms include *tecomates* and round-sided or outcurving-side bowls, dishes with flat bottoms, outsloping sides, and everted rims, as well as vertical-side and outcurving-side dishes. In addition, the pre-Mamom ceramic inventory also includes censers, effigy bowls, and mushroom stands. Differences among pre-Mamom regional groups include ideosyncratic vessel forms and jar handles. Surface finish is largely shared across groups. This is generally an orange-brown or buff dull finish, and red, black, and more rarely white slips. Some vessel forms such as wide-everted-rim dishes or the tecomate are common in all groups. The tecomate neckless jar is common throughout the Maya highlands and Pacific coast, as well as in the Gulf coast and in the highlands of Mexico during Early to Middle Preclassic periods, and it indicates wide-ranging interactions among neighboring regions. White-slipped ceramic types are only known in limited percentages in the western Peten pre-Mamom samples and may also indicate interaction with the west, primarily with the Chiapas highlands where this surface color is more frequent.

Noting these similarities does not necessarily lead one to conclude that the farmers migrating into the lowlands brought ceramic technology and styles from other regions. The so-called donor areas could variably be identified with highland Chiapas (Lowe 1977), or the Guatemalan or Honduran and Salvadoran highlands (Sharer and Gifford 1970; Fash 1991). The fact that a new interrelated group of ceramics existed in the intermediate area between the highlands and the lowlands, such as at Sakajut in the Alta Verapaz highlands (Sedat and Sharer 1972), appeared to strengthen the case for migration. Therefore, all subsequent innovations in Maya culture were also thought to have been transmitted from the highlands to the lowlands through migrations.

In reality, however, the similarities among the Peten pre-Mamom stylistic groups are greater than between any of these and other styles outside of the Maya lowlands. A closely related "donor area" has not been found. It is therefore unlikely that these styles were introduced into the lowlands as an already developed complex by a migrating group. Rather, these diverse stylistic forms are more likely to represent a combination of spontaneous local developments (out of pre-ceramic archetypes) and of symbolic expressions widely shared through interregional interactions on a variety of other media (mostly perishable) prior to the adoption of ceramics.

The greatest amount of overlap among the four pre-Mamom stylistic groups of the Maya lowlands is found in the motifs incised on the vessel surfaces and these are important on a number of levels. The abstract signs typically include the flame eyebrow, k'an-cross, cleft head, double-line break, music brackets, "shark tooth" or bloodletter, and avian serpent motifs (Cheetham 2005). The recently discovered pre-Mamom ceramics from Holmul and Cival, which now represent the largest available sample, also display woven mat, crossed bands, and U-shaped motifs (Fig. 6.4).

Outside of the Maya region, these motifs are found on ceramics of the late Early Preclassic and early Middle Preclassic periods in highland Mexico, Oaxaca, Gulf coast, highland and coastal Chiapas, Guatemala, and El Salvador. The vessels on which these signs occur are also generally similar to flat-based bowls and the previously mentioned wide-everted-rim dishes from the Maya region. Flannery and Marcus (1994) propose that patterned distribution of certain motifs on specific ceramic types (Gray and Yellow-white) within the Oaxacan community of San Jose Mogote reflected clan divisions. Such divisions were clearly marked in the distribution of two sets of symbols, which they group into abstract sky-monster and were-jaguar deity complexes. The first includes the flame eyebrow, music brackets, and crossed bands motifs as *pars pro toto* elements of a sky deity, which is avian- and serpent-like at times. The were-jaguar set includes the double-line break and cleft head motifs as elements connected with the cleft in the earth or, in other words, the place of emergence of the Maize God (Flannery and Marcus 1994). During the San Jose phase the first set of signs was common on Leandro Gray ware while the second set occurred almost exclusively on Atoyac Yellow-white ware. However, the distribution of such symbols and ceramics also could follow status boundaries among different households within the same community.

The evidence of status differentiation in artifacts, burial, or other contexts during the pre-Mamom phases is very elusive in the Maya lowlands. The structures associated with these ceramics at Cahal Pech, Blackman Eddy, and some of the ritual caches from this period, as at Uolantun (Puleston 1973) and Seibal (Willey 1970a), indicate few if any status distinctions within early communities. The high-quality of the ceramics and their symbolic decorations may be the one indication that they were restricted in use to a small group within the community.

The symbols on pre-Mamom ceramics are direct antecedents to iconographic symbols used to identify rain and other deities in later Preclassic and Classic period ritual art. In Preclassic contexts, the deity is actually combining avian and serpent elements and has been named the Principal Bird Deity by scholars (Bardawil 1976). It is a deity of the sky, mainly a solar deity, sometimes equated to Itzamnaah, but also related to other celestial elements such as rain and lighting. The so-called shark tooth is actually a representation of a bloodletter, a symbol that in later Maya iconography refers to the ritual of bloodletting to venerate deities and ancestors. The k'an cross, cleft head, double-line break motifs, and related variants of the so-called were-jaguar complex are separate elements that refer to the four parts plus the center of the Maya cosmos. The k'an cross is also an opening in the earth and between the worlds of the living and the supernatural. Seen in profile view, the k'an cross is sometimes depicted in abstact forms as a v-shaped cleft or a step-fret motif. The Cival jade offering (described below) is a good compendium of k'an cross symbolism. As a whole, these motifs represent all the parts of the cosmos, its center-opening and as such the birthplace of the Maize God. Finally, the mat motif is a well-known Maya and Mesoamerican symbol of political power. These sets of motifs (sky and earth/maize) appear prominently in Late Preclassic and Classic period iconography with minor stylistic modifications on monumental scultpture and other permanent media (Estrada-Belli 2006b). One set of contexts in which they appear are cross-shaped offerings such as the jade axe offerings of Seibal and Cival that also include other objects with maize symbolism. Other examples that combine Maize God and avian motifs closer in time to these are the pectoral worn by the ruler on Cival Stela 2 and the headdress worn by a Maize God figure in Cival's Mural 1 (Estrada-Belli 2006b) and on the West Wall of the San Bartolo mural depicting a coronation ceremony of the Maize God himself (Hurst 2005; Saturno, Stuart, et al. 2005). Avian and serpent imagery is also prevalent on friezes and "mask" relief sculptures at Nakbe, Cerros, Uaxactun, and other sites where they identify the deity to which the pyramid—and thus the temple—are dedicated. These themes, the avian head or head with serpent-head wings, are repeated on the friezes of Classic-period temple buildings as well as on carved stelae as the ruler's

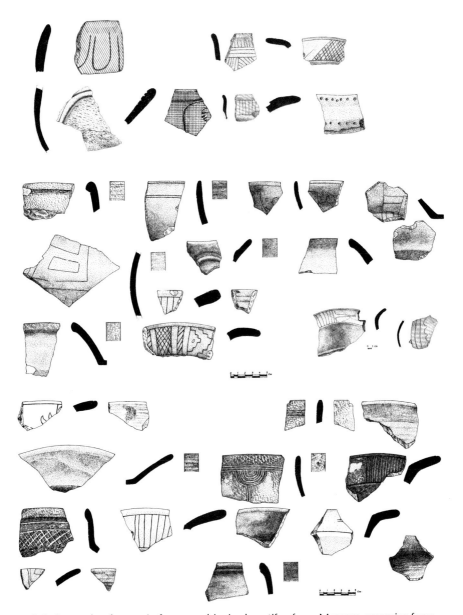

6.4. A sample of ceramic forms and incised motifs of pre-Mamom ceramics from the Holmul region.

headdress and are the most common symbols of royalty (Andrews 1995; Freidel and Schele 1988a; Hansen 1992a).

In sum, while we lack direct material evidence for status distinctions among the earliest pottery-using lowland Maya at the beginning of the Middle Preclassic (1100–850 BCE), the motifs depicted on pre-Mamom ceramics include a set of symbols that evoke the same celestial deities, the solar and rain gods related to the birth of the Maize God, which later will be associated with elite and specifically with royal ritual art. The wide geographical distribution of the early symbols across Mesoamerica reflects a set of religious beliefs that pre-dated social differentiation but were eventually singled out by emerging elites within narratives that legitimized the concentration of power in the hands of rulers. Because the similarities in form and decoration are greater among groups within the Maya lowlands than with any outside region, these similarities cannot be due to a flow of foreign populations or ideas into the area, but to spontaneous processes. The contextual evidence for these symbols at lowland sites suggests pre-Mamom ceramics, at least initially, were used as special ritual goods within communities as part of the processes in which status differentiation might have been developing or expressed on permanent media. In this view, the first appearance of ceramics in the Maya lowlands at ca. 1000 BCE should be seen not as the first sign of peasant migrants entering the region but as evidence of social ranking.

SUDDEN CIVILIZATION? HIGHLAND-TO-LOWLAND MIGRATIONS "RELOADED"

The University of Pennsylvania Tikal project from 1957 to 1970 (Shook 1957; Coe 1990) produced the greatest amount of data on the Preclassic of any other project. The massive North Acropolis trench exposed temples and tombs that preceded the accepted beginning date of the Classic period and pointed to the Late Preclassic period as the phase of most rapid development and artistic manifestations of Maya civilization (W. Coe 1965a). Tikal's data were complemented by other large-scale excavations at Altar de Sacrificios (Willey 1973a) and Seibal (Willey et al. 1982) and large-scale surveys in the Belize River valley (Willey 1965) providing further evidence of the antiquity of the elements of Maya civilization in the lowlands but also added new fuel to migration theories on the origins of Maya civilization in some respects.

At that time, masonry architecture, polychrome ceramics, and hieroglyphic writing were used as the defining characteristics of Classic Maya civilization (Morley 1946). Vaulted temple buildings, however, had been found in Preclassic contexts in Tikal's North Acropolis. These were lavishly decorated with mural paintings of ancestral figures, clearly anticipating dynastic iconography of the Classic period. In addition, richly furnished tombs were found in the plazas between these early temples suggesting that the antecedents to Classic Maya civilization existed centuries prior to the appearance of carved monuments with hieroglyphic texts and Long Count dates.

Tikal's North Acropolis excavations produced detailed, abundant, and consistent data that have since been held as evidence that the institution of kingship made its first appearance shortly prior to the end of the Late Preclassic period. Today, as thirty years ago, many scholars view the Late Preclassic period as an era of rapid growth leading to the so-called crystallization of divine kingship and other state-level institutions in the 1st century of the Christian Era (Adams and Culbert 1977; Willey 1977). As a corollary of this now problematic assumption, the passage from village farming communities to Classic Maya civilization was seen as a sudden phenomenon. It had allegedly happened after a long period of little or no change, the Middle Preclassic period from 1100 to 400 BCE. Once again, there were attempts to find the sources of rapid change outside of the lowlands.

Polychrome ceramic decoration was thought to be a key stylistic and technological innovation that appeared at the end of the Late Preclassic period and became the hallmark of Classic Maya civilization. It was believed to be an important indicator if not a factor of significant changes in the structure of lowland Maya society, in spite of the existence of equally sophisticated techniques of ceramic decoration centuries earlier. The earliest set of lowland polychrome ceramics were first excavated at Holmul in 1911 and thus named the "Holmul I" style (Merwin and Vaillant 1932). The polychrome decoration consisted of abstract symbols and stylized supernatural forms in red, black, and yellow on an orange slip background. New vessel forms included bowls, dishes, and vases with mammiform supports, and a Z-angle profile. At first, both painted style and vessel forms appeared unrelated to previous types of Preclassic decoration, which favored monochrome slips and simpler forms. James Gifford hypothesized that new people had arrived in the Belize River valley bringing the Holmul I ceramic assemblage or knowledge of it from some other region (Willey and Gifford 1961). The introduction of such new status objects would parallel the rapid increase in social distinction within local communities evident from architecture and burials. With it, the knowledge of writing and other manifestations of Classic civilization also made their appearance in the lowlands.

Increasingly, the Holmul I ceramic style appeared to be irregularly distributed in the lowlands and to cluster mostly in eastern Peten and Belize (Pring 1977). To the south, mammiform vessels and polychrome decorations were found at Altar de Sacrificios and Seibal and marked a separate cluster of this style (Shook and Smith 1950). Vessel tetrapod forms and orange slip decorations somewhat related to the lowland style were known from the Guatemalan highlands. Based on similar stylistic details and antiquity, Sharer and Gifford (1970) suggested that the polychrome style had been brought into the lowlands by groups of highland migrants, perhaps from the overpopulated centers of Kaminaljuyu and Chalchuapa. The new wave of migrants was said to have followed the same routes as the much earlier migrant farmers who brought Xe ceramics and agriculture to the lowlands. This was believed to be a response to increased competition over resources by an overextended highland population, as the size of Kaminaljuyu, Chalchuapa, and other southern area sites attested.

Aside from highland overpopulation, another possible stimulus for this migration was the eruption of the Ilopango volcano in El Salvador that could have sent waves of refugees north and west (Sharer and Gifford 1970). The date of the volcanic eruption has been since reassessed at 400–550 CE (Dull et al. 2001), making it an unlikely cause. This re-dating was perhaps one of several deadly blows to the migration theory. Subsequently, in-depth ceramic analyses determined that the early polychrome style did not constitute a complete complex but rather a set of fine-quality and special function types that complemented the later phases of the Late Preclassic Chicanel ceramic complex (Brady et al. 1998). More significantly, petrographic analyses of paste recipes (Callaghan 2008) revealed that in order to create the new polychrome style, long-established Late Preclassic clay recipes were used. It was therefore unlikely that this style and technology had been brought into the lowlands as a set and more likely to be a local development perhaps inspired by contemporary highland examples.

The period in which the Holmul I style was used, from 50 to 250 CE bridging the transition from Preclassic to Classic periods, was believed to be the time in which Classic Maya civilization "crystallized" (Gifford 1965), which rendered essential a clear understanding of its place of origin. However, the significance of the cultural and social changes taking place during this transition were more assumed than borne out by hard data. Even in the face of widespread ceramic influences from the highlands, Gordon Willey (1977) pointed out that the Late Preclassic period was a time of true growth in population as well as in cultural complexity in the lowlands. The Holmul I style ceramics emerged at the end of this period and in connection with no population increase but rather a decline. Willey also noted that some areas such as the northern plains (Dzibilchaltun) experienced a population decline, while other areas continued their progress towards the early Classic with a total lack of Holmul I style ceramics (Ball 1977).

"Protoclassic" or Holmul I style ceramics were clearly present at Tikal (Culbert 1977). The highland-inspired polychrome techniques and the Usulutan-like (highland-inspired) resist or double-slip painting technique at Tikal marked a gradual increase in sophistication and in overall status differentiation beginning in the Late Preclassic period. Willey (1977) believed, as did Morley before him (1946), that the existence of early carved dates (Cycle 8, i.e., pre-376 CE) primarily in the Tikal zone was of paramount importance for an understanding of the process of development of Classic Maya civilization. While the "idea" of the stela cult and polychrome decoration may have come from the highlands, he believed these were innovations of a local emerging elite centered at Tikal. Once formed, the Tikal kingdom assumed an expansive mode, attempting to build an "empire" in the Peten. This would have explained the introduction of elite innovations at Tikal first, such as the carving of early monuments and the radiating distribution of early dated monuments at sites in the central Tikal zone and surrounding areas to the east (Holmul, Xultun, and Belize), west (Usumacinta region), and south (Pasion region). This zone also largely overlapped with the spotty distribution of Holmul I ceramic styles, while also including northern Belize, as Hammond noted (1977), probably because of its strategic resources and river routes to the sea. Long-distance trade connections were also believed to be radiating out of Tikal during the Protoclassic and Early Classic period due to the evident increased complexity of the Tikal social system (Willey 1977).

It was probably not coincidental, Willey (1977) noted, that the earliest signs of Teotihuacan interest in the Maya lowlands were found at places along the lowland routes, such as Altun Ha on the Belizean coast (Pendergast 1971). Possibly, he suggested, the distant central highland city of Teotihuacan could have had an influential role in the formation of Classic Maya states.

Sanders and Price (1968) and Spinden (1928) had proposed earlier that Classic Maya society was a case of secondary state formation stimulated by the area of primary state formation in Mesoamerica, the Central Highlands of Mexico. This process was viewed from an evolutionary perspective. They postulated that Late Preclassic centers such as Kaminaljuyu, deemed to be capitals of Maya chiefdoms, were transformed into state-organized societies after the arrival of elite traders from Teotihuacan. Similarly, subsequent incursions of Teotihuacan traders and accompanying warriors into the Peten region would have transformed the Preclassic Tikal chiefdom system into an early Classic Maya state. The evidence of Teotihuacan-style temple architecture and richly furnished tombs in Early Classic Kaminaljuyu (Kidder et al. 1946) was interpreted as a enclave of foreign elite merchants at that site. Similarly, the mounting evidence of Teotihuacan-style architecture and ceramics at Tikal inspired many scholars to envision a strong Teotihuacan influence on the locals at the opening of the Classic period (W. Coe 1965a; Coggins 1975; Proskouriakoff 1993). Later it would be found that Teotihuacan artifacts and architectural styles at Tikal predated those of Kaminaljuyu by perhaps a century, seriously challenging this hypothesis (Laporte and Fialko 1990; Braswell 2003b).

THE TIDES TURN FOR THE PRECLASSIC MAYA

Although the multiple theories suggesting that lowland Maya civilization was spawned by migrations from the highlands had met their demise, interregional interaction remained an important mechanism for understanding developmental processes within the Maya area and more generally within Mesoamerica. Survey and excavations in the northern Maya highlands documented the distribution of Preclassic occupation in the Alta and Baja Verapaz, regional development in the key Salama Valley, and defined overland routes connecting the southern highland and lowland regions. This evidence highlights the importance of Preclassic highland-lowland interaction to the growth and development of both regions (Sharer and Sedat 1973, 1987). At the northern end of the Maya lowlands in modern day Yucatan, an area that was previously thought to be devoid of Preclassic occupation revealed some of the densest concentrations of settlement beginning in the early Middle Preclassic and continuing in the Late Preclassic period, including early ceremonial centers such as Xtobo (Anderson 2011; Andrews et al. 2008; Glover et al. 2008; Rissolo and Amador 2004). Moreoever, the role of regional and interregional interaction in the development of lowland Maya civilization took on new meaning as the monumental architecture and carved art (stylistically linked to the Maya highlands and Pacific coast regions) of El Mirador and other large Preclassic centers in northern Guatemala were uncovered in the last 20 years of the 20th century (Estrada-Belli 2011).

When Ian Graham first mapped the site of El Mirador in 1962, the site's largest pyramid, the Danta pyramid, was believed to be a natural hill and was used as a navigational landmark by airplane pilots. For many, it was difficult to fathom that the largest Maya center had existed entirely before the Classic period. Excavations by the Peabody Museum of Harvard University first in 1970 (Marcus n.d.), then by Brigham Young University (Matheny 1987; Matheny and Matheny 2011), and again by Harvard University (Demarest 1984) demonstrated it beyond any doubt. Research at El Mirador and nearby sites continues to date led by Richard Hansen/ FARES, providing staggering evidence of the complexity of Preclassic Maya society (Hansen 1990, 1998, 2005; Hansen and Balcarcel 2008) predating any influence from the highland regions of Guatemala and Central Mexico.

Ian Graham's El Mirador map showed a vast ceremonial core stretching on an upland area for over 2 km from east to west and more than 1 km from north to south. This area was completely paved and punctuated by massive temple complexes. The largest of these is the 73 m high Danta complex at the east end of the site. The 53 m high Tigre Complex stands at the opposite end of a perfect E-W axial line crossing the site. A large moat and embankment encircles the central part of the site, as well. As many as 15 pyramid complexes at El Mirador follow the so-called triadic arrangement on east-west (such as Danta and Tigre) or north-south axes (such as Monos and Tres Micos). An elevated complex of temples and other buildings dominates the central area and is known as the Central Acropolis. To the north of this is one of the largest E-Groups in the Maya lowlands—the Leon Group. At the east end of the site was the Danta temple-pyramid complex, the largest at the site, and the largest by volume, measuring 600 m at its base, in the ancient world.

El Mirador was not only a Preclassic city of unprecedented dimensions, it was also the center of a network of large centers connected by a system of paved causeways within a large area now known as the Mirador Region. The causeway system itself highlights the central role played by the massive city of El Mirador, as it integrated many large centers around itself to form perhaps the largest rather than the first political system in Maya history during the Late Preclassic period (see below; Hansen 2005).

The Mirador Region centers of Tintal, Wakna, El Porvenir, La Muralla, Zacatal, and La Florida reached their building apex during the Late Preclassic becoming the largest centers in the lowlands at the time. Tintal, the largest of these, extended over an area about one third of El Mirador's ceremonial core. All these centers were suddenly abandoned, as was El Mirador (Hansen 2005), at the onset of the Classic period. Most of them remain largely unexplored today (although see Hansen, this volume) and are testimony to how much more there is to be known about the Preclassic period.

An even more surprising new fact was added to our evidently limited knowledge of the Preclassic lowland Maya when it was found that ceremonial architecture at Nakbe largely predated that of El Mirador, being mostly attributed to the late Ox (Mamom) phase (600–350 BCE; Hansen 1992a, 1998). The earliest public buildings at the site, the ball court, and the E-Group plaza date to that period.

In Richard Hansen's (2005) view, several centers had emerged in competition with one another in the Middle Preclassic period in the Mirador Region, and Nakbe perhaps was the largest among them. The relative homogeneity in the ceramics of this epoch, the Mamom-phase pottery recognized by most archaeologists, may actually reflect something that ran deeper than stylistic emulation: increased political integration in the Maya lowlands at this time, with Nakbe as the most important ritual center in the Mirador Region, possibly extending its religious and political influence elsewhere in the lowlands. It seems reasonable to propose that this process was a preamble to the more evident centralization and integration that is evident in architecture, ceramics, and ritual practices during the Late Preclassic period. El Mirador seems to have overshadowed all other centers and extended its trade connections far and wide across the Yucatan peninsula as reflected by the homogeneity of the Chicanel-style pottery and possibly by the spread of the Triadic Group pyramid complex across the region.[1]

Other large centers with Late Preclassic monumental architecture became known outside of the Mirador Region. These were Cerros (Freidel 1982) and Lamanai (Pendergast 1981) in northern Belize, Becan in southern Quintana Roo (Webster 1976), San Bartolo (Saturno, Taube, et al. 2005a) and Cival in northeastern Peten (Estrada-Belli, Bauer, et al. 2003; Estrada-Belli, Grube, et al. 2003) and El Palmar to the west of Tikal (Houston et al. 2010). All these sites display a primary Late Preclassic occupation followed by permanent or temporary abandonment. Some of these—Cerros, Becan, and Cival—feature large defensive works such as moats or stone walls and palisades (Fig. 6.2, 6.5). In addition, significant Late Preclassic building components were only recognized after deep excavations at Seibal (Willey et al. 1982), Altar de Sacrificios (Adams 1971), Calakmul (Carrasco and Colón González 2005), Rio Azul (Adams 1999), Yaxha, Naranjo, Caracol (Chase and Chase 1999), and Cahal Pech (Awe 1992).

The political geography of the Late Preclassic Maya lowlands and the great uniformity in architecture and art were without a doubt the result of intensive interaction across the Yucatan Peninsula. The similarities in art and architecture and the great homogeneity of the Chicanel phase ceramics across lowland regions combined with El Mirador's sheer size have led Hansen (Hansen and Guenter 2005) to speak of El Mirador as the first Maya state. While this point is currently debated, the El Mirador massive temples, carved monuments, and hieroglyphs seem at least to demonstrate that the Preclassic Maya state was no longer a chimera, and Preclassic civilization no longer a contradiction in terms (Hammond 1992; Sharer 1992).

THE RISE OF THE FIRST LOWLAND STATES

Until recently, some scholars held that the lowland Maya lacked several important characteristics of "civilization" prior to 300 CE. The most important trait is kingship or some other state-like centralized political institution. The key problem has been the lack of direct evidence of the existence of Preclassic kings, mainly royal tombs. Up to this point it has been customary to see the Classic period custom of burying rulers in richly furnished tombs below funerary temple-pyramids as a universal characteristic of kingship. When such centrally located tombs failed to appear at Preclassic sites, in spite of intensive excavation, we concluded that the Preclassic

Maya must have had some other form of government that did not require lavish interments of the deceased ruler, such as chiefdoms or corporate systems. It was thought that they had been ruled probably by a class of religious leaders, a theocracy, such as the one that was postulated to have ruled over Classic period Teotihuacan (J. Thompson 1970) or by a system similar to the *multepal*, an assembly of lineage leaders that ruled northern Yucatan's statelets prior to the Spanish conquest (Roys 1957:6; Marcus 1993:118–20). According to this view, the Maya were ruled by assembly until the end of the Late Preclassic period when kinghip was introduced. The replacement of a form of corporate system by an individualized system of governance would certainly represent a major "conjuncture" with widespread ramifications within a society in economic, ritual, and power relations that should be accompanied by visible changes in the material record (Knapp 1992). But the questions remain as to what changes did take place in the archaeological record at the onset of the Classic period and what do they mean?

PRECLASSIC ROYAL BURIALS AT TIKAL AND THE SEARCH FOR THE DYNASTY'S FOUNDER

Once again, the 1960s were a great decade for Maya archaeology. The University of Pennsylvania Tikal excavations were turning up evidence that challenged any earlier assumption about the lack of individualized rule in Maya society prior to the Classic period (Coe 1990). Elaborate Preclassic burials and tombs were placed in axial positions under the basal platform of temples, as if the latter served for worship of the interred individual. The earliest burials in this architectural complex date to the Middle Preclassic, and many more elaborate tombs appeared in the Late Preclassic period. Among them, Burial 85 dating to about 100 CE was outstanding for its rich furnishing and has been identified with the Tikal dynastic founder Yax Ehb Xook (Coggins 1975; Coe 1990; C. Jones 1991; Martin and Grube 2000; Martin 2003, and this volume).

This tomb lies at the bottom of a deep (2.5 m) shaft below a temple structure (Str. 5D-sub2) reaching into the bedrock. In the vault was a bundled individual with a jade mask with the royal *hun* diadem and 26 vessels. Some of these were decorated with Usulutan resist technique and modeled effigy spouts. Some of them appear to be imports from Kaminaljuyu

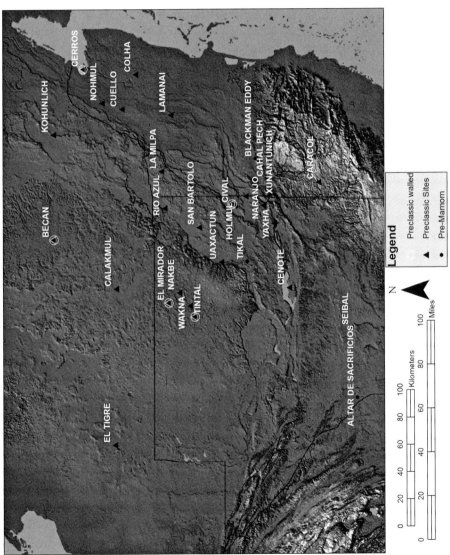

6.5. Map of Maya Lowlands showing major Preclassic sites mentioned in the text and presence/absence of defensive works.

(Culbert 2003). There were also shell and jade ornaments, stingray spines, and codex-like gesso fragments. Interestingly, while this tomb was certainly outstanding for its wealth, it was not associated with a period of major construction or remodeling of the ritual space of the acropolis. Instead it was one of many high-status burials placed in this location since the Middle Preclassic (Coe 1990).

Burial 166 contained an old woman and a bundled young woman with 21 elaborate vessels (Culbert 1993). This could have been a queen and/or queen mother interment related to Burial 85. Another predecessor of Burial 85 was interred on the eastern side of the acropolis plaza at roughly the same time (Burial 167), or shortly prior to 100 CE. In it were three individuals—a male, a female and a child with rich offerings. These tombs of the end of the Late Preclassic period were but a sample of several earlier interments in this location within the main acropolis. No significant breaks in the layout or volume of the North Acropolis around 100 CE occurred when the "founder" took the throne. Instead, the elites buried in the North Acropolis were the inheritors of high-status from a long line of rulers, reaching back at least to the beginning of the Late Preclassic.

Indeed, after the deposition of Burial 85 the North Acropolis was dramatically improved by construction some time after the founder's death, signaling a change in scale of ritual buildings (Coe 1990). Burial 125 held one of the rulers responsible for this period of prosperity. Elsewhere at Tikal, the Mundo Perdido plaza received important renovations and began to accommodate high-status burials after 200 CE (Laporte and Fialko 1990).

Given these archaeological facts, it is not clear why later kings referred to Yax Ehb Xoc as the dynasty founder. It is possible that the period following the founder's reign represents the beginning of a time of unprecedented prosperity at Tikal rather than a *conjuncture* in which major changes were made to the ancient Maya system of governance. The point here is that we should probably not take this date or period as a watershed moment in the development of Maya political systems, but in Tikal's history specifically. Indeed the epoch of much more significant changes or the *conjuncture* in the record of the North Acropolis must be identified with the placing of the first elite burial and erection of the first platform atop it, probably to venerate a deceased ruler, in the Middle Preclassic period (Coe 1990).

PRECLASSIC ROYAL BURIALS AND THE 100 CE "CONJUNCTURE" ACROSS THE LOWLANDS

Outside of Tikal, elaborate burials have been found at many Preclassic sites. There is however an overall scarcity of well-furnished burials such as Tikal Burial 85 before ca. 100 CE, in spite of an abundance of other impressive traits of complexity such as monumental architecture and royal iconography that predate such tombs. Most glaring is the absence of burials from some of the greatest sites of this period, such as El Mirador. However, Late–Terminal Preclassic tombs have been found at Wakna, Tintal, Cival, Seibal, Rio Azul, Holmul, and Altun Ha, among the best known (Krejci and Culbert 1995; Estrada-Belli 2004b). A number of relatively richly furnished Preclassic burials also come from some of the smaller sites of this period. Not surprisingly, the smaller lowland sites have received more research than the larger ones of the central lowlands mostly because of their size and accessibility (northern Peten, and adjoining areas of Campeche and Quintana Roo, Mexico, remain relatively inaccessible).

One must not rule out the possibility that different burial practices may have been in operation in the centuries prior to the end of the Preclassic period that did not require the construction of a temple-pyramid above the burial and the arrangement of offerings on the scale seen in the Classic period. There is a good possibility that generations of Preclassic rulers were buried in residential contexts in relatively elaborate settings, but these remain undetected under less obvious constructions, as is the case in smaller sites. Placement of a ruler in a public ritual area would constitute an exception to the norm during the Preclassic period.

Some of the best examples of early burials of high-ranking individuals come from residential contexts at Cuello, Belize. Here, indicators of social status have been found in burials dating to the earliest phases of the Middle Preclassic (1000–800 BCE) and include jade and shell ornaments associated with children as well as adults. Several high-status burials appear in a sequence in specific residential loci over periods of time. Among them is Burial 160 (500–400 BCE). While the cist and the accompanying vessels were simple, there were deer bone tubes incised with the royal mat design and a human cranium fragment fashioned into an effigy pectoral. The locus of these burials had special significance for this community which centuries later erected a ceremonial platform supporting a small pyramid temple above it (Hammond et al. 1992).

The recent discoveries of rich burials at San Bartolo and at K'o in northeastern Peten offer significant examples of Preclassic elite mortuary practices. Both were found under residential platforms (Pellecer 2006; Tomasic and Bozarth 2011). In the San Bartolo burial, a cist sealed by horizontal slabs contained six vessels, including an unusual orange effigy censer and effigy bowls decorated with Usulutan-style wavy lines, similar to examples from the Kaminaljuyu area, and other plain Late Preclassic vessels. With the body was also a small jade statuette similar to "royal" diadem jewels found at Cerros and Nohmul, Belize (Freidel et al. 2002; Justeson et al. 1988). The K'o burial, dated to 350 BCE by C-14, was in a double-chambered chultun under a Late Preclassic house platform. The interred was accompanied by eight vessels, including a black effigy censer of an ancestor wearing the foliated *hun* jewel, symbol of royalty in the Classic periods. The special objects from both interments, the figurine and the censers, depict royal insignia worn by the king portrayed in the San Bartolo West Wall Mural around 100 BCE.

SITE PLANNING, MONUMENTAL ARCHITECTURE, AND COSMOLOGY OR THE MAKING OF MAYA CIVILIZATION

In addition to monumentality, large-scale site planning and cosmological arrangements have been attributed to state-level societies. One obvious commonality in the layout of lowland sites with undisturbed Late Preclassic architecture, such as El Mirador, Tintal, Nakbe, Wakna, Cival, San Bartolo, and Cerros among many, is the general arrangement along an E-W axis. That pattern was maintained and expanded upon during centuries of building activity. A primary east-west pattern also has been noted at early sites in neighboring regions of highland Chiapas, which has engendered some discussion of migrations or highland influences on the early developments of lowland Maya civilization (Lowe 1977, 1981, 1989a)—a point to which we shall return.

Another commonality of Preclassic sites, especially in the central lowland region (Peten, southern Campeche, Quintana Roo, and Belize), is the presence of two distinct types of building arrangements. These are known as E-Groups and Triadic Groups and are known to have served different ritual functions. Both have widespread distribution at large and small sites. E-Groups are generally formed by a western pyramid with radial stairways and an elongated platform with one or three small substructures on the east side of the plaza. Their name is derived from the first group of this kind to be recognized—Group "E" of Uaxactun (A.L. Smith 1950). Triadic Groups are normally situated on an elevated platform and are formed by a main pyramidal temple flanked by two smaller ones facing each other. The most common orientation of Triadic Groups is west-facing, although orientations to the other cardinal directions are not uncommon, especially at sites where multiple Triadic Groups are present (such as El Mirador, Nakbe, Cerros, and Cival).

E-Group architectural arrangements appear to have greater antiquity than the Triadic Group. Both types appear to be expanded upon during the Late Preclassic and Early Classic periods. But the earliest examples of E-Groups have been dated to the Middle Preclassic period (ca. 800–600 BCE) at Nakbe, Tikal (Mundo Perdido), Cival, and Cenote (Hansen 1998; Chase and Chase 1999). Triadic Groups, on the other hand, appear first in the Late Preclassic period (e.g., at El Mirador, Nakbe, Tintal, Wakna, Tikal, Uaxactun, Calakmul, Caracol, Lamanai, Cerros, Cival, and many others) and are also known in the northern Yucatan region (Hansen 1998; Andrews 1965; Anderson 2011). The greatest number of Triadic Groups are found at El Mirador, where the largest in size can also be found.

Triadic Groups are commonly found at the extreme ends of a site's axial lines. E-Groups tend to be located most commonly near the center of the site's ceremonial area (e.g., at El Mirador, Tikal, and Cival), but also occur at the axial extremes (e.g., Nakbe). Often, E-Groups are found to occupy the most prominent and broad hilltop and form the central focus of later site planning for ceremonial centers and communities.

A good example of coherent site orientation and planning followed throughout Middle and Late Preclassic times is found at the recently mapped center of Cival, Peten. Its ceremonial core occupies an artificially leveled 0.5 km^2 hilltop (Fig. 6.2). The site core is dominated by four major pyramidal complexes at axial extremes. The tallest is the eastern Triadic Group (Group 1, 33 m high), followed by the North Pyramid (21 m high), the West (Structure 20, 19 m high), and South Pyramids (12 m high). At the very center of the orthogonal axes connecting these groups is the E-Group plaza. Its western radial pyramid (18 m high) faces a 130 m long eastern platform supporting an outset central building. Two smaller (4 m high) rectangular buildings close the north and south ends of the plaza.

Just to the north of the plaza is a ball court which was first built in the Late Preclassic and follows the general north-south axis perpendicular to the E-Group's axis. Deep excavations have documented that the entire area enclosed by these complexes was leveled by massive amounts of fill in the Middle Preclassic period (probably ca. 800 BCE), followed by a series of subsequent floors laid out in the Late Preclassic period.

To the north on a separate knoll is a smaller E-Group plaza with an 8 m high western pyramid facing a 48 m long platform. This complex was built in the Late Preclassic period as the site expanded out from the initial main hill core to occupy what was previously a residential site.

The map shows that Cival's east-west axis was followed throughout the Late Preclassic by most residential and ritual construction. The orientation and patterned distances between major buildings along the site's axes denote consistent planning.

In simplified form, the E-Group's western-pyramid-facing-eastern-platform layout is also seen outside the lowlands. Known early Middle Preclassic examples occur in highland Chiapas (e.g., Chiapa de Corzo, Finca Arizona, San Isidro) (Lowe 1977, 1981; Chapter 5, this volume) and can even be detected in the layout of some sites in Pacific coastal and highland Guatemala (e.g., Takalik Abaj) (Popenoe de Hatch 2002a). Once more, similar traits have been taken to reflect possible migrations or diffusion from highland to lowland regions (Lowe 1981, 1989a; Clark and Hansen 2001). However, these occurrences also signal interregional interaction, and as research progresses there are increasing indications of the originality of lowland Maya ritual site planning and of the greater antiquity of E-Groups in the lowlands.

THE ANTIQUITY OF E-GROUPS, PUBLIC RITUALS, AND ROYAL SYMBOLS

It is the uprecedented wealth in ritual offerings and the scale of public works at Cival that are currently the best indicators of the emergence of centralization of ritual and power early in the Middle Preclassic period. Cival's earliest E-Group plaza floors document one of the largest and oldest such complexes in the lowlands (Estrada-Belli 2002, 2003; Estrada-Belli, Grube et al. 2003). The first version of this E-Group's eastern platform was created by modifying the bedrock surface of the hilltop on which it is located. Altogether, the Cival eastern platform (Structure 7) and its central outset structure (Structure 12) were remodeled six times, the last two dating in the Terminal Preclassic period 0–250 CE.

At Cival, the northern and southern sight lines of the E-Group point to sunrise on the days of the passage of the sun through the zenith (May 9, August 3) and the antizenith (February 1, November 12), an alignment shared only with a select few other sites of great antiquity in the lowlands (Aveni et al. 2003). The first passage of the sun at its zenith in the southern lowlands roughly corresponds with the advent of the rainy season, around May 10. The second passage of the sun at its zenith occurs on August 2, in connection with the arrival of a second wave of monsoons in the Maya lowlands. Through the use of these devices the lowland Maya were able to maintain the congruence of the ritual *tzolkin* and solar *haab* calendars with the pace of the seasonal and agricultural cycles (Girard 1966). Thus, E-Group plazas with their buildings aligned to the cardinal position and their E-W alignments underscored the quadripartite construct of the calendar and served as the cosmological central locus for rituals related to it. Consistently, that alignment once established with the construction of the E-Group in the Middle Preclassic was carefully followed in subsequent building episodes and accompanied by the placement of offerings. The recurring rituals reinforced the importance of these human-made spaces as reflecting the Maya's immutable cosmological landscapes and vision.

The Earliest Public Rituals

Evidence of public rituals of great antiquity is often found in E-Groups. The earliest offerings come in the form of cists, stone boxes, or lip-to-lip vessel pairs dating to the Middle Preclassic period. These offerings are often placed along the group's east-west axis. Centuries later those same locations were chosen to erect the first carved monuments, as at Tikal and Uaxactun (Laporte and Fialko 1990). In the Early Classic period, the E-Group remained a site's primary ritual space where the commemorations of *k'atun* cycle completions (k'atuns 8.14 through 8.17) were celebrated on monuments with a ruler's dedicatory inscription for the first time.

The earliest evidence of ritual activity in Cival's E-Group dates to sometime between 800 and 600 BCE.[2] A cache of 5 water jars, 5 upright celts, and 109 jade pebbles was carefully placed in a three-level k'an cross–shaped pit dug into the bedrock (Figs. 6.6, 6.7; Estrada-Belli, Bauer et al. 2003; Estrada-Belli 2006b). This cache included an extraordinary amount of wealth and complexity of elements for this time period. The second event was the burial of a large defaced stela across the centerline of the eastern platform, also during the Middle Preclassic period. Subsequently, at the beginning of the Late Preclassic period, a low rectangular platform was built on the axial line abutting the eastern platform's stairway. A carved stela (Stela 2) bearing the striding image of a ruler was erected at the center of the platform (Fig. 6.8). Subsequently, the platform was enlarged and three large timber posts were placed in cardinal arrangement around the stela (Fig. 6.9).

The symbolism of the early offering (Cache 4) in the Cival E-Group plaza recalls the cardinal placement of the five rain gods above the primordial sea (the jars), the central position of the Maize God in the universe (the jade axe/corn symbols) (see Taube 2005), and the role of water to give life to the Maize God as the basic ordering elements of the Maya cosmos. Maize God iconography is also present in the avian pectoral worn by the ruler on Stela 2.

The Maize God as the *axis mundi*, the giver of sustenance to the people, was the ideal alter-ego for Classic Maya rulers as it was manifested in royal media and paraphernalia. But now we see it first expressed in the Middle Preclassic period at sites such as Cival, and at E-Group plazas across the lowlands. A slightly earlier example of this type of cache (900–700 BCE) is found at Seibal (Willey 1970a). Earlier expressions of this cosmology related to the life cycle of the Maize God, rain, earth, and sun can be found on the earliest lowland ceramics of 1000 BCE.

The Earliest Monumental Art and Royal Ideology

Civàl's Preclassic Stela 2 stylistically predates the earliest monuments from Nakbe and El Mirador (Fig. 6.8; Estrada-Belli 2003). A vessel found in its offertory cache suggests a date of 300–200 BCE. It is carved in simple low-relief outlines. The figure wears a bird-head pectoral with three plaques decorated with incised diagonal lines indicating that in reality they would be fashioned in jade. This avian motif is worn by rulers as a pectoral or a headdress on numerous Preclassic monuments, at Kaminaljuyu, Abaj Takalik, in the Maya highlands, on the Pacific coast, and the Gulf coast of Mexico (La Mojarra, Stela 1) (Parsons 1986; Winfield Capitaine 1988). It is also worth noting that this stela's tapered shape recalls upturned jade

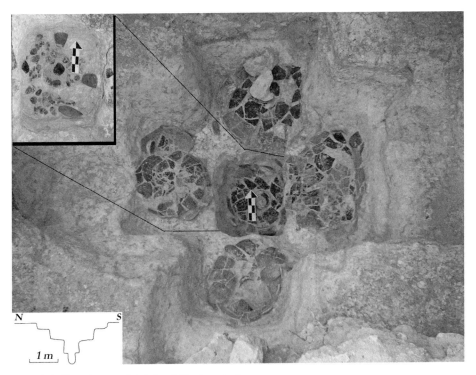

6.6. Plan view and details of Cival cache four.

celts such as those in the cruciform cache below the same plaza, reinforcing the conceptual associations between jade, maize, and ruler as *axis mundi* (Taube 2005).

At Cival, the date of the first portrait of a ruler coincides with the construction of the earliest Triadic Group (Figs. 6.10, 6.11). Its main temple was decorated with monumental sculpture. In the southern lowlands, some of the best-known examples of Preclassic monumental sculpture on Triadic Groups are found at El Mirador, Nakbe, Calakmul, Tikal, Uaxactun, San Bartolo, Cerros, and Cival. These often represent the so-called Principal Bird Deity (PBD) or other deities of difficult identification, usually described as solar deities but including elements of rain, such as the Cival examples, resulting in a composite celestial deity. Some anthropomorphic masks can be readily identified as the young Maize God (e.g., at Calakmul) (Carrasco and Colón González 2005). The main theme of the Cival masks was the rising

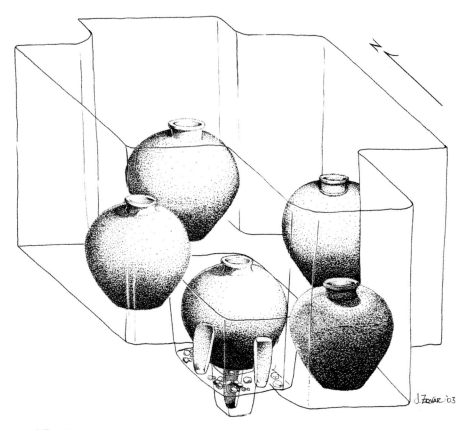

6.7. Artistic reconstruction of the multi-level components of Cival Cache 4. Art by Joel Zovar.

sun and the birth of the Maize God. Above the solar god masks, figures of the Maize God, some with royal headdresses, others with PBD / avian headdresses, were found painted inside the upper temple room (see Estrada-Belli 2011: fig. 5.22, 5.23). These figures are dated by C-14 to about 200 BCE (Estrada-Belli 2006b).[3] The themes expressed by the monumental sculptures seem to revolve around the places and actors of the world creation and the birth of the Maize God. To a certain extent, the iconography of the earliest Maya temples is an elaboration on a theme first depicted as simple incised motifs on the pre-Mamom ceramics discussed above, and so it represents an elaboration of pre-existing ritual symbols on a new medium.

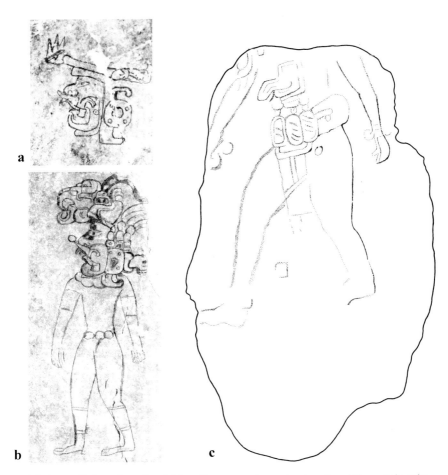

6.8. Low relief carving of a striding figure wearing avian-head and three jade celts as a pectoral. Drawing by Nikolai Grube.

SUMMARY AND CONCLUSIONS

E-Group plazas, large ritual caches, and monumental sculptures constitute the earliest evidence in the Maya lowlands of monumentality and complexity in public rituals and, by inference, the appearance of centralized power. E-Groups and their associated rituals appear in the Middle Preclassic period, ca. 800–700 BCE. They are found in a wide area across the southern lowlands, from the Mirador Region to the Maya Mountains. These plazas were the monumental settings for rituals related to the creation of the Maya cosmos, the agricultural cycle, and the Maize God as the *axis mundi*, which

6.9. Artistic reconstruction of Cival's E-Group plaza's eastern platform and its outset central building (Structures 7 and 13[center]) Stela 2 is located on a low rectangular platform in connection with the eastern platform stairways central axis and is flanked by three large wooden posts (ca. 1 m in diameter).

eventually became the prototype of kingship. Nakbe was perhaps the greatest ceremonial center in the lowlands of its time, but other sites were built in large scale as well. Later architecture certainly obscures the exact extent and form of early buildings even at purely Preclassic sites such as Cival. At the beginning of the Late Preclassic period (ca. 300 BCE), each center's population and resources increased as agricultural practices also improved. Ever larger temple complexes were erected, and the themes of creation and birth of the Maize God were elevated as the symbols of worldly power on a monumental scale. The greatest monumental complexes of this time were erected in the Mirador Region, at El Mirador, Tintal, and Wakna (Hansen 1998, and this volume).

Late Preclassic Cival was but one among many major centers outside the Mirador Region in which monumental construction took place. Its ceremonial center measures less than half that of El Mirador, as the majority of other centers do. The huge disparity in size among Preclassic centers and the location of the five largest so close to El Mirador should be meaningful. It could represent a huge and highly integrated political system stretching from the Mirador Region over much of the lowlands.

The distances are not prohibitive enough to deny El Mirador's reach over the lowlands. Archaeologists have been using the highly factional Classic Maya as a measure of reference for the Preclassic Maya. The Classic Maya were never unified under a single ruler, although they came close to unification at the end of the Classic period. In other regions of the world early unification is not uncommon and was often followed by fragmentation, as in southern Mesopotamia where the Uruk hegemony was followed by the proto-dynastic period of political fragmentation of Bronze Age Sumer (Oppenheim 1964). Much more research needs to be done on the political geography of the Late Preclassic to test models of El Mirador–centered hegemony over other polities. Much will depend on the evidence from other large centers in the Mirador Region. We are much less equipped to discuss a lowland-wide political geography of the Middle Preclassic period, but clearly we ought to consider that besides Nakbe there were other sizable ritual centers at that time—Cival, Tikal, Cenote, and other sites with early E-Groups being just a few known to us, not to mention yet-to-be-uncovered sites. These early centers could not exist in isolation given all their shared characteristics and probably had close political relationships with one another.

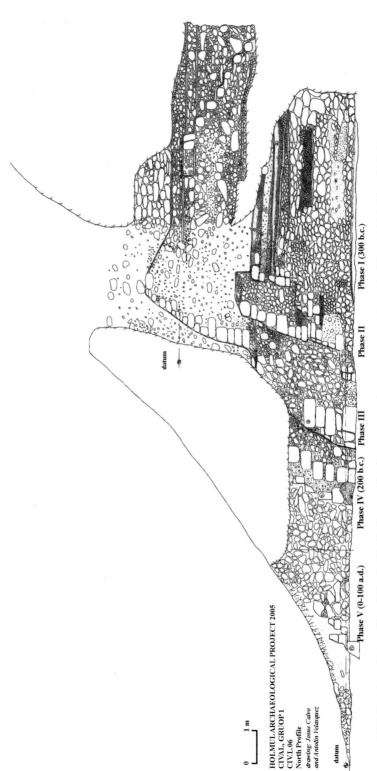

0   1 m

datum

datum

Phase V (0-100 a.d.)   Phase IV (200 b.c.)   Phase III   Phase II   Phase I (300 b.c.)

6.10. Stratigraphic profile of Cival's Triadic Group. The five construction stages span the period from 300 BCE to 100 CE.

6.11. Photo of monumental stucco mask on Cival's Triadic Group Structure 1, phase IV, dated by radiocarbon to ca. 200 BCE.

The progression from E-Group plaza rituals in the Middle Preclassic period to the monumental art of Late Preclassic period triadic temples seen in the Cival record provides a particularly compelling case for the continuity of ideological programs and of the associated concept of kingship from the Middle to the Late Preclassic periods. In spite of variation in sculptural art across the lowlands, from the Middle Preclassic on the theme of the creation and birth of the Maize God continued to be the message of lowland Maya ideology in ever-changing media. Far from being a period in which lowland Maya culture remained stagnant and impervious to stimuli from its neighbors, the Middle Preclassic period was perhaps a period of greater innovation in Maya culture-history.

The significance of the so-called Preclassic to Classic cultural transition may have been overemphasized. This is in part because the highland-centric perspective has dominated Maya archaeology, and accidents of discovery have favored the Late Preclassic period at a few widely spaced centers. In part, this may also be because too much importance has been given to the appearance of items of civilization such as writing and polychrome ceramics. Cross-culturally, writing often postdates state-level organization. Some of the world's largest states lacked writing altogether. In any case, there is evidence of writing in the Preclassic period, at least by 400–300 BCE (Saturno et al. 2006) as in other regions in Mesoamerica. Kingship, craft specialization, long-distance trade, monumental architecture, and public rituals, as a whole, are better indicators of a society's complexity than any individual feature taken singly, such as writing. When does this complex set of features appear in lowland society?

The transition from the Preclassic to the Classic period is often cited as such a moment. It is characterized by changes in the balance of power between cities that had been established a long time before. But in spite of the fall of El Mirador, we see a continuation of ritual and burial practices of rulers into the Classic period throughout the lowlands. Royal interments are increasingly individualistic in character as time progresses and first appear in public settings at the turn of the Christian Era in the Mirador Region and at Tikal. No real systemic change is apparent in the transition from the Middle Preclassic to the Late Preclassic period either. Rather, there appears to be a change in scale of the architecture, of the resources disposed of, and in the development of writing.

The real *conjuncture*, then, has to be found at the beginning of the Middle Preclassic period. The visible material correlates signal profound changes in sociopolitical organization, including large-scale public rituals, the consolidation of the ritual needs of neighboring villages into a central place by the conversion of hilltops into open ceremonial spaces, the appropriation of rituals associated with the ideology of the Maize God as life-giver that turned it into a symbol of central authority, and the creation of a network of competing centers of ritual and political power across the Maya lowlands. Long-distance trade of high-value items and other kinds of interactions with centers outside of the Maya region are also evident in the Middle Preclassic period beginning in 800 BCE, as attested by the presence of Motagua Valley jade at Cival (Seitz et al. 2001; Taube et al. 2011) and as far away as West Mexico (see Chapter 3).

Therefore, the interactions within the Maya lowlands among ritual centers as early as the Middle Preclassic period may have played a greater role in shaping what we refer to as Maya Civilization than may have interactions with other regions. The motives of these intense near-neighbor interactions are probably not the trade in necessities as Rathje's (1972) model suggested, nor in exotic items as in later revisions of that core-periphery theory (Freidel et al. 2002), but probably in a variety of symbolic-value items, most of which were made from materials locally available but fashioned with expert craftsmanship and esoteric knowledge. Pre-Mamom ceramics were fashioned locally and were decorated with fine symbols by expert hands. The symbols were not exotic in any way to the Maya. They represented values broadly understood across Mesoamerica expressed with esoteric sophistication.

In viewing the interactions among Mesoamerican regions, perhaps past generations of archaeologists have overemphasized the geographic and cultural distances, as well as diffusion and migration as mechanisms of change. If we view Preclassic Mesoamerica as a coherent cultural area rather than a patchwork of different cultural and ethnic traditions perhaps we could easily move beyond migration theories towards a more nuanced understanding. Regular interactions among different Mesoamerican peoples with very similar ideological and organizational systems had indeed taken place since the Early Preclassic period in spite of our datasets' imperfect chronological alignments and area coverage.

ENDNOTES

6.1. The Chicanel ceramic complex and the Mamom ceramic complex were first defined at Uaxactun by Robert E. Smith (1950).

6.2. A piece of charcoal recovered from the floor that sealed the Cival cache produced a 1-sigma result of 790–760 and 680–550 calibrated years BCE (2-sigma result of 800–520 cal. BCE; sample; 2520 + 40 BP C-14 years; CIV.T08.43, Beta 213528).

6.3. A piece of carbon found embedded in the stucco lining of the masks below the temple returned an uncalibrated date of 2170 ± 40 years b.p., a calibrated 1-sigma date of 260–160 BCE, and a calibrated 2-sigma of 360–90 BCE (Beta 1995-70 calibrated with Oxcal v.2.0). The temple rooms containing the painted figures were erected as part of the same construction episode as the masks.

7

Early States in the Southern Maya Region

MICHAEL LOVE

The lack of evidence has not deterred Mesoamericanists from making propositions about state origins. (Wright, 1977)

The analysis of early state formation is entering a new era in which scholars focus less on what a state is and more on how it is. Under the processualist rules for the investigation of state origins, dominant since the 1960s, scholars were urged to develop criteria for statehood, translate them into archaeologically observable patterns, and then evaluate the evidence to determine at what point in time a given society moved up the evolutionary ladder. One problem with those rules is that there is no single definition of a state that satisfies everyone (Claessen and Skalník 1978; Cohen 1978). Attempts have been made to adjust criteria, or to define sub-classifications such as the archaic state, the typical state, the city-state, the territorial state, or (everyone's favorite) the inchoate state, but still no consensus emerged, except in the most general of characterizations.

Playing by the new rules of the game, according to Norman Yoffee, we should propose analytical constructs, rather than classificatory dogmas, and focus our attention on "how social roles were altered and/or abandoned and new ones adopted or created in the development of the earliest cities, states, and civilizations" (2005:181). As anxious as I am to play by the new rules, and even to expand them by an explicit ban on sports metaphors, I admit a certain nostalgia for the nomological clarity of unqualified statements such as those that states have minimal populations of hundreds of thousands (Johnson and Earle 2000), states must exhibit at least four levels of regional hierarchy (Wright and Johnson 1975), or all states have palaces for their rulers (Flannery 1998).

Any paper, or any conference, purporting to be about state origins seemingly assumes from the outset that states can be identified (even if not defined) and that such identification somehow increases our understanding of the society or societies under study. However, that may not be the case, as classification can mislead as well as enlighten. Among the several myths of early states discussed by Yoffee perhaps the most salient is that "the earliest states were basically all the same kind of thing" (2005:5). Yoffee quite rightly observes that early states differed greatly in size, structure, cohesiveness, and culture, so that by labeling a given social formation as a state, we may in fact obscure more than we elucidate. While I can't endorse Yoffee's Rule that "if you can argue whether a society is a state or isn't, then it isn't" (Yoffee 2005:41), I do concur that our focus should be on analyzing social life and social relationships, rather than focusing too rigidly on definitions.

This chapter discusses two instances of social change in the Southern Maya Region during the Late Preclassic period. In both cases that changes result in the formation of a state of some kind, but the states were different in their size, their form, and in their developmental histories. The differences may be just as interesting as the similarities, and we may learn more about the two cases, and early states in general, by focusing on those differences rather than on whether one or the other conforms to some idealized form of the state. Perhaps more importantly, the social changes that took place in the Late Preclassic period illustrate the value of statehood as an analytical concept, showing why we should continue to use the term even if we cannot agree upon a definition of "the state." In the course of this chapter I will indicate what I consider to be important aspects of state systems and how such systems contrast with less complex forms of society and government, but my emphasis will be on analyzing social change rather than engaging in a classificatory exercise.

THE SOUTHERN MAYA CITY STATES AND CITY-STATE CULTURE

In an earlier paper (Love 2011), I defined the highlands and Pacific coast of Guatemala, El Salvador, and Chiapas, Mexico, as an interaction zone of early city-states during the Late Preclassic period. I labeled the region as the "Southern City-State Culture" or SCSC. My characterization drew upon Mogen Hansen's discussion of city-states and city-state culture, in which he observed that early states develop in networks of economically and culturally linked urban centers (Hansen 2000). The model shares some similarities with Colin Renfrew's 1975 definition of Early State Modules, but Hansen addressed cultural interaction among the states as well as their economic networks, and did not impose the uniformity of structure and size that Renfrew proposed. For Mesoamerica, analysis of the cultural dimension is fundamental in that many elements of high culture (following the definition of Baines and Yoffee 1998) were shared among those interacting cities, shaping the formation of elite identities that cut across ethnic and linguistic divisions (Love 2011). Hansen's model works very well for the highlands and Pacific coast, where a number of urban centers became early states that were linked by both economic exchange and cultural interaction. Like Yoffee (2005) Hansen distinguishes politics (the state) from culture (the civilization that is shared among several states).

The cities within the Southern City-State Culture include Kaminaljuyu, Takalik Abaj, El Ujuxte, and Izapa. Each of those cities was both an urban center and the capital of a regional polity that reached statehood. Other cities, such as Chalchuapa, Chiapa de Corzo, Chocolá, Cotzumalguapa (which includes both El Baúl and Bilbao), and San Andrés Semetebaj were probably urban and may also have been state-level polities, but presently there is not enough evidence to be certain.

In the present chapter I wish to make a more detailed examination of the two cases where evidence for the development of the state is strongest: Kaminaljuyu and El Ujuxte. Although I label each as a city-state, there are significant differences between the two in size, wealth, the structure of their regional polities, and their historical backgrounds. The two cities occupied very different environments, with Kaminaljuyu in the central highlands of Guatemala and El Ujuxte the southwestern coastal plain just a few kilometers from the ocean (Fig. 7.1). Despite the differences, there are also significant similarities beyond the classification "city-state." Each crossed the threshold to statehood in the Late Preclassic period. Each was an important node in the trade networks linking the central Guatemalan highlands to the Pacific coastal plain. The elite of each city participated in aspects of high culture that were an important part of Southern City-State Culture, and Mesoamerica as a whole. Also, for each example there is sufficient evidence on either side of the cusp of statehood to analyze what changes took place during the transition, with multiple lines of evidence from regional surveys and household excavations, as well as data on economy, ideology, and rituals.

THE POLITICAL AND CULTURAL GEOGRAPHY OF THE SOUTHERN MAYA REGION

Having qualified the theme of my chapter regarding the definition of early states, I will add the further qualification that the territory we call the Southern Maya Region may not have been Maya, at least not all of it. It is very doubtful that all portions of the territory were occupied by Mayan speakers, and many different branches of the Mayan language family had developed by the Late Preclassic period (Josserand 2011). Although the largest cities, including Kaminaljuyu and Takalik Abaj, display cultural traits that were part of Maya high culture, they also display links to non-Maya Central America and to the Isthmian region, the latter being a region probably occupied predominantly by speakers of Mixe-Zoquean languages. The Southern Maya Region was a zone of cultural interaction, migration, and long-distance trading routes, so that many of the largest cities may well have been polyglot and multi-cultural (Love 2004, 2011). Hypothetical dichotomies, such as a highland Maya region and a Mixe-Zoquean coastal plain, are much too simplistic and ultimately unhelpful, implying that people within those zones were "all one thing." Many forms of identity probably crossed whatever linguistic boundaries may have existed, so that we cannot be sure even to what extent language structured interaction or formed the basis of social identity within any single city, let alone the entire region. With those stipulations, I will adopt the term "Southern Maya Region" here solely for parsimony.

Trends toward social complexity in this region begin as early, if not earlier, than anywhere else in Mesoamerica. At what point the developmental trajectory crossed the link to statehood in the region can be debated and depends much upon definitions. The social and political formations of the latter Middle Preclassic (ca. 600–400 BCE) and early Late Preclassic (ca. 400–200 BCE) defy easy classification and highlight the deficiencies of neo-evolutionary categories. The trajectories of social and political change,

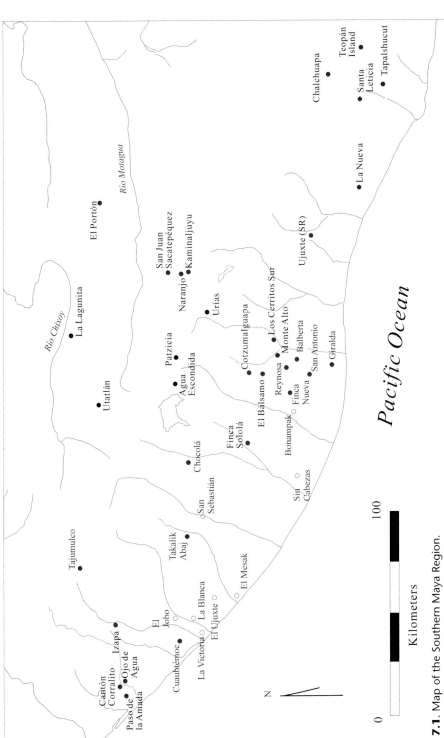

7.1. Map of the Southern Maya Region.

which include population growth, urbanization, increasing political central-ization, economic intensification, and changing ideological structures, may be best examined through the case studies that follow.

THE ORIGINS OF THE EARLY STATE IN SOUTHWESTERN GUATEMALA

The antecedents to the rise of El Ujuxte as a state in the Late Preclassic are lengthy, stretching back to the early complex societies of the Mazatán region of Chiapas (Blake 2011; Clark and Blake 1994; Clark and Pye 2006, 2011; Lesure 2011; Love 2007; Rosenswig 2010, 2011). At ca. 900 BCE, the beginning of the Middle Preclassic, the demographic and political center of the greater Soconusco shifted eastward from Mazatán to the Río Naranjo, located in present-day Guatemala, evidenced by a dramatic growth in popu-lation and a regional system that was much larger and more hierarchically structured than anything previously seen (Fig. 7.2). This striking change in regional organization is punctuated with the rise of La Blanca as a city and regional paramount (Fig. 7.3). La Blanca was one of Mesoamerica's largest settlements during the Middle Preclassic, with some of the most impressive early architecture in southern Mesoamerica. The city covered nearly 300 ha and its polity extended over 300 km^2, with more than 80 settlements and a multi-tiered settlement hierarchy (Blake et al. 1995; Love 2002c; Love and Guernsey 2011; Rosenswig 2005, 2010).

I will discuss the case of La Blanca in some detail because it is impor-tant to understand what changes took place during the transition from the Middle to the Late Preclassic, which is where I choose to locate the transi-tion to statehood in the regional sequence.

The Regional System of La Blanca

The La Blanca polity had at least three and perhaps as many as five levels, depending upon how finely one wishes to divide settlements that lack monumental architecture and how one interprets the relationships between the second and third levels of the hierarchy. The nature of the regional capital, La Blanca, is discussed below. The second level consists of two centers, El Infierno and La Zarca, which each have one large public mound over 15 m in height. Izapa may also have been a secondary center of La Blanca during the Conchas phase (Love 2002c). A third level consists of settlements with smaller public buildings, whose remains are mounds roughly 5–6 m in height (Rosenswig 2010, 2011). The fourth level is composed of villages with 2 to 10 residences, and the fifth level is formed by isolated residential mounds.

It is uncertain to what extent this formal settlement hierarchy reflects political organization. The third level of the hierarchy, identified by Rosenswig (2010), is exemplified by Cuauhtémoc, which had a single public mound approximately 5 m in height. All the third-level sites lie on the western edge of the La Blanca polity, and their relationship to the secondary centers is uncertain. The third-tier sites may have been dependent on La Zarca or El Infierno, directly under the aegis of La Blanca, or politically independent.

La Blanca as an Early City

The core of La Blanca is a ceremonial precinct of about 100 ha. Areas of habitation extend over at least 280 ha, but surface materials are found over more than 300 ha. The exact boundaries of La Blanca are difficult to determine because of the extensive damage to the site caused by road construction in 1972–73. Road grading and filling certainly destroyed habitation mounds in the southern sector of the site, but may also have spread surface materials over a wide area. Only extensive excavation in the future will be able to determine the precise limits of the site.

The Central Precinct of La Blanca was an impressive ceremonial zone, which was leveled and raised with several meters of fill, perhaps as many as five at its north end. The first construction episode took place at the end of the Conchas A sub-phase, at about 900 BCE. The Central Precinct includes the West Acropolis, the East Acropolis, Mound 1, and several smaller public mounds (Mounds 3, 5, 25, and the now-destroyed Stela Mound). The smaller public mounds and the two acropolises serve to form four plazas around Mound 1: the Great Plaza to the north, the Sunken Plaza to the east, and the West and South Plazas. The major mounds and plazas are aligned with an axis that passes through Mound 1 to the peak of the Tajumulco volcano, the tallest volcano in Central America with an elevation of 4221 m. Not coincidentally, this axis of 22 degrees azimuth is very close to the 21 degree axis documented for the Valley of Guatemala's major centers in the Middle and Late Preclassic periods (Shook 1952).

The largest ceremonial construction at the site, Mound 1, was one of the earliest monumental temple pyramids in Mesoamerica. The mound origi-

Before 900 BCE

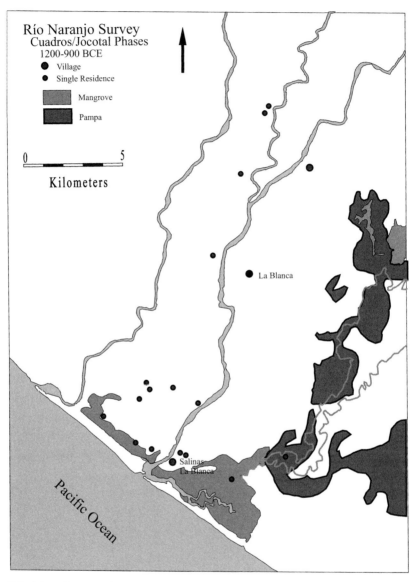

7.2. Map showing the increase in settlement in the Rio Naranjo survey region during the Early and Middle Preclassic periods.

After 900 BCE

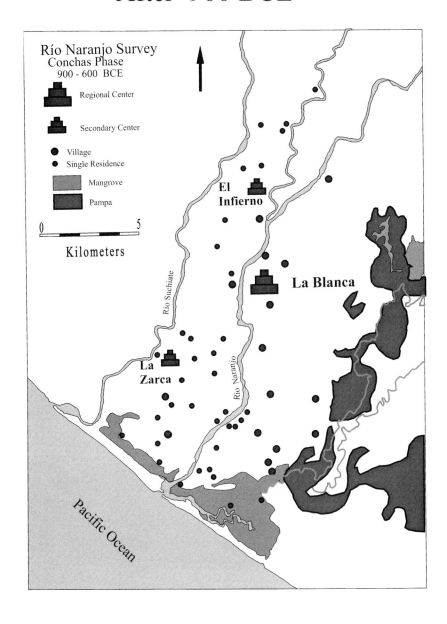

Río Naranjo Survey
Conchas Phase
900 - 600 BCE

Regional Center

Secondary Center

● Village
• Single Residence

Mangrove

Pampa

0   5
Kilometers

El
Infierno

La Blanca

Río Suchiate

La
Zarca

Río Naranjo

Pacific Ocean

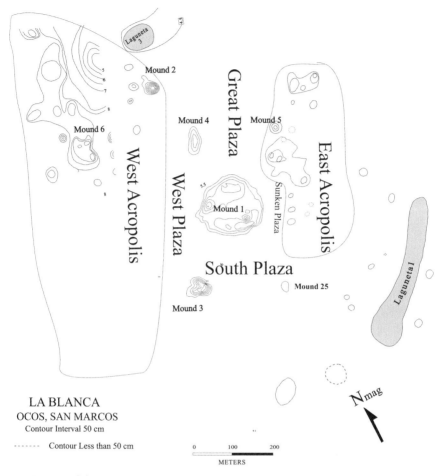

7.3. Map of the central zone of La Blanca.

nally stood over 25 m in height, and measured 150 x 100 m at its base. It was built without stone, using a sophisticated rammed earth technique with a capping layer of selected dark brown clay. The great bulk of the mound was raised in a single construction episode, with subsequent enlargements accomplished by the application of relatively thin strata of earth. Mound 1 was largely destroyed in 1972 for road construction, but investigations in 2003, 2004, and 2008 found that its base survives to an overall depth of 4.5 m. Ceramics within the earliest phase of construction indicate that Mound 1 was built during the Conchas B sub-phase, sometime soon after 900 BCE (Love et al. 2005).

Only two fragments of stone sculpture are known from La Blanca (Love 2010; Love and Guernsey 2011). Monument 1 is a head carved in the Olmec style, representing either an anthropomorphic supernatural or a human with animal-like characteristics. Monument 2 is a knee fragment from a standing human figure. Other stone monuments, notably a stela, are rumored to have been present in the West Plaza, but have not been located. Other important, but smaller, art works from the site may include the Young Lord sculpture (Reilly 1987) and a saurian image now in the Museo del Libro in Antigua, Guatemala (Fields and Reents-Budet 2005a). The most unique sculptural monument from La Blanca may be Monument 3 (Fig. 7.4), an earthen altar in the shape of a quatrefoil (Love and Guernsey 2007; Love et al. 2006). All these sculptures reflect the participation of La Blanca in the Olmec sphere of interaction.

Household Differentiation at La Blanca

Excavations in residential zones at La Blanca show significant social differentiation at the household level (Love 1991, 2006; Love and Guernsey 2011). Elite households are marked by high densities of prestige goods, including jade, mica jewelry, and fine-paste ceramics decorated with elaborate iconography. The iconography includes supernatural beings, such as were-jaguars and other "Olmec" creatures, along with what may be calendrical symbols that closely resemble Lamat and Ajaw glyphs. The elite residences also have higher densities of obsidian and greater numbers of cores, suggesting that they controlled long-distance exchange.

Economic intensification provided the material base for the expansion of elite power during the Middle Preclassic and the means to finance monumental public works. Key elements of intensification were the increased consumption of maize and the use of the domestic dog as a protein source (Blake et al. 1992; Love 1999a, 2002b; Rosenswig 2005; Wake and Harrington 2002), both of which reflect a maximizing strategy of gaining the most calories for each unit of labor expended in food procurement (Love 1999a).

Social and ideological factors were also key aspects of elite power at La Blanca. High densities of animal bone in La Blanca Mound 9, two to four times that found at other residences, may indicate elite sponsorship of feasts (Love 2006; Barge 2012). Such feasts may have been held in conjunction with rituals associated with Monument 3. Rosenswig (2005, 2007) proposes that there was a significant shift in feasting patterns from the Early to the

Middle Preclassic, and he believes that elites gained greater control over feasting activities as a means to solidify their political power. However, the distribution of fancy serving vessels at La Blanca appears to be widespread, indicating that most, if not all, households held some kind of feast (Fauvelle 2010). However, the kind of feasts held at elite households may have differed from those of others in scale and perhaps in the kinds of food served (Barge 2012).

Other types of household rituals involved the use of altars, incensarios, and ceramic figurines (Love and Guernsey 2011). The precise nature of domestic rituals is unclear, but many interpret Preclassic figurines as representative, especially of ancestors (Cyphers 1993b; Grove and Gillespie 2002; Guernsey 2012; Marcus 1998b). Joyce (2003) found that figurines also were used in public contexts adjacent to residential zones and proposed that they were used to mark milestones in individual lives, such as transitions between age groups. Whatever their meaning, handmade ceramic figurines are omnipresent and dense in the residences of La Blanca, indicating the great importance of household ritual in Middle Preclassic times.

What Kind of Polity Was La Blanca?

Under the old rules of the game, we would debate the nature of La Blanca's settlement hierarchy, and we might make a log/normal plot of settlement rank versus size in order to "objectively" determine just how many tiers there were in the regional hierarchy. Then we could look at the evidence for social stratification, and the degree of economic centralization, before making a final decision on whether La Blanca was a state. With apologies to Yoffee, there is a lot to argue about in this case.

There are many aspects of the La Blanca polity that are state-like. First, there is evidence of a strong centralized government. The most conservative classification would see three levels of hierarchy in La Blanca's regional system and the most liberal might see five. The concentration of population in the Río Naranjo region, drawing population from both the Mazatán zone to the west and the Río Jesus zone to the east, may be evidence of coercive resettlement (Love 2002c). The massive mobilization of labor to construct the acropolis and Mound 1 may also be evidence of a strong centralized government. Despite recent theoretical developments proposing that monumentality is not necessarily indicative of centralized power (summarized in Rosenswig and Burger 2012), the strong central planning

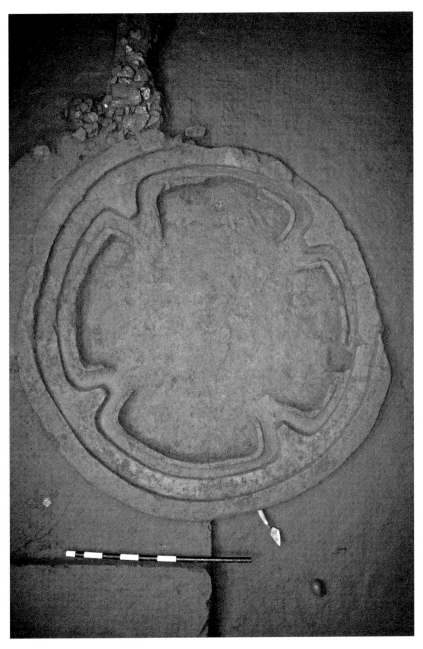

7.4. Photograph of La Blanca Monument 3.

exhibited at La Blanca bears the hallmarks of elite culture: sophisticated engineering (standardized orientations, standardized measurement, precise leveling, selected materials, and the sophisticated rammed-earth construction technology), ideological unity and significance (the central axis aligned to astronomical and geographical targets), and the incorporation of elite residences (the East Acropolis) as part of the Central Precinct.

The evidence for significant social stratification at La Blanca is strong and shows a clear division between elites and non-elites. The differences in wealth between the East Acropolis residences and others at the site show a great gap between elites and non-elites. Jade, the best indicator of household wealth at La Blanca, appears in much higher quantities in the residences of the East Acropolis, especially Operations 32 and 37, which are adjacent to the Sunken Plaza (Love and Guernsey 2011).

Many Mayanists either place great emphasis on the first appearance of rulership (Estrada-Belli 2011) or equate it with the development of the state (Kaplan 2002). La Blanca shows the presence of an ideology of rulership in the form of the quatrefoil, Monument 3, which is clearly linked to Middle Preclassic systems of elite power. The quatrefoil symbolizes a portal to the supernatural and was long-lived in Mesoamerica, being consistently linked to elite power and the ability of rulers to communicate with the supernatural (Guernsey 2010). Further, representations of supernatural figures, such as the were-jaguar, and symbols such as the Ajaw and Lamat, are limited to elite residences at La Blanca. Figurines from elite residences may depict rites of transformation, some of which parallel imagery better attested in monumental art in which rulers took on the qualities of supernatural beings (Guernsey 2006:82).

By framing the evidence in a certain light, one could represent La Blanca as a small state. But in the end, I come down against viewing La Blanca, or any other Middle Preclassic polity, in that light. In my view, the city looks like the capital of a state, but its regional system did not reach the status of a state-level polity. Yes, there was rulership, but that in and of itself is not indicative of a state system of government. Nor is social stratification in and of itself definitive, because divisions based on wealth may also appear in pre-state societies (Fried 1960). Mechanisms of financing governmental and public infrastructure were apparently limited to the ability to draw upon the labor of the populace. Further, I view the size of the system and the complexity of the governmental apparatus as key to defining the existence of a state. On that measure, the La Blanca polity does not seem to be large or complex enough to be called a state. The second-level centers do not appear to be large settlements with significant administrative complexes; they lack public buildings other than their principal mounds, so that they may have acted merely as ritual centers rather than governmental ones.

Despite the evidence of a pronounced social hierarchy, control over labor, and an ideology of rulership, then, it would be hyperbole to call La Blanca a state because the institutions of government were poorly developed. The La Blanca polity did, however, successfully subjugate a large hinterland from which it could draw labor and resources. In that respect it established the basis for centralized power that was to become more pronounced and more developed in the years that followed its decline.

THE GROWTH OF SOCIAL COMPLEXITY AND THE FORMATION OF AN EARLY STATE AT EL UJUXTE

After 600 BCE, La Blanca declined to be a small village of approximately 20 ha, although its large temples may have continued to be used for some time as pilgrimage sites, judging by the amount of Late Preclassic and Classic period ceramics found on their slopes. Late Preclassic burials are found as intrusive features in abandoned Conchas phase housemounds, perhaps a sign of veneration and respect for what the city had been and for the sacred location that it continued to be. There may have been a brief period during which the region lacked political centralization (Love 2002b), but by 500 BCE a successor to La Blanca developed just over 10 km to the east. That site, El Ujuxte, became a large urban center by the Late Preclassic period and the capital of a system that was much larger and more complex than that of La Blanca.

El Ujuxte as a City

Occupation at El Ujuxte (Fig. 7.5) began in the second half of the Middle Preclassic at about 600 BCE, and the major axes of the site's grid may have been laid out at that time. Major constructions at the site have not been extensively excavated, but evidence from the Central Plaza excavations show that constructions there began during the Caramelo phase (600–400 BCE), with offerings placed at the origin point of the site axes.

Primary deposits dating to the Caramelo phase have been found in only 2 of the 16 residential areas tested, so that the overall size of the site at that time may not have been terribly large. The division of the Caramelo and Cataluña phases is based on frequencies of ceramic wares, so surface remains cannot be unambiguously attributed to one phase or the other. Hence, a secure estimate of the site size in its early occupation cannot be given at the present time.

By the Cataluña phase (400–200 BCE), El Ujuxte consisted of a nuclear zone covering at least 4 km². Surface remains, indicating extended habitation zones, cover over 6 km². If the mound group at the site of Valle Lirio is included as part of the site, its total area exceeds 8 km². Within this area are over 200 mapped mounds and many more unmapped ones that, during our five years of fieldwork, were located on private farms to which we were unable to obtain access.

El Ujuxte was built on a grid plan. The longest axis of the grid (north to south) aligns with the rising of the bright star Capella. With the exception of the Chabela Group, all buildings at the site, both public and residential, share the same orientation with their longer axes on an azimuth of 35 degrees east of magnetic north. Burials also align with the site grid, although the orientation of the head may be toward any one of the four grid directions. Major streets within the city run east to west.

The alignment of Mound 1 with the summit of Mound 2a (the tallest mound on the Mound 2 Acropolis) coincides with the point of summer solstice sunrise over the peak of the volcano Santa María. Other alignments mark the zenith passage sunrise, winter solstice, and the rising of the Pleiades (Poe 2000). The ceremonial core of the site, then, marks important passages of the sun: the 260-day zenith passage cycle and the 365-day solar year.

The Chabela group, located northwest of the Mound 2 platform, has a distinct alignment of 89 degrees azimuth. This alignment coincides with the rising of the constellation Gemini on the northern horizon. The significance of this event is uncertain, other than the fact that the rising of Gemini occurs on this line-of-site just before sunrise, as well as the rising of Orion. Significantly, the main site axis and the axis of the Chabela Group intersect at the principal mound of the Valle Lirio group, some 2.5 km south of Mound 2, showing a considerable amount of engineering skill as well as astronomical knowledge.

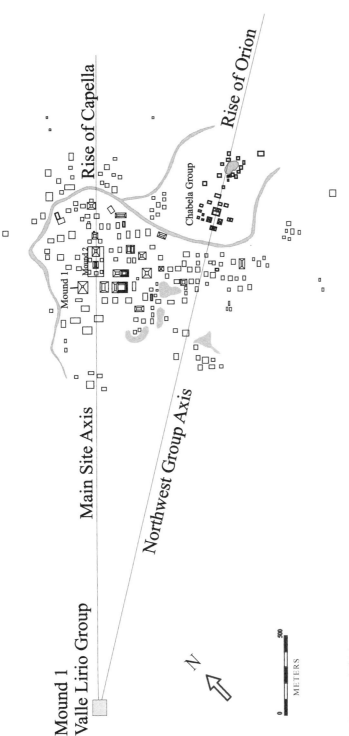

7.5. Map of El Ujuxte.

The Regional System of El Ujuxte

The El Ujuxte polity was both larger and more complex than the Middle Preclassic La Blanca polity. First, it was twice as large, covering approximately 600 m², stretching from the Río Naranjo to somewhere between the Río Ocosito and the Río Samalá (Fig. 7.6). Second, it encompassed at least five and possibly six levels of hierarchy. Below El Ujuxte, the second tier consists of at least four centers, each of which covers over 1 km². Each of the secondary centers has public architecture that copies that of El Ujuxte. The largest of the secondary centers is Chiquirines Viejo with a central complex that replicates precisely the El Ujuxte pattern of an acropolis surmounted by seven mounds with its largest mound to the west. The remaining secondary centers have the acropolis with seven mounds, but lack the large pyramid to the west. Tertiary centers have at least two large "public" mounds at opposite ends of a plaza, those mounds being no more than 6 m in height. Fourth-level centers have a single "public" mound, 5–6 m in height. The fifth and sixth levels of the hierarchy consist of large and small villages without public architecture.

The size and complexity of the regional system are the most important factors in considering the El Ujuxte polity to be a state. The scale and sophistication of the secondary centers shows them to be significant administrative centers, while their replication of El Ujuxte´s acropolis plan shows them to be part of its political system. To date, none of these secondary centers has been excavated, so there are no data regarding the economic relationship between El Ujuxte and the lesser cities. There are, however, good data from El Ujuxte itself about the economic and ideological systems that formed the basis of its power.

Making a State: Economics and Ideology at El Ujuxte

The early state that took shape at El Ujuxte was in part an outgrowth of the La Blanca polity and in part a dramatic reorganization of its predecessor. In an earlier paper (Love 2002b), I analyzed the transition as an episode of political cycling, in which centralized power had to be re-established, in an altered form, following the collapse of the La Blanca polity. Elites seeking power, I proposed, consciously modified aspects of the previous system in order to enhance their power and make it more enduring. In the process, they created both economic and ideological institutions that gave rise to a state system of government. In what follows, I will both summarize and

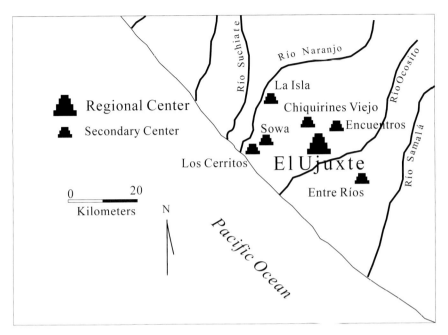

7.6. Map showing the extent of the regional system of El Ujuxte.

amplify aspects of that earlier paper. My focus here is on the institutions of power and of government, so I will not address another topic of that paper, the transformation of agency. The modification of daily practice and its implications for agency and resistance were as important to the creation of the state as was the institutionalization of power, but space does not allow me to treat that topic here.

Social Differentiation and Economic Organization

If regional data inform us about the nature of government at El Ujuxte, it is excavation data from households and public spaces that tell us about the basis of social power. Excavations at El Ujuxte sampled 16 residential structures. A principal components analysis of variability in the household assemblages is shown in Figure 7.7. The plot shows the relationship between five variables used to rank households at El Ujuxte: the size of the platform on which the residence was constructed (ranging from 1 to 6 m in height), the ratio of obsidian prismatic blades to casual obsidian tools, the

Factor Loadings Plot

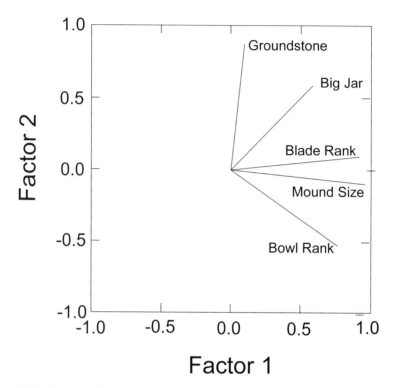

7.7. Diagram showing a principal components analysis of household variability at El Ujuxte.

number of large storage jars, the size (rim diameter) of food service bowls, and the ratio of formal grinding tools to utilized cobble tools.

Using these variables, Mound 35 (excavated by Operation 12) is the highest ranked residence at the site. The plan of Mound 35 (Fig. 7.8) suggests that it was a palace structure. It is a multi-tiered elongated platform running west to east along the small stream that passes through the center of the site. Two test pits placed in the structure showed a unique facing of white/gray clay and earth on the penultimate construction episode. Low mounds around the structure appear to be part of an elite compound, and within one of these structures the small pendant was found. This pendant, perforated for hanging, conforms to the "Bib" headdress identified by Freidel (pers. comm., 2003) as one of the insignia of Preclassic rulers of the Maya lowlands, and suggests that the compound in and around Mound 35 may have been the residence of the ruler(s) of El Ujuxte.

The complete elite compound (which includes Operations 11 and 13 in addition to Operation 12) ranks highest on nearly all measures of household status. Figure 7.9 shows a plot of two such variables: Blade Rank (the ratio of prismatic blades to casual obsidian tools) to Big Jar rank (the frequency of large storage vessels). What this plot shows is that the greatest incidence of storage vessels is found in the residences of highest rank. This and other evidence we have in hand shows that the economy of El Ujuxte was much more centralized and elite-dominated than that of La Blanca. The elite had much more control over subsistence surpluses and long-distance exchange of both basic and exotic materials. In addition, it appears from the obsidian data that the El Ujuxte elite took steps to eliminate independent exchange networks that may have promoted household autonomy, such as those that procured small nodules for the production of casual obsidian tools.

Ideology

Ideological change at El Ujuxte is manifested in two important aspects of ritual practice. First, there is a dramatic reduction in household ritual. Second, there is a concomitant rise in public ritual at specific locations such as the Mound 2 platform and the Central Plaza.

Household Ritual

As discussed above, during Middle Preclassic times at La Blanca two classes of materials were most strongly linked to household ritual: ceramic figurines and feasting vessels. The forms of household ritual linked to those materials suffered a dramatic decline at Late Preclassic El Ujuxte. At La Blanca the frequency of figurine heads per cubic meter of excavation ranges from 1.4 to 3.9, depending on the household and the subphase. At El Ujuxte, however, their frequency is about 0.02 fragments of all figurine parts (heads and bodies) per cubic meter of excavation, with most of the 19 figurine fragments recovered coming from the Caramelo phase deposits. Clearly, a dramatic change took place, and figurine use plummeted after 600 BCE.

At La Blanca, feasting vessels, which I define as the elaborately decorated Cuca Red on Buff bowls (Love 2002c), were found in all households.

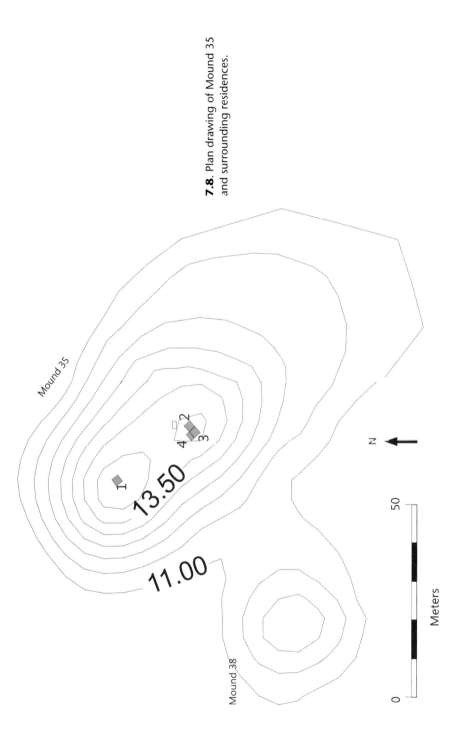

7.8. Plan drawing of Mound 35 and surrounding residences.

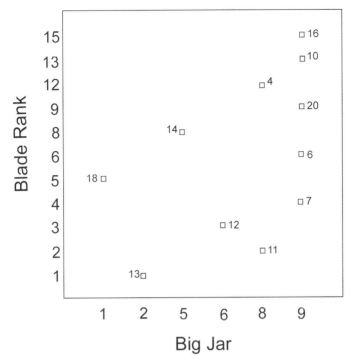

7.9. Plot of blade rank and storage jar rank for El Ujuxte residences demonstrating that that the highest incidence of storage vessels is found in the residences of highest rank.

An analysis of serving vessel size (limited to flat-bottomed bowls with out-leaning walls) showed no significant differences across households (Fau-velle 2010) for any ceramic ware. At El Ujuxte, however, the frequency of feasting vessels (defined in this instance as out-leaning bowls with diam-eters more than 1 standard deviation above the mean) is strongly correlated with household rank. As shown in Figure 7.10, these data suggest that at El Ujuxte feasting became largely restricted to elite households. Feasting prob-ably did not completely disappear from lesser-ranked households, but was curtailed and became much more the prerogative of the elite.

At the same time that these two important aspects of household ritual were reduced, ritual in the public sectors of the site was amplified, an asser-tion supported by two lines of evidence. First, the formality of architectural arrangements in the core of El Ujuxte is striking, and the large plazas front-ing the stage-like Mound 2 platform suggest public spectacles with large au-

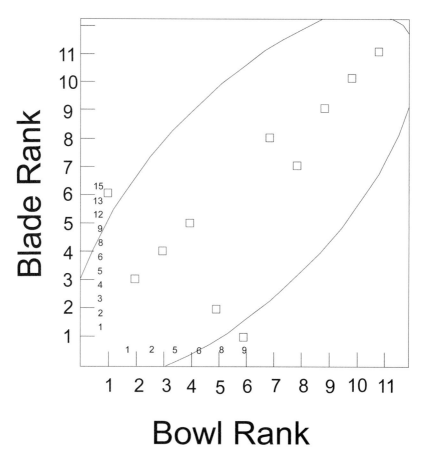

7.10. Spearman's rank correlation for blade rank and feasting bowl rank for El Ujuxte residences showing that the frequency of feasting vessels correlates strongly with household rank.

diences. Second, the number of caches excavated in the Central Plaza indicates a scale of public ritual that vastly exceeded that of previous times.

The remains of four floors, and hints of a fifth, were found during the Central Plaza excavations at El Ujuxte. Associated with each floor were offerings in the form of caches of ceramic vessels and other materials. The greatest number of offerings was associated with the Pitahaya phase renovation of the plaza, which took place at about 100 BCE. The Pitahaya phase offerings were placed along the east/west axis of the site, on the centerline of Mound 1. Within a 4x4 m exposure, we recovered 131 vessels in 30 discrete caches (Love and Balcárcel 2000). The caches include pebbles of contrasting materials (igneous stone and pumice) that may have been used in divinatory rituals similar to those of modern day-keepers, as well as stingray spines used for letting blood. Two caches, Features 27 and 28, include numerous small dishes, 3 large bowls, and 2 ceramic crosses in each (Figure 7.11).

El Ujuxte does not possess the massive sculptural programs of sites such as Kaminaljuyu, Takalik Abaj, and Izapa. Nonetheless, the ritual caches, the site grid, and the astronomical alignments all suggest that the elite of El Ujuxte expressed the same ideological statements favored by other elite, and carried out rituals similar to those depicted on the sculpture of other sites (Guernsey 2010; Guernsey and Love 2005). The elite, presumably in the person of a ruler, appropriated rituals that had formerly been private and made them public in a spectacle where an elite interpretation of ideology was presented (Love 1999b, 2002b).

This interpretation becomes more credible when we examine the evidence for the new ideological claims made by the elite at El Ujuxte. At La Blanca, and in earlier times, rulers derived their identity and power from linking themselves to themes of supernatural communication and fertility. In particular, there is a focus on communication with the supernatural realm (Love and Guernsey 2007) as attested by the Monument 3 quatrefoil, or reiterated in the overall site plan, which was aligned to the volcano Tacaná, another symbolic portal to the underworld. The elite at El Ujuxte, however, make much broader claims based on grandiose visions of celestial and cosmological order. The site as a cosmogram was concerned with solar cycles and celestial phenomena and sought to create a city that was in harmony with those cycles. The elite evidently controlled a growing body of astronomical and calendrical knowledge and used it to construct a mythology of creation and an ideology of power. Like the rulers at San Bartolo who commissioned murals replete with cosmological significance (Taube et al. 2010), the rulers of El Ujuxte quite literally structured their site with the symbols and messages of cosmological order. The caches—with their cruciform-shaped plaques, divinatory pebbles, and stingray spines—may have symbolized the actions of divine sacrifice at the time of creation, so that the ruler replicated the ritual actions that brought the present creation into being. This ideology of rulership, dramatically different from and much more grandiose than that of Middle Preclassic times, became the template for rulers in southern Mesoamerica for the next 1000 years.

The power of the elite at El Ujxute, and the state-level system of government that sustained it, rested on two pillars of equal importance: economics and ideology. Economically, the elite of El Ujuxte expanded the power developed under the hegemony of La Blanca by gaining greater control over the production and distribution of key resources, thereby undermining household autonomy. Ideologically, they also undermined household autonomy by bringing ritual into greater public view, where they controlled the agenda. In this setting they presented a new interpretation of rulership, one in which the ruler was presented as the center point for maintaining cosmological order.

The new order brought into being at El Ujuxte and other Late Preclassic centers was apparently efficacious. The political system of El Ujuxte was more successful than that of previous centralized polities in that it was larger, more complex, and longer enduring than any political system of the Early or Middle Preclassic. It survived for over 600 years in an increasingly complex and competitive social landscape, close by the large centers of Izapa and Takalik Abaj. Eventually, El Ujuxte, like much of the Southern Maya Region, was caught in the enigmatic Late Preclassic collapse whose causes are yet to be fully understood.

COMPLEXITY IN THE PRECLASSIC PERIOD
IN THE VALLEY OF GUATEMALA

The story of social complexity in Preclassic highland Guatemala has for many years been considered synonymous with Kaminaljuyu. Late Preclassic Kaminaljuyu was one of the most magnificent cities of ancient Mesoamerica and is justifiably recognized for its Preclassic art and architecture. It has taken over 30 years to discard the label of chiefdom placed on the Preclassic city by the Pennsylvania State project (Michels 1979a), but recent research has made it clear that Late Preclassic Kaminaljuyu was a large urban settlement and likely the paramount of a state-level regional polity. New investigations have also clarified the Middle Preclassic period in the Valley of Guatemala and revealed both antecedents, and possible early competitors, to Kaminaljuyu. Fresh data from outside the Valley of Guatemala provide information about the limits of the Kaminaljuyu polity, preventing the pendulum from swinging too far away from the "chiefdom" label and too far toward viewing the city as an expansionistic territorial state.

7.11. Photographs of artifacts recovered from Features 27 and 28 in the Central Plaza excavations at El Ujuxte.

The Settlement History of the Valley of Guatemala

Reconstructing the settlement history in the Central Highlands of Guatemala is a difficult task and requires the judicious use of a number of sources. Many of the projects that have studied Kaminaljuyu and the Valley of Guatemala have used different methods of ceramic analysis and developed distinctive classificatory schemes yielding conflicting ceramic chronologies (Ohi 1994b; Shook and Popenoe de Hatch 1999; Wetherington 1978). I have adopted the chronology proposed by Shook and Popenoe de Hatch (1999) and attempted to match the studies of others to that framework. A close reading is needed to make correct phase assignments in terms of that chronology, and even with close reading the data from some sources are simply not usable.

The most intensive survey of the Valley of Guatemala and the adjoining Canchón plateau, immediately to the southwest, was undertaken by the Pennsylvania State University Kaminaljuyu project (Michels 1979b; Michels and Wetherington 1979; Murdy 1984), but the study by Shook (1952) is still in many ways the most useful. The Pennsylvania State settlement data, though laudable in a great many respects, are complicated by several factors. Foremost is the heavy reliance upon obsidian hydration dating for making chronological assignments. In addition to the general problems inherent in obsidian hydration as a chronometric technique, even under the best of circumstances (Braswell 1992; Ridings 1996), the assessments of Murdy's valley-wide survey are made more problematic by the use of a small number of dates derived from surface materials. Dates derived from these assays often have been contradicted by subsequent investigations. A good example is the site of Naranjo, dated by the Pennsylvania State project to the Terminal Formative, when the occupation at the site is, in fact, Middle Preclassic (Arroyo 2006, 2010a). Further examples are provided by excavations of the Kaminaljuyu San Jorge (Popenoe de Hatch 1997), Miraflores II (Valdés and Popenoe de Hatch 1996), and A-IV-1 (Velásquez and Hermes 1992) projects, where ceramic dating contradicts the chronological assignments of the Pennsylvania State obsidian hydration dates. A further problem is that the ceramic chronology used by the Pennsylvania State project varies significantly from that now commonly accepted, not only in the time spans assigned to ceramic phases, but in the elimination of the Majadas and Santa Clara phases.

Figure 7.12 shows a relative measure of population history for the Valley of Guatemala and the Canchón plateau, deriving the number of sites per phase from Murdy (1984) and Shook (1952). I have drawn upon Murdy's data to the greatest extent possible by ignoring the dates from obsidian hydration and using only ceramic data reported in Appendix C of his dissertation. That procedure reduces by half the number of Preclassic sites that he reports, but makes dating of the remaining sites much more secure. Further, the data indicate only the presence of pottery from a given phase, and not its spatial distribution, meaning that site size for a given phase cannot be estimated.

The reconstructed demographic history of the region shows only scattered small settlements during the Early Preclassic Arévalo phase (ca. 1200–900 BCE). The similarity of Arévalo ceramics to Pacific coast assemblages is often interpreted to mean that the first agricultural colonists of the valley derived from the coast (Arroyo et al. 2007; Popenoe de Hatch 1991; Robinson et al. 2002). The great leap in population occurred in the Las Charcas phase, when the number of sites increased six-fold. The number of sites declined in the Providencia and Verbena phases, but Shook's data suggest that sites in those phases were larger than in Las Charcas, often much larger,

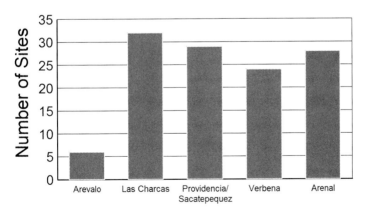

Preclassic Valley of Guatemala/ Canchon Plateau Sites

Number of sites excluding Kaminaljuyu

Phases

Data from Murdy (1985) Appendix C

7.12. Graph showing the number of sites identified for each phase of the Preclassic period in the Valley of Guatemala.

so that overall population probably grew, albeit by an unknown amount. Most importantly, we know that the area of occupation at Kaminaljuyu increased significantly during those two phases, strengthening the conclusion that valley-wide population continued to grow until the end of the Preclassic period.

The growth of population in the Las Charcas phase coincides with evidence for a noticeable increase in socio-political complexity and ceremonial activity. Figure 7.13 shows the distribution of population within the Valley of Guatemala and also indicates sites with public architecture and stone monuments. Sites with confirmed (excavated) public architecture from this time period include Kaminaljuyu (Shook 1951), Mulatto (Martínez Hidalgo 2003[1999]; Martínez Hidalgo et al. 2003[1998]), Naranjo (Arroyo 2006), and Rosario Naranjo (Jacobo 2003[1992]). At Mulatto a series of low platforms, ca. 2 m in height, form an octagon around a plaza, and a solitary mound, 6 m in height, is close by (Martínez Hidalgo 2003[1999]; Martínez Hidalgo et al. 2003[1998]). Small platforms in formal arrangements were also constructed at Kaminaljuyu by this time, as documented by the Miraflores II project (Martínez et al. 1996). An enigmatic but massive structure called the Gran Muro was found near Mound B-I-1. The wall, of unknown function, measured 7.5 m in height, and was traced for a length of 50 m before it passed under modern housing (Ohi 1994b). Small pyramidal structures were also present at Kaminaljuyu and Naranjo. Shook documented several more sites (Virginia, Arcos, Portillo, Charcas, Cieneguilla, and others) with small pyramidal mounds (6 m in height and less) and occupations that include the Las Charcas phase. But because these sites were occupied in subsequent periods, the unexcavated pyramidal structures cannot be dated securely to Las Charcas alone. The long, sinuous earthwork known as Montículo de la Culebra was also begun during the Las Charcas phase with the construction of low clay platforms. Martínez Hidalgo and Cabrera Morales (1999) state that the early construction of the La Culebra included a canal or canals with hydraulic functions. If that interpretation is correct, intensive agriculture within the Valley of Guatemala began much earlier than previously suspected. La Culebra will be discussed at greater depth in a following section.

Although Kaminaljuyu was an extensive settlement in the Las Charcas phase, Naranjo (Fig. 7.14) was the largest and most impressive of all the sites known for that period in the valley (Arroyo 2006, 2010a; Popenoe de Hatch 2002b; Shook 1952). Naranjo has a pyramidal mound 7 m

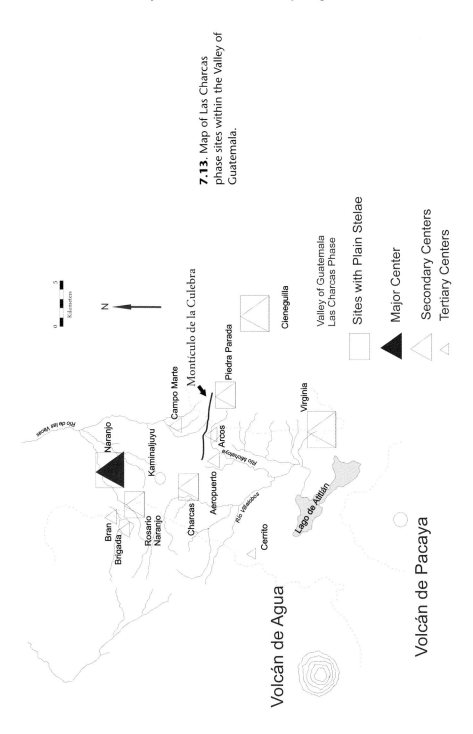

7.13. Map of Las Charcas phase sites within the Valley of Guatemala.

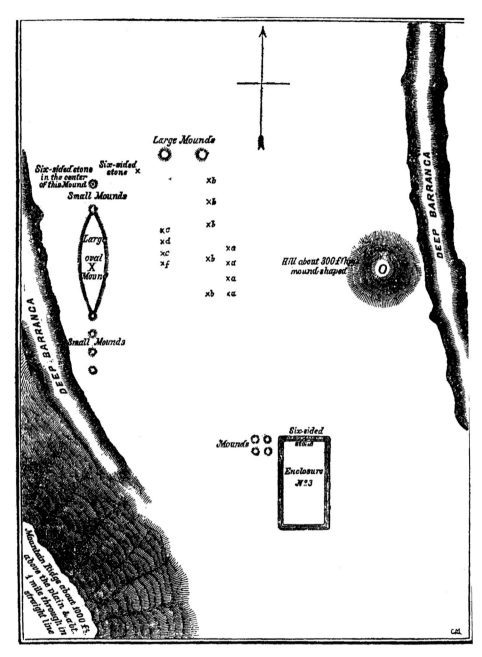

7.14. Map of Naranjo.

in height, a number of low platform mounds, and 34 plain monuments (stelae and basalt columns) aligned in three rows within the plaza east of the largest mounds (Arroyo 2006, 2010b; Pereira Figueroa et al. 2006). A fourth row was recently discovered on the west site of the large mounds (Arroyo 2010b). The unsculpted columnar basalt monuments may have been imported from over 30 km distance, and ritual offerings were found associated with many of them. Although the plain monuments dominate at Naranjo, there are vestiges of low-relief carving on one of the stelae, and three sculpted monuments documented at the house of the owner of the property may have come from the site (Arroyo 2006:5). Habitation areas, previously unknown at the site, were excavated by Arroyo, and the map of the site shows areas of habitation that exceed 100 ha (Arroyo 2010b: 49).

Naranjo's principal occupation dates to the Las Charcas phase (850–600 BCE) and continued into Providencia times (600–400 BCE), but population declined at the beginning of the Late Preclassic Verbena phase. Naranjo ceramics and figurines share similarities with complexes from the Pacific coast, including the use of some stylistically Olmec motifs, and attest to strong cultural relationships with both the central and western Guatemalan coastal zones (Arroyo and Paiz 2010).

Within Kaminaljuyu, Las Charcas phase occupation was significant all around the borders of Lake Miraflores, but especially heavy on the north side of the lake (Fig. 7.15). Public constructions, pyramidal mounds of 6–7 m in height, were erected at C-III-6, C-III-9, and C-III-10 (Shook 1951; Popenoe de Hatch 1991). Recent excavations have found substantial Las Charcas deposits east and south of the lake (de León and Alonzo 1996), as well as occupations north of the mapped mounds at the Parque la Democracia (Velásquez 2006). There was early platform mound construction in the A-IV-1 group, although probably for domestic purposes (Suasnávar Bolaños and Flores 1992; Velásquez 1993; Velásquez and Hermes 1992).

The Miraflores II project recovered substantial evidence of Las Charcas phase occupation south of Lake Miraflores, in the Miraflores plaza, during the Middle Preclassic as well (Popenoe de Hatch 2000, 2002b; Valdés 1997). Ceramic materials from the Las Charcas phase were found in four mounds, along with domestic features such as floors, hearths, and trash pits. East of the Miraflores plaza, habitation was scattered, but extended to approximately 400 m east of the mapped mounds, where Las Charcas phase deposits were recorded by the Carnegie near the modern Roosevelt Hospital (Kidder 1961).

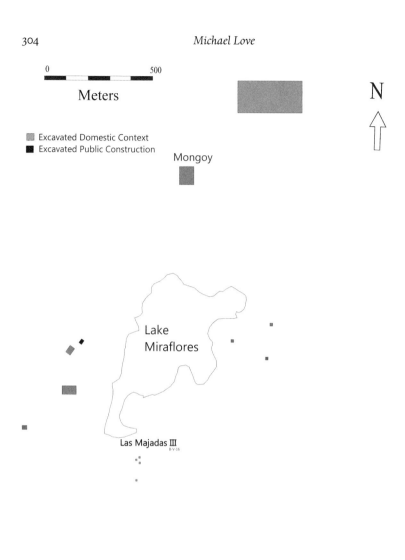

7.15. Map showing the Las Charcas phase occupation at Kaminaljuyu.

The relationship of Kaminaljuyu and Naranjo during the Las Charcas phase is enigmatic. Whether they were competitors, collaborators, or both part of the same expansive settlement is unclear. Both had public architecture during the Las Charcas phase, as well as extensive habitation areas, but it is as yet undetermined whether the remains in and around Kaminaljuyu were continuous or were, rather, a cluster of distinct habitation zones. Further, it cannot be determined at present whether any of the plain stelae known from Kaminaljuyu were erected during Las Charcas times, marking it as a political and ritual center. If Kaminaljuyu was a center, it may be that it emerged from a competitive landscape to win out over its neighbors and become the single dominant site within the Valley of Guatemala. If not, then Naranjo was probably the dominant site within the valley during the first half of the Middle Preclassic, and its habitants, and presumably its rulers, may have been part of the Kaminaljuyu florescence in the Providencia phase.

The Providencia Phase

The Providencia phase was a time of growing populations and increasing political centralization. Kaminaljuyu grew in size and may have eclipsed other Las Charcas phase settlements, including Naranjo, Piedra Parada, Santa Isabel, and Virginia. The distributions of population, major architecture, and stone monuments are shown in Figure 7.16. Kaminlajuyu was almost certainly the largest site in the valley by this time, with an extent of over 200 ha. The construction of large buildings increased steadily throughout this period (Escobedo et al. 1996; Popenoe de Hatch 1991), and the tradition of low-relief sculpture was begun. The earliest known low-relief sculpture from the site, Stela 9, was found by Ed Shook in a secure Majadas/Early Providencia phase context. A remarkable burial accompanied by 33 trophy skulls (Velásquez 1990) signals a dramatic change in social relations and the emergence of pronounced inequality. A small platform was built between Mound C-IV-1 and C-IV-4, and the "Edificio Quemado" was constructed at B-I-1 (Ohi 1994a). Figure 7.17 shows locations where public architecture and domestic occupations of the Providencia phase at Kaminaljuyu have been identified.

It is during the Providencia phase that the first irrigation systems linked to Lake Miraflores were built with the construction of the eponymous Miraflores canal (Barrientos Q. 1997a, 1999, 2000; Popenoe de Hatch 1997, 2002b). This early canal was 3.0 m wide, 5.8 m deep and at least 250 m in length (based on what has survived modern disturbances to the canal's original course). It is thought to have drawn water from Lake Miraflores for agricultural fields located south of the main architectural center. The extent of these fields, their composition, and the plants that might have been grown there are all unknown at present time. Popenoe de Hatch thinks it

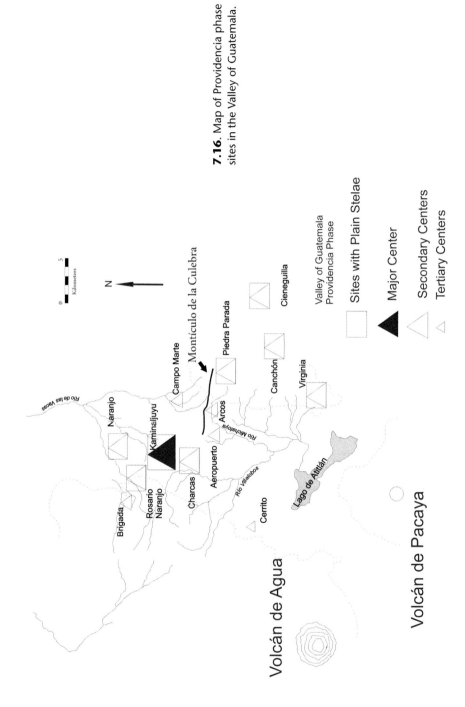

7.16. Map of Providencia phase sites in the Valley of Guatemala.

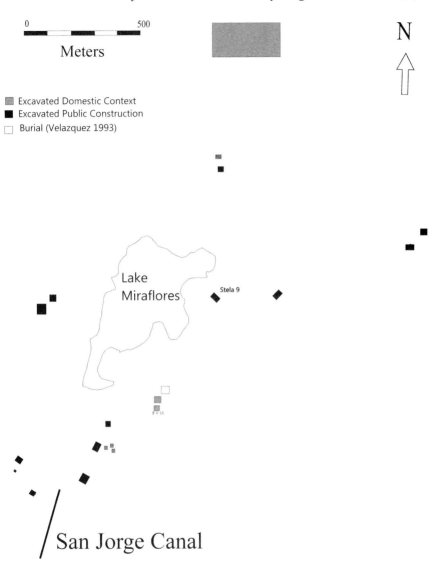

7.17. Map of Providencia phase occupation and construction at Kaminaljuyu.

unlikely that staple crops were grown in the irrigated fields, but rather believes that they were used for the cultivation of foods supplemental to the diet, such as vegetables, spices, and root crops (Popenoe de Hatch 1997:96). However, the scale and sophistication of the canal seem inconsistent with such a small scale of cultivation.

A significant enlargement of the Montículo de la Culebra was undertaken at this time (Martínez Hidalgo and Cabrera Morales 1999; Ortega et al. 1996; Ortega G. 2001; Ortega G. and Ito 2001). This structure raised the mound to a height exceeding 5 m, with a series of steps on both north and south faces. There is no firm evidence that the tumulus functioned as an aqueduct at this time, but given the evidence of a hydraulic function for prior and subsequent phases of construction, that proposition, among others, needs to be considered seriously.

The Late Preclassic Kaminaljuyu State

As the preceding discussion makes clear, political centralization, economic intensification, and the growth of social hierarchy were all underway within the Valley of Guatemala during the Middle Preclassic period. There may have been several political and ritual centers in the Valley of Guatemala during the Middle Preclassic, but by the end of the Providencia phase Kaminaljuyu clearly was in the ascendancy while other centers waned. Naranjo, Piedra Parada, Rosario Naranjo, and Mulatto declined or were abandoned completely by the start of the Late Preclassic Verbena phase. The timing of these events suggests that both population and political power became consolidated at Kaminaljuyu, although the murky dating of southern valley sites, such as Virginia and Santa Isabel, leaves unresolved the extent to which that is the case. Figure 7.18 shows the settlement distribution for the Valley of Guatemala in the Late Preclassic.

Although Kaminaljuyu was a large city and a major power during the Providencia phase, it was during the Late Preclassic Verbena and Arenal phases (ca. 400 BCE–100 CE) that it reached its peak in population, and its elite reached the fullest heights of political and economic power. A number of recent projects at Kaminaljuyu have greatly enhanced our knowledge of the Late Preclassic city (Ohi 1994b; Ohi et al. 1997; Popenoe de Hatch 1997, 2000; Valdés 1997; Velásquez 2006). All of these projects have found substantial Late Preclassic period materials throughout and beyond the mapped portion of the site, and clarified the urban nature of the city in the Verbena and Arenal phases.

The Carnegie map covers approximately 5 km² within which more than 200 structures were recorded. The map, of course, includes constructions of all time periods, but the total extent during the Late Preclassic is difficult to estimate. Michels (1979b) estimates the site covered a total area of ap-

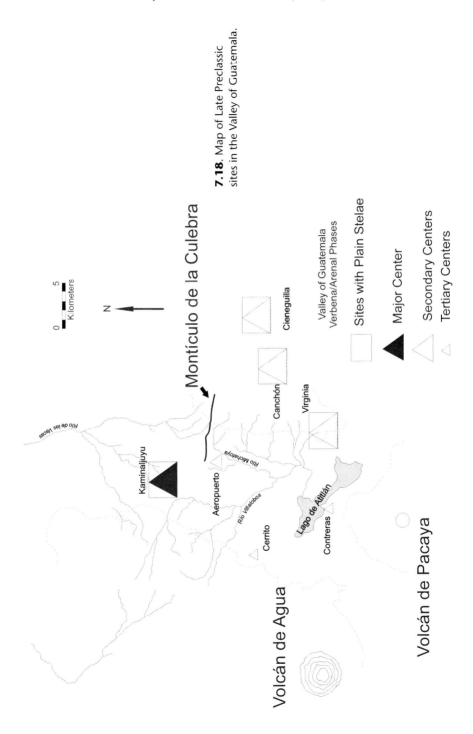

7.18. Map of Late Preclassic sites in the Valley of Guatemala.

proximately 7.5 km², but that figure represents its Late Classic maximum. Kaplan (2002, 2011) estimates at least 10 km² for the Late Preclassic city and argues that sites often considered separate and distinct settlements, such as Cruz de Cotio to the west, Rosario Naranjo to the north, Cementerio to the east, and Charcas to the south, should be considered part of Kaminaljuyu proper. Including all those sites would raise the city's expanse to over 14 km². Ponciano (2000) believes that all occupation north of the Montículo de la Culebra was part of an integrated Kaminaljuyu.

My own estimates are based on the following premises. The southern edge of the site seems to be well delimited close to the mapped portion of the site. The sparse remains found on the southeast quadrant of the Carnegie map by the Pennsylvania State testing program (Michels 1979c) and the trajectory of the documented Miraflores and San Juan canals seemingly indicate a large agricultural zone forming the southern and southeastern boundaries of the site. Large *barrancas* form natural boundaries to the southwest and east, leaving the only doubt about the city's extent to be its northern limit. In that direction there is good evidence for residential areas north of the mound areas mapped by the Carnegie (Velásquez 2006). Excavations within the Parque la Democracia, approximately 200 m north of Mound C-I-6, found evidence of Preclassic habitation in the absence of visible mounds. On the basis of that evidence, we might stipulate that habitation stretched north to the barranca 100 m from Parque la Democracia. It is possible, perhaps even probable, that such habitation areas lay between the mapped mounds of Kaminaljuyu and the site of Ross, which is only a few hundred meters from the northwest edge of the Kaminaljuyu map. Shook (1952) clearly considered Ross to be part of Kaminaljuyu, despite its distinctive name. However, there is little basis to extend the city's northern limit beyond Ross. It is more than a full kilometer from Ross to Rosario Naranjo, with no empirical basis to speculate that settlement extended across that expanse. It is also a full kilometer from the eastern edge of the Carnegie site map to Cruz Cotio and Garland, again without empirical evidence of intervening settlement.

While it is surely possible that the site was larger, present evidence makes it unlikely that the urban core of Kaminaljuyu exceeded 8 km² during the Late Preclassic (Fig. 7.19), including the roughly 25 ha occupied by Lake Miraflores. Ponciano's arguments for a greater Kaminaljuyu extending to the Montículo de la Culebra certainly have merit, but the present evidence does not demonstrate continuous occupation across that large expanse, which

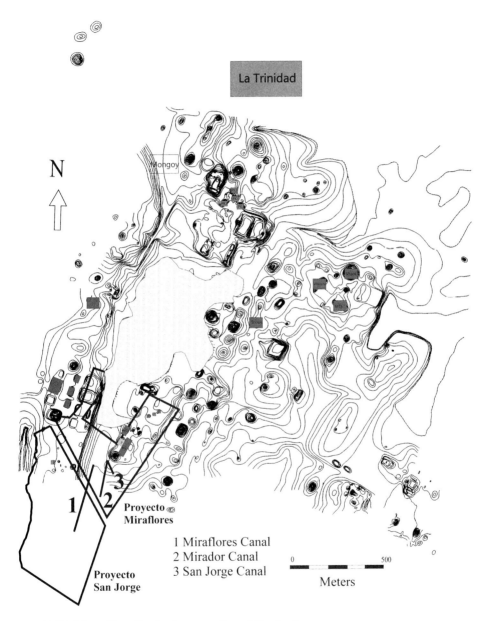

7.19. Map of Late Preclassic occupation at Kaminaljuyu.

would encompass over 30 km². As detailed below, there is no problem, in my opinion, in viewing all of this area as politically subject to Kaminaljuyu, which may render debate about precise limits moot. But to view it all as one uninterrupted urban expanse is hyperbolic. Even at 8 km², however, Kaminaljuyu can comfortably be described as urban and among the largest of Mesoamerican cities in the Late Preclassic.

Within the central core of Kaminaljuyu, extensive monumental constructions were raised. Ponciano (2000) estimates that 70 percent of the structures visible at Kaminaljuyu were constructed in the Preclassic period, although many were extensively modified during the site's demographic maximum in the Late Classic. Mound E-III-3, the largest mound at the site, was built in the Late Preclassic and stood over 21 m tall (Shook and Kidder 1952). Formal plaza arrangements, including an E-group within zone A-IV (Murdy 1990; Valdés 1997), covered over 2 km².

Irrigation and Intensive Agriculture

During the Verbena phase, around 400 BCE, the Miraflores canal was filled in and replaced by the larger San Jorge canal and the smaller Mirador canal (Barrientos Q. 1997a, 1999, 2000; Popenoe de Hatch 2002b; Valdés 1998). The canals functioned up until approximately 100 CE, when Lake Miraflores went dry. The San Jorge canal subsequently was filled during the Santa Clara phase (Barrientos Q. 2000). Smaller ditches have been located perpendicular to the San Jorge canal, which diverted water from the major canals to agricultural fields still attested by areas of organically rich soils and preserved furrows (Barrientos Q. 2000; Valdés and Popenoe de Hatch 1996); a system of raised fields has also been proposed (Barrientos Q. 1997a; Popenoe de Hatch 1997). The Late Preclassic canal system was both larger and more technically sophisticated than the Miraflores canal, including features to control the volume and the speed of the water (Barrientos Q. 1997b), implying that the scale of intensive agricultural production was increased relative to the earlier system.

The intensification of production via the enlarged canal system was almost certainly undertaken under the control of a central authority. What are interpreted as administrative buildings lie along the course of the San Jorge canal. Near the agricultural fields, two Arenal phase contexts, Cocina 1 and Cocina 3, revealed evidence of large-scale food preparation (Popenoe de Hatch 1997), probably for the feeding of large work parties.

Our view of how much economic intensification took place at Kaminaljuyu during the Late Preclassic hinges on whether the Montículo de la Culebra was used as an aqueduct. In the colonial period, the Pinula aqueduct used La Culebra as the base for a brick-lined canal that carried water to Guatemala City (Navarrete and Luján Muñoz 1986). The extant ruins of the La Culebra tumulus run a length of approximately 4.5 km, beginning in the hills southwest of modern Guatemala City and continuing at least to La Aurora, the location of the modern zoo. Ohi (2001) believes that La Culebra ran an additional 1.4 km and terminated near Kaminaljuyu Mounds A and B, but that opinion is untested by archaeological excavation. As mentioned above, although construction of La Culebra began in the Las Charcas phase and was expanded in the Providencia phase, its largest episode of construction was during the Arenal phase, when portions of the tumulus reached 7 m in height. Two recent projects have found remnants of a stone-lined canal along the summit of this structure (Ortega et al. 1996; Ortega G. 2001; Ortega G. and Ito 2001; Valle 2007), indicating a hydraulic function.

Despite these exciting data, the interpretation of La Culebra as a Late Preclassic aqueduct should not be granted lightly. First, Navarrete and Luján (1986) note that it is uncertain whether La Culebra was a single continuous structure, for the earliest colonial written records and plans present it as a series of mounds following the same alignment, rather than being a single structure. It is possible that what had been a continuous structure was pierced and broken after the Preclassic period, but we cannot be certain. Second, the dating of the canal at the top of the Verbena phase structure is not secure. Martínez Hidalgo and Cabrera Morales (1999) report that materials within the canal were mixed and included Classic period remains. That observation is not fatal, as it isn't unreasonable to find later material in an abandoned channel, but it does beg for further investigation. Third, even if the canal did carry water, it may not have been for agricultural purposes. Sophisticated hydraulic systems are known at other Late Preclassic sites in the southern region, including Chocolá, Takalik Abaj, and Izapa (Gómez Rueda 1995; Kaplan and Valdés 2004; Marroquín 2005). These hydraulic systems were not agricultural, but seem to have controlled water largely for symbolic and ritual reasons (and probably also practical reasons such as drainage). The location of La Culebra is precisely atop the continental divide; water falling to the south drained into Lake Atitlán, while water falling to the north drained to the Río Las Vacas and thence to the Río Motagua. Location, therefore, may have had tremendous symbolic, even cosmological, meaning that motivated the construction and use of the canal for the manipulation of water.

That La Culebra functioned as an aqueduct from its inception in the Las Charcas period to the end of the Late Preclassic is a strong and tantalizing possibility, but probably can never be proven. Given the evidence of large and sophisticated canal construction at Kaminaljuyu proper, the engineering of such a project would have been well within the capabilities of Late Preclassic society in the Valley of Guatemala. Like so much of Kaminaljuyu and its hinterland, La Culebra is now so badly damaged that we may never be able to garner sufficient evidence to decide the matter one way or the other.

RECONSTRUCTING SOCIAL AND POLITICAL STRUCTURES AT LATE PRECLASSIC KAMINALJUYU

All of the evidence above makes clear that Late Preclassic Kaminaljuyu was a large city, with impressive ceremonial/public architecture, and a large population supported by intensive agriculture. But what was the nature of political and social organization at the site and within the Valley of Guatemala? Survey data are confused, and data from domestic contexts have not been published in a way that would allow a reconstruction of household life (as opposed to just examining "domestic deposits"). Some broad characteristics of the regional system can be gleaned from extant data, however, and these are supplemented by burial data. Information on exchange systems provides some further insight. Finally, the presence of an enormous sculptural corpus and early hieroglyphic texts is suggestive, but not decisive.

Settlement Patterns during the Late Preclassic

Within the Valley of Guatemala, the population grew substantially during the Late Preclassic period. Much of the growth took place in Kaminaljuyu itself, and additional settlements, both large and small, developed within its immediate environs.

Outside of Kaminaljuyu, the most significant growth took place just north of Lake Amatitlán. There, a number of large sites developed with large mounds arranged in parallel plazas. The sites of Virginia, Santa Isabel,

Cieneguilla and Canchón all have such arrangements; Virginia and Santa Isabel also have plain stelae. The dating of these sites is of varying reliability; only recently has Santa Isabel been excavated and the results await publication (Arroyo pers. comm., 2012). The data from Piedra Parada show that the twin plaza site plan was present by the Las Charcas phase, but it may have endured until the end of the Preclassic period in the southern valley. Ceramic data indicate that Virginia and Canchón were occupied during the Late Preclassic, but there are no ceramic data for Cieneguilla. The surface ceramics from Santa Isabel do not include Late Preclassic materials, but the data are from small lots, so they may not be definitive (Murdy 1984; Shook 1952).

We can, for the sake of argument, consider the idea that this southern cluster represents a polity or polities that are independent of Kaminaljuyu. The case for that position is that throughout the Preclassic sequence there are large sites south of the Montículo de la Culebra, with some degree of separation from the sites north of La Culebra. Unfortunately, the imprecise dating of Cieneguilla and Virginia, sites with both major architecture and plain stelae, does not allow us to examine this theory in detail. Arguing against the idea that these major sites are independent of Kaminaljuyu is the evidence for intense interaction between people of Kaminaljuyu and those of the Escuintla area. Medrano (2000) suggests that people and goods flowed freely through the Palín pass, the main route to the coast, which lies immediately west of Lake Amatitlán. Bove's (2011) map of sites with plain stelae suggests a route of highway-like scale between Kaminaljuyu and the coast of Escuintla. Such interaction does not seem likely if the southern valley was governed by a group independent of or hostile to Kaminaljuyu's rulers.

If we hypothesize that the "southern cluster" sites were Kaminaljuyu dependencies, then we can propose a five-tiered hierarchy for the valley, with Kaminaljuyu as the first tier and the multi-plaza sites as the second. Below those come the sites with multiple large mounds and plain monuments, such as Cerrito, Charcas, and possibly Bran (Murdy 1984; Shook 1952). A fourth tier would include sites with large mounds but no large sculpture (I exclude the numerous "mushroom stones" from the category of "large sculpture"), and the fifth would consist of non-mound sites. We might think of combining the third and fourth tiers, but even a four-tier hierarchy suggests a complex system of government compatible with a state, especially when that hierarchy covers 1200 km². The common ground plans, the orientation of the site axes, and the absence of stelae representing rulers outside of Kaminaljuyu all suggest that the entire region was dominated by Kaminaljuyu.

Despite my desire to label the Kaminaljuyu polity as a state, I wish to avoid statements that attribute absolute control over all aspects of social and economic life to the elite of Kaminaljuyu. I don't believe there is evidence to show that economic production and distribution, or even ritual, were overseen by "The Kaminaljuyu State." I do, however, think that there is evidence that the elite of Kaminaljuyu had effective power over many aspects of life at the secondary and tertiary centers of the valley.

Social Inequality

Domestic excavation data from Kaminaljuyu and for the Valley of Guatemala as a whole exist, but are not published in a form that allows a quantitative analysis of household differentiation. It might be possible in the future to statistically analyze the numerous bell-shaped pits and their refuse contexts, if all the collections have been preserved. The possible identification of elite residential structures by the A-IV-1 Project (Velásquez and Hermes 1996) is intriguing, but the published data allow little more than general comparison with other residential zones at the site. The excavations there recovered high-status burials, large numbers of storage vessels, and evidence of the production of greenstone and obsidian artifacts (Suasnávar Bolaños 1993; Valdés and Popenoe de Hatch 1996).

From excavation data, the best evidence for social inequality comes from the numerous burials excavated by the many Kaminaljuyu projects. Published burial data include the Carnegie excavations (Shook and Kidder 1952), the Grupo A-IV-1 Project (López 1993), the San Jorge Project, the Miraflores II Project (Valdés 1997), the El Mulatto site excavations (Martínez Hidalgo 2003[1999]; Martínez Hidalgo et al. 2003[1998]), the Mongoy project (Ohi and Ohi 1994), and others.

The Mound E-III-3 excavations revealed the richest Preclassic burials known in the Maya territory, and undoubtedly represent the remains of Kaminaljuyu rulers. Both Tomb I and Tomb II were large, multi-tiered burial chambers constructed using massive wooden timbers. Although heavily damaged before they were excavated by Ed Shook, Tomb I contained over 298 ceramic vessels and 47 additional objects, and Tomb 2 contained 157 ceramic vessels and at least 50 other objects (Figs. 7.20, 7.21). Both date to the Arenal phase.

Another interment in Mound D-IV-2, excavated by Stephen Borhegyi, is accompanied by 71 ceramic vessels, jade, and stone mortars (Murdy 1984). Because of an obsidian blade found "in the neck" of the individual (Murdy 1984), Borhegyi interpreted the feature as a dedicatory sacrifice. Without forensic analysis of the skeleton, however, that conclusion is unconfirmed, and it may well be that the feature is a third high-status burial.

A fourth possible elite burial is the "Tumba Miraflores," excavated by Gustavo Espinoza and described by Murdy (1984). That burial's offerings, if they are such, included Silhouette Sculpture 2, 11 prismatic basalt columns set along the side walls, 17 small ceramic vessels, a large obsidian blade, a complete human skull, an incomplete human skull (the cranial vault) painted red, 6 beads of clay, jade, and sulphur. All those elements rested on a cap of fired clay near the top of the pit containing the primary burial.

Other burials at Kaminaljuyu range from relatively affluent (more than a dozen offerings) to relatively impoverished (no offerings), so that the complete data from Late Preclassic burials demonstrate a wide social gap between rulers and the mass of Kaminaljuyu's populace.

Sculpture

The Late Preclassic florescence at Kaminaljuyu is also marked by an enormous sculptural corpus encompassing many styles, including early Maya stelae with hieroglyphic inscriptions, silhouettes, altars, and potbelly figures. The earliest securely dated text is from Stela 10, excavated by Ed Shook in a Verbena phase context, and dating to no later than 200 BCE if the Shook/Hatch chronology is correct. Curiously, there are no known Long Count dates on any of the sculptures at Kaminaljuyu, although both Altars 1 and 2 have a format much like Takalik Abaj Stelae 1 and 2, which suggests that their eroded central panels did at one time include such inscriptions.

The sculptural corpus of Kaminaljuyu is both large and diverse. Parson's (1986) catalog lists 127 sculptures, Ariadne Prater's catalog (2007) exceeds 250 pieces, and the total may exceed 300 (Ponciano 2000). The extraordinary size of the Kaminaljuyu corpus exceeds that known from anywhere else in Late Preclassic Mesoamerica, and its great diversity has been interpreted as evidence of a multi-ethnic community (Graham 1979; Love 2004; Proskouriakoff 1971).

Michael Love

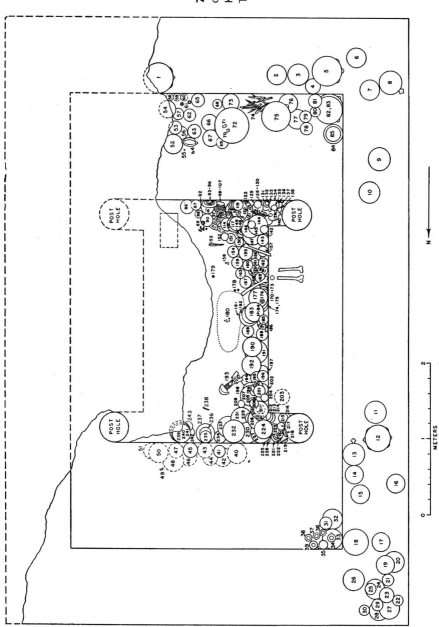

7.20. Plan drawing of Kaminaljuyu Tomb 1.

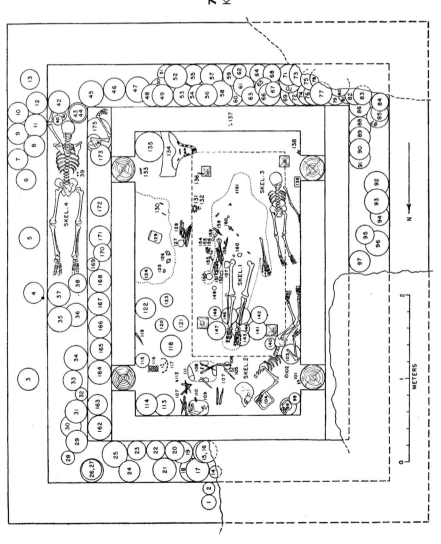

7.21. Plan drawing of Kaminaljuyu Tomb 2.

The role of art, especially the representation of rulers, in the construction of an early Maya ideology of rulership has received much attention. The subject matter of the Kaminaljuyu corpus is highly varied, but several themes are represented with great frequency. The first is that of the presentation of subjects to rulers (Doering and Collins 2010; Fahsen 2002). In these scenes, kneeling individuals are shown before rulers who are enthroned or standing with full regalia. Fahsen (2002) interprets the kneeling individuals as captives, but Guernsey (pers. comm., 2006) and Doering and Collins (2010, following Guernsey) note that their postures and gestures may reflect respect and submission, but not necessarily capture. The second theme is deity impersonation, in which rulers are depicted with costumes and/or masks representing divine beings. These latter representations embodied new ideologies of rulership based upon creation mythologies that anticipate some narratives found in the *Popol Vuh* text (Guernsey 2006; Guernsey Kappelman 2001, 2002).

Kaplan (2001, 2002) argues that these sculptures are evidence of early sacred kingship at the site and thus imply the existence of a state-level political system. As previously noted, I believe that it is a fundamental mistake to equate rulership with the state. Rulership in Mesoamerica has a long history that precedes clear evidence of states, and titles of rulership can be used by governing polities of greatly varying sizes (Martin and Grube 2000). Nor can a state-level political system be assumed solely on the basis of ideological statements by the elite, whether representational or textual. It is the nature of such ideologies to aggrandize and exaggerate. There are many examples of rulers who dress up in costumes, proclaiming themselves to be divine, while governing political systems that are, fundamentally, something less complex than states, whether we call them chiefdoms, Middle Range Societies, or something else (Krader 1968). However, I take the sculptures and texts to represent evidence for firm social stratification and the presence of a Late Preclassic elite that possessed economic wealth, political power, and literacy.

Kaminaljuyu and the Valley of Guatemala: A Summary

Centralized political power in the hands of the elite is well documented at Kaminaljuyu in the Late Preclassic period by the mass of public construction, monument erection, and intensive irrigation-based systems of subsistence production. Social stratification is documented by extreme differences in grave offerings and by the ideology presented in sculpted monuments. However, these traits, of themselves, do not define a state. States, even those that we label as city-states, are regional political systems. Even the classic city-states of Greece and Sumeria controlled hinterlands, and it is worth recalling that the original definition of the state as a four-tiered hierarchy was based upon the Sumerian polities that we call city-states. The more extensive "territorial state" (Trigger 1993, 2003) is a different type of entity and may, in fact, be considered a type of empire. Moreover, the most significant distinction between states and simpler forms of government may best be thought of as one of bureaucracy (Service 1975). States have more complex systems of government that involve the formation of institutions for administration. In the absence of written records, and perhaps even with them, a regional settlement system is the best evidence for the existence of such administrative structures (Spencer and Redmond 2004). The most convincing evidence, therefore, for a Kaminaljuyu state in the Late Preclassic comes from its control of a stratified regional settlement hierarchy that encompassed all of the Valley of Guatemala. The distribution of sites with large public mounds, plain stelae, and other monuments within the Valley of Guatemala suggests that these sites were second, third, and fourth tiers of control. Regrettably, there is still much we do not know about how the Kaminaljuyu polity operated both economically and politically, but its status as a state should be in doubt no longer.

Kaminaljuyu's Influence Outside of the Valley of Guatemala

Having presented the case for a state-level political system within the Valley of Guatemala, it remains to examine whether Kaminaljuyu's political influence extended beyond the valley's limits. Kaminaljuyu is posited by some (for example Kaplan 2001, 2002, 2011) to be the center of a larger polity that encompassed most, if not all, of the Miraflores Ceramic Sphere. I argue here, however, that the Miraflores Sphere was a region of cultural and economic interaction, but not an integrated political system, within the large Southern City-State Culture.

Despite the general perception that Kaminaljuyu was a dominant force in the Guatemalan highlands during the Late Preclassic period, there is no evidence that it exerted direct political control outside of the Valley of Guatemala. In fact, the areas immediately west of the Valley of Guatemala show less evidence of interaction with Kaminaljuyu's population in the Late Preclassic than in previous periods (Braswell and Robinson 2011; Love 2011; Popenoe de Hatch 1997). During the Providencia phase, the ceramics of

Chimaltenango and Sacatepequez are very similar to those of Kaminaljuyu, hence the often-used Providencia/Sacatepquez phase name. At the beginning of the Verbena period, however, the ceramics of those regions show increasing divergence from Kaminaljuyu, with fewer shared attributes and little evidence of direct exchange (Popenoe de Hatch 1997; Shook and Popenoe de Hatch 1999). Economic data also indicate decreasing interaction between Kaminaljuyu and its neighbors to the west. During the Providencia phase, Kaminaljuyu ceases to receive obsidian from the San Martín Jilotepeque source, which had previously provided 12% of the obsidian consumed (Braswell and Amador 1999). From that time on, obsidian from San Martín Jilotepeque flowed exclusively to the west, through the highlands and to Pacific piedmont sites, where it represented a majority of the obsidian at San Andrés Semetebaj, Takalik Abaj, and sites in the Chiapas highlands (Love 2011).

While Kaminaljuyu's economic contacts and cultural influences extended along trade routes into the northern highlands (Sharer and Sedat 1987) and even farther into the Maya lowlands, all indicators are that its primary economic networks, cultural contacts, and possible political influence lie to the south and the east, within the Miraflores Ceramic Sphere (Demarest and Sharer 1986; Demarest 2011) and the larger Southern City-State Culture (Love 2011). In addition to the shared ceramic styles within this zone, the obsidian exchange network of El Chayal reached to the coast and thence to the west, toward the Soconusco. It should be noted, however, that the sites of western El Salvador within the Miraflores Ceramic Sphere, such as Chalchuapa, derived the bulk of their obsidian from the Ixtepeque source, indicating their own economic independence from Kaminaljuyu.

Kaminaljuyu sat in a prime location to control the exchange of many products across the Central Guatemalan cordillera. In addition to obsidian, other important items that flowed through the trade systems certainly included jade and possibly cacao (Popenoe de Hatch 1997). Cotton textiles and salt from the coastal plain might also have flowed into the highlands via Kaminaljuyu. While individuals at Kaminaljuyu may have profited from the trade networks that intersected at the site, there is no evidence that the Kaminaljuyu state organized the production and distribution of the commodities that passed through the Valley of Guatemala. Recent survey in the area of the El Chayal quarries shows no evidence of large sites, workshops, or control facilities (Mejía Amaya and Suyuc Ley 1998, 2000). There is some limited evidence of jade working in the A-IV-4 area and of prismatic blade manufacturing in the Miraflores II project area (Suasnávar Bolaños 1993), but no indications that such work was centrally organized, nor that it was of large scale. There is much better evidence for organized production on the Escuintla coast (Bove 2011), reinforcing the model that Kaminaljuyu's elite benefited from trade, but did not control it. Kaminaljuyu may have been either an *entrepôt* (Abu-Lughod 1991) or a port of trade (Brown 1977; Chapman 1971) for traders moving across the continental divide rather than a producer of finished goods.

The shared ceramic styles of regions within the Miraflores Sphere resulted from a complex set of interactions between individuals and groups throughout the central highlands of Guatemala and those living on the Pacific coast. Sourcing studies over a long period have shown that ceramics in the Miraflores sphere were not traded over great distances (Demarest 2011). These studies in tandem indicate that the Miraflores Ceramic Sphere was not formed by the simple imitation of Kaminaljuyu ceramics at other sites but through the exchange of ideas in both directions, as some important Miraflores types originated on the coast.

Similarly, the potbelly style of sculpture, sometimes linked to the Miraflores Ceramic Sphere and read as a marker of Kaminaljuyu influence, had its center of greatest occurrence on the coast of Escuintla (Guernsey 2012; Rodas 1993). The distribution of the form extends far beyond the area of the Miraflores Sphere into Chiapas and beyond (Guernsey 2012; Scott 1988), but overlaps with the early Southern Maya style of relief sculpture only in some locations, such as Kaminaljuyu and the Late Preclassic piedmont centers of Cotzumalguapa, Chocolá, and Takalik Abaj. In short, Kaminaljuyu is often seen as the source of cultural traits that in fact originated at many different points within the Southern City-State Culture.

Bove (2011) has recently critiqued the idea that the Miraflores Ceramic Sphere was based on the political hegemony of Kaminaljuyu. He notes first that the distribution of the Miraflores Sphere ceramic types is not uniform throughout the coast of Escuintla.

If the "Miraflores political sphere" stretched from Kaminaljuyu to the small Finca Arizona site eighty-five km directly south on the coast how did it bypass Los Cerritos-Sur? Los Cerritos-Sur is a huge Middle-Terminal Formative regional center only fifty-six km directly south of Kaminaljuyu and strategically located to control movement at the foot of the two major passes into the central highlands. Los Cerritos-Sur has numerous obsidian workshops, monumental sculpture in the Monte Alto style of potbellies and heads but no Kaminaljuyu style sculpture or any other indication of Kaminaljuyu political, social, economic, or ideological control (Bove 2011: 113).

Most importantly, Bove sees the political systems of coastal Escuintla as consisting of a number of small polities, without overarching integrative mechanisms:

> In central Escuintla the sites are regularly distributed. Although there are significant size differences, Thiessen diagrams...suggest a high degree of spatial regularity and by inference, economic competition. Rank-size curves...of this and the ensuing Late-Terminal Preclassic period are convex suggesting that no single site dominates the region (Bove 2011:102).

The regional system described by Bove is not what one would expect if Escuintla were part of a Kaminaljuyu territorial state *cum* empire. Instead, the data suggest that the Miraflores Ceramic Sphere was the product of factors other than political integration.

The distribution of Maya-style stelae along the piedmont, especially at Cotzumalguapa, Chocolá, and Takalik Abaj, is also often discussed as though it demonstrates a homogenous "Southern Maya" regional culture. But iconographic similarities merely demonstrate elite interaction, not political integration. Obviously, there were elite interactions across the entire region that are reflected in writing, calendrics, and iconography (Guernsey 2006), but those interactions extend across ethnic lines and go far beyond the Southern Maya Region, into the Maya lowlands, and as far as the Gulf Coast. Politically, however, the landscape of the Late Preclassic southern zone was fragmented, with polities of varying size and varying degrees of centralization.

DOS CIUDADES, UN CAMINO: THE GROWTH OF SOCIAL COMPLEXITY AND THE ORIGINS OF THE STATE IN THE SOUTHERN MAYA REGION

The development of social complexity in the Southern Maya Region was a process played out over a period of 1500 years. It was not a tale of smooth, consistent growth, but rather a process punctuated by episodic collapse and subsequent reintegration. The two cases studied show the diversity of forms that a state society, even when restricted to a subcategory of city-state, can take. Research into this region and this topic is not yet mature, the data are uneven, and there are many gaps in our knowledge, but the general outlines of regional prehistory are now taking form.

In the coastal case, El Ujuxte developed following the collapse of elite power at La Blanca, more or less as a direct successor and without a host of direct competing centers. During the transition from the Middle to the Late Preclassic, the elite of El Ujuxte established dominance over a large region of the coast, going beyond the prior model of La Blanca in size and scope. The El Ujuxte polity endured longer than any previous polity in the region, perhaps as long as 600 years. In the Guatemalan highlands, the development of the Kaminaljuyu polity was more gradual through the course of the Middle Preclassic, with a dramatic growth in size at the onset of the Late Preclassic, when Kaminaljuyu emerged out of a crowded political landscape within the Valley of Guatemala. A number of early competitors to Kaminaljuyu were present in the Middle Preclassic, but eventually were eclipsed or perhaps subjugated.

In both cases, El Ujuxte and Kaminaljuyu, we see clear evidence of increasing elite power in the Late Preclassic period. Wealth became increasingly concentrated, the labor expended in monumental construction surged, and subsistence production was intensified. An ideology linking rulership to divine forces of creation and renewal was manifested, although in varying ways, through monuments, architecture, and ritual. At Kaminaljuyu, but not El Ujuxte, the existence of early texts attests to the creation of new forms of knowledge that further cemented elite authority.

The household data from El Ujuxte point to greater elite control over various aspects of the economy. At Kaminaljuyu we lack systematic household data, and also lack clear information about the basis and extent of elite power beyond the ability to harness labor and support artists. We do not understand fully the extent of the Kaminaljuyu elite's involvement in economic production and long-distance exchange. That is, we do not know whether elites actively organized the economy or merely facilitated it. We also do not fully understand the extent to which the intensification of subsistence production through irrigation technology contributed to the city's wealth.

It is clear from these two examples that the early states of the Southern City-State Culture were not all the same thing. Kaminaljuyu and El Ujuxte, along with Takalik Abaj, Izapa, and other early states, were all subject to the same broad historical patterns of Preclassic Mesoamerica, but each had a distinctly local history. Despite their intellectual, cultural, and economic ties, each has something different to teach us about the nature of early states.

To close, I will return to the opening thoughts of this essay, and ask what is the value of the state as a concept? How does identifying Kaminaljuyu, El Ujuxte, and other cities as states increase our understanding of them? Does saying that the early city-states formed a network of economic and cultural interaction elucidate or obscure their nature?

I see value in the concept of a state, even if we discard other aspects of the neo-evolutionary model and even if we acknowledge that early states were not all the same thing. If used properly, the concept of state allows us to recognize just how distinctive they were compared to the societies that preceded them, as summarized in the following passage from Morton Fried (1960:36):

> the notion of the state is something more than formally organized society, or even the aggregate of institutions and apparatus of social control at some specified level of complexity. Central to the concept of a state...is an order of stratification, specifically a system whereby different members of society enjoy invidiously different rights of access to the basic productive necessities of life...Indeed the state is something more than this—a formal organization of power including but going beyond the social control functions of kinship. This formal organization of power has as its central task the protection (and often the extension) of the order of stratification.

The concept of a state allows us to analyze political structure apart from the development of class and from the practices of "high culture" that reinforce and legitimate class distinctions. Once those concepts are separated we can more productively, and more profoundly, address the "how" about social life, culture, and the structures of political power. Within the present study, the concept of state helps us to recognize the importance of the transition from the Middle Preclassic to the Late Preclassic within the Southern Maya Region and beyond. Social inequality, titles of rulership, and high culture existed earlier, but it was in the Late Preclassic period that "this formal organization of power" reached an unprecedented level that dramatically altered how people lived their lives. Undoubtedly, the "how" questions are ultimately more interesting than arguments over terminology, but in this case, the "what" and the "how" are bound up together. Understanding the "how" of early Mesoamerican states and the "how" of many dimensions of social life ultimately begins with a good argument about what a state is and when it comes to be.

ACKNOWLEDGMENTS

I thank the participants in the 2007 Penn Museum Conference for their comments on the first draft of this essay. Bob Sharer, Loa Traxler, and two anonymous reviewers provided helpful comments for the revisions. Fred Bove also read an earlier draft and offered very cogent suggestions for improvement. I am indebted to Fred's analysis of Escuintla settlement patterns for insight into the nature of the Kaminaljuyu polity. I am equally indebted to Bárbara Arroyo for sharing the results of her research at both Naranjo and Kaminaljuyu. My knowledge of Kaminaljuyu has also benefitted from discussions with Marion Popenoe de Hatch and the late Juan Antonio Valdés. I thank Julia Guernsey for sharing her considerable insights into Preclassic Mesoamerica and for helping to develop many of the ideas presented here and in other works. I am also grateful for her close editing of the text. Any errors in grammar, spelling, or organization were caused by my subsequent "massaging" of the text. Investigations at La Blanca and El Ujuxte were carried out under the auspices of the Instituto de Antropología e Historia de Guatemala; I thank the personnel of the Departamento de Prehispánicos y Coloniales for their help and support. Research at El Ujuxte was supported by National Science Foundation Grants (SBR-9807304, SBR-96171123, SBR-9510991), with additional support from the Heinz Foundation, the Wenner-Gren Foundation for Anthropological Research, Sonoma State University, and the Universidad del Valle de Guatemala. Financial support for the excavations at La Blanca came from the New World Archaeological Foundation, the Wenner-Gren Foundation for Anthropological Research, the National Geographic Society, the Mesoamerica Center in the Department of Art and Art History at the University of Texas at Austin, and National Science Foundation Grant BCS-0451024. A grant from the Foundation for the Advancement of Mesoamerican Studies, Inc. helped support the analysis of materials associated with La Blanca Monument 3.

8

Cultural and Environmental Components of the First Maya States: A Perspective from the Central and Southern Maya Lowlands

RICHARD D. HANSEN

Archaeology is the only discipline that can tell us how government began, the nature of the world's first governments, and the role those governments played in the organization of their respective political systems. (Haas 1982:216)

Archaic states are stratified into a series of classes including full-time occupational specialists, and are topped by a highly centralized, hierarchical government that rules a territory with more or less defined boundaries. (Sharer 1994:139)

The search for a comprehensive understanding of the development of social and political complexity in Mesoamerica has attracted considerable interest and prompted significant debate. Much of the controversial posturing that has surrounded this topic can be attributed to the lack of adequate or uniform definitions, incomplete data, faulty or inadequate interpretations of available data, and the exploitation of obscure semantics to justify specific theoretical positions. Recent archaeological investigations throughout the Maya lowlands have provided new data pertaining to the sophistication and complexity of early Maya "civilization." The resultant information, reviewed here in diachronic format and in synchronic contexts, provides an empirical foundation for conclusions and hypotheses that can be further investigated and tested.

This chapter proposes that the first lowland Maya states began to emerge in the Middle Preclassic period (ca. 1000–400 BCE), perhaps jointly with the developments at La Venta, and flourished during the Late Preclassic period (ca. 300 BCE–150 CE), led by developments in the Mirador Basin of northern Guatemala, and southern Campeche, Mexico. The resultant hypotheses derived from a series of multi-disciplinary investigations suggest: (1) The Preclassic lowland Maya developed one of the first states in Mesoamerica through a sequentially defined process that evolved into a four-tier hierarchy of settlement distribution and socio-political organization within a specific territorial area; (2) the origins of states in Mesoamerica, and in particular within the Mirador Basin, are found in the Middle Preclassic period, between ca. 1000 and 400 BCE, with more expansive states appearing by the latter part of the Middle Preclassic and the early Late Preclassic periods (ca. 400–200 BCE); (3) lowland Maya states were the result of autochthonous processes likely inspired and spurred by competitive ideologies and peer polity interactions, consistent with other models of political and economic evolution; (4) in a two-way process other Mesoamerican societies, including those on the Gulf and Pacific coasts and in the Mexican Highlands (see Chapters 3–5, this volume), provided important ingredients to contemporaneous Mesoamerican social and political identities which the lowland Maya adopted, adapted, and integrated in their social memory, while contributing some of their own innovations to other Mesoamerican societies in the process; (5) the economic, architectural, and ideological components of early lowland Maya society provided the cultural foundations for later Maya states in the Classic period.

The explanations for the rise of social and political complexity in Mesoamerica and, in particular, in the Maya lowlands have implications of global concern. The objectives of such paradigms are (1) to define the evidence for the emergence of Maya states; (2) evaluate extant models for the emergence of Maya states; and (3) to refine or replace models for the emergence of Maya states (see Chapter 1, this volume).

State formation in Mesoamerica has received considerable attention, often resulting in varied or opposing perspectives (e.g., Sahlins and Service 1960; Krader 1968; Sanders and Price 1968; Marcus 1976; Wright 1977, 1978, 1986; Jones and Kautz 1981; Johnson and Earle 1987; Sanders and Webster 1988; Yoffee 1988, 2005; Flannery 1972, 1995; Feinman and Marcus 1998; Flannery and Marcus 2000; Spencer and Redmond 2004; Blomster et al. 2005; Flannery et al. 2005; Stoltman et al. 2005; Hansen 2005; Neff 2006; Neff et al. 2006a, 2006b; Sharer et al. 2006; Sharer 2007; Hansen and Suyuc-Ley 2011). However, there also appear to be areas of common ground. For example, many theoretical discussions of the evolution of complex societies accept the development of "big men" or "chiefs" from simple "egalitarian" societies that existed with less-complex economic structures (e.g., Service 1962, 1975; Lindstrom 1984; Johnson and Earle 1987; Gregg 1991; Earle 1997). Such discussions often propose that in the initial stages of societal development individuals attained higher rank or status on the basis of skills, talents, personal wealth, merchant acumen, or other capabilities that propelled them into administrative or leadership roles, becoming "accumulators" or "aggrandizers" (Hayden and Gargett 1990; Clark and Blake 1994; Rathje 1971, 1972, 2000). Status and rank differentiations of individuals and, subsequently, lineages have been posited as a response to societal restraints or opposition to the accumulation of personal power, and to maintain or expand wealth and power structure (see Clark and Blake 1994; Earle 1991b, 1997). In time, elevated status apparently became invested in specific lineages or similar groups, and leadership positions acquired by achievements became subordinate to those inherited from lineage or group membership, sanctioned and recognized by the remainder of society. The formation of such hierarchical power structures has universal anthropological implications, but the testing of such developmental processes can only be obtained from areas where developmental sequences can be defined from diachronic and synchronic perspectives furnished by detailed archaeological research (Haas 1982:216).

Mesoamerica is an area in which the process of socio-political and economic complexity can be critically evaluated (e.g., Adams 1977; Clark 1991, 1994). The relatively close proximity of resources and the linguistic and environmental diversity within Mesoamerica provide test cases for defining the chronology and causal factors of evolving complexity. Although the well-known "mother culture" model calls for a single origin or point of influence for all Mesoamerican civilizations (e.g., Clark 1990), examination of numerous examples throughout the world suggests that states generally do not emerge in isolation, a subject that prompts a discussion of "primary states" versus "secondary states," and the formation of "Sister States" (see below). The "mother culture" model has been criticized (Hammond 1988; Flannery and Marcus 1994, 2000; Marcus and Flannery 1996; Clark and Hansen 2001; Hansen 2005) for conclusions unsupported by available data, including assumptions of primacy based on inexact chronologies with leeways of 100 to 200 years or more, while ignoring chronologies and comparable developments in other areas. Further problems lie in wrangling over semantics and definitions, especially when it comes to defining the first appearance of states in Mesoamerica. Most of these problems and issues were noted in the 1970s and 80s. In the volume, *The Transition to Statehood in the New World* (Jones and Kautz 1981), each chapter was followed by "a discussion of certain definitional problems that still plague the archaeology of state formation, concluding, perhaps unfashionably, that definitions should be as fully grounded empirically as they are logically constructed from theoretical premises" (Jones and Kautz 1981:3).

It is highly likely that Maya states emerged by a far more complex process than can be comprehended by previously proposed models. An improved understanding of this process must rely on the application of more sophisticated archaeological methodologies, including greater utilization of multi-disciplinary approaches, more advanced technologies, improved chronometric strategies, and investigations conducted on a regional scale. Long-term, comprehensive regional investigations hold many advantages including a broader, multi-disciplinary perspective based on multiple lines of evidence. Wide-reaching and in-depth investigations enable the evaluation and testing of multiple hypotheses, identification of multi-causal factors, and the definition of alternative models for the rise of complexity within specific regions (Sharer et al. 2006).

While long-term comprehensive investigations have been conducted in the Maya lowlands since the mid 20th century, only recently has this kind of research focused on the critical Preclassic era. These Preclassic archaeological and ecological investigations, such as those in the Mirador Basin of northern Guatemala and in several other regions of the Maya lowlands (e.g., Estrada-Belli et al. 2004a, 2004b, 2006a; Andrews and Robles 2004; Anderson 2011), have revolutionized our understanding of the origins of Maya states. We now have evidence for the centralization of social, economic, and political systems and the emergence of a hierarchical sociopolitical structure, as well as the institution of sacred kingship. The results of these archaeological and ecological studies provide the foundation for models and hypotheses that can be further tested. The Mirador Basin was, apparently, a crucial core of these Preclassic developments in the Maya lowlands. As presented below, the rise to social and political complexity in this region was a process that derived from a combination of economic, environmental, and ideological components enabled by agricultural productivity, specialized production systems, the mobilization of labor, extensive communication and interaction systems—especially evident in a causeway network linking major and minor polities into a cohesive unit—and the manipulation of architectural art and religious ideology.

Over the past two decades, research in the Basin has led to a hypothesis that state level organizations first emerged in northern Peten and southern Campeche during the Middle Preclassic period (ca. 1000–400 BCE). This hypothesis is based on evidence for the Middle Preclassic development of centralized administrative hierarchies within a specific territorial area. Beyond the Mirador Basin, surveys and settlement studies in Peten, Campeche, northern Yucatan, and Quintana Roo have identified an astonishing number of Middle Preclassic settlements with probable tiered hierarchies by this period (Robles-Castellanos and Andrews 2003, 2004; Robles-Castellanos 2004; Andrews and Robles 2004; Rissolo and Ochoa 2002; Sprajc 2002, 2003, 2002–2004, 2005a, 2005b, 2005c; Sprajc and Grube 2008; Estrada-Belli et al. 2006; Anderson 2011; A. Andrews, pers. comm. 2006; K. Reese-Taylor, pers. comm. 2011). These early settlements are in areas thought to be vacant in the Middle Preclassic period less than two decades ago.

The appearance of complex political, social, and economic institutions in the Maya lowlands, in a process comparable to developments seen on the Gulf coast and in the highlands of Mexico (Clark and Hansen 2001; Garber et al. 2002; Hansen 1992a, 1992c, 1998, 2001a, 2005, 2012a; Hansen and Guenter 2005; Hansen and Balcarcel 2008; Hansen, Howell et al. 2008; Hansen and Suyuc-Ley 2011; Marcus and Flannery 1996; Reilly 1994; see also Chapters 3–5, this volume). The dynamic processes of the formation of state-level administrative hierarchies can best be understood through the observation of the earlier stages of this development and by understanding the political, geographical, and economic environment in which it originated (see also Clark 1991; Clark and Blake 1994; Earle 1997:14).

During the Late Preclassic period (ca. 300 BCE–150 CE), the process of political, social, and economic centralization reached its apogee. Initial data from El Mirador and other lowland sites such as Edzna, Cerros, Cuello, and Colha promoted the notion that Maya sacred kingship and related institutions that have traditionally defined Maya civilization began in the Late Preclassic period (e.g., Freidel 1981, 1985, 1986b; Hansen 1982, 1984; Matheny 1986a, 1986b, 1987; Freidel and Schele 1988a, 1988b; Fields 1989; Reese-Taylor 1996; Kappelman 1997). Subsequent research, however, suggests that the architectural and cultural florescence of the Late Preclassic period represents the culminating manifestations of the growth of complexity, including the presence of sacred kingship, which began centuries earlier during the Middle Preclassic (Hansen 1992a, 2012a; Hansen and Guenter 2005; see also Estrada-Belli, Bauer et al. 2003; Bauer 2005a, 2005b; Estrada-Belli 2006).

The process of Preclassic state development in the Maya lowlands has a particular focus in the Mirador Basin of northern Guatemala (Hansen and Suyuc-Ley 2011), although it is clear that other lowland regions, including the sites of Holmul, Cival, and San Bartolo, were also important players, either in their own developmental trajectories or as part of a Mirador hegemony. The diachronic processes of economic, architectural, and ideological complexity indicate the autochthonous manner by which the first Maya states emerged. It did not require contact with, or inspiration from, the Olmec to enlighten the Maya on these developmental processes, particularly since they were already in place on a pan-Mesoamerican scale. What this highly sophisticated development did require, however, was an acute awareness of the ideological systems and associated political, economic, and religious symbolism which created a competitive agenda to propel the Maya, as well as other Mesoamerican societies, into increasing displays of political and economic prowess by the late Middle Preclassic period. The great Olmec capital of La Venta and the monumental capitals in the Mirador Basin were emerging simultaneously. However, the cultural emulations and variations between these societies are more consistent with a "peer-polity" and "competitive neighbor" process of development than a "mother-daughter" relationship. The developmental consequences of competing ideologies among major powers have been evident in the 20th century as well as in ancient times. Throughout history, social competition has driven technological, political, economic, and scientific innovations forward and thereby promoted the growth and increasing complexity of societies.

GEOGRAPHICAL AND HISTORICAL CONTEXTS

The Mirador Basin is located in the extreme north-central area of the department of Peten, Guatemala, and the extreme southern part of Campeche

(Fig. 8.1). The Basin is circumscribed by a narrow range of karstic hills on the north, east, and south, with lower and less pronounced elevations on its western edge. These natural features form a rounded, triangular-shaped depression characterized by a high percentage of what are now tree-covered seasonal swamps known as *bajos* (Fig. 8.2). Primary drainage near the sites of El Mirador, Wakna, and Nakbe extends towards the Candelaria River to the northwest, which ultimately drains into the Laguna de Terminos of the Gulf coast. This drainage system is important as it signals a possible route to, and a possible point of contact with, the Gulf coast cultures and other regions of Mexico.

The landscape of the Basin is dominated by the low-lying bajos that are partially the result of the natural elevated circumscription of the area, which creates hydraulic pressure and stagnation of water within the basin (Fig. 8.3). The stunted-tree-covered swamps form approximately 60 percent of the surface area of the Basin, and a comprehensive study of the Basin's flora has detailed the evolutionary format of vegetative types, as well as specific floral communities that may have bearing on settlement patterns (Castañeda and Hansen 2007, 2008, 2016). The soils found in this delimited area are distinct from all other soils in the northern Peten, consisting of clayey types known as Uaxactun, Macanche, and Yaloch soils of poor to medium fertility at present (Simmons et al. 1959; FYDEP 1968; Stevens 1964). Additionally, bajos contain rare and uncommon minerals such as todorokite, identified in magnesium oxide nodules (Dixon et al. 1994).

Early explorations of the Mirador Basin, including those of Ian Graham in the 1960s, Heinrich Berlin in the 1950s, and even earlier explorations by the Carnegie Institution in the 1920s and 30s, resulted in the identification of a few of the major sites within its confines, including Calakmul, Uxul, Balakbal, El Mirador, Nakbe, Naachtun, La Muralla, and La Iglesia (Morley 1938; Ruppert and Denison 1943; Berlin 1951; Graham 1967). To date, an additional 51 major and minor sites have been identified, tested, and mapped by the Mirador Basin Project on the Guatemalan side of the Basin (Hansen et al. 2006; Hansen, Howell et al. 2008; Hansen et al. 2009; Hansen and Suyuc-Ley 2002, 2007, 2010; Mejía 2006, 2008; Mejía, Hansen et al. 2010; Mejía et al. 2007; Mejía et al. 2008; Mejia, Aguilar et al. 2010). In addition, the effort to locate major and minor sites by Ivan Sprajc and Nikolai Grube has proven productive in southern Campeche, Mexico (Sprajc 2002, 2003, 2005a, 2005b, 2005c, 2005d; Sprajc and Grube 2008).

GULF OF MEXICO
Archeological sites of Maya culture
National border
Mexican National border
National highway
Corals
Marshland
N
0
100 km
CAMPECHE BAY
CARIBBEAN
MEXICO
Y U C A T A N
Yucatan
Quintana Roo
Campeche
Tabasco
Puuc
Chenes
Isla Cerritos
Punta Holchit
Cabo Catoche
Isla Contoy
Isla Mujeres
El Rey
Isla Cancun
El Meco
Cancun
Progreso
Xcambo
Dzilam Gonzales
Tizimin
Culuba
27 m
Komchen
Motul
Dzibilchaltun
Punta Boxcohuo
Merida
Ake
Izamal
Ek Balam
Balankanche Caves
Kantunil
Valladolid
Chochola
Acanceh
Punta Nimun
Maxcanu
Mayapan
Ikil
Chichen Itza
Chichimila
Yaxuna
Xcaret
Cozumel
Isla de Cozumel
Coba
Oxkintoc
Ticul
Mani
Uxmal
Mulchic
Tancah
Punta Celarain
Tulum
Jaina
Xcalumkin
Kabah
Loltun
Punta Nitun
Hecelchakan
Labna
Sayil
Muyil
Xlapak
Campeche
Okop
Senor
Santa Rosa Xtampak
Punta Morro
Seyba Playa
Edzna
Dzibilnocac
Chunhuhub
Felipe Carrillo Puerto
Punta Pajaros
129 m
Champoton
Tabasqueno
Villa de Guadalupe
Hochob
Reforma Agraria
212 m
Punta Xicalango
Laguna de Terminos
Ciudad del Carmen
Francisco Escarcega
Nadzcaan
Balamku
Becan
Chicanna
Xpujil
Morocoy
Dzibanche
Chetumal
Punta Herradura
Banco Chinchorn
Frontera
Paraiso
Comalcalco
Grijalva
Usumacinta
Hormiguero
Rio Bec
Kohunlich
Santa Rita
Cerros
Corozal District
Hondo
Pulltrouser Swamp
Noh Mul
365 m
Cardenas
Villahermosa
Benito Juarez
Calakmul
Los Alacranes
Cuello
Orange Walk
Ambergris Caye
Uxul
Villa El Triunfo
La Milpa
New River Lagoon
San Pedro
Balancan
Macuspana
El Mirador
Naachtun
Rio Azul
Lamanai
Altun Ha
Caye Caulker
Caye Chapel
Long Caye
Teapa
Tortuguero
Emiliano Zapata
San Pedro
Nakbe
Orange Walk District
Xultun
Belize City
Turneffe Islands
Northern Caye
Palenque
Pomona
Tenosique de Pino Suarez
Uaxactun
Belize District
Northern Lagoon
Blackbird Caye
Lighthouse
Rio Chancala
Agua Azul cascades
Nakum
Belize
Belmopan
El Peru
El Zotz
Tikal
Naranjo
Southern Lagoon
Half Moon Caye
Tecpatan
Piedras

8.1. Map of the Maya area in Mesoamerica showing the general location of the Mirador-Calakmul Basin (modified after Grube 2001:10).

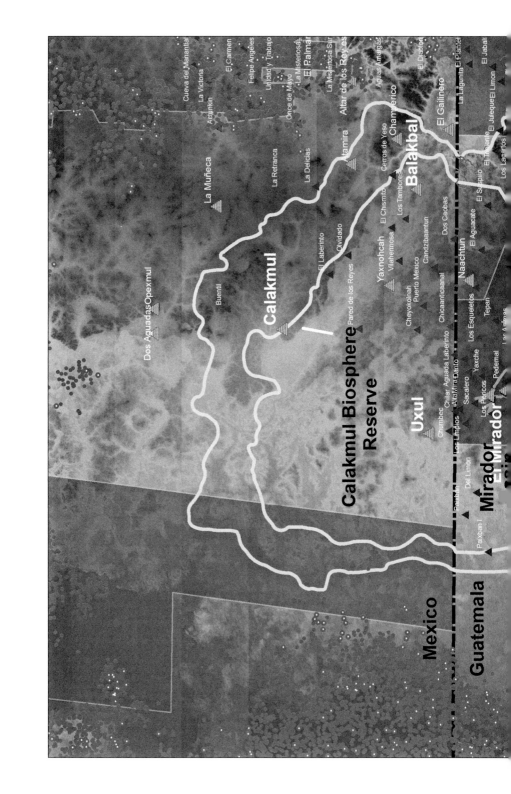

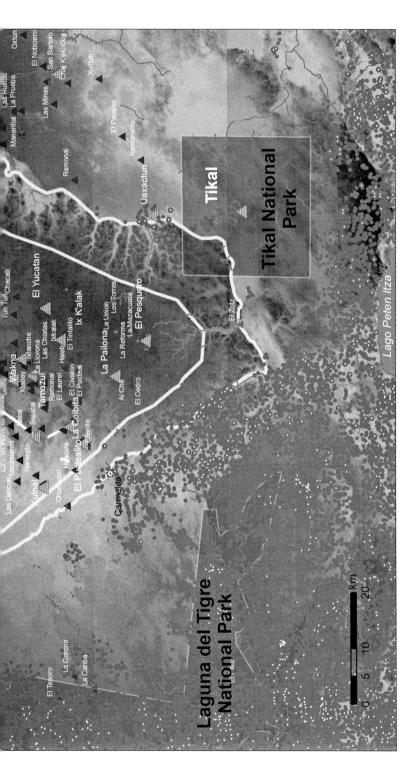

8.2. Map of the Mirador-Calakmul Basin area showing the concentration and density of known large and early sites within the geographical borders of the karstic ridge that surrounds the system (identified by the two lines) (Map by Josephine Thompson, ©FARES 2011).

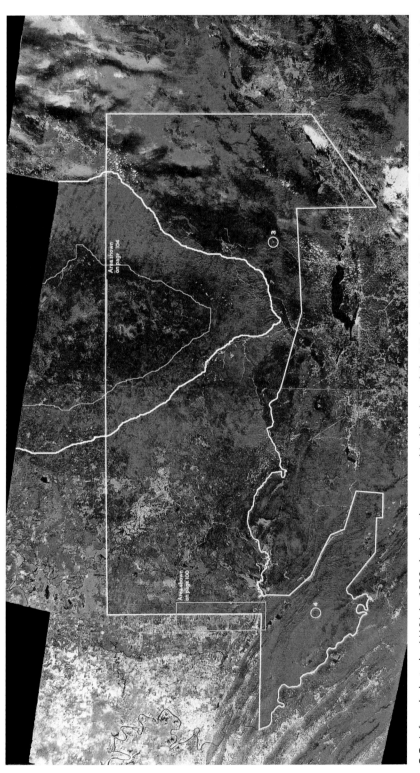

8.3. Infrared photo by NASA in 1992 showing the geographical borders of the Mirador-Calakmul basin system. The high upland forest is sharply defined by deforestation areas (upper left) and the *bajo* vegetation of north central Peten and southern Campeche (modified after Stuart 1992: 98–99).

Overall, mapping teams using traditional methods, Total Station instruments, and GPS technology have located an extraordinary concentration of major and minor settlements dating to the Middle and Late Preclassic periods and the Late Classic period within the Basin, representing one of the highest settlement densities yet recorded in the Maya area (Mejía 2012). Recent mapping of 650 square kilometers of the Mirador Basin with high resolution LiDAR has dramatically improved our knowledge of the settlement distribution and communication systems evident in the area. Mapping and explorations accompanied by test pit excavations have increased the chronological and spatial characterization of settlements. The concentration of sites appears to be much greater within the geographical confines of the Basin than in the areas surrounding the Basin. Furthermore, the remains of the Basin's monumental Middle and Late Preclassic cities contain structures that rival the largest in the Western Hemisphere. Yet, in contrast to complex societies throughout the remainder of the ancient world, the precocious political and economic development that occurred in the Mirador Basin coalesced in the region most distant from riverine or coastal areas of any in the Maya lowlands.

The Mirador Basin Project has conducted extensive investigations that provide detailed chronological assessments of sites and associated architecture. The architectural sampling strategies have included large public buildings (i.e., Matheny et al. 1980; Hansen 1984, 1990, 1992a, 1998, 2000; Hansen and Balcarcel 2008; Matheny 1986a, 1986b, 1987; Stutz-Landeen 1986; Howell and Copeland 1989; Velasquez-Fergusson 2011), as well as a stratified sample of Preclassic and Classic residences of varying sizes (Nielsen 1980; Dahlin et al. 1980; Demarest et al. 1984; Balcarcel 1999; Balcarcel and Lopez 2001; Castellanos 2008; Meagher and Schrodt 2009). This work has allowed a more comprehensive perspective on the precocious Preclassic occupation and the accompanying cultural and environmental changes on a regional scale (Hansen 1998; Balcarcel 1999; Balcarcel and Lopez 2001, 2002, 2004; Balcarcel et al. 2004; Mejía 2006, 2008).

ENVIRONMENTAL CONTEXT

The recovery of archaeological and ecological materials in stratified contexts has allowed for the definition of environmental and cultural events in distinct time periods. For example, studies of pollen sequences (50 samples) and as-

sociated AMS carbon dates (12) from more than 17 vertical m of highly stratified cylindrical cores from a series of deep-water lakes and aguadas along
the western edge of the Basin have defined occupation spans (settlement
onset and abandonment) and cultigens at specific points in time that coincide
with the archaeological record (Wahl 2000, 2005; Hansen et al. 2002; Wahl et
al. 2005; Wahl et al. 2006; Wahl, Byrne et al. 2007). Since the prevailing winds
come from the east, it is likely that pollen of taxa from grasses (*Poaceae*),
weeds (*Asteraceae*), forest species (*Melastomataceae-Combretaceae-Urticaceae*),
and agricultural products (*Zea*) in these cores are indicators of agricultural
and biological occurrences within the Basin to the east. While there are disputes about the capacity of certain pollens to travel with winds, the record
is remarkably similar in all three sample locations, suggesting a continuity in
the vegetation record. Furthermore, there is direct correlation of the presence of pollen (or lack thereof) to non-carbonate inorganic sediment deposits, indicating increased sedimentation due to deforestation and agricultural activity, as determined by magnetic susceptibility. The stratified pollen
samples reflect a consistent record of 8,500 years, and the associated results
of sediment chemistry, organic content, and magnetic susceptibility analyses
should accurately portray the Basin's cultural and ecological sequences.

The Mirador Basin pollen data indicate that the area had shifted from
grassland savannas to moist tropical forest by at least 8,400 cal years BP
(Wahl et al. 2006). The first evidence of maize pollen at the lake of Puerto
Arturo dates to a median age of 4,600 BP with a 2-sigma age range of 4440–
4750 BP (Wahl et al 2006:385; Wahl, Byrne et al. 2007:817).[1] This maize
pollen sample is associated with the appearance of *Ambrosia*, a common
agricultural weed of the sunflower family, indicating that there were agricultural disturbances in the area by about 2650 BCE. The cultural remains
of this early occupation have only recently been identified below the earliest platforms and architecture at Nakbe, but it is now evident that the area
was marked by a human presence at this time. The samples also contain a
relatively high amount of *Poaceae*, sedges and grasses commonly found in
wetland marshes (*civales*). This suggests that the bajos, which were likely
lakes during the Pleistocene period, were primarily wetland marshes by the
time of Maya occupation. By ca. 3400–3200 cal. years BP (1420–1270 BCE
cal.—CAMS #94186), permanent Maya settlement is suggested by a dramatic decrease in forest taxa, an abrupt increase in *Zea mays* pollen, plus *Am-
aranthaceae* and *Asteraceae-Ambrosia* pollen, common weeds associated with

agricultural disturbances (Wahl, Byrne et al. 2007:817). These data have a strong correlation with the chronometric data from archaeological excavations, where a cluster of dates (n=12) for the earliest sedentary occupation at Nakbe range between 1235 and 760 BCE (uncal. C-14 years; calibrated dates push the range to between 1465 BCE and 923 BCE) (Hansen 2005), indicating a sedentary occupation and subsistence by about the same time as incipient occupation was occurring in the Gulf Coast region.

CULTURAL CONTEXT

Thus the beginnings of permanent occupation of the Mirador Basin occurred by ca. 1000 BCE, with a primary concentration of activity at the sites of Nakbe and El Mirador (Hansen 1998, 2001a, 2005; Clark et al. 2000; Clark and Hansen 2001). There is evidence for early Middle Preclassic occupation at the sites of Wakna, Xulnal, and La Florida as well (Fig. 8.2). The initial sedentary occupation at Nakbe corresponds to a period dubbed the "early Ox" phase. Ceramics from this earliest occupation are sparse and consist of red-rimmed unslipped tecomates, incised body sherds, incised rims, and thumbnail-impressed bowls and tecomate forms. Chert blades were also produced at this initial stage. We do not yet have evidence of obsidian importation or other evidence of outside contact in this period, but this may be a sampling problem. It appears that there was a limited occupation at Nakbe (primarily in the East Group, Fig. 8.4) that utilized hard-packed clay floors and postholes carved in bedrock. It is clear that soon thereafter, between 1000 and 800 BCE, Nakbe was a permanent, sedentary village with structures built on low platforms.

Although a hierarchical political and economic structure is difficult to identify at this early juncture without broader horizontal exposure of residences and associated deposits—often buried by later Preclassic architecture—it is clear that nucleated settlement had begun by the early Middle Preclassic period. As noted above, pollen and stable isotope data (Jacob 1994; Hansen et al. 2002) indicate that seasonal swamps around Nakbe and El Mirador were open, grass-covered wetland civales or marshes (Hansen et al. 2002; see also Dunning et al. 2002). Fossil remnants of these systems are still found in the large bajo to the east of Nakbe, the central regions of the Basin, and in the extreme southern area of the Basin near El Pesquero. These marshes would have had a myriad of natural resources, including abun-

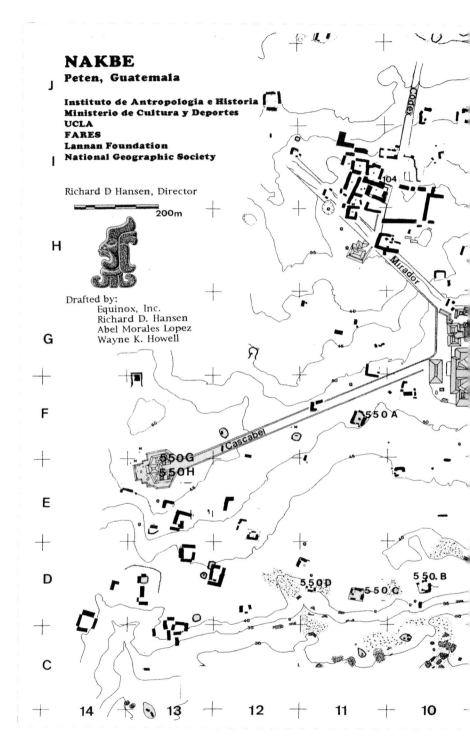

8.4. Map of Nakbe, Mirador Basin-RAINPEG Project (after Hansen et al. 2002:285, © FARES 1998).

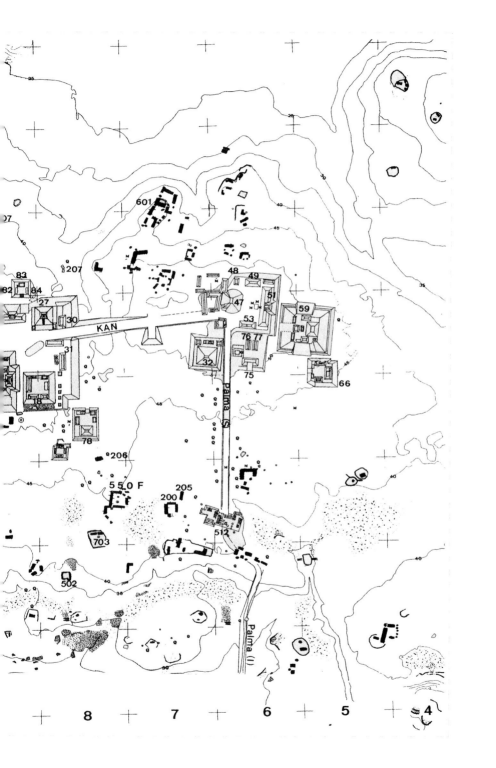

dant birds, turtles, reptiles, shellfish, deer, and peccaries. Even more crucial were deposits of wetland mud in the marshes, rich in nutrients and organic matter. Excavations by John Jacob, Tom Schreiner, Kara Nichols, Enrique Hernandez, and David Wahl in bajos throughout the Mirador Basin have identified this rich layer, now buried by extensive sedimentation (Fig. 8.5). In addition, the natural landscape would have provided farmers areas to cultivate without having to clear large and extensive forest cover. A similar pattern is seen at Tikal, where the majority of early Middle Preclassic (Eb) materials were found near the Bajo de Santa Fe (W. Coe 1965a, 1965b) or, as in the case of the Central Lakes area, near lacustrine resources (Rice 1976b). At both Nakbe and El Mirador (and presumably at other sites in the Basin as well), food production was expanded by transporting rich muck to other areas, thus replicating the fertile system found in the marshes. The perennially wet marshes ultimately became the economic engines of the Mirador

8.5. Dr. Thomas Schreiner investigating what appears to be the buried A-horizon of the original *bajo* surface prior to intense sedimentation (Photo by R.D. Hansen).

Basin that launched the hierarchical structure evident in succeeding periods of Maya occupation of the region.

THE FOUNDATIONS OF LOWLAND STATES IN THE EARLY MIDDLE PRECLASSIC PERIOD (CA. 1000–600 BCE)

Economic surpluses are fundamental to the growth of complex societies. When surpluses of labor, food, and other resources are associated with a rich ideological system of shared beliefs and ritual behavior, economic capabilities are converted into power. This economic power is reflected in growing populations, social stratification (including elites, religious specialists, artisans, and other manufacturing specialists), mobilization of labor for monumental constructions, development of infrastructure for public benefit (i.e., reservoirs, causeways, terrace systems, canals), feasting and socially cohesive interactions, importation of exotic goods, security, and enforcement of civil and legal controls.

In the Mirador Basin, as throughout Mesoamerica, the underlying economic foundation of Preclassic society was agriculture (Flannery et al. 1967; Siemens and Puleston 1972). As defined above, perennially wet marshes attracted early maize farmers by about 2650 BCE, most likely by exploiting their rich muck soils. By ca. 800 to 600 BCE (the middle Ox phase at Nakbe), structures with vertical stone walls, wattle-and-daub residences, and monumental platforms were being constructed throughout the site. Additionally, elsewhere in the Basin, Middle Preclassic occupations with similar characteristics have been located at Wakna, La Florida, Xulnal, and most recently in the northern sector of El Mirador. Early Middle Preclassic masonry consists of small, roughly shaped stones hewn from limestone quarries and transported to construction areas. Masonry walls were then covered with a rather primitive lime and clay plaster or a chalky, powdered lime plaster, while floors consisted primarily of packed clay, sascab, or thin lime plaster.

One characteristic clearly differentiates early lowland Maya settlements from their neighbors on the Gulf coast. While major lowland Maya sites were organized on an east-west axis, contemporary Olmec centers such as La Venta were laid out along a north-south axis. An east-west causeway was constructed between the two dominant architectural groups of early lowland Maya sites, as if to emphasize their alignment and orientation (Figs. 8.4 and 8.6). Furthermore, ritual structures were laid out to meet specific align-

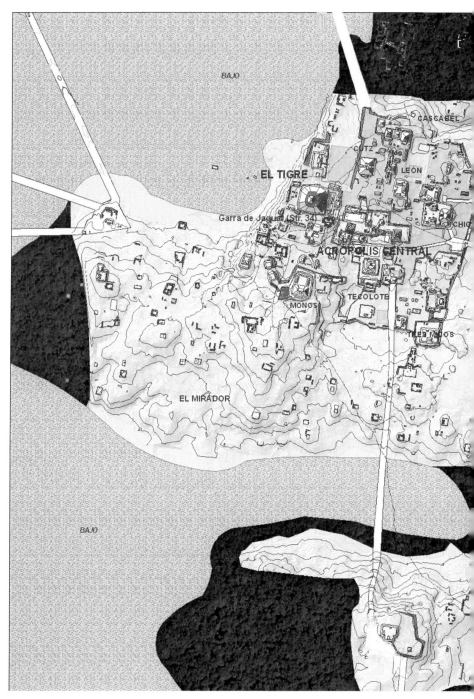

8.6. Map of the central civic center of El Mirador (Map by Josephine Thompson, © FARES 2010).

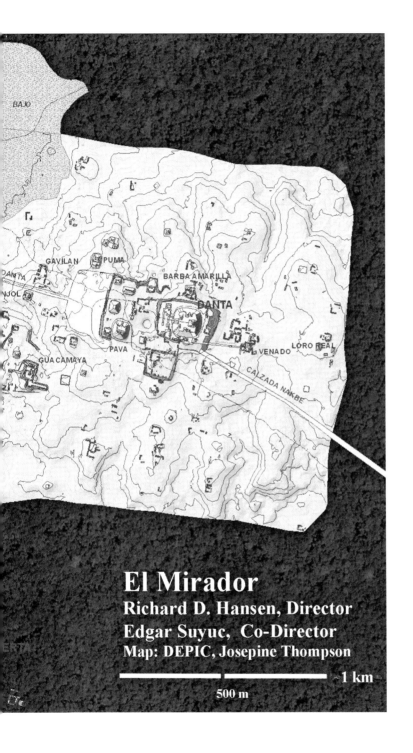

El Mirador

Richard D. Hansen, Director
Edgar Suyuc, Co-Director
Map: DEPIC, Josepine Thompson

500 m

1 km

ment requirements, indicating that their construction and placement was a planned process, probably associated with important astronomical/solar features (see Sprajc 2005d, 2008; Sprajc et al. 2009).

The scale of construction activities within the Mirador Basin indicates that large labor forces were being marshaled for public construction projects during the Middle Preclassic period. Constructions from this period were located in both the East Group and West Group at Nakbe, and within the Cascabel, Leon, Sacalero, Monos, and Central Acropolis Groups at El Mirador (Fig. 8.6). At both sites, evidence for nucleated settlement exceeded an area of 50 to 100 h.[2]

Pottery from this period (800–600 BCE) at Nakbe and El Mirador is clearly within the Middle Preclassic pre-Mamom and Mamom tradition. Diagnostics include figurines, incised bowls, cylinder seals, pre-slip and post-slip incised tecomates, painted stucco-on-slipped monochromes, chamfered bowls with bichrome and dichrome slips, incised and chamfered resist types, along with Palma Daub types with streaky, linear, or blotchy bands of light red, black, and/or orange wash (Fig. 8.7). The dominance of these ceramics and their known distribution within the Basin (and beyond, in some cases) helps identify specific contacts and influences during certain periods. Ceramic studies supervised by Donald Forsyth (Brigham Young University) indicate that early Middle Preclassic ceramics from Nakbe and El Mirador (Early and Middle Ox and Monos Complexes) are typologically more similar to pottery from Uaxactun than from Tikal. They are also more similar to the Xe-Escoba-San Felix Mamom phases in the Pasión and Usumacinta region than with Belize or Yucatan (Forsyth 1989, 1992, 1993a, 1993b:40–41). This suggests that residents had stronger links with sites to the south and southwest of the Basin than to the north, east, or southeast.

Ceramic figurines are found in all levels associated with the Middle Preclassic periods from Nakbe and El Mirador (Fig. 8.8). Figurine forms include solid and hollow masculine bodies, feminine torsos, punctate eyes and nipples, as well as zoomorphic creatures. Ron Bishop (Smithsonian Institution) analyzed the chemical composition of figurines from Middle Preclassic Uaxactun and Nakbe, and identified three Nakbe figurines in the Uaxactun collections; however, no Uaxactun materials have yet been identified in Nakbe samples (Bishop n.d.; Hansen 2001a). Bishop's discovery indicates that Middle Preclassic figurine production was primarily by local artisans for local consumption, rather than being exported from a single

8.7. Middle Preclassic ceramics from Structure 200 in the Cascabel Group at El Mirador (Photo by R.D. Hansen).

source. The overwhelming typological similarities and prevalence of figurines throughout the Middle Preclassic Maya area is a clear indicator of pan-Mesoamerican interaction that allowed the spread of ideas and ideologies that were incorporated at local levels.

Within the Mirador Basin, there is evidence for leadership and status distinctions during the Middle Preclassic period (800–400 BCE). The existence of leadership positions is suggested by the control of labor and expenditures for the "public good," as suggested by the construction of monumental platforms, pyramidal structures, dams, reservoirs, canals, raised fields, and causeways, as well as the construction of specialized ritual structures of consistent form and standardized format, such as E-Group complexes. The existence of status distinctions comes from evidence of variations in residence size and architectural sophistication, and the introduction of symbol systems that distinguished groups and differentiated elites from the masses.

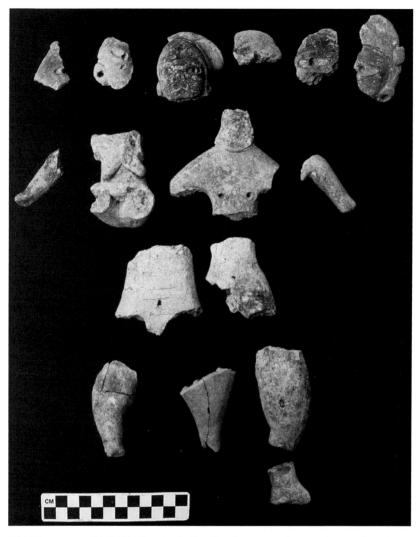

8.8. The range of Middle Preclassic figurine fragments from primary deposits at Nakbe (Photo by R.D. Hansen).

Differential status also can be seen in the importation and distribution of exotic goods from the Maya highlands (obsidian, jade, basalt, granite) and coasts (shells, coral, parrot fish), stone monuments, and other indicators of rank and status such as jade- or hematite-inlaid human incisors (Mata Amado and Hansen 1992) and cranial deformation.

By the early Middle Preclassic period, shells were being imported into the Mirador Basin and made into ornaments, including anthropomorphic and zoomorphic forms, as well as circular disks and earspools. Other imports included sea urchins and freshwater clams (Feldman 2001). *Strombus* shells imported from the Caribbean are especially prevalent at Nakbe and other Middle Preclassic lowland sites during this time (Fig. 8.9). The majority of these shells were drilled with a single perforation, leaving the spines and natural protuberances intact. The shells are exclusive to the ca. 1000–600 BCE era, and have not been found in any deposits of subsequent periods throughout the Mirador Basin. Similar shells have been recovered from early Middle Preclassic contexts at Tikal (Laporte and Valdes 1993), Uaxactun (Ricketson and Ricketson 1937), and in Belize at Colha (Dreiss 1994), Blackman Eddy (Garber et al. 2002), Pacbitun (Hohmann and Powis 1996), and Cahal Pech (Awe 1992; Lee and Awe 1995; Cheetham 1999, 2005). At Cahal Pech and Pacbitun, shells in various stages of manufacture were

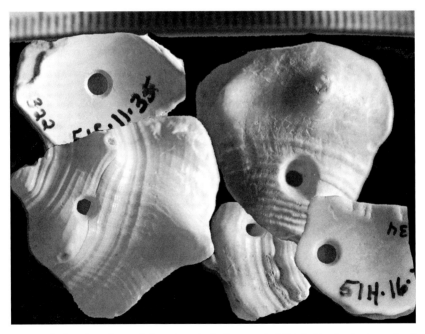

8.9. Drilled and perforated *Strombus* shells from early Middle Preclassic deposits at Nakbe. These shells have never been recovered from any contexts of the subsequent periods of time in the Mirador Basin, and may have been a form of early currency (Photo by J. Woods).

found in association with awls, drills, and cutting implements, suggesting a workshop industry prior to export to sites of the interior lowlands (Awe 1992; Lee and Awe 1995; Hohman and Powis 1996). Despite their prevalence, they have yet to be identified in Middle Preclassic burial contexts or as jewelry. Retention of the spines suggests that they were not used as body ornaments. The unique presence of *Strombus* shells in early Middle Preclassic ritual and elite deposits indicates an important status or economic indicator or, perhaps, a currency like the Kula rings of the south Pacific where possession and heirloom status of shells was often as important as ornamentation (Malinowski 1961:88–89).

While sharing some imported exotic status markers like jade with other areas of Mesoamerica, there are several items that are unique to specific regions during the Middle Preclassic. For example, *Strombus* shell has not been found in the Gulf coast lowlands at La Venta or San Lorenzo. By the same token, hematite mirrors and ilmenite beads, so common at Olmec centers, are not evident in the Mirador Basin or elsewhere in the Middle Preclassic Maya lowlands. Such disparities suggest that the lowland Maya had developed an autochthonous value and symbol system independent from their Mesoamerican neighbors.

There are other examples that suggest the primacy of localized developmental trajectories in the Maya lowlands, such as obsidian trade and specialized lithic production systems. During the Middle Preclassic, obsidian was imported into the Mirador Basin primarily from San Martin Jilotepeque in the Maya highlands (Kunselman 2000). In contrast, the Olmec centers of San Lorenzo and La Venta relied on a different trade network for their supply, importing obsidian from Orizaba (Guadalupe Victoria), El Chayal, and the Basin of Mexico (Coe and Diehl 1980:391; Cyphers 1996:66). The lowland Maya shifted to depending heavily on the El Chayal obsidian source from San Martin Jilotepeque at about 300 BCE (Nelson 1985:645; Nelson and Howard 1986; Fowler et al. 1989), after the Olmec political and economic system disintegrated.

The archaeological evidence suggests that in the early phases of settlement, obsidian tool production was orchestrated within the Basin rather than imported as finished products.[3] This was a likely strategy by local elites to support local craft specialists and to control skill crafting, production, and distribution of exotic commodities, behavior common to incipient hierarchies throughout the world (Helms 1993:34; see also Fraser and Cole

1972). The importation of exotic commodities via trade networks served to demonstrate variations in economic status, establish political legitimacy, allow authoritative benevolence, create demand for skilled crafting, and display long-distance managerial skills (see Helms 1993).

Specialist production of local chert tools was also evident at the small site of La Florida, located in the Mirador Basin south of Tintal. This site had dense deposits of chert debitage, dating to the Middle Preclassic, Late Preclassic, and Late Classic periods, due to a rich source of eroded chert nodules from an adjacent arroyo (Hansen and Suyuc-Ley 2002). Evidence of Middle Preclassic occupation at La Florida was found in residence constructions, chultuns, small platforms, and a standing weathered stela, suggesting that the site was of some importance at this early time.

The appearance of long-distance trade items used for ritual or economic purposes does not always imply a more complex cultural trajectory, since such trade may precede social stratification (Helms 1993:213). But exotic commodities highlight an important contrast between the ordinary masses and those responsible for the political and economic organization of merchant relations, varied ethnic groups, and skilled artisan development and distribution systems (Helms 1993:14; Clark and Blake 1994). Such administrative responsibility demonstrated authority and the implementation and maintenance of prestige that justified and stoked the formation of rank and status differences (Helms 1993:68).

Middle Preclassic long-distance trade and socio-economic contact is consistent with interaction sphere (Freidel 1981) and peer-polity interaction models (Renfrew and Cherry 1986; Renfrew 1986). By this time, if not earlier, there are clear indicators of status and personal wealth in the Maya lowlands. Physical characteristics and personal status indicators such as woven mat symbols, skull deformation (forehead flattening; Fig. 8.10), and dental inlays (hematite disks; Fig. 8.11) appear during this time (Mata Amado and Hansen 1992). Figurines depicting the three-pronged "Jester God" were recovered from early Middle Preclassic deposits at Nakbe (Hansen 2001a:55), suggesting that the iconography of rulership and Maize God symbolism, evident in contemporaneous Olmec societies, was also present in lowland Maya society.

Ritual paraphernalia was an important legitimization strategy. Large slab altars were placed on centerlines of important structures, as with Altar 4 and Stela 1 at Nakbe (Fig. 8.12). A small blue-green jade bead had

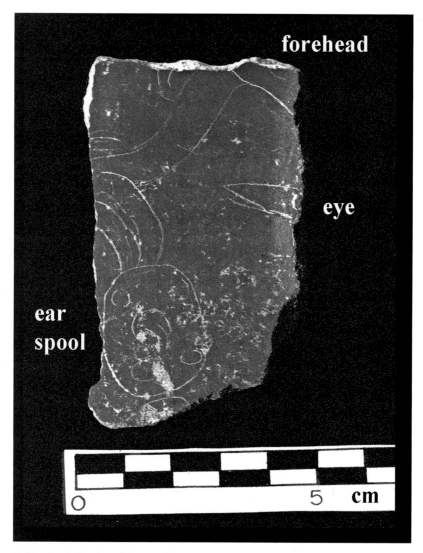

8.10. An incised Middle Preclassic Juventud Red sherd from Structure 59 at Nakbe, showing the eye, portions of the ear spool, and the deformed forehead of a person, indicating early status differentiation by cranial deformation (Photo by R.D. Hansen).

been placed on Altar 4, a pan-Mesoamerican practice of associating monuments with offerings, as noted at other Middle Preclassic Maya sites such as Cuello, Belize (Hammond 1977a, 1985a). The woven mat or *pop* motif,

8.11. A Middle Preclassic human incisor from Op. 51 C at Nakbe (ca. 800 BCE) with an inlaid hematite disk in the tooth (Photo by R.D. Hansen).

associated with royalty and deity figures in later times, is found incised on Middle Preclassic ceramics (Fig. 8.13). The presence of monuments, exotic imported offerings, and the woven mat motif all indicate that the symbols of the institution of kingship and hierarchical administrative control coalesced in the Mirador Basin during the earlier phases of the Middle Preclassic period (Hansen 2012a).

8.12. *facing page* Area of Op. 51 at Nakbe at the western base of Structure 51, showing the Middle Preclassic Altar 4 in the center line axis of the plaza, which had been sealed under a Middle Preclassic floor adjacent to an earlier phase of the elongated platform on the east side of the plaza. A Late Classic burial platform was erected on the left side, and a large standing stela, Stela 1, had been extracted from its earlier position in the platform (Photo by C.D. Bieber).

8.13. *above* Woven mat motifs (*pop* elements), symbols of Maya regal authority, found incised on Middle Preclassic ceramics from Nakbe (Photo by R.D. Hansen).

FORMATION OF LOWLAND STATES IN THE LATE MIDDLE PRECLASSIC PERIOD (CA. 600–400 BCE)

By the late Ox and Monos phases at Nakbe and El Mirador (ca. 600–400 BCE), monumental pyramidal structures up to 24 m high and faced with masonry were constructed at Nakbe, Xulnal, El Pesquero (see below), and El Mirador on massive platforms measuring 3 to 8 m high. Excavations suggest that similar large constructions appeared at Wakna, Tintal, and to a lesser height in La Florida. At El Mirador, several areas were known to have monumental architecture by the Middle Preclassic period, including the Cascabel area, Leon Group, the Sacalero Group, the Sacalero Causeway, the Central Acropolis, and the Monos pyramid area.[4] The first of three major phases of a ball court was built at Nakbe during this period, indicating institutionalized involvement in a pan-Mesoamerican cultural tradition (Velásquez 1999; Hansen 1998, 2001a).

Agricultural Intensification

By late Middle Preclassic times, if not earlier, vast quantities of bajo soils were transported throughout the sites of Nakbe and El Mirador (and possibly Xulnal and El Pesquero) and deposited in terrace constructions, containment dams, and specialized fields (Martínez et al. 1999; Bozarth 2000; Hansen et al. 2000; Bozarth and Hansen 2001; Hansen et al. 2002; Hansen 2012b:257, fig. 11.14). Terrace constructions bordered by stone walls and filled with imported muck formed gardens next to elite residence compounds. One of these, Nakbe Group 18, is likely a Middle Preclassic royal palace compound (Martínez and Hansen 1993; Clark and Hansen 2001) (see Fig. 8.4). The large platform of Group 18 had a 20 m x 120 m terrace on its southern flank that supported the cultivation of maize, squash, gourds, and palms (Bozarth 2000; Bozarth and Hansen 2001; Hansen et al. 2002). Additional imported mud fields have been identified throughout the site centers of Nakbe and El Mirador (Hansen et al. 2002:289). Excavations of unusual linear formations in the Bajo Carrizal, located to the southwest and west of El Mirador, by the Mirador Basin Project suggest that these features were most likely Preclassic raised agricultural fields on a massive scale (Schreiner et al. 2008). Pending additional investigations in these bajos, it is likely that a chinampa-style system was in effect in the Middle and Late Preclassic periods, suggested by the extended parallel rows of differential vegetation in the bajos (Fig. 8.14).

8.14. Aerial view of the series of elongated, parallel, elevated features in the Bajo Carrizal, found to the southwest of El Mirador. The features appear to have been an ancient chinampa-like system (Photo by E. Hernandez).

The discovery of fields of imported soil, check dams, and artificial terrace constructions suggests that lowland Maya society in the Mirador Basin was supported by intensive agriculture by at least the late Middle Preclassic period if not earlier. The production capabilities of these agricultural features fueled an unprecedented population increase for the Maya lowlands, and furnished the economic surpluses to propel the "aggrandizing" elite into more powerful positions within an even more complex sociopolitical organization that took shape during the succeeding Late Preclassic period.

Residential and Public Architecture

Excavations in residential areas and civic centers provide a glimpse of the socioeconomic gradations within Nakbe, El Mirador, and El Pesquero societies during the late Middle Preclassic period. Excavations by Beatriz Balcarcel at Nakbe revealed a late Middle Preclassic elite residence platform near a series of imported-mud agricultural terraces (Operation 502). The platform measured 20 x 17 m and was faced by large cut-stone blocks placed end to end in a pattern consistent with this period (see below) (Fig. 8.15). The west face had a single broad stairway that led towards the terraces and fields. The platform had a stucco floor and supported the remains of masonry residential structures on its east side. Postholes indicate several additional perishable residences on the same platform (Balcarcel 1999). The elite character of this Middle Preclassic platform, with its large stone blocks, thick lime plaster floor, and broad stairway, differs markedly from the remains of simple huts or even the single-coursed stone platforms found in other residential areas in the vicinity, and demonstrates the economic and social variations reflected by contemporaneous structures within Nakbe.

Group 18, the largest of the elite residential complexes at Nakbe, revealed a likely royal palace dating to the late Middle Preclassic period (Martínez and Hansen 1993; Clark and Hansen 2001:16–18). Group 18 was located on the primary platform of the West Group, immediately east of the platform that supports Structure 1, the largest structure at the site (Fig. 8.4). An inset stairway is located on the northern face of the Group 18 platform, oriented towards the more public gathering area near the Kan Causeway. The platform measures 80 m^2 with a height of up to 4 m. Several structures line its perimeter, providing an additional 2 to 3 m in height.

Water collection was of prime importance at Nakbe, El Mirador, Wakna, Tintal, and other large Mirador Basin sites. Entire plazas were designed to channel and direct water flows into managed reservoirs. This can be observed with Structure 32 of the Nakbe East Group, which was designed to collect and channel water into a specially constructed, rectangular reservoir located adjacent to the ball court to the east of the building. The entire plaza complex to the west of the Leon Group at El Mirador functioned to channel water toward the large reservoirs to the west at the base of the 30 m escarpment.

So-called E-Groups are among the most significant architectural complexes found in the Preclassic Maya lowlands (Hansen 1992a, 1992b, 1992c, 1998:63ff; Chase and Chase 1995; Aveni et al. 2003). This architectural form may represent the mythological *wak chan* of Maya cosmology, the residence of First Father and the site of the planting of the three primordial stones of creation (Hansen 1992a, 1998:68ff; 2000). The architectural form consists of an elongated north-south platform on the east side of a plaza, with a dominant pyramidal structure on the west that frequently, but not always, possessed quadripartite stairways. The final form of Middle Preclassic E-Group constructions at Xulnal and Nakbe correlates with contemporaneous buildings at Tikal (Str. 5C-54 "Lost World") and Uaxactun (Group D; Acevedo, pers. comm. 1996; Laporte and Valdés 1993; Laporte and Fialko 1993a, 1995), as well as those in more distant highland Chiapas, such as Chiapa de Corzo, Mirador-Chiapas, and La Libertad (Mason 1960a; Agrinier 1970; Clark 1988:8). The data from the lowlands suggest a long and consistent evolutionary development, with the best-documented sequence observed in Tikal's Lost World Pyramid (5C-54) by Juan Pedro Laporte and Vilma Fialko (Laporte and Fialko 1993a, 1995:47–51).

The earliest E-Group in the Tikal sequence (Structure 5C-54-1) dates to the Eb ceramic phase, or ca. 800 BCE (Laporte and Fialko 1993a:16–20; Cheetham et al. 2003). Two carbon dates from the Nakbe E Group (Structure 51 Sub 1) indicate it is probably slightly later than this Tikal example, but likely as early as 780 BCE (Hansen 2005:58). A similarly early structure was identified in the E-Group at the site of Cival by Estrada-Belli (2003, 2006; see Estrada-Belli, this volume). The Tikal, Cival, and Nakbe examples are earlier than the E Group at La Venta (Structures D-1 and D-8), which dates to about 500–400 BCE (Rebecca González Lauck, pers. comm. 1998; González Lauck 1996:75). Thus, it seems likely that the E-Group complex is a lowland Maya innovation that was subsequently adopted on the Gulf coast, Pacific coast, and in the Maya highlands.

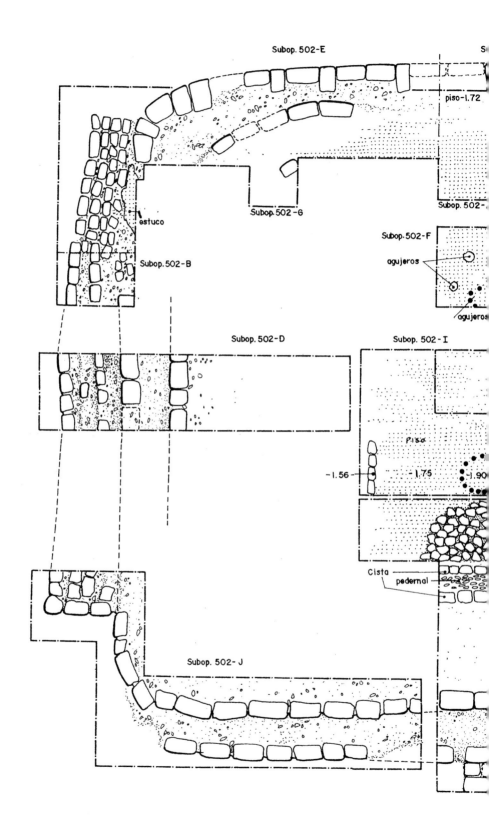

Subop. 502-E

S

piso-1.72

Subop. 502-

Subop. 502-6

estuco

Subop. 502-B

Subop. 502-F

agujeros

agujeros

Subop. 502-D

Subop. 502-I

Piso

-1.56

-1.75

-1.90

Cisto

pedernal

Subop. 502-J

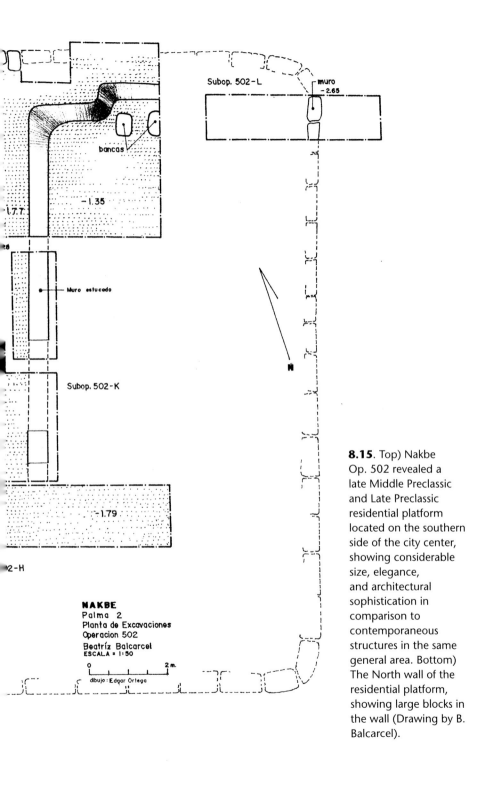

Subop. 502-L

muro
−2.65

bancas

−1.35

17.7.

Muro estucado

Subop. 502-K

−1.79

2-H

N

NAKBE
Palma 2
Planta de Excavaciones
Operacion 502
Beatríz Balcarcel
ESCALA = 1:50

0   2 m.

dibujo : Edgar Ortega

8.15. Top) Nakbe Op. 502 revealed a late Middle Preclassic and Late Preclassic residential platform located on the southern side of the city center, showing considerable size, elegance, and architectural sophistication in comparison to contemporaneous structures in the same general area. Bottom) The North wall of the residential platform, showing large blocks in the wall (Drawing by B. Balcarcel).

Some of the most radical changes during the late Middle Preclassic period occurred in masonry construction patterns (see Hansen 1998). The small, roughly hewn flat stones used to construct vertical walled platforms in earlier periods measured roughly 25 x 28 x 8 cm (Fig. 8.16). By the late Middle Preclassic these had been replaced by massive, finely hewn stone blocks measuring nearly 1 m long by 50 cm high and 50 cm wide (Fig. 8.17). These larger stones were placed in the walls of public structures with the long axis exposed, maximizing the use of stone and indicating a clear specialization in the labor force required to quarry and transport the material (Woods and Titmus 1994a, 1996; Hansen et al. 1997; Hansen 1998). Experimental data obtained by James Woods and Gene Titmus in quarry excavations at Nakbe indicated there were several levels of craft specializations involved in making the stone tools used to cut and shape megalithic blocks. There were additional quarrying strategies to cut the blocks, as well as varied labor specializations involved in shaping the blocks themselves, each requiring approximately 34 man-hours to produce (Woods and Titmus 1996:484–85). The presence of monumental architecture built from megalithic blocks (600–1000 pounds per block) provides good evidence for a centralized political authority that commissioned and executed the projects (see Helms 1993:78–81). These monumental projects gave rise to architectural innovations, including the apron molding (a sloping projection over sharp inset at the base of a façade), a design that lasted for over a thousand years as a hallmark of Maya buildings.

The use of lime stucco is another defining characteristic of lowland Maya architecture, in addition to monumental masonry. Lime stucco was used in vast quantities. It was applied to the interiors and exteriors of walls of public and private structures, residences, platforms, temples, causeways, and to plaza surfaces. Great amounts of labor were required to quarry and transport the limestone, firewood, and water to make lime plaster, indicating the need for centralized political and economic control over the production, distribution, and utilization of labor and costly resources (Schreiner 2001, 2002, 2003; E. Hansen 2000; E. Hansen et al. 1995).

All of these construction strategies were utilized in monumental Middle Preclassic architecture at El Mirador, Nakbe, Xulnal, and particularly at El Pesquero. A fortuitous discovery at El Pesquero in 2009 of an intact Middle Preclassic structure buried within a later, Late Preclassic structure has revealed the extraordinary complexity of such early architecture, with roof

8.16. Early Middle Preclassic platform (800–700 BCE) at Nakbe, showing the vertical walls, thin plaster, and small, crudely hewn stones (Photo by R.D. Hansen).

8.17. Massive elongated blocks (measuring 1.4 x .5 x .45 m) in Structure 200 of the Cascabel Group at El Mirador, which appeared at the latter part of the Middle Preclassic period (600–400 BCE). This architectural material signaled the advent of quarry specialists in the Mirador Basin. Note the rectangular earspool indicating architectural art, defined by dots (Photo by R.D. Hansen).

combs, corner masks, and a unique form of vaulted chamber (Mejía et al. 2010) (Figs. 8.18 and 8.19). Recent explorations and excavations at the site of Yaxnocah, located to the north of El Mirador and south of Calakamul in Campeche, have also identified monumental Middle Preclassic architecture (Kathryn Reese-Taylor, pers. comm. 2011).

Another architectural innovation confirmed to date to at least the late Middle Preclassic period is the creation of architectural art, consisting of monumental masks and associated panels, as evident in El Mirador Structure 200 and Structure 34 Sub 1 (Fig. 8.20). One of the most frequent iconographic elements is the presence of the J-scroll-and-bracket motif, a feature also noted on a late Middle Preclassic structure at Rio Azul (Valdez 1995).

Early Causeways

The late Middle Preclassic period was marked by the construction of the Basin's first causeways, known as *sacbeob* or "white roads." Four and possibly five sacbeob have been identified at Nakbe from this period—the Kan, Palma, Kancito, the Northern Nakbe, and Mirador causeways—and evidence for similar antiquity has been found for the Sacalero, Tintal, and Nakbe casueways at El Mirador. The Kan, Palma, and Sacalero causeways connect early architectural groups within Nakbe and El Mirador, while the Mirador, Nakbe, and Tintal causeways link the sites of Nakbe, El Mirador, and Tintal. The earliest levels of these causeways date to the late Middle Preclassic period (600–400 BCE) (Suasnávar 1994; Suasnávar and Hansen 1997; Hernandez and Schreiner 2006), indicating that organized labor had been marshaled into intra-site and extensive inter-site communication systems within the Basin (see Fig. 8.2). These causeways were elevated, modified, and repaved during the Late Preclassic and additional causeways constructed (e.g., the Danta Causeway) with thick plastered floors, measuring 23 to 50 cm thick (Suasnávar 1994; Suasnávar and Hansen 1997; Suasnávar 1994; Schreiner and Hernandez 2008, 2009; Hernandez et al. 2007; Hernandez 2008). The massive size of these major causeways, some of which extended to more than 24 km in length, and range from 24 to 40 m wide (the Sacalero causeway near the Cascabel Group at El Mirador is 50 m wide) and 2 to 6 m high, incorporated massive amounts of labor and materials in their construction and their periodic maintenance. Excavations by the Mirador Basin Project, under the supervision of Tom Schreiner and Enrique Hernandez, in the Tintal-Mirador causeway have demonstrated the use of

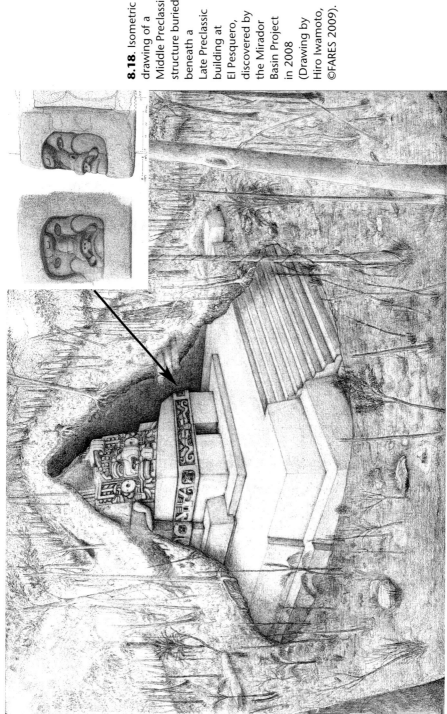

8.18. Isometric drawing of a Middle Preclassic structure buried beneath a Late Preclassic building at El Pesquero, discovered by the Mirador Basin Project in 2008 (Drawing by Hiro Iwamoto, ©FARES 2009).

8.19. Ceramics recovered from the floor and fill of Structure 1-Sub at El Pesquero, Mirador Basin (Photo by R.D. Hansen).

2.88 million m³ of construction fill in the Tintal causeway alone, with a total of up to 10,000 m³ of costly lime mixes per kilometer to form the plastered surfaces (Hernandez et al. 2008). The organizational skills required for the labor and construction of such massive features, plus the quantities of fill and processed lime resources required both centralized control and the political, economic, and social cohesion between nearly every major Preclassic center of the Basin. The causeways increased the productive potential of both managerial elites and agricultural labor by allowing quicker and easier transport of products and commodities (Chase and Chase 2001).

8.20. Late Middle Preclassic mask on the façade of El Mirador Structure 34 Sub 1 (Drawing by G. Valenzuela, ©FARES 2009).

They also served as water management systems, religious procession ways, and perhaps even as boundary markers (Suasnávar and Hansen 1994; Shaw 2001; Hernandez and Schreiner 2006). These massive constructions consolidated a large work force laboring for the "common good of society," allowed increased social and economic interactions between neighboring polities, and contributed to the overall organic solidarity of the population, all factors crucial to avoiding fissioning or rebellion against an emerging power structure (Bandy 2004).[5]

The architectural development and public works projects established during the late Middle Preclassic period suggest an increasingly centralized hierarchical power structure was emerging or had emerged in the major centers of the Mirador Basin. As Sharer and Traxler propose (Chapter 1, this volume), the evidence for the existence of the institution of sacred kingship by the Late Preclassic era at San Bartolo and elsewhere in the Maya lowlands (Chapters 11 and 12, this volume) makes it reasonable to propose that early versions of Maya kings were ruling at the larger Middle Preclassic centers in the lowlands, such as Nakbe, Xulnal, Tintal, El Pesquero and El Mirador in the Mirador Basin. Part of this developmental process involved legitimization through the erection and portrayal of human figures on massive stelae, large subsistence and economic projects (raised field and terrace agriculture systems, causeways, reservoirs, dams, canals, and quarries), and the construction of impressive structures and platforms of ideological and social importance.

The presence of the Middle Preclassic causeways is perhaps the strongest evidence for the beginnings of a state-level society in the Mirador Basin, because it implies a cohesion of the major sites into a single, centralized organization with relatively easier access of products and services. This is suggested, in part, by the uniformity of ceramics, lithics, architecture, and trade commodities. While it is likely that the rulers of the Middle Preclassic centers of the Mirador Basin operated in concert, as Sharer and Traxler suggest (Chapter 1, this volume), centralized control would have been facilitated if greater authority was vested in one ruler, perhaps a ruler of Nakbe or El Mirador, who like later Classic Maya kings may have exercised the power to "oversee" inaugurations of subordinate rulers and other events in the Basin's capitals (see Martin and Grube 2000).

Early Stone Monuments

In a variety of societies in ancient Mesoamerica, manifestations of power are perhaps most easily observed in stelae and other stone monuments erected at sites where the political and economic authority could commission such works. During the Classic Maya period, hundreds of these monuments, termed *lakamtun* or "banner stones" (Stuart 1996), were placed in important plazas or in front of temples, palaces, and/or public buildings commemorating historical and other chronologically significant events. Such displays of political and religious authority were presided over by the *K'uhul Ajaw* or "sacred king" (Martin and Grube 2000). The antiquity of the stela cult extends far into the Middle Preclassic period, to at least ca. 1000–800 BCE on the Gulf coast, at Chalcatzingo in the central Mexican highlands, and in the Valley of Oaxaca (see Chapters 3 and 4, this volume), if not earlier (Cyphers 1997b, 2004a). Cyphers has proposed that the majority of the sculpture dates to the "apogee" of San Lorenzo between 1200 and 800 BCE (1996; see also Chapter 4, this volume). Yet these monuments cannot be accurately dated due to disturbances by later occupants of the site and the fact that "the overwhelming majority of San Lorenzo sculptures have no stratigraphic associations whatsoever…" (Coe and Diehl 1980:294; see also Graham 1989, 1991; Hansen 2005:53).

The early rulers of Chalcatzingo and polities in both the Maya and
Oaxacan regions probably became acutely aware of the social and political
advantages of monument carvings and dedications, but the Olmec clearly
exploited sculptural manifestations of personified power and associated ideologies most successfully. Interestingly, early Olmec rulers apparently relied
on in-the-round portraiture (colossal heads and full figures of tabletop
altars), while the early rulers of Chalcatzingo, and those in the Maya area,
favored stelae with low-relief portraits (Grove, Chapter 3, this volume).

In the Mirador Basin, extensive research has revealed carved monuments that correspond to much of the established chronological sequences
of the area.[6] Examination of Preclassic monuments in their original context
has been limited, however, because the majority of Preclassic stelae, altars,
and carved fragments were re-erected or moved by the Late Classic occupants of the Mirador Basin.[7] In spite of the lack of original context for many
monuments, their stylistic format and surrounding archaeological context
permit a rough chronological seriation.

The presence of carved monuments in the Mirador Basin is less common
than one would surmise due to activities of later societies. At present, the
earliest-known carved monument in the Mirador Basin is thought to be Stela
1 at the site of La Isla, located on a patch of elevated terrain in the bajo between Nakbe and El Mirador (Fig. 8.21). This standing stela was discovered
with a thin altar (Altar 2) of uncertain age on the west side of a 5 m high
structure. Excavations by the Mirador Basin Project, supervised by James
Woods, indicated that the monument was likely reset by later occupants.
Stela 1 measures 1.67 m high, and is a slightly contorted, unshaped boulder
with an incised, upward-peering crocodilian creature bearing a bifurcated
flame eyebrow, an elevated nose assemblage, and shark-like maxillary teeth.
The form of the sculpture, the unmodified nature of the stone, and the early
iconography suggest a Middle Preclassic date. The monument's association
with the vast bajo between Nakbe and El Mirador is significant, as this is an
area of initial settlement exploiting the rich wetland marshes of the region.

The most securely dated monuments in the Mirador Basin are Nakbe
Altar 4 and La Florida Stela 1. Nakbe Altar 4 was discovered *in situ* on a
sascab floor at the base of a Middle Preclassic platform that formed the site's
eastern E-Group structure (Fig. 8.22). It was sealed by Middle Preclassic fill
(Lot 16) and two damaged Middle Preclassic floors (Floors 5 and 6). The
monument was placed precisely on the centerline of the eastern E-Group

8.21. Middle Preclassic Isla Stela 1 (Photo by R.D. Hansen).

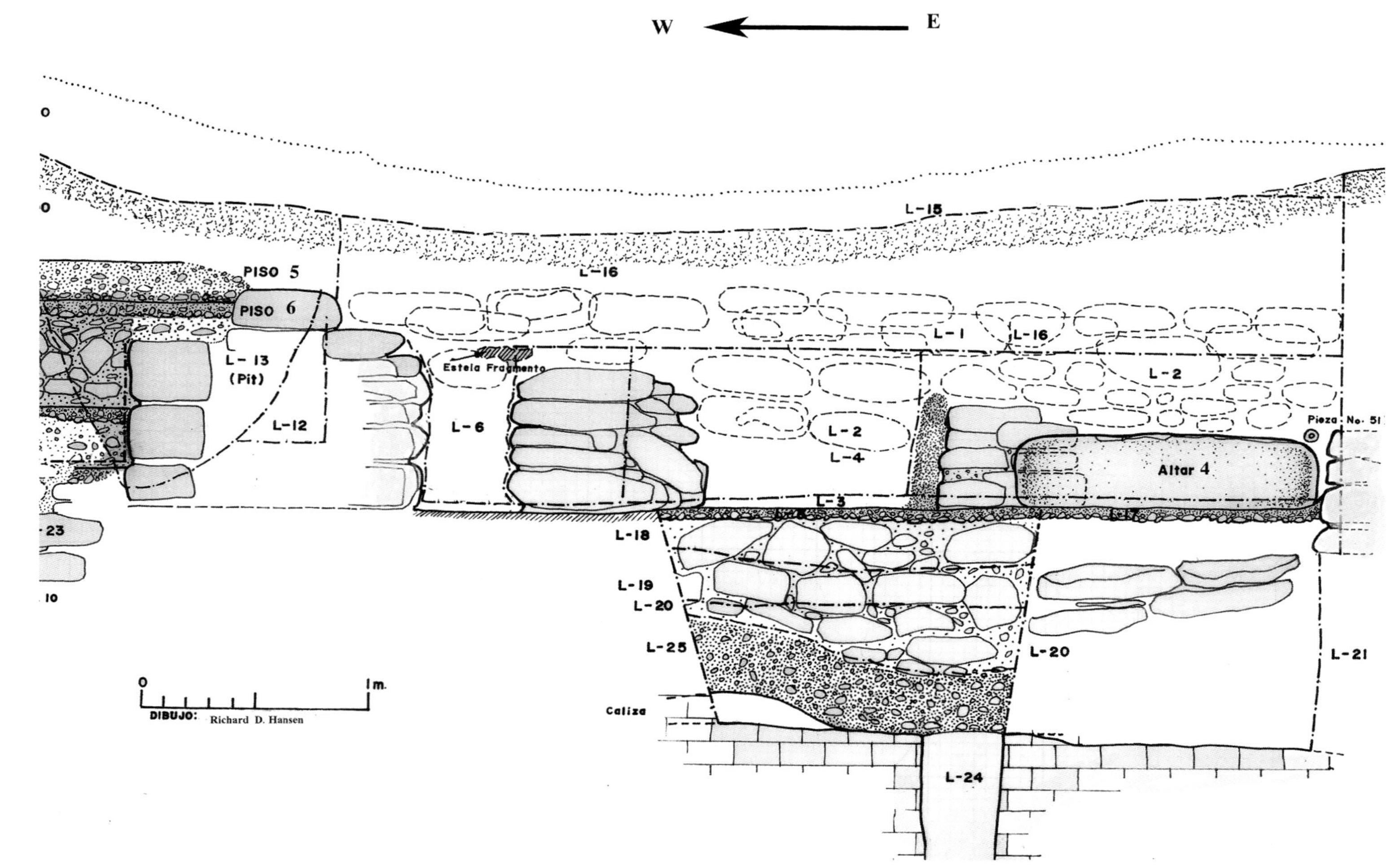

W

E

L-15
L-16
L-2
L-16
L-1
L-2
L-4
L-3
Altar 4
Pieza No 51
L-21
L-20
L-24
L-18
L-19
L-20
L-25
Caliza
Estela Fragmento
L-6
PISO 5
PISO 6
L-12
L-13 (Pit)
23
10

DIBUJO: Richard D. Hansen

0   1 m.

structure, indicating a consistency with Mesoamerican patterns of ritual placement of monuments. A single, small blue-green stone bead was found several centimeters above the center of the stone. The monument had been buried by a later Middle Preclassic platform faced by large, poorly mortared stones. On the basis of both ceramic and C-14 analyses, the monument dates to around 800–600 BCE (uncalibrated) (Beta 31755, Beta 31756, UCLA 2830, UCLA 2833; see Hansen 2005).

La Florida Stela 1 is an uncarved (or perhaps severely eroded) monument, and also dates to the Middle Preclassic era. It is a little more than a meter high in its current deteriorated state, and had been erected and later buried in a Middle Preclassic platform (Fig. 8.23). Associated Mamom ceramics suggest a date between 600 and 400 BCE.

Nakbe Monument 8 (Fig. 8.24) is a less securely dated Preclassic carved monument. A large, semi-circular monument, measuring 1.65 m wide, 1.5 m high, and roughly 0.70 m thick, it was discovered upside down near a large Middle and Late Preclassic palace construction on the southern side of the massive Structure 59 in Nakbe's East Group. This location is near a concentration of quarries and approximately 200 m southeast of the East Group ball court. It's possible the monument was associated with the ball court (dating to the late Middle Preclassic and early Late Preclassic periods; Velásquez 1999; Hansen 2001a:55), perhaps as a marker. However, there is also evidence that it was a throne, possibly dating to the time of the Middle Preclassic Nakbe East Group.

The principal scene on Nakbe Monument 8 shows two downward-peering saurian heads, one on each side, emanating from large rectangular ear flares with four bosses. Both heads have J-scroll and bracket elements appended to the end of the snout. The heads are joined by a band consisting of a series of scrolls that curve away from each other and the centerline of the monument. This band represents an ancestral sky band element found in later Maya art. The dual-headed serpent bar forms the serpent wing motif of the celestial bird, or Principal Bird Deity, on numerous early monuments associated with royal power in the southern Maya area, such as Takalik Abaj Altars 12 and 13, Izapa Stelae 18 and 23, and Kami-

8.22. *facing page* Profile drawing of Nakbe Op. 51 C, 51 I, 51 I, 51 H, showing Middle Preclassic Altar 4 directly on a Middle Preclassic floor and sealed by Middle Preclassic fill (Lot 16) and what remained of two Middle Preclassic floors (Floor 5, 6) (Drawing by R.D. Hansen).

8.23. La Florida Stela 1, a monument which had been sealed in Middle Preclassic fill (Photo by R.D. Hansen).

8.24. Nakbe Monument 8, a possible throne stone, believed to date to the late Middle Preclassic (Drawing by R.D. Hansen).

naljuyu Altar 9 (Kappelman 1997; Guernsey 2006). The dual-headed saurian image has been depicted as a supernatural throne for the gods (see Kerr 1138 with Itzamnaah seated on a dual-headed serpent throne), forming a metaphor for a ruler posturing as a divine mediator (Fig. 8.25).

At a later time, a cross-shaped element, or *k'an* cross, was pecked near the upper center of the stone, along with a curious series of pecked basins placed along the lower edge of the stone. The *k'an* cross appears to have been intrusively pecked, perhaps as a semi-homophonous reference to the original name of the ancient polity, the Kan Kingdom, which controlled the Mirador Basin in the Preclassic period (see discussion below). There is, however, a phonetic distinction between *ka'an* or *chaan* (meaning "sky")

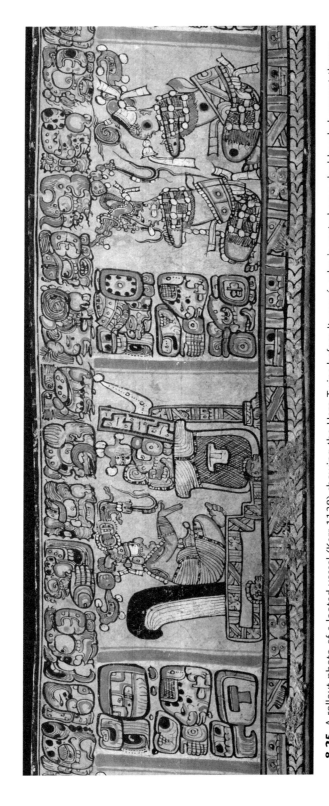

8.25. A rollout photo of a looted vessel (Kerr 1138) showing the Hero Twins before Itzamná, who is seated on a dual headed serpent throne (Photo © Justin Kerr, Vol. 1, 1998, No. 1138).

and *kan* or *chan* ("serpent"), perhaps indicating that if the *k'an* cross on Nakbe Monument 8 were a homophone or phonetic reference, it was done by someone who was basically illiterate.

The emphasis on deity portraits is a pan-Mesoamerican theme, suggesting that the emerging elite may have been promoting a religious ideology to justify growing differences in wealth, rank, or power, a strategy commonly employed by emergent state societies throughout the world (see R. Hansen 2000). It appears that human portraits appeared slightly later than those of deities in the Mirador Basin, as is evidenced by Nakbe Monument 2, Nakbe Stela 1, and Tintal Stela 1. Early Maya and Zapotec sculptures often depict deities in contrast to the predominance of human portraits among the Olmec and at Chalcatzingo in the Mexican highlands (Grove, Chapter 3, and Cyphers, Chapter 4, this volume), variations that illustrate important synchronic cultural differences.

Nakbe Monument 2 (Fig. 8.26) was placed on a floor within a room on Structure 52, a 1 m high Late Classic platform placed on the centerline axis in front of Middle Preclassic Structure 51 in Nakbe's East Group. Monuments 2 and 3 were placed secondarily in fragmented form and were associated with dense quantities of Late Classic ceramics, burned copal, and a few obsidian blades. Monument 2 consists of a limestone slab fragment with lined trefoil elements attached to a square cartouche with four carved dots on the corners, forming a quincunx, similar to elements in Olmec and early Maya art. This motif was apparently attached to a human profile head, with a major portion of the face carefully pecked away in antiquity. The profile face is associated with a "question mark" scroll and an early earflare assemblage, indicating consistency with early pan-Mesoamerican iconography. Along with Nakbe Monument 3, the edges of Monument 2 are carved with a series of concentric semi-circles and lines (Fig. 8.26). While unusual in the Maya lowlands this is consistent with early monuments from the Pacific coastal and piedmont regions, as well as early Zapotec sculpture (e.g., San Jose Mogote Stela 1).[8]

CHANGES AT THE END OF THE MIDDLE PRECLASSIC PERIOD (CA. 500–400 BCE)

There were important changes marking increased centralization of authority at Nakbe by the end of Middle Preclassic period, between 500 and

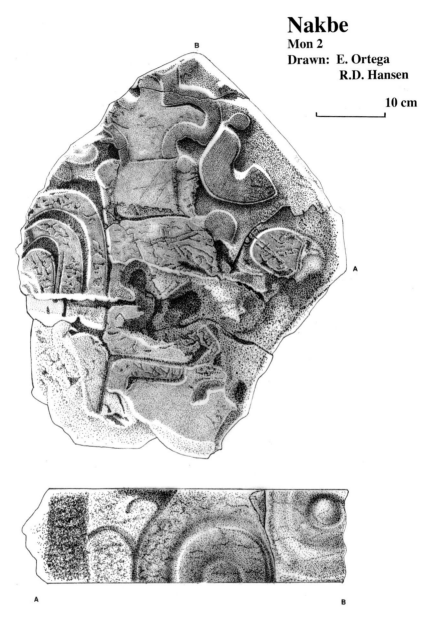

Nakbe
Mon 2
Drawn: E. Ortega
R.D. Hansen

10 cm

8.26. Middle Preclassic Nakbe Monument 2 (Drawing by E. Ortega and R.D. Hansen).

400 BCE. Large-scale architectural programs were enacted that involved the construction of new monumental terraced pyramids, causeways, ritually significant architectural formats, and radical changes in quantity and quality of construction materials, such as limestone block size, shape, and form. The utilization of artificial agricultural terraces indicates further intensification of food production, and the establishment of causeways to facilitate intersite commerce suggests that the political and administrative hierarchy was moving towards a more complex and centralized system. Specific architectural forms of ritual and ideological importance, such as the Middle Preclassic E-Groups, were constructed to their maximum Preclassic height and volumes not only at Nakbe (and possibly El Mirador, Wakna, and Xulnal), but also at Tikal. These and other ritually significant architectural forms suggest a manipulation of religious ideology (Hansen 1992a, 2000). The impressive size of architecture and the control of a vast labor pool suggest that religious authority was one of the catalysts for political centralization and organic social solidarity, as well as the intensification of socio-political and economic power of an emerging ruling elite (Hansen 1990, 1992a, 2000; Demarest and Conrad 1992; see also Kolb 1994).

By the end of the Middle Preclassic period, or perhaps by the beginning of the Late Preclassic (ca. 400–300 BCE), stelae in the Mirador Basin assumed their largest size and format of any subsequent or previous period (Hansen 1992a, 1992b, 1992c, 1995, 2001a). These monuments depict Preclassic kings, portraits of anthropomorphic deities, or a combination of the two, together with all of the trappings of royal power. Carved monuments such as Tintal Stela 1, Nakbe Stela 1, and perhaps fragmented Pedernal Monument 2 average about 4 to 5 m in height and approximately 2 m wide. In contrast to earlier sculptures in the Mirador Basin, several of these monuments were carefully carved on both sides with standing human figures, either as royal portraits or as deity impersonators. Similar carved human portraits dating to this time have been found at Cival, Peten (Estrada-Belli, Grube et al. 2003; Estrada-Belli et al. 2006), and Actuncan, Belize (Grube and McGovern 1995; Grube and Martin 2001).

In contrast to subsequent or previous monuments in the Mirador Basin, these monuments were carved from exotic stones. In the case of Nakbe Stela 1, the stone was of an extremely hard, non-local crystalline limestone. Tintal Stela 1 was carved from red sandstone imported from the distant Altar de Sacrificios area (Schreiner n.d.).[9] At contemporaneous La Venta,

the Olmec also utilized a variety of exotic stones, including schist, serpentine, and gneiss (as opposed to the more common basalt), for the monuments placed around Pyramid C-1 (González Lauck 1994:98; see also Clark,
Chapter 5, this volume).

Tintal Stela 1 (Fig. 8.27) was first found by Ian Graham and a preliminary
drawing was published by Justeson and Mathews (1983). The sculpture had
been reset in the middle of a 3 m high Late Classic vaulted structure exposed by looters. The stela was associated with a round stone altar that may
have been contemporaneous with the stela, and, as at Nakbe, Pedernal, and
Holmul, had been the scene of extensive ritual behavior, which included the
burning and smashing of numerous whole vessels, including drums, bowls,
and vessels typically used to hold liquids (Chinja Impressed type). The stone
had been intentionally mutilated in antiquity, with deep pecking in the center
causing the over 7-ton monument to snap in half, nearly obliterating the iconography. The visible image portrayed what appears to be a single standing
human protagonist and a kneeling personage, with only the lower portions
of the legs visible with ankle knots and flared tassels, similar to those at San
Bartolo, Uaxactun, and Nakbe. The base of the monument has the remnants
of a large earlier carving of unusual form, perhaps part of an original boulder
sculpture. In addition, extensive Preclassic "graffiti" was carved on the base,
which survived because of its burial below floor levels. An important Early
Classic burial and associated funerary offerings were discovered at the base
of this monument (Hansen et al. 2006), suggesting that the monument had
been re-erected and placed in its present position during Early Classic times.

Nakbe Stela 1 was found in 45 fragments and had been intentionally
smashed in antiquity (see Hansen and Guenter 2005; Fig. 8.28). The sculpture depicts two standing, barefoot individuals dressed in royal regalia with
elaborate headdresses, belt heads with plaques, and large inset earflare-like
spools, consistent with other known early examples such as the Loltun cave
carving (Freidel and Schele 1988a, 1988b). The figure on the left is indicating upwards with his left hand, index finger extended, toward a profile
head appended to the headdress of the individual on the right. There is a
strong iconographic relationship between the appended headdress figure
and God E, the Maize God, in Olmec and Maya cosmology (Taube 1996a,
2004; Fields 1989, 1991; Freidel 1990; Hansen 1992a). The identity of this
individual as the Maize God is also confirmed in the San Bartolo murals
(O'Neill 2002; Kaufmann 2003; Saturno, Taube et al. 2005a).

8.27. A portion of Tintal Stela 1, showing the lower feet of a standing individual and a kneeling figure to the right. The massive sandstone monument is 2.17 m wide at the base line of the sculpture (Photo by C.D. Bieber).

8.28. Nakbe Stela 1, reassembled from 45 fragments (Drawing by R.D. Hansen and J.L Hansen).

While there is no doubt that the portrayed individuals on Stela 1 are dressed in royal regalia, the question is, Who were they? My original assessment was that they were either a representation, or a personification, of the Hero Twins of the *Popol Vuh* (Hansen 1992a, 2000). However, many known dual figures on other early monuments (e.g., Polol Altar 1, Kaminaljuyu Altar 1, Takalik Abaj Stela 5, El Baul Stela 1, and later monuments, such as Palenque Tablet of the Sun, Copan Altar Q, Altar L, and Motmot Marker) appear to commemorate transfers of power, as in showing an incoming ruler with a predecessor or founding father (Sharer 1994:106). It is possible then that Nakbe Stela 1 depicts a Maya ruler acknowledging a predecessor, one with considerable status, as the figure on the right has at least six appended plaques (versus three on the lefthand figure). Furthermore, the plaques on the figure on the right have an unusual projection, not unlike the form of a chest plaque found in Comitan, Chiapas (Lowe 1989b, 1994:125). While some have suggested that Olmec rulers actually intruded into the Maya lowlands, as possibly commemorated on Nakbe Stela 1 (Clark et al. 2000:494–95), this author contends that the monument represents a later ruler acknowledging a right to reign through a link to the founding ruler of the dynasty, shown in an ideologically acceptable format, such as the "Hero Twin" myth. The intrusive appearance of the Olmec in the Pacific coastal regions is striking, as noted by marked changes in ceramics and figurines (e.g., Lesure 2000, 2004), a phenomenon not evident in the Mirador Basin sites. Nevertheless, the possibility exists that the monument could portray the arrival of a foreign ruler in somewhat the same speculative manner as La Venta Stela 3 or the "Alvarado Stela" in the National Museum in Mexico are occasionally interpreted as representing the intrusion of a Maya ruler into the Gulf coast lowlands.[10]

It is suggested here that the similarities between the sizes and forms of the La Venta monuments and the great sculptures in the Mirador Basin are not coincidental, but are the product of a vigorous ideological competitiveness (see Lowe 1977, 1981, 1989a). The massive size, celtiform shape, and use of exotic stone in the Mirador Basin appear to match a similar trajectory of stelae manufacture in the Olmec heartland areas at about the same time (see Porter 1992). Monuments such as La Venta Stela 1, Stela 2, Stela 3, Monument 25, and Monument 26 provide strong comparisons in the similar changes in size, form (celtiform), the importation of exotic (non-local) stone, and rich iconographic themes. The La Venta monuments, along with

Nakbe Stela 1, also correlate with the emphasis on legitimacy during political centralization, a process known in numerous emergent complex societies (see Kolb 1994). The parallel development during this era in both the Gulf coast and Maya lowlands may be quite adequately explained by Renfrew's Peer Polity Interaction model (Renfrew 1986; see also Hansen 2005).

The discovery by William Saturno of the murals at San Bartolo, Guatemala, can perhaps refine the dating of the iconography of Nakbe Stela 1 and Tintal Stela 1. The similarities of the knot bundles on the ankles, the Maize God head, and the dress of the protagonists on Nakbe Stela 1 to the scenes in the San Bartolo murals are striking. Further iconographic connections are found on El Mirador Stela 4, which has two kneeling female figures with beaded ankles and breechcloths similar to the San Bartolo figures. Recent C-14 dating of the murals places them around 100 BCE (Saturno et al. 2005b), which is more compatible, stylistically, with the later El Mirador Stela 4, which dates to the Late Preclassic period.[11]

It is suggested here, however, that Nakbe Stela 1 and Tintal Stela 1 are earlier than the San Bartolo murals and El Mirador Stela 4 and most likely date to the late Middle Preclassic–early Late Preclassic period. This conclusion is based on: (a) Middle Preclassic archaeological contexts for monuments at Nakbe; (b) the diminutive size and the presence of early glyph panels on known Late Preclassic monuments in the Basin; (c) the use of exotic stone and the large size of the monuments that appears to coincide with the size and composition of monuments in the Olmec heartland; and (d) the thematic elements of the sculpture, which appear to be earlier than the Late Preclassic.

In summary, the Middle Preclassic period witnessed the introduction of sculptured stone monuments, demographic increases, agricultural intensification, and major architectural development, including causeways, reservoirs and agricultural systems, which created the demand for procurement and transport of architectural fill, limestone quarry specialization, lime production, and stucco utilization. There were major transformations in the size and form of limestone blocks used in architectural constructions. The cultural innovations were fueled by a differential access to wealth, organized exploitation of natural resources, implementation of systematic agriculture methods, and an increasing focus on labor intensification and specialist production systems. The result of these transformations served to consolidate the economic and political power of an emerging administrative elite. The evidence indicates that by the end of the Middle Preclassic period monuments depicting individual rulers began to appear at Nakbe and other sites in the Basin. These monuments significantly contributed to a powerful display of legitimization and would have impacted elite control over commoner subjects.

APOGEE OF LOWLAND STATES IN THE LATE PRECLASSIC PERIOD (CA. 400 BCE–150 CE)

The brief period between the Middle Preclassic and the Late Preclassic period (ca. 400–300 BC) does not appear to have been a simple transition. Pollen data from core samples obtained by the Mirador Basin Project from three lakes in the western Mirador Basin indicate that native forest had returned to the area during this particular narrow span of time, suggesting a temporary disruption of occupation (Wahl 2005; Wahl et al. 2005, 2006; Wahl, Byrne et al. 2007; Wahl, Schreiner et al. 2007). This observation has limited archaeological corroboration, suggested by the decomposition and weathering on Mirador Str. 34 Sub 1 prior to its burial by the Late Preclassic Str. 34. This "hiatus" was short-lived, however, based on associated archaeological and pollen data. Excavations indicate that within a short time, rulers in the Mirador Basin commissioned new monumental architecture of unprecedented size by the beginning of the Late Preclassic period (ca. 300 BCE). Structures between 40 and 72 m in height and measuring up to 600 x 300 m at the base were constructed throughout the Mirador Basin during this time, especially evident at large sites such as El Mirador, Nakbe, Wakna, Tintal, Xulnal, Lechugal, Paixban, Tazumal, and numerous smaller sites with radically new architecture (Hansen 1990:171–72; 1998, 2000).

In addition to an emphasis on monumentality, the manipulations by the emergent political, religious, and economic elite further consolidated the demand for and control of extensive labor systems in the early Late Preclassic period through the incorporation of both new and old ideological content in architectural formats. This included the establishment of the Triadic Architectural Pattern, one of the most consistent formats at the major sites in the Mirador Basin (Fig. 8.29). Triadic architecture became ubiquitous in the Late Preclassic Maya lowlands, and the form was adopted over a wide geographical area. El Mirador, itself, has at least 24 major triadic groups within the civic center, with more being discovered as the mapping extends

8.29. Tigre Complex at El Mirador (modified from drawing by Studio C, Guatemala; Courtesy of Fernando Paiz).

to the peripheral regions. The triadic arrangement is most likely related to the concept of the "Celestial Hearth" and the reference to Creation (see Hansen 1990, 1992a, 1998:77–81). Its use in subsequent periods, such as the Cross Group at Palenque, Caana Pyramid at Caracol, and the Early Classic Structures 5D-22, -23, and -24 at Tikal, was a conscious reference to the past and its ideological meaning.

The placement of structures was planned with considerable precision, perhaps to conform to celestial and solar cosmograms. Archaeologist Carlos Morales detected a series of strategic alignments of buildings, forming parallel and perpendicular alignments, and isosceles triangle associations (Morales-Aguilar and Hansen 2005; Sprajc et al. 2009). Structure placements appear to have allowed shadows of tall buildings to fall on specific buildings on important days of the calender year, particularly the equinoxes (Hansen n.d.). Structures were also placed with specific alignments that correlate to solar movements and patterns (Sprajc et al. 2009).

The Late Preclassic Maya at El Mirador also utilized a form of atavism, a reversion to the ideology and thinking of former times. This is particularly evident on the first platform of Danta Pyramid (Fig. 8.30), where four smaller triadic structures form a square at each corner of the basal platform, with a fifth point represented by the eastern bar-like structure of the E-Group constructed on the platform, all forming a "quincunx" design consistent with Olmec and early Mesoamerican ideologies (Reilly 1994a 1994b, 1995a, 1995b; Taube 2004:13). In Mesoamerican art the antiquity of the quincunx, with a symbolic *axis mundi* in the center, extends well into the Middle Preclassic periods in the Olmec, Zapotec, and Maya areas, forming one of the ideological staples of early Mesoamerican cosmology (see Reilly 1994a, 1994b; Bauer 2005a, 2005b; Estrada-Belli 2006a). The incorporation of such ancient ideological content in architectural formats indicates that the administrative elite adhered to a vibrant religious ideological system, one capable of invoking and controlling vast amounts of labor, tribute, and economic and political power.

In addition, architectural sculptures rendered in deep relief consisting of deity portraits continued to be placed on facades flanking structure stairways. Monumental sculpture on building facades from the Middle Preclassic and early Late Preclassic periods were carved in minute detail in stone prior to applications of stucco (Nakbe Structure 1, Nakbe Structure 27, El Mirador Structure 200, El Mirador Structure 34 Sub1). Late Preclassic architectural sculpture, such as that on El Mirador Structure 34, Danta Pyramid, and La Pava Acropolis at El Mirador, utilized thick molded stucco placed over large stone armatures with only minimal prior stone carving.

As monumental architecture increased in size, the size of stone stelae appears to have decreased dramatically, supporting the notion that the architecture became a literal and figurative extension of the stela (Hansen 2007). The decrease in stone sculpture from heights of 4 to 5 m to monuments less than 1 m in height was a dramatic shift in social and political emphasis that is not well understood. One possibility is that this decrease in size may reflect a change in the means used to commemorate kingship. The size decrease is further accentuated by the fact that no monuments have been located in their original locations in front of major Late Preclassic structures in the Mirador Basin—locations where the Classic Maya would have placed monuments in great abundance. The possible exceptions are the mutilated Monument 21 located in a secondary context at the base of the triadic Cutz Complex in the Grand Plaza at El Mirador (Fig. 8.31) and a stela and altar at the western base of Danta Pyramid, although the dates of the placement of these monuments are uncertain.

The reduced size of the monuments also correlates with the introduction of hieroglyphic texts that were carefully incised in fine lines on the monuments and other portable objects during the Late Preclassic and Ter-

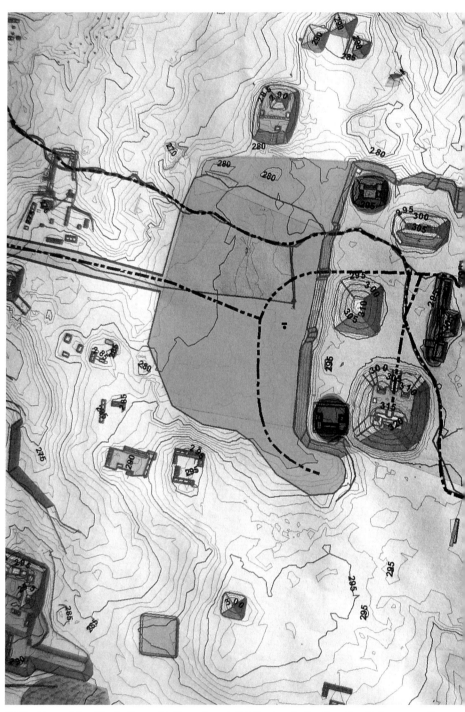

8.30. Map of the Danta Pyramid Complex at El Mirador, indicating the Quincunx pattern identified by R. Hansen on the first platform of the building (Map by DEPIC; Josephine Thompson, © FARES 2009).

8.31. A fragment of the badly mutilated El Mirador Monument 21, located at the base of the triadic Cutz Complex in the Grand Plaza at the site (drawing by G. Valenzuela).

minal Preclassic periods (ca. 100 BCE–250 CE). El Mirador Stela 2 has one of the earliest incised hieroglyphic texts yet known from the Mirador Basin (Hansen 1991, 1995, 2001a). This consists of a band of incised glyphs with several phonetic elements still visible in the badly weathered and perhaps intentionally mutilated glyphs. Stela 1 from El Chiquero was, in its intact form, less than 90 cm in height, but a text panel, which had been carefully scraped off in antiquity, is located on the lower half of the monument (Fig. 8.32a, b). The badly weathered Monument 3 at Pedernal, located southeast of El Mirador, has two standing figures in elaborate royal dress, on each side of a glyph panel (Fig. 8.32c). This composition is similar to early sculptures in the southern Maya area, such as Takalik Abaj Stela 5, and the southern Peten on Polol Altar 1. The text had been almost entirely removed by the Maya, with the exception of a single glyph that was nestled in a slight cavity of the stone.

Small Terminal Preclassic (ca. 150–250 CE) monuments have been discovered by Nikolai Grube east of Naachtun at the site of La Toronja (Grube and Martin 2001:II–43) and in the Bajo de la Juventud near Tikal. The Hauberg Stela (Schele 1985; Guenter 2002) is of similar form and format and is believed to date as early as ca. 199 CE (Schele 1985) or slightly later in the Early Classic period (Guenter, pers. comm. 2004).

A hierarchal pattern in human burials is evident in the Mirador Basin during the Late Preclassic period. The small number of earlier burials is probably the result of archaeological sampling. Formal Middle Preclassic burials have been identified throughout the Maya lowlands, as at Cuello (Hammond 1977a, 1985a; Robin 1989) and in the Maya highlands, as at Los Mangales (Sharer and Sedat 1987:147). Middle Preclassic burials have also been recovered at Nakbe (Op. 32, Op. 52), but formal tomb constructions are still undetected. The Late Preclassic elite tombs recovered in the North Acropolis at Tikal (Coe and McGinn 1963; W. Coe 1965a, 1965b) are believed to represent early royalty. In the Mirador Basin, elaborate Late Preclassic tombs such as those in Wakna Structure 3 (Fig. 8.33) were placed in a triadic pattern, replicating the triadic format of the architecture (Hansen 1998:90–95).[12] An informant (the actual looter of the major tombs at Wakna) showed this author three burial chambers in Structure 3 with Late Preclassic pottery (Fig. 8.34) still *in situ*. According to the informant, a total of 23 pounds of jade (sold by the pound) had been extracted from the principal chamber in the central structure of the triadic platform (Hansen 1998:90–91).

The massive scale of Late Preclassic architecture found within the Mirador Basin leaves little doubt that political and economic power was highly centralized. The presence of carved monuments with portraits and texts, and the existence of large tombs within major structures, all point to the consolidation of power under the authority of individual rulers (Hansen 2012a; see also Martin, Chapter 12, this volume). Given the explicit depiction of a royal inauguration on the San Bartolo murals, it is clear that the Late Preclassic rulers of that site, together with those in the Mirador Basin and elsewhere, were ancestral versions of the Classic period sacred kings who held power at a series of capitals across the Maya lowlands.

The Late Preclassic kings of the El Mirador Basin oversaw the mobilization of labor in unprecedented numbers to construct and maintain a variety of public works designed to serve both the practical and esoteric needs

a

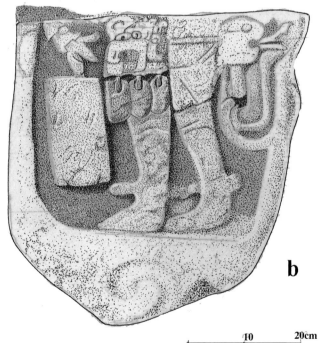

b

10   20cm

El Chiquero Stela 1
Drawn: E. Ortega, R. Hansen

c

30 cm

8.32. a, b) *facing page* El Chiquero Stela 1 from the Late Preclassic; c) *above* Pedernal Monument 3 from the Late Preclassic (Photo by C. Sherriff).

of their subjects. Calculations of the energetics of construction programs based on extensive experiments conducted by the Mirador Basin Project have determined that as many as five million man-days of labor were needed to construct the Tigre Complex (Hansen 1990), and ten to twelve million man-days of labor were needed to construct the massive Danta Pyramid (both at El Mirador), depending on quarry locations.[13]

Plazas, like that immediately west of the Leon Pyramid (the massive E-Group building in El Mirador's Central Group), were designed as catchment systems for water collection and management in artificial reservoirs at the site. A system of reservoirs in the Grand Central Acropolis at El Mirador was constructed to collect water from adjacent plastered buildings. The sophisticated sluice and pool systems of these reservoirs were enhanced with finely modeled stucco decorations just above the water line. Depicting

8.33. Tomb 1 of Wakna, which had been looted prior to 1990, when an informant took the author to see the site. Preclassic ceramics were still in the chamber when it was found, but, according to the informant, the jade artifacts had been removed and sold. Note the structural similarities of the vault construction to a Cimi phase tomb in Structure 5D-86 at Tikal and a tunnel in Structure J at Monte Alban (Hansen 1998: 95) (Photo by H. Mejia).

8.34. Arranging ceramics fit for a king, Guatemalan archaeologist Beatriz Balcarcel prepares the vessels that were recovered from the looted Late Preclassic tombs at Wakna for photography (Photo by R.D. Hansen).

nearly the entire pantheon of Maya cosmology, these decorations include several variant images of Itzamná in avian form, an undulating feathered serpent with aquatic references, aquatic elements, repeated images of the rain deity Chak, and what appears to be the Hero Twins of the Popol Vuh, with one transporting a decapitated head. Such rich iconographic details, lining Preclassic sunken plazas and reservoirs, are a testament to an over-arching sophistication governed by (and governing) a broad ideological base (Fig. 8.35; Argyle 2010; Argyle and Hansen 2010, 2016; Hansen n.d.).

A massive defensive wall, now about 8 m high in its ruined state, was erected along three sides of the central area of El Mirador, with the fourth side framed by a 30 m escarpment (Medina 2012; see Fig. 8.6). A defensive 15 m deep moat system recently has been discovered to the east of Danta Pyramid at El Mirador. In addition, a major moat system has been discovered at the sites of Xulnal and Tintal surrounding a large portion of the civic centers of the sites (Fig. 8.36). These wall and moat systems suggest the need for restricted areas, most likely defensive constructions, to protect the cities and their occupants from an external but undetermined threat.

While first constructed in the Middle Preclassic, the extensive causeways linking the major sites within the Basin were renewed and expanded during the Late Preclassic period. Satellite cities such as La Ceibita, located to the south of Tintal, were connected by causeways to the larger centers, and even smaller peripheral communities were connected by causeways to the satellite cities. This network is a testament to inter-site and intra-site interaction that enabled commerce, trade, tribute, food distribution, military support, and communication to flourish during the Late Preclassic period. Reflecting this interaction, neutron activation analyses of Preclassic and Classic ceramics from numerous sites within the Basin by Ron Bishop and Dorie Reents-Budet are beginning to show intense interaction and ceramic exchange within the Basin (Bishop, pers. comm. 2011; Reents-Budet et al. 2011).

The evidence for Late Preclassic complexity and centralization of authority, apparent from long-term archaeological research in the Mirador Basin, is replicated, albeit on a smaller scale, at a number of other sites in the Maya lowlands. This evidence forms the backdrop for, and is symptomatic of, what has been previously dubbed the "Chicanel State" (Hansen 1982, 1984, 1990), referring to the widespread, uniform ceramic sphere that extended throughout the lowlands during the Late Preclassic period (see Forsyth 1989, 1992, 1993a, 1993b). The uniformity of the Late Preclassic

8.35. Frieze decorating what was originally a sunken plaza and subsequently renovated as a series of pools and water collection reservoirs with rich iconographic images, depicting important elements of Maya cosmology (Photo by R.D. Hansen, ©FARES 2010).

Tintal Central Area

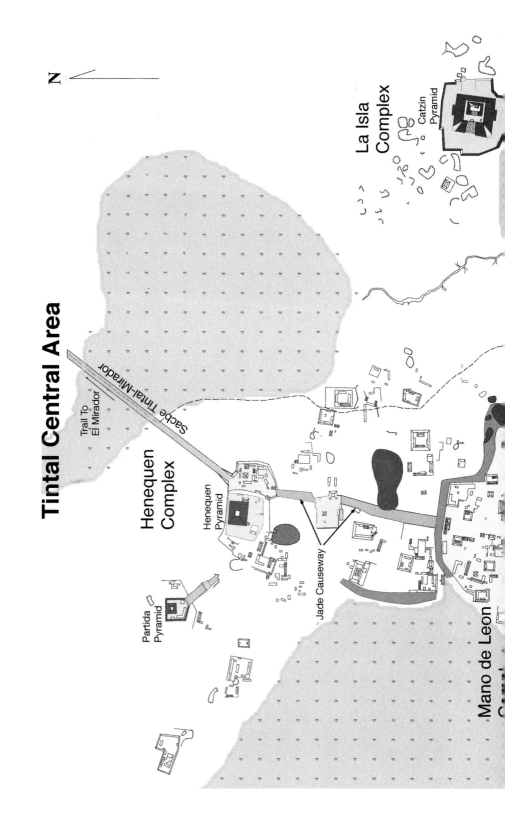

N

La Isla Complex

Catzin Pyramid

Trail To El Mirador

Sacbe Tintal-Mirador

Henequen Complex

Henequen Pyramid

Partida Pyramid

Jade Causeway

Mano de Leon

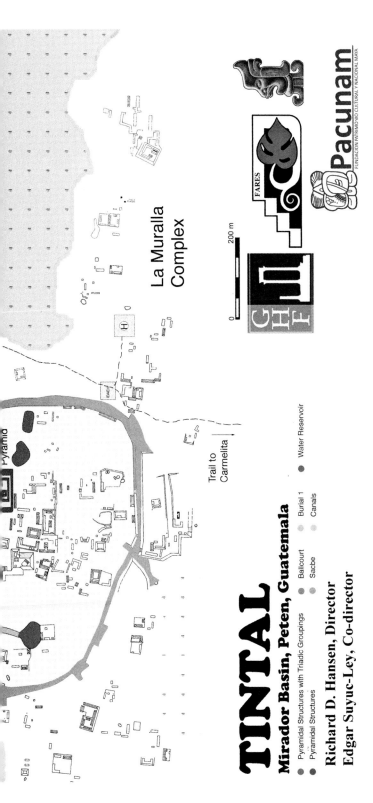

La Muralla Complex

Trail to Carmelita

TINTAL
Mirador Basin, Peten, Guatemala

● Pyramidal Structures with Triadic Groupings ● Ballcourt ● Burial 1 ● Water Reservoir
● Pyramidal Structures ● Sacbe ● Canals

Richard D. Hansen, Director
Edgar Suyuc-Ley, Co-director

0   200 m

FARES

Pacunam
FUNDACIÓN PATRIMONIO CULTURAL Y NATURAL MAYA

8.36. Map of a portion of the civic center of Tintal, Mirador Basin (Map by H. Mejia, E. Hernandez, J. Thompson, ©FARES 2011).

Chicanel Ceramic Sphere was never matched in any previous or subsequent periods of Maya history, and the implications are that a state mechanism provided the impetus and social, political, and economic vehicles in ceramic exchange extending over the entire Maya area from the tip of the Yucatan Peninsula to Honduras.

Preclassic Sacred Kings

As already mentioned, the evidence also points to the presence of kingship as the ultimate authority within this sophisticated Middle and Late Preclassic socio-political development (R. Hansen 2000, 2001a, 2012a). But the identification of the specific protagonists behind this system has been more elusive than the infrastructure they created. Perhaps one of the most promising avenues has been the insightful research by Simon Martin (1997; Grube and Martin 2001) and Stanley Guenter (2004, 2007, n.d.) on the 17 known codex-style vases painted in the Late Classic period between ca. 670 and 740 CE. These vessels, now in private collections, present what appears to be a retrospective dynastic history (Martin 1997:862; Guenter 2004, 2007) of a series of rulers of the Kan or "Snake" Kingdom. While some of the 17 vessels present only portions of the dynastic sequence, each documents a consistent series of rulers' names and dates of accession, even though recorded by different scribes. There are no known Classic period rulers that correlate with the sequential listings and the *tzolkin* and *haab* dates recorded on the codex-style vases (Martin 1997:862). The range of recorded dynastic accessions of kingship proposed by Guenter is compatible with the archaeological evidence, with dynastic accessions occurring between about 400 BCE and 20 CE (Guenter 2004, 2007, n.d.), precisely corresponding to the apogee of the proposed state within the Mirador Basin. Current research also suggests possible correlations with rulers on the codex-style vases. For example, Ruler 13 of the accession sequence, identified as Yuknoom Yich'ak'kak, who acceded to the throne on 8 Kaban 5 Xul, may be represented on the jaguar paw stucco panels on Structure 34 at El Mirador (Fig. 8.37). Guenter's proposed dates for this Late Preclassic ruler are consistent with both the ceramic and C-14 data (Beta 1965) of Structure 34 (see Hansen 1984, 1990).

Assuming the codex-style vessels record retrospective history, 2 of the 19 recorded dynastic protagonists were afforded the Kaloom'te title (Ruler 2 and Ruler 19, see Kerr #K6751; Martin 1997:846; Guenter n.d.), the highest

8.37. Reconstruction drawing of El Mirador Structure 34, also known as the Jaguar Paw Temple (Drawing by Studio C, Guatemala; Courtesy of Fernando Paiz and T.W. Rutledge).

title afforded any Maya king (Martin and Grube 2000:17). The Kaloom'te title appears to have been reserved for paramount kings or "conquerors," and the juxtaposition of the accession of these individuals with evidence of social upheavals at La Venta and the Gulf coast region may be more than coincidence. The last recorded king of the dynastic sequence appears to have been depicted on El Mirador Monument 18 as a downward peering ancestor figure (Guenter n.d., 2004; Chambers and Hansen 1996). He is also possibly retrospectively depicted on a Late Classic vase found in a burial under the summit floor of Structure 104 in the Codex Group at Nakbe (Hansen 2001b; Fig. 8.38).

The Mirador Basin and the Kan Polity

An elite burial located at the base of Tintal Stela 1 (ca. 300–400 CE) contained a mosaic jade mask with the largest fragment consisting of a highly polished trilobed jade, marked with an incised glyph and three U-shaped elements on the upper lobes (Hansen et al. 2006; Fig. 8.39). The incised glyph is an early version of T516, phonetically read as *ajaw*. The small serpent, which can be read as *kan*, located on the upper prefix of the glyph has been noted by Guenter, Grube, and Martin to be on the Hauberg Stela (glyph B-2; Fig. 8.40a), and on Tikal Stela 5 as a regal title for the mother of the great Yik'in Chan K'awiil (glyph D-9; Fig. 8.40b), suggesting that the Late Classic ruler of Tikal, Jasaw Chan K'awiil, took a wife from a site within the ancestral Snake (Kan or Kaan) Kingdom (Hansen, Howell et al. 2008).

An indication that the Mirador Basin was indeed the ancient site of the great Kan state was found in 2003 on 6 x 5 m bedrock carving excavated by project co-director Edgar Suyuc-Ley at La Muerta, a southern suburb of El Mirador. Suyuc-Ley's discovery revealed a medium relief sculpture of a series of superimposed profile deity heads carved in the bedrock (Fig. 8.41). In addition to extensive natural weathering, it appears that some of the carving had been intentionally mutilated long ago. The carved profile deity heads are oriented to the north, towards the center of El Mirador and towards a series of six glyphs in a vertical column. The glyphs are badly weathered, but sufficient details remain to allow tentative identification. The first glyph is part of a *tzolkin* date, with the number severely eroded. Photos and analyses with various lighting angles suggest that the glyph is most likely a *chicchan* day name, followed by two additional glyphs that are not understood, but must be a verbal phrase. These are followed by

8.38. Vase recovered from a burial in the summit of Structure 104 in the Codex Group at Nakbe. The image, an open-mouth serpent on a jaguar-skin throne, has similarities to the name of the 19th ruler of the dynastic sequence recorded on codex style vases (Photo by F.R. Hillman).

5   10 cm

8.39. Large tri-lobed, polished jade from a burial at the base of Tintal Stela 1, with a T516 *ajaw* glyph incised on the face. Note the serpent figure (*kan*) on the upper left of the glyph block. Width of jade is 6.62 cm (Photo by R.D. Hansen).

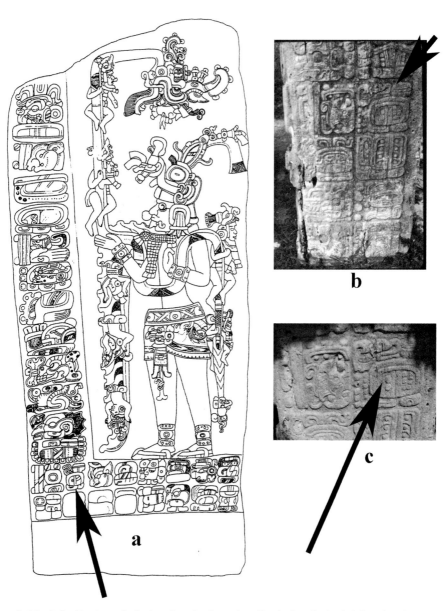

8.40. a) the Hauberg Stela showing the *kan-ajaw* (Snake-Lord) glyph (after drawing by L. Schele (Schele 1985); b,c) East face of Tikal Stela 5, noting that the mother of the Late Classic ruler Yik'in Chan K'awiil of Tikal was a *kan ajaw*, a woman from a site somewhere in the *Kan* polity (*Yokman*) that married Hasaw Chan K'awiil (Photo by R.D. Hansen).

8.41. La Muerta Monument 1, a bedrock carving (6 x 5 m) in a southern suburb of El Mirador, dating to the Terminal Preclassic-Early Classic periods (Photo by R.D. Hansen).

two more glyphs forming what is believed to be a nominal phrase. The final glyph is the distinctive snake or *kan* glyph with the *ajaw* prefix (see Hansen, Suyuc-Ley et al. 2008:58; Fig. 8.42). This evidence, combined with the Tintal jade glyph, suggests that the Mirador Basin was home to the original Kan site, birthplace of the Maize God, and perhaps the original

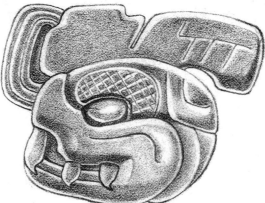

8.42. Lower glyph on the bedrock panel of La Muerta Monument 1, showing the *k'ujul kan ajaw* title (Photo by R.D. Hansen ©FARES 2003; Drawing by E. Ortega).

Tamoanchan site, the ancestral reference for generations of subsequent Maya societies (Hansen and Guenter 2005; Guenter 2005, 2007; Hansen, Suyuc-Ley et al. 2008:61–62).[14]

The Kan lords had apparently achieved an immortality worthy of being recorded in retrospective histories on Late Classic pots and carved in stone, and leaving, as a testament to their administrative prowess, the jungle-shrouded architecture of the great ancestral cities of the Basin. It was this legacy that encouraged the kings of great Maya cities within the Basin, such as Calakmul, and at Dzibanche in Quintana Roo, to be explicitly identified with the Kan Kingdom. Maya kings of Calakmul even assumed some of the ancestral royal names recorded on the codex-style vessels, a practice also observed at Tikal and Yaxchilan.

CONCLUSION

The Mirador Basin data suggest that Maya kingship was a process closely linked with the economic capabilities of the region, with control of a large and ample labor force, and ideological incentives (religious. political, economic) that persuaded and coerced the masses to accommodate royal institutions and bureaucracy (Hansen 1992a, 2000, 2012a). If our conclusions are correct, by the late Middle Preclassic period the rulers of small state systems emerged in the Mirador Basin and embarked on the formation of perhaps the first expansive state in the Maya lowlands, the Kan Kingdom, with its presumed capital at Nakbe or El Mirador. By the early Late Preclassic period, however, the development of the state saw its apogee and El Mirador emerged as the major polity in terms of size and central position. From their beginnings, the centralized and cohesive nature of the earliest polities was characterized by the construction of causeways, which linked the major and minor cities of the Basin into a common economic and political alliance, with satellite communities joined to both major and minor sites. This precocious formation made possible the construction of the largest platforms, palaces, and pyramidal structures in most of the major sites in the Mirador Basin, and allowed the growth of the cities to be among the largest in the Maya world, centuries before the time of Christ.

The monuments and constructions of the Mirador Basin are the silent witnesses of a unique saga of human history, beginning in the early Middle Preclassic period and reaching a peak of development until a dramatic, demographic decline occurred at the end of the Late Preclassic period (Hansen 1984, 1990, 1992a, 2001a; Hansen, Howell et al. 2008; Hansen 2012b; Balcarcel et al. 2010). It is now apparent that the Preclassic kings of the Mirador Basin ruled over the first and most powerful states in the Maya lowlands. In the process, they created an architectural environment unrivaled in the Maya lowlands at any period of time.

Although there were likely subsequent rulers at various periods in the Mirador Basin, the entire area appears to have suffered large-scale depopulation by about 150 CE. This finding is corroborated by the pollen data that records the disappearance of maize pollen and agricultural weeds and the return of tropical forest species, also evident in the isotope signatures of the flora (Hansen et al. 2002). These detailed data, which are consistent from several sources along the western edge of the Mirador Basin, suggest the reality of this depopulation event chronologically, biologically, and culturally (Wahl 2005a; Wahl et al. 2005; Wahl et al. 2006, Wahl, Byrne et al. 2007; Hansen 2012b). As the tropical forest returned to cover the great Preclassic structures, a later modest and dispersed population returned in the Late and Terminal Classic periods, particularly in sites in the southern part of the Basin, residing in modest structures among the ruins of the former splendor (Hansen 1996, 2001b). The northern part of the Basin, however, erupted again in a formidable display of power with the emergence of Dzibanche and, ultimately, Calakmul as an expansive state system that dominated much of the political, economic, and social scenarios of the Late Classic Maya lowlands.

After the fall of the Preclassic states throughout the Maya lowlands, it appears that the ruins of the great cities of the Mirador Basin were the object of pilgrimages for centuries thereafter. This is indicated by the presence of Classic era incense burners on the summit of the largest pyramids, as well as several examples of Postclassic ceramics and figurines on structures or in burials (Hansen, Howell et al. 2008). Recent excavations at the site of Naachtun have demonstrated a strong Early Classic and Terminal Classic presence at the site, suggesting that perhaps some of the occupants from the interior of the Basin had migrated to Naachtun (Nondedeo et al. 2012). The floresence at Dzibanche in the Early Classic period and, subsequently, at Calakmul, which became a dominant state during the Late Classic period, is likely reflective of the polity that existed centuries earlier farther south in the same cultural and environmental system. It is noteworthy, however, that the name of Calakmul was not *Kan* or *Kaan*, but rather *Ox te'tuun* or *Chiik Naab* (Martin and Grube 2000:104). It is likely that the Kan title was a reference to the Preclassic polity that had provided the legacy and legitimacy for the Basin rulers at Calakmul.

Meanwhile, the occupants of many of the abandoned Preclassic sites during the Late Classic period included artists and scribes, living in modest structures, who produced the unique codex-style ceramics (Robicsek and Hales 1981; Hansen et al. 1991; Hansen, Howell et al. 2008; Reents-Budet et al. 2011) that they exported to other sites within the Basin such as Calakmul (Reents-Budet et al. 2011). Neutron activation analysis of these materials and comparison with more than 36,000 other samples show that codex-style ceramics are unique in composition and restricted in manufacture to the Mirador Basin (Reents-Budet et al. 2011). They present detailed supernatural and mythological scenes in finely painted lines on bowls, plates, and vases. But they also record a fascinating sequence of kings believed to be the dynasty of the Preclassic Kan rulers, who once presided over the first state-level polity in the Maya lowlands. This legacy, both of the rulers and the ruled, and the associated cultural and natural dynamics of statehood and kingship formed the primordial foundation for the first Maya states.

ENDNOTES

8.1. A maize pollen (*Zea mays*) grain, recovered from a sealed lake deposit (Puerto Arturo) was associated with sediments between two AMS carbon dates of 3320 and 1279 BCE (calibrated). The sample has an estimated calibrated date of 4650 BP (2700 BCE) according to the fine-grained stratigraphic sequence, suggesting that an early corn-growing occupation may have occurred somewhere in the Basin (Wahl 2005). We now have additional evidence for an early agricultural presence in three of the small lakes along the western edge of the Basin, where AMS dates show a consistent presence of *Zea mays* and agricultural weeds by 2600 BCE (Wahl et al. 2006, 2007; Wahl et al. 2014; Wahl et al. 2015). Deep deposits under early Middle Preclassic platforms at Nakbe have revealed post holes, and stone debitage that date to approximately the same period.

8.2. The distribution of early Middle Preclassic settlements may have been severely distorted by subsequent quarrying activity over vast portions of Nakbe, particularly to the south of the East Group and areas between the East and West Groups. I conclude, based on the size and distribution of monumental architecture at Nakbe, and test excavations throughout the peripheral areas, that Middle Preclassic residences and platforms covered the entire site. A similar situation probably occurred in the Cascabel and Sacalero areas of El Mirador, now known to date to the Middle Preclassic periods. Further sampling at more distant locations from the site center should resolve this issue.

8.3. The presence of cortex on recovered obsidian waste flakes and core shatter indicates that some San Martin Jilotepeque obsidian was transported into Nakbe and El Mirador in raw nodule form, and there is ample evidence of early-stage reduction debitage. Other possible cortex sources may have been on the distal ends of cores and possibly large imported flakes, but evidence suggests that obsidian was transported with cortex and initially worked at the sites into prismatic blades. Chemical analyses by Ray Kunselman of 85 samples of Middle Preclassic obsidian blades and flakes from sealed contexts show a strong concentration (66%) of Middle Preclassic obsidian from San Martin Jilotepeque, with 32% from El Chayal, and 1% from Ixtepeque (Kunselman 2000). Percentages may change with the pending analyses of more obsidian fragments from Middle Preclassic contexts at Nakbe and El Mirador, but comparisons with other sites suggest that SMJ percentages are likely to increase.

8.4. At Nakbe, El Mirador, El Pesquero, Xulnal, and other sites in the Mirador Basin, the late Middle Preclassic period is characterized by large bowls with extremely wide everted rims (up to 10 cm wide) and waxy monochrome slips. In addition, slightly inverted-rim bowls with incised exteriors suggest a standardization of vessel forms, slips, and manufacturing modes. Woven mat motifs continue to be incised on vessel exteriors, indicating an enduring presence of the symbols of royalty.

8.5. Similar economic and social parallels can be observed in U.S. history. When the transcontinental railroad was completed in 1869, it served as a major stimulus in the economic and social integration of the country. Today, the rail system and the interstate freeway systems allow for social and economic interaction across the entire country.

8.6. The greatest percentage of monuments identified in the Basin are uncarved stones that appear to have been relocated from their original settings by Late Classic populations and reset, often near elite residences as a form of stela cult. Many of the stones are in a deteriorated state, without detectable carved or incised designs, since they frequently are still standing and exposed to the elements. It is also possible that many were originally covered with a lime plaster. These monuments are found along causeways (Nakbe Stela 12), near residential constructions (Nakbe Mons. 5, 6, 7, Stelae 10, 11), near major architecture (Nakbe Mon. 8, Stela 9; El Mirador Stela 19, Altar 20, Mon. 21), and even incorporated into architecture (El Mirador Mons. 5–11; La Florida Stela 1). They are also placed directly on platforms of buildings (Pedernal Stela 1, Altar 6). In some cases, stelae were placed without architectural associations (La Muerta Stela 2). Fragments of carved monuments are often found in rubble or along collapsed walls (El Mirador Stela 12), or were recovered from looters' camps (Zacatal Mon. 2).

8.7. Monuments at Pedernal, Tintal, and Nakbe were associated with smashed Late Classic ceramics consisting of drums, plates, bowls, and restricted orifice, liquid storage vessels (Chinja Impressed). Tintal Stela 1 was associated with incensarios and evidence of incense burning. Nakbe Monuments 2 and 3 were set inside Structure 52 where copal incense was found and bloodletting appears to have occurred (Hansen 1992a).

8.8. A series of Preclassic sculptures from coastal Chiapas had edges carved with both realistic and abstract figures (see Lee 1990). In like manner, San Jose Mogote Monument 3 had carving that extended over the side of the stone (Marcus and Flannery 1996:129).

8.9. Chemical and compositional analyses and subsequent comparisons with other red sandstone sources in the Maya area revealed that the stone for Tintal Stela 1 came from the lower Pasión and upper Usumacinta areas (Schreiner 1992). It appears that the sandstone slab weighing over 6.42 metric tons (Sidrys 1978:174), for which additional fragments have now been identified, came from the Altar de Sacrificios region, approximately 110 km away, 150 km by riverine routes. Its date of transport is uncertain, but it was most likely moved into the Mirador Basin during the Middle Preclassic and subsequently discovered, venerated, and ultimately mutilated during the Late Classic. The monument was recarved from an earlier sculpture, a practice known in Middle Preclassic times throughout Mesoamerica (e.g., Cyphers 1994).

8.10. The appearance of Olmec-style artifacts has been noted at a variety of sites, although evidence that these artifacts originated in the Olmec heartland is becoming increasingly evident (Blomster et al. 2005). At Mazatán, Chiapas, Clark noted the abrupt change in human figurine forms from the Ocos local style to the deformed crania of "Olmec" figurines (Clark 1990:51). Similarly, Richard Lesure found that the Soconusco region of Chiapas and Guatemala had a rapid decline in realistic ceramic animal effigies, thought to be associated with local traditions about 1000 BCE, while representations of stylized mythical creatures and symbols became common on incised vessels associated with the Olmec art (Lesure 2000, 2004). Changes in ceramics (from red serving wares to black or white wares) in Pacific coast societies have been correlated with emulation and/or contact with the Gulf coast Olmec (Clark and Pye 2000b:234). Architecturally, structural patterns and spatial organization of sites potentially accessible to direct Olmec occupation follow the north-south axis orientation of Olmec sites, as evident for examples at Finca Acapulco (Lowe 1977:285), San Isidro (Lowe 1989b), La Libertad (Lowe 1989b:382), and La Venta (see González Lauck 1996:74). These transformations may corroborate arguments that Olmec influence pervaded the Soconusco sometime around 1000 BCE, and coincided with shifts in social, political, and economic organizations.

A second visible shift is ostensibly between 900 and 600 BCE in which an Olmec presence is suggested by the appearance by small portable objects such as figurines, plaques, and jade celts. The viable trade and transportation routes along the Pacific coast made participation easier for the coastal societies in the broader interactions with the Olmec (Clark and Pye 2000b), yet the widespread availability of such objects from trade complicates their significance as evidence for Olmec influence or presence.

8.11. The result of examination of the San Bartolo ceramics by Donald Forsyth and this author concurs with Saturno's dating of the murals. The fill that covered the murals cannot be much earlier than 100 BCE or later than about the time of Christ. This suggests either that Nakbe Stela 1 is later than the late Middle Preclassic–early Late Preclassic period, or Preclassic iconographic depictions of figures like those in the murals remained fairly constant over several hundred years, as attested by studies of Olmec Maize God images on celts and other portable objects (Taube 1996a). I prefer the latter position because of the radical architectural, demographic, and iconographic changes in the Maya lowlands during the latter part of the Late Preclassic period. For example, text panels are not found on large late Middle Preclassic–early Late Preclassic stelae in the lowlands. Texts appear later, but only on monuments of extremely reduced size, characteristic of Terminal Preclassic sculpture.

8.12. Extensive excavations on Nakbe Structure 13, similar in size and shape to Wakna Structure 3, failed to locate burials in the same locations as those found at Wakna. Patterns of Late Preclassic royal burials are still enigmatic.

8.13. Recent mapping of the Danta Complex provided the first accurate map of the massive structure. Calculations of volumetric comparisons were based on the extensive experimental programs enacted by the Mirador Basin-RAINPEG project.

8.14. The Mirador Basin is also a candidate for being the legendary Tamoanchan place (Hansen, Howell et al. 2008). Tamoanchan was the mythological birthplace of political dynasties throughout all of Mesoamerica. "Tamoanchan" is not a Nahuatl or Mixe-Zoque word, but a Maya word meaning "Land of Rain or Mist" (Thompson 1950:115). The Tamoanchan place is associated with "primeros pobladores" (Sahagun 1955 (I):14) or the "house of descent, place of birth...where gods and men originated" (Seler 1904:220). Sahagun further explains that the Tamoanchan place was in the province of Guatemala (1955 (I):307), and associated with the land of mists, rain, and water. The long-abandoned Mirador Basin is a viable candidate for the mythical place of origin because of its swampy marshland landscape.

9

Rethinking the Role of Early Economies in the Rise of Maya States: A View from the Lowlands

ELEANOR M. KING

Economic exploitation is thus the clearest manner to demonstrate that political power was being exercised. (Rosenswig and Kennett 2008:137)

It has become axiomatic in studies of the rise of states to assume that emerging elites differentiated themselves from their contemporaries by centrally controlling key economic sectors. Because a state is, by definition, a centralized, hierarchical political entity, many theorists conclude that all aspects of the society were similarly organized (cf. Smith 2003). Besides, there is an unspoken feeling that, while people may not live on bread alone, control over the production and distribution of that bread—the economy— is an easy, obvious, and sure way to extend one's power. There are many variations on the theme of centralized economic control; however, a general model can be sketched, citing Mesoamerican examples.

Increased population leads to increased food production and the generation of a surplus, controlled by a fortunate few, the incipient elite. Either the rise in population itself (Love 1999a), the increase in production (Price 1984), or both (Clark and Blake 1994) are thought to be stimulated by these elite, who may have privileged access to critical resources such as land and water (McAnany 1995; Scarborough 1998; Lucero 1999, 2006). Surplus, in turn, sparks the development or intensification of craft specialization, also controlled by the incipient elite (Brumfiel and Earle 1987). Specialized production then promotes regional and trans-regional trade networks that tie emerging political centers together (Sanders and Santley 1983). Thus, early elites living in central places control both production and distribution of essential goods. These range from crops and utilitarian items used in all households, such as stone tools, to prestige items made of prized, often "exotic" materials like jade, primarily consumed by the elite. Few scholars claim the elite managed *all* sectors of the economy. They leave room for low-level agricultural and craft production in the control of incipient commoners—those on their way to becoming less equal. Some horizontal bartering or exchange among this group is also presumed to exist. Generally, though, rising elites are thought largely to control both the means and mode of production (Marx and Engels 1970, 1972)—that is both the land, labor, and technology of production and the social relationships that organize and deploy that labor. The degree to which Maya elite power relied on control of the economy at various sites is still being debated. However, the point here is that most Mayanists would agree that the elite relied to *some* degree on economic control, and that this control was *ipso facto* hierarchical and centralized (Scarborough and Valdez 2009; McAnany 2010:4), as befits our prevailing notions of the archaic state (Smith 2003, cited in McAnany 2010:16).

Most investigations of the rise of complexity follow this model, whether iterated or not. Not surprisingly, then, they start with the question "What resources did the elite control?" and proceed from there. This is what Anne Pyburn (2004) has called a "bad" question, like the famous "When did you stop beating your wife?" Bad questions frame the investigation so that no contradictory evidence can be presented (Pyburn 2004:19). By assuming an incipient elite exerted centralized control over the economy, we only look for what and whom they controlled and when. Conversely, all fresh data is interpreted circularly in that light so that nothing new can be learned. For the Maya, the thrust of theories on the rise of complexity since the first origins conference 30 years ago (Adams 1977) has been mostly to push back the beginnings of sociopolitical differentiation to earlier and earlier times. Only the dates have changed. The framing of the debate and the evidence used to support different theories remain very much the same. A better question might be "Why do we assume the elite controlled the economy to begin with?" I propose it has to do with our ingrained worldview.

According to Sahlins (1996), much of our Western worldview is still inextricably linked to early Judaeo-Christian ideas. The key moment in that tradition is the fall of Adam and his expulsion with Eve from Paradise. Because Adam and Eve sinned by wanting something they could not have, their descendants were condemned forever to have to satisfy their own desires. As Augustine put it, "the punishment was the crime" (Sahlins 1996:397). This idea of needs-driven man, woefully subject to his own physical and mental limitations from which he is freed only at death, dominated medieval and Renaissance thinking. Hobbes, Locke, and the materialist philosophers of the Enlightenment, however, brought a new twist to this worldview. Where previous scholars had seen bodily needs as "the original evil and a source of vast sadness," the new wave of thinkers saw these needs as simply "natural" or at least a "necessary evil"—a rational response to the unavoidable human condition (Sahlins 1996:398). In the hands of Adam Smith, needs even become the supreme source of social virtue, and for Bernard de Mandeville they were the source of society itself. As Sahlins (1996:38) puts it: "*O, felix culpa*!...Out of Sin came Society. Men congregate in groups and develop social relations either because it is to their respective advantage to do so or because they discover that other men can serve as means to their own ends." Sahlins dubs this pragmatic, Western view of the world "utilism," which he defines as "need-and-scarcity-driven behavior" (Sahlins 1996:397; cf. McAnany 2010:8–10). He points out that it lies behind capitalism and has been a driving force in shaping the world as we know it. Utilism is the basis for our "native" or folk (Hallowell 1965) anthropology—the principle by which we weigh and understand the actions of all peoples regardless of how they themselves might conceptualize the world and human actions. Sahlins even daringly suggests, albeit in a footnote, that there is a connection between the "triple libido" discussed by Augustine and some of our most powerful and enduring social theories. Augustine identified three principal "human lusts": for temporal goods, for carnal pleasures, and for domination. Sahlins asks, "Is it too crude to point out that the three main Western theories of human social behavior or of the formation of society would invoke the same desires: gain (Marx), sex (Freud), and power (Nietzsche, Foucault)?" (Sahlins 1996:397–98). Whether or not we can go that far, it seems clear that utilism is behind our views of past elites and their behavior. It is *the* principle guiding our questions on the rise of the state, early economies, and resource allocations, or, to borrow

Jameson's term (1991; cited in McAnany 2010), it is the "cultural logic" that frames our research.

For the Maya and other truly "foreign" societies this background assumption is problematic because it does not allow us to discover other, non-Western principles of sociopolitical organization (see also Clark 2007b:21; Sharer and Golden 2004). The Maya, in particular, have suffered from this as they are frequently compared to societies that conform more to our Western views of complexity and are found wanting. Compounding the problem of utilism is our equally Western tendency to conflate the concepts of "hierarchy" and "order." We tend to see organization as possible only in hierarchical terms. Thus, society for us is organized only when it is hierarchically organized—a concept still with us from the Greeks. For us, the opposite of hierarchy, then, is not horizontality but chaos (Crumley 1987; see Scarborough and Valdez 2009 for additional discussion of our cultural bias towards hierarchy). Utilism and hierarchy together make it very difficult for us even to conceive of a different kind of social order, one perhaps not strictly geared to desires for domination, temporal goods, and carnal pleasures, and not necessarily hierarchical (see McAnany 2010 for an extensive discussion of other motivations).

To remedy this situation, I will attempt to adopt a less biased stance and examine the evidence we have on early Maya economies from a non-hierarchical and, hopefully, non-utilist or perhaps less utilist perspective. In the much longer paper I prepared for the conference (King 2007), I examined economic indicators of the pre-state to state transition throughout the ancient Maya world. Here I will focus on the Peten and northern Belize. My goal is to evaluate what the data, such as they are, actually tell us. Please note, though, that many of the arguments made here can be extended to other parts of the Maya area that had different resources and different economies.

Three questions are relevant to an economic discussion: (1) what resources were used by people in the Maya area prior to and during the development of complexity? (2) how were they used? and (3) how were they valued? These questions can best be answered by looking at the main sectors of economic activity recognized by anthropologists: production, distribution, and consumption. I should note that McAnany (2010:8*ff*.), in summarizing discussions of prehistoric economies, has suggested that these three categories may not even apply to pre-capitalistic societies. According to some scholars, they do not properly reflect and configure the way that such economies worked.

McAnany (2010) herself shows how inextricably linked social relationships and ritual activities were with economic ones in the Maya world. I would argue, however, that using these three categories as simple descriptors of distinct types of economic activity does not preclude the inclusion of other factors in ancient economic processes. In the absence of more emic divisions, they provide useful heuristic domains, well-understood in anthropology, that enable us to separate out different types of activities for comparison and discussion rather than considering the mass of data altogether. With that in mind, responses to the first two questions posed above can be found in the accumulating data on agricultural and craft production, as well as patterns of exchange. Consumption, too, often neglected in archaeological studies, can give us critical insights into what and how resources were used (Pyburn 2008; Metcalfe et al. 2009). Even more importantly, consumption can help us get at the far more elusive question of value. Lesure (1999) and Graham (2002) have reminded us that many raw materials and finished objects assume a range of values that can vary according to circumstances, including location, time period, and use. Flad and Hruby (2007), Clark (2007b), and McAnany (2010:203) emphasize the fungibility between different categories of goods— alienable / inalienable, utilitarian / prestige—depending on how they are consumed and, as Speal (2009) points out, circulated. Pyburn (2008) concurs, stressing that value was actively construed and advertised by human agents, notably the Maya elite. Thus, we need to focus on how agents used artifacts in order to determine their value (Clark 2007b; see also McAnany 2010 for discussion of this point). One way to do so is through archaeological context. Several scholars have convincingly argued that tight contextualization of economic indicators rather than broad "presence/absence" criteria will indicate their relative importance. This observation seems to hold true whether we are dealing with faunal and botanical evidence (Shaw 1991, 1999; Metcalfe et al. 2009) or "high-end" goods such as jade or shell jewelry (Krejci and Culbert 1995; Buttles 2002). By looking at the full spectrum of variation in the contexts of where specific goods are found in specific regions, then, we should be able to derive some idea of their relative value. Because values may have changed over time, we need to compare contexts that are as nearly contemporaneous as our broad time frames will allow.

The development of complexity represents a process, however, not a single event. For the Maya, as far as we now know, this development spanned from the Middle Preclassic (1000–400 BCE), when initial differentiation occurred, to the beginning of the Late Preclassic (400 BCE–250 CE), when the first true states appear. To highlight the process rather than the end product I adopt a diachronic perspective. I will focus on that chronological range with the understanding that the development of the state was not uniform throughout the Maya world. In addition, the "Maya state" was not a single, monolithic entity. Not only were early Maya states often differently configured, but they changed from the Preclassic through the Classic. To understand the origins of states and the nature of complexity, then, we also need to understand its *transformation* over time.

For purposes of this study I define a complex society systemically as one made up of differentiated and interrelated parts, integrated into one sociopolitical unit governed by a hierarchy of authority. Different roles in such a society are differently valued, and status is at least in part ascribed rather than achieved. This definition thus encompasses both early Maya communities where functional distinctions and incipient stratification are first evident and later ones where centralized authority and diverse social roles and institutions are well established.

To avoid falling into the usual Western intellectual ruts, I use a heterarchical rather than hierarchical view of Maya complexity. Heterarchy has been defined by Crumley (1987, 1995, 2003) and developed by others (e.g., King and Potter 1994; Ehrenreich et al. 1995; King 2000; Scarborough et al. 2003; Metcalfe et al. 2009; Scarborough and Valdez 2009) as a model of sociopolitical organization that allows for the interplay between both vertical or hierarchical and non-vertical or horizontal elements within a society. It thus gives equal analytical weight to "inequality" and "heterogeneity" (McGuire 1983) in the development and expression of complexity. Structures are "heterarchical when each element is either unranked relative to other elements or possesses the potential for being ranked in a number of ways" (Crumley 1987:158). Power, for instance, can be hierarchical, as when one city in a society holds dominion over another. It can also "be counterpoised rather than ranked," however, as when three cities of equivalent size and importance have different power bases—military, commercial, political (Crumley 1995:3). As Crumley (1987, 1995) points out, there is nothing intrinsically hierarchical about complexity *per se*; oak trees, crystals, and symphonies have complex structures that cannot really be described as vertically organized. In human populations rigidly hierarchical systems may contain egalitarian subsystems, just as egalitarian systems may contain hidden hierarchies (e.g., gender; Flanagan 1989). Critical to the argument here is the fact that heterarchy does not negate hierarchy, it subsumes it—a point often lost on scholars either following Crumley's lead or objecting to the model (e.g., Smith and Schreiber 2005:205). In Crumley's terms (1987:163), true complexity is actually the interplay between hierarchy and heterarchy "across space, through time, and in the human mind."

The beauty of this model is manifold. First, it does not privilege hierarchy—our Western sense of order—at the expense of other possible organizations. That allows us to ask the "good" question of how authority was configured rather than the "bad" question of what the elites controlled. Heterarchy also allows us to disentangle the various threads making up Maya society. We can thus envision economic, political, and religious systems that *may* or may *not* have operated independently of each other. In other words, heterarchy forces us to prove rather than assume that complex functions were centralized and conflated into a single hierarchical structure. This flexibility is key for understanding Maya economies, which even in the Late Classic (600–900 CE), when Maya states were well developed, never seem synchronized with sociopolitical and religious organization (King 2000). We can also unravel different components of these economies and examine their interplay, as Scarborough and Valdez (2009) and McAnany (2010) have recently demonstrated. In addition, heterarchy allows us to deal with the regional and temporal variations that seem to plague the research on early states. Where hierarchy does not accommodate variability, heterarchy does. Thus we can acknowledge differences in how and when new polities emerged in differing parts of the Maya area and look at them as part of a larger pattern of complexity. Finally, heterarchy conforms more closely to the new models of self-organizing systems arising from complexity theory in the sciences (Kauffman 1993; Lansing 2003), allowing us to place social systems within the context of other types of complex systems. I would stress, however, that heterarchy, like hierarchy, does not *explain* complex behavior, it merely *describes* it. We still have to sort out what motivates that behavior.

EARLY MAYA ECONOMIES: A SELECTIVE OVERVIEW

Maya economies, like the economies of most early states, were agrarian, in this case based on the cultivation of maize. Agriculture is thought to have grown slowly out of localized foraging economies of the late Archaic

(8000–2000 BCE) that practiced limited forms of cultivation. While these economies were largely undifferentiated in the Early Preclassic (2000–1000 BCE), when farming was first widely adopted, by the Middle Preclassic we begin to see marked differences in goods and productive strategies that culminate in the Late Preclassic florescence of Maya states. Most theorists believe that the increasing variability observed in the Preclassic reflects the control of a newly emerging elite over the basic means of production— land, labor, and technology, as in our archetypical economic model (cf. Scarborough and Valdez 2009; Smith 2003). Added to that suite for the Maya should be water, a critical resource during the dry season. It deserves special mention, because of the recent theoretical emphasis on its management as a source of elite power (e.g., Scarborough 1998; Lucero 1999, 2006; Lucero and Fash 2006).

"Control" is notoriously difficult to address archaeologically, as there are few tangible signs of elites exerting it. Scholars generally use the co-occurrence of several traits to suggest its presence. Thus, we often infer land ownership, for example, from the existence of differentiated agricultural lands, some richer than others, the evidence of their continuous and intensive exploitation, and the simultaneous presence of large, "elite" architecture nearby. Similarly, control over technology, for instance craft production, is inferred from the distribution and location of workshops in relation to elite households and central spaces. As mere association is not enough (Clark 2003), other clues include tracing the ways craft products move from producers to non-producers. Elite control over labor is even harder to ascertain. It is manifest in public works such as roads and temples, which are presumed to have been built by a labor force larger than an extended kin unit. Total man-hours per volume of monumental construction (Abrams 1994) or the general requirements of intensive forms of cultivation (Harrison and Turner 1978; Turner and Harrison 1983) have been used to suggest a system of *corvée* labor and commoner-to-elite work indebtedness for the Maya. Interpreting these kinds of activities as evidence for elite control assumes that appropriation of labor was key for early elites. Without followers they would have been unable to create or build the power base necessary for expanded social control. Some scholars even suggest that the elite not only reaped the benefit of labor obligations from subordinates, but also actively reorganized and mobilized that labor in new ways (Sharer and Traxler 2006:180–82), changing the social relations through which labor was deployed (Wolf 1982:75). In other words, they controlled the mode as well as the means of production. Another consideration is that control can be less obvious than through direct orders. Incentives or rewards represent more subtle means of getting people to do your bidding. These are difficult to define archaeologically, though, and fall within the larger purview of how authority is accepted, naturalized, and perpetuated (McAnany 2010:16).

It is beyond the scope of this chapter to devise new ways to measure elite control over the means and mode of production. I will therefore fall back on the methods available with the caveat that they are often inadequate. I will also leave to others the task of figuring out how a kin-based labor system might have been appropriated and transformed by an emerging elite (see Chapter 10 for one such model) and what made commoners buy into the system (see McAnany 2010). Instead, I will explore how well our overarching economic scenario actually applies to the lowland regions selected. I will examine the complete economic cycle of production, distribution, and consumption, with an emphasis on what these activities can tell us about elite control over the means of production. I will address mode of production in my conclusions. Due to space limitations, I will not discuss all aspects of this economic triad in detail. I will focus on just two lowland production systems, subsistence and lithics. Food and water are essential to questions of land tenure, crop production (staple and special), and control over labor. They are also the basis for the generation of surplus, which enables support for non-agriculturalists and *corvée* work forces. Maya lithics have been well studied and leave a strong archaeological signature. They will serve to exemplify the economics of technology. I will then look briefly at how these products were distributed by the Maya and, finally, consumed.

Production: Food and Water

Conventional wisdom has it that farming in the Maya area was first adopted from the highlands by already settled populations of intensive foragers inhabiting the Pacific and Belizean coasts. From there cultivation is thought to have been taken inland by people moving up the rivers. Recent evidence, however, has suggested that some cultivars, such as maize, may actually have had a lowland origin and that Early Preclassic lifeways were far more variable than presumed (Pohl et al. 1996, 2007; Piperno et al. 2007; Lohse et al. 2006; Neff et al. 2006c). Some populations (Pacific coast) appear to have been settled whereas others (Belize) were not, and different groups relied differentially on agriculture. This early variability had important implications for the rise of Maya states.

In the central lowlands increasing data on early agriculture has given us a picture of contrasting developments (see Chapters 6 and 10, this volume). Pollen research in Belize has shown early evidence for habitat disturbances with cultigens (maize and manioc) appearing between 3400 and 3000 BCE (Jones 1991, 1994; cited in Lohse et al. 2006). Cultivation seems to have been more common around wetlands such as Cob, Cobweb, and Pulltrouser Swamps after 2400 BCE (Lohse et al. 2006), and farming became widespread in the Early Preclassic (Jones 1994; Pohl et al. 1996; cited in Lohse et al. 2006). This conclusion is supported by use-wear studies of constricted unifaces, the diagnostic artifact of the late Early Preclassic, which suggest they were used for land-clearing and perhaps hoeing (Gibson 1991; Hudler and Lohse 1994; cited in Lohse et al. 2006). Faunal analyses in turn suggest that, by the beginning of the Middle Preclassic, the species available reflect a long-disturbed habitat and, specifically, destruction of high-canopy rainforest (Shaw 1991, 1999). However, the degree to which the early inhabitants of Belize actually relied on agriculture is debatable. Early Preclassic settlement data are lacking, despite MacNeish's discovery of a few stratified early tool deposits on the coastal plain (Leslie Shaw, pers. comm. 2007) and the presence of early pit and posthole features on Caye Coco (Rosenswig 2004; cited in Lohse et al. 2006). It seems that most of Belize's inhabitants were still mobile foragers who practiced wetland margin agriculture as part of a broad subsistence round. How much they relied on maize even after they settled into farming is also in doubt, as maize counts remain low at various sites throughout the Preclassic (Miksicek 1991; Tykot et al. 1996; Powis et al. 1999; White and Schwarcz 1989; Henderson 2003). Indeed, both floral and faunal analyses suggest that wild foods remained an important part of the diet at this time (Henderson 2003; Shaw 1991, 1999).

Settled, pottery-using villages only appeared at the end of the Early Preclassic in Belize. The earliest are found in the Belize River Valley at Cahal Pech and Blackman Eddy, dating to between 1200 and 1100 BCE (Awe 1992; Garber 2004; Garber et al. 2004b; Healy and Awe 1995; Powis et al. 1999). In the north the dates are generally slightly later, though initial dates as early as 1200 BCE have been postulated for Cuello (Kosakowsky and Pring 1998). The recent consensus seems to be, however, that the first pottery-using villages appeared at Colha (Hester 1996), K'axob (McAnany et al. 2003), and

Cuello between 1000 and 600 BCE. It seems likely, then, that for a significant period of time mobile and settled horticulturalists co-existed in Belize.

It is unclear why settlement happened earlier in the Belize Valley, but there is evidence that agriculture and sedentism in the north responded to climate fluctuations. Several scholars have reported significant changes in the water table (Folan et al. 1983; Miksicek 1991; Pohl et al. 1996). Overall, sea levels have risen steadily 125 m since the beginning of the Holocene (Luzzader-Beach and Beach 2009), creating new wetland habitats in coastal areas (Pohl et al. 1996) and a higher water table (Luzzader-Beach and Beach 2009). However, this trend seems to have been reversed when the climate was cooler and drier (Miksicek 1991). One such regression happened in the Early Preclassic, with sea levels and water tables reaching their nadir between 1500 and 1000 BCE (Pohl 1996:364). In northern Belize drier conditions resulted in the exposure of significant new tracts of fertile, organically rich soils at wetland margins. Unsurprisingly, cultivation around these areas increases dramatically during this time, though the horticulturalists remain mobile. The pendulum then swung the other way, with water tables rising again around 1000 BCE and drowning the habitual wetland fields (Pohl et al. 1996). Near Cobweb Swamp, horticulturalists reacted by draining and modifying these fields in the early Middle Preclassic, leaving the first evidence for intensive agricultural practices in this area (Jacob 1992, 1995). To better keep up their fields, they decided to settle nearby, establishing the first village at Colha under the site core around 900 BCE (King and Potter 1994; Hester 1996). A high degree of cultural continuity in lithic techniques and forms suggests that the settlers were descendants of the original foraging cultivators rather than intruders (Iceland 1997). Sedentism at Colha thus seems to have followed or at least to have been coeval with agricultural intensification. The establishment of other sites in northern Belize, such as Cuello (Miksicek 1991) and K'axob (McAnany et al. 2003), also coincides with the rising water tables, though neither site is specifically associated with intensified agriculture. Cuello's location not far from Pulltrouser Swamp and K'axob's right on that swamp (Harrison and Turner 1978; Harrison 1990; McAnany et al. 2003), however, suggest that it could well have been an important factor in settling.

It is tempting to see agricultural intensification as the root of subsequent elite differentiation in the north, but the correlation is far from clear. The early Middle Preclassic communities there, like village communities throughout Belize at this time, were egalitarian. In fact Cliff and Crane (1989) have argued for Cerros that the Maya worked hard to suppress evidence of their differences until the Late Preclassic. It seems more likely, then, that we are dealing initially with what Pyburn (1998, 2008) has called "smallholders" and Lohse "householders" (Lohse 2002; Lohse and Valdez 2004)—small family farmers working to keep what they had. Social differences do emerge, but slightly later during the Middle Preclassic, when there is evidence at Colha, for example, of both horizontal and vertical differentiation. Distinct activity areas have been identified, including one that combined large hearths, plaster floors, and a high percentage of *tecomates* (neckless jars) for some unknown purpose (Roemer 1979). In other sectors, numerous burin spall drills, found in association with shell beads, suggest that bead manufacture as well as lithic production might have been important "cottage industries" at this time (Potter 1980:189; 1991). This variation in activity across the site strongly calls to mind Sheets's (2000) description of Late Classic Ceren in El Salvador, where households of comparable status showed evidence for horizontal specialization and interdependence. Similar specializations in shell ornament production have been documented for Cahal Pech and Pacbitun in the Belize River Valley (Lee and Awe 1995; Hohmann and Powis 1996; cited in Powis et al. 1999) and at Kichpanha in northern Belize, not far from Colha, where tool production is also found (Leslie Shaw, pers. comm. 2007). The beginnings of hierarchical differentiation appear at Colha in the replacement of domestic architecture in the site center by large, open platforms used for well-furnished burials and caches (Potter 1980, 1982; Buttles 2002), in a pattern McAnany (1995) has elaborated for K'axob and Garber (2004) for Blackman Eddy, slightly earlier. Whether the burials at Colha belonged to farmers, chertworkers, beadmakers, tecomate-users, or another group, however, remains moot. There is no clear-cut economic basis to incipient elite power. The same could be said for similar small communities now documented throughout northern Belize. Internal differentiation and incipient stratification hint at the beginnings of complexity but the economic tie-ins are unclear.

By the Late Preclassic clear stratification had emerged at northern Belizean sites, but it still does not seem to have been based on direct elite control over land and crop production. At K'axob, a longitudinal study by Henderson (2003) focused on the expanding size of farming households beginning in the Late Preclassic. Her results suggest that what she calls "large corporate households" developed quite slowly at the site and show significant autonomy in terms of indicators ranging from diet to goods. She concludes that the elite here controlled neither the land, nor the crops, nor the mode of production. Rather, the farmers did, though the elite may have had some overarching authority that could specify what they required (cf. Pyburn 2008 for a similar view of Late Classic households). Henderson's (2003) study is particularly significant because K'axob is one of the communities perched on the edge of Pulltrouser Swamp and associated with the raised fields there at that time (McAnany 1995; McAnany et al. 2003).Similarly, Scarborough and Valdez (2009) have documented the proliferation of small communities along the escarpments overlooking the Rio Bravo in the Three Rivers Region of Belize at this time. They argue that, from the beginning, these were interdependent, resource-specialized communities with economies based more on horizontal exchange than allegiance and tribute to the larger regional centers.

In the Peten interior a different pattern of land use and development prevailed from early on. There the importance of permanent water for Maya agricultural economies is evident. Pollen analysis from the edge of the Mirador Basin suggests that forest clearance and maize cultivation there may have begun as early as 2750 BCE, although the first permanent structures date only to 1000 BCE (Wahl et al. 2006). Perhaps the earliest horticulturalists in the Peten, then, were similar to their mobile counterparts in Belize, though there is little evidence, as yet, of their existence. The palynological consensus is that the period of significant human impact on the Peten environment begins around 1200 BCE (Brenner et al. 2002; Dunning et al. 2002; Hansen et al. 2002; Wahl et al. 2006), contemporaneous with settled villages in the Belize Valley (Lohse et al. 2006). It seems probable that these pioneers were already settled horticulturalists, based on the ceramics they left behind and the evidence from soil analyses. Work by several scholars has convincingly argued that early Maya occupations in the central lowlands focused on what were originally perennial wetlands, some with open water, which would have provided a ready source of water for storage and use during the dry season (Dunning 1995; Dunning et al. 2002, 2006; Hansen et al. 2002; Wahl et al. 2006; Beach et al. 2008). Access to water was crucial for settlement in this area, as the interior of the Peten is a karstic plain with internal drainage but no permanent rivers (Beach et al. 2006:6). Farming of wetland margins was underway by the early Middle Preclassic throughout this region, at a time when maximal rainfall across the southern lowlands (Brenner et al. 2000; Pope et al. 2000; cited in Dunning et al. 2002) would have helped establish permanent water sources (Dunning et al. 2002). In fact, the densest known area of early settlement in the Peten is the Mirador Basin where 70 percent of the land has been estimated to be *bajo* (Jacob 1994; cited in Hansen 2005), or wetland, now seasonal but once perennial (Dunning 1995; Dunning et al. 2002, 2006).

The earliest known occupation in the Mirador Basin is at Nakbe, where the remains of structures probably made of pole and thatch are associated with packed earthen floors. These constructions were swiftly replaced in the early Middle Preclassic (1000–800 BCE) by more substantial structures (Hansen 1993, 1994, 1998, 2005). By 600–500 BCE Nakbe covered an esti-mated 40–50 ha. There was also marked evidence of social differentiation at this time. Variation in the size and sophistication of residences, now made of stone and associated with paved plazas, suggests unequal access to resources. This conclusion is supported by the uneven distribution of decorated ceram-ics and figurines and by skeletal evidence for cranial deformations and dental incrustations in selective burials. Significantly, certain design motifs such as the mat, associated with elites, first appear at this time (Hansen 1993, 2005). The first large public platforms were erected during the middle of the Middle Preclassic, suggesting incipient elite access to and control over labor (Hansen 2005:63). By the Late Middle Preclassic monumental construction was well underway, with large platforms covering thousands of square meters and the first major architecture, including an E-group, placed around well-defined plazas on a pronounced east-west axis (Hansen 1993, 2005). The uniformity and large size of the blocks used as well as architectural innovations such as apron moldings and evidence for specialized quarrying techniques all sug-gest the existence of stone-working specialists (Forsyth 1993c; Woods and Titmus 1996; Hansen 1994, 2005). During this period, too, the first carved stone monuments are found, including stelae and altars, though some altars may have been used as early as 600 BCE (Hansen 2005). Aqueducts and other hydraulic systems as well as massive causeways connecting Nakbe to other sites in the Mirador Basin similarly date to 600–400 BCE (Hansen 1993). By this time the centralization and sociopolitical differentiation that are hall-marks of the state were clearly well underway in the Peten. They would continue to evolve into the first full-fledged Maya states of the Late Preclas-sic at Nakbe, nearby El Mirador, and other locations (Hansen 1990, 2005).

In this area it is easier to identify a possible economic reason for elite success. The prime areas around the wetlands could have been privately owned, just as Coe and Diehl (1980) postulated for the river levees on the Olmec Gulf coast. Soils research suggests that, while the dry uplands would have been productive, the initial organic content of the fertile wetland margins would have made them even more so. As Wahl et al. (2006) observe, they could easily have been farmed by ditching and draining techniques already known to the pioneers. However, there does not seem to be any archaeological evidence to support the idea of private ownership. There are no houses squarely located on plots, no barriers between plots, and no other such property markers.

The intensification of agriculture shows more promise as a basis for incipient elite control. Excavations adjacent to a palace complex in the Nakbe site center have revealed an artificial garden terrace system where fertile mud "imported" from the neighboring wetlands was used to grow maize, squash, and gourds (Hansen et al. 2002). The date of this fill is uncertain, but 2.5 m of it lies over a floor level with Middle Preclassic ceramics (Hansen et al. 2002:286) as a *terminus post quem*. The bulk of the fill could thus be Late Preclassic, when states were already well developed. There are indications of earlier levels of imported mud (Hansen et al. 2002), but how substantial and pervasive they are is unclear. Certainly, the emerging soils and climate information suggests that true intensification and the organizational changes it connotes are not coeval with the initial development of complexity. Instead, intensification seems to have been the gradual result of long-term human impacts on the environment, and seems to have reached a peak only in the latter part of the Late Preclassic. Indeed, in much of the Peten aggressive farming during the Early and Middle Preclassic seems to have precipitated deforestation and massive erosion. Aggraded soils filled in the wetlands, turning them into seasonal swamps (Dunning 1995; Dunning et al. 2002, 2006). This process was accelerated in the Late Preclassic by a gradual, if erratic, drying that culminated in a time of maximum desiccation around 100 CE (Dunning et al. 2002:278). The extensive terracing at Nakbe may have begun in the Middle Preclassic, but seems to have become prominent only in the Late Preclassic as inhabitants tried to counter the destruction of their productive environment. Similar terracing has been recorded at Calakmul on the *bajo* margins at this time (Gunn et al. 2000; cited in Dunning et al. 2002). It is also in the Late Preclassic that we begin to see deliberately engineered reservoirs in the site cores, presumably to replace the dwindling open water resources (Scarborough 1993; cited in Dunning et al. 2002). These human efforts ultimately proved futile, however. Even terracing could not prevent further destruction; at Nakbe at least one Late Preclassic terrace surface lies buried beneath massive colluviation (Dunning et al. 2002:276). Drying and infilling degraded the perennial wetlands beyond recovery, causing the abandonment of many of the precocious Peten states by 150 CE (Hansen et al. 2002). This devastation was not universal in the Yucatan interior. In the south, around places such as Laguneta Tamarandito in the Petexbatun area, probably a combination of more careful management (Dunning 1995) and different micro-environmental conditions (Beach et al. 2006) were able to forestall large-scale erosion and enable continued exploitation of wetland margins.

Subsistence Summary

The contrast between northern Belize and the Peten highlights both similarities in the nature of basic subsistence resources in the Maya lowlands and the variability in their exploitation. Farming communities in both areas relied on wetland margin agriculture, which, in fact, had provided the initial impetus to settlement. In Belize, however, where water sources are abundant, there was a conscious choice to focus on horticulture at the expense of other activities in the seasonal round. In the river-deprived Peten, on the other hand, settlement focused early around perennial wetlands. Though mobile horticulturalists may have roamed there initially, their activities would perforce have been confined to the areas nearby permanent water sources, where they rapidly established themselves. In both areas intensification seems to represent an effort to improve endangered soils, but with vastly different timing and results. In Belize intensification occurred when early farmers attempted to rescue wetland margins from rising groundwater, and sedentism followed. Presumably they remained nearby to monitor and maintain the fields. While it is tempting to see early "owners" of these improved lands as the initially differentiated elite at places such as Colha and K'axob, the correlation is far from clear. The existence of other resources and specializations suggests alternate elite candidates. The presence of terraced fields adjacent to communities that lacked significant monumental structures in the Rio Bravo area (Scarborough and Valdez 2009) also argues against the importance of agricultural intensification for elite development.

In the Peten, the concentration of early farmers on the limited prime land at the margins of wetlands seems to conform to the classic scenario of limited resources appropriated by emerging elites. However, true intensification seems to happen there much later at sites like Nakbe, in reaction to problems caused by human action, compounded by climatic change. In neither case can we state unequivocally that intensification was part of an elite strategy, deliberate or not, to seize and manipulate advantageous lands for their own benefit.

Comparing these two regions demonstrates that there was considerable variability in subsistence throughout the Maya area. People residing in different places had access to the same general suite of resources, but these were locally variable and uniquely configured. They may have exploited them in similar ways but the results were as varied as the individual localities themselves (cf. Scarborough and Valdez 2009). This truism merits restating in light of continued scholarly insistence on the importance of intensive agricultural methods or hydraulic management in the rise of Maya states. The correlation is just not that simple. It rests primarily on the idea that larger populations would have needed food and water and that the managerial requirements of intensifying food production and/or supplying water would have promoted the concentration of power in the hands of a few (cf. Flannery 1972 on linearization in social systems, where lower order controls are bypassed by a higher control). In Belize intensification did indeed precede the development of complexity, but it cannot be said to have "caused" it. While permanent settlements supported more people than mobile camps, sites remained small throughout the Middle Preclassic when elites first emerged. In the Mirador Basin, on the other hand, the existence of limited water resources coupled with fertile soil seems to have promoted concentrated population growth in select places. While clearly a large population can spur state development, here again there is no direct correlation between intensive agriculture and sociopolitical differentiation. Intensification, in fact, seems to have been more a consequence of complex development than its cause, as Late Preclassic farmers tried to mitigate the damage done by their forbearers. By that time, Nakbe was already a powerful center on the wane and El Mirador was in its full glory. The dedication with which the farmers struggled to maintain their fields in the face of major erosion suggests that these fields had become too important to abandon—probably because population peaked in the Basin at this time (Wahl et al. 2006). Interestingly, a parallel situation prevailed in Belize where progressive erosion from the Middle to the Late Preclassic rendered wetland margin fields less productive (Jacob 1992, 1995). Human overexploitation of local fauna compounded the crisis, which peaked in the early Late Preclassic. Shaw (1991, 1999) has argued that, as a result, the residents of Colha, at least, were forced to rely on their social networks for provisioning rather than increasing use of an already depleted habitat. I have suggested elsewhere (King 2003) that it is this strategy rather than intensification that promoted stratification and centralization of an already differentiated society at Colha in the Late Preclassic, a point to which I shall return.

Specialized Production: Lithics

Craft production has long been associated with the development of complexity. The very existence of specialization implies the kind of organic solidarity (Durkheim 1933) and interdependence that complex social systems signify (King 2000; McAnany 2010). To use Flad and Hruby's (2007) terms, while "product specialization" can even be found in egalitarian communities, "producer specialization" has been viewed as a hallmark of complexity since the days of V. Gordon Childe (Clark 2007b). It implies a level of interdependence that precludes autonomous functioning and supports the emergence of a new class of people not involved in day-to-day food or technical production. This new group may be horizontally differentiated from the producers, fulfilling other functions (e.g., religious specialists). More commonly, though, they are deemed to be vertically differentiated—elite appropriators and/or managers of productive work. Thus, our concept of craft specialization and functional interdependence in a complex society automatically drapes itself over a sociopolitical hierarchy (King 2000:7–11). Taking a heterarchical approach to this problem, however, requires asking rather than assuming to what extent craft resources and production were actually controlled by incipient elites. Again, what were the available resources, how were they distributed, and how did the Maya exploit them over time? Recently, discussions of craft specialization have emphasized a practice approach that attempts to contextualize craft production and use and sees a continuum of circulating items from gifts (unalienable) to commodities (alienable) (Flad and Hruby 2007; Clark 2007b). Specialization *per se* is not my focus here, however, but rather its role in traditional theories of complexity. Craft production in this context can be viewed as product specialization that develops into producer specialization over time. I will focus on lithic production, an archaeologically visible and clearly specialized craft system, to examine this process. While stone tool making followed its own unique pathways, as did each craft system (King 2000, 2007), it can speak to the general issues raised by specialization in relation to emerging complexity.

In the Maya area a long-established chipped stone industry made tools from local resources that varied by region. In the lowlands, chert and chalcedony of various grades predominated, as these materials occur naturally in limestone formations. Imported obsidian is also found in the lowlands, mostly in the form of prismatic blades and blade cores. Jade was similarly imported, but from early on was used for special-purpose rather than everyday items. Finally, a smaller lowland pecked and groundstone industry focused on production of *manos*, *metates*, and other items from both local and imported materials. I will focus here on chert/chalcedony, as these materials represent the bulk of lithic tools used in the lowlands. Obsidian and jade have been much researched as items of long-distance trade, so I will discuss them below under distribution. Groundstone, although a significant trade item, has been comparatively little studied. I will therefore omit it from my discussion.

Chert/chalcedony is widely distributed throughout the central lowlands, but varies greatly in quality from place to place. In the Peten at Tikal large, high-quality nodules of chert were plentiful (Moholy-Nagy 1976, 1991). While no workshops were excavated, the range of manufacturing debris present, from unretouched flakes to manufacturing failures, confirms that the entire production sequence took place locally. Consumption seems to have been primarily local as well, given the numbers of used tools and flakes found and the small amount of non-local chert in the assemblage (Moholy-Nagy 1991). However, there is no way of telling how much chert Tikal may have exported to nearer or farther neighbors in the form of nodules, preforms, or finished products. Moholy-Nagy (1991) suggests incipient specialist production may have begun at the site towards the end of the Middle Preclassic, as tool types increase significantly. By the Late Preclassic lithic innovations such as stemmed artifacts (bifaces and bifacial points) and the improved quality of the tools suggest a well-developed and already specialized lithic industry. Interestingly, the small quantity of chert imports increases at this time, too. However, the lack of workshop information makes it impossible to assess how production was organized. Was it in the hands of the elite or the specialists themselves? How closely tied were the elite and the specialists? Who controlled the distribution of chert products? These questions remain to be resolved.

In the Mirador Basin to the northwest, a different situation prevailed. There chert occurs mostly in small nodules of inferior quality, found in the *bajos* (Woods and Titmus 1996). Preliminary assessment of decortication flakes from Nakbe has suggested that the chert was recovered locally on the surface (Woods and Titmus 1996), rather than mined. It was used primarily in the production of general utility bifaces and a range of other utilitarian tools that parallel the types documented for El Mirador as well (Woods and Titmus 1996; Fowler 1987). Some of the chert, particularly for larger tools, seems to have been imported. Indeed, Woods and Titmus (1996:486) argue that the need for better quality material would have helped foster early specialization at Nakbe. They suggest that individual nodules were imported and that the cost of transporting chert of an appropriate size and quality would have encouraged a high level of skill. No one would want to see material wasted, particularly during the crucial first stage of creating a blank, the most difficult part of the reduction process (Woods and Titmus 1996:486). It is perhaps not surprising, then, that eccentrics, which require making a "nearly flawless biface" much larger than the end product, are rare at Nakbe (Woods and Titmus 1996:487). Here the evidence for specialization is significantly more indirect than at Tikal, especially given the small overall number of tools (276) reported and, again, the absence of workshops. While reduction of local chert no doubt took place at the Mirador Basin sites, it is quite possible that manufactured tools were imported from elsewhere—perhaps even Tikal. It certainly does not look as though lithic production *per se* played a great role in the Preclassic economy. There are no published clues as to its development over time, so it seems likely it stayed at a rather constant level of expertise and investment. Better evidence for a specialized craft comes from one of the uses to which the general utility bifaces were put, which was stone quarrying (Forsyth 1993c; Woods and Titmus 1996; Hansen 2005). However, the degree to which that was under the "control" of elites simply because it was a specialized craft and because the stone was mostly used in monumental constructions is debatable. As Clark (2003) has pointed out, to infer "control" we need more than mere juxtaposition of data. It is also not clear how control of a craft aimed completely at local elite consumption would have given the latter the early "edge" they needed, according to the classic theory, to dominate others at the site. Indeed, quarrying for monuments would seem to have been a by-product rather than a cause of complexity, a way to solidify and perpetuate incipient differences (see McAnany 2010:141–57).

In northern Belize circumstances were different still. There an abundance of high-quality chert, localized in what Shafer and Hester (1983) have called Belize's "chert-bearing zone," permitted the development of an important toolmaking industry in the Preclassic, centered on the site of Colha. Located at the northern end of the zone, Colha was a locus for chertworking activity from the Archaic on (Iceland et al. 1995; Hester 1996; Iceland 1997). By the Middle Preclassic, significant numbers of both expedient and recognizable formal tools were produced, including the burin spall drills previously noted. Use-wear analyses suggest that each form served multiple functions (Potter 1991). The wide range of forms, their variability in function, and the lack of workshops indicate that lithic production was not yet fully specialized at this time. However, the already high level of craftsmanship suggests it was well on its way (Potter 1991). By the Late Preclassic, the production system had changed dramatically. Distinct lithic workshops appear at this time inter-mingled with residences in three "manufacturing zones" near the site core (King 2000:102, 158, 190). Production was a highly standardized, two-stage process. Large numbers of tool blanks were prepared in off-site quarries and taken back to the workshops, where they were fashioned into a narrow range of formal tools, including oval bifaces, tranchet bit tools, blades, and eccentrics (Shafer 1979, 1982, 1991; Shafer and Hester 1979, 1983). All work-shops appear to have produced the same four tools, but some may have spe-cialized in producing more of one particular form (Shafer 1991:38). These tools were traded widely in Belize and beyond, with some found as far away as Tikal (Moholy-Nagy 1991) and El Mirador (Sharer and Traxler 2006:262) in the Peten. Two "consumer zones" can be identified. One was a "primary" area extending 75 km in radius around Colha for utilitarian artifacts like the oval bifaces, the other a "peripheral" area 200 km in radius for elite items, such as macroblades and eccentrics (Shafer and Hester 1983; Hester and Shafer 1994). In fact, it would be fair to say that Colha dominated lowland tool production at this time. Its tools apparently even replaced local prod-ucts in sites where there were pre-existing lithic industries, such as at Blue Creek in northern Belize (Barrett 2004, 2006).

The indications are strong that the Colha elite were directly involved in all aspects of lithic production and distribution during the Late Preclassic. The aggregation of workshops into manufacturing zones, the similarity in their output, and the clear separation between quarry and workshop activities argue for an overarching production strategy at this time. While the proximity of workshops to the site core does not by itself indicate control (Clark 2003), that fact combined with chertworker involvement in elite activities supports the idea of centralized management. There is strong evidence that a skilled blade-maker participated in the placement of at least one important cache in a core temple during this period (Potter 1992; King and Potter 1994).

Despite Colha's dominance of Late Preclassic lithic production and trade, lithic procurement systems in northern Belize at other sites may have been more variable than expected. There are indications that Colha not only exported formal tools but also macroflake or macroblade blanks that were made into tools by the consumers themselves (McSwain 1989, 1991a, 1991b; Santone 1993). Also, inhabitants of sites such as Cuello near the chert-bearing zone may have procured their own nodules (McSwain 1991a, 1991b). There are such broad similarities across chert formations that there is still no sure way to determine where in the chert-bearing zone individual items originated (Cackler et al. 1999; Chiarulli 2006). It is possible, then, that dual systems of procurement existed, with sites both importing tools and preforms from Colha and gathering their own chert from the zone. Several sites within the "primary consumer zone" seem also to have retained local lithic procurement systems focused on other resources. Blue Creek did, albeit at a reduced level (Barrett 2004, 2006). So did Cuello, whose inhabitants continued to use a local chalcedony (McSwain 1991a). It seems clear that at any given site in Belize in the Late Preclassic there were several different ways to procure lithics. Sites could receive finished products from Colha directly via long-distance or regional trade, they could receive unworked nodules from Colha or other parts of the chert-bearing zone, which they would work themselves into expedient tools, they could procure and work these raw materials for themselves, or they could procure and work generally poorer-quality lithic materials closer to hand (see Speal 2009 for further discussion of variability in procurement). Some of these choices reflect different valuations of the material and different "costs," a point that I will address in the conclusions.

Summary of Lithic Production

The variability visible in subsistence is, unsurprisingly, recapitulated in lithic production strategies across the central lowlands. While in some places, such as the chert-bearing zone of Belize, localized resources seem to have lent themselves to centralized control, complexity was not a necessary consequence of their exploitability. At Tikal, which abounds in good chert, there is no evidence for anywhere near the same level of organization and sheer volume of production as at Colha. That lack of development is noteworthy in light of the poor-quality chert found at other northern Peten sites. One might expect chertworking to have played a more important role in Tikal's rise to power. Conversely, an absence of good chert does not seem to have impeded the growth of Nakbe and El Mirador, which dwarfed Tikal and Colha alike in the Preclassic. Arguably, some of their power could have come from controlling stone imports, but the volume of that trade seems insignificant in their economies. By the same token, Colha was never the Maya giant our economic models might predict nor did its dominion over the lithic trade continue into the Classic. Why not? If elites rise to power by controlling a critical resource, what is wrong with chert? And if chert was indeed the basis for Colha power, why did it fail in the long run? Though Colha ruled lowland lithic production in the Late Preclassic, that development happened late. Why? After all, the inhabitants of the site had been sitting on the same important resource since the end of the Early Preclassic. While the beginnings of sociopolitical differentiation are already visible in the Middle Preclassic, they are overshadowed by what was going on at Nakbe at that time. They also did not approach the level of stratification evident at Colha later on. Additionally, it is not clear that the emerging elites relied economically on tool production. While chertworking was important, it was not, as seen, the *only* activity at the site and perhaps not even as significant as intensive farming. What, then, was early differentiation at Colha based on and did that basis change over time? Finally, even when centralized control existed it was not necessarily complete. The lithic industry in Belize even at the height of Colha's power was variable and probably opportunistic, with each community deciding for itself the appropriate mix of procurement strategies. Ultimately, we need to remember that the Maya, like all of us, made choices. These were made by incipient elites and commoners both, separately and together. Such decisions are further reflected in patterns of distribution and consumption, discussed below.

Distribution

Distribution includes different kinds of exchanges, from reciprocal to redistributive (including tribute) to market, following Polanyi's (1968) classic scheme. It can be difficult to distinguish between these archaeologically, as "foreign" goods, or ones not produced at a site, could have arrived there through any one of those means (cf. Clark 2003). Bearing that in mind, I will focus on trade, which includes reciprocal exchanges such as bartering and market exchange, because of its importance to the Maya. The concept of "market" is useful here despite the non-capitalist context, *pace* Polanyi, because, as Smith (2004) has argued, we need to be able to refer to commercial exchange when dealing with ancient or proto-states. Markets are near invisible in the archaeological record of the Maya and documenting their existence and development remains a critical issue for further research if we are to understand the nature of trade in this area (see King and Shaw 2007; Dahlin 2003, 2009; Dahlin et al. 2007; Shaw 2012). For the present, I will assume that markets are as old as the world and that some kind of at least informal market system must have existed from early on in the Maya area.

Trade, especially long-distance trade, has long been seen as an anchor of elites among the Maya. Control of exotic goods and/or trade routes is often argued to trigger sociopolitical differentiation. Incipient entrepreneurs are thought to use their access to special contacts and special goods to control distribution, thereby seizing and securing permanent power (e.g., Rathje 1972; Freidel et al. 2002). While it is clear that trade was key in early Maya societies, our top-down approach and our tendency to zero in on long-distance trade obscures some important patterns, lately emerging. Below, I will summarize some of the significant data on trade, focusing on how resources moved around, whom they went to, and who moved them.

Three levels of trade can be distinguished for the Maya area, which may be loosely termed local, regional, and long-distance (cf. Speal 2009 on lithic trade). Local trade is the hardest to document, as materials from neighboring sites tend to resemble each other; however, it is occasionally identifiable. Barrett (2004, 2006), for example, was able to distinguish tools produced within the Blue Creek settlement area from regional and long-distance imports. The problem here, of course, is determining the mechanism by which these tools moved and whether that changed over time, which it might have. In the Middle Preclassic, when social differentiation was not well developed, these lithics could have been bartered; later on they seem to have been redistributed. Barrett (2006) notes that there is a drop in local tool use from the Middle Preclassic to the Late Preclassic in the Blue Creek area, due to imports from Colha. Contrary to what one might expect, most of the waste and tools associated with local production show up in elite contexts in the Late Preclassic. To Barrett (pers. comm. 2007) this suggests an elite monopoly over the local production process at that time. The same problem of distribution mechanism applies to Cahal Pech where some kind of local exchange might be inferred indirectly from dietary data. Powis et al. (1999) document differences in Middle Preclassic maize consumption there between residents of an outlying settlement and two more central groups at the site. They propose that the higher rates of consumption in the site core reflect higher status, which suggests that maize came in as tribute and was redistributed. However, an alternative explanation could be that the center residents had a different diet because they did not provision themselves directly. The inhabitants of one group, for example, were shell ornament craftsmen, who might have exchanged their product locally for food. There is no reason to postulate elite involvement in this process.

Trade on a regional level is easier to see and has been well documented. Maya communities were probably never self-sufficient (Love 1999a; Barrett 2006). From the earliest times, communities located in different areas relied on each other for essential products. Thus, early Middle Preclassic inland villages in Belize regularly received fish and shellfish from the coast, probably in exchange for farm produce. This kind of intra-regional trade very likely developed out of even older patterns of exchange during the Archaic period between different foraging populations. By the time of initial social differentiation, probably no one in Belize lived only off what the surrounding land and water could provide. The goods procured tend to show up in a broad range of contexts within sites, suggesting that they were widely available to all consumers. Thus, marine edibles are found throughout the sites of Colha, Cuello, and Cahal Pech at this time (Shaw 1991, 1994; Wing and Scudder 1991; Powis et al. 1999). Barter or market exchange rather than elite redistribution best explains their dissemination.

In other cases, however, it is more difficult to distinguish between trade and tribute among neighboring sites, as Rosenswig and Kennett (2008:139) have pointed out. Sometimes, regional trade was more uneven, with particular goods only going to the elite. This was the case for Colha's stemmed macroblades and certain ceramics like the spouted vessels used for cacao

(Powis et al. 2002). The difficulty here is in determining whether these circulated as part of a gift exchange of inalienable goods or as part of a redistributive economy that led to a concentration of alienable objects in the hands of the elite. Compounding the problem is the fact that categories such as inalienable/alienable and gift/commodity are fungible (Flad and Hruby 2007; Clark 2007b). They do not connote essential qualities of the objects themselves, but rather identify how certain objects are used in specific circumstances (Flad and Hruby 2007:9), or even how they reached a site (Speal 2009:108). Valuation can also be a reflection of scarcity. Thus, marine shell beads, prized by the elite at inland sites, did not have the same importance at coastal sites like Cerros, where stone beads were preferred (Rosenswig and Kennett 2008:141). Scarcity was not always a factor, however. Moholy-Nagy (1997:296; cited in McAnany 2010:231) points out that in Classic period Tikal, obsidian, a long-distance good, was found in common domestic contexts whereas prized eccentrics were made from local chert. Hence, the same object and the same source material could be viewed differently in different contexts or at different times. In the examples above, both spouted vessels and stemmed macroblades are found in ritual (burials, caches) and elite contexts; however, they also occur in other, less prestigious locations (Shafer 1991; Powis et al. 2002). They could thus have moved through local economies both laterally, as gifts among the elite, and vertically, down a specific hierarchical chain within a polity, thereby affirming the legitimacy of the sociopolitical hierarchy (Potter and King 1995). Alternatively, they could have been more widely traded and appropriated for specific ritual uses by the elite. Our data and conceptual categories are not yet fine enough to determine how goods circulated.

Equally pertinent, we cannot at present distinguish between different kinds of regional market systems and possible changes in them over time (Barrett 2006; cf. Minc 2006, 2009). We also cannot gauge with any accuracy the impact of politics on how and where trade items moved. At Cerros, for example, participation in a regional network seems to have affected access to lithic products as much as relative location to source materials, given that the site had percentages of Colha imports similar to those found at Chau Hiix, which was closer to the source (Chiarulli 2012). Participation in the network, however, seems in turn to have been affected by the political status of the site, so that the relative quantity of imports at Cerros waxed and waned along with the site's political fortunes (Speal 2009:99). These changes might reflect changing political alliances and competition among rival sites, as speculated by Rosenswig and Kennett (2008). It is possible, alternatively, that regional marketing and exchange systems may have been coterminous with larger territorial boundaries, as has been argued for the Late Classic (Speal 2009; cf. Minc 2009), and that these shifted over time. These are all issues that remain to be resolved. For present purposes, what seems likely is that, while some regionally traded prestige items may have reinforced elite power, they were not the foundation on which it was built. Their limited numbers and possible status as gifts, at least in some contexts, argue against that. They are a concomitant of, but not a cause for, complexity.

Long-distance trade, especially in obsidian, jade, groundstone, spondylus, salt, and ceramics, has been the subject of intense discussion and theorizing in the Maya area. Again, I will focus on lithics, specifically obsidian and jade, as representative of wider patterns of exchange.

Obsidian is perhaps the best known. In the lowlands it was always an exotic, originating in specific sources, whose products can be identified by trace-element analysis. Numerous studies over the years have established the provenience of lowland obsidian artifacts from sources in the Guatemalan highlands (San Martin Jilotepeque, El Chayal, Ixtepeque, San Luis, and La Esperanza) and central Mexico (Pachuca). They have also suggested the probable coastal and overland routes by which objects traveled (Hammond 1972b, 1976; Dreiss and Brown 1989). Obsidian trade is assumed to have been down-the-line (Dreiss and Brown 1989) from center elite to center elite, with objects moving progressively away from the source in a dendritic system that eventually reached most households (Smith 1976; Minc 2006:85). The pattern produced by such systems can be similar to that produced by redistributive exchange, especially as we lack data on how obsidian trickled out to rural settlements. Recent studies, however, suggest that obsidian moved as a trade good, because of where products from different sources are found. While specific sources definitely predominated at different times (Dreiss and Brown 1989; Brown et al. 2004), it is clear that several sources were always available at any given moment within the same area. In the Peten at Nakbe (Hansen 2005:62) and El Mirador (Fowler et al. 1989), San Martin Jilotepeque predominated in the Middle Preclassic, but by the early Late Preclassic at El Mirador at least, El Chayal was more important (Fowler et al. 1989). This switch replicates a pattern that is widespread throughout the lowlands (Nelson et al. 1978, 1983; Nelson and Clark 1990; Brown et al. 2004), but not uniform. At sites such as Tikal, San Martin Jilotepeque materials were still dominant during the Late Preclassic (Fowler et al. 1989). In the northern Peten, then, there seem to have been several sources available simultaneously, which were variably used by different sites. The same thing can be seen on an even more localized scale in northern Belize. There Hammond (1991b:198) reports that Cuello during the Late Preclassic imported mostly Ixtepeque materials, along with lesser amounts from El Chayal and a small mix of other sources. Nearby Colha at the same time, however, showed a significant continued reliance on San Martin Jilotepeque materials, though they no longer dominate the assemblage (Brown et al. 2004:231). These data suggest that no "down-the-line" center had a monopoly on distribution over a whole region. Residents of the lowlands seem to have had some choice in what they got. This situation might conform more to a market model than a redistributive one. Other evidence for elite management of obsidian, such as the location of obsidian workshops in site centers (e.g., at El Mirador; Hansen 1990:209) remains unconvincing in the absence of clear lines of control. Again, we need to sharpen our analytic categories and archaeological correlates if we really want to determine obsidian's role in elite power strategies (see Clark 2003 for further discussion). Finally, even if obsidian was managed by the elite, its importance in the emergence of complexity is moot. While it is found in the Middle Preclassic, its availability increases significantly in the Late Preclassic at a time of state consolidation. In other words, the obsidian procurement system, whatever it was, while present before, was more widely integrated into economies corresponding to already differentiated sociopolitical systems. Of course the importation of highland obsidian from the Middle Preclassic onwards indicates that the lowland Maya were part of an interregional trade network that doubtless served as a conduit for the exchange of information with the Maya highlands and other areas of Mesoamerica. It is this interregional interaction rather than control over the obsidian trade that more likely had an impact on the development of complexity (see Chapter 6, this volume).

A similar story is emerging for jade, which is even more localized to a few sources located in Guatemala and lower Central America. At Cuello INA analysis of a group of jades revealed four known sources, but slightly over half of the objects remained ungrouped (Hammond 1991c:201–2). Potentially, each of these could represent a different source, suggesting the site had access to many different suppliers. A review of the samples by time period (Hammond 1991c:200) shows that during the Middle Preclassic and Late Preclassic several sources are represented, thereby paralleling the situation with obsidian. Jade also shows a similar variability in context. While it is associated with rituals and the elite, Krejci and Culbert (1995) found that it occurred more regularly in small housemounds than large ones during the Preclassic. Again, it seems that we are missing the mechanisms by which this material traveled from source to site to consumer. Like the obsidian trade, the jade trade seems not to have been a catalyst for, but an expression of, elite status.

Distribution Summary

Distinct levels of trade can be distinguished in the Maya area that must have overlapped and intersected in interesting ways. Local, regional, and long-distance goods were all essential to Maya communities, which seem to have been integrally linked from the beginning. If we consider the amount of foodstuffs that were regularly exchanged, they were never completely self-sufficient, even at their most egalitarian stage at the end of the Early Preclassic/beginning of the Middle Preclassic. This interdependence increased as time went on. Trade patterns were complicated and variable, though, and changed over time. Even long-distance trade, which focused on a finite group of materials from specific sources, does not seem to have operated in as straightforward a manner as many of our models presume. Thus, there is variability in the ways that lowland sites, for example, acquired prized highland exotics such as jade and obsidian, possibly even those within the same polity. Similar differences are hinted at in the way local and regional goods moved, though their circulation has been less well explored.

Given this diversity and the lack of specific data on how goods moved (Barrett 2006), it is difficult to assess the role trade might have played in the emergence of Maya elites. In some cases it seems to have been important, in others it did not. For sites in northern Belize like Blue Creek, which straddled the end of a navigable river stretch (Barrett 2004, 2006; Barrett and Guderjan 2006), or Cerros, which commanded a section of coast, trade was probably key in the development of local elites. Rosenswig and Kennett (2008) have argued that it was also important in the positioning of other sites in northern Belize, but in the cases they cite (e.g., Colha, Kichpanha) there were other factors at work, too. In communities where trade was paramount, simple differential access to a wider range of goods might have helped create initial disparities and eventual stratification. The same argument has long been applied to Tikal and other sites strategically placed in the Peten interior (Sharer and Traxler 2006). However, the extent to which trade was a criterion for complexity in most sites remains moot. There is no doubt, for example, that the Colha elite controlled chert production and probably its initial export from the site in the Late Preclassic. The pathways chert products followed in regional trade after that are less certain, though. While they could have been exchanged directly with other centers and redistributed out from central markets, they could also have proceeded along different, less centralized routes. The way they traveled to consumers in neighboring sites was also probably different from the way they traveled to customers farther away, and may have been influenced, as noted, by political (Speal 2009) or other non-economic factors. What we really need to do is model the different levels of trade in a common framework, so we can better evaluate their impact. While it is beyond the scope of this chapter to do so, I would note that Minc (2006) has recently provided just such a model, reviewing the archaeological implications of different market systems in an approach that is more specific than Hirth's (1998) distributional analysis. Suffice it to observe for now that different types of trading systems may have existed at different scales. Thus, even if long-distance trade was structured one way, local and regional trade may have followed separate organizational pathways. Trade at one level probably did influence trade at another, but we should assume neither congruence nor continuity over time. Classically, we tend to presuppose that emerging Maya polities were "locally focused" with only prestige goods crossing boundaries (Barrett 2006:119). This kind of pattern corresponds to Minc's (2006:84) "solar system," where political control and economic interaction are spatially coterminous. Such a system is characterized by poor articulation between neighboring solar systems and sharp discontinuities in commodity flow at their boundaries. However, the data already presented strongly argue that this was not the case from very early on in the Middle Preclassic. Thus, patterns remain to be demonstrated rather than assumed at all levels of trade.

Consumption

Consumption in the Maya area is poorly understood, as it is rarely a direct topic of inquiry. As Pyburn (2008) has reminded us, however, it is an important domain to consider, if we want to understand why incipient commoners decided to accept their status (see also Lohse 2013, Metcalfe et al. 2009, and Clark 2007b). Traditionally, Maya goods have been divided into two broad categories: utilitarian items or basic goods that are found in every household, and prestige or luxury items that were used primarily by the elite. In point of fact many archaeologists have shown this division is not so simple (see Hruby and Flad 2007 for recent discussions). Artifacts can vary in their valuation, as already noted (Flad and Hruby 2007; Clark 2007b; Speal 2009; Rosenswig and Kennett 2008; McAnany 2010). Also, many of the so-called elite goods are found in commoner households as well, just in lesser quantities. Thus, jade, a quintessential prestige item, is found in lowland burials suggesting a range of statuses, particularly in the Preclassic. In 365 burials from Belize, the Peten, and the Pasión area, Krejci and Culbert (1995) noted that the quantity rather than the presence of jade distinguished true elites from others. The same observation applied to shell ornaments and obsidian flakes and blades, though the latter were generally less common than either jade or shell in burials. Furthermore, it was not until the Terminal Preclassic/Early Classic that tombs of the high elite— "royal" burials—are found, with large quantities of objects clearly distinguishing them from everyone else (Krejci and Culbert 1995:103–6). Only, too, in the Early Classic do items such as earflares become restricted to the richest burials (Krejci and Culbert 1995:106, 111). Krejci and Culbert conclude that there were fewer differences among Preclassic burials than there were later on. Burials in small platforms had the same materials as burials in large platforms, though the larger ones generally had the wealthier burials. These patterns confirm that the significant transition for the Maya in terms of elaborate status was not in the Preclassic, when states first arose, but during the 4th and 5th centuries CE (Krejci and Culbert 1995:108, 114), when power perhaps became configured in a whole new way.

Krejci and Culbert's (1995) overview shows that, at the time incipient elites were forming, everyone seemed to have access to the same range of goods, at least for important ritual functions, albeit in different quantities. The similarity in burial furnishings—what people considered appropriate or necessary for the occasion (Krejci and Culbert 1995)—suggests a strong common value system uniting Maya society. While several authors have proposed such a value system existed (e.g., Sharer and Traxler 2006), it is often interpreted, following Marxist arguments, as a political-religious ideology imposed from above. The apparent uniformity in burial practices suggests that on an emic level at least that was not the case. Indeed, one would expect at least some variation between non-elite and elite where a particular "state" religion is overlaid onto folk practices.

Not all items were similarly shared, though. The spouted vessels associated with cacao consumption, for example, seem to occur mostly in elite contexts throughout the Preclassic (Powis et al. 2002), so presumably they were the prime consumers not only of the pots but also of their contents. Consumption of items also changed over time. Thus, at Blue Creek, lithics produced from local materials seem to have been available to the whole community in the Middle Preclassic. In the Late Preclassic, though, they appear mostly in elite contexts (Jason Barrett, pers. comm. 2007). At the same time, in the Late Preclassic almost half of the lithics used at Blue Creek come from Colha. Their finer chert and distant origin might lead us to expect their occurrence in elite rather than commoner contexts. Instead, and unlike locally made tools, they are found throughout the settlement. Clearly, there were different considerations of value involved in consumption that must be disentangled if we are to understand the nature of elite power, a point elaborated below.

EARLY MAYA ECONOMIES AND THE ORIGINS OF COMPLEXITY: AN ASSESSMENT

Review of the evidence on the early economies of the Maya reveals two important points. First is the unsurprising fact that economic conditions were highly variable throughout the area. After all, it is the most diverse region ecologically and geographically in Mesoamerica (Sharer and Traxler 2006). Maya sites could not just adopt a more complex lifestyle from their Mesoamerican neighbors and transpose it wholesale. Nor was one Maya site able simply to imitate another, following the kind of basic model we used to envision for pristine and secondary states. The roots of social differentiation were complicated, differing from place to place and region to region. Certainly, no single economic factor, not even the most popular—control over land/water, control over scarce resources, control over trade—can explain why complexity developed. Instead, if we look at what happened, where it happened, and when it happened, we find different constellations of factors involved at different sites. These may have *supported* the development of complexity without necessarily causing it. For some early centers we can even single out one main factor that might have accelerated this process. However, it would be foolish to assume that other factors, social and religious as well as economic, were not also at work. At Nakbe and El Mirador wetland farm land may have been a premium resource, with access to it giving certain residents an advantage over others. At Tikal trade may have been operative. In Belize, at Colha, a monopoly on chert resources is what finally propelled the elite to power, though social differentiation began earlier, maybe on another basis. The case of Colha underscores, too, that sociopolitical differentiation was variably timed throughout the Maya area. These temporal differences cannot be explained simply in terms of one place lagging behind the next. Colha, for instance, was fully involved from early on in local, regional, and, eventually, long-distance trade and communication networks. Nonetheless, strong status distinctions there, like elsewhere in Belize, did not appear until the Late Preclassic.

This temporal variability underscores what the archaeological record seems to be telling us over and over: people made economic and other choices and they made them repeatedly. These choices in turn constrained their future options, opening up new choices, closing off others. The mobile horticulturalists who first settled at Colha chose to focus on their fields rather than their broader seasonal round. This decision had consequences in the development of both horizontal and vertical differentiation—specialization in different tasks and the emergence of an initial elite. People were also affected by the decisions of others. They were interdependent (cf. McAnany 2010:205–6). Thus, for example, while Henderson (2003:488) does not believe regional elites controlled staple crop production at K'axob, she observes that the development and maintenance of regional political hierarchies would have had consequences for the way K'axob households managed their own economic prosperity (see also Scarborough and Valdez 2009). Henderson's example stresses the point, discussed elsewhere by Lohse (2013; Lohse and Valdez 2004) and Scarborough and Valdez (2009), that all the decisions were not made by the elite. Commoners made them as well. It is the interaction between elite and commoner, strategy and choice that we see played out in the archaeological record (Lohse 2013; McAnany 2010:2). Pyburn (2008) echoes this sentiment, proposing that incipient elites would have had to "advertise" their view of what was desirable to incipient commoners and convince them to accept it. That would have involved more negotiation than coercion (Scarborough and Valdez 2009).

These considerations suggest that at the heart of our enterprise of un-raveling complexity lies a question of values. Ultimately, how Maya author-ity was configured rests on what motivated the Maya—what they valued. What led them to make the choices they did? Economically, specifically, why were certain resources/objects deemed more desirable than others? How did that valuation affect Maya development? While it is impossible to question the ancient Maya directly, we can pry some idea of value from the archaeological and ethnohistoric record. Looking at what was valued and how it was used may give us some ideas on why it was prized and what effect it had, which we can then test against other parts of the record.

From the review of economic factors, it is clear that the Maya valued wetland margins for farming and accessible, open water for drinking. They also prized well-made tools from good-quality materials. We can add to that list items not discussed here, including decorated ceramics and marine re-sources such as the hard-to-get *Spondylus* and more common conch. They valued certain foods, such as cacao, for which they developed special spouted containers, also valued. Most precious, perhaps, were the jades and "social jades" (Hammond et al. 1977; cited in Hammond 1991c), greenstones used like jade, which were an important part of burial kits and also served in other rituals, as evidenced by caches throughout the Maya world (Krejci and Culbert 1995). I propose that what tied this disparate list together was an underlying value on *labor*—with the meaning here of "work invested." I do not mean this in the traditional economic sense of "value added," though it may be hard for us to disentangle our Western notions from what the Maya thought. As Clark (2007b:27) has pointed out, labor is part of the normal calculus we go through to determine an object's value, which also includes "intrinsic" properties such as raw materials and other "added" ones such as transport distances and skill in crafting. This notion comes to us from John Locke, who inextricably linked labor to our definition of personal property. Indeed, for Locke property is created by the fusion of natural materials with labor (cited in Clark 2007b:28). This new "product" then becomes some-thing to negotiate with and dispose of as the individual wishes—a strategy for acquiring goods and, in the context of state development, power. I doubt the Maya saw it this way. It is unclear to what extent private property—as opposed to group or kin-based ownership—even existed in Maya society. How free the individual was to manipulate commodities or even gifts is thus unknown (for another view of resource ownership see Chapter 10, this volume). Perhaps more importantly, the Maya sliced up their cognitive universe differently than we do ours and the dichotomy of humans *versus* nature that we so clearly perceive was not a sharp boundary in their view (King 1984). The idea of mixing human labor with nature's bounty would not have struck them as producing a fundamentally new product, nor one that could necessarily be appropriated, commoditized, or alienated. Labor, however, was important to them. I have argued elsewhere (King 1984) that it was a key organizing concept at the time of the Conquest and afterwards among the Yucatec Maya, where it was a basis for what I have identified as corporate groups, *tzuculob*. These entities represented small communities or *parcialidades, barrios*/parts of a town (Barrera Vásquez 1980), similar to the *chinamit-molab* units of Postclassic highland Guatemala (Hill and Monaghan 1987). *Tzuculob* seem to have been kin-based but not exclusively, as groups had a residential component as well. Members owed their labor to the group, and what was corporately owned was the property that labor produced. While the group controlled this labor force, it would again be a mistake to see labor itself in Western terms as an alienable commodity (cf. Earle 2000). Labor obligations are better viewed as part of a whole system of mutual obligations, including ritual and social ones (see McAnany 2010), that tied group members together. In that sense labor was both a *cargo* or burden individuals bore (King 1984) and a right they expected from others.

The implication of this idea for the rise of complexity is that authority was configured around labor—obligations of labor from commoner to elite and, conversely, from elite to commoner. Okoshi (1995:24; cited in Izquierdo 2004:63) tells us from his reading of Yucatecan texts that the strength of the ruler lay not in possession of territory but in his ability to mobilize labor. Wealth and power were thus directly proportional to the human resources a ruler had access to (Izquierdo 2004:63). These were probably structured along kinship (Izquierdo 2004; Chapter 10, this volume) and *tzucul* (King 1984) lines. The ruler, too, had obligations, however, to take care of his people and to mediate with the gods (King 1984; Izquierdo 2004), "maintaining in equilibrium the forces of nature, making communal life possible" (Izquierdo 2004:63; my translation). These duties were part of his "social persona," or intrinsic identity *qua* ruler (see Chapter 10, this volume). Indeed, Okoshi's (1995) analysis of the Yucatecan terms for governing "recognizes that the Maya concept of governing in the lowlands was 'to care for,' 'to serve' [in order] to achieve harmony between people"

(Izquierdo 2004:64; my translation). This proposition is not entirely new; among Mayanists the idea that the arrangement between elites and commoners had to be reciprocal and mutually beneficial has long competed with the idea that elites simply exploited those beneath them. What I am suggesting is the principle motivating that arrangement. I would go further and suggest that elite and commoner were not the only ones involved in this equation. The gods had their role to play as well. They had their own labor obligations to fulfill, their own burden to bear, which humans helped them achieve through ritual and sacrifice (King 1984).

There is ample evidence from documents that the post-Conquest Maya extended this value to their economy, prizing labor over actual property (Farriss 1984:270–74; King 1984). Indeed, the only land that was privately owned by the Maya in early colonial Yucatan was terrain that had been improved in some way by an input of human labor. That included saltflats and *hoyas*, the moist fertile depressions on the margins of cenotes that are ideally suited to intensive cultivation of cacao and fruit trees. The water sources themselves were owned, too, by the elite (Farriss 1984:180). There was scant surface water in northern Yucatan and considerable labor would have been involved in maintaining water holes and diverting water around them for human needs, such as farming. The remainder of the land was tilled by all members of a community, elite and commoner alike, based on hereditary usufruct rights (Farriss 1984:273). While it was possible to buy and sell pieces of land, these were not undeveloped. They usually comprised *milpa* in its first or second year, or other kinds of fields. As Farriss (1984:278) notes, "one owned what was worth owning, which was not the land itself but the improvements on it." What had value were cleared milpa plots, orchards, houses, henequen plants, and the like. They belonged to the person or group who had done the work, even if they were on community land. What a buyer actually paid for, then, was not the property being sold but the labor invested in its creation. Indeed, the amount of work that went into the property determined its purchase value (Farriss 1984:274). This same principle is reflected in the archaeological list above. Wetland fields and water sources require year-round work; specialized obsidian and chert tools demand a substantial and skilled labor investment; special ceramics represent careful and painstaking detail work; and resources from afar are laborious to acquire. Most of all, jade requires considerable work both to obtain and to carve, as no stone is tougher (King 2003). Of course, labor was not the only value imbued in objects, which often materialized multiple concepts. Jade, for example, carried an importance based on its association with the watery Underworld and its powerful denizens. Even unworked and easy to acquire materials such as stream cobbles or quartz crystals could be important ideological objects. The discussion of this dimension of valuation, however, belongs more properly in considerations of the ideological factors contributing to the rise of complexity (see Chapter 11, this volume). While acknowledging that the several dimensions were probably inseparable to the Maya, here I examine the implications of the value placed on labor.

Given the importance of labor, it is not surprising that it was valued and manipulated economically, and what helped support complexity were things that required work. Thus, the different trajectories we see in different regions of the Maya area resulted in part from differences in the enterprises where labor was locally invested—farming, tool production, or trade. I have argued elsewhere (King 2003) that they also derived from the way work was organized, which affected the choices elite and commoner alike were able to make. I will explore this idea briefly by looking at the distinctive trajectory the evolution of complexity took at Colha. Here, both the timing and the consequences of social differentiation are of particular interest. I will then frame my analysis in term of heterarchy and extend it with observations of other sites, to provide a model for how early states may have developed. I would note that while the initial impetus towards more developed complexity at Colha could be interpreted in a utilist framework, as needs- and scarcity-driven behavior, the overall trajectory, which I am concerned with here, cannot. In addition, as McAnany (2010) reminds us, the fact that pre-capitalist economies were differently construed does not mean that the actors in them never operated out of self-interest or in reaction to externally stringent circumstances.

At Colha the key juncture in the development of complexity is the transition from the Middle Preclassic to the Late Preclassic. It is at this time that the local population seems to have experienced a food crisis. Rising water tables coupled with overhunting created food shortages for local residents, who were faced with either intensifying their current practices or finding what Shaw (1991, 1999) has called a social solution to their problem by exploiting regional trade networks. They apparently chose to do the latter, beefing up their tool production. Indeed, there is evidence from at least one household in the site center of a shift in economic orientation towards greater involvement in lithic production/management at that time (Shaw 1999). Using Arnold's (1993) model of complex development among hunters and gatherers on California's Channel Islands, I have argued that the chertworkers at Colha were in a unique position to capitalize on the crisis. They had the specialized knowledge, skills, and materials to produce quality stone tools. It is likely they also owned the means of production, that is, the workshops and even the quarry sites where blanks were made, as these would fit into the category of resources "improved" by human labor. They were thus in a position to divert goods and wealth to their own ends in political economic parlance (cf. Chapter 10, this volume, on entrepreneurs). Alternatively, one could say they fulfilled their obligations to the community by using their skilled labor to bring in needed supplies. In short, they were able to dominate the burgeoning regional trade in foodstuffs and lithics at the site and to establish themselves in the center, from which they controlled production. In the Late Preclassic, then, the chertworkers *were* the elite at the site (King 2003; King and Potter 1994).

Their power did not last into the Classic, because the organizational requirements of lithic production coupled with outside forces worked against them. In the Early Classic incursions by powerful neighbors from the Peten, suggested by evidence at several sites (Pyburn et al. 1998), disrupted regional trade patterns and political stability. Many northern Belizean centers suffered, including Colha, as witnessed by their reduced and often ephemeral Early Classic occupations. While many sites recuperated and rose again to prominence in the Late Classic, Colha did not. In part, people probably got used to relying on other lithic resources, which, as seen, were already being exploited. In part, too, the organization of lithic manufacture has a centrifugal effect that is hard to counter. As Epstein (1990) has pointed out, one or at most a few individuals can handle all stages of lithic production. Thus, lithic household groups would tend to be informally organized, something that is reflected in the Late Classic settlement pattern visible on the Colha surface, where informal household groupings (Ashmore 1981) predominate. These types of groups have been equated by Wilk (1988) with loosely organized multifamily units, who are semi-independent economically (King 2000:148–52). In their Late Preclassic heyday the chertworkers at Colha dominated important resources and labor-intensive trade items, so they were able to continue in their pivotal and privileged role. They could even centralize production and mobilize their members to work in a two-stage process, albeit mostly in parallel and redundant capacities. When times changed and trade was disrupted, the resources they controlled were no longer as critical. They were not then in a position to translate their labor to dominate other venues such as farming. To do so would have required them to transcend their semi-solitary status and reorganize to muster more of a family workforce than might have been at their disposal. They probably would have been loath, as well, to give up their signature specialization. Indeed, as McAnany (2010:199–252) points out, working a particular material and producing a particular craft product is a key part today (and probably in the past as well) of a Maya craftperson's identity, even when the product and the activity themselves do not provide substantial revenue or other rewards. It *is* who they are. For the chertworkers at Colha, the problem may have been compounded by a lack of easy access to land. While they may have owned quarries, it is likely that much of the available land, especially the most productive, was already being farmed by others. As a result, chertworking families could no longer serve to renew the ranks of the elite. At the same time, the established elite, while retaining their position in the community, may not have been able to advance any further. Interestingly, chertworkers remained on a par economically and socially with other Colha commoner residents, including intensive farmers, during the Classic (King 2000:143–48). Apparently, the labor value of their product still gave them a certain cachet.

In terms of a heterarchical model of complexity, Colha's trajectory from Late Preclassic through Early Classic is an example of what Crumley (2003) has called "hyperhierarchy" and its consequences. She uses this term to describe societies that are able to consolidate power and merge "distinct hierarchies (e.g., religious, political, economic) into…hypercoherence" (2003:138), a term she borrows from Flannery (1972). Such a society, for example, was the Roman Empire. These kinds of hierarchies work well for decision-making, as there is a clear chain of command. However, they are less flexible when adapting to what is called "surprise" or chaos in self-organizational terminology, that is tensions/events that are beyond their control. In those situations, heterarchical structures, which rely on multiple lines of information and are flexible to adapt, thrive better (Crumley 2003). I propose that the unique combination of circumstances that put the chertworkers at Colha in the catbird's seat at the beginning of the Late Preclassic promoted hypercoherence at the site. It seems clear that political, economic, and religious hierarchies were merged at that time, if we remember that chertworkers not only lived in the center but participated in ceremonies there (Potter 1992; King and Potter 1994). This hyperhierarchical organization made the elite at Colha relatively inflexible to respond to a prolonged economic and political crisis at the onset of the Early Classic. Their inability to react was subsequently aggravated by the organizational constraints of lithic production itself, as noted, which made recovery difficult.

This same pattern can be discerned at the end of the Late Preclassic in the Peten. Early social differentiation at sites like Nakbe and El Mirador was probably predicated, as discussed, on access to prime agricultural land. This resource would most likely have been owned because it would have required continuous labor, even in the absence of intensive strategies, to produce the multiple crops per year that were possible. Ownership of this land would thus have provided early elites at these sites with the impetus chertworking did for Colha's elite, albeit earlier. The organizational requirements of farming would have favored larger labor pools than chertworking (Epstein 1990; King 2000:148–52), initially of kin, who were reciprocally obligated to help with the work. The lack of water on the Peten plateau may have precipitated matters by constraining the mobility of the population as it grew in the Middle Preclassic, putting pressure on resources and exacerbating the differences between those who had access to good land and those who did not. One result may have been an extension of reciprocal obligations from kin to non-kin, including affines (Chapter 10, this volume), or from near kin to more distant (Izquierdo 2004) or even fictive kin (Chapter 10), thereby setting the stage for the development of a true social hierarchy.

The fact that these sites grew to hyperhierarchy is suggested by the sheer scale of monumental construction and the apparent coherence between their religious, political, and economic sectors. The accelerating environmental crisis during the Late Preclassic, combining both changes in climate and their own failure to curb erosion, would have precipitated an organizational crisis. Such a "surprise" is precisely the kind of problem hypercoherent systems are least able to solve (Crumley 2003; see also Flannery 1972). Despite the size of the farming labor pools, there was nothing to turn that labor to. With the disappearance of the perennial wetlands and open water (Dunning et al. 2002; Beach et al. 2006; Beach et al. 2008) these sites lost their prime attractiveness, thereby perhaps impelling some of the population movements that caused such severe repercussions in Belize. Nakbe seems to have been largely abandoned after this time, and while El Mirador was reoccupied in the Late Classic, it never regained its former glory (Hansen 2005). At other Peten sites, such as San Bartolo, comparable problems led also to abandonment at the end of the Late Preclassic (Thomas Garrison, pers. comm. 2007). Not all the Peten centers succumbed to this crisis, however. Others, like Tikal, which were perhaps more heterarchically organized and had other strings to their bows (e.g., tool production and trade), were able to weather the difficulties. Indeed, in the void left by the demise of its principal rivals, Tikal was able to flourish, achieving unprecedented heights of power in the Early Classic. Concentration of water management in the hands of the elite (Scarborough 1993, 1998), following the depletion of natural water resources, would have helped intensify social stratification there and created the conditions for Tikal's Classic rise.

A question remaining, however, is why Maya states in general never again seem to have achieved the level of hypercoherence they did in the Late Preclassic. While Crumley (2003) has argued that a certain level of hyperhierarchy hampered states in the Late Classic and helped precipitate the infamous Collapse, economic, political, and religious structures were not as congruent then as they were early on (King 2000). Tikal, for example, may have succumbed at the end, but it was able to recuperate from major political blows during the mid Classic and achieve considerable Late Classic prominence. The same relative flexibility can be seen at other sites.

Two factors may help explain these patterns. First, population in the Late Preclassic was sparser and may have been easier to control and cohere, though not everywhere, as some communities appear to have remained more independent (Scarborough and Valdez 2009). Networks between sites might also have been easier to maintain, as there were comparably fewer of them. Increased demographic pressure in subsequent time periods may have promoted increased competition and more heterarchical structures for survival (Leslie Shaw, pers. comm. 2007). More numerous resource-specialized communities would also have provided a strong alternative economy that supported hinterland populations through the vicissitudes experienced by the large urban centers and hindered centralized control (Scarborough and Valdez 2009). Second, the very nature of the Maya value system may have mitigated against hypercoherency, certainly economically. Placing a value on labor rather than on tangible assets such as land or objects leads to varied results (King 2003). Thus, a piece of land worked for milpa may rise in value, but what is it worth the next year when it lies fallow? Different activities require differential investments of labor and different types of labor organization. Variable inputs of labor will result in variable values placed on the fruits of that work, but this will not produce a straightforward ranked system of products, because of the way work is structured. As in the case of the Colha chertworkers, the actual organization of labor will affect how much of an impact the product of that labor will have on the larger society. Thus, a productive process that involves many hands and can easily be centrally controlled, such as agriculture, will lead to a different production and distribution system than one characterized by semi-independent labor, which is harder to harness. An emphasis on labor, then, by its very nature calls forth heterarchical structures.

In the Late Preclassic smaller populations and intensive exploitation of single resources may have been able to override the heterarchical tendencies of a labor-based system. In some cases, the enterprise in which labor was invested and how it was structured might even have *promoted* hierarchy. This factor may help explain the unparalleled size of the early Peten sites. As cross-cultural studies tell us, access to and control over land is one of the most stable ways to promote and ensure sociopolitical stratification. Ownership of the work-improved lands in the central Peten resembles hereditary property/tangible asset ownership elsewhere in the world. As much or more than ownership, however, mobilization of labor on a large scale, first from near kin, then from extended kin and even non-kin, probably allowed a more typical hierarchical pattern of social relationships to develop. That does not mean that elites "controlled" this labor in a classic Western economic sense, at least initially, but rather that they had access to it and could mobilize it in return for upholding their part of the bargain. As time went on, naturalization and perpetuation of authority, for instance through monumental construction (McAnany 2010:141–57), may have changed the initial elite to non-elite relations to a more permanent form of subjugation, and perhaps even a different mode of production (Sharer and Traxler 2006:180–82). However, mutual labor obligations and reciprocal duties would still have ensured that persuasion was an important factor (Scarborough and Valdez 2009), even at the most centralized sites. Thus, while early hypercoherence in this area resembles that found in similar, agrarian-based early states around the world, it had its own unique form. Disruptions at the end of the Preclassic led to a reconfiguration and during the Classic a rising population furnished enough of a brake that the labor-based system's innate heterarchical tendencies could not be surmounted. Who is to say, too, that Classic peoples did not remember the disasters that befell their ancestors? They may have preferred to diversify rather than put all their energies into fields that had never regained their original fertility.

I would close with two points. First, we cannot hope to understand the Maya if we do not leave room in our models for variation over time and space. I have tried to demonstrate here that a heterarchical rather than a hierarchical view of complexity allows for just this kind of flexibility. Second, if ever we hope to recover traces of non-Western and pre-colonial organizations, the Maya states are good candidates. As Pyburn (2004) has pointed out, our ethnographic and historical models are otherwise tainted by colonial and other influences that have inevitably infused Western biases into the record. We should be prepared, then, to encounter seriously different value systems and different structural configurations as we examine the more remote past and take them into account. McAnany (2010) has shown us one such path towards doing so in discussing Maya economies over time in their inextricably embedded social, political, and ritual contexts. The model proposed here is another attempt to do so, restricted here to the context of the developing states. Linking a value placed on labor with a heterarchical organizational structure, it is perforce speculative. It is also inevitably based in part on biased colonial documents, from which I have tried to glean the subtext. As McDavid (2007:2), citing philosopher William James, notes, however, "theories provide instruments, not answers." She adds that, "our work must be evaluated as less a solution than as a program for more work." In that spirit, I offer my model not as the last word but as a first step towards understanding the early prominence of a truly remarkable group of people.

ACKNOWLEDGMENTS

My thanks go to the conference organizers for inviting me and to the conference participants for a stimulating and fun week-long discussion. It was a pleasure to have the luxury of sitting, thinking, and exchanging ideas in pleasant surroundings. I would also like to thank them for comments on my final draft that helped sharpen the discussion. John Clark and Dana Anthony provided detailed commentaries on my original paper that were immeasurably helpful in prodding my thinking. Norman Hammond and Jerry Sabloff also gave me important feedback that sharpened the results. Jason Barrett, Timothy Beach, Beverly Chiarulli, Liwy Gracioso, Thomas Hester, Jon Lohse, Sheryl Luzzader-Beach, Anne Pyburn, Harry Shafer, Leslie Shaw, and Fred Valdez, Jr., all gave me key information for both the article and the Maya Weekend presentation. I appreciate their ready support. Stephen Epstein helped me clarify my thinking and elegantly streamlined my prose. Two anonymous reviewers for the volume provided comments and suggestions that helped me clarify my argument. To all of them I offer my deepest thanks. This chapter was finalized in 2013. Any remaining errors or flaws, however, belong to the usual suspect.

10

Middle Preclassic Maya Society: Tilting at Windmills or Giants of Civilization?

MARCELLO A. CANUTO

In order to become the master, the politician poses as the servant.

—Charles de Gaulle

Society is a masked ball, where every one hides his real character, and reveals it by hiding.

—Ralph Waldo Emerson

INTRODUCTION

Among the greatest challenges of the study of Formative period (2000 BCE–200 CE) Mesoamerica is the explanation for the causes of social complexity. It is by now a commonly held notion that by the Late Formative period (ca. 400 BCE), there existed a handful of coeval regional states in Mesoamerica (Grove 1981a). In the specific case of the lowland Maya area, by 400 BCE, its inhabitants were living in large cities (such as Cival and Nakbe) that functioned as regal centers from which an *ajaw* (holy lord) governed a centralized regional state.

In general terms, this period saw the development of social interactions bespeaking institutionalized power differentials not only between groups but also within them (Love 1999b; see Mann 1986). Recent research now demonstrates that institutions of formal power in the Maya region date to as early as the Late Formative (henceforth, when referring to the Maya region, the preferred term *Preclassic* will be used) period (Estrada-Belli 2006a; Hansen 2005; Love 1999a; McAnany 2002; Saturno et al. 2006, among others). Nevertheless, evidence for precocious complexity *per se*—such as the existence of and justification for "natural lords" (Roys 1941:649) dating to periods earlier in time than scholars originally thought—renders the causal processes of that complexity no less nebulous. In fact, evidence of precocity only forces scholarly focus onto even earlier and less understood periods of time. Consequently, to interpret the developments of the Late Preclassic period in the Maya area, this chapter must focus on the developments that preceded it—that is, those dating to the Middle Preclassic period (1000–400 BCE).

This task will prove challenging for the simple reason that current data from the lowland Maya area are far more limited and patchy than what has been gathered in the rest of contemporaneous Mesoamerica. Given that nearly half a century of research have not sufficed to forge consensus among scholars as to how and why the first regional states emerged elsewhere in Mesoamerica (Blomster et al. 2005; Flannery 1968; Flannery et al. 2005; Stoltman et al. 2005; Neff et al. 2006a; Neff et al. 2006b; Schele 2000), it would seem a fool's errand, or more romantically, a quixotic quest to attempt an interpretation of how social complexity arose in the Maya area given the current state of knowledge. However, as pointed out by Clark (2007a), much of the data regarding the Maya area is as robust (or weak) as that which hails from Oaxaca or the Gulf coast. It is under that banner that this chapter tilts at the Middle Preclassic Maya in hopes of finding giants of a later civilization rather than mundane windmills.

In any event, regardless of regional focus, any diachronic study of this kind is prone to suggesting that an early manifestation of some later pattern functioned as its precursor. To avoid McAnany's "leading assumptions" (2002:230), local developments must be understood *sui generis*—as logical outcomes of and wholly relevant to the local environment in which they occur and without recourse to their eventual function as prerequisites for later developments. For instance, the custom of burying kin members below a residential floor during the Middle Preclassic period (e.g., McAnany et al. 1999) should not be assumed to represent the precursor of later Classic-period rites of dynastic ancestor worship. Although the Middle Preclassic burial ritual might prove relevant to later institutions of statecraft, its initial manifestation might have carried very different meanings for its participants. To assume otherwise would be to succumb to the allure of teleology.

THE STUDY OF EARLY COMPLEXITY AND MESOAMERICA

For the Maya lowlands, the study of the rise of ancient complexity must explain the alchemy that transmutated a particular blend of social practices, developed in sedentary subsistence farming communities, into ideologies of hereditary inequality and divine rulership. Specifically, this chapter addresses the potential drivers of social complexity in the lowland Maya area of the Preclassic period by focusing on the social relations that shaped the everyday lives of this area's inhabitants. In other words, how did social forms of identity, interaction, and organization of the Preclassic Maya condition the development of socio-political complexity?

Several attempts to address these questions for the southern lowland Maya provide useful information and models (Adams 1977; Grube 1995; Powis 2005). Nevertheless, the heavy theoretical lifting on the question of socio-political complexity in early Mesoamerica has been shouldered by research in areas outside the lowland Maya area, mainly Oaxaca (Blanton et al. 1996; Blanton, Kowalewski et al. 1993; Flannery 1968, 1972; Marcus and Flannery 1996; Sanders and Nichols 1988; Spencer and Redmond 2004), the Pacific coast (Cheetham 2006; Clark 1997; Clark and Blake 1994; Clark and Pye 2000a; Love 1999b; Matheny 1986a), and central Mexico (Sanders 1962a, 1968; Sanders, Parsons et al. 1979; Sanders and Price 1968). Research in the Gulf coast (Clark 2007a; Cyphers Guillén 1996, 1997b, 1999; Diehl and Coe 1995; Love 1999b; Symonds 2000) and Honduras (Cummins 2007; Joyce 2003; Joyce and Henderson 2001) have also contributed to the interpretation of the early rise of complexity in Mesoamerica. It is therefore only logical that this chapter looks to the models and research from these areas first.

Research in Mesoamerica has adopted several distinct paradigms to model socio-political complexity: culture ecology, neo-evolutionary processualism, and agency theory. Furthermore, although these models are derived from regionally focused field research, they are proposed as broader explanations of the pan-Mesoamerican phenomenon of the rise of complexity during the Formative period. Since such models are not inherently hobbled or hedged by their proponents as explanations for a particular time and place, their applicability to the Maya area of the Preclassic period can be assessed.

Culture Ecology: Fruitful Complexity

Derived from models applied to the Near East or South Asia (Adams 1966), culture ecology models in Mesoamerica sought explanations for complexity in the human-nature interface, especially as it relates to subsistence adaptations. The natural conditions found in Mesoamerica, such as variable soil fertility, water supply, stone tool technology, and the absence of pack animals, establish baseline delimiters of the environment's carrying capacity. Only certain Mesoamerican environments—generally identified as the highlands—were thus pliable to intensive forms of agriculture and only in those did human societies have the chance to sustain complex forms of socio-political organization.

In the case of the valley of Mexico, irrigation was a necessity given that rainfall and permanent water sources were sparse and insufficient. In fact, the environmental conditions of the Basin of Mexico were considered so similar to those of Mesopotamia that the hydraulic hypothesis used to explain complexity in the Fertile Crescent was thus applied (Sanders 1962a, 1968, 1973; Sanders and Nichols 1988; Sanders et al. 1979; Sanders and Price 1968). Specifically, this model suggests that irrigation and trade were required to coalesce a state-level society defined by dense populations and surplus management.

Irrigation alone did not prompt higher orders of social organization, however. The region's ecological diversity also induced a level and intensity of non-local trade and communication that required the development of certain organizational principles of its inhabitants. Considering this ecological system, the agricultural adaptation required, and the concomitant development of trade-exchange networks, the long-term human response would have been the development of small city-states. Over time, with continued exchange of needed resources, the Basin of Mexico became the center of large conglomerations of symbiotically related city-states.

For the Formative period in Mesoamerica's lowland regions such as the Maya and Olmec areas, however, this paradigm has been applied in relatively simplistic ways (see Sanders 1962b, 1963, 1973, 1977). Since lowland environments do not follow the precepts of the highlands, the development of the Olmec and Preclassic Maya were not interpreted as evidence for socio-political complexity (see below for more detailed discussion). Recently, more sophisticated applications of this paradigm to later Classic-period lowland Maya society have proven fruitful. There has been a growing appreciation for how certain lowland natural resources, such as water (Davis-Salazar 2003; Lucero 2002, 2006; Scarborough 1998) and land (Dunning and Beach 1994; Fedick and Ford 1990; Ford 1990, 2004), were limited and patchy. Although the Maya lowlands do not present conditions highly analogous to those of arid regions throughout the world, the uneven distribution of certain resources provides some justification for considering the role of a managerial class administering and redistributing them.

Similar studies have been recently applied to the Olmec region (Cyphers and Zurita-Noguera 2006a) in an effort to explain the rise of San Lorenzo as uniquely precocious. It is therefore possible to consider that culture ecology could prove relevant to the interpretation of Preclassic lowland Maya complexity. Any new deployment of this paradigm, however, would have to guard against the reductionism of past applications, which dismissed the Maya lowlands as too impractical for autochthonous complexity.

Neo-evolutionary Processualism: It's in the System

A systems approach proved quite useful for the interpretation of early Mesoamerican complexity. Framed by Flannery (1972), this paradigm would be used to interpret the development of complexity in the Oaxaca valley from hunter-gatherer to Monte Alban's militaristic expansion (Flannery 1976, 1986; Flannery and Marcus 1983). The systems approach was established to argue against prime mover models that pinned full responsibility for complexity on a single factor, such as population pressure, warfare, or irrigation.

The systems approach, alternatively, was a multi-variate analysis that identified several relationships between independent aspects of cultural systems such as subsistence technology, food supply, population levels, and exchange systems. Connected through feedback loops, changes to one aspect of society would be met by responses and changes in related aspects of society. In this paradigm, the impact of several independent socio-environmental variables would have triggered evolutionary mechanisms such as "promotion" that encouraged processes of system centralization, that is, socio-political complexity.

These models emphasize materialist causes for change—that is, those vaguely defined socio-environmental variables. The impetus for change is seen as external to the system, suggesting that socio-political complexity would fail to develop in an otherwise homeostatic system. Early applications of this paradigm discounted human agency as relevant to systemic change.

In its more sophisticated form, systems theory recognized the impact of individual agents on long-term social processes (Clark and Blake 1994; Cowgill 2000; Flannery 1999; Flannery and Marcus 1976a). The models note that within systems of inter-regional exchange, increasing population, and changing subsistence technology, there exist individuals whose "actions were based on empirical observations, interpreted in light of a coherent body of logic... [that made] sense as a series of related and internally consistent responses based on the same set of underlying principles" (Flannery and Marcus 1976a). Therefore, within the processes of system centralization, certain individuals played important and archaeologically visible roles in the promotion of cultural systems.

Archaeology has traditionally viewed these individuals as "agents of process," affecting change only through the manipulation of material goods (i.e., wealth) (Blanton et al. 1996; Earle 1997). Seen in another way, big men are agents of change insofar as they attempt control of staple or wealth finance systems. In the ethnographic record, it is clear that big men are not so limited (Godelier and Strathern 1991); rather they can command allegiance and rise to prominence by many means other than the control over the production and distribution of material goods (Harrison 1987; Lindstrom 1984; Modjeska 1982). Some big men enact non-materialist strategies, such as claiming to "command attractive explanatory systems" (Lindstrom 1984:284)—that is, an ideology—that can prove mutually advantageous for leader and follower.

For the Preclassic lowland Maya, the materialist systems approach has proven useful and commonly (though not thoroughly) applied (see discussion below). Furthermore, there is some new evidence relating to the adoption of a new subsistence adaptation—widespread maize farming (Neff et al. 2006c; Pohl et al. 1996; Pope et al. 2001; Rue et al. 2002; Wahl et al. 2006)—that would have wrought major environmental changes to the lowland area. Systems theory would suggest that changes consequent to the widespread adoption of maize farming would trigger several feedback loops involving population levels, surplus management, and tool production that could have triggered evolutionary mechanisms that led to system centralization. Furthermore, heads of household involved in the management of new stores of food surplus could have become agents of change, centralizing agrarian communities through the control of this staple good.

Agency: *Ecce Homo*!

The dissatisfaction with the processualist "individual" led to the search for more nuanced approaches to ancient agency. A series of models that focused on forceful agents of the past were proposed (Clark and Blake 1994; Hayden and Gargett 1990; Hayden 1995; Rathje 2002). Variously termed as "aggrandizers," "accumulators," "strategizing individuals," "coalition-builders," or "emergent elites," these individuals were seen as capable of altering social relationships through the manipulation of material culture and ideology.

In the case of Mesoamerica, these individuals likely represented the structurally favored "family leader" or "shaman." These individuals—to be referred to here as *entrepreneurs*—deploy tactics to promote and then sustain relations of prerogative between themselves and others. The model imbues the entrepreneur with the strategic foresight to instigate the production of "unusual quantities" of specialty items, such as *chicha*, for events of conspicuous consumption and public munificence that reproduce (but also modify) local social relations. Most equivalent to the ethnographic "big man," these entrepreneurs engaged in a Maussian gift-giving dynamic (Mauss 1954) that altered social relations and valuations by influencing the habits of production.

Through events of concerted social action—such as feasts (Dietler and Hayden 2001), production of specialty items, the construction of public buildings (Rathje 2002), and sporting events (Clark and Blake 1994; Hayden and Gargett 1990; Hill and Clark 2001)—entrepreneurs sought local integration and consolidation of their emergent status. These activities also provided contexts for continued interaction or competition between different big men (Brumfiel 1992; Brumfiel and Fox 1994). Such elite or factional competition could spur further centralization, surplus-production, and social distinction.

Entrepreneurs thus created conditions of both material and ideological indebtedness, fealty, obligation, and competition that resulted in conditions of inequality among members of a single social group. An obvious consequence of material production being so induced is that the archaeological record of such societies exhibits an increase in portable exotic goods, public spaces, and communal buildings: "the range of prestige technologies, is constrained only by the materials available, the ingenuity of the crafts-man, and the degree of power that aggrandizers are capable of acquiring" (Hayden 1995:258).

A failing of these practice-oriented approaches is that these "agents" are imbued with such discretionary knowledge that their eventual development into an elite seems inevitable. Agents are privileged with competences in highly specialized practices that are themselves learned and are therefore to be regarded as social products rather than as innate individual capabilities. In other words, this model for the development of early complexity raises the question of how do "special agents" learn and then enact their prac-tices? Should those practices not be accessible to anyone within the social group that produces, abides, and provides the social contest for them—why one agent and not another? How do specific individuals develop any com-petence at all in the deployment of the society-changing strategies above and beyond "the multiplicities of players [pursuing] separate interests, in divergent ways" (Clark 2000b:109)?

For the Preclassic lowland Maya, evidence for the repeated and cumula-tive action of such agents is visible in the regional distribution of ceramic fine wares (see discussion below). The widespread distribution of fineware serving vessels suggests that the inter-group prestation exchange was re-gional in scale (Clark and Cheetham 2003). Perhaps through mechanisms of "competitive generosity," specialty items were traded far and wide as group leaders competed with one another in efforts to consolidate their intra-group position of prominence.

Summary

Several broad paradigms have been developed for Formative Mesoamer-ica, culture ecology for the Basin of Mexico, neo-evolutionary evolutionism for Oaxaca, and agency theory for the Pacific coast. For the lowland Maya area, however, no distinct model has been developed. Rather aspects and elements of these paradigms have been applied to the Maya lowlands with some degree of success. Nevertheless, a comprehensive explanation for the rise of complexity in the Preclassic lowland Maya area is missing. What fol-lows here is a review of the application of these paradigms to the Preclassic Maya lowlands.

INITIAL VIEWS ON EARLY COMPLEXITY IN
THE MAYA LOWLANDS

Over the past half-century of research in the Maya lowlands, it has become clear that the character and complexity of the Preclassic period has been underappreciated. The absence of direct research on the Preclassic periods led to generalizations of cultural development drawn from culture ecology or neo-evolutionary theories that simplified if not reduced the more than 1000-year Preclassic period history into the general categories of "tribal" or "egalitarian society." While these attributions might not be entirely inapplicable or inaccurate, they do suffer from a degree of imprecision that renders them impractical *per se*. However, the first attempts to characterize the Preclassic Maya provide some clues as to how best to proceed with the study of this period.

A New Horizon

Evidence of the Preclassic lowland Maya was recovered in the earliest phases of formal research in the area. For instance, the Carnegie excavations of Str. E-VII sub of Uaxactun (Ricketson 1937) revealed early evidence for Late Preclassic monumentality and socio-political complexity among the lowland Maya. Moreover, as a consequence of this work, Smith (1955) was able to provide researchers with a clear and ubiquitous marker of Preclassic Maya occupation—the red monochrome ceramics associated with the earliest contexts at Uaxactun. Though their absolute dating remained unknown, Smith called the red monochrome ceramics found in the earliest stratigraphic contexts at Uaxactun (underlying masonry structures) *Mamom*, and those in contexts associated with the buildings, *Chicanel*.

Furthermore, Willey and collaborators (1965) at Barton Ramie in Belize developed a comprehensive sequence of Preclassic period Maya society that supported and then supplemented the initial work by Smith (1955) at Uaxactun. They recognized a prevalence of red-paste wares in the stratigraphically early contexts of several other Classic Maya centers, namely Xunantunich (then known as "Benque Viejo") and San José (Thompson 1939, 1940), Barton Ramie (Willey, Bullard et al. 1965) and San Estevan (Bullard 1965). Eventually, even earlier ceramics were encountered at Barton Ramie (Early Jenney Creek phase; Willey, Bullard et al. 1965) and at Tikal (Eb phase; Coe 1990). By the late 1960s, therefore, there was already good evidence that settlement during the Middle Preclassic period would prove substantial. In fact, McAnany (2004:3) notes that the Preclassic period discoveries of these early projects were comprehensive enough in Belize to demonstrate a settlement pattern favoring estuarine and wetland environments that subsequent research later confirmed.

Soon after, other research projects recovered material related to the Mamom phase or earlier. In the southwestern area of the Peten, research at the Classic centers of Seibal (Sabloff 1975; Willey 1970b) and Altar de Sacrificios (Adams 1971) recovered evidence of the Preclassic period occupations that appeared to be even earlier than Mamom (and therefore contemporaneous with the Early Jenney Creek and Eb ceramics). The ceramic phases dating to these occupations were named Xe (Altar de Sacrificios) and Real Xe (Seibal) and attributed to 900–600 BCE (Willey 1970b:318; 1973a). A few years later, research in the highland Guatemalan region of Verapaz recovered material similar to these lowland Xe traditions (Sedat and Sharer 1972). These discoveries were further complemented by work in the Rio Bec region at Becan, Chicanna, and Xpujil (Adams and Culbert 1977:16) that also recovered examples of early ceramics of the Mamom tradition.

Tribal Ecology

Despite much of this research, Sanders and Price (1968:111) suggested that during the Middle and Late Preclassic periods (the Mamom and Chicanel ceramic phases), Maya society exhibited tribal forms of organization— that is, "sedentary agricultural settlements," "lacking community stratification," and maybe "socially autonomous" (1968:110). This blindness to the data available likely results from an unerring commitment to a culture ecology model that had little room for autochthonous complexity in the Mesoamerican lowlands.

To explain socio-political complexity in this region, Sanders invokes Vogt's (1961) religious participation model in which lineage heads reserved control over certain areas, serving as regulators of the economic system. This complexity, however, would have been limited by the distribution of fertile "intensifiable" soil types (Sanders 1977); their patchy distribution led to clustering of the population in certain areas of the lowlands that were to eventually host the largest of Classic Maya centers (such as Tikal and Calakmul).

Despite this hierarchy-inducing ecological variability, however, the Maya lowlands still presented a much more constant landscape than do the Mesoamerican highlands (Sanders 1973). According to Sanders, therefore, the Peten's relative ecological evenness inhibited the establishment and development of political units larger than small ceremonial centers. Although relatively richer, the few areas where soil would have allowed the production of greater food surpluses did not gain enough of an advantage over the peripheries to wield stable and long-term control (as in the case of highland Mexico). Rather, lowland areas were seen as having managed to support only small ceremonial centers surrounded by agrarian hamlets of limited population. Furthermore, whatever developments might have occurred in the lowland regions were secondary to and derivative of lowland-highland interaction

At least, now, it can be averred that research on the question of the Preclassic Maya since Sanders and Price's (1968) initial evaluation has proved them mistaken (Clark and Cheetham 2003; Clark and Hansen 2001; Hammond 2000; Hansen 1998; Saturno et al. 2006; Sharer and Traxler 2006). It is clear that more complex systems of socio-political organization—paramount chiefdoms or early states—had developed by the Middle and Late Preclassic periods. Nevertheless, the question of the Peten's varying fertility provides an important factor to consider when interpreting the distribution of the earliest concentrated settlements in the lowland Preclassic Maya area.

Land-hungry Peasants

Considering the notable presence of Preclassic period material throughout the lowlands, Adams's *Origins of Maya Civilization* (1977) provided the first synthetic consideration of the Preclassic period Maya. By that time, there was a consensus among scholars that the excavations at Tikal, Altar de Sacrificios, Uaxactun, Becan, and Dzibilchaltun had convincingly demonstrated the existence of socio-political complexity in the Late Preclassic Maya lowlands. In fact, Hammond (1977b:65) made the point that "our relatively small exposures of and samples from Middle Preclassic levels have led to a failure to realize that the increasing complexity of Maya society which we now accept for the Late Preclassic may have begun more than half a millennium earlier."

Growing evidence of Middle Preclassic (1000–400 BCE) lowland settlement triggered debate over the origins of these initial settlers. The Early

Preclassic (2000–1000 BCE) predecessors were regarded as pioneering settlers of either Maya or Mixe-Zoquean stock (Lowe 1977:247), sparsely settled (Coe 1977:195) throughout the lowlands. This vague information so paled in relation to the Early Preclassic evidence from neighboring areas that the "absence of Early Preclassic occupation in the Petén and Yucatán began to look exceptional" (Hammond 1991d:5).

Since the Early and Middle Preclassic periods were initially characterized by several distinct ceramic traditions—Xe at Seibal, Swasey at Cuello (Hammond 1977b:50), and Eb at Tikal (Culbert 1977:29)—it seemed possible that the Early Preclassic lowland landscape was populated by different groups. For instance, some (Adams 1970; Hammond 1977b:61) suggested that Xe and Swasey phase occupations in the Petexbatun region and in Belize developed as a consequence of hunter-gatherer groups following aquatic and near-riverine resources. In the case of the Xe occupation, the original settlers could have come southward from the Gulf coast, and the lower Grijalva and Usumacinta regions. Alternatively, Willey (1977:386) suggested that the Xe ceramic complex derived from highland ceramic traditions (see Sharer and Gifford 1970).

Independent of these questions of "origins," however, the Middle Preclassic Maya (of whatever ceramic stripe) were generally viewed as developing a progressively more specialized adaptation to the lowland tropical region they were colonizing. Though the Xe, Eb, and Swasey sites were few, they suggested to Willey that Middle Preclassic Maya lived in dispersed small farming villages composed of perishable residences built either directly on the ground or on slightly elevated platforms with little or no public architecture. They would have formed "simple, egalitarian societies" (1977:387).

The Middle Preclassic colonization was rapid and led to "widely dispersed and meager hamlets" (Puleston and Puleston 1971b:335). This rapidity was largely impelled by the settlers' adoption of a land-extensive farming system that resulted in an ever-expanding frontier (Adams 1971:155). As prime estuarine regions filled with settlement, population pressure (either in the form of other migratory settlers or as descendent groups, or both) would have triggered inter-community competition, if not struggle (Rice 1976b). Given a sociopolitical system with little regional integration, the withdrawal of groups to uninhabited areas was likely a favored option. This secondary exploitation created a two-level settlement hierarchy (Hammond 1977b) and triggered a series of new subsistence adaptations in response to the changes in the environment being exploited by these Preclassic *peteneros* (Puleston and Puleston 1971b). Overall, the Middle Preclassic Maya were modeled as forest agriculturalists living in decentralized autonomous communities prone to "local cleavages at the expense of regional organization" (Sahlins 1968:31).

Resource-deprived Lowlanders

The Middle Preclassic period was thus understood as "a spiraling interaction continuum of gradual population growth, community enlargement, and tribal segmentation" (Ball 1977:123). Although population growth, *per se*, was not always directly recognizable in the sparse evidence at hand, the application of a general culture ecology (see Boserup 1965) model to explain differential population growth throughout the lowlands during the Middle Preclassic period was suggested (Ball 1977; Sanders 1973, 1977; Webster 1977). Whether or not accepted as sufficient explanations, these studies did establish the notion of a "Central Zone" to identify (if not explain) the existence of an area within the Maya lowlands where there was a higher concentration of large centers.

Those scholars who went beyond culture-ecology and behavior-driven-by-soil-types models adopted more complex, multi-variate models that included an appreciation for socio-economic adaptations. These approaches did not discard the notions of population pressure, differential carrying capacities, and resource availability as relevant to the rise of complexity in the lowland region. However, they introduced various other socio-environmental factors such as regional exchange (Rathje 1971, 1977) and agricultural intensification (Netting 1977; Rathje 1972; Sanders 1977) as germane to the Middle Preclassic period. The main thrust of these models was to explain the rise of large Classic period centers, such as Tikal and Calakmul, in the "Central Zone." This area was understood as presenting a series of environmental advantages (soil fertility) and disadvantages (absence of critical resources) that would have impelled intra-zonal organization and hierarchy to manage. As a result, the "Central Zone" came to be interpreted as engaged in core-periphery relations with the rest of the Maya area that involved the exchange of raw materials from the highlands for manufactured lowland goods.

Given the heavily materialist perspective of early research in the question of lowland Maya complexity, it is of little surprise that limited attention was paid to any ideological factors for socio-political complexity (Willey 1977:416). In fact, this early phase of Maya society was characterized more in terms of technological achievement (such as pottery making), adaptive strategies (such as swidden farming and settlement location), and trade contacts (resource procurement), than for its ideo-religious characteristics. Perhaps Rice (1976b:445) provides the most apropos description of the Maya for this early period:

> One can imagine social and ceremonial leadership growing with population size, the subsistence system, and participation in trade. As land pressure begins to limit subsistence options in terms of both space and labor investment, internal control and planning become major concerns. Identical development in surrounding regions would bring leaderships into increasing contact, if not conflict, both testing and reinforcing bases of power, while formalizing local and regional territories and hierarchies.

The leader in this reconstruction is conceived primarily as foreman managing resources, striking trading partnerships, and accumulating some wealth as payment for the successful distribution of goods throughout the community.

These "boot-strap" models for socio-political complexity were derived directly from neo-evolutionary models (Flannery 1972) coming into vogue at the time. Given their anti-diffusionist posture, these models accommodated foreign influence only through strict economical mechanisms, and therefore left little room for other, perhaps more dramatic, forms of contact with the early lowland Maya. However, some of the more important regions exhibiting coeval or more pronounced socio-political complexity were to be found in regions of similar environmental conditions, such as the Pacific coast (Lowe 1977; Quirarte 1977) or the Gulf coast (Coe 1977), which would not have found any advantage to the types of economic relations posited by core-periphery models, rendering materialist explanations somewhat incomplete.

From Kings to Shamans

The discovery that the massive constructions of El Mirador, namely the gargantuan Danta and Tigre architectural complexes dated to the Late Preclassic (Graham 1962; Hansen 1998; Matheny 1980, 1986b), suggested that by this period, lowland Maya society had developed a centralized political hierarchy (Hammond 1992; Sharer 1992). Complementary discoveries of Late Preclassic period monumental constructions at Tikal (Laporte 1995; Laporte and Fialko C. 1990) and Uaxactun (Valdés 1993) suggested that this complexity was regional, much like its later Classic period successor. To wit, Freidel and Schele (1988a:549) were the first to suggest that the single most visible attribute of Classic period society—the institution of divine rulership known as *ajaw*—was indeed constitutive of Late Preclassic Maya society from the 1st century BCE onward as well.

Since the authors were interested in the development of this institution, they developed an explanatory model that, by necessity, focused on the Middle Preclassic period. In the same way that Rice (1976b:445) suggested the Middle Preclassic leader was "a centralized authority [that] served to minimize conflict and disruption" (Rice 1976b:445), Freidel and Schele (1988a:549) claimed that "the institution of *ahaw*...was invented to accommodate severe contradictions in Maya society between the ethos of egalitarianism and an actual condition of flourishing elitism brought on by successful trade and interaction between the Lowland Maya and their hierarchically organized neighbors over the course of the Preclassic era" (Freidel and Schele 1988a:549). According to Freidel (1979), these regional economies were driven by goods of culturally specific value (exotics, information, and finished products) rather than bulk goods, such as salt, basalt, and obsidian (Rathje 1971, 1972, 1977).

Freidel suggested that a Middle Preclassic regional commercial network resulted in intra-community inequality which, in turn, would have required ideological justification. Furthermore, this justification would have had to deploy an idiom resonant with predominantly peasant traditions of the time. Given the exotic nature of the goods needing justification, Freidel and Schele claimed that there developed "an institution of kingship that appealed more to the principle of personal charismatic power endowed in the role of the shaman than to the principles of lineage and genealogy" (Freidel and Schele 1988a:550). In other words, Late Preclassic rulers did not descend from "managerial" ancestors charged with logical administration of resources. Rather, they descended from early rulers who constituted "a political ideology emphasizing personal charismatic power and ritual roles of a village-level specialist" (Freidel and Schele 1988a:550).

This model derived from a materialist paradigm that interprets complexity as a consequence of new "needs" arising from the growing scale of local economies. Nevertheless, the big men of the Middle Preclassic could also be seen as incidental accumulators of material wealth; in Freidel and Schele's model, their major role was the monopolization of ideological power which "was manifested in a material form that [could] be manipulated centrally and experienced in common" (Earle 1997:10). To some degree, this model presages agent-oriented models applied to the Pacific coast (Clark and Blake 1994).

Summary

Preliminary research on the Preclassic Maya was able to establish important culture-historical benchmarks that identified the period—the Middle Preclassic period (1000–400 BCE)—for the study of the rise of socio-political complexity in the lowlands. However, given the few and insufficient data from this period, only general models of Middle Preclassic Maya society were developed. Drawing from a smattering of paradigms applied elsewhere in Mesoamerica, the models idealized the Preclassic Maya as autonomous and egalitarian farmers living in small villages scattered throughout the lowlands. These villages were presumably composed of several extended families whose primary activities included subsistence agriculture, although there was some evidence of special function activities.

What characterized much of Middle Preclassic Maya society derived from the adaptation of subsistence agriculture strategies to the lowland environment. To this cultural "blank," some scholars posited several factors—ideology, trade, war, and environmental limitations—as causes for change. It would seem that initial research in the Preclassic period worked backwards, perhaps by necessity, from the Classic period "answers" to the Preclassic period "questions." In large part, Middle Preclassic Maya society was "reverse engineered"; that is, attributes from later periods were combined with general principals of social process to backwards-model an earlier society.

Subsequent to these initial studies, a specialized interest in these questions helped to design research projects aimed specifically at elucidating the development of the Middle Preclassic period. These projects provided a plethora of data (rather than models); a short summary of the salient results follows.

MIDDLE PRECLASSIC MAYA COME FRONT AND CENTER

More sophisticated models for the Middle Preclassic period became possible as scholars designed research focused directly on the "earliest Maya" (Hammond 1977b) at sites such as Cuello (Hammond 1991a), Cerros (Freidel 1979; Robertson and Freidel 1986), Colha (Shafer and Hester 1983), and Lamanai (Pendergast 1981). In the past thirty years, research on the Preclassic Maya has flourished to such an extent that several areas within the lowland Maya area provide compelling data on the Middle Preclassic period. Moreover, taken together, these data provide enough regional information to posit regional models of socio-political development.

Specifically, the areas for which detailed data have been gathered are: (1) the Rio Hondo and the New River region of northern Belize, including the sites of Cerros (Freidel 1979), Cuello (Hammond 1991a), K'axob (McAnany 2004), Colha (Shafer and Hester 1983), Nohmul (Hammond 1985b), and San Estevan (Bullard 1965); (2) the Belize River Valley, including the sites of Barton Ramie, Cahal Pech (Awe 1992), and Blackman Eddy (Brown 1997); (3) the central Peten, including the sites of Nakbe (Clark and Hansen 2001), Tintal, Wakna, El Mirador (Matheny 1986b), Uaxactun (Hendon 1999), and Tikal (Laporte 1995); (4) the Petexbatun area, including the sites of Seibal (Willey 1990), Altar de Sacrificios (Smith 1972), and Itzan (Johnston 2006); and finally (5) the Copan region (for more detail see Canuto 2002, 2004; Crangle 1994; Cummins 2007; Hall and Viel 1994, 2004; Longyear 1952; Sharer et al. 2011; Viel 1993a, 1993b, 2006; Viel and Hall 1998, 1999). Data from these sites is supplemented by much more information gathered from other sites where Preclassic materials have been recovered incidentally during the investigations of other time periods. Furthermore, the research on this period is ongoing and data is rapidly accumulating, so it is reasonable to expect that the next decades of research will bring many more and surprising results.

In the most general of terms, these data demonstrate that the socio-political complexity in the Maya lowlands had developed far earlier than the Late Preclassic period (Awe 1992; Clark and Cheetham 2003; Clark and Hansen 2001; Clark et al. 2000; Garber et al. 2004a; Hammond 1986, 1992; Hansen 1998; Healy, Cheetham et al. 2004). In the space provided, it proves impossible, however, to summarize the data gathered on the Middle Preclassic period from all these efforts. However, the research on two regional phenomena related to all Middle Preclassic sites in the Maya lowlands will be summarized, namely (1) the recent evidence for the widespread adoption of agriculture in the region, and (2) the distribution and chronology associated with the various Middle Preclassic ceramic types. These data will provide a baseline for the development of a social model explaining the Middle Preclassic rise of socio-political complexity in the Maya lowlands.

Early Preclassic Period: Precocious Pre-ceramic Horticulturalists

Early models of the Early and Middle Preclassic periods postulated farmers filtering into the central Peten following riverine and estuarine environments inland from the surrounding regions. In the last decade of research, multiple palynological studies have greatly refined this view both in terms of dates and scale. Paleoecological studies of areas neighboring the lowland Maya area—the Pacific coast (Neff et al. 2006c) and the eastern Gulf coast (Pope et al. 2001; Rust and Leyden 1994)—have demonstrated that domesticated corn was being used as early as 5000–3500 BCE. The development of a horticultural adaptation that took specific advantage of estuarine / riverine environments developed on the Pacific Coast as early as 2000 BCE.

In northern Belize, furthermore, the same data suggest that domesticated maize was in use by 3400 BCE, and indicators of agriculture-induced deforestation was ongoing by 2500 BCE (Jones 1994; Pohl et al. 1996). In the southwestern area of the Petexbatun, initial deforestation was also dated to ca. 2000 BCE (Dunning et al. 1997; Dunning et al. 1998). Among the regions occupied by the lowland Maya, the only outlier to this pattern is the southeastern Maya area around Copan where major deforestation seems to date to ca. 900 BCE (Rue et al. 2002; see also McNeil et al. 2010).

These data from the margins of the central lowlands suggest that populations to the west, south, and east (but not the southeast) of the central Peten had adopted the horticulturalist adaptation nearly a millennium before the Middle Preclassic period. Consistent with this earlier time frame, paleoecological studies in the central Peten (Curtis et al. 1998; Hansen et al. 2002; Islebe et al. 1996; Leyden 2002; Vaughan et al. 1985; Wahl et al. 2006; Wahl, Byrne et al. 2007) demonstrate that major deforestation in this area dates to ca. 2000–1000 BCE, reaching its peak at ca. 500 BCE. These data are compatible with the horticulturalist-incursion model in that as "agriculturalists made their way up-river, it would have been a small step for them to adapt floodplain agricultural strategies to the edges of wetlands" (Wahl et al. 2006:386).

It would seem that these data indicate the existence of an Early Preclassic pre-ceramic occupation in the Peten undertaking horticultural practices nearly a millennium before the Middle Preclassic period. Evidence for such an occupation in Belize has already been recovered (Iceland 2005; Iceland and Hester 1996), and, given the paleoecological data, it is likely that evidence for a more widespread distribution of this occupation will soon follow. Even if not substantial, the indication of a long-term Early Preclassic sedentary population within the Maya lowlands renders more feasible the possibility of widespread complexity developing in the first half of the 1st millennium BCE (see Iceland 2005).

Middle Preclassic Period: Early Regional Interaction

The beginning of the Middle Preclassic period of the Maya lowlands can now generally be appreciated as broadly correlated with the development of ceramic production. However, paleoecological data of this period suggest that agricultural activity was greatly increasing. For instance, deforestation of the central lowlands was accelerating, reaching its peak ca. 700–500 BCE (Wahl, Byrne et al. 2007), while intensive manipulation of wetland areas in northern Belize was also commencing (Pohl et al. 1996). In other words, consistent with the data for an extensive pre-ceramic occupation, the palynological and ceramic data suggest that regional exchange networks and agricultural intensification techniques date to the pre-Mamom phase of the Middle Preclassic period.

Recent recovery of pre-Mamom phase ceramics from sites like Cahal Pech and Blackman Eddy has triggered a reclassification of the disparate pre-Mamom ceramic complexes from central Belize into a single "horizon" (Cheetham 2005; Clark and Cheetham 2003). Cheetham (2005:28) proposes the "Cunil horizon" based on a broad set of similarities, such as specialized forms (colander bowls, mushroom stands, chalice-shaped censers, pot stands, wide-everted-rim plate, and *tecomates*), pottery-making techniques (dull slips, patchy coloration, fine-tip etching), and decorative motifs (*k'an* cross, zigzag, shark tooth, music bracket, cleft, flame eyebrow, and the avian serpent). Pre-Mamom phase ceramics have been classified into four regional ceramic interaction complexes (Clark and Cheetham 2002; see Chapter 6, this volume, for further discussion of these early ce-

ramics). These are Xe ceramics in the southwestern Petexbatun region, Eb
and Ox ceramics in central Peten, Cunil ceramics in central Belize, and
Swasey ceramics in northern Belize.

Comparison of these four complexes show that their utilitarian wares
are distinct from one another while their fine-ware assemblages are similar.
Clark and Cheetham (2003) suggest that the distinctiveness of the utilitarian
assemblages indicates local groups were in place in their particular area (Petexbatun, Mirador Basin/central Peten, central Belize, and northern Belize)
long before they adopted pottery. As a consequence, these groups developed
local tool-making traditions that would have been reflected in their earliest
ceramic assemblages (Clark and Gosser 1995), a conclusion consistent with
the recent paleoclimatological data discussed above. As for the similarities
among the fine wares, interregional interaction of group leaders would account for the widespread distribution of similar types. They conclude that
the pre-Mamom lowland Maya landscape was populated by distinct "tribes"
engaged in interregional exchanges of elite goods.

It is important to note, furthermore, that the southeastern Maya area
sequence is entirely different. It is clear that during the Cunil horizon, inhabitants of the Copan region were indeed conversing in the pan-Mesoamerican symbols of the day (Gordon and Uir phase ceramics at Copan and
Chotepe at Puerto Escondido). However, these fine wares, though marked
with "Olmec-style" imagery, were not similar to those of the lowland tradition. Therefore, though groups in the southeastern region were likely not
in intensive contact with those in the central Peten, their degree of socio-
political complexity was likely commensurate.

Summary

Hammond (2000:209) suggested that the Mamom ceramic sphere
argued "for a high degree of interaction between regions…a common set
of ideas about material culture is accepted across the lowlands and into
the highland zone." New data, however, suggest that most lowland Maya
groups, during the early Middle Preclassic period (ca. 1000–700 BCE), were
already integrated into the pan-Mesoamerican symbol system of the time.
In fact, this shared symbol system "attests to a shared tradition and frequent
interaction, it indicates a common belief system predating the Mamom
era" (Cheetham 2005:31). These data suggest that the early Middle Preclassic period was far from being a time of quiet tribal existence; rather, there

appears to be great ferment in all corners of the Maya area (see Ball and Taschek 2003; Cheetham 2005; Clark and Cheetham 2003).

To wrangle the disparate data on the Middle Preclassic for this essay proves challenging, as they have been gathered from multiple efforts using distinct approaches and to answer different research questions. However unrelated the data might be, they do help define in the broadest of terms a Middle Preclassic "narrative" useful for general model building. What follows, then, is a model that attempts to explain how the integration of multiple Middle Preclassic groups led to the first evidence of lowland Maya socio-political complexity.

MODELING THE EARLY MAYA COMPLEXITY: IT TAKES A VILLAGE

What is needed for the Middle Preclassic period is a model for the most important social innovation of the period—the agrarian community. Expressed in another way: "Proto-Mesoamerican tribes, as do all tribes, faced the dilemma of aggregation. Tribal peoples have manifold reasons for getting together with others, but crowds are *trouble*" (Clark and Cheetham 2003:312, *emphasis added*). In classic social theory, traditional social anthropology, and modern sociology, aggregation, spatial proximity, and interaction are the empirical prerequisites for the formation of the social group broadly termed "community" (Arensberg 1961; Durkheim 1984; Redfield 1955). The development of a full model for the rise of social complexity in Middle Preclassic Maya society needs to contend with how and why "crowds are trouble."

It is suggested here that the emergence of hereditary rank, hierarchy, and differentiation is fundamentally a social question. There is no single external factor, such as climate change, environmental limitation (Carneiro 1972), or population pressure (Sanders and Price 1968), that satisfyingly explains why human groups change the form and scope of their social interactions vis-à-vis one another. Importantly, an increasing archaeological interest in modeling ancient communities (Canuto and Yaeger 2000; Rogers and Smith 1995; Schwartz and Falconer 1994; Wilk and Ashmore 1988; Wills and Leonard 1994) provides some support for this view.

The transformations of social structure and the creation of social personas during the Middle Preclassic resulted in the incorporation of new forms of praxis into daily social life. New identities, new goods, new statuses, new responsibilities therefore changed the way in which people, through shared common quotidian practice, would have established a sense of common identity. The nature of community was changing, requiring a more complex conjunction of what Watanabe calls "place, people, and premise" (1992:12). In fact, the great majority of the data from the Middle Preclassic period speak to these same social processes: the formation of corporate hierarchies (premise), the elaboration of personhood (people), and place-making (place).

For each process, distinct archaeological proxies—such as architectural monumentality, spatial plans of sites, exchange of exotic goods, personal adornment, burial practices, and sacrificial offerings—attest to the salience of these particular processes in different contexts. Despite a growing and coherent set of data, the Middle Preclassic period is overwhelmingly understudied. Perforce, these data are patchy, discontinuous, and limited. For this reason, the model proposed here should be understood as a working hypothesis, subject to radical change as more research is done. What follows is a discussion of how social practices led to the development of hierarchical corporate groups, accommodated a growing number of non-kin-based social personas, and established special "places" of power and social memory. On the whole, I suggest an *emergent lineage-community* model to interpret the social transformations evident in the Middle Preclassic period.

The Legacy of Lineage: A Forest of Caciques

To begin, models of this type should be drawn from a wealth of ethnographic and ethnohistoric data from the region. This research has demonstrated that descent groups were important to both the modern and colonial Maya (Beals 1932; Bunzel 1952; Carmack 1981; Edmonson 1982; Gossen and Leventhal 1993; Holland 1964a, 1964b; Hopkins 1988; Landa 1941; Roys 1957; Tedlock 1982; J. Thompson 1970; Vogt 1961, 1968; Wauchope 1938; Wisdom 1940). One challenge, however, is the question of lineality—whether patrilineal, matrilineal, double-descent, or even cognatic—which remains unsolved since even the ethnographic record is equivocal (Sharer 1993). The debates on the prehispanic Maya descent rules amply show the variability of their system (Coe 1965d; Fox and Justeson 1986; Haviland 1977; Hopkins 1988; Marcus 1983b; Mathews and Schele 1974; Scholes and Roys 1948; Stuart and Schele 1986).

This approach also requires adapting the synchronic models of ethnographic and ethnohistoric examples to the Middle Preclassic period, which lasted more than half a millennium. The long-term diachronic perspective of archaeology tends to emphasize "social process" and ignore the humanist scale of practice. For this reason, a dynamic *emergent lineage model* is developed. Data from the Preclassic period are used to develop a model that is "kinship based, where one's position within the social group is defined by abilities such as age, knowledge, hunting prowess and so forth" (Lange 1992:109–11), but that also accounts for processual change over centuries.

Families First

The first step would be to establish basic principles of how these early "tribal" groups would have been organized. Comprehensive ethnographic and ethnohistoric research has suggested that the basic social group among modern and colonial Maya (Farriss 1984:132; Wilk 1988:137–41) was the co-residential group composed of consanguineal and affinal kin—like an extended family marked by the inclusion of both spouses and children (Murdock 1949:41–42). This extended family was maintained through postmarital residence proscriptions. Among modern Maya groups, co-residence rules vary from region to region—there appears to be a general distinction between a patrilocal pattern among both highland Guatemalan and lowland Yucatecan groups, and first a uxorilocal and then a neo/patrilocal pattern among Cholan peoples (Wilk 1988:141).

Ethnographic research shows that such groups present a pattern of emergent clustering around originally dispersed homesteads (see Hudson 1969). Derived from the domestic developmental cycle (Fortes 1958), an "accretionary family-growth model" (Tourtellot 1988a:97) is based on specific lineal and locality rules among modern Maya groups. In fact, many modern Maya settlements exhibit a residential pattern in which nuclear families descendant from an original family prefer to remain proximal to the residence of the husband's parents (Hanks 1990; Redfield and Villa Rojas 1934; Wisdom 1940)—a patrilineal and patrilocal pattern. Therefore, over time, the imposition of such residential rules combined with the natural generational growth of a single nuclear family, would foster the development of a spatially clustered set of different households.

Although the evidence from the Preclassic period does not speak to the details of post-marital locality or overall lineality, the earliest phases at Cuello (Hammond 1991d; Wilk and Wilhite 1991) and at Cahal Pech (Awe 1992; Healy, Cheetham et al. 2004) suggest the existence of what has been called a "generationally extended family residential group" (Canuto 2002; Sharer 1993:97; Yaeger 2000). The growth of the domestic structures through the earliest phases of these sites also falls within the patterns of the natural generational growth of a kin-based group with specific lineage-derived locality rules. The settlement data from the surrounding settlement at Cahal Pech suggest that each nearby knoll was the seat of a separate extended family group. It would therefore not be outlandish to suggest that most of the Cunil horizon and contemporary sites of the terminal Early Preclassic were large co-residing kin groups.

Extended over multiple generations, such lineal-locality rules would pro-scribe an indefinitely expanding cluster. Ethnographic research, however, has shown that this developmental cycle does not extend far beyond four generations (Wisdom 1940:149; LaFarge 1947:114–15; Vogt 1969:129–34) before the extended family group as a jural unit disintegrates: "Upon [the] death [of the original family], the last link which binds the family together is lost, and the family as a unit breaks up. Each household inherits equally of the family property, and each household head becomes the head of his new family group" (Wisdom 1940:249–50). With the expiration of this founding family and their nuclear household, the larger residential group disperses its corporate holdings among the descendant families and devolves into a non-corporate group of loosely affiliated smaller families. These cadet families then begin to develop into separate residential kin groups of their own as their former affiliations become less representative of their identity and de-terminative of their resources.

While the extent of an Early Preclassic pre-ceramic period has yet to be defined (Clark and Cheetham 2003; Iceland 2005) for the Maya lowlands, there is the possibility that this form of aggregation and its subsequent dis-solution through group fissioning would have characterized centuries of Maya occupation in the lowlands. In fact, due to economic constraints, eco-logical factors, and the posited social structure, dispersal of households on the landscape might be the "default" setting of Maya settlement (Drennan 1988). Maya extensive agricultural practices (e.g., long-fallow cycle swid-den agriculture) focused household labor requirements locally on dispersed areas and made residence near agricultural plots advantageous (Drennan 1988). In fact, the lack of standardization of agricultural intensification efforts implies local, individual control of agricultural strategies (Dunning and Beach 1994). Thus, dispersal helps maximize agricultural productivity and minimize labor costs of the extended family.

Although settlement fissioning occurs for various reasons, it also allows households a modicum of control against competition from the descendants of the founding family (McAnany 1995). Considering the low archaeological impact this type of occupation would make, it is possible that the thus-far archaeologically invisible Early Preclassic lowland Maya settlements might have take this form. Socially guided mechanisms of intergenerational dispersal of horticulturalists could lead to the extensive environmental impact that has been recorded by palynological data.

Family Names

The jural dissolution of the larger extended family seen in contexts such as the Chortí *sian otot* (Wisdom 1940) represents the limits of descent-based affiliations and their eventual eclipse by intragenerational alliances (marriages) that fragment the original descent-based group into smaller units. Over time, there is evidence that these newly unaffiliated families might maintain a loose system of horizontal cooperation and interaction (Gillespie 2000b), but their identity as a single localized lineage is subverted by the dominance of the individual marriage alliances that compose the larger group. As much as descent rules can foster settlement clustering and nucleation, the formation of equally important marriage alliances can encourage the opposite process of settlement fissioning.

This process would lead to a dispersal of settlement with a diffused form of descent group affiliation. For the Yucatan, one such system, based on patronyms, was noted by Landa (1941). As an organizational principle, the patronym was associated with rights, obligations, privileges, and marriage proscriptions, fostering the development of non-localized exogamous paternal sibs (Beals 1932:473; Haviland 1968, 1972)—also known as patriclans (Hopkins 1988)—rather than strict lineages. Similar organizational principles were recognized among the Itzá and the Pokomam (Miles 1957). Roys recognized that the native term *ch'ibal* (1939:35, 40) was a possible referent for this form of association. Recent research (Restall 1997) on the Colonial period in the Yucatan has demonstrated that the ch'ibal was co-terminous with the local town, the *kah* (Gillespie 2000b; Restall 1997:17; contra Roys 1957:4). In other words, there was no formal organization of the ch'ibal members outside the limits of the local community.

A sib community or clan (Keesing 1972) would posit a co-residing group of descent-related families, but would not result in the internal stratification of its constituent members based on their consanguineal relation to an apical ancestor. In fact, the Yucatec *ch'ibalob* consisted of both elites and non-elites and were hardly egalitarian, but these intragroup distinctions did not derive from asymmetrical kinship relations within the ch'ibal—they resulted from the personal or nuclear family control over land and resources. In fact, because the specific lineal connections between members remained ambiguous, the sib community was not constituted according to the strict genealogical accounting of rights and privileges to the resources of the group. To this extent, therefore, the sib was not corporate because it did not control communal resources that required redistribution and adjudication. The lack of corporateness undermined the need for residential proximity (see Yaeger 2000:291) because of a minimized need to physically claim and secure access to centrally distributed resources. In fact, there is more of a need to directly oversee and control the individually held resources of the family. Consequently, the spatial definition of a sib community remained dependent upon an individual household's adaptive strategies rather than on a group-based behavior.

The data required to assess the applicability of this model—regional settlement patterns and comparative household inventories—is difficult to collect for the Preclassic period. However, there is the suggestion of this type of organization at Cuello through much of the Middle Preclassic period (Wilk and Wilhite 1991:129), as well as at Copan (Cummins 2007:123; Fash 1986:76–79; Viel and Hall n.d.). Given the absence of a strong central locus for the settlement and a prevalence for evenly distributed settlement, it would seem likely that settlement patterns reflected strategies optimal for individual households rather than for a larger group. If true, Cuello and Copan throughout much of the Middle Preclassic were characterized by generationally limited, residential kin groups distributed over the landscape with a passive sense of group identity.

At Copan, the Gordon phase platforms would reflect a degree of centralization—a central public plaza space—where various family members of different sibs would be buried with their particular descent-group identifying iconography. In such a context, the social landscape could accommodate social stratification (as a function of individual family strategies) without subsequently requiring the architectural elaboration of a particular civic-ceremonial center. In these cases, furthermore, marriage alliances between members of cadet families would result in social fissioning, as founding families could not muster sufficient social incentives to induce nucleation. At Copan, the eclectic mix of ceramic styles throughout the Middle Preclassic (Cummins 2007; Viel 2006) reflects a degree of household autonomy with respect to their participation in exchange networks.

The slow development of Cuello's central household combined with the settlement data indicating an even distribution of settlement suggest a similar process was extant for much of the Swasey and Bladen phases. The architectural elaborations recorded at the central household of Cuello fall well within the range of the social stratification sustained by the generational development of a residential kin group. It would be roughly at 600 BCE when the central courtyard architecturally reflects a degree of centralization and corporatism not typical of a sib community (Gerhardt and Hammond 1991:106).

It is important that the attribution of sib community not be misunderstood as an evolutionary phase. At all times, a social group's social structure depends on the relative influence of the complementary forces of kin affiliations and marriage alliances. As suggested by several ethnographers (Redfield and Villa Rojas 1934; Vogt 1976; Wisdom 1940), the generational dissolution of an extended family is triggered by alliances of marriage within subsequent generations that allow members eventually to disassociate and establish their own smaller extended families.

A sib can develop as a consequence of this cycle perpetuated over time. There were likely many different types of corporate groups throughout the Middle Preclassic period. Nevertheless, the loosely organized groups visible in the archaeological record during the early Middle Preclassic period do seem consistent with a *sib-like* organization. Furthermore, the spread of regionally distinct ceramic types attests to the development of several local networks of exchange of limited reach.

First Families

However, in specific cases during the Middle Preclassic period, descent affiliations and family accumulation of privilege and resources *were not* counter-balanced by marriage alliances and residential dispersal. When the marriage alliances of descendant generations were eclipsed by the descent affiliations of the spouse (the husband, in a patrilineal system), the generational transference of privileges over resources and labor did not result in their dispersal, but rather in their concentration within a single descendant family. In those instances the developmental cycle of founding, growth, disassociation, and re-founding was broken and the material record was thereby impacted. The subsequent and repeated clustering of residences near the household of the "first-generation family" helped develop a vertical hierarchy controlled by the heads of the original family who enjoyed easy access to the labor and products of the related descendent families (Sanders 1989). How and why certain areas might exhibit this pattern might involve some type of "aggrandizer"; this question will be discussed further below.

In these cases, the descent rules maintained the integrity of a lineage for multiple generations. Therefore, the direct descendants of a lineage founder had privileged access to lineage resources and resided in larger, more elaborate residences (Tourtellot 1988a, 1988b). Lesser members, off-shoot families, and recent additions did not conscript labor equally and thus had smaller, "humbler" residences. Furthermore, the founding family lived not only in the larger residential compounds but also in those with the longest time-spans, while cadet families had shallower time-depth (Tourtellot 1988a, 1988b).

At Blackman Eddy, Cahal Pech, and Cuello (Hammond, Bauer et al. 2002), access to the founding residential group was successively restricted. The architectural formalization of the residential space physically separated it from surrounding residences, a trend that indicates a special function for that residential complex, by association to its inhabitants. This formalization is also accompanied by the construction of specialized buildings within the residential space, such as a sweat bath at Cuello (Hammond and Bauer 2001), round structures at several sites (Aimers et al. 2000; Hendon 1989, 1999; Willey et al. 1965:51–59), and linear triadic complexes at Cahal Pech (Healy, Cheetham et al. 2004) and Blackman Eddy (Garber et al. 2004c). With these constructions, the leading family signaled that certain activities were its prerogative.

The construction of these buildings was accompanied by dedicatory events (Healy, Cheetham et al. 2004:121) and feasts (Hammond et al. 1995:125; Joyce 2003:250; Powis et al. 2002) that further enforced the singular nature of this residence. Feasting likely involved the sharing of exotic goods, such as cacao-based drinks, as evinced by the fragmentary remains of spouted vessels (Powis et al. 2002). The recovery of blood-letting para-phernalia—at Blackman Eddy (Garber et al. 2004c)—also suggests that ritual events were associated with these feasts. Moreover, the dedicatory caches often included imported goods such as jadeite, obsidian flakes, and marine shell objects. Overall, these events reflected a command over labor and goods (Abrams 1987, 1994; Sanders 1989) and control over agricultural production (e.g., Brumfiel 1987; Brumfiel and Earle 1987; McAnany 1989).

Even though these events were likely inclusive, their periodic nature would establish a temporal delimitation to the physical proximity of the social group. Consequently, intragenerational clustering would have miti-gated the attenuation of interfamily interaction, guaranteed representation of cadet families within the larger group, and provided access to resources distributed through a shared descent-based ideology (see Haviland 1968; Hopkins 1988; McAnany 1995; Rice 1988). Therefore, settlement nucle-ation—perhaps even beyond the environmental capacity of the region—was advantageous to all members.

This strategy of social intensification would have led to the creation of a localized group represented by the sharing of ideas, goods, and resources that would also have required relations to other like areas to remain viable over generations. Therefore, as social alliance networks extended between distinct population aggregates, so would networks of social obligation and sumptuary goods exchange have expanded. If the social relations of mul-tiple "first families" throughout the Maya lowlands promoted exchange of goods and ideas over a wide area, it might have resulted in the sharing of serving vessels as seen in the early Middle Preclassic period (Clark and Cheetham 2003).

First Fathers

Although monumental funerary buildings likely made their initial ap-pearance during the Late Preclassic period (see Freidel and Schele 1989:242), the veneration of ancestors was practiced much earlier "as part of emer-gent Preclassic communal identity and territorial possession" (Hammond, Bauer et al. 2002). The evidence for ancestor respect—perhaps as a means to claim property and rights—during the Middle Preclassic comes in the form of burials located under house or patio floors (Hammond et al. 1991; Robin 1989), burials intruded into already built ceremonial buildings (Aimers et al. 2000; Healy, Cheetham et al. 2004), specially treated burials (Healy, Cheetham et al. 2004), and ritual objects made from human bone (Hammond, Saul et al. 2002).

These examples suggest that several strategies of ancestor veneration were used to provide reasons to recognize a jural prerogative of the descent group over resources: "subfloor and shrine burials represent vital links in the chain of inheritance; thus, the placement of individuals in these residential contexts involved elaborate ritual" (McAnany 1995:161). In the absence of a formal legal system, an effective form of claiming, maintaining, and demonstrating rights over property and place is through the burial of one's ancestors in those areas. The development of generationally sustained descent groups was likely in large part due to widespread acceptance of the inherent rights and interdictions that underwrote the practice of ancestor veneration. The case of multiple burials in the Gordon platforms at Copan perhaps further illustrates a difference of social structure in the southeast Maya area during the Early and Middle Preclassic in which the social groups were not vested with jural control over household resources (much like sibs).

What is missing, however, from the range of evidence for ancestor worship in the Middle Preclassic is the centrally located monumental mortuary structure. Interestingly, this absence might be limited to the lowland Maya of this time, since a monumental Middle Preclassic mortuary structure was excavated in the Salama Valley in the northern Maya highlands (Sharer and Sedat 1987:127–41). For the lowland area, however, none of the central structures dating to this period—such as Str. B1 at Blackman Eddy (Brown and Garber 2005; Brown and Garber 2008; Garber et al. 2004c), Str. B4 at Cahal Pech (Aimers et al. 2000; Healy, Cheetham et al. 2004; Powis et al. 1999), and Str. 51 at Nakbe (Hansen et al. 2002)—can be considered a monumental funerary shrine. In fact, all these structures had predominantly ritual functions, perhaps as stages for public performances. For some, the subsequent addition or intrusion of burials highlights the importance of associating certain people with public, ritual, central, or civic buildings. Over time, the repeated association of a single structure with the burial of particular individuals legitimized the notion of a special mausoleum for future ancestors. The tendencies notwithstanding, the location of one's interment in the Middle Preclassic remained largely a function of one's accomplishments in life.

Future Ancestors

The descent groups of the Middle Preclassic were in no way as formally defined as lineages found elsewhere in the Maya region, such as the *amak* of the ethnohistoric Quiche (Carmack 1981:59, 161; Fox and Cook 1996:811–12). As the basic social unit of the Quiche, it was centered around a *tinamit* (Carmack 1981:65) where "the lineage house, the altar and temple for the patron deity, and the residence of the lineage head were built." The different *amak* were segmentary in nature as they united "in loose unions of political groups to combat a common enemy" (Carmack 1981:60). No such nested organization is evident for the Middle Preclassic.

However, the evidence does suggest increasing regional interaction—every Middle Preclassic center thus far studied has evidence of precious materials such as shells and jade (as well as utilitarian goods such as obsidian). These suggest long-distance trade was commonplace, which is consistent with the interregional prestation of serving vessels (Cheetham 2005). It is clear that the various descent groups developing throughout the region were engaged in reciprocal gift-giving (Demarest 1992a; Freidel 1986c; Hoopes 1985; Lincoln 1985; Rathje 1972; Sabloff 1986; Schortman and Nakamura 1991). It is possible that specially orchestrated exchanges were designed to forge alliances, pay dowries, perform ritual celebrations, or establish trade agreements that would create a separate regional exchange system in which only a handful of people could participate.

Such external alliances weaken the lineage's vertical integration because they create horizontal affiliations between families based on equivalent status and wealth (de Montmollin 1989, 1995; Marcus 1976a, 1992b, 1993) that result in the development of regionally dispersed endogamous social classes. Horizontally integrating mechanisms, like marriage, trade, or political alliances, led to the creation of institutions and practices that differ from and even undermine descent groups (Sanders 1989:102). In fact, the founding family of any lineage eventually came to have more in common with founding families of other lineages than with the families of their own lineage.

The internally stratified social descent-based group thus begins to reflect a social organization of both kin-based affiliations manifested through descent rules and personal alliances cemented through marriage or even fictive kin. This combination leads to a form of social integration in which "political and economic interests, on the verge of invading the social field, have not yet overstepped the 'old ties of blood'" (Levi-Strauss 1982:186). In this manner, the integration of a stratified descent-based social group is based more on alliances, affiliations, and contractual relationships to the central household in which "nothing prevents the substitution of affinity for blood ties whenever the needs arises" (Levi-Strauss 1982:187; see Gillespie 2000b). This house-society model (Gillespie 2000b, 2000c; Joyce 2000; Joyce and Gillespie 2000) suggests that social groups were not bound to either residential or descent rules: the house "perpetuates itself through the transmission of its name, its goods, and its titles through a real or imaginary line, considered legitimate as long as this continuity can express itself in the language of kinship or of affinity and, most often, of both" (Lévi-Strauss 1987:151).

The Middle Preclassic data demonstrate that several social groups were adapting old forms of social organization (residential kin groups) to new forms of organization better suited to sustain a more complex set of social relations. After the widespread settlement of the region and adoption of pottery, after social strategies of periodic residential fissioning were discarded, the aggregation of people into villages led to the development of new types of social groups. These changes were not necessary, just chosen. The question to ask is Who chose them? And, who could opt out of them?

Ecce Personae, or the "Way of Masks"

Lineage-based models applied to the question of social complexity in the Preclassic period suggest that inequalities inherent to the system of kinship were primary to the development of socio-political inequality. However, the development of complex descent groups was not the only mechanism impelling social change during the Middle Preclassic period. Although the proscriptions and prescriptions of a lineage-based social structure were the medium within which agents interacted, schemed, and negotiated during the Middle Preclassic, there developed a series of other forms of social action that would have provided impetus for structural change. The most commonly appreciated form of social action derives from the individual agent (Clark and Blake 1994; Cowgill 2000; Flannery 1999; Flannery and Marcus 1976a) who realizes strategies of long-term impact to social relations. This and other types of agents developed non-kin-based forms of social interaction in the Middle Preclassic.

The Amplification of Kinship

The nature of "special agents" as individuals can be reworked in order to re-establish the historical and cultural moorings to which they are necessarily tethered. In this vein, Gillespie (2001) has suggested a focus on the concepts of "personhood," society, and collective representations in which emphasis is placed on the enactment of social relationships through (daily) practice. In this formula, actors as "persons" rather than as "individuals" are constrained by the expectations of others regarding their particular role and capabilities. The social persona "is often encompassed by a title or name and materialized by insignia, totem crests, or badges of office. They signify a category of being that may be coextensive with specific groups, property, and places" (Gillespie 2001:82).

Akin to Mauss' *personage* (1985), the social persona embodies rights, both jural and moral, that the individual appropriates. In this fashion, one's social persona is not just a social role (see Radcliffe-Brown 1952)—the individual "has not simply put on the mask but has taken upon himself the identity it proclaims. For it is surely only by appropriating to himself his socially given personhood that he can exercise the qualities, the rights, the duties and the capacities that are distinctive of it" (Fortes 1973:311).

The consideration of "personhood" within society also unlinks social status from social position (contra Binford 1971; Gillespie 2001; see Goodenough 1965; contra Saxe 1970) and thereby allows for the existence of such categories as a "juvenile" whose burial might reflect the embodiment of that persona by any particular individual satisfying the requirements of such a personage. In other words, material goods associated with juveniles could evince only social differentiation rather than also social hierarchy. In this framework, social complexity results in the assignation of social personas to fewer and fewer individuals. In this framework, a singular special individual does not instigate change, rather it is the social group that creates those social persons whose roles allow (maybe even call) for social innovation.

Importantly, archaeological research has access to several material indices of the ancient embodiment of social persons. For instance, a critical dimension of personhood is its relationship to the human body; specifically, embodiment constructs the social persona (Fisher and Loren 2003; Meskell 1999, 2000). Through dress, ornamentation, gesture, and posture, "an individual has the ability to 'put on a social skin' allowing for self-identification as a member of a larger or different social or interest groups" (Fisher and

Loren 2003:225). It is through embodiment that any particular individual finally dons (literally and figuratively) the attributes of their social persona.

Therefore, data such as clothing, personal ornamentation, burial materials, and figural representations (whether ceramic or rupestrian) can provide some information on the representation of past social identities. For Preclassic Mesoamerica, then, the existence of figurines within household contexts, for instance, can indeed refer to the development of household-based rituals (Cyphers Guillén 1993b; Marcus 1999). However, these (and many other) items can also be seen as media for the representation of social identities or personas from that period (Joyce 2003)—they "provide a basis for constructing preliminary hypotheses about emic definitions of social categories and the relationship between them" (Lesure 1997:247).

For the Middle Preclassic, it would appear that there were several socially recognized personas that engaged primarily in social relations not included in kin/descent groups. There were surely more; some may even have been limited to specific groups. However, any model of the social development of the Middle Preclassic period must incorporate the manner in which individuals could have manipulated these various roles over time. A few of the more prominent roles are discussed here, namely lineage heads, elders, nubile women, children/youth, adult women, ritual specialists, ballplayers, warriors, and architects.

Elders, Lineage Heads, Nubile Women

A society that permits the social dynamics that result in the surplus production of prestige goods *also* provides the social logic for a person to play the role of negotiator or advisor to the various centers of production. Rather than the lineage head having to create new social relations (as entrepreneur), he works under the expectations associated with his particular persona. As part of his duties, the lineage-head-as-negotiator might be responsible for the social collective at periodic intergroup gatherings (such as feasts). If a "lineage head" remains so contained within the proscriptions of his descent group, how does change occur?

This idea of lineage head as representative is perhaps vestigially preserved in the term *ajaw*, which means "he who shouts" (Houston and Stuart 2001)—that is, the person who speaks for a group. It seems plausible to suggest that the meaning of the "ruler" title relates to the special function or role of the social persona. Considering that entrepreneurs would have sponsored communal activities (such as feasts or ballgames), their role in those activities would likely have involved some degree of public speaking, whether in the form of incantations, proclamations, narrations, or dialogues. It is possible that public oration was a critical role of the lineage head—yet such a function leaves a great deal of room for individual achievement and distinction.

Beyond public performance, a lineage head might also find some ability to achieve distinction through the different ways in which a surplus of fine goods can be used. Leach wrote: "Kachins do not look upon moveable property as capital to be invested, they regard it rather as an adornment to the person" (1954:142). In such a case, he becomes the bearer of these goods, his body adorned with finery representing the social collective that produced them. The insignia of the group's prestige worn by a single person cannot themselves be exchanged freely—"insignia cannot become object of exchange in any conventional sense; giving one away would be tantamount to abandoning one's social identity entirely" (Graeber 1996:5). This finery is his "mask," and his role is to promote the prestige and power of his entire group vis-à-vis neighboring groups, through the display of his *persona*.

This form of personal adornment is demonstrated repeatedly in the burial contexts of the Preclassic period wherein insignia made of mundane materials are found but which symbolize an individual's specialized role. Mat motifs found on bone are associated with burials at Cuello (Gerhardt and Hammond 1991:106), and mat motifs on ceramics from Nakbe (Hansen 2001a:54; 2005:63) indicate the existence of a widely shared symbolic system marking special personages by ca. 500 BCE (if not earlier). Certainly other exotic materials—jadeite and shell ornaments, inlaid jade teeth—were all used to mark the leader in culturally recognized "finery," providing the appropriate display of the group's status as represented on a single person.

However, for the purpose of exchange, other objects of value must be produced that can, in fact, circulate, without impinging on the person's (and by extension, the group's) carefully crafted and displayed identity. Such objects, furthermore, must bear some generic value separate and divisible from the giver's identity. The evidence at a Middle Preclassic residential cluster from Cahal Pech, known as the Cas Pek group, suggests a heavy household investment in the production of shell ornaments. Also, the inhabitants of Group E at Uaxactun (Hendon 1999; Ricketson 1937) engaged in similar activities. Given the ubiquity of shell ornamentation in burials throughout the Middle Preclassic and the material's "exotic" nature, these objects could represent items of both intrinsic and symbolic value. The head of the descent group associated with this residential group would have been responsible for coordinating their production.

The example of wampum trade (Beauchamp 1898, 1901; Foster 1985; Hammel 1983; Holmes 1883) provides an informative analogy to the relevance of shell production in the Middle Preclassic period. Although wampum was treated as currency by European traders, the Iroquois vested it with the power to transform social relations. They would present "treaty belts" of wampum at events during which leaders from different groups would strike peace treaties. For the Iroquois, because objects made with wampum had to accompany meta-discursive speech of conciliation and community integration (see Urban 1996), the objects enabled changes to intergroup social relations and rendered those negotiations successful.

Wampum was both a bulk currency of generic value and integral to goods of cultural value to the group investing in their manufacture. Wherein a negotiator could prove his mettle would be in the faithful and successful execution of his duties with respect to the function of wampum acquisition and negotiation-making. From wampum acquisition to treaty-belt manufacture, however, the leader had to cajole or negotiate with members of his own group. These intragroup negotiations were undertaken with the premise—rather than pretense—that greater production would ensure greater success. Thus, prestige was afforded not only for the accumulation of generic wampum (wealth) but also for the successful exchange of (prestige) wampum.

Therefore, the development of early social networks (such as lineage) that required some type of negotiator role (lineage head) instigated the production of (1) objects of personal prestige (pendants, insignia, jewelry, headdresses, clothing) that helped define the group (lineage) as distinct from others, and (2) objects that could shuffle between "different domains of value" (Graeber 1996:13; such as beads, vessels, cloth, and cacao beans)— that is, objects that the receivers could revalue according to different criteria. Importantly, such generic items did not necessarily get democratically redistributed. In the case of wampum, for instance, although some was distributed to spectators (Beauchamp 1898:11; Fenton 1998:128; Michelson 1974), the majority of it was divided among the community leaders (Graeber 2001:130), i.e., the lineage heads.

It might be in this fashion that the jade and shell beads common in Preclassic period burials at Copan, Cahal Pech (Healy, Cheetham et al. 2004), K'axob (McAnany 2002), and Cuello (Hammond 1991d) were traded—that is, as objects of generic value that were then reconstituted into unique objects reflecting specific meanings associated with social personas. Also, the trade of *Strombus* shell (originating in the Caribbean) to Nakbe (Hansen 1992a:173–74; Hansen 2005) and Uaxactun (Hendon 1999; Ricketson 1937) might reflect an item of generic value that was then reworked into local systems of symbolic value; in this fashion it would have functioned both as currency and ornamentation. The production of finery and the exchange of goods in the Middle Preclassic period was part of a social network of reciprocal prestation that enabled groups to maintain contact, exchange information, and negotiate accords, alliances, and marriages, rather than a materialist system of wealth accumulation and consumption). The brokers of such exchanges could control the changing valuation of their traded items and thereby derive from the socially sanctioned exchange process some degree of personal authority.

Lesure (1997) provides an example of activities for which lineage heads (or, elders) might prove necessary using figurines from the Mokaya region. He notes the presence of two main categories: unmarried women and village elders. The female figurines are generic in shape and have little in the way of specific detail to suggest they represent anything other than the general category of a "young woman." Contrastingly, the elder rotund males are represented with many more attendant details: they are seated, defined by costume, marked with ornamentation signifying particular social stations, roles, and functions. Interestingly, by 1100 BCE, the figure of the elder seems to fall out of the figurine repertoire and is replaced by figurines of seated nude males striking chiefly postures that suggest the onset of hereditary ranking (Clark 1994:42; for an equivalent model for Oaxaca see Marcus 1999). Lesure suggests the Early Preclassic manufacture of elder male and nubile woman figurines alludes to social negotiation inherent to marriage alliances and associated bride-price. The eventual replacement of the "elder" with the younger "chief" could represent the co-option of marriage negotiations by the maximal lineage head in lieu of several lineage leaders (elders).

Lineage leaders would act in their capacities as group representatives, donning the insignia of group and status conferred on them by their group at particular events. While their insignia of office (which brought with it socially defined rank) were likely defined by group prescriptions, it would be in the exchange of other generically valued materials where a "chief" could affect alterations and thereby prove himself as not the "passive bearer of personhood" (Fortes 1973:287), but an agent of some influence. Those of succeeding generations, having learned from experience, personal exposure, and family memory, quickly gained a competence in discharging such duties that could provide them the necessary distinction (*sensu* Bourdieu 1990) at an earlier age. In this light an exchange of nubile women (unmarked figurines of generic value) would be the "commodity" over which lineage heads were afforded the luxury of some manipulation, creativity, and innovation.

Elders, Women, and Children

If figurines reflect stereotypic social personas (Flannery and Marcus 1976a:382; Joyce 2003; Lesure 1997; Marcus 1999; Oliveros 1974) rather than individual portraits (see Gillespie 2001 for equivalent treatment of Classic Maya monuments), they can reflect emic social distinctions. Two clear distinctions drawn during the Middle Preclassic period are gender and age.

In the northern Honduran coastal regions, members of several distinct farming communities—Playa de los Muertos, Puerto Escondido, Las Honduritas—engaged in the production of figurines (Joyce 2003; Joyce and Henderson 2001; Kennedy 1981; Popenoe 1934) that constituted a single canon of representation (Joyce 2003:250), though apparently produced in different locales throughout the core area (Agurcia F. 1977:8). Joyce notes that these figures represent stereotypes of life-cycle events—the transition to adulthood or old age, or to other moral ideals—such as the decorated seated body. Joyce (2003:259) also notes that by the Middle Preclassic, the greater detail of these figural representations does not necessarily denote the greater individualism of a wealthier society, but rather the elaboration of forms by which the decorated adult could be embodied.

Importantly, Joyce (2003) also relates several figurine types and their associated ornamentation to burials of the same category found at Playa de los Muertos (Popenoe 1934). She thereby suggests a relationship between the idealization of identity in life via figurines and in death through mortuary practices. In this way, mortuary contexts are linked to the representation of social personas rather than to explicit individuals. Ornamentation, dress, and associated burial goods are not just examples of accumulated wealth, but are markers identifying the person (as adult, woman, man, chief, lineage member) in death. The existence, moreover, of gender/age-appropriate ornamentation speaks to the materialization of social personas and renders slightly more complex the age-old interpretation of juvenile burial goods as reflecting the existence of ascribed status.

These interpretations resonate with burial data from the Middle-to-Late Preclassic period K'axob (McAnany et al. 1999), where age differentiation was marked in juvenile burials (Storey and McAnany 2006). Most interestingly, limestone spheres (*yuntun*) and small bowls are exclusively found with children, while objects common to adult burials (such as large open bowls) were not found at all. Beyond their discrimination by age, there exists evidence suggesting gender differentiation of sub-adults as well. Data from Cuello (Robin 1989; Robin and Hammond 1991; Saul and Saul 1991) and Dos Hombres (Trachman and Valdez 2006) suggest that along with the jade and shell beads accompanying sub-adults, there seemed to be a correlation between females (of any age) and *Spondylus* bivalve pendants located in the pelvic region. There is some suggestion, however, that such materials were markers of ascribed status (rather than identity), especially when associated with sub-adults (Hammond et al. 1991:362).

Apart from body decoration, there is also evidence of bodily modification, such as cranial shaping (Hansen 2005:63; Saul and Saul 1991:154) This evidence speaks to the practice of inscribing aesthetics of beauty onto the body that due to their permanence are archaeologically visible. It is more than likely that cranial shaping represents one of many forms of bodily decoration that Early and Middle Preclassic Maya engaged in to mark individuals as specific persons. In fact, at Nakbe, there is also evidence dating to the Middle Ox phase (800–600 BCE) of dental incision and imported hematite inlays (Hansen 2005:63; Mata Amado and Hansen 1992). Similar decoration is found at Cahal Pech (Healy, Cheetham et al. 2004:120), Altar de Sacrificios (Willey 1973a:28), and Seibal (Tourtellot 1990: table 1). Furthermore, roller stamps were recovered from the fill of a Middle Preclassic version of Str. B1 at Blackman Eddy (Brown 1997) and at Cuello (Hammond 1991b:180; 2006). These items suggest that less permanent forms of bodily decoration were also well within the range of acceptable practices at this time. Both cranial shaping and tattooing would have provided mechanisms to symbolize different social personas.

The existence of these nuanced roles and social personas suggests the development of an increasingly complex domestic context. Decoration, ornamentation, body posture, and skeletal modification were all used to distinguish individuals by roles, which were defined only partly by age and sex. Although age and sex are the most widespread forms of social distinction, the Middle Preclassic data suggests that these distinctions were becoming increasingly materially elaborated. The material culture associated with these personas—figurines, stamps, clothing, shells, jadeite, hematite—suggest that a complex suite of practices of exchange, production, and expertise underpinned the formation of these social personas. These data suggest that the social relations that composed the domestic sphere of society expanded to create non-kin-based social roles.

Religious Specialists

The religious specialist, or shaman, represents another social persona that develops in this period. Much has been said regarding the presence and relevance of such figures in contemporaneous Olmec society (Furst 1995; Reilly 1995a). Therefore, the idea that such individuals would be of equal relevance to the understanding of Middle Preclassic Maya communities seems plausible. In fact, Late Preclassic kingship in the Maya lowlands was initially interpreted as based on the assumed prevalence of charismatic shamans from previous periods (Freidel and Schele 1988a).

In terms of the ritual toolkit from the Middle Preclassic, there is some evidence for the use of specialized materials. At Cahal Pech, the round structures considered to be public stages for ritual were covered with copal (Aimers et al. 2000). Figurines from several sites appear to represent individuals undergoing spirit possession. A blood-letting tool and a stingray spine at Blackman Eddy (Garber et al. 2004c) also attest to some degree of ritual activity. Finally, an enigmatic burial consisting of a shell mask and trumpet from Uaxactun (Hendon 1999:107) might be evidence of a ritual specialist. In terms of the costuming, Hendon (1999:107) suggests: "the role of shell objects as valuable and symbolically important costume elements or offerings gives significance to the abundance of shell found in the Group E Middle Preclassic midden deposits."

Finally, several bark-beaters have been recovered from Middle Preclassic contexts at Cuello (Hammond 2006) and K'axob (McAnany and López Varela 1999). Since these objects were used for the manufacture of bark paper, they were, in later periods, associated with scribal and ritual activities. Even though there is little evidence of writing in this period, the manufacture of paper could indicate ritual activity. This paper could have been used to collect blood for ritual burning, or to provide a surface for designs from cylinder seals.

These materials hardly provide enough information to constitute a comprehensive interpretation of the shaman's role in Middle Preclassic society. However, they do strongly suggest the existence in Middle Preclassic Maya society of a shaman or ritual specialist who commanded some degree of local authority—certainly enough to obtain items of foreign origin. The ability to maintain contact with and manipulate the products of distant places is seen as reflective of a command over the sacred world as well (Helms 1994).

One question that remains irresolvable given the current nature of the evidence is the extent to which the ritual specialist was a permanent member of local groups or an itinerant specialist. In the latter case, their peregrinations would allow them contact with and access to foreign goods, thereby rendering them "more than shamans…questing for knowledge and spiritual power. They took on the role of trading partners and the social elite in a regional economy" (Freidel 1995:4). Considering modern ethnographic examples (see Vogt 1969), it is just as likely that small villages would have counted on a particular shaman for the community.

Perhaps in the dispersed community of Copan, the shaman represented the most centralizing figure of the region (Cummins 2007). The development of an esoteric knowledge and access to exotic goods resulted in social authority. The shaman would be the center of non-kin-based social relations—and for much of Copan's history, perhaps the only social figures of the kind. In other parts of the Maya lowlands, the ritual specialist would have numbered among several social personas whose social relations would have stepped out of the idiom of kinship and descent.

Ballplayers, Warriors, Architects

In neighboring regions such as the Pacific coast, the ballgame was played in formal courts from the middle of the 2nd millennium BCE onward (Hill and Clark 2001). Some of the earliest ball courts in the Maya lowlands date to the Late Preclassic, from northern Belize, Cerros (Scarborough et al. 1982), and Colha (Eaton and Kunstler 1980), and the Copan region (Los Achiotes; Canuto 2002) where Middle Preclassic populations existed. In addition, ball courts recently documented in the northern Maya lowlands, dating to the Middle and Late Preclassic (Anderson 2011), suggest that masonry ball court architecture perhaps had a deeper history in that region. The game itself, as modern ethnographic studies (Leyenaar 1978, 2001) show, can be played without permanent architectural markings and could therefore have been played for centuries without leaving much of an architectural signature.

Evidence drawn from ethnohistoric sources suggests the game gave leave to a series of other activities, such as gambling among spectators, social competition between rival groups, and sponsorship of ball court construction and events (Hill and Clark 2001). The ballgame would enforce differences between centers while fostering a sense of *communitas* among the groups within a single center. The game, the related rituals, and the accompanying activities legitimized the meaningfulness of the center as a source of social identity. It is perhaps quite unlikely that there existed full-time ballplayers in the Middle Preclassic of the Maya lowlands; however, it is not impossible to consider this activity as part of community-level practices that provided the opportunity for distinction and status through a series of relationships completely foreign to the household or descent group. Whether the individual in the Middle Preclassic was considered a social persona (as in the *aj pitz* of the Classic period) remains unlikely; nevertheless, it is possible that the game's early disciples did fashion forms of social interaction within the social group that were not kin based.

Another social persona seen with regularity in later Maya periods is the warrior. On mural paintings, painted vessels, figurines, and stone monuments, the warrior is ubiquitous in the Classic period. For the Middle Preclassic period, however, there is some evidence of inter-center strife (Brown and Garber 2003), but no concomitant expression of a particular warrior class. While it is unlikely, like the ballplayer, that such a social persona was developed to be a full-time responsibility, it is possible that such a cadre of individuals was developing during this period and providing an opportunity for distinction and accomplishment outside the parameters of kinship social relations.

Finally, the monumental constructions at Nakbe speak to an increasing level of specialization in the arts of construction. The quarrying techniques, the apron-moulding innovations, and the monumentally sized buildings are all indications that some degree of expertise, perhaps resulting from full-time involvement, was developing by the end of the period.

Since the "architect" does not exist as a social category even during the Classic period, the attribution of a technical specialty as a social persona might not be warranted. However, the social relations that they likely engaged in when coordinating labor crews, designing buildings, and planning resource acquisition were likely not to have been encompassed by kin or descent relations.

Summary

It is clear from these examples that Middle Preclassic society in the Maya lowlands was infused with different personas, actors, roles, and personages. Whether they were distinguished by age, gender, or both, heavy symbolic investment was made to develop and sustain these types of distinctions in society. There existed no faceless peasants susceptible to the manipulations of a singular individual. Rather, multiple social roles were developed that were charged with expectations that required individuals to fashion new non-kin-based relations. These social personas were not necessarily identified in the figural or plastic arts of the time. Nevertheless, throughout the Middle Preclassic period, an increasing number of social roles, greater attendant social expectations, and the ever-narrowing pool of competent individuals capable of meeting those expectations conspired to create offices, ranks, and status groups whose idiom of social integration was separate from those of kinship and descent.

Polity Is Where the Heart Is

Recalling Watanabe's "place, people, and premise" (1992:12) alliterative trinity, it is clear that "premise" (kin-based social structure) and "people" (social roles) were in flux during the Middle Preclassic period. As a consequence, there was an added premium placed on the creation, elaboration, and reproduction of "place." In fact, the development of place appears critical to the concomitant development of corporate hierarchies and non-kin-based personas in the Middle Preclassic period.

Place-making was accomplished through the repeated construction of a domestic complex in one place. At Cuello and Cahal Pech, for instance, the progressive formalization of central patios created a central locale. Furthermore, the decorative elaboration of structures composing these residential complexes—such as the red paint at Cahal Pech, the red painted plaster at Altar de Sacrificios, the apron molding at Nakbe, and the architectural masks at Blackman Eddy—was a strategy to centralize activity in one place. Place-making also involved a cycle of ritual practices—reverential dedication, feasting, and ritual termination—that accompanied the construction, use, and cancellation of these centrally located architectural complexes that would have provided other opportunities for community formation. Moreover, the scale of the constructions (especially those of Nakbe) at these places involved some degree of communal labor, suggesting that the construction events also involved community building.

Non-domestic structures were also constructed as part of the domestic residential complexes at Cuello, Cahal Pech, and Blackman Eddy. Sites such as Tikal, Uaxactun, Nakbe, and Cival had ritual structures in the settlement center surrounded by sufficient open space to accommodate crowds. Every Middle Preclassic site had some feature that involved either ancestor burials, sacrificial victims, or dedicatory offerings in public / open areas (see Chapter 6, this volume). These activities created public stages (see Inomata 2006b) for ceremony, feasting, ritual, and exchange. The Middle Preclassic round structures found throughout the lowlands—Cahal Pech, Altun Ha, Colha, Uaxactun (to name a few)—have been interpreted as raised stages for the communal viewing of important rituals (Aimers et al. 2000:82). These sites "can be seen as engines for the creation of time, through the repetition at them of ritualized acts" (Gosden and Lock 1998:6).

Place-making also involved the inverted practices of site destruction. Evidence from Blackman Eddy (Brown and Garber 2003) of the violent dismantling and burning of one of the central ceremonial buildings, the mass burial of primarily young adult males and the burial of two decapitated sacrificial victims in the fill of a major construction event at Cuello (Hammond 1991d), and the caching of a decapitated head in a bowl at Cahal Pech (Aimers et al. 2000) suggest that Middle Preclassic life was punctuated by violent events that led not only to architectural elaboration but also destruction of emergent central places. Although the evidence is far too limited to suggest some regional organization of these events, it does speak to the development of rivals, challengers, factions, and even enemies

As sites of display, performance, and persuasion, Middle Preclassic centers were where explicit community identities were forged. The communal labor required to build these central locales triggered a common sense of belonging that might even have crossed descent group boundaries. Through an increasingly complex network of social personas calling for group action, subsequent rituals, performances, and gatherings at these spaces would further inculcate a sense of the social collective, especially as a function of social memory. Connerton (1989) notes that the development of collective memory is sustained within the rubric of performance that enacts a master narrative that conveys proto-typical behavior and synchronizes it among the larger social group. In other words, as Connerton states, "to study the social formation of memory is to study those acts of transfer that make remembering in common possible" (1989:39).

Public display was useful to the development of tradition: "By engaging in persuasive display, then, all one is really doing is calling on others to imitate actions that are implicitly being said to have already been carried out in the past" (Graeber 1996:9). The chiefly postures, the paraphernalia of office, and the specialized ritual objects were displayed to develop and enact a master narrative that fostered the development of an idealized, imagined community marked empirically by "place" and the periodic spatial contiguity of "people" at communal gatherings, and not necessarily based on descent affiliation. To this extent therefore the Middle Preclassic center was becoming the heart of a symbolic community—a group that thought themselves into difference, a polity.

NOT WINDMILLS, BUT PRECLASSIC PERIOD GIANTS

The data relating to the Middle Preclassic period is suggestive but hardly conclusive; more research will only provide better opportunities to construct a much more comprehensive model for the development of Maya social complexity. This essay focused on internal, socially driven change—that which arises from the continuous interplay of structure and practice. Clearly there are external factors such as the environment, neighboring groups, demographic factors that likely played important roles in the manner in which the Middle Preclassic Maya developed over nearly a millennium before the Late Preclassic period. My focus on the internal mechanisms of change was not meant to indicate the irrelevance of these other potential factors. However, it is rare that material conditions of existence trigger only one predictable social response; and Maya society was no different.

In this chapter, I suggest that the shift away from the logic of kinship and descent occurred in the Middle Preclassic period. However, I took pains—with an outline of an *emergent lineage-community* model—to demonstrate that this change was an amplification rather than wholesale rejection of past forms of social organization. Furthermore, the model also explains how lowland Maya social inequality did not require external impetus for its development. Rather, the changes that would be the foundation stones for a Late Preclassic social structure based on divine kingship, polities, and a regional political economy were deliberately extracted from the quarry of kinship and descent group relations during the preceding centuries of the Middle Preclassic period.

Ideology and the Early Maya Polity

SIMON MARTIN

While the last two decades have produced a sizeable influx of new data on the Preclassic Maya, we still find ourselves asking rather fundamental questions about the milieu from which the earliest polities emerged. Growing appreciation of the sophistication and scale of Preclassic achievements has understandably provoked renewed questions as to the political, cultural, and economic innovations that gave rise to them. Our greater understanding of succeeding Classic-era societies—whose material remains are far more plentiful, and where iconographic and epigraphic studies have proved especially productive—has only thrown the *terra obscura* of the Preclassic into greater relief.

The charge of this essay is to discuss the ideological underpinnings of early Maya polities. Wider interest in the topic has its roots in the turn away from materialistic explanations in archaeology toward cultural factors and, more specifically, the exploration of past mentalities. There is still a vein of thinking that views ideology as the tool of a self-serving and exploitative elite, but most scholars now prefer to see it in broader and more complex terms as a structural component active at all levels of society (see Demarest 1992b). In a dramatic migration from ideology's once peripheral status, some have come to see it as a primary factor in social formation, including the founding of early states (e.g., Chang 1983). The issue of ideology in early Maya polities has attracted the interest of a number of writers, each with their own datasets and research questions (e.g., Coe 1981a; Estrada-Belli 2006a; Freidel 1981, 1992; Freidel and Schele 1988a, 1988b; Grove and Gillespie 1992; Guernsey 2006; Hansen 1992a; Love 1999b; Reese 1996; Schele 1985; Schele and Miller 1986:103–10; Stuart

2005; Willey 1973b, 1977:416–17). The task at hand is to examine the issue in light of current evidence, to see in what ways our understanding might be expanded, refined, or revised.

"Ideology" will be treated here in its narrow sense as a system of beliefs that encompass the moral and spiritual basis for governance. Lying at the nexus between the religious and political worlds, ideology is always something more than a formulation of power; it actively generates social cohesion and identity. Hand-in-hand with the emergence of more populous and internally differentiated communities—with their inherent potential for divisiveness—came both the institutions of political order and the ideas that gave them validity. While the minds of people were never "empty," a blank slate on which new constructs could be written (Carneiro 1972:198), the scale and complexity of these societies would minimally require a reconfiguration of existing understandings. One of the recurring features of an ideology is its ability to adapt to changing circumstances, while at the same time presenting itself as natural, traditional, and immutable. The world over, these systems work by harnessing supernatural forces that, as unimpeachable sources of authority and legitimacy, are used to frame pragmatic goals. The distinction between sacred and the secular begins to loses its meaning within the bounds of ideology, since its aim is a "total vision."

SOCIAL EVOLUTION AMONG THE MAYA

The archaeological understanding of Maya social development has been enhanced and elaborated in recent years, but despite some regional variability its trajectory remains much the same. Permanent settlements and their agrarian hinterlands were established during the Early Preclassic (2000–1000 BCE), initially in coastal zones but ultimately penetrating all parts of the highlands and the lowland peninsula. In the Middle Preclassic (1000–400 BCE) there are increasing signs of interaction with contemporary societies in western Mesoamerica, and cultural traits that we see as distinctively Maya become evident. Monumental construction becomes a feature of the larger settlements taking shape at this time, and signs of social differentiation increase. The Late Preclassic (400 BCE–200 CE) saw a marked escalation of these trends, with the building of architecture on a scale comparable to, and often exceeding, that seen elsewhere in Mesoamerica. A century or two into the 1st millennium CE, however, a range of centers, including the very largest, were abandoned, and their immediate regions suffered a precipitous fall in population—justifiably dubbed the "Preclassic collapse."

Over the next two or three centuries some of the surviving centers, plus others newly founded, developed a set of new forms and practices—most notably an emphasis on monuments with hieroglyphic texts—that characterize the Classic period (200–900 CE). After a slow start in the Early Classic (200–600 CE), when the population may have taken time to surpass Late Preclassic levels, the pace of development quickened as the Classic phenomenon spread from the central lowlands to more peripheral parts of the Maya realm—with the notable exception of the highlands and Pacific piedmont. During the Late Classic (600–800 CE) populations reached their peak and the lowland landscape was largely filled by a sizeable number of distinct, structurally autonomous political centers. With few signs of an impending crisis, this system experienced its own unraveling at the onset of the Terminal Classic (800–900 CE)—with abandonment beginning in the central lowlands, but overtaking the northern zone by century's end.

We can essentially take two positions regarding the Preclassic–Classic transition, characterized (or caricatured) here as *revolution* versus *evolution*. The first takes the evidence of distinction between the two eras as indicative of fundamental and far-reaching change. Here the onset of the Classic follows a profound cultural failure and marks a seismic shift in the governing principles of polities, one which gave rise to new and significantly different forms. The counterview takes the position that many if not all features of the Classic tradition were present within the Preclassic and, while major changes took place, the continuities are as important as the disjunctions. It perceives an on-going dynamic in which periods of stability and growth are interspersed with less predictable bouts of turbulence and transformation—a form of "punctuated equilibrium" if you will. I shall return to these contrasting paradigms, since ideology takes a pivotal role in each: either as the means to effect a radical metamorphosis, or as an adaptive response to social crises.

The labels "Preclassic" and "Formative" were coined as part of an overt evolutionary scheme and serve to define this period in contrast to the succeeding "Classic" (Willey and Phillips 1958:149–50). For all the weaknesses of this perspective it expresses a certain truth, in that we continue to investigate the earlier and least-known eras by reference to later, best-known ones. There are many ways in which we can, and do, study the Preclassic period "on its own terms"; but if we are interested in symbolic systems, then it is both legitimate and practical to trace form and practice back in time. This is not to presume that ideas are static and unchanging, only that where continuities of symbolic expression are evident our initial assumption—to be confirmed by further testing—should favor corresponding continuities of thought over disjunction (cf. Kubler 1962; Willey 1973b). If evolution better describes the transition, then we should be able to interpret important aspects of Preclassic ideology from what we know of the Classic. If, on the other hand, revolution better describes the situation we may find ourselves in a foreign land, obliged to reconstruct an ideological program solely from Preclassic materials.

SOURCES ON EARLY MAYA IDEOLOGY

Ideologies are so extraordinarily complex, so densely woven from abstract and unstated understandings, what hope can we have of retrieving those of long-extinct cultures? Our access to past mentalities is effectively restricted to symbolic expressions: be they the explicit communications of art and writing or the more implicit signals we might detect in the design or spatial dimensions of architecture and ritual deposits. The relationships between artifacts and the ideas that inspired them are never direct or unproblematic. To achieve any success we must rely on closely argued, comparative approaches—eschewing, as much as we can, intuitive responses necessarily grounded in our own time and culture. The obstacles remain considerable. The base of excavated material is restricted, the artistic conventions complex, the examples of writing are both scarce and hard to comprehend. Yet research over the past two decades has cumulatively added to our knowledge of Maya symbol systems and, within appropriate parameters, there are good opportunities for further progress.

The most iconic examples of Preclassic art are undoubtedly the collection of large stucco-modeled façades applied to public buildings, almost always paired on either side of a central stairway. They include examples excavated at El Mirador, Nakbe, Cerros, Uaxactun, Lamanai, Cival, Tikal, Calakmul, Chakanbakan, and Itzamkanac (Carrasco and Colón 2005; Coe 1990; Cortés de Brasdefer 1994; Estrada-Belli 2006a; Freidel 1986b; Hansen 1992a; Pendergast 1981; Ricketson and Ricketson 1937; Valdés 1987, 1988; Vargas 2001). The freestanding stela first emerged in western Mesoamerica during the Middle Preclassic, appearing in the Maya lowlands at El Mirador, Nakbe, Cival, Cuello, and San Bartolo, and in the highlands and piedmont at Izapa, Takalik Abaj, El Baúl, Chocolá, Chalchuapa, El Naranjo, El Jobo, and El Portón, among others (Arroyo 2010b; Estrada-Belli 2006a; Guernsey, Clark, and Arroyo 2010; Hammond 1982; Hansen 1991, 1992a; Jones 1986; Norman 1973, 1976; Parsons 1986, 1988; Porter 1992; Sharer and Sedat 1973; Stuart 2005). These centers and several more also have a range of three-dimensional sculptures, to which we might add rock carvings, such as the one in Loltun Cave (Thompson 1897). The earliest stelae were either plain or decorated in some fugitive medium— paint or possibly even stucco—but later ones were carved with mythological scenes or depictions of rulers. These portrait stelae subsequently acquired dates and hieroglyphic texts, introducing a pattern that would characterize the whole of the succeeding Classic period. Some smaller, portable objects—especially items of adornment in greenstone, bone, or shell—can be assigned to the Preclassic on stylistic grounds, although few have known provenience or dating information (e.g., Coe 1973b:25–27; Schele and Miller 1986:79, 82–83, 119–20, 227; Mora-Marín 2001; Fields and Reents-Budet 2005b:191). A few paintings from the Preclassic have been uncovered in deep excavations (e.g., Coe 1990; Valdés 1995), with the most dramatic by far being the recent finds at San Bartolo, Guatemala (Saturno 2009; Saturno, Taube, and Stuart 2005a; Taube et al. 2010).

The following sections take differing iconographic and epigraphic approaches to the issue of ideology. They will focus on selected themes and explore the relationships between theology and authority in early Maya polities, with a collective discussion of their implications at the end.

Iconography: Cult of the Great Bird

A striking feature of Preclassic art is the frequency with which we see avian imagery, either in overtly mythological contexts or in the costuming of lords. New discoveries and identifications have greatly expanded this pattern, which must now be seen as pan-regional in scope. Most or all can be linked to the Principal Bird Deity, first described by Lawrence Bardawil (1976). This character emerges in the Middle Preclassic and can be identified in several Mesoamerican zones (Cortez 1986:17; Taube et al. 2010:33, 35–39; Nielsen and Helmke, forthcoming). At the late Olmec site of Tres Zapotes, Stela D presents this avian god within a celestial program that would be repeated throughout the Maya area (Norman 1976b:28; Quirate 1976:77–78; Cortez 1986; Taube 1996b:92–94) (Fig. 11.1a). We see the bird inverted—equipped with arms to highlight its anthropomorphic qualities—and emerging from the mouth of a monstrous, front-facing jaguar head. In Karl Taube's analysis, this feline aspect to the sky is seen in other examples of Olmec iconography, for example on La Venta Altar 4 and on the "Olmec-style" painted mural from Oxtotitlan (Fig. 11.1b, c). Prominent features are its flared fangs, elements that would be abstracted into hooked devices over the coming centuries. At Tres Zapotes a bicephallic, blunt-nosed serpent hangs down of either side to frame the image of three lords. Its heads seem to emerge from behind the jaguar's earflares, although in earlier times the body of the snake is held in its jaws.[1]

This descending Principal Bird Deity motif appears in the Maya low-lands at San Bartolo, not only in the murals but also on a stucco frieze on the outside of the building that houses them (Taube et al. 2010: fig. 23b) (Fig. 11.2a). In the Pacific piedmont it occurs on stelae at Takalik Abaj and Izapa (Figs. 11.2b, 11.4b). Here the celestial symbolism from Tres Zapotes is repeated, although the retreat of the jaguar's face now leaves the fangs and earflares—rather like the smile of the Cheshire Cat—as disembodied motifs. This program continues to evolve in Maya hands, transforming some devices and introducing others. The earflares, for example, come to enclose the face nicknamed the "Shiner"—identified by its squint eyes, T-shaped tooth, and "mirror" markings, or by its attenuated form, a simple diagonal line (Stuart 1988:201–3; Saturno, Taube and Stuart 2005a:38–41; Taube 2007) (Figs. 11.2c, 11.3a).[2] Emerging evidence suggests that this motif conveys ideas of brilliance and luster associated with jade and other polished stones. A symbol of preciosity, it also seems to capture notions of radiance, perhaps explaining why it is sometimes replaced by the *k'in* "sun" sign (Fig. 11.2b). It is unlikely to be coincidental that the Classic Maya sun god K'inich Ajaw carries features of the Shiner, including its squint eyes and T-tooth. In an important transitory stage of the sky motif attested on Takalik Abaj Altar 12, the Shiner head is transferred to the fanged-band, joining a group of embedded emblems that also include the sun and stars to produce one of the earliest known examples of the Classic sky-band (Fig. 11.2d). The serpent heads terminating the device remain here, but by Classic times they are replaced by those of eagles (Taube 2007). The bi-cephallic serpent continues as an independent element that the Principal

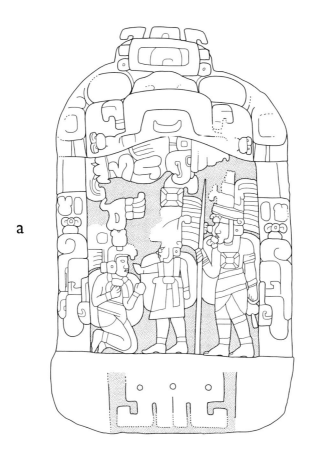

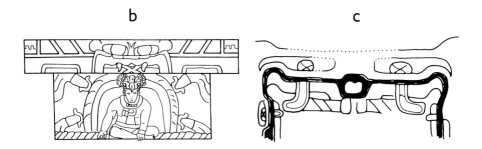

11.1. Origins of the Maya sky-band: a) Tres Zapotes Stela D (drawing by Simon Martin after James Porter); b) La Venta Altar 4 (drawing by Kent Reilly); c) Oxtotitlan Mural (detail) (drawing by Karl Taube).

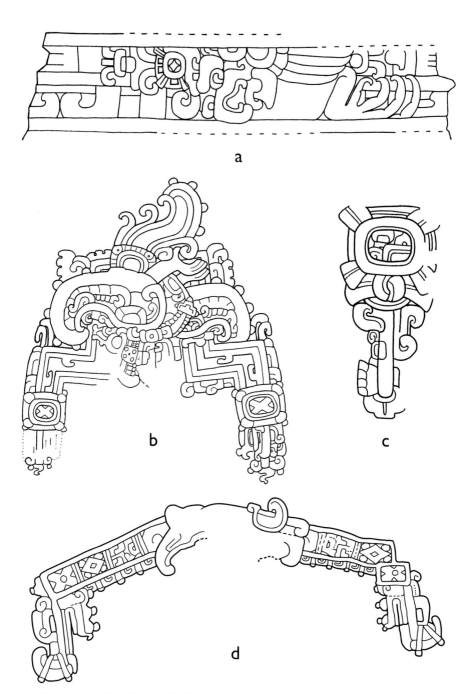

11.2. Descending Principal Bird Deity and evolution of the sky-band: a) San Bartolo Structure 1-sub (exterior stucco frieze) (drawing by Karl Taube); b) Takalik Abaj Altar 13 (drawing by Karl Taube); c) Kaminaljuyu Altar 9 (detail) (drawing by Karl Taube); d) Takalik Abaj Altar 12 (detail) (drawing by Simon Martin after James Porter).

Bird Deity holds in its beak (Fig. 11.4a), becoming a standard accoutrement in its Classic representations.

These elements allow us to interpret the façade masks such as those of Nakbe and Cerros, where the bird's head is framed by the same celestial devices (Hansen 1992a; Reese 1996) (Fig. 11.3a, b). In fact, identical features appear in battered form at Uaxactun, Tikal, Lamanai, and elsewhere—where what is often called the "long-lipped head" is in fact the beaked visage of the great bird.[3]

It is hard to over-emphasize the importance of the San Bartolo murals as a window into early Maya cosmology and foundational myths (Saturno 2009; Saturno, Taube, and Stuart 2005a; Taube et al. 2010). No other artwork, from any period, sets itself the task of visualizing the structure of the Maya universe and the core narratives of its creation. What we find is startlingly familiar: the same characters and the same events recur throughout the Classic era, with certain features that continue into the Postclassic and even the Colonial periods. Much is oriented around the story of the Maize God and the cycle of corn cultivation—a central paradigm of life and death in Mesoamerica. His birth, death, and rebirth are all represented, and he is revealed as the agent behind several key primordial events, including the origin of human sustenance. Another major theme establishes the four corners of the world with the placement of cosmic trees. Before each a young lord performs a penis perforation and makes an offering appropriate to the direction at hand, following a sequence of fish, deer, turkey, and incense repeated in the same context in the Dresden Codex, which was created well over a millennium later (Taube et al. 2010:28). On the crown of each tree sits a Principal Bird Deity—with subtle distinctions that appear to define separate aspects—each presiding over a cardinal quadrant of the cosmos (Fig. 11.4a).

Scholars have long associated the Principal Bird Deity with the monstrous bird Wuqub Kaqix "Seven Macaw" described in the 16th-century K'iche' epic of the Popol Vuh (Tedlock 1985; Christenson 2003). The initial evidence for this came from Izapa, whose monuments present not the familiar royal portraits but fragments of myth frozen in stone (Norman 1976b:327). The scene on Izapa Stela 2 has been linked to the episode in which the Hero Twins shoot the arrogant bird—a solar imposter—from its tree, while Stela 25 shows the plot point in which the bird rips off the arm of one brother, both episodes described in the Popol Vuh (Lowe, Lee,

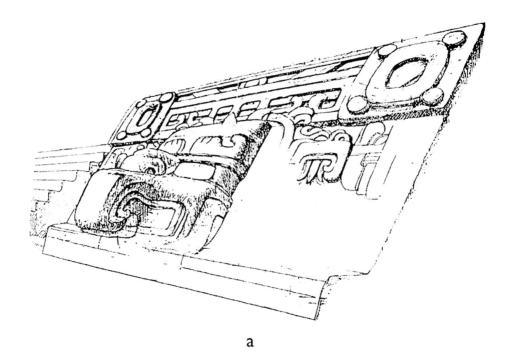

a

b

11.3. Principal Bird Deity masks: a) Façade mask of Nakbe Str.1 (drawing by Terence Routledge, courtesy of Richard D. Hansen); b) Façade mask of Cerros Structure 5C-2nd Upper (drawing by Linda Schele).

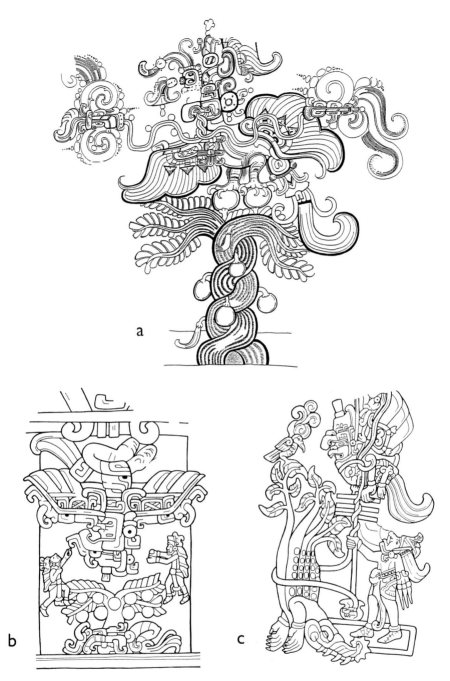

11.4. Principal Bird Deity in narrative: a) San Bartolo Str.1 sub-1 West Wall (drawing by Heather Hurst); b) Izapa Stela 2 (drawing by Ayax Moreno, New World Archaeological Foundation [NWAF]); c) Izapa Stela 25 (drawing by Ayax Moreno, NWAF).

and Martínez 1982) (Fig. 11.4b, c). There the brother is called Hunahpu "One Lord," making him the direct descendent of the prototypical ruler Juun Ajaw "One Lord" who features strongly in Classic Maya art and writing. Indeed, the very same tale can be traced right through the Classic era (Coe 1989b; Cortez 1986; Guernsey 1997; Robicsek and Hales 1982:56–57; Stone 1983), with varying degrees of visual elision between the Principal Bird Deity and his manifestation as a macaw (Martin 2006a).

Should the façade images of the great bird be taken as emblematic depictions or as *pars pro toto* narratives? Aid here comes from an Early Classic building façade, the remarkable entablature of Rosalila, a now-buried version of Copan Structure 16 (Agurcia 2004). All four of its sides feature stucco-modeled bird deities which combine features of a quetzal and macaw with the head of the sun god K'inich Ajaw—a direct reference to the name of the Copan dynastic founder K'inich Yax K'uk' Mo' "Radiant First Quetzal Macaw" (Fig. 11.5). Something more than an attractive combination of prestigious birds and the Sun God, the name seems to be derived from and celebrate a particular myth or symbolic relationship connected to the Principal Bird Deity (Martin 2006a).[4] Rosalila presents us with a complex engagement between mythology and royal identity—seemingly part of a contrived equivalence that sets founders in a special supernatural context (of which see more below) (Fash 1991; D. Stuart 1992). The narrative sense here emerges from the pictured descent of the Rosalila birds—their serpent head wings are inverted and, where they survive, their wing feathers are swept upward.[5] They appear to swoop down from a mountain depicted on the roof-comb—in whose center we see a form of the Shiner familiar from Preclassic façades.

The descent of the Principal Bird Deity is described in inscriptions from the Classic period, where the verb employed is **EHM** "to descend, go down" (Zender 2005:8–11). On one unprovenienced painted vessel it clearly refers to the defeat of the bird god, captioning a scene in which it is shot from its tree by a blowgun pellet fired by Juun Ajaw (Robicsek and Hales 1982:56–57). This is widely taken to be an explicit counterpart to the downfall of Wuqub Kaqix in the Popol Vuh. On another vessel the *ehm* term marks a further descent of the bird, this time motivated by a duck-billed wind deity (see Kerr 2000:1010)—although Juun Ajaw and his brother are involved here too, attending the court of God D in some unknown portion of the story. The dates ascribed to both *ehm* events are suspiciously similar

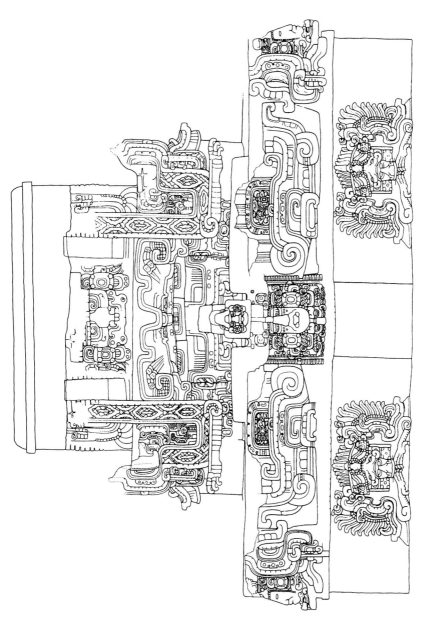

11.5. Copan Structure 16, Rosalila Phase (drawing by Barbara Fash).

and could well indicate that the same event is described (Zender 2005:11). The self-same duck-billed figure appears some 800 years earlier on the West Wall of the San Bartolo mural, where he dances and calls out to attract the bird's attention and offers up some rounded object, apparently a gift or lure (Taube et al. 2010:48–49). The following scene is incomplete but shows the Maize God dressed in a bird costume in the act of spearing something (Saturno 2009:127). His victim survives only as the tip of a flailing claw, but presumably this identifies it as the great bird (Saturno 2007a), specifying an additional defeat, this time at the hands of a "disguised" Maize God.[6] This could well relate to a scene recovered in fragments from a demolished portion of the paintings, which shows the once-mighty bird deity limp and lifeless, hung over the back of the one of the young lords who otherwise offer sacrifices to the world quarters, themselves related to Juun Ajaw "One Lord" (Saturno 2009:123, fig. 9; Taube et al. 2010:19, fig.12). Some versions of the story may be elaborated, others truncated, and the second instance could simply be the prologue to the bird's misfortune. It is also possible that there are multiple stories involving the descent of the great bird, which might easily, for example, be a trope for recurring cosmological events.

The identification of kings with the Principal Bird Deity is also reflected in the masks, headdresses, and feather displays that turn them into embodiments of the great bird (Cortez 1986; Guernsey 1997, 2006:91–117). Kaminaljuyu Stela 11 (Fig. 11.6a) is perhaps the most notable early example of lords costumed in this way, but as Bardawil first noted, such attire forms a continuum across the two epochs, and kings continue to don masks of the great bird in the Classic Period—although by that time only as part of a wider repertoire of divine identities.[7]

To proceed further is to ask complex and difficult questions about the nature and meaning of the great bird and, most especially, its relationship to God D—the famed "paramount god" of the Maya, long equated with the Colonial period Itzamna (Seler 1990[1887]:98). It was Nicholas Hellmuth (1987:303–12) who first explicitly established the connection, noting that the elderly God D wears the same set of diagnostic motifs as the Principal Bird Deity. He further suggested that the old god transforms himself into the bird, an apotheosis that follows his symbolic death (1987:365). Several authors have expanded on this view of the bird as an avatar, manifestation, or co-essence of God D. Julia Guernsey has produced a comprehensive study of the monuments at Izapa and includes an extended section on

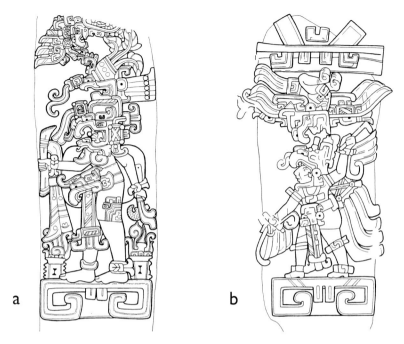

11.6. 11.6. a) Kaminaljuyu Stela 11; b) Izapa Stela 4 (drawings by Ayax Moreno, NWAF).

the Principal Bird Deity (2006:91–117). She argues that performance and transformation are central themes on Izapa stelae, and that the physical impersonation of the bird through costume and dance evokes the metamorphosis of God D into the Principal Bird Deity. In this way, images showing the bird with a full or partial humanoid face in its jaws show rulers engaged in role-playing.

Yet figures such as that on Izapa Stela 4, with his tied-on wings beneath a descending Principal Bird Deity—here again with a human face between its jaws—may instead refer to the San Bartolo tale (Fig. 11.6b). Thus, rather than a king impersonating the bird, we might have the Maize God in his bird costume, pictured shortly before the spearing event. Furthermore, recent epigraphic work has certain implications for the nature and identity of God D. There is now evidence to indicate that the entity we call God D is a visual fusion between the Principal Bird Deity and the aged deity known as God N. A small but transparent set of glyphic spellings separates the two names and demonstrates that an intricate relationship between them lies at the heart of this complex (Bassie 2002; Martin 2006b). Their very deliberate combination fits a wider pattern of divine hybridity for the Maya that I have described as *theosynthesis*, which in this case involves the aged deity as a presence that pervades or unifies different domains of the universe (Martin, n.d.-a).

Another feature that requires a brief discussion is the linkage between the Principal Bird Deity and the Shiner. Few Preclassic images of the great bird lack the Shiner's face on their chests, where it serves to signal its lustrous, shiny qualities (Figs. 11.2a, 11.4b, 11.4c, 11.6a). In one form or another this motif is applied to the bird throughout the Classic and Postclassic—usually by means of the aforementioned squint eyes and the "mirror" devices on its head and body. This attribute is so consistent and long-lived, one might wonder if the concept survived to the time of the Popol Vuh. Passages here describe the bright, shining qualities of Wuqub Kaqix at length, as the bird boasts of being both the sun and moon (see Christenson 2003:92). It is these pretensions that draw the ire of the Hero Twins and provoke their attack. On Takalik Abaj Altar 30 he bears a *k'in* "sun" symbol in place of the shining head (see Guernsey 2006: fig. 5.3)—a more overt reference, perhaps, to his assuming the role of the sun.[8]

This rather detailed excursion into the iconography of the Principal Bird Deity supports and confirms earlier work, and establishes, I believe, three major points. The first is the prominence accorded to this creature and its mythic narratives. It is by no means the only supernatural theme presented on early monuments, but it easily is the most dominant and diverse in its representations. If we are to understand ideology within Late Preclassic Maya polities then we will need to take on the question of the great bird. The second is the tremendous consistency with which these ideas and their expressions are represented throughout the region. Ranging over great distances and diverse topographical and ecological zones, images of the great bird display a coherence that is not simply pan-Maya, but pan-Mesoamerican. Lastly, there are strong signs that the bird maintained its ideological currency beyond the great transition, retaining its vigor in the rhetoric of Early Classic kings, continuing in some form right up to the Colonial period. At the same time, it was plainly of most relevance to the rulers of the earliest Maya regimes. Who were these rulers and what were their qualities? Here we must turn to epigraphy for the data it can provide.

Epigraphy: Lords, Divinity, and Dynasty

Writing, which is to say a system that encodes language in graphic form, offers a tool of considerable ideological potential. Texts can crystallize oral performance and memory, storing ideas and messages that can be conveyed across space and time—at times traversing continents and millennia. The realization of language as script does more than simply expand its communicative range; it generates unique forms of discourse with their own characteristics, qualities, and connotations. Regardless of the original spur to its invention and its other functions within society, the regimes behind early complex societies consistently used writing to sustain and augment their power. Preclassic Maya texts should provide a window into the self-representation of the governing elite.

Unfortunately our sample of assuredly Preclassic Maya inscriptions is very small, numbering little more than two dozen examples at the present time.[9] Maya writing evolved over the two millennia that it was used, and many of the earliest signs bear little or no resemblance to those we know from later periods. At least some of this obscurity may be the product of the collapse in 100–200 CE. The extinction of some, possibly dominant, script communities could have led surviving ones to innovate to meet the new challenges of a changed political and cultural environment (Houston 2007a). Compounded by the limited sample, this means that paleographic analysis cannot tell very much about the development of style or its relative dating. With the exception of Long Count dates at El Baúl of 36 CE and at Takalik Abaj of 103 and 126 CE —each of which introduces now-illegible inscriptions—we are effectively adrift in time. A further obstacle to reading is the morphosyntactical simplicity of early texts, which lack the elaboration and precision we see in later periods (Houston 2004). Preservation is another problem. Although we have inscriptions on Preclassic stelae at El Mirador, Chalchuapa, El Portón, Takalik Abaj, and Kaminaljuyu—as well as others on the aforementioned portable objects—almost every one is damaged or incomplete. As a cumulative result of all these factors, we lack sound knowledge about the origins and function of writing during the Preclassic.

The single most significant contribution to Preclassic Maya epigraphy has come, once again, from San Bartolo (Houston 2006; Saturno, Stuart, and Beltrán 2006; Saturno, Stuart, and Taube 2005). The two extant walls of Structure 1 sub-1 contain a number of isolated captions referring to actors or events in the scenes. The dating of this building to around 100 BCE offers the first real fix for Preclassic paleography. A fragment from a still earlier mural has since been recovered from sealed fill, establishing that there was a fully formed Maya script in use some centuries before (currently set at 400–200 BCE) (Saturno, Stuart, and Beltrán 2006:1282) (Fig. 11.7). The San Bartolo texts are as hard to read as any others from this era, but it is notable that the two longest, including the earliest, include the term **AJAW** "lord" (Lounsbury 1973) (Fig. 11.8a, b).

The *ajaw* term also appears on several portable objects from the Preclassic. Despite the poverty of the corpus, this is statistically significant and suggests that "lords" (they are human in all cases we can identify) were key subjects for early inscriptions (Fig. 11.8c-f).[10] The term *ajaw* (plural *ajawo'ob*) survives to this day, most notably in the Maya highlands where it refers to the *principales*, the indigenous nobility whose hereditary rights were confirmed by the Spanish authorities in the 16th century. It is not an office *per se*, but a rank distinction held by a number of noble lines. There is firm evidence from copious references in the Classic period that it had the same role in earlier times, and referred to groups of elite collaterals. One member of this group, usually a scion of the highest-ranking line, served as the paramount lord or king of any given polity (of which more below).

11.7. Text from San Bartolo dating to 400–200 BCE (drawing by David Stuart).

The best known of the early references to *ajaw* comes from a greenstone pectoral that now resides in the Dumbarton Oaks Collection in Washington, DC (Coe 1966b; Freidel and Schele 1988b; Schele and Miller 1986:119–20) (Fig. 11.9). It does not include a date, but refers to a lord or ruler by name, seemingly in the context of his accession to power. In an accompanying portrait he is shown wearing the fully panoply of Mesoamerican kingship. Jade jewels form a headdress that lies over, or incorporates, the core emblem of *ajaw* rank: a white *amate*-cloth headband—called in the texts *sak hu'un* "white paper"—which is usually decorated with one or

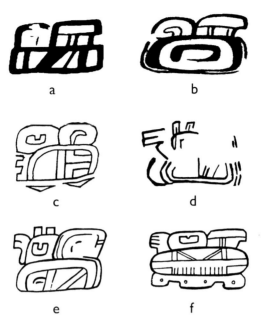

11.8. Early **AJAW** compounds: a) San Bartolo Fragment (drawing by David Stuart); b) San Bartolo Str.1 sub-1, West Wall (drawing by David Stuart); c) "Spoon" in the Jade Museum, Costa Rica (drawing by David Mora-Marín); d) Jaguar Figurine in the Yale University Art Gallery (drawing by David Mora-Marín); e) Celt in the Dumbarton Oaks Collection (drawing by David Mora-Marín); f) Slate disk in the Jade Museum, Costa Rica No.6528 (drawing by David Mora-Marín).

more red stripes.[11] The earliest versions consist of a cord tied around the temples, over the crown, and under the chin. Such bands are often embellished by one or more "Jester Gods" (Fields 1989, 1991; Freidel 1990; Taube 1998). Often taken as a mark of kingship, they can in fact be used by any holder of *ajaw* rank, at least by Late Classic times (this is especially clear in the murals of Bonampak, where a line of visitors in capes each wears a headband bearing their own Jester emblem), and are also worn by certain deities. Appearing in a variety of forms, from a simple trefoil to fully anthropomorphic being, the Jester God is a complex entity which has been linked to generative forces and the sprouting of maize—with its tri-lobed head sometimes shown as shoots or leaves. More often, however, its closest affinities seem to be with the material of paper itself, the processed bark of the fig tree, and here it is best seen as a supernatural embodiment of this material and its rich symbolic meanings. Its varieties are more clearly dis-

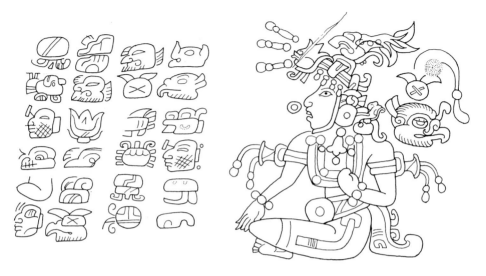

11.9. Dumbarton Oaks Pectoral (drawing by Linda Schele).

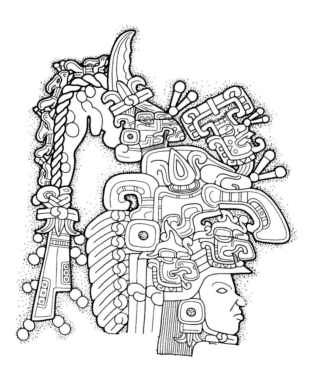

11.10. La Mojarra Stela 1 (detail) (drawing by George Stuart).

cerned in the early period, where the band over the crown regularly sports one that is fused with the Principal Bird Deity, while the band over the brow shows another merged with either a shark or the Maize God, sometimes in triple form, spaced out along the band (Hansen 1992a:146–48; Stuart 2004a; Taube 1998:454–56; Taube et al. 2010:65–66).[12] The whole assembly is of great antiquity and widely spread through Mesoamerica—an excellent example appears on La Mojarra Stela 1 (Fig. 11.10), dated to 153 CE or a little later—but it is also a recurrent feature of lordly portraits from the Olmec region or in what we perceive as Olmec style (Fields 1989).

Impressive persistence in the symbolism of kingship emerges from San Bartolo, where the mythic program surrounds an accession ceremony that matches in every important regard another produced as much as 800 years later (Fig. 11.11a, b). In both, an aged character wearing a patterned cape—usually a distinctive feature of the Underworld ruler God L—presents a headdress crown to an enthroned young lord (at San Bartolo he wears his own bird headdress). Thus, not only are the title and its particular regalia legacies from distant times, the specific rituals of investiture associated with them are equally ancient and charged with cosmic significance (Saturno 2009; Taube et al. 2010:60–69). This allows us to talk about an archetypal idea of kingship that spans the Preclassic to Classic eras and produces a formidable argument for institutional continuity.[13]

In the San Bartolo murals this is one of a pair of investiture scenes in which royal emblems are presented to lords enthroned on scaffolds. The other more clearly occurs within a narrative thread of the Maize God and directly follows his apparent spearing of the great bird. It shows the still-feathered Maize God offering a jewel in the form of the Jester God, the personification of paper called *huun*, in a form merged with the Principal Bird Deity. The recipient, seated on a jaguar skin of rulership, is evidently another form of the Maize God himself. Though without clear parallel elsewhere, this must constitute another core mythic underpinning to kingship in which the corn deity gains a special status after his successful "hunt."

Stylistically, the regalia at San Bartolo bears close comparison to that on the Dumbarton Oaks pectoral (Fig. 11.9), suggesting a rough placement for the latter to around 100 BCE. Returning to the pectoral text, it has a further contribution to make in its rendering of **CH'AB x-x ya-AK'AB li**, which evidently provides an early form of *(u)ch'ab yak'abil* "(his) creation, his darkness" (seen over the last four glyphs of the second paired column).

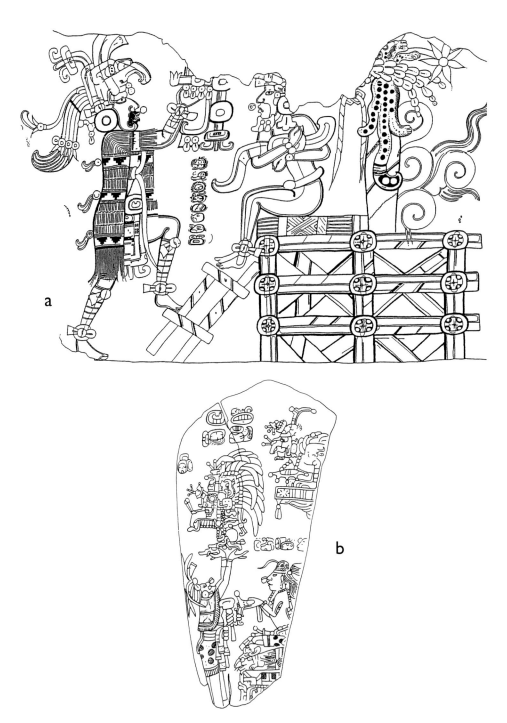

11.11. Accession scenes: a) San Bartolo Str.1 sub-1 West Wall (drawing by Heather Hurst); b) Bone in the Dallas Museum of Art (drawing by Karl Taube).

This same couplet recurs throughout the Classic as a mystical possession of kings, and it even survived into the historical period, appearing, much changed, as a magical formula in incantations from 18th-century Yucatan (Roys 1965:xv). David Stuart (2005:278) has argued that it formerly represented some special inner force or essence of the ruler, strongly linked to his procreative powers. Significantly, captured kings are said to have "no creation, no darkness," suggesting the nullifying effect that imprisonment, humiliation, and possible disfigurement had on his ability to form a conduit for divine power.

This role of kingship as a channel for supernatural power, with rulers acting as interfaces between people and gods, was first articulated in the 1980s (Freidel 1992; Freidel and Schele 1988a, 1988b; Schele 1985; Schele and Freidel 1990; Schele and Miller 1986). This view was built on interpretations of the Jester God motif, especially as it appeared on monumental sculptures such as those uncovered at Cerros, as well as scenes of "god-conjuring" and visionary experience. Additional impetus arrived from the decipherment of the God C portrait glyph and its accompanying "water group" as **K'UH** "god" (Ringle 1988; Stuart, Houston, and Robertson 1999). This term takes an adjectival role in the "emblem glyph"—the personal title held by a polity ruler—which could now be read *k'uhul x ajaw* "Divine/Holy Lord of X" (where "x" is the name of a polity or particular dynastic house) (Mathews 1991:24–26). Studies of greater depth and comparative reach followed and refined many aspects of the role of Maya kings in the supernatural maintenance of their realms (Houston and Stuart 1996).

Evidence for "holy lords" in the Preclassic is equivocal. The earliest certain reference appears in the form of an emblem glyph on the Hauberg Stela, a diminutive monument carrying a date in 197 CE (Schele 1985; Schele, Mathews, and Lounsbury 1990)—although some elements of its style could indicate a retrospective reference. The full "holy" form of the emblem glyph is rare during the Early Classic, suggesting that the expansion of this status began only after about 500 CE (Houston and Stuart 1996:295). This would coincide with a notable acceleration in polity formation at that time.

The **AJAW** sign has a complex graphic evolution in which its components were simplified, elaborated, and reworked over time (Lacadena 1995; Freidel, Reese-Taylor, and Mora-Marín 2002:54–61). It has been argued that the "tuft"-like element at the top left corner of some early forms is part of the brow design of deities and signals the **K'UH** term (Freidel, Reese-

Taylor, and Mora-Marín 2002:58) (Fig. 11.12a). Interpreted as a *Spondylus* motif, in most contexts it seems to work just as easily as whiskers or hair. It is prominent in the Shiner head (Fig. 11.12b), including its unions with, or manifestations as, the sun god (Fig. 11.12c). A strikingly similar example comes from the newly excavated mask at Cival (Estrada-Belli 2006a:65–69), where the tuft appears together with the squared protrusions at top, as well as the enclosed U-shaped device (Fig. 11.12d). The picture is still indistinct, but some early compounds featuring *ajaw* seem to have included elements used in the Shiner portrait, a feature that survives into the Early Classic but then disappears. A *k'uhul ajaw* reading for this form would require further examination and a greater understanding of sign development in the initial stages of Maya writing than we presently have. One should note that during the Early Classic we see *ajaw* glyphs that also carry a "tuft" design in

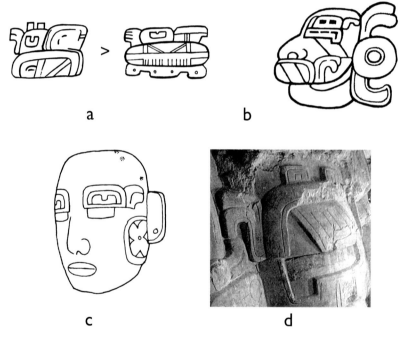

11.12. a) Early **AJAW** compounds on a Preclassic celt in the Dumbarton Oaks Collection and an Early Classic slate disk in the Jade Museum, Costa Rica No.6528 [here inset with **[PA']CHAN-na** "sky"] (drawings by David Mora-Marín); b) God C' head on San Bartolo Str.1 sub-1, North Wall (drawing by Heather Hurst); c) Greenstone figurine from Uaxactun (drawing after Linda Schele); d) Close-up of Cival Mask 2 (photograph in Estrada-Belli 2006:Fig.12a).

contexts where they must be read alone (e.g., Tikal Stela 31, J2 [Jones and Satterthwaite 1982: fig. 51]).

A further category of relevant epigraphic data comes from retrospective texts produced in the Classic era. For some time, epigraphers have been aware of limited references to dates and events from the Preclassic—some very remote and perhaps no more than legendary, others lying within the spans of the great centers such as El Mirador, and within striking distance of the "founders" of the Classic polities (Grube 2004; Grube and Martin 2001; Guenter 2005; Martin 1997; Stuart 2004a, 2004b). Some of the more notable of these appear at Copan and Pusilha, which both tie the 8.6.0.0.0 K'atun-ending of 159 CE to a character nicknamed "Foliated Ajaw" (Fig. 11.13a). He is associated with a place dubbed "Chi-Altar" on all occasions. These texts include what seem to be fully supernatural contexts painted on codex-style ceramics (Grube 2004:127–28). The Chi-Altar locale is also named in connection with dynastic founders at Yaxchilan and Tikal. Tikal mentions it again in association with the similarly named "Foliated Jaguar," the actor

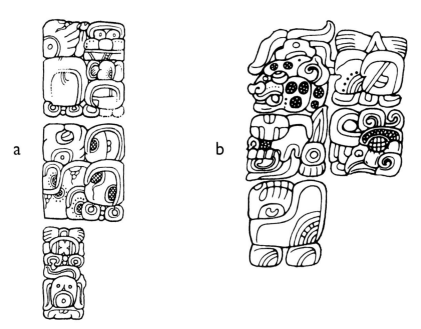

a

b

11.13. a) Foliated Ajaw on Copan Stela I (Drawing by Barbara Fash); b) Foliated Jaguar on Tikal Stela 31 (drawing by William Coe).

11.14. Celt in the Dumbarton oaks Collection, Washington DC (drawing by Linda Schele).

of an event, now lost, that fell before 8.14.0.0.0 or 317 CE (Fig. 11.13b). This same name appears on both an early celt and an "ancestral" belt ornament on an unprovenienced stela (Martin 2003:6–7), and it serves the same role on a celt now at Dumbarton Oaks (Fig. 11.14). An important historical text on the back of this stone is missing its upper part, but seems to describe a K'atun anniversary, although not one that can yet be fixed in time (Schele and Miller 1986:82–83).[14] We have no further leads on the location of Chi-Altar, but its absence from contemporary events in the Classic could be consistent with the idea that it was one of the great sites abandoned at the close of the Preclassic—El Mirador being an obvious, although not at all the only, candidate.

These references, falling at the very cusp of the Preclassic-Classic transition, bring us to a vital issue: the foundation of royal dynasties—sometimes viewed as *the* defining distinction between the two eras. Peter Mathews was the first to recognize the Classic "successor count" that was used to number polity rulers in sequence and trace their line back to a founder king (Mathews 1975; Riese 1984; Stuart and Schele 1986). In some cases foundations can be placed to a particular day; in others we can do no more than make estimates based on the length of the given sequence. Current evidence suggests that the Tikal dynasty, for example, was established around 90 CE—well within the Late Preclassic—enduring in fairly robust form until at least 794 CE, and probably rather later (Martin 2003:5, n.6; Martin and Grube 2000:27). The initial date sits well with archaeological evidence of a new momentum in construction activity at the site. Other starting points can be fixed at centers such as Copan and Palenque, in 427 and 431 CE respectively, and seem to reflect the belated expansion of the Classic system to "frontier" zones.

Yet it would be wrong to think that the farthest these counts take us is the 1st century CE or later. Naranjo, for example, puts the accession of its 35th king at 546 CE. Using an average of 22.5 years per reign—a figure derived from the dated sequences at Copan and Palenque, but one that also emerges from 881 years of British royal history (Martin 1997:853–54)—the start of the Naranjo dynasty would fall around 200 BCE. This could, of course, be a fictive claim, but there are Preclassic remains at Naranjo, and we know that near-neighbor Yaxha was an especially massive early site, so the archaeological antiquity of this region is not at issue. A greater objection would be the divine attributes of the founding king, who is associated with wildly different, extraordinarily ancient time frames. Even so, we see an emerging pattern in which dynastic founders were "more than mortal," and their identities could in some sense merge with the deities whose names they took—as suggested in the Copan case mentioned earlier. It is not uncommon for ancestors of special renown to be ascribed supernatural status by their successors and to be absorbed into a "state mythology" (see Proskouriakoff 1978:116–17; Houston and Stuart 1996:296).

Extended dynastic sequences are also claimed by Altar de Sacrificios, whose 36th king was in power in 633 CE (Graham 1972: fig. 27; Houston 2007b), and Tamarindito, whose 25th king ruled at some point between 698 and 726 CE (Houston 1993:114, fig. 4.17). Following the 22.5-year reign estimate that would take us to about 154 BCE and 158–186 CE respectively. One king list appears on a group of codex-style vessels produced ca. 700 CE that, at its longest, describes nineteen rulers of the "Snake" polity, each ascribed a full *k'uhul ajaw* emblem. Despite the presence of well-known royal names, their sequencing cannot be reconciled with the monument record of Calakmul or other sites that refer to "Snake" kings, and if real, the series must largely predate them. Using the aforementioned reign-length estimate, the list should constitute about 400 years of history and thus presumably intrudes into the Preclassic era (Martin 1997). Two sherds of codex-style pottery bearing this same list have recently been excavated in the main palace group at Calakmul (Martin, n.d.-b). The Late Classic court that commissioned these vessels must have viewed these characters as legitimate precursors who validated the position of their ruler and his regime.

Before moving on, brief mention should be made of a title carried by two of our putative Preclassic kings—Ruler 2 of the Kan dynasty and Foliated Jaguar of Chi-Altar—who are named as *kaloomte'*. This seems to have been a political rank above that of *ajaw* that was held only by the most powerful kings in the Classic era (at least until an evident debasement of royal titles occurred in the Terminal Classic). It has yet to be identified on a genuinely early monument, but if its placement in the Preclassic holds true it could have much to reveal about the early political system. During the Classic, holders of the *kaloomte'* title were overlords who integrated a system of early polities into loose hegemonies (Martin and Grube 2000), and the origin of this landscape might yet lie in earlier centuries.

It is hard to draw too many conclusions from the scanty and disparate remnants of Preclassic writing we currently have, although some themes do emerge. The presence of the *ajaw* glyph shows a degree of continuity between the Preclassic and Classic, and there is enough of a supporting context—in terms of accompanying rituals and regalia—to suggest that it was the same or very similar in character. The king's possession of "creation" and "darkness" shows the persistence of concepts regarding the ruler's manipulation of spiritual power. The duties and life events of kings, the celebration of K'atun endings and K'atun anniversaries, are described for the Preclassic and prefigure such ceremonies and notions of time in the Classic. Moreover, we may also need to consider the possibility that some royal dynasties reach back into Late Preclassic times, and that whatever else the Classic phenomenon represents, it might not be safe to take the inception of royal lines as its defining feature.

DISCUSSION: RELIGION, KINGSHIP, AND THE EARLY POLITY

It goes without saying that ancient societies, like the subjects of so many scientific endeavors, can never be seen, touched, or heard directly. Ideology must be counted among the most elusive of their features. Its nature can only be discerned by inference, by chasing the shadows and reflections of notions long disappeared. Having gathered some of the most relevant sources, what can we say about the guiding ideas behind Preclassic Maya society? What connections, if any, can we draw between ideology and the character of the polities that created and employed it?

The unity of representation and the consistency of content, across large tracts of territory and through extended periods of time, both argue for a coherent and well-embedded political philosophy by Late Preclassic times. It is equally clear that this emerged from interaction with neighboring cultures, although the degree to which autochthonous developments blended with imported ones is still unclear. The most prominent mythological subject, the Principal Bird Deity, was just as familiar to the users of Isthmian script at La Mojarra as it was to the users of Maya glyphs at San Bartolo. The rulers of Izapa, which may have straddled a linguistic and cultural border, would have had little difficulty in creating a multi-ethnic rhetoric on their monuments—everyone, it seems, spoke much the same ideological language.

But what does such ubiquity tell us? We still need a model to explain exactly why this character and its story resonated so deeply. Much of what we know, or think we know, emerges from the dialogue between the corpus of Precolumbian images and sections of the Popol Vuh.[15] To be sure, this document is no direct and unalloyed voice from antiquity; it strongly reflects the interests and agendas of its writers and the early Colonial culture of the 16th century. Yet used as a comparative source it has proved very productive in interpreting at least some earlier artworks and texts. We may see this again where a quite separate iconographic argument concerning the Shiner indicates that the Principal Bird Deity shone brightly like polished stone—just as described for Wuqub Kaqix.

We must return at this point to the central dichotomy of the Principal Bird Deity: his role as an enemy to be vanquished on the one hand, and his co-identity with the beneficent and lordly God D on the other. Authors have negotiated this problem in different ways, but no solution easily satisfies all the contexts required. Constance Cortez advances one of the more interesting views by equating the bird to a humbled prisoner or trophy, and his display on buildings with a permanent public record of the triumph of order over chaos. The defeated bird is in this manner: "a symbol of misplaced hubris…it is not the heroic bird that is worshipped, but rather the concept and image of the bird subjugated" (1986:72–73).

However, this view does not sit well with much that we see in Classic iconography, where the Principal Bird Deity often appears at the apex of the sky or, in one of its quadripartite forms, at the summit of a cosmic tree. In these instances it evidently takes an honored role in the cosmos and forms part of the stable world-order of present time. Here we might see the bird restored to the sky after its failure to usurp solar powers during the previous creation—which is where the Popol Vuh places the defeat of Wuqub Kaqix. The contrasting personas of the Principal Bird Deity would in this way be time-specific: one is the tyrant of a previous era, the other the reformed benefactor of the current one (Joel Skidmore, pers. comm. 2005). The great façade masks of the Preclassic would represent this second stage in the cycle, with the bird returned, but contained, in its proper celestial realm. The prime agent of this reversal is, of course, Juun Ajaw—the prototype for all earthly kings.

The early emphasis on these narratives could be rooted in the particular claims to power made by the first regimes. That Maya kings saw themselves as embodiments and replications of Juun Ajaw is widely acknowledged—the association between *ajaw* "lord" and *juun ajaw* "one lord" is plain enough, while the white paper headband is one of Juun Ajaw's main diagnostic features. It follows that the adventures of Juun Ajaw and his brother serve as a model for the "good king"—who, among other things, venerates his ancestors, plays ball, is clever and courageous, and is willing to sacrifice himself (see Coe 1989b). Defeating the solar imposter counts as one of his great triumphs in making the earth fit for humankind (Tedlock 1985), and it would not be surprising if kings portrayed themselves as like-in-kind victors over the great bird. The theme continued in the Classic, although now as only one among numerous religious allusions that served to reinforce the role of kings and kingship.

This takes us to the meaning of *ajaw*-ship in early polities and the second great challenge we face in understanding Preclassic ideology: to situate the ruler within his particular constellation of powers, privileges, and responsibilities. The royal portraits of the Classic, idealized and formulaic though they are, give us at least a simulacrum of the Maya king. In the Preclassic, by contrast, the king is barely glimpsed and herein lies much of the visceral disjunction we feel with the early period. Hammond (1991a:269) has suggested that the emergence of carved monuments with portraits and texts may be epiphenomenal to the emergence of the elites they promote—their inception little more, indeed, than a new rhetorical fashion. It is true that archaeology has not as yet found much in the way of Preclassic monuments with portraits and texts with dates in the lowlands—in contrast to the highlands and Pacific coast (see Chapter 7, this volume)—but perhaps only because they are relatively few in number and deeply buried. One unprovenienced stone of unknown date, now in the Ethnografisch Museum in Antwerp, Belgium, exhibits traits of Olmec-style and ranks among the earliest Maya monuments with a hieroglyph inscription (Boot 2006; Taube 2004:46) (Fig. 11.15).

David Freidel and Linda Schele were the first to develop an explicit historical model for the development of early Maya kingship (1988a, 1988b). In their analysis, the surge in social complexity that took place in the Late Preclassic was sparked by a redefinition of the *ajaw* office, which was re-

11.15. Stela in the Antwerp Museum (drawing Karl Taube).

quired to resolve mounting social contradictions. Formerly, the term had described an egalitarian group, a brotherhood of lords with charismatic, shamanic roles in the community. But under the influence of incipient dynasts from the highlands, it was transformed into a more hierarchical order that restricted access to the supernatural world of deities and deified ancestors. Yet these new *ajaw* still retained many of their old charismatic features and failed to develop a system of institutionalized descent. As cities became more populous and harder to control, this flaw caused a structural failure, producing the wider collapse of Late Preclassic society. The success of the Classic system lay in its deep regard for the hereditary principle.

This conjecture is bold and usefully stimulates debate, but is built on sparse data. The finds at San Bartolo alone dispute the notion that sophisticated developments in the lowlands required highland input. The spread of elite culture in the Preclassic from highlands to lowlands—often characterized in the transfer of the "stela cult"—has been a long-held assumption among Mayanists. While this model may yet prove to be true, there can be no doubt that the accessibility of rich Preclassic remains in the highlands—which are often unencumbered by later, overlying settlement—has been a major influence. Only when the deepest levels of more lowland sites have been explored will we get a firm sense in which direction ideas flowed, or to what degree profited from coeval development.

A fine example of the relatively pristine conditions of some highland sites is offered by the site of El Naranjo, just outside Guatemala City. Bárbara Arroyo (2010b) has recently investigated important Middle Preclassic remains there, which include an extensive ceremonial plaza equipped with long rows of plain, but often well-fashioned, stela-altar pairs. Arroyo hypothesizes that the stones are K'atun markers and thus precursors to the same system practiced in the Classic period (pers. comm. 2006). "Plain" monuments are a feature of all periods of Maya history, but the engraving of permanent portraits and texts on what seem once to have been anonymous time-markers could be seen as the "co-opting" of age-old ceremonial behavior by a new breed of kings. Chronologically oriented rites and ceremonies remained the dominant theme and purpose of monuments throughout the Classic (Stuart 1996, 2005), with kings using them to freeze and fix in the memory their own personal performance. However, this development clearly originates within the Late Preclassic, as both highland and lowland examples attest, and cannot be seen as a distinguishing feature of Classic culture.

The body of evidence concerning dynastic foundation in the Classic period is growing steadily, and we have at least a broad idea of royal self-definition in that period. The central component was not necessarily one of direct lineal descent from the founder. Such strict rules would surely break down in the volatile world of Maya militarism, and there is evidence that the "successor count" traverses ruptures in strict patrilineal descent (Martin 2003:29). This is not to question the importance of bloodline among Classic dynasts—but the lack of proper family trees makes it hard to chart the rules of legitimate succession. The essential feature more concerns the activation of a "kingship" in a particular place and in some ritually distinct manner.

It is this divinely sanctioned event that is in some sense embodied and perpetuated in the "emblem glyph."

This view differs somewhat from those who have taken this sanctity as a personal quality of kings, whose rites of initiation make them not simply the sole intermediary between gods and humankind, but elevates them to a quasi-divine status (e.g., Schele and Miller 1986:110). The "divine king" has been a feature of the landscape since the time of Frazer, although students of kingship have increasingly moved away from the concept. Today, most instances of the "king-as-living god" are seen as misreadings (see Feeley-Harnik 1985:276; Ray 1991:22–53). Some meaning, I suspect, lies in the almost total confinement of the "holy lord" epithet within emblem glyphs. There are very few examples outside this context, and they are mostly very late—as if the idea was taken up only when kings were reaching for more exalted descriptions of themselves, a phenomenon we see with the spread of once-restricted epithets at the end of the Late Classic. Thus, no ruler is crowned a *k'uhul ajaw* on his accession; he simply becomes an *ajaw*. This might support the idea that the subject of the "holiness" is more the kingship than the king.[16] The source of this divine sanction is most likely traced not to the blessing of a general pantheon or Supreme Being, but more directly to a tutelary deity or group of such deities. It is they who witness the king's accession, serve as his patrons in war, and receive his sacrifices (see Houston and Stuart 1996).

If these features were truly restricted to the Classic Maya, then the Preclassic was "pre-dynastic" and the *ajawo'ob* of that time achieved power outside a system of lineal descent and/or without the expressed sanction of the gods represented by the *k'uhul ajaw* title. I have already noted some cause to be cautious on these fronts, but the continuity in royal rituals like those exhibited at San Bartolo give further pause to wonder about so dramatic a change in practice and meaning between two eras. It is conceivable that the Preclassic hosted more than one political model and that early manifestations of "Classic-style" kingship were initially confined to a few major centers. Continuities in governmental system between the two eras have certainly been suggested before—although the present challenge is to discern the processes involved with more clarity and certainty than hitherto possible.

An important consequence of work in the 1980s was the shift to "kingship" as an object of analysis (e.g., Schele and Miller 1986; Freidel 1992; Freidel and Schele 1988a, 1988b; Stuart 1988; Schele and Freidel 1990). This offered a global comparative framework and largely sidestepped an on-going debate about the taxonomy of Maya polities—in short, whether one or the other should be designated a "chiefdom" or a "state," following the well-known developmental schema (Service 1962; Willey and Phillips 1958). This volume accepts the general character of Preclassic polities as "states" and does not concern itself with "neo-evolutionary" typologies of this kind (see Chapters 1 and 2, this volume). Yet we cannot entirely pass over this intellectual history, since it has had a significant impact on the perceived capabilities and organizational prowess of the early Maya polity, perhaps most notably in our view of El Mirador—the proverbial "elephant in the room" of the Preclassic.

If we are in the business of drawing inferences from disparities in the archaeological record (e.g., volumetric assessment, settlement density, and population assessments, with their implications for energetics and economic resources), then El Mirador's physical remains alone are testimony to its importance in the region (see Chapter 8, this volume). Those directing its fortunes succeeded in constructing a city larger than those built by the Maya in subsequent centuries (larger even, it is said, than the total building mass at Teotihuacan). They either motivated or compelled a labor-force from a wide area, or were sufficiently persuasive to achieve similar results with a local populace working over longer periods (or simply more intensively). However it was achieved, we are left with the paradox that the city with the biggest monumental architecture, set among a smaller and more dispersed regional population, is viewed by many scholars as developmentally inferior to the many less grandiose cities that followed it.[17] Is it facetious to wonder if the evolutionary trajectory should not be inverted, and the Classic seen as a devolved landscape inhabiting what had once been a rather grander territory? Before we go too far down this line of reasoning, it is well to remember that several other Preclassic giants lie in the forest barely touched by investigation—we still have much to learn about the basic landscape of this epoch.

FINAL REMARKS

What remains of our competing revolutionary and evolutionary paradigms? It is doubtful that descriptions of this kind can ever adequately capture the nature of a complex, multi-faceted phenomenon such as the Preclassic collapse and the subsequent development of Classic society. Each of many research questions might legitimately favor one perspective over the other and yet fail to capture the essence of the whole. There can be no question that there was a dramatic extirpation that left many large centers all but deserted—leaving many Classic societies to grow up around their ruins in the style of Medieval Romans, constantly aware of the relics of a fallen precursor. Political changes such as these were plainly revolutionary, but if we restrict the question to one of ideology, as we must, the boundary more closely resembles an evolutionary model.

The Principal Bird Deity did not disappear at the end of the Preclassic, but continued in its twin representations as a constituent of the great ruler of the sky and as a monster whose defeat was an essential prologue to humankind's appearance on earth. Its thematic dominance did decline, however, and the emphasis in imagistic and, perhaps, conceptual terms switched to God D over the course of the Classic (although this hybrid personality could be seen to be a feature of the complex from the very beginning). The regalia and rituals of lordship were consistent from at least 100 BCE onwards, and if the underlying nature and responsibilities of the *ajaw* changed, it is not visible in the iconographic record. The term *ajaw* itself was in use from at least the first part of the Late Preclassic onwards (400–200 BCE), although its specific sense in that single early example is currently unknown.

The continuity of these features across the transition to the Classic era suggests that whatever calamity sealed the fate of the great Preclassic cities, it did not lead to a wholesale rejection of their ideology. None of the major symbols of rulership were expunged, nor were the gods associated with kingly authority deserted in search of more efficacious alternatives. Classic kings remade themselves in the image of their forefathers, wore their crowns, underwent their rituals, and thought themselves imbued by the same procreative powers. The primary markers with which we isolate Classic elite culture were all developed in the Late Preclassic. More uncertain is the evidence for dynastic rule and sacred kingship in the Preclassic. Some data is suggestive, but all of it falls short of proof. Yet, even if "holy lords" were indeed restricted to the Classic, the material to hand indicates that their emergence was not heralded by a radically different inventory of rites, ceremonies, and symbols.

The fragile political structure some envisage for the Late Preclassic seems hard to reconcile with the tremendous physical achievements in constructing centers like El Mirador, as well as their substantial period of occupation. Could so massive a phenomenon as El Mirador go unremarked in the inscriptions of later centuries? Given the great interest shown by Classic kings in historical precedents and sources of ancient power, it would be surprising if so. However, history does not, in any real sense, yet exist for the Preclassic. We can only hope that the scattered clues we have, together with fortuitous discoveries in the field, will one day coalesce into some more substantial understanding. San Bartolo stands as a cautionary reminder of how one totally unexpected find can transform our understanding. It tells us so much only because we know so little.

ENDNOTES

11.1. This motif appears in the Oxtotitlan painting, although it is more clearly seen on La Venta Monument 80, where the body of the serpent is visually compared to a rope (Taube 1996b:93, fig. 13f).

11.2. This character was first identified by David Stuart, who initially called it the "God C-Sun God," before devising the "Shiner" name (1988:201–3, pers. comm. 2007). The same motif has been read *tzuk* (Freidel, Schele, and Parker 1993:140, 432), although this stems from a misunderstanding of its use in phonetic spellings (where a gourd combined with the Shiner serves as the syllable **tzu**—derived from *tzuh* "gourd"). In the Early Classic the glyph **K'UH** "god" (God C) is embellished with attributes of the Shiner (e.g., Schele 1985: fig. 4a), with rare examples recurring in the Late Classic (e.g., Stuart 1988: fig. 5.30b). In Preclassic art it appears as a façade mask in its own right— as at Cerros and Cival—and, again, this sometimes reappears in the Late Classic, for example as a balustrade at Pomona (Estrada-Belli 2006a; Saturno, Taube and Stuart 2005a:38–41;Taube 2007).

11.3. A more fragmentary adobe version is also seen at Kaminaljuyu (Guernsey 2006), while it appears on stone monuments at El Mirador, Izapa, Kaminaljuyu, Takalik Abaj, Palo Gordo, Monte Alto (Guernsey 2006; Hansen 1991, 1992a; Reese 1996; Lowe, Lee, and Martinez 1982).

11.4. The mythic model for this name is set out in more detail on the façade of the Margarita structure, an earlier version of Copan Structure 16 now buried beneath Rosalila (Bell, Canuto, and Sharer 2004: plate 2b). It features a sky-band with a large inverted sky-serpent, to which Chaak clings, holding a fiery lightning axe, also facing down. The center of the composition presents a pair of entwined birds, a quetzal and a macaw, equipped with serpent-head wings and god faces in their mouths (in this case clearly sun gods). Elsewhere, these same birds sport supernatural wings and the distinctive jewels of the Principal Bird Deity, giving good grounds to believe that they represent aspects or avatars of the great god (see Fields and Reents-Budet 2005b:217; Hellmuth 1987: fig. 31). Widely taken to be an embodied hieroglyph naming the Copan founder K'inich Yax K'uk Mo', or "Radiant First Quetzal Macaw"—whose tomb lies at the base of Structure 16—there is reason to believe that the Margarita scene portrays some myth from which the Copan king's name was derived (Martin 2006a). The same or a closely similar theme appears on the Late Preclassic stucco façade of Calakmul Structure Sub-II (Carrasco 2005; Carrasco and Colón 2005; Carrasco and Rodríquez 2003), where we also find a surrounding sky-band, falling Chaak, and two versions of the Principal Bird Deity with deity heads in its mouths.

11.5. The latter noted in Hansen 1992a:138.

11.6. The remains of the putative claw are small, but match the yellow color of the bird deity, with more similarity to the narrow feet of Individuals 2 and 4 rather than to the heavily taloned Individuals 8 and 10, with the greatest resemblance to those of the "dead" bird (Taube et al. 2010: fig. 7, fig. 12).

11.7. To choose a few among many examples, we see the Principal Bird Deity as a headdress on Tikal Stela 31 (Jones and Satterthwaite 1982: fig. 51c), Quirigua Monument 26 (Jones 1983), and Caracol Stela 16 (Beetz and Satterthwaite 1981: fig. 15a).

11.8. A fine depiction of God D in his dual personality of the elderly God N and the Principal Bird Deity appears on the lid of an Early Classic blackware vessel (see Hellmuth 1987; Fields and Reents-Budet 2005:147). The old man sits on a motif that resembles a flower or sun sign.

11.9. Judgments here are necessarily subjective. I have chosen to exclude a number of well-known early texts that appear to come from the Protoclassic—a nebulous period that more properly belongs to the initial stages of the Early Classic than the last throes of the Late Preclassic.

11.10. The term also appears in some supernatural names and titles during the Classic period (such as the name of the Hero Twin *Juun Ajaw* or the Sun God *K'inich Ajaw*).

11.11. There is also an *ik hu'un* "black paper" band that serves a similar function but may have a different significance (Stuart 2004a).

11.12. The first of these is probably related to those cases where the bird wears a trefoil diadem, as on the upper façades at Cerros.

11.13. Proskouriakoff (1960:455) first linked "niche" scenes to accession ceremonies on the monuments of Piedras Negras—although their distinctive feature is really a "cosmic throne" that features the celestial starry crocodile and, at times, a ladder ascending its stepped dias. A debate has since arisen as to whether these scenes depict royal accessions or instead calendrical period-ending ceremonies. Piedras Negras Stela 6 presents this theme in conjunction with a text recording the "first" period-ending event for Ruler 3 (Stuart and Graham 2003:36), while Stela 11 shows the enthroned ruler holding an incense bag inscribed with the day of the appropriate period ending commemorated in its text (see Taube et al. 2010: fig. 40a, b). On the other hand, Piedras Negras Stela 33 (Maler 1901: plate 26) is directly acccompanied by a text dated to the inauguration of Ruler 2, which appears to caption the scene, unlike a much smaller text, placed lower in the scene, that records the period ending.

11.14. The phrase concerned seems to anticipate an anniversary with **TZUTZ-ma U?**-"K'atun" *tzutz-[j]-oom u-?* "he will end his K'atun" (see Houston 2004:305). The Dumbarton Oaks celt also features an early *ajaw* sign with a "God C variant" brow motif. In a standard formula the polity or dynasty name should precede it, but here it is badly effaced. The visible portion is not inconsistent with the Chi-Altar compound, but we can go no further than that. A better candidate for the Chi-Altar term on a portable jade object comes from the jade figurine now in the Yale University Art Gallery (Coe 1973b:25). Here at A7-B7 we see a hand and an indented sign that vaguely resembles the "altar" glyph. David Mora-Marín's rendering shows a probable **ji** sign that functions as a complement to the "altar" glyph elsewhere (Mora-Marín 2001: fig. 23).

11.15. There are other, Classic-era images that depict the battle between Juun Ajaw/Hunahpu and the great bird (Stone 1983; Coe 1989b; Guernsey 2006).

11.16. Maya rulers certainly underwent transforming rites that set them apart from their people and invested them with special powers and responsibilities. Yet this is some distance short of the "living god" conjectured by some authors.

11.17. It has been interpreted as the capital of a "state" by some (e.g., Matheny 1986a; Sharer 1992) and as a "chiefdom" by others (e.g., Blanton, Feinman, Kowalewski and Peregrine 1996; Marcus 1983b, 2003).

References

Abrams, Elliot M. 1987. Economic Specialization and Construction Personnel in Classic Period Copan, Honduras. *American Antiquity* 52(3): 485–99.

———. 1994. *How the Maya Built Their World: Energetics and Ancient Architecture*. Austin, TX: University of Texas Press.

Abu-Lughod, Janet L. 1991. *Before European Hegemony: The World System A.D. 1250–1350*. New York, NY: Oxford University Press.

Adams, Richard E.W., ed. 1977. *The Origins of Maya Civilization*. Albuquerque, NM: University of New Mexico Press.

———. 1970. Suggested Classic Period Occupational Specialization in the Southern Maya Lowlands. In *Monographs and Papers in Maya Archaeology*, ed. William R. Bullard Jr., pp. 489–98. Papers of the Peabody Museum of Archaeology and Ethnology, vol. 61. Cambridge, MA: Peabody Museum of Archaeology and Ethnology, Harvard University.

———. 1971. *The Ceramics of Altar de Sacrificios, Guatemala*. Peabody Museum of Archaeology and Ethnology Papers, 63(1). Cambridge, MA: Peabody Museum of Archaeology and Ethnology, Harvard University.

———. 1986. Río Azul: Lost City of the Maya. *National Geographic Magazine* 169(4): 420–51.

———. 1999. *Río Azul: An Ancient Maya City*. Norman, OK: University of Oklahoma Press.

Adams, Richard E.W., and T. Patrick Culbert. 1977. Origins of Civilization in the Maya Lowlands. In *The Origins of Maya Civilization*, ed. Richard E.W. Adams, pp. 3–24. Albuquerque, NM: University of New Mexico Press.

Adams, Richard E.W., and Richard C. Jones. 1981. Spatial Patterns and Regional Growth Among Classic Maya Cities. *American Antiquity* 46:301–22.

Adams, Richard E.W., and Woodruff D. Smith. 1981. Feudal Models for Classic Maya Civilization. In *Lowland Maya Settlement Patterns*, ed. Wendy Ashmore, pp. 335–49.

Albuquerque, NM: University of New Mexico Press.

Adams, Robert McC. 1966. *The Evolution of Urban Society: Early Mesopotamia and Prehispanic Mexico*. Chicago, IL: Aldine.

———. 2000. Scale and Complexity in Archaic States. Review of *Archaic States*, Gary M. Feinman and Joyce Marcus, eds. *Latin American Antiquity* 11(2): 187–93.

Agrinier, Pierre. 1964. *The Archaeological Burials at Chiapa de Corzo and Their Furniture*. Papers of the New World Archaeological Foundation, No. 16. Provo, UT: New World Archaeological Foundation, Brigham Young University.

———. 1970. *Mound 20, Mirador, Chiapas, Mexico*. Papers of the New World Archaeological Foundation, No. 28. Provo, UT: New World Archaeological Foundation, Brigham Young University.

———. 1975. Un Complejo Cerámico, Tipo Olmeca, del Preclásico Temprano en El Mirador, Chiapas. In *Balance y Perspectiva de la Antropología de Mesoamérica y el Norte de México*. 2:21–34. Sociedad Mexicana de Antropología.

———. 1984. *The Early Olmec Horizon of Mirador, Chiapas, Mexico*. Papers of the New World Archaeological Foundation, No. 48. Provo, UT: New World Archaeological Foundation, Brigham Young University.

———. 2000. *Mound 27 and the Middle Preclassic Period at Mirador, Chiapas, Mexico*. Papers of the New World Archaeological Foundation, No. 58. Provo, UT: New World Archaeological Foundation, Brigham Young University.

———. 1989. Mirador-Plumajillo, Chiapas, y Sus Relaciones con Cuatro Sitios del Horizonte Olmeca de Veracruz, Chiapas y la Costa de Guatemala. *Arqueología* 2:19–36.

———. 2013. *Mound 1 at Ocozocoautla, Chiapas, Mexico*. Papers of the New World Archaeological Foundation, No. 76. Provo, UT: New World Archaeological Foundation, Brigham Young University.

Agrinier, Pierre, David Cheetham, and Gareth W. Lowe. 2000. Appendix 1: Three Early Ceramic Complexes from Miramar, Chiapas, Mexico. In *Mound 27 and the Middle Preclassic Period at Mirador, Chiapas, Mexico*, ed. Pierre Agrinier, pp. 177–214. Papers of the New World Archaeological Foundation, No. 58. Provo, UT: New World Archaeological Foundation, Brigham Young University.

Agrinier, Pierre, and Gareth W. Lowe. 1960. The Mound 1 Tombs and Burials. In *Mound 1, Chiapa de Corzo, Chiapas, Mexico*, ed. Gareth W. Lowe and Pierre Agrinier, pp. 39–54. Papers of the New World Archaeological Foundation, No. 8. Provo, UT: New World Archaeological Foundation, Brigham Young University.

Agurcia F., Ricardo. 1977. Playa de los Muertos Figurines. M.A. thesis, Department of Anthropology, Tulane University.

————. 2004. Rosalila, Temple of the Sun-King. In *Understanding Early Classic Copan*, ed. Ellen E. Bell, Marcello A. Canuto, and Robert J. Sharer, pp. 101–111. Philadelphia, PA: University of Pennsylvania Museum of Archaeology and Anthropology.

Aimers, James J., Terry G. Powis, and Jaime J. Awe. 2000. Prehistoric Round Structures in the Upper Belize River Valley. *Latin American Antiquity* 11(1): 71–86.

Anderson, David S. 2011. Xtobo, Yucatan, Mexico, and the Emergent Preclassic of the Northern Maya Lowlands. *Ancient Mesoamerica* 22:301–22.

Andrews, Anthony, and Fernando Robles Castellanos. 2004. An Archaeological Survey of Northwest Yucatan, Mexico. *Mexicon* 26(1): 7–14.

Andrews, E. Wyllys V. 1965. *Progress Report of the 1960–1964 Field Seasons, National Geographic Society-Tulane University Dzibilchaltun Program*. Middle American Research Institute. New Orleans, LA: Tulane University.

————. 1990. The Early Ceramic History of the Lowland Maya. In *Vision and Revision in Maya Studies*, ed. Flora S. Clancey and Peter D. Harrison, pp. 1–19. Albuquerque, NM: University of New Mexico Press.

Andrews, E. Wyllys V., George J. Bey, and Christopher Gunn. 2008. Rethinking the Early Ceramic History of the Northern Maya Lowlands: New Evidence and Interpretations. Paper presented at the 74th Annual Meeting of the Society for American Archaeology, Vanucouver, B.C.

Andrews, E. Wyllys V., and Norman Hammond. 1990. Redefinition of the Swasey Phase at Cuello, Belize. *American Antiquity* 55(3): 570–84.

Andrews, E. Wyllys V., and William M. Ringle. 1992. Los Mayas Tempranos en Yucatan: Investigaciones Arqueológicas en Komchen. *Mayab* 8:5–17.

Andrews, George F. 1995. *Pyramids and Palaces, Monsters and Masks: The Golden Age of Maya Architecture. The Collected Works of George F. Andrews*. Lancaster, CA: Labyrinthos.

Arensberg, Conrad M. 1961. The Community as Object and as Sample. *American Anthropologist* 63:241–64.

Argyle, J. Craig. 2010. Lost Paneles y Rasgos Asociados al Manejo de Agua en la Gran Acropolis de El Mirador: Operación 610-O. In *Exploraciones Arqueológicas en la Cuenca Mirador*, ed. Héctor E. Mejía, Richard D. Hansen, and Edgar Suyuc-Ley, pp. 539–56. Report filed with the Instituto de Antropología e Historia, Guatemala. Proyecto Cuenca Mirador. Idaho State University: Foundation for Anthropological Research and Environmental Studies (FARES).

Argyle, J. Craig, and Richard D. Hansen. 2010. La Cosmovisión de Estuco: Los Paneles Estucados del Sistema Hidráulico del Mirador. In *La Cosmovisión a Través del Tiempo: Tres Mil Anos de Historia Maya*. III Convención Mundial de Arquelogia

Maya, 2010. Casa Convento Concepcion, Antigua, Guatemala. 18–20 Junio, 2010.

———. 2016. The Preclassic Frieze of the Great Central Acropolis at El Mirador: Resource Allocation and Myth Recounted in Stucco. In *2016 Mirador: Research and Conservation in the Ancient Kaan Kingdom*, ed. Richard D. Hansen and Edgar Suyuc, pp. 131–52. Corporacion Litografica, Guatemala: Foundation for Anthropological Research and Environmental Studies (FARES).

Arieta, Virginia. 2009. Densidad Poblacional Olmeca: El Caso de una Terraza Doméstica en San Lorenzo, Veracruz. M.A. thesis, Facultad de Filosofia y Lestras, Universidad Nacional Autónoma de México, México.

Arnold, Jeanne E. 1993. Labor and the Rise of Complex Hunter-Gatherers. *Journal of Anthropological Archaeology* 12:75–119.

Arnold, Philip J., III. 1995. Ethnicity, Pottery and the Gulf Olmec of Ancient Veracruz, Mexico. *The Biblical Archaeologist* 58(4): 191–99.

———. 2003. Early Formative Pottery from the Tuxtla Mountains and Implications for Gulf Olmec Origins. *Latin American Antiquity* 14(1): 29–46.

Arqueología Mexicana. 2001. Hallazgo de un Altar Olmeca, El Marquesillo, Veracruz. *Arqueología Mexicana* 54:15.

Arroyo, Bárbara, ed. 2010. *Entre Cerros, Cafetales, y Urbanismo en el Valle de Guatemala: Proyecto de Rescate Naranjo*. Academia de Geografia e Historia de Guatemala, Publicación Especial No. 47. Guatemala: Serviprensa.

———. 2006. Proyecto Arqueológico de Rescate Naranjo: Informe Final. Guatemala: Departamento de Monumentos Prehispánicos y Coloniales, Instituto de Antropología e Historia.

———. 2007. Informe Final: Proyecto Arqueológico de Rescate Naranjo. Report submitted to the Dirección General del Patrimonio Cultural y Natural, Guatemala City.

———. 2010a. Descripción del Sitio y Excavaciones. In *Entre Cerros, Cafetales, y Urbanismo en el Valle de Guatemala: Proyecto de Rescate Naranjo*, ed. Bárbara Arroyo, pp. 35–56. Publicación Especial No. 47. Academia de Geografia e Historia de Guatemala: Guatemala City.

———. 2010b. Monumentos. In *Entre Cerros, Cafetales, y Urbanismo en el Valle de Guatemala: Proyecto de Rescate Naranjo*, ed. Bárbara Arroyo, pp. 57–101. Publicación Especial No. 47. Academia de Geografia e História de Guatemala: Guatemala City.

Arroyo, Bárbara, and Lorena Paiz. 2010. Cerámica. In *Entre Cerros, Cafetales, y Urbanismo en el Valle de Guatemala: Proyecto de Rescate Naranjo*, ed. Bárbara Arroyo, pp. 103–83. Publicación Especial No. 47. Academia de Geographia e História de Guatemala: Guatemala City.

Arroyo, Bárbara, Karen Pereira, Margarita Cossich, Lorena Paiz, Edgar Arévalo, Mónica De León, Carlos Alvarado, and Fabiola Quiroa. 2007. Proyecto de rescate Naranjo: Nuevos datos del Preclásico en el valle de Guatemala. In *XX Simposio de Investigaciones Arqueológicas en Guatemala, 2006*, ed. Juan Pedro Laporte, Bárbara Arroyo, and Hector E. Mejía, pp. 861–74. Guatemala: Ministerio de Cultura y Deportes, Instituto de Antropología e Historia, Asociación Tikal, y Fundación Arqueológica del Nuevo Mundo.

Ashmore, Wendy A. 1981. Some Issues in Method and Theory in Lowland Maya Settlement Archaeology. In *Lowland Maya Settlement Patterns*, ed. Wendy Ashmore, pp. 37–70. Albuquerque, NM: University of New Mexico Press.

Aveni, Anthony F., Anne S. Dowd, and Benjamin Vining. 2003. Maya Calendar Reform? Evidence from Orientations of Specialized Architectural Assemblages. *Latin American Antiquity* 14(2): 159–78

Avíles, María. 2000. The Archaeology of Early Formative Chalcatzingo, Morelos. Report submitted to the Foundation for the Advancement of Mesoamerican Studies, Crystal River, FL. http://www.famsi.org/reports/94047/index.html, accessed April 2007.

Awe, Jaime. 1992. Dawn in the Land Between the Rivers: Formative Occupation at Cahal Pech, Belize and Its Implications for Preclassic Development in the Maya Lowlands. Ph.D. diss., Institute of Archaeology, University College, London.

Bachand, Bruce R., and Lynneth Lowe. 2011. Chiapa de Corzo y los Olmecas. *Arqueología Mexicana* 107:74–83.

Baines, John, and Norman Yoffee. 1998. Order, Legitimacy and Wealth in Ancient Egypt and Mesopotamia. In *Archaic States*, ed. Gary M. Feinman and Joyce Marcus, pp. 199–260. Santa Fe, NM: School of American Research Press.

Balcarcel, Beatriz. 1999. Excavaciones en Residencias Preclásicas de Nakbe, Peten. In *XII Simposio de Investigaciones Arqueológicas en Guatemala, 1988*, ed. Juan Pedro Laporte, Hector L. Escobedo, and Ana Claudia Monzón de Suasnávar, pp. 337–51. Guatemala: Ministerio de Cultura y Deportes, Instituto de Antropología e Historia, Asociación Tikal.

Balcarcel, Beatriz, and Francisco Lopez. 2001. Excavaciones y Rescate de la Estructura 1 de La Florida, Peten. Paper presented at the 15th Simposio de Investigaciones Arqueologicas, Guatemala City, July 16–20.

———. 2002. Excavaciones y rescate de la Estructura 1, La Florida, Peten. In *Investigaciones Arqueológicas y Ecológicas en la Cuenca Mirador: Rescate y Excavaciones en el sitio La Florida: Informe Final de la Temporada 2001–2002*, ed. Richard D. Hansen and Edgar O. Suyuc-Ley, pp. 60–120. Guatemala: Departamento de Monumentos

Prehispánicos y Coloniales, Instituto de Anthropología e Historia.

Balcarcel, Beatriz, Francisco Lopez, and Silvia Alvarado. 2004. Excavaciones en el sitio La Muerta, Grupo Laberinto, Peten, Guatemala. In *Investigación, Conservación y Desarrollo en El Mirador, Peten, Guatemala: Informe Final de la Temporada 2003*, ed. Richard D Hansen and Edgar Suyuc-Ley, pp. 321–411. Guatemala: Departamento de Monumentos Prehispánicos y Coloniales, Instituto de Antropología e Historia.

Balcarcel, Beatriz, Stephanie Schrodt, Richard D. Hansen, and Gustavo Martinez. 2010. El Ultimo Suspiro Ceramico del Preclásico Tardio en la Zona Cultural Mirador. In *XXIII Simposio de Investigaciones Arqueológias en Guatemala. 2009*, ed. Bárbara Arroyo, Adriana Linares Palma, and Lorena Paiz Aragón, pp. 1125–40. Museo Nacional de Arquelogia y Etnologia, Ministerio de Cultura y Deportes, Instituto de Antropología e Historia, Asociación Tikal.

Balkansky, Andrew K. 1999. Settlement Pattern Studies in the Mixteca Alta, Oaxaca, 1966–1996. In *Settlement Pattern Studies in the Americas: Fifty Years since Viru*, ed. Brian R. Billman and Gary M. Feinman, pp. 191–202. Washington, DC: Smithsonian Institution Press.

Ball, Joseph W. 1977. Rise of the Northern Maya Chiefdoms: A Socioprocessual Analysis. In *The Origins of Maya Civilization*, ed. Richard E.W. Adams, pp. 101–32. Albuquerque, NM: University of New Mexico Press.

———. 1993. Pottery, Potters, Palaces, and Polities: Some Socioeconomic and Political Implications of Late Classic Maya Ceramic Industries. In *Lowland Maya Civilization in the 8th Century A.D.*, ed. Jeremy A. Sabloff and John Henderson, pp. 243–72. Washington, DC: Dumbarton Oaks Research Library and Collection.

Ball, Joseph W., and Jennifer T. Taschek. 2003. Reconsidering the Belize Valley Preclassic: A Case for Multiethnic Interactions in the Development of a Regional Culture Tradition. *Ancient Mesoamerica* 14(2): 179–217.

Bandy, Matthew S. 2004. Fissioning, Scalar Stress, and Social Evolution in Early Village Societies. *American Anthropologist* 106(2): 322–33.

Barba de Piña Chan, Beatriz. 1956. Tlapacoya: un sitio preclásico de transición. *Acta Antropológica* 1:1. México, DF: Escuela Nacional de Antropología e Historia.

Bardawil, Lawrence W. 1976. Principal Bird Deity in Maya Art: An Iconographic Study of Form and Meaning. In *The Art, Iconography, and Dynastic History of Palenque. Proceedings of the Segunda Mesa Redonda de Palenque, December 14–21, 1974*, ed. Merle Greene Robertson, pp. 195–210. Pebble Beach, CA: Robert Louis Stevenson School, Pre-Columbian Art Research.

Barge, Meghan. 2012. Vertebrate Consumption and Feasting at La Blanca, Guatemala. M.A. thesis, Dept. of Anthropology, California State University, Northridge.

Barrera Vásquez, Alfredo. 1980. *Diccionario Maya Cordemex. Mérida*, Yucatan, Mexico: Ediciones Cordemex.

Barrett, Jason W. 2004. Construction Hierarchy Through Entitlement: Inequality in Lithic Resource Access among the Ancient Maya of Blue Creek, Belize. Ph.D. diss., Dept. of Anthropology, Texas A&M University.

———. 2006. Rethinking Long-Distance Exchange and the Economic Interdependence of Maya Sites During the Late Preclassic Period: The View from Northern Belize. *Research Reports in Belizean Archaeology* 3:113–28.

Barrett, Jason W., and Thomas H. Guderjan. 2006. An Ancient Maya Dock and Dam at Blue Creek, Rio Hondo, Belize. *Latin American Antiquity* 17(2): 227–39.

Barrientos Q., Tomás. 1997a. Desarrollo Evolutivo del Sistema de Canales Hidráulicos en Kaminaljuyu, Guatemala. Tesis de Licenciatura, Departamento de Arqueología, Universidad del Valle de Guatemala, Guatemala.

———. 1997b. Evolución tecnológica del sistema de canales hidráulicos en Kaminaljuyu y sus implicaciones socio-políticas. In *X Simposio de Investigaciones Arqueológicas en Guatemala*, ed. Juan Pedro Laporte and Hector L. Escobedo, pp. 61–69. Guatemala: Museo Nacional de Arqueología y Etnología.

———. 1999. Interpretación Para Una Sociedad Hidráulica en Kaminaljuyú Miraflores. *U Tz'ib* 2:16–23.

———. 2000. Kaminaljuyu: ¿Una Sociedad Hidráulica? In *XIII Simposio de Investigaciones Arqueológicas en Guatemala*, ed. Juan Pedro Laporte, Hector L. Escobedo, Ana Claudia Monzón de Suasnávar, and Bárbara Arroyo, pp. 29–55. Guatemala: Ministerio de Cultura y Deportes, Instituto de Antropología e Historia, Asociación Tikal.

Barthel, Thomas S. 1968. El Complejo 'Emblema'. *Estudios de Cultura Maya* 7:159–93.

Bassie, Karen. 2002. Maya Creator Gods. *Mesoweb*, http://www.mesoweb.com/features/bassie/CreatorGods/CreatorGods.pdf, accessed April 2007.

Bathgate, David. 1980. Cultural-Ecological Adaptation at Santa Marta (Tr-19): A Preclassic Village in the Upper Grijalva Basin, Chiapas, Mexico. M.A. thesis, Dept. of Anthropology, Brigham Young University.

Bauer, Jeremy. 2005a. El Pasado Preclásico y Monumental de Holmul: Resultados de las Temporadas de Excavación 2003 y 2004 en Cival, Peten. In *XVII Simposio de Investigaciones Arqueológicas en Guatemala*, ed. Juan Pedro Laporte, Bárbara Arroyo, Hector Escobedo, and Héctor Mejía, pp. 201–14. Ministerio de Cultura y Deporte: Guatemala City.

———. 2005b. Between Heaven and Earth: The Cival Cache and the Creation of the Mesoamerican Cosmos. In *Lords of Creation: The Origins of Sacred Maya Kingship*, ed. Virginia M. Fields and Dorie Reents-Budet, pp. 28–29. Los Angeles County Museum of Art. Scala Publishers: London.

Baus, Carolyn, and Patricia Ochoa. 1989. El Estilo Tlatilco y su Relacion con el Occidente de Mexico. In *El Preclásico o Formativo: Avances y Perspectivas*, ed. Martha Carmona Macias, pp. 319–32. México, DF: Museo Nacional de Antropología, Instituto Nacional de Antropología e Historia.

Beach, Timothy, Nicholas Dunning, Sheryl Luzzader-Beach, D.E. Cook, and Jon Lohse. 2006. Ancient Maya Impacts on Soils and Soil Erosion. *Catena* 66(2): 166–78.

Beach, Timothy, Shery Luzzader-Beach, Nicholas Dunning, and Duncan Cook. 2008. Human and Natural Impacts on Fluvial and Karst Systems of the Maya Lowlands. *Geomorphology* 101(1-2):308–331.

Beals, Ralph L. 1932. Unilateral Organizations in Mexico. *American Anthropologist* 34(3): 467–75.

Beauchamp, William M. 1898. Wampum Used in Council and as Currency. *American Antiquarian* 20(1): 1–13.

———. 1901. Wampum and Shell Articles Used by the New York Indians. *New York State Museum Bulletin* 41(8): 319–480.

Becker, Marshall J. 1979. Priests, Peasants, and Ceremonial Centers: The Intellectual History of a Model. In *Maya Archaeology and Ethnohistory*, ed. Norman Hammond and Gordon R. Willey, pp. 3–20. Austin: University of Texas Press.

Beetz, Carl P., and Linton Satterthwaite. 1981. *The Monuments and Inscriptions of Caracol, Belize*. University Museum Monograph 45. Philadelphia, PA: University Museum, University of Pennsylvania.

Bell, Ellen E., Marcello A. Canuto, and Robert J. Sharer, eds. 2004. *Understanding Early Classic Copan*. Philadelphia, PA: University of Pennsylvania Museum of Archaeology and Anthropology.

Bell, Ellen E., Robert J. Sharer, Loa P. Traxler, David W. Sedat, Christine W. Carrelli, and Lynn A. Grant. 2004. Tombs and Burials in the Early Classic Acropolis at Copan. In *Understanding Early Classic Copan*, ed. Ellen E. Bell, Marcello A. Canuto, and Robert J. Sharer, pp. 131–58. Philadelphia, PA: University of Pennsylvania Museum of Archaeology and Anthropology.

Bennyhoff, James A. 1966. Chronology and Periodization: Continuity and Change in the Teotihuacan Ceramic Tradition. In *Teotihuacan: Onceava Mesa Redonda*, pp. 19–29. México: Sociedad Mexicana de Antropología.

Benson, Elizabeth, ed. 1968. *Dumbarton Oaks Conference on the Olmec*. Washington, DC: Dumbarton Oaks Research Library and Collections.

Berlin, Heinrich. 1946. Archaeological Excavations in Chiapas. *American Antiquity* 21:19–28.

———. 1951. Breves Estudios Arqueologicos: El Peten, Guatemala. *Antropología e Historia de Guatemala* 3(2): 1–8.

———. 1958a. El Glifo 'Emblema' en las Inscripciones Mayas. *Journal de la Societé des Americanistes* 47:111–19.

———. 1958b. El Asiento de Chiapa. *Anales de la Sociedad de Geografía e Historia* 31:19–33.

Bernal, Ignacio. 1969. *The Olmec World*, trans. Doris Heydon and Fernando Horcasitas. Berkeley, CA: University of California Press.

Bernal-García, María Elena. 1994. Tzatza: Olmec Mountains and the Ruler's Ritual Speech. In *Seventh Palenque Roundtable, 1989,* ed. Merle Greene Robertson and Virginia Fields, pp. 113–24. San Francisco, CA: The Pre-Columbian Art Research Institute.

Beverido Pereau, Francisco. 1970. San Lorenzo Tenochtitlán y la Civilización Olmeca. M.A. thesis, Facultad de Antropología, Universidad Veracruzana.

———. 1987. Breve Historia de la Arqueología Olmeca. *La Palabra y el Hombre* 64:161–94.

Binford, Lewis R. 1971. Mortuary Practices: Their Study and Their Potential. In *Approaches to the Social Dimension of Mortuary Practices*, James A. Brown, pp. 6–29. Memoirs of the Society for American Archaeology, No. 25. Washington, DC: Society for American Archaeology.

Bishop, Ronald. n.d. Neutron Activation Studies on Middle Preclassic Figurines, Nakbe, Guatemala. Archived material, Rupert, ID: Foundation for Anthropological Research & Environmental Studies.

Blake, Michael. 1991. An Emerging Early Formative Chiefdom at Paso de La Amada, Chiapas, Mexico. In *The Formation of Complex Society in Southeastern Mesoamerica*, ed. William R. Fowler, pp. 27–46. Boca Raton, FL: CRC Press.

———. 2011. Building History in Domestic and Public Space at Paso de la Amada: An Examination of Mounds 6 and 7. In *Early Mesoamerican Social Transformations: Archaic and Formative Lifeways in the Soconusco Region,* ed. Richard G. Lesure, pp. 97–18. Berkley: University of California Press.

Blake, Michael, Brian S. Chisholm, John E. Clark, Barbara Voorhies, and Michael W. Love. 1992. Prehistoric Subsistence in the Soconusco Region. *Current Anthropology* 33:83–94.

Blake, Michael, John E. Clark, Barbara Voorhies, George Michaels, Michael W. Love, Mary E. Pye, Arthur Demarest, and Bárbara Arroyo. 1995. Revised Chronology for the Late Archaic and Formative Periods on the Pacific Coast of Southeastern Mesoamerica. *Ancient Mesoamerica* 6:161–83.

Blanton, Richard E., Gary M. Feinman, Stephen A. Kowalewski, and Linda M. Nicholas. 1999. *Ancient Oaxaca*. New York, NY: Cambridge University Press.

Blanton, Richard E., Gary M. Feinman, Stephen A. Kowalewski, and Peter N. Peregrine. 1996. A Dual-Processual Theory for the Evolution of Mesoamerican Civilization. *Current Anthropology* 37(1): 1–14.

Blanton, Richard E., Stephen A. Kowalewski, Gary Feinman, and Jill Appel, eds. 1981. *Ancient Mesoamerica: A Comparison of Change in Three Regions*. New York, NY: Cambridge University Press.

Blanton, Richard E., Stephen A. Kowalewski, Gary Feinman, and Jill Appel. 1982. *Monte Alban's Hinterland, Part 1: the Prehispanic Settlement Patterns of the Central and Southern Parts of the Valley of Oaxaca, Mexico*. Memoirs of the Museum of Anthropology 15. Ann Arbor, MI: Museum of Anthropology, University of Michigan.

Blanton, Richard E., Stephen A. Kowalewski, Gary M. Feinman, and L.M. Finsten, eds. 1993. *Ancient Mesoamerica: A Comparison of Change in Three Regions*, 2nd ed. Cambridge: Cambridge University Press.

Blomster, Jeffrey P., Hector Neff, and Michael D. Glascock. 2005. Olmec Pottery Production and Export in Ancient Mexico Determined through Elemental Analysis. *Science* 307(5712): 1068–72.

Boas, Franz. 1921. *Álbum de Colecciones Arqueológicas, 1911–1912*. Mexico: Escuela Internacional de Arquelolgía y Etnología Americana.

Boksenbaum, Martin William, Paul Tolstoy, Garman Harbottle, Jerome Kimberlin, and Mary Neivens. 1987. Obsidian Industries and Cultural Evolution in the Basin of Mexico before 500 B.C. *Journal of Field Archaeology* 14:65–75.

Boot, Erik. 2006. Early Maya Writing on an Unprovenanced Monument: The Antwerp Museum Stela. *Mesoweb*, http://www.mesoweb.com/articles/boot/Antwerp.pdf, accessed April 2007.

Borhegyi, Stephan F.D. 1965. Archaeological Synthesis of the Guatemalan Highlands. In *Handbook of Middle American Indians, vol. 2*, ed. Robert Wauchope, pp. 3–58. Austin, TX: University of Texas Press.

Borstein, Joshua A. 2001. Tripping Over Colossal Heads: Settlement Patterns and Population Development in the Upland Olmec Heartland. Ph.D. diss., Dept. of Anthropology, Pennsylvania State University.

———. 2005. Epiclassic Political Organization in Southern Veracruz, Mexico: Segmentary versus centralized integration. *Ancient Mesoamerica* 16(1): 11–21.

———. 2008. El Papel de Laguna de los Cerros en el Mundo Olmeca. In *Ideología*

Política y Sociedad en el Periodo Formativo: ensayos en homanaje al doctor David C. Grove, ed. Ann Cyphers and Kenneth G. Hirth. México, D.F.: Universidad Nacional Autónoma de México, Instituto de Investigaciones Antropológigas.

Boserup, Ester. 1965. *The Conditions of Agricultural Growth: The Economics of Agrarian Change under Population Pressure*. Chicago, IL: Aldine Publishing Co.

Bourdieu, Pierre. 1990. *The Logic of Practice*. Cambridge: Polity Press.

Bove, Frederick J. 1978. Laguna de los Cerros: An Olmec Central Place. *Journal of New World Archaeology* 2(3): 1–56.

———. 2011. The People with No Name: Some Observations of the Plain Stelae of Pacific Guatemala (and Chiapas) with Respect to Issues of Ethnicity and Rulership. In *The Southern Maya in the Late Preclassic*, ed. Michael Love and Jonathan Kaplan, pp. 77–114. Boulder: Colorado University Press.

Bozarth, Steven R. 2000. Analisis de Fitolitas de Opalo en un Jardín de la Realeza de Nakbe, Sitio Maya Preclasico, Guatemala. In *Investigaciones Arqueológicas y Ecológicas en la Cuenca Mirador, 1998: Informe de la Temporada de Campo*, ed. Richard D. Hansen and Judith Valle, pp. 567–98. Proyecto Regional de Investigaciones Arqueológicas del Norte del Peten, Guatemala, UCLA RAINPEG, Foundation for Anthropological Research and Environmental Studies, Idaho.

———. 2007. Phytolith Analyses of the Mirador Basin. Paper presented at the 72nd Annual Meeting of the Society for American Archaeology, Austin, April 26.

Bozarth, Steven R., and Richard D. Hansen. 2001. Estudios Paleo-Botánicos de Nakbe: Evidencias Preliminares de Ambiente y Cultivos en el Preclásico. In *XIV Simposio de Investigaciones Arqueologicas en Guatemala*, ed. Juan Pedro Laporte, Ana Claudia Monzón de Suasnávar, and Bárbara Arroyo, pp. 419–36. Guatemala: Ministerio de Cultura y Deportes, Instituto de Antropología e Historia, Asociación Tikal.

Brady, James E., Joseph W. Ball, Ronald L. Bishop, Duncan C. Pring, Norman Hammond, and Rupert A. Housle. 1998. The Lowland Maya 'Protoclassic': A Reconsideration of Its Nature and Significance. *Ancient Mesoamerica* 9(1): 17–38.

Braswell, Geoffrey E. 1992. Obsidian-hydration Dating, the Coner Phase, and Revisionist Chronology at Copán, Honduras. *Latin American Antiquity* 3:130–47.

———. 2003a. Introduction: Reinterpreting Early Classic Interaction. In *The Maya and Teotihuacan: Reinterpreting Early Classic Interaction*, ed. Geoffrey E. Braswell, pp. 1–43. Austin, TX: University of Texas Press.

———. 2003b. Dating Early Classic Interaction between Kaminaljuyu and Central Mexico. In *The Maya and Teotihuacan: Reinterpreting Early Classic Interaction*, ed. Geoffrey E. Braswell, pp. 1–43. Austin, TX: University of Texas Press.

Braswell, Geoffrey E., and Fabio E. Amador. 1999. Intercambio y Producción durante el Preclásico: La Obsidiana de Kaminaljuyú-Miraflores II y Urías, Sacatepéquez. In *XII Simposio de Investigaciones Arqueológicas en Guatemala*, ed. Juan Pedro Laporte, Hector L. Escobedo, and Ana Claudia Monzón de Suasnávar, pp. 905–10. Guatemala: Ministerio de Cultura y Deportes, Instituto de Antropología e Historia, Asociación Tikal.

Braswell, Geoffrey E., and Eugenia J. Robinson. 2011. The Eastern Cakchiquel Highlands During the Preclassic Period. In *The Southern Maya in the Late Preclassic: The Rise and Fall of an Early Mesoamerican Civilization*, ed. Michael Love and Jonathan Kaplan, pp. 287–315. Boulder: Colorado University Press.

Bray, Warwick. 1972. The City State in Central Mexico at the Time of the Spanish Conquest. *Journal of Latin American Studies* 4:161–85.

Brenner, Mark, Michael F. Rosenmeier, David A. Hodell, and Jason H. Curtis. 2002. Paleolimnology of the Maya Lowlands: Long-term Perspectives on Interactions Among Climate, Environment, and Humans. *Ancient Mesoamerica* 13:141–57.

Brockington, Donald L. 1967. *The Ceramic History of Santa Rosa, Chiapas, Mexico.* Papers of the New World Archaeological Foundation, No. 23. Provo, UT: New World Archaeological Foundation, Brigham Young University.

Brodie, Fawn M. 1992. *No Man Knows My History: The Life of Joseph Smith.* New York, NY: Alfred A. Knopf.

Brown, David O., Meredith L. Dreiss, and Richard E. Hughes. 2004. Preclassic Obsidian Procurement and Utilization at the Maya Site of Colha, Belize. *Latin American Antiquity* 15(2): 222–40.

Brown, Kenneth L. 1977. The Valley of Guatemala: A Highland Port of Trade. In *Teotihuacan and Kaminaljuyu: A Study in Prehistoric Culture Contact*, ed. William T. Sanders and Joseph W. Michels, pp. 205–395. University Park, PA: The Pennsylvania State University.

Brown, M. Kathryn. 1997. Investigations of Middle Preclassic Public Architecture at the Site of Blackman Eddy, Belize. http://www.famsi.org/reports/96052/index.html, accessed February 2010.

Brown, M. Kathryn, and James F. Garber. 2003. Evidence of Conflict During the Middle Formative in the Maya Lowlands: a View from Blackman Eddy, Belize. In *Ancient Mesoamerican Warfare*. M. Kathryn Brown and Travis W. Stanton, eds, pp. 91–108. Walnut Creek, CA: AltaMira Press.

Brown, M. Kathryn, and James F. Garber. 2005. The Development of Middle Formative Public Architecture in the Maya Lowlands: The Blackman Eddy, Belize, Example. In *New Perspectives on Formative Mesoamerican Cultures*, ed. Terry G. Powis, pp. 39–49. BAR International Series, 1377. Oxford: British Archaeological Reports.

Brown, M. Kathryn, and James F. Garber. 2008. Establishing and Re-using Sacred Place: A Diachronic Perspective from Blackman Eddy, Belize. In *The Use and Perception of Abandoned Structures in the Maya Lowlands*, ed. Travis W. Stanton and Aline Magnoni, pp. 147–70. Boulder, CO: University Press of Colorado.

Brumfiel, Elizabeth M. 1987. Elite and Utilitarian Crafts in the Aztec State. In *Specialization, Exchange, and Complex Societies*, ed. Elizabeth M. Brumfiel and Timothy K. Earle, pp. 102–18. Cambridge: Cambridge University Press.

———. 1992. Distinguished Lecture in Archaeology: Breaking and Entering the Ecosystem—Gender, Class, and Faction Steal the Show. *American Anthropologist* 94(3): 551–67.

Brumfiel, Elizabeth M., and Timothy K. Earle. 1987. Specialization, Exchange, and Complex Societies: An Introduction. In *Specialization, Exchange, and Complex Societies*, ed. Elizabeth M. Brumfiel and Timothy K. Earle, pp. 1–9. Cambridge: Cambridge University Press.

Brumfiel, Elizabeth M., and John W. Fox, eds. 1994. *Factional Competition and Political Development in the New World*. Cambridge: Cambridge University Press.

Bryant, Douglas D., and John E. Clark. 1983. Los primeros Mayas Precolumbinos de la Cuenca Superior del Rio Grijalva. In *Homenaje a Frans Blom: Anthropologia e Historia de los Mixe-Zoques y Mayas*, ed. Lorenzo Ochoa and Thomas A. Lee Jr., pp. 223–39. Mexico, DF: Centro de Estudios Mayas, Universidad Nacional Autonoma de Mexico.

———. 2005a. Late Preclassic Ceramics. In *Ceramic Sequence of the Upper Grijalva Region, Chiapas, Mexico, Part 1*. ed. Douglas D. Bryant, John E. Clark, and David Cheetham, pp. 265–282. Papers of the New World Archaeological Foundation, No. 67. Provo, UT: New World Archaeological Foundation, Brigham Young University.

———. 2005b. Protoclassic Ceramics. In *Ceramic Sequence of the Upper Grijalva Region, Chiapas, Mexico, Part 1*, ed. Douglas D. Bryant, John E. Clark, and David Cheetham, pp. 283–349. Papers of the New World Archaeological Foundation, No. 67. Provo, UT: New World Archaeological Foundation, Brigham Young University.

Bullard, William R. Jr. 1965. *Stratigraphic Excavations at San Estevan, Northern British Honduras*. Royal Ontario Museum Occasional Paper 9. Toronto: Royal Ontario Museum.

Bunzel, Ruth. 1952. *Chichicastenango: A Guatemalan Village*. American Ethnological Society Publication 22. Seattle, WA: University of Washington Press.

Burger, Richard L. 1987. Unity and Heterogeneity within the Chavin Horizon. In *Peruvian Prehistory*. Richard W. Keatinge, ed, pp. 99–144. Cambridge: Cambridge University Press.

———. 1992. *Chavin and the Origins of Andean Civilization*. London: Thames and Hudson.

Buttles, Palma J. 2002. Material and Meaning: A Contextual Examination of Select Portable Material Culture from Colha, Belize. Ph.D. diss., Dept. of Anthropology, The University of Texas at Austin.

Cackler, Paul R., Michael Glasscock, Hector Neff, Harry Iceland, K. Anne Pyburn, Dale Hudler, Thomas Hester, and Beverly Mitchum-Chiarulli. 1999. Chipped Stone Artifacts, Source Areas, and Provenance Studies of the Northern Belize Chert-Bearing Zone. *Journal of Archaeological Science* 26:389–97.

Callaghan, Michael G. 2006. Cerámica del Proyecto Arqueológico Holmul, Muestras de 2004 y 2005. In *Investigaciones Arqueológicas en la Region de Holmul, Petén, Guatemala. Informe preliminar de la Temporada 2005*, ed. Francisco Estrada-Belli, pp. 225–328. http://vanderbilt.edu/estrada-belli/holmul/reports/, accessed February 2007.

———. 2008. Technologies of Power: Ritual Economy and Ceramic Production in the Terminal Preclassic Period Holmul Region, Guatemala. Ph.D. diss., Vanderbilt University.

Campbell, Lyle R. 1988. *The Linguistics of Southeast Chiapas, Mexico*. Papers of the New World Archaeological Foundation, No. 50. Provo, UT: New World Archaeological Foundation, Brigham Young University.

Campbell, Lyle R., and Terrence S. Kaufman. 1976. A Linguistic Look at the Olmecs. *American Antiquity* 41(1): 80–89.

Canto Aguilar, Giselle, and Victor Mauricio Castro Mendoza. 2007. Los señores de Zazacatla, Morelos. *Arqueología Mexicana* 85:16–19.

Canuto, Marcello A. 2002. A Tale of Two Communities: The Role of the Rural Community in the Socio-Political Integration of the Copan Drainage in the Late Preclassic and Classic Periods. Ph.D. diss., Dept. of Anthropology, University of Pennsylvania.

———. 2004. The Rural Settlement of Copan: Changes through the Early Classic. In *Understanding Early Classic Copan*, ed. Ellen E. Bell, Marcello A. Canuto, and Robert J. Sharer, pp. 29–53. Philadelphia, PA: University of Pennsylvania Museum of Archaeology and Anthropology.

Canuto, Marcello A., and Jason Yaeger, eds. 2000. *The Archaeology of Communities: A New World Perspective*. London: Routledge.

Carmack, Robert M. 1981. *The Quiché Mayas of Utatlan*. Oklahoma City, OK: University of Oklahoma.

Carneiro, Robert L. 1970. A Theory on the Origin of the State. *Science* 169(3947):733–738.

————. 1972. From Autonomous Villages to the State, a Numerical Estimation. In *Population Growth: Anthropological Implications*, ed. Brian Spooner, pp. 64–77. Cambridge, MA: MIT Press.

————. 1977. Comment on 'Shifts in Production and Organization: A Cluster Interaction Model.' *Current Anthropology* 18(2): 222–23.

————. 1981. The Chiefdom as Precursor of the State. In *The Transition to Statehood in the New World*, ed. Grant D. Jones and Robert R. Kautz, pp. 37–79. Cambridge: Cambridge University Press.

Carr, Robert F., and James E. Hazard. 1961. *Map of the Ruins of Tikal, El Peten, Guatemala*. Tikal Report No. 11. Philadelphia, PA: University Museum, University of Pennsylvania.

Carrasco V., Ramón. 2005. The Sacred Mountain: Preclassic Architecture in Calakmul. In *Lords of Creation: The Origins of Sacred Maya Kingship*, ed. Virginia M. Fields and Dorie Reents-Budet, pp. 62–66. Los Angeles, CA: Los Angeles County Museum of Art and London: Scala Publishers.

Carrasco V., Ramón, and Marinés Colón González. 2005. El Reino de Kaan y la Antigua Ciudad Maya de Calakmul. *Arqueología Mexicana* 13(75): 40–47.

Carrasco V., Ramón, and Omar Rodríguez C. 2003. La Antigua Ciudad Maya de Calakmul: Una Respectiva. *Revista de Universidad Nacional Autónoma de México* 623:48.

Caso, Alfonso. 1942. Definición y Extensión del Complejo 'Olmeca.' In *Mayas y Olmecas: Segunda Reunión de Mesa Redonda sobre Problemas Antropológicos de México y Centroamérica*, pp. 43–46. México: Sociedad Mexicana de Antropología.

————. 1947. *Calendario y Escritura de las Antiguas Culturas de Monte Alban*. Mexico, DF: Mexico.

————. 1965. ¿Existió un Imperio Olmeca? *Memorias de El Colegio Nacional* 5(3): 11–60.

Castañeda, Cesar, and Richard D. Hansen. 2016. Cultural Development and Change of Vegetation in the Mirador System. In *2016 Mirador: Research and Conservation in the Ancient Kaan Kingdom*, ed. Richard D. Hansen and Edgar Suyuc, pp. 37–62. Corporacion Litografica, Guatemala: Foundation for Anthropological Research and Environmental Studies (FARES).

————. 2007. Estudios Botanicos en la Cuenca Mirador: Desarrollo de Vegetación y su Significado Cultural. In *XX Simposio de Investigaciones Arqueológias en Guatemala*, ed. Juan Pedro Laporte, Bárbara Arroyo, and Hector E. Mejía, pp. 111–20. Guatemala City, Guatemala: Museo Nacional de Arquelogia y Etnologia, Ministerio de Cultura y Deportes, Instituto de Antropología e Historia, Asociación Tikal, Fundación Arqueologica del Nuevo Mundo.

————. 2008. Relación Entre Cambio Cultural y Vegetación en la Cuenca Mirador,

Norte de Guatemala. In *Revista de la Universidad del Valle de Guatemala No. 18*, pp. 90–100.

Castellanos, Carlos. 2008. Algunas Consideraciones para el Estudio de Areas Habitacionales: El Caso de las Estructuras No Visibles en El Mirador, Peten. *Abstractos del XXII Simposio de Investigaciones Arqeulógicas en Guatemala*, p. 91. Ministerio de Cultura y Deportes, Instituto de Antropología e Historia, Museo Nacional de Arqueología y Etnologia, Asociación Tikal.

Castillo, Mangas, María Teresa, Luis Córdoba Barradas, and Raúl García Chávez. 1993. Un aldea del Formativo en San Miguel Amantla, Azcapotzalco, D.F. In *A propósito del Formativo*, ed. Ma. Teresa Castillo Mangas, pp. 59–71. México, DF: Subdirección de Salvamento Arqueológico, Instituto Nacional de Antropología e Historia.

Chambers, Mary Elizabeth, and Richard D. Hansen. 1996. El Monumento 18 de El Mirador: El Contexto Arqueológico y la Iconografia. In *IX Simposio de Investigaciones Arqueológicas en Guatemala*, ed. Juan Pedro Laporte and Hector L. Escobedo, pp. 313–29. Guatemala: Ministerio de Cultura y Deportes, Instituto de Antropología e Historia, Asociacion Tikal.

Chang, Kwang-chih. 1983. *Art, Myth, and Ritual: The Path to Political Authority in Ancient China*. Cambridge, MA: Harvard University Press.

Chapman, Anne M. 1971. Commentary On: Mesoamerican Trade and Its Role in the Emergence of Civilization. In *Observations on the Emergence of Civilization in America*, ed. Robert F. Heizer and John A. Graham, pp. 196–211. Contributions of the University of California Archaeological Research Facility, vol. 11. Berkeley, CA: University of California Department of Anthropology.

Chase, Arlen F., and Diane Z. Chase. 1995. External Impetus, Internal Synthesis, and Standardization: E Group Assemblages and the Crystalization of Classic Maya Society in the Southern Lowlands. In *The Emergence of Lowland Maya Civilization: The Transition from the Preclassic to Early Classic*, ed. Nikolai Grube, pp. 87–101. Acta Mesoamericana, 8. Möckmühl, Germany: Verlag Anton Saurwein.

———. 1996. More Than Kin and King: Centralized Political Organization Among the Late Classic Maya. *Current Anthropology* 37(5): 803–10.

———. 1999. External Impetus, Internal Synthesis, and Standardization: E-Group Assemblages and the Crystallization of Classic Maya Society in the Southern Lowlands. In *The Emergence of Lowland Maya Civilization*, ed. Nikolai Grube, pp. 87–102. Acta Mesoamericana, vol. 8. Mockmuhl, Germany: Verlag Anton Surwein.

———. 2001. Ancient Maya Causeways and Site Organization at Caracol, Belize. *Ancient Mesoamerica* 12:273–81.

Chase, Diane Z., Arlen F. Chase, and William Haviland. 1990. The Classic Maya City:

Reconsidering the 'Mesoamerican Urban Tradition'. *American Anthropologist* 92:499–506.

Cheetham, David. 1998. Interregional Interaction, Symbol Emulation, and the Emergence of Socio-Political Inequality in the Central Maya Lowlands. M.A. thesis, Dept. of Anthropology, University of British Columbia.

———. 2005. Cunil: A Pre-Mamom Horizon in the Southern Maya Lowlands. In *New Perspectives on Formative Mesoamerican Cultures*, ed. Terry G. Powis, pp. 27–38. BAR International Series, 1377. Oxford: BAR International Series.

———. 2006. The Americas' First Colony: A Possible Olmec Outpost in Southern Mexico. *Archaeology* 59(1): 42–46.

———. 2007. Cantón Corralito, Objects from a Possible Gulf Olmec Colony. Report to the Foundation for the Advancement of Mesoamerican Studies, Inc. http//:www.famsi.org/reports/05021/index.html, accessed January 2011.

———. 2010. Cultural Imperatives in Clay: Early Olmece Carved Pottery from San Lorenzo and Cantón Corralito. *American Mesoamerica*. 21:165–85.

Cheetham, David, Donald W. Forsyth, and John E. Clark. 2003. La Ceramica Pre-Mamom de la Cuenca del Rio Belize y del Centro de Peten: Las Correspondencias y sus Implicaciones. In *XVI Simposio de Investigaciones Arqueologicas en Guatemala*, ed. Juan Pedro Laporte and Hector L. Escobedo, pp. 615–34. Guatemala: Ministerio de Cultura y Deportes, Instituto de Antropología e Historia, Asociación Tikal.

Cheetham, David, and Thomas A. Lee, Jr. 2005. Cerámica Zoque Temprana en Chiapa de Corzo: Secuencia, Transición y Relaciones Externas. In *Anuario 2004*, pp. 287–315. Tuxtla Gutierrez, Chiapas, Mexico: Centro de Estudios Superiores de Mexcio y Centroamerica, Universidad de Ciencias y Artes de Chiapas.

Chiarulli, Beverly A. 2006. Preliminary Analyses of Lithic Artifacts and Debitage Recovered from Chau Hiix During the 2003 and 2005 Field Seasons. In *Report on the 2005 Field Season at Chau Hiix*. Report submitted by K. Anne Pyburn to the Dept. of Archaeology, Belmopan, Belize.

———. 2012 Producers, Consumers, and Traders: Lithic Industries at Cerros and Chau Hiix, Belize. *Lithic Technology* 37(2): 95–110.

Childe, V. Gordon. 1950. The Urban Revolution. *Town Planning Review* 21:3–17.

———. 1951. *Man Makes Himself*. London: Watts Press.

Christenson, Allen J. 2003. *Popol Vuh: The Sacred Book of the Maya*. New York, NY: O Books.

Cioffi-Revilla, Claudio, and Todd Landman. 1999. Evolution of Maya Polities in the Ancient Mesoamerican System. *International Studies Quarterly* 43:559–98.

Claessen, Henry J.M., and Peter Skalník. 1978. The Early State: Theories and Hypotheses. In *The Early State*, ed. Henry J.M. Claessen and Peter Skalník, pp. 3–29. The Hague: Mouton.

Clark, John E. 1987. Politics, Prismatic Blades, and Mesoamerican Civilization. In *The Organization of Core Technology*, ed. Jay K. Johnson and Carol A. Morrow, pp. 259–84. Boulder, CO: Westview Press.

———. 1988. *The Lithic Artifacts of La Libertad, Chiapas, Mexico: An Economic Perspective*. Papers of the New World Archaeological Foundation, No. 52. Provo, UT: New World Archaeological Foundation, Brigham Young University.

———. 1990. Olmecas, Olmequismo y Olmequización en Mesoamerica. *Arqueología* 3:49–56.

———. 1991. The Beginnings of Mesoamerica: Apologia for the Soconusco Early Formative. In *The Formation of Complex Society in Southeastern Mesoamerica*, ed. William R. Fowler, pp. 13–26. Boca Raton, FL: CRC Press.

———. 1993. Una Reevaluación de la Entidad Política Olmeca: ¿Imperio, Estado o Cacicazgo? In *Segundo and Tercer Foro de Arqueología de Chiapas*, Thomas A. Lee, Jr., pp. 159–69. Tuxtla Gutiérrez: Instituto Chiapaneco de Cultura.

———. 1994. The Development of Early Formative Rank Societies in the Soconusco, Chiapas, Mexico. Ph.D. diss., Dept. of Anthropology, University of Michigan, Ann Arbor.

———. 1996. Craft Specialization and Olmec Civilization. In *Craft Specialization and Social Evolution: In Memory of V. Gordon Childe*, ed. Bernard Wailes, pp. 187–99. Philadelphia, PA: University of Pennsylvania Museum of Archaeology and Anthropology.

———. 1997. The Arts of Government in Early Mesoamerica. *Annual Review of Anthropology* 26:211–34.

———. 2000a. Los Pueblos de Chiapas en el Formativo. In *Las Culturas de Chiapas en el Periodo Prehispánico*. Durdica Segota, ed, pp. 36–59. Mexico, DF: Consejo Estatal para la Cultura y las Artes de Chiapas, Consejo Nacional para la Cultura y las Artes.

———. 2000b. Towards a Better Explanation of Hereditary Inequality: A Critical Assessment of Natural and Historic Human Agents. In *Agency in Archaeology*, ed. Marcia-Anne Dobres and John E. Robb, pp. 92–112. London: Routledge.

———. 2001. Ciudades Tempranas Olmecas. In *Reconstruyendo la Ciudad Maya: El Urbanismo en las Sociedades Antiguas*, ed. Andres Ciudad Real, Ma. Josefa I. Ponce de León, and Ma. del Carmen Martínez Martínez, pp. 183–210. Madrid: Sociedad Española de Estudios Mayas.

———. 2003. A Review of Twentieth-Century Mesoamerican Obsidian Studies. In

Mesoamerican Lithic Technology, ed. Kenneth G. Hirth, pp. 15–54. Salt Lake City, UT: University of Utah Press.

———. 2004a. Mesoamerica Goes Public: Early Ceremonial Centers, Leaders, and Communities. In *Mesoamerican Archaeology: Theory and Practice*, ed. Julia A. Hendon and Rosmary Joyce, pp. 43–72. Malden, MA: Blackwell.

———. 2004b. The Birth of Mesoamerican Metaphysics: Sedentism, Engagement, and Moral Superiority. In *Rethinking Materiality: The Engagement of Mind with the Material World*, ed. Elizabeth DeMararis, Chris Gosden, and Colin Renfrew, pp. 205–24. Cambridge: McDonald Institute for Archaeological Research, University of Cambridge.

———. 2005a. Archaeology, Relics and Book of Mormon Belief. *Journal of Book of Mormon Studies* 14(2): 38–49.

———. 2005b. Ceramics as History. In *Ceramic Sequence of the Upper Grijalva Region, Chiapas, Mexico, Part 2*, ed. Douglas D. Bryant, John E. Clark, and David Cheetham, pp. 651–56. Papers of the New World Archaeological Foundation, No. 67. Provo, UT: New World Archaeological Foundation, Brigham Young University.

———. 2007a. Mesoamerica's First State. In *The Political Economy of Ancient Mesoamerica: Transformations During the Formative and Classic Periods*, ed. Vernon L. Scarborough and John E. Clark, pp. 11–46. Albuquerque, NM: University of New Mexico.

———. 2007b. In Craft Specialization's Penumbra: Things, Persons, Action, Value, and Surplus. In *Rethinking Craft Specialization in Complex Societies: Archaeological Analyses of the Social Meaning of Production*, ed. Zachary X. Hruby and Rowan K. Flad, pp. 20–35. Archaeological Papers of the American Anthropological Association, No. 17. Arlington, VA: American Anthropological Association.

———. 2008. Cities and Towns of the Olmec. In *Encyclopedia of the History of Science, Technology, and Medicine in Non-Western Cultures, Volume 1*, 2nd ed., ed. Helaine Selin, pp. 554–58. New York, NY: Springer Verlag.

———. 2009. El Origin del Estado en Mesoamérica. In *Las Sociedades Complejas del Occidente de México en el Mundo Mesoamericano: Homenaje al Dr. Phil C. Weigand*, ed. E. Williams, L. López Mestas, and R. Esparza, pp. 373–91. Zamora: El Colegio de Michoacán.

———. 2014. A Census of Western Chiapas Sites. In *A Brief Reconnaissance of Three Chiapas Municipalities*, by F. Peterson. Papers of the New World Archaeological Foundation, No. 73, pp. 183–216. Provo, UT: New World Archaeological Foundation, Brigham Young University.

Clark, John E., and Michael Blake. 1989. El Origen de la Civilización en Mesoamérica.

In *El Preclásico o Formativo: Avances y Perspectivas*, ed. M. Carmona Macias, pp. 385–403. México: Instituto Nacional de Arqueología e Historia.

———. 1994. The Power of Prestige: Competitive Generosity and the Emergence of Rank Societies in Lowland Mesoamerica. In *Factional Competition and Politial Development in the New World*, ed. Elizabeth M. Brumfiel and John W. Fox, pp. 17–30. Cambridge: Cambridge University Press.

Clark, John E., and David Cheetham. 2002. Mesoamerica's Tribal Foundations. In *The Archaeology of Tribal Societies*, ed. William A. Parkinson, pp. 278–339. Archaeological Series, International Monographs in Prehistory. Ann Arbor, MI: University of Michigan.

———. 2005. Cerámica del Formativo de Chiapas. In *La Producción Alfarera en el México Antiguo, Volume I*, ed. Beatriz L. Merino Carrión and Ángel García Cook, pp. 285–433. Colección Cientíca, No. 484. Mexico, DF: Instituto Nacional de Antropología e Historia.

Clark, John E., and Arlene Colman. 2012. Structure of the Mesoamerican Universe, from Aztec to Olmec. In *Enduring Motives: The Archaeology of Tradition and Religion in Native America*, ed. Linea Sundstrom, pp. 15–59. Tuscaloosa: University of Alabama Press.

———. 2013. Olmec Things and Identity: A Reassessment of Offerings and Burials at La Venta, Tabasco. *Archeological Papers of the American Anthropological Association. Special Issue: The Inalienable in the Archaeology of Mesoamerica* 23:14–37.

Clark, John E., and Dennis Gosser. 1995. Reinventing Mesoamerica's First Pottery. In *The Emergence of Pottery: Technology and Innovation in Ancient Societies*, ed. William K. Barnett and John W. Hoopes, pp. 209–21. Washington, DC: Smithsonian Institution.

Clark, John E., Julia Guernsey, and Bárbara Arroyo. 2010. Stone Monuments and Preclassic Civilization. In *The Place of Stone Monuments: Context, Use, and Meaning in Mesoamerica's Preclassic Transition*, ed. J. Guernsey, J.E. Clark, and B. Arroyo, pp. 1–26. Washington, DC: Dumbarton Oaks.

Clark, John E., and Richard D. Hansen. 2001. The Architecture of Early Kingship: Comparative Perspectives on the Origins of the Maya Royal Court. In *Royal Courts of the Ancient Maya. Volume 2: Data and Case Studies*, ed. Takeshi Inomata and Stephen D. Houston, pp. 1–45. Boulder, CO: Westview Press.

Clark, John E., Richard D. Hansen, and Tomas Pérez Suarez. 2000. La zona maya en el Preclásico. In *Historia antigua de México: vol. 1. El México antiguo, sus áreas culturales, los orígenes y el horizonte Preclásico*, ed. Linda Manzanilla and Leonardo López Luján, pp. 437–510. México, D.F.: Instituto Nacional de Antropología e Historia,

Universidad Nacional Autónoma de México.

Clark, John E., and John G. Hodgson. 2008. Olmec Sculpture from Coastal Chiapas, Mexico. *Thule: Rivista Italiana di Studi Americanistici* 22/23–24/25:41–99.

Clark, John E., and Thomas A. Lee, Jr. 1984. Formative Obsidian Exchange and the Emergence of Public Economies in Chiapas, Mexico. In *Trade and Exchange in Early Mesoamerica*, ed. Kenneth Hirth, pp. 235–74. Albuquerque, NM: University of New Mexico Press.

———. 2007. The Changing Role of Obsidian Exchange in Central Chiapas. In *Archaeology, Art, and Ethnogenesis in Mesoamerican Prehistory: Papers in Honor of Gareth W. Lowe*, ed. Lynneth S. Lowe and Mary E. Pye, pp. 109–59. Papers of the New World Archaeological Foundation, No. 68. Provo, UT: New World Archaeological Foundation, Brigham Young University.

Clark, John E., Thomas A. Lee Jr., and Douglas D. Bryant. 2005. Introducing the Grijalva Maya Project. In *Ceramic Sequence of the Upper Grijalva Region, Chiapas, Mexico*, ed. Douglas D. Bryant, John E. Clark, and David Cheetham, pp. 1–20. Papers of the New World Archaeological Foundation, No. 67. Provo, UT: New World Archaeological Foundation, Brigham Young University.

Clark, John E., Thomas A. Lee Jr., and Tamara Salcedo. 1989. The Distribution of Obsidian. In *Ancient Economies of the Soconusco: The Prehistory and History of the Economic Development in the Coastal Lowlands of Chiapas, Mexico*, ed. Barbara Voorhies, pp. 268–84. Salt Lake City, UT: University of Utah Press.

Clark, John E., and Gareth W. Lowe. 2013. Izapa History. In *Middle and Late Preclassic Izapa: Ceramic Complexes and History*, by G.W. Lowe, S.M. Ekholm, and J.E. Clark. Papers of the New World Archaeological Foundation, No. 79. Provo, UT: New World Archaeological Foundation, Brigham Young University.

Clark, John E., and Mary E. Pye, eds. 2000a. *Olmec Art and Archaeology in Mesoamerica*. Washington, DC: National Gallery of Art.

———. 2000b. The Pacific Coast and the Olmec Question. In *Olmec Art and Archaeology in Mesoamerica*, ed. John E. Clark and Mary E. Pye, pp. 217–51. Washington, DC: National Gallery of Art.

———. 2006. Los orígenes del privilegio en el Soconusco, 1650 AC: Dos décadas de investigación. In *XIX Simposio de Investigaciones Arqueológicas en Guatemala, 2005*, ed. Juan Pedro Laporte, Bárbara Arroyo, and Hector E. Mejía, pp. 9–20. Guatemala: Ministerio de Cultura y Deportes, Instituto de Antropología e Historia, Asociación Tikal, Fundación Arqueológica del Nuevo Mundo.

———. 2011. Revisiting the Mixe-Zoque: A Brief History of the Preclassic Peoples of Chiapas. In *The Southern Maya in the Late Preclassic: The Rise and Fall of an Early*

Mesoamerican Civilization, ed. Michael Love and Jonathan Kaplan, pp. 24–45. Boulder: Colorado University Press.

Clark, John E., and Tomás Pérez Suárez. 1994. Los Olmecas y el Primer Milenio de Mesoamérica. In *Los olmecas en Mesoamérica*, ed. John Clark, pp. 261–75. México, DF: Citibank.

Clewlow, C. William, Jr., Richard A. Cowan, James F. O'Connell, and Carlos Beneman. 1967. *Colossal Heads of the Olmec Culture.* Contributions of the University of California Archaeological Research Facility No. 4. Berkeley, CA: University of California.

Cliff, Maynard B., and Cathy J. Crane. 1989. Changing Subsistence Economy at a Late Preclassic Maya Community. In *Prehistoric Maya Economies of Belize*, ed. Patricia A. McAnany and Barry L. Isaac, pp. 295–324. Research in Economic Anthropology Supplement 4. Greenwich, CN: JAI Press, Inc.

Cobean, Robert H., Michael D. Coe, Edward A. Perry, Jr., Karl K. Turekian, and Dinkar P. Kharkar. 1971. Obsidian Trade at San Lorenzo Tenochtitlán, Mexico. *Science* 174(4010): 666–71.

Cobean, Robert H., James R. Vogt, Michael D. Glascock, and Terrance Stocker. 1991. High-Precision Trace-Element Characterization of Major Mesoamerican Obsidian Sources and Further Analysis of Artifacts from San Lorenzo Tenochtitlán, Mexico. *Latin American Antiquity* 2(1): 69–91.

Coe, Michael D. 1957. The Khmer Settlement Pattern: A Possible Analogy with That of the Maya. *American Antiquity* 22(4): 409–10.

———. 1961. *La Victoria: An Early Site on the Pacific Coast of Guatemala.* Papers of the Peabody Museum of Archaeology and Ethnology vol. 53. Cambridge, MA: Peabody Museum of Archaeology and Ethnology, Harvard University.

———. 1965a. The Olmec Style and Its Distribution. In *Handbook of Middle American Indians. Vol. 3: Archaeology of Southern Mesoamerica, Part 2*, ed. Gordon R. Willey, pp. 739–75. Austin, TX: University of Texas Press.

———. 1965b. Archaeological Synthesis of Southern Veracruz and Tabasco. In *Handbook of Middle American Indians. Vol. 3: Archaeology of Southern Mesoamerica, Part 2*, ed. Gordon R. Willey, pp. 679–715. Austin, TX: University of Texas Press.

———. 1965c. *The Jaguar's Children: Pre-Classic Central Mexico.* New York, NY: Museum of Primitive Art.

———. 1965d. A Model of Ancient Community Structure in the Maya Lowlands. *Southwestern Journal of Anthropology* 21(2): 97–114.

———. 1966a. *The Maya.* Ancient Peoples and Places, vol. 52. New York, NY: Praeger.

———. 1966b. *An Early Stone Pectoral from Southeastern México.* Studies in Pre-Columbian Art and Archaeology, No. 1. Washington, DC: Dumbarton Oaks, Trustees for Harvard University.

———. 1968. America's *First Civilization: Discovering the Olmec*. New York, NY: American Heritage.

———. 1972. Olmec Jaguars and Olmec Kings. In *The Cult of the Feline: A Conference in Pre-Columbian Iconography*, ed. Elizabeth P. Benson, pp. 1–18. Washington, DC: Dumbarton Oaks Research Library and Collections.

———. 1973a. Mormons and Archaeology: An Outside View. *Dialogue, a Journal of Mormon Thought* 8(2): 40–48.

———. 1973b. *The Maya Scribe and His World*. New York, NY: The Grolier Club.

———. 1977. Olmec and Maya: A Study in Relationships. In *The Origins of Maya Civilization*, ed. Richard E.W. Adams, pp. 183–95. School of American Research Advanced Seminar Series. Albuquerque, NM: University of New Mexico Press.

———. 1981a. Religion and the Rise of Mesoamerican States. In *The Transition to Statehood in the New World*, ed. Grant D. Jones and Robert R. Kautz, pp. 157–71. Cambridge: Cambridge University Press.

———. 1981b. San Lorenzo Tenochtitlán. In *The Handbook of Middle American Indians. Supplement 1: Archaeology*, ed. Jeremy A. Sabloff, pp. 117–46. Austin, TX: University of Texas Press.

———. 1989a. The Olmec Heartland: Evolution of Ideology. In *Regional Perspectives on the Olmec*, ed. Robert J. Sharer and David C. Grove, pp. 68–84. School of American Research Advanced Seminar Series. New York, NY: Cambridge University Press.

———. 1989b. The Hero Twins: Myth and Image. In *The Maya Vase Book: A Corpus of Rollout Photographs of Maya Vases, Volume 1*, ed. Justin Kerr, pp. 161–84. New York, NY: Kerr Associates.

———. 2005. *The Maya*. 7th ed. Ancient Peoples and Places. New York, NY: Thames and Hudson.

Coe, Michael D., and Richard A. Diehl. 1980. *In the Land of the Olmec*. 2 vols. Austin, TX: University of Texas Press.

Coe, Michael D., and Louis A. Fernandez. 1980. Appendix 2: Petrographic Analysis of Rock Samples from San Lorenzo. In *In the Land of the Olmec, vol. 1*, ed. Michael D. Coe and Richard A. Diehl, pp. 397–404. Austin, TX: University of Texas Press.

Coe, William R. 1962a. Priestly Power and Peasant Corn: Excavations and Reconstructions at Tikal, Probably the Greatest Lowland Maya Center—Part I. *The Illustrated London News, Archaeological Section* 2077:103–6.

———. 1962b. Excavations and Splendid Finds at Mayan Tikal, Guatemala—Part II. *The Illustrated London News, Archaeological Section* 2078:135–37.

————. 1965a. Tikal, Guatemala, and Emergent Maya Civilization. *Science* 147(3664): 1401–19.

————. 1965b. Tikal: Ten Years of Study of a Maya Ruin in the Lowlands of Guatemala. *Expedition* 8(1): 4–56.

————. 1990. *Excavations in the Great Plaza, North Terrace and North Acropolis of Tikal.* 6 vols. Tikal Report 14. Philadelphia, PA: University of Pennsylvania Museum of Archaeology and Anthropology.

Coe, William R., and John J. McGinn. 1963. Tikal: The North Acropolis and an Early Tomb. *Expedition* 5(2): 24–32.

Coe, William R., and Robert Stuckenrath. 1965. Comment. In *Samuel A. Barrett: A Memorial*, pp. 70. The Kroeber Anthropological Society Papers No. 33. Berkeley, CA: The Kroeber Anthropological Society.

Coggins, Clemency C. 1975. Painting and Drawing Styles at Tikal: An Historical and Iconographic Reconstruction. Ph.D. diss., Dept. of Fine Arts, Harvard University.

Cohen, Mark N. 1981. The Ecological Basis for New World State Formation: General and Local Model Building. In *The Transition to Statehood in the New World*, ed. Grant D. Jones and Robert R. Kautz, pp. 105–22. Cambridge: Cambridge University Press.

Cohen, Ronald. 1978. Introduction. In *Origins of the State: The Anthropology of Political Evolution*, ed. Ronald Cohen and Elman R. Service, pp. 1–20. Institute for the Study of Human Issues: Philadelphia.

Cohen, Ronald, and Elman R. Service, eds. 1978. *Origins of the State: The Anthropology of Political Evolution*. Philadelphia, PA: Institute for the Study of Human Issues.

Colman, Arlene. 2010. The Construction of Complex A at La Venta, Tabasco: A History of Buildings, Burials, Offerings, and Stone Monuments. M.A. thesis, Dept. of Anthropology, Brigham Young University. Provo, Utah.

Con Uribe, María José. 1976. Síntesis de los Trabajos Realizados en el Salvamento Arqueológico de la Presa de la Angostura, Chiapas. In *Las Fronteras de Mesoamérica: XIV Mesa Redonda de la Sociedad Mexicana de Antropología*, pp. 173–180. Mexico: La Sociedad Mexicana de Antropología.

Connerton, Paul. 1989. *How Societies Remember*. Cambridge: Cambridge University Press.

Cordova F. de A., Carlos, Ana Lillian Martin del Pozzo, and Javier López Camacho. 1994. Paleolandforms and Volcanic Impact on the Environment of Prehistoric Cuicuilco, Southern Mexico City. *Journal of Archaeological Science* 21:585–96.

Córdova Tello, Mario, and Carolina Meza Rodríguez. 2007. Chalcatzingo, Morelos: un discurso sobre piedra. *Arqueología Mexicana* 87:60–65.

Cortés de Brasdefer, Fernando. 1994. Los Mascarones de Chakanbakan. *Mexicon* 16(2): 32–34.

Cortez, Constance. 1986. The Principal Bird Deity in Preclassic and Early Classic Maya Art. M.A. thesis, Dept. of Art and Art History, University of Texas at Austin.

Covarrubias, Miguel. 1942. Origen y Desarrollo del Estilo Artístico Olmeca. In *Mayas y Olmecas: Segunda Reunión de Mesa Redonda sobre Problemas Antropológicos de México y Centroamérica*, pp. 46–49. México: Sociedad Mexicana de Antropología.

———. 1943. Tlatilco, Archaic Mexican Art and Culture. *Dyn* 4-5:40–46.

———. 1946a. El Arte Olmeca o de La Venta. *Cuadernos Americanos* 28(4): 153–79.

———. 1946b. *Mexico South, the Isthmus Of Tehuantepec*. New York, NY: A.A. Knopf.

———. 1950. Tlatilco: El arte y la cultura preclásica del valle de México. *Cuadernos Americanos* 9(3): 149–62.

———. 1957. *Indian Art of Mexico and Central America*. New York, NY: Alfred A. Knopf.

Cowgill, George L. 1974. Quantitative Studies of Urbanization at Teotihuacan. In *Mesoamerican Archaeology: New Approaches*, ed. Norman Hammond, pp. 363–96. London, England: Duckworth.

———. 1992. Towards a Political History of Teotihuacan. In *Ideology and Pre-Columbian Civilizations*, ed. Arthur A. Demarest and Geoffrey W. Conrad, pp. 87–114. Santa Fe, NM: School of American Research Press.

———. 2000. Rationality and Contexts in Agency Theory. In *Agency in Archaeology*, ed. Marcia-Anne Dobres and John E. Robb, pp. 51–60. London: Routledge.

Cowgill, Ursula M., G. Evelyn Hutchinson, A.A. Racek, Clyde E. Golden, Ruth Patrick, and Matsuo Tsukada. 1966. *The History of Laguna de Petenxil, A Small Lake in Northern Guatemala*. Memoirs of the Connecticut Academy of Arts and Sciences, vol. 17. New Haven, CT: Connecticut Academy of Arts and Sciences.

Crangle, Sebastian. 1994. The Protoclassic Period of Copan. B.A. Honors Thesis, University of Queensland.

Crumley, Carole L. 1987. A Dialectical Critique of Hierarchy. In *Power Relations and State Formation*. Thomas C. Patterson and Christine W. Gailey, eds, pp. 155–68. Washington, D.C.: American Anthropological Association.

———. 1995. Heterarchy and the Analysis of Complex Societies. In *Heterarchy and the Analysis of Complex Societies*, ed. Robert M. Ehrenreich, Carole L. Crumley, and Janet E. Levy, pp. 1–6. Archaeological Papers of the American Anthropological Association, No. 6. Arlington, VA: American Anthropological Association.

———. 2003. Alternative Forms of Social Order. In *Heterarchy, Political Economy, and the Ancient Maya. The Three Rivers Region of the East-Central Yucatán Peninsula*, ed. Vernon L. Scarborough, Fred Valdez Jr., and Nicholas Dunning, pp. 136–45. Tucson, AZ: The University of Arizona Press.

Culbert, T. Patrick. 1977. Early Maya Development at Tikal, Guatemala. In *The Origins of Maya Civilization*. Richard E. W. Adams, ed, pp. 27–43. Albuquerque, NM: University of New Mexico Press.

———, ed. 1991a. *Classic Maya Political History: Hieroglyphic and Archaeological Evidence*. Cambridge: Cambridge University Press.

———. 1991b. Polities in the Northern Peten, Guatemala. In *Classic Maya Political History: Hieroglyphic and Archaeological Evidence*, ed. T. Patrick Culbert, pp. 128–46. Cambridge: Cambridge University Press.

———. 2003. The Ceramics of Tikal. In *Tikal: Dynasties, Foreigners, & Affairs of State*, ed. Jeremy A. Sabloff, pp. 47–81. Santa Fe, NM: School of American Research Press.

Cummins, Daniel. 2007. Formative Copan: The Ritual Transformation of an Early Mesoamerican Village. Ph.D. diss., School of Social Science, University of Queensland.

Curtis, Jason H., David A. Hodell, Mark Brenner, Richard A. Balser, Gerald A. Islebe, and Henry Hooghiemstra. 1998. A Multi-Proxy Study of Holocene Environmental Change in the Maya Lowlands of Peten, Guatemala. *Journal of Paleolimnology* 19:139–59.

Cyphers Guillén, Ann. 1984. The Possible Role of Women in Formative Exchange. In *Trade and Exchange in Early Mesoamerica*, ed. Kenneth G. Hirth, pp. 115–23. Albuquerque, NM: University of New Mexico Press.

———. 1987. Ceramics. In *Ancient Chalcatzingo*, ed. David C. Grove, pp. 200–251. Austin, TX: University of Texas Press.

———. 1993a. Escenas Escultóricas Olmecas. Antropológicas 6:47–52.

———. 1993b. Women, Rituals, and Social Dynamics in Ancient Chalcatzingo. Latin American Antiquity 4(3): 209–24.

———. 1994. Olmec Sculpture. *National Geographic Research and Exploration* 10(3): 294–305.

———. 1996. Reconstructing Olmec Life at San Lorenzo. In *Olmec Art of Ancient Mexico*, ed. Elizabeth P. Benson and Beatriz de la Fuente, pp. 61–71. Washington, DC: National Gallery of Art.

———. 1997a. La Arquitectura Olmeca en San Lorenzo Tenochtitlán. In *Población, Subsistencia y Medio Ambiente en San Lorenzo Tenochtitlán*, ed. Ann Cyphers, pp. 91–117. México DF: Instituto de Investigaciones Antropológicas, Universidad Nacional Autónoma de México.

———. 1997b. Olmec Architecture at San Lorenzo. In *Olmec to Aztec: Settlement Pat-*

terns in the Ancient Gulf Lowlands, ed. Barbara L. Stark and Philip J. Arnold III, pp. 96–114. Tucson, AZ: University of Arizona Press.

———. 1997c. El Contexto Social de Monumentos en San Lorenzo. In *Población, Subsistencia y Medio Ambiente en San Lorenzo Tenochtitlán*, ed. Ann Cyphers, pp. 163–94. Mexico, DF: Instituto de Investigaciones Antropologicas, Universidad Nacional Autonoma de Mexico.

———. 1999. From Stone to Symbols: Olmec Art in Social Context at San Lorenzo Tenochtitlán. In *Social Patterns in Pre-Classic Mesoamerica*, ed. David C. Grove and Rosemary A. Joyce, pp. 155–81. Washington, D.C.: Dumbarton Oaks Research Library and Collections.

———. 2004a. *Escultura Olmeca de San Lorenzo Tenochtitlán*. Mexico DF: Instituto de Investigaciones Antropologicas, Universidad Nacional Autonoma de Mexico, Coordinacion de Humanidades.

———. 2004b. Escultura Monumental Olmeca: Temas y Contextos. In *Acercarse y Mirar: homenaje a Beatriz de la Fuente*, ed. María Teresa Uriarte and Leticia C. Staines, pp. 51–74. México: Universidad Nacional Autónomo de México.

———. 2008. Los tronos y la configuración del poder olmeca. In *Ideología Política y Sociedad en el Periodo Formativo: ensayos en homanaje al doctor David C. Grove*, ed. Ann Cyphers and Kenneth G. Hirth. México, D.F.: Universidad Nacional Autónoma de México, Instituto de Investigaciones Antropológigas.

———. 2009. Bad-year Economics and the San Lorenzo Olmec. Conference presented at Dumbarton Oaks, Washington DC, November 5, 2009.

———. n.d.-a La cerámica de San Lorenzo Tenochtitlán. Unpublished ms, in possession of the author.

———. n.d.-b Las excavaciones en San Lorenzo Tenochtitlán. Unpublished ms, in possession of the author.

Cyphers Guillén, Ann, and Anna Di Castro. 1996. Los Artefactos Multiperforados de Ilmenita de San Lorenzo. *Arqueología* 16:3–14.

———. 2009. Early Olmec Architecture and Imagery. In *The Art of Urbanism: Mesoamerican Kingdoms Represented Themselves in Architecture and Imagery*, ed. William L. Fash, Jr., and Leonardo López Luján, pp. 21–52. Washington, DC: Dumbarton Oaks Research Library and Collections.

Cyphers Guillén, Ann, Alejandro Hernández-Portilla, Marisol Varela-Gómez, and Lilia Grégor-López. 2006. Cosmological and Sociopolitical Synergy in Preclassic Architectural Complexes. In *Precolumbian Water Management: Ideology, Ritual, and Power*, ed. Lisa J. Lucero and Barbara W. Fash, pp. 17–32. Tucson, AZ: University of Arizona Press.

Cyphers Guillén, Ann, and Artemio López Cisneros. 2007. El Luchador: Historia Antigua y Reciente. *Arqueología Mexicana* 15(88): 66–70.

Cyphers, Ann, Timothy Murtha, Joshua Borstein, Judith Zurita-Noguera, Roberto Lunagómez, Stacey Symonds, Gerardo Jiménez, Mario Arturo Ortiz, and José Manuel Figueroa. 2008–2007. Arqueología Digital en la Primera Capital Olmeca, San Lorenzo. *Thule* 22-25:121–44. Centro Studi Americanistici 'Circolo Amerindiano,' Perugia, Italia.

Cyphers, Ann, Timothy Murtha, Judith Zurita Noguera, Gerardo Jiménez, Elvia Hernández Guevara, Brizio Martínez Gracia, Virginia Arieta Baizabal, Roberto Lunagómez, Joshua Borstein, Stacey Symonds, Mario Arturo Ortiz, and José Manuel Figueroa. 2014. *Atlas Digital de la Zona Arqueológica de San Lorenzo, Veracruz.* México: Instituto de Investigaciones Antropológicas, Universidad Nacional Autónoma de México, México.

Cyphers Guillén, Ann, and Mario A. Ortiz. 2000. Geomorphology and Ancient Cultural Landscapes of Southern Veracruz. In *Mounds, Modoc and Mesoamerica: Papers in Honor of Melvin L. Fowler*, ed. Steven R. Ashler, pp. 99–110. Springfield, IL: Illinois State Museum.

Cyphers Guillén, Ann, and Judith Zurita-Noguera. 2006a. A Land that Tastes of Water. In *Precolumbian Water Management: Ideology, Ritual, and Power*, ed. Lisa J. Lucero and Barbara W. Fash, pp. 33–50. Tucson, AZ: University of Arizona Press.

———. 2006b. Monumentality at San Lorenzo. Paper presented at the 71st Annual Meeting of the Society for American Archaeology, San Juan, Puerto Rico, April 29.

———. 2007. Tempranos conceptos cosmológicos en San Lorenzo. Paper presented at the Encuentro Pueblos y Fronteras, San Cristóbal de las Casas.

———. 2012. Early Olmec Wetland Mounds: Investigating Energy to Produce Energy. In *Early New World Monumentality*, ed. R.L. Burger and R.M. Rosenswig, pp. 138–73. Gainsville: The University Press of Florida.

Dahlin, Bruce H. 1984. A Colossus in Guatemala: The Preclassic Maya City of El Mirador. *Archaeology* 37(5): 18–25.

———. 2003. Chunchicmil: A Complex Economy in NW Yucatan. *Mexicon* 25(5): 129–38.

———. 2009. Ahead of Its Time? The Remarkable Early Classic Maya Economy of Chunchicmil. *Journal of Social Anthropology* 9(3): 341–67.

Dahlin, Bruce H., John E. Foss, and Mary Elizabeth Chambers. 1980. Project Acalches: Reconstructing the Natural and Cultural History of a Seasonal Swamp at El Mirador, Guatemala: Preliminary Results. In *El Mirador, Peten, Guatemala: An Interim Report*, ed. Ray T. Matheny, pp. 37–57. Papers of the New World Archaeological Foundation, No. 45. Provo, UT: New World Archaeological Foundation, Brigham Young University.

Dahlin, Bruce H., Christopher T. Jensen, Richard E. Terry, David R. Wright, and Timothy Beach. 2007. In Search of Ancient Maya Market. *Latin American Antiquity* 18(4): 363–84.

Davis-Salazar, Karla L. 2003. Late Classic Maya Water Management and Community Organization at Copan, Honduras. *Latin American Antiquity* 14(3): 275–99.

De la Fuente, Beatriz. 1992. Order and Nature in Olmec Art. In *The Ancient Americas: Art from Sacred Landscapes*, ed. Richard Townsend, pp. 122–33. Chicago, IL: Art Institute of Chicago.

de León, Francisco, and Juan A. Alonzo. 1996. Lago Miraflores, núcleo de actividad humana de Kaminaljuyu. In *IX Simposio de Investigaciones Arqueológicas en Guatemala*, ed. Juan Pedro Laporte and Hector L. Escobedo, pp. 411–18. Guatemala: Ministerio de Cultura y Deportes, Instituto de Antropología e Historia, Asociación Tikal.

de Montmollin, Olivier. 1989. *The Archaeology of Political Structure: Settlement Analysis in a Classic Maya Polity*. Cambridge: Cambridge University Press.

———. 1992. Patrones Fronterizos de los Reinos Mayas del Clásico en los Altos Tributarios del Río Grijalva. *Arqueología* 7:57–67.

———. 1995. *Settlement and Politics in Three Classic Maya Polities*. Monographs in World Archaeology No. 24. Madison, WI: Prehistory Press.

Delgado, Agustín. 1965a. *Archaeological Reconnaissance in the Region of Tehuantepec, Oaxaca, Mexico*. Papers of the New World Archaeological Foundation, No. 18. Provo, UT: New World Archaeological Foundation.

———. 1965b. *Excavations at Santa Rosa, Chiapas, Mexico*. Papers of the New World Archaeological Foundation, No. 17. Provo, UT: New World Archaeological Foundation.

Demarest, Arthur A. 1984. The Harvard El Mirador Project, 1982–1983. Preclassic Ceramics of El Mirador: Preliminary Results and Ongoing Analysis. *Mesoamerica* 7:53–92.

———. 1989. The Olmec and the Rise of Civilization in Eastern Mesoamerica. In *Regional Perspectives on the Olmec*, ed. Robert J. Sharer and David C. Grove, pp. 303–44. School of American Research Advanced Seminar Series. New York, NY: Cambridge University Press.

———. 1992a. Ideology in Ancient Maya Cultural Evolution: The Dynamics of Galactic Polities. In *Ideology and Pre-Columbian Civilizations*, ed. Arthur A. Demarest and Geoffrey W. Conrad, pp. 135–157. Santa Fe, NM: School of American Research Press.

———. 1992b. Archaeology, Ideology, and Pre-Columbian Cultural Evolution: The Search for an Approach. In *Ideology and Pre-Columbian Civilizations*, ed. Arthur A. Demarest and Geoffrey W. Conrad, pp. 1–13. School of American Research Advanced Seminar Series. Santa Fe, NM: School of American Research Press.

———. 1996. Closing Comment on the Maya State. *Current Anthropology* 37(5): 821–30.

———. 2004. *Ancient Maya: The Rise and Fall of a Rainforest Civilization*. Cambridge: Cambridge University Press.

———. 2011. The Political, Economic, and Cultural Correlates of Late Preclassic Southern Highland Material Culture: Evidence, Analyses, and Controversies. In *The Southern Maya in the Late Preclassic*, ed. Michael Love and Jonathan Kaplan, pp. 345–86. Boulder: Colorado University Press.

Demarest, Arthur A., and Robert J. Sharer. 1986. Late Preclassic Ceramic Spheres, Culture Areas, and Cultural Evolution in the Southeastern Highlands of Mesoamerica. In *The Southwest Maya Periphery*, ed. Patricia Urban and Edward Schortman, pp. 194–223. Austin, TX: University of Texas Press.

Demarest, Arthur A., and Geoffrey W. Conrad, eds. 1992. *Ideology and Pre-Columbian Civilizations*. School of American Research Advanced Seminar Series, Santa Fe, NM: SAR Press.

Demarest, Arthur A., Robert Sharer, William Fowler, Jr., Eleanor King, and Joyce Fowler. 1984. Las Excavaciones, Proyecto El Mirador de la Harvard University, 1982–1983. *Mesoamerica Ano* 5(7): 14–52.

Di Castro, Anna. 1997. Los Bloques de Ilmenita de San Lorenzo. In *Población, Subsistencia y Medio Ambiente en San Lorenzo Tenochtitlán*, ed. Ann Cyphers, pp. 153–60. Mexico, DF: Instituto de Investigaciones Antropológicas, Universidad Nacional Autónoma de México.

Di Castro, Anna, and Ann Cyphers. 2006. Iconografía de la cerámica de San Lorenzo. *Anales del Institutito de Investigaciones Estéticas* 28(89): 29–58.

Di Castro, Anna, Ann Cyphers, and Marisol Varela. 2008. Los Espejos de San Lorenzo. In *Homenaje al Doctor Jaime Litvak King*, ed. P. Schmidt, E. Ortiz, and J. Santos, pp. 167–76. México: Instituto de Investigaciones Antropológicas, Universidad Nacional Autónoma de México, México.

Diehl, Richard A. 1976. Pre-Hispanic Relationships between the Basin of Mexico and North and West Mexico. In *The Valley of Mexico: Studies in Pre-Hispanic Ecology and Society*, ed. Eric R. Wolf, pp. 249–86. Albuquerque, NM: University of New Mexico Press.

Diehl, Richard A. 1981. Olmec Architecture: A Comparison of San Lorenzo and La Venta. In *The Olmec and Their Neighbors: Essays in Memory of Matthew W. Stirling*, ed. Michael D. Coe, David C. Grove, and Elizabeth P. Benson, pp. 69–81. Washington, DC: Dumbarton Oaks Research Library and Collections.

———. 1989. Olmec Archaeology: What We Know and What We Wish We Knew. In *Regional Perspectives on the Olmec*, ed. Robert J. Sharer and David C. Grove, pp. 17–32. Cambridge: Cambridge University Press.

———. 2004. *The Olmecs: America's First Civilization*. Ancient Peoples and Places. New York, NY: Thames and Hudson.

Diehl, Richard A., and Michael D. Coe. 1995. Olmec Archaeology. In *The Olmec World: Ritual and Rulership*, pp. 11–26. Princeton, NJ: The Princeton University Art Museum.

Dietler, Michael, and Brian D. Hayden, eds. 2001. *Feasts: Archaeological and Ethnographic Perspectives on Food, Politics, and Power*. Washington, DC: Smithsonian Institution Press.

Dixon, J.B., J.S. Jacob, and G.N. White. 1994. Todorokite in Manganese Oxide Nodules of a Guatemalan Vertisol. Paper presented at the Soil Science Society of America Meeting, Seattle, October 31–November 4.

Doering, Travis F. 2002. Obsidian Artifacts from San Andres, La Venta, Tabasco, Mexico. M.A. thesis, Dept. of Anthropology, Florida State University.

———. 2007. An Unexplored Realm in the Heartland of the Southern Gulf Olmec: Investigations at El Marquesillo, Veracruz, Mexico. Ph.D. diss., Dept. of Anthropology, University of South Florida.

Doering, Travis F., and Lori D. Collins. 2010. Revisiting Kaminaljuyu Monument 65 in Three-Dimensional High Definition. In *The Place of Stone Monuments: Context, Use, and Meaning in Mesoamerica's Preclassic Transition*, ed. Julia Guernsey, John E. Clark, and Barbara Arroyo, pp. 259–282. Washington, DC: Dumbarton Oaks Research Library and Collections.

Dreiss, Meredith L. 1994. The Shell Artifacts of Colha: The 1983 Season. In *Continuing Archeology at Colha, Belize*, ed. Thomas R. Hester, Harry J. Shafer, and Jack D. Eaton, pp. 177–99. Studies in Archeology 16, Texas Archeological Research Laboratory. Austin: University of Texas Press.

Dreiss, Meredith L., and David O. Brown. 1989. Obsidian Exchange Patterns in Belize. In *Prehistoric Maya Economies in Belize*, ed. Patricia A. McAnany and Barry L. Isaac, pp. 57–90. Research in Economic Anthropology, Supplement 4. Greenwich, CN: JAI Press, Inc.

Drennan, Robert D. 1984. Long-Distance Movement of Goods in the Mesoamerican

Formative and Classic. *American Antiquity* 49(1): 27–43.

———. 1988. Household Location and Compact Versus Dispersed Settlement in Pre-hispanic Mesoamerica. In *Household and Community in the Mesoamerican Past*, ed. Richard R. Wilk and Wendy A. Ashmore, pp. 273–93. Albuquerque, NM: University of New Mexico Press.

Drucker, Philip. 1952. *La Venta, Tabasco: A Study of Olmec Ceramics and Art*. Bureau of American Ethnology Bulletin 153. Washington, DC: Smithsonian Institution Bureau of American Ethnology.

———. 1981. On the Nature of Olmec Polity. In *The Olmec and Their Neighbors: Essays in Memory of Matthew W. Stirling*, ed. Michael D. Coe, David C. Grove, and Elizabeth P. Benson, pp. 29–47. Washington, DC: Dumbarton Oaks Research Library and Collections.

Drucker, Phillip, and Eduardo Contreras. 1953. Site Patterns in the Eastern Part of the Olmec Territory. *Journal of the Washington Academy of Sciences* 43(12): 389–96.

Drucker, Philip, and Robert F. Heizer. 1965. Commentary on W.R. Coe and Robert Stuckenrath's Review of 'Excavations at La Venta, Tabasco, 1955.' In *Samuel A. Barrett: A Memorial*, pp. 37–69. The Kroeber Anthropological Society Papers No. 33. Berkeley, CA: The Kroeber Anthropological Society.

Drucker, Philip, Robert F. Heizer, and Robert J. Squier. 1959. *Excavations at La Venta Tabasco, 1955*. Bureau of American Ethnology Bulletin 170. Washington, DC: Smithsonian Institution Bureau of American Ethnology.

Dull, Robert A., John R. Southon, and Payson Sheets. 2001. Volcanism, Ecology and Culture: A Reassessment of the Volcán Ilopango TBJ Eruption in the Southern Maya Realm. *Latin American Antiquity* 12(1): 25–44.

Dunham, Peter S. 1990. Coming Apart at the Seams: The Classic Development and the Demise of Maya Civilization; A Segmentary View from Xnaheb, Belize. Ph.D. diss., Dept. of Anthropology, State University of New York at Albany.

Dunham, Peter S., and Peter Mathews. 1992. The Segmentary State and the Classic Lowland Maya: A 'New' Model for Ancient Political Organization. Paper presented at the conferences at Cleveland State University, October 14th–18th.

Dunning, Nicholas P. 1995. Coming Together at the Temple Mountain: Environment, Subsistence and the Emergence of Lowland Maya Segmentary States. In *The Emergence of Lowland Maya Civilization. The Transition from the Preclassic to the Early Classic*, ed. Nikolai Grube, pp. 61–69. Möckmül, Germany: Verlag Anton Saurweir.

Dunning, Nicholas P., and Timothy Beach. 1994. Soil Erosion, Slope Management, and Ancient Terracing in the Maya Lowlands. *Latin American Antiquity* 5(1): 51–69.

Dunning, Nicholas P., Timothy Beach, and Sheryl Luzzadder-Beach. 2006. Environmental Variability Among Bajos in the Southern Maya Lowlands and Its Implications for Ancient Maya Civilization and Archaeology. In *Precolumbian Water Management. Ideology, Ritual, and Power*, ed. Lisa J. Lucero and Barbara W. Fash, pp. 81–99. Tucson, AZ: The University of Arizona Press.

Dunning, Nicholas P., Timothy Beach, and David Rue. 1997. The Paleoecology and Ancient Settlement of the Petexbatun Region, Guatemala. *Ancient Mesoamerica* 8:255–66.

Dunning, Nicholas P., Sheryl Luzzadder-Beach, Timothy Beach, John G. Jones, Vernon Scarborough, and T. Patrick Culbert. 2002. Arising from the Bajos: The Evolution of a Neotropical Landscape and the Rise of Maya Civilization. *Annals of the Association of American Geographers* 92(2): 267–83.

Dunning, Nicholas P., David Rue, Timothy Beach, Alan Covich, and Afred Traverse. 1998. The Paleoecology of Laguna Tamarindito, El Petén, Guatemala. *Journal of Field Archaeology* 25:139–51.

Durkheim, E. 1933[1893]. *The Division of Labor in Society*, trans. G. Simpson. New York, NY: Macmillan.

Durkheim, Emile. 1984[1893]. *The Division of Labor in Society*. New York, NY: The Free Press.

Earle, Timothy K, ed. 1991. *Chiefdoms: Power, Economy, and Ideology*. SAR Advanced Seminar Series. Cambridge: Cambridge University Press.

———. 1976. A Nearest-Neighbor Analysis of Two Formative Settlement Systems. In *The Early Mesoamerican Village*, ed. Kent V. Flannery, pp. 196–223. New York, NY: Academic Press.

———. 1987. Chiefdoms in Archaeological and Ethnohistorical Perspective. *Annual Review of Anthropology* 16:279–308.

———, ed. 1991a. *Chiefdoms: Power, Economy, and Ideology*. SAR Advanced Seminar Series. Cambridge: Cambridge University Press.

———. 1991b. The Evolution of Chiefdoms. In *Chiefdoms: Power, Economy, and Ideology*, ed. Timothy K. Earle, pp. 1–15. SAR Advanced Seminar Series. Cambridge: Cambridge University Press.

———. 1997. *How Chiefs Come to Power: The Political Economy in Prehistory*. Stanford, CA: Stanford University Press.

———. 2000. Archaeology, Property, and Prehistory. *Annual Review of Anthropology* 29:39–60.

Eaton, Jack. D., and Barton Kunstler. 1980. Excavations at Operation 2009, a Maya Ballcourt. In *The Colha Project: Second Season, 1980 Interim Report*, ed. Thomas R.

Hester, Jack D. Eaton, and Harry J. Shafer, pp. 121–32. San Antonio, TX: Center for Archaeological Research.

Edmonson, Munro S. 1982. *The Ancient Future of the Itza: The Book of Chilam Balam of Tizimin*. Austin, TX: University of Texas Press.

Ehrenreich, Robert, Carole L. Crumley, and Janet E. Levy, eds. 1995. *Heterarchy and the Analysis of Complex Societies*. Archaeological Papers of the American Anthropological Association No. 6. Arlington, VA: American Anthropological Association.

Ekholm, Susanna. 1969. *Mound 30a and the Early Preclassic Sequence of Izapa, Chiapas, Mexico*. Papers of the New World Archaeological Foundation, No.25. Provo, UT: New World Archaeological Foundation, Brigham Young University.

———. 1989. Las Figurillas Preclásicas Cerámicas de Izapa, Chiapas: Tradición Mixe-Zoque. In *Preclasico o Formativo: Avances y Perspectivas*, ed. Martha Carmona Macias, pp. 333–52. Mexico, DF: Museo Nacional de Antropología, Instituto Nacional de Antropología e Historia.

———. 1993. La Escultura Más Temprana Excavada en Izapa, Chiapas. In *Antropología, Historia e Imaginativa: En Homenaje a Eduardo Martínez Espinosa*, ed. Carlos Navarrete and Cristina Álvarez A., pp. 67–76. Mexico: Gobierno del Estado de Chiapas, Consejo Estatal de Fomento a la Investigacion y Difusion de la Cultura.

Elferink, Jan G.R. 2000. Aphrodisiac Use in Pre-Columbian Aztec and Inca Cultures. *Journal of the History of Sexuality* 9(1/2): 25–36.

Epstein, Stephen M. 1990. Operation 4044 Preliminary Excavation Report, Colha, Belize. Unpublished ms.

Escobedo, Héctor L., Mónica Urquizú, and Jeanette Castellanos. 1996. Nuevas Investigaciones en Kaminaljuyu: Excavaciones en los Montículos A-V-II y A-VI-I. In *IX Simposio de Investigaciones Arqueológicas en Guatemala*, ed. Juan Pedro Laporte and Héctor L. Escobedo, pp. 419–36. Guatemala: Ministerio de Cultura y Deportes, Instituto de Antropología e Historia, Asociación Tikal.

Estrada-Belli, Francisco. 2002. Anatomía de una Ciudad Maya: Holmul. Resultados de Investigaciones Arqueológicas en 2000 y 2001. *Mexicon* 24(5): 107–12.

———. 2003. Anatomía de Holmul: Su ciudad y Territorio. In *XVI Simposio de Investigaciones Arqueológicas en Guatemala*, ed. Juan Pedro Laporte, Bárbara Arroyo, Héctor Escobedo, and Héctor E. Mejía, pp. 265–74. Guatemala City: Museo Nacional de Arqueología y Etnología.

———. 2004a. Cival, La Sufricaya and Homul: The Long History of Maya Political Power and Settlement in the Holmul Region. Paper presented at the II Belize Archaeology Symposium, Belize City, July 7.

———. 2004b. Investigaciones Arqueológicas en la Region de Holmul, Petén, Guatemala. Informe Preliminar de la Temporada 2004. http://www.vanderbilt.edu/estrada-belli/holmul/reports, accessed February 2007.

———. 2006a. Lightening Sky, Rain, and the Maize God: The Ideology of Preclassic Maya Rulers at Cival, Peten, Guatemala. *Ancient Mesoamerica* 17(1): 57–78.

———. 2006b. Investigaciones Arqueológicas en la Region de Holmul, Petén, Guatemala. Informe Preliminar de la temporada 2005. http://www.vanderbilt.edu/estrada-belli/holmul/reports, accessed February 2007.

———. 2011. *The First Maya Civilization: Ritual and Power before the Classic Period.* Routledge: New York.

Estrada-Belli, Francisco, Jeremy Bauer, Michael Callaghan, Nina Neivens, Antolin Velasquez, and Josue Calvo. 2006. Las Epocas Tempranas en el Area de Holmul, Peten. In *XIX Simposio de Investigaciones Arqueologicas en Guatemala*, ed. Juan Pedro Laporte, Bárbara Arroyo, and Héctor E. Mejía, pp. 639–48. Guatemala: Ministerio de Cultura y Deportes, Instituto de Antropología e Historia, Asociación Tikal.

Estrada-Belli, Francisco, Jeremy Bauer, Molly Morgan, and Angel Chavez. 2003. Symbols of Early Maya Kingship at Cival, Petén, Guatemala. *Antiquity Online* 77(298). http://antiquity.ac.uk/projgall/estrada_belli/index.html, accessed September 2009.

Estrada-Belli, Francisco, Nikolai Grube, Marc Wolf, Kristen Gardella, and Claudio Lozano Guerra-Librero. 2003. Preclassic Maya Monuments and Temples at Cival, Peten, Guatemala. *Antiquity* 77(2960): 1–4.

Estrada-Belli, Francisco, and David Wahl. 2010. Prehistoric Human-Environment Interactions in the Southern Maya Lowlands: The Holmul Region Case. http://www.bu.edu/holmul/reports/Holmul_NSF_human_environment_interactions.pdf, accessed November 2010.

Evans, Susan T., and Janet Catherine Berlo. 1992. Teotihuacan, an Introduction. In *Art, Ideology, and the City of Teotihuacan*, ed. Janet Catherine Berlo, pp. 1–26. Washington, DC: Dumbarton Oaks.

Fahsen, Federico. 2002. Who Are the Prisoners in Kaminaljuyú Monuments? In *Incidents of Archaeology in Central America and Yucatán: Studies in Honor of Edwin M. Shook*, ed. Michael W. Love, Marion Popenoe de Hatch, and Héctor L. Escobedo, pp. 360–74. Lanham, MD: University Press of America.

Farriss, Nancy. 1984. *Maya Society Under Colonial Rule: The Collective Enterprise of Survival.* Princeton, NJ: Princeton University Press.

Fash, William L. 1986. History and Characteristics of Settlement in the Copán Valley, and Some Comparisons with Quiriguá. In *The Southeast Maya Periphery*, ed. Patricia A. Urban and Edward M. Schortman, pp. 72–93. Austin, TX: University of Texas Press.

———. 1987. The Altar and Associated Features. In *Ancient Chalcatzingo*, ed. David C. Grove, pp. 82–94. Austin, TX: University of Texas Press.

———. 1991. *Scribes, Warriors and Kings: The City of Copán and the Ancient Maya*. London: Thames and Hudson.

Fash, William L., and Robert J. Sharer. 1991. Sociopolitical Developments and Methodological Issues at Copán, Honduras: A Conjunctive Perspective. *Latin American Antiquity* 2(2): 166–87.

Fauvelle, Mikael. 2010. Feasting and Social Complexity at La Blanca, Guatemala. Unpublished M.A. thesis, Dept. of Anthropology, California State University, Northridge.

Fedick, Scott L., and Anabel Ford. 1990. The Prehistoric Agricultural Landscape of the Central Maya Lowlands: An Examination of Local Variability in a Regional Context. *World Archaeology* 22:18–33.

Feeley-Harnik, Gillian. 1985. Issues in Divine Kingship. *Annual Review of Anthropology* 14:273–313.

Feinman, Gary M., and Joyce Marcus, eds. 1998. *Archaic States*. Santa Fe, NM: School of American Research Press.

Feinman, Gary M., and Linda M. Nicholas. 1999. Reflections on Regional Survey: Perspectives from the Guirún Area, Oaxaca. In *Settlement Pattern Studies in the Americas: Fifty Years since Virú*, ed. Brian R. Billman and Gary M. Feinman, pp. 172–90. Washington, DC: Smithsonian Institution Press.

Feldman, Lawrence. 2001. Nakbe Shell Species. Unpublished ms, Foundation for Anthropological Research and Environmental Studies, Idaho.

Fenton, William N. 1998. *The Great Law and the Longhouse: A Political History of the Iroquois Confederacy*. Norman, OK: University of Oklahoma Press.

Fields, Virginia M. 1989. The Origins of Divine Kingship among the Lowland Classic Maya. Ph.D. diss., Institute of Latin American Studies, University of Texas, Austin.

———. 1991. The Iconographic Heritage of the Maya Jester God. In *Sixth Palenque Round Table*, ed. Merle Greene Robertson and Virginia M. Fields, pp. 167–74. Norman, OK: University of Oklahoma Press.

Fields, Virginia M., and Dorie Reents-Budet. 2005a. Late Preclassic Expressions of Authority on the Pacific Slope. In *Lords of Creation: The Origins of Sacred Maya Kingship*, ed. Virginia M. Fields and Dorie Reents-Budet, pp. 37–43. Los Angeles, CA: Los Angeles County Museum of Art.

————, eds. 2005b. *Lords of Creation: the Origins of Sacred Maya Kingship.* Los Angeles, CA: Los Angeles County Museum of Art.

Fisher, Genevieve, and Diana D. Loren. 2003. Embodying Identity in Archaeology. *Cambridge Archaeological Journal* 13:225–30.

Flad, Rowan K., and Zachary X. Hruby. 2007. 'Specialized' Production in Archaeological Contexts: Rethinking Specialization, the Social Value of Products, and the Practice of Production. In *Rethinking Craft Specialization in Complex Societies: Archaeological Analyses of the Social Meaning of Production*, ed. Zachary X. Hruby and Rowan K. Flad, pp. 1–19. Archaeological Papers of the American Anthropological Association, No. 17. Arlington, VA: American Anthropological Association.

Flanagan, James G. 1989. Hierarchy in Simple 'Egalitarian' Societies. *Annual Review of Anthropology* 18:245–66.

Flannery, Kent V., ed. 1976. *The Early Mesoamerican Village.* New York, NY: Academic Press.

————, ed. 1986. *Guilá Naquitz: Archaic Foraging and Early Agriculture in Oaxaca, Mexico.* New York, NY: Academic Press.

————. 1968. The Olmec and the Valley of Oaxaca. In *Dumbarton Oaks Conference on the Olmec*, Elizabeth Benson, pp. 79–110. Washington, DC: Dumbarton Oaks Research Library and Collection.

————. 1972. The Cultural Evolution of Civilizations. *Annual Review of Ecology and Systematics* 3:399–426.

————. 1982. Review of *In the Land of the Olmec. American Anthropologist* 84(2): 442–47.

————. 1994. Childe the Evolutionist: A Perspective from Nuclear America. In *The Archaeology of V. Gordon Childe: Contemporary Perspectives*, ed. D. R. Harris, pp. 101–12. Chicago: The University of Chicago Press.

————. 1995. Prehistoric Social Evolution. In *Research Frontiers in Anthropology*, ed. C. Ember and M. Ember, pp. 1–26. Englewood Cliffs, New Jersey: Prentice-Hall.

————. 1998. The Ground Plan of Archaic States. In *Archaic States*, ed. Gary M. Feinman and Joyce Marcus, pp. 15–57. Santa Fe, NM: School of American Research Press.

————. 1999. Process and Agency in Early State Formation. *Cambridge Archaeological Journal* 9(1): 3–21.

————. 2006. On the Resilience of Anthropological Archaeology. *Annual Review of Anthropology* 35:1–13.

Flannery, Kent V., Andrew K. Balkansky, Gary M. Feinman, David C. Grove, Joyce Marcus, Elsa M. Redmond, Robert G. Reynolds, Robert J. Sharer, Charles S. Spencer, and Jason Yaeger. 2005. Implications of New Petrographic Analysis for the

Olmec 'Mother Culture' Model. *Proceedings of the National Academy of Sciences* 102(32): 11219–23.

Flannery, Kent V., Anne T. Kirkby, Michael J. Kirkby, and Aubrey W. Willams Jr. 1967. Farming Systems and Political Growth in Ancient Oaxaca. *Science* 158(3800): 445–54.

Flannery, Kent V., and Joyce Marcus, eds. 1983. *The Cloud People: Divergent Evolution of the Zapotec and Mixtec Civilizations.* New York, NY: Academic Press.

———. 1976a. Formative Oaxaca and the Zapotec Cosmos. *American Scientist* 64(4): 374–83.

———. 1976b. Evolution of the Public Building in Formative Oaxaca. In *Cultural Change and Continuity: Essays in Honor of James Bennett Griffin*, ed. Charles E. Cleland, pp. 205–21. New York, NY: Academic Press.

———. 1994. *Early Formative Pottery of the Valley of Oaxaca, Mexico.* Memoirs of the Museum of Anthropology 27. Ann Arbor, MI: Museum of Anthropology, University of Michigan.

———. 2000. Formative Mexican Chiefdoms and the Myth of the 'Mother Culture.' *Journal of Anthropological Archaeology* 19:1–17.

Folan, William J., Joel Gunn, Jack D. Eaton, and R.W. Patch. 1983. Paleoclimatological Patterning in Southern Mesoamerica. *Journal of Field Archaeology* 10:453–68.

Ford, Anabel. 1990. Maya Settlement in the Belize River Area: Variations in Residence Patterns of the Central Maya Lowlands. In *Precolumbian Population History in the Maya Lowlands*, ed. T. Patrick Culbert and Don S. Rice, pp. 167–81. Albuquerque, NM: University of New Mexico Press.

———. 2004. Integration among Communities, Center, and Regions: The Case from El Pilar. In *The Ancient Maya of the Belize Valley: Half a Century of Archaeological Research*, ed. James F. Garber, ed, 238–56. Gainesville, FL: University Press of Florida.

Forsyth, Donald W. 1989. *The Ceramics of El Mirador, Peten, Guatemala.* Papers of the New World Archaeological Foundation, No. 63. Provo, UT: New World Archaeological Foundation, Brigham Young University.

———. 1992. Un Estudio Comparativo de la Cerámica Temprana de Nakbe. In *IV Simposio de Arqueología Guatemalteca*, ed. Juan Pedro Laporte, Héctor L. Escobedo, and Sandra Villagran de Brady, pp. 45–56. Guatemala: Ministerio de Cultura y Deportes, Instituto de Antropología e Historia, Asociación Tikal.

———. 1993a. La Cerámica Arqueológica de Nakbe y El Mirador, Peten. In *III Simposio de Arqueología Guatemalteca*, ed. Juan Pedro Laporte, Héctor.L. Escobedo, Sandra Villagran de Brady, pp. 111–40. Guatemala: Ministerio de Cultura y Deportes, Instituto de Antropología e Historia, Asociación Tikal.

———. 1993b. The Ceramic Sequence at Nakbe. *Ancient Mesoamerica* 4:31–53.

———. 1993c. La Arquitectura Preclásica en Nakbe: Un Estudio Comparativo de Dos Períodos. In *VI Simposio de Investigaciones Arqueológicas en Guatemala, 1992*, ed. Juan Pedro Laporte, Hector L. Escobedo, and Sandra Villagrán de Brady, pp. 131–42. Guatemala City, Guatemala: Museo Nacional de Arqueología y Etnología. Ministerio de Cultura y Deportes, Instituto de Antropología e Historia, Asociación Tikal.

Fortes, Meyer. 1958. Introduction. In *The Developmental Cycle in Domestic Groups*, ed. Jack Goody, pp. 1–14. Cambridge: Cambridge University Press.

———. 1973. On the Concept of the Person among the Tallensi. In *La Notion de Personne en Afrique Noir*, ed. Germaine Dieterlen, pp. 283–319. Paris: Editions du Centre National de la Recherche Scientifique.

Foster, Robert J. 1985. Production and Value in the Enga Tee. *Oceania* 55:182–96.

Fowler, William R. Jr., ed. 1991. *The Formation of Complex Society in Southeastern Mesoamerica*. Boca Raton, FL: CRC Press.

———. 1987. *Analysis of the Chipped Stone Artifacts of El Mirador, Guatemala*. Notes of the New World Archaeological Foundation No. 5. Provo, UT: New World Archaeological Foundation, Brigham Young University.

Fowler, William R. Jr., Arthur A. Demarest, Helen V. Michel, Frank Asaro, and Fred Stross. 1989. Sources of Obsidian from El Mirador: New Evidence on Preclassic Maya Interaction. *American Anthropologist* 91(1): 158–68.

Fox, John W. 1987. *Maya Post-Classic State Formation: Segmentary Lineage Migration in Advancing Frontiers*. Cambridge: Cambridge University Press.

———. 1988. Hierarchization in Maya Segmentary States. In *State and Society: The Emergence and Development of Social Hierarchy and Political Centralization*, ed. John Gledhill, Barbara Bender, and Mogens Trolle Larsen, pp. 103–112. London: Routledge.

———. 1989. On the Rise and Fall of Tuláns and Maya Segmentary States. *American Anthropologist* 91:656–81.

Fox, John W., and Garrett W. Cook. 1996. Constructing Maya Communities: Ethnography for Archaeology. *Current Anthropology* 37(5): 811–21.

Fox, John W., Garrett W. Cook, Arlen F. Chase, and Diane Z. Chase. 1996. Questions of Political and Economic Integration: Segmentary Versus Centralized States Among the Ancient Maya. *Current Anthropology* 37:795–801.

Fox, John W., and John Justeson. 1986. Classic Maya Dynastic Alliance and Succession. In *Supplement to Handbook of Middle American Indians Vol. 4*, ed. Victoria Bricker and R. Spores, pp. 7–34. Austin, TX: University of Texas Press.

Fox, Richard G. 1977. *Urban Anthropology: Cities in Their Cultural Settings*. Englewood Cliffs, NJ: Prentice Hall.

Fraser, Douglas, and Herbert M. Cole. 1972. Art and Leadership: An Overview. In *African Art and Leadership*, ed. Douglas Fraser and Herbert M. Cole, pp. 295–328. Madison, WI: University of Wisconsin Press.

Freidel, David A. 1979. Culture Areas and Interaction Spheres: Contrasting Approaches to the Emergence of Civilization in the Maya Lowlands. *American Antiquity* 44(1): 36–54.

———. 1981. Civilization as a State of Mind: The Cultural Evolution of the Lowland Maya. In *The Transition to Statehood in the New World*, ed. Grant D. Jones and Robert R. Kautz, pp. 188–227. Cambridge: Cambridge University Press.

———. 1982. The Maya City of Cerros. *Archaeology* 35(4): 12–21.

———. 1985. Polychrome Facades of the Lowland Maya Preclassic. In *Painted Architecture and Polychrome Monumental Sculpture in Mesoamerica*, ed. Elizabeth Boone, pp. 5–30. Washington, D.C.: Dumbarton Oaks.

———. 1986a. Maya Warfare: An Example of Peer Polity Interaction. In *Peer Polity Interaction and Socio-political Change*, ed. Colin Renfrew and John F. Cherry, pp. 93–108. Cambridge: Cambridge University Press.

———. 1986b. The Monumental Architecture. In *Archaeology at Cerros, Belize, Central America: Volume 1, An Interim Report*, ed. Robin A. Roberston and David A. Freidel, pp. 1–21. Dallas, TX: Southern Methodist University Press.

———. 1986c. Terminal Classic Lowland Maya: Successes, Failures, and Aftermath. In *Late Lowland Maya Civilization*, ed. Jeremy A. Sabloff and E. Wyllys Andrews V, pp. 409–30. Albuquerque, NM: University of New Mexico Press.

———. 1990. The Jester God: The Beginning and End of a Maya Royal Symbol. In *Vision and Revision in Maya Studies*, ed. Flora S. Clancy and Peter D. Harrison, pp. 67–78. Albuquerque, NM: University of New Mexico Press.

———. 1992. The Trees of Life: Ahau as Idea and Artifact in Classic Lowland Maya Civilization. In *Ideology and Pre-Columbian Civilizations*, ed. Arthur A. Demarest and Geoffrey W. Conrad, pp. 116–33. Santa Fe, NM: School of American Research Press.

———. 1995. Preparing the Way. In *The Olmec World: Ritual and Rulership*, ed. Jill Guthrie, pp. 3–9. Princeton, NJ: Princeton University Art Museum.

———. 2000. Mystery of the Maya Façade. *Archaeology* 53(5): 24–28.

Freidel, David A., Kathryn A. Reese-Taylor, and David Mora-Marín. 2002. The Origins of Maya Civilization: The Old Shell Game, Commodity, Treasure, and Kingship. In *Ancient Maya Political Economies*, ed. Marilyn A. Masson and David A. Freidel, pp. 41–86. Walnut Creek, CA: Altamira Press.

Freidel, David A., and Linda Schele. 1988a. Kingship in the Late Preclassic Maya Lowlands: The Instruments and Places of Ritual Power. *American Anthropologist* 90(3): 547–67.

———. 1988b. Symbol and Power: A History of the Lowland Maya Cosmogram. In *Maya Iconography*, ed. Elizabeth Benson and Gillett Griffin, pp. 44–93. Princeton, NJ: Princeton University Press.

———. 1989. Dead Kings and Living Temples: Dedication and Termination Rituals among the Ancient Maya. In *Word and Image in Maya Culture: Explorations in Language, Writing, and Representation*, ed. William Hanks and Don Rice, pp. 233–43. Salt Lake City, UT: University of Utah Press.

Freidel, David A., Linda Schele, and Joy Parker. 1993. *Maya Cosmos: Three Thousand Years on the Shaman's Path*. New York, NY: Harper Collins.

Fried, Morton H. 1960. On the Evolution of Social Stratification and the State. In *Culture in History: Essays in Honor of Paul Radin*, ed. Stanley Diamond, pp. 713–31. New York, NY: Columbia University Press.

———. 1968. State: The Institution. In *International Encyclopedia of the Social Sciences*, vol. 15, ed. David L. Sills, pp. 143–50. New York, NY: Macmillan and Free Press.

———. 1978. The State, the Chicken and the Egg, or What Came First. In *Origins of the State: The Anthropology of Political Evolution*, ed. Ronald Cohen and Elman R. Service, pp. 35–48. Philadelphia, PA: Institute for the Study of Human Issues.

Fritz, John M. 1986. Vijayanagara: Authority and Meaning of a South Indian Imperial Capital. *American Anthropologist* 88:44–55.

Furst, Peter T. 1968. The Olmec Were-Jaguar Motif in the Light of Ethnographic Reality. In *Dumbarton Oaks Conference on the Olmec*, ed. Elizabeth P. Benson, pp. 143–74. Washington, DC: Dumbarton Oaks Research Library and Collections.

———. 1995. Shamanism, Transformation, and Olmec Art. In *The Olmec World: Ritual and Rulership*, ed. Jill Guthrie, pp. 69–82. Princeton, NJ: Princeton University Art Museum.

FYDEP. 1968. Mapa de los Suelos de El Peten. Proyecto de Evaluación Forestal FAO-FYDEP. Fomentos y Desarrollo del Peten. Instituto Geográfico Nacional: Guatemala City.

Gámez Eternod, Lorena. 1993. Crecimiento del sitio de Tlapacoya, Estado de México, durante el Horizonte Formativo. In *A propósito del Formativo*, ed. Ma. Teresa Castillo Mangas, pp. 11–32. México, DF: Subdirección de Salvamento. Arqueológico, Instituto Nacional de Antropología e Historia.

Gamio, Manuel. 1942. Franz Boas en México. *Boletín Bibliográfico de Antropología* 6:35–42.

Garber, James, ed. 2004. *The Ancient Maya of the Belize Valley: Half a Century of Archaeological Research*. Gainesville, FL: University Press of Florida.

Garber, James F., Christopher J. Hartman, and M. Kathryn Brown. 2002. The Kanocha Phase (1200–850 B.C.) on Structure B1: Results of the 2001 Field Season at Blackman Eddy. In *The Belize Valley Archaeology Project: Results of the 2001 Field Season*, ed. James F. Garber, M. Kathryn Brown, and Christopher J. Hartman, pp. 42–75. San Marcos: Southwest Texas State University.

Garber, James F., M. Kathryn Brown, Jaime J. Awe, and Christopher J. Hartman. 2004a. Middle Formative Prehistory of the Central Belize Valley: An Examination of Architecture, Material Culture, and Sociopolitical Change at Blackman Eddy. In *The Ancient Maya of the Belize Valley: Half a Century of Archaeological Research*, ed. James F. Garber, pp. 25–47. Gainesville, FL: University Press of Florida.

———. 2004b. The Terminal Early Formative Kanocha Phase (1100–900 B.C.) at Blackman Eddy. In *Archaeological Investigations in the Eastern Maya Lowlands: Papers of the 2003 Belize Archaeology Symposium*, ed. Jaime Awe, John Morris, and Sherilyne Jones, pp. 13–25. Research Reports in Belizean Archaeology, vol. 1. Belmopan, Belize: The Institute of Archaeology, National Institute of Culture and History.

Garber, James F., M. Kathryn Brown, W. David Driver, David M. Glassman, Christopher J. Hartman, F. Kent Reilly, and Lauren A. Sullivan. 2004c. Archaeological Investigations at Blackman Eddy. In *The Ancient Maya of the Belize Valley*, ed. James F. Garber, pp. 48–69. Gainesville, FL: University Press of Florida.

Garber, James F., Christopher J. Hartman, and M. Kathryn Brown. 2000. The Kanocha Phase (1200–850 B.C.) on Structure B1: Results of the 2001 Field Season at Blackman Eddy. In *The Belize Valley Archaeology Project: Results of the 2001 Field Season*, ed. James F. Garber, M. Kathryn Brown, and Christopher J. Hartman, pp. 42–75. San Marcos, TX: Southwest Texas State University.

García Cook, Ángel. 1981. The Historical Importance of Tlaxcala in the Cultural Development of the Central Highlands. In *The Handbook of Middle American Indians, Supplement 1: Archaeology*, ed. Jeremy A. Sabloff, pp. 244–76. Austin, TX: University of Texas Press.

García Moll, Roberto. 1979. Un Relieve Olmeca en Tenosique, Tabasco. *Estudios de Cultura Maya* 12:53–59.

García Moll, Roberto, Daniel Juárez Cossío, Carmen Pijoan Aguade, María Elena Salas Cuesta, and Marcela Salas Cuesta. 1991. *Catálogo de Entierros de San Luis Tlatilco, México: Temporada IV*. Serie Antropología Fisica-Arqueología. México, DF: Instituto Nacional de Antropología e Historia.

Geertz, Clifford. 1973. *The Interpretation of Cultures*. New York, NY: Basic Books.

———. 1980. *Negara: The Theater State in Nineteenth-century Bali*. Princeton, NJ: Princeton University Press.

Gerhardt, Juliette C., and Norman Hammond. 1991. The Community of Cuello: The Ceremonial Core. In *Cuello: An Early Maya Community in Belize*, ed. Norman Hammond, pp. 98–117. Cambridge: Cambridge University Press.

Gibson, Eric C. 1991. A Preliminary Functional and Contextual Study of Constricted Adzes from Northern Belize. In *Maya Stone Tools: Selected Papers from the Second Maya Lithic Conference*, ed. Thomas R. Hester and Harry J. Shafer, pp. 229–37. Monographs in World Archaeology No. 1. Madison, WI: Prehistory Press.

Gifford, James. 1965. Ceramics. In *Prehistoric Maya Settlement Patterns in the Belize Valley*, ed. Gordon R. Willey, William R. Bullard, John B. Glass, and James Gifford, pp. 319–90. Papers of the Peabody Museum of Archaeology and Ethnology vol. 54. Cambridge, MA: Peabody Museum of Archaeology and Ethnology, Harvard University.

Gillespie, Susan D. 1994. Llano del Jícaro: An Olmec Monument Workshop. *Ancient Mesoamerica* 5:231–42.

———. 1999. Olmec Thrones as Ancestral Altars: The Two Sides of Power. In *Material Symbols: Culture and Economy in Prehistory*, ed. John E. Robb, pp. 224–53. Center for Archaeological Investigations, Occasional Paper No. 26. Carbondale, IL: Southern Illinois University.

———. 2000a. The Monuments of Laguna de los Cerros and Its Hinterland. In *Olmec Art and Archaeology in Mesoamerica*, ed. John Clark and Mary Pye, pp. 95–115. Washington, DC: Center for Advanced Study, National Gallery of Art.

———. 2000b. Rethinking Ancient Maya Social Organization: Replacing Lineage with House. *American Anthropologist* 102(3): 467–84.

———. 2000c. Beyond Kinship: An Introduction. In *Beyond Kinship: Spatial and Material Reproduction in House Societies*, ed. Rosemary A. Joyce and Susan D. Gillespie, pp. 1–21. Philadelphia, PA: University of Pennsylvania Press.

———. 2001. Personhood, Agency, and Mortuary Ritual: A Case Study from the Ancient Maya. *Journal of Anthropological Archaeology* 20:73–112.

———. 2008. History in Practice: Ritual Deposition at La Venta, Complex A. In *Memory Work: Archaeologies of Material Practices*, ed. B. J. Mills and W. H. Walker, pp. 109–36. Santa Fe: SAR Press.

———. 2011. Archaeological Drawings as Re-presentations: The Maps of Complex A, La Venta, Mexico. *Latin American Antiquity* 22:3–36.

———. n.d. Chalcatzingo Monument 34: A Formative Period Southern Style Stela in the Central Mexican Highlands. Unpublished ms, Dept. of Anthropology, University of Florida, Gainesville.

Girard, Rafael. 1966. *Los Mayas: su civilización, su historia, su vinculaciones continentales.* Mexico, D.F.: Libromex Editores.

Glover, Jeffrey B., Dominique Rissolo, Joseph W. Ball, and Fabio E. Amador. 2008. Who Were the Middle Preclassic Settlers of Quintana Roo's North Coast? New Evidence from Vista Alegre. *Mexicon* 33:69–73.

Godelier, Maurice and Marilyn Strathern, eds. 1991. *Big Men and Great Men: Personifications of Power in Melanesia.* Cambridge: Cambridge University Press.

Goman, Michelle, and Roger Byrne. 1998. A 500-Year Record of Agriculture and Tropical Forest Clearance in the Tuxtlas, Veracruz, Mexico. *The Holocene* 8(1): 83–98.

Gómez Rueda, Hernando. 1995. Exploración de sistemas hidráulicos en Izapa. In *VIII Simposio de Investigaciones Arqueológicas en Guatemala*, ed. Juan Pedro Laporte and Héctor L. Escobedo, pp. 9–18. Guatemala: Ministerio de Cultura y Deportes, Instituto de Antropología e Historia, Asociación Tikal.

———. 1996a. *Las Limas, Veracruz y otros Asentamientos Prehispánicos de la Región Olmeca.* Mexico: Instituto Nacional de Antropología e Historia.

———. 1996b. Izapa: Organización Espacial de un Centro del Formativo en la Costa Pacífica de Chiapas. *IX Simposio de Investigaciones Arqueológicas en Guatemala, 1995*, ed. Juan Pedro Laporte and Héctor L. Escobedo, pp. 549–63. Guatemala: Museo Nacional de Arqueología y Etnología.

Gonzalez, Silvia, Alejandro Pastrana, Claus Siebe, and Geoff Duller. 2000. Timing of the Prehistoric Eruption of Xitle Volcano and the Abandonment of Cuicuilco Pyramid, Southern Basin of Mexico. In *The Archaeology of Geological Catastrophes*, ed. W.J. McGuire, D.R. Griffiths, P.L. Hancock, and I.S. Stewart, pp. 205–24. Geological Society Special Publication No. 171. London, England: Geological Society.

González Cruz, Arnoldo, and Martha Cuevas García. 1998. *Canto versus Canto: Manufactura de Artefactos Líticos en Chiapa de Corzo, Chiapas.* Colección Científica, No. 376. Mexico, DF: Instituto Nacional de Antropología e Historia.

González Lauck, Rebecca. 1988. Proyecto Arqueológico La Venta. *Arqueología* 4:121–65.

———. 1990. The 1984 Archaeological Investiations at La Venta, Tabasco. Ph.D. diss., Dept. of Anthropology, University of California, Berkeley.

———. 1994. La Antigua Ciudad Olmeca en La Venta, Tabasco. In *Los Olmecas en Mesoamérica*, ed. John E. Clark, pp. 93–111. Mexico, DF: Citibank.

———. 1995. La Venta: Una Gran Ciudad Olmeca. *Arqueologia Mexicana* 2(12): 38–42.

———. 1996. La Venta: An Olmec Capital. In *Olmec Art of Ancient Mexico*, ed. Elizabeth P. Benson and Beatriz de la Fuente, pp. 73–81. Washington, DC: National Gallery of Art.

———. 1997. Acerca de Pirámides de Tierra y Seres Sobrenaturales: Observaciones Preliminares en Torno al Edificio C-1, La Venta, Tabasco. *Arqueología, Segunda Epoca* 17:79–97.

———. 2001. La Venta (Tabasco, Mexico). In *Archaeology of Ancient Mexico and Central America: An Encyclopedia*, ed. Susan T. Evans and David L. Webster, pp. 798–801. New York, NY: Garland.

———. 2004. Observaciones en Torno a los Contextos de la Escultura Olmeca en La Venta. In *Acercarse y Mirar: Homenaje a Beatriz de la Fuente*, ed. María Teresa Uriarte and Leticia Staines Cicero, pp. 75–106. Mexico, DF: Instituto de Investigaciones Estéticas, Universidad Nacional Autonoma de Mexico.

———. 2006. La Venta. In *Olmecas, Mayas y Otras Culturas: Tabasco y la Zona Arqueológica de Palenque*. Mexico, DF: Consejo Nacional para La Cultura y Las Artes, Instituto Nacional de Antropología e Historia.

———. 2007. El Complejo A, La Venta, Tabasco. *Arqueología Mexicana* 15(87): 49–54.

———. 2010a. Pre-Olmec and Olmec Architecture. In *Pre-Columbian Architecture in Mesoamerica*, ed. M. T. Uriarte, pp. 71–82. New York: Abbeville Press Publishers and INAH.

———. 2010b. The Architectural Setting of Olmec Sculpture Clusters at La Venta, Tabasco. In *The Place of Stone Monuments: Context, Use, and Meaning in Mesoamerica's Preclassic Transition*, ed. J. Guernsey, J.E. Clark, and B. Arroyo, pp. 129–48. Washington DC: Dumbarton Oaks.

Goodenough, Ward H. 1965. Rethinking 'Status' and 'Role': Toward a General Model of the Cultural Organization of Social Relationships. In *The Relevance of Models for Social Anthropology*, ed. Michael Banton, pp. 1–24. ASA Monographs, No. 1. London: Tavistock.

Gosden, Chris and Gary Lock. 1998. Prehistoric Histories. *World Archaeology* 30(1):2–12.

Gossen, Gary H., and Richard M. Leventhal. 1993. The Topography of Ancient Maya Religious Pluralism: A Dialogue with the Present. In *Lowland Maya Civilization in the Eighth Century A.D.*, ed. Jeremy A. Sabloff and John S. Henderson, pp. 185–217. Washington, DC: Dumbarton Oaks Research Library and Collection.

Grabar, Andre. 1965. *Christian Iconography: A Study of Its Origins*. Bollingen Series, 35. Princeton, NJ: Princeton University Press.

Graeber, David. 1996. Beads and Money: Notes Toward a Theory of Wealth and Power. *American Ethnologist* 23:1–32.

———. 2001. *Toward an Anthropological Theory of Value: The False Coin of Our Own Dreams.* New York, NY: Palgrave MacMillan.

Graham, Alan. 1976. Studies in Neotropical Paleobotany. II. The Miocene Communities of Veracruz, Mexico. *Annals of the Missouri Botanical Garden* 63(4): 787–842.

Graham, Elizabeth. 2002. Perspectives on Economy and Theory. In *Ancient Maya Political Economies*, ed. Marilyn Masson and David Freidel, pp. 398–416. Walnut Creek, CA: Altamira Press.

Graham, Ian. 1962. Cinco Meses en el Petén: Recorrido y Observaciones sobre Notables Sedes de la Arqueología. *El Imparcial*, July 24.

———. 1967. *Archaeological Explorations in El Peten, Guatemala.* Middle American Research Institute Publication No. 33. New Orleans, LA: Tulane University.

Graham, John A. 1972. *The Hieroglyphic Inscriptions and Monumental Art of Altar de Sacrificios.* Papers of the Peabody Museum of Archaeology and Ethnology 64(2). Cambridge, MA: Peabody Museum of Archaeology and Ethnology, Harvard University.

———. 1979. Maya, Olmecs, and Izapans at Abaj Takalik, Guatemala. *Actes du XLII Congres du Americanistes, Paris* 8:179–88.

———. 1982. Antecedents of Olmec Sculpture at Abaj Takalik. In *Pre-Columbian Art History: Selected Readings*, ed. Alana Cordy-Collins, pp. 7–22. Palo Alto, CA: Peek Publications.

———. 1989. Olmec Diffusion: A Sculptural View from Pacific Guatemala. In *Regional Perspectives on the Olmec*, ed. Robert J. Sharer and David C. Grove, pp. 227–46. Cambridge: Cambridge University Press.

———. 1991. Through the Looking Glass: A Rejoinder to Coe and Diehl's Reply to Hammond. In *The Review of Archaeology* 12(2): 39–45.

Green, Dee F. 1969. Book of Mormon Archaeology: Myths and Alternatives. *Dialogue* 4(2): 71–80.

Green, Dee F., and Gareth W. Lowe. 1967. *Altamira and Padre Piedra, Early Preclassic Sites in Chiapas, Mexico.* Papers of the New World Archaeological Foundation, No. 15. Provo, UT: New World Archaeological Foundation, Brigham Young University.

Greengo, Robert E., and Clement W. Meighan. 1976. Additional Perspective on the Capacha Complex. *Journal of New World Archaeology* 1(5): 15–23.

Gregg, Susan A., ed. 1991. *Between Bands and States.* Center for Archaeological Investigations, Occasional Paper 9. Carbondale, IL: Southern Illinois University.

Grove, David C. 1968. The Preclassic Olmec in Central Mexico: Site Distribution and

Inferences. In *Dumbarton Oaks Conference on the Olmec*, ed. Elizabeth P. Benson, pp. 179–85. Washington, DC: Dumbarton Oaks Research Library and Collection.

———. 1970. *The Olmec Paintings of Oxtotitlán Cave, Guerrero, Mexico*. Studies in Pre-Columbian Art and Archaeology No. 6. Washington, DC: Dumbarton Oaks Research Library and Collections.

———. 1973. Olmec Altars and Myths. *Archaeology* 26:128–35.

———. 1974a. The Highland Olmec Manifestation: A Consideration of What It Is and What It Isn't. In *Mesoamerican Archaeology: New Approaches*, ed. Norman Hammond, pp. 109–28. Austin, TX: University of Texas Press.

———. 1974b. *San Pablo, Nexpa, and the Early Formative Archaeology of Morelos*. Vanderbilt University Publications in Anthropology 12. Nashville, TN: Vanderbilt University.

———. 1981a. The Formative Period and the Evolution of Complex Culture. In *The Handbook of Middle American Indians, Supplement 1: Archaeology*, ed. Jeremy A. Sabloff, pp. 373–91. Austin, TX: University of Texas Press.

———. 1981b. Olmec Monuments: Mutilation as a Clue to Meaning. In *The Olmec and Their Neighbors: Essays in Memory of Matthew W. Stirling*, ed. Elizabeth P. Benson, pp. 48–68. Washington, DC: Dumbarton Oaks Research Library and Collections.

———. 1984. *Chalcatzingo: Excavations on the Olmec Frontier*. New York, NY: Thames and Hudson.

———. 1987a. Chalcatzingo in a Broader Perspective. In *Ancient Chalcatzingo*, ed. David C. Grove, pp. 434–42. Austin, TX: University of Texas Press.

———, ed. 1987b. *Ancient Chalcatzingo*. Austin, TX: University of Texas Press.

———. 1989a. Olmec: What's in a Name? In *Regional Perspectives on the Olmec*, ed. Robert J. Sharer and David C. Grove, pp. 8–14. New York, NY: Cambridge University Press.

———. 1989b. Chalcatzingo and Its Olmec Connection. In *Regional Perspectives on the Olmec*, ed. Robert J. Sharer and David C. Grove, pp. 122–47. New York, NY: Cambridge University Press.

———. 1994. La Isla, Veracruz, 1991: A Preliminary Report with Comments on the Olmec Uplands. *Ancient Mesoamerica* 5:223–30.

———. 1997. Olmec Archaeology: A Half Century of Research and its Accomplishments. *Journal of World Prehistory* 11:51–101.

———. 1999. Public Monuments and Sacred Mountains: Observations on Three Formative Period Sacred Landscapes. In *Social Patterns in Preclassic Mesoamerica*, ed. David C. Grove and Rosemary Joyce, pp. 255–90. Washington, DC: Dumbarton Oaks Research Library and Collection.

———. 2000a. Faces of the Earth at Chalcatzingo: Serpents, Caves, and Mountains in Middle Formative Period Iconography. In *Olmec Art and Archaeology in Meso-america*, ed. John Clark and Mary Pye, pp. 277–95. Washington, DC: Center for Advanced Study, National Gallery of Art.

———. 2000b. The Pre-Classic Societies of the Central Highlands of Mexico. In *The Cambridge History of the Native Peoples of the Americas*, ed. Richard E.W. Adams and Murdo J. McLeod, pp. 122–55. New York, NY: Cambridge University Press.

———. 2005. Los Monumentos de la Terraza 6 de Chalcatzingo, Morelos. *Arqueología* 35:23–32.

———. 2006. Chalcatzingo y la 'cultura Tlatilco' en el Preclásico de Morelos. In *Ar-queología e historia del Centro de México: Homenaje a Eduardo Matos Moctezuma*, ed. Leonardo López Luján, David Carrasco, and Lourdes Cué, pp. 103–13. México, DF: Instituto Nacional de Antropología e Historia.

———. 2007a. Cerro Sagrados Olmecas: Montañas en la Cosmovisión Mesoameri-cana. *Arqueología Mexicana* 87:30–35.

———. 2007b. Stirrup Spout Vessels and Carved Stone Monuments: The Many Faces of Interregional Interactions in Formative Period Morelos. In *Archaeology, Art, and Ethnogenesis in Mesoamerican Prehistory: Papers in Honor of Gareth W. Lowe*, ed. Lyn-neth S. Lowe and Mary E. Pye, pp. 209–27. Papers of the New World Archaeo-logical Foundation No. 68. Provo, UT: New World Archaeological Foundation, Brigham Young University.

Grove, David C., and Jorge Angulo V. 1987. A Catalog and Description of Chalcatzin-go's Monuments. In *Ancient Chalcatzingo*, ed. David C. Grove, pp. 114–31. Austin, TX: University of Texas Press.

Grove, David C., and Susan D. Gillespie. 1992. Ideology and Evolution at the Pre-State Level: Formative Period Mesoamerica. In *Ideology and Pre-Columbian Civilizations*, ed. Arthur A. Demarest and Geoffrey W. Conrad, pp. 15–36. Santa Fe, NM: School of American Research Press.

———. Middle Formative Domestic Ritual at Chalcatzingo, Morelos. In *Domestic Ritual in Ancient Mesoamerica*, ed. Patricia Plunkett, pp. 11–19. Cotsen Institute of Archae-ology Monograph 46. Los Angeles, CA: Cotsen Institute of Archaeology at UCLA.

Grove, David C., Susan D. Gillespie, Ponciano Ortiz, and Michael Hayton. 1993. Five Olmec Monuments from the Laguna de los Cerros Hinterland. *Mexicon* 15(5): 91–95.

Grube, Nikolai. 1995. *The Emergence of Lowland Maya Civilization: The Transition from the Preclassic to the Early Classic*. Acta Mesoamericana, vol. 8. Möckmühl, Ger-many: Anton Saurwein.

————. 2000. The City-States of the Maya. In *A Comparative Study of Thirty City-State Cultures*, ed. Mogens Herman Hansen, pp. 547–65. Copenhagen: Kongelige Danske Videnskabernes Selskab.

————. 2001. Proluge. In *Maya: Divine Kings of the Rain Forest*, ed. Nikolai Grube, pp. 10–17. Cologne, Germany: Konemann Press.

————. 2004. El Origin de la Dinastía Kaan. In *Los Cautivos de Dzibanché*, ed. Enrique Nalda, pp. 114–31. Mexico, DF: Instituto Nacional de Antropología y Historia.

Grube, Nikolai, and Simon Martin. 2001. The Coming of Kings: Writing and Dynastic Kingship in the Maya Area Between the Late Preclassic and the Early Classic. In *Notebook for the XXVth Maya Hieroglyphic Forum at Texas*. Austin, TX: Department of Art History, University of Texas.

Grube, Nikolai, and James McGovern. 1995. A Preclassic Stela from Actuncan, Cayo District, Belize. Paper presented at the 60th Annual Meeting of the Society for American Archaeology. Minneapolis, MN.

Guderjan, Thomas H. 2004. Public Architecture, Ritual, and Temporal Dynamics at the Maya Center of Blue Creek, Belize. *Ancient Mesoamerica* 15:235–50.

Guenter, Stanley. 2002. La Estela Hauberg y el Reino Preclásico Kan. In *Investigaciones Arqueológicas y Ecológicas en la Cuenca Mirador: Rescate y Excavaciones en el sitio La Florida, Informe Final de la Temporada 2001–2002*, ed. Richard D. Hansen and Edgar O. Suyuc-Ley, pp. 305–19. Guatemala: Departamento de Monumentos Prehispánicos y Coloniales, Instituto de Antropología e Historia.

————. 2004. Gobernantes Preclásicos de la Cuenca Mirador. Paper presented at the XVIII Simposio de Investigaciones Arqueológicas, Guatemala, July 21.

————. 2005. Altar Chi: Una Capital Real del Preclásico. Paper presented at the XIXth Simposio de Investigaciones Arqueologicas en Guatemala, Guatemala City, July 18–22.

————. 2007. Discovering the Snake Kingdom: The Epigraphy of the Mirador Basin. Paper presented at the 72nd Annual Meeting of the Society for American Archaeology, Austin, April 26.

————. n.d. The Painted King List and the Origins of the Snake Kingdom. In *The Kan Kingdom: Essays on the Mirador-Calakmul Cultural and Natural System, Volume 1*, ed. Richard D. Hansen, Edgar Suyuc-Ley, and Stanley P. Guenter. FARES Foundation, University of Francisco Marroquin.

Guernsey, Julia. 1997. Of Macaws and Men: Late Preclassic Cosmology and Political Ideology in Izapan-style Monuments. Ph.D. diss., Dept. of Art and Art History, University of Texas at Austin.

————. 2006. *Ritual and Power in Stone: The Performance of Rulership in Mesoamerican*

Izapan-Style Art. Austin, TX: University of Texas Press.

———. n.d. The Iconography of the Quatrefoil. Unpublished ms., Dept. of Art and Art History, University of Texas at Austin.

———. 2010. A Consideration of the Quatrefoil Motif in Preclassic Mesoamerica. *Res* 57/58:75–96.

———. 2012. *Sculpture and Social Dynamics in Preclassic Mesoamerica.* New York: Cambridge University Press.

Guernsey, Julia, John E. Clark, and Bárbara Arroyo. 2010. *The Place of Stone Monuments: Context, Use, and Meaning in Mesoamerica's Preclassic Transition.* Washington DC: Dumbarton Oaks.

Guernsey, Julia and Michael Love. 2005. Late Preclassic Expressions of Authority on the Pacific Slope. In *Lords of Creation: The Origins of Sacred Maya Kingship*, ed. Virginia M. Fields and Dorie Reents-Budet, pp. 37–43. Los Angeles, CA: Los Angeles County Museum of Art.

Guernsey Kappelman, Julia. 2001. Sacred Geography at Izapa and the Performance of Rulership. In *Space, Power, and Poetics in Ancient Mesoamerica*, ed. Rex Koontz and Kathryn Reese-Taylor, pp. 81–111. Boulder, CO: Westview Press.

———. 2002. Carved in Stone: the Cosmological Narratives of the Late Preclassic Izapan-style Monuments from the Pacific Slope. In *Heart of Creation: The Mesoamerican World and the Legacy of Linda Schele*, ed. Andrea Stone, pp. 66–82. Tuscaloosa, AL: University of Alabama Press.

Gunn, Joel D., J.E. Foss, William J. Folan, and M. del Rosario Dominguez Carrasco. 2000. Environments of Elevated Cities in the Interior Yucatan Peninsula. Paper presented at the 65th Annual Meeting of the Society for American Archaeology, Philadelphia, April 5–9.

Gussinyer, Jordi. 1972. Rescate Arqueológico en la Presa de la Angostura (Primera Temporada). *Boletín del Instituto Nacional de Antropología e Historia, Epoch II* (1): 3–14.

Gutiérrez, Gerardo, and Mary E. Pye. 2011. Conexiones Iconográficas Entre Guerrero y Guatemala Desde el Periodo Formativo Medio: Hacia un Entendimiento de la Ruta de Comunicación de la Mar del Sur. In *Contlalco y La Coquera: Arqueología de dos sitios tempranos del municipio de Tlapa, Guerrero*, ed. G. Gutiérrez, A. Vera, M.E. Pye, and J.M. Serrano, pp. 127–46. Mexico: Municipio de Tlapa de Comofort, Letrantigua Editorial.

Haas, Jonathan. 1981. Class Conflict and the State in the New World. In *The Transition to Statehood in the New World.* Grant D. Jones and Robert R. Kautz, eds, pp. 80–104. Cambridge: Cambridge University Press.

———. 1982. *The Evolution of the Prehistoric State*. New York, NY: Columbia University Press.

Hall, Jay, and René Viel. 1994. Searching for the Preclassic Maya at Copán, Honduras: Results of the 1993 University of Queensland Field Season. In *Archaeology in the North*, ed. Marjorie Sullivan, Sally Brockwell, and Ann Webb, pp. 381–93. Darwin: NARU, Australian National University.

———. 2004. The Early Classic Copán Landscape: A View from the Preclassic. In *Understanding Early Classic Copan*, ed. Ellen E. Bell, Marcello A. Canuto, and Robert J. Sharer, pp. 17–28. Philadelphia, PA: University of Pennsylvania Museum of Archaeology and Anthropology.

Hallowell, A. Irving. 1965. The History of Anthropology as an Anthropological Problem. *Journal of the History of the Behavioral Sciences* 1:24–38.

Hammel, George R. 1983. Trading in Metaphors: The Magic of Beads. In *Proceedings of the 1982 Glass Trade Bead Conference*, ed. Charles Hayes, pp. 5–28. Research Records, 16. Rochester, NY: Research Division, Rochester Museum and Science Center.

Hammond, Norman. 1972a. Locational Models and the Site of Lubaantun: A Classic Maya Centre. In *Models in Archaeology*, ed. David L. Clarke, pp. 757–800. New York, NY: Methuen.

———. 1972b. Obsidian Trade Routes in the Mayan Area. *Science* 178:1092–3.

———. 1973. British Museum-Cambridge University Corazal Project, 1973 Interim Report. Unpublished ms., Cambridge University Centre of Latin American Studies. Cambridge, UK.

———. 1974. The Distribution of Late Classic Maya Major Ceremonial Centers in the Central Area. In *Mesoamerican Archaeology: New Approaches*, ed. Norman Hammond, pp. 313–34. London: Duckworth.

———. 1975. *Lubaantun, A Classic Maya Realm*. Peabody Museum Monographs 2. Cambridge, MA: Harvard University Peabody Museum of Archaeology and Ethnology.

———. 1976. Maya Obsidian Trade in Southern Belize. In *Maya Lithic Studies: Papers from the 1976 Belize Field Symposium*. Special Report No. 4, ed. Thomas R. Hester and Norman Hammond, pp. 71–82. San Antonio, TX: Center for Archaeological Research, The University of Texas at San Antonio.

———. 1977a. The Earliest Maya. *Scientific American* 236(3): 116–33.

———. 1977b. Ex Oriente Lux: A View from Belize. In *The Origins of Maya Civilization*, ed. Richard E.W. Adams, pp. 45–76. Albuquerque, NM: University of New Mexico Press.

————. 1982. A Late Formative Period Stela in the Maya Lowlands. *American Antiquity* 47(2): 396–403.

————. 1985a. The Emergence of Maya Civilization. *Scientific American* 255(2): 106–15.

————. 1985b. *Nohmul: A Prehistoric Community in Belize; Excavations 1973–1983.* BAR International Series, 250. Oxford: British Archaeological Reports.

————. 1986. New Light on the Most Ancient Maya. *Man* 21:399–413.

————. 1988. Cultura Hermana: Reappraising the Olmec. *Quarterly Review of Archaeology* 9(4): 1–4.

————. 1991a. Inside the Black Box: Defining Maya Polity. In *Classic Maya Political History: Hieroglyphic and Archaeological Evidence*, ed. T. Patrick Culbert, pp. 253–84. Cambridge: Cambridge University Press.

————. 1991b. Obsidian Trade. In *Cuello: An Early Maya Community in Belize*, ed. Norman Hammond, pp. 197–98. Cambridge, England: Cambridge University Press.

————. 1991c. Jade and Greenstone Trade. In *Cuello: An Early Maya Community in Belize*, ed. Norman Hammond, pp. 199–203. Cambridge, England: Cambridge University Press.

————. 1991d. The Maya and Their Civilization. In *Cuello: An Early Maya Community in Belize*, ed. Norman Hammond, pp. 1–7. Cambridge: Cambridge University Press.

————. 1992. Preclassic Maya Civilization. In *New Theories on the Ancient Maya*, ed. Elin C. Danien and Robert J. Sharer, pp. 137–44. Philadelphia, PA: University Museum, University of Pennsylvania.

————. 2000. Maya Lowlands: Pioneer Farmers to Merchant Princes. In *Cambridge History of the Native Peoples of the Americas. Vol. 2: Mesoamerica, part 1*, ed. Richard E.W. Adams and Murdo J. MacLeod, pp. 197–249. Cambridge: Cambridge University Press.

————. 2006. Early Symbolic Expression in the Maya Lowlands. *Mexicon* 28(2): 25–28.

Hammond, Norman, Arnold Aspinall, Stuart Feather, John Hazelden, Trevor Gazard, and Stuart Agrell. 1977. Maya Jade: Source Location and Analysis. In *Exchange Systems in Prehistory*, ed. Timothy K. Earle and Jonathan E. Ericson, pp. 35–67. New York, NY: Academic Press.

Hammond, Norman, and Jeremy R. Bauer. 2001. A Preclassic Maya Sweatbath at Cuello, Belize. *Antiquity* 75(290): 683–84.

Hammond, Norman, Jeremy R. Bauer, and Jody Morris. 2002. Squaring Off: Late Middle Preclassic: Architectural Innovation at Cuello, Belize. *Antiquity* 76:327–28.

Hammond, Norman, Amanda Clarke, and Sarah Donaghey. 1995. The Long Goodbye: Middle Preclassic Maya Archaeology at Cuello Belize, 1993. *Latin American Antiquity* 6:120–28.

Hammond, Norman, Amanda Clark, and Cynthia Robin. 1991. Middle Preclassic Buildings and Burials at Cuello, Belize: 1990 Investigations. *Latin American Antiquity* 2:352–63.

Hammond, Norman, Francisco Estrada-Belli, and Amanda Clarke. 1992. Middle Preclassic Maya Buildings and Burials at Cuello, Belize. *Antiquity* 66(253): 955–64.

Hammond, Norman, Duncan Pring, Rainer Berger, V. Roy Switzer, and Alan P. Ward. 1976. Radiocarbon Chronology for Early Maya Occupation at Cuello, Belize. *Nature* (44): 92–110.

Hammond, Norman, Julie M. Saul, and Frank P. Saul. 2002. Ancestral Faces: A Preclassic Maya Skull-Mask from Cuello, Belize. *Antiquity* 76:951–52.

Hanks, William F. 1990. *Referential Practice: Language and Lived Space Among the Maya.* Chicago, IL: University of Chicago Press.

Hansen, Eric F. 2000. Ancient Maya Burnt Lime Technology: Cultural Implications of Technological Styles. Ph.D. diss., Institute of Archaeology, University of California, Los Angeles.

Hansen, Eric F., Richard D. Hansen, and Michele R. Derrick. 1995. Los Análisis de los Estucos y Pinturas Arquitectónicos de Nakbe: Resultados Preliminares de los Estudios de los Métodos y Materiales de Producción. In *VIII Simposio de Arqueología Guatemalteca*, ed. Juan Pedro Laporte and Héctor L. Escobedo, pp. 543–60. Guatemala: Ministerio de Cultura y Deportes, Instituto de Antropología e Historia, Asociacion Tikal.

Hansen, Mogen H. 2000. Introduction: The Concepts of City-State and City-State Culture. In *A Comparative Study of Thirty City-State Cultures: An Investigation Conducted by the Copenhagen Polis Centre*, ed. Mogen H. Hansen, pp. 11–34. Historik-filosofiske Skrifter 21. Kongelige Danske.

Hansen, Richard D. 1982. Excavations in the Tigre Pyramid Area, El Mirador, Guatemala: A New Evaluation of Social Process in the Preclassic Maya Lowlands. In *Abstracts of the 44th International Congress of Americanists*. England: University of Manchester. Summarized in *Past and Present in the Americas: A Compendium of Recent Studies*, J. ed. Lynch, 1984, pp. 133–34. Manchester, England: Manchester University Press.

———. 1984. Excavations on Structure 34 and the Tigre Area, El Mirador, Peten, Guatemala: A New Look at the Preclassic Lowland Maya. MA thesis, Dept. of Anthropology, Brigham Young University.

———. 1990. *Excavations in the Tigre Complex, El Mirador, Peten, Guatemala.* Papers of the New World Archaeological Foundation, no. 62. Provo, UT: New World Archaeological Foundation, Brigham Young University.

———. 1991. An Early Maya Text from El Mirador, Guatemala. In *Research Reports on Ancient Maya Writing*, 37. Washington, DC: Center for Maya Research.

———. 1992a. The Archaeology of Ideology: A Study of Maya Formative/Preclassic Architectural Sculpture at Nakbe, Peten, Guatemala. Ph.D. diss., Dept. of Anthropology, University of California, Los Angeles.

———. 1992b. Proyecto Regional de Investigaciones Arqueológicas del Norte de Peten, Guatemala: Temporada 1990. In *IV Simposio de Arqueología Guatemalteca*, ed. Juan Pedro Laporte, Héctor L. Escobedo, and Sandra Villagran de Brady, pp. 1–36. Guatemala: Ministerio de Cultura y Deportes, Instituto de Antropología e Historia, Asociación Tikal.

———. 1992c. El Proceso Cultural de Nakbe y el Area del Peten Nor-Central: Las Epocas Tempranas. In *V Simposio de Investigaciones en Guatemala*, ed. Juan Pedro Laporte, Héctor L. Escobedo, and Sandra Villagran de Brady, pp. 81–96. Guatemala: Ministerio de Cultura y Deportes, Instituto de Antropología e Historia, Asociación Tikal.

———. 1993. Investigaciones Arqueológicas en el Sitio Nakbe: Los Estudios Recientes. In *VI Simposio de Investigaciones Arqueológicas en Guatemala, 1992*, ed. Juan Pedro Laporte, Héctor L. Escobedo, and Sandra Villagrán de Brady, pp. 115–22. Guatemala City, Guatemala: Museo Nacional de Arqueología y Etnología. Ministerio de Cultura y Deportes, Instituto de Antropología e Historia, Asociación Tikal.

———. 1994. Las Dinámicas Culturales y Ambientales de los Orígines Mayas: Estudios Recientes del Sitio Arqueológico Nakbe. In *VII Simposio de Investigaciones Arqueológicas en Guatemala, 1993*, ed. Juan Pedro Laporte and Héctor L. Escobedo, pp. 369–87. Guatemala City, Guatemala: Museo Nacional de Arqueología y Etnología. Ministerio de Cultura y Deportes, Instituto de Antropología e Historia, Asociación Tikal.

———. 1995. Yax Te Tun: The Incipient Development, Context, and Cultural Implications of Early Monuments in the Maya Lowlands. Paper presented at the 94th Annual Meeting of the American Anthropological Association, Washington DC. November 15–19.

———. 1996. El Clásico Tardío del Norte de Peten. *U tz'ib* 2(1): 1–15.

———. 1998. Continuity and Disjunction: The Pre-Classic Antecedents of Classic Maya Architecture. In *Function and Meaning in Classic Maya Architecture*, ed. Stephen D. Houston, pp. 49–122. Washington, DC: Dumbarton Oaks Research Library and Collection.

————. 2000. Ideología y Arquitectura: Poder y Dinámicas Culturales de los Mayas del Período Preclásico en las Tierras Bajas. In *Arquitectura e Ideología de los Antiguos Mayas: Memoria de la Segunda Mesa Redonda de Palenque*, ed. Silvia Trejo, pp. 71–108. Mexico, DF: Instituto Nacional de Antropología e Historia.

————. 2001a. The First Cities: The Beginnings of Urbanism and State Formation in the Maya Lowlands. In *Maya: Divine Kings of the Rainforest*, ed. Nikolai Grube, Eva Eggebrecht, and Matthias Seidel, pp. 50–65. Cologne: Könemann.

————. 2001b. Marvels of the Ancient Maya, Guatemala: The Past Engages the Future. *Archaeology*, Sept./Oct.:51–58.

————. 2005. Perspective on Olmec-Maya Interaction in the Middle Formative (Preclassic) Period. In *New Perspectives on Formative Mesoamerican Cultures*, ed. Terry G. Powis, pp. 51–72. BAR International Series, 1377. Oxford: British Archaeological Reports.

————. 2007. Yax Lakamtun: Perspectives of the First Monuments in the Maya Lowlands and the Implications for the Ideological Systems of the Preclassic Maya. Paper presented at the *The Place of Sculpture in Mesoamerica's Preclassic Transition*. Dumbarton Oaks Pre-Columbian Symposium, Antigua, Guatemala. October 5–6, 2007.

————. 2012a. Kingship in the Cradle of Maya Civilization. In *Fanning the Sacred Flame: Mesoamerican Studies in Honor of H.B. Nicholson*, ed. Matthew A. Boxt and Brian Dervin Dillon, pp. 139–71. Boulder, CO: University Press of Colorado.

————. 2012b. The Beginning of the End: Conspicuous Consumption and Environmental Impact of the Preclassic Lowland Maya. In *An Archaeological Legacy: Papers in Honor of Ray T. Matheny*, ed. Joel Janetski, Deanne Gurr, and Glenna Nielson-Grimm, pp. 241–85. Provo, UT: Brigham Young University Press.

————. n.d. *Maya Genesis: The Nature and Cultural Process in the Cradle of Maya Civilization*. Book ms. In preparation.

Hansen, Richard D., and Beatriz Balcarcel. 2008. El Complejo Tigre y la Acropolis Central de El Mirador durante el Preclásico Medio y Tardio. In *XXI Simposio de Investigaciones Arqueológicas en Guatemala, 2007*, ed. Juan Pedro Laporte, Bárbara Arroyo, and Héctor E. Mejía, pp. 339–48. Guatemala City, Guatemala: Museo Nacional de Arqueologia y Etnologia, Ministerio de Cultura y Deportes, Instituto de Antropología e Historia, Asociación Tikal, Fundación Arqueológica del Nuevo Mundo.

Hansen, Richard D., Beatriz Balcarcel, Edgar Suyuc, Héctor E. Mejía, Enrique Hernandez, Gendry Valle, Stanley P. Guenter, and Shannon Novak. 2006. Investigaciones Arqueológicas en el Sitio Tintal, Peten. In *XIX Simposio de Investigaciones Arqueológicas en Guatemala*, ed. Juan Pedro Laporte, Bárbara Arroyo, Héctor E.

Mejía, pp. 683–94. Guatemala: Ministerio de Cultura y Deportes, Instituto de Antropología e Historia, Asociación Tikal.

Hansen, Richard D., Ronald L. Bishop, and Federico Fahsen. 1991. Notes on Maya Codex-Style Ceramics from Nakbe, Peten, Guatemala. *Ancient Mesoamerica* 2:225–43.

Hansen, Richard D., Steven Bozarth, John Jacob, David Wahl, and Thomas Schreiner. 2002. Climatic and Environmental Variability in the Rise of Maya Civilization: A Preliminary Perspective from Northern Peten. *Ancient Mesoamerica* 13:273–95.

Hansen, Richard D., Donald W. Forsyth, James C. Woods, Eric F. Hansen, Thomas Schreiner, and Gene L. Titmus. 1997. Developtmental Dynamics, Energetics, and Complex Interactions of the Early Maya of the Mirador Basin, Guatemala. Abstracts of the 62nd Annual Meeting. Society for American Archaeology, pp. 102. Nashville, Tennessee.

Hansen, Richard, and Stanley P. Guenter. 2005. Early Social Complexity and Kingship in the Mirador Basin. In *Lords of Creation: The Origins of Sacred Maya Kinship*, ed. Virginia M. Fields and Dorie Reents-Budet, pp. 60–61. Los Angeles, CA: Los Angeles County Museum of Art.

Hansen, Richard D., Wayne K. Howell, and Stanley P. Guenter. 2008. Forgotten Structures, Haunted Houses, and Occupied Hearts: Ancient Perspectives and Contemporary Interpretations of Abandoned Sites and Buildings in the Mirador Basin, Guatemala. In *Ruins of the Past: The Use and Perception of Abandoned Structures in the Maya Lowlands*, ed. Travis W. Stanton and Aline Magnoni, pp. 25–64. Boulder: University Press of Colorado.

Hansen, Richard D., Gustavo Martinez, John Jacob, and Wayne K. Howell. 2000. Cultivos Intensivos: Sistemas Agrícolas de Nakbe. In *Investigaciones Arqueológicas y Ecológicas en la Cuenca Mirador, 1998: Informe de la Temporada de Campo*, ed. Richard.D. Hansen and J. Valle, pp. 687–700. Proyecto Regional de Investigaciones Arqueológicas del Norte del Peten, Guatemala. Rupert, ID: Foundation for Anthropological Research & Environmental Studies.

Hansen, Richard D., and Edgar Suyuc-Ley, eds. 2002. *Excavaciones Arqueológicas y Ecológicas en la Cuenca Mirador: Rescate y Excavaciones en el sitio La Florida, Informe Final de la Temporada 2001–2002*. Guatemala: Departamento de Monumentos Prehispanicos y Coloniales, Instituto de Antropología e Historia.

———, eds. 2007. Investigaciones en la Zona Cultura y Natural Mirador: Resumen General de la Temporada de Campo 2006. In *Proyecto Arqueológico Cuenca Mirador: Investigacion y Conservación en los Sitios Arqueológicos El Mirador, La Muerta, Tintal, La Tortuga, Tamazul, La Llorona, Camarón, El Desencanto, Lechugal, Icotea, Los Chuntos, y El Laurel, Informe 2006*, ed. Nora Maria López, pp. iii–vii. Report filed with the Ministerio de Cultura y Deportes, Instituto de Antropología e Historia (IDAEH). Rupert, ID: FARES Foundation, Idaho State University.

———, eds. 2010. Investigaciones en la Cuenca Mirador, Temporada 2008. In *XXIII Simposio de Investigaciones Arqueológicas en Guatemala, 2009*, ed. Bárbara Arroyo, Adriana Linares Palma, and Lorena Paiz Aragón, pp. 559–66. Guatemala City, Guatemala: Museo Nacional de Arqueologia y Etnologia, Ministerio de Cultura y Deportes, Instituto de Antropología e Historia, Asociación Tikal.

———, eds. 2011. L'émergence de l'Etat dans le Monde Maya: Une vue du Basin de Mirador. In *Maya: de l'aube au Crepuscule, Collections Nationales de Guatemala*, Dominique Michelet, ed, pp. 32–37. Musée de quai Branly, Somogy: Editions d'art.

Hansen, Richard D., Edgar Suyuc-Ley, and Héctor Mejía. 2008. Mirador Basin 2008. A Field Report of the 2008 Season. Global Heritage Fund. http://www.global-heritagefund.org/where/mirador/progress2008/mirador_progress2008.html, accessed September 25, 2009.

———, eds. 2009. Investigaciones Multidisciplinarias en El Mirador: Informe Final de la Temporada 2008, Vol. I & II. Report filed with the Ministerio de Cultura y Deportes, Instituto de Antropología e Historia, Departmento de Monumentos Prehispanicos y Coloniales, Guatemala City. Proyecto Cuenca Mirador. 1144 pp. Rupert, ID: Idaho State University, FARES Foundation.

Harrison, Peter D. 1990. The Revolution in Ancient Maya Subsistence. In *Vision and Revision in Maya Studies*, ed. Flora S. Clancy and Peter D. Harrison, pp. 99–113. Albuquerque, NM: University of New Mexico Press.

Harrison, Peter D., and Billy Lee Turner II, eds. 1978. *Prehispanic Maya Agriculture*. Albuquerque, NM: University of New Mexico Press.

Harrison, Simon. 1987. Magical and Material Politics in Melanesia. *Man* 24:1–20.

Haug, Gerald H., Konrad A. Hughen, Daniel M. Sigman, Larry C. Peterson, and Ursula Röhl. 2001. Southward Migration of the Intertropical Convergence Zone Through the Holocene. *Science* 293(5533): 1304–8.

Haviland, William A. 1968. *Ancient Lowland Maya Social Organization*. Middle American Research Institute Publication 26, pp. 93–117. New Orleans, LA: Tulane University.

———. 1972. A New Look at Classic Maya Social Organization at Tikal. *Ceramica de Cultura Maya* 8:1–16.

———. 1977. Dynastic Genealogies from Tikal, Guatemala. *American Antiquity* 42:61–67.

———. 1997. On the Maya State. *Current Anthropology* 38:443–45.

Hayden, Brian. 1995. Pathways to Power: Principles for Creating Socioeconomic Inequalities. In *Foundations of Social Inequality*, ed. T. Douglas Price and Gary M.

Feinman, pp. 15–86. New York, NY: Plenum.

Hayden, Brian, and Rob Gargett. 1990. Big Man, Big Heart? A Mesoamerican View of the Emergence of Complex Society. *Ancient Mesoamerica* 1:3–20.

Healan, Dan M. 1997. Pre-Hispanic Quarrying in the Ucareo-Zinapecuaro Obsidian Source Area. *Ancient Mesoamerica* 8:77–100.

Healy, Paul F., and Jaime J. Awe. 1995. Radiocarbon Dates from Cahal Pech, Belize: Results from the 1994 Field Season. In *Belize Valley Preclassic Maya Project: Report on the 1994 Field Season*, ed. Paul F. Healy and Jaime J. Awe, pp. 198–206. Occasional Papers in Anthropology No. 10. Peterborough, Ontario: Trent University Department of Anthropology.

Healy, Paul F., David Cheetham, Terry Powis, and Jaime Awe. 2004. Cahal Pech, Belize: The Middle Formative Period. In *The Ancient Maya of the Belize Valley: Half a Century of Archaeological Research*, ed. James F. Garber, pp. 103–24. Gainsville, FL: University of Florida Press.

Healy, Paul F., Bobby Hohmann, and Terry Powis. 2004. The Ancient Maya Center of Pacbitun. In *The Ancient Maya of the Belize River Valley: Half a Century of Archaeological Research*, ed. James F. Garber, pp. 207–28. Gainsville, FL: University Press of Florida.

Heizer, Robert F. 1960. Agriculture and the Theocratic State in Lowland Southeastern Mexico. *American Antiquity* 26(2): 215–22.

———. 1966. Ancient Heavy Transport, Methods and Achievements. *Science* 153(3738): 821–30.

———. 1967. Analysis of Two Low Relief Sculptures from La Venta. In *Contributions of the University of California Archaeological Research Facility* 3:25–55.

———. 1968. New Observations on La Venta. In *Dumbarton Oaks Conference on the Olmec*, ed. Elizabeth P. Benson, pp. 9–40. Washington, DC: Dumbarton Oaks Research Library and Collection.

Heizer, Robert F., and James A. Bennyhoff. 1958. Archaeological Investigation of Cuicuilco, Valley of Mexico, 1957. *Science* 127:232–33.

———. 1972. Archaeological Investigations at Cuicuilco, Mexico, 1957. In *National Geographic Society Research Reports 1955–1960*, pp. 93–104. Washington, DC: National Geographic Society.

Heizer, Robert F., John A. Graham, and Lewis K. Napton. 1968. The 1968 Excavations at La Venta. *Contributions of the University of California Archaeological Research Facility* 5:127–54.

Hellmuth, Nicholas M. 1987. *Monster und Menschen in der Maya-Kunst*. Graz: Akademische Druck- und Verlagsanstalt.

Helms, Mary W. 1993. *Craft and the Kingly Ideal: Art, Trade, and Power*. Austin, TX: University of Texas Press.

———. 1994. Chiefdom Rivalries, Control, and External Contacts in Lower Central America. In *Factional Competition and Political Development in the New World*, ed. Elizabeth M. Brumfiel and John W. Fox, pp. 55–60. New Directions in Archaeology. Cambridge: Cambridge University Press.

Henderson, Hope. 2003. The Organization of Staple Crop Production at K'axob, Belize. *Latin American Antiquity* 14(4): 469–96.

Hendon, Julia A. 1989. Elite Household Organization at Copan, Honduras: Analysis of Activity Distribution in the Sepulturas Zone. In *Household and Communities: Proceedings of the 21st Annual Chacmool Conference*, ed. Scott MacEachern, David J. W. Archer, and Richard D. Garvin, pp. 371–80. Calgary: Archaeological Association, University of Calgary.

———. 1991. Status and Power in Classic Maya Society: An Archeological Study. *American Anthropologist* 93(4): 894–918.

———. 1999. The Preclassic Maya Compound as the Focus of Social Identity. In *Social Patterns in Preclassic Mesoamerica*, ed. David Grove and Rosemary Joyce, pp. 97–125. Washington, DC: Dumbarton Oaks Research Library and Collection.

Hermes, Bernard. 1993. Dos Reportes del Laboratorio Cerámico: Vasijas Miniatura y Adiciones Tipológicas para la Epoca Preclásica. In *Tikal y Uaxactun en el Preclásico*, ed. Juan Pedro Laporte and Juan Antonio Valdés, pp. 47–52. Mexico, DF: Universidad Nacional Autonoma de Mexico.

Hernandez, Enrique. 2008. Sitios Asociados a la Calzada Tintal-Mirador: Sitio Arqueológico El Arroyon. In *Informe Final de Investigaciones 2007: Investigacion y Conservación en los Sitios Arqueológicos de la Zona Cultural y Natural Mirador*, ed. Nora Lopez, Richard D. Hansen, and Edgar Suyuc, pp. 1084–103. Formal report filed with the Departamento de Monumentos Prehispánicos y Coloniales, Instituto de Antropología e Historia, Ministerio de Cultural y Deportes, Guatemala City. Rupert, Idaho: FARES Foundation.

Hernandez, Enrique, and Thomas Schreiner. 2006. Exploraciones y Excavaciones del Sacbe Tintal-Mirador, Peten, Guatemala. In *Investigacion y Conservacion en los sitios arqueológicos El Mirador, La Muerta, Wakna, El Porvenir, El Guiro, La Iglesia, La Sarteneja, Chab Ché y la Ceibita: Informe Final de la Temporada 2005*, ed. Edgar Suyuc Ley and Richard D. Hansen, pp. 318–57. Rupert, ID: Foundation for Anthropological Research & Environmental Studies.

Hernandez, Enrique, Thomas Schreiner, and David Wahl. 2007. The Tintal-Mirador Causeway: A Monumental Prehispanic Sacbe in the Mirador Basin, Guatemala.

Paper presented at the 72nd Annual Meeting of the Society for American Archaeology, Austin, April 26.

————. 2008. El Sacbe entre Tintal y El Mirador, y su Implicación para los Antiguos Pobladores Mayas. *Abstractos del XXII Simposio de Investigaciones Arqueológicas en Guatemala*, p. 48. Ministerio de Cultura y Deportes, Instituto de Antropología e Historia, Museo Nacional de Arqueología y Etnología, Asociación Tikal.

Herrera, R. Sergio, Hector Neff, Michael D. Glascock, and J. Michael Elam. 1999. Ceramic Patterns, Social Interaction and the Olmec: Neutron Activation Analysis of Early Formative Pottery in the Oaxaca Highlands of Mexico. *Journal of Archaeological Science* 26(8): 967–87.

Hester, Thomas R. 1996. The Colha Project, Preceramic to Preclassic: A Survey of Major Results, 1979–1994. *Proceedings of the First International Symposium on the Maya*, ed. Juan Luis Bonor. Belmopan, Belize: Department of Archaeology.

Hester, Thomas R., Robert N. Jack, and Alice Benfer. 1973. Trace Element Analysis of Obsidian from Michoacan, Mexico: Preliminary Results. *Contributions of the University of California Archaeological Research Facility* 18:167–76.

Hester, Thomas R., and Harry J. Shafer. 1994. The Ancient Maya Craft Community at Colha, Belize, and Its External Relationships. In *Archaeological Views from the Countryside. Village Communities in Early Complex Societies*, ed. Glenn M. Schwartz and Steven E. Falconer, pp. 48–63. Washington, DC: Smithsonian Institution Press.

Hicks, Frederick, and Charles E. Rozaire. 1960. *Mound 13, Chiapa de Corzo, Chiapas, Mexico*. Papers of the New World Archaeological Foundation, No. 10. Provo, UT: New World Archaeological Foundation, Brigham Young University.

Hill, Robert M., and John Monaghan. 1987. *Continuities in Highland Maya Social Organization*. Philadelphia, PA: University of Pennsylvania Press.

Hill, Warren D., Michael Blake, and John E. Clark. 1998. Ball Court Design Dates Back 3,400 Years. *Nature* 392:878–79.

Hill, Warren D., and John E. Clark. 2001. Sports, Gambling, and Government: America's First Social Compact? *American Anthropologist* 103(2): 331–45.

Hirth, Kenneth G. 1978. Interregional Trade and the Formation of Prehistoric Gateway Communities. *American Antiquity* 43:35–45.

————. 1987a. Formative Period Settlement Patterns in the Río Amatzinac Valley. In *Ancient Chalcatzingo*, ed. David C. Grove, pp. 343–67. Austin, TX: University of Texas Press.

————. 1987b. Río Amatzinac Survey: Site Descriptions. In *Ancient Chalcatzingo*, ed. David C. Grove, pp. 509–24. Austin, TX: University of Texas Press.

———. 1998. The Distributional Approach. *Current Anthropology* 39(4): 451–76.

———. 2009. Intermittent Crafting and Multicrafting at Xochicalco. *Archaeological Papers of the American Anthropological Association* 19(1): 75–91.

Hohmann, Bobbi, and Terry G. Powis. 1996. The 1995 Excavations at Pacbitun, Belize: Investigations of the Middle Formative Occupation in Plaza B. In *Belize Valley Preclassic Maya Project: Report on the 1995 Field Season*, ed. Paul F. Healy and Jaime Awe, pp. 98–117. Trent University Occasional Papers in Anthropology 12. Peterborough, ON: Trent University.

Holland, William. 1964a. Conceptos Cosmologicos Tzotziles como una Base para Interpretar la Civilizacíon Maya Prehispánica. *América Indigena* 24(1): 11–27.

———. 1964b. Contemporary Tzotzil Cosmological Concepts as a Basis for Interpreting Prehistoric Maya Civilization. *American Antiquity* 29:301–6.

Holmes, William H. 1883. Art in Shell of the Ancient Americans. In *Second Annual Report of the Bureau of American Ethnology 1880–1881*, pp. 185–305.

Hoopes, John W. 1985. Trade and Exchange. In *A Consideration of the Early Classic Period in the Maya Lowlands*, ed. Gordon R. Willey and Peter Mathews, pp. 145–60. Albany, NY: Institute for Mesoamerican Studies, State University of New York.

Hopkins, Nicholas A. 1984. Otomanguean Linguistic Prehistory. In *Essays in Otomanguean Cultural History*, ed. J. Katherine Josserand, Marcus Winter, and Nicholas A. Hopkins, pp. 25–64. Vanderbilt University Publications in Anthropology, No. 31. Nashville, TN: Anthropology Section, Department of Sociology and Anthropology, Vanderbilt University.

———. 1988. Classic Mayan Kinship Systems: Epigraphic and Ethnographic Evidence for Patrilineality. *Estudios de Cultura Maya* 17:87–121.

Hosler, Dorothy, Sandra L Burkett, and Michael J. Tarkanian. 1999. Prehistoric Polymers: Rubber Processing in Ancient Mesoamerica. *Science* 284(5422): 1988–91.

Houston, Stephen D. 1993. *Hieroglyphs and History at Dos Pilas: Dynastic Politics of the Classic Maya*. Austin, TX: University of Texas Press.

———. 1997. Estados Débiles y Estructura Segmentaria: La Organización Interna de las Entidades Políticas Mayas. *Apuntes Arqueológicos* 5(1): 67–92.

———. 2004. Writing in Early Mesoamerica. In *The First Writing: Script Invention as History and Process*, ed. Stephen D. Houston, pp. 274–309. Cambridge: Cambridge University Press.

———. 2006. An Example of Preclassic Mayan Writing? *Science* 311:1249–50.

———. 2007a. Maya Writing as an Evolving Practice. Paper presented at the Advanced Seminar at the School of Advanced Research, Santa Fe, April 15–19.

———. 2007b. Apasionado: Cities and Monuments of the Lower Pasión River. Paper presented at the 31st Maya Meetings at Texas, Austin, March 9–11.

Houston, Stephen D., Edwin Román, Timothy Beach, Rafael Cambranes, Laura Gámez, Jose Garrido, Thomas Garrison, Arturo Godoy, Zachary Hruby, Sheryl Luzzadder-Beach, Varinia Matute, Zachary Nelson, Griselda Pérez, Griselda Quiroa, Armando Rodríguez, Andrew Scherer, and Walker Caitlin. 2010. Un paisaje inconstante: Crecimiento, ruptura y renovación en la región de El Zotz, Guatemala. In *XXIII Simposio de Investigaciones Arqueológicas en Guatemala, 2009*, ed. Bárbara Arroyo, A Linares, and, Lorena Paiz, pp. 486–96. Museo Nacional de Arqueologia y Etnologia, Guatemala, Guatemala.

Houston, Stephen D., and David Stuart. 1996. Of Gods, Glyphs and Kings: Divinity and Rulership among the Classic Maya. *Antiquity* 70:289–312.

———. 2001. Peopling the Classic Maya Court. In *Royal Courts of the Ancient Maya. Volume 1: Theory, Comparison, and Synthesis*, ed. Takeshi Inomata and Stephen D. Houston, pp. 54–83. Boulder, CO: Westview Press.

Howell, Wayne K., and Denise Ranae Evans Copeland. 1989. *Excavations at El Mirador, Peten, Guatemala: The Danta and Monos Complexes*. Papers of the New World Archaeological Foundation, Nos. 60 & 61. Provo, UT: New World Archaeological Foundation, Brigham Young University.

Hruby, Zachary X., and Rowan K. Flad, eds. 2007. *Rethinking Craft Specialization in Complex Societies: Archaeological Analyses of the Social Meaning of Production*. Archaeological Papers of the American Anthropological Association, No. 17. Arlington, VA: American Anthropological Association.

Hudler, Dale B., and Jon C. Lohse. 1994. A Functional and Contextual Study of Unifacial Chert Tools in Belize. Paper presented at the 59th Annual Meeting of the Society for American Archaeology, Los Angeles, April 20–24.

Hudson, John C. 1969. A Location Theory for Rural Settlement. *Annals of the Association of American Geographers* 59:365–81.

Hurst, Heather. 2005. San Bartolo, Petén: Técnicas de pintura Mural del Preclásico Tardío. In *XVIII Simposio de Investigaciones Arqueológicas en Guatemala, 2004*, vol. 2, ed. Juan Pedro Laporte, Bárbara Arroyo and Hector E. Mejía, pp. 639–46. Guatemala City: Ministerio de Cultura y Deportes, Asociación Tikal, IDAEH, FAMSI.

Iannone, Gyles. 2002. Annales History and the Ancient Maya State: Some Observations on the 'Dynamic Model,' *American Anthropologist* 104:68–78.

Iceland, Harry B. 1997. The Preceramic Origins of the Maya: The Results of the Colha Preceramic Project in Northern Belize. Ph.D. diss., Dept. of Anthropology, The University of Texas at Austin.

———. 2005. The Preceramic to Early Middle Formative Transition in Northern

Belize: Evidence for the Ethnic Identity of the Preceramic Inhabitants. In *New Perspectives on Formative Mesoamerican Cultures*, ed. Terry G. Powis, pp. 15–26. BAR International Series, 1377. Oxford: British Archaeological Reports.

Iceland, Harry B., and Thomas R. Hester. 1996. Earliest Maya? Origins of Sedentism and Agriculture in the Maya Lowlands. In *The Prehistory of the Americas*, ed. Thomas R. Hester, L. Laurencich-Minelli, and S. Salvatori, pp. 11–17. XIII National Congress of Prehistoric and Protohistoric Sciences. Forli: A.B.A.C.O. Edizioni.

Iceland, Harry B, Thomas R. Hester, Harry J. Shafer, and Dale Hudler. 1995. The Colha Preceramic Project: A Status Report. *The Newsletter of the Friends of the Texas Archeological Research Laboratory* 3(2):11–15.

Inomata, Takeshi. 2001. The Classic Maya Palace as a Political Theatre. In *Reconstruyendo la Ciudad Maya: El Urbanismo en las Sociedades Antiguas*, ed. Andrés Ciudad Ruiz, Ma. Josefa Iglesias Ponce de León, Ma. Del Carmen Martínez Martínez, pp. 341–61. Madrid: Sociedad Española de Estudios Mayas.

———. 2006a. Politics and Theatricality in Mayan Society. In *Archaeology of Performance: Theaters of Power, Community, and Politics*, ed. Takeshi Inomata and Lawrence S. Coben, pp. 187–221. Walnut Creek, CA: AltaMira Press.

———. 2006b. Plazas, Performers, and Spectators: Political Theaters of the Classic Maya. *Current Anthropology* 47(5): 805–42.

———. 2012. La Fundación y el Desarrollo Político Durante el Periodo Preclásico en Ceibal. In *La Cuenca del Río Pasión: Estudios de Arqueología y Epigrafía Maya*, ed. M.E. Vega and L.S. Lowe, pp. 33–56. Mexico: UNAM.

Inomata, Takeshi, and Stephen D. Houston, eds. 2001a. *Royal Courts of the Ancient Maya. Volume One: Theory, Comparison, and Synthesis.* Boulder, CO: Westview Press.

———, eds. 2001b. *Royal Courts of the Ancient Maya. Volume Two: Data and Case Studies.* Boulder, CO: Westview Press.

Inomata, Takeshi, Daniela Triadan, and Otto Rodrigo Román. 2010. La Transformación y Continuidad de Ritos Durante el Período Preclásico en Ceibal, Guatemala. In *El Ritual en el Mundo Maya: de lo Privado a lo Público*, ed. M.J. Iglesias Ponce de León, A. Ciudad Real, and M. Sorroche Cuerva, pp. 29–48. Madrid, Spain: Sociedad Española de Estudios Mayas.

Islebe, Gerald A., Hooghiemstra Henry, Mark Brener, Jason H. Curtis, and David A. Hodell. 1996. A Holocene Vegetation History from Lowland Guatemala. *The Holocene* 6:265–71.

Izquierdo y de la Cueva, Ana. 2004. Unidad y Fragmentación del Poder Entre los Mayas. *Estudios de Cultura Maya* 25:57–76.

Jack, Robert N., and Robert F. Heizer. 1968. Finger-Printing of Some Mesoamerican Obsidian Artifacts. *Contributions of the University of California Archaeological Research Facility* 5:81–100.

Jack, Robert N., Thomas R. Hester, and Robert F. Heizer. 1972. Geologic Sources of Archaeological Obsidian from Sites in Northen and Central Veracruz, Mexico. *Contributions of the University of California Archaeological Research Facility* 16:117–22.

Jackson, Thomas L., and Michael W. Love. 1991. Bladerunning: Middle Preclassic Obsidian Exchange and the Introduction of Prismatic Blades at La Blanca, Guatemala. *Ancient Mesoamerica* 2:47–59.

Jacob, John S. 1992. The Agroecological Evolution of Cobweb Swamp, Belize. Ph.D. diss., Dept. of Soil and Crop Sciences, Texas A&M University.

———. 1994. Evidencias para Cambio Ambiental en Nakbe, Guatemala. In *VII Simposio de Investigaciones Arqueológicas en Guatemala, 1993*, ed. Juan Pedro Laporte and Héctor L. Escobedo, pp. 275–80. Guatemala City: Museo Nacional de Arqueología y Etnología, Ministerio de Cultura y Deportes, Instituto de Antropología e Historia, Asociación Tikal.

———. 1995. Ancient Maya Wetland Agricultural Fields in Cobweb Swamp, Belize: Construction, Chronology, and Function. *Journal of Field Archaeology* 22(2): 175–90.

Jacobo, Alvaro L. 2003[1992]. Resultados Preliminares de las excavaciones de rescate arqueológico en el área sur de la laguna El Naranjo, Kaminaljuyu. In *Kaminaljuyu en el Simposio de Investigaciones Arqueológicas en Guatemala*, ed. Juan Pedro Laporte and Hector E. Mejía, pp. 83–94. Guatemala: Ministerio de Cultura y Deportes, Instituto de Antropología e Historia, Asociación Tikal.

Jaime Riverón, Olaf. 2003. El Hacha Olmeca: Biografía y Paisaje. M.A. thesis, Instituto de Investigaciones Antropológicas, Universidad Nacional Autonoma de Mexico.

Jameson, Fredric. 1991. *Postmodernism, or, The Cultural Logic of Late Capitalism.* Durham, NC: Duke University Press.

Jansen, Maarten. 2004. Archaeology and Indigenous Peoples: Attitudes Towards Power in Ancient Oaxaca. In *A Companion to Archaeology*, ed. John Bintliff, pp. 235–52. Oxford: Blackwell Publishing.

Jiménez Delgado, Gerardo. 2008. Control de Recursos y el Surgimiento de Jerarquías Sociales en el Territorio Olmeca: El Patrón de Asentamiento del Periodo Formativo en la Región Jáltipan-Minatitlán. In *Sociedad e Ideología en el periodo Formativo, Homenaje al Doctor David C. Grove*, ed. A. Cyphers and K. Hirth, pp. 177–202. México: Instituto de Investigaciones Antropológicas, Universidad Nacional Autónoma de México, México.

Jiménez, Oscar. 1990. Geomorfología de la Región de La Venta, Tabasco: Un Sistema Fluvio-lagunar Costero del Cuaternario. *Arqueología* 3:5–16.

Jiménez Moreno, Wigberto. 1966. Mesoamerica before the Toltecs. In *Ancient Oaxaca*, ed. John Paddock, pp. 1–82. Stanford, CA: Stanford University Press.

Johnson, Allen W., and Timothy Earle. 1987. *The Evolution of Human Societies: From Foraging Group to Agrarian State*. Stanford, CA: Stanford University Press.

Johnson, Allen W., and Timothy Earle. 2000. *The Evolution of Human Societies: From Foraging Group to Agrarian State*. Stanford, CA: Stanford University Press.

Johnston, Kevin J. 2006. Preclassic Maya Occupation of the Itzan Escarpment, Lower Río de la Pasión, Petén, Guatemala. *Ancient Mesoamerica* 17:177–201.

Jones, Christopher. 1983. Monument 26, Quiriguá, Guatemala. In *Quiriguá Report II*, ed. Edward Schortman and Patricia Urban, pp. 118–28. Philadelphia, PA: University Museum, University of Pennsylvania.

———. 1986. Ruler in Triumph: Chocola Monument 1. *Expedition* 28(3): 3–13.

———. 1991. Cycles of Growth at Tikal. In *Classic Maya Political History: Hieroglyphic and Archaeological Evidence*, ed. T. Patrick Culbert, pp. 102–28. School of American Research Advanced Seminar Series. Cambridge: Cambridge University Press.

Jones, Christopher, and Linton Satterthwaite. 1982. *The Monuments and Inscriptions of Tikal: The Carved Monuments*. Tikal Report No. 33, Part A. University Museum Monograph 44. Philadelphia, PA: University Museum, University of Pennsylvania.

Jones, Grant D., and Robert R. Kautz, eds. 1981. *The Transition to Statehood in the New World*. Cambridge: Cambridge University Press.

Jones, John G. 1991. Pollen Evidence of Prehistoric Forest Manipulation and Maya Cultivation in Belize. Ph.D. diss., Dept. of Anthropology, Texas A&M University.

———. 1994. Pollen Evidence for Early Settlement and Agriculture in Northern Belize. *Palynology* 18:205–211.

Joralemon, Peter David. 1971. *A Study of Olmec Iconography*. Studies in Pre-Columbian Art and Archaeology No. 7. Washington, DC: Dumbarton Oaks Research Library and Collections.

———. 1976. The Olmec Dragon: A Study in Pre-Columbian Iconography. In *Origins of Religious Art and Iconography in Preclassic Mesoamerica*, ed. Henry B. Nicholson, pp. 27–71. UCLA Latin American Studies Series, Volume 31. Los Angeles, CA: UCLA Latin American Center Publications.

———. 1996. In Search of the Olmec Cosmos: Reconstructing the World View of Mexico's First Civilization. In *Olmec Art of Ancient Mexico*, ed. Elizabeth P. Benson and Beatriz de la Fuente, pp. 51–59. Washington, DC: National Gallery of Art.

Josserand, J. Kathryn. 2011. Languages of the Preclassic Period Along the Pacific Coastal Plains of Southeastern Mesoamerica. In *The Southern Maya in the Late Preclassic*, ed. Michael Love and Jonathan Kaplan, pp. 141–74. Boulder: Colorado University Press.

Joyce, Arthur A., and Marcus Winter. 1996. Ideology, Power, and Urban Society in Pre-Hispanic Oaxaca. *Current Anthropology* 37(1): 33–47.

Joyce, Rosemary A. 2000. Heirlooms and Houses: Materiality and Social Memory. In *Beyond Kinship: Social and Material Reproduction in House Societies*, ed. Rosemary A. Joyce and Susan D. Gillespie, pp. 89–212. Philadelphia, PA: University of Pennsylvania Press.

———. 2003. Making Something of Herself: Embodiment in Life and Death at Playa de los Muertos, Honduras. *Cambridge Archaeological Journal* 13:248–61.

Joyce, Rosemary A., and Susan D. Gillespie, eds. 2000. *Beyond Kinship: Social and Material Reproduction in House Societies*. Philadelphia, PA: University of Pennsylvania Press.

Joyce, Rosemary A., and John S. Henderson. 2001. Beginnings of Village Life in Eastern Mesoamerica. *Latin American Antiquity* 12:5–23.

Joyce, Rosemary A., and Julia A. Hendon. 2000. Heterarchy, History, and Material Reality: Communities in Late Classic Honduras. In *The Archaeology of Communities: A New World Perspective*, ed. Marcello A. Canuto and Jason Yaeger, pp. 143–60. London: Routledge.

Justeson, John S., and Peter Mathews. 1983. The Seating of the Tun: Further Evidence Concerning a Late Preclassic Lowland Maya Stela Cult. *American Antiquity* 48(3): 586–93.

Justeson, John S., William M. Norman, and Norman Hammond. 1988. The Pomona Flare: A Preclassic Maya Hieroglyphic Text. In *Maya Iconography*, ed. Elizabeth Benson and Gillette Griffin, pp. 94–151. Princeton, NJ: Princeton University Press.

Kaplan, Jonathan. 2001. Algunas Consideraciones del Apogeo Miraflores en el Preclásico Tardío de Kaminaljuyú. In *XIV Simposio de Investigaciones Arqueológicas en Guatemala*, ed. Juan Pedro Laporte, Ana Claudia Monzón de Suasnávar, and Bárbara Arroyo, pp. 39–46. Guatemala: Ministerio de Cultura y Deportes, Instituto de Antropología e Historia, Asociación Tikal.

———. 2002. From Under the Volcanoes: Some Aspects of the Ideology of Rulership at Late Preclassic Kaminaljuyú. In *Incidents of Archaeology in Central America and Yucatán: Studies in Honor of Edwin M. Shook*, ed. Michael W. Love, Marion Popenoe de Hatch, and Hector L. Escobedo, pp. 311–57. Lanham, MD: University Press of America.

———. 2011. Miraflores Kaminaljuyu: Corpse and Corpus Delicti. In *The Southern Maya in the Late Preclassic: The Rise and Fall of an Early Mesoamerican Civilization*, ed. Michael Love and Jonathan Kaplan, pp. 237–85. Boulder: Colorado University Press.

Kaplan, Jonathan, and Juan Antonio Valdés. 2004. Chocolá, an Apparent Regional Capital in the Southern Maya Preclassic: Preliminary Findings from the Proyecto Arqueológico Chocolá (PACH). *Mexicon* 26:77–86.

Kappelman, Julia Guernsey. 1997. Of Macaws and Men: Late Preclassic Cosmology and Political Ideology in Izapan-Style Monuments. Ph.D. diss., Dept. of Art and Art History, University of Texas, Austin.

Kauffman, Stuart A. 1993. *The Origins of Order: Self-Organization and Selection in Evolution*. New York, NY: Oxford University Press.

Kaufman, Terrence. 1974. *Idiomas de Mesoamérica*. Guatemala City: Editorial José de Pineda Ibarra y Ministerio de Educación.

———. 1976. Archaeological and Linguistic Correlations in Mayaland and Associated Areas of Meso-America. *World Archaeology* 8:101–18.

Kaufmann, Carol. 2003. Sistine Chapel of the Early Maya. *National Geographic* 204(6): 72–77.

Keatinge, Richard W. 1981. The Nature and Role of Religious Diffusion in the Early Stages of State Formation: An Example from Peruvian Prehistory. In *The Transition to Statehood in the New World*, ed. Grant D. Jones and Robert R. Kautz, pp. 172–87. Cambridge: Cambridge University Press.

Keesing, Roger M. 1972. Simple Models of Complexity: The Lure of Kinship. In *Kinship Studies in the Morgan Centennial Year*, ed. Priscilla Reining, pp. 17–31. Washington, DC: The Anthropological Society of Washington.

Kelly, Isabel. 1980. *Ceramic Sequence in Colima: Capacha, an Early Phase*. Anthropological Papers of the University of Arizona 37. Tucson, AZ: University of Arizona Press.

Kennedy, Nedenia C. 1981. Formative Period Ceramic Sequence from Playa de los Muertos, Honduras. Ph.D. diss., Dept. of Anthropology, University of Illinois.

Kerr, Justin. 2000. *The Maya Vase Book: A Corpus of Rollout Photographs of Maya Vases, Volume 6*, ed. Barbara and Justin Kerr. New York, NY: Kerr Associates.

Kidder, Alfred V. 1950. Introduction. In *Uaxactun, Guatemala: Excavations 1931-1937, by A. L. Smith*. Carnegie Institution of Washashington Publication 588. Washington, DC: Carnegie Institution of Washington.

———. 1961. Archaeological Investigations at Kaminaljuyu, Guatemala. *Proceedings of the American Philosophical Society* 105:559–70.

Kidder, Alfred V., Jesse D. Jennings and Edwin M. Shook. 1946. *Excavations at Kaminaljuyu*. Carnegie Institution of Washington Publication 561. Washington, DC: Carnegie Institution of Washington.

Killion, Thomas, and Javier Urcid. 2001. The Olmec Legacy: Cultural Continuity and Change in Mexico's Southern Gulf Coast Lowlands. *Journal of Field Archaeology* 28(1/2): 3–25.

King, Brian C. 2002. Ceramic Characterization Analysis at Tres Zapotes, Veracruz, Mexico. Paper presented at the 67th Annual Meeting for the Society for American Archaeology, Denver, March 20–24.

King, Eleanor M. 1984. Tzucul, Cuch, and Sacrifice: A Study of the Late Postclassic Social Organization among the Yucatec Maya. Unpublished ms.

———. 2000. The Organization of Late Classic Lithic Production at the Prehistoric Maya Site of Colha, Belize: A Study in Complexity and Heterarchy. Ph.D. diss., Dept. of Anthropology, University of Pennsylvania.

———. 2003. Craft Politics and Labor Relations: The Role of Specialization in the Development and Maintenance of Maya Polities. Paper presented at the 67th Annual Meeting of the Society for American Archaeology, Denver, April 11.

———. 2007. Labor's Love Lost: A Reconstruction of the Early Maya Economy. Paper prepared for the University of Pennsylvania Museum International Research Conference, Philadelphia, April 9–13.

King, Eleanor M., and Daniel Potter. 1994. Small Sites in Prehistoric Maya Socioeconomic Organization: A Perspective from Colha, Belize. In *Archaeological Views from the Countryside. Village Communities in Early Complex Societies*, ed. Glenn M. Schwartz and Steven E. Falconer, pp. 64–90. Washington, DC: Smithsonian Institution Press.

King, Eleanor M., and Leslie C. Shaw. 2007. In Search of Maya Markets. Paper presented at the 72nd Annual Meeting of the Society for American Archaeology, Austin, April 25–29.

Knapp, A. Bernard. 1992. *Archaeology, Annales and Ethnohistory*. Cambridge, UK: Cambridge University Press.

Knight, Charles. 2003. Obsidian Production, Consumption, and Distribution in Tres Zapotes: Piecing Together the Political Economy. In *Settlement Archaeology and Political Economy at Tres Zapotes, Veracruz, Mexico*, ed. Christopher A. Pool, pp. 69–89. Cotsen Institute of Archaeology Monograph 50. Los Angeles, CA: Cotsen Institute of Archaeology, University of California.

Kolb, Michael J. 1994. Monumentality and the Rise of Religious Authority in Precontact Hawai'i. *Current Anthropology* 34(5): 521–48.

References 613

Kosakowsky, Laura J. 1987. *Preclassic Maya Pottery at Cuello, Belize*. Anthropological Papers of the University of Arizona, 47. Tucson, AZ: University of Arizona Press.

Kosakowsky, Laura J., and Duncan Pring. 1991. Ceramic Chronology and Typology. In *Cuello: An Early Maya Community in Belize*, ed. Norman Hammond, pp. 60–69. Cambridge, UK: Cambridge University Press.

———. 1998. The Ceramics of Cuello, Belize: A New Evaluation. *Ancient Mesoamerica* 9(1): 55–66.

Kowalewski, Stephen A. 1990. The Evolution of Complexity in the Valley of Oaxaca. *Annual Review of Anthropology* 19:39–58.

Krader, Lawrence. 1968. *Formation of the State*. Englewood Cliffs, NJ: Prentice-Hall.

Krejci, Estella, and T. Patrick Culbert. 1995. Preclassic and Classic Burials and Caches in the Maya Lowlands. In *The Emergence of Lowland Maya Civilization. The Transition from the Preclassic to the Early Classic*, ed. Nikolai Grube, pp. 103–16. Möckmül, Germany: Verlag Anton Saurweir.

Kruger, Robert P. 1996. An Archaeological Survey in the Region of the Olmec: Veracruz, Mexico. Ph.D. diss., Dept. of Anthropology, University of Pittsburgh.

Kubler, George. 1961. *The Art and Architecture of Ancient America*. Baltimore, MD: Penguin Books.

———. 1962. *The Shape of Time*. New Haven, CT: Yale University Press.

Kunselman, Raymond, 2000. Yacimiento Mesoamericano de Obsidiana: Estudios de Utilización, Conexiones y Contactos en Nakbe. In *Investigaciones Arqueológicas y Ecológicas en la Cuenca Mirador, 1998: Informe de la Temporada de Campo*, ed. Richard.D. Hansen and J. Valle, pp. 630–44. Proyecto Regional de Investigaciones Arqueológicas del Norte del Peten, Guatemala. Rupert, ID: Foundation for Anthropological Research & Environmental Studies.

Lacadena, Alfonso. 1995. Evolución Formal de las Grafias Escriturarias Mayas: Implicaciónes Historicas y Culturales. Ph.D. diss., Dept. of American History II (Anthropology of America) Universidad Complutense de Madrid.

LaFarge, Oliver. 1947. *Santa Eulalia: The Religion of a Cuchumatan Indian Town*. Chicago, IL: University of Chicago Press.

Landa, Diego de. 1941. *Relación de las Cosas de Yucatan*. Papers of the Peabody Museum, vol. 18. Cambridge, MA: Peabody Museum, Harvard University.

Lane MacFeeters, Marcianna. 1998. Producción Campesina de Maíz en San Lorenzo Tenochtitlán: Implicaciones para la Arqueología Olmeca. Ph.D. diss., Facultad de Filosofía y Letras, Universidad Nacional Autónoma de México.

Lange, Frederick W. 1992. Search for Elite Personages and Site Hierarchies in Greater Nicoya. In *Wealth and Hierarchy in the Intermediate Area*, ed. Frederick W. Lange, pp. 109–40. Washington, DC.: Dumbarton Oaks Research Library and Collection.

Lansing, J. Stephen. 2003. Complex Adaptive Systems. *Annual Review of Anthropology* 32:183–204.

Laporte, Juan Pedro. 1995. Preclásico a Clásico en Tikal: Proceso de Transformación en Mundo Perdido. In *The Emergence of Lowland Maya Civilization*, ed. Nikolai Grube, pp. 17–34. Acta Mesoamericana 8. Möckmühl: Anton Sauerwein.

Laporte, Juan Pedro, and Vilma Fialko. 1990. New Perspectives on Old Problems: Dynastic References for the Early Classic at Tikal. In *Vision and Revision in Maya Studies*, ed. Flora S. Clancy and Peter D. Harrison, pp. 33–66. Albuquerque, NM: University of New Mexico Press.

———. 1993a. El Preclásico de Mundo Perdido: Algunos Aportes sobre los Orígenes de Tikal. In *Tikal y Uaxactun en el Preclásico*, ed. Juan Pedro Laporte and Juan Antonio Valdés, pp. 9–47. Mexico, DF: Universidad Nacional Autonoma de Mexico.

———. 1993b. Análisis Cerámico de Tres Depósitos Problemáticos de Fase Eb, Mundo Perdido, Tikal. In *Tikal y Uaxactun en el Preclásico*, ed. Juan Pedro Laporte and Juan A. Valdés, pp. 53–69. México, DF: Instituto de Investigaciones Antropológicas, Universidad Nacional Autónoma de México.

———. 1995. Un Reencuentro con Mundo Perdido, Tikal, Guatemala. *Ancient Mesoamerica* 6:41–94.

Laporte, Juan Pedro, and Juan Antonio Valdés, eds. 1993. *Tikal y Uaxactun en el Preclásico*. Mexico, DF: Instituto de Investigaciones Antropológicas, Universidad Nacional Autonoma de Mexico.

Leach, Edmund. 1954. *Political Systems of Highland Burma*. Cambridge: Cambridge University Press.

Lee, David, and Jaime J. Awe. 1995. Middle Formative Architecture, Burials, and Craft Specialization: Report on the 1994 Investigations at the Cas Pek Group, Cahal Pech, Belize. In *Belize Valley Preclassic Maya Project: Report on the 1995 Field Season*, ed. Paul F. Healy and Jaime Awe, pp. 95–115. Trent University, Occasional Papers in Anthropology. Peterborough, Ontario, Canada.

Lee, Thomas A. Jr. 1969a. Archaeological Salvage at Chiapa de Corzo, Chiapas, Mexico. Preliminary Report submitted to the Instituto Nacional de Antropología y Historia, Mexico City.

———. 1969b. Salvamento Arqueológico en Chiapa de Corzo. *Boletín del Instituto Nacional de Antropología e Historia* 38:17–22.

———. 1969c. *The Artifacts of Chiapa de Corzo, Chiapas, Mexico*. Papers of the New World Archaeological Foundation, No. 26, Provo, UT: New World Archaeological Foundation, Brigham Young University.

———. 1974a. *Mound 4 Excavations at San Isidro, Chiapas, Mexico.* Papers of the New World Archaeological Foundation, No. 34. Provo, UT: New World Archaeological Foundation, Brigham Young University.

———. 1974b. The Middle Grijalva Chronology and Ceramic Relationships: A Preliminary Report. In *Mesoamerican Archaeology: New Approaches*, ed. Norman Hammond, pp. 1–20. Austin, TX: University of Texas Press.

———. 1978. Informe Preliminar de la 2a. Temporada de Campo, Febrero-Junio, 1978, del Proyecto de la Zona Guajilar-Niágara. Report submitted to the Instituto Nacional de Antropología y Historia, Mexico City.

———. 1982. Dos Esculturas Olmecas del Valle del Río Grijalva. *Revista Mexicana de Estudios Antropológicos* 28:67–77.

———. 1989. Chiapas and the Olmec. In *Regional Perspectives on the Olmec*, ed. Robert J. Sharer and David C. Grove, pp. 198–226. Cambridge: Cambridge University Press.

———. 1990. Un nuevo complejo de escultura en la Planicie Costera de Chiapas. *Arqueologia* 3:57–66.

———. 1993. Evidencia Olmeca en el Dominio de Chiapa de Corzo. *Segundo y Tercer Foro de Arqueología de Chiapas*, ed. Thomas A Lee Jr., pp. 228–35. Chiapas, Mexico: Gobierno del Estado de Chiapas, Consejo Estatal de Fomento a la Investigacion y Difusion de la Cultura, and Instituto Chiapaneco de Cultura.

———. n.d. *Archaeological Salvage at Chiapa de Corzo, Mound 17.* Unpublished ms, New World Archaeological Foundation, Brigham Young University.

Lee, Thomas A., Jr., and John E. Clark. 2013. *Minor Excavations in Lower Izapa.* Papers of the New World Archaeological Foundation, No. 78. Provo, UT: New World Archaeological Foundation, Brigham Young University.

———. 2015. Excavations along the Totopac and Grijalva Rivers. In *Reconnaissance and Excavations in the Malpaso Basin, Chiapas, Mexico*, ed. T.A. Lee, C. Navarrete, and J. E. Clark. Papers of the New World Archaeological Foundation, No. 74. Provo, UT: New World Archaeological Foundation, Brigham Young University.

Lee, Thomas A., Jr., Carlos Navarrete, and John E. Clark, eds. 2015. *Reconnaissance and Excavations in the Malpaso Basin, Chiapas, Mexico.* Papers of the New World Archaeological Foundation, No. 74. Provo, UT: New World Archaeological Foundation, Brigham Young University.

Lesure, Richard G. 1997. Figurines and Social Identities in Early Sedentary Societies of Coastal Chiapas, Mexico, 1550–800 B.C. In *Women in Prehistory: North America and Mesoamerica*, ed. Cheryl Classen and Rosemary A. Joyce, pp. 227–48. Philadelphia, PA: University of Pennsylvania Press.

―――. 1999. On the Genesis of Value in Early Hierarchical Societies. In *Material Symbols: Culture and Economy in Prehistory*, ed. John E. Robb, pp. 23–55. Center for Archaeological Investigations, Occasional Paper No. 26. Carbondale, IL: Southern Illinois University.

―――. 2000. Animal Imagery, Cultural Unities, and Ideologies of Inequality in Early Formative Mesoamerica. In *Olmec Art and Archaeology in Mesoamerica*, ed. John E. Clark and Mary E. Pye, pp. 193–216. Washington, DC: National Gallery of Art.

―――. 2004. Shared Art Styles and Long-Distance Contact in Early Mesoamerica. In *Mesoamerican Archaeology*, ed. Julia A. Hendon and Rosemary A. Joyce, pp. 73–96. Oxford, UK: Blackwell Press.

―――. 2011. Paso de la Amada as a Ceremonial Center. In *Early Mesoamerican Social Transformations: Archaic and Formative Lifeways in the Soconusco Region*, ed. Richard G. Lesure, pp. 119–45. Berkeley: University of California Press.

Levi-Strauss, Claude. 1982. *The Way of the Masks*. Seattle, WA: University of Washington Press.

―――. 1987. *Anthropology and Myth*. Oxford: Basil Blackwell.

Leyden, Barbara W. 2002. Pollen Evidence for Climatic Variability and Cultural Disturbance in the Maya Lowlands. *Ancient Mesoamerica* 13:85–101.

Leyenaar, Ted J.J. 1978. *Ulama, the Perpetuation in Mexico of the Pre-Spanish Ball Game Ullamaliztli*. Leiden: Brill.

―――. 2001. Modern Ballgames of Sinaloa: A Survival of the Aztec Ullamaliztli. In *The Sport of Life and Death: The Mesoamerican Ballgame*, ed. E. Michael Whittington, pp. 122–29. New York, NY: Thames and Hudson.

Lincoln, Charles E. 1985. Ceramics and Ceramic Chronology. In *A Consideration of the Early Classic Period in the Maya Lowlands*, ed. Gordon R. Willey and Peter Mathews, pp. 55–94. Institute for Mesoamerican Studies Publication, 10. Albany, NY: State University of New York.

Lindstrom, Lamont. 1984. Doctor, Lawyer, Wise Man, Priest: Big-Men and Knowledge in Melanesia. *Man* 19:291–309.

Lohse, Jon C. 2002. Late Classic Maya Commoners and Political Economic Strategies: 'Smallholders' versus 'Householders.' Unpublished ms.

―――. 2013. Classic Maya Political Ecology, Class Histories, and Political Change in Northwestern Belize. In *Classic Maya Political Ecology*, ed. Jon C. Lohse, pp. 1–24. Los Angeles, CA: Cotsen Institute of Archaeology Press.

Lohse, Jon C., Jaime Awe, Cameron Griffith, Robert M. Rosenswig, and J. Fred Valdez. 2006. Preceramic Occupations in Belize: Updating the Paleoindian and Archaic Record. *Latin American Antiquity* 17(2): 209–26.

Lohse, Jon C., and Fred Valdez Jr. 2004. *Ancient Maya Commoners*. Austin, TX: University of Texas Press.

Longyear, John M. 1952. *Copan Ceramics: A Study of Southeastern Maya Pottery*. Carnegie Institute of Washington Publication 597. Washington, DC: Carnegie Institute of Washington.

López, Roberto F. 1993. Un ensayo sobre patrones de enterramiento y evidencias de sacrificio humano en Kaminaljuyu, Guatemala. In *VI Simposio de Investigaciones Arqueológicas en Guatemala*, ed. Juan Pedro Laporte, Héctor L. Escobedo, and Sandra Villagrán de Brady, page nos.? Guatemala: Ministerio de Cultura y Deportes, Instituto de Antropología e Historia, Asociación Tikal.

López Jiménez, Fanny, and Víctor Esponda Jimeno. 1998. Arqueología del Valle de Cintalapa y Jiquipilas, notas preliminares. In *Cultura y Etnicidad Zoque*, ed. Dolores Aramoni, Thomas A. Lee, and Miguel Lisbona, pp. 27–46. Chiapas, Mexico: Universidad Autónoma de Chiapas and Universidad de Ciencias y Artes del Chiapas.

———. 1999. Reconocimiento Arqueológico en el Valle de Cintalapa y Jiquipilas, Chiapas. In *Río La Venta, Tesoro de Chiapas*, pp. 193–202. Padova, Italy: Tipolitografia Turra.

Loughlin, Michael, and Christopher A. Pool. 2006. Olmec to Epi-Olmec in the Eastern Lower Papaloapan Basin. Paper presented at the 71st Annual Meeting of the Society for American Archaeology, San Juan, Puerto Rico, April 26–39.

Lounsbury, Floyd. 1973. On the Derivation and Reading of the ben-ich Prefix. In *Mesoamerican Writing Systems*, ed. Elizabeth P. Benson, pp. 99–143. Washington, DC: Dumbarton Oaks Research Library and Collections.

Love, Michael W. 1991. Style and Social Complexity in Formative Mesoamerica. In *The Formation of Complex Society in Southeastern Mesoamerica*, ed. William R. Fowler Jr., pp. 47–76. Boca Raton, LA: CRC Press.

———. 1993. Ceramic Chronology and Chronometric Dating: Stratigraphy and Seriation at La Blanca, Guatemala. *Ancient Mesoamerica* 4:31–53.

———. 1999a. Economic Patterns in the Development of Complex Society in Pacific Guatemala. In *Pacific Latin America in Prehistory*, ed. Michael Blake, pp. 89–100. Pullman, WA: Washington State University Press.

———. 1999b. Ideology, Material Culture, and Daily Practice in Pre-Classic Mesoamerica: A Pacific Coast Perspective. In *Social Patterns in Pre-Classic Mesoamerica*, ed. David C. Grove and Rosemary A. Joyce, pp. 127–53. Washington, DC: Dumbarton Oaks Research Library and Collection.

———. 2002a. Ceramic Chronology of Preclassic Period Western Pacific Guatemala and Its Relationship to Other Regions. In *Incidents of Archaeology in Central America and Yucatán: Essays in Honor of Edwin M. Shook*, ed. Micahel Love, Marion Pope-noe de Hatch, and Héctor L. Escobedo, pp. 51–73. Lanham, MD: University Press of America, Inc.

———. 2002b. Domination, Resistance and Political Cycling in Formative Period Pacific Guatemala. In *The Dynamics of Power*, ed. Maria O'Donovan, pp. 214–37. Occasional Paper No. 30. Center for Archaeological Investigations, Southern Illinois University, Carbondale, IL.

———. 2002c. *Early Complex Society in Pacific Guatemala: Settlements and Chronology of the Río Naranjo, Guatemala*. Papers of the New World Archaeological Foundation, No. 66. Provo, UT: New World Archaeological Foundation, Brigham Young University.

———. 2004. Etnicidad, Identidad y Poder: Interacción entre los Maya y sus Vecinos en el Altiplano y Costa del Pacífico de Guatemala en el Preclásico. In *XVII Simposio de Investigaciones Arqueológicas en Guatemala*, ed. Juan Pedro Laporte, Bárbara Arroyo, Héctor L. Escobedo, and Héctor E. Mejía, pp. 449–60. Guatemala: Ministerio de Cultura y Deportes, Instituto de Antropología e Historia, Asociación Tikal.

———. 2006. Middle Formative Household Diversity at La Blanca, Guatemala. Paper presented at the 71st Annual Meetings of the Society for American Archaeology, San Juan, Puerto Rico, April 26–30.

———. 2007. Recent Research in the Southern Highlands and Pacific Coast of Mesoamerica. *Journal of Archaeological Research* 15:275–328.

———. 2010. Thinking Outside the Plaza: Varieties of Preclassic Sculpture in Pacific Guatemala and Their Political Significance. In *The Place of Stone Monuments in Mesoamerica's Preclassic Transition: Context, Use and Meaning*, ed. Julia Guernsey, John E. Clark, and Bárbara Arroyo, pp. 149–75. Washington, DC: Dumbarton Oaks.

———. 2011. City States and City-State Culture in the Southern Maya Region. In *The Southern Maya in the Late Preclassic: The Rise and Fall of an Early Mesoamerican Civilization*, ed. Michael Love and Jonathan Kaplan, pp. 47–76. Boulder: Colorado University Press.

Love, Michael W., and Beatriz Balcárcel. 2000. Ofrendas rituales en la Plaza Central de Ujuxte. In *Trabajos de Análisis del Proyecto Ujuxte*, ed. Michael W. Love and Donaldo Castillo Valdéz, pp. 64–75. Unpublished report submitted to the Instituto de Antropología e Historia de Guatemala.

Love, Michael W., and Julia Guernsey. 2007. Monument 3 from La Blanca, Guatemala: A Middle Preclassic Earthen Sculpture and its Ritual Associations. *Antiquity* 81:920–32.

————. 2011. La Blanca and the Soconusco Middle Formative. In *Early Mesoamerican Social Transformations: Archaic and Formative Lifeways in the Soconusco Region*, ed. Richard G. Lesure, pp. 170–88. Berkeley: University of California Press.

Love, Michael W., Julia Guernsey, Sheryl Carcuz, and Molly Morgan. 2006. El monumento 3 de La Blanca, San Marcos: Una nueva escultura del Preclásico Medio. In *XIX Simposio de Investigaciones Arqueológicas en Guatemala, 2005*, ed. Juan Pedro Laporte, Bárbara Arroyo, and Héctor E. Mejía, pp. 51–62. Guatemala: Ministerio de Cultura y Deportes, Instituto de Antropología e Historia, Asociación Tikal, Fundación Arqueológica del Nuevo Mundo.

Love, Michael W., and Thomas L Jackson. 1998. Intercambio y Consumo de la Obsidiana en la Costa Sur Occidental durante el Preclásico Medio. In *Taller Arqueología de la Región de la Costa Sur de Guatemala*, ed. Christa Schieber de Lavarreda, pp. 95–108. Guatemala: Ministerio de Cultura y Deportes, Instituto de Antropología e Historia.

Love, Michael W., Donaldo Castillo Valdéz, René Ugarte, Brian Damiata, and John Steinberg. 2005. Investigaciones Arqueológicas en el Montículo 1 de La Blanca, Costa Sur de Guatemala. In *XVIII Simposio de Investigaciones Arqueológicas en Guatemala*, ed. Juan Pedro Laporte, Bárbara Arroyo, and Héctor E. Mejía, pp. 959–69. Guatemala: Ministerio de Cultura y Deportes, Instituto de Antropología e Historia, Asociación Tikal, Foundation for the Advancement of Mesoamerican Studies, Inc.

Lowe, Gareth W. 1959. *Archaeological Exploration of the Upper Grijalva River, Chiapas, Mexico*. Papers of the New World Archaeological Foundation, No. 2. Orinda, CA: New World Archaeological Foundation.

————. 1960. *Mound 1, Chiapa de Corzo, Chiapas, Mexico*. Papers of the New World Archaeological Foundation, No. 8. Provo, UT: New World Archaeological Foundation, Brigham Young University.

————. 1962a. Algunos Resultados de la Temporada 1961 en Chiapa de Corzo, Chiapas. *Estudios de Cultura Maya* 2:185–96.

————. 1962b. *Mound 5 and Minor Excavations, Chiapa de Corzo, Chiapas, Mexico*. Papers of the New World Archaeological Foundation, No. 12. Provo, UT: New World Archaeological Foundation, Brigham Young University.

————. 1964. Burial Customs at Chiapa de Corzo. In *The Archaeological Burials at Chiapa de Corzo and Their Furniture*, ed. Pierre Agrinier, pp. 65–75. Papers of the New World Archaeological Foundation, No. 16. Provo, UT: New World Archaeological Foundation, Brigham Young University.

————. 1967. Current Research, Eastern Mesoamerica. *American Antiquity* 32:135–41.

———. 1969. Current Research, Eastern Mesoamerica. *American Antiquity* 34:353–57.

———. 1972. Quarterly Report to the NWAF Board of Directors, May 20. Unpublished ms, HBL Library, Brigham Young University.

———. 1975. *The Early Preclassic Barra Phase of Altamira, Chiapas.* Papers of the New World Archaeological Foundation, No. 38. Provo, UT: New World Archaeological Foundation, Brigham Young University.

———. 1977. Mixe-Zoque as Competing Neighbors of the Early Lowland Maya. In *The Origins of Maya Civilization*, ed. Richard E. W. Adams, pp. 197–248. Albuquerque, NM: University of New Mexico Press.

———. 1978. Eastern Mesoamerica. In *Chronologies in New World Archaeology*, ed. R.E. Taylor and Clement W. Meighan, pp. 331–93. New York, NY: Academic Press.

———. 1981. Olmec Horizons Defined in Mound 20, San Isidro, Chiapas. In *The Olmec and Their Neighbors*, ed. Elizabeth Benson, pp. 235–55. Washington, DC: Dumbarton Oaks Research Library and Collection.

———. 1989a. Algunas Aclaraciones sobre la Presencia Olmeca y Maya en el Preclásico de Chiapas. In *Preclasico o Formativo: Avances y Perspectivas*, ed. Martha Carmona Macias, pp. 363–84. Mexico, DF: Museo Nacional de Antropología and Instituto Nacional de Antropología e Historia.

———. 1989b. The Heartland Olmec: Evolution of Material Culture. In *Regional Perspectives on the Olmec*, ed. Robert J. Sharer and David C. Grove, pp. 33–67. Cambridge: Cambridge University Press.

———. 1991. Buscando una Cultura Olmeca en Chiapas. *Primer Foro de Arqueología de Chiapas*, pp. 111–30. Chiapas, México: Gobierno del Estado de Chiapas y Instituto Chiapaneco de la Cultura, Tuxtla Gutiérrez.

———. 1994. Communidades de Chiapas Relacionadas con los Olmecas. In *Los Olmecas en Mesoamérica*, ed. John Clark, pp.113–27. México, DF: Citibank.

———. 1995. Presencia Maya en la Cerámica del Preclásico Tardío en Chiapa de Corzo. In *Memorias del Segundo Congreso Internacional de Mayistas*, pp. 321–41. Mexico: Universidad Nacional Autónomo de México, Instituto de Investigaciones Filológicas, Centro de Estudios Mayas.

———. 1998a. *Los Olmecas de San Isidro en Malpaso, Chiapas.* Mexico, DF: Instituto Nacional de Antropología e Historia and Chiapas, Mexico: Centro de Investigacioned Humanisticas de Mesoamerica and el Estado de Chiapas.

———. 1998b. *Mesoamérica Olmeca: Diez Preguntas.* Colección Científica, No. 370. Mexico, DF: Instituto Nacional de Antropología e Historia.

———. 1999. *Los Zoques Antiguos de San Isidro.* Chiapas, Mexico: Libros de Chiapas, Consejo Estatal para la Cultura y las Artes de Chiapas, Tuxtla Gutiérrez.

————. 2007. Early Formative Chiapas: The Beginnings of Civilization in the Central Depression of Chiapas. In *Archaeology, Art, and Ethnogenesis in Mesoamerican Prehistory: Papers in Honor of Gareth W. Lowe*, ed. Lynneth S. Lowe and Mary E. Pye, pp. 63–108. Papers of the New World Archaeological Foundation, No. 68. Provo, UT: New World Archaeological Foundation, Brigham Young University.

Lowe, Gareth W., and Pierre Agrinier. 1960. *Mound 1, Chiapa de Corzo, Chiapas, Mexico*. Papers of the New World Archaeological Foundation, No. 8. Provo, UT: New World Archaeological Foundation, Brigham Young University.

Lowe, Gareth W., Susanna Ekholm, and John E. Clark. 2013. *Middle and Late Preclassic Izapa: Ceramic Complexes and History*. Papers of the New World Archaeological Foundation, No. 79. Provo, UT: New World Archaeological Foundation, Brigham Young University.

Lowe, Gareth W., Thomas A. Lee Jr., and Eduardo Martínez Espinosa. 1982. *Izapa: An Introduction to the Ruins and Monuments*. Papers of the New World Archaeological Foundation, No. 31. Provo, UT: New World Archaeological Foundation, Brigham Young University.

Lowe, Gareth W., and J. Alden Mason. 1965. Archaeological Survey on the Chiapas Coast, Highlands, and Upper Grijalva Basin. In *Handbook of Middle American Indians, Vol. 2*. ed. Gordon R. Willey, pp. 195–236. Austin, TX: University of Texas Press.

Lowe, Lynneth S. 1998. *El Salvamento Arqueológico de la Presa de Mal Paso, Chiapas: Excavaciones Menores*. Mexico, DF: Universidad Nacional Autonoma de Mexico.

Lucero, Lisa J. 1999. Water Control and Maya Polities in the Southern Maya Lowlands. In *Complex Polities in the Ancient Tropical World*, ed. Elisabeth A. Bacus and Lisa J. Lucero, pp. 35–50. Archaeological Papers of the American Anthropological Association, No. 9. Arlington, VA: American Anthropological Association.

————. 2002. Collapse of the Classic Maya: A Case for the Role of Water Control. *American Anthropologist* 104(3): 814–26.

————. 2006. *Water and Ritual: The Rise and Fall of Classic Maya Rulers*. Austin, TX: University of Texas Press.

Lucero, Lisa J., and Barbara W. Fash, eds. 2006. *Precolumbian Water Management: Ideology, Ritual, and Power*. Tucson, AZ: University of Arizona Press.

Lunagómez Reyes, Roberto. 2010. Recientes Investigaciones Arqueológicas en la Región de Medias Aguas, Veracruz. In *50 Años de Arqueología en la Universidad Veracruzana*, ed. Y. Lira López, pp. 127–40. Xalapa: Universidad Veracruzana.

Luzzader-Beach, Sheryl, and Timothy Beach. 2009. Arising from the Wetlands: Mechanisms and Chronology of Landscape Aggradation in the Northern Coastal Plain of Belize. *Annals of the Association of American Geographers* 99(1):1–26.

Lynch, John, ed. 1984. *Past and Present in the Americas: A Compendium of Recent Studies.* Manchester: Manchester University Press.

Majewski, Teresita. 1987. Excavations at Telixtac and Huazulco. In *Ancient Chalcatzingo*, ed. David C. Grove, pp. 368–75. Austin, TX: University of Texas Press.

Maler, Teobert. 1901. *Researches in the Central Portion of the Usumatsintla Valley: Report of Explorations for the Museum 1898–1900.* Memoirs of the Peabody Museum of Archaeology and Ethnology 2(1). Cambridge, MA: Harvard University.

Malinowski, Bronislaw. 1961. *Argonauts of the Western Pacific.* New York, NY: E.P. Dutton & Company.

Mann, Michael. 1986. *The Sources of Power: A History of Power from the Beginning to A.D. 1760, vol. 1.* Cambridge: Cambridge University Press.

Manzanilla, Linda. 2001. State Formation in the New World. In *Archaeology at the Millennium: A Sourcebook*, ed. Gary M. Feinman and T. Douglas Price, pp. 381–413. New York, NY: Kluwer Academic/Plenum Publishers.

Marcus, Joyce. n.d. Report of the Peabody Museum 1970 expedition to El Mirador. Unpublished ms. Peabody Museum of Archaeology and Ethnology, Harvard University.

———. 1973. Territorial Organization of the Lowland Classic Maya. *Science* 180(4089): 911–16.

———. 1974. The Iconography of Power among the Classic Maya. *World Archaeology* 6(1): 83–94.

———. 1976a. *Emblem and State in the Classic Maya Lowlands: An Epigraphic Approach to Territorial Organization.* Washington, DC: Dumbarton Oaks Research Library and Collection.

———. 1976b. The Size of the Early Mesoamerican Village. In *The Early Mesoamerican Village*, ed. Kent V. Flannery, pp. 79–90. New York: Academic Press.

———. 1983a. On the Nature of the Mesoamerican City. In *Prehistoric Settlement Patterns: Essays in Honor of Gordon R. Willey*, ed. Evon Z. Vogt and Richard M. Leventhal, pp. 195–242. Albuquerque, NM: University of New Mexico Press.

———. 1983b. Lowland Maya Archaeology at the Crossroads. *American Antiquity* 48(3): 454–88.

———. 1989. Zapotec Chiefdoms and the Nature of Formative Religions. In *Regional Perspectives on the Olmec*, ed. Robert J. Sharer and David C. Grove, pp. 148–97. Cambridge: Cambridge University Press.

———. 1992a. Political Fluctuations in Mesoamerica. *National Geographic Society Research and Exploration* 8:392–411.

————. 1992b. Royal Families, Royal Texts: Examples for the Zapotec and Maya. In *Mesoamerican Elites: An Archaeological Assessment*, ed. Diane Z. Chase and Arlen F. Chase, pp. 221–41. Norman, OK: University of Oklahoma Press.

————. 1993. Ancient Maya Political Organization. In *Lowland Maya Civilization in the Eighth Century A.D.: A Symposium at Dumbarton Oaks 7th and 8th October 1989*, ed. Jeremy A. Sabloff and John S. Henderson, pp. 111–71. Washington, DC: Dumbarton Oaks Research Library and Collection.

————. 1995. Where Is Lowland Maya Archaeology Headed? *Journal of Archaeological Research* 3(1): 3–53.

————. 1998a. The Peaks and Valleys of Ancient States: An Extension of the Dynamic Model. In *Archaic States*, ed. Gary M. Feinman and Joyce Marcus, pp. 59–94. Santa Fe, NM: School of American Research Press.

————. 1998b. *Women's Ritual in Formative Oaxaca: Figurine-Making, Divination, Death, and the Ancestors*. Ann Arbor, MI: University of Michigan, Museum of Anthropology.

————. 1999. Men's and Women's Ritual in Formative Oaxaca. In *Social Patterns in Preclassic Mesoamerica*, ed. David Grove and Rosemary Joyce, pp. 67–96. Washington, DC: Dumbarton Oaks Research Library and Collection.

————. 2003. Recent Advances in Maya Archaeology. *Journal of Archaeological Research* 11(2): 71–148.

Marcus, Joyce, and Gary M. Feinman. 1998. Introduction. In *Archaic States*, ed. Gary M. Feinman and Joyce Marcus, pp. 3–13. Santa Fe, NM: School of American Research Press.

Marcus, Joyce, and Kent V. Flannery. 1996. *Zapotec Civilization: How Urban Society Evolved in Mexico's Oaxaca Valley*. London: Thames and Hudson.

Marroquín, Elizabeth. 2005. El manejo de agua en Tak´alik Ab´aj, Retalhuleu: La evidencia de canales prehispánicos. In *XVIII Simposio de Investigaciones Arqueológicas en Guatemala*, ed. Juan Pedro Laporte, Bárbara Arroyo, and Héctor E. Mejía, pp. 997–1008. Guatemala: Ministerio de Cultura y Deportes, Instituto de Antropología e Historia, Asociación Tikal, Foundation for the Advancement of Mesoamerican Studies, Inc.

Martin, Simon. 1997. The Painted King List: A Commentary on Codex-style Dynastic Vases. In *The Maya Vase Book: A Corpus of Roll-out Photographs of Maya Vases, Volume 5*, ed. Justin Kerr, pp. 846–63. New York, NY: Kerr Associates.

————. 2000. *Chronicle of the Maya Kings and Queens: Deciphering the Dynasties of the Ancient Maya*. London: Thames and Hudson.

————. 2003. In Line of the Founder: A View of Dynastic Politics at Tikal. In *Tikal:*

Dynasties, Foreigners, and Affairs of State, ed. Jeremy A. Sabloff, pp. 3–45. School of American Research Advanced Seminar Series. Santa Fe, NM: School of American Research Press.

———. 2006a. Sun Bird: The Symbolism of Macaws in Ancient Maya Art. Paper presented at The Peabody Museum Weekend of the Americas, Cambridge, October 14th.

———. 2006b. The Old Man of the Maya Universe: Towards an Understanding of God N. Paper presented at the 30th Maya Meetings at Texas, Austin, March 14–19.

———. n.d. a. The Old Man of the Universe: A Unitary Presence within Ancient Maya Religion. In *Maya Archaeology 3*, ed. Charles Golden, Stephen D. Houston, and Joel Skidmore. San Francisco: Precolumbia Mesoweb Press. Forthcoming.

———. n.d. b. Reading Calakmul: Recent Epigraphic Finds of the Proyecto Arqueológico de Calakmul. In *Memoria de al IV Mesa Redonda de Palenque: Arqueología, Imagen y Texto*. Instituto Nacional de Antropología e Historia, Mexico City. Forthcoming.

Martin, Simon, and Nikolai Grube. 1995. Maya Superstates. *Archaeology* 48(6): 41–46.

———. 2000. *Chronicle of the Maya Kings and Queens: Deciphering Dynasties of the Ancient Maya*. London: Thames and Hudson.

———. 2008. *Chronicle of the Maya Kings and Queens*, 2nd ed. London: Thames and Hudson.

Martínez Donjuán, Guadalupe. 1986. Teopantecuanitlán. In *Primer Coloquio de Arqueología y Etnohistoria del Estado de Guerrero*, pp. 55–80. Mexico City, Mexico: Instituto Nacional de Antropología e Historia and the Gobierno del Estado de Guerrero.

———. 1994. Los olmecas en el estado de Guerrero. In *Los Olmecas en Mesoamérica*, ed. John E. Clark, pp. 143–63. México, DF: Citibank, México.

———. 2010. The Sculpture from Teopantecuanitlan, Guerrero, Mexico. In *The Place of Stone Monuments in Mesoamerica's Preclassic Transition: Context, Use, and Meaning*, ed. J. Guernsey, J.E. Clark, and B. Arroyo, pp. 55–76. Washington DC: Dumbarton Oaks.

Martínez Espinosa, Eduardo. 1959. Una Nueva Escultura Olmeca de Tonalá, Chiapas. *Instituto de Ciencias y Artes de Chiapas* 3:79–81.

———. 1982[1971]. Una Pieza Olmec de Chiapa de Corzo. *Revista Mexicana de Estudios Antropológicos* 28:103–7.

Martínez Hidalgo, Gustavo. 2003[1999]. Desarrollos locales de los sitios periféricos de Kaminaljuy: una perspectiva desde el sitio El Mulato. In *Kaminaljuyu en el Simposio de Investigaciones Arqueológicas en Guatemala*, ed. Juan Pedro Laporte and Héctor

E. Mejía, pp. 338–47. Guatemala: Ministerio de Cultura y Deportes, Instituto de Antropología e Historia, Asociación Tikal.

Martínez Hidalgo, Gustavo, and Richard D. Hansen. 1993. Excavaciones en el Complejo 59, Grupo 66 y Grupo 18, Nakbe, Peten. In *III Simposio de Arqueología Guatemalteca*, ed. Juan Pedro Laporte, Héctor.L. Escobedo, and Sandra Villagran de Brady, pp. 73–86. Guatemala: Ministerio de Cultura y Deportes, Instituto de Antropología e Historia, Asociación Tikal.

Martínez Hidalgo, Gustavo, Richard D. Hansen, John Jacob, and Wayne Howell. 1999. Nuevas Evidencias de los Sistemas de Cultivo del Preclasico en la Cuenca El Mirador. In *XII Simposio de Investigaciones Arqueológicas en Guatemala, 1998*, ed. Juan Pedro Laporte, Héctor L. Escobedo, and Ana Claudia Monzón de Suasnávar, pp. 327–36. Guatemala: Ministerio de Cultura y Deportes, Instituto de Antropología e Historia, Asociación Tikal.

Martínez Hidalgo, Gustavo, and Tania Cabrera Morales. 1999. El Montículo de la Culebra: Monumento fachada de la arqueología del Valle de Guatemala. In *XII Simposio de Investigaciones Arqueológicas en Guatemala*, ed. Juan Pedro Laporte, Héctor L. Escobedo, and Ana Claudia Monzón de Suasnávar, pp. 477–84. Guatemala: Ministerio de Cultura y Deportes, Instituto de Antropología e Historia, Asociación Tikal.

Martínez Hidalgo, Gustavo, Tania Cabrera Morales, and Nancy Monterroso. 1996. Urbanismo y diseño arquitectónico en la plaza Mirador de Kaminaljuyu, Guatemala. In *IX Simposio de Investigaciones Arqueológicas en Guatemala*, ed. Juan Pedro Laporte and Héctor L. Escobedo, pp. 397–409. Guatemala: Ministerio de Cultura y Deportes, Instituto de Antropología e Historia, Asociación Tikal.

Martínez Hidalgo, Gustavo, Tania Cabrera Morales, and Patricia Ixcot. 2003[1998]. Algunos aspectos relacionados con los sitios periféricos de Kaminaljuyu: El caso del montículo de San Carlos. In *Kaminaljuyu en el Simposio de Investigaciones Arqueológicas en Guatemala*, ed. Juan Pedro Laporte and Héctor E. Mejía, pp. 280–92. Guatemala: Ministerio de Cultura y Deportes, Instituto de Antropología e Historia, Asociación Tikal.

Martínez Muriel, Alejandro. 1976. Distribucción de la Población Prehispánica en el Vaso de la Presa de la Angostura, Chiapas. In *Las Fronteras de Mesoamérica: XIV Mesa Redonda de la Sociedad Mexicana de Antropología*, pp. 181–90. Mexico: La Sociedad Mexicana de Antropología.

———. 1988. Prehistoric Rural Population Trends in Central Chiapas, Mexico. Ph.D. diss., Dept. of Anthropology, University of California, Los Angeles.

Martínez Muriel, Alejandro, and Carlos Navarrete. 1978. El Salvamento Arqueológico en el Estado de Chiapas. *Revista Mexicana de Estudios Antropológicas* 24(3): 229–55.

Marx, Karl, and Friedrich Engels. 1970[1846]. *The German Ideology: Part One with Selections from Parts Two and Three, Together with Marx's Introduction to a Critique of Political Economy*, ed. C.J. Arthur. New York, NY: International Publishing.

———. 1972[1848]. The Communist Manifesto. In *Karl Marx Essential Writings*, ed. Frederick L. Bender, pp. 240–63. New York, NY: Harper and Row.

Mason, J. Alden. 1960a. *Mound 12, Chiapa de Corzo, Chiapas, Mexico*. Papers of the New World Archaeological Foundation, No. 9. Provo, UT: New World Archaeological Foundation, Brigham Young University.

———. 1960b. *The Terrace to North of Mound 13, Chiapa de Corzo, Chiapas, Mexico*. Papers of the New World Archaeological Foundation, No. 11. Provo, UT: New World Archaeological Foundation, Brigham Young University.

Mastache, Alba Guadalupe. 1988. El trabajo de lapidaria en el estado de Guerrero, una artesanía actual inspirada en formas prehispànicas. *Arqueología* 2:197–216. México, DF: Instituto Nacional de Antropología e Historia.

Mata Amado, Guillermo, and Richard D. Hansen. 1992. El Diente Incrustado Temprano de Nakbé. In *V Simposio de Investigaciones Arqueológicas en Guatemala*, ed. Juan Pedro Laporte, Héctor L. Escobedo, and Sandra Villagrán de Brady, pp. 115–18. Guatemala: Ministerio de Cultura y Deportes, Instituto de Antropología e Historia, Asociación Tikal.

Matheny, Ray T., ed. 1980. *El Mirador, Peten, Guatemala: An Interim Report*. Papers of the New World Archaeological Foundation, No. 45. Provo, UT: New World Archaeological Foundation, Brigham Young University.

———. 1986a. Early States in the Maya Lowlands During the Late Preclassic Period: Edzna and El Mirador. In *City-States of the Maya: Art and Architecture*, ed. Elizabeth P. Benson, pp. 1–44. Denver, CO: Rocky Mountain Institute for Pre-Columbian Studies.

———. 1986b. Investigations at El Mirador, Petén, Guatemala. *National Geographic Research* 2:332–53.

———. 1987. El Mirador: An Early Maya Metropolis Uncovered. *National Geographic* 172(3): 316–39.

Matheny, Ray T., Deanne L. Gurr, Donald W. Forsyth, and R. Richard Hauck. 1983. *Investigations at Edzná, Campeche, Mexico. Volume 1, Part 1: The Hydraulic System*. Papers of the New World Archaeological Foundation, No. 46. Provo, UT: New World Archaeological Foundation, Brigham Young University.

Matheny, Ray T., Richard D. Hansen, and Deanne L. Gurr. 1980. *Preliminary Field Report, El Mirador, 1979 Season*. Papers of the New World Archaeological Foundation, No.

45. Provo, UT: New World Archaeological Foundation, Brigham Young University.

Matheny, Ray T., and Deanna G. Matheny. 2011. Introduction to Investigations at El Mirador, Peten, Guatemala. *El Mirador Series, Part I.* Provo, UT: New World Archaeological Foundation.

Mathews, Peter. 1975. The Lintels of Structure 12, Yaxchilán, Chiapas. Paper presented at the 16th Annual Conference of the Northeastern Anthropological Association, Middletown.

———. 1985. Maya Early Classic Monuments and Inscriptions. In *A Consideration of the Early Classic Period in the Maya Lowlands*, ed. Gordon Willey and Peter Mathews, pp. 5–54. Institute for Mesoamerican Studies Publication 10. Albany, NY: State University of New York.

———. 1991. Classic Maya Emblem Glyphs. In *Classic Maya Political History: Hieroglyphic and Archaeological Evidence*, ed. T. Patrick Culbert, pp. 19–29. Cambridge: Cambridge University Press.

Mathews, Peter, and Linda Schele. 1974. Lords of Palenque: The Glyphic Evidence. In *Primera Mesa Redonda de Palenque (part 1)*, pp. 63–76. Pebble Beach, CA: The Robert Louis Stevenson School.

Mathews, Peter, and Gordon R. Willey. 1991. Prehistoric Polities of the Pasion Region: Hieroglyphic Texts and Their Archaeological Setting. In *Classic Maya Political History: Hieroglyphic and Archaeological Evidence*, ed. T. Patrick Culbert, pp. 30–71. Cambridge: Cambridge University Press.

Mauss, Marcel. 1954. *The Gift: Forms and Functions of Exchange in Archaic Societies.* London: Cohen and West.

———. 1985. A Category of the Human Mind: The Notion of Person, the Notion of Self. In *The Category of the Person: Anthropology, Philosophy, History*, ed. Michael Carithers, Stephen Collins, and Steven Lukes, pp. 1–25. Cambridge: Cambridge University Press.

McAnany, Patricia A. 1989. Economic Foundations of Prehistoric Maya Society: Paradigms and Concepts. In *Prehistoric Maya Economies of Belize*, ed. Patricia A. McAnany and Barry L. Isaac, pp. 347–72. Research in Economic Anthropology, Supplement, 4. Greenwich: JAI Press.

———. 1995. *Living with the Ancestors: Kinship and Kingship in Ancient Maya Society.* Austin, TX: University of Texas Press.

———. 2002. A Social History of Formative Maya Society. In *La Organización Social entre los Mayas Prehispánicos, Coloniales y Modernos*, ed. Vera Tiesler Blos, Rafael Cobos, and Merle G. Robertson, pp. 227–240. México, D.F.: Instituto Nacional de Antropología e Historia.

———. 2004. Situating K'axob within Formative Period Lowland Maya Archaeology. In *K'axob: Ritual, Work, and Family in an Ancient Maya Village*, ed. Patricia A. McAnany, pp. 1–9. Monumenta Archaeologica, 22. Los Angeles, CA: Cotsen Institute of Archaeology, University of California, Los Angeles.

———. 2010. *Ancestral Maya Economies in Archaeological Perspective*. Cambridge, England: Cambridge University Press.

McAnany, Patricia A., Kimberly A. Berry, and Ben S. Thomas. 2003. Wetlands, Rivers, and Caves: Agricultural and Ritual Practice in Two Lowland Maya Landscapes. In *Perspectives on Ancient Maya Rural Complexity*, ed. Gyles Iannone and Samuel V. Connell, pp. 71–81. Los Angeles, CA: Cotsen Institute of Archaeology, University of California at Los Angeles.

McAnany, Patricia A., and Sandra L. López Varela. 1999. Re-creating the Formative Maya Village of K'axob: Chronology, Ceramic Complexes, and Ancestors in Architectural Context. *Ancient Mesoamerica* 10(1): 147–68.

McAnany, Patricia A., Rebecca Storey, and Angela K. Lockard. 1999. Mortuary Ritual and Family Politics at Formative and Early Classic K'axob, Belize. *Ancient Mesoamerica* 10(1): 129–46.

McDavid, Carol. 2007. Revisiting the 'Prospects for Public Participation in African American Archaeology': A Pragmatic Model for Evaluating Approaches and Results. Paper presented at the 78th Annual Meeting of the Texas Archaeological Society, San Antonio, October 26–28.

McDonald, Andrew J. 1974. Middle Preclassic Ceremonial Centers in Southern Chiapas. Paper presented at the 41st International Congress of Americanists, Mexico City, September 2–7.

———. 1977. Two Middle Preclassic Engraved Monuments at Tzutzuculi on the Chiapas Coast of Mexico. *American Antiquity* 42:560–66.

———. 1983. *Tzutzuculi: A Middle-Preclassic Site on the Pacific Coast of Chiapas, Mexico*. Papers of the New World Archaeological Foundation, No. 47. Provo, UT: New World Archaeological Foundation, Brigham Young University.

———. 1999. Middle Formative Pyramidal Platform Complexes in Southern Chiapas, Mexico: Structure and Meaning. Ph.D. diss., Dept. of Anthropology, University of Texas at Austin.

———. n.d. Ocozocoautla Report. Unpublished ms., New World Archaeological Foundation, Brigham Young University.

McElrath, Dale. 1973. Report of Preliminary Investigations at the Site of Perseverancia, Chiapas, Mexico. Unpublished ms., New World Archaeological Foundation, San Cristobal, Mexico.

McGuire, Randall H. 1983. Breaking Down Cultural Complexity: Inequality and Heterogeneity. In *Advances in Archaeological Method and Theory, vol. 6*, ed. Michael B. Schiffer, pp. 91–142. New York, NY: Academic Press.

McNeil, Cameron L, David A. Burney, and Lida Pigott Burney. 2010. Evidence Disputing Deforestation as the Cause for the Collapse of the Ancient Maya Polity of Copan, Honduras. *Proceedings of the National Academy of Sciences* 107(3):1017–1022.

McSwain, Rebecca. 1989. Production and Exchange of Stone Tools among Preclassic Maya Communities: Evidence from Cuello, Belize. Ph.D. diss., Dept. of Anthropology, University of Arizona.

———. 1991a. Chert and Chalcedony Tools. In *Cuello: An Early Maya Community in Belize*, ed. N. Hammond, pp. 160–73. Cambridge: Cambridge University Press.

———. 1991b. Chert Trade. In *Cuello: An Early Maya Community in Belize*, ed. Norman Hammond, pp. 192–95. Cambridge: Cambridge University Press.

Meagher, Alison, and Stephanie Schrodt. 2009. Pozos de Sondeo: Operaciones 108 B, 108 C, 108 G, 108J, 108 M, El Mirador, Temporada 2008. In *Investigaciones Multidisciplinarias en El Mirador: Informe Final de la Temporada 2008, Vol. 1 & II*, ed. Héctor Mejía, Richard D. Hansen, and Edgar Suyuc-Ley, pp. 647–61. Report filed with the Ministerio de Cultura y Deportes, Instituto de Antropología e Historia, Departamento de Monumentos Prehispanicos y Coloniales, Guatemala. Proyecto Cuenca Mirador. Idaho State Universtiy: Foundation for Anthropological Research and Environmental Studies (FARES).

Medellín, Alfonso. 1960. Monolitos Inéditos Olmecas. *La Palabra y El Hombre* 16:75–97.

Medina, Paulo H. 2012. Maya Warfare: Implications of Architecture that Infers Violence in the Preclassic Maya Lowlands. M.A. thesis, Dept. of Anthropology, California State University, Los Angeles.

Medrano Busto, Sonia. 2000. Escuintla y Kaminaljuyu: Integración de dos Regiones. In *XIII Simposio de Investigaciones Arqueológicas en Guatemala*, ed. Juan Pedro Laporte, Héctor L. Escobedo, Ana Claudia Monzón de Suasnávar, and Bárbara Arroyo, pp. 95–114. Guatemala: Ministerio de Cultura y Deportes, Instituto de Antropología e Historia, Asociación Tikal.

Mejía, Héctor E. 2006. Rumbo a Paxban. In *Investigacion y Conservacion en los Sitios Arqueológicos El Mirador, La Muerta, Wakna, El Porvenir, El Guiro, La Iglesia, La Sarteneja, Chab Ché y la Ceibita: Informe Final de la Temporada 2005*, compilado por Edgar Suyuc Ley y Richard D. Hansen, pp. 217–20. Rupert, ID: Idaho State University, Foundation for Anthropological Research and Environmental Studies.

———. 2008. Desarrollo y Estructura de las Ciudades al sur de El Mirador, Peten.

In *XXI Simposio de Investigaciones Arqueológicas en Guatemala, 2007*, ed. Juan Pedro Laporte, Bárbara Arroyo, and Héctor E. Mejía, pp. 543–64. Guatemala City, Guatemala: Museo Nacional de Arqueologia y Etnologia, Ministerio de Cultura y Deportes, Instituto de Antropología e Historia, Asociación Tikal, Fundación Arqueológica del Nuevo Mundo.

———. 2012. Patron de Asentamiento en la Cuenca Mirador. In *XXV Simposio de Investigaciones Arqueológicas en Guatemala 2011*, ed. Bárbara Arroyo, Lorena Paiz Aragón, and Héctor Mejía. Guatemala City, Guatemala: Museo Nacional de Arqueologia y Etnologia, Ministerio de Cultura y Deportes, Instituto de Antropología e Historia, Asociación Tikal, Fundación Arqueológica del Nuevo Mundo.

Mejía, Héctor E., Boris Aguilar, Julio Cotom, Hiro Iwamoto, and Antonio Portillo. 2010. Rescate Arqueológico en El Pesquero: Un Sitio de Rango Intermedio en el Limite Sur de la Cuenca Mirador. In *XXIII Simposio de Investigaciones Arqueológicas en Guatemal, 2009*, ed. Bárbara Arroyo, Adriana Linares Palma, and Lorena Paiz Aragón, pp. 567–82. Guatemala City, Guatemala: Museo Nacional de Arqueologia y Etnologia, Ministerio de Cultura y Deportes, Instituto de Antropología e Historia, Asociación Tikal.

Mejía, Héctor, Richard D. Hansen, and Edgar Suyuc-Ley, eds. 2010. *Exploraciones Arqueologicas en la Cuenca Mirador, 2009*, p. 754. Report filed with Instituto de Antropología e Historia, Guatemala. Proyecto Cuenca Mirador. Rupert, ID: Idaho State University, Foundation for Anthropological Research and Environmental Studies (FARES).

Mejía Amaya, Héctor E., and Edgar Oswaldo Suyuc-Ley. 1998. La Industria de Obsidiana de El Chayal. In *XI Simposio de Investigaciones Arqueológicas en Guatemala*, ed. Juan Pedro Laporte and Hector L. Escobedo, pp. 561–73. Guatemala: Ministerio de Cultura y Deportes, Instituto de Antropología e Historia, Asociación Tikal.

Mejía Amaya, Héctor E., and Edgar Oswaldo Suyuc Ley. 2000. Ri Chay Abaj Proyecto Geológico-Arqueológico El Chayal. *U Tz'ib* 1:1–48.

Mejía, Héctor E., Antonio Portillo, Julio Cotom, and Miguel Pereira. 2008. Programa de Reconocimiento Regional: Exploraciones Arqueológicas en las Concesiones Forestales de La Gloria y Cruce La Colorada, San Andres, Peten. In *Informe Preliminar Temporada 2008: Investigación y Conservación en los Sitios Arqueológicos de la Zona Cultural y Natural Mirador 2008*, ed. Nora Lopez, Richard Hansen, and Edgar Suyuc, pp. 18–30. Preliminary report filed with the Instituto de Antropología e Historia de Guatemala, Monumentos Prehispánicos y Coloniales, Ministerio de Cultural y Deportes, Guatemala. Rupert, Idaho: Foundation for Anthropological Research and Environmental Studies (FARES).

Mejía, Héctor, Gendry Valle, Fancisco Casteñeda, and Enrique Hernandez. 2007. Sobreviviendo a la Selva: Patron de Asentamiento en la Cuenca Mirador. In *XX Simposio de Investigaciones Arqueológicas en Guatemala*, ed. Juan Pedro Laporte, Bárbara Arroyo, and Héctor E. Mejía, pp. 241–64. Guatemala City, Guatemala: Museo Nacional de Arqueologia y Etnologia, Ministerio de Cultura y Deportes, Instituto de Antropología e Historia, Asociación Tikal, Fundación Arqueologica del Nuevo Mundo.

Melgar, José María. 1869. Antigüedades Mexicanos. *Boletín de la Sociedad Mexicana de Geografia y Estadistica* 2:292–97.

Merwin, Raymond E., and George Vaillant. 1932. *The Ruins of Holmul*. Memoirs of the Peabody Museum of American Archaeology and Ethnology, Vol. 3, No. 2. Cambridge, MA: Peabody Museum.

Meskell, Lynn. 1999. *Archaeologies of Social Life: Age, Sex, Class, Etc. in Ancient Egypt*. Oxford: Blackwell.

———. 2000. Writing the Body in Archaeology. In *Reading the Body: Representations and Remains in the Archaeological Record*, ed. Alison E. Rautmann, pp. 13–21. Philadelphia, PA: University of Pennsylvania Press.

Metcalfe, Jessica Z., Christine D. White, Fred J. Longstaffe, Gabriel Wrobel, Della Collins Cook, and K. Anne Pyburn. 2009. Isotopic Evidence for Diet at Chau Hiix, Belize: Testing Regional Models of Hierarchy and Heterarchy. *Latin American Antiquity* 20(1): 15–36.

Michels, Joseph, ed. 1979a. *The Kaminaljuyu Chiefdom*. University Park, PA: The Pennsylvania State University.

———. 1979b. A History of Settlement at Kaminaljuyú. In *Settlement Pattern Excavations at Kaminaljuyu, Guatemala*, ed. Joseph Michels, pp. 277–306. University Park, PA: The Pennsylvania State University.

———, ed. 1979c. *Settlement Pattern Excavations at Kaminaljuyu, Guatemala*. University Park, PA: The Pennsylvania State University.

Michels, Joseph, and Ronald K. Wetherington. 1979. The Kaminaljuyu Test Trenches: Component Assemblage Definition and Phasing. In *Settlement Pattern Excavations at Kaminaljuyu, Guatemala*, ed. Joseph Michels, pp. 619–740. University Park, PA: The Pennsylvania State University.

Michelson, Gunther. 1974. Upstreaming Bruyas. In *Papers in Linguistics from the 1972 Conference on Iroquois Research*, ed. Michael K. Foster, pp. 36–46. Mercury Series Paper, 10. Ottowa: Ethnology Division, National Museum of Man.

Miksicek, Charles H. 1991. The Ecology and Economy of Cuello. In *Cuello: An Early Maya Community in Belize*, ed. Norman Hammond, pp. 70–84. Cambridge: Cambridge University Press.

Milbrath, Susan. 1979. *A Study of Olmec Sculptural Chronology*. Washington, DC: Dumbarton Oaks Research Library and Collection.

Miles, S. W. 1957. The Sixteenth-Century Pokom-Maya: A Documentary Analysis of Social Structure and Archaeological Setting. *Transactions of the American Philosophical Society* 47(4):733–781.

Miller, Don E. 1976a. Excavations at La Libertad: A Late Preclassic Ceremonial Center in Chiapas, Mexico. Unpublished ms., New World Archaeological Foundation, Brigham Young University.

———. 1976b. La Libertad Burials. Unpublished ms., New World Archaeological Foundation, Brigham Young University.

———. 1979. Elite Domestic Structures at La Libertad, Chiapas, Mexico. Paper presented at the 43rd International Congress of Americanists, Vancouver, August 13–17.

———. 2014. *Excavations at La Libertad, a Middle Formative Ceremonial Center in Chiapas, Mexico*. Papers of the New World Archaeological Foundation, No. 64. Provo, UT: New World Archaeological Foundation, Brigham Young University.

Miller, Don E., Douglas Donne Bryant, John E. Clark, and Gareth W. Lowe. 2005. Middle Preclassic Ceramics. In *Ceramic Sequence of the Upper Grijalva Region, Chiapas, Mexico, Part 1*, ed. Douglas D. Bryant, John E. Clark, and David Cheetham, pp. 141–264. Papers of the New World Archaeological Foundation, No. 67. Provo, UT: New World Archaeological Foundation, Brigham Young University.

Millet Camara, Luis Alfonso. 1979. Rescate Arqueológico en la Región de Tres Zapotes, Veracruz. Senior thesis, Dept. of Archaeology, Escuela Nacional de Antropología e Historia, Mexico.

Millon, René. 1960. The Beginnings of Teotihuacan. *American Antiquity* 26(1): 1–10.

———. 1973. *Urbanization at Teotihuacán, Mexico. Vol. 1, The Teotihuacan Map: Text*. Austin, TX: University of Texas Press.

———. 1981. Teotihuacan: City, State, and Civilization. In *The Handbook of Middle American Indians, Supplement 1: Archaeology*, ed. Jeremy A. Sabloff, pp. 198–243. Austin, TX: University of Texas Press.

Millon, René, Bruce Drewitt, and James A. Bennyhoff. 1965. The Pyramid of the Sun at Teotihuacán: 1959 Investigations. *Transactions of the American Philosophical Society*, 55(6). Philadelphia, PA.

Minc, Leah D. 2006. Monitoring Regional Market Systems in Prehistory: Models, Methods, and Metrics. *Journal of Anthropological Archaeology* 25(1): 82–116.

———. 2009. Style and Substance: Evidence for Regionalism Within the Aztec Market System. *Latin American Antiquity* 20(2): 343–74.

Modjeska, Nicholas. 1982. Production and Inequality: Perspectives from Central New Guinea. In *Inequality in New Guinea Highlands Societies*, ed. Andrew Strathern, pp. 50–108. Cambridge: Cambridge University Press.

Moholy-Nagy, Hattula. 1976. Spatial Distribution of Flint and Obsidian Artifacts at Tikal, Guatemala. In *Maya Lithic Studies: Papers from the 1976 Belize Field Symposium*, ed. Thomas R. Hester and Norman Hammond, pp. 91–108. San Antonio, TX: Center for Archaeological Research, The University of Texas at San Antonio.

———. 1991. The Flaked Chert Industry at Tikal, Guatemala. In *Maya Stone Tools: Selected Papers from the Second Maya Lithic Conference*, ed. Thomas R. Hester and Harry J. Shafer, pp. 21–29. Monographs in World Archaeology No. 1. Madison, WI: Prehistory Press.

———. 1997. Middens, Construction Fill, and Offerings: Evidence for the Organization of Classic Period Craft Production at Tikal, Guatemala. *Journal of Field Archaeology* 24(3): 293–313.

Mora, Raziel. 1971. Informe de las excavaciones realizadas durante la primera temporada de trabajos de salvamento arqueológico, efectuadas en la presa de la angostura, Edo. de Chiapas. Unpublished report for INAH and NWAF.

Mora-Marín, David. 2001. Late Preclassic Inscription Documentation Project. Report to the Foundation for the Advancement of Mesoamerican Studies, Inc. http//:www.famsi.org/reports/99049/index.html, accessed April 2007.

———. 2005. Kaminaljuyu Stela 10: Script Classification and Linguistic Affiliation. *Ancient Mesoamerica* 16:63–87.

Morales-Aguilar, Carlos, and Richard D. Hansen. 2005. El orden del espacio en la arquitectura Preclásica de El Mirador, Peten, Guatemala. Paper presented at the I Congreso Centroamericano de Arqueología en El Salvador, San Salvador, El Salvador.

Morley, Sylanus G. 1938. *Inscriptions of Peten*. Washington, DC: Carnegie Institute of Washington.

———. 1946. *The Ancient Maya*. Stanford, CA: Stanford University Press.

Mueller, Andreas D., Gerald A. Islebe, Michael B. Hillesheim, Dustin A. Grzesik, Flavio S. Anselmetti, Daniel Ariztegui, Mark Brenner, Jason H. Curtis, David A. Hodell, and Kathryn A. Venz. 2009. Climate Drying and Associated Forest Decline in the Lowlands of Northern Guatemala During the Late Holocene. *Quaternary Research* 71(2): 133–41.

Murdock, George Peter. 1949. *Social Structure*. New York, NY: Macmillan.

Murdy, Carson N. 1984. Prehistoric Man-Land Relationships Through Time in the Valley of Guatemala. Ph.D. diss., Dept. of Anthropology, Pennsylvania State University.

Murdy, Carson N. 1990. Tradiciones de arquitectura prehispánica en el valle de Guatemala. *Anales de la Academia de Geografía e Historia de Guatemala* 64:349–98.

Murtha, Timothy, and Ann Cyphers. n.d. Spatial and Temporal Modeling of the San Lorenzo Plateau. Unpublished ms, in possession of the author.

Navarrete, Carlos. 1959a. *A Brief Reconnaissance of the Tonala Region, Chiapas, Mexico.* Papers of the New World Archaeological Foundation, No. 4. Orinda, CA: New World Archaeological Foundation.

———. 1959b. *Explorations at San Agustin, Chiapas, Mexico.* Papers of the New World Archaeological Foundation, No. 3. Orinda, CA: New World Archaeological Foundation.

———. 1966. *The Chiapanec History and Culture.* Papers of the New World Archaeological Foundation, No. 16. Provo, UT: New World Archaeological Foundation, Brigham Young University.

———. 1974. *The Olmec Rock Carvings at Pijijiapan, Chiapas, Mexico and Other Olmec Pieces from Chiapas and Guatemala.* Papers of the New World Archaeological Foundation, No. 35. Provo, UT: New World Archaeological Foundation, Brigham Young University.

———. 1978. The Prehispanic System of Communications between Chiapas and Tabasco. In *Mesoamerican Communication Routes and Cultural Contacts,* ed. Thomas A. Lee Jr. and Carlos Navarrete, pp. 75–106. Papers of the New World Archaeological Foundation, No. 40. Provo, UT: New World Archaeological Foundation, Brigham Young University.

Navarrete, Carlos, Rubén Cabrera, Eduardo Martínez, and Jorge Acuña Nuricumbo. 1992. El Maritano, un sitio del Preclásico Inferior vuelto a ocupar: Malpaso, Chiapas. *Anales de Antropología* 29:115–76.

Navarrete, Carlos, Thomas A. Lee Jr., and Carlos Silva Rhoads. 1993. *Un Catálogo de Frontera: Esculturas, Petroglifos y Pinturas de la Región Media del Grijalva, Chiapas.* Mexico, DF: Centro de Estudios Mayas, Universidad Nacional Autonoma de Mexico.

Navarrete, Carlos, and Jorge Luján Muñoz. 1986. *El Gran Montículo de la Culebra en el Valle de Guatemala.* Mexico, DF: Universidad Autónoma de México, Academia de Geografía e Historia de Guatemala.

Navarrete, Carlos, and Eduardo Martínez. 1961. Investigaciones Arqueológicas en el Río Sabinal, Chiapas. *Magazine of the Instituto de Ciencias y Artes de Chiapas* 5:49–83.

Neff, Hector. 2006. The Olmec and the Origins of Mesoamerican Civilization. *Antiquity* 80(309): 714–16.

Neff, Hector, Jeffrey P. Blomster, Michael D. Glascock, Ronald L. Bishop, M. James

Blackman, Michael D. Coe, George L. Cowgill, Ann Cyphers, Richard A. Diehl, Stephen Houston, Arthur A. Joyce, Carl P. Lipo, and Marcus Winter. 2006a. Smokescreens in the Provenance Investigation of Early Formative Mesoamerican Ceramics. *Latin American Antiquity* 17(1): 104–18.

Neff, Hector, Jeffrey P. Blomster, Michael D. Glascock, Ronald L. Bishop, M. James. Blackman, Michael D. Coe, George L. Cowgill, Richard A. Diehl, Stephen Houston, Arthur A. Joyce, Carl P. Lipo, and Marcus Winter. 2006b. Methodological Issues in the Provenance Investigation of Early Formative Mesoamerican Ceramics. *Latin American Antiquity* 17(1): 54–76.

Neff, Hector, Deborah M. Pearsall, John G. Jones, Bárbara Arroyo, Shawn K. Collins, and Dorothy E. Freidel. 2006c. Early Maya Adaptive Patterns: Mid–Late Holocene Paleoenvironmental Evidence from Pacific Guatemala. *Latin American Antiquity* 17(3): 287–315.

Neff, Hector, Frederick J. Bove, and José Vicente Genovez. 2006d. El clima y la naturaleza de la ocupación del Postclásico en la Costa Sur de Guatemala. In *XIX Simposio de Investigaciones Arqueológicas en Guatemala, 2005*, ed. Juan Pedro Laporte, Bárbara Arroyo, and Héctor E. Mejía, pp. 137–42. Guatemala: Ministerio de Cultura y Deportes, Instituto de Antropología e Historia, Asociación Tikal, Fundación Arqueológica del Nuevo Mundo.

Nelson, Ben A., J. Andrew Darling, and David A. Kice. 1992. Mortuary Practices and the Social Order at La Quemada, Zacatecas, Mexico. *Latin American Antiquity* 3(4): 298–315.

Nelson, Fred W., Jr. 1985. Summary of the Results of Analysis of Obsidian Artifacts from the Maya Lowlands. *Scanning Electron Microscopy* 1985(2): 631–49.

———. 1988. Appendix 4: Trace Element Analysis of Obsidian Artifacts. In *The Lithic Artifacts of La Libertad, Chiapas, Mexico: An Economic Perspective*, ed. John E. Clark, pp. 271–76. Papers of the New World Archaeological Foundation, No. 52. Provo, UT: New World Archaeological Foundation, Brigham Young University.

Nelson, Fred W., Jr., and John E. Clark. 1990. Determination of Exchange Patterns in Prehistoric Mesoamerica. In *Nuevos Enfoques en el Estudio de la Lítica*, ed. María de los Dolores Soto de Arechavelta, pp. 153–76. Mexico, DF: Universidad Nacional Autónoma de México.

———. 1998. Obsidian Production and Exchange in Eastern Mesoamerica. In *Rutas de Intercambio en Mesoamerica: III Coloquio, Pedro Bosch Gimpera*, ed. Evelyn C. Rattray, pp. 277–333. Mexico, DF: Universidad Nacional Autonoma de Mexico.

Nelson, Fred W., Jr., and David S. Howard. 1986. *Trace Element Analysis of Obsidian Artifacts from El Mirador, Guatemala*. Notes of the New World Archaeological

Foundation, No. 3. Provo, UT: New World Archaeological Foundation, Brigham Young University.

Nelson, Fred. W., Jr., David A. Phillips, Jr., and Alfredo Barrera Rubio. 1983. Trace Element Analysis of Obsidian Artifacts from the Northern Maya Lowlands. In *Investigations at Edzná, Campeche, Mexico*, ed. Ray T. Matheny, Deanne L. Gurr, Donald W. Forsyth, and F. Richard Hauck, pp. 204–19. Papers of the New World Archaeological Foundation, No. 46. Provo, UT: New World Archaeological Foundation, Brigham Young University.

Nelson, Fred W., Jr., Raymond V. Sidrys, and Richard D. Holmes. 1978. Trace Element Analysis by X-Ray Fluorescence of Obsidian Artifacts from Guatemala and Belize. In *Excavations at Seibal: Artifacts*, ed. Gordon R. Willey, pp. 153–61. Memoirs of the Peabody Museum of Archaeology and Ethnology, Vol. 14, No. 1. Cambridge, MA: Harvard University.

Netting, Robert M. 1977. Maya Subsistence: Mythologies, Analogies, Possibilities. In *Origins of Maya Civilization*, ed. Richard E. W. Adams, pp. 299–333. Albuquerque, NM: University of New Mexico Press.

Niederberger, Christine B. 1976. *Zohapilco, cinco milenios de ocupación humana en un sitio lacustre de la cuenca de México*. Colección Científica 30. México, DF: Instituto Nacional de Antropología e Historia.

———. 1987. *Paleopaysages et Archeologie Pre-Urbaine du Bassin de Mexico*. Collection Etudes Mésoaméricaines, No. 11. México, DF: Centre d'Etudes Mexicaines et Centramericaines.

———. 1996. The Basin of Mexico: A Multimillennial Development Toward Cultural Complexity. In *Olmec Art of Ancient Mexico*, ed. Elizabeth P. Benson and Beatriz de la Fuente, pp. 83–93. Washington, DC: National Gallery of Art.

———. 2000. Ranked Societies, Iconographic Complexity, and Economic Wealth in the Basin of Mexico toward 1200 B.C. In *Olmec Art and Archaeology in Mesoamerica*, ed. John E. Clark and Mary E. Pye, pp. 169–91. Washington, DC: National Gallery of Art.

Nielsen, Glenna. 1980. Salvage of Looters' Trenches, El Mirador. In *El Mirador, Peten, Guatemala: An Interim Report*, ed. Ray T. Matheny, pp. 25–36. Papers of the New World Archaeological Foundation, No. 45. Provo, UT: Brigham Young University.

Nielsen, Glenna. 1990. Central Plaza Excavations at El Mirador, Peten, Guatemala: Operations 18 and 27. Ph.D. diss., Dept. of Anthropology, University of Utah.

Nielsen, Jesper, and Christopher Helmke. n.d. La Caída del Gran Ave Celestial: Un Mito Cosmogónico del Clásico Temprano en el México Central. In *Teotihuacan:*

Medios de Comunicación y Poder en la Ciudad de los Dioses, ed. Nikolai Grube and Ingrid Kummels. Forthcoming.

Nondedeo, Philippe, Carlos Morales, Alejandro Patiño, Melanie Forne, Chloe Andrieu, Julien Sion, Dominique Michelet, Charlotte Arnauld, Celine Gillot, Monica de Leon, Julio Cotom, Eva Leminnier, Gregory Pereira, and Isaac Barrientos. 2012. Prosperidad Economica en Naachtun: Resultados de las dos Primeras Temporadas de Investigación. In *XXV Simposio de Investigaciones Arqueológicas en Guatemala*, ed. Bárbara Arroyo, Lorena Paiz, and Héctor Mejía, pp. 227–35. Guatemala City, Guatemala: Museo Nacional de Arqueologia y Etnologia, Ministerio de Cultura y Deportes, Instituto de Antropología e Historia, Asociación Tikal.

Norman, V. Garth. 1973. *Izapa Sculpture. Part I: Album*. Papers of the New World Archaeological Foundation, No. 30. Provo, UT: New World Archaeological Foundation, Brigham Young University.

———. 1976. *Izapa Sculpture: Part 2: Text*. Papers of the New World Archaeological Foundation, No. 30. Provo, UT: New World Archaeological Foundation, Brigham Young University.

Ochoa, Lorenzo. 1983. El Medio Usumacinta: Un Eslabón en los Antecedentes Olmecas de los Mayas. In *Antropología e Historia de los Mixe-Zoques y Mayas: Homenaje a Frans Blom*, ed. Lorenzo Ochoa and Thomas A. Lee, pp. 147–74. Mexico, DF: Universidad Nacional Autonoma de Mexico.

Ochoa, Lorenzo, and Martha Ivón Hernández. 1977. Los Olmecas y el Valle del Usumacinta. *Anales de Antropología* 14:75–90.

Ochoa Castillo, Patricia. 2003. *Tlatilco: el lugar donde hay cosas ocultas*. Saltillo, Coahuila, México: Centro Cultural Vito Alesasio Robles.

Ohi, Kuniaki. 1994a. Cronología de Mongoy, Kaminaljuyu. In *Kaminaljuyú, 1991–1994*, ed. Kuniaki Ohi, pp. 365–68. Tokyo: Museo de Tabaco y Sal.

———, ed. 1994b. *Kaminaljuyú, 1991–1994*. Tokyo: Museo de Tabaco y Sal.

———. 2001. Prefacio. In *La Culebra, Kaminaljuyú*, ed. Kuniaki Ohi, pp. xxiii. Tokyo: Museo de Tabaco y Sal.

Ohi, Kuniaki, Noboyuki Ito, Shione Shibata, and Hiroshi Minami. 1997. Los resultados de las investigaciones arqueológicas en Kaminaljuyu. In *X Simposio de Investigaciones Arqueológicas en Guatemala*, ed. Juan Pedro Laporte and Héctor L. Escobedo, pp. 93–100. Guatemala: Museo Nacional de Arqueología y Etnología.

Ohi, Kuniaki, and Blanca Ohi. 1994. Los Entierros de Mongoy, Kaminaljuyu. In *Kaminaljuyú, 1991–1994*, ed. Kuniaki Ohi, pp. 259–81. Tokyo: Museo de Tabaco y Sal.

Okoshi Harada, Tsubasa. 1995. Gobierno y Pueblo Entre los Mayas Yucatecos Posclásicos. *Revista Universidad de México* 534/535:22–27.

Oliveros, José Arturo. 1974. Nuevas Exploraciones en El Opeño, Michoacán. In *The Archaeology of West Mexico*, ed. Betty Bell, pp. 182–201. Ajijic, Jalisco, México: Sociedad de Estudios Avanzados del Occidente de México.

———. 2004. *Hacedores de Tumbas en El Opeño, Jacona, Michoacán*. Michoacán, México: El Colegio de Michoacán.

Oliveros, José Arturo, and Magdalena de los Ríos Paredes. 1993. La Cronología de El Opeño, Michoacán: Nuevos Fechamientos por Radio-Carbono. *Arqueología* 9-10:45–48.

O'Neill, Tom. 2002. Uncovering a Maya Mural. *National Geographic* 201(4): 70–75.

Oppenheim, A. 1964. *Ancient Mesopotamia: Portrait of a Dead Civilization*. Chicago: University of Chicago Press.

O'Rourke, Laura C. 2002. Las Glaeras and San Lorenzo: A Comparative Study of Two Early Formative Communities in Southern Veracruz, Mexico. Ph.D. diss., Dept. of Anthropology, Harvard University.

Ortega, Edgar. 2001. Proyecto de Rescate Arqueológico Shadai, Montículo de la Culebra, Kaminaljuyu. In *La Culebra, Kaminaljuyú*, ed. Kuniaki Ohi, pp. 14–30. Tokyo: Museo de Tabaco y Sal.

Ortega, Edgar, and Noboyuki Ito. 2001. Notas de Campo en la Culebra, Kaminaljuyu. In *La Culebra, Kaminaljuyú*, ed. Kuniaki Ohi, pp. 31–46. Tokyo: Museo de Tabaco y Sal.

Ortega, Edgar, José Samuel Suasnávar Bolaños, Juan Luis Velásquez, and Julio A. Roldán. 1996. El Montículo La Culebra, Kaminaljuyú: Proyectos de Rescate Arqueológico. In *IX Simposio de Investigaciones Arqueológicas en Guatemala*, ed. Juan Pedro Laporte and Hector L. Escobedo, pp. 461–76. Guatemala: Museo Nacional de Arqueología y Etnología.

Ortiz, Mario Arturo, and Ann Cyphers. 1997. La Geomorfología y las Evidencias Arqueológicas en la Región de San Lorenzo Tenochtitlán, Veracruz. In *Población, Subsistencia y Medio Ambiente en San Lorenzo Tenochtitlán*, ed. Ann Cyphers, pp. 31–54. Mexico, DF: Instituto de Investigaciones Antropologicas, Universidad Nacional Autonoma de Mexico.

Ortíz, Ponciano. 1975. La Cerámica de los Tuxtlas. M.A. thesis, Dept. of Anthropology, Universidad Veracruzana, Jalapa, Veracruz, Mexico.

Ortíz, Ponciano, and María del Carmen Rodríguez. 1989. Proyecto Manatí 1989. *Arqueología* (época 2)1:23–52.

———. 1994. Los Espacios Sagrados Olmecas: El Manatí, un Caso Especial. In *Los Olmecas en Mesoamérica*, ed. John E. Clark, pp. 68–91. Mexico, DF: Citibank.

———. 1999. Olmec Ritual Behavior at El Manatí: A Sacred Space. In *Social Patterns in Pre-Classic Mesoamerica*, ed. David C. Grove and Rosemary A. Joyce, pp. 225–54. Washington, DC: Dumbarton Oaks Research Library and Collection.

———. 2000. The Sacred Hill of El Manatí: A Preliminary Discussion of the Site's Ritual Paraphernalia. In *Olmec Art and Archaeology in Mesoamerica*, ed. John E. Clark and Mary E. Pye, pp. 75–93. Washington, DC: National Gallery of Art.

———. 2008. Los Monumentos de La Merced: Iconografía y Contexto. *Thule: Rivista Italiana di Studi Americanistici* 22/23-24/25: 145–82.

Ortíz, Ponciano, María del Carmen Rodríguez, and Alfredo Delgado. 1997. *Las Investigaciones Arqueológicas en el Cerro Sagrado Manatí*. Xalapa, Veracruz: Universidad Veracruzana and Instituto Nacional de Antropología e Historia.

Paillés, H. Maricruz. 1980. *Pampa El Pajón: An Early Estuarine Site, Chiapas, Mexico*. Papers of the New World Archaeological Foundation, No. 44. Provo, UT: New World Archaeological Foundation, Brigham Young University.

Palerm, Ángel. 1972. Sistemas de Regadío Prehispánico en Teotihuacán y en el Pedregal de San Angel. In *Agricultura y Civilización en Mesoamérica*, ed. Ángel Palerm and Eric Wolf, pp. 95–108. México, DF: Instituto Nacional de Antropología e Historia.

Parsons, Lee Allen. 1986. *The Origins of Maya Art: Monumental Stone Sculpture of Kaminaljuyu, Guatemala, and the Southern Pacific Coast*. Studies in Pre-Columbian Art and Archaeology No. 28. Washington, DC: Dumbarton Oaks Research Library and Collection.

———. 1988. Proto-Maya Aspects of Miraflores-Arenal Monumental Stone Sculpture from Kaminaljuyu and the Pacific Coast. In *Maya Iconography*, ed. Elizabeth Benson and Gillett Griffin, pp. 6–43. Princeton, NJ: Princeton University Press.

Pastrana, Alejandro. 1997. Nuevos Datos Acerca de la Estratigrafía de Cuicuilco. *Arqueología* 18:3–16.

Paynter, Robert. 1989. The Archaeology of Equality and Inequality. *Annual Review of Anthropology* 18:369–99.

Pellecer, Monica. 2006. El Grupo Jabalí: Un Complejo Arquitectónico de Patrón Triadico en San Bartolo, Peten. Paper presented at the XIX Simposio de Investigaciones Arqueológicas en Guatemala, Guatemala City, July 18–22.

Pendergast, David M. 1971. Evidence of Early Teotihucan-Lowland Maya Contact at Altun Ha. *American Antiquity* 36(4): 455–60.

———. 1981. Lamanai, Belize: Summary of Excavation Results, 1974–1980. *Journal of Field Archaeology* 8(1): 29–53.

———. 1984. Review: Recent Research on Maya Lowland Prehistory. *Latin American Research Review* 19(3): 232–39.

Pereira Figueroa, Karen, Bárbara Arroyo, and Margarita Cossich. 2006. Las estelas

lisas de Naranjo, Guatemala. Paper presented at the XX Simposio de Investigaciones Arqueológicas en Guatemala, Guatemala City, July 24–28.

Pérez Campa, Mario A. 2007. Preclásico Tardío (400 a.C–200 d.C). *Arqueología Mexicana* 86:40–43.

Peterson, Fredrick A. 1961. Lost Cities of Chiapas. *Science of Man* 1:52–56, 91–93.

———. 1963. *Some Ceramics from Mirador, Chiapas, Mexico*. Papers of the New World
Archaeological Foundation, No. 15. Provo, UT: New World Archaeological Foundation, Brigham Young University.

———. 2014. *A Brief Reconnaissance of Three Chiapas Municipalities*. Papers of the New
World Archaeological Foundation, No. 73. Provo, UT: New World Archaeological Foundation, Brigham Young University.

Piña Chan, Román. 1955. *Las Culturas Preclásicas de la Cuenca de México*. México: Fondo
de Cultura Económica.

Piña Chan, Román, and Luis Cavarrubias. 1964. *El Pueblo del Jaguar (Los Olmecas Arqueológicos)*. México: Consejo Para la Planeación e Instalación del Museo Nacional
de Antropología.

Pinkowski, Jennifer. 2006. A City by the Sea: Early Urban Planning on Mexico's Pacific
Coast. *Archaeology* 59(1): 46–49.

Piperno, Dolores R., Jorge Enrique Moreno, Jose Iriarte, Irene Holst, Matthew Lach-
niet, John G. Jones, Anthony J. Ranere, and R. Castanzo. 2007. Late Pleistocene
and Holocene Environmental History of the Iguala Valley, Central Balsas Watershed of Mexico. *Proceedings of the National Academy of Sciences of the United States
of America* 104(29): 11874–81.

Pires-Ferreira, Jane W. 1975. *Formative Mesoamerican Exchange Networks, with Special
Reference to the Valley of Oaxaca*. Ann Arbor, MI: University of Michigan.

———. 1976. Shell and Iron-Ore Minor Exchange in Formative Mesoamerica, with
Comments on Other Commodities. In *The Early Mesoamerican Village*, ed. Kent V.
Flannery, pp. 311–25. New York, NY: Academic Press.

Pires-Ferreira, Jane W., and B.J. Evans. 1978. Mössbauer Spectral Analysis of Olmec
Iron Ore Mirrors: New Evidence of Formative Exchange Networks in Mesoamer-
ica. In *Cultural Continuity in Mesoamerica*, ed. David L. Browman, pp. 101–54. The
Hague: Mouton Publishers.

Plunket, Patricia, and Gabriela Uruñuela. 1998. Preclassic Household Patterns Preserved Under Volcanic Ash at Tetimpa, Puebla, Mexico. *Latin American Antiquity*
9:287–309.

Poe, William C. 2000. Site Organization at Ujuxte and Neighboring Sites. Paper presented at the 65th Annual Meeting of the Society for American Archaeology,

Philadelphia, April 5–8.

Pohl, Mary. 2005. *Olmec Civilization at San Andres, Tabasco, Mexico*. Research Reports at FAMSI. http://www.famsi.org/reports/01047/index.html, accessed September 2009.

Pohl, Mary D., Dolores R. Piperno, Kevin O. Pope, and John G. Jones. 2007. Microfossil Evidence for Pre-Columbian Maize Dispersals in the Neotropics from San Andrés, Tabasco, Mexico. *Proceedings of the National Academy of Sciences of the United States of America* 104(16): 6870–75.

Pohl, Mary D., Kevin O. Pope, John G. Jones, John S. Jacob, Dolores R. Piperno, Susan D. deFrance, David L. Lentz, John A. Gifford, Marie E. Danforth, and J. Kathryn Josserand. 1996. Early Agriculture in the Maya Lowlands. *Latin American Antiquity* 7(4): 355–72.

Pohl, Mary D., Kevin O. Pope, and Christopher L. von Nagy. 2002. Olmec Origins of Mesoamerican Writing. *Science* 298:1984–87.

Polanyi, Karl. 1968. *Primitive, Archaic and Modern Economies: Essays of Karl Polanyi*, ed. George Dalton. Garden City, NY: Anchor Books.

Ponciano, Erick M. 2000. La Concepción de Kaminaljuyú con Una Ciudad en el Altiplano Central del Valle de Guatemala Durante el Periodo Formativo. In *XIII Simposio de Investigaciones Arqueológicas en Guatemala*, ed. Juan Pedro Laporte, Héctor L. Escobedo, Ana Claudia Monzón de Suasnávar, and Bárbara Arroyo, pp. 1–10. Guatemala: Ministerio de Cultura y Deportes, Instituto de Antropología e Historia, Asociación Tikal.

Pool, Christopher A. 2000. From Olmec to Epi-Olmec at Tres Zapotes, Veracruz, Mexico. In *Olmec Art and Archaeology in Mesoamerica*, ed. John E. Clark and Mary E. Pye, pp. 137–53. Washington, DC: National Gallery of Art.

———. 2003. Centers and Peripheries: Urbanization and Political Economy at Tres Zapotes. In *Settlement Archaeology and Political Economy at Tres Zapotes, Veracruz, Mexico*, ed. Christopher A. Pool, pp. 90–98. Cotsen Institute of Archaeology Monograph 50. Los Angeles, CA: Cotsen Institute of Archaeology, University of California.

———. 2006a. Current Research on the Gulf Coast of Mexico. *Journal of Archaeological Research* 14:189–241.

———. 2006b. The Early Horizon at Tres Zapotes: Implications for Olmec Interaction. Paper presented at the 71st Annual Meeting of the Society for American Archaeology, San Juan, Puerto Rico, April 26–30.

———. 2007. *Olmec Archaeology and Early Mesoamerica*. Cambridge: Cambridge University Press.

————. 2009. Asking More and Better Questions: Olmec Archaeology for the Next *Katun*. *Ancient Mesoamerica* 20:241–52.

————. 2010. Stone Monuments and Earthen Mounds: Polity and Placemaking at Tres Zapotes, Veracruz, Mexico. In *The Place of Sculpture in Mesoamerica's Preclassic Transition: Context, Use, and Meaning*, ed. Julia Guernsey, John E. Clark, and Bárbara Arroyo, pp. 97–126. Washington, DC: Dumbarton Oaks Research Library and Collection.

Pool, Christopher A., Ponciano Ortiz Ceballos, María del Carmen Rodríguez Martínez, and Michael L. Loughlin. 2010. The Early Horizon at Tres Zapotes: Implications for Olmec Interaction. *Ancient Mesoamerica* 21:95–105.

Pool, Christopher A., and Michael A. Ohnersorgen. 2003. Archaeological Survey and Settlement at Tres Zapotes. In *Settlement Archaeology and Political Economy at Tres Zapotes, Veracruz, Mexico*, ed. Christopher A. Pool, pp. 7–31. Cotsen Institute of Archaeology Monograph 50. Los Angeles, CA: Cotsen Institute of Archaeology, University of California.

Pope, Kevin O., Mary D. Pohl, John G. Jones, David L. Lentz, Christopher von Nagy, Francisco J. Vega, and Irvy R. Quitmyer. 2001. Origin and Environmental Setting of Ancient Agriculture in the Lowlands of Mesoamerica. *Science* 292:1370–73.

Popenoe, Dorothy. 1934. Some Excavations at Playa de los Muertos, Ulua River, Honduras. *Maya Research* 1:62–86.

Popenoe de Hatch, Marion. 1991. Kaminaljuyu: Un Resumen General Hasta 1991. *U Tz'ib* 1:2–6.

————. 1997. *Kaminaljuyu/San Jorge: Evidencia Arqueológica de la Actividad Económica en el Valle de Guatemala 300 a.C. a 300 d.C.* Guatemala: Universidad del Valle de Guatemala.

————. 2000. Kaminaljuyu Miraflores II: La Naturaleza del Cambio Político al Final del Preclásico. In *XIII Simposio de Investigaciones Arqueológicas en Guatemala*, ed. Juan Pedro Laporte, Héctor L. Escobedo, Ana Claudia Monzón de Suasnávar, and Bárbara Arroyo, pp. 11–27. Guatemala: Ministerio de Cultura y Deportes, Instituto de Antropología e Historia, Asociación Tikal.

————. 2002a. Evidencia de un Observatorio Astronomico en Abaj Takalik. In *XV Simposio de Investigaciones Arqueológicas en Guatemala*, ed. Juan Pedro Laporte, Bárbara Arroyo and Héctor Escobedo, pp. 437–58. Guatemala City: Museo Nacional de Arqueología y Etnología.

————. 2002b. New Perspectives on Kaminaljuyú, Guatemala: Regional Interaction During the Preclassic and Classic Periods. In *Incidents of Archaeology in Central America and Yucatán: Studies in Honor of Edwin M. Shook*, ed. Michael W. Love,

Marion Popenoe de Hatch, and Héctor L. Escobedo, pp. 277–96. Lanham, MD: University Press of America.

Popenoe de Hatch, Marion, Erick M. Ponciano, Tomás Q. Barrientos, Mark Brenner, and Charles Ortloff. 2002. Climate and Technological Innovation at Kaminaljuyu, Guatemala. *Ancient Mesoamerica* 13:103–14.

Popenoe de Hatch, Marion, Christa Schieber de Lavarreda, and Miguel Orrego Corzo. 2011. Late Preclassic Developments at Takalik Abaj, Department of Retalhuleu, Guatemala. In *The Southern Maya in the Late Preclassic*, ed. Michael Love and Jonathan Kaplan, pp. 203–36. Boulder, CO: University Press of Colorado.

Popenoe de Hatch, Marion, and Edwin M. Shook. 1999. La Arqueología de la Costa Sur. In *Epoca Precolombina. Tomo I, Historia General de Guatemala*, ed. Marion Popenoe de Hatch, pp. 171–90. Guatemala: Asociación de Amigos del País, Fundación para la Cultura y el Desarrollo.

Porter, James B. 1989. Olmec Colossal Heads as Recarved Thrones: 'Mutilation,' Revolution, and Recarving. *RES* 17/18:23–30.

———. 1992. 'Estelas Celtiformes': Un Nuevo Tipo de Escultura Olmeca y sus Implicaciones para los Epigrafistas. *Arqueología* 8:3–13.

Porter, Muriel Noe. 1953. *Tlatilco and the Pre-Classic Cultures of the New World*. Viking Fund Publications in Anthropology 19. New York, NY: Wenner Gren Foundation for Anthropological Research.

Potter, Daniel R. 1980. Archaeological Investigations at Operation 2012. In *The Colha Project Second Season, 1980 Interim Report*, ed. Thomas R. Hester, Jack D. Eaton, and Harry J. Shafer, pp. 173–84. Venice, Italy: Center for Archaeological Research, The University of Texas at San Antonio, and Centro Studi e Ricerche Ligabue.

———. 1982. Some Results of the Second Year of Excavation at Operation 2012. In *Archaeology at Colha, Belize: The 1981 Interim Report*, ed. Thomas R. Hester, Harry J. Shafer, and Jack D. Eaton, pp. 98–122. Venice, Italy: Center for Archaeological Research, The University of Texas at San Antonio, and Centro Studi e Ricerche Ligabue.

———. 1991. A Descriptive Taxonomy of Middle Preclassic Chert Tools at Colha, Belize. In *Maya Stone Tools: Selected Papers from the Second Maya Lithic Conference*, ed. Thomas R. Hester and Harry J. Shafer, pp. 21–29. Monographs in World Archaeology No. 1. Madison, WI: Prehistory Press.

———. 1992. Strata 55 and the Evolution of Lowland Maya Blood Ritual. Paper presented at the 57th Annual Meeting of the Society for American Archaeology, Pittsburgh, April 8–12.

Potter, Daniel R., and Eleanor M. King. 1995. A Heterarchical Approach to Lowland Maya Socioeconomies. In *Heterarchy and the Analysis of Complex Societies*, ed. Robert M. Ehrenreich, Carole L. Crumley, and Janet E. Levy, pp. 17–32. Archaeological Papers of the American Anthropological Association, No. 6. Arlington, VA: American Anthropological Association.

Powis, Terry G., ed. 2005. *New Perspectives on Formative Mesoamerican Cultures*. BAR International Series, 1377. Oxford: British Archaeological Reports.

Powis, Terry, Ann Cyphers, Nilesh Gaikwad, Louis Grivetti and Keong Cheong. 2011. Cacao Use and the San Lorenzo Olmec. *Proceedings of the National Academy of Sciences*. *Proceedings of the National Academy of Sciences* 108(21): 8595–600.

Powis, Terry G., Norbert Stanchly, Christine D. White, Paul F. Healy, Jaime J. Awe, and Fred Longstaffe. 1999. A Reconstruction of Middle Preclassic Maya Subsistence Economy at Cahal Pech, Belize. *Antiquity* 73(280): 364–76.

Powis, Terry G., Fred Valdez Jr., Thomas R. Hester, W. Jeffrey Hurst, and Stanley M. Tarka Jr. 2002. Spouted Vessels and Cacao Use among the Preclassic Maya. *Latin American Antiquity* 13(1): 85–116.

Prater, Ariadne. 2007. Kaminaljuyu Stone Sculpture: Indicators of Time, Place and Function. Paper presented at the Dumbarton Oaks Conference, "The Place of Sculpture in Mesoamerica's Preclassic Transition: Context, Use, and Meaning," Antigua, Guatemala, October 5–6.

Price, Barbara J. 1970. Review of *Dumbarton Oaks Conference on the Olmec*. *American Antiquity* 35(3): 392–94.

———. 1971. Prehispanic Irrigation Agriculture in Nuclear America. *Latin American Research Review* 6(3): 3–60.

———. 1977. Shifts in Production and Organization: A Cluster-Interaction Model. *Current Anthropology* 18:209–33.

———. 1978. Secondary State Formation: An Explanatory Model. In *Origins of the State: The Anthropology of Political Evolution*, ed. Ronald Cohen and Elman R. Service, pp. 161–86. Philadelphia, PA: Institute for the Study of Human Issues.

———. 1984. Competition, Productive Intensification, and Ranked Society: Speculations from Evolutionary Theory. In *Warfare, Culture, and Environment*, ed. R. Brian Ferguson, pp. 209–40. Orlando, NJ: Academic Press.

Prindiville, Mary, and David C. Grove. 1987. The Settlement and Its Architecture. In *Ancient Chalcatzingo*, ed. David C. Grove, pp. 63–81. Austin, TX: University of Texas Press.

Pring, Duncan. 1977. Influence or Intrusion? The Proctoclassic in the Maya Lowlands. In *Social Process in Maya Prehistory*, ed. Norman Hammond, pp. 135–65. New York, NY: Academic Press.

———. 1979. The Swasey Complex of Northern Belize: A Definition and Discussion. In *Studies in Ancient Mesoamerica*, ed. John A. Graham, pp. 215–29. Berkeley, CA: University of California, Berkeley.

Proskouriakoff, Tatiana. 1960. Historical Implications of a Pattern of Dates at Piedras Negras. *American Antiquity* 25:454–75.

———. 1971. Early Architecture and Sculpture in Mesoamerica. In *Observations on the Emergence of Civilization in Mesoamerica*, ed. Robert F. Heizer and John A. Graham, pp. 141–56. Contributions of the University of California Archaeological Research Facility, No. 11. Berkeley, CA: University of California.

———. 1978. Olmec Gods and Maya God-Glyphs. In *Codex Wauchope*, ed. Marco Giardino, Barbara Edmonson and Winifred Creamer, pp. 113–17. New Orleans, LA: Tulane University.

———. 1993. *Maya History*. Austin, TX: University of Texas Press.

Puleston, Dennis E. 1973. Ancient Maya Settlement and Environment at Tikal: Implications for Subsistence Models. Ph.D. diss., Dept. of Anthropology, University of Pennsylvania.

Puleston, Olga S., and Dennis E. Puleston. 1971a. A Processual Model for the Rise of Classic Maya Civilization in the Southern Lowlands. *Atti del XL Congresso Internazionale degli Americanisti*, pp.119–124. Genoa: Tilger.

———. 1971b. An Ecological Approach to the Origins of Maya Civilization. *Archaeology* 24(4): 330–37.

Pulido Méndez, Salvador. 1993. Xico, Estado de México, en el Preclásico. In *A propósito del Formativo*, ed. Ma. Teresa Castillo Mangas, pp. 33–44. México, DF: Subdirección de Salvamento Arqueológico, Instituto Nacional de Antropología e Historia.

Pyburn, K. Anne. 1998. Consuming the Maya. *Dialectical Anthropology* 23:111–29.

———. 2004. Introduction: Rethinking Complex Society. In *Ungendering Civilization*, ed. K. Anne Pyburn, pp. 1–46. New York, NY: Routledge.

———. 2008. Pomp and Circumstance Before Belize: Ancient Maya Commerce and the New River Conurbation. In *The Ancient City: Perspectives from the Old and New World*, ed. Joyce Marcus and Jeremy Sabloff, pp. 247–72. Santa Fe, NM: School of American Research.

Pyburn, K. Anne, Boyd Dixon, Patricia Cook, and Anna McNair. 1998. The Albion Island Settlement Pattern Project: Domination and Resistance in Early Classic Northern Belize. *Journal of Field Archaeology* 25(1): 37–62.

Pye, Mary E., and John E. Clark. 2006. Los Olmecas son Mixe-Zoques: Contribuciones de Gareth W. Lowe a la Arqueología del Formativo. *Presencia Zoque: Una Aproximación Multidisciplina*, ed. Dolores Aramoni, Thomas A. Lee, and Miguel Lisbona, pp. 207–22. Chiapas, Mexico: Universidad de Ciencias y Artes de Chiapas.

Pye, Mary E., and Gerardo Gutiérrez. 2007. The Pacific Coast Trade Route of Mesoamerica: Iconographic Connections between Guatemala and Guerrero. In *Archaeology, Art, and Ethnogenesis in Mesoamerican Prehistory: Papers in Honor of Gareth W. Lowe*, ed. Lynneth S. Lowe and Mary E. Pye, pp. 229–46. Papers of the New World Archaeological Foundation, No. 68. Provo, UT: New World Archaeological Foundation, Brigham Young University.

Pye, Nanette. 1976. The Fire-Serpent and Were-Jaguar in Formative Oaxaca: A Contingency Table Analysis. In *The Early Mesoamerican Village*, ed. Kent V. Flannery, pp. 272–82. New York, NY: Academic Press.

Quirarte, Jacinto. 1976. The Relationship of Izapan-Style Art to Olmec and Maya Art: A Review. In *Origins of Religious Art and Iconography in Preclassic Mesoamerica*, ed. Henry B. Nicholson, pp. 73–86. UCLA Latin American Studies Series, Volume 31. Los Angeles, CA: UCLA Latin American Center Publications.

———. 1977. The Ballcourt in Mesoamerica: Its Architectural Development. In *Pre-Columbian Art History: Selected Readings*, ed. Alana Cordy-Collins and Jean Stern, pp. 191–212. Palo Alto, CA: Peek Publications.

Raab, Mark L., Matthew A. Boxt, Datherine Bradford, Brian A. Stokes, and Rebecca B. González Lauck. 2000. Testing at Isla Alor in the La Venta Olmec Hinterland. *Journal of Field Archaeology* 27(3): 257–70.

Radcliffe-Brown, Alfred R. 1952. *Structure and Function in Primitive Society*. New York, NY: The Free Press.

Ramírez, Felipe, Lorena Gámez, and Fernán González. 2000. *Cerámica de Temamatla*. México, DF: Instituto de Investigaciones Antropológicas, Universidad Nacional Autónoma de México.

Rathje, William L. 1971. The Origin and Development of Lowland Classic Maya Civilization. *American Antiquity* 36(3): 275–85.

———. 1972. Praise the Gods and Pass the Metates: A Hypothesis of the Development of Lowland Rainforest Civilizations in Mesoamerica. In *Contemporary Archaeology: A Guide to Theory and Contributions*, ed. Mark P. Leone, pp. 365–92. Carbondale, IL: Southern Illinois University.

———. 1977. The Tikal Connection. In *The Origins of Maya Civilization*, ed. Richard.E.W. Adams, pp. 373–82. Albuquerque, NM: School of American Research, University of New Mexico Press.

———. 2000. The Nouveau Elite Potlatch: One Scenario for the Monumental Rise of Early Civilizations. Paper presented in the Ancient Maya Political Economies: Essays in Honor of William Rathje. SAA Annual Meeting, Philadelphia, April 2000.

————. 2002. The Nouveau Elite Potlatch: One Scenario for the Monumental Rise of Early Civilizations. In *Ancient Maya Political Economies*, ed. Marilyn A. Masson and David A. Freidel, pp. 31–40. Walnut Creek, CA: Altamira Press.

Ray, Benjamin C. 1991. *Myth, Ritual, and Kingship in Buganda*. New York, NY: Oxford University Press.

Redfield, Robert. 1955. *The Little Community: Viewpoints for the Study of a Human Whole*. Chicago, IL: University of Chicago Press.

Redfield, Robert, and Alfonso Villa Rojas. 1934. *Chan Kom*. Carnegie Institute of Washington Publication 448. Washington, DC: Carnegie Institute of Washington.

Reents-Budet, Dorie, Sylviane Boucher le Landais, Yoly Palomo Carrillo, Ronald Bishop and James Blackman. 2011. Cerámica del Estilo Códice: Nuevos Sitios de Producción y Patrones de Distribución. In *XXIV Simposio de Investigaciones Arqueologicas en Guatemala, 2010*, ed. Bárbara Arroyo, Lorena Paiz Aragón, Adriana Linares Palma, and Ana Lucia Arroyave, pp. 841–56. Guatemala City, Guatemala: Museo Nacional de Arqueologia y Etnologia, Ministerio de Cultura y Deportes, Instituto de Antropología e Historia, Asociación Tikal.

Reese, Kathryn V. 1996. Narratives of Power: Late Formative Public Architecture and Civic Center Design at Cerros, Belize. Ph.D. diss., Dept. of Anthropology, University of Texas, Austin.

Reese-Taylor, Kathryn V., and Debra S. Walker. 2002. The Passage of the Late Preclassic into the Early Classic. In *Ancient Maya Political Economies*, ed. Marilyn A. Masson and David A. Freidel, pp. 87–122. Walnut Creek, CA: Altamira Press.

Reilly, F. Kent, III. 1987. The Ecological Origins of Olmec Symbols of Rulership. M.A. thesis, Dept. of Art and Art History, University of Texas at Austin.

————. 1989. The Shaman in Transformation Pose: A Study of the Theme of Rulership in Olmec Art. *Record of the Art Museum, Princeton University* 48(2): 4–21.

————. 1990. Cosmos and Rulership: The Function of Olmec-Style Symbols in Formative Period Mesoamerica. *Visible Language* 24(1): 12–37.

————. 1994a. Visions to Another World: Art, Shamanism, and Political Power in Middle Formative Mesoamerica. Ph.D. diss., Institute of Latin American Studies, University of Texas, Austin.

————. 1994b. Cosmologia, Soberanismo y Espacio Ritual en la Mesoamérica del Formativo. In *Los Olmecas en Mesoamerica*, ed. John E. Clark, pp. 239–59. Mexico, DF: El Equilibrista.

————. 1995a. Art, Ritual, and Rulership in the Olmec World. In *The Olmec World: Ritual and Rulership*, ed. Jill Guthrie, pp. 27–46. Princeton, NJ: Princeton University Art Museum.

———. 1995b. The Axis Mundi. In *The Olmec World: Ritual and Rulership*, ed. Jill Guthrie, pp. 225–32. Princeton, NJ: Princeton University Art Museum.

———. 1999. Mountains of Creation and Underworld Portals: The Ritual Function of Olmec Architecture at La Venta, Tabasco. In *Mesoamerica Architecture as Cultural Symbol*, ed. Jeff Karl Kowalske, pp. 14–39. New York, NY: Oxford University Press.

Renfrew, Colin. 1975. Trade as Action at a Distance: Questions of Integration and Communication. In *Ancient Civilization and Trade*, ed. Jeremy A. Sabloff and C.C. Lamberg-Karlovsky, pp. 3–59. University of New Mexico Press: Albuquerque.

———. 1982. Polity and Power: Interaction, Intensification, and Exploitation. In *An Island Polity: The Archaeology of Exploitation in Melos*, ed. Colin Renfrew and Malcolm Wagstaff, pp. 264–90. Cambridge: Cambridge University Press.

———. 1986. Introduction: Peer Polity Interaction and Socio-political Change. In *Peer Polity Interaction and Socio-political Change*, ed. Colin Renfrew and John F. Cherry, pp. 1–18. Cambridge: Cambridge University Press.

Renfrew, Colin, and John F. Cherry, eds. 1986. *Peer Polity Interaction and Socio-political Change*. Cambridge: Cambridge University Press.

Restall, Matthew. 1997. *The Maya World: Yucatec Society and Culture, 1550–1850*. Stanford, CA: Stanford University Press.

Rice, Don S. 1976a. A Historical Ecology of Lakes Yaxha and Sacnab, El Peten, Guatemala. Ph.D. diss., Dept. of Anthropology, Pennsylvania State University.

———. 1976b. Middle Preclassic Maya Settlement in the Central Maya Lowlands. *Journal of Field Archaeology* 3(4): 425–46.

———. 1988. Classic to Postclassic Maya Household Transitions in the Central Peten, Guatemala. In *Household and Community in the Mesoamerican Past*, ed. Richard R. Wilk and Wendy A. Ashmore, pp. 227–47. Albuquerque, NM: University of New Mexico Press.

Rice, Prudence M. 1979. Introduction and the Middle Preclassic Ceramics of Yaxha-Sacnab, Guatemala. *Cerámica de Cultura Maya* 10:1–36.

Ricketson, Oliver G. 1937. Part I: The Excavations. In *Uaxactun, Guatemala, Group E 1926–1931*, pp. 1–180. Carnegie Institution of Washington Publication 477. Washington, DC: Carnegie Institution of Washington.

Ricketson, Oliver G., and Edith B. Ricketson. 1937. *Uaxactun, Guatemala: Group E 1926–1931*. Carnegie Institution of Washington Publication 477. Washington, DC: Carnegie Institution of Washington.

Ridings, Rosanna. 1996. Where in the World Does Obsidian Hydration Work? *American Antiquity* 61:136–48.

Riese, Berthold. 1984. Hel Hieroglyphs. In *Phoneticism in Maya Hieroglyphic Writing*, ed. John S. Justeson and Lyle Campbell, pp. 263–86. Institute for Mesoamerican Studies, Publication 9. Albany: University of New York.

Ringle, William M. 1988. *Of Mice and Monkeys: The Value and Meaning of T1016, the God C Hieroglyph*. Research Reports on Ancient Maya Writing 18. Washington, DC: Center for Maya Research.

———. 1999. Pre-Classic Cityscapes: Ritual Politics among the Early Lowland Maya. In *Social Patterns in Pre-Classic Mesoamerica*, ed. David C. Grove and Rosemary A. Joyce, pp. 183–223. Washington, DC: Dumbarton Oaks Research Library and Collection.

Rissolo, Dominique, and Fabio E. Amador. 2004. Evaluación cerámica preliminar de investigaciones recientes en el noreste de la Península de Yucatán, México: Reconsiderando el Preclásico Medio en las Tierras Bajas Mayas del Norte. In *XVII Simposio de Investigaciones Arqueológicas en Guatemala, 2003*, ed. Juan Pedro Laporte, Bárbara Arroyo, pp. 357–66. Museo de Arqueologia y Etnologia de Guatemala, Guatemala.

Rissolo, Dominique, and Jose Manuel Ochoa Rodriguez. 2002. A Reassessment of the Middle Preclassic in Northern Quintana Roo. Paper presented at the 67th Annual Meeting of the Society for American Archaeology, Denver, March 20–24.

Rivero Torres, Soñia. 1992. *Laguna Miramar, Chiapas, México: Una Aproximación Histórico-Arqueológico de los Lacandones desde el Clásico Temprano*. Chiapas, Mexico: Gobierno del Estado de Chiapas and Instituto Chiapaneco de Cultura.

Robertson, Robin A., and David A. Freidel, eds. 1986. *Archaeology at Cerros, Belize, Central America. Volume I: An Interim Report*. Dallas, TX: Southern Methodist University Press.

Robicsek, Francis, and Donald M. Hales. 1981. *The Maya Book of the Dead: The Ceramic Codex*. Charlottesville, VA: University of Virginia Art Museum.

———. 1982. *Maya Ceramic Vases from the Late Classic Period: The November Collection of Maya Ceramics*. Charlottesville, VA: University of Virginia Bayly Memorial Museum of Art.

Robin, Cynthia. 1989. *Preclassic Maya Burials at Cuello, Belize*. BAR International Series, 480. Oxford: British Archaeological Reports.

———. El Antiguo-Nuevo Paradigma Sobre la Cronologia y la Indole del Origen de la Civilizacion Maya en el Norte de la Peninsula de Yucatan. Paper presented at The Origins of Lowland Maya Civilization, First Boundary End Conference on Ancient America, 2004.

Robin, Cynthia, and Norman Hammond. 1991. Ritual and Ideology. In *Cuello: An*

Early Maya Community in Belize, ed. Norman Hammond, pp. 204–34. Cambridge: Cambridge University Press.

Robinson, Eugenia J., Patricia Farrel, Kitty Emery, Dorothy Freidel, and Geoffrey E. Braswell. 2002. Preclassic Settlements and Geomorphology in the Highlands of Guatemala: Excavations at Urías, Valley of Antigua. In *Incidents of Archaeology in Central America and Yucatán: Studies in Honor of Edwin M. Shook*, ed. Michael W. Love, Marion Popenoe de Hatch, and Héctor L. Escobedo, pp. 251–76. Lanham, MD: University Press of America.

Robles-Castellanos, Fernando. 2004. El Antiguo-Nuevo Paradigma sobre la Cronologia y la Indole del Origen de la Civilizacion Maya en el Norte de la Peninsula de Yucatan. Paper presented at the 1st Boundary End Conference on Ancient America, Asheville, NC, May 27–29.

Robles-Castellanos, Fernando, and Anthony P. Andrews, eds. 2003. *Reconocimeinto Arqueologico de la Esquina Noroeste de la Peninsula de Yucatan y Primeras Aproximaciones a los temas de Investigacion*. Mexico, DF: Instituto Nacional de Antropología e Historia.

———. 2004. Proyecto Costa Maya: Reconocimiento arqueológico de la esquina noroeste de la península de Yucatán. In *XVII Simposio de Investigaciones Arqueológicas en Guatemala, 2003*, ed. Juan Pedro Laporte, Bárbara Arroyo and Héctor Mejía, pp. 47–66. Guatemala: Ministerio de Cultura y Deportes, Instituto de Antropología e Historia, Asociación Tikal.

Rodas, Sergio. 1993. Catalogo de Barrigones de Guatemala. *U Tz'ib* 1:1–36.

Rodríguez, Marci Lane, Rogelio Aguirre, and Javier González. 1997. Producción Subsistencia y Medio Ambiente en San Lorenzo Tenochtitlán. In *Población, Subsistencia y Medio Ambiente en San Lorenzo Tenochtitlán*, ed. Ann Cyphers, pp. 55–73. Mexico, DF: Instituto de Investigaciones Antropologicas, Universidad Nacional Autonoma de Mexico.

Rodríguez, Maria del Carmen, and Ponciano Ortíz. 1997. Olmec Ritual and Sacred Geography at Manatí. In *Olmec to Aztec: Settlement Patterns in the Ancient Gulf Lowlands*, ed. Barbara L. Stark and Philip J. Arnold III, pp. 68–95. Tucson, AZ: University of Arizona Press.

———. 2000. A Massive Offering of Axes at La Merced, Hidalgotitlán, Veracruz, Mexico. In *Olmec Art and Archaeology in Mesoamerica*, ed. John E. Clark and Mary E. Pye, pp. 154–67. Washington, DC: National Gallery of Art.

Roemer, Erwin Jr. 1979. Excavations at Operation 2006, a Lithic Workshop. In *The Colha Project 1979: A Collection of Interim Papers*, ed. Thomas R. Hester, pp. 99–107. San Antonio, TX: Center for Archaeological Research, The University of Texas at San Antonio.

Rogers, J. Daniel, and Bruce D. Smith, eds. 1995. *Mississippian Communities and House-holds*. Tuscaloosa, AL: University of Alabama Press.

Rosenswig, Robert M. 2004. The Late Archaic Occupation of Northern Belize: New Archaeological Excavation Data. In *Archaeological Investigations in the Eastern Maya Lowlands: Papers of the 2003 Belize Archaeology Symposium*, ed. Jaime Awe, John Morris, and Sherilyne Jones, pp. 267–77. Research Reports in Belizean Archaeology, vol. 1. Belmopan, Belize: The Institute of Archaeology, National Institute of Culture and History.

———. 2005. From the Land Between Swamps: Cuauhtémoc in an Early Olmec World. Ph.D. diss., Dept. of Anthropology, Yale University.

———. 2006. Sedentism and Food Production in Early Complex Societies in the Soconusco, Mexico. *World Archaeology* 38:329–54.

———. 2007. Beyond Identifying Elites: Feasting as a Means to Understand Early Middle Formative Society on the Pacific Coast of Mexico. *Journal of Anthropological Archaeology* 26:1–27.

———. 2010. *The Beginnings of Mesoamerican Civilization: Inter-regional Interaction and the Olmec*. New York: Cambridge University Press.

———. 2011. An Early Mesoamerican Archipelago of Complexity. In *Early Mesoamerican Social Transformations: Archaic and Formative Lifeways in the Socnusco Region*, ed. Richard Lesure, pp. 242–71. Berkeley: University of California Press.

———. 2009. Early Mesoamerican Garbage: Ceramic and Daub Discard Patterns from Cuauhtémoc, Soconusco, Mexico. *Journal of Archaeological Method and Theory* 16(1): 1–32.

Rosenswig, Robert M., and Richard L. Burger. 2012. Considering New World Monumentality. In *Early New World Monumentality*, ed. Richard L. Burger and Robert M. Rosenswig, pp. 3–22. Gainesville, FL: University Press of Florida.

Rosenswig, Robert M., and Douglas J. Kennett. 2008. Reassessing San Estevan's Role in the Late Formative Political Geography of Northern Belize. *Latin American Antiquity* 19(2): 123–45.

Roys, Ralph L. 1939. *The Titles of Ebtun*. Carnegie Institution of Washington Publication 505. Washington, DC: Carnegie Institution of Washington.

———. 1940. *Personal Names of the Maya of Yucatan*. Contributions to American Anthropology and History, 31. Carnegie Institution of Washington Publication 523. Washington, DC: Carnegie Institution of Washington.

———. 1941. *The Xiu Chronicle*. Cambridge, MA: Peabody Museum of Archaeology and Ethnology, Harvard University.

———. 1957. *The Political Geography of the Yucatan Maya*. Carnegie Institution of Washington Publication 613. Washington, DC: Carnegie Institution of Washington.

———. 1965. *The Ritual of the Bacabs*. Norman, OK: University of Oklahoma Press.

Rue, David J., David Webster, and Alfred Traverse. 2002. Late Holocene Fire and Agriculture in the Copan Valley, Honduras. *Ancient Mesoamerica* 13:267–72.

Ruppert, Karl, and John H. Denison Jr. 1943. *Archaeological Reconnaissance in Campeche, Quintana Roo, and Peten*. Carnegie Institution of Washington Publication 543. Washington, DC: Carnegie Institution of Washington.

Rust, William F. 1987. A Settlement Survey of La Venta, Tabasco, Mexico. Preliminary Report of the 1986 Season. Unpublished ms., Instituto Nacional de Antropología e Historia, Mexico, DF.

———. 1988. Informe Preliminar de la Temporada de Campo 1987. Unpublished ms., Instituto Nacional de Antropología e Historia, Mexico, DF.

———. 1992. New Ceremonial and Settlement Evidence at La Venta, and Its Relation to Preclassic Maya Cultures. In *New Theories on the Ancient Maya*, ed. Elin C. Danien and Robert J. Sharer, pp. 123–29. Philadelphia, PA: University Museum, University of Pennsylvania.

Rust, William F., and Barbara W. Leyden. 1994. Evidence of Maize Use at Early and Middle Preclassic La Venta Olmec Sites. In *Corn and Culture in the Prehistoric New World*, ed. Sissel Johannessen and Christine Hastorf, pp. 181–201. Boulder, CO: Westview Press.

Rust, William F., and Robert J. Sharer. 1988. Olmec Settlement Data from La Venta, Tabasco. *Science* 242:102–4.

———. 2006. Riverine Resource Concentration at La Venta. Paper presented at the 52nd annual Congress of Americanists, Seville, July 17–26.

———. n.d. Riverine Resource Concentration at La Venta. In *The Evolution of Olmec Societies*, ed. John E. Clark, Robert L. Carneiro, and Regina de los Angeles Montaño Perches. Cambridge: Cambridge University Press. Forthcoming.

Sabloff, Jeremy A. 1975. *Excavations at Seibal, No. 2, Ceramics*. Memoirs of the Peabody Museum of Archaeology and Ethnology, vol. 13. Cambridge, MA: Peabody Museum of Archaeology and Ethnology, Harvard University.

———. 1986. Interaction among Classic Maya Polities: A Preliminary Examination. In *Peer-Polity Interaction and Socio-political Change*, ed. Colin Renfrew and John F. Cherry, pp. 109–16. Cambridge: Cambridge University Press.

Sabloff, Jeremy A., and C.C. Lamberg-Karlovsky. 1975. *Ancient Civilization and Trade*. Albuquerque, NM: University of New Mexico Press.

Sahagún, Fray Bernardino de. 1955. *Florentine Codex: General History of the Things of New Spain, Part 13, Book 12*, trans. by C. E. Dibble and A.J.O. Anderson. Santa Fe,

NM: School of American Research and the University of Utah.

Sahlins, Marshall. 1968. *Tribesmen*. Englewood Cliffs: Prentice-Hall.

———. 1996. The Sadness of Sweetness: The Native Anthropology of Western Cosmology. *Current Anthropology* 37(3): 395–665.

Sahlins, Marshall D., and Elman R. Service. 1960. *The Evolution of Culture*. Ann Arbor: University of Michigan Press.

Sánchez Vásquez, María de Jesús, Róman Aurelio Chávez Torres, Francisco Javier Ortuño Cos, and Eneida Baños Ramos. 1993. Consideraciones generals del Preclásico Medio en Zacatenco, D.F. In *A propósito del Formativo*, ed. Ma. Teresa Castillo Mangas, pp. 73–83. México, DF: Subdirección de Salvamento Arqueológico, Instituto Nacional de Antropología e Historia.

Sanders, William T. 1962a. Cultural Ecology of Nuclear Mesoamérica. *American Anthropologist* 64(1): 34–44.

———. 1962b. Culture Ecology of the Maya Lowlands, Part I. *Estudios de Cultura Maya* 2:79–121.

———. 1963. Culture Ecology of the Maya Lowlands, Part II. *Estudios de Cultura Maya* 3:203–41.

———. 1968. Hydraulic Agriculture, Economic Symbiosis and the Evolution of States in Central Mexico. In *Anthropological Archaeology in the Americas*, pp. 88–107. Washington, DC: The Anthropological Society of Washington.

———. 1973. The Cultural Ecology of the Lowland Maya: A Reevaluation. In *The Classic Maya Collapse*, ed. T. Patrick Culbert, pp. 325–65. Albuquerque, NM: University of New Mexico Press.

———. 1977. Environmental Heterogeneity and Evolution of Lowland Maya Civilization. In *Origins of Maya Civilization*, ed. Richard E.W. Adams, pp. 287–98. Albuquerque, NM: University of New Mexico Press.

———. 1981a. Classic Maya Settlement Patterns and Ethnographic Analogy. In *Lowland Maya Settlement Patterns*, ed. Wendy Ashmore, pp. 351–69. Albuquerque, NM: University of New Mexico Press.

———. 1981b. Ecological Adaptation in the Basin of Mexico: 23,000 B.C. to the Present. In *The Handbook of Middle American Indians, Supplement 1: Archaeology*, ed. Jeremy A. Sabloff, pp. 147–97. Austin, TX: University of Texas Press.

—— 1989. Household, Lineage, and the State in 8th-century Copan. In *House of the Bacabs, Copan: A Study of the Iconography, Epigraphy, and Social Context of a Maya Elite Structure*, ed. David L. Webster, pp. 89–105. Studies in Precolumbian Art and Archaeology, 29. Washington, DC: Dumbarton Oaks Research Library and Collection.

Sanders, William T., and Deborah L. Nichols. 1988. Ecological Theory and Cultural Evolution in the Valley of Oaxaca. *Current Anthropology* 29:33–80.

Sanders, William T., Jeffrey R. Parsons, and Robert S. Santley. 1979. *The Basin of Mexico: Ecological Processes in the Evolution of a Civilization.* New York, NY: Academy Press.

Sanders, William T., and Barbara J. Price. 1968. *Mesoamerica: The Evolution of a Civilization.* New York, NY: Random House.

Sanders, William T., and Robert S. Santley. 1983. A Tale of Three Cities: Energetics and Urbanization in Prehispanic Central Mexico. In *Prehistoric Settlement Patterns: Essays in Honor of Gordon R. Willey,* ed. Evon S. Vogt and Richard M. Leventhal, pp. 243–91. Albuquerque, NM: University of New Mexico Press.

Sanders, William T., and David L. Webster. 1978. Unilinealism, Multilinealism and the Evolution of Complex Societies. In *Social Archaeology: Beyond Subsistence and Dating,* ed. Charles L. Redman, Mary Jane Berman, Edward V. Curtain, William T. Langhorne, Jr., Nina M. Versaggi, and Jeffry C. Wanser, pp. 249–302. New York, NY: Academic Press.

———. 1988. The Mesoamerican Urban Tradition. *American Anthropologist* 90 (3): 521–46.

Santley, Robert S. 2004. Prehistoric Salt Production at El Salado, Veracruz, Mexico. *Latin American Antiquity* 15(2): 199–221.

Santley, Robert S., Philip J. Arnold III, and Thomas P. Barrett. 1997. Formative Period Settlement Patterns in the Tuxtla Mountains. In *Olmec to Aztec: Settlement Patterns in the Ancient Gulf Lowlands,* ed. Barbara L. Stark and Philip J. Arnold III, pp. 174–205. Tucson, AZ: University of Arizona Press.

Santone, Lenore M. 1993. Demand Structure, Transport Costs, and Patterns of Interregional Exchange: Aspects of the Prehistoric Lithic Economy of Northern Belize. Ph.D. diss., Dept. of Anthropology, The University of Texas at Austin.

Saturno, William A. 2007a. The Dark at the End of the Tunnel: Considering Politics and Political Interaction in the Maya Preclassic. Paper prepared for the University of Pennsylvania Museum International Research Conference, Philadelphia, April 9–13.

———. 2007b. San Bartolo and the Preclassic Maya Lowlands. Paper presented at the 25th University of Pennsylvania Museum Maya Weekend, Philadelphia, April 13–15.

———. 2009. Centering the Kingdom, Centering the King. In *The Art of Urbanism: How Mesoamerican Kingdoms Represented Themselves in Architecture and Imagery,* ed. William L. Fash and Leonardo López Luján, pp. 111–34. Washington DC:

Dumbarton Oaks.

Saturno, William A., David Stuart, and Boris Beltrán. 2006. Early Maya Writing at San Bartolo, Guatemala. *Science* 311(5765): 1281–83.

Saturno, William A., David Stuart, and Karl Taube. 2005. La Identificación de las Figuras del Muro Oeste de Pinturas Sub-1, San Bartolo, Petén. In *XVIII Simposio de Investigaciones Arqueológicas en Guatemala, 2004*, vol. 2, ed. Juan Pedro Laporte, Bárbara Arroyo, and Hector F. Mejía, pp. 647–56. Guatemala: Ministerio de Cultura y Deportes, Asociación Tikal, IDAEH, FAMSI.

Saturno, William A., Karl A. Taube, and David Stuart. 2005a. *The Murals of San Bartolo, El Petén, Guatemala, Part 1: The North Wall.* Ancient America, no. 7. Barnardsville, NC: Center for Ancient American Studies.

————. 2005b. *Los Murales de San Bartolo, El Petén, Guatemala, Parte 1: El Mural del Norte.* Ancient America, no. 7. Barnardsville, NC: Center for Ancient American Studies.

Saul, Fank P., and Julie M. Saul. 1991. Preclassic Population of Cuello. In *Cuello: An Early Maya Community in Belize*, ed. Norman Hammond, pp. 134–58. Cambridge: Cambridge University Press.

Saxe, Arthur A. 1970. Social Dimensions of Mortuary Practices. Ph.D. diss., Dept. of Anthropology, University of Michigan.

Scarborough, Vernon L. 1993. Water Management for the Southern Maya Lowlands: An Accretive Model for the Engineered Landscape. In *Economic Aspects of Water Management in the Prehispanic New World*, ed. Vernon L. Scarborough and Barry Isaac, pp. 17–68. Research in Economic anthropology Supplement 7. Greenwich, CN: JAI Press.

————. 1998. Ecology and Ritual: Water Management and the Maya. *Latin American Antiquity* 9 (2): 135–59.

Scarborough, Vernon L., Beverly Mitchum, Sorraya Carr, and David Freidel. 1982. Two Late Preclassic Ballcourts at the Lowland Maya Center of Cerros, Northern Belize. *Journal of Field Archaeology* 9(1): 21–34.

Scarborough, Vernon L., Fred Valdez Jr., and Nicholas Dunning. 2003. *Heterarchy, Political Economy, and the Ancient Maya. The Three Rivers Region of the East-Central Yucatán Peninsula.* Tucson, AZ: The University of Arizona Press.

Scarborough, Vernon L., and Fred Valdez, Jr. 2009. An Alternative Order: The Dualistic Economies of the Ancient Maya. *Latin American Antiquity* 20(1): 207–27.

Schele, Linda. 1985. The Hauberg Stela: Bloodletting and the Mythos of Maya Rulership. In *The Fifth Palenque Round Table, 1983, Vol. VII*, ed. Merle Greene Robertson and Virginia M. Fields, pp. 135–49. San Francisco, CA: Pre-Columbian Art Research Institute.

———. 1995. The Olmec Mountain and the Tree of Creation in Mesoamerican Cosmology. In *The Olmec World: Ritual and Rulership*, pp. 105–17. Princeton, NJ: Art Museum, Princeton University in association with Harry N. Abrams.

———. 2000. Sacred Landscape and Maya Kingship. In *The Breakout: The Origins of Civilization*, ed. Martha Lamberg-Karlovsky, epp. 45–55. Peabody Museum Monographs, No. 9. Cambridge, MA: Peabody Museum of Archaeology and Ethnology, Harvard University.

Schele, Linda, and David Freidel. 1990. *A Forest of Kings: The Untold Story of the Ancient Maya*. New York, NY: William Morrow and Company.

Schele, Linda, and Peter Mathews. 1991. Royal Visits and Other Intersite Relationships among the Classic Maya. In *Classic Maya Political History: Hieroglyphic and Archaeological Evidence*, ed. T. Patrick Culbert, pp. 226–52. Cambridge: Cambridge University Press.

Schele, Linda, Peter Mathews, and Floyd Lounsbury. 1990. *Re-dating the Hauberg Stela*. Texas Notes on Precolumbian Art, Writing, and Culture 1. Austin, TX: Center of the History and Art of Ancient American Culture, Art Department, University of Texas at Austin.

Schele, Linda, and Mary Ellen Miller. 1986. *The Blood of Kings: Dynasty and Ritual in Maya Art*. Fort Worth, TX: Kimbell Art Museum.

Scholes, France V. and Ralph L. Roys. 1948. *The Maya Chontal Indians of Acalan-Tixchel: A Contribution to the History and Ethnography of the Yucatan Peninsula*. Carnegie Institute of Washington Publication 560. Washington, DC: Carnegie Institute of Washington.

Schortman, Edward M., and Seiichi Nakamura. 1991. A Crisis of Identity: Late Classic Competition and Interaction on the Southeast Maya Periphery. *Latin American Antiquity* 2(4): 311–36.

Schreiner, Thomas. 1992. Possible Sources of Red Sandstone Used for Tintal Stela 1: Progress Report. Archived material, Foundation for Anthropological Research and Environmental Studies, Rupert ID.

———. 2001. Fabricación de Cal en Mesoamerica: Implicaciones para los Mayas del Preclásico en Nakbe, Peten. In *XIV Simposio de Investigaciones Arqueologicas en Guatemala*, ed. Juan Pedro Laporte, Ana Claudia Monzón de Suasnávar, and Bárbara Arroyo, pp. 405–18. Guatemala: Ministerio de Cultura y Deportes, Instituto de Antropología e Historia, Asociación Tikal.

———. 2002. Traditional Maya Lime Production: Environmental and Cultural Implications of a Native American Technology. Ph.D. diss., Dept. of Architecture, University of California, Berkeley.

———. 2003. Aspectos Rituales de la Producción de Cal en Mesoamérica: Evidencias y Pespectivas de las Tierras Bajas Mayas. In *XVI Simposio de Investigaciones Arqueológicas en Guatemala, 2002,* ed. Juan Pedro Laporte, Bárbara Arroyo, Héctor L. Escobedo, and Héctor E. Mejía, pp. 487–94. Guatemala: Ministerio de Cultura y Deportes, Instituto de Antropología e Historia, Asociación Tikal.

———. n.d. Possible Sources of Red Sandstone Used for Tintal Stela 1. In *The Kan Kingdom: Essays on the Mirador-Calakmul Cultural and Natural System,* ed. Richard D. Hansen, Edgar Suyuc-Ley, and Stanley P. Guenter. Guatemala: University of Francisco Marroquin Press. In preparation.

Schreiner, Thomas, and Enrique Hernandez. 2008. Investigaciones en el Sacbe Tintal, Mirador y Naranjita, 2008. In *Informe Preliminar Temporada 2008: Investigación y Conservación en los Sitios Arqueológicos de la Zona Cultural y Natural Mirador 2008,* ed. Nora Lopez, Richard Hansen, y Edgar Suyuc, pp. 120–23. Preliminary report filed with the Instituto de Antropología e Historia de Guatemala, Monumentos Prehispánicos y Coloniales, Ministerio de Cultural y Deportes, Guatemala. Rupert, Idaho: Foundation for the Anthropological Research and Environmental Studies (FARES).

———. 2009. Excavaciones y Prospeccion Arqueologica en el Sacbe Tintal-Mirador: Excavacion en el Bajo Carrizal, Op. 500 F y La Naranjita Op. 500 G. In *Investigaciones Multidisciplinarias en El Mirador: Informe Final de la Temporada 2008, Vols. 1 & II,* Tomo II, ed. Héctor Mejía, Richard D. Hansen, and Edgar Suyuc-Ley, pp. 217–42. Proyecto Cuenca Mirador. Report filed with the Ministerio de Cultura y Deportes, Instituto de Antropología e Historia, Departamento de Monumentos Prehispanicos y Coloniales, Guatemala City. Rupert, ID: Idaho State University, Foundation for Anthropological Research and Environemental Studies (FARES).

Schreiner, Thomas, David Wahl, and Enrique Hernandez. 2008. Investigaciones Preliminares en el Bajo Carrizal, Cuenca Mirador, Peten, Guatemala. In *Informe Final de Investigaciones 2007: Investigacion y Conservación en los Sitios Arqueológicos de la Zona Cultural y Natural Mirador,* ed. Nora Lopez, Richard D. Hansen, and Edgar Suyuc, pp. 1113–26. Formal report filed with the Departamento de Monumentos Prehispánicos y Coloniales, Instituto de Antropología e Historia, Ministerio de Cultural y Deportes, Guatemala City. Rupert, ID: Idaho State University: Foundation for Anthropological Research and Environmental Studies (FARES).

Schulze, Carlos Heinrich, John Duncan Keppie, Amabel Ortega-Rivera, Fernando Ortega-Gutiérrez, and James K. W. Lee. 2004. Mid-Tertiary Cooling Ages in the Precambrian Oaxacan Complex of Southern Mexico: Indication of Exhumation and Inland Arc Migration. *Revista Mexicana de Ciencias Geológicas* 21(2): 203–11.

Schwartz, Glenn M., and Steven E. Falconer, eds. 1994. *Archaeological Views from the Countryside*. Washington, DC: Smithsonian Institution Press.

Scott, John F. 1988. Potbellies and Fat Gods. *Journal of New World Archaeology* 7:25–36.

Sedat, David W., and Robert J. Sharer. 1972. Archaeological Investigations in the Northern Maya Highlands: New Data on the Maya Preclassic. In *Studies in the Archaeology of Mexico and Guatemala*, ed. John A. Graham, pp. 23–35. Contributions of the University of California Archaeological Institute. Berkeley, CA: Department of Anthropology, University of California, Berkeley.

Seitz, Russell, George E. Harlow, Virginia B. Sisson, and Karl Taube. 2001. 'Olmec Blue' and Formative Jade Sources: New Discoveries in Guatemala. *Antiquity* 75:687–688.

Seler, Eduard. 1904. Mexican Picture Writing of Alexander von Humboldt. In *Mexican and Central American Antiquities, Calendar Systems, and History*, pp. 127–229. Bureau of American Ethnology, Bulletin 28. Washington, DC: Smithsonian Institution.

———. 1990[1887]. *Collected Works in Mesoamerican Linguistics and Archaeology*, 2nd ed., ed. J. Eric S. Thompson and Francis B. Richardson. 5 vols. Culver City, CA: Labyrinthos.

Serra Puche, Mari Carmen. 1988. *Los Recursos Lacustres de la Cuenca de México Durante el Formativo*. México, DF: Instituto de Investigaciones Antropológicas, Universidad Nacional Autónoma de México.

———. 1989. El Sur de la Cuenca Durante el Formative. In *El Preclasico o Formative: Avances y Perspectivas*, ed. Martha Carmona Macias, pp. 279–86. México, DF: Instituto Nacional de Antropología e Historia.

Serra Puche, Mari Carmen, and Ludwig Beutelspacher. 1994. *Xochitécatl*. México, DF: Instituto Nacional de Antropología e Historia.

Service, Elman R. 1962. *Primitive Social Organization*. New York, NY: Random House.

———. 1975. *Origins of the State and Civilization: The Processes of Cultural Evolution*. New York, NY: W.W. Norton and Company.

Shafer, Harry J. 1979. A Technological Study of Two Maya Lithic Workshops at Colha, Belize. In *The Colha Project 1979: A Collection of Interim Papers*, ed. Thomas R. Hester, pp. 28–78. San Antonio, TX: Center for Archaeological Research, The University of Texas at San Antonio.

———. 1982. Maya Lithic Craft Specialization in Northern Belize. In *Archaeology at Colha, Belize: The 1981 Interim Report*, ed. Thomas R. Hester, Harry J. Shafer, and Jack D. Eaton, pp. 31–38. Venice, Italy: Center for Archaeological Research, The University of Texas at San Antonio and Centro Studi e Ricerche Ligabue.

———. 1991. Late Preclassic Formal Stone Tool Production at Colha, Belize. In *Maya*

Stone Tools: Selected Papers from the Second Maya Lithic Conference, ed. Thomas R. Hester and Harry J. Shafer, pp. 31–44. Monographs in World Archaeology No. 1. Madison, WI: Prehistory Press.

Shafer, Harry J., and Thomas R. Hester. 1979. Lithic Research at Colha: An Overview. In *The Colha Project 1979: A Collection of Interim Papers*, ed. Thomas R. Hester, pp. 18–27. San Antonio, TX: Center for Archaeological Research, The University of Texas at San Antonio.

———. 1983. Ancient Maya Chert Workshops in Northern Belize, Central America. *American Antiquity* 48:519–43.

Sharer, Robert J., ed. 1978. *The Prehistory of Chalcuapa, El Salvador. 3 Vol.* University Museum Monograph 36. Philadelphia, PA: University of Pennsylvania Press.

Sharer, Robert J. 1982. In the Land of Olmec Archaeology. *Journal of Field Archaeology*. 9(2): 253–67.

———. 1989a. The Olmec and the Southeast Periphery of Mesoamerica. In *Regional Perspectives on the Olmec*, ed. Robert J. Sharer and David C. Grove, pp. 247–71. Cambridge: Cambridge University Press.

———. 1989b. Olmec Studies: A Status Report. In *Regional Perspectives on the Olmec*, ed. Robert J. Sharer and David C. Grove, pp. 3–7. Cambridge: Cambridge University Press.

———. 1991. Diversity and Continuity in Maya Civilization: Quirigua as a Case Study. In *Classic Maya Political History*, ed. T. Patrick Culbert, pp. 180–98. Cambridge: Cambridge University Press.

———. 1992. The Preclassic Origin of Lowland Maya States. In *New Theories on the Ancient Maya*, ed. Elin C. Danien and Robert J. Sharer, pp. 131–36. University Museum Monograph 77. Philadelphia, PA: University Museum, University of Pennsylvania.

———. 1993. The Social Organization of the Late Classic Maya: Problems of Definition and Approaches. In *Lowland Maya Civilization in the Eighth Century A.D.*, ed. Jeremy A. Sabloff and John S. Henderson, pp. 91–110. Washington, DC: Dumbarton Oaks Research Library and Collection.

———. 1994. *The Ancient Maya*. Stanford University Press. Palo Alto: California.

———. 2007. Early Formative Pottery Trade and the Evolution of Mesoamerican Civilization. *Antiquity* 81(311): 201–3.

Sharer, Robert J., Andrew K. Balkansky, James H. Burton, Gary M. Feinman, Kent V. Flannery, David C. Grove, Joyce Marcus, Robert G. Moyle, T. Douglas Price, Elsa M. Redmond, Robert G. Reynolds, Prudence M. Rice, Charles S. Spencer, James B. Stoltman, and Jason Yaeger. 2006. On the Logic of Archaeological Inference:

Early Formative Pottery and the Evolution of Mesoamerican Societies. *Latin American Antiquity* 17(1): 90–103.

Sharer, Robert J., Marcello A. Canuto, and Ellen E. Bell. 2011. Before the Classic in the Southeastern Area: Issues of Organizational and Ethnic Diversity in the Copan Valley. In *The Southern Maya in the Late Preclassic: The Rise and Fall of an Early Mesoamerican Civilization*, ed. Michael Love and Nathan Kaplan, pp. 317–41. Boulder, CO: University of Colorado Press.

Sharer, Robert J., and James C. Gifford. 1970. Preclassic Ceramics from Chalchuapa, El Salvador, and Their Relationships with the Maya Lowlands. *American Antiquity* 35(4): 441–62.

Sharer, Robert J., and Charles W. Golden. 2004. Kingship and Polity: Conceptualizing the Maya Body Politic. In *Continuities and Changes in Maya Archaeology: Perspectives at the Millennium*, ed. Charles W. Golden and Greg Borgstede, pp. 23–50. New York, NY: Routledge.

Sharer, Robert J., and David C. Grove, eds. 1989. *Regional Perspectives on the Olmec*. Cambridge: Cambridge University Press.

Sharer, Robert J., and David W. Sedat. 1973. Monument 1, El Portón, Guatemala, and the Development of Maya Calendrical and Writing Systems. *University of California Archaeological Research Facility Contribution* 18:177–94.

Sharer, Robert J., and David W. Sedat. 1987. *Archaeological Investigations in the Northern Maya Highlands, Guatemala: Interaction and the Development of Maya Civilization*. University Museum Monograph 59. Philadelphia, PA: University Museum, University of Pennsylvania.

Sharer, Robert J., and Loa P. Traxler. 2006. *The Ancient Maya*. 6th ed. Stanford, CA: Stanford University Press.

Shaw, Justine M. 2001. Maya Sacbeob: Form and Function. *Ancient Mesoamerica* 12:261–72.

Shaw, Leslie C. 1991. The Articulation of Social Inequality and Faunal Resource Use in the Preclassic Community of Colha, Belize. Ph.D. diss., Dept. of Anthropology, University of Massachusetts at Amherst.

———. 1999. Social and Ecological Aspects of Preclassic Maya Meat Consumption at Colha, Belize. In *Reconstructing Ancient Maya Diet*, ed. Christine D. White, ed, pp. 83–100. Salt Lake City, UT: University of Utah Press.

———. 2012. The Elusive Maya Marketplace: An Archaeological Consideration of the Evidence. *Journal of Archaeological Research* 20(2): 117–55.

Sheets, Payson. 2000. Provisioning the Ceren Household. *Ancient Mesoamerica* 11:217–30.

Shook, Edwin M. 1951. Guatemala. *Carnegie Institution of Washington Yearbook* 50:240–44.

———. 1952. Lugares arqueológicos del altiplano meridional central de Guatemala. *Antropología e Historia de Guatemala* IV:3–40.

———. 1957. The Tikal Project. *University Museum Bulletin* 21:36–52.

Shook, Edwin M., and Alfred V. Kidder. 1952. Mound E-III-3, Kaminaljuyu, Guatemala. *Carnegie Institution of Washington, Contributions to American Anthropology and History* 53:33–127.

Shook, Edwin M., and Marion Popenoe de Hatch. 1978. The Ruins of El Balsamo. *Journal of New World Archaeology* 3(1): 1–37.

———. 1999. Las Tierras Altas Centrales: Períodos Preclásico y Clásico. In *Epoca Precolombina, Tomo I, Historia General de Guatemala*, ed. M. Popenoe de Hatch, pp. 289–318. Guatemala: Asociación de Amigos del País, Fundación para la Cultura y el Desarrollo.

Shook, Edwin M., and Robert E. Smith 1950. Descubrimientos Arqueológicos en Poptún. *Antropología e Historia de Guatemala* 2:3–15.

Sidrys, Raymond. 1978. Megalithic Architecture and Sculpture of the Ancient Maya. In *Papers on the Economy and Architecture of the Ancient Maya*, ed. Raymond Sidrys, pp. 155–83. Institute of Archaeoloyg Monograph VIII. Los Angeles, CA: University of California, Los Angeles.

Siebe, Claus. 2000. Age and Archaeological Implications of Xitli Volcano, Southwestern Basin of Mexico-City. *Journal of Volcanology and Geothermal Research* 104:45–64.

Siemens, Alfred H., and Dennis Puleston. 1972. Ridged Fields and Associated Features in Southern Campeche: New Perspectives on the Lowland Maya. *American Antiquity* 37(2): 228–39.

Simmons, Charles, S., Jose Manuel T. Tarano, and Jose Humberto Pinto. 1959. *Clasificación de Reconocimiento de los Suelos de la República de Guatemala*. Guatemala: Ministerio de Educación Pública.

Sinopoli, Carla. 2001. Empires. In *Archaeology at the Millennium: A Sourcebook*, ed. Gary M. Feinman and T. Douglas Price, pp. 439–71. New York, NY: Kluwer Academic/Plenum Publishers.

Sisson, Edward B. 1970. Settlement Patterns and Land Use in the Northwestern Chontalpa, Tabasco, Mexico: A Progress Report. *Cerámica de Cultura Maya* 6:41–65.

———. 1976. Survey and Excavation in the Northwestern Chontalpa, Tabasco, Mexico. Ph.D. diss., Dept. of Anthropology, Harvard University.

Smith, A. Ledyard. 1950. *Uaxactún, Guatemala: Excavations of 1931–1937*. Carnegie Institution of Washington Publication 588. Washington, D.C.: Carnegie Institution of Washington.

———. 1972. *Excavations at Altar de Sacrificios: Architecture, Settlement, Burials, and Caches.* Papers of the Peabody Museum of Archaeology and Ethnology 62(2). Cambridge, MA: Peabody Museum of Archaeology and Ethnology, Harvard University.

———. 1982. *Excavations at Seibal, No. 1, Department of Peten, Guatemala: Major Architecture and Caches.* Memoirs of the Peabody Museum of Archaeology and Ethnology, Vol. 15. Cambridge, MA: Peabody Museum of Archaeology and Ethnology, Harvard University.

Smith, Adam T. 2003. *The Political Landscape: Constellation of Authority in Early Complex Polities.* Berkeley, CA: University of Californai Press.

Smith, Carol A. 1976. *Regional Analysis.* New York, NY: Academic Press.

Smith, Michael E. 1989. Cities, Towns, and Urbanism: Comments on Sanders and Webster. *American Anthropologist* 91:454–60.

———. 2004. The Archaeology of Ancient State Economies. *Annual Review of Anthropology* 33:73–102.

Smith, Michael E., and Katharina J. Schreiber. 2005. New World States and Empires: Economic and Social Organization. *Journal of Archaeological Research* 13(3): 189–229.

Smith, Robert E. 1950. *Ceramic Sequence at Uaxactun, Guatemala.* 2 vols. Middle American Research Institute Publication 20. New Orleans, LA: Middle American Research Institute, Tulane University.

———. 1955. *Ceramic Sequence at Uaxactún, Guatemala.* Middle American Research Institute Publication 20. New Orleans, LA: Middle American Research Institute, Tulane University.

Sociedad Mexicana de Antropología, ed. 1942. *Mayas y Olmecas: Segunda Reunión de Mesa Redonda.* México: Sociedad Mexicana de Antropología.

Solari, Luigi A., J. Duncan Keppie, Fernando Ortega Gutiérrez, Kenneth L. Cameron, and Robert López. 2004. ~990 MA Peak Granulitic Metamorphism and Amalgamation of Oaxaquia, Mexico: U-PB Zircon Geochronological and Common PB Isotopic Data. *Revista Mexicana de Ciencas Geológicas* 21(2): 212–25.

Sorenson, John L. 1956. *An Archaeological Reconnaissance of West-Central Chiapas, Mexico,* pp. 7–19. New World Archaeological Foundation, Publication No. 1. Orinda, CA: New World Archaeological Foundation.

———. 2000. *Mormon's Map.* Provo, UT: The Foundation for Ancient Research and Mormon Studies, Brigham Young University.

Soustelle, Jacques. 1984. *The Olmecs: The Oldest Civilization in Mexico.* Garden City, NY:

Double-day and Company.

Southall, Aidan W. 1956. *Alur Society: A Study in Processes and Types of Domination.* Cambridge: Heffer and Sons.

Speal, C. Scott. 2009. The Economic Geography of Chert Lithic Production in the Southern Maya Lowlands: A Comparative Examiation of Early Stage Reduction Debris. *Latin American Antiquity* 20(1): 91–119.

Spencer, Charles S. 1980. *The Cuicatlan Cañada and Monte Alban: A Study of Primary State Formation.* New York, NY: Academic Press.

———. 2003. War and Early State Formation in Oaxaca, Mexico. *Proceedings of the National Academy of Sciences* 100:11185–87.

Spencer, Charles S., and Elsa M. Redmond. 2004. Primary State Formation in Mesoamerica. *Annual Review of Anthropology* 33:173–99.

Spinden, Herbert J. 1928. *Ancient Civilizations of Mexico and Central America.* 3rd ed. New York, NY: New York American Museum of Natural History.

Sprajc, Ivan. 2002. *Archaeological Reconnaissance in Southeastern Campeche, Mexico: 2001 Field Season Report.* Report submitted to the Foundation for the Advancement of Mesoamerican Studies. http://www.famsi.org/reports/00016/index.html, accessed December 2007.

———. 2003. *Archaeological Reconnaissance in Southeastern Campeche, Mexico: 2002 Field Season Report, with Appendices by Daniel Juarez Cossio, Adrian Baker Pedroza, and Nikolai Grube.* Report submitted to the Foundation for the Advancement of Mesoamerican Studies (FAMSI). http://www.famsi.org/reports/01014/index.html, accessed December 2007.

———. 2002–2004. Maya Sites and Monuments in SE Campeche, Mexico. *Journal of Field Archaeology* 29(3-4): 385–407.

———. 2005a. *Archaeological Reconnaissance in Southern Campeche, Mexico: 2004 Field Season Report.* Report submitted to the Committee for Research and Exploration (NGS#7592-04). Washington, DC: National Geographic Society.

———. 2005b. *Archaeological Reconnaissance in Southern Campeche, Mexico: 2005 Field Season Report.* Report submitted to the Committee for Research and Exploration (NGS #7756-04). Washington, DC: National Geographic Society.

———. 2005c. Astronomical Alignments in the Recently Discovered Archaeological Sites of Southern Campeche, Mexico: A Preliminary Report. Paper presented at the 13th Annual Conference of the European Society of Astronomy and Culture, Sardinia, Italy, June 28–July 3.

———. 2005d. More on Mesoamerican Cosmology and City Plans. Latin American Antiquity 16 (2): 209–16. Society for American Archaeology.

———. 2008. Alineamientos Astronómicos en la Arquitectura. In *Reconocimiento Arqueológico en el Sureste del Estado de Campeche, México: 1996–2005*, ed. Ivan Sprajc, pp. 233–42. Paris Monographs in American Archaeology 19, BAR International Series. Oxford: Archaeopress.

Sprajc, Ivan, and Nikolai Grube. 2008. Arqueología del Sureste de Campeche: una Síntesis. In *Reconocimiento arqueológico en el sureste del estado de Campeche, México: 1996–2005*, ed. Ivan Sprajc, pp. 263–75. Paris Monographs in American Archaeology 19, BAR International Series. Oxford: Archaeopress.

Sprajc, Ivan, Carlos Morales-Aguilar, and Richard D. Hansen. 2009. Early Maya Astronomy and Urban Planning at El Mirador, Peten, Guatemala. *Anthropological Notebooks*, Vol. 15 (3), pp. 79–101. Slovenia: Slovene Anthropological Society. Electronic document, http://www.drustvo-antropologov.si/anthropological_notebooks_eng.html, http://www.drustvoantropologov.si/AN/PDF/2009_3/Anthropological_Notebooks_XV_3_Sprajc.pdf.

Spranz, Bodo. 1970. *Die Pyramiden von Totimehuacan, Puebla (Mexico)*. Weisbaden, Germany: Steiner Franz Verlag.

Stark, Barbara L. 1974. Geography and Economic Specialization in the Lower Papaloapan, Veracruz, Mexico. *Ethnohistory* 21(3): 199–221.

———. 1999. Formal Architectural Complexes in South-Central Veracruz, Mexico: A Capital Zone? *Journal of Field Archaeology* 26(2): 197–225.

———. 2000. Framing the Gulf Olmecs. In *Olmec Art and Archaeology in Mesoamerica*, ed. John E. Clark and Mary E. Pye, pp. 31–53. Washington, DC: National Gallery of Art.

Stark, Barbara L, and Philip J. Arnold III. 1997. Introduction to the Archaeology of the Gulf Lowlands. In *Olmec to Aztec: Settlement Patterns in the Ancient Gulf Lowlands*, ed. Barbara L. Stark and Philip J. Arnold III, pp. 3–32. Tucson, AZ: University of Arizona Press.

Stark, Barbara L., Lynnette Heller, and Michael A. Ohnersorgen. 1998. People with Cloth: Mesoamerican Economic Change from the Perspective of Cotton in South-Central Veracruz. *Latin American Antiquity* 9(1): 7–36.

Stein, Gil. 2001. Understanding Ancient State Societies in the Old World. In *Archaeology at the Millennium: A Sourcebook*, ed. Gary M. Feinman and T. Douglas Price, pp. 353–79. New York, NY: Kluwer Academic/Plenum Publishers.

Stevens, Rayfred L. 1964. The Soils of Middle America and Their Relation to Indian Peoples and Cultures. In *Handbook of Middle American Indians. Vol. 1: Natural Environment and Early Cultures*, ed. Robert C. West, pp. 265–315. Austin, TX: University of Texas Press.

Stirling, Matthew W. 1940a. Great Stone Faces of the Mexican Jungle. *National Geographic* 78(3): 309–34.

—— 1940b. *An Initial Series from Tres Zapotes, Veracruz, Mexico*. National Geographic Society Mexican Archaeology Series 1(1).Washington, DC: National Geographic Society.

———. 1943a. La Venta's Green Stone Tigers. *National Geographic* 84(3): 321–28.

———. 1943b. *Stone Monuments of Southern Mexico*. Bureau of American Ethnology Bulletin 138. Washington, DC: Bureau of American Ethnology.

———. 1947. On the Trail of La Venta Man. *National Geographic* 91:137–72.

———. 1955. *Stone Monuments of the Río Chiquito, Veracruz, Mexico*. Bureau of American Ethnology, Bulletin 157. Washington, DC: Smithsonian Institution.

———. 1957. *An Archaeological Reconaissance of Southeastern Mexico*. Bureau of American Ethnology, Bulletin 164. Washington, DC: Smithsonian Institution.

———. 1968. Three Sandstone Monuments from La Venta Island. *Contributions of the University of California Archaeological Research Facility, Studies in Mesoamerican Archaeology* 5:35–39.

Stirling, Matthew W., and Marion Stirling. 1942. Finding Jewels of Jade in a Mexican Swamp. *National Geographic* 82(5): 635–61.

Stokes, Brian A. 1999. Lithic and X-ray Fluorescence Analysis of Obsidian Blades from Isla Alor: An Olmec and Post-Olmec Residential Site Near La Venta, Tabasco, Mexico. M.A. thesis, Dept. of Anthropology, University of California, Northridge.

Stoltman, James B., Joyce Marcus, Kent V. Flannery, James H. Burton, and Robert G. Moyle. 2005. Petrographic Evidence Shows that Pottery Exchange Between the Olmec and Their Neighbors Was Two-Way. *Proceedings of the National Academy of Sciences* 102(32): 11213–18.

Stone, Andrea. 1983. The Zoomorphs of Quirigua, Guatemala. Ph.D. diss., Dept. of Art and Art History, University of Texas at Austin.

Storey, Rebecca, and Patricia A. McAnany. 2006. Children of K'axob: Premature Death in a Formative Maya Village. In *The Social Experience of Childhood in Ancient Mesoamerica*, ed. Traci Ardren and Scott R. Hutson, pp. 53–72. Boulder: University Press of Colorado.

Strelow, David, and Lisa LeCount. 2001. Regional Interaction in the Formative Southern Maya Lowlands: Evidence of Olmecoid Stylistic Motifs in a Cunil Ceramic Assemblage from Xunantunich, Belize. Paper presented at the 66th Annual Meeting of the Society for American Archaeology, New Orleans, April 18–22.

Stuart, David. 1984. Royal Auto-Sacrifice among the Maya: A Study of Image and Meaning. *Res* 7/8:6–20.

————. 1988. Blood Symbolism in Maya Iconography. In *Maya Iconography*, ed. Elizabeth Benson and Gillett Griffin, pp. 175–221. Princeton, NJ: Princeton University Press.

————. 1992. Hieroglyphs and Archaeology at Copán. *Ancient Mesoamerica* 3:169–84.

————. 1996. Kings of Stone: A Consideration of Stelae in Ancient Maya Ritual and Representation. *Res* 29/30:148–71.

————. 2004a. La Concha Decorada de la Tumba del Templo del Búho, Dzibanché. In *Los Cautivos de Dzibanché*, ed. Enrique Nalda, pp. 132–40. Mexico, DF: Instituto Nacional de Antropología y Historia.

————. 2004b. The Beginnings of the Copan Dynasty: A Review of the Hieroglyphic and Historical Evidence. In *Understanding Early Classic Copan*, ed. Ellen E. Bell, Marcello A. Canuto, and Robert J. Sharer, pp. 215–47. Philadelphia, PA: University of Pennsylvania Museum of Archaeology and Anthropology.

————. 2005. Ideology and Classic Maya Kingship. In *A Catalyst for Ideas: Anthropological Archaeology and the Legacy of Douglas W. Schwartz*, ed. Vernon L. Scarborough, pp. 257–85. School of American Research Advanced Seminar Series. Sante Fe, NM: School of American Research Press.

Stuart, David, and Ian Graham. 2003. *Corpus of Maya Hieroglyphic Inscriptions, Vol. 9, Part 1: Piedras Negras*. Cambridge, Massachusetts: Peabody Museum of Archaeology and Ethnology, Harvard University.

Stuart, David, and Stephen Houston. 1994. *Classic Maya Place Names*. Dumbarton Oaks Studies in Pre-Columbian Art and Archaeology 33. Washington, DC: Dumbarton Oaks Research Library and Collection.

Stuart, David, Stephen D. Houston and John Robertson. 1999. Recovering the Past: Classic Mayan Language and Classic Maya Gods. Notebook to the XXIIIrd Linda Schele Forum on Maya Hieroglyphic Writing, Austin, March 13–14.

Stuart, David and Linda Schele. 1986. Yax-K'uk'-Mo', The Founder of the Lineage of Copan. Copan Notes 6. Copán Mosaics Project and the Instituto Hondureño de Antropología e Historia, Copán, Honduras.

Stuart, George. 1992. Maya Heartland Under Seige. *National Geographic*. 182(5): 94–107.

Stutz-Landeen, Ellen. 1986. Excavations on a Late Preclassic Plaza Unit at El Mirador, Peten, Guatemala. M.A. thesis, Dept. of Anthropology, Brigham Young University.

Suasnávar Bolaños, José Samuel. 1993. Presencia de Piedra Verde en el Grupo A-IV de Kaminaljuyu. In *VI Simposio de Investigaciones Arqueológcas en Guatemala, 1994*, ed. Juan Pedro Laporte and Héctor L. Escobedo. Guatemala: Ministerio de Cultura y

Deportes, Instituto de Antropología e Historia, Asociación Tikal.

———. 1994. Las Calzadas de Nakbe. In *VII Simposio de Investigaciones Arqueológicas en Guatemala, 1993*, ed. Juan Pedro Laporte, Héctor L. Escobedo, and Sandra Villagran de Brady, pp. 335–48. Guatemala: Ministerio de Cultura y Deportes, Instituto de Antropología e Historia, Asociación Tikal.

Suasnávar Bolaños, José Samuel, and Rosa María Flores. 1992. Plataformas Preclásicas y Rasgos Asociados en el Grupo A-IV-1 de Kaminaljuyu. In *V Simposio de Investiga ciones Arqueológicas en Guatemala*, ed. Juan Pedro Laporte, Héctor L. Escobedo, and Sandra Villagrán de Brady, pp. 13–24. Guatemala: Ministerio de Cultura y Deportes, Instituto de Antropología e Historia, Asociación Tikal.

Suasnávar Bolaños, José, and Richard D. Hansen. 1997. Cause and Causeway in Northern Peten. Paper presented at the 62nd Annual Meeting of the Society for American Archaeology, Nashville, April 2–6.

Sugiyama, Saburo. 1992. Rulership, Warfare, and Human Sacrifice at the Ciudadela: An Iconographic Study of Feathered Serpent Representations. In *Art, Ideology, and the City of Teotihuacan*, ed. Janet C. Berlo, pp. 205–30. Washington DC: Dumbarton Oaks Research Library and Collection.

———. 2005. *Human Sacrifice, Militarism, and Rulership: Materialization of State Ideology at the Feathered Serpent Pyramid, Teotihuacan*. Cambridge: Cambridge University Press.

Sullivan, Timothy. 2009. The Social and Political Evolution of Chiapa de Corzo: A Regional Analysis of the Development of a Middle Formative through Early Classic Mesoamerican Political Center. Ph.D. diss., Dept. of Anthropology, University of Pittsburgh, Pittsburgh.

Symonds, Stacy C. 2000. The Ancient Landscape at San Lorenzo Tenochtitlán, Veracruz, Mexico: Settlement and Nature. In *Olmec Art and Archaeology in Mesoamerica*, ed. John E. Clark and Mary E. Pye, pp. 44–73. Washington, DC: National Gallery of Art.

Symonds, Stacey C., Ann Cyphers, and Roberto Lunagómez. 2002. *Asentamiento Prehispánico en San Lorenzo Tenochtitlán*. México: Universidad Nacional Autónoma de México.

Symonds, Stacey C., and Roberto Lunagómez. 1997. Settlement System and Population Development at San Lorenzo. In *Olmec to Aztec: Settlement Patterns in the Ancient Gulf Lowlands*, ed. Barbara L. Stark and Philip J. Arnold III, pp. 144–73. Tucson, AZ: University of Arizona Press.

Tambiah, Stanley J. 1977. The Galactic Polity: The Structure of Traditional Kingdoms in Southeast Asia. *Annals of the New York Academy of Sciences* 293:69–97.

Taube, Karl A. 1996a. The Olmec Maize God: The Face of Corn in Formative Meso-america. *Res 29/30*:39–81.

———. 1996b. The Rainmakers: The Olmec and Their Contribution to Mesoameri-can Belief and Ritual. In *The Olmec World: Ritual and Rulership*, pp. 83–103. Prince-ton, NJ: Art Museum, Princeton University in association with Harry N. Abrams.

———. 1998. The Jade Hearth: Centrality, Rulership, and the Classic Maya Temple. In *Function and Meaning in Classic Maya Architecture*, ed. Stephen D. Houston, pp. 427–78. Washington, DC: Dumbarton Oaks Research Library and Collection.

———. 2004. *Olmec Art at Dumbarton Oaks*. Pre-Columbian Art at Dumbarton Oaks, No. 2. Washington, DC: Dumbarton Oaks Research Library and Collection.

———. 2005. The Symbolism of Jade in Classic Maya Religion. *Ancient Mesoamerica* 16(1): 23–50.

———. 2007. In the World of the Sun: Solar Imagery and Symbolism among the Clas-sic Maya. Paper presented at the 31st Maya Meetings at Texas, Austin, March 9–11.

Taube, Karl A., Zachary Hruby, and Luis A. Romero. 2011. Ancient Jade Workshops: Archaeological Reconnaissance in the Upper Río El Tambor, Guatemala. In *The Techology of Ancient Maya Civilization: Political Economy and Beyond in Lithic Studies*, ed. Zachary Hruby, G.E. Braswell, and O.F. Chinchilla Mazariegos, pp. 143–50. Sheffield: Equinox.

Taube, Karl A., William A. Saturno, David Stuart, and Heather Hurst. 2010. *The Murals of San Bartolo, El Petén. Part 2: The West Wall*. Ancient America 10. Bar-nardsville, NC: The Boundary End Archaeology Research Center.

Taube, Karl A., William A. Saturno, and David Stuart. n.d. *Initial Report of the San Bartolo Murals, Part 2, The West Wall*. Ancient America Series. Barnardsville, NC: Center for Ancient American Studies.

Tedlock, Barbara. 1982. *Time and the Highland Maya*. Albuquerque, NM: University of New Mexico Press.

Tedlock, Dennis. 1985. *Popol Vuh: The Mayan Book of Myth and History*. New York, NY: Simon and Schuster.

Tejada Bouscayrol, Mario, and Ronald W. Lowe. 1993. El Monumento 1 de Ocozo-coautla. In *Segundo y Tercer Foro de Arqueología de Chiapas*, pp. 88–115. Chiapas, Mexico: Gobierno del Estado de Chiapas, Consejo Estatal de Fomento a la Inves-tigacion y Difusion de la Cultura, and Instituto Chiapaneco de Cultura.

Tello, Julio. 1943. Discovery of the Chavin Culture in Peru. *American Antiquity* 9(1): 135–60.

Thompson, Edward H. 1897. *Cave of Loltun, Yucatan: Report of Explorations for the Museum, 1888–89 and 1890–91*. Memoirs of the Peabody Museum of American

Archaeology and Ethnology 1(2). Cambridge, MA: Harvard University.

Thompson, J. Eric S. 1939. *Excavations at San José, British Honduras*. Carnegie Institute of Washington Publication 506. Washington, DC: Carnegie Institute of Washington.

———. 1940. *Late Ceramic Horizons at Benque Viejo, British Honduras*. Carnegie Institute of Washington Publication 528. Washington, DC: Carnegie Institute of Washington.

———. 1941. Dating of Certain Inscriptions of Non-Maya Origin. *Theoretical Approaches to Problems, No. 1*. Washington, DC: Carnegie Institution.

———. 1954. *The Rise and Fall of Maya Civilization*. Norman, OK: University of Oklahoma Press.

———. 1970. *Maya History and Religion*. Norman, OK: University of Oklahoma Press.

Thompson, Richard A. 1970. Stochastics and Structure: Cultural Change and Social Mobility in a Yucatec Town. *Southwestern Journal of Anthropology* 26:354–74.

Thomson, Charlotte W. 1987. Chalcatzingo Jade and Fine Stone Objects. In *Ancient Chalcatzingo*, ed. David C. Grove, pp. 295–304. Austin, TX: University of Texas Press.

Tolstoy, Paul. 1971. Recent Research into the Early Preclassic of the Central Highlands. *Contributions of the University of California Archaeological Research Facility* 11:25–28. Berkeley, CA.

———. 1989a. Coapexco and Tlatilco: Sites With Olmec Materials in the Basin of Mexico. In *Regional Perspectives on the Olmec*, ed. Robert J. Sharer and David C. Grove, pp. 85–121. School of American Research Advanced Seminar Series. New York, NY: Cambridge University Press.

———. 1989b. Western Mesoamerica and the Olmec. In *Regional Perspectives on the Olmec*, ed. Robert J. Sharer and David C. Grove, pp. 275–302. School of American Research Advanced Seminar Series. New York, NY: Cambridge University Press.

Tolstoy, Paul, Suzanne K. Fish, Martin W. Boksenbaum, Kathryn Blair Vaughn, and C. Earle Smith. 1977. Early Sedentary Communities of the Basin of Mexico. *Journal of Field Archaeology* 4(1): 91–106.

Tolstoy, Paul, and Louise I. Paradis. 1970. Early and Middle Pre-Classic Cultures in the Basin of Mexico. *Science* 167:344–51.

Tomasic, John, and Steven Bozarth. 2011. New Evidence from a Preclassic Tomb at K'o, Guatemala. Paper presented at the Annual Meetings of the Society for American Archaeology, Sacramento, CA.

Tourtellot, Gair. 1988a. Developmental Cycles of Households and Houses at Seibal. In *Household and Community in the Mesoamerican Past*, ed. Richard R. Wilk and

Wendy A. Ashmore, pp. 97–120. Albuquerque, NM: University of New Mexico Press.

———. 1988b. Mapping Community Patterns at Sayil, Yucatan, Mexico: The 1985 Season. *Journal of New World Archaeology* 7(2-3): 1–24.

———. 1990. Population Estimates for Preclassic and Classic Seibal, Peten. In *Precolumbian Population History in the Maya Lowlands*, ed. T. Patrick Culbert and Don S. Rice, pp. 83–102. Albuquerque, NM: University of New Mexico Press.

Tozzer, Alfred M., trans. 1941. *Landa's Relación de las Cosas de Yucatan: A Translation.* Papers of the Peabody Museum, vol. 18. Cambridge, MA: Harvard University.

———. 1957. *Chichen Itza and Its Cenote of Sacrifice: A Comparative Study of Contemporaneous Maya and Toltec.* Memoirs Peabody Museum of Archaeology and Ethnology, vols. 11 and 12. Cambridge, MA: Peabody Museum.

Trachman, Rissa M., and Fred Valdez Jr. 2006. Identifying Childhood among the Ancient Maya: Evidence Toward Social Reproduction at the Dancer Household Group in Northwestern Belize. In *The Social Experience of Childhood in Ancient Mesoamerica*, ed. Traci Ardren and Scott R. Hutson, pp. 73–102. Boulder: University Press of Colorado.

Treat, Raymond. 1969. Excavations at Vistahermosa, Chiapas, Mexico. M.A. thesis, Dept. of Anthropology, Universidad de las Americas, Puebla, Mexico.

———. 1986. *Early and Middle Formative Sub-mound Refuse Deposits at Vistahermosa, Chiapas.* Notes of the New World Archaeological Foundation, No. 2. Provo, UT: New World Archaeological Foundation, Brigham Young University.

Trigger, Bruce G. 1974. The Archaeology of Government. *World Archaeology* 6(1): 95–106.

———. 1993. *Early Civilizations: Ancient Egypt in Context.* Cairo: American University in Cairo Press.

———. 2003. *Understanding Early Civilizations.* New York: Cambridge University Press.

———. 2004. Cross-Cultural Comparison and Archaeological Theory. In *A Companion to Social Archaeology*, ed. Lynn Meskell and Robert W. Preucel, pp. 43–65. Oxford: Blackwell.

Turner, Billy Lee, II, and Peter D. Harrison, eds. 1983. *Pulltrouser Swamp: Ancient Maya Habitat, Agriculture, and Settlement in Northern Belize.* Austin, TX: University of Texas Press.

Turner, Ellen Sue, Norman I. Turner, and Richard E. W. Adams. 1981. Volumetric Assessment, Rank Ordering, and Maya Civic Centers. In *Lowland Maya Settlement Patterns*, ed. Wendy Ashmore, pp. 37–70. Albuquerque, NM: University of New Mexico Press.

Tykot, Robert H., Nikolaas J. Van der Merwe, and Norman Hammond. 1996. Stable Isotope Analysis of Bone Collagen, Bone Apatite and Tooth Enamel in the Reconstruction of Human Diet: A Case Study from Cuello, Belize. In *Archaeological Chemistry: Organic, Inorganic, and Biochemical Analysis*, ed. M. V. Orna, pp. 355–65. Washington, DC: American Chemical Society.

Urban, Greg. 1996. *Metaphysical Community*. Austin, TX: University of Texas Press.

Uruñuela, Gabriela, Patricia Plunket, and Ma. Amparo Robles. 2006. New Evidence on the Beginnings of the Great Pyramid at Cholula. In *Cholula: The Great Pyramid*, ed. Felipe Solís, Gabriela Uruñuela, Patricia Plunket, and Martín Cruzand Dionisio Rodríguez, pp. 177–89. México: Conaculta-Instituto Nacional de Antropología e Historia.

Vaillant, George C. 1930. *Excavations at Zacatenco*. Anthropological Papers of the American Museum of Natural History 32(1). New York, NY: American Museum of Natural History.

———. 1931. *Excavations at Ticoman*. Anthropological Papers of the American Museum of Natural History 32(2). New York, NY: American Museum of Natural History.

———. 1935. *Excavations at El Arbolillo*. Anthropological Papers of the American Museum of Natural History 35(2). New York, NY: American Museum of Natural History.

Valdés, Juan Antonio. 1987. Uaxactún: Recientes Investigaciones. *Mexicon* 8(6): 125–28.

———. 1988. Los Mascacrones Preclássicos de Uaxactún: El caso del Grupo H. In *Primer Simposio Mundial sobre Epigrafía Maya*, pp. 165–81. Guatemala: Asociación Tikal.

———. 1993. Arquitectura y Escultura en la Plaza Sur del Grupo H, Uaxactun. In *Tikal y Uaxactun en el Preclásico*, ed. Juan Pedro Laporte and Juan Antonio Valdés, pp. 96–126. Mexico, DF: Instituto de Investigaciones Antropológicas, Universidad Nacional Autonoma de Mexico.

———. 1995. Desarrollo Cultural y Señales de Alarma entre los Mayas: El Preclássico Tardío y la Transición Hacia el Clásico Temprano. In *The Emergence of Lowland Maya Civilization: The Transition from the Preclassic to the Early Classic*, ed. Nikolai Grube, pp. 71–85. Acta Mesoamericana 8. Möckmühl: Verlag Anton Saurwein.

———. 1997. El Proyecto Miraflores dentro del Marco Preclásico de Kaminaljuyu. In *X Simposio de Investigaciones Arqueológicas en Guatemala*, ed. Juan Pedro Laporte and Hector L. Escobedo, pp. 81–92. Guatemala: Museo Nacional de Arqueología y Etnología.

———. 1998. Kaminaljuyu, Guatemala: descubrimientos Recientes sobre Poder y el

Manejo Hidráulico. In *Memorias del Tercer Congreso Internacional de Mayistas*, pp. 752–770. Mexico, D.F.: Universidad Nacional Autónoma de México.

Valdés, Juan Antonio, and Marion Popenoe de Hatch. 1996. Evidencias de poder y control social en Kaminaljuyu: proyecto arqueológico Miraflores II. In *IX Simposio de Investigaciones Arqueológicas en Guatemala*. Juan Pedro Laporte and Hector L. Escobedo, eds, pp. 377–396. Guatemala: Ministerio de Cultura y Deportes, Instituto de Antropología e Historia, Asociación Tikal.

Valdez, Fred, Jr. 1995. Religion and Iconography of the Pre-Classic Maya at Río Azul, Peten, Guatemala. In *Religión y sociedad en el area Maya*. Varela Torrecilla, Juan L. Bonor V., and Yolanda Fernández Marquínez, eds, pp. 211–217. Caja Madrid: Sociedad Española de Estudios Mayas, Instituto de Cooperación Iberoamericana.

Valle, Judith. 2007. Rescate arqueológico en Montículo de la Culebra y el Acueducto de Pinula: Dos monumentos en agonia. In *XX Simposio de Investigaciones Arqueológicas en Guatemala, 2006*. Juan Pedro Laporte, Bárbara Arroyo, and Hector E. Mejía, eds, pp. 823–833. Guatemala: Ministerio de Cultura y Deportes, Instituto de Antropología e Historia, Asociación Tikal, y Fundación Arqueológica del Nuevo Mundo.

VanDerwarker, Amber M. 2006. *Farming, Hunting, and Fishing in the Olmec World*. Austin, TX: University of Texas Press.

Vargas, Ernesto. 2001. *Itzamkanac y Acalan: Tiempos de Crisis Anticipando el Futuro*. Mexico, DF: Instituto de Investigaciones Antropológicas, Universidad Nacional Autónoma de México.

Vaughan, Hague H., Edward S. Deevey, and S. E. Garrett-Jones. 1985. Pollen Stratigraphy of Two Cores from the Peten Lake District, with an Appendix in Two Deep-Water Cores. In *Prehistoric Lowland Maya Environemnt and Subsistence Economy*. Mary Pohl, ed, pp. 73–89. Cambridge, MA: Harvard University Press.

Velásquez, Juan Luis. 1993. La Secuencia de Ocupación del Grupo A-IV-1: Un Grupo Preclásico de Kaminaljuyu. In *VI Simposio de Investigaciones Arqueológicas en Guatemala*. Juan Pedro Laporte, Hector L. Escobedo, and Sandra Villagrán de Brady, eds, pp. 377–390. Guatemala: Ministerio de Cultura y Deportes, Instituto de Antropología e Historia, Asociación Tikal.

———. 1999. Excavaciones en el Juego de Pelota de Nakbe y Grupos Residenciales. In *XII Simposio de Investigaciones Arqueológicas en Guatemala, 1998*. Juan Pedro Laporte, Hector L. Escobedo, and Ana Claudia Monzón de Suasnávar, eds, pp. 353–359. Guatemala: Ministerio de Cultura y Deportes, Instituto de Antropología e Historia, Asociacion Tikal.

———. 2006. La transición cerámica del Preclásico Tardío al Clásico Temprano: Una visión desde La Trinidad-Kaminaljuyu. In *XIX Simposio de Investigaciones Arque-*

ológicas en Guatemala, 2005. Juan Pedro Laporte, Bárbara Arroyo, and Hector L. Escobedo. Guatemala: Ministerio de Cultura y Deportes, Instituto de Antropología e Historia, Asociación Tikal, y Fundación Arqueológica del Nuevo Mundo.

Velásquez , Juan Luis, and Bernard Hermes. 1992. Proyecto A-IV-1, Kaminaljuyu: Los materiales y sus implicaciones Teóricas. In *V Simposio de Investigaciones Arqueológicas en Guatemala*. Juan Pedro Laporte, Hector L. Escobedo, and Sandra Villagrán de Brady, eds, pp. 25–30. Guatemala: Ministerio de Cultura y Deportes, Instituto dc Antropología e Historia, Asociación Tikal.

———. 1996. El proceso evolutivo del centro de El Salvador: su secuencia de ocupación y relaciones. In *IX Simposio de Investigaciones Arqueológicas en Guatemala*. Juan Pedro Laporte and Hector L. Escobedo, eds, pp. 619–648. Guatemala: Ministerio de Cultura y Deportes, Instituto de Antropología e Historia, Asociación Tikal.

Velásquez-Fergusson, Maria Laura. 2011. La Ocupación entre los Períodos Preclásico Tardio al Clásico Tardio: Una Perspectiva desde la Estructura 4D3-4, Complejo Tigre, El Mirador, Peten, Guatemala. Thesis for Licenciada en Arqueologia, Escuela de Historia, Area de Arqueologia, Universidad de San Carlos de Guatemala.

Velson, Joseph F., and Thomas C. Clark. 1975. Transport of Stone Monuments to the La Venta and San Lorenzo Sites. *Contributions of the University of California Archaeological Research Facility* 24:1–39.

Viel, René H. 1993a. Copan Valley. In *Pottery of Prehistoric Honduras: A Regional Perspective*. John S. Henderson and Margaret Beaudry-Corbett, eds, pp. 12–18. Los Angeles, CA: Institute of Archaeology, University of California, Los Angeles.

———. 1993b. *Evolución de la Cerámica de Copán, Honduras*. Tegucigalpa: Instituto Hondureño de Antropología e Historia.

———. 2006. The Ceramic Chronology of Copan: A Plotted History and Some Revisionist Reflections. In *An Archaeological Life: Papers in Honour of Jay Hall*. Sean Ulm and Ian Lilley, eds, pp. 203–212. Research Report Series, 7. Brisbane: Aboriginal and Torres Strait Islander Studies Unit, University of Queensland.

Viel, René H., and Jay Hall. 1998. The Chronology of Copán, Honduras: An Update and Discussion. Paper presented at the 63rd Annual Meeting of the Society for American Archaeology, Seattle, March 25–29.

———. 1999. El Periodo Formativo de Copán, Honduras. In *XII Simposio de Investigaciones Arqueológicas en Guatemala*. Juan P. Laporte, Héctor L. Escobedo, and Ana Claudia Monzón de Suasnávar, eds, pp. 99–106. Guatemala: Ministerio de Cultura y Deportes, Instituto de Antropología e Historia, Asociación Tikal.

———. n.d. The Chabij and Bijac Phases Revisted: A Definition of the Protoclassic Period at Copan, Honduras. Unpublished MS, in possession of the author.

Villamar Becerril, Enrique. 2002. Estudio Osteológico y Tafonómico de Entierros Olmecas del Periodo Preclásico de San Lorenzo, Veracruz. Licenciatura thesis, Universidad Autónoma de México.

Vogt, Evon Z. 1961. Some Aspects of Zinacantan Settlement Patterns and Ceremonial Organization. *Estudios de Cultura Maya* 1:131–145.

———. 1968. Some Aspects of Zinacantan Settlement Patterns and Ceremonial Organization. In *Settlement Archaeology*. Kwang-chih Chang, ed, pp, pp. 154–171. Palo Alto, CA: National Press Books.

———. 1969. *Zinacantan: A Maya Community in the Highlands of Chiapas*. Cambridge, MA: Harvard University Press.

———. 1976. *Tortillas for the Gods*. Cambridge, MA: Harvard University Press.

von Nagy, Christopher L. 1997. The Geoarchaeology of Settlement in the Grijalva Delta. In *Olmec to Aztec: Settlement Patterns in the Ancient Gulf Lowlands*. Barbara L. Stark and Philip J. Arnold III., eds, pp. 253–277. Tucson, AZ: University of Arizona Press.

———. 2003. Of Meandering Rivers and Shifting Towns: Landscape Evolution and Communities with the Grijalva Delta. Ph.D. dissertation, Department of Anthropology, Tulane University.

von Nagy, Christopher L., Mary D. Pohl, and Kevin O. Pope. 2002. Ceramic Chronology of the La Venta Olmec Polity: The View from San Andrés, Tabasco. Paper presented at the 67th Annual Meeting of the Society for American Archaeology, Denver, March 20–24.

von Nagy, Christopher L., Maria B. Tway, Mary D. Pohl, and Kevin Pope. 2000. Informe: Estudios sobre la Cerámica y otros Artifactos del Sitio San Andrés (Barí 1), Municipio de Huimanguillo, Tabasco, México. Anexo al informe general del año 1999. Report submitted to the Instituto Nacional de Antropología y Historia, Mexico City.

Wahl, David. 2000. A Stratigraphic Record of Environmental Change from a Maya Reservoir in the Northern Peten, Guatemala. M.A. thesis, Department of Geography, University of California, Berkeley.

———. 2005. Climate Change and Human Impacts in the Southern Maya Lowlands: A Paleoenvironmental Perspective from the Northern Peten, Guatemala. Ph.D. dissertation, Department of Geography, University of California, Berkeley.

Wahl, David, Roger Byrne, and Lysanna Anderson. 2014. An 8700 Year Paleoclimate Reconstruction from the Southern Maya Lowlands. *Quaternary Science Reviews* 103(214):19–25.

Wahl, David, Roger Byrne, Thomas Schreiner, and Richard Hansen. 2006. Holocene

Vegetation Change in the Northern Peten and its Implications for Maya Prehistory. *Quaternary Research* 65(3): 380–389.

———. 2007. Palaeolimnological Evidence of Late-Holocene Settlement and Abandonment in the Mirador Basin, Peten, Guatemala. *The Holocene* 17(6): 813–820.

Wahl, David, Francisco Estrada-Belli, and Lysanna Anderson. 2013. Mais, clima y fuego en la región de Holmul, Peten, Guatemala. In *XXVI Simposio de Investigaciones Arqueologicas en Guatemala*. Bárbara Arroyo and Héctor E. Mejía, eds. Musco Nacional de Arqueologia y Etnologia, Guatemala.

Wahl, David, Richard D. Hansen, Roger Byrne, Lysanna Anderson, and Thomas Schreiner. 2015. Holocene Climate Variability and Anthropogenic Impacts from Lago Paixban, a Perennial Wetland in Peten, Guatemala. *Global and Planetary Change* August 2015.

Wahl, David, Thomas Schreiner, and Roger Byrne. 2005. La secuencia Paleo-ambiental de la Cuenca Mirador en Peten. In *XVIII Simposio de Investigaciones Arqueológicas en Guatemala, 2004*. Juan Pedro Laporte, Bárbara Arroyo, and Héctor E. Mejía, eds, pp. 53–58. Guatemala: Ministerio de Cultura y Deportes, Instituto de Antropología e Historia, Asociacion Tikal.

Wahl, David, Thomas Schreiner, Roger Byrne, and Richard Hansen. 2007. A Paleoecological Record from a Late Classic Maya Reservoir in the North Petén. *Latin American Antiquity* 18(2): 212–222.

Wake, Thomas A. and Lady R. Harrington. 2002. Vertebrate Faunal Remains from La Blanca, Guatemala. In *Early Complex Society in Pacific Guatemala: Settlements and Chronology of the Rio Naranjo, Guatemala*. Papers of the New World Archaeological Foundation, No. 66. Michael W. Love, ed, pp. 237–252. Provo, UT: New World Archaeological Foundation, Brigham Young University.

Warren, Bruce W. 1959. New Discoveries in Chiapas, Southern Mexico. *Archaeology* 12:98–105.

———. 1961a. A Chiapa de Corzo Sherd Report. *Katunob* 2(1): 14–17.

———. 1961b. The Archaeological Sequence at Chiapa de Corzo. In *Los Mayas del Sur y sus Relaciones con los Nahuas Meridionales, VIII Mesa Redonda, San Cristobal de las Casas, Chiapas*, pp. 75–83. Chiapas, Mexico: Sociedad Mexicana de Antropología.

———. 1978. The Sociocultural Development of the Central Depression of Chiapas, Mexico: Preliminary Considerations. Ph.D. dissertation, Department of Anthropology, University of Arizona.

Watanabe, John M. 1992. *Maya Saints and Souls in a Changing World*. Austin, TX: University of Texas Press.

Wauchope, Robert. 1938. *Modern Maya Houses: A Study of their Archaeological Signifi-*

cance. Carnegie Institution of Washington Publication 502. Washington, D.C.: Carnegie Institution of Washington.

Webster, David L. 1974. *Fortifications of Becan, Campeche, Mexico.* Middle American Research Institute, publication 31. New Orleans, LA: Tulane University.

———. 1975. Warfare and the Origin of the State: A Reconsideration. *American Antiquity* 40:464–470.

———. 1976. *Defensive Earthworks at Becan, Campeche, Mexico : Implications for Maya Warfare.* Middle American Research Institute Publication 41. New Orleans, LA: Middle American Research Institute, Tulane University.

———. 1977. Warfare and the Evolution of Maya Civilization. In *The Origins of Maya Civilization.* Richard E. W. Adams, ed, pp. 335–372. School of American Research Advanced Seminar Series. Albuquerque, NM: University of New Mexico Press.

———. 1998. Warfare and Status Rivalry: Lowland Maya and Polynesian Comparisons. In *Archaic States.* Gary M. Feinman and Joyce Marcus, eds, pp. 311–352. Santa Fe, NM: School of American Research Press.

Webster, David L., Ann Corinne Freter, and Nancy Gonlin. 2000. *Copán: The Rise and Fall of an Ancient Maya Kingdom.* Orlando, FL: Harcourt Brace.

Webster, David L., and William Sanders. 2001. La Antigua Ciudad Mesoamericana: Teoría y Concepto. In *Reconstruyendo La Ciudad Maya: El Urbanismo en Las Sociedades Antiguas.* Andrés Ciudad Ruiz, M. Josefa Iglesias Ponce de León, and M. del Carmen Martínez Martínez, eds, pp. 43–64. Madrid: Sociedad Española de Estudios Mayas.

Wedel, Waldo R. 1952. Structural Investigations in 1943. In *La Venta, Tabasco: A Study of Olmec Ceramics and Art.* Philip Drucker, ed, pp. 34–79. Bureau of American Ethnology Bulletin 153. Washington, D.C.: Bureau of American Ethnology.

Weiant, Clarence W. 1943. *An Introduction to the Ceramics of Tres Zapotes, Veracruz, Mexico.* Smithsonian Institution Bureau of American Ethnology, Bulletin 139. Washington, D.C.: Smithsonian Institution.

Wendt, Carl J. 2003a. Early Formative Domestic Organization and Community Patterning in the San Lorenzo Tenochtitlán Region, Veracruz, Mexico. Ph.D. dissertation, Department of Anthropology, Pennsylvania State University.

———. 2003b. Buried Occupational Deposits at Tres Zapotes: The Results of an Auger Testing Program. In *Settlement Archaeology and Political Economy at Tres Zapotes, Veracruz, Mexico.* Christopher A. Pool, ed, pp. 32–46. Cotsen Institute of Archaeology Monograph 50. Los Angeles, CA: Cotsen Institute of Archaeology, University of California.

———. 2009. The Scale and Structure of Bitumen Processing in Early Formative

Olmec Households. *Archaeological Papers of the American Anthropological Association*. 19(1): 33–44.

Wendt, Carl J, and Ann Cyphers. 2008. How the Olmec used Bitumen in ancient Mesoamerica. *Journal of Anthropological Archaeology* 27: 175–191.

Wendt, Carl J., and Shan-Tan Lu. 2006. Sourcing Archaeological Bitumen in the Olmec Region. *Journal of Archaeological Science* 33:89–97.

West, Robert C., Norbert P. Psuty, and Bruce G. Thom. 1969. *The Tabasco Lowlands of Southeastern Mexico*. Technical Report No. 17. Baton Rouge LA: Coastal Studies Institute.

Wetherington, Ronald K. 1978. The Ceramic Chronology of Kaminaljuyu. In *The Ceramics of Kaminaljuyu*. Ronald K. Wetherington, ed, pp. 115–149. University Park, PA: The Pennsylvania State University.

Whalen, Michael E. 1983. Reconstructing Early Formative Village Organization in Oaxaca, Mexico. *American Antiquity* 48(1): 17–43.

Whaley, Gordon W. 1946. Rubber, Heritage of the American Tropics. *The Scientific Monthly* 62(1): 21–31.

White, Christine D., and Henry P. Schwarcz. 1989. Ancient Maya Diet: As Inferred from Isotopic and Chemical Analysis of Human Bone. *Journal of Archaeological Science* 16:451–474.

Wicke, Charles R. 1971. *Olmec: An Early Art Style of Pre-Columbian Mexico*. Tuscon, AZ: University of Arizona Press.

Wilk, Richard R. 1988. Maya Household Organization: Evidence and Analogies. In *Household and Community in the Mesoamerican Past*. Richard R. Wilk and Wendy A. Ashmore, eds, pp. 135–151. Albuquerque, NM: University of New Mexico Press.

Wilk, Richard R., and Wendy A. Ashmore, eds. 1988. *Household and Community in the Mesoamerican Past*. Albuquerque, NM: University of New Mexico Press.

Wilk, Richard R., and Harold L. Wilhite Jr. 1991. The Community of Cuello: Patterns of Household and Settlement Change. In *Cuello: An Early Maya Community in Belize*. Norman Hammond, ed, pp. 118–133. Cambridge: Cambridge University Press.

Willey, Gordon R. 1953. *Prehistoric Settlement Patterns in the Virú Valley, Peru*. Smithsonian Institution Bulletin 155. Washington, D.C.: Smithsonian Institution Bureau of American Ethnology.

———. 1965. *Prehistoric Maya Settlements in the Belize Valley*. Papers of the Peabody Museum of Archaeology and Ethnology, vol. 54. Cambridge, MA: Peabody Museum.

————. 1970a. *The Real Xe Ceramics of Seibal, Peten, Guatemala*. Monographs and Papers in Maya Archeology 61. Cambridge, MA: Peabody Museum of Archaeology and Ethnology, Harvard University.

————. 1970b. Type descriptions of the ceramics of the Real Xe Complex, Seibal, Petén, Guatemala. In *Monographs and Papers in Maya Archaeology, vol. 61*. William R. Bullard, ed, pp. 313–355. Cambridge, MA: Peabody Museum of Archaeology and Ethnology, Harvard University.

————. 1973a. *The Altar de Sacrificios excavations: General Summary and Conclusions*. Papers of the Peabody Museum of Archaeology and Ethnology, vol. 64, No. 3. Cambridge, MA: Peabody Museum.

————. 1973b. Mesoamerican Art and Iconography and the Integrity of the Mesoamerican Ideological System. In *The Iconography of Middle American Sculpture*. Ignacio Bernal, Michael D. Coe, George Kubler, Gordon R. Willey, and J. Eric Thompson, eds, pp. 153–162. New York, NY: Metropolitan Museum of Art.

————. 1977. Rise of Maya Civilization; A Summary View. In *The Origins of Maya Civilization*. Richard E. W. Adams, ed, pp. 383–423. Albuquerque, NM: University of New Mexico Press.

————. 1978. *Excavations at Seibal, No. 1, Artifacts*. Memoirs of the Peabody Museum of Archaeology and Ethnology, Vol. 14. Cambridge, MA: Peabody Museum of Archaeology and Ethnology, Harvard University.

————. 1990. General Summary and Conclusions. In *Excavations at Seibal, Department of Peten, Guatemala*. Gordon R. Willey, ed. Memoirs of the Peabody Museum, 17. Cambridge, MA: Peabody Museum of Archaeology and Ethnology, Harvard University.

Willey, Gordon R., William R. Bullard Jr., John B. Glass, and James C. Gifford. 1965. *Prehistoric Maya Settlements in the Belize Valley*. Papers of the Peabody Museum of Archaeology and Ethnology, vol. 54. Cambridge, MA: Peabody Museum of Archaeology and Ethnology, Harvard University.

Willey, Gordon R., and James Gifford. 1961. Pottery of the Holmul I Style from Barton Ramie, British Honduras. In *Essays in Pre-Columbian Art and Archaeology*. Samuel K. Lothrop, ed, pp. 151–170. Cambridge, MA: Harvard University Press.

Willey, Gordon R., and Philip Phillips. 1958. *Method and Theory in American Archaeology*. Chicago, IL: University of Chicago Press.

Willey, Gordon R., and Jeremy A. Sabloff. 1980. *A History of American Archaeology*. 2nd edition. San Francisco, CA: W. H. Freeman.

Willey, Gordon R., A. Leyard Smith, Gair Tourtellot III, and Ian Graham. 1975. *Excavations at Seibal, No. 1, Introduction, The Site and its Setting*. Memoirs of the Peabody Museum of Archaeology and Ethnology, Vol. 13. Cambridge, MA: Peabody Museum of Archaeology and Ethnology, Harvard University.

Willey, Gordon R., A. Ledyard Smith, and Jeremy A. Sabloff. 1982. *Excavations at Seibal, Department of Peten, Guatemala*. Peabody Museum of Archaeology and Ethnology, Harvard University. Cambridge, MA: Harvard University Press.

Williams, Howell, and Robert F. Heizer. 1965. Sources of Stones Used in Prehistoric Mesoamerican Sites. *Contributions of the University of California Archaeological Research Facility* 1:1–39.

Wills, W. H. and Robert D. Leonard, eds. 1994. *The Ancient Southwestern Community*. Albuquerque, NM: University of New Mexico Press.

Winfield Capitaine, Frederick 1988. *La Estela 1 de La Mojarra*. Research Reports on Ancient Maya Writing Publication 16. Washington, D.C.: Center for Maya Research.

Wing, Elizabeth S., and Sylvia Scudder. 1991. The Exploitation of Animals. In *Cuello: An Early Maya Community in Belize*. Norman Hammond, ed, pp. 84–97. Cambridge, England: Cambridge University Press.

Winter, Marcus. 1989. *Oaxaca: The Archaeological Record*. Mexico, DF: Editorial Minutiae Mexicana.

———. 1994. Los Altos de Oaxaca y los Olmecas. In *Los Olmecas en Mesoamerica*. John E. Clark, ed, pp. 119–141. Mexico, D.F.: El Equilibrista.

———. 2004. *Oaxaca: The Archaeological Record*. 2nd edition. Oaxaca, Mexico: Editorial Minutiae Mexicana.

———. 2007. Recent Archaeological Investigations of Preclassic Occupations in the Southern Isthmus of Tehuantepec. In *Archaeology, Art, and Ethnogenesis in Mesoamerican Prehistory: Papers in Honor of Gareth W. Lowe*. Lynneth S. Lowe and Mary E. Pye, eds, pp. 193–207. Papers of the New World Archaeological Foundation, No. 68. Provo, UT: New World Archaeological Foundation, Brigham Young University.

Wisdom, Charles. 1940. *The Chorti Indian of Guatemala*. Chicago, IL: University of Chicago Press.

Wolf, Eric R. 1982. *Europe and the People Without History*. Berkeley, CA: University of California Press.

Woods, James C., and Gene L. Titmus. 1994a. Piedra en Piedra: Perspectivas de la Civilización Maya através de los Estudios Líticos. In *VII Simposio de Investigaciones Arqueológicas en Guatemala, 1993*. Juan Pedro Laporte and Hector L. Escobedo, eds, pp. 349–368. Guatemala: Ministerio de Cultura y Deportes, Instituto de Antropología e Historia, Asociacion Tikal.

———. 1994b. Stone on Stone: Perspectives of Maya Civilization from Lithic Studies.

Eighth Palenque Round Table. Martha J. Macri and Jan McHargue, eds, pp. 479–489. San Francisco, CA: The Pre-Columbian Art Research Institute.

———. 1996. Stone on Stone: Perspectives of Maya Civilization from Lithic Studies. In *Eighth Palenque Round Table, 1993.* Merle Greene Robertson, Martha J. Macri, and Jan McHargue, eds, pp. 479–489. San Francisco, CA: Pre-Columbian Art Research Institute.

Wright, Henry T. 1977. Recent Research on the Origin of the State. *Annual Review of Anthropology* 6:279–397.

———. 1978. Toward an Explanation of the Origin of the State. In *Origins of the State: The Anthropology of Political Evolution.* R. Cohen and E. R. Service, eds, pp. 49–68. Philadelphia: Institute for the Study of Human Issues.

———. 1986. The Evolution of Civilizations. In *American Archaeology, Past and Future: A Celebration of the Society for American Archaeology, 1935–1985.* David D. Meltzer, John A. Fowler, and Jeremy A. Sabloff, eds, pp. 323–365. Washington, D.C.: Smithsonian Institution Press.

Wright, Henry T., and Gregory A. Johnson. 1975. Population, exchange and Early State Formation in Southwestern Iran. *American Anthropologist* 77:267–289.

Yaeger, Jason. 2000. Changing Patterns of Social Organization: The Late and Terminal Classic Communities at San Lorenzo, Cayo District, Belize. Ph.D. dissertation. Department of Anthropology, University of Pennsylvania.

Yoffee, Norman. 1988. The Collapse of Ancient Mesopotamian States and Civilizations. In *The Collapse of Ancient States and Civilizations.* Norman Yoffee and George L. Cowgill, eds, pp.44–68. Tucson: University of Arizona Press.

———. 2005. *Myths of the Archaic State: Evolution of the Earliest Cities, States, and Civilizations.* Cambridge: Cambridge University Press.

Zeitlin, Judith F. 1978. Community Distribution and Local Economy on the Southern Isthmus of Tehuantepec: An Archaeological and Ethnohistorical Investigation. Ph.D. dissertation, Department of Anthropology, Yale University.

Zeitlin, Robert N. 1978. Long-Distance Exchange and the Growth of a Regional Center on the Southern Isthmus of Tehuantepec, Mexico. In *Prehistoric Coastal Adaptations: The Economy and Ecology of Maritime Middle America.* Barbara L. Stark and Barbara Voorhies, eds, pp. 183–210. New York, NY: Academic Press.

———. 1979. Preclassic Exchange on the Southern Isthmus of Tehuantepec, Mexico. Ph.D. dissertation, Department of Anthropology, Yale University.

———. 1982. Toward a More Comprehensive Model of Interregional Commodity Distribution: Political Variables and Prehistoric Obsidian Procurement in Mesoamerica. *American Antiquity* 47:260–275.

———. 1990. The Isthmus and the Valley of Oaxaca: Questions about Zapotec Imperialism in Formative Period Mesoamerica. *American Antiquity* 55:250–261.

———. 1993. Pacific Coastal Laguna Zope: A Regional Center in the Terminal Formative Hinterlands of Monte Albán. *Ancient Mesoamerica* 4:85–101.

———. 1994. Accounting for the Prehistoric Long-Distance Movement of Goods with a Measure of Style. *World Archaeology* 26(2): 209–234.

———. 2001a. Laguna Zope (Oaxaca, Mexico). In *Archaeology of Ancient Mexico and Central America: An Encyclopedia*. Susan T. Evans and David L. Webster, eds, pp. 393–94. New York, NY: Garland Publishing.

———. 2001b. Oaxaca and Tehuantepec Region. In *Archaeology of Ancient Mexico and Central America: An Encyclopedia*, Susan T. Evans and David L. Webster, eds, pp. 537–546. New York, NY: Garland Publishing.

Zeitlin, Robert N., and Arthur A. Joyce. 1999. The Zapotec-imperialism Argument: Insights from the Oaxaca Coast. *Current Anthropology* 40:383–92.

Zender, Marc U. 2005. The Raccoon Glyph in Classic Maya Writing. *PARI Journal* 5(4): 6–11.

Zurita, Judith, and Ann Cyphers. 2008. El Contexto Arqueológico de un Monumento Olmeca. Poster presentation at the Congreso Interno, Instituto de Investigaciones Antropológicas, Universidad Nacional Autónoma de México, October 7–10, 2008.

200

SOLUTIONS FOR INTERIOR DESIGN
SOLUTIONS DE DESIGN D'INTÉRIEUR
LÖSUNGEN ZUR RAUMGESTALTUNG
TIPS VOOR JE INTERIEUR

© 2009 **booQs** publishers bvba
Godefriduskaai 22
2000 Antwerp
Belgium
Tel.: +32 3 226 66 73
Fax: +32 3 226 53 65
www.booqs.be
info@booqs.be

ISBN: 978-94-60650-11-6
WD: D/2009/11978/012
(Q012)

Editorial coordination: Simone K. Schleifer
Assistant to editorial coordination:
Aitana Lleonart
Editor & texts: Àlex Sánchez Vidiella
Art direction: Mireia Casanovas Soley
Design and layout coordination:
Claudia Martínez Alonso
Layout: Print Plates
Translation: Cillero & De Motta
Cover photo: © Kei Sugino

Editorial project:

LOFT publications
Via Laietana, 32, 4.º, of. 92
08003 Barcelona, Spain
Tel.: +34 932 688 088
Fax: +34 932 687 073
loft@loftpublications.com
www.loftpublications.com

Printed in China

200

SOLUTIONS FOR INTERIOR DESIGN
SOLUTIONS DE DESIGN D'INTÉRIEUR
LÖSUNGEN ZUR RAUMGESTALTUNG
TIPS VOOR JE INTERIEUR

014

068

176 230 304

Modern interior design aims to create spaces suited to occupants' lifestyles. Home interiors are a reflection of the spirit of our time, of how we live and how we work. This book compiles examples of modern homes, categorized by rooms, in order to illustrate the trends and influences inspiring interior design.

The decoration of our homes reveals our interests and our personality. Our homes are our refuge, the place where we escape from the stress in our everyday lives. In an age where we are exposed to a constant barrage of information and different influences, we like to think of our homes as a place where we only allow the parts of this cultural barrage that interest us.

Our homes therefore become an expression of our reaction and interpretation of this information. And, among other trends, the minimalist approach has appeared as a breath of fresh air for a society that is overwhelmed by information and speed.

Some modern interior designs achieve a unique interaction with our environment, which offers art and technologies and a richness and diversity of cultures. Elements such as graphic, industrial, and fashion design, together with music and visual arts have all contributed to creating meaningful and attractive spaces.

In general terms, we can observe three important traits of modern rooms: comfort, quality, and harmony. Everyone wants to be comfortable in their own home. The rooms in this compilation exude relaxation, pampering, and the friendly interaction of the individuals who share their atmosphere.

This volume gathers together examples that illustrate numerous ideas, all attractive as well as creative.

L'objectif de la décoration d'un intérieur moderne est de créer des espaces qui s'adaptent aux styles de vie de leurs occupants. Les intérieurs reflètent l'état d'esprit de notre époque, notre mode de vie et de travail. Dans ce livre, on découvre des exemples de maisons actuelles, classées par pièces, qui illustrent les tendances et les influences qui ont inspiré leur décoration intérieure.

La décoration d'un logement révèle nos centres d'intérêts et notre personnalité. Notre domicile est notre refuge, le lieu où nous échappons au stress quotidien. À une époque où nous nous exposons inévitablement à un bombardement constant d'information et d'influences diverses, il est réconfortant de penser que notre maison est un espace où nous recevons uniquement les personnes qu'il nous plaît d'inviter.

Par conséquent, nos maisons deviennent l'expression de notre réaction et de notre interprétation de toute cette information. Parmi toutes ces tendances, l'optique minimaliste a fait son apparition, elle apporte une bouffée d'air frais dans une société étouffée par les suggestions et la vitesse.

Certaines décorations d'intérieurs modernes ont réussi à interagir de manière particulière avec notre environnement, ce qui apporte une richesse et une diversité artistique, culturelle et technologique. Le design graphique, industriel ou de mode d'une part, mais également la musique et les arts visuels, ont contribué à créer des espaces éloquents et visuellement plaisants.

En général on peut observer trois caractéristiques principales dans les pièces modernes : le confort, la qualité et l'harmonie. Nous voulons tous nous sentir bien chez nous. Les pièces véhiculent une sensation de détente et de confort et favorisent l'établissement d'une relation agréable entre les personnes qui sont plongées dans cette même ambiance.

Ce volume rassemble des modèles classés par pièces pour illustrer de nombreuses idées, toutes visuellement attrayantes et créatives.

Das Ziel moderner Innenarchitektur besteht darin, Bereiche zu schaffen, die sich dem Lebensstil ihrer Bewohner anpassen. Die Räume spiegeln neben dem Geist unserer Zeit auch unseren Lebens- und Arbeitsstil wieder. In diesem Buch werden Beispiele aktueller Häuser vorgestellt, nach Räumen gegliedert, um die Trends und Einflüsse zu zeigen, die ihre Innengestaltung inspiriert haben.

Die Gestaltung unseres Heims enthüllt unsere Interessen und unsere Persönlichkeit. Unser Heim ist der Zufluchtsort, an dem wir uns dem alltäglichen Stress entziehen. Zu einer Zeit, in der wir unweigerlich einer konstanten Bombardierung mit Informationen und den verschiedensten Einflüssen ausgesetzt sind, beruhigt der Gedanke, mit unserem Heim über einen Bereich zu verfügen, zu dem wir nur willkommenen Menschen Zugang gewähren.

So werden unsere Häuser Ausdruck dafür, wie wir all diese Informationen auslegen und darauf reagieren. Unter den vielfältigen Trends ist eine minimalistische Betrachtungsweise entstanden, die einen Hauch frische Luft in eine Gescllschaft bringt, die unter dem Druck der Geschwindigkeit und verwirrender Bezugspunkte steht.

Einigen modernen Innengestaltungen ist es gelungen, auf besondere Art mit unserer Umwelt zu interagieren und damit ein Mehr an künstlerischer, kultureller und technologischer Vielfalt einzubringen. Grafik-, Industrie- und Modedesign wie auch Musik und visuelle Künste haben dazu beigetragen, aussagekräftige und optisch attraktive Räume zu schaffen.

Generell sind drei bedeutende Züge in modernen Räumen zu erkennen: Komfort, Qualität und Harmonie. Wir alle möchten uns in unserem eigenen Haus wohl fühlen. Entspannung und Komfort ausstrahlende Räume fördern eine angenehme Beziehung unter den Menschen, die sich dieses Ambiente teilen.

Dieser Band enthält nach Räumen gegliederte Beispiele zur Illustration zahlreicher optisch attraktiver und kreativer Ideen.

Het doel van de moderne binnenhuisarchitectuur is het creëren van ruimten die zich aanpassen aan de levensstijl van de inwoners. De interieurs laten de geest van onze tijd, onze leef- en werkwijze zien. In dit boek worden voorbeelden van actuele huizen getoond, geclassificeerd volgens het type vertrek, die de tendensen en invloeden illustreren die het interieurontwerp hebben geïnspireerd.

De inrichting van ons huis onthult onze interesses en onze persoonlijkheid. Ons huis is ons toevluchtsoord, de plek waar we aan de dagelijkse stress ontsnappen. In een tijdperk waarin we constant worden gebombardeerd met informatie en verschillende invloeden, troosten we ons met de gedachte dat ons huis een ruimte is waar we zelf bepalen wie we er toelaten.

Bijgevolg zijn onze huizen de uiting van onze reactie op en de interpretatie van al deze informatie geworden. Onder de vele trends dook de minimalistische benadering op die voor een frisse wind heeft gezorgd in een samenleving die wordt overstelpt met referenties en snelheid.

Sommige moderne interieurs zijn erin geslaagd op een bijzondere manier op ons milieu in te werken, wat rijkdom en artistieke, culturele en technologische diversiteit met zich meebrengt. Zowel grafisch, industrieel als modeontwerp, evenals muziek en beeldende kunsten hebben bijgedragen aan de creatie van sprekende en visueel aantrekkelijke ruimten.

Over het algemeen vallen in moderne vertrekken drie belangrijke kenmerken op: comfort, kwaliteit en harmonie. We willen ons in ons eigen huis allemaal op ons gemak voelen. De vertrekken stralen ontspanning en geriefelijkheid uit en bevorderen bovendien een prettige relatie tussen de personen die deze ruimten delen.

In dit boek staan voorbeelden, volgens vertrek geclassificeerd, die talrijke, visueel aantrekkelijke en creatieve ideeën laten zien.

ENTRANCES & STAIRS > VESTIBULES ET ESCALIERS

DIELEN UND TREPPEN > HALLEN EN TRAPPEN

Entrances, hallways and staircases should be well lit and maintained, and deserve the same attention to detail and design as any other domestic space, since they are the spaces that receive most traffic.

Eingänge, Dielen und Treppen sollten über gute Beleuchtung verfügen und leicht in Ordnung zu halten sein. Diese Bereiche verdienen hinsichtlich Design und Details die gleiche Aufmerksamkeit wie alle anderen Räumlichkeiten, da sie außerdem den meisten Verkehr verzeichnen.

Les entrées, les vestibules et les escaliers doivent être correctement éclairés et entretenus. Ces espaces méritent la même attention en termes de design et de détails que tout autre espace de la maison, d'autant plus que ce sont les plus fréquentés de la maison.

Hallen en trappen dienen goed verlicht te zijn en goed te worden onderhouden. Deze ruimten verdienen dezelfde aandacht wat het ontwerp en de details betreft als elke andere kamer in huis, aangezien zij vaak de meest bezochte ruimten van de woning zijn.

01

Enclosing the entrance hall with a glass wall opens the home's threshold to the exterior and is immediately inviting.

Si le vestibule est délimité par une paroi en verre, la porte d'entrée s'ouvrira sur l'extérieur provoquant une sensation de bienvenue.

Wird die Diele mit einer Glaswand abgegrenzt, öffnet sich die Haustür nach außen hin und vermittelt einen einladenden Eindruck.

Als de hal met een glaswand begrensd wordt, geeft de huisdeur uit op het exterieur wat een gastvrije indruk wekt.

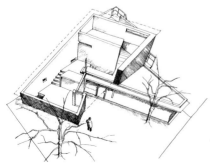

02 *Front doors can be as embellished or as minimalist as the architecture of your home dictates.*

Les portes principales peuvent être aussi baroques ou minimalistes que l'architecture du reste de la maison.

Die Haustüren können so barock oder minima-
listisch wie die Architektur Ihres Hauses sein.

De hoofddeuren kunnen net zo barok of mini-
malistisch zijn als de architectuur van uw huis.

03 Constructing bespoke concrete staircases can be complicated. Make sure the design adheres to building regulations.

La construction d'un escalier en béton sur mesure peut s'avérer complexe. Vérifiez que le design respecte les normes de construction.

Der Bau einer maßgeschneiderten Betontreppe kann kompliziert sein. Prüfen Sie, ob die Konstruktion die Bauvorschriften erfüllt.

De bouw van een betonnen trap op maat kan gecompliceerd zijn. Controleer of het ontwerp voldoet aan de bouwnormen.

04

Straight-run stairs have no turns or angles, and are the simplest form of stairway to install.

Les escaliers qui ne tournent pas ou n'ont pas d'angles sont les plus simples à installer.

Treppen ohne Wendungen oder Winkel sind am einfachsten einzubauen.

Trappen zonder draaiingen of hoeken zijn het gemakkelijkst om te installeren.

05

As seen in traditional Japanese architecture, even a shallow pond can create an evocative exterior pathway to a home.

Comme l'a démontré l'architecture tradition-nelle japonaise, même un bassin peu profond peut constituer un passage extérieur.

Wie schon die traditionelle japanische Architektur gezeigt hat, kann bereits ein flacher Teich einen inspirierenden Außenflur hervorbringen.

Zoals de traditionele Japanse architectuur heeft aangetoond kan zelfs een ondiepe vijver een wandelpad creëren dat tot de verbeelding spreekt.

06 Although it needs re-touching quite regularly, paint is a cheap and effective finish for concrete stairs.

Même s'il faut y apporter une retouche de temps en temps, la peinture reste une finition économique et pratique pour les marches en béton.

Obwohl die Farbe regelmäßig nachbearbeitet werden muss, stellt sie eine günstige und wirksame Ausführung der Betontreppenstufen dar.

Een goedkope en efficiënte manier om betonnen treden af te werken is ze te verven, hoewel dit wel regelmatig onderhouden moet worden.

07

Adjustable blinds permit as much light exposure to the interior of your home as you desire.

*Les stores réglables peuvent révéler l'intérieur
de la maison si on le souhaite.*

*Regulierbare Jalousien können nach Belieben
Einblick ins Hausinnere gewähren.*

*Door middel van verstelbare rolgordijnen kunt
u naar wens de lichtinval regelen en een blik op
het interieur toelaten.*

08

A 'floating' effect can be achieved by covering your steps in a contrasting material or color.

On peut obtenir un effet de suspension si l'on habille les marches de matériaux ou de couleurs offrant un contraste.

Anhand der Treppenstufenverkleidung mit Kontrastmaterialien oder –farben kann ein schwebender Eindruck erzielt werden.

Als contrastrijke materialen en kleuren gebruikt worden voor de bekleding van de treden, kan men een hangeffect krijgen.

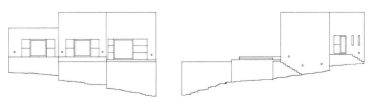

09 *For very narrow spaces, hanging and sus-pended staircases are not suitable.*

Les escaliers suspendus ne sont pas recom-mandés pour des espaces très étroits.

Hänge- und Schwebetreppen sind für sehr enge Platzverhältnisse nicht empfehlenswert.

Hangtrappen zijn niet aan te raden voor zeer smalle ruimten.

10

In contemporary homes, halls and stairways should be clutter-free in order to create a sense of seamless connection and flowing spaces.

Dans les maisons modernes, les vestibules et les escaliers doivent rester dégagés pour créer une continuité et une mobilité parfaites.

In den heutigen Häusern müssen Dielen und Treppen frei gezeigt werden, um perfekte Verbindung und Mobilität zu erreichen.

In moderne huizen dienen hallen en trappen vrij te zijn van obstakels om voor een perfecte verbinding en mobiliteit te zorgen.

11 *Installing a large window next to an entrance lets in light and brings in the outside.*

L'installation d'une grande fenêtre à côté d'une entrée permet de laisser pénétrer la lumière et de capter des fragments de l'extérieur.

Der Einbau eines großzügigen Fensters neben dem Eingang lässt Licht einfallen und Fragmente von außen aufnehmen.

De installatie van een groot raam naast de ingang zorgt ervoor dat het licht kan binnendringen en dat fragmenten kunnen opgevangen worden van wat er zich buiten afspeelt.

12

Stairs and doors can be visually pleasing and still comply with safety criteria.

Les escaliers et les portes peuvent être à la fois beaux à voir et répondre aux exigences de sécurité.

Treppen und Türen können einen angenehmen Anblick bieten und trotzdem die Sicherheitsanforderungen erfüllen.

Trappen en deuren kunnen er aantrekkelijk uitzien en toch voldoen aan de veiligheidseisen.

13

These floating stairs are the perfect choice for this classic minimalist lounge room.

L'escalier suspendu est un choix approprié pour ce salon aux lignes minimalistes classiques.

Die Hängetreppe ist eine angemessene Wahl für dieses Wohnzimmer mit klassischen minimalistischen Linien.

De hangtrap is een geschikte keuze voor deze zitkamer met klassieke minimalistische lijnen.

14

Concertina glass doors are ideal for terraces and decks.

Les portes vitrées en accordéon sont parfaites pour accéder à la cour et à la terrasse.

Glastüren im Akkordeonstil sind ideale Eingänge für Innenhof und Terrasse.

De glazen harmonicadeuren zijn ideaal als toegang tot een patio of terras.

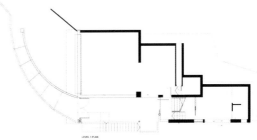

LEVEL 1 PLAN

053

15

A short flight of steps generally doesn't need a balustrade or any other safety feature.

En règle générale, une petite volée de marches n'a pas besoin de rambarde ni d'aucun autre type d'élément de sécurité.

Ein kleiner Treppenabschnitt erfordert norma-lerweise weder Geländer noch sonstige Sicher-heitselemente.

Een korte trap vereist gewoonlijk geen leuning of een andere soort beveiliging.

16 Hardwearing, industrial carpet is ideal for heavy traffic stairs and halls.

Les tapis résistants, de type industriel, sont la solution idéale pour les escaliers et les vestibules très fréquentés.

Widerstandsfähige Teppiche industrieller Art sind ideal für Treppen und Dielen mit hohem Durchgangsverkehr.

Stevige industriële vloerbekleding is ideaal voor trappen en voor inkomhallen die vaak betreden worden.

17

Spiral staircases, generally made of metal, are growing in popularity, especially for small spaces.

Les escaliers en colimaçon, traditionnellement fabriqués en métal, sont de plus en plus populaires, tout particulièrement dans les espaces restreints.

Wendeltreppen, die normalerweise mit Metall hergestellt werden, werden besonders für kleine Bereiche immer beliebter.

Wenteltrappen, meestal van metaal, worden steeds populairder, vooral voor kleine ruimten.

18

These aluminum-framed jalousie (louvered) windows perfectly compliment the simple U-shaped stairs.

Ces persiennes, avec leur encadrement en aluminium, viennent compléter à la perfection ces escaliers simples en forme de « U ».

Diese Jalousien mit Aluminiumrahmen sind eine perfekte Ergänzung zur einfachen Treppe in U-Form.

Deze jaloezieën met aluminium kozijn passen perfect bij de eenvoudige U-vormige trappen.

LIVING ROOMS > SALONS

WOHNZIMMER > WOONKAMERS

The living room is one of the most important spaces in a house because it is the meeting point for the family. Sometimes it is also the largest room in the house, and so creating character using decorative details can prove a challenge.

Das Wohnzimmer als Familientreffpunkt ist einer der wichtigsten Räume im Haus. In manchen Fällen ist es auch das größte Zimmer, so dass es schwierig sein kann, ihm anhand dekorativer Details den gewünschten Charakter zu verleihen.

Le salon est l'une des pièces les plus importantes de la maison car elle se transforme en point de rencontre familiale. Souvent, c'est aussi la plus grande pièce, c'est pourquoi conférer un caractère à cet espace par des détails de décoration peut s'avérer difficile.

De woonkamer is een van de belangrijkste vertrekken van de woning, aangezien deze ruimte het ontmoetingspunt van het gezin is. Soms is het ook de grootste Kamer, vandaar dat het soms moeilijk is om dit vertrek aan de hand van decoratieve details een eigen karakter te geven.

19

In this house the owners have chosen a comfortable sofa complemented with yellow 'butterfly' chairs that echo the tone of the wall tapestry.

Dans cette habitation, on a choisi un canapé confortable complété par des fauteuils papillons qui s'accordent avec le ton du mur.

In dieser Wohnung hat man sich für ein bequemes Sofa entschieden. Es wird durch Fledermaussessel ergänzt, die zum Farbton der Wand passen.

In deze woning is gekozen voor een comfortabele bank en gele vlinderstoelen, die met de kleur van het wandtapijt combineren.

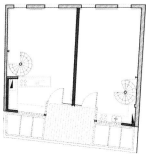

20

It is useful to know how the living room is going to be used before starting to decorate to find a style that suits the owners' personal tastes.

Savoir à quel usage on destine le salon peut se révéler utile avant de procéder à sa décoration, on obtiendra ainsi un style plus personnel.

Vor dem Dekorieren des Wohnzimmers ist es angebracht, sich zu überlegen, wie es genutzt werden soll, um durch die Dekoration einen persönlicheren Stil zu erreichen.

Het kan nuttig zijn om eerst na te gaan welke bestemming we aan onze woonkamer geven, alvorens haar in te richten. Zo kan een persoonlijke stijl worden gevonden.

21 It is important to feel content and relaxed in a living room so gentle colors, such as these, are an excellent option.

Dans le salon, il est important de pouvoir s'amuser et se détendre. Les couleurs douces, comme celles-ci, constituent un bon choix.

Im Wohnzimmer sind Genuss und Entspannung wichtig. Ruhige Farben – wie in diesem Beispiel – sind eine gute Wahl.

Het is belangrijk om in de woonkamer te genieten en te ontspannen. Rustige kleuren, zoals de kleuren in dit voorbeeld, zijn een goede optie.

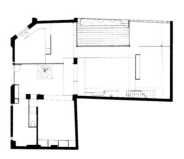

22

Natural wood floors and strong colors are a great way to create a space with contrasts, which is also warm.

Les sols en bois naturel de couleurs foncées sont une bonne alternative quand on veut obtenir un espace contrasté et chaleureux à la fois.

Naturholzböden mit kräftigen Farben sind eine gute Alternative für einen kontrastreichen und gleichzeitig gemütlichen Raum.

Vloeren van natuurlijk hout in intense kleuren zijn een goed alternatief wanneer men een contrustrijkc ruimte wil creëren die tegelijkertijd een warme sfeer uitstraalt.

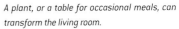

23

A plant, or a table for occasional meals, can transform the living room.

Une plante, ou une table pour boire ou manger de manière occasionnelle peuvent transformer votre salon.

Eine Pflanze oder ein Tisch, um nebenbei etwas zu sich nehmen zu können, können unser Wohnzimmer verwandeln.

Een plant of een tafel voor occasionele maaltijden kunnen onze woonkamer een andere uitstraling geven.

24

Here, juxtaposed linked spaces are connected by using the same parquet flooring and unifying the colors.

Dans ce cas, la juxtaposition des espaces est obtenue grâce à l'utilisation du même parquet et à l'homogénéisation des couleurs.

In diesem Fall entsteht die Verbindung der Bereiche durch den Einsatz des gleichen Parketts
und homogener Farben.

In dit geval wordt een harmonieuze opeenvol-
ging van ruimten verkregen door het gebruik
van dezelfde parketvloer en homogene kleuren.

25

The way the living room is used will require a certain lighting, whether natural or artificial.

Certaines exigences se présenteront, en fonction de la vocation du salon, concernant l'éclairage, qu'il soit naturel ou artificiel.

Je nach Verwendungszweck des Wohnzimmers entstehen unterschiedliche Anforderungen hinsichtlich natürlicher und künstlicher Beleuchtung.

Al naargelang het gebruik dat aan de woonkamer wordt toegekend, worden bepaalde eisen gesteld aan de natuurlijke en kunstmatige verlichting.

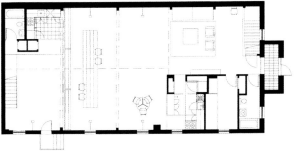

26

While bright, strong colors provide vitality and depth in living rooms, lighter tones produce serenity.

Alors que les couleurs vives et soutenues confèrent de la vitalité au salon, les tons plus clairs apportent davantage de sérénité.

Während glänzende und kräftige Farben dem Wohnzimmer viel Vitalität verleihen, bringen hellere Töne mehr Ruhe ein.

Terwijl sprekende en intense kleuren de woonkamer meer vitaliteit geven, brengen lichtere kleuren meer rust.

27

Windows in living rooms should let in plenty of light, but a system should be installed to cover them when necessary.

Les fenêtres du salon doivent garantir une bonne illumination même s'il faut disposer de systèmes adéquats pour réduire la lumière naturelle lorsque cela s'avère nécessaire.

Wohnzimmerfenster müssen gute Beleuchtung ermöglichen. Es müssen aber auch angemessene Systeme vorhanden sein, um die Tageslichteinstrahlung bei Bedarf reduzieren zu können.

De ramen van de woonkamer moeten een goede verlichting mogelijk maken, maar ze moeten ook over geschikte systemen beschikken om de natuurlijke verlichting zo nodig te reduceren.

28

The bedroom in this house is unusually located behind a concrete wall that separates it from the living room.

La disposition de la chambre de cette habitation est peu conventionnelle puisqu'elle se trouve derrière un mur en béton qui la sépare du salon.

Die Schlafzimmeranordnung dieser Wohnung ist recht ungewöhnlich, da es hinter einer Betonwand liegt, die es vom Wohnzimmer trennt.

De opstelling van de slaapkamer van deze woning is niet erg gebruikelijk. Zij bevindt zich namelijk achter een betonnen muur waarmee deze ruimte van de woonkamer wordt gescheiden.

29

Maintaining some elements of the original architecture, such as the wooden doors and interior concrete posts, gives this living room character.

Maintenir certains éléments de l'architecture originale donne du caractère au salon, comme ici, avec les portes en bois et les colonnes en béton.

Die Bewahrung einzelner Elemente der ursprünglichen Architektur verleiht dem Wohnzimmer Charakter, wie in diesem Beispiel die Holztüren und Betonsäulen.

Het behoud van enkele elementen van de oorspronkelijke architectuur geeft de woonkamer een persoonlijke uitstraling, zoals de houten deuren en de betonnen kolommen in dit voorbeeld.

30

Using light tones and cool materials, such as transparent surfaces, increases spatial fluidity.

L'emploi de tons clairs et de matières froides, comme des surfaces transparentes, permettent de fluidifier l'espace.

Helle Farbtöne und kalte Werkstoffe als transparente Flächen begünstigen ein fließendes Raumgefühl.

Het gebruik van lichte kleuren en koude materialen, zoals doorzichtige oppervlakken, zorgt ervoor dat de ruimten beter in elkaar overvloeien.

31

This attic has been located under the slope of the roof to make the most of the space and of the light coming in through the skylights.

Dans cet appartement sous les toits, le salon se trouve sous l'inclinaison de la mansarde afin de tirer parti de la niche du toit et de la lumière provenant des lucarnes.

In dieser Dachgeschosswohnung befindet sich das Wohnzimmer unter der Dachschräge, um den Dachfreiraum und das Licht der Dachluken zu nutzen.

In dit appartement bevindt de woonkamer zich onder het schuine zolderdak waarbij optimaal gebruik gemaakt wordt van de open ruimte van het dak en van het licht dat via de dakramen binnenvalt.

32

The kitchen often occupies a prime location that connects directly to the living room.

La cuisine se trouve souvent dans un espace central qui conduit directement au salon.

Die Küche befindet sich häufig im mittleren Be- De keuken bevindt zich vaak in een centrale
reich, der unmittelbar zum Wohnzimmer führt. ruimte die direct aan de woonkamer grenst.

33

The materials in each room emphasize the warmth the owners wanted.

Dans chaque pièce, les matériaux mettent l'accent sur l'aspect chaleureux que recherchent les propriétaires.

In jedem Raum wird anhand der Materialien die
von den Besitzern gesuchte Wärme betont.

In elk vertrek benadrukken de materialen de
warmte waar de eigenaars naar op zoek zijn.

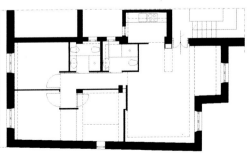

34

Neutral drapes are a good choice to separate living and dining rooms in small spaces.

Des rideaux de couleur neutre constituent une bonne solution pour ces espaces réduits où l'on souhaite séparer la salle à manger du salon.

Vorhänge in neutralen Farben sind eine gute Lösung bei reduzierten Platzverhältnissen, wo das Esszimmer vom Wohnzimmer getrennt werden soll.

Gordijnen in een neutrale kleur vormen een goede oplossing voor kleine ruimten waar men de eetkamer van de woonkamer wil scheiden.

35   When spaces are renovated, the original distri-   En réhabilitant les espaces on peut rompre la
      bution can be changed in order to place the liv-   distribution originale et placer le salon princi-
      ing room in the optimum location.   pal à l'endroit le mieux indiqué.

Beim Umbau der Räume kann man die ur-
sprüngliche Aufteilung aufheben und das
Hauptwohnzimmer an einen geeigneteren
Platz verlegen.

Bij verbouwingen kan de originele indeling worden doorbroken en kan voor de woonkamer de
meest ideale plek worden gezocht.

FUTURO PRIMIT

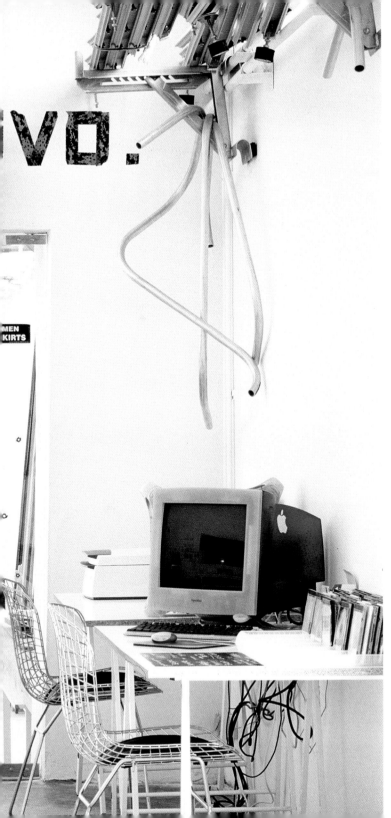

36

Any room is suitable for graphic art; this will add visual richness to the house.

On peut placer dans n'importe quelle pièce un objet de décoration graphique qui enrichit visuellement la maison.

In allen Räumen lässt sich die Wohnung durch graphische Mittel optisch bereichern.

Elk vertrek is geschikt voor een grafisch ontwerp die de woning visueel verrijkt.

37

When spaces are linked but a wall interrupts the visual connection, using white walls and ceilings can help to harmonize views.

Lorsque les espaces semblent se succéder entre des murs qui font obstacle à la connexion visuelle, le blanc des murs et le plafond contribue à harmoniser les plans.

Wenn die Räume wie zwischen Mauern, die die optische Verbindung unterbrechen, verkettet erscheinen, unterstützt weiße Farbe auf Wänden und Decken die Harmonisierung der Grundrisse.

Wanneer bij opeenvolgende ruimten de visuele verbinding door een muur belemmerd wordt, zorgt de witte kleur van de muren en het plafond voor harmonie.

38

An irregularly distributed house can make the rooms seem smaller and darker. To avoid this, choose furniture with dual functions.

Une distribution irrégulière de la maison peut donner l'impression que les pièces sont plus petites. Pour éviter cela, il faut choisir un mobilier deux en un.

Eine unregelmäßige Aufteilung der Wohnung kann dazu führen, dass die Räume kleiner erscheinen. Um das zu vermeiden, muss man sich für Mobiliar mit Doppeleinsatz entscheiden.

Een onregelmatige indeling van de woning kan ervoor zorgen dat de kamers kleiner lijken. Om dit te vermijden, kiest men best voor meubilair met dubbele functies.

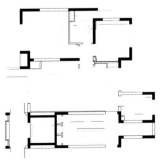

39

Rather than hiding spaces behind drapes, fill areas with glass surfaces.

Si l'on souhaite éviter de dissimuler des espaces derrière des rideaux, on peut entourer le volume de surfaces vitrées.

Sollen hinter Gardinen versteckte Bereiche vermieden werden, kann der Raum mit Glasflächen verkleidet werden.

Als men wil vermijden dat ruimten achter gordijnen aan het zicht worden onttrokken, kan glas gebruikt worden.

133

40

The living room is separated from the dining room and kitchen by a glass partition that insulates it from any noise.

Le salon est séparé de la salle à manger et de la cuisine par une paroi vitrée qui l'isole du bruit.

Das Wohnzimmer ist durch einen Glaswandschirm, der es von allen Geräuschen isoliert, vom Esszimmer und von der Küche getrennt.

De woonkamer is van de eetkamer en keuken gescheiden door middel van een glaswand die deze van elk geluid afschermt.

41

An elongated table provides more space for large dinner parties and helps to define the separation between the dining and living rooms.

Une longue table permettra de disposer d'un plus vaste espace pour de nombreux convives, et délimitera la zone de la salle à manger par rapport au salon.

Ein länglicher Tisch bietet mehr Platz für meh-
rere Gäste und grenzt den Esszimmerbereich
gleichzeitig vom Wohnzimmer ab.

Een lange tafel biedt meer plaats aan meerdere
tafelgenoten en begrenst de eetkamer ten op-
zichte van de woonkamer.

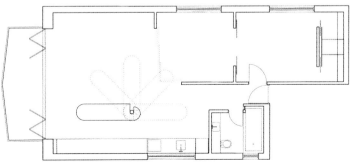

139

42

When white becomes a second skin covering the entire space, it guarantees the area has an open feeling.

Lorsque c'est le blanc qui recouvre intégralement l'espace, la luminosité à l'intérieur est garantie.

Ein komplett weiß verkleideter Raum garantiert die Lichtdurchlässigkeit des Inneren.

Door een ruimte volledig wit aan te kleden wordt de doorschijnendheid van het interieur gegarandeerd.

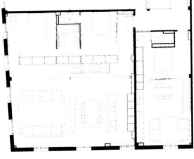

143

43

The L-shaped kitchen houses the hob, the sink, the work table and the storage compartments, ending in a table that creates a work space.

La cuisine en forme de L est équipée d'une plaque de cuisson, d'un évier, d'un plan de travail et de placards de rangement.

Die Küche in L-Form umfasst Induktionskoch-
feld, Spülbecken, Arbeitstisch und Vorratsabteile.

De L-vormige keuken beschikt over een induc-
tiekookplaat, een wasbak, een aanrecht en op-
bergruimten.

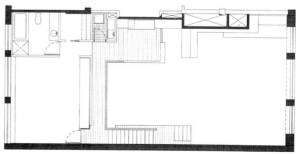

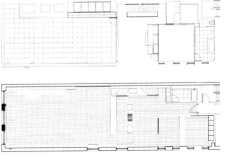

44

Keeping spaces free from superfluous decorative elements enables easy circulation between rooms.

Lorsque les espaces sont dépourvus d'éléments décoratifs superflus, la circulation entre les pièces en est facilitée.

In Bereichen ohne überflüssige Dekorationselemente verläuft der Verkehr zwischen den Räumen bequemer.

Als overbodige decoratieve elementen uit de ruimten worden gelaten, is het comfortabeler om van de ene naar de andere kamer te gaan.

45 To avoid the ordinary and add a touch of light and freshness, introduce a note of color to deconstruct the predominant color scheme.

On peut choisir d'introduire une touche de couleur qui rompt avec la base chromatique prédominante.

Man kann sich für die Einfügung eines Farb-
tons entscheiden, der die vorherrschende
Farbgrundlage unterbricht.

Men kan ervoor kiezen hier en daar wat kleur
aan te brengen zodat de overheersende
kleurbasis wordt doorbroken.

46

Industrial properties provide open spaces with many layout possibilities.

Les espaces industriels proposent des plans ouverts avec différentes options de distribution.

Industriebereiche garantieren offene Grundrisse mit unterschiedlichen Aufteilungsmöglichkeiten.

Industriële ruimten garanderen open ruimten met verschillende indelingsmogelijkheden.

47

The glazed walls afford views of the countryside and are a great idea if the architecture allows them.

Les parois vitrées renvoient des images du paysage et sont recommandées lorsque l'architecture le permet.

Glasumfriedungen bringen Landschaftsbilder zurück und sind empfehlenswert – vorausgesetzt, dass sie von der Architektur her möglich sind.

Glazen afsluitingen verschaffen uitzicht op het landschap en zijn aan te raden, mits de architectuur dit toestaat.

157

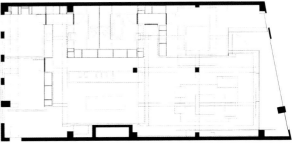

48

To create a certain independence between the areas, warm spaces have been alternated with sparsely decorated rooms.

Pour garantir une certaine indépendance entre les espaces, on alterne des espaces chauds avec des espaces à la décoration très épurée.

Um eine gewisse Selbständigkeit unter den Räumen zu gewähren, wechseln sich warme Bereiche mit anderen, dekorativ sehr reinen Bereichen ab.

Om een zekere onafhankelijkheid tussen de verschillende zones te creëren, werden warme ruimten afgewisseld met schaars gedecoreerde kamers.

49

The glazed walls, offering great views over the garden, create a connection between the exterior and interior spaces.

Les baies vitrées qui donnent sur le jardin établissent le lien entre intérieur et extérieur.

Glasumfriedungen mit Blick auf den Garten gewährleisten den Dialog zwischen Innen- und Außenbereich.

De glazen afsluitingen met uitzicht op de tuin garanderen de dialoog tussen binnen en buiten.

50

When trying to create a feeling of freedom, install large windows to produce a sense of space.

Si l'on recherche une sensation de liberté, les grandes fenêtres fourniront un effet d'amplitude.

Auf der Suche nach Freiheit bieten große
Glasflächen den Eindruck von Weite.

Als men op zoek is naar een gevoel van vrijheid
dan zorgen grote ramen voor een ruimte-effect.

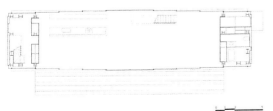

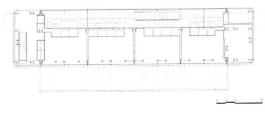

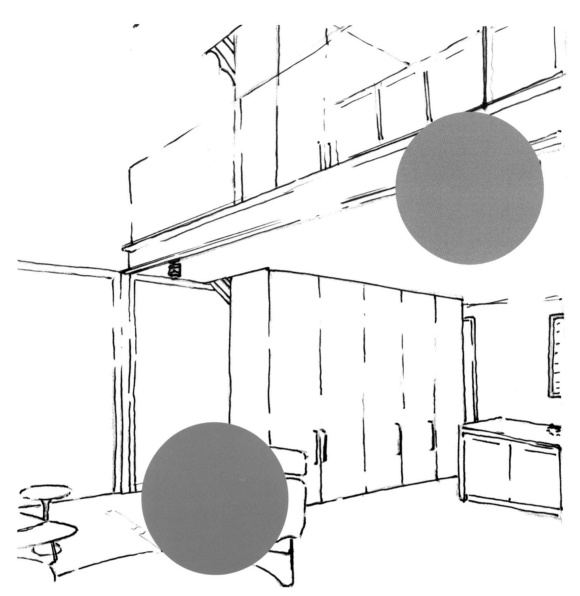

51

The expressive possibilities of artificial light are infinite, well-placed spotlights can help to define different areas.

Les nuances de la lumière artificielle sont infinies. La disposition des sources de lumière peut servir à délimiter différentes zones.

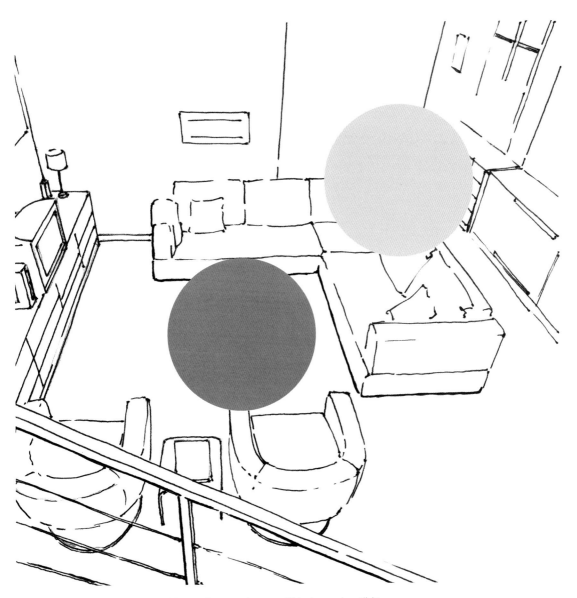

Die Ausdrucksmöglichkeiten künstlichen Lichts sind unendlich. Die Anbringung von Strahlern kann die Abgrenzung unterschiedlicher Bereiche unterstützen.

De expressieve mogelijkheden van kunstlicht zijn oneindig. Het plaatsen van spotlights kan helpen om bepaalde zones te begrenzen.

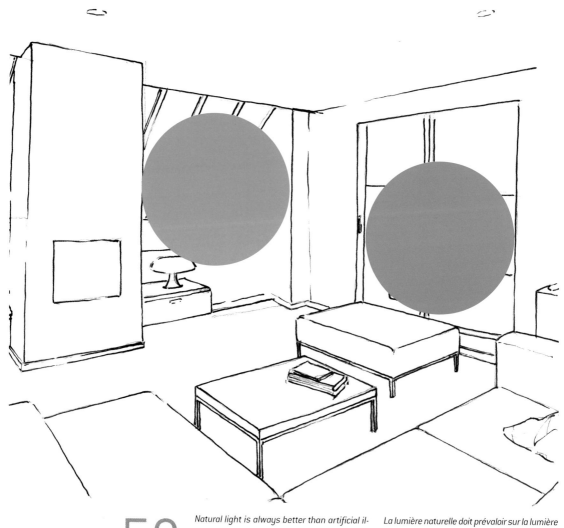

52

Natural light is always better than artificial illumination, since it is cheaper, healthier and more ecological.

La lumière naturelle doit prévaloir sur la lumière artificielle car cette dernière est plus chère et moins respectueuse de l'environnement.

Tageslichtbeleuchtung soll vor künstlicher Beleuchtung stehen, da Letztere teurer und umweltschädlicher ist.

Natuurlijk licht moet voorrang krijgen op kunstlicht, want dit laatste is duurder en minder milieuvriendelijk.

53

There are a huge range of contemporary seating options: chaise lounges, armchairs, sofas, stools, big cushions.

Les alternatives contemporaines en termes de meubles pour s'asseoir sont multiples : transats, fauteuils, canapés, poufs et même gros coussins.

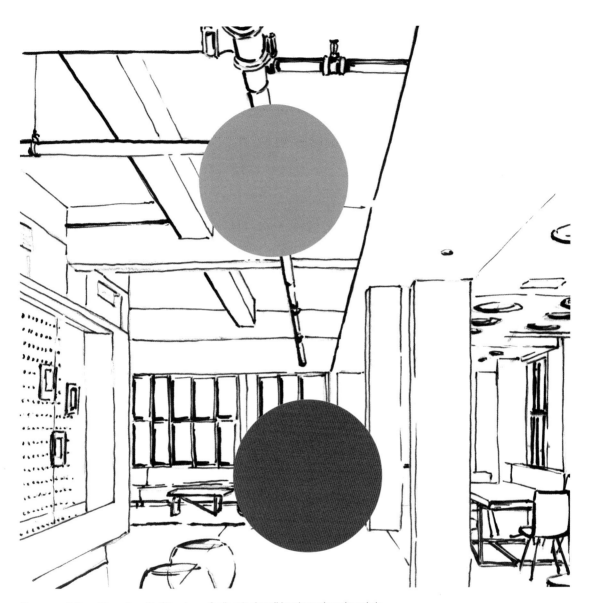

Die gegenwärtigen Alternativen für Sitzgelegenheiten sind zahlreich: Chaiselongues, Sessel, Sofas, Puffs und sogar große Kissen.

Er zijn vele eigentijdse alternatieve zitmeubels: chaises longues, fauteuils, banken, poefs en zelfs grote kussens.

175

DINING ROOMS > SALLES À MANGER

ESSZIMMER > EETKAMERS

Dining rooms are traditionally considered to be the most formal part of the home. Perhaps the space with the most rigid function, dining rooms were traditionally only used on special occasions. Trends in the way we eat have led us to re-think the dining room and incorporate it into the main body of the home.

Esszimmer galten als formellster Teil des Hauses. Da ihnen ihre Aufgabe im Haus am strengsten zugewiesen war, wurden sie nur zu besonderen Gelegenheiten genutzt. Aufgrund der Änderung unserer Essgewohnheiten wurde ihr Design neu durchdacht, und sie wurden mit in den Hauptbereich des Hauses aufgenommen.

Les salles à manger sont considérées comme la partie la plus formelle de la maison. S'agissant de l'espace dont la fonction est la plus strictement déterminée, elle n'était souvent utilisée que pour des occasions particulières. Nos changements d'habitudes concernant les repas nous ont conduits à repenser son design et à l'intégrer à la partie principale de la maison.

Eetkamers werden beschouwd als het formeelste deel van het huis. Aangezien het de huiselijke ruimte met de onbuigzaamste functie was, werd de eetkamer slechts op bijzondere ogenblikken gebruikt. De veranderingen in onze eetgewoonten hebben ons ertoe aangezet om het ontwerp ervan te herformuleren en ze op te nemen in het belangrijkste deel van het huis.

54

An outdoor, semi-enclosed dining area is ideal, since it allows residents to take advantage of all weather conditions.

Un coin salle à manger extérieur partiellement couvert est idéal, car on peut l'utiliser en toute saison.

Ein teilüberdachter Essbereich außerhalb ist ideal, da er zu allen Jahreszeiten genutzt werden kann.

Een gedeeltelijk afgedekte eethoek buiten is ideaal, want deze kan tijdens elk jaargetijde worden gebruikt.

55

Don't clutter your dining table with chairs. Place the minimum number to meet your everyday needs and store away the spares.

N'entourez pas la table de votre salle à manger d'une multitude de chaises. Disposez la quantité minimum nécessaire au quotidien et rangez le reste.

Überhäufen Sie den Esszimmertisch nicht mit unzähligen Stühlen. Stellen Sie nur so wenige auf, wie Sie täglich verwenden, und bewahren Sie den Rest auf.

Zet niet te veel stoelen rond uw eettafel. Zet alleen het aantal stoelen neer dat u voor uw dagelijkse behoeften nodig heeft en bewaar de rest.

56

Even if they are located in the same space, dining and living rooms should be clearly defined.

Même lorsqu'ils se trouvent dans le même espace, la salle à manger et le salon doivent être clairement définis.

Auch wenn sie im gleichen Raum liegen, müssen Ess- und Wohnzimmer genau definiert sein.

Hoewel ze zich in dezelfde ruimte bevinden dienen de eet- en zithoek duidelijk van elkaar te onderscheiden zijn.

57

A dining table centerpiece should be easy to remove, clean, and striking, such as this set of ceramic vessels.

Le centre d'une table de salle à manger doit être facile à dégager, comme c'est le cas avec cet ensemble de récipients en céramique.

Die Dekoration eines Esszimmertischs muss, wie dieser Satz aus Keramikbehältern, leicht abgeräumt werden können.

De voorwerpen op een eettafel, zoals deze aardewerken vazen, moeten gemakkelijk weggeruimd kunnen worden.

185

58

If possible, place your dining table close to a natural source of light. Extra illumination should be specific, preferably using overhanging lamps.

Si vous pouvez, placez la table de la salle à manger près d'une source de lumière naturelle. L'éclairage complémentaire doit être ponctuel et de préférence suspendu.

Stellen Sie den Esstisch, wenn möglich, in der Nähe einer Tageslichtquelle auf. Die zusätzliche Beleuchtung sollte nur bei Bedarf zum Einsatz kommen und vorzugsweise hängend sein.

Zet, indien mogelijk, de tafel van de eethoek dichtbij een bron van natuurlijk licht. Gebruik alleen indien nodig aanvullende verlichting, bij voorkeur een hanglamp.

189

59

Dining room furniture is the least flexible in the entire home, but that doesn't mean it can't be eclectic. Try experimenting with old and new.

Le mobilier de la salle à manger est le moins flexible de toute la maison, ce qui ne signifie pas qu'il ne puisse pas être éclectique. Essayez les combinaisons d'éléments neufs et anciens.

Das Esszimmermobiliar bietet zwar die geringste Flexibilität im ganzen Haus, was aber nicht bedeutet, dass es nicht eklektisch sein kann. Experimentieren Sie, indem Sie neue und antike Elemente kombinieren.

Het meubilair van de eetkamer is het minst flexibele van het hele huis, wat niet hoeft te betekenen dat het niet eclectisch kan zijn. Experimenteer door nieuwe en oude meubels met elkaar te combineren.

60

Dining and lounge areas can also be defined with furniture. Here an elongated sofa acts as a dividing wall.

La distinction entre la salle à manger et le salon peut aussi s'effectuer grâce au mobilier. Dans ce cas, le canapé sert de séparation.

Die Unterscheidung zwischen Ess- und Wohnzimmer kann auch anhand des Mobiliars erfol-
gen. In diesem Fall übernimmt das Sofa die
Trennung.

Het onderscheid tussen de eet- en zithoek kan
ook met behulp van meubels worden gemaakt.
In dit geval fungeert de bank als scheiding.

193

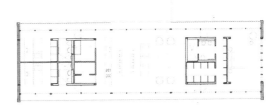

61

For large dining tables, folding chairs are ideal as they can be easily put away when not in use.

Les chaises pliantes sont idéales pour les grandes tables de salle à manger car on peut les ranger facilement lorsqu'on ne les utilise pas.

Klappstühle sind ideal für große Esstische, da sie bei Nichtgebrauch leicht aufbewahrt werden können.

Klapstoelen zijn ideaal voor grote eettafels, aangezien die gemakkelijk kunnen worden opgeborgen als ze niet worden gebruikt.

62

When dining and kitchen areas are connected, a harmonious décor can be achieved by complimenting the colors and textures of the main pieces of furniture.

Si votre cuisine et votre salle à manger communiquent, vous pourrez réaliser une décoration harmonieuse en complétant les couleurs et les textures des meubles principaux.

Wenn Ihre Küche und Ihr Esszimmer miteinander verbunden sind, können Sie durch einander ergänzende Farben und Texturen der größeren Möbel eine harmonische Gestaltung erreichen.

Als uw keuken en eetkamer met elkaar in verbinding staan, dan krijgt u een harmonieuze inrichting door de kleuren en texturen van de voornaamste meubels op elkaar af te stemmen.

63 *Choose your dining table according to your needs. Singles and couples will rarely need a table to seat more than four diners.*

Choisissez la table de la salle à manger selon vos besoins. Les personnes seules ou en couple auront besoin tout au plus d'un modèle à quatre places.

Wählen Sie den Esstisch entsprechend Ihres Bedarfs. Alleinlebende Personen oder Paare brauchen meist höchstens ein Modell mit vier Sitzgelegenheiten.

Kies de eettafel al naargelang uw behoeften. Personen die alleen of met een partner wonen hebben hoogstens een model voor vier plaatsen nodig.

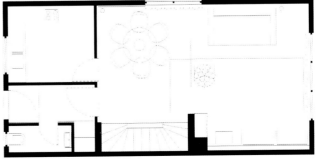

64

A wide range of low seating options, such as cushions and stools, is now available in order to meet today's demand for less formal modes of dining.

Le marché propose une vaste gamme de sièges bas, de type coussin ou pouf qui permettent de s'asseoir à table de manière moins formelle.

Auf dem Markt gibt es ein breites Angebot an niedrigen Sitzgelegenheiten wie Kissen oder Puffs, mit denen man sich ungezwungener an den Tisch setzen kann.

Er is een ruim aanbod lage stoelen, in de vorm van kussens of poefs, op de markt verkrijgbaar. Hiermee kan men tegemoet komen aan de vraag naar minder formeel tafelen.

65

In corporate dining rooms, the emphasis needs to be on adaptability.

Dans les salles à manger d'entreprise, les besoins les plus fondamentaux sont liés à l'adaptabilité.

In Kantinen ist es besonders wichtig, dass sie anpassungsfähig sind.

In eetzalen van bedrijven moet de nadruk liggen op de versatiliteit.

66

The dining experience will benefit from natural light and good views, even if this means placing the table away from the kitchen area.

Le repas devra bénéficier de la lumière naturelle et des vues extérieures même si cela implique de placer la table loin de la cuisine.

Beim Essen sollten Tageslicht und Aussicht genutzt werden, auch wenn der Tisch dafür von
der Küche entfernt aufgestellt werden muss.

Tijdens de maaltijd dient men te profiteren van
natuurlijk licht en uitzicht, ook al betekent dit
dat de tafel ver van de keuken neergezet moet
worden.

211

67

Glass-top tables are suitable for formal dining, but should be avoided for families.

Les tables avec surface en verre sont idéales pour des repas formels mais il vaut mieux y renoncer dans des maisons familiales.

Tische mit Glasplatten sind ausgezeichnet für förmliche Essen, sollten aber in Familienhäusern vermieden werden.

Tafels met glazen tafelbladen zijn ideaal voor formele etentjes, maar in huizen met gezinnen dienen ze te worden vermeden.

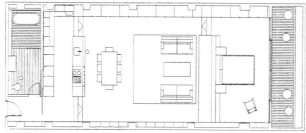

215

68

If space allows, a dining area in a kitchen enables diners and cooks to converse.

Si l'espace le permet, un coin salle à manger dans la cuisine permet aux convives et aux cuisiniers de communiquer pendant les préparatifs.

Wenn es die Platzverhältnisse zulassen, bietet ein Essbereich in der Küche Möglichkeit für den Kontakt zwischen Gästen und Köchen bei der Zubereitung.

Als de ruimte het toelaat zorgt een eethoek in de keuken ervoor dat tafelgenoten en koks tijdens de bereiding van de maaltijd met elkaar kunnen converseren.

69

A common mistake is thinking that a coffee table will suffice. Look at ways to free up space. One such option would be using a foldaway bed.

C'est une erreur fréquente de penser qu'une table au centre suffira. Envisagez différentes manières d'aménager l'espace, comme avec ce lit pliant.

Ein häufiger Fehler besteht darin, zu glauben, dass ein Sofatisch ausreicht. Erwägen Sie verschiedene Arten, Platz zu gewinnen, wie in diesem Fall mit einem Klappbett.

Het is een gebruikelijke vergissing om te denken dat een salontafel volstaat. Bestudeer verschillende manieren om ruimte te creëren, zoals met dit opklapbed.

70

As urban apartments become smaller, fold-away tables are enjoying a renaissance.

Comme les appartements en ville sont de plus en plus petits, les tables pliantes sont de nouveau en vogue.

Da die Wohnungen in den Städten immer kleiner werden, sind Klapptische wieder modern geworden.

Doordat stadsappartementen steeds kleiner worden, zijn vouwtafels weer in de mode.

71

The dining table can be placed against the kitchen furnishings or in its own area.

On peut choisir de mettre une table de salle à manger proche des meubles de la cuisine ou de la placer dans un coin à part.

Man kann zwischen einem Esstisch wählen, der an die Küchenmöbel angebaut ist oder getrennt in einer Ecke aufgestellt wird.

Men kan kiezen voor een eettafel die vastgemaakt is aan de keukenmeubels of men kan deze in een aparte hoek neerzetten.

72

To prevent heat and smoke from reaching the dining room, the kitchen is enclosed in an L-shape with an extractor fan.

Pour éviter que la fumée et les fortes températures de la cuisine ne parviennent à la salle à manger, la cuisine est fermée en forme de L avec une hotte aspirante.

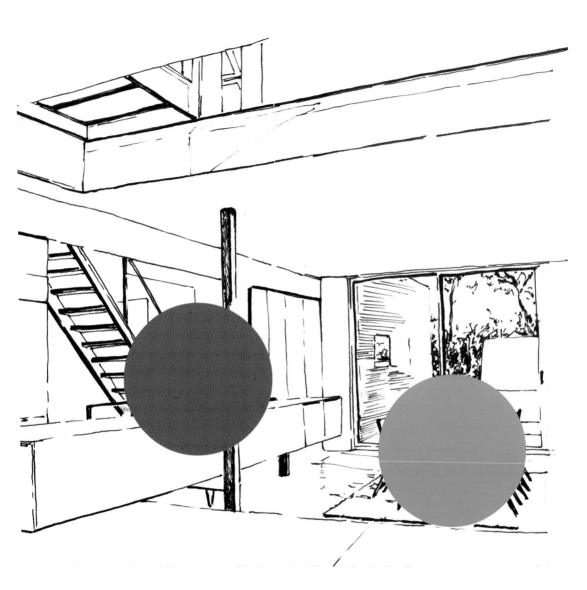

Um zu vermeiden, dass Rauch und hohe Kochtemperaturen bis ins Esszimmer gelangen, wird die Küche in L-Form mit einer Dunstabzugshaube abgeschlossen.

Om te voorkomen dat de rook en hoge temperaturen uit de keuken de eetkamer bereiken, wordt de L-vormige keuken van een afzuigkap voorzien.

73

Separations between areas are functional when they are practical, simple and light.

Les séparations entre les pièces sont fonctionnelles lorsqu'elles sont légères, discrètes et pratiques.

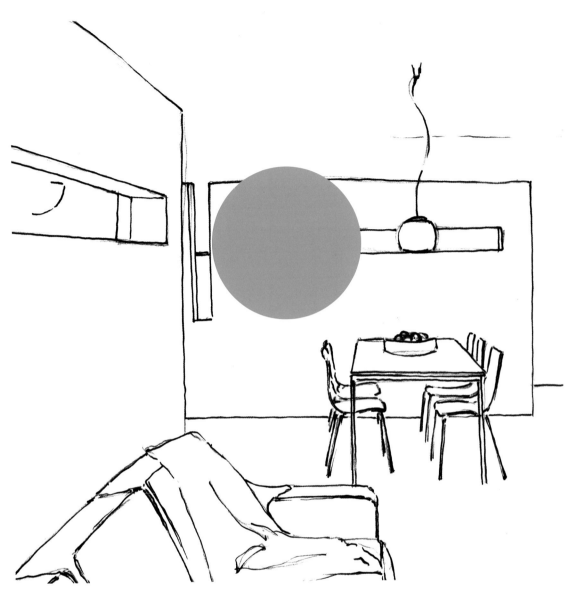

Die Abtrennungen zwischen Bereichen sind funktionell, wenn sie leicht, wenig sperrig und praktisch sind.

Scheidingswanden tussen verschillende delen zijn functioneel wanneer ze licht, onopvallend en praktisch zijn.

LIVE & WORK SPACES > VIVRE ET TRAVAILLER

LEBEN UND ARBEITEN > WONEN EN WERKEN

Today, the option of working at home is more widespread than ever. The projects featured here explore the spaces for living and working chosen by architects, artists, designers and other freelance professionals who have opted for this lifestyle.

Heutzutage ist die Möglichkeit der Heimarbeit weiter verbreitet als nie zuvor. Die im Folgenden vorgestellten Projekte zeigen Lebens- und Arbeitsbereiche von Architekten, Künstlern, Designern und anderen Berufsgruppen, die sich für diesen Lebensstil entschieden haben.

Aujourd'hui la possibilité de travailler à domicile se généralise plus que jamais. Les projets présentés par la suite explorent les espaces pour vivre et travailler proposés par des architectes, des artistes, des designers et autres professionnels qui ont opté pour ce style de vie.

Vandaag de dag is thuiswerk een algemener verschijnsel dan ooit tevoren. De projecten die hierna worden getoond, laten woon- en werkruimten van architecten, kunstenaars, ontwerpers en andere professionals zien die voor deze levensstijl hebben gekozen.

74

When designing a work area it is important to consider the activity which will take place there in order to create a space that is suitable for the job.

Au moment de la création de la zone de travail, il faut tenir compte du type d'activité exercée pour obtenir un espace fonctionnel.

Beim Entwurf des Arbeitsbereichs ist die Art der auszuführenden Tätigkeit für die Gestaltung eines funktionellen Bereichs zu beachten.

Bij het ontwerpen van de werkruimte moet rekening gehouden worden met het type activiteit die er beoefend zal worden om een functionele ruimte te creëren.

75

The space allocated for the work area needs plenty of natural light. It is also advisable to include an area in which to relax.

Il faudra que l'espace de la zone de travail reçoive beaucoup de lumière naturelle. Il est bon d'y aménager une zone pour se détendre.

Der Arbeitsbereich erfordert reichlich Tageslicht. Auch ein Bereich zum Entspannen ist angebracht.

De werkruimte heeft veel natuurlijk licht nodig. Het is wenselijk om te beschikken over een ruimte waar men zich kan ontspannen.

76

Flexible spaces that combine domestic and work activities should have multifunctional structures which define the areas.

Les espaces qui rassemblent activités domestiques et travail doivent bénéficier de structures multifonctionnelles afin de délimiter les zones.

Die Räume, in denen private Beschäftigungen und Beruf kombiniert werden, müssen Mehrzweckstrukturen zur Abtrennung der Bereiche nutzen.

In ruimten waar het werk met huiselijke activiteiten gecombineerd wordt dient gebruik gemaakt te worden van multifunctionele structuren die de zones begrenzen.

77

These high ceilings have allowed space a shelving structure that extends horizontally to the mezzanine.

De hauts plafonds ont permis de créer une trame d'étagères qui s'étendent horizontalement jusqu'à la mezzanine.

Hohe Decken haben ein Fachwerk aus Regalen möglich gemacht, die waagerecht bis zum Zwischengeschoss verlaufen.

Dankzij de hoge plafonds was het mogelijk om een samenstel van boekenkasten te creëren dat zich horizontaal uitstrekt tot aan de mezzanine.

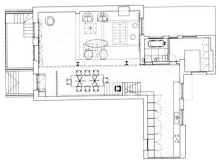

78

The skylights are opened by an electric mechanism, allowing the space to be ventilated.

Les lucarnes s'ouvrent à l'aide d'un mécanisme électrique de manière à ventiler l'espace.

Die Dachluken können anhand elektrischer Vorrichtungen zur Raumbelüftung geöffnet werden.

De dakramen worden door middel van een elektrisch mechanisme geopend. Hierdoor kan de ruimte worden geventileerd.

79

Mezzanines can only be installed when the main space is not vital and can be divided.

Les mezzanines ne sont envisageables que dans des lieux où l'espace principal n'est pas vital et peut être compartimenté.

Zwischengeschosse sind nur dort möglich, wo der Hauptraum nicht unerlässlich ist und aufgeteilt werden kann.

De mezzanines zijn enkel mogelijk op plaatsen waar de hoofdruimte niet vitaal is en kan worden onderverdeeld.

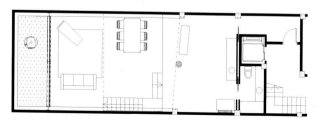

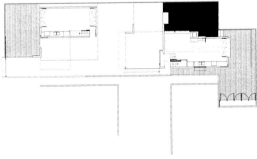

80

Industrial spaces often have interesting structures that are worth leaving exposed.

Les espaces industriels présentent souvent des structures intéressantes que l'on peut laisser apparentes.

Industriebereiche bieten häufig interessante Strukturen, die man sichtbar lassen sollte.

Industriële ruimten hebben vaak interessante structuren die gezien mogen worden.

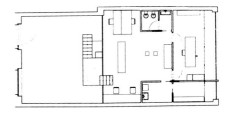

81

Insetting storage units in walls is one possible solution for combining living and working spaces.

Une solution pour conjuguer zone de vie et zone de travail consiste à encastrer les unités de rangement dans un des murs.

Eine Lösung zur Kombination von Lebens- und
Arbeitsbereich ist die Eingliederung der Aufbe-
wahrungseinheiten in eine der Wände.

Een oplossing om een woon- en werkzone te
combineren is om één van de wanden te voorzien van inbouwkasten.

82

In this case, the former is on the mezzanine and the latter is on the main floor.

Dans ce cas, la partie privée se trouve sous la mezzanine, tandis que la zone de travail se trouve à l'étage principal.

In diesem Fall liegt der Privatbereich auf dem Zwischengeschoss, während der Arbeitsbereich auf dem Hauptgeschoss liegt.

In dit geval bevindt de privézone zich op de mezzanine, terwijl de werkzone op de hoofdverdieping is gelegen.

83

Easily movable installations, such as drapes or sliding panels, help create visual continuity.

Les séparations mobiles pratiques, comme les rideaux ou les panneaux coulissants, favorisent la continuité visuelle.

Leicht bewegliche Einrichtungen wie Gardinen oder Schiebepaneele begünstigen die optische Kontinuität.

Voorzieningen die gemakkelijk te verplaatsen zijn, zoals gordijnen en schuifpanelen, bevorderen de visuele continuïteit.

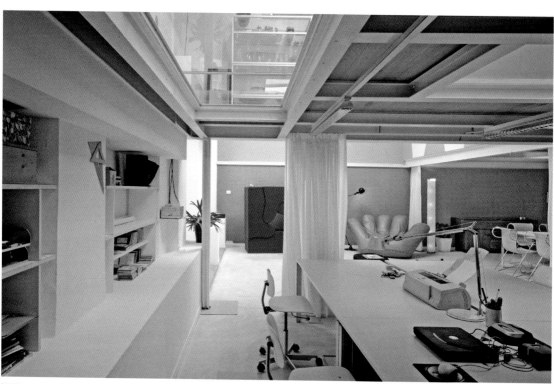

84

In this loft, the latter has been placed on a mezzanine to separate private and public living spaces.

Dans ce loft, la maison proprement dite se trouve sous la mezzanine afin de maintenir une séparation entre la vie privée et la vie publique.

In diesem Loft liegt das eigentliche Haus im Zwischengeschoss, um das Privatleben vom öffentlichen Leben getrennt zu halten.

In deze loft bevindt het woongedeelte zich op de mezzanine, zodat het privégedeelte wordt afgeschermd van het openbare deel.

85

A good way to create atmosphere in work spaces is to install comfortable seating that encourages more informal, relaxed conversation with clients.

Pour créer une atmosphère dans les zones de travail on peut choisir des sièges confortables qui permettent de discuter avec ses clients de manière détendue.

Bei der Gestaltung der Arbeitsbereiche kann man bequeme Sitzmöglichkeiten wählen, um mit den Kunden entspannt Gespräche führen zu können.

Om in de werkzones sfeer te scheppen, kan gekozen worden voor comfortabele stoelen zodat op ontspannen wijze gesprekken met de klanten gevoerd kunnen worden.

86   *Double-height shelves or dual-function pieces enable boundaries to be marked between the work area and the rest of the home.*

Des étagères à double hauteur ou des pièces avec plus d'une fonction permettent d'établir la limite entre la zone de travail et le reste de la maison.

Regale mit doppelter Höhe oder Mehrzwecke-
lemente ermöglichen die Trennung zwischen
Arbeitsbereich und restlicher Wohnung.

Dubbelhoge boekenkasten of meubelstukken
met meer dan één functie kunnen de grens
tussen de werkzone en de rest van de woning
bepalen.

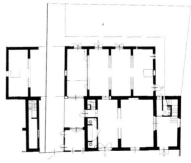

87

A wall separates the kitchen from the work area and serves as a headboard for the foldaway bed.

Un mur sépare la cuisine de la zone de travail et sert de tête de lit pour le lit pliant.

Eine Wand trennt die Küche vom Arbeitsbereich und dient als Kopfteil für das Klappbett.

Een wand scheidt de keuken van de werkzone en fungeert als hoofdeinde van het vouwbed.

88   *The ergonomics of the work space must be taken into account to optimize productivity and create a feeling of wellbeing.*

L'ergonomie est l'un des aspects dont il faut tenir compte : dans la zone de travail il est primordial d'assurer son bien-être.

Ein wichtiger Aspekt ist die Ergonomie: am Arbeitsplatz muss das Wohlbefinden gewährleistet sein.

Eén van de dingen waarmee rekening gehouden dient te worden is de ergonomie: op de werkplek dient het welzijn te worden gegarandeerd.

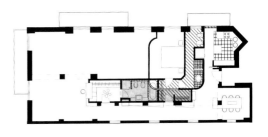

89 Keeping the space well ventilated and avoiding biomechanical stress helps optimize productivity and creativity.

Le fait de disposer d'un espace ventilé et d'éviter le stress biomécanique aide à optimiser la productivité et la créativité.

Gute Raumbelüftung und Vermeidung von bio-
mechanischem Stress optimieren Produkti-
vität und Kreativität.

De ruimte goed ventileren en biomechanische
stress vermijden, helpen onze productiviteit en
creativiteit te optimaliseren.

90

Sometimes filing units, such as these stainless steel shelves, can be integrated into the living room.

Parfois, les meubles de rangement, comme ces étagères en acier inoxydable, peuvent s'intégrer au salon.

In manchen Fällen können die Aufbewahrungsmöbel, wie in diesem Fall die Edelstahlregale, ins Wohnzimmer integriert werden.

Soms kunnen opbergmeubels, zoals deze roestvrij stalen boekenkasten, deel uitmaken van de woonkamer.

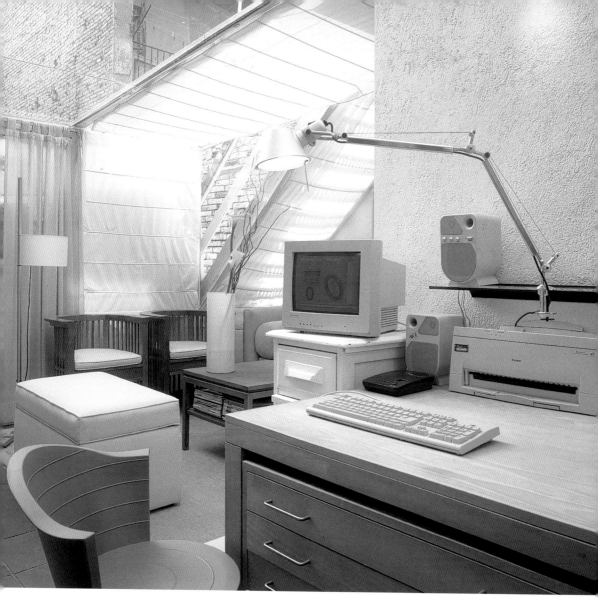

91 *If the climate allows, placing the work area in natural surroundings is a good option.*

Si les conditions le permettent, une bonne option consiste à situer la zone de travail dans un cadre naturel.

Wenn es die Umstände erlauben, ist die Anordnung des Arbeitsbereichs in einer natürlichen
Umgebung eine gute Option.

Als de omstandigheden het toestaan is het een
goed idee om de werkruimte in een natuurlijke
omgeving te plaatsen.

92

Placing a rocking chair or a piece of restored
furniture in the library area adds warmth.

*Pour obtenir davantage de chaleur dans la par-
tie bibliothèque, on opte pour des rocking-
chairs ou tout autre type de mobilier restauré.*

*Um mehr Wärme im Bereich der Bibliothek zu
schaffen, hat man sich für Schaukelstühle oder
andere restaurierte Möbel entschieden.*

*Om de bibliotheek gezelliger te maken, wordt
ervoor gekozen om er een schommelstoel of
een ander gerestaureerd meubelstuk neer te
zetten.*

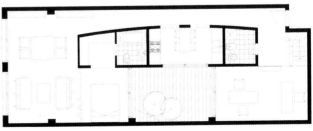

93

The work table should be large enough to enable the work tools to be freely placed.

Les dimensions de la surface de la table doivent permettre de poser les éléments de travail de manière flexible.

Die Tischplatte muss groß genug sein, um eine
flexible Anordnung der Arbeitselemente zu
ermöglichen.

Het tafelblad dient groot genoeg te zijn, zodat
men er de voor het werk nodige spullen op flexibele wijze neer kan zetten.

94

A mezzanine was constructed to allow access to books on the upper shelves.

La construction d'une mezzanine permet de consulter les livres qui se trouvent dans la partie haute de la bibliothèque.

Der Bau eines Zwischengeschosses ermöglicht den Zugang zu den Büchern im oberen Regalteil.

De constructie van een mezzanine maakt het mogelijk om de boeken die zich bovenaan in de boekenkast staan te raadplegen.

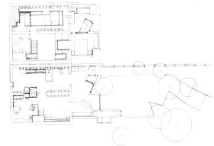

95

The work area is located at one end below the staircase in order to facilitate circulation and prevent visual obstacles.

Pour faciliter le parcours intérieur et éviter les obstacles visuels, la zone de travail se situe à une extrémité et en bas des escaliers.

Um die Wege innerhalb zu erleichtern und optische Hindernisse zu vermeiden, wurde der Arbeitsbereich an ein Ende unter der Treppe gelegt.

Om de verplaatsing binnenshuis te vergemakkelijken en visuele obstakels te vermijden wordt de werkzone onder de trap geplaatst.

96

It is advisable to install auxiliary surfaces, such as meeting tables or folding wings attached to the work desk.

Il est pratique de disposer de surfaces supplémentaires qui s'adaptent à la table de travail ou qui disposent de pans pliables adaptés.

An den Arbeitstisch anpassbare Hilfsflächen oder Arbeitstische mit Klappflügeln können sich als praktisch erweisen.

Het is wenselijk om over hulpvlakken te beschikken die op de werktafel aangesloten kunnen worden. Ook is een uitvouwbare tafel een goede optie.

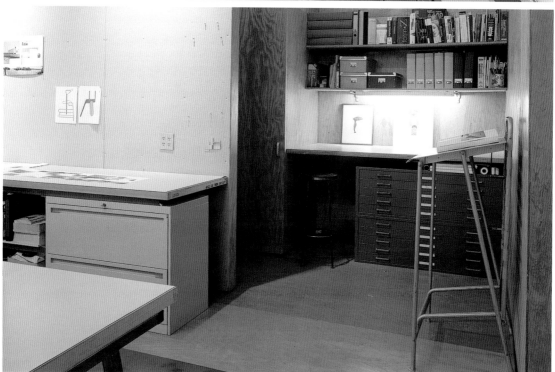

97

Closets and filing cabinets should be installed to meet the needs of each work station, but storage in transit areas should be avoided.

La présence de placards et de classeurs dépendra des besoins du travail tout en évitant le rangement dans des zones de transit.

Schränke und Ablagen hängen vom Bedarf der Arbeit ab, wobei die Aufbewahrung in Durchgangsbereichen vermieden werden sollte.

Op elke werkplek is er behoefte aan opberg- en archiefkasten maar deze worden best vermeden op plaatsen waar men vaak langs loopt.

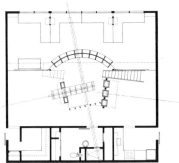

KITCHENS > CUISINES

KÜCHEN > KEUKENS

Our burgeoning food and nutrition culture has led to greater importance being placed on the kitchen than ever before; it has gone beyond a mere place to prepare food to become one for meeting, conversing and bonding.

Die Verbreitung der Kochkultur hat dem Küchenbereich eine bisher unbekannte Wichtigkeit verliehen. Die Küche ist mehr als nur ein Ort, an dem das Essen zubereitet wird. Sie ist heute ein Raum für Treffen, Gespräche und Beziehungspflege.

La prolifération de la culture gastronomique a doté la zone de la cuisine d'une importance qu'elle n'avait jamais eue jusqu'à présent. La cuisine est plus qu'un lieu où préparer un repas. Actuellement c'est un espace pour se réunir, pour discuter et pour créer des liens.

De proliferatie van de gastronomische cultuur heeft ervoor gezorgd dat de keuken een belangrijkere rol speelt dan ooit tevoren. De keuken is meer dan alleen een plek om het eten klaar te maken. Tegenwoordig is het een ruimte om bijeen te komen, te praten en banden te leggen.

98

Choosing the same material for both flooring and fittings (in this case wood) ensures an uninterrupted flow of space.

Le choix du même matériau pour le sol et les accessoires, ici le bois, garantit une continuité spatiale.

Die Auswahl des gleichen Materials – in diesem Fall Holz – für Boden und Zubehör gewährleistet räumliche Kontinuität.

De keuze van hetzelfde materiaal voor de vloer en accessoires - in dit geval hout - garanderen de continuïteit van de ruimte.

99

Doing away with doors and incorporating cut-away walls can integrate the kitchen into the rest of the home while still defining its separate function.

La suppression des portes permet d'intégrer la cuisine au reste de la maison sans atténuer sa fonction indépendante.

Durch die Entfernung der Türen kann die Küche in den Rest des Hauses integriert werden, ohne jedoch dadurch ihre eigenständige Funktion abzuschwächen.

Het weglaten van deuren zorgt ervoor dat de keuken deel uitmaakt van de rest van het huis zonder haar onafhankelijke functie teniet te doen.

100 Customized pieces, such as this spectacular, freestanding cabinet, should be considered if your budget and space allow.

Un meuble fait sur mesure, comme ce buffet modulaire, peut être envisagé, si votre budget vous le permet.

Maßgeschneiderte Teile – wie dieser Anrichte-tisch im Baukastenstil – sind zu empfehlen, wenn es das Budget erlaubt.

Als uw budget dit toelaat, kunnen op maat ge-maakte meubels, zoals dit modulaire buffet, worden gebruikt.

101

Using different types of wood and wood finishes can create a warm yet dramatic interplay.

L'emploi de divers types et finitions en bois peut créer un ensemble accueillant et spectaculaire à la fois.

Der Einsatz unterschiedlicher Holzarten und –ausführungen kann eine gemütliche und gleichzeitig spektakuläre Zusammenstellung schaffen.

Het gebruik van verschillende houtsoorten en -afwerkingen kan een gezellig en tevens spectaculair geheel creëren.

102   Be aware of the standard dimensions of kitchen fixtures when planning.

Au moment de la planification, tenez compte des dimensions standard des installations de votre cuisine.

Bei der Planung müssen die Standardabmes-
sungen der Kücheneinrichtungen beachtet
werden.

Houd bij de planning rekening met de stan-
daardafmetingen van de keukenapparatuur.

103

The union of cooking and dining areas has been the most prominent change in kitchen design in recent decades.

Le changement le plus remarquable dans le design des cuisines des dernières décennies a été la réunion de la cuisine et de la salle à manger.

Die herausragendste Änderung im Küchendesign der letzten Jahrzehnte bestand in der Verbindung zwischen Küche und Esszimmer.

De afgelopen decennia was de open keuken de opvallendste verandering in het keukendesign.

104

Organize the distribution of your kitchen according to space available.

Organisez la distribution de votre cuisine selon l'espace dont vous disposez.

Planen Sie die Aufteilung Ihrer Küche entsprechend des verfügbaren Raums.

Deel uw keuken in volgens de ruimte waarover u beschikt.

105

Even if you use the same type of base wood, an infinity of color variations can be achieved through staining.

Même si vous utilisez le même bois de base, il est possible d'obtenir des variations chromatiques au moyen de bois teintés.

Auch beim Einsatz des gleichen Holzes als Grundlage können anhand getönter Hölzer Farbvariationen geschaffen werden.

Zelfs als u hetzelfde basishout gebruikt, is het mogelijk om door middel van getint hout kleurschakeringen te verkrijgen.

106

Enamel paint reflects light and makes a space seem larger.

La peinture émaillée réfléchit la lumière et agrandit l'espace.

Lackfarben reflektieren das Licht und lassen den Raum größer erscheinen.

Lakverf weerspiegelt het licht en zorgt ervoor dat de ruimte groter lijkt.

107

Polished stone makes an ideal kitchen flooring for its elegance and durability.

Élégante et durable, la pierre polie constitue la matière idéale pour un sol de cuisine.

Aufgrund seiner Eleganz und Lebensdauer ist polierter Stein das ideale Material für Küchenböden.

Vanwege zijn elegantie en duurzaamheid is gepolijste steen het ideale materiaal voor de keukenvloer.

334

108

Lacquered surfaces, such as the cupboards in this kitchen, add depth and color.

Les surfaces vernies, comme les armoires de cette cuisine, ajoutent profondeur et couleur.

Lackierte Flächen – wie diese Küchenschränke – bringen Tiefe und Farbe ein.

Gelakte oppervlakken, zoals de kasten van deze keuken, voegen diepgang en kleur toe.

109

Galvanized steel need not look industrial, especially when combined with other elements in organic materials, such as wood or stone.

L'acier galvanisé ne donne pas nécessairement un aspect industriel, encore moins combiné avec le bois ou la pierre.

Verzinkter Stahl muss nicht unbedingt eine in-
dustrielle Optik ausstrahlen – insbesondere
dann nicht, wenn er mit Holz oder Stein kombiniert wird.

Verzinkt staal hoeft er niet industrieel uit te
zien, helemaal niet als het met hout of steen
wordt gecombineerd.

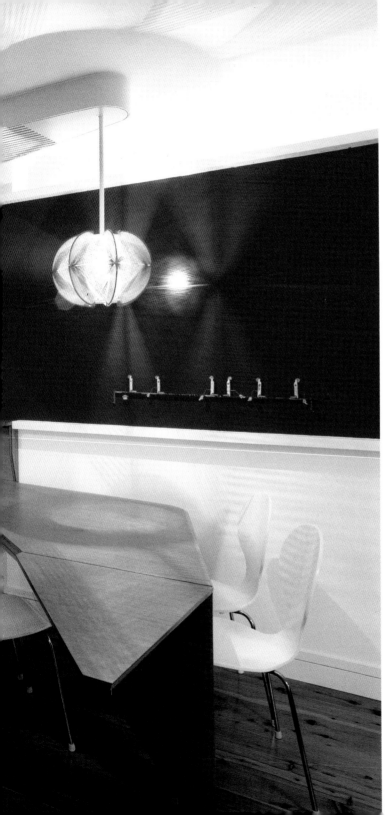

110

If your kitchen cannot accommodate a conventional right-angled table, explore other types such as this expandable model.

Si vous ne pouvez pas installer la traditionnelle table rectangulaire dans votre cuisine, recherchez d'autres modèles comme cette table extensible.

Wenn Sie in Ihrer Küche keinen herkömmlichen rechteckigen Tisch aufstellen können, sollten Sie andere Modelle, wie diesen Ausziehtisch, testen.

Als in uw keuken geen traditionele rechthoekige tafel past, overweeg dan andere modellen zoals deze uitschuifbare tafel.

111

Don't rule out color in the kitchen. Choices need not be permanent.

Ne lésinez pas sur les couleurs dans la cuisine. Vos choix ne sont jamais définitifs.

Sparen Sie nicht mit Farben in der Küche. Die
Entscheidungen müssen nicht endgültig sein.

Wees niet zuinig met kleuren in de keuken. De
gemaakte keuzes hoeven niet permanent te
zijn.

345

112

Brick walls need not look rustic if they are combined with contemporary interiors.

Les murs en brique ne confèrent pas un aspect rustique s'ils accompagnent un intérieur moderne.

Backsteinwände wirken nicht rustikal, wenn sie mit aktuellen Innenausstattungen kombiniert werden.

Bakstenen muren hebben geen landelijke uitstraling als ze met een actueel interieur worden gecombineerd.

113

Self-contained modules create 'spaces within spaces' and can add volume to even the smallest of kitchens.

Les modules indépendants créent des espaces à l'intérieur de l'espace et peuvent apporter du volume aux petites cuisines.

Eigenständige Module schaffen Räume innerhalb von anderen Räumen und können sogar in kleinsten Küchen Raum zur Verfügung stellen.

Onafhankelijke modules creëren ruimten binnen andere ruimten en kunnen zelfs de kleinste keuken van volume voorzien.

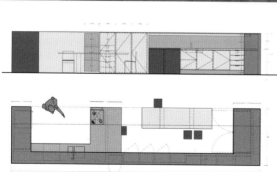

114

Display only what is needed day to day and store the rest away in cupboards, drawers or pantries.

Ne laissez à la vue que ce que vous utilisez tous les jours et rangez le reste dans des armoires, des tiroirs ou des garde-manger.

Lassen Sie nur das stehen, was Sie täglich brauchen, und bewahren Sie den Rest in Schränken, Schubladen oder Abstellkammern auf.

Stal alleen uit wat dagelijks wordt gebruikt en bewaar de rest in kasten, laden of provisiekamers.

115

As the kitchen is arguably, the most frequently used part of the home it makes sense to place it where there is plenty of natural light.

La cuisine est la pièce de la maison la plus utilisée. Il est donc logique de l'installer là où la lumière naturelle est la plus abondante.

Die Küche ist der meistgenutzte Teil des Hauses. Daher ist es logisch, dass sie dort eingerichtet wird, wo das meiste Tageslicht einfällt.

De keuken is het meest gebruikte deel van het huis. Het is dan ook logisch om de keuken op een plaats te installeren waar veel natuurlijk licht binnenvalt.

116

As shown above, a discreet extractor has been cleverly fed through an exterior wall in the absence of natural ventilation.

Comme on peut le voir, à l'étage supérieur, on a astucieusement branché un extracteur discret, en raison de l'absence d'aération naturelle.

Hier ist zu sehen, wie wegen fehlender natürlicher Belüftung im oberen Bereich eine dezente Dunstabzugshaube ganz erfinderisch angeschlossen wurde.

Omdat er geen natuurlijke ventilatie is, is er, zoals u kunt zien, aan de bovenkant op vindingrijke wijze een onopvallende afzuiger aangesloten.

117

In some cases, the extractor can be made into a feature, such as this L-shaped model.

Dans certains cas, l'extracteur peut devenir un élément de la décoration, comme ce modèle en forme de L.

In manchen Fällen kann die Dunstabzugshaube – wie bei diesem Modell in L-Form – zum Dekorationselement werden.

Soms kan de afzuigkap een decoratief element zijn, zoals dit L-vormige model.

118

Lighting plays an important role in the kitchen. Angle lights to illuminate work, eating and storage areas.

Dans la cuisine, la lumière joue un rôle très important. Les lumières obliques éclairent le coin préparation, l'espace repas et celui du rangement.

In der Küche spielt die Beleuchtung eine wichtige Rolle. Schräge Lampen beleuchten Anrichte-, Ess- und Vorratsbereich.

In de keuken speelt het licht een zeer belangrijke rol. Indirecte verlichting voorziet de bereidingszone, de ruimte waar gegeten wordt en de opbergruimte van licht.

119 *Hardwearing, flexible and mobile outdoor furniture can often make ideal kitchen furniture.*

Le mobilier extérieur, résistant, flexible et mobile, peut constituer une option idéale pour les cuisines.

Widerstandsfähige, flexible und bewegliche Möbel für Außenbereiche können eine ideale Option für Küchen sein.

Het bestendige, flexibele en verplaatsbare buitenmeubilair kan een ideale optie voor de keuken zijn.

120

Linoleum can provide an economic and stylish floor covering solution.

Le linoléum peut s'avérer une solution économique et élégante pour couvrir vos sols.

Linoleum kann eine günstige und elegante Lösung als Bodenbelag darstellen.

Linoleum kan een goedkope en elegante oplossing voor uw vloer zijn.

121

Warmth can be added to an all-white, minimalist kitchen with wooden flooring and accessories.

Une cuisine minimaliste, de couleur blanche nucléaire, peut se combiner avec un sol et des accessoires en bois.

Eine minimalistische, strahlend weiße Küche kann gut zu Boden und Zubehör aus Holz passen.

Een minimalistische, zuiver witte keuken kan gecombineerd worden met een vloer en accessoires van hout.

374

375

122

When contemplating an auxiliary kitchen, choose streamlined, discreet furniture and accessories that will not interfere with the rest of the décor.

Si vous envisagez d'aménager une arrière-cuisine, choisissez un mobilier fonctionnel et discret n'interférant pas avec le reste de la décoration.

Wenn Sie die Möglichkeit einer Zusatzküche erwägen, sollten Sie sich für funktionelles und dezentes Mobiliar entscheiden, das die übrige Dekoration nicht beeinträchtigt.

Als u de mogelijkheid overweegt om een bijkeuken te maken, kies dan functioneel en bescheiden meubilair dat geen storend effect heeft op de rest van de inrichting.

123

Advances in technology and design techniques mean that kitchens can now be installed in almost any type of dwelling.

Les avancées de la technologie et du design permettent de monter une cuisine dans presque n'importe quelle maison.

Technologische und gestalterische Fortschritte ermöglichen den Einbau einer Küche in praktisch allen Wohnungsarten.

Dankzij de vorderingen op het gebied van technologie en design kan in praktisch elk type woning een keuken worden gemonteerd.

124

Accessories such as faucets or lights can become features in their own right if correctly chosen and placed.

Les accessoires comme les luminaires ou les robinets peuvent se transformer en décoration s'ils sont choisis et placés de manière adéquate.

Zubehörteile wie Wasserhähne und Lampen können sich in Dekorationselemente verwandeln, wenn sie angemessen ausgewählt und angebracht werden.

Accessoires, zoals kranen of lichten, kunnen decoratieve elementen worden als ze succesvol worden uitgekozen en aangebracht.

387

125

Preparation areas can be discreetly defined by using curtains and other vertical coverings.

Les zones de préparation peuvent être délimitées de manière discrète par des rideaux ou tout autre type de parois verticales.

Anrichtebereiche lassen sich anhand von Vorhängen und anderen senkrechten Verkleidungen dezent definieren.

De bereidingszones kunnen discreet omlijnd worden door gordijnen en andere verticale bekledingen.

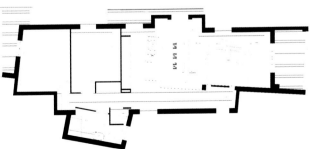

126

The old rules governing the design of cupboards and other modules have been broken because the kitchen now takes prime place in the home.

En ayant transformé la cuisine en lieu principal de la maison, on a brisé les anciennes normes qui régissaient le design des placards et des modules.

Dadurch, dass sich die Küche in den wichtigsten Bereich des Hauses verwandelt hat, gelten die ehemaligen Designregeln für Schränke und Module nicht mehr.

Aangezien de keuken de belangrijkste plek van het huis geworden is, zijn de oude regels voor het ontwerp van kasten en modules doorbroken.

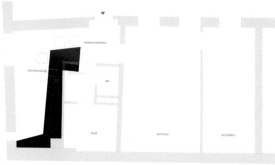

127

Ample mirrors and the long panel above the preparation area create the optical illusion of a much larger space.

Les larges miroirs et le long panneau au-dessus de la zone de préparation créent l'illusion optique d'un plus grand espace.

Großzügige Spiegel und lange Paneele über dem Anrichtebereich erwecken den optischen Eindruck, dass mehr Platz vorhanden ist.

De grote spiegels en het lange paneel boven de bereidingszone zorgen ervoor dat de ruimte groter lijkt.

128

This neat, easy-to-reach wine rack nestles beneath the freestanding counter module.

Cet ingénieux porte-bouteilles d'accès aisé se trouve sous le module indépendant utilisé comme plan de travail.

Dieser erfinderische und leicht zugängliche Flaschenständer befindet sich unter dem eigenständigen Modul, das als Arbeitsfläche verwendet wird.

Dit gemakkelijk bereikbare en vindingrijke flessenrek bevindt zich onder de onafhankelijke module die wordt gebruikt als werktafel.

129

When there is limited space for the dining table, placing a counter close to the cooking area is a practical idea.

Une solution recommandée lorsqu'on a peu d'espace pour la table de la salle à manger, c'est de l'intégrer aux meubles de la cuisine.

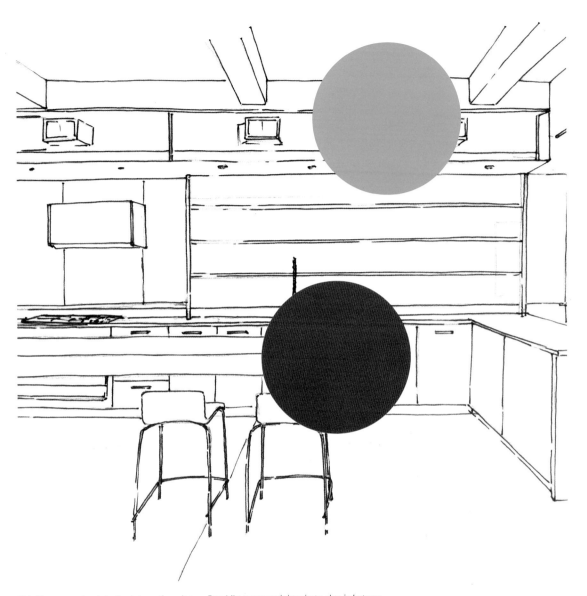

Bei Platzmangel wird die Integration des Küchentischs in die Küchenmöbel empfohlen.

Beschikt u over weinig ruimte, dan is het een goede oplossing om de eettafel op te nemen in het keukenmeubilair.

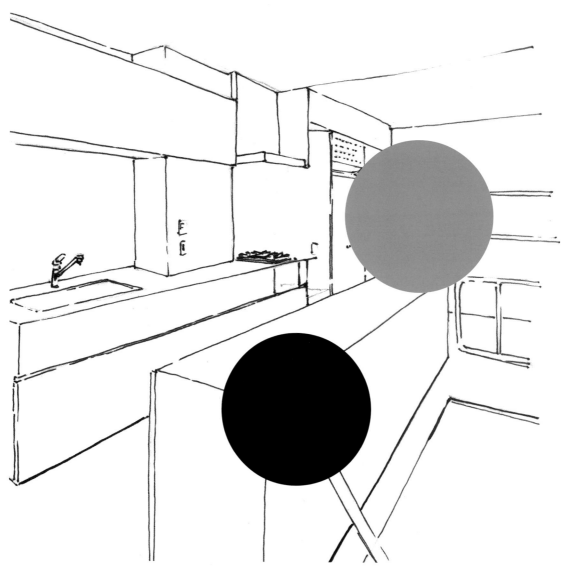

130

A good ventilation system is important in a kitchen. There are a multitude of different kinds available, combining technology and design.

Il est important de disposer d'un bon système d'aération dans la cuisine. On trouve sur le marché une multitude de versions qui allient technologie et design.

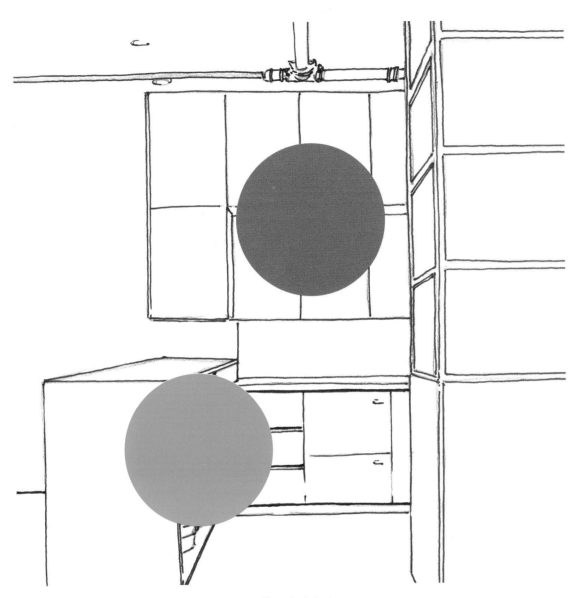

In der Küche ist ein gutes Belüftungssystem wichtig. Auf dem Markt werden zahlreiche Ausführungen angeboten, die Technologie und Design verbinden.

Het is belangrijk om in de keuken over een goed ventilatiesysteem te beschikken. Er zijn op de markt vele uitvoeringen verkrijgbaar die technologie en design combineren.

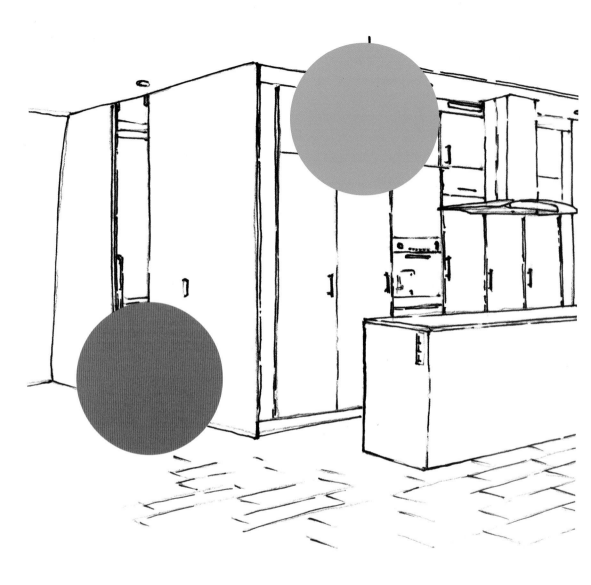

131

The type of ceiling will determine the best lighting system for the kitchen. Halogen lamps are generally the best choice.

Le type de plafond déterminera le système le plus adapté pour éclairer la cuisine. Les halogènes semblent être la meilleure option

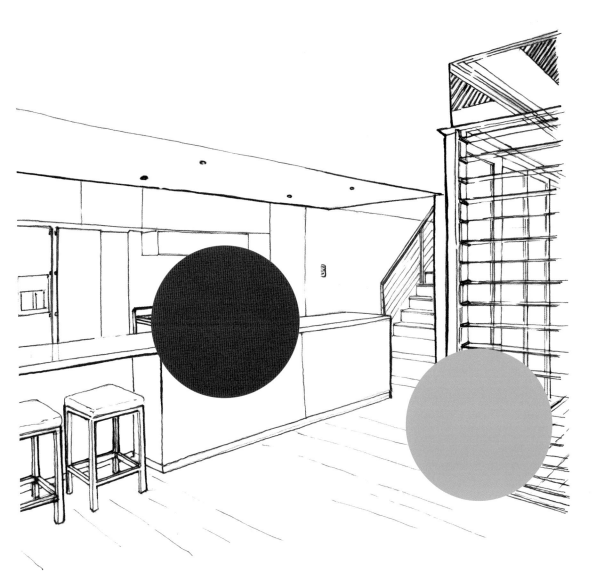

Die Art der Decke bestimmt das geeignetste Beleuchtungssystem für die Küche. Halogenleuchten scheinen die beste Lösung zu sein.

Het type plafond zal bepalen welk het beste verlichtingssysteem voor de keuken is. Halogeenlampen lijken de beste optie.

BEDROOMS > CHAMBRES

SCHLAFZIMMER > SLAAPKAMERS

It is a well known fact that we spend a third of our lives sleeping. It is therefore safe to say that, along with the bathroom, the bedroom is the most personal space in the home and it should be the quietest area. Children's bedrooms offer much more scope for creativity.

Bekanntlich verbringen wir ein Drittel unseres Lebens mit Schlafen. So ist das Schlafzimmer der persönlichste Raum einer Wohnung und sollte der ruhigste Ort des Hauses sein. Kinderschlafzimmer lassen der Kreativität den meisten Spielraum.

Nous savons qu'on passe un tiers de notre vie à dormir. Au regard de cette information, on peut donc dire que la chambre est l'espace le plus personnel d'une maison et doit être le lieu le plus calme dans une habitation. Les chambres des enfants sont celles qui offrent les plus grandes possibilités pour développer votre créativité.

Het is bekend dat we een derde deel van ons leven slapend doorbrengen. Volgens dit gegeven kunnen we zeggen dat de slaapkamer de persoonlijkste ruimte van een woning is en dat dit het rustigste vertrek van het huis dient te zijn. Kinderslaapkamers bieden de beste mogelijkheden voor de ontwikkeling van uw creativiteit.

132

The bedroom is the most personal space in the home, and the bed is its most important element.

La chambre est l'espace le plus personnel de la maison et le lit l'élément le plus important.

Das Schlafzimmer ist der persönlichste Raum
im Haus und das Bett das wichtigste Element.

De slaapkamer is de persoonlijkste ruimte van
het huis en het bed het belangrijkste onderdeel.

133

In studio and loft apartments, match your bed linen to the general color scheme and install an enclosed closet.

Dans les studios et les appartements de type loft, assortissez la literie au schéma chromatique général et installez une penderie encastrée.

In Atelier- und Loftwohnungen ist es empfehlenswert, die Bettwäsche mit dem allgemeinen Farbenmuster zu kombinieren und einen Wandschrank einzubauen.

Stem in éénkamerflats en lofts het beddengoed af op het algemene kleurengamma en breng een ingebouwde kleerkast aan.

134 Every bedroom needs a bedside or auxiliary table next to the bed for books, a lamp and other objects.

Les chambres doivent comprendre à côté du lit une table de nuit ou une petite table adjacente pour mettre des livres, une lampe ou d'autres objets.

Zu den Schlafzimmern gehört neben dem Bett ein Nachtschränkchen oder ein Beistelltisch für Bücher, eine Lampe oder andere Gegenstände.

In slaapkamers moet naast het bed een nachtkastje of bijzettafeltje worden geplaatst voor boeken, een lamp of andere voorwerpen.

135

Japanese futon beds have grown in popularity over the years, since they are great for small, open-plan spaces.

Au fil du temps, les futons japonais sont devenus de plus en plus populaires. Ils s'adaptent aux espaces réduits et aux plans ouverts.

Im Laufe der Jahre sind die japanischen Futons immer beliebter geworden. Sie passen sich kleinen Räumen und offenen Grundrissen an.

In de loop der jaren zijn de Japanse futons steeds populairder geworden. Zij passen goed in kleine open ruimten.

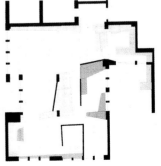

136

An adjacent or en-suite bathroom is desirable for any bedroom.

Il est recommandé d'avoir une salle de bains adjacente ou intégrée à toutes les chambres.

Für alle Schlafzimmer ist es ratsam, über ein anliegendes bzw. En-suite-Bad zu verfügen.

Voor gelijk welke slaapkamer is een aangrenzende of en suite badkamer wenselijk.

423

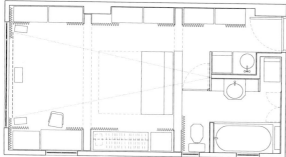

137   The position and angle of the bed are impor-   La disposition de la chambre est importante et
tant; many believe they can even affect the   de nombreuses personnes pensent que cela
quality of your sleep.   peut même affecter la qualité du sommeil.

Die Anordnung des Betts ist wichtig. Viele Leute glauben sogar, dass diese Anordnung Auswirkungen auf die Schlafqualität hat.

De opstelling van het bed is belangrijk en veel mensen geloven zelfs dat deze de kwaliteit van de nachtrust kan beïnvloeden.

138 Because of its restful nature, the use of color in the bedroom should be restrained.

Étant donné que la fonction d'une chambre c'est de pouvoir s'y reposer, l'utilisation de la couleur doit être modérée.

Da die Funktion des Schlafzimmers darin besteht, sich dort ausruhen zu können, sollte
Farbe moderat eingesetzt werden.

Aangezien de slaapkamer fungeert als rust-
plaats, is het raadzaam het gebruik van kleuren te beperken.

139

Decorating bedrooms provides a great opportunity to play with textures: experiment with bed linen, cushions and drapes.

La décoration des chambres offre une bonne opportunité pour jouer avec les textures : faites des essais avec la literie, les coussins et les rideaux.

Die Schlafzimmergestaltung bietet eine gute Möglichkeit, mit Texturen zu spielen: Experimentieren Sie mit der Bettwäsche, den Kissen und den Vorhängen.

Bij de inrichting van slaapkamers kan met texturen gespeeld worden: experimenteer met beddengoed, kussens en gordijnen.

435

140

Location-specific lighting is important. Whether beside the bed or overhead, lamps should not cast shadows, as this will inhibit reading.

L'éclairage local est important. Que ce soit à côté du lit ou au-dessus, les lampes ne doivent pas projeter d'ombre.

Lokale Beleuchtung ist wichtig. Egal ob neben oder über dem Bett, die Lampen sollten keine Schatten werfen.

De plaatselijke verlichting is belangrijk. Of de lampen zich nu aan de zijkant van het bed of erboven bevinden, zij mogen geen schaduwen werpen.

141

Personalizing a bedroom can be fun and easy. Murals, collages and even graffiti can all be used to make walls with flair.

La personnalisation d'une chambre peut être une activité divertissante et aisée. On peut utiliser des peintures murales, des collages et même des graffitis.

Die persönliche Gestaltung eines Schlafzimmers kann lustig und einfach sein. Man kann Wandgemälde, Collagen und sogar Graffitis einsetzen.

Een slaapkamer een persoonlijk tintje geven kan een leuke en eenvoudige activiteit zijn. Er kunnen muurschilderingen, collages en zelfs graffiti worden gebruikt.

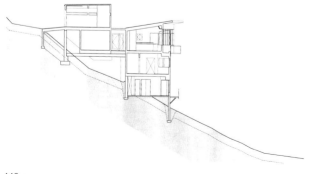

440

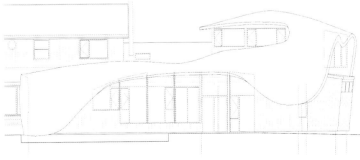

441

142

In reduced space dwellings, foldaway beds can be a good choice.

Dans les habitations peu spacieuses, les lits pliants peuvent constituer une bonne option.

In Wohnungen mit wenig Platz können Klappbetten eine gute Wahl sein.

In woningen met weinig ruimte kunnen vouwbedden een goede optie zijn.

143

Big cushions can also form a soft 'headboard' and have the added advantage of providing good neck support.

Les gros coussins peuvent aussi former un traversin moelleux et présentent l'avantage d'offrir un bon appui pour le cou.

Große Kissen können ein weiches Kopfteil bilden und bieten außerdem den Vorteil einer guten Nackenstütze.

De grote kussens kunnen ook worden gebruikt als zacht hoofdkussen en bieden tevens steun in de nek.

144

Sofa beds are useful, but should generally only be used for guests and not as the main bed.

Les canapés-lits sont utiles, même s'ils ne doivent être utilisés que pour les invités, jamais comme lit principal.

Bettcouchs sind nützlich, sollten aber nur für Gäste und nicht als Hauptbett verwendet werden.

Slaapbanken zijn nuttig, hoewel ze alleen gebruikt zouden moeten worden voor logés en nooit om er dagelijks op te slapen.

145

Day beds can be used for guests and to provide an extra sofa in the living area.

Les invités peuvent aussi dormir dans des transats utilisés comme canapé complémentaire dans le salon.

Gäste können auch auf Chaiselongues schlafen. Diese können wiederum als Zusatzsofa für das Wohnzimmer verwendet werden.

Logés kunnen eveneens op chaises longues slapen, die ook weer als extra bank in de zitkamer kunnen worden gebruikt.

451

146

Make up beds simply: nothing beats crisp white cotton sheets and perhaps a splash of color in the pillow or blanket.

Préparez les lits simplement : il n'y a rien de mieux que des draps en coton blanc et une touche de couleur pour l'oreiller ou la couverture.

Gestalten Sie die Betten einfach: nichts ist besser als weiße Baumwolllaken und ein Hauch Farbe am Kopfkissen oder auf der Decke.

Maak de bedden eenvoudig op: er bestaat niets beters dan witte katoenen lakens en wat kleur in het kussen of de deken.

147

Bursts of light at your bedside are important, whether from overhanging lamps or lamps placed on tables.

L'éclairage à côté du lit est fondamental, que ce soit des appliques ou des lampes de chevet.

Die Beleuchtung neben dem Bett ist wichtig – egal ob mit Hängelampen oder anhand von Lampenschirmen auf den Nachtschränkchen.

De verlichting naast het bed is belangrijk. Het kunnen hanglampen zijn of op nachtkastjes staande lampen.

148

Attic bedrooms are particularly cozy and alluring. Place the bed underneath the skylight.

Les chambres d'un appartement sous les toits sont particulièrement chaleureuses et accueillantes. Placez le lit sous la lucarne.

Zimmer in Dachgeschossen sind besonders warm und gemütlich. Stellen Sie das Bett unter die Dachluke.

Slaapkamers op de zolderverdieping zijn bijzonder gezellig en knus. Zet het bed onder het dakraam.

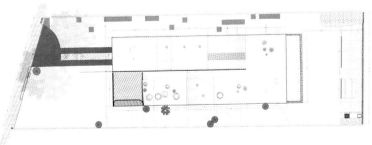

459

149

Whether minimalist or more elaborate, your bedroom is your own private sanctuary.

Indépendamment du style que vous choisissez, la chambre est votre sanctuaire personnel et son accès est restreint.

Ungeachtet des gewählten Stils ist das Schlafzimmer Ihr persönliches Heiligtum und nicht jedem zugänglich.

Het maakt niet uit welke stijl u kiest, de slaapkamer is uw persoonlijk heiligdom waartoe maar weinig mensen toegang krijgen.

150 *Storing clothing requires good organization, with rails, shelves and drawers.*

Le rangement de votre garde-robe requiert une bonne organisation, avec des penderies, des rayons et des tiroirs.

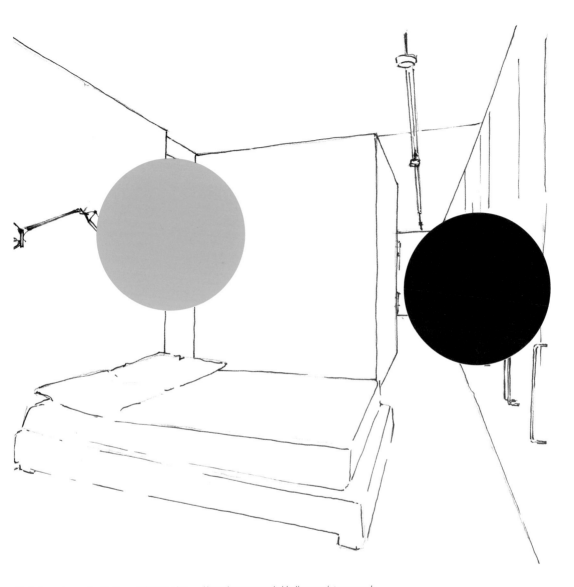

Die Aufbewahrung der Kleidung erfordert eine gute Organisation mit Stangen, Fächern und Schubladen.

Het opbergen van de kleding vereist een goede organisatie met stangen, planken en laden.

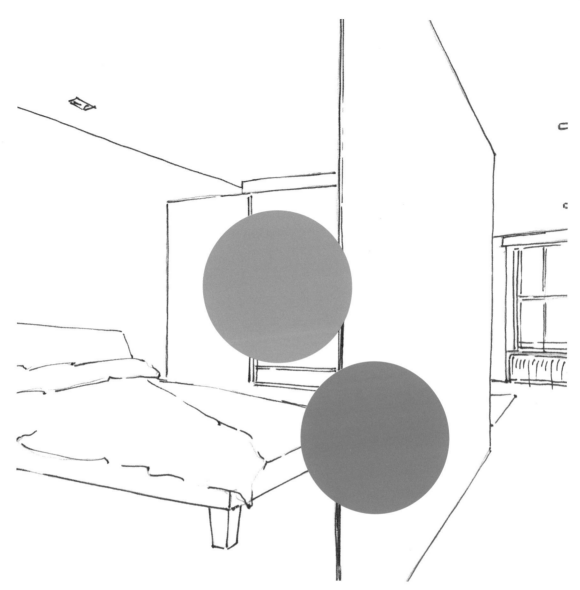

151

When creating a suite with a bedroom, a bath-room and a small living area, the dimensions of the room must be taken into account.

Si vous voulez une chambre du type en-suite, avec la salle de bains et un petit espace à vivre, il faut mesurer les espaces dont vous disposez.

Soll ein Schlafzimmer im Suite-Stil mit Bad und kleinem Aufenthaltsraum entstehen, so muss die verfügbare Größe des Raums in Betracht gezogen werden.

Wilt u een slaapkamer in suitestijl creëren met een badkamer en een kleine zitruimte, dan dient beoordeeld te worden over welke afmetingen we beschikken.

152

Separating spaces with movable partition walls enables a home to adapt to changing needs.

La séparation des espaces au moyen de cloisons mobiles permet d'adapter l'habitation aux besoins du moment.

Räumliche Abtrennungen mit mobilen Wänden ermöglichen die Anpassung der Wohnung an den jeweiligen Bedarf.

Dankzij de scheiding van de ruimten door middel van verplaatsbare schotten kan de woning aangepast worden aan de behoeften van elk moment.

BATHROOMS > SALLES DE BAINS

BADEZIMMER > BADKAMERS

Today's culture of well-being and the proliferation of spas have encouraged many designers to transfer these principles to domestic spheres. Although its use remains mainly functional, the bathroom need not be merely a space for daily ablutions.

Die Wellnesskultur und die steigende Zahl der Kuranlagen haben viele Designer dazu bewegt, solche Prinzipien auch in den häuslichen Bereich zu übertragen. Das Bad bewahrt zwar weiterhin seinen funktionellen Verwendungszweck, was aber nicht bedeutet, dass es nur ein Bereich für die tägliche Hygiene sein muss.

La culture du bien-être et la prolifération des stations balnéaires ont poussé de nombreux designers à tenter de transmettre ces principes à la sphère domestique. Même si l'utilisation de la salle de bains reste fonctionnelle, pourquoi ne pas en faire plus qu'un simple espace consacré à l'hygiène quotidienne.

De welzijnscultuur en de proliferatie van welnesscentra hebben ervoor gezorgd dat veel ontwerpers proberen deze principes naar de huiselijke sfeer over te brengen. Hoewel het gebruik van de badkamer functioneel blijft, hoeft het niet alleen maar een ruimte voor de dagelijkse hygiëne te zijn.

153

A Zen-like tranquility can be achieved by using natural stone and a minimal color palette.

On peut obtenir une tranquillité zen en utilisant la pierre naturelle et une gamme de couleurs restreinte au maximum.

Zen-Ruhe wird durch den Einsatz von Naturstein und eine möglichst knapp gehaltene Farbpalette erzielt.

Er kan rust in zenstijl worden bereikt door het gebruik van natuursteen en een minimaal kleurengamma.

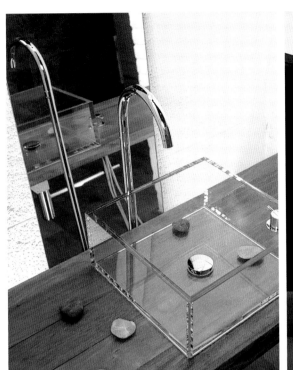

154 *Here a piece of period furniture has been placed among modern steel shelves and fittings, juxtaposing old and new.*

Ici, un meuble d'époque se trouve entres des étagères modernes en acier, créant une juxtaposition d'éléments anciens et modernes.

In diesem Fall steht ein antikes Möbelstück zwischen modernen Stahlregalen und schafft die Verbindung antiker und moderner Elemente.

In dit geval wordt een antiek meubelstuk tussen moderne stalen rekken geplaatst, zodat een combinatie van oude en moderne elementen ontstaat.

155

Long, narrow bathrooms can benefit from large mirrors and keeping the core materials to an absolute minimum.

Les salles de bains longues et étroites peuvent utiliser à volonté des miroirs larges et réduire au minimum les matériaux principaux.

Lange und schmale Badezimmer können durch großzügige Spiegel und eine möglichst weitgehende Reduzierung der wichtigsten Materialien begünstigt werden.

In lange, smalle badkamers kunnen grote spiegels een gunstig effect hebben en kunnen de hoofdmaterialen tot een minimum beperkt worden.

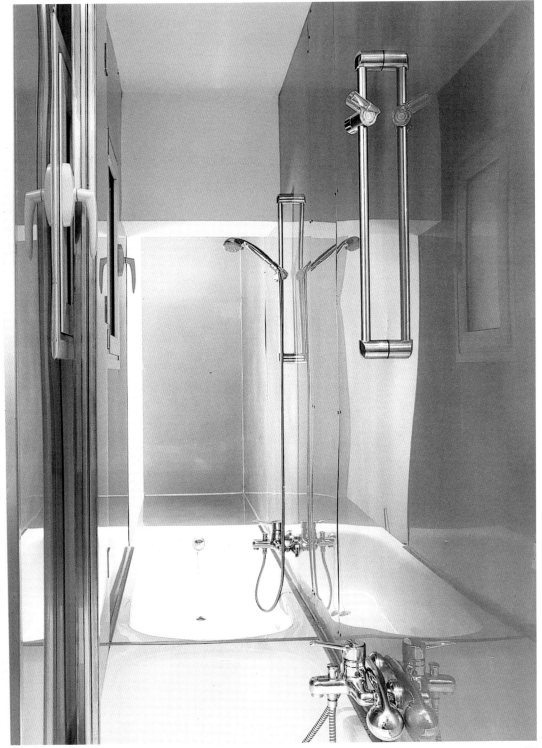

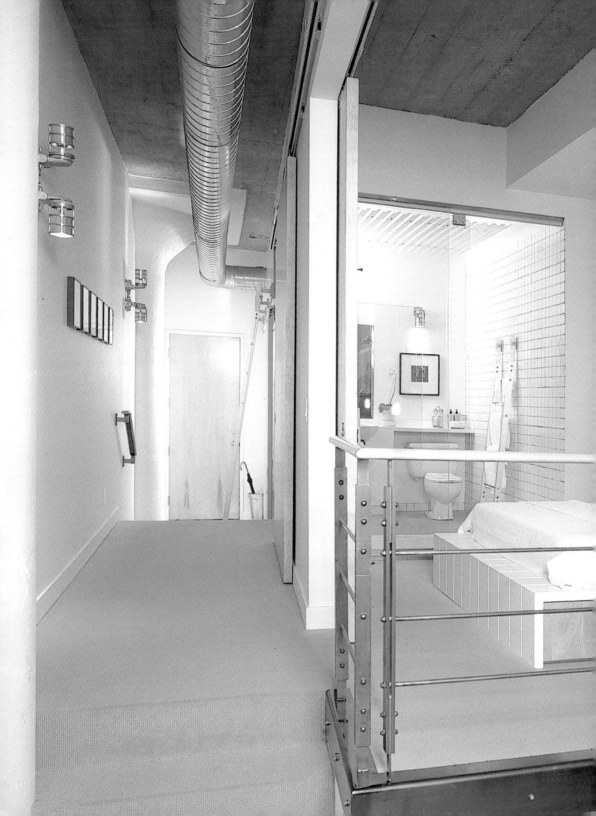

156

Opening up bathrooms to the rest of the home via glass installations provides light and space.

L'ouverture des salles de bains au reste de la maison par le biais de dispositifs en verre apporte lumière et espace.

Die Öffnung der Badezimmer anhand von Glasinstallationen zum Rest des Hauses hin vermehrt Licht und Raum.

Het openen van de badkamers naar de rest van het huis door middel van glaswanden zorgt voor licht en ruimte.

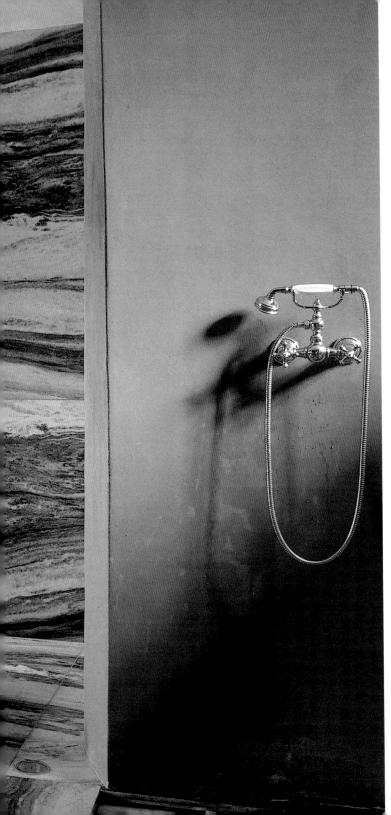

157

Here, the architects have decided to leave a section of the original wall exposed, creating a textural interplay between stone and marble.

Les architectes ont décidé de laisser apparent une partie du mur d'origine, ce qui crée une interaction de textures entre le marbre et la pierre.

Die Architekten haben entschieden, einen Teil der ursprünglichen Wand sichtbar zu lassen. Dadurch entsteht eine Wechselwirkung zwischen Marmor und Stein.

De architecten hebben besloten om een deel van de oorspronkelijke muur bloot te laten en een interactie van texturen tussen het marmer en de steen te creëren.

158

Derivatives of what we commonly call 'plastic' can offer inexpensive, practical and imaginative solutions.

Les dérivés de la matière, communément appelée plastique, peuvent nous apporter des solutions abordables, pratiques et imaginatives.

Materialderivate, die allgemein als Kunststoff bekannt sind, können erschwingliche, praktische und erfindungsreiche Lösungen bieten.

Derivaten van het materiaal, dat in het algemeen bekendstaat als plastic, kunnen betaalbare, praktische en fantasierijke oplossingen verschaffen.

159

An endless variety of colors, forms and textures are available.

Toutes les possibilités sont à votre portée grâce à un grand nombre de couleurs, de formes et de textures.

Dank einer unendlichen Vielfalt an Farben, For-
men und Texturen stehen Ihnen alle Möglich-
keiten offen.

U beschikt over allerlei mogelijkheden dankzij
oneindig veel kleuren, vormen en texturen.

493

160 *An open-plan bathroom can free up space for features such as this generous walk-in shower.*

La salle de bains au plan ouvert peut libérer de l'espace pour intégrer des éléments comme cette douche à accès latéral.

Das Badezimmer mit offenem Grundriss kann Platz zur Integration von Elementen – wie in diesem Fall einer Dusche mit Seiteneingang – bieten.

De open badkamer kan kan plaats vrijmaken om er elementen zoals deze ruime instapdouche in onder te brengen.

161

In loft dwellings, consider sectioning off the bathroom area with a screen or freestanding partition.

Dans les habitations de type loft, on doit envisager l'idée de séparer le coin salle de bains à l'aide d'un panneau ou d'une séparation verticale.

In Lofts sollte man die Idee erwägen, den Badezimmerbereich mit einem Paneel oder einer senkrechten Teilung abzutrennen.

In lofts dient rekening gehouden te worden met het idee dat het badkamergedeelte dient te worden afgeschermd met een paneel of verticale scheidingswand.

162

Freestanding bathroom furniture, such as this vanity unit, can make a bathroom feel more spacious.

Le mobilier modulaire de la salle de bains, comme ce cabinet de toilette (en-haut) peut offrir une impression d'espace dans une pièce.

Badezimmermöbel im Baukastenstil, wie dieser Toilettentisch (oben), lassen den Raum größer wirken.

Het modulaire meubilair van de badkamer, zoals deze wastafel (boven), kan ervoor zorgen dat het vertrek ruimer lijkt.

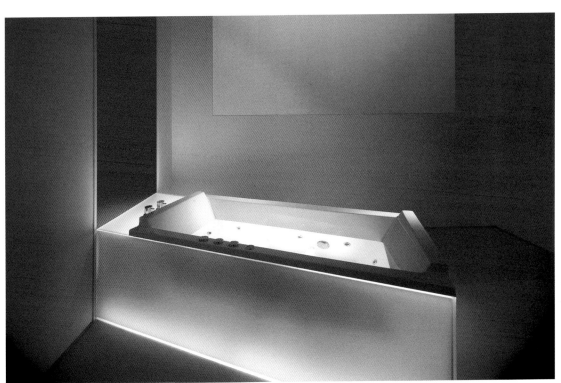

163

On the mezzanine floor of this loft home, a second bathroom is kept free from adornment and furniture, heightening its purely functional role.

Sous la mezzanine de cette maison de type loft, on trouve une deuxième salle de bains, sans décoration ni meubles, qui vise à remplir sa fonction basique.

Im Obergeschoss dieses Lofthauses gibt es ein zweites Bad ohne Verzierungen und Möbel, um damit seine grundlegende Funktion zu betonen.

Op de tussenverdieping van deze loft bevindt zich een tweede badkamer zonder versieringen en meubels. Hierdoor komt de basisfunctie ervan beter naar voren.

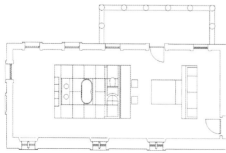

506

164

Depending on the level of privacy you need, choosing to not enclose the shower area can save a great deal of space in small bathrooms.

En fonction du niveau d'intimité que vous souhaitez, vous pourrez éviter de fermer la partie douche et disposer ainsi d'un espace plus vaste.

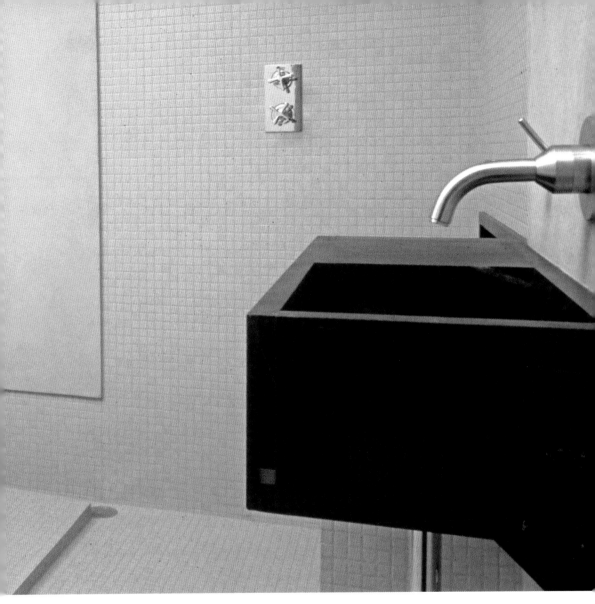

Je nach gewünschter Privatsphäre besteht die Möglichkeit, auf den Abschluss des Duschraums zu verzichten und damit mehr Platz zu gewinnen.

Op grond van het gewenste privacyniveau is het mogelijk om af te zien van een gesloten douche en zo meer ruimte te krijgen.

165

Common in Arabian bathhouse architecture, sunken baths are particularly alluring.

Les baignoires, très courantes dans l'architecture des salles de bains arabes, sont situées à un niveau inférieur, ce qui offre un charme tout particulier.

Die in der Architektur arabischer Bäder sehr
häufigen Badewannen auf niedrigerer Ebene
sind besonders attraktiv.

Badkuipen die op een lager niveau zijn aangebracht, een gewoonte in de architectuur van de
Arabische baden, zijn bijzonder aantrekkelijk.

511

166

If you have the space, a double washbasin is ideal for large households.

Si vous avez de la place, un lavabo double est idéal dans les grandes maisons.

Bei ausreichend Platz ist ein doppeltes Wasch-becken in großen Wohnungen ideal.

Als u over ruimte beschikt dan is een dubbele wastafel voor grote huisgezinnen ideaal.

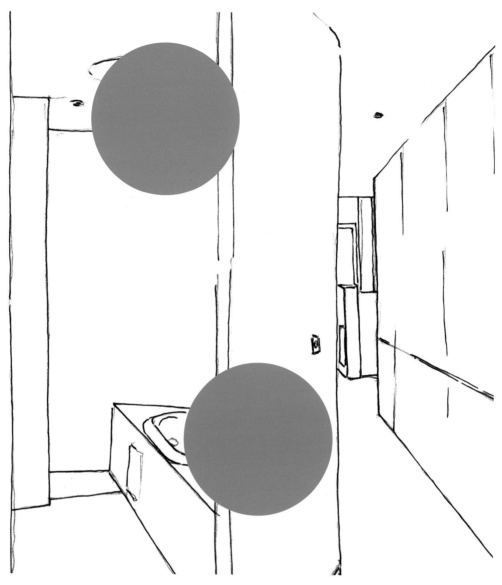

167

Companies have ingenious methods for installing bathroom fittings, including pieces by prestigious designers, to adapt to any space.

Les entreprises disposent de formules innovantes pour installer les sanitaires dans n'importe quel type d'espace, y compris des pièces signées par des designers prestigieux, afin de s'adapter à n'importe quel espace.

Die Firmen bieten neuartige Formeln für den Einbau der Sanitäreinrichtungen in alle Bereiche. Auch Einrichtungen berühmter Designer können an jeden Raum angepasst werden.

De sanitairfabrikanten bieden nieuwe formules om sanitair in elk type ruimte te installeren. Er worden zelfs artikelen van prestigieuze ontwerpers aangeboden die aan elke ruimte kunnen worden aangepast.

515

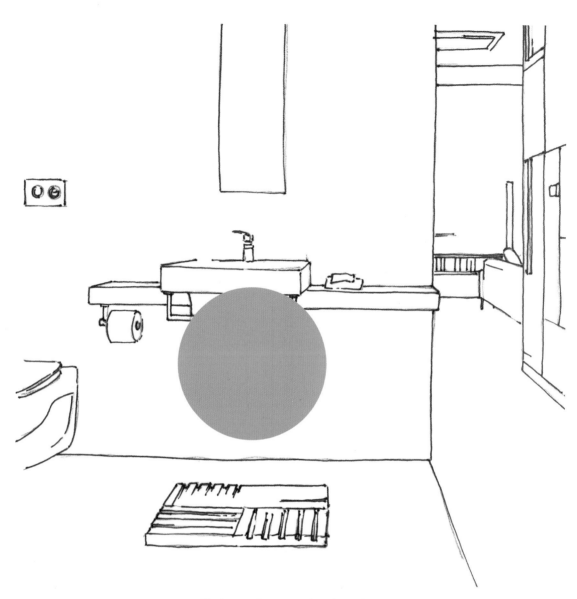

168

Simple, natural geometry adorns the modern bathroom, where relaxation and a harmonious style prevail.

Les géométries simples se retrouvent dans la salle de bains où dominent la relaxation et l'harmonie esthétique.

Einfache Geometrien entsprechen dem Badezimmer, wo Entspannung und ästhetische Harmonie vorherrschen.

Eenvoudige vormen passen bij een badkamer waar ontspanning en esthetische harmonie overheersen.

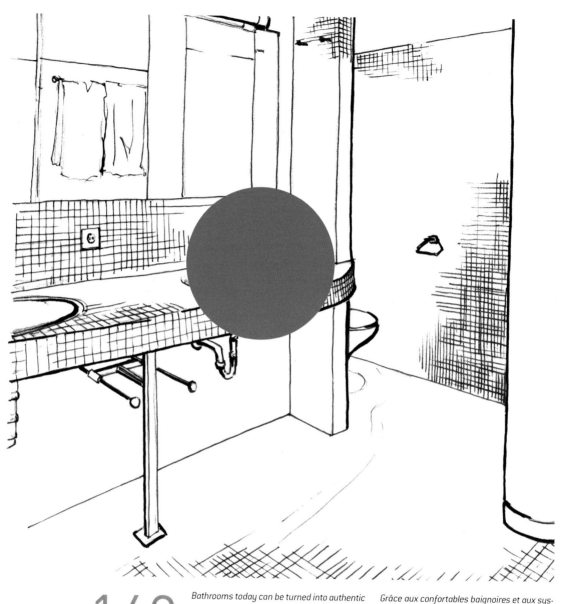

169 Bathrooms today can be turned into authentic home spas through installing comfortable baths and hydrotherapy systems.

Grâce aux confortables baignoires et aux systèmes d'hydro-massage, les salles de bains d'aujourd'hui peuvent se devenir de véritables spas à domicile.

Dank komfortabler Badewannen und Hydro-massageanlagen können die heutigen Bade-zimmer zu echten Heimwellnessanlagen werden.

Dankzij de comfortabele baden en hydromas-sagesystemen kunnen badkamers vandaag de dag veranderen in ware huisspa's.

ALL IN ONE SPACES > TOUT EN UN

ALLES IN EINEM > ALLES IN ÉÉN

All in one living spaces, such as studios, make maximum use of the room available. One of the trends most commonly employed to create a feeling of open-plan spaciousness is to knock down partition walls, eliminating separate rooms and joining, for instance, the dining room and kitchen. This makes properties seem much larger.

Les habitations de type studio mettent à profit l'espace disponible de manière optimale. L'une des techniques les plus utilisées pour donner une sensation d'amplitude consiste à éliminer toute cloison, et supprimer des pièces ou les réunir, comme la salle à manger et la cuisine. On obtient ainsi l'impression que l'habitation est plus grande.

In Atelierwohnungen wird der verfügbare Raum optimal genutzt. Eine der häufigsten Techniken, um den Eindruck von mehr Platz zu erwecken, besteht darin, Wände einzureißen, Zimmer zu entfernen oder Räume wie Esszimmer und Küche zu verbinden. Dadurch erreicht man, dass die Wohnung viel größer erscheint.

In éénkamerflats wordt optimaal gebruik gemaakt van de beschikbare ruimte. Eén van de meest gebruikte technieken om een gevoel van ruimte te geven is het afbreken van een tussenwand, het elimineren van kamers of het samenvoegen van vertrekken, zoals de eetkamer en keuken. Zo lukt het om het huis veel groter te laten lijken.

170

The aim in this loft was to adapt numerous functions, ingeniously organized to maximize the space available.

Dans ce loft, on a voulu adapter de multiples fonctions ingénieusement organisées pour maximiser l'espace disponible.

Die Idee dieses Lofts bestand darin, zahlreiche
erfinderisch organisierte Funktionen anzupassen, um den verfügbaren Raum zu maxi-
mieren.

De bedoeling van deze loft was vele op vindingrijke wijze georganiseerde functies aan te
passen om de beschikbare ruimte te maxima-
liseren.

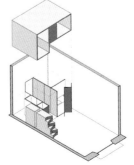

171

Using multifunctional pieces, such as this staircase, enable different functions of the house to be organized in just one element.

L'utilisation d'éléments multifonctionnels, comme cet escalier, permet d'organiser différentes fonctions de la maison dans une seule pièce.

Der Einsatz von Mehrzweckelementen – wie diese Treppe – macht es möglich, verschiedene Funktionen der Wohnung in einem Raum anzuordnen.

Dankzij het gebruik van multifunctionele elementen, zoals deze trap, is het mogelijk om in één vertrek verschillende functies van de woning onder te brengen.

172

Many studios are located in renovated properties where the new space has been adapted to
the existing infrastructure.

De nombreux studios se trouvent dans des habitations remodelées, où les nouveaux espaces
s'adaptent aux infrastructures existantes.

Viele Atelierwohnungen befinden sich in um-
gebauten Häusern, wo sich die neuen Bereiche
an die vorhandenen Infrastrukturen anpassen.

Veel éénkamerflats bevinden zich in gereno-
veerde woningen, waar de nieuwe ruimten zich
aanpassen aan de bestaande infrastructuren.

173

The introduction of auxiliary structures enables very organized designs that can be adapted to suit the client's taste.

L'introduction de structures auxiliaires fournit des plans très organisés qui s'adaptent aux goûts du client.

Die Verwendung von Hilfsstrukturen ermöglicht sehr gut organisierte, den Kundenwünschen angepasste Programme.

Dankzij de introductie van hulpstructuren zijn goede opstellingen ontstaan die zijn aangepast aan de smaak van de klant.

174 *The more protected zones of the house can be a good place to put areas for entertainment and resting.*

Les parties les plus protégées de la maison peuvent constituer une bonne option pour abriter les espaces de distraction et de détente.

Die am besten geschützten Bereiche der Woh-
nungen bieten sich als Unterhaltungs- oder Ru-
hezonen an.

De meest beschermde zones van de woning
kunnen gebruikt worden als ruimten voor ver-
maak en rust.

175

The spaces in less frequently used areas can be hidden by drapes, creating greater privacy.

Grâce à l'utilisation de rideaux, les espaces situés dans des parties peu habituelles peuvent bénéficier d'une plus grande intimité, et ainsi passer inaperçues.

Anhand von Vorhängen können Räume in recht
ungewöhnlichen Bereichen eine höhere Privatsphäre bieten und sogar unauffällig bleiben.

Dankzij het gebruik van gordijnen kunnen
ruimten in weinig gebruikte zones meer privacy genieten, alsmede onopgemerkt blijven.

176

Function, structure, color, ergonomics and materials are factors to be considered when selecting elements for a house.

La fonction, la structure et la couleur sont des facteurs dont il faut tenir compte au moment du choix du mobilier.

Bei der Auswahl des Mobiliars sind Funktion, Struktur und Farbe zu beachten.

Functie, structuur en kleur zijn factoren waarmee rekening dient te worden gehouden wanneer het meubilair wordt uitgekozen.

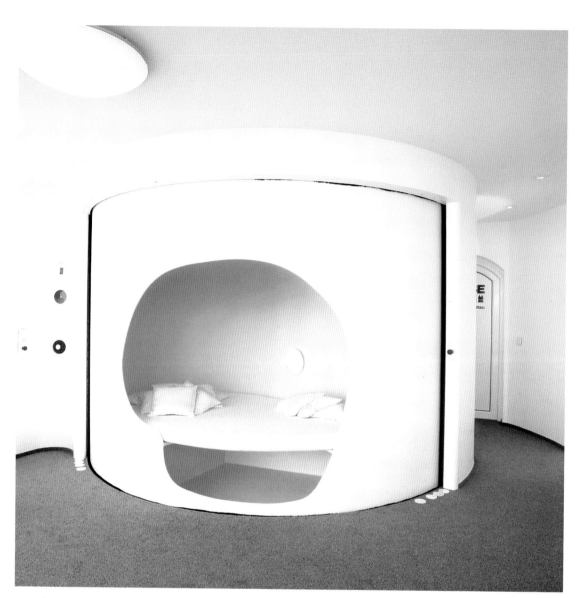

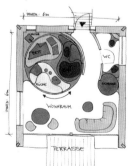

540

177

One option is to choose a large sink that protrudes from the bathroom wall and to place a mirror at eye-level.

On peut opter pour un grand lavabo qui dépasse des murs de la salle de bains et rehausser le miroir au niveau des yeux.

Man kann sich für ein großes Becken entscheiden, das aus der Badezimmerwand hervorragt, und den Spiegel auf Augenhöhe anheben.

Men kan kiezen voor een grote wasbak die zich onderscheidt van de badkamermuur en de plaatsing van een spiegel ter hoogte van de ogen.

178

Create a space with character by incorporating graphic elements such as this Japanese-style decoration.

On peut obtenir un espace doté de caractère en intégrant des éléments graphiques, comme cette décoration de type japonaise.

Durch die Aufnahme graphischer Elemente wie dieser japanischen Dekoration ist es möglich, Bereiche mit Charakter zu schaffen.

Het is mogelijk om een karaktervolle ruimte te creëren dankzij de integratie van grafische elementen, zoals deze Japanse versiering.

179

In this case, an island has been placed in the middle as the centerpiece, enabling circulation around it.

Ici, on a choisi une île comme élément principal, et la circulation s'organise autour de cette dernière.

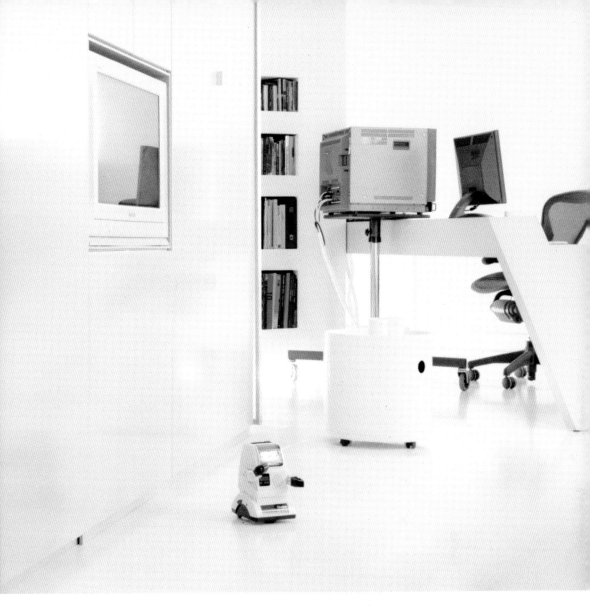

In diesem Fall hat man sich für eine Insellö-
sung als Hauptelement entschieden. Der Verkehr verläuft um die Insel herum.

In dit geval koos men als hoofdelement een ei-
land, waar men omheen kan lopen.

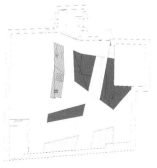

180

The living room, dining room and work spaces normally occupy the same room in studios.

Dans les studios, le salon, la salle à manger et l'espace de travail se trouvent généralement dans la même pièce.

In Atelierwohnungen teilen sich Wohnzimmer, Esszimmer und Arbeitsraum normalerweise das gleiche Ambiente.

In éénkamerflats worden salon, eetkamer en werkplek meestal in dezelfde ruimte ondergebracht.

181

Tables with a basic rectangular shape, on a support with wheels, are more flexible as they are easy to move and have multiple uses.

Les tables à roulettes garantissent une plus grande flexibilité grâce à leur transport facile et à leurs fonctions multiples.

Tische mit Rädern bieten dank ihres einfachen Transports und ihrer mehrfachen Einsatzmöglichkeiten höhere Flexibilität.

Tafels met wieltjes zorgen voor meer flexibiliteit omdat ze gemakkelijk te verplaatsen zijn en op vele manieren gebruikt kunnen worden.

182

This small house makes use of all available space without enclosing areas by using unnecessary partition walls.

Cette habitation aux dimensions réduites tire profit de tout l'espace sans s'enfermer derrière des cloisons inutiles.

Diese Wohnung mit reduzierten Abmessungen nutzt den gesamten Raum, ohne sich in unnötige Wände einzuschließen.

Deze kleine woning benut alle ruimte zonder onnodige tussenwanden.

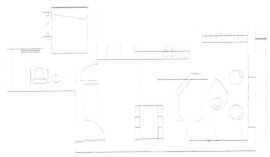

559

183

*Graphic installations are the clear protago-
nists in an apartment space that is inspired
by cartoons.*

*Dans cet appartement, les motifs graphiques
deviennent les héros d'un espace inspiré des
dessins animés.*

In diesem Appartement werden die graphi-
schen Motive zu Hauptdarstellern eines an Zei-
chentrickfilmen inspirierten Bereichs.

In dit appartement spelen grafische motieven
een belangrijke rol in een ruimte die is geïnspireerd op tekenfilms.

184

Roofs can be converted into stylish, habitable spaces for urban nomads.

Les toits de certains bâtiments se transforment en espaces habitables, parfaits pour les nomades urbains.

Die Dächer einiger Gebäude erweisen sich als ausgezeichnete Wohnräume für städtische Nomaden.

De daken van sommige gebouwen worden omgebouwd tot bewoonbare ruimten, ideaal voor stadsnomaden.

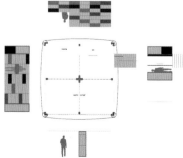

185

Wallpaper is making a big comeback. Today, there are a whole range of colors, textures and patterns on the market.

La tapisserie est revenue massivement et présente une combinaison de couleurs, de textures et de dessins intéressants.

Tapeten sind wieder ganz stark im Kommen und bieten interessante Farb-, Textur- und Musterkombinationen.

Behang is weer helemaal in. Er zijn interessante combinaties van kleuren, texturen en dessins verkrijgbaar.

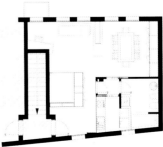

186

An innovative bedroom can be created by choosing a structure that houses the bed and storage space.

Une option pour créer une chambre originale consiste à choisir une structure qui abrite le lit et l'espace suffisant pour le rangement.

Eine Option für ein originelles Schlafzimmer besteht in einer Struktur, die Bett und ausreichenden Aufbewahrungsraum umfasst.

Een manier om een originele slaapkamer te creëren is te kiezen voor een structuur die zowel het bed als de nodige opbergruimte omvat.

187

Multifunctional elements are the best way to solve the problem of limited spaces. Fitted closets and furniture that is easy to move help adapt the space to different functions.

Les armoires encastrées et le mobilier facile à manipuler permettront d'adapter l'espace aux différentes fonctions.

Wandschränke und leicht handzuhabende Möbel helfen dabei, den Raum an die verschiedenen Funktionen anzupassen.

Inbouwkasten en gemakkelijk te hanteren meubels helpen bij het aanpassen van de ruimte aan verschillende functies.

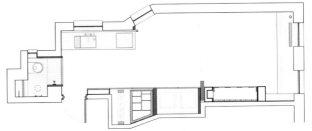

188

When one space contains different areas it is important to create a multipurpose environment where the furniture adapts to meet different needs.

Les concepteurs de ce projet ont utilisé la dernière technologie pour adapter les fonctions de l'habitation à une pièce extrêmement petite.

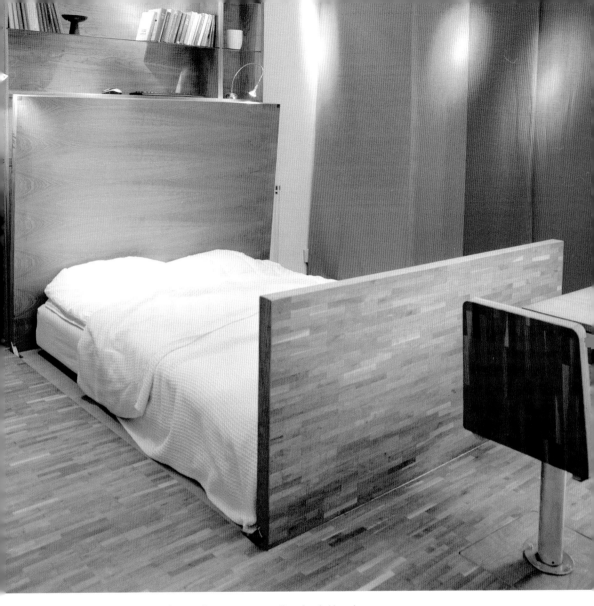

Die Designer dieses Projekts haben neuartigste Technologien eingesetzt, um die Funktionen der Wohnung einem außerordentlich kleinen Raum anzupassen.

De ontwerpers van dit project hebben de modernste technologie gebruikt om de functies van de woning af te stemmen op een buitengewoon kleine kamer.

189

When space allows, a mezzanine enables space to be vertically distributed in order to create privacy in some areas.

Lorsque l'espace le permet, une mezzanine distribue les pièces verticalement pour favoriser les espaces privés.

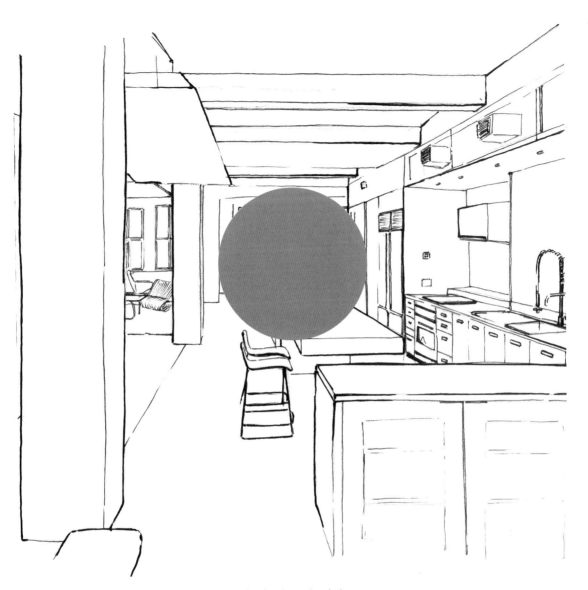

Wenn es die Räumlichkeiten zulassen, teilt ein Zwischengeschoss die Räume senkrecht zugunsten von Privatbereichen auf.

Wanneer de ruimte het toelaat deelt een mezzanine de vertrekken verticaal in, wat gunstig is voor de privéruimten.

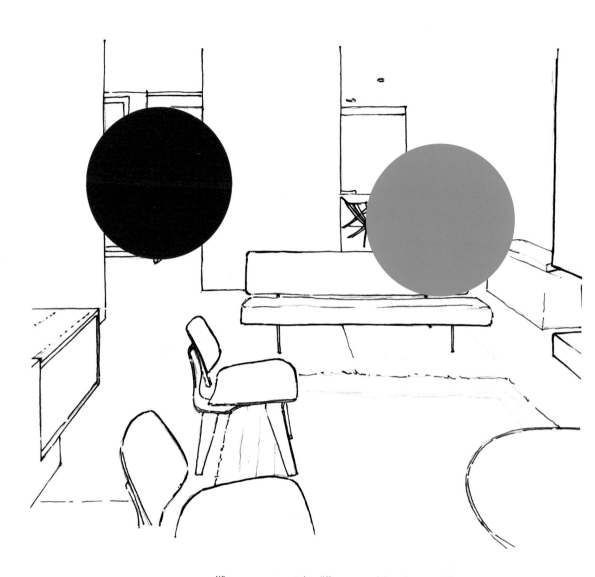

190

When one space contains different areas it is important to create a multipurpose environment where the furniture adapts to meet different needs.

Lorsque différents espaces se trouvent dans une seule pièce, il faut faire en sorte que les meubles s'adaptent selon les besoins.

Liegen verschiedene Bereiche im gleichen Ambiente, müssen die Möbel ihre Funktionen dem jeweiligen Bedarf anpassen.

Wanneer verschillende vertrekken in één ruimte overvloeien, moet ervoor gezorgd worden dat de meubels al naar gelang de behoeften van functies kunnen wisselen.

OUTSIDE SPACES > ESPACES EXTÉRIEURS

AUSSENBEREICHE > BUITENRUIMTEN

Newly built constructions often integrate outside spaces into the design, or at least have an ample balcony. People with outside spaces often don't use them to their full potential; balconies are frequently neglected, and decks and terraces are filled with junk.

Generell bieten neue Gebäude Terrassen und Innenhöfe oder bauen zumindest einen großzügigen Balkon ein. Oftmals werden sie von ihren Eigentümern jedoch nicht optimal genutzt: Balkone werden häufig vernachlässigt, und Innenhöfe und Terrassen füllen sich mit selten gebrauchtem Gerümpel.

En général, les constructions récentes intègrent le design de terrasses et de cours, ou tout au moins, prévoient un généreux balcon. Mais fréquemment les personnes qui en possèdent n'en tirent pas le meilleur parti : les balcons sont souvent négligés et les cours et terrasses se remplissent de vieilleries peu utilisées.

Over het algemeen zijn moderne gebouwen uitgerust met terrassen en patio's of in ieder geval met een groot balkon. Maar vaak profiteren de mensen die erover beschikken er niet optimaal van: balkonnen worden vaak niet verzorgd en patio's en terrassen worden gevuld met weinig gebruikte spullen.

191 Hard-wearing polished stone or ceramic tiles make ideal terrace flooring, especially if the space is exposed to the elements.

Les carreaux en pierre polie et en céramique constituent un sol parfait pour la terrasse, surtout lorsqu'il est exposé aux intempéries.

Platten aus poliertem Stein und Keramik stellen einen idealen Terrassenboden dar, insbesondere, wenn dieser der Witterung ausgesetzt ist.

Tegels van gepolijst steen en keramiek zijn ideaal voor de betegeling van terrasvloeren, vooral wanneer deze aan de weersomstandigheden worden blootgesteld.

587

192

Create privacy on urban decks by using partition walls and elevated elements.

Vous gagnez en intimité sur les terrasses urbaines avec des murs de séparation et des éléments élevés.

Schaffen Sie anhand von Trennwänden und hohen Elementen Privatsphäre auf städtischen Terrassen.

Op stadsterrassen krijgt men meer privacy door er scheidingswanden en hoge elementen te plaatsen.

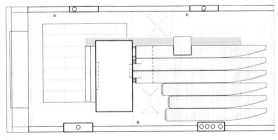

193

Dramatic wall decorations, ceramic art, sculpture and water features can all work well in exterior spaces.

Dans les espaces extérieurs on retrouve aussi des éléments impressionnants comme des murs, des œuvres en céramique, des sculptures et des points d'eau.

In Außenbereichen machen sich auch spektakuläre Elemente wie Wände, Keramikwerke, Skulpturen und Wasserstellen gut.

In buitenruimten functioneren opvallende elementen zoals wanden, keramieken bouwwerken, beeldhouwwerken en waterpunten ook.

194

This simple skirting board of natural pebbles, chosen to emphasize the space's sea vistas, frames the deck's dimensions.

Ce simple socle en pierres naturelles, choisi pour accentuer les vues de la mer, entoure le périmètre de la terrasse.

Dieser einfache Sockel aus Natursteinchen, der ausgewählt wurde, um den Blick aufs Meer zu betonen, rahmt die Abmessungen der Terrasse ein.

Deze eenvoudige plint van natuursteentjes, gekozen om het zeezicht te benadrukken, omkadert het terras.

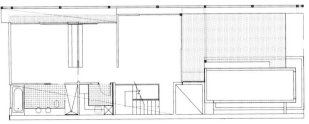

195

A balcony is not a storeroom; keep clutter away as it will discourage you from using the space.

Un balcon n'est pas un débarras et il faudrait donc qu'il reste dégagé, sinon, on n'est plus tenté de l'utiliser.

Ein Balkon ist kein Abstellraum und sollte nicht zugestellt werden, da er dann nicht zur Verwendung einlädt.

Een balkon is geen rommelhok. Het balkon moet dan ook opgeruimd blijven, anders wordt u niet aangemoedigd om het te gebruiken.

196

Choose a retractable canopy or study the sun's trajectory and opt for a partial roof.

Choisissez un store rabattable ou étudiez la position du soleil et installez un toit qui puisse l'abriter partiellement.

Wählen Sie eine Klappmarkise oder entscheiden Sie sich entsprechend der Sonnenstellung
für ein Dach mit Teilabdeckung.

Kies een opvouwbaar zonnescherm of kijk naar
de positie van de zon en kies voor een afdak
dat gedeeltelijk overdekt.

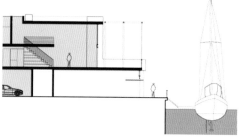

197

Acrylic fences and partitions make ideal, safe, contemporary deck and balcony enclosures.

Les clôtures et les séparations en acrylique constituent des moyens sûrs et modernes de fermeture, idéals pour les terrasses et les balcons.

Umzäunungen und Acrylabtrennungen stellen ideale, sichere und zeitgenössische Abschlüsse für Terrassen und Balkons dar.

Omheiningen en scheidingswanden van acryl zijn ideale, veilige en eigentijdse balkon- en terrasafsluitingen.

198

Entertaining outdoors needs the same amenities you would encounter inside; a sink and food preparation area, cooking facilities and comfortable furniture.

Pour des soirées en extérieur, on attend le même confort qu'à l'intérieur : un évier, un coin cuisine et du mobilier confortable.

Für Veranstaltungen im Freien ist der gleiche Komfort wie innerhalb erforderlich: Spülbecken, Kochbereich und bequeme Möbel.

Voor een gezellig avondje buiten zijn dezelfde gemakken nodig als binnen: een gootsteen, een ruimte om te koken en comfortabel meubilair.

199

Glass curtain walls and windows are the most effective way to integrate your deck into the rest of your home.

Les surfaces en verre sont la manière la plus efficace d'intégrer la terrasse au reste de la maison.

Glasflächen sind die wirksamste Art, die Terrasse in den Rest des Hauses zu integrieren.

Glaswanden zijn de efficiëntste manier om het terras deel te laten uitmaken van de rest van de woning.

200

This highly effective installation has been achieved using nothing more than bamboo trunks of varying lengths, arranged ad-hoc against a metal panel.

Cette installation si efficace a été obtenue uniquement à partir de pousses de bambou de différentes longueurs, alignées contre une plaque en métal.

Diese so wirksame Einrichtung entstand nur anhand von unterschiedlich langen Bambusstämmen, die gegen eine Metallplatte ausgerichtet wurden.

Deze efficiënte installatie werd verkregen door eenvoudigweg bamboestengels van verschillende lengtes tegen een metaalplaat te plaatsen.

DIRECTORY > RÉPERTOIRE
ADRESSENVERZEICHNIS > ADRESSENBESTAND

A-Cero
A Coruña, Spain
www.a-cero.com

Agustí Costa
Berga, Spain
www.agusticosta.com

Ai Wei Wei
www.aiweiwei.com

Air Projects
Barcelona, Spain
www.air-projects.com

Aires Mateus & Asociados, LDA
Lisbon, Portugal
www.airesmateus.com

Akira Sakamoto Architect & Associates
Osaka, Japan
www.akirasakamoto.com

Arantxa Garmendia, David Maturen
Zaragoza, Spain
davidmaturen@hotmail.com

Architectuur Centrale Thijs Asselbergs
Haarlem, The Netherlands
www.architectuurcentrale.nl

Architecture Workshop Ltd.
Wellington, New Zealand
www.archwksp.co.nz

Attilio Stocchi
Milan, Italy
www.saette.it

Audrey Matlock Architects
New York, USA
www.audreymatlock.com

Avi Laiser & Amir Schwarz
Tel Aviv, Israel
avi@avix.co.il

Barclay & Crousse Architecture
Paris, France
www.barclaycrousse.com

Bearth & Deplazes Architekten AG
Chur, Switzerland
www.bearth-deplazes.ch

Belmont Freeman Architects
New York, USA
www.belmontfreeman.com

Beriot, Bernardini & Gorini
Madrid, Spain
beriot-bernardini@arrakis.es

BO6 Architectenbureau
Gendt, The Netherlands
www.bo6.nl

Bone-Levine Architects
New York, USA
www.bonelevine.net

BP Architectures
St. Kilda, Australia
www.bparchitects.com.au

Brunete Fraccaroli Arquitetura e Interiores
São Paulo, Brazil
www.brunetefraccaroli.com.br

Carles Gelpí & Arroyo
Barcelona, Spain
www.cga.cat

Casadesus
Molins de Rei, Spain
www.casadesusdisseny.com

Cassandra Complex
North Melbourne, Australia
www.cassandracomplex.com.au

Cha & Innerhofer Architecture + Design
New York, USA
www.paulchaarchitect.com

Chroma AD
New York, USA
www.chromaad.net

Cecconi Simone Inc.
Toronto, Ontario, Canada
www.cecconisimone.com

Claesson Koivisto Rune Arkitektkontor
Stockholm, Sweden
www.claesson-koivisto-rune.se

Claudio Caramel
Padova, Italy
www.claudiocaramel.it

Claudio Nardi Architects
Firenze, Italy
www.claudionardi.it

Cloud 9
Barcelona, Spain
www.e-cloud9.com

Conrad Bercah & W Office West Architecture Workroom
Atlanta, GA, EE.UU.
www.westarchitecture.com

Conran & Partners
London, United Kingdom
www.conranandpartners.com

Crepain Binst Architecture
Antwerp, Belgium
www.crepainbinst.be

Criação e Estudios de Arquitectura e Engenharia

David Boyle
Pretty Beach, Australia
davidboylearch@bigpond.com

Deborah Berke & Partners Architects LLP
New York, USA
www.dberke.com

Delson or Sherman Architects
Brooklyn, USA
www.delsonsherman.com

Desai/Chia Architecture
New York, USA
www.desaichia.com

Dorotea Oliva
Buenos Aires, Argentina
www.doroteaoliva.com

Driendl Architects
Vienna, Austria
www.driendl.at

Eduard Samsó
Barcelona, Spain
samso@coac.net

Elizabeth Alford
alford@mail.utexas.edu

Enric Miralles & Benedetta Tagliabue/EMBT
Barcelona, Spain
www.mirallestagliabue.com

Eric Cobb Architects
Seattle, USA
www.cobbarchitects.com

Fabrizio Leoni
Cagliari, Italy
fabrizio_leoni@hotmail.com

Felicity Bell
London, United Kingdom
www.felicitybell.com

Filippo Bombace
Rome, Italy
www.filippobombace.com

FOB Architects & FOB Association
Kyoto, Japan
www.fob-web.co.jp

Foreign Office Architects
London, United Kingdom
www.f-o-a.net

Franc Fernández
Barcelona, Spain
www.francfernandez.com

Francesc Rifé
Barcelona, Spain
www.rife-design.com

Fréderic Jung & Claudine Dreyfus

Gaëlle Hamonic & Jean-Christophe Masson
Paris, France
www.hamonic-masson.com

Garofalo Architects
Chicago, USA
www.garofaloarchitects.com

Gary Chang/EDGE (HK) Ltd
Quarry Bay, Hong Kong, China
www.edge.hk.com

GCA Arquitectes Associats
Barcelona, Spain
www.gcaarq.es

Gluckman Mayner Architects
New York, USA
www.gluckmanmayner.com

Greg Gong
Victoria, Australia
omegagg@ihug.com.au

Guillermo Arias, Luis Cuartas
Bogotá, Colombia
info@octubre.com.co

Gus Wüstemann
Barcelona, Spain
www.guswustemann.com

Guthrie & Buresh Architects
West Hollywood, CA, USA
guthrieburesh@sciarc.edu

Haehndl & Coll

Hank M. Chao/MoHen Design International
Wulumuqi S. Rd., Shanghai, China
www.mohen-design.com

Hecker, Phelan & Guthrie
Richmon, Victoria, Australia
www.hpg.net.au

Hiroyuki Arima/Urban Fourth
Fukuoka, Japan

Hobby A.
Salzburg, Austria
www.hobby-a.at

Holzer Klober Architekturen GmbH
Zürich, Switzerland
www.holzerklober.ch

Hugh Broughton Architects
London, United Kingdom
www.hbarchitects.co.uk

Ian Moore Architects
Rushcutters Bay, Sydney, Australia
www.ianmoorearchitects.com

Ibarra Rosano Design Architects
Tucson, Arizona, USA
www.ibarrarosano.com

Ippolito Fleitz Group
Stuttgart, Germany
www.ifgroup.org

Javier Hernández Mingo
Madrid, Spain
tiri71@hotmail.com

Jean-Pierre Lévêque/Brenac & González
Bastille, Paris, France
www.brenac-gonzalez-architectes.com

Joan Bach
Barcelona, Spain

John Harvey
Chislehurst, Kent, United Kingdom
www.johnharvey.biz

Johanna Grawunder
www.grawunder.com

Jonathan Clark Architects
London, United Kingdom
www.jonathanclarkarchitects.co.uk

Kanika R'Kul/Leigh & Orange
King's Road, Hong Kong, China
www.leighorange.com

Kar-Hwa Ho
New York, USA
kho@kpf.com

Karin Léopold & François Fauconnet
Paris, France
www.leopold-fauconnet.com

Katsufumi Kubota/Kubota Architect Atelier
Yamaguchi, Japan
www.katsufumikubota.jp

Kazuyo Sejima, Ryue Nishizawa/SANAA
Shinagawa-ku, Tokyo, Japan
www.sanaa.co.jp

Ken Shuttleworth
London, United Kingdom
www.kenshuttleworth.com

Kengo Kuma & Associates
Tokyo, Japan
www.kkaa.co.jp

Laura Agnoletto & Marzio Rusconi Clerici
Milan, Italy

Lazzarini Pickering Architetti
Rome, Italy
www.lazzarinipickering.com

Legorreta & Legorreta
Lomas de Reforma, México D.F.
www.legorretalegorreta.com

Lena Schacherer, Ivo Dolezalek
Vienna, Austria

Luigi Colani
Karlsruhe, Germany
www.colani.de

Manuel Ocaña del Valle
Madrid, Spain
manuelocana@telefonica.net

Martínez Lapeña Torres Arquitectes
Barcelona, Spain
jamlet@arquired.es

McDowell & Benedetti
London, United Kingdom
www.mcdowellbenedetti.com

Michael Carapetian

Miquel Batlle, Michèle Orliac
Barcelona, Spain
michele-miquel@telefonica.net

MINIM Arquitectos
Barcelona, Spain
www.minim.es

Molnar Freeman Architects
Woollahra, Australia
www.molnarfreeman.com

Moneo Brock Studio
Madrid, Spain
www.moneobrock.com

Moriko Kira Architect
Amsterdam, The Netherlands
www.morikokira.nl

Neal R. Deputy Architect, Inc.
Miami Beach, USA
nrdai@aol.com

Non Kitch Group
Koksijde, Belgium
nonkitchgroup@hotmail.com

Nonzero Architecture
Santa Monica, USA
www.nonzeroarch.com

Oishi Kazuhiko Architecture Atelier
Fukuoka, Japan
www.members.jcom.home.ne.jp/oishi.architect

Oriol Roselló, Lucía Feu
Banyoles, Spain
www.bangolo.com

Pablo Chiappori
Buenos Aires, Argentina
www.lacortedeco.com

Patrizia Sbalchiero
Milan, Italy

Peanutz Architekten
Berlin, Germany
www.peanutz-architekten.de

Pedro Mora, Marta Sánchez-Bedoya, Luis Martín y Aznar/Saadvanced
Moratilla de los Meleros (Guadalajara), Spain
www.saadvanced.com

Peter Tyberghien
Gent, Belgium
peter@tyberghien.be

Philippe Starck/Duravit
Paris, France
www.starck-bath.com

Philippe Stuebi Architekten GmbH
Zürich, Switzerland
www.philippestuebi.ch

Pipe Dreams

Plasma Studio
London, United Kingdom
www.plasmastudio.com

Proctor Rihl
London, United Kingdom
www.procter-rihl.com

PTW Architects
Sydney, Australia
www.ptw.com.au

Ramon Esteve
Valencia, Spain
www.ramonesteve.com

Ramon Pintó
Barcelona, Spain
ramonpinto@coac.es

Randy Brown Architects
Omaha, USA
www.randybrownarchitects.com

Resolution: 4 Architecture
New York, USA
www.re4a.com

Robert Grodski & Associates Pty. Ltd.
Prahan, Victoria, Australia
info@grodskiarchitects.com.au

Roger Hirsch Architect, Myriam Corti
New York, USA
www.rogerhirsch.com

Safdie Rabines Architects
San Diego, USA
www.safdierabines.com

SCDA Architects
Singapore
www.scdaarchitects.com

SCT Estudio de Arquitectura
Palma de Mallorca, Spain
www.sctarquitectos.com

Schappacher White Ltd.
New York, USA
www.schappacherwhite.com

Shigeru Ban
Tokyo, Japan
www.shigerubanarchitects.com

Shinichi Ogawa & Associates
Tokyo, Japan
www.shinichiogawa.com

Shuhei Endo
Osaka, Japan
www.paramodern.com

Silvia Rademakers, Virginia Palleres

Simon Conder Associates
London, United Kingdom
www.simonconder.co.uk

SJB Interiors
Southbank, Australia
www.sjb.com.au

Slade Architecture
New York, USA
www.sladearch.com

Staughton Architects
Melbourne, Australia
www.starch.com.au

Stéphan Bourgeois

Stéphan Chamard

Stephan Varady
Sydney, Australia
svarady@bigpond.com

Stephen Chung/Urbanica
Boston, USA
www.urbanicaboston.com

Stone Design
Madrid, Spain
www.stone-dsgns.com

Studio Aisslinger
Berlin, Germany
www.aisslinger.de

Studio Damilano
Borgo San Dalmazzo, Italy
www.damilanostudio.com

Studio Pescia

Studio Rodighiero Associati
Castiglione D/S, Mantua, Italy
www.sra.it

Takao Shiotsuka Atelier
Oita-shi, Oita, Japan
www.shio-atl.com

Tang Kawasaki Studio
New York, USA
www.tangkawasaki.com

Tezuka Architects, Masahiro Ikeda
Tokyo, Japan
www.tezuka-arch.com

Tomoyuki Utsumi/Milligram Studio Architectural Practice
Tokyo, Japan
www.milligram.ne.jp

Tyler London
London, United Kingdom
www.tylerlondon.com

Vincent James, Paul Yaggie/ VJAArchitects
Minnesota, USA
www.vjaa.com

Waro Kishi & K. Associates
Kyoto, Japan
www.k-associates.com

White Architects, White Design
Gothenburg, Sweden
www.white.se

William Smart/Smart Design Studio
Surry Hills NSW, Australia
www.smartdesignstudio.com

Xavier Gomà

PHOTO CREDITS > CRÉDITS PHOTOGRAPHIQUES
FOTONACHWEIS > FOTOVERANTWOORDING

Adam Butler
P. 426, 432, 435 (Top)

Alberto Muciaccia
P. 258 - 262

Alberto Peris Caminero
P. 104, 106 (Top Left)

Alberto Piovano
P. 186, 189

Alejandro Bahamón
P. 544 - 547

Alejo Bagué
P. 412

Alexander Von Reiswitz/Frank Seehausen
P. 491

Alfonso Postigo
P. 476 - 479

Almond Chu
P. 422 - 425

Andrea Martiradonna
P. 250 - 253, 482, 483, 585

Andreas Llg
P. 372 - 375

Ángel Baltanás
P. 522 - 527

Angelo Kaunat
P. 498

Antonio De Lucca & Allessandro Lui
P. 566 - 571

Barclay & Crousse
P. 178

Ben Wrigley
P. 594, 596

Bill Timmerman
P. 332 - 335

Bjorg Arnasdottir
P. 572 - 575

Björg
P. 270

Bruno Helbling
P. 364

Bruno Klomfar
P. 328 - 331

Carlos Domínguez
P. 338, 492, 493, 506, 507 (Bottom Right)

Caroline Mayer
P. 392 - 395

Catherine Tighe
P. 86, 88 (Bottom Center, Bottom Right), 89, 90, 306, 308

Chris Ott
P. 597

Chris Tubbs
P. 254

Christopher Wesnofske
P. 96 - 99

Claudio Lazzarini & Carl Pickering
P. 206, 208, 210 (Top)

Conran & Partners
P. 414

D. Malhâo, J.P. Silva, F. Mateus
P. 44

Daici Ano
P. 504, 507 (Top Left, Top Right, Bottom Left)

Dao Lou Zha
P. 344, 345

Darius Ramazani
P. 202, 203

David Cardelús
P. 231, 256, 282, 283

David Hecht/Tannerhecht
P. 600 - 603

David Joseph
P. 590, 591

David M. Joseph
P. 305

Davide Virdis
P. 266 - 269

Desai/Chia Architecture
P. 94, 95

Dessi & Monari
P. 418 - 421

Don F. Wong
P. 34

Duravit
P. 500, 501, 503 (Top)

Eduard Hueber
P. 310, 312

Eduardo Consuegra
P. 36, 38 (Top), 39, 494, 495

Eric Roth
P. 144 - 147

Eugeni Pons
P. 232 - 237, 348 - 351

Fabien Baron
P. 78 - 81, 472, 437 (Bottom)

Farshid Assadi
P. 300 - 303

Garofalo Architects
P. 441

Gorgotza & Llorella
P. 542, 543

Hanse Haus
P. 538 - 541

Henry Bourne/Speranza
P. 274 (Bottom), 275

Hervé Abbadie
P. 70 - 77, 316, 319 (Top Left, Top Right, Bottom Left, Bottom Right)

Hiroyuki Hirai
P. 28 - 31, 167 - 169, 502, 503 (Bottom)

Jacek Kucy
P. 508

Jan Verlinde
P. 154, 158, 610

Jan Verlinde, Ludo Nöel
P. 92

Joan Mundó
P. 140 - 143

John Ellis
P. 184

John Gollings
P. 156, 159, 160, 352 - 357, 530 - 533

John Wheatley
P. 592

Reach for the Stars

Reach for the Stars

1996–2006: Fame, Fallout and Pop's Final Party

Michael Cragg

NINE
EIGHT
BOOKS

NEB 015

First published in the UK in 2023 by Nine Eight Books
An imprint of Bonnier Books UK
4th Floor, Victoria House, Bloomsbury Square, London, WC1B 4DA
Owned by Bonnier Books, Sveavägen 56, Stockholm, Sweden

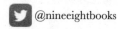 @nineeightbooks

@nineeightbooks

Hardback ISBN: 978-1-7887-0724-4
eBook ISBN: 978-1-7887-0725-1

A CIP catalogue record for this book is available from the British Library.

Publishing director: Pete Selby
Senior editor: Melissa Bond

Nine Eight Books would like to thank
Peter Stoneman for additional editorial support.

Cover design by Steve Leard
Typeset by IDSUK (Data Connection) Ltd
Printed and bound in Great Britain by Clays Ltd, Elcograf S.p.A

1 3 5 7 9 10 8 6 4 2

Nine Eight Books is an imprint of Bonnier Books UK
www.bonnierbooks.co.uk

Contents

Spoken-word intro

I'm going to start with a confession. As a closeted teenager in the early '00s I did some things I am ashamed of. I went to see the Libertines. I was a fan of post-*Kid A* Radiohead. I once went to Ireland to see Travis only to be hit on the head by warm beer and, at one point, an inflatable armchair. For a while, I thought hiding in indie music would help me keep my secret for a bit longer when in fact it just fed my covert obsession; glorious, shiny, ludicrous pop. I'd secretly gorge on the Latin flavours of 'Spice Up Your Life' or get a delicious sugar rush from 'Don't Stop Movin''. Later I'd sit with my proudly pop-obsessed uni housemate and listen to 'hard-edged' ladband Five and the high street R&B of Blue, before hitting the local indie club. I'd carelessly align myself with the throng of *NME* readers trying to justify their love of Girls Aloud or the Sugababes via the prism of credibility ('It's pretty good for a pop song!!!'), when in fact I owned all their albums and distinctly remember singing along to the former's pearlescent six-minute epic 'Untouchable' in a full-length mirror, willing myself to be who I was.

Perhaps because I only lived this UK pure pop boom – instigated by the Buffalo boot-stomping swagger of the Spice Girls in 1996, which is where this book starts – on the periphery, when I started writing about music as a journalist years later, I immersed myself fully. As pop shifted through the gears over the following two decades, taking in post-ironic synthpop, Lady Gaga, gloom wobble dubstep, drop-obsessed EDM and Billie Eilish-adjacent mope-pop before settling on a sort of generic streaming-friendly dance-pop sound, I often found myself harking back to the weightlessness of, say, Liberty X's 'Just a Little' or Five's 'Keep On Movin'' or A1's 'Caught in the Middle'. Like most people, this rose-tinted nostalgia – hey, this book is about the late '90s and early '00s, get used to it – ramped up as a pandemic-ravaged world went into lockdown. Gazed upon from a modern world seemingly on fire, this prelapsarian era suddenly represented even more of a refreshing change. A time before the threat of nuclear war, climate crisis, global financial collapse, social media, culture wars, Piers Morgan's TV career, TikTok and, of course, the pandemic.

Musically, the shiny, irony-free, edge-less, story-telling '90s and '00s anthems also stick out among the darker, slower, generally heavier feel of recent pop. Featuring early input from some of today's biggest hitmakers, from Stargate (Beyoncé, Rihanna) to Steve Mac (Ed Sheeran, Sam Smith) to Max Martin (Ariana Grande, the Weeknd), '00s pop's uncomplicated perfection still feels imbued with more life than a lot of the Logic-created music that's lazily finessed for playlist domination today. The Spice Girls' ragged 'Wannabe', for example, turned the beauty of female friendship into a battle cry in a lad-heavy, post-Britpop

Britain. Their doctrine, critiqued ad nauseam in recent years, felt rightfully joyous away from the harping naysayers who years later could hop on the ubiquitous bird app to poke holes in everything.

Post-'Wannabe', Billie Piper harnessed the Spice Girls' bolshiness on her debut single 'Because We Want To', allowing young girls in particular a place to rebel, even if the stakes were as low as a stereo being a bit too loud. Boybands, buffeted by the success of Take That and lush enough to escape into, veered between mushy, love-hearts-in-your-exercise-book ballads (Westlife) and hip-thrusting, arm-waggling up-tempos either delivered by perma-smiling Ken dolls (A1) or rough-around-the-edges *EastEnders* characters (Five).

It was also a pre-social media world, untethered from the discourse, ruled over by long-lost cultural markers: music TV shows from *CD:UK* to *Popworld*; pop magazines from *Smash Hits* to *Big!*; by Radio 1 roadshows and the hysterical annual *Smash Hits* Poll Winners Party; by CD singles (the iTunes Store didn't launch in the UK until June 2004) sent skywards by the death of Princess Diana in 1997 and Elton John's hastily repurposed candle-based tribute. It was a time when a well-placed tabloid story could win an all-important chart war and, for better or worse, a misplaced quote (Lee Ryan, elephants, 9/11 – need I say more?) could actually help, not hinder (in the UK at least), a career away from the permanence of Twitter. Singles, aided by bargain-bin mecca Woolworths, were still king, with a top-ten placing paramount for fear of being dropped. It was also a time when January's quiet period would see a sudden influx of releases by acts desperate to improve on their previous single stalling at, say, number nineteen (I'm looking at you, allSTARS*).

A decade in pop is a lifetime, however. So this book finishes in 2006, a year when a lot of those previously mentioned cultural markers started to disappear. *Top of the Pops* was axed, as was *CD:UK*. Simon and Miquita left *Popworld*, while their irreverent forebear *Smash Hits* – grappling with a sudden dearth of pop stars and skewing towards TV talent – printed its final issue. As the internet began to swallow up print media and started creating a whole new stratum of disarmingly 'real' pop stars via sites like MySpace, the TV landscape also changed. Launched in 2004 by Simon Cowell – who had spent the decade moving from behind-the-scenes A&R for the likes of Westlife and Five to oddly dressed TV panto villain – *The X Factor* built on the success of 2001's *Popstars* and the following year's double whammy of *Pop Idol* and *Popstars: The Rivals*.

Suddenly, the mechanisms behind the manufactured pop juggernaut were being completely laid bare. Not only could we see the sausage being made, but we were in charge – or made to think we were in charge – of its ingredients. The power was with the viewers-turned-voters; where in the past pop stars such as Rachel Stevens represented the girl-next-door-done-good archetype, a beacon of relatability with a sheen of glamorous untouchability to keep the pop star mythos going, now the public decided which girl next door got their chance and that distanc-ing, untouchable sheen had to go. Relatability was key, as was authenticity, which in the end would give way to the influx of chart-dominating, straight-faced singer-songwriters like Adele, Ed Sheeran and Emeli Sandé – what journalist Peter Robinson referred to in 2011 as 'The New Boring'.

The harsh critiques previously given behind closed doors by (mostly) men in suits were now being codified on TV talent shows into a new way of talking about wide-eyed hopefuls. Eventually those (mostly) men in suits became the true stars, eclipsing the show's winners and losers. The public, used to seeing warts and worse on the increasingly popular *Big Brother*, also needed (sob) stories, a journey, an angle. Years of drama school training followed by a sideways step into a pop band wasn't enough. The public needed to be there every step of the way and slowly became distrustful of slick, ready-made acts in matching outfits doing the same choreography (or ANY choreography: see One Direction). On the surface, *The X Factor* aimed at discovering unbridled talent away from the media-trained shiny pop of old, only to balk at any sudden movements lest it harm the brand. The light entertainment TV format also meant audiences were likely to forget about the contestants once the show was over and the conveyor belts cranked into gear again; a narrative established from the outset via Hear'Say on the original TV talent show experiment, *Popstars*. From that point forward, the permanent smiles started to fray at the edges and the pop bubble quickly calcified into a trap.

All of this shiny, happy, factory-formed pop, be it Steps, S Club or Same Difference, was catnip to critics who, in a pre-poptimism era, saw music loved by children, girls, gay men, large amounts of the population, as inferior. Something to be grown out of. Something certainly less worthy than whatever they were listening to, despite the fact that seemingly weightless music is far easier to anchor with your own all-important meaning than something defined as X or Y from the start. Rather than accept that two competing ideas can both offer up positives and negatives, the pop vs indie debate became a war. Frankly, in book-form at least, it feels like the indie side has had its say. Part of why I wanted to do this book in an oral history format was to add some extra weight to a hugely important period of UK music that often felt ignored in the stream of chin-stroking think pieces on Britpop, the post-Strokes UK indie resurgence or the post-MySpace Arctic Monkeys chatter.

Reach for the Stars is about celebrating not just the (often, but not always) immaculate pop but also the pop stars themselves at a time when pop really did mean '. . . as in popular'. The reason I focused solely on the UK (with a dash of Ireland) is because, post-Spice Girls, a wave of pop crashed onto these shores. Girl-bands, boybands, mixed gender groups, solo artists – every week seemed to bring with it a new act to become obsessed with. And this was an era of proper fan obsession, too – none of this casual £9-a-month streaming nonsense; this was a time of hammering phone lines, queuing outside record-shop signings, cutting out clippings, snapping up merchandise.

I also wanted to give the pop stars themselves the chance to speak. Often asked in playful interviews at the time to discuss who they fancied or what colour best describes them or their favourite sandwich filling, their voices weren't always hugely important outside of singing. On these pages they can recall the highs, the lows and the endless hours spent in minivans being whisked to local radio stations. I wanted to reflect on the joy of that period – and nearly everyone I spoke to got misty-eyed remembering this incredibly unique, all-in-this-together time in pop – but also, with hindsight, to highlight some of the trickier moments, including the side-lining of Black artists into 'urban' categories, the lack of care around mental health and the climate of fear around pop stars coming out.

Obviously part of being a pop star in this period was to walk that thin line between characterful funster and media-trained robot. Everyone had to learn to whack on a smile, even if behind the scenes punches were being thrown (Five), inter-band alliances were being formed (Steps) and toilet windows were definitely not being climbed out of (Sugababes). Which is why, all these years later, it's fun to see the perma-smiling facade thrown onto the fire. Truth bombs are joyfully dropped from great heights, augmented by supporting input from a host of the era's defining songwriters, producers, music video directors, journalists, record label bosses, PRs, fashion experts, TV hosts and talent show judges.

In fact, it was one of the latter, Louis Walsh, who had this to say to me at the start of our tetchy ten-minute phoner: 'No one's going to read this.'

Please let's not live in a world where Louis Walsh is right.

Now here's a story from A to Z: Who's who?

Alex Needham: Formerly of *Smash Hits*, *The Face* and *NME*. Currently arts editor of *The Guardian*.

Alexis Petridis: Former editor of *Select* magazine and current head pop and rock critic of *The Guardian*.

Andy Margetson: Director of S Club 7's TV series *Miami 7* and *L.A. 7*, as well as various S Club music videos.

Andy McCluskey: Member of OMD and the co-founder, songwriter and producer behind Atomic Kitten.

Antony Costa: A quarter of Supersexual hitmakers Blue.

Ashley Bird: Former editor of hirsute rock bible *Kerrang!*

Barry Stone: Songwriter, producer and one half of Jewels & Stone.

Bradley McIntosh: The swinging one from S Club 7.

Brian Dowling: *Big Brother* season two winner and former co-host of *SM:TV*.

8

Brian Higgins: Songwriter, producer and head honcho of ludicrous hit factory Xenomania.

Cameron McVey: Songwriter and producer who basically rescued the Sugababes' *One Touch*.

Carolyn Owlett: One-third of the 'hip-hop Supremes', the 411.

Ceri Evans: Better known as UK garage producer and remixer Sunship.

Chantelle Fiddy: Journalist, editor and debut album-era Craig David stan.

Charlie Adelman: Manager and American Steps super-fan.

Chris Cowey: Television producer who worked at *Top of the Pops* from 1997 to 2003.

Chris Herbert: Manager behind Five, Girl Thing, Hear'Say, Triple 8 and more. Also put the Spice Girls together before being given the boot.

Christian Ingebrigtsen: The blond Norwegian one from excellently coiffured boyband A1.

Claire Richards: Steps' main vocalist and inventor of culinary classic, Pasta a la Clara.

Colin Barlow: Former co-managing director, Polydor.

Craig David: UK garage and R&B legend.

Craig McLean: Culture journalist who had the balls to pop Hear'Say on the cover of *The Face*.

Daizy Agnew: Former member of just-slightly-behind-the-curve girlband, Girls Can't Catch.

Dania Pasquini: One half of music video director duo, Max & Dania.

Darcus Beese: Former A&R director, Island Records.

David Lim: '00s pop super-fan and co-host of podcast *Right Back at Ya!*

Dean Piper: Former celebrity journalist for the *People* and the *Mirror*.

Emma Bunton: AKA the living legend that is Baby Spice.

Felix Howard: Songwriter and musician whose credits include the Sugababes, V and Amy Winehouse.

Geri Halliwell: AKA the living legend that is Ginger Spice.

Gregg Masuak: Music video director.

Hallgeir Rustan: Former member of ubiquitous Norwegian production team, Stargate.

Hannah Robinson: Songwriting icon.

Hannah Verdier: Journalist and former editor at *Smash Hits*.

Holly-Jade Johnston: '00s boyband super-fan.

Hugh Goldsmith: Former managing director, RCA, and founder of Innocent Records and later Brightside Records.

Iain James: Songwriter and former member of just-behind-the-curve boyband, Triple 8.

Ian 'H' Watkins: Mr Hyperactive and Steps' loveable class clown.

Jamelia: 'Window Shopping' hitmaker and living legend.

James Bourne: One third of baggy jeans enthusiasts, Busted.

James Masterson: Chart geek who runs the Chart Watch website.

JB Gill: A quarter of Jack the Lad Swing exponents, JLS.

Jenessa Williams: Journalist and long-term McFly stan.

Jenny Frost: Formerly of Eurovision contestants Precious before being snapped up by Atomic Kitten.

Jeremy Joseph: Owner of the G-A-Y nightclubs. Important to note that our forty-minute interview took place while he was running through London.

Jo O'Meara: The Voice in S Club 7.

Jodi Albert: Former Girl Thing member turned *Hollyoaks* actor. Also married to Kian from Westlife.

Joe McElderry: Winner of *The X Factor* in 2009 and Rage Against the Machine's biggest fan . . .

Joe Stone: Writer, editor and the Spice Girls' biggest fan.

Joel Babbington: '00s pop super-fan and co-host of podcast *Right Back at Ya!*

Jon Shave: Songwriter, producer and Xenomania alumnus.

Jonathan Bown: Former assistant editor at *Smash Hits*.

Jony Rockstar: Songwriter and producer famed for his work with the Sugababes.

Jordan Paramor: *Smash Hits* and *Heat* journalist who also penned a number of pop annuals.

Justine Bell: Former A&R coordinator, Innocent Records.

Karl Twigg: Songwriter and producer partly responsible for some of Steps' most incredible moments.

Keisha Buchanan: The Sugababes' longest-serving member and vocal powerhouse.

Keith Semple: Former One True Voice vocalist who now fronts two rock bands, SEMPLE Band and the Cyberiam.

Kelli Young: Cane-wielding member of Liberty X.

Kevin McDaid: Former member of actually-really-great lost boyband, V.

Kimberley Walsh: Sultry-voiced member of Girls Aloud.

Laura Snapes: *The Guardian*'s deputy music editor and '00s pop superfan.

Lauren Cochrane: Senior fashion writer at *The Guardian*.

Lee Brennan: Cute-as-a-button lead singer with 911.

Lee Latchford-Evans: Steps' much-needed everyman.

Lee Thompson: Former head of music at Viking FM and later at music TV channel, The Box.

Lisa Scott-Lee: Steps' chief cheerleader and post-irony icon.

Liz McClarnon: One third of Atomic Kitten.

Louis Walsh: Slightly tetchy Boyzone and Westlife manager turned TV talent show judge.

Louise Nurding: Former member of Eternal turned solo star.

Lucie Cave: Former Trouble TV presenter turned *Heat* magazine editor-in-chief.

Malcolm McLean: '00s pop super-fan and author of 2019's *Freak Like Me: Confessions of a 90s Pop Groupie*.

Mark Beaumont: Premier indie music journalist.

Marvin Humes: Former member of VS and linchpin of occasional condom manufacturers JLS.

Max Giwa: The other half of music video director duo, Max & Dania.

Mel B: AKA the living legend that is Scary Spice.

Melanie Blatt: All Saints' silken-voiced centrepiece.

Melanie C: AKA the living legend that is Sporty Spice.

Miranda Cooper: Xenomania's lyrical genius and former Gina G backing dancer.

MNEK: Producer, songwriter, singer and '00s pop fan.

Mutya Buena: Sugababe 4 Life and the greatest singer of her generation.

Myleene Klass: Former member of TV talent show experiment, Hear'Say.

Nadine Coyle: 'The Voice' of Girls Aloud.

Natalie Appleton: One quarter of All Saints.

Natasha Hamilton: Husky-voiced member of Gareth Southgate's favourite girlband, Atomic Kitten.

Nicola Roberts: Every cool person's favourite Girls Aloud member.

Nicole Appleton: Spoken word exponent and member of All Saints.

Nigel Dick: Music video director and auteur behind S Club's film, *Seeing Double*.

Nikki Whelan: '00s pop super-fan with a basement full of merchandise.

Oritsé Williams: JLS's most thoughtful member.

Paul Flynn: Journalist, author and advice-giving legend.

Pete Selby: Former music retail buyer who once peed next to a boyband member.

Pete Waterman: Music industry impresario who signed Steps and later became a reluctant TV talent show judge.

Pete Whelan: '00s pop super-fan with a basement full of merchandise.

Peter Bradshaw: *The Guardian*'s film critic.

Peter Loraine: Former editor of *Top of the Pops* magazine turned marketing genius at Polydor turned label and management company owner.

Peter Robinson: Journalist, editor, author, Girls Aloud super-fan and founder of Popjustice.

Richard 'Biff' Stannard: Responsible for some of the biggest and best songs from this period.

Richard X: Producer, songwriter and professional pop agitator.

Rick Nowels: Songwriter and producer who worked with both Mel C and Geri on their solo material.

Ritchie Neville: Five's biggest heartthrob, i.e. he had curtains.

Sam Bloom: Former member of TV stars and chart also-rans, allSTARS*.

Savan Kotecha: Simon Cowell's favourite songwriter.

Scott Robinson: Five's spiky-haired bad boy with a heart of gold.

Sean Conlon: The soul of Five.

Sean Smith: One half of *X Factor* 2007 third-place runners-up, Same Difference.

Shayne Ward: Basically saved *The X Factor* by winning series two in 2005.

Shirley Manson: Iconic Garbage frontwoman and eventual Spice Girls fan.

Siobhán Donaghy: The Sugababes' ethereal, most effortlessly cool member.

Simon Ellis: The former musical director for the Spice Girls turned S Club 7 hitmaker.

Simon Jones: Pop PR legend.

Sophie Ellis-Bextor: Indie darling turned slayer of Posh Spice turned excellent pop practitioner.

Stef D'Andrea: Jeepster records founder and Belle and Sebastian apologist.

Steve Anderson: One of the few people with a Girls Aloud production credit outside of Xenomania.

Steve Brookstein: (Rightfully?) bitter winner of the first *X Factor* series.

Stuart Kershaw: Member of OMD and the co-founder, songwriter and producer behind Atomic Kitten.

Su-Elise Nash: One third of R&B/garage crossover hitmakers, Mis-Teeq.

Tanya Boniface: Singer of above-average R&B-pop hits such as the 411's 'Dumb'.

Tisha Martin: Singer of above-average R&B-pop hits such as the 411's 'On My Knees'.

Tom Findlay: Co-creator of the immaculate 'Song 4 Mutya (Out of Control)'.

Tom Fletcher: Bespectacled leader of McFly and (very briefly) former member of Busted.

Tony Lundon: Former member of 'Move Ya Body' hitmakers Liberty X.

Una Healy: Irish *Popstars* survivor and former member of the Saturdays.

Yvie Burnett: Louis Walsh's sidekick and former *X Factor* vocal coach.

1

Glorious wannabes:
The arrival of the Spice Girls

On 13 February 1996, in a nondescript conference room in Manchester, four twenty-something men deflated UK pop. Gary, Mark, Howard and Jason, resplendent in fifty shades of beige and with their grown-out boyband feather-cut fringes now grazing their eyebrows, confirmed Take That were over. 'Unfortunately the rumours are true, "How Deep Is Your Love" is going to be our last single together,' intoned designated band newsreader Gary. Sat in front of a suitably depressing makeshift backdrop resembling a hung-out-to-dry maroon bedsheet, he stuck the knife in deep: 'From today, Take That is no more.'

Having ushered in a new wave of boybands – from 911 to Bad Boys Inc to original Irish stool-botherers Boyzone – The That, as *Smash Hits* hailed them, were bowing out near the top. Long gone were the leather-clad, jelly-wrestling videos of yore. Having cemented their side-step into Serious Artistes with 1995's impeccable 'Back for Good' and having lost rogue member Robbie Williams to the wilds of Glastonbury, it had already felt like the fun was starting to drain away. That they bowed out with a cover felt like the ultimate 'will this do?' ahead of what many predicted would be Gary's swift rise up the solo ranks to be anointed the next George Michael.

Mired in Britpop's afterbirth, the UK music scene in 1996 was a bloke-heavy swirl of guitar-led authenticity, coke-sweat and lad mags. If women's voices were heard at all it was via the clutched pearls of media commentators' faux shock at the rise of ladette culture or through the prism of sex on the pages of magazines aimed at men. At the time, UK pop's biggest female artist was bop merchant and *FHM* regular Louise Nurding, a former member of Eternal whose credentials as the UK's biggest girlband at the time shouldn't be underplayed. Their New Jack Swing-infused R&B sound, however, was quickly bettered by American girlbands such as TLC, SWV and En Vogue.

By the summer of 1996, however, everything had changed. Pop's barren wasteland, still mourning the loss of Take That, was re-turfed by three pairs of Buffalo boots, one pair of scuffed trainers and the *click clack* of two black stilettos. Up against a tetchy pop climate, blinkered record industry groupthink ('girls don't buy music by girls!') and a wave of increasingly tepid dick soup, Geri, Emma, Mel B, Victoria and Melanie C created a global pop culture movement that shifted everything from pop to politics; merch to marketing; feminism to fashion. The Spice

Girls were the launchpad for everything that followed in the late '90s and early '00s, kickstarting a sugar rush of pure pop that brought back boybands, cemented the status of grade-A girlbands and, over in America, laid the foundations for the arrival of Britney Spears.

Like all great epoch-defining moments, it started in a modest semi-detached house in Maidenhead.

'There wasn't a girlband that was sassy, sexy, cool'

In February 1994, Heart management, AKA father-and-son duo Bob and Chris Herbert, put an advert in entertainment trade magazine The Stage. *They were looking for 'streetwise, outgoing, ambitious and dedicated' 18–23-year-olds for a 'choreographed, singing/dancing, all-female pop act for a recording deal'.*

Chris Herbert, Spice Girls former manager: I was interested in A&R and wanted to try to get myself a position within that department in a major label. That's when I thought about putting a band together and from there that should leap-frog me into the industry. So it was purely selfish reasons at the time. Looking at the marketplace off the back of the success of Take That and Boyzone, literally every record company was following suit. The message was loud and clear about just signing boybands. I was looking at it going, 'That's all very good, but boybands only appeal to 50 per cent of the market; it's female bias.' Up until that point you just had Eternal, but there wasn't a girlband that was sassy, sexy, cool, aspirational, fun.

'*Geri is a self-confessed bullshitter and we were all along for the ride*'

Approximately 400 women showed up for Heart management's auditions. Melanie C chose to cover 'I'm So Excited' and missed the second audition with tonsillitis. Geri, on the other hand, missed the first audition but managed to talk her way into the second. Eventually, Geri, Melanie C, Mel B, Victoria and Michelle Stephenson became the band, Touch. Three months into living, recording and rehearsing together, Stephenson exited stage right and a replacement had to be found.

Chris Herbert: I wanted to cast it like the TV show *Friends*. They were such a mismatch of characters but it covered the full spectrum. You'd never put them in a room together but they worked collectively anyway. So if you could cast it in the same way as those TV shows and get a girl that represented every single colour of the spectrum then you're going to open the net even wider.

Melanie C: I remember the very early days more clearly than I do the crazy days. We were all so ambitious and determined to succeed. And excited because things were starting to happen. All of our dreams were being realised.

Mel B: I didn't think about what was out there or what someone else was doing or what Britpop was. One of the biggest television highlights of the week was *Top of the Pops*. The biggest moment was when I saw this incredible mixed-race woman Neneh Cherry owning the stage singing 'Buffalo Stance' in 1988. I'd never seen someone who looked a bit like me on *Top of the Pops*. That was massive. I was just focused on what we were doing and how well we could do it, how different we could be and how good we could be.

Geri: Before the Spice Girls I was working as a solo artist. I'd met the other girls but we weren't a band yet and I remember thinking, 'What way do I go?' I went to ask this DJ, who was quite well up in the food chain, and he said to me: 'Girlbands never work.' He actually said that. But I went with what I felt. I really loved the girls and the idea of what we were doing.

Chris Herbert: Geri is just pure cheek and tenacity and charm. She missed that first audition. Every time I spoke to her it was all really positive and 'yeah, I'm going to be there'. Then the day before she'd come up with an excuse like she had laryngitis or she'd been on a skiing holiday and burnt her face. Whether or not that was tactical, it worked. I was so far through the process that I just said, 'Look, come down, we're doing a workshop and I've got it down to my shortlist.' She bowled through the doors and I thought, 'You make up for a lack of talent with your character and your campness and everything about you.' She added another element – it's not all about talent; it's about the full package.

Melanie C: Our original management had an investor and he had a house in Maidenhead of all places, so we all moved in. I suppose it was quite good because it kept us out of too much trouble. It was a pretty modest semi and we drove off every day to this little church hall to do choreography, vocal lessons and to have meetings with producers and songwriters.

Emma: I'd just missed out on playing Bianca in *EastEnders*. I was down to the last four. So I'd just found out about that and

I was devastated. I was at college and a singing teacher asked if I'd ever thought of being in a band. She said, 'Well, I'm working with some girls and one of them wants to go back to uni so they're looking for another girl.' She told me to go and meet these two managers, I sang for them and they asked me when I could move in with the girls.

Chris Herbert: Michelle was a very good singer but she didn't fit in. There was the girls and then there was Michelle. She had a lot on her plate – her mother wasn't well, which I didn't know at the time – but she was very introverted. We decided to let her go and look for someone else. Pepi Lemer, who was their vocal coach, mentioned she was doing coaching with this girl, who was really sweet. So I went and saw her and in walked Emma. I thought she was brilliant. Then the girls met her and literally as soon as she walked in they were like sisters.

Mel B: I remember after Michelle [Stephenson] left, we all went to meet Emma, who turned up with her mum Pauline. She looked really cute but also you could see she had this little edge and we all knew instantly she was the one to complete the band. And we were right.

Emma: As soon as I met them we had an instant connection.

Melanie C: When Emma came in, that's when the dynamic shifted and we started to believe we had something really special. It was a real chemistry between the five of us.

Geri: She was eighteen years old. There's a big difference between an eighteen-year-old and a 22-year-old; you've just seen a tiny bit more. So I've always felt very protective of Emma. She was instantly my little sister and I immediately felt like that towards her. I still do.

Emma: I'll never forget Geri driving and looking at me at the same time and being convinced she was going to kill me. Instant connection with Mel B; we ordered a takeaway that first night. But I got homesick very quickly and I was still really young. So I thought, 'Right, either hide this and feel a bit sad or just speak to them all.' Literally the first night I went, 'I'm really homesick and miss my mum,' and of course that bonded us and they were all amazing. I felt fine after that.

Mel B: I shared a room with Mel C. I'd done a season in Black-pool when I was sixteen and lived by myself for a few months but Melanie had spent a year at dance college away from home and she was really good at a lot of practical things. She taught me how to do my washing – to separate the whites from the col-oureds for washes. And Victoria was always really good at look-ing after her clothes, hanging them up when most of us just had clothes in a pile on the floor. That's why me and Geri 'borrowed' her outfits when she went home at the weekend. She never said anything even though she must have known.

Melanie C: We did actually have a cleaning rota. I think I probably did the lion's share because that's my nature. But since I was twenty-two I've always had a cleaner. Also, being Sporty Spice, you don't really have to iron much.

Emma: Mel C or Geri would have taken the bins out. Practical Spice.

Mel B: We all took it in turns.

Emma: Mel B used to cook corned beef and rice, which was a step up from my beans on toast. We used to make Victoria clean the bathroom.

Chris Herbert: Geri was like mother hen; she had everyone organised and they had a routine in terms of what their schedule was every day. If you went into that house there were Take That posters everywhere, they were like young girl fans on a mission, living out a dream. There was an energy there.

Mel B: I remember going into nightclubs at pound-a-pint weekends with Geri. It would be just the two of us – always dressed in matching hot-pants and long socks. The thing that would make me die laughing is the way Geri would act as if we were stars already. At one point every evening, she'd go up to the DJ, get on the mic and announce to everyone: 'Ladies and gentlemen, Touch are in the house.' It was just me and her; no one knew who the hell we were. I'd just burst out laughing.

Melanie C: Geri is a self-confessed bullshitter, right, and we were all along for the ride. We would go to clubs and go up to the bouncer and say, 'We're a girlband, we're on the guest list,' and they'd say, 'No, you're not.' Somehow we'd convince them to let us in.

Emma: We'd go out on a Wednesday. It was drum 'n' bass night and we'd go to that. Me and Mel B used to love it and then Geri would come and try to get into it as well. Geri was doing all her voguing and we'd be like, 'What is going on?'

Biff Stannard, songwriter and producer: They were nurtured. It wasn't so much that they were told what to do but because they had time living together they figured it out for themselves. It's so rare. There were other bands that lived together, like Five did later on, and what they learned was which ones hated each other. So it can be counterproductive.

Chris Herbert: For this to be authentic and convincing they had to be like sisters. That was only ever going to happen by chucking them in a house together and seeing what manifested. It could have gone horribly wrong but actually it was the making of that band. During the best part of a year that's where Girl Power was really born and they just became this unstoppable unit. All the DNA happened there.

Emma: [We were] very confident together, like, 'We're going to make this happen.' We even wrote a song called 'We're Gonna Make This Happen'. So it was just thinking it, feeling it, going for it, having each other's backs; we just felt like we could do it.

Chris Herbert: They had the ability to sing and dance but they hadn't necessarily considered being in a band, so there was a lot of work to be done in terms of getting them to perform like a proper fully fledged act. I had to drill them every day: rehearsing the same four songs, the same choreography, doing vocal lessons. In Geri's case, she was a bit of a wooden horse in terms of her dancing ability, so she would go down to Pineapple Studios and have dance classes in the evening. I should think it was pretty bloody boring for them. But I'd still say to this day they were at their best vocally back then.

I needed to get them to the point where they could showcase that to the best in the industry.

Mel B: I had absolutely no doubt we were going to make it. Our original managers kept telling us we weren't ready and we'd be constantly pestering them to get people down from record companies to come and see us. When they did we'd be the ones taking phone numbers and networking.

Emma: We were asking for a contract and they were like, 'We're not sure how ready we are for that, we don't know how good you are yet.' By the time they wanted a contract we felt strong on our own.

Melanie C: We wanted things to be moving quicker. We wanted something solid. And we were skint. I was signing on and claiming housing benefit before we were put in this house. We wanted a little bit more stability.

Chris Herbert: My biggest tussle was with Geri. I love Geri to bits, I think she's brilliant, and I've not worked with anyone else who is as focused and ambitious, but she definitely lacked in other areas. I didn't think they were ready and Geri wanted the quicker route. I wanted to get them ready for a showcase, then I wanted to assemble their creative team, then once we had the writers and producers I wanted to get to the studio and craft the best part of the album. Then take that to a record label. As time went on, Geri was getting frustrated. She and I would argue because she wanted us to get a song off the shelf and take it to a label to get a singles deal. I'm not going to deny [this process] was very frustrating for them, but I felt it was necessary.

Melanie C: It was a really bold and brave move [to leave Chris and Bob Herbert]. But we just felt like they didn't understand what we had. I'm sure some of it was naïvety and maybe foolishness, but everything we ever dreamed of, we made happen. We needed management that shared that vision and we felt like we were maybe being held back because they were being realistic. They were like, 'Girls, don't run before you can walk,' and we were like, 'No, no, we're ready to go.'

Chris Herbert: I wanted to get them under contract and the girls wanted to be under contract. My partners at the time included my father and a financial backer called Chic Murphy. Chic was a bit of an old-school promoter and manager and his view was that any one of these girls is interchangeable. Do not make them feel secure. As long as they are feeling insecure, they're going to be fighting for their position and you'll be getting their A game. He was vehemently against putting them under contract and I was fighting for it. In the end, I got them to draw up a contract and we issued that contract to the girls and their lawyers. What I didn't realise was there was a bit of stalling tactics going on because during the course of that [process] the rot had set in and the girls were starting to think more independently. They had met people in the industry who were saying, 'You girls are the next big thing,' everything they wanted to hear, so that contract never got signed. That's how they got away. Big lesson learned.

Steve Anderson, songwriter and producer: I think the Spice Girls were so needed at the time. It was the anti to everything else that was going on. Biff tells a story of how he went for a meeting with Jason Donovan and it happened to be at the same studio the Spice Girls were at. He walked out of his meeting and Mel B literally jumped on his back and said, 'Who are you and what do you do?' A week later they wrote 'Wannabe'.

Biff Stannard: They interrogated everyone they met – 'Are you married? Gay? Straight?' Everything was asked. Like they were shining a bright light in your face. As soon as I said I'd done 'Steam' by East 17, which they loved, Mel dragged me into the showcase and introduced me as 'Biff – he wrote "Steam"', and it went from there. Everyone else was asked to leave, which was very flattering at the time, and they just performed three or four songs for me. It's a bit like that Adele thing; you're just really entertained by them instantly. Really funny. Watching their bond and how they got on was really magnetising.

'"Wannabe" is a punk record'

Hugely passionate, fiercely determined and brilliantly bonkers, the newly christened Spice (the 'Girls' bit was added later after record label bigwigs kept referring to them as 'those Spice Girls') needed a single that somehow encapsulated all those qualities. It was the job of Biff and his co-writer and co-producer Matt Rowe to try to keep up with them in the studio, with 'Wannabe' one of their first completed songs. Later, at new label Virgin Records' behest, the song would go through various different guises, even relegated from debut-single status at one point.

Melanie C: Matt and Biff had a tiny little writing room at [east London studios] Strongroom. All five of us bundled into this tiny space with them and we were just so full of energy and excitement. We were so close that we all had our silly little sayings and Biff just wanted to get that on tape. There were no rules; just go with it. 'Wannabe' was written very quickly. We didn't know it would ever see the light of day – it was us just experimenting, having fun and being the Spice Girls.

Biff Stannard: It sounds like a night out. I just remember thinking, 'If I was a straight guy, I would be so intimidated by them.' They were making me feel borderline uncomfortable because they were so in your face – and let's be honest, all gay men love women like that – so I idolised them instantly. I wanted them to write about that. About what a force of nature they were. 'Wannabe' is like a punk record. It's about how they make men feel. I remember having a lie-down after a session and waking up and Matt had written a Post-it note on the tape saying, 'Press play and listen to this.' I remember thinking, 'Bloody hell, that's good.' The demo pretty much is what the final version became.

Mel B: For the record, I wrote the rap in the toilet.

Geri: I remember Mel B coming out with 'zig-a-zig-ah'. She's got that fantastic thing as a writer where she can come up with the final bit that can give a song its personality. That *zing*.

Emma: For me, ['zig-a-zig-ah'] is definitely a bit naughty. It's not quite as naughty as what Mel B would say.

Mel B: Never going to tell. It's whatever you want it to be.

Biff Stannard: Of course 'zig-a-zig-ah' is about sex! I think people figured it out because whenever they'd perform it Mel B would always do that thing with her legs, which looks pretty sexual.

Geri: I remember thinking on the chorus it had to be 'got to get wid my friends' because 'wid' was just cool. I was much more about the cake of a song – the repetitive chant of the song. It was written effortlessly.

Biff Stannard: They were like the band you'd always dream of working with. They knew exactly who they were and what they wanted to be, so therefore I knew exactly in my head how it should sound. This was back when you'd get artists for three days or a whole week; it was a real pleasure. You don't get that any more. So we did the trilogy of songs – 'Wannabe' on day one, 'Feed Your Love' on day two and '2 Become 1' on day three. Then there was three or four sessions after that where we did 'Mama' and 'If You Can't Dance'. It was quite easy because they're all songwriters, then there's me and Matt, so you have seven songwriters in the room.

Geri: I can't remember who did what [on 'Wannabe']; it was more about the spilling of a vibe on the page. Writing by yourself fulfils you in a different way because you're really expressing how you feel and you can get more reflective, but when writing with the other Spicies you can feed off each other.

Biff Stannard: Victoria was there for the writing and the recording of the vocals on the 'Wannabe' demo, but she wasn't there for the mastering of the vocals. She was at the dentist, I think.

Geri: I think she was either shopping or . . . bless her . . . some of us . . . I don't know what to say. She wasn't there.

Emma: I thought she was at a wedding. One of them she was at a wedding.

Melanie C: She was there when it was written and demoed. I don't think she was there when we were mastering. There was an absence at some point.

Mel B: When we split from our first managers, we just didn't stop pushing and pushing. We found out Simon Cowell was a big deal in the industry, drove up to London really early and jumped out on him singing 'Wannabe' along to our tape. He said: 'Sorry, girls, I don't think you're quite right,' and went into his office. We've both laughed about that since because he was so very wrong.

Hugh Goldsmith, former managing director of RCA: We were actually very close to signing the Spice Girls before Virgin pipped us to the post. [Their new manager] Simon Fuller was a great friend of Mike [McCormack, RCA's former director of A&R], Jeremy [Marsh, former president, BMG Music Division] and I, and we were already working with him on other artists signed to RCA. As a result, we got to know the girls well when they were talking to potential label homes and, following a memorable Spice Girls showcase in Jeremy's kitchen, we were massively keen to sign them. However, it was a huge deal financially and unfortunately we weren't able to compete with the offer Virgin were prepared to make. We were gutted.

Geri: We'd written an album and ['Wannabe'] was the strange family member that was just there. We knew we had to either lead with it or it would never come out. The record company didn't want to go with it. I walked in on a meeting and heard them saying they wanted us to have a strong R&B flavour and I remember standing there saying, 'We want this song, we want this song.' It was scary, but we had the confidence to stand by it. I fought with [co-managing director] Ashley Newton, who wanted the production of 'Wannabe' to be very R&B. I remember having arguments on the phone time and time again, saying that we were dead in the water if we tried to compete with the Americans at R&B. We had to be who we were. It was very un-airbrushed. It was like a rabble and a collection of voices and feelings and expressions.

Emma: Geri came to me and she was like, 'I think we've got a bit of a problem, I don't think they want the first single to be "Wannabe".' I was adamant that 'Wannabe' had to be the first single. We loved 'Say You'll Be There', which I think they wanted, but 'Wannabe' was like getting a punch in the face. It was *pow*, it was the moment. It had to be first. It was Geri and I that really pushed for that and we did it. Of course we did. Our poor record company didn't have a leg to stand on.

Biff Stannard: We were really involved in those discussions because we were such good mates by that point. They were still learning [about the music industry] so they would ring us and Geri would say, 'They want this or that.' But they had creative control contractually. Simon Fuller got them such a great deal where they, along with Simon, got to pick the singles so they would have been able to override Virgin anyway contractually via lawyers. If you're in a room with them and they say the single is 'Wannabe', you're not going to say no.

Emma: That's what was so lovely about it, because we weren't corrupted by the industry. We didn't know who we should or shouldn't be speaking to. I loved that about us. It's about the heart of the Spice Girls. It still feels very pure.

Biff Stannard: They used to dress me up in the studio. They just got really bored and they'd dress me up in make-up while we were making '2 Become 1'. With that song, Matt Rowe and Geri were having a fling of sorts and I think Matt had written the first two lines lyrically. It was a very '90s thing of having the third single be a ballad. Then the ballads turned into a big thing for them. No one goes for a wee at a Spice Girls gig during the ballads, do they?

Joe Stone, journalist and superfan: I didn't massively care about the ballads, but definitely having that safe-sex message [in '2 Become 1'] fuelled my capacity at that age to be a know-it-all. They gave you the tools to really make adults uncomfortable, like I'd say, 'Obviously this is about wearing a condom, it's really important to practise safe sex.'

Biff Stannard: I think it was me and Emma who really wanted to get that line [about safe sex] in. Back then you'd think there would be some kind of pushback but the whole band thought it was great. I think it's really sweet the way she sings that line. I've often wondered if people did start wearing condoms more because of that.

'Suddenly we had something really important we had to do'

Having battled for 'Wannabe' to be the lead single, the girls faced another problem; a music industry with the adage 'if it ain't broke don't fix it' tattooed across its forehead in 60ft letters. The last pop act to truly cross over in the UK had been Take That, leading to a slew of oddly hairless boybands. Cute, energetic and prone to a perfectly timed hip thrust, they spoke directly to pop's core fanbase, AKA teenage girls and gay men. On paper, a new girlband who weren't making R&B were headed straight for the dumper. Even pop magazines were hedging their bets, with Big! *calling them 'a poppier version of Eternal' and predicting a chart peak of eighteen in an early review of 'Wannabe'. That would pale into insignificance compared to* Smash Hits' *initial reaction, however. For the Spice Girls, this only solidified a band mantra that would soon morph into a new religion complete with empowered devotees.*

Alex Needham, former deputy editor, *Smash Hits*: They came in one afternoon and did their act, were sort of flirtatious and full of energy, very in your face, and then they put 'Wannabe' on the cassette player and performed around us. I remember finding it so toe-curling. Geri might have even tried to sit in my lap.

Jordan Paramor, former features editor, *Smash Hits*: This wasn't unusual. One guy brought in his Bontempi organ to play us his music. And we'd get calls saying Ultra were waiting in reception or Bad Boys Inc would pop in. Robbie Williams popped in a lot, too. I just remember these girls coming in, putting their tape on and dancing and singing around us. They were just so confident. I remember sitting there thinking, 'Woah, I could never do that.'

Alex Needham: It became a scandal later because Kate [Thornton, then editor] didn't even come out of her office to watch the performance, which was obviously terrible diplomacy on her part. Anyway, they cleared off and we didn't hear much more about them. I was in charge of printing the song lyrics [in the magazine] and I don't think I even did 'Wannabe'.

Biff Stannard: They got a whiff early on that *Smash Hits* weren't interested. They sort of started the demise of *Smash Hits* because they ostracised them purposely and *Top of the Pops* magazine championed them.

Peter Loraine, former editor, *Top of the Pops* magazine: The record company were like, 'You must write about them, it's going to be huge.' And we were in two minds because other than Eternal there was no one else like that. We knew from our mail bag, and via research groups, that it was all teenage girls that liked boys; they liked boy pop stars. They saw it as 'they're going to get my boy'. So it was going to take something different.

Geri Halliwell: They said they couldn't put us on the cover of magazines because they wouldn't sell any copies.

Alex Needham: Kate's whole direction for the magazine was that she was interested in Britpop, so she wanted us to put the Bluetones on the cover. She was interested in Oasis; that's who she thought *Smash Hits* should be covering. It was a bit of a disconnect.

Peter Loraine: If you were a reader of that magazine and the Bluetones walked past you in the street you wouldn't have known who they were. So they were going in a different direction from us. But we were open-minded about the Spice Girls.

Jordan Paramor: Take That had split, East 17 were on the way out. It was all going a bit wrong. There were a lot of indie bands around, so Shed Seven, the Bluetones, Oasis, Blur.

Peter Loraine: Myself and Susie Boone, who was the deputy editor, went to have lunch with [the Spice Girls] one day at a restaurant in Portobello. We arrived first and it was a bit like a scene out of a film because there was a genuine screech of a car pulling up downstairs. Before [meeting us] they gathered around and did some kind of 'we can do this' chant. They were everything everybody always says they were – loud, funny, entertaining, very bullish. Then they burst into song. This was mainly led by Geri. At one point she leaned over to me and said, 'We know you don't like us.' And I was like, 'That's really not true.' 'Well, we've been told you're in two minds about writing about us,' and I said, 'Well, yes, but the reason is that at the moment most of our readers like reading about boys.' Then with 'Wannabe', and with Girl Power, they spun it and they very clearly knew how they were going to do something different.

Mel B: You have to remember, me, Vic and Mel C came from a dance background and Emma went to Sylvia Young, so all of us had been going to auditions since we were really young and you learn that rejection is just part of the job. I even auditioned to be part of the von Trapp family in a theatre production of *The Sound of Music* despite my mum saying, 'They will just want white, blond kids, Melanie.' We were all used to having to prove ourselves again and again and Geri was just a born hustler – she had so much drive and confidence so we just thought, 'Right, let's go bang on the next door.'

Melanie C: We always felt we were more like a New Kids on the Block or a Take That, but we didn't put two and two together and go, 'Oh, we're girls, that's an issue.' We went into it thinking it was a level playing field and very quickly we learned that it wasn't.

Lee Thompson, former head of music, Viking FM, Hull: There was a guy who I worked with, Steve Jordan, and he'd had these five whirling dervish girls come in one day to be interviewed for the evening show. They were talking over each other, it was like they'd had no media training whatsoever, but that was the charm of the Spice Girls. Steve's words to me as they left were, 'That's the last we'll see of those girls.' This was just before 'Wannabe' came out. When you spoke to people at Virgin at the time they had no idea that 'Wannabe' was going to be this massive global hit.

H from Steps: At the time, Britpop was dominating the charts – I mean I loved a bit of Britpop – and there was a massive knee-jerk reaction to pure, classic, cheesy pop. And that's what the Spice Girls did – they came out unashamedly with a massive Girl Power banger. Even though you couldn't use them as a template for us as a band, they definitely brought pop back. They made it much easier for us to knock on people's doors and go, 'HI!'

Jeremy Joseph, owner, G-A-Y: The first show the Spice Girls ever did was at G-A-Y. It's funny because they'd just got to number one with 'Wannabe' but they did five or six songs. We try to make sure the shows we put on are just the hits and the new single. But with the Spice Girls, it was really interesting that every song got this amazing reaction. People were going mad for songs they'd never heard before.

Joel Babbington, co-host of *Right Back at Ya!* podcast: I was five when the Spice Girls came out and for me growing up in a low-income household in Essex, which could be a bleak time, it made it all feel so optimistic. Just a beam of joy that was shone into my house. It was that pure escapism. Like, I want to live in the world they're in.

Melanie C: We never set out to be this feminist, Girl Power movement, but because record labels had mentioned [girlbands don't sell], magazines had mentioned it, we were like, 'Fuck this, we've got a point to prove.' We're here and we're going to do this for the girls. Thank God for that sexism because it gave us an opportunity to change things. We wanted to have fun, we wanted to go out there, we wanted to make music, we wanted to perform, we wanted to be famous, but suddenly we had something really important we had to do.

Biff Stannard: I was watching some old interviews they did recently where they would take journalists to task about some sexist remarks they made. It was very easy to mock the Girl Power feminism side but it was a big thing back then. And [especially] coming off the back of the whole *Loaded* generation with lad culture. They were fearless.

Geri: [Girl Power] was an organic thing that existed within us already. I'd heard Shampoo say [the phrase Girl Power] and I thought, 'Oh, that's good.' That phrase epitomised what we stood for. It was about celebrating each other and celebrating the generation. It doesn't have to be sharp elbows – it's pulling you up rather than putting you down.

Jordan Paramor: Feminism started to really come to the fore more – before that if you were a feminist you were just seen as an angry old woman. The Spice Girls gave women permission to go, 'No, it's Girl Power, we're amazing.' It influenced the whole next generation of girls growing up.

Laura Snapes, journalist, editor and superfan: A combination of going to a girls' school and Girl Power really bolstered my world view of 'boys suck and girls are much better'. A very seven-year-old way to see the world. I had no conception of what feminism was.

Jordan Paramor: Ladette culture was still going but it was morphing into something else. Ladette was more, 'You have to like Oasis, you have to go to gigs and drink pints and keep up with the lads.' Then the Spice Girls came along and changed the landscape. You knew they were going out and partying, but they were doing it in a different way. They weren't drinking pints; they were drinking really nice wine at the Met Bar.

Nicole Appleton, All Saints: I always saw [ladette] as meaning that you drank pints, and I didn't drink pints! That's why I didn't like it. I'd drink Champagne and margaritas. I was a Champette.

Jordan Paramor: Everything got a bit classier, because it had been a bit grubby and grimy. I think a lot of young people didn't feel cool enough to feel part of that Britpop, ladette world, but the Spice Girls came along and it was like, 'Okay, well I can be part of this.'

Paul Flynn, journalist and author: That was one of the beauties of the Spice Girls – they could appeal to girls but they also had a lad mag quality to them. They were the girls you'd see in clubs, or versions of that. There was something quite elite suburban about them; gobby, funny. And, apart from Geri, they were all regional.

Melanie C: We were at the BRITs in February 1996, so we still hadn't released anything, and Virgin Records invited us. We had a few drinks, as one does at the BRITs, especially in the '90s, and there were words between myself and Victoria. I think I told her where to go and so the next day I was in really big trouble. I didn't think I'd done anything wrong. That for me was a huge turning point because it made me very controlling of myself. This was my dream as much as anybody else's and to think I could fuck it up for me, fuck it up for the other girls, completely freaked me out. It set me on that road of not ever finding myself in that situation again. I became very disciplined, to the point of it becoming a bit of an issue later on in my career.

Laura Snapes: As I got older and I started reading about the Spice Girls in grown-up media, as opposed to kids' media, you'd get to see what their lives were, or supposedly were, and just the horrible ways they were treated in the media.

Melanie C: Early on, certain things were said, even before we were in the public eye, that made me feel very conscious about my size. It was something that never affected me until I was in the public eye and I became so hyper-sensitive being photographed, going to shoots and being criticised and commented on constantly. I was striving for perfection for fear of not being good enough. I went into a tailspin of trying to become what I visually thought a pop star should look like in the '90s.

Laura Snapes: I remember the tabloids' fixation with Mel C's sexuality very precisely. Reading about them through that lens gave me a more keenly developed sense of how women were expected to be in the public eye and that's a deeper seed sowing for a developed sense of feminism.

'You could see my nipples and the video was banned in India'

Released on 26 June 1996, 'Wannabe' spent seven weeks at number one in the UK, finishing the year as the country's second biggest-selling single behind the Fugees' 'Killing Me Softly'. On the European Hot 100, it was number one for nine weeks, eventually replaced by the band's second single, 'Say You'll Be There'. In America – the lucrative but often elusive market for most UK pop acts at that time – 'Wannabe' spent a month at number one, while global sales of their debut album, Spice, *quickly rocketed past the 20 million mark. Their household name status was assisted by their very own pop superhero nicknames; Posh, Sporty, Scary, Baby and Ginger. The ride to global domination was a bumpy one, however, with 'Wannabe''s messy, chaotic, backflip-heavy video – filmed in London's King's Cross after a proposed shoot in Barcelona fell through – nearly scrapped in favour of something more polished. Once again, the band knew best.*

41

Gregg Masuak, video director: I had actually been approached by the record company to remake the 'Wannabe' video, which they hated. As did I when I first saw it – I thought it was bullshit. They didn't want it to represent the girls. Now it's such an iconic video, we all love it, because it just was shit and stupid but in a really good way. And perfectly them. So I was bummed when the management and the band told the record company to fuck off; they weren't going to remake it. But I'm really pleased that stupid, shit video is out there.

Geri: We were protective of [the 'Wannabe' video]. Plus we were so busy by that point that we couldn't shoot another one anyway.

Jordan Paramor: They made pop fun again. It's that simple. Boyzone were really nice guys, but they weren't wearing Union Jack dresses or jumping on tables. They were sitting on stools.

Mel B: My hair caused controversy [in the 'Wannabe' video], because the stylists wanted to straighten it and I refused. I wanted to go out there in my 'fro. I wanted to be who I was. I was given some Alexander McQueen trousers and a designer top I hated. I ran out and bought a cheap yellow top for a couple of quid, came back with it and put it on – without a bra. The problem was St Pancras Station was pretty derelict at the time and freezing cold so you could see my nipples and the video was banned in India.

Brian Higgins, songwriter and producer: We'd just started Xenomania and I started to hear a murmur about the Spice Girls and, me being as competitive as I am, I didn't want

42

to like it. But when I saw them interviewed I couldn't believe it. I thought they were incredible. I just thought, 'I don't know any girls like that.' So intimidating and sexy and frightening and confident. Once I put that with the record and heard 'Say You'll Be There', I just thought, 'Oh my God, this is incredible.'

Louise Nurding: I remember being in south-east Asia on tour and hearing about this new girlband that were releasing a record and going, 'I wonder how that will do.' I thought the video was interesting and exciting. Then a couple of weeks later I remember going, 'Oh my God, it's blowing up.' I thought it was so good for young girls and women in the pop industry, that they were shifting that amount of records and creating that amount of excitement.

Paul Flynn: It just exploded in a way that hadn't happened before – Take That were such a slow burn. When the girl version of it appeared, it was right out of the box enormous. What I thought was so clever about 'Wannabe' was that one line about 'getting with my friends'. That as a message to send out to school-age kids was always going to have repercussions for years. Pop songs were all about heartbroken women, or women chasing love, and 'Wannabe' was like, 'No, my friends are more important.'

Geri: I think when you're in a girlband you suddenly feel bulletproof. I think women naturally like hanging out with each other, like a pride of lions. I think it's much easier to defend someone else rather than yourself. Still today, I feel protective over our friendship.

Melanie C: I think because we had each other, and the dynamic of the band, it made us very courageous. When you're in a band like that and you become successful, all of a sudden you feel very protective over each other. Especially at the time. Women were being spoken to in a way that would never happen today. Because I had that strength from, say, Mel B and Geri together, we all just got carried along with that. We wouldn't stand for anything. We were Spice sisters.

Chris Cowey, executive producer, *Top of the Pops*: 'Wannabe' was brilliantly written, brilliantly produced. The video was superb. And *Top of the Pops* played a massive part in that whole marketing thing because their nicknames were down to Peter Loraine, who was the editor of *Top of the Pops* magazine.

Peter Loraine: During that initial lunch in Portobello I said that we would write about them and, to do something that's bespoke to the magazine, why don't we give them nicknames? They loved that. Fast forward a few weeks later and we were doing our first photoshoot with them and [all the nicknames] slotted into place. But we didn't make a big deal out of it – we were working on a piece and there were a few of us in the room, probably about three or four people, and together we all came up with the names. So it was my idea that we would do the nicknames but the names just came about from what we were calling them among ourselves.

Emma: I loved mine. I'll say it a thousand times, I really love mine. I've always been like that.

Mel B: I thought Scary Spice was funny. I didn't feel it defined me because I knew who I was and I also thought it was quite handy to have people being a bit scared . . . but that's not who I really am.

H from Steps: We tried to kind of do that – so I was Hyperactive Steps, Claire was Smiley Steps, Lee was Sporty Steps, Faye was Curly Steps, Lisa was Party Steps. It was like, 'Why are we trying to do this?' They had to put you in a box to appeal to that young audience.

Paul Flynn: It was pop working at its most potent. It's the people that look like you, that sound like you, but a bit better. And the possibility of fame and riches, of hanging out with important and powerful people and going to amazing places – all those dreams that the '80s instilled in us. Oasis were the same; they wore the same clothes as their fans but slightly better. It was very working class, too. Even Victoria Beckham is what you'd call nouveau riche. I always thought that Posh Spice was a really funny name for her. I remember my friend slept with someone and said, 'Oh my God, he was so rich he's got more than one type of cheese in his fridge,' and that's what Posh Spice is.

Peter Loraine: There was not a moment where any of us thought it would ever mean a thing to anybody outside the pages of the magazine. But the late Linda Duff, who was the gossip editor of the *Daily Star*, was an old *Smash Hits* journalist from the mid-'80s and she loved pop music. She phoned me up and said, 'I've just read your Spice Girls piece, it's hilarious, I'm going to use these nicknames in the *Daily Star* this week.' So they started calling them by the *Top of the Pops* names. Fast-forward about six months and Simon Fuller phones and says, 'We've just landed in New York and there are hundreds of kids at the airport and they're all just screaming "BABY", "SPORTY", "SCARY".'

Melanie C: With some of us, they don't know our real names.

Peter Loraine: People always say, 'Did the magazine get paid for the idea?', and no, we didn't, but what did happen was that the band were so ferociously loyal to the magazine. We could ring up Virgin Records and say, 'We'd really like Mel C to wear a football shirt because it's the World Cup and would she do it with Spike from 911?' It was great for the magazine – we beat *Smash Hits* and we became the UK's biggest-selling music magazine and the UK's biggest-selling teen magazine. Everything changed as a result of the Spice Girls. Before them our magazine had a ceiling – we couldn't really sell more than 200,000 copies because I believed we were getting almost every teenage pop fan that was interested. Then with the Spice Girls it suddenly went really young.

James Masterson, UK chart geek: From the late '80s to the early '90s, the whole idea of a singles market was in decline. The CD revolution had arrived and the music industry was very excited and had jumped on it straight away. But the idea that kids would purchase CDs wasn't really being contemplated. What you start to see around about '93 and '94 is this gradual transition away from vinyl. By 1995, things gradually started to move in the direction of the CD generation and there was this realisation that the music industry couldn't take for granted the idea that a generation would simply grow up buying pop music. So the industry did need to skew younger and focus in on that. The Spice Girls fit perfectly because they were dressed in primary colours, very bright, very bubbly, and they were nicely poised to take advantage of the fact that the CD single revolution was just about getting into gear.

Peter Loraine: The record sales in that demographic went up; the magazine went from selling 200,000 copies to a Spice Girls cover selling 300,000. So we started putting them on the cover for consecutive months.

'She said she tied her hair up with a pair of knickers'

By the start of 1997, the Spice Girls were the biggest pop culture phenom- enon since the Beatles. Their first three singles had all peaked at number one, as had their album. The rate of their success meant they were asked to become the face of nearly every product imaginable, even helping to launch an entire new TV channel.

Gregg Masuak, video director, 'Who Do You Think You Are': My first meeting with them was a wardrobe call and they just exploded like a barrel full of monkeys into the room. You'd never heard so much chatter coming from every angle, from every direction, about everything possible known to man- kind. They were really fun. But they were so pressed for time and management were busy building in all these deals. In fact, it was announced that the girls had all become millionaires on the day of the shoot. So that added to their joy.

Peter Loraine: They were so entertaining to speak to. You'd get an hour to interview them and what you'd try to do is three

47

interviews. So one for September, one for October, one for November. Then we'd have five minutes left and it would be, 'Right, let's see how posh Posh Spice is.' Things like, 'Has your dad got a lawnmower that he drives around the garden and sits on?', and she'd go, 'Oh, actually, yes, he does.' If only two of them were available you never thought, 'Oh, please don't let it be X or Y because they're boring.' They were all as brilliant as each other.

Gregg Masuak: When Channel 5 launched it was the Spice Girls that were the first thing shown on the channel and so I did all those initial commercials. But it was only Posh Spice who wanted to have a bucket of water thrown at her. She was like, 'I'll do that, no worries.'

Peter Loraine: We used to divide it up, who would interview each person, and I used to do Victoria. She was so funny. Half the time I'm not even sure she knew she was being funny. She told me one day she'd got up really early and had been pulled over by the police because she was driving too fast. She said she tied her hair up with a pair of knickers as she had to get out of the car.

Chris Cowey, producer, BRIT Awards 1997: They were so clear about what they wanted to do. But they had this veneer of carefree fun about them. None of us knew Geri was going to come out in *that* dress. I got a real roasting from someone at a lecture I did at an American university for over-sexualising women because of the crotch shot of Geri. I had to explain that it wasn't intended as that – there was a ramp that led up onto the stage and the camera was at the bottom looking up. We genuinely didn't know Geri was going to come out in that dress so the camera configuration was arranged in advance. It was then unavoidable we'd see her knickers.

Geri: Charging around the world and being interviewed and all those things, that can be draining. I remember going to Asia and we'd be so jet-lagged that we felt drunk. We'd go straight into promo and we were so tired we'd just laugh.

Melanie C: [The schedule] was absolutely insane. I found an old Filofax – so '90s – and I was having a flick through it and it was like, 'New York, London, Dublin, Taiwan'. The amount of countries and continents we were in in a week was ridiculous. Obviously it's one of those situations where the more experienced people around you were like, 'This isn't going to last forever,' so it was go, go, go.

Gregg Masuak: There was so little time [shooting 'Who Do You Think You Are'] that we needed to race through it. We had to send over an incomplete edit to management to say, 'This is what we still have to do,' and they just went ahead and approved it. Without my approval. To this very day what the world has seen is an incomplete version. It's indicative of the arrogance of hubris; of managers of pop stars who actually don't have the creativity to make things as good as they should be, and could be, with the power to say, 'Yeah, this is done.' Simon Fuller can go fuck himself. Like he cares.

Biff Stannard: We wrote [second album *Spiceworld*'s lead single] 'Spice Up Your Life' in two hours and we recorded it and had it confirmed as the first single in four. There were five mics in a row and I recorded it Motown-style with them all singing. So if Mel B was a bit loud – ha! – I'd get her to step back a bit. And Emma could come forward a bit. We sent it to Simon and he came back within an hour saying, 'That's the first single,' so the pressure was off. But then they said, 'Oh, we're going to make a movie at the same time.'

'We were in danger of becoming a joke musically'

Everything about the Spice Girls' early success felt like it was on fast-forward. Released just fourteen months after their debut album, November 1997's Spiceworld *(14 million global sales) was quickly followed a month later by the Golden Raspberry-winning film of the same name. In America, where* Spice *had only been released in February that year, it meant they had two albums on the* Billboard *Hot 100 at the same time, a fact that led to criticisms of money-grabbing. An accusation not helped by the fact that their perma-smiling visages adorned everything from lollipops to cameras to mopeds. Around that time the band also sacked Simon Fuller as their manager, a move that tipped mounting criticisms over into a very British build-them-up-and-tear-them-down backlash. In the UK, it had been brewing ever since Geri had the temerity to not only plant a big red kiss on Prince Charles's cheek – breaking royal protocol – but also squeeze his bum.*

Biff Stannard: They had announced the second album was coming that November [in 1997] and we hadn't even started.

Melanie C: We were shooting the movie, so we had a mobile studio onset. I remember 'Stop' was written [with Andy Watkins and Paul Wilson, AKA Absolute] onset. The movie took six weeks to film, which is crazy. The album took longer.

Biff Stannard: They'd turn up in the outfits from the film. They were soldiers one day or they'd come as Spice Girls in their full get-up. It was really weird. Then we'd have to create that mood where we had to write a song.

Melanie C: I love speaking to Biff because he fills in so many gaps, because that time was crazy.

Biff Stannard: We were at Abbey Road for about three or four months, but we only did three or four songs in that period because you'd sometimes only get them for an hour. There are frog sounds on 'Never Give Up on the Good Times' because we were so bored, so we'd embellish and embellish. I'm a massive New Order fan and there's a frog on their *Low-Life* album and I remember thinking, 'I really want to put frogs on this song.' There were big burly security guards in the studio literally tapping their watches, waiting to take them to shoot the film. It was like, 'Hang on a minute, the reason you're here and they're making the film is because of what we did in a tiny room a year ago.'

Melanie C: Biff's so mild-mannered, he's such a big softie, so for him to lose his rag was a big deal. That would have made us all sit up.

Biff Stannard: I asked them really politely to leave and then thought, 'Fuck this,' and we moved to a smaller vocal room and sat on the floor with a guitar and wrote 'Viva Forever'. That's the only time I got frustrated with the situation. It had all got so big and we were all going a bit mad.

Lee Brennan, 911: I dated Emma around the end of 1997. It all had to be perfectly timed with her tour manager and my tour manager. She'd fly in from somewhere and be like, 'I'm landing here, you need to be at that gate at that time and there will be paparazzi so you need to duck down.' It was crazy. With 911, we didn't have people chasing us all the time. But as soon as there was any inkling of 'Is this guy seeing a Spice Girl?', they were following me everywhere. We went to Ireland for a week and that was mental. There were a few fights with photographers because they just don't give a shit, half of them. I think they sent an undercover guy to stay in the same hotel as us.

Melanie C: I think in the initial meetings we had with Simon Fuller we talked about wanting to do a film. Some of the first trips we took to LA were to have meetings with Disney and different studios.

Mel Blatt, All Saints: For me, that was the main thing with the Spice Girls that I had a problem with. It's a way of life now, but they were kind of the first people to put their names on everything, like every day, everywhere, everywhere, everywhere. Using that to promote themselves as well. That's what I had a problem with, so when we were being compared to them I was like, 'No, no, no.' We write our own music, we're here to perform, we're not selling anything. We wanted to be a band, just a band.

Shirley Manson, Garbage: I felt that the creation of the Spice Girls was a hideously cheap effort by a bunch of old white men in the music industry, invested in exploiting the injection of female rebellion into mainstream pop. The whole campaign felt very manipulative, transparent and cynical to me at the time. It wasn't ['Girl Power' as a slogan] that bothered me at all, but the pretence of it. I never felt that these girls were in charge of their songwriting, their style or their imaging. The power remained solely with the men who were managing, writing and producing their career. The 'girls' held no power whatsoever from where I was sitting. It all felt so fake to me.

Melanie C: One of the big factors in leaving Simon Fuller was to do with the endorsements. Each of us girls have different reasons, but for me I've always wanted to sing and make music and perform live, but there was a point where the endorsements had just completely overtaken everything we were doing music-wise. We were in danger of becoming a joke musically. That was part of the reason I started to lose faith in Simon as a manager because it was taking us in a direction I didn't feel was right for the band.

Alex Needham: It's the acts who have a sense of joy about it, and authenticity, which the Spice Girls had in spades, that do well. I feel like it was their own creation, as much as they were marketed heavily. Looking retrospectively, you can tell the ones who were being ordered about from the ones who did have some agency. The Spice Girls were selling so many records that they felt confident in sacking Simon Fuller right in the middle of it and taking ownership of it – they had the moxie to turn around and say, 'I don't think it should be done like this.'

Melanie C: Things became really difficult once Simon had gone. For whatever reason, whether it's a patriarchal thing of 'the man that made you' – which isn't true because we came to Simon fully formed and he helped facilitate what we wanted to achieve – it was a very interesting turn from the tabloid media. They really tried to knock us down, like, 'How dare they succeed without a man at the helm?'

'I took myself to bed for at least forty-eight hours'

At the start of 1998, the Spice Girls embarked on their first concert tour, starting off in Europe before eventually heading over to America. On 26 May, the band landed back in the UK after two shows in Helsinki. Promo for new single 'Viva Forever' was scheduled for the next day via a performance in front of Carol Smillie on the National Lottery Live *show. Only Geri didn't turn up. She was, according to Melanie C at the time, not feeling great but would be back soon. The next day, however, as the rest of the band flew to Oslo to continue with the tour, Geraldine announced via her lawyer that she had left the Spice Girls. Consequently the news meant that the official England World Cup song, '(How Does It Feel to Be) On Top of the World', released a day later and featuring the girls alongside the dulcet tones of Space, Ocean Colour Scene and Echo and the Bunnymen, was to be the last Spice Girls song recorded with Halliwell until 2007. It peaked at number nine.*

Emma Bunton: It was odd. Jade [Jones, Damage vocalist and Emma's husband] was on the flight [back to the UK] with us and I remember [Geri] saying, 'I'm going now. Bye, everyone.' I actually thought, 'That's weird,' and Jade picked up on it, too.

He was like, 'You never say goodbye to each other, you'll be seeing her again in four hours.' I didn't know, obviously, but I thought it was odd.

Melanie C: I got the bloody short straw, didn't I, having to fucking say, 'Get well soon, Geri' [on *National Lottery Live*]. I'm the worst person to do that because I'm the worst liar, but we truly believed she'd come back. We thought she was having a bit of a wobble. There'd been times in the past where people had walked away from the band in the heat of the moment. So we hoped she'd be back, but no, she was definitely gone for good . . . Well, until 2007.

Simon Ellis, musical director on the Spiceworld tour: I was walking the streets of Oslo at about 4 p.m. and I got the call saying, 'Geri's left,' and I was like, 'What do you mean she's left?' They were like, 'She's left the band.' We had a show that night, so I said, 'Right, get the girls down to rehearsals,' and we literally sat around the piano, the four girls that were left and me, and we went through the songs saying, 'You're singing that bit, you're doing that bit.' The girls all knew Geri's parts anyway, so it was kind of easy. The main concern was that somebody was going to forget that Geri wasn't there and they'd look around and think, 'Why isn't she singing her part?'

Mel B: It felt very weird but the four of us had these real show-biz backgrounds and we all knew the show had to go on, but of course it just didn't feel right on that day.

Chris Cowey: Before Geri left, we did their final performance on *Top of the Pops* and you could tell she didn't want to know. She was looking all frumpy and disinterested. It was very obvious that there was some kind of schism going on there.

Alex Needham: It's an inevitability with bands, isn't it? You're tired, you're spending all day with each other, you're getting on each other's tits. It's just a fact of life. Then there's all the other unpleasant stuff – like their ex-boyfriend speaks to a paper about what they were like in bed and their family sells stories – and all of that takes its toll. You can't trust anyone.

Emma: We talk about it now and I've had it out with her, because I love Geri. We have a great relationship and we did back then, but I just felt like she'd left me.

Joe Stone: Geri leaving was truly devastating for me. I'd lost two or three grandparents at that point and it had really not touched the sides in comparison. They had played such a massive part in my childhood. It also felt in conflict with everything they'd led me to believe, which was friendship never ends. I took myself to bed for at least forty-eight hours. I was having food brought to me – I was inconsolable. To try to soothe me, my mum was like, 'Oh, there will be something else that you love just as much as the Spice Girls,' and she suggested that I could become a B*Witched fan. I remember fucking losing it at that point.

Melanie C: It was really hard to come to terms with and we were all very upset by it. She had her reasons and she was very unhappy and having a hard time, so of course with time we've come to forgive her. And she has since apologised . . . On stage at Wembley in front of 70,000 people. Very Geri. I think she might have felt her time was done with the Spice Girls, but we didn't. Also, we had an American tour to fulfil. Our biggest fear at the time was that it would jeopardise that tour because they were expecting five girls.

Biff Stannard: I'm a massive Pet Shop Boys fan, especially lyrically, and we always thought it would be great to call the last song on an album 'Goodbye'. And that felt like quite a Neil and Chris thing to do. I think that's initially what [1998 single 'Goodbye'] was, rather than about Geri, but later when we met up with them [on tour] in Nashville and we were talking more, it changed. The middle eight that Victoria sings is definitely about Geri.

'I feel like a lot of the pop girls we know and love owe part of their career to them'

Recording for the band's third and final (SO FAR!) album started in mid-1999 with long-term collaborators Biff Stannard and Matt Rowe. Sessions with Eliot Kennedy (who previously co-wrote Pepsi advert soundtrack 'Step to Me' in 1997) and white-hot R&B futurist Rodney Jerkins followed, but recording was interrupted by various solo endeavours and an eight-date 'we're still friends, you guys!' UK Christmas tour. The album was finally finished in July 2000, with fans voting via the World Wide Web to call the album Third Time Around. *Ignoring democracy, the band went with* Forever – *a title anchored by cover art featuring the band members desperately gripping each other's hands as if tied to a chain-link fence – and it was released on 1 November 2000. In a much-publicised chart battle, the album was beaten to number one by sensible coat enthusiasts Westlife. In America the album stalled at thirty-nine. A month later, promotion for the album ceased, bringing the band's whirlwind four-year career to an end . . . That was until they reunited in 2007 for a greatest hits album, which included a new single, 'Headlines (Friendship Never Ends)', and world tour.*

Melanie C: I think we all felt that whatever came next needed to have a change of direction. That's when we worked with Jimmy Jam & Terry Lewis and Rodney Jerkins, so we felt it was time to try something a little different with *Forever*.

Laura Snapes: I barely remember any of the songs on *Forever* outside of 'Holler'.

Emma: 'Holler''s a banger.

Joe Stone: I just thought *Forever* was dog shit. I've never been the type of fan where you just uncritically consume everything they do.

Gregg Masuak, director 'Let Love Lead the Way': There were two singles and I got the ballad, which sucked. I was in the States when they asked me and it always felt like, 'Can Gregg do it? He's got two days and £100k less than the other videos.' It was nice to see them but it was much more grown-up than my previous experience. When I did the Channel 5 commercials with them, Victoria was talking about this footballer she had a crush on; then by the time I did that video she's on the phone talking about what designer shit Brooklyn was going to wear that day.

Lucie Cave, editor-in-chief, *Heat* magazine: Victoria and David were just unbelievable. Her and Jade Goody would be our biggest sellers. You wanted to know everything about her life. I remember Geri fuelled many a *Heat* interview and cover. You'd follow these people through their love lives and their bodies.

Dean Piper, former celebrity journalist: I cocked up once with Emma Bunton. We were in ['fancy' central London club] Funky Buddha and we were drinking. I remember we smoked half a packet of B&H and she was quite pissed and we had an open chat about the Spice Girls. They'd not long broken up, so I was like, 'Come on, when are you going to get back together?' I then went into the loo, took out my Nokia 3210 and I wrote down the whole thing and texted it to one of my colleagues and said, 'Just keep this for me tomorrow.' Then I did an exclusive in the *People* newspaper like, 'Emma Bunton opens up about the Spice Girls'. She was furious. Obviously. I'd completely broken her trust.

Gregg Masuak: I always thought Emma got the short end of the stick in terms of the persona she had to play. Just be really cute and innocent. The others got to let loose and they had the ability to be more physical. So I nicknamed her Grumpy Spice because she always had to be aware of herself and not swear or go wild in case somebody blew the lid off the fact she's not a baby. But when I saw her on set for this video she was much more comfortable presenting herself. When Emma's stylist got the whole brief wrong we had to improvise and so she's just wearing a roll of fabric that's all safety-pinned together. It's not a dress; it's just a piece of fucking fabric that's been draped around her. She's fucking awesome. She didn't complain.

Emma: I was at a difficult point [during the reunion in 2007], because I'd literally just had my baby. I took Beau on tour at three months. I didn't know what to expect really. My body wasn't back in shape; my hips weren't in the right place to be up on stage performing. I look back on it fondly but I probably wouldn't do it again with a three-month-old.

Biff Stannard: We wrote [2007's final single] 'Headlines' separately, so we never had that chemistry. Matt had to fly to America to record Mel B and Victoria and then I did the other three in the UK. It was very difficult at that point to get five people back into that headspace again.

Joe Stone: I think the biggest shock when you talk about their legacy is that they've got the legacy they've got. They're still such a part of popular culture. I don't think any other band has been so globe-conquering but lasted for such a short period.

Laura Snapes: My hope is that it remains a legacy. They're not an act that should have any purchase with seven-year-olds today, because it is of its time. It depresses me when they try to elongate it and stretch it into something it's not. There's always this 'was it feminist or was it capitalist?' thing, but it can very easily be both. They created a world and a sense of belonging that you really wanted to be part of. Especially if you were a shy little kid. All you could see was five women becoming the biggest thing on the planet. They seemed funny and naughty and everywhere and it just implicitly says that you too can be funny and naughty and have mates and be everywhere.

Shirley Manson: I feel differently about them now, looking back. I realise how much they influenced an entire generation of young girls into embracing the idea that they were powerful and could embody any identity within the spectrum of their gender. I realise it was a timely and beautiful experiment that served its purpose with thrust, joy and vigour; I also realise how influential a pop band the Spice Girls were and the immense love they engender to this day. At the time, I couldn't see the positives. I was too obsessed with judging the artifice.

Geri: The music is the legacy – if it's still being played and still being liked then that's wonderful. Let's look at talent shows, for example, you sometimes get amazing voices but it doesn't connect. Why is that? It's because if you don't have that real connection with a personality that's dripping into the song, it doesn't stay with you and it doesn't stick. The testament of a great song is: 'Does it still sound good twenty years later? Do you still want to hear it?'

Melanie C: The best thing for us girls is seeing the change in how female artists are viewed and the opportunities that seem to have opened up for women in music. Now feels like the golden age of being a Spice Girl because so many amazing female artists were Spice Girls fans. It's lovely to hear how they were inspired and empowered by us.

Mel B: Our legacy is our audience. We brought fun back but we also had something to say by celebrating everyone for their differences; gay, straight, Black, white, brown, bi, small, whatever you were, you were welcome to our party. We were – and we still are – all about inclusivity, about Girl Power, about standing up for who you are. In a way we were quite ahead of our time when it came to mixing music and feminism and that makes me proud. Our fans make me proud, the girls make me proud.

After 2007–08's hugely successful, full-band line-up comeback tour (the 47-date jaunt made over $200 million), each member continued with their solo projects, be it TV, fashion, more albums or *Strictly Come Dancing*. In 2012, the band reunited to perform at the closing ceremony of the London Olympics as part of the *A Symphony of British Music* celebrations, whizzing around the Olympic Stadium on top of five black cabs to a mash-up of 'Wannabe' and 'Spice Up Your Life'. That heady rush was quickly punctured by Beady Eye covering Oasis's 'Wonderwall'. Posh, Baby, Scary, Sporty and Ginger reformed again briefly later that year at the premiere of their ill-fated jukebox musical, *Viva Forever!*. Written by their 'Who Do You Think You Are' co-star Jennifer Saunders, it was panned by critics and closed after seven months.

The band then almost destroyed any lingering post-Olympics goodwill via the ill-fated GEM project, announced in July 2016 to celebrate the twentieth anniversary of 'Wannabe'. Featuring Geri, Emma and Mel B (hence that acronym), the accompanying video – seemingly filmed on three iPhones – had all the high-gloss production value of a fan-made YouTube tribute to a recently deceased pet. A day later a new song called 'Song for Her' leaked, but, as Emma would later tell me, 'We'd been in the studio again but that was not our focus.' In 2019, and minus Victoria this time, the band reformed for a sold-out UK stadium tour that grossed over $78 million from just thirteen shows. The reunion chimed with a slew of famous fans waxing lyrical about their childhood heroes, be it Adele, Emma Stone, all of HAIM, Charli XCX and Little Mix.

While their biggest hit spoke of dismissing nostalgia – if you want a future, forget the past, etc. – its timelessness lives on. In December 2020, Spotify released a list of the ten most streamed '90s songs by female artists in the year 2020 and nestled above Britney's '. . . Baby One More Time' sat 'Wannabe'. A knockabout, curiously unhinged belter created by a bunch of wannabes that ended up shifting the world on its axis.

* Geri Halliwell quotes taken from my interview for *Beat* magazine, issue 19, summer 2016
* Emma Bunton quotes taken from my interview for *Guardian Guide*, 23 March 2019
* All Saints quotes taken from my interview for *Guardian Guide*, 21 July 2018

2

Who do you think you are?
The Spice Girls go solo

Unlike most bands that split up – sorry, 'go on hiatus' – all five members of the Spice Girls embarked on solo careers. For Mel B, Emma, Victoria and Melanie C, releases were scattered in between recording and releasing the final Spice Girls album. In fact, for Mel B – who was the first member to go solo with 1998's excellent, Missy Elliott-assisted banger 'I Want You Back' – this caused a problem when her R&B-leaning album *Hot*, featuring production from Rodney Jerkins and Jimmy Jam & Terry Lewis, arrived less than a month before the Spice Girls' R&B-leaning album *Forever*, featuring production from Rodney Jerkins and Jimmy Jam & Terry Lewis. *Hot* stalled at number twenty-eight.

They also all had to try to steer clear of Geri, whose debut album *Schizophonic*, unleashed in 1999, spawned three number-one singles. Melanie C, meanwhile, had to balance flogging her rock and alt-pop-leaning *Northern Star* album, released in late 1999, with recording and promotion for *Forever*, while Emma and Victoria both sensibly waited until 2001 to properly launch their respective solo adventures. Both did, however, release collaborations in 1999 and 2000, with Emma's Tin Tin Out-assisted cover of 'What I Am' battling with Geri's 'Lift Me Up' for chart supremacy (Geri 'won') and later Victoria's garage anthem 'Out of Your Mind' featuring True Steppers and Dane Bowers going toe to toe with Spiller and Sophie Ellis-Bextor's 'Groovejet (If This Ain't Love)'. In the end Victoria's tune didn't punish enough people, peaking in the runner-up spot.

Between them the five members of the Spice Girls scored twenty-eight solo UK top-ten singles, which even the sniffiest of critics will agree is not to be sniffed at.

'Someone threw a Weetabix at me'

Jeremy Joseph: Geri wasn't sure who her fanbase was going to be but she knew she had an audience at G-A-Y who loved her. [Her performing 'Look at Me'] was an amazing moment. George Michael came to support her. The reaction was phenomenal. I think she felt that security that she needed. When you're in a band, the other members are your security blanket; leaving a band, you lose that.

Joe Stone: Around the time of single releases, I got a lot of nerves for Geri. They'd had such a run of success that things like [lead single] 'Look at Me' only getting to number two did seem devastating.

Simon Jones, Geri's former PR: There was so much hype. I think everyone was overly confident – Geri was on the cover of every paper every single day – that the label assumed it would be number one. They didn't feel like they needed to do [the classic singles trick] of releasing two CDs and in the end Boyzone kept it off the top. It was super close and, if we had had a CD2, it wouldn't have even been a conversation. I remember getting the midweeks on a Tuesday morning and it not being number one and thinking, 'This is a disaster.'

Laura Snapes: I do think Geri Halliwell is a Dadaist pop genius for some of the stuff she came up with. Like that time at the BRITs [in 2000] when she came out in between the inflatable legs or the video for 'Look at Me', which Taylor Swift must have seen before making the 'Look What You Made Me Do' video, because she also has a funeral for herself.

Simon Jones: The 'Look at Me' video is genius. I remember being in a meeting and Geri said, 'We're going to kill off Ginger Spice in the video,' knowing that those images would then be picked up in all the papers.

Malcolm McLean, author of *Freak Like Me: Confessions of a 90s Pop Groupie*: We went to Geri's house the day after her twenty-seventh birthday. She came out to see us and it had rained loads so she went in and got a T-shirt and towel out. I had to get changed in front of her. I loved the fact that Geri Halliwell was giving me a towel and a T-shirt from her house, but I also had to take my top off in front of her. I still have the T-shirt. But it's really shit and I wore it to death and people would be like '. . . that's the T-shirt'.

Simon Jones: With Geri, there always had to be a stunt and an angle. Geri is the best PR of all time. She doesn't need the money, obviously, but if Geri ever needed another career she could be a PR. Her ability to get herself talked about was amazing.

Dean Piper: I heard on the grapevine that Geri decided she wanted to go through Soho on a unicorn. And her PR at the time went, 'Right . . .' And she went, 'What do you mean? I've seen them in films, just get me a unicorn.' She allegedly thought unicorns existed. She's absolutely brilliant.

Simon Jones: As far as I know that's not true. There are so many stories about Geri. She's incredible. There *was* an Old Compton Street moment around [2004's] 'Ride It' single. It was, 'What are we going to do?' And she was like, 'Why don't I ride a horse down Old Compton Street?' We were going to arrive at G-A-Y so Jeremy [Joseph] was part of it all.

Jeremy Joseph: I think I can take credit for this one. We were looking for mad ideas and I knew she was obsessed with horses, so the idea was 'How about riding a horse down Old Compton Street?' The whole point was to bring London to a standstill. You wanted to maximise everything. If Geri is front page of every paper riding a horse or performing at G-A-Y, then other artists are going to go, 'I want to do that.' It's a snowball effect.

Simon Jones: I had to get a sign made that said, 'Ride It, out now', or something. Awful when you think about it now – so cheap. So I'm standing there trying to fix this sign when she's on the horse and she says, 'Right, let's go,' and I'm like, 'Hang on, the sign's not attached.'

Rick Nowels, songwriter and producer: Working with Geri was fabulous. She's as fun as you'd imagine her to be. She's got a great wit, a great mind. A lot of the sort of conceptual stuff in the Spice Girls' songs came from her – she's a big-picture, positive person. I love our song 'Scream If You Wanna Go Faster'; it should have been the hit. It was going to be the first single and then she did a dance version of 'It's Raining Men'. 'Scream If You Wanna Go Faster' would have given her more of an identity as a cool artist and as a singer-songwriter. 'It's Raining Men' is a cheap shot.

Melanie C: I loved my time with the Spice Girls but it was quite intense and overwhelming and there was always an element of compromise. For me to go out and do things my way was really refreshing for me. At that age, you're discovering who you are and very quickly I was thrown into this arena where lots of people were having an opinion on who I was. I'd read something and I wouldn't recognise that person. I'd be like, 'Is that me? Is that who they want me to be? Is that who I should be?' Sporty Spice in an interview was very different to Sporty Spice on stage. There were all these different things to get your head around.

Biff Stannard: I remember I was really drunk and I was trying to copy Blur's 'Beetlebum' on the guitar. Badly. [Melanie C] walked in when I was playing and just started singing that melody [to debut solo single] 'Goin' Down'. Matt [Rowe] was drunk on the floor. It's quite a sleazy song. The choice of that song as the first single would have been intentional.

Melanie C: I had a bit of a bee in my bonnet at the time. I was quite frustrated about being put in a box. Now I'm older and wiser I get it, but at the time I was really frustrated because I knew there was more to me than just being Sporty Spice.

Biff Stannard: To be fair to Mel, she was a massive fan of Blur, which is probably why I was learning that song. It was a natural sound for her to make. It didn't feel contrived to have loads of guitars on songs with her.

Rick Nowels: I had a manager named Steven Budd in the UK and he called me and said, 'You've got a meeting with Mel C.' I was pretty starstruck. That's a Spice Girl. They were big like the Beatles. She came over to LA not too long after and we sat down and we wrote, and the first song we did was 'Northern Star'.

Melanie C: It was phenomenal. I was having this opportunity to work with these people who'd worked on my favourite album of all time, which was Madonna's *Ray of Light*.

Rick Nowels: *Ray of Light* was a culturally iconic album. So everybody who worked on that album was golden for a bit after that. All cool artists looked at that album for a source of direction and inspiration. It's easy for the record company, like, 'Let's go to the hippest people'. Any project there is you always want the coolest names and the coolest people.

Melanie C: You were not allowed to get out of your lane in the '90s. I was quite naïve – I went out [at V99 festival] thinking, 'My band's great, I'm great, the tunes are great,' and then just had a really divided appreciation from the audience. It was probably the hardest gig I've ever done – someone threw a Weetabix at me, and you need a bloody strong arm because those Weetabix are light – but I'm really grateful for it. It was like a baptism of fire, you know. It set me on this road of earning my stripes as a live performer.

Rick Nowels: I call Geri and Mel C the Lennon and McCartney of the Spice Girls. They're both fantastic songwriters.

Joe Stone: People talked about the Spice Girls as a band being overexposed, which is fair, but I think fatigue really set in with the solo careers. There were five campaigns running simultaneously. There was a real drop in quality because they're the best example of a group being more than the sum of their parts. And that was incredibly exposing when they fractured off into their solo careers.

MNEK, songwriter, producer and '00s pop fan: I grew up at a time when one of the Spice Girls was always releasing something. If Mel B wasn't here doing her solo single, Mel C was with Lisa Left Eye, Victoria was wearing a lip ring, Emma was in the fucking desert and Geri was out there going rogue.

Melanie C: Obviously, starting my career in the Spice Girls, you go from zero to a hundred in no time. We were flying first class, private jets on tour, five-star hotels. Then it came to my solo career and my first album was very successful; second album the troubles started, and then when I was dropped from Virgin Records it was like, 'What now?' So I set up my own label. I wanted to do the exact opposite of everything I'd done so far. I did get in a tour bus and stay in shitty hotels and play some dives. I think it was the making of me as a performer. That made me feel worthy of my position.

David Lim, co-host, *Right Back at Ya!* podcast: That Victoria versus Sophie [Ellis-Bextor] chart battle was brilliant. Obviously the Posh machine was turned up to 100. It was so crucial to be in the tabloids, as well as the constant TV appearances you had to do. Now it's like, where do we get a performance? Where do we get fun personality stuff? It's just BuzzFeed challenges.

Sophie Ellis-Bextor: It was insane. It was even on the news.

Joe Stone: It felt high stakes. My favourite factoid about that is that apparently Victoria was demanding the sale figures were faxed to her every three hours. That feels incredibly late '90s, early '00s.

Laura Snapes: I cried when Groovejet beat 'Out of Your Mind' to number one. Very unfair. I would copy everything they did, even down to their crushes. I've never found David Beckham attractive but, because Victoria did, he became my de facto crush.

Sophie Ellis-Bextor: I think the worst bit was that, when I was number one, I'd agreed to do a Radio 1 roadshow in Plymouth on my own. When I finally got home, I didn't have any food or drink in so I went to the local pub and asked for a glass of Champagne but they didn't have any, so I had a pint and then I started to fall asleep halfway through it. That's how I celebrated.

Joel Babbington: Victoria Beckham had one of the biggest-selling singles of that year, and in any other week it would have been number one, but she was labelled a flop.

Joe Stone: For her first solo single proper, 'Not Such an Innocent Girl', they tried to manufacture another chart battle between her and Kylie with 'Can't Get You Out of My Head', but by that point there was no battle. It got to number six. It really quickly went from everything looking like it could be number one to settling for a top ten.

Nigel Dick, director, Mel B's 'Tell Me' video: You had to stick a pin up [Mel B's] bum a bit because I remember she kept arriving saying she'd only had two hours' sleep. She also told me a few other things that perhaps being a gentleman I should not share. So you just go, 'Yes, thank you very much for sharing, now let's get to work.' She was part of this band of bubbly, sexy girls, so the minute it starts rolling she starts delivering. The trick is to focus her on delivering the maximum Mel B-ness, whatever that is.

Mel B: On 'Tell Me' I had a 10-foot wind machine and complete creative input so it was fantastic.

Nigel Dick: I think subconsciously if you get the brief and they say we've got five loaves and two fish then you come up with an idea that suits that. If they say we've got £350,000, or whatever it was for Mel B, then automatically you go bigger. You want to show the bucks on the screen. I think I stole the idea of the big wind machine from a fashion spread I saw. It's a prop; it gives you something to use to direct – 'Okay, darling, stand here, look fabulous and sing the song.'

Emma: I worked with Tin Tin Out first, which felt like a nice stepping stone.

James Masterson: November 1999 and it was Spice Girl versus Spice Girl, Geri [with 'Lift Me Up'] vs Emma. That was the most extraordinary week because by some strange coincidence the tabloids found out that Geri was having a fling with Chris Evans. It started at the beginning of that week and then magically they split up around the Thursday or Friday. It was a great example of the synergy at play, where the antics of these people were suddenly on the front pages of newspapers with a chart battle going on behind it.

Emma: To be able to get back in the studio with Biff [for 'What Took You So Long'] was really enjoyable.

Biff Stannard: 'What Took You So Long' was really good fun. I'd had that title for a while. It wasn't because she was late; she was always on time. I remember that being a really happy moment when it went to number one. We went out and celebrated.

Gregg Masuak, director, 'What Took You So Long': Poor Emma. We kept on wanting to go to the tropics, but we always ended up somewhere so fucking cold. It was the desert but it was winter time and she was dressed in nothing. I had this idea she would be there at night and all the wolves were going to come and find her and gather around. They were trained but wild. It was only afterwards that she came to me and said, 'This is great, because my biggest fear in the world is dogs.' When you're terrified of dogs you jump in the middle of a ring of wolves – that's Emma.

As the chart placings started to diminish, the artists forever known as Scary, Baby, Ginger and Posh gradually shifted their focus away from music. Families were added to, TV careers were cemented, successful fashion labels were launched and a library's worth of books were written. Only Sporty has remained fully committed to the pop grindstone, releasing her eighth album, *Melanie C*, in 2020. It became her first album since 2003 to enter inside the UK top ten.

* Emma Bunton quotes taken from my interview for *Guardian Guide*, 23 March 2019

* Sophie Ellis-Bextor quotes taken from my interview for *The Guardian*, 12 March 2014

3

A slam dunk?
Five make a splash

Having helped form, and then been sacked by, the Spice Girls, managers Bob and Chris Herbert quickly turned their attention to boybands. With no Take That and with the ballad-obsessed Boyzone hogging the spotlight, the pair felt pop was missing a proper all-dancing, all-singing, attitude-heavy ladband. In America, where Spice Girls mania was still just around the corner, the precisely curtained Backstreet Boys – who had started their careers in Europe in 1996 pushing big-chorused, R&B-lite bangers created by Swedish hitmakers Max Martin and Denniz PoP – were starting to take off. Keen to fill the gap in the market in the UK, while gliding along in the transatlantic slipstream of the Backstreet Boys, the managers placed an advert in *The Stage* in early 1997. While Take That and the recently signed 911 had slogged it out on schools tours and at club nights before landing major label deals, Five (or 5ive if you're a purist) signed with BMG/RCA under the watchful eye of a certain Simon Cowell.

'Boyzone were going to bring you flowers and Five were going to fuck you down the side alley'

Formed in May 1997, Five, AKA Ritchie Neville, Scott Robinson, J Brown, Sean Conlon and Abs Love, released their debut single 'Slam Dunk (Da Funk)' *— created, like half of their 1998 debut album,* Five, *by Martin and PoP in Stockholm — just six months later. Their eleven UK top-ten singles, three top-five albums and two arena tours spanned less than a four-year period. That it ended in burnout, depression and fist fights was hardly surprising given their lightspeed ascent. But it all started out via five lads — including singers, rappers and novice dancers — standing out from an initial crowd of 3,000 wannabes that featured a pre-fame Russell Brand among their number.*

Chris Herbert: When I did the Spice Girls I actually made a mood board and I pretty much had all the characters you see today on that board. I did the same with Five and it was urban, more street, a bit more hip-hop-influenced, rappy. In terms of styling it was baseball and basketball, very American influenced.

Hugh Goldsmith: In my last few months at RCA, I introduced Simon Cowell to Chris Herbert, who I'd met socially one weekend. Chris, of course, had put the Spice Girls together and seemed quite down at the time, having been left by the girls, who then went on to find new management and become hugely successful. We gave Chris £10,000 to spend on sourcing talent for a new act that we all agreed he would eventually manage. That act would become Five.

Chris Herbert: The idea really was Boyzone were going to bring you a bunch of flowers and Five were going to fuck you against a wall down the side alley. Girls love a bad boy and boys could relate to it. Musically it was going to be harder and tougher and more appealing to girls and boys alike.

Scott Robinson: It was an audition I'd found in *The Stage* and it was looking for the Spice Boys. I remember wearing a grey Kappa tracksuit – I'm from Essex – and some white Reebok Classics. I had a cropped haircut that I gelled down, which looked horrific. Also, despite being seventeen, I had been out drinking the night before and my dad came into my room to wake me up saying, 'You've got to go to this audition.' I was like, 'Dad, I can't go, I'm hungover, I don't want to be in the Spice Boys anyway.' He thought it could be my big break.

Ritchie Neville: I didn't look it, but I was a little grunge-y kid; I was into Nirvana, Pearl Jam and Stone Temple Pilots. It was either that or I was into dance music. Pop was a bit of a dirty word to me. I turned up and it was a media circus. There was press there and a Spice Girls tribute band performing. I was in this queue just going, 'What the hell is this?'

Sean Conlon: I saw Abs at my audition. He had some sun-glasses on and looked a little bit like how Peter Andre used to dress. He really stood out from the whole queue.

Scott: I went to London and auditioned at Pineapple Studios. There were thousands of people and I was number twenty-two and J was number twenty-one. I heard his audition and then I went in and did mine. Next we went into another room where we had to dance and that's where I thought it was game over.

Ritchie: The audition process itself was like a cattle market. Ushering ten in at a time, super rushed. I walked into one of the dance studios and some music came on and I turned around and there were people windmilling and going for it. I felt really awkward. So I just very lightly moved, feeling very self-conscious about it all. Within a minute they turned the music off and if you got a piece of paper it meant you went to the next part, which was singing.

Scott: I remember thinking, 'But I can't dance.' It looks like I could in the videos and on stage but that's because a choreographer has drummed it into me. So I just stood there nodding my head a little bit as if I had a pint in my hand. J was breakdancing right in the middle, which is hilarious because he went on to really not like fame and stuff like that. He was never as confident with the singing, because he's a rapper, so he wanted to prove himself with the dancing. Everyone was standing in a semi-circle and J was in the middle doing head-spins.

Sean: I performed one of my own songs. At the time, that's all I was doing, just writing songs. I never really had any aspirations to be in a band or even to be famous. I had no idea the band was going to be as big as it was. I thought it would be an introduction into the industry, like I'd meet somebody and be able to write songs. I never thought about being famous. Plus I was only fifteen so it was more like a stepping stone for me.

Ritchie: I did George Michael's 'Freedom', which was a bit of a speciality as I'd done it in a singing competition at school.

Scott: [Russell Brand] was there. He denies that now. Which is funny because he's done some dodgy things in his career and auditioning for Five isn't the worst thing he's done.

Ritchie: After that first audition it was a kind of, 'Don't call us, we'll call you.' I thought they were going to call the house phone and so I remember one lunch time about a week after the auditions, I called Mum from the payphone at school to check to see how quickly she would answer. And she didn't answer! I got home that night and told her. She laughed and was like, 'Rich, do you honestly think if they wanted you in their big new band that they're only going to call once?'

Sean: When we got into the second audition and they put us together as a five, something clicked. You could feel it.

Scott: The second audition was at a place called Nomis Studios and that was where it started to hot up. They put us into groups. Every other group was a group of four, because the original idea was for the band to have four members. We were the only group of five. They were trying to see which one of us they could kick out. I remember J in tears in the toilet thinking it would be him to go. He was like, 'I'm the oldest, I'm more of a rapper than a singer.' They gave us a track to learn so that every group did the same song and Abs very cleverly wrote a rap for it and J did the same. We were the only band that had done something different.

Ritchie: At the time, pop bands had always been five people, so they wanted to do something different and have four people. But they couldn't decide which one of us to lose, so they kept it as five. Which is one of the reasons we called ourselves Five.

Scott: That audition process was meant to go on for weeks and weeks, but on that very day they sent everyone else home.

Sean: You did start to get a feeling like, 'Hang on, this could be a little bit bigger than I thought.'

Scott: I remember Simon Cowell was there and he said, 'You're the band, I'm signing you to RCA Records on a five-album deal, this is happening very soon.'

Ritchie: He was definitely a presence and a character. I remember whispers of like, 'Yeah, that's the guy from the record label.'

Sean: We didn't have the struggle that other bands have where they're gigging for years and trying to get a deal. It was on a plate for us really.

Ritchie: I could see the potential in every single one of us and I knew the fire I had in my belly, so when the songs started coming and they were really good I was like, 'We could seriously take the world here.' We had everything we needed. We could have set up our lives forever.

Scott: We auditioned in the May and by Christmas we were top ten in the charts with 'Slam Dunk (Da Funk)'. Our first show ever was the Radio 1 roadshow in Weston-super-Mare. When we pulled up, Peter Andre was at the gate signing autographs and I remember wondering if anyone would want our autograph one day. Then after we'd done our performance people were asking for our autograph and we didn't have one. I was just using the one I put on my bank card. Our second ever performance was the *Smash Hits* Poll Winners Party in front of 15,000 people. We never looked back from that moment. It was so quick that it was too quick actually. That's why it didn't last.

'I'd ask for a score to get some Stellas from the offie'

A key element in the Spice Girls' early success was their genuine bond. It was one fostered via months of living together in a small terraced house, a literal move organised by Bob and Chris Herbert to set a solid foundation. Keen to see if lightning would strike twice, the Five boys – aged between fifteen (Sean) and twenty-one (J) – were quickly moved into a council house in Surrey. In terms of the narrative around the band as 'the bad boys of pop', the move was genius. In terms of their relationships and their health vis-à-vis cleanliness and sanitation, it was a disaster.

Sean: I didn't think anything of it when I first moved. I just thought, 'I'm going to do music, it all makes sense.' So I had my clothes packed in one hand and my keyboard in the other. Then I went on the train, met Scott and J at Euston Station and the next minute we're in the house. Then it starts to become pretty daunting.

Ritchie: I nearly didn't move in. I was doing my A levels, it was the last year, so I was a bit like, 'I've come all this way, I should really finish them.' My parents agreed. But I didn't want to be left behind if I moved in three months later – they would have had a lot of experiences already and I'd be playing catch-up. One day I put on Radio 1 and Ultra Naté's 'Free' came on. Being a little spiritual, I was like, 'That's a sign': you're free to do what you want to do. I went home and told my mum I had to go and she understood.

Scott: I wasn't particularly an old seventeen-year-old. I'd been away from home once for Edinburgh Festival when I was in a musical and I struggled then. You didn't really have time to catch your breath. It was a three-bedroom house, so me and Abs shared, but he was never there because he had a girlfriend at the time. I would see my girlfriend Kerry, who is now my wife, at the weekends. Sean had a tiny little box room and then Rich and J shared. It was funny but it was mental. Put five young teenagers in a house with no parents and see what happens. There's a lot of drinking, but also a lot of work. We worked so hard.

Sean: We had a lot of moments when we really did get on but there were bits of testosterone and bits of friction here and there. Just lads living together trying to find their feet. It wasn't always great but we did have some laughs.

Scott: Individually, people had problems with J. He was going through the same pressures but at a different age and dealing with them differently. It was difficult for all of us. I'd looked up to J for quite a while until I started to realise he was manipulating and using me a little bit.

Chris Herbert: They probably became caricatures of themselves because we said this is what we're doing and this is the image, so their reputation started following them wherever they went.

Scott: We were the band that liked a drink. But so did Westlife. They're Irish boys; they can fucking drink. They were just not saying they were having a drink; they were being good boys. So we got tarred as the ladband, but we were still a boyband. We were just a bit cooler. And we still are.

Pete Whelan, '00s pop superfan: I think a lot of it was image and gimmick. I know there was a bit of fighting between them but I think there was an element of, 'If we present them as tough, they're not just another generic boyband like Westlife.'

Peter Robinson, journalist and editor of Popjustice: I wonder how much of the bad-boy image was real. You had Take That and East 17 and then you had Westlife and Five, which is basically the same thing. The difference the second time around was Five and Westlife were A&R-ed by the same person, Simon Cowell, and on the same record label, so it's very easy to manage it. Having them knocking around at the same time probably did each of them a favour.

Lee Thompson: It was contrived, but then actually they started living up to that persona and then some. They came in for an interview one time, probably about '98 or '99. We were in a Mexican restaurant afterwards and they were fighting with each other. The guy from the label was like, 'I can't do anything about this, that's the way they are.' I remember two of them going outside to fight.

Sean: [Management and label] wanted the edgy style of band for sure. A lot of boybands were really contrived and controlled. Because the fans that were into boybands were predominantly young teenagers, they were very conscious about what parents would think. But then with us I think initially they wanted an edgy band but they tried to contrive it in another way with the TV show.

Chris Herbert: We launched them off [ITV documentary series] *Neighbours from Hell*. It was all about warring neighbours. I had put them into a house in a place called Heatherside in Camberley and the boys were warring with this gang there. We were like, 'This is brilliant.' There were neighbours up in arms and I thought, 'This is perfect for this show.' So we rung them and said, 'Look, we've got this band, do you want to put them on?', and that's how we did it. It fed perfectly into the narrative we were trying to create.

Ritchie: They wanted a band with edge and that's what they bloody well got. None of us are people that will be bossed around. So then if you put five of those people together all the time and then they start annoying each other . . . We're all very strong characters so eventually there's going to be those eruptions. We were young, we didn't have that level of maturity.

Scott: I'm not even joking, at one point we ran out of plates because no one was washing them so we chucked them away. Then we went to the supermarket and bought paper plates and plastic cutlery so that we could dispose of it. So you'd have a microwave meal and then dash the plate in the bin. People would say juvenile but I'd say genius. That place was a cesspit.

Chris Herbert: It was dreadful. I sent my cleaners down there and they refused to clean the place.

Ritchie: We were travelling around a lot so it wasn't like you could stay in and cook. We put on loads of weight later on as we'd just be having McDonald's and KFC. I was getting tubby. I remember there was a piece in the tabloids calling me 'beefy'. I remember that really hitting home, like, 'Beefy?!' I didn't realise. I went and looked in the mirror and I'd definitely put on weight.

Sean: I didn't have a clue [about living alone]. I hadn't cooked, I hadn't washed my own clothes. I was literally just a child.

Scott: Later they moved us into a really plush five-bedroom house. But it's funny because we were fucking paying for that house. We were thinking, 'Look at us, wahey,' and we'd get picked up in nice cars and say, 'Can you wait an hour, mate?', and they'd keep the meter running.

Ritchie: Even our parents didn't understand [our record contract]. It was a recipe for disaster because music industry contracts are really complicated. I had the perception that if you make it big enough you will be a millionaire. I thought I would end up with £50 million and a yacht.

Scott: We had a lawyer but I didn't really know what a lawyer was. I'd seen one on the telly, so we asked a couple of questions. But basically when we got into that band, even when money was coming in, we were given £100 a week to live on. I had had a couple of jobs as a pot collector at a local social club, then I ran a burger wagon, so I was always trying to make money. Sean was fifteen. He'd never seen £100. I remember him going, 'Have I got to share it?'

Sean: I thought I'd won the lottery then.

Ritchie: Sean was quite good with money and he was also quiet about it. He wouldn't advertise the fact he'd saved it; he'd keep his mouth closed. I would always hit up Scott, like, 'I can't even eat.' That first year was a struggle.

Scott: Sean used to hoard it. After about five weeks I'd spent all my money on beer. I would go into Sean's room and he'd go, 'I've not spent any, still got £500.' I'd ask for a score to get some Stellas from the offie.

Sean: I wouldn't say I hoarded it. But I was careful with it. Scott enjoyed it a little bit more, I suppose.

Scott: It wasn't until we started to get a bit wiser – not wise enough, I might add – that we'd say, 'Have we got any money?' They'd say, 'You've got some coming in,' and I'd look at my bank account and be like, 'You weren't joking.' So I'd go and buy a Merc.

'We weren't saying that it wasn't a hit record, but it just sounded like everybody else'

With the Backstreet Boys joining the Spice Girls in kickstarting American radio's renewed interest in pure pop, Five were flown out to Cheiron Studios in Stockholm to work with Denniz PoP and Max Martin. Known for fusing top-tier ABBA melodies with a very Swedish approximation of R&B, PoP and Martin – alongside songwriter and rapper Herbie Crichlow and producer Jake Schulze – crafted a sound that suited both Five's penchant for rapping over more hard-edged 'funk' beats (the word 'funk' appears approximately 678 times on debut album Five) and, via the ballads, highlighted Scott *and Ritchie's doe-eyes. In the UK, the band worked with Biff Stannard and Julian Gallagher, as well as Tim Lever and Mike Percy of '80s synthpop experimentalists Dead or Alive fame. The latter two, alongside Eliot Kennedy, co-created the album's second single 'When the Lights Go Out', which would later become the band's first (and only) US top-ten hit. Along the way they also turned down a boyband classic and very nearly got their hands on one of pop's biggest ever singles, '. . . Baby One More Time'.*

Sean: I didn't even have a passport. I had to get one really quickly so I could even go [to Sweden].

Scott: It's so difficult because you're seventeen so you don't really know who these [producers] are. I knew they were a big deal. I knew I was in the room with people who knew what they were doing.

Ritchie: We didn't understand it at all. We knew they'd worked with Ace of Base. The Backstreet Boys were big but they hadn't had the mega hits like 'I Want It That Way'. We knew 'Quit Playing Games' and actually that was one of my guilty pleasures.

Sean: If I'm brutally honest I didn't really know who they were. Scott was into Backstreet Boys but I'd never sort of got into that.

Scott: I remember talking to Denniz and he was playing me some of the new songs the Backstreet Boys had coming up. I remember phoning one of my mates and going, 'You'll never guess what, I've just listened to the new Backstreet Boys album before it's even been finished.'

Sean: I listened to Seal, Roachford, Sade and singers like that. I wasn't the type of person who read interviews and I didn't even always know who the people were that sang the songs. I was only interested in the music.

Scott: We had to fight [to be able to write songs on the debut album]. We wanted to have our stamp on the music. We were the only boyband out there at the time that it was okay to like if you were a guy. It wasn't that embarrassing to go, 'You know what, Five are pretty cool.' I've got no problem with Westlife's music, I think it's very good, but if you were a lad and you were a Westlife fan you would take that to the grave. You're not shouting that from the rooftops and saying, 'Oh, yeah, I love "Flying Without Wings", what a tune.'

Biff Stannard: They were bad boys, like East 17. It was almost like anti-pop. They were just so naughty. Sometimes people have said to me, 'Was it a sort of casting couch thing?' But they're not my type at all. I just remember thinking they were feisty, really good writers as well, and there was friction in the studio and sometimes that leads to really good results. That was the first thing Simon [Cowell] threw at me that I thought was really good.

Scott: Denniz was a big part in nurturing what we were doing and the rapping. Him and Herbie Critchlow pretty much invented the way Abs and J went on to rap. J was a Tupac-type rapper when he joined the band and then him and Abs started doing these phone raps like the Beastie Boys.

Biff Stannard: I remember J was a bit self-conscious about [the rapping]. It was different with Tony in East 17 – you could get away with that kind of cadence of rapping. I still hear a lot of people who sound like J in modern rap actually.

Scott: When Denniz passed away [of stomach cancer in August 1998, aged thirty-five] it was quite hard to pick yourself up after that. We still worked over in Sweden with Max [Martin] and he had learned everything from Denniz. He then did alright for himself.

Biff Stannard: Lovely Denniz. That hit them quite hard because they were getting there with him. It was hard for me to fill his shoes, because I was a massive fan. I was intimidated by that. I was the first person they'd met afterwards and they were a bit, not wary, but, 'What's this going to be like?'

Sean: It was sad, although I never got terribly close to Denniz, if I'm brutally honest. They were quite business-like [in the studio] and quite mechanical. I'm not saying that's a bad thing – that's how they've got success – but that's just the truth.

Scott: At one point Simon offered Max Martin his Aston Martin to have '. . . Baby One More Time' [for us].

Chris Herbert: I'll tell you the story. Clive Davis had signed the boys in America to Arista and Clive had also signed TLC. Max was trying to pitch the song for TLC and he asked us to give it to Clive. We played it for him and he was like, 'It's not right.' We were listening to it and we were like, 'You could make this into a guys' song as well.' So we said to Max that we'd love to use it for Five. It took some convincing. Even to the point where Simon said, 'Look, I'll buy you a brand-new 500 Sl Mercedes for the song.' So Max agreed.

Ritchie: We were that tougher boyband, so you could imagine guys singing that chorus and it being a tougher pop song.

Chris Herbert: We played it to the guys and at the end it was deathly quiet and we said, 'What do you think?' In front of Max, they went, '. . . It's fucking wank!' Max was so insulted by it. I managed to convince Max again that we could win the boys over, but by this point Max was like, 'I've got this other girl who is going to sing it.' I asked who it was and he said it was a girl called Britney and that she was an up-and-coming new artist. I said, 'But the boys have just had a top-ten hit in America [with 'When the Lights Go Out'], you must be mad not to give us this song.' Anyway, Britney Spears did it.

Scott: Everyone always goes, 'Oh, do you regret you didn't get it?', but just because it was a hit with Britney didn't mean it would have been a hit with Five. I think Rich would have looked good in a school uniform, but I don't think it would have had the same effect.

Ritchie: I thought that was quite brave of Max because it was a guaranteed hit with us. Britney had only just been signed. All is fair in love and war. Simon would have probably said, 'Okay, well what else have you got, then?'

Biff Stannard: There's another really good story about Max using a massive snare sound and Simon telling him to turn it down. Apparently Max just hung up on him. 'Isn't the snare a bit loud?' 'No, bye.'

Hallgeir Rustan, former member of Stargate: Simon Cowell always knew what he wanted. At that time, we used DHL to send the mixes and every delivery took three or four days. There was one mix where Simon wasn't happy with the snare drum sound. Several mixes were sent via DHL but Simon still didn't like it. He got on a plane and flew to our studio in Trondheim. We listened to fifty or sixty different snare drums. Finally we ended up with the snare drum that was in the first mix. Everybody's happy.

Chris Herbert: Five didn't learn from their mistakes because we had almost the exact same scenario with 'Bye Bye Bye'.

Scott: The hook was there but the rest of the chorus was different. I said, 'Do you know what, this isn't a Five song. It doesn't sound like us, give it to NSYNC.' They did and obviously they finished the verses without us. Could Five have sung it in that vein and done quite well? Probably. But it wouldn't have felt right to us.

Sean: When we first went to Cheiron, it was a bit Backstreet Boys but edgier, with some rapping and more of a hip-hop influence. When we got further on, we started doing some of the writing and we started to stumble on something boybands hadn't really done before. Songs like 'If Ya Gettin' Down', 'Let's Dance', 'Keep On Movin''. Although we had some songs that were still very American and boyband-y, we were also creating something British. We were just putting our foot down at that point. We weren't saying that ['Bye Bye Bye'] wasn't a hit record, but it just sounds like everybody else. Give it to one of them.

Peter Robinson: Five were the sort of band, a bit like Girls Aloud later, who felt like they could do all sorts of nonsense and do something exciting. So, if they sample Joan Jett or do a song based around the *Battlestar Galactica* theme or do a song that samples *Grease*, it makes sense. I went to Simon Cowell's office during Five's reign and he played me a cover they'd done of 'Pour Some Sugar on Me' by Def Leppard, which never came out. They seemed like the kind of band where you'd go, 'Okay, fair, that makes sense.'

Scott: Our first single in the States, 'When the Lights Go Out', went top ten.

Lee Brennan: 'When the Lights Go Out' was written by John McLaughlin for us. It was meant to be the first song from our second album, but Simon Cowell got his mitts on it. I don't know how. We'd learned the song and then suddenly we were told it was no longer our song.

Scott: I remember being too exhausted to be overly excited [by US success]. We could have been massive in the States if we'd have been given enough time. We were spread too thin over too many territories.

Ritchie: They wanted us everywhere all at once. Most bands take off in the UK, then Europe, they might go to Asia, and then after a few years, if they get really successful, America comes knocking. Whereas the whole world knocked for us at the same time. It sounds like fun and it was, but it was genuinely us waking up on a coach and not knowing what continent we were on.

Chris Herbert: It burnt them out. In hindsight, I would never do that again. We took on too much too soon. There was a point where you looked at the world and there wasn't a territory they weren't selling records in. We got a Disney special, which was the holy grail. They'd done it with NSYNC, they'd done it with Britney, and we got one along with B*Witched.

Sean: I look back on that time with a little bit of sadness really because we could have been so much bigger in the US. We had the top-ten record, we played Times Square, it was really starting to happen. We just couldn't find our feet and that's when everything started to become dysfunctional and there were frictions within the band. And then frictions between the band and management. Then the band and the label. Frictions everywhere.

Ritchie: Some of the guys, who will remain nameless, would piss high-level people off. Like high-level ITV producers, high-level BBC producers. Radio 1 people. You'd be like, 'Boys, keep it together.' We had America on a plate. But it was like a self-destruct button with some people. Like, 'I'm going to do everything I can to fuck this up. I'm going to be obnoxious and rude, I'm going to disappear at a huge photoshoot with a major US magazine.' To the point where the label came in and were like, 'You fucking British guys are a bunch of twats and you can fuck off.'

'I would say there were a few tussles and other times I was physically attacked'

From the very start, Five's bad-boy image always seemed to co-exist with the music. In fact, an advert for the Five *album, in conjunction with Woolworths, played into this sense of major label-endorsed rebellion. Billed as the 'I've seen the light' promotion, fans were encouraged, while buying Five's debut, to hand in an old CD by a rival band ('Let's face it we've all made mistakes', ran the blurb). In return, fans would get a free four-track bonus CD and a signed certificate. The reality of this ladband image, however, would slowly start to take over. Strangers thrust into a house together a week after being told they were in a band, their early disagreements soon grew into full-blown fist fights. What had started as a spark for creating exciting pop songs soon morphed into a situation where they would have to be kept apart in the studio. Suddenly the age gaps between various members became insurmountable chasms.*

Biff Stannard: Part of being a producer is being a babysitter; it's not just about doing beats. They'd lived in the house together and they were fighting like dogs from the beginning. Just at each other's throats. To the point where you'd work with a three and a two, never all five at one time. I don't think I ever worked with them as a five-piece more than once or twice. They did have a security person with them, but he was off getting them drugs or whatever.

Ritchie: No drugs. There was occasionally, possibly a little bit of spliff.

Hallgeir Rustan: When we had a meeting with Simon Cowell he told us about the boys and that the chemistry inside the group was perhaps not the best. He recommended we work with the vocalists, Scott and Ritchie, first because if we took the whole group in the studio it could lead to fighting.

Scott: You're overworked and everything starts to fracture because you're tired. You put teenagers and early twenty-somethings together and it's carnage. So yeah, there would be rows that would break into fights. And J would always be in the middle of that. There were points where a couple of us would be recording and then we'd go and the other three would come in.

Ritchie: I personally harbour no ill-will or resentment to J or Abs. I would want nothing more than to hear that they're happily getting on with their lives and that they're cool. J was quite a domineering character and he wanted things done his way. He was willing to get that point across in a physical way sometimes. Sometimes.

Simon Jones, former PR for *SM:TV* and *CD:UK*: They definitely had fist fights down at *CD:UK*. They had to be separated a couple of times. And it would always be threatening to kick off with other bands as well. They were punching each other. I remember watching it in the corridors. You had the two studios and in between there was the café area where loads of the bands would just hang out. So stories would naturally occur, which we'd then give to the tabloids. I'm sure I gave that story about Five having a fight to them because it mentioned *SM:TV* and *CD:UK*, so I'd done my job.

Ritchie: I would say there were a few tussles and other times I was physically attacked. There were fist fights and tussles that spilled out into corridors. Some physicality went on.

Biff Stannard: They were just really laddy. It was drinking and it was banter. They kind of gave the impression they didn't really give a fuck whether it was a hit or not or whether it sold.

Jeremy Joseph: At first I was a bit wary of doing [Five at G-A-Y]. I didn't know whether they were suitable. They started a bit rough around the edges and then, as it was getting a bit poppier, we started doing them and it worked. But it wasn't actually until I'd spoken to Ritchie I realised their attitude wasn't as bad boy as they were being portrayed. That's what changed my view of them.

Paul Flynn: Things are so massively different now, but when I worked at *Attitude*, there were two conversations you'd have with the straight acts we'd put on the cover; one was, 'How much flesh are they willing to show?' A hot boy would sell the magazine like nothing else could. It was pre-internet, pre-being able to see everything you want all the time. The other question was, 'How are they with gay people? What do they think about gay people? Are they going to feel uncomfortable?' You literally had to gauge the temperature. Can you imagine having that conversation now? The one we loved in the office was J. So we just did him on the cover [in May 2000]. He didn't show flesh, but he did do vest. It was quite Russian roulette as to what would happen on the day [with straight pop stars]; you had to go through a little dance each time.

Dania Pasquini, one half of video directors Max & Dania: We did lots of videos for them, from the beginning right through to their last ever video. In general they were a good bunch of guys. I never personally saw or witnessed anything other than good fun and them being up for it. They were clever, funny, witty, up-for-it guys. They had attitude when a lot of boybands didn't at that time.

Max Giwa, the other half of video directors Max & Dania: They were these bad boys who just wanted to be raucous and have a great time with girls so we were like, 'Brilliant, bring it on.' We just created a world around them.

Hannah Verdier, pop journalist: Five were always problematic from the start. They hated it all. Ritchie was alright, but they hated each other. The first time I met them I was at *Just Seventeen* and we had to play five-a-side football against them. The writer who was supposed to do it was sick on the day because she knew what they were like and I was a keen sub-editor so I said I would go. They were utterly horrible.

Alex Needham: They always seemed massively overworked. When it's something you really believe in and you're putting your heart and soul into it, you're probably a bit more cheerful. When you're just turning up and you've got to be a certain whacky character when you're eighteen and you find it all totally cringeworthy, then you turn up, do it and clear off.

Scott: We wanted to be the band that were honest. We wanted to be the band that said, 'Yeah, I was pissed last night, I've got a hangover.' Just be real because people connect with that much more. When Westlife are on the TV going, 'No sex before marriage and I've never had a drink in my life,' and then it would cut to an interview with Five and me going, 'What day is it because

I was hammered last night, what's going on?' That was more relatable.

Ritchie: Bearing in mind we came from the generation that were drinking cider down the park, it was like, 'Well, where did you grow up?' Obviously they were lying.

Jordan Paramor: Five didn't hide the fact they didn't get along. If you interviewed Take That or Boyzone, they might have had a blazing row beforehand, but you wouldn't know that on the shoot. But Five didn't tow the party line like other bands did. If one of them was annoying, they'd snap at them and they wouldn't really care if we put that in *Smash Hits*. They were always arguing. You could tell J was really uncomfortable about it all.

Holly Jade-Johnson, boyband super-fan: They were a bit rough. I remember on the *Smash Hits* roadshow they definitely seemed more like they were going to go to jail pretty soon. Or had been in jail.

Biff Stannard: I used to like it when they argued; it would be interesting to try to work it into the songs. That energy. You did them so quickly and you'd play them back to Simon Cowell and he'd go, 'That's shit,' and your heart would sink. Then the next one he'd go, 'Single.' So ruthless. But it worked and 'Keep On Movin'' is still one of my favourite songs I've ever done.

Paul Flynn: I don't know how I know this, someone must have put it on as a joke or something, but 'Keep On Movin'' sounds amazing on ecstasy. The chord progression is built for ecstasy.

'Westlife, Five and A1 were all gauging who got the biggest screams on the tour'

While their boyband peers had been shlepping up and down the country doing gay club nights or popping up in shopping centres in order to get attention, Five appeared fully formed, backed by industry heavyweights and with a string of early hits under their elastic waistbands. It meant there was a certain confidence about them that didn't always go down too well. That arrogance and immediate success drew the attention of not only the pop magazines, but also the tabloids, a situation that was sent into overdrive by the fact that Ritchie – the band's heartthrob – was in a relationship with fellow pop star Billie Piper.

Scott: Back in the day, there was a little bit of arrogance, like, 'Oh, no, I'm better than them. We're number one and they're not.' I get on really well with Peter Andre now, but I remember back in the '90s when we first met thinking, 'You're a twat.'

Lee Brennan: They came on the *Smash Hits* Poll Winners Party tour with us and won the Best New Act award. It was like, 'Who the hell are these guys?', just creating chaos backstage. Right from the start, before they'd even released a song, they were sure of themselves and didn't give a crap who anybody else was, even if you'd had number-one singles. They were groomed, they were styled, their hair was bang on, plus they had the songs.

Lucie Cave, former presenter on Trouble: We used to cover the *Smash Hits* tour and I remember Westlife, Five and A1 were all real rivals because they'd be gauging who got the biggest screams on the tour. There was loads of jealousy behind the scenes. Everyone just got really pissed every night. They would do their thing on stage and then everyone would go back to the hotel and stay up until 5 a.m. Then there would be fans there, so God knows what was going on.

Christian Ingebrigtsen, A1: There were definitely boyband rivalries. With Five in particular because they were the tough guys. So we were always happy if we headlined over them. Obviously. We weren't really good friends with Five back then; we never really spoke to them. Westlife were as big as they were but they were always nice backstage.

Lucie Cave: Five could get away with being moody with you and you sort of expected that from them, but Westlife had to be switched on all the time. They were getting pretty tired by the end of the tour because they had to be these golden boys in all white.

Nikki Whelan, '00s pop superfan: Scott from Five was always rude.

Scott: Back then, the fans didn't want to have a conversation with you as if you were a normal person. I had my face and my neck scratched, like I was bleeding because they just wanted to say, 'I've got Scott's hair under my nails, yay!' Once I had my shoe stolen by a fan. We were on tour in Italy and we were about to go on stage and the stylist is going, 'Scott, where's your shoe?' I knew whoever stole my trainer was in the audience. So I went out on stage and said, 'You might have noticed I've got one shoe on, but I am not going to sing "Until the Time Is Through" until I get my trainer back.' From the very back of the arena, followed by a spotlight, this trainer got carried across people's hands.

Sean: I was so overwhelmed with the fame and the people dressed as pop stars, I sort of went into my shell. I just didn't feel comfortable with it, so I'd sit quietly on my own a lot. It was only when we did *The Big Reunion* [in 2013] and we got to meet other bands that I started to feel more comfortable. I realised they felt like me too but everyone responded differently. I was more withdrawn. Like, this feels out of control so I'm just going to sit in this corner.

Ritchie: In the environment I was in day in day out, it wasn't always a very nice place to be. It was aggressive and there was a lot of confrontation. Then you've got the pressures of learning to be famous at seventeen and eighteen. I've never felt as lonely as I felt at that age. Every day was: 'You've got to get through this, this is the beginning of your life, it's not always going to be like this, one day the band won't exist.' Billie was going through the same thing, but alone. More often than not the people that work for you, they don't give a fuck about you. At least with Five, when we weren't rowing, we might have a deep conversation in the van and talk about stuff. I don't think she had that.

Scott: The record company wanted you to hide [relationships from fans] but I didn't want to. I was so in love with Kerry that I wanted to shout it from the rooftops. They were saying, 'You're going to alienate the fans,' but I wanted them to know that I wasn't there for them. So, after a while of them saying no, I just announced it in an interview. I was bored of being told what to do.

Ritchie: I remember being backstage in Germany somewhere in a corridor and having this really odd moment with Billie. We didn't really know each other, we just walked up to each other, said hello and hugged. But neither of us let go. We ended up standing there and having this tender, lovely hug for about four minutes. We were each other's solace. I knew I could trust her and I could tell her anything and she's not going to sell her story. I moved into a flat and I remember being absolutely made up. Five had lived together for nearly two years and I was like, 'I can't spend another moment with these boys, they're doing my tits in.' Billie was still living out of a hotel and it was doing her head in so I suggested she move in with me while she was look-ing for her own flat. We ended up living together for two years; she never left.

Laura Snapes: I was aware Ritchie Neville went out with Billie Piper and that that made her unpopular. Looking back, he looks like Julian Clary – hardly a teen heartthrob.

Nikki Whelan: When I was younger I did get defensive about [them having relationships]. I went through a phase of not liking Billie because of it, which is ridiculous. But I love her now. It was that immaturity.

Ritchie: Our management knew, her management knew, the labels knew. Cowell and [director of Innocent Records, Billie's label] Hugh Goldsmith knew each other, because Hugh was part of RCA when we signed with them. So they were friends. They had conversations about it and it was about controlling how it came out. It was a case of, 'This is going to come out, so instead of them doing it how they want to do it, why don't we work with them?'

A SLAM DUNK?

Hugh Goldsmith: In her book [2006's *Growing Pains*], Billie says I advised her that 'going out' with a popular boyband member could potentially harm her popularity and also attract unwanted aggression from jealous fans of whoever that artist might be. Naturally, we were all concerned about the impact Billie dating Richie might have on her career, but, more importantly, we most certainly did not want to see her get hurt in any way.

Jordan Paramor: I remember [Billie] coming on stage at the *Smash Hits* Poll Winners' Party after the news broke and getting booed.

Ritchie: We were nervous about it. We knew the first show after coming out about the relationship would be bad, but actually it was worse than we thought it would be. The booing was awful. It wasn't just a few people – most of that arena booed her. When you really love someone, it's hard. You have a couple of those relationships in your life if you're lucky and, at the time, especially with what was going on in our lives, I totally loved her. That was really difficult to watch. It was hard for her, but actually it didn't affect her record sales and it didn't affect her career.

Hugh Goldsmith: Innocent was a small, tightly knit team and we had a strong family vibe between us and with our artists. So we were all absolutely gutted to witness Billie being booed by a sector of Five fans on the *Smash Hits* tour and our hearts went out to her. Understandably, Billie was devastated by what happened and things got even worse, in the next few months, as jealous fans started sending hate mail to her fan club and to the teen magazines. Billie's confidence was knocked badly by the whole experience. Our label view on all the nastiness was that it would eventually die down if Billie lay low for a while. So her focus then swung primarily on to starting the next album as well as doing promotion outside the UK.

Jeremy Joseph: For a nightclub, the licence was eighteen and over, but on stage the licence doesn't apply. We did Billie when she was sixteen. She had her head screwed on. She was older than her years. She started with this teen girl market, but girls were never really going to like Billie because she's competition. Our audience didn't care that she was dating someone from Five. She was an example of the label going, 'Right, we're losing this audience, what audience will work for her?' You watched her go from bubblegum pop to more adult dance.

'Simon basically shut down the entire Eiffel Tower for Girl Thing'

By the summer of 2000, Five were the biggest boyband in the country. Their first two albums had shifted 6.5 million copies worldwide, they'd sold a million albums in America alone and 1999's Invincible *had given them two UK number-one singles in the shape of ecstasy fave 'Keep On Movin'' and the ludicrous Queen collaboration, 'We Will Rock You'. Happy with the success of the so-called Spice Boys, and perhaps still smarting from their sacking from the Spice Girls, in 1998, Chris and Bob Herbert set about forming Girl Thing, recruiting Jodi Albert, Michelle Barber, Anika Bostelaar, Linzi Martin and Nikki Stuart. Signed to RCA by Simon Cowell – who had once turned down Scary et al., let's not forget – they were pitched somewhere between the rebellious Five and the personality-packed Spice Girls, but with an All Saints 'edge'. They launched in the summer of 2000 with shouty anthem 'Last One Standing', which, thanks to the truckloads of cash being poured into the project, was assumed to be a given for the number-one spot. The band even recorded a number of radio interviews and idents pre-emptively heralding their debut chart-topper. In the end, the single peaked at eight, while the follow-up single, 'Girls on Top', crashed out at twenty-five. Their self-titled album, which featured their original version of the soon-to-be-massive 'Pure and Simple', was only released in Australia.*

Chris Herbert: We were incredibly arrogant by this point. We'd had a real run of success, Simon Cowell and I, and we believed our own hype. I think we had all the characters in there and the songs were pretty good, but we overhyped it. The expectations of this band were that they were going to eclipse the Spice Girls and Five combined.

Jeremy Joseph: They were playing off a sort of, 'Let's do a girl version of Five.' Actually, all you're trying to do is copy one success and move it onto another and it doesn't work.

Biff Stannard: It just felt really contrived. I thought Simon was really interesting, but wasn't sure about the band. So I produced two songs on their album. Simon is unlike any other person I've ever met. His whole thing is trying to capture the zeitgeist just after it's happened but he was a bit late with them. He got better at it as time went on.

Jordan Paramor: I did their media training. It was too transparent. Too contrived. You could see what they were trying to do and you can't take the public for fools. It's no different to

Boyzone slipping into Take That's shoes or Westlife coming along later to replace Boyzone. But Girl Thing missed the boat.

Jodi Albert: We got to appear on the cover of *Smash Hits* magazine before we even released our first single. That was incredible.

Hannah Verdier: We went all out with the build-up a few weeks before, like, 'Hey there's this new pop band,' and then put them on the cover. I can remember really clearly the midweeks coming in and they weren't anywhere near number one.

Chris Herbert: We had all the front covers of the magazines booked with them celebrating their number one before we'd even charted.

Hannah Verdier: The management wanted us to be best friends with them. Like, 'Right, you're going to go in and make friends.' We had to hang out with them.

Jodi Albert: We went to Paris to launch the band in front of the world's press. They basically shut down the entire Eiffel Tower for Girl Thing. Journalists were flown in from across the world and put up in an amazing hotel in Paris. We performed five tracks and then we sat down to do interviews. The treatment was amazing.

Chris Herbert: We had the girls performing at the top with Union Jacks flying off it. It was a bit cringey.

Alex Needham: Girl Thing were just a catastrophic, million-pound flop, weren't they? Not a bad first single, though.

Chris Herbert: Because the first Girl Thing single hadn't charted at number one it was deemed a failure. Simon was in a tailspin because it had knocked his ego. Mine, too. But he'd taken it quite badly and was probably getting the wrath of the label because he'd spent so much money on the launch of this band.

James Masterson: It's always thrown back at him as his greatest failure. They released one single that went in at number eight in their first week and for any brand-new act that would be a good achievement, but Simon Cowell said that was a disaster. There's an example of how it was all focused on that first week.

'I just needed a little bit of help'

When sessions for what would become Five's third album, 2001's Kingsize, *started, it was clear that the band were disintegrating. While the album's lead single 'Let's Dance' gave them another chart-topper, the video only featured four members. The two follow-up singles – 'Closer to Me' and the Grease-sampling 'Rock the Party' – featured videos made up of cobbled-together footage and animation, respectively. A perfunctory greatest hits album called* Greatest Hits *followed in November and peaked at number nine.*

Hallgeir Rustan: I think the friction within the band made it difficult to hold together. When everyone thinks they are the alpha male then it's going to cause problems.

Chris Herbert: I knew the band were exhausted. But they were also becoming hard work as well. I couldn't recognise whether it was pure exhaustion, whether they were suffering mentally, or whether they were just playing up. It was a combination of all those things. There was also a bit of bullying going on.

Sean: For me, it was a struggle from the beginning unfortunately. We had some really good laughs in Sweden when we were recording the first album, then after it came out there were internal struggles. We had just come back to do a new album and I was really struggling with anxiety, feeling overwhelmed. We didn't really have any help, you know, so the other guys in the band said I should go and see a counsellor. Back then, it was unheard of. It's not like now. So I went to see a counsellor, saw a psychologist and they were the ones who signed me off and said he's not mentally healthy enough to come back and work.

Ritchie: We'd started the promotion for 'Let's Dance' and they paired me with Sean to sit with the journalist. The journalist asked, 'How are you guys doing?', and you don't go, 'To be honest with you, mate, I'm fucking tired,' you just go, 'Yeah, I'm good, thanks.' Sean sat there with his head down and he was like, 'Yeah, yeah, I'm fucking good, man,' and he just kept repeating, 'Soooo fucking good, I'm soooo fucking good.' Then he got up and walked off. He didn't come back and I did the interview. Afterwards I went to the tour manager and he was like, 'He's in the van, he's going home, he needs a bit of time.' I still didn't understand it at this point. We were specifically told not to call him. We were told he didn't want to be bothered by anyone or anything, he just wants space. So we respected that. Then he never came back.

Chris Herbert: Sean comes across as a hard northerner but is really really soft and he's the youngest in the band, so, although externally he was playing a character, internally he was in real turmoil. Trying to come to terms with this newfound success and fortune and fame and schedules. I knew he was going downhill but it came very suddenly.

Scott: We had to lie and tell anyone that asked that Sean had glandular fever. We knew that he was having a breakdown and he'd left. But the label wanted to make sure that *Kingsize* was going to sell so they said we couldn't tell anyone.

Sean: Now they would have said it was to do with mental health and you'd get a bit more care, but back then it was more, 'Mental health issues? Hang on a second, you're selling millions of albums, you're making money, how could you have any mental health issues?' That's how it was.

Scott: If that was now, the single release would have been put back and we would have had a break. And the band would never have broke up.

Ritchie: Most people only see the videos, where you're selling a dream. It's a happy place. But you might have been crying before that take and the make-up artist says, 'Come on, you've got puffy eyes, let's get that sorted,' and then you're back in dreamland. That's where you realise that money ultimately means absolutely nothing. It's about where you're at inside yourself as a human being that dictates how happy you are.

Sean: The label were in a rush and they didn't want to wait, so they convinced the band to use a cardboard cut-out of me [in the video for 'Let's Dance'].

Dania Pasquini: At that time, we were playing with what we do and we were taking the mickey out of ourselves, the whole industry, out of Simon. [That video] opens with the band going in to meet someone who was meant to be Simon Cowell. You can see their sense of humour in that video because they created those characters, they brought that to the table. You can't fake that.

Ritchie: We had a bit to say about that video idea because that was our life. We'd go into these meetings and be like, 'Who the fuck are these people?' We'd be in Simon Cowell's office and he'd go off to speak to someone and so we'd be like, 'Go on, go through his desk.' We were taking his drawers out and he had all these books on psychology and body language. Or you'd be in the room and just when you'd catch eyes with him he'd give you the quickest little wink. It was as if that wink was to say, 'You're my baby.' Unbeknown to him, afterwards we'd all get in the van and be like, 'Did you get a wink today?' If someone didn't, you'd be like, 'Yeah, I'm his baby today.' Everyone got a wink at some point. That's why the spoof thing happened in the video because that was how it felt.

Max Giwa: Sean wasn't available so we had a cardboard cut-out of him. That was a send up. They all embraced it and took it on board.

Dania Pasquini: [The cut-out] was our idea. We were paying homage to the fact that he couldn't be there. We wanted to include him and, because the whole video was about irony and poking fun at the industry, we thought it was fitting. But I didn't understand that he was having a hard time then. I have a different view of it now.

110

Sean: It did hurt a little bit. It was kind of like the label saying, 'Well, he's so miserable anyway and he's not smiling and he's so quiet that he might as well have been a cardboard cut-out.' That's what it felt like to me.

Scott: It was awful. Sean can't even watch that video because that's just fucking wrong.

Sean: From the video directors' point of view, they had a job to do. What are they going to do? There's a band member missing, they've got their career and they've just got to carry on. They didn't know me personally.

Scott: I was also struggling. My eldest son was in intensive care because he was born six weeks early. He was really poorly and I remember a call when I was at the hospital looking after him saying, 'You've got to go on *CD:UK* and perform,' and I was like, 'I couldn't give a fuck, I'm not doing it.'

Chris Herbert: I can't remember that, no. Towards the end, there was trauma most days. It was very, very difficult. The ending of that band was really messy. I realise now that Scott was also really struggling mentally.

Scott: In the end, I ended up doing the performance. I was crying in the corridor and I think Rich looked at the boys and said, 'This is done.'

Ritchie: There was a lot going on. We'd also done a show in Belgium and I had sprained my ankle. So we were a band called Five with four members, doing a song called 'Let's Dance' but I was doing it on a stool. Then Scott just broke down in the corridor and I remember him saying, 'I just can't do this any more.' He was crying so much that he couldn't really talk. And J and I sat either side with our arms around him and I distinctly remember looking across at J and going, 'It's done, isn't it?' You can have as many number-one singles as you like but we were looking at two out of five members being basically unwell.

Sean: Simon Cowell was quite bitter about it back then. I don't hold anything against him; he was younger and he had his eye on the prize. There wasn't any mental health awareness. I'm sure he would deal with it differently now. Or I'd like to think he would. But back then he was quite bitter. I think he looked at me like, 'How could I not appreciate everything I'd been given by him?' He thought I was throwing it back in his face and being unappreciative because so many other kids would have loved to be doing what I was doing. But I just needed a little bit of help. I literally went from school to the next minute being on TV and really famous, but still a child. I handled it the best that I could, but it didn't go too brilliantly.

Chris Herbert: Richard Griffiths, who headed up BMG at the time, later went on to manage One Direction and I remember sitting down with him and he said, 'We're treating One Direction in a very different way to how we treated Five, because we learned how not to do it with them.'

'Liam Gallagher got a Bop It! out of his bag'

While Five's pop-star journey ended horribly, the band have continued in various guises throughout the years. After The Big Reunion in 2013, which J only appeared in briefly, they continued as a four-piece, before Abs left in 2014.

A SLAM DUNK?

In 2022, Scott, Sean and Ritchie released a new album, Time, *still under the Five moniker despite the obvious numerical discrepancy. Like a lot of the pop stars from that era, for Scott, Ritchie and Sean it's the positive memories that have slowly drifted back to the surface. A time of huge concerts in front of hundreds of thousands of fans, of unexpected collaborations and of drunken evenings playing inane games with the lead singer of Oasis.*

Scott: The first memory that jumps out is being on stage with Queen at Party in the Park in front of 200,000 people, performing 'We Will Rock You', which obviously went to number one. The Queen version only got to number two, so Five beat Queen at their own game. Just coming off stage and Brian May saying he prefers our version because it's faster. I remember he said to me, and I'll never forget it, 'I always knew that "We Will Rock You" was a number-one record, I just didn't know it would happen now.' Really cool.

Ritchie: My ultimate favourite moment was actually a private one. We were doing 'We Will Rock You' and we were at Roger Taylor's house. He had this rehearsal studio and we'd done a few passes at the song and were having a tea break. The mic was still up so I just sang the opening lines of Jimi Hendrix's 'Hey Joe'. Then Brian started joining in with the guitar, then Roger's picked up the sticks and the three of us jammed the entire song. It was such a lovely moment. Yes, it's Rich from Five, the number-one boyband, and it's Queen, the absolute legends, but we were just three guys that really loved music.

Sean: This is going to be a bit of a let-down because most people talk about things like playing in front of 250,000 people, but my moment is laying in the little house we had in Surrey. We'd just signed the record deal and been to a label party. I remember laying in this little box room, still getting my £100 a week, and I couldn't believe we'd actually signed a record deal. For me that was it. It felt like anything was possible. All I wanted to do was music and it felt like it was really going to happen.

Scott: The other memory that sticks out is being very drunk with Liam Gallagher in Rio, where we'd performed on the same stage in front of 250,000 at Rock in Rio. I was with Sean, Rich, my wife, Kerry, and Liam Gallagher. He was playing an Oasis album that was about to come out and every song he had written he was like, 'Ah, fucking hell, man, this is an absolute banger, this is amazing.' Then every one Noel had written he'd say, 'This one's fucking shite.' Noel didn't speak to us at all – we weren't cool enough. But Liam was down for it, he invited us into the room for a few drinks.

Sean: Do you know what, I really, really liked Liam. He gets a bit of a bad rap from back in the day, but what I liked about him was, given the genre of music he's in, like the indie music, he could have been snobby with us. There was a lot of that at the time. He wouldn't get any sort of medals from the serious music press for hanging out with Five, but he didn't care. He just said, 'Sit down, have a drink.'

Scott: This is so not rock 'n' roll, but Liam then got a Bop It! out of his bag and was like, 'Shall we have a fucking bang on this, it's a brilliant game?' So we're standing around playing Bop It!, pissed. It's my favourite pub story. My mates will go, 'Tell the Bop It! Liam Gallagher story.'

Ritchie: At the time, it was really hard, but it's almost like it's giving back now. It's nice now.

Sean: I definitely don't regret being in the band. I wish that I could have found the strength to not have to leave. I wish we could have carried on. But it's not a regret because I had to do it. If I could change anything, I would put myself in a better place to handle it, you know.

4

Thank Steps for the Music

The Spice Girls' all-encompassing success instantly broadened pop's appeal, making consumers of a pre-teen, or tween, market who had previously ignored the lure of two-track cassette singles. It also made space for something more cartoonish in UK pop, while also making unfathomable success seem more attainable. Their sense of carefree magic wasn't necessarily as evident in the boybands that also peppered the pop landscape, however. Irish balladeers Boyzone would shortly usher in Irish balladeers Westlife and, while they both knew their way around a key change and looked delicious in a sensible black M&S roll-neck, the heady bounce and pep of that sugar-rush pop was absent.

That is until Steps – AKA Ian 'H' Watkins, Lee Latchford-Evans, Claire Richards, Faye Tozer and Lisa Scott-Lee – arrived in November 1998 via the ludicrous fiddle-heavy, line-dancing techno curio '5,6,7,8'. If the Spice Girls seemed like a gang you might want to join, Steps were the Butlin's Red Coats you initially wanted to avoid. Six months after '5,6,7,8' swept the UK school disco scene, Irish leg-wagglers B*Witched unleashed their own fiddle-heavy banger 'C'est La Vie' and suddenly fun was back in dysfunctional pop.

Keen to find a 'mixed Spice', AKA a pop act with both male and female members, '5,6,7,8' scribes Steve Crosby and Barry Upton, alongside manager Tim Byrne, had turned to pop's post-Spice Girls Bible, *The Stage*, in order to find their band. What was initially supposed to target the burgeoning line-dancing market (!), with little hopes of longevity, soon expanded into a hugely successful, ABBA-aping success story that's still going strong twenty-five years later.

'One of the girls, who was quite deep and spiritual, said it hurt her soul to sing "5,6,7,8"'

Claire from Steps: I actually signed my first record deal for a girlband called TSD on my eighteenth birthday. I had been doing karaoke every weekend at a pub and it was through people I'd met and knew that I heard about this girlband that was being put together. I went [to the audition] with my mum because I was only seventeen. We just chatted for ages and at the end they said, 'Do you want to do it, then?', and I said, 'Yeah, okay.'

H from Steps: Back then there was no *X Factor*, there was no *Britain's Got Talent* or *The Voice*, so the way we used to get jobs was via *The Stage*. Everyone was auditioning for either girlbands or boybands. So this one advert jumped out because it was looking for boy and girl members. I've got the original advert somewhere and it says, 'auditions for sassy, sexy twenty-year-olds'. I thought, 'Well, I can do that.' We all sent our CVs in and I embellished mine quite a lot because all I'd done was been a Red Coat at that point. So through a process of elimination Lisa and I plus three other members got the audition. That was the first line-up that was shopped around. Nobody took any interest.

Claire: When [TSD] didn't work out, I was devastated. I was temping at the time, doing reception work, and my mum said, 'Right, come on, you're miserable, let's start sending out your tapes and photos.' So I kept buying *The Stage* and looking at the adverts and sending off my cassette and picture to everybody. Most of the time using the Burger King head office's franking machine to send them.

H: The original three members left, basically because they didn't want to be line-dancing pop stars. We were so uncool. I love cheesy pop and I couldn't believe my luck. I'd come from a very small village in Wales and to me I'd hit the jackpot even though we hadn't done anything at that point.

Claire: I don't know how many applications I sent off but, I am not joking, Steps is the only one that called me for an audition. Myself, Lee and Faye were all at the same audition. H and Lisa had been in the band with three other people for about six months. For whatever reason, all three of those people decided it wasn't for them. I remember H telling me later that one of the girls, who was quite deep and spiritual, said it hurt her soul to sing '5,6,7,8'. Clearly I'm not that deep.

H: Claire has always been a lot more mature, so I thought she was twenty-eight when we first met.

Claire: Little shit.

H: I always thought she was an old soul, which is ridiculous because she's actually the baby of the band.

Claire: I do think he thought I looked older because I had really short hair and it probably aged me a little bit. But I was bloody nineteen! How dare he.

'I remember going from Blue Peter rehearsals straight to the dole office'

Once the final line-up was secured, the five-piece initially went their separate ways. There was no group house and, unlike other bands that followed later, there was no record deal in place. 'Normal' jobs still needed to be done in between showcases for labels. After dominating pop in the UK in the '80s and early '90s via his PWL label, be it with Kylie, Jason or 2 Unlimited, music impresario Pete Waterman was somewhat cast adrift by 1997. Kylie had gone indie, Jason had gone completely and 2 Unlimited had found there were indeed limits. After one very short showcase led to a very low offer, however, the fortunes for both Steps and Waterman were about to change.

H: Some of us couldn't afford mobile phones – I think Claire had one – but the rest of us wrote postcards to each other. We were penpals, basically. We weren't on a retainer, because we weren't signed. The people looking after us at the time didn't pay us a wage. It was all up in the air; we didn't know what was around the corner, so we were all rabbits in headlights when it started. It was pipe dreams.

Claire: Lisa was finishing a job at Butlin's, Lee was still at college. I don't know what H was doing. Faye was working at the Hilton on Park Lane, and actually she carried on for a while. There was no money at the start. Then we started rehearsing at Pinnacle leisure centre in Epsom. Believe it or not we rehearsed for the showcases for two weeks. Two weeks for one routine.

H: We had our showcase in Nomis Studios. We invited lots of record companies and heads of A&R – Simon Cowell came to see us on that same day and said no to us. He didn't want us. Years afterwards when we were doing the same show as West-life, Simon came over to me and said, 'I made a mistake, I'm sorry.' But Pete [Waterman] just got it.

Claire: I think Simon had been to see the other formation of the group. I think they'd done a few showcases and hadn't been signed. The only showcase [the new line-up] did was at Battery Studios and that was for Tina Wisby and Steve Jenkins, who were the head of Jive, and Pete Waterman. Pete had a licensing deal with Jive at the time, so technically we were signed through Pete's label Eastern Bloc Unity Label and it all went through Jive.

Pete Waterman: An old friend of mine rang me and said he'd got a group and they wanted to audition for us. To be honest, I went out of politeness. One thing I can tell you now is I wasn't interested in a line-dancing group. My mother-in-law at the time had been telling me for at least a year that the way to make money was a line-dancing record and when your head of A&R is your mother-in-law you've got a real problem. So I had avoided it like the plague.

H: Pete was this legendary figure that shaped my childhood. My bedroom wall was Bananarama, Kylie, Jason, and Rick Astley. All of these icons, their careers were launched by this man, this god. And he was a pop god.

Claire: I was a PWL kid. That was exactly the kind of music I listened to and was obsessed with as a teenager. Pete just seemed to get it immediately. We'd all raided our wardrobes and found matching outfits and basically just mimed and did the dance routines. We didn't even pretend to sing it. I've heard him tell the story that as soon as he heard me sing he just knew – but he didn't hear me sing on that day!

Pete Waterman: They did '5,6,7,8' and instantly I'd forgotten about the line-dancing thing, I just watched them and Claire was brilliant.

Karl Twigg, Steps songwriter and producer: Straight away you could tell they were stars. 911 came in as well and you had the main guy who looked like one of Ant and Dec, don't know which one. Straight away you thought, 'Hang on, these guys are going to make it.' But Pete didn't take them on.

Lee Brennan: I don't think Pete had much time for us really. I think he just thought, 'Here's another act trying to do it.' Didn't want to sign us.

Pete Waterman: [Steps] had done the rounds of all the record companies because Tim [Byrne], who was their manager, was packaging them as Mixed Spice. I guess what worked for me was because I had just gone in to be polite, it sort of whacked me and I went, 'Wow, that's amazing.' I forgot all about the cowboy hats and I just thought they were really good. But I was in a hurry, so I said to Steve, 'Listen, sign 'em, give him £500 for the record and I'll make it at the weekend.' If they'd have had another offer they wouldn't have taken mine because I was so matter of fact about it. So I went back to the office, played the demo [of '5,6,7,8'] to a couple of producers and members of the staff and they all thought it was awful. Dreadful. I said, 'Sorry, but it's a hit.' The two producers wouldn't put their name on it at first; they wanted nothing to do with it. So I said, 'Put Pete Waterman on twice the size you normally would, then.'

Karl Twigg: That is complete and utter . . . truth. I tell you what it was, when Mark [Topham, Steps songwriter and producer] and I first got to PWL we'd been in jazz funk bands. And we'd gone from that to '5,6,7,8'. We still knew all the guys from those other bands, so we were like, 'Fucking hell, what are they all going to say when they hear this?' The funny thing is, when we did [Steps' 2000 number-one bop] 'Stomp' later on, all the musicians we knew played on that song. So even they succumbed to the lure of Steps.

Pete Waterman: There was so much belligerence against me putting this record out that the producers really wanted to take the mickey out of me. But you can't wind me up – once I think a record is a hit the more perverse you want to be the more I'm going to like it. So when I went in they'd really modernised it, and really techno-ed it as opposed to line-dance-ed it. Thinking they were going to offend me. If anything they'd made it more palatable for me. I did come up with the techno idea, but not as techno as they went.

Karl Twigg: I would never have made a record to piss him off. You put your heart and soul into it.

H: We're opening up old wounds now – I'm over it, I promise – but in the original version of '5,6,7,8', I sang the whole middle eight. Lisa did the answer phrase bit. But the lyrics were so bad, oh my gosh. I'm so glad it was cut in the end.

Karl Twigg: There were some parts in the middle of it that Pete wanted to keep that just sounded like 'I Should Be So Lucky'. I had a massive row with him while we were making it. I took that part out. I just ripped the original version they bought in to pieces.

H: The label saw us as a one-off novelty record. Like 'The Birdie Song' or 'Agadoo'. They didn't believe in us that much to invest money in the future. But our peers, like B*Witched or Five or S Club, they had millions of pounds invested in them as groups that would have longevity.

Claire: I was lucky I still lived at home with my mum and dad, so any money I got I spent on clothes. Everybody else had to pay rent. Every now and then we'd get per diems, so the first time someone handed us that little wad of cash it was like, 'Oh my God!' For a long time, that's all we really lived on. If we earned any money from any gigs we did, it just covered our expenses.

It was a good year and a half before we earned any proper money at all.

H: I remember going from *Blue Peter* rehearsals straight to the dole office to get our Jobseeker's Allowance, me and Lee. We lived together. We weren't getting paid. So yeah, we were on TV but we were also signing on. Nobody recognised us back then so it was fine.

Claire: By this point, H especially had so much faith in the fact '5,6,7,8' was going to be a massive hit. And, being signed to an actual label, we felt like there was something behind it. Even at that point, it was still just meant to be a line-dancing band. Pete knew it was going to be the hit that got us noticed, but it wasn't his intention to follow through with that sound. We've got a stash of line-dancing hits just waiting to be released!

Pete Waterman: The real gem of the story is one of my mates was Tony Wilson from Factory Records. He did evening shows for Granada and I did [ITV's late-night clubbing show] *The Hitman and Her*. We had a mutual respect for each other. He rang me and said, 'Waterman, everybody's after your guts,' and I went, 'Why?', and he said, 'Because you've killed country music, you're a pariah.' Then he said they'd got so much hate mail, could we do a programme with you? It was a Wednesday-night slot on Granada and it was like, 'You bring your band on and let these people have a go at you.' So we did the show, everybody was having a go at me, but the audience just went through the roof. By Saturday I had a call from the lady who ran Saturday morning TV for the BBC saying, 'Could we have this group on?'

H: All I knew was that I was in a pop band and I was going to be on the front of *Smash Hits* magazine and on *Top of the Pops* and that's all I cared about.

Claire: [At that time] there was Aqua and the Vengaboys and we could have gone down that road, I think, but Pete managed to change it to become something in between all of that. Even though it was all very upbeat and up-tempo, if you listen to our songs they're all quite depressing. It was our image that meant people really saw us as that kiddy band. We'd perform everything with a big smile and a dance routine. People just hadn't seen anything like it. There is a very big element of escapism when it comes to Steps.

H: Also, don't forget, Pete had spent a long time in the pop wilderness – he'd had major hits in the '80s, but there'd been a spell of time where there were tumbleweeds. He didn't know where he was going. He had a lot to prove.

Karl Twigg: He was a byword for bad music. When we got [to PWL] it was the uncoolest place to be.

Pete Waterman: ['5,6,7,8'] sold 500,000 copies. It's probably the biggest-selling single never to enter the top ten. The whole fact it was selling was staggering. We kept looking at it and thinking, 'This is incredible.' It was selling right across the board, not just the stores that reported to the charts. Steps were the only group where we never discounted any of their records. We never did discounts to Woolworths or anybody. We kept that right up until the very end – if you want it, you've got to buy it.

Claire: In those days, everybody worked hard to break an artist because back then you had to. In a night, we'd probably do an under-18s, then do something early evening and then do a nightclub. Imagine being in a nightclub and that fiddle starts up. The outfit I wore in the '5,6,7,8' video was the outfit I wore for every single club gig for months and months. Bearing in my mind my outfit was red PVC trousers and a red mesh top, neither of which are very washable. So yeah, you could probably smell me coming most of the time. When we got *Top of the Pops* we begged them, 'Please please please can we have a new outfit.'

H: '5,6,7,8' became this monster nobody could stop. We released the record in November and it stuck around for a few months and it was in January when Pete said, 'Right, we can do something more with this.' Then negotiations took place. At the time, we were line-dancing pop stars but it was Pete's idea to turn us into, and I quote, 'ABBA on speed'. He always saw us as more than 'The Birdie Song'. Everyone laughed at us, everyone wanted to get rid of us, but we kept coming back. It was like COVID; you couldn't get rid of us – it was a pop pandemic.

'All of S Club 7 were sleeping underneath the make-up tables'

Given Steps' manager Tim Byrne had started his career working on the Smash Hits *Poll Winners' Party and its associated tour, Steps were quickly thrown into the 'live' circuit of nationwide roadshows. With six-week lead times for singles and a plethora of magazines (*Smash Hits, Big!, Top of the Pops, J-17, *etc.), regional radio and TV shows to appear on, pop acts would often* *find themselves bumping into each other multiple times a week. A community slowly built; a petri dish of bonding and bickering between power naps.*

Claire: The vibe was very different [back then]. Everybody knew everybody. I remember at the *Smash Hits* Poll Winners' Party, it was always the girls in one room and the boys in the other, so obviously H and Lee would be in with Five and 911 and Westlife. We'd be in with B*Witched and Billie Piper and the girls from S Club 7. Everybody got on really well. We all had a laugh. I find that in pop now everybody keeps themselves to themselves. No one really mixes any more.

Lee Brennan: They'd set up little curtained-off areas and we'd all be chatting over the curtains. We'd all be in a sports hall getting changed together. I think once everybody got really, really busy it would be like passing ships in the night. You'd see someone coming offstage and be like, 'Hey, how you doing, mate? Can't stop, going to another thing somewhere else.' It became this crazy whirlwind.

H: I still class some of my dear friends now as people I met from bands during that period. I've known some of them for twenty-five years and unless you've lived it you don't understand it. We shared dressing rooms at the *Smash Hits* Poll Winners' Party, so we'd be with S Club and we were all knackered getting our make-up done. They were sleeping underneath the make-up tables. I remember Tina and Jon literally sleeping on my feet. It was crazy. I remember Adam Rickett coming in to change – my ears pricked up then, I can tell you. It's a cliché but it was an incredible rollercoaster that will never happen again like that.

Bradley McIntosh, S Club 7: When we were around other bands at, say, the *Smash Hits* afterparty, we always felt like they all knew each other and we didn't know them as well. We were often in America doing the TV shows. So we'd feel like outsiders.

H: All Saints were the coolest band. They'd walk in a room and everybody wanted to see them, whereas we'd be changing behind a cardboard divider with our coat-hanger head mics.

Claire: For a while, I definitely thought I was cooler than I was. I'd be like, 'I wear Maharishi trousers and I wear shell-toed trainers, I must be cool.' I *so* wanted to be in All Saints. I think it took me a long time to realise what Steps is. I think I was fighting against what Steps was but now I'm not at all. Steps is exactly us.

H: We had a record company and we had people looking after us, but we didn't have people throwing money at us. Honestly, I think that's why we did so well [financially], because we were young but we weren't stupid. We knew that money was going to have to be coming from somewhere. That money was going to be recouped. Whereas, no disrespect to other bands, maybe they weren't as savvy and sassy as us. We weren't teenagers, we'd had jobs and we'd worked in the business, so even though we didn't understand record contracts we knew somebody was paying for it and that was probably going to be us.

'Her mum's ringing up saying, "You're not taking drugs, are you, Claire?"'

While '5,6,7,8' peaked at number fourteen and dug its scootin' boots in by hanging around the UK top forty for over three months, Steps were still dismissed as one-hit wonders in waiting. While a bank of line-dancing songs gathered dust in a cupboard somewhere, there was one song that was about to change everything. August 1998's 'One for Sorrow', which 'channelled' ABBA's 'The Winner Takes It All', became their first bona-fide smash (it would have been number one were it not for those pesky Welsh polemicists Manic Street Preachers and their snappily titled 'If You Tolerate This Then Your Children Will Be Next'), setting a template of hi-NRG yet wistful pop that the band would become synonymous for. Oh, and covers – lots of covers.

Claire: ['One for Sorrow'] started to prove to people that we weren't going anywhere and that we could release serious music.

Pete Waterman: Karl [Twigg] and Mark [Topham] played me 'One for Sorrow' at a meeting with the management and the band. I was very worried about whether we were ready to go with that song at that time. So I said, 'No, we need something before that,' so we did 'Last Thing on My Mind', which should have been a hit for Bananarama [in 1992], but at that point they were past their sell-by date. It was a long way from outside the top ten to a number one, so we needed an interim record. When 'One for Sorrow' came out, it was just a record that was like, 'Wow.'

Jeremy Joseph: With Steps you're watching a band evolve at G-A-Y. There was a moment where suddenly we saw an enduring pop act and it was with 'Last Thing on My Mind'. They performed '5,6,7,8' and got an okay reaction. Then they did 'Last Thing on My Mind' and the reaction was stronger. You could see for an adult audience that they were turning into a proper band.

Claire: I used to just hang around the studio and wait until I was needed because I was told, 'Don't go home.' But I didn't really have a life either because I didn't have a boyfriend and I lived at home with my mum and dad.

Karl Twigg: Their schedule was insane. We were trying to finish Claire's vocal [on 'One for Sorrow'] because the next day they would be off and we wouldn't see them again for sixteen weeks. [One night] she was recording at 2.30 a.m. and her mum's ringing up saying, 'You're not taking drugs, are you, Claire?'

Claire: She was saying, 'What are they giving you? What is it that's making you stay awake?' I was like, 'Mum, I'm twenty, I think I can stay awake.' Most of the time we'd have little naps during the day. I used to have this coat that looked like a sleeping bag so I'd put the hood over my head and you'd just have this little lump of duvet.

Karl Twigg: [Mark and I] did used to have the odd spliff, one every sort of fifteen minutes . . . No, it wasn't that bad.

H: Oh, that would explain a lot. I would have flagged that. I was such an angel back then. But I was smoking cigarettes a lot, just because at the time everybody knows we weren't singing live. It was the thing to do – we were basically pop drag queens. We used to lip synch for our lives.

Karl Twigg: All we did was muck about and laugh [in the studio]. That is it. H would come in in the morning and fucking nipple-cripple me. I'd be like, 'You fucker.'

H: Yeah, just little nipple cramps. That was my general good morning, to the girls as well . . . I'm joking!

Claire: With ['One for Sorrow'] I always thought it was because I was the only one [in the studio], so that was why I sang the whole song. But I've been told different since.

Lisa from Steps: Years ago it was difficult when somebody was given more [lines], but how I look at it now that I've had kids and grown up, I'm proud of the vocal and it's a great song. I'm proud that she's in our band.

Karl Twigg: I don't want to say that she carried the band, but I think at the beginning her voice was so unique and powerful. To the point where after recording '5,6,7,8' we said to Claire, 'Give us a call if this doesn't work out.' But the minute we finished ['One for Sorrow'], we were just looking at each other like, 'Let's have another listen, is it really what we think it is?' I love that record.

Claire: Pete used to do this thing where he'd sit us in the studio and listen to the whole album back to back and then he'd play what the next single was going to be. It was 'One for Sorrow' and I started crying.

Pete Waterman: We could have had a number one with that song if we'd have done discounting. If we were number one or number three we didn't care because we wanted to build the fanbase. If you didn't like Steps you didn't like Steps full stop. It wasn't like we were going to convince you by knocking 10p off the price of the record.

Claire: Later I was trying to make a point that every time we released a single we would be number two but we would have sold more copies than most other number ones of that year. It was probably my mistake for using Westlife as an example – well, it obviously was – and I just said, 'Next week Westlife could release a song and sell 10,000 and they'll be number one.' They took it that I was specifically picking them out. Then Louis Walsh was on the radio going into one about Steps and then Westlife wouldn't talk to us for ages. It was really weird.

H: [Follow-up] 'Tragedy' was also a really strange one because it was another single that stuck around, so we were in the pop consciousness. Probably for the wrong reasons because they just wanted us to go away. 'Tragedy' was chosen because it was part of the TV show *Bee Gees Mania* and our manager at the time, Tim Byrne, he bagsied 'Tragedy' for us. The dance routine originally was more like Kevin McAllister in *Home Alone*, like slapping each side of our faces, but we said no.

Claire: ['Tragedy'] was the first number one of 1999, so that made it more special. It had felt like it was never going to happen. Back then those chart positions were so important. It was the difference between your record company keeping you or getting dropped.

Peter Loraine, former artist development manager, Polydor: For my first job at Polydor I was tasked with putting together a Bee Gees tribute album. So I spoke to Tim and together we decided they would do 'Tragedy'. Very exciting. Two days later Tim phones back and he says, 'It's not going to happen, I can't get Pete Waterman to do it, he thinks it's a terrible idea, sorry.' My boss was Lucian Grainge, who is now head of Universal for the world, and he asked me how I was getting on with the Bee Gees album and I said, 'Robbie's in, 911, Louise, but Steps have said no.' Lucian picked up the phone, ordered a car and we drove to PWL and we went in for a meeting with Pete. Lucian said, 'This is my new person, he's doing this, you need to do this for us, at least try it out.' So Pete kind of rolls his eyes and agrees. And it went to number one!

Pete Waterman: I was never not behind it. Not true. I was approached to do this album with the Bee Gees and we agreed to do a Steps track as long as it was 'Tragedy' and that we could have the single rights and they could have it on the album. That was the only negotiation. I can even tell you when I did that deal – I was walking down the platform at Euston Station to catch the train to Liverpool. I know exactly where I was when I rang Tim Byrne and said, 'Right, I've agreed that deal, we've got the singles rights and they can have the track for the album free of charge.'

Peter Loraine: Then *Abbamania* [the ABBA tribute album] came after the Bee Gees one.

Pete Waterman: The thing was, ABBA were like [production hit factory] Stock Aitken Waterman. People hated ABBA. The whole thing came about because Elvis Costello and myself were on a very late-night television show and Bono made this derogatory remark, which he always denies, about ABBA. And we just said, 'Sorry, this is one the greatest pop bands of all time.' At that time, nobody played ABBA. I then got called by London Weekend Television and we talked the producer Bob Massie into using pop groups like B*Witched, Steps and all that [for a TV special] and that's literally how that whole ABBA thing broke open. It was huge and I think there were four singles taken from that album that were hits. ABBA saw us as these outcasts that history had almost erased, so [it was comforting for them] when one of these guys, Pete Waterman, comes along and says, 'Welcome to the club, I know what it's like to be hated because I'm hated more than you are.'

Steve Anderson: When 'One for Sorrow' came out everyone was like, 'Oh, it's a bit like ABBA,' but what that did was remind people about ABBA. A few weeks after the release of 'One for Sorrow', ABBA's *Greatest Hits* went to number one. It was before *Mamma Mia!*, all of that. He did it again when Steps did 'Stomp' and there was a sticker on the sleeve like 'respect to Nile Rodgers and Bernard Edwards'. It was a Chic record. But then people started getting more interested in Chic.

Karl Twigg: Yeah, I think that [sticker] might have been Pete's idea. They still sued us anyway so we probably shouldn't have put the sticker on there. I think that drew more attention to it. 'I'll show you how to get past this, lads.' Yeah, cheers, Pete. They got a percentage of the song.

Pete Waterman: You can't just put this record out without paying homage to the person you've nicked it from. I'll sort the publishing out with Nile Rodgers, but you've got to credit the fact it was their idea. You can't just take somebody's track and then say, 'Well, it's in homage.' If it is then great, but pay the bleeding bloke.

'The reaction was, "Who the fucking hell is Belle and Sebastian?"'

The BRIT Awards have always prized themselves on their unique collaborations, and the 1999 show was no exception. In years to come, we'd witness Florence Welch twirling around Dizzee Rascal and Rihanna looking perplexed near the Klaxons, but on that chilly February night an ill-fated supergroup made a right old racket that would go down in award show infamy. But enough about David Bowie and Placebo's 'unique' take on '20th Century Boy'; let's focus instead on Steps, Cleopatra, Billie Piper, B*Witched and Tina Cousins donning their finest highly flammable satin flares for the four-part medley 'Thank ABBA for the Music'. If that riled up the 'real music' gatekeepers, they would soon get their own back when milky tea-drinking students Belle and Sebastian caused the biggest award show controversy since Jarvis Cocker waggled his bony posterior near a Jesus-aping Michael Jackson.

Claire: There was a real snobbery around pop, and us, and what they think we are. People like the Spice Girls, you can't ignore that volume of success, so they had to acknowledge them in a way, but everybody else was doing really well behind them but was never given as much attention. We were selling more records and selling out more arenas than quite a lot of those acts who got their moment.

Pete Waterman: They used all the acts doing ABBA to get the audience, because that was the big thing at the time – B*Witched,

Steps and all that, it was enormous. They knew there were no big acts to get the kids watching TV so they put them on. But it was more, 'Get them on and get them off as quick as possible.'

Louise: When you were in that environment it wasn't so much about the music. It was about your ability to draw a crowd on the red carpet. I'm sure your cooler bands would look down their noses a bit more, but ultimately there is no difference. If you're selling enough records to keep on making albums then you're doing something right, regardless of your style of music. Also, everyone loves a good pop song.

H: That night was crazy. It was definitely us versus them. The room was full of the coolest people in the world and there was us. I filmed all the rehearsals, so there's Lisa and I watching Cher. Backstage footage of Stephen Gately playing the slot machines and us rehearsing with Billie Piper. I just couldn't believe my luck – this iconic show and they had us on there. And they didn't really do pop. Those cool cats, the bigwigs, they don't like pop.

Claire: It was one of the first public votes using the internet [for British Breakthrough Act]. We were being told constantly that we were going to win. No one told us what order the awards were going to be done in and I'd been ill with tonsillitis so had missed most of the day's rehearsal. Everybody that was in that category was in our performance pretty much. So we were all stood backstage [ready to perform] and someone went, 'Is that our award [being read out]? We found out we hadn't won and then we had to go out and do ABBA Mania.

Peter Robinson: I was there that night and I don't think the problem with that performance was the lack of rehearsal. In terms of saying thank you to someone, it's a bit like putting a ribbon on a shit and posting it through a letterbox.

Stef D'Andrea, joint owner of Belle and Sebastian's former label, Jeepster: We got an invitation from the BPI. We thought it was a bit peculiar. Radio 1 were promoting [the award] and saying you can vote for your favourite via phone voting and via the very new form of internet voting. A lot of Belle and Sebastian's fans were fourteen to twenty. The two youngest people at Jeepster at the time were nineteen or twenty years old, and a chap who worked with us called David understood where the internet was going. He had started Sinister List, the band's mailing list, which the fans would join and have these great long chats. So the suggestion came from one of these chat rooms – why don't we spread the word to all the Belle and Sebastian fans to vote via Radio 1's website?

Mark Beaumont, indie scribe for *Melody Maker* and *NME*: It was the first show of strength of the internet because the BRITs were the establishment stronghold and here was Belle and Sebastian using the weight of their fanbase to break the stranglehold of pop. I think it was the first high-profile example of the internet being used to shift culture. There was a real feeling that [the alternative indie scene] had broken through over the course of Britpop in the mid '90s. With the alternative music scene at that point, there was a sense that they did deserve to be there and at that top table. We got used to that feeling that we could break the charts on a regular basis. There was a certain amount of entitlement there.

Claire: No one had even heard of Belle and Sebastian.

H: Who were they again? Who?!

Pete Waterman: Had I heard of them before? No. Had anyone? No. Did I care? No. I felt sorry for Steps.

Karl Twigg: I was there. I was on the table with them. The reaction was, 'Who the fucking hell is Belle and Sebastian?'

Stef D'Andrea: Technically Steps had more fans, but as we know with pop fans they're very overnight things and they don't tend to maintain fans. Belle and Sebastian have still got a strong fanbase twenty-five years later, but Steps, like most pop bands, didn't last.

Claire: I remember Pete Waterman and Steve Jenkins going crazy and causing a real stink because if it wasn't us who should have won, Five were in that category, Cleopatra. It was all the new pop of the time. No one could believe it.

Peter Robinson: I remember a sort of pandemonium. Not because Steps hadn't won it but just the fact that Belle and Sebastian had. And they weren't like [fellow nominees] Cornershop, who had had a hit record. The way they galvanised their fanbase was the sort of thing a band like Steps would be doing years later.

Pete Waterman: I wasn't surprised [when Steps lost]. I'd made it quite plain that I thought the BRIT Awards were basically the major labels patting themselves on the back and that was proved.

Stef D'Andrea: We were literally one man and his dog. Me and my friend started [the label]. We were in a tiny rented office in west London, we had two teenagers working for us and that was it. It was probably the last shocking moment at the BRITs really, after the Jarvis incident and the John Prescott Chumbawamba thing [Prescott received a cold shower at the 1998 awards]. It was going to be on the front page of *The Sun* the next day but wound up on page three because some other celebrity nonsense happened, but it was on the front page of *The Sun* in Scotland.

Pete Waterman: To me [the BRITs] shot themselves in the foot because you couldn't deny it – everybody could see it at that point. I didn't have to say anything any more, did I? Steps not winning – how does that work? Sometimes you stay quiet because it looks wrong if you say anything because the public can see it for themselves. Everybody that year just went, 'What?'

Stef D'Andrea: There were various people either congratu-lating us on the night or saying snide things. Just, 'Who are you? I've never heard of you?' I realised how much it mattered to people. It's harder to imagine that now because award ceremo-nies just go over people's heads, like the charts do. In the '90s, the charts and award ceremonies were so big. We did end up on *Top of the Pops* in 2000 when we had a single called 'Legal Man'. We came into view of the pop artists again because that pop group with seven people in it were there. I realised by standing next to them that all seven of them seemed to be identical in height. They must have gone, 'Right, we want it so that when they're on screen you don't have to go from small to tall.' It was like they were made by a machine.

H: There was a lot of controversy around it and Pete went to town.

Stef D'Andrea: We then went back to our office and suddenly all these phone calls started coming in from the *Mail* and *The Sun*, asking for comment. It was like, 'What? Who is Pete Waterman? What is he saying?' When I told the band about it they all pissed themselves laughing. After all the stink started with Pete Waterman and the newspapers, they thought they'd really cracked it. They thought they'd uncovered a con because 12 per cent of the votes came from one computer and that was basically old men not understanding the internet. If you go back to 1998 and you're at a university like Glasgow or Edinburgh, there's like 25,000 students there and you've got a library with these things called computer terminals you can go on the internet with. So 25,000 students would have access to a handful of terminals. They didn't understand how the voting worked.

Pete Waterman: To apologise for the year before, you then dream up a new category [Best Live Act]. How does that work? I thought that was nonsense. That was an even bigger insult than not giving them the award in the first place.

H: When we did win that award a year later, they told us to pay to get a physical copy of it. So it was £500 each and everyone paid for their one, but I said, 'No, stick your BRIT Award,

I don't want one, thank you.' I'm not paying for something I've won.

Mark Beaumont: It was fantastic Belle and Sebastian managed to bag the award through canniness and the passion of their fans, but if you see the indie versus pop thing as a bit of a battle, which to some degree it was, it woke the pop world up to the potential of what could be done with the internet. Over time, they certainly weaponised that.

Pete Waterman: If nobody loves you, you don't care, do you? If people hate you, then you know there will be no good reviews written about you so you don't have to read reviews or care what people think. There's no point, you know where you stand.

Mark Beaumont: I remember Steps came to the *NME* Awards in 2001 and I was sent on a ridiculous job by the editor. There was a programme on at the time called *Banzai* and there was a guy on it called Shakey-Hands Man and his job was to shake hands with people for as long as possible. So I was sent out to be the Shakey-Hands Man at the *NME* awards and Faye from Steps – what a lovely woman – she literally shook my hand until I wanted to stop. She had no problem whatsoever with very lengthy handshakes. I was quite fond of Steps really. At that time, as much as there was a sense of triumph in the underground alternative music reaching the charts, there was also a bit of respect there.

Chris Cowey: You have to park your own personal musical tastes to one side and do what's right for the audience. I had to learn to appreciate S Club 7 and Steps and try to find the television gold in it. Even getting bands like Steps to sing live, you know, some of them had great voices. Also, I used to always try to focus on *Top of the Pops* refuseniks, of which there were a few. I would say to the Radioheads of this world, 'Look, every time you don't do the show, that means I have to put Steps on.'

Claire: *Top of the Pops* was my absolute dream come true. When I was a kid my nan's husband worked as a security guard at the BBC and he took me there one day and showed me round. I remember watching Bonnie Tyler rehearsing in the studio and just thinking, 'This is everything I've ever wanted.' Then we went to the canteen and had beans and chips and that is exactly what I ate the first time we did *Top of the Pops*.

Lee Thompson, head of music, The Box: One of our biggest acts were Steps. They were brilliant because they knew that if you put a simple dance routine in the video and then when the single comes out you open up the booklet and it tells you how to do it, it's that perfect synergy. Very clever. That's why Steps were so huge and so successful without Radio 1 play. You'd never find a Steps song on the Radio 1 playlist or even on a commercial radio playlist at that point.

Paul Flynn: I was reviewing Steps for the *Manchester Evening News* and I took my friend who really loved them. It was a bit of a step too far for me. Quite literally. But, you know, I'd take Steps over Travis any day of the week. They were playing the Manchester Apollo and I was the row in front of Pete Waterman and he had a banner that said, 'Steps we fucking love you'. And it looked like he'd made it himself.

Pete Waterman: What? No, not me. Definitely not me. Let me tell you, I've done a lot of things in my life, but a Steps concert with a banner? Definitely not. It was my doppelgänger.

'They probably thought, "Are they children's entertainers? Is this comedy?"'

By the summer of 1999, Steps had scored five top-ten singles in the UK, while debut album Step One *had shifted close to 1.5 million copies. They also found themselves on the same label as both Britney Spears and the Backstreet Boys. It made sense, therefore, for Steps and their matching outfits to traverse the Atlantic and see if their easily digestible dance routines and hi-NRG pop could seduce audiences used to pneumatic precision and Swedish-made, high-gloss bangers. The fact that they were all wearing yellow pedal pushers wasn't going to faze them.*

Charlie Adelman, US Steps fan: I first heard the music of Steps when I was eleven years old at my first Britney Spears concert. Steps opened and it was 'One for Sorrow' that got me into them. I remember hearing it at the show and being like, 'Oh, I love this.' Then they did 'Tragedy' and my dad said, 'This is an abomination, they've ruined the Bee Gees.' I had never heard the original at that point.

Claire: We didn't want to go [to America]. We were doing so well in the UK and we were quite savvy when it came to what things were going to cost us. They wanted us to re-shoot videos and we didn't really want to do that. I'm glad we did it. It was good for us, but it was a weird experience.

143

H: We were bonafide pop stars . . . Actually, I hate that word 'stars'; I prefer tarts. So we were pop tarts in our own right by 1999. We were riding high, we'd had massive success, so I didn't think of Britney as anything different to somebody that was doing the same job as us. When we were just starting out, we were headlining a gig in Singapore for the record company and Britney was our support, which is crazy. She was so lovely and I remember we were dicking around in the pool after, just being stupid. And because of that she asked us to support her on her American tour.

Claire: H loved that tour . . .

H: I became great mates with her. For some reason, she took a shine to me – probably because I've got a big gob. She loved the British accent. I wore pedal pushers at the time and she loved them. She also loved the Paul Frank T-shirts that I used to wear and I remember drawing a little map for her to tell her how to get to the Paul Frank shop in Covent Garden. We got on really well, so [on the tour] she invited me to fly on her private jet, which didn't go down very well with the others. Come on, I'm not going to turn that down! I'm not going to go on a sleeper bus, with no sleep.

Claire: We didn't really have to sleep on the bus anyway, because by the time we came off stage we would drive a couple of hours and be in the next place. H never really wanted to do that so somehow he got himself well in there with old Britney.

H: I remember [the US] reaction was horror. They were used to NSYNC, the Backstreet Boys and obviously Britney. We'd turn up looking like tropical fruits in banana yellow doing 'Love's Got a Hold of My Heart' and they'd be like, 'What the fuck is this?' They probably thought, 'Are they children's entertainers? Is this comedy?' But we did a big Disney special and there was a massive spike and 'Tragedy' did really well, I think.

Charlie Adelman: I remember on the sticker for the *Step One* album here the quote was from the *New York Times* review and it was something like, 'If the '90s belonged to the Spice Girls, the '00s belong to Steps.' But if Steps had blown up in the US my passion for it may not have sustained. I was far less into S Club 7 because they were on TV every week and everyone knew who they were. They were cheesy and lame and everyone knew that. Steps I could get away with because people didn't really know.

Claire: Do you know what, some audiences were great, but in the middle of America I'd say nine times out of ten there'd be lots of open mouths. People just not entirely sure what was going on.

Charlie Adelman: Britney was the first modern pop artist I was into and Steps were just so different from that. It was fun to have Britney, this over-the-top, promiscuous pop star, who for an eleven-year-old boy felt very edgy, but then Steps were like a modern take on the old queens I'd grown up listening to.

Pete Waterman: I stepped away at that point because I knew the Americans wouldn't understand Steps, and they didn't. They went and did some very strange things and I wasn't prepared to do that. I just didn't get it. The Americans saw Steps and thought they were a cabaret band.

H: Because we'd spent so much time in America, the other territories that we were riding high in suffered. So we had to make a decision between carrying on in America or maintaining what we have. The general consensus was to maintain what we had. At this point we were knackered, we were burnt out. We'd just started to realise that we could say no to things. We were very much pop puppets. But we were workaholics as well. We all knew that if we didn't work hard we wouldn't get results. Other bands rested on their laurels or they'd take months off because they were knackered, but we were literally on the whole time. We used to do two weeks at Wembley arena with matinees. No other band did matinees.

Jordan Paramor, author, *Steps: In Private*: Quite often Faye and Lisa would be up for a drink afterwards, maybe H, so we'd go to the bar. Claire not always. Lee was a bit more head down. Faye loved a party. There were hilarious times where I would be chasing Faye down the corridor trying to get her to speak to me. They were so easy and lovely to deal with. I've been around some people that I would not like to go on tour with, quite frankly.

Sam Bloom, all STARS*: I don't remember us spending that much time with Steps when we supported them. They are a bit older than us so they were in a slightly different age bracket. They were also in a different fame bracket, too.

Claire: There were a lot more magazines and more TV shows to do back in those days and we would do absolutely everything that we could.

H: I remember it was the 1999 MTV Europe Awards in Dublin and I was hanging out with Britney and Christina. I had a stinking cold, I was so ill. So I was going home early. I was in the limo rank and next door to me was Missy Elliott and then Alicia Silverstone was the other side of me giving me tissues. Missy Elliott had her arm around me at one point saying, 'You'll be okay.' I was like, 'This is fucking some surreal shit.' I'd just been chatting to Britney and Christina and now Missy Elliott's got her arm around me and Alicia Silverstone is giving me tissues. What the fuck? And I went home to a Lemsip.

'It's not enough to say, "Oh, the tabloids were homophobic"; everyone was'

The idea of 'manufactured pop' heavily implies laser-focused, conveyor-belt perfection. Band members have jumped through hoops, passed various tests and been selected based on their ability to make uncomplicated sense to as many people as possible. It's a straight line from the band to the fans; no tangents, no kinks, no sudden movements. The platonic ideal of a pop act is that everyone is available to be fancied at all times. This is very important for men whose attractiveness and constant availability snares the core female pop fans who, it was heavily assumed, would not accept a deviation from the single and straight. For H – who saw friend Stephen Gately come out via The Sun *in 1999 ('Music experts and fans are predicting Boyzone's career will continue to prosper' ran a worried BBC article at the time) – that meant living as a gay man within the band but not being publicly out until 2007, six years after the band split. For Lee, and the female members of Steps, it meant hiding relationships.*

H: There came a time when the band all knew [I was gay], where I'd told them, and from then onwards they had my back.

As we were evolving as a group and getting more well-known, the interest from the tabloids was growing. Also, magazines like *Smash Hits* and *Top of the Pops* would always ask, 'Who do you fancy?', and Lisa would always go, 'He's only got eyes for me.' It was a way of shutting the conversation down. To make a joke out of it. In hindsight, you could still say Britney Spears was fit and mean it, but not want to play with her boobs.

Claire: We all just backed him up, whatever he said. Firstly, it wasn't our situation to discuss. It was very rare that we were asked [about our sexuality], if ever really. But we all knew, so within the five of us we didn't need to keep things hidden. But it was all a bit more sneaky in those days, so nobody would come out and ask him in an interview. We all know now what went on back then with people getting stories and things, so I think we all did well within us to keep a lid on it. And quite rightly he told his story himself when he was ready.

H: We lived in a very different day and age. We had to appeal to our market, which was perceived as the teen market. I kind of got away with it – I was never a sex object. I was never a sex bomb. I was always the cheeky blond one with blue eyes and big gob, so I masked a lot of the interest in me with that. I deflected it.

Alex Needham: Sexuality was almost irrelevant because the audience was so young. We probably would ask people who they fancied, which is slightly cringey that we would do that to people we knew were gay. Although we didn't always know. I remember asking Ricky Martin whether he fancied Mel B, which is quite embarrassing now.

Jordan Paramor: We all knew [H was gay]. There was so much stuff we were privy to. Obviously we hadn't put it in the magazine. We weren't out to stitch anybody up. We were mates with them, we'd go out with them. There was a really nice element of trust between magazines and pop stars because when we were on the roadshow the things that went on in terms of people getting off with each other, people sneaking into people's bedrooms. It was hilarious. But none of it went into the magazine. People weren't privy to what was going on behind the scenes because it was the happy, joyous world of pop. You didn't do that. That's why we got such brilliant access and people trusted us.

Joel Babbington: It felt like Steps were the band where we didn't know anything about their personal lives. They were literally Steps the pop stars and nothing else.

Claire: We all had to pretend we were single and we weren't allowed to tell anybody if we did have partners for fear of upsetting the fans. I think back then they never really gave people enough credit to understand that people like us had lives outside of work. Faye had a boyfriend, Lisa had a boyfriend, Lee often had a girlfriend. But the general rule of thumb was that if you were in a band you had to pretend you were young, free and single. That's not reality. We have come a long way since then thankfully. It doesn't feel right for someone to tell the world whether they're straight or gay. Why should you? But back then it was such a burden for so many people. I remember when it happened to Stephen Gately, you're forced in a way to tell everybody about your private life.

Jordan Paramor: It still breaks my heart when I think about Stephen Gately. It kills me that he was forced into coming out in the papers. He then wanted to do a second interview to talk about it, with a magazine. So I did an interview with him for *Smash Hits* and we sat and had a glass of wine just the two of us in this bar. He spoke to me really emotionally about it and I ran everything past him afterwards to make sure he was happy. He wanted to explain things more to the fans and expand on what had been said in the paper. He was such a young boy to have that happen to him.

Paul Flynn: The broad thinking was, up until Gately, that if you had a gay member of your band it's going to damage the brand. The girls aren't going to like it. Of course we know that's nonsense and has been proven to be nonsense since. But around then George Michael came out, famously with the LA sting, and that did kill his career in America. American radio did stop playing his records. When I started working at *Attitude* the industry was openly homophobic. It almost wore it as a badge of pride, and that spills down to people's lives in very direct ways. It's not enough to say, 'Oh, the tabloids were homophobic'; everyone was. The country was terrible, the climate was terrible.

H: It's sounds really vacant, but I'd always wanted to be a pop star. It was the thing I always aspired to because I loved pop music. It was the place I went to lose myself, because I was a young gay boy in a rural village and there wasn't anybody like me. I was bullied and I was made to feel very different and I lost myself in my bedroom wall. That's all I knew. Getting a mention in *Smash Hits*, let alone being on the cover or being on

Top of the Pops, was a massive middle finger at all of the bullies who taunted me and called me names because I was different. It was a massive fuck you, to be fair. And it's still a massive fuck you. After twenty-five years, I have a huge smile on my face and they're doing fuck all.

'In hindsight we should have gone on a break, like Ross and Rachel'

Steps' third album, Buzz, *released at the end of 2000, saw them start to experiment with new producers, specifically Max Martin affiliate Jörgen Elofsson, who gifted them the immaculate 'It's the Way You Make Me Feel'. Despite that album adding four top-five hits to their tally, the band spent most of 2001 denying they were splitting up. Things weren't helped by the announcement of a greatest hits album and accompanying tour, a chapter-ending move that typically foreshadowed the end for any pop band. Despite hearing constant denials and receiving another tranche of Steps merch for Christmas, fans had a rude awakening on 26 December 2001. As the front cover of* The Sun *put it: 'STEPS SPLIT'. Little did they know at the time, H and Claire had actually informed the band of their decision to leave four days earlier.*

H: We were going to keep it quiet for a few more months and work it all out and then do a statement. But the tabloids leaked the story, so that was the news everyone woke up to that day. We were scrambling for damage limitation because it was 'Steps ruin Christmas'. Crazy, right? The fucking *Sun*.

Joe McElderry, winner, *The X Factor*, 2009: Steps was my first concert ever. It was the last tour they did before they split up. I remember just being in complete awe. Now I live not far from Faye Tozer and we're friends, so I like to tell her on a regular basis that I am still an obsessive stalker fan of hers.

H: An element of it was that we were very tired and we needed a break. The real story was we hated each other. Not hated, that's a strong word, but we were sick of each other. We were tired. And we didn't want our surnames to be Steps. We wanted to live and enjoy what we'd worked hard for. In hindsight we should have gone on a break, like Ross and Rachel. But you can't re-write history.

Claire: When you're in that kind of world there are highs and lows anyway, but it's quite a toxic environment to have to live in twenty-four hours [a day], seven days a week. Anybody that lives their job 24/7 is going to come a cropper at some point.

Lisa: I woke up the next morning thinking, 'I'm not in a pop group any more.' I didn't have a job; I didn't have the guys. It was really scary.

Lee from Steps: I was like, 'They'll change their minds.'

Lisa: H and Claire went off to form a duo, so there was the three of us who were like, 'What the fuck happened?'

Claire: I also had the pressure of basically starving myself for four and a half years because I was told I had to lose weight on day one of being in Steps. I always felt like I was the fat one because I'd been told I was fat. I was nineteen, I was a size 12 and I had a bum and hips. When you're that young you don't understand that, no matter how much you try, if you don't look like Kate Moss naturally, you're never going to look like Kate Moss. You're just going to be ill. If anybody told me to lose weight now I would go and order a burger and a cake. But I was in my early twenties and that is the age of a person where you develop your adult personality. However you experience life then is how you carry it forward as an adult. I got to twenty-four or twenty-five and I had no clue who I was. I had no clue how I could continue doing what we were doing. A really good rest might have done the job, but then if we hadn't stopped when we did there wouldn't be Steps now.

Karl Twigg: It was a shame. I thought that if Steps had got through that album and held it together for a bit longer they could have carried on.

Pete Waterman: Towards the end the management were completely ruling the roost. They broke the group up. That was just simply the management wanting to break the group into two things – H & Claire and then Steps. And it never worked.

H: No, [splinter group H & Claire] was a natural progression. There were lots of people's noses out of joint that thought that was planned, but no.

'I thought something else would start pretty soon'

While H and Claire, AKA H & Claire, scored three top-ten singles, their debut album, 2002's Another You and Another Me, *stalled at number fifty-eight and they were dropped. While Faye Tozer scored a UK top ten with Russell Watson, and Lee Latchford-Evans starred in an Edinburgh fringe play called* Wolfboy, *a 'psychological sexual thriller', the only other person to properly try their luck with music outside of the band was Lisa Scott-Lee, whose perceived edginess — she often matched her chunky multi-coloured hair dye to her dental braces — had won her a legion of fans. In 2003, she unleashed electropop behemoth* Lately, *which peaked at number six (number four in the midweeks). After her two follow-up singles stalled outside the top ten, however, she embarked on an MTV fly-on-the-wall documentary in 2005 called* Totally Scott-Lee *(subtitle:* Desperately Seeking Fame*). The now ironically reappraised cult classic, complete with desperate in-built catchphrase '. . . but I'm B-List at Capital', focused on new single 'Electric', which, as per the show's rules, had to go top ten or she'd quit the music industry. It peaked at number thirteen and that was that.*

Claire: The year of H & Claire was great. We had such a great time. We achieved a lot and we earned a lot of money as well.

H: I remember at the time we had the biggest record deal for people from an existing band. It was crazy. We set records for that deal and we didn't have to pay any of that back; it was great.

Lisa: I just wish [the MTV documentary] would go away. I'm a performer; that's all I want to do. It wasn't about me trying to be a big solo star. It's weird because when we do our signings now, people have T-shirts on with this 'B-List at Capital' thing, which I don't understand.

Claire: [H and I] had worked really hard, we were co-presenting *SM:TV* at the same time, we were gigging constantly, but the album just didn't connect, we did a gig at Euro Disney and then we were dropped. I was devastated. It was great to feel like we had a career beyond Steps, but I don't know if I realised that would be it for pretty much ten years. I thought something else would start pretty soon.

A decade later, in 2011, the band reformed for a no-holds-barred four-part Sky Living documentary, *Steps: Reunion*, in which they went over every detail of their career and eventual demise. In October, they chucked out another greatest hits album, *The Ultimate Collection*, which included all the hits plus a gloriously on-the-nose version of ABBA's 'Dancing Queen'. The album entered at number one, with the band also scooting around the UK on a thirty-date arena tour. High on the excitement, they released 2012's unloved Christmas album, *Light Up the World*. After another tour, the band finally did a Ross and Rachel and took a break, returning in 2017 with new management (via Peter Loraine's Fascination) and new music in the shape of the thundering, *Vice*-approved single 'Scared of the Dark'. The accompanying album, *Tears on the Dancefloor*, as well as 2020's *What the Future Holds*, both showcased the DNA of Steps – big melodies, big vocals, even bigger key changes – but with a semi-modern twist. They also both peaked at number two and were both accompanied by huge arena tours. In 2022, their third greatest hits, *Platinum Collection*, released to celebrate their twenty-fifth anniversary, entered at number one.

* Lisa Scott-Lee and Lee Latchford-Evans quotes taken from my interview for *Guardian Guide*, 6 January 2018

5
From Billie to Blue:
The influence of Innocent Records

In early 1992, Take That were alarmingly close to being handed their P45s by their label, RCA. Their debut single, 'Do What U Like', complete with a homoerotic video featuring jelly being vigorously applied to bare buttocks, had peaked at eighty-two. Their two follow-up singles, 'Promises' and 'Once You've Tasted Love', hadn't fared much better. With budgets extended and the all-important media demanding a hit before they'd feature the band again, a new tactic was needed. For Hugh Goldsmith, former songwriter turned publisher of pop-culture magazine *Sky* turned newly appointed marketing director at RCA, the band needed a way of speaking directly to their fanbase.

Utilising the then-untested database marketing business, Hugh and RCA encouraged fans at Take That's shows to hand over their addresses. Over 8,000 fans signed up and were swiftly sent information on the band's next single, 'It Only Takes a

Minute', in the hope the move would reach enough people for the band to land an all-important top twenty and therefore a *Top of the Pops* appearance. The plan worked and that fourth single – complete with a look that was less G-A-Y foam party and more fingerbanging behind the boxing gym – entered at sixteen. After an appearance on *Top of the Pops*, the song crashed into the top ten, eventually peaking at number seven. The rest, as they say, is history.

When Virgin Records, coffers bulged by Spice Girls swag, were looking to launch their own pop label imprint from scratch, they turned to Goldsmith, who had also helped, along with Simon Cowell, turn two lantern-jawed *Soldier Soldier* actors into hitmakers, Robson & Jerome. Launched in 1997, Innocent Records' first signing would arrive a year later in the shape of Billie Piper. From there, Goldsmith would sign ex-*EastEnder* Martine McCutcheon, whose immaculate ballad 'Perfect Moment' topped the charts in 1999, before scoring more chart success with '00s pop mainstays Atomic Kitten and Blue.

With no existing catalogue to fall back on and knowing full well the amount of money needed to launch pop acts, Goldsmith knew he had to avoid the Take That grind and hit the ground running.

'Even before Billie was famous, when you were with her, people looked'

Hugh Goldsmith: My first call from Paul Conroy, Virgin's President, came in March 1997. At this point, I was managing director of RCA. Paul explained that Virgin wanted to expand more into the world of pop, having had a hugely successful time with the Spice Girls, who were now fully established as a world-dominating pop phenomenon. Paul asked me whether I would be interested in setting up a new pop label and I jumped at the chance. My first task on setting up Innocent was to put together my team. Even though I was keen to have a more hands-on involvement in A&R than I'd had at RCA, it was imperative that I should find a great head of A&R and I did, in the form of Cheryl Robson, who I poached from Chrysalis Publishing. It was Cheryl's idea that we should look for a young solo female and she mentioned Madonna as a reference. Quite soon after we started our search, I was reading the latest issue of *Music Week* and leaping out from a *Smash Hits* ad was someone who seemed to embody the essence of Girl Power in every fibre of her being. I had a strong feeling she might be the person we were looking for.

Jodi Albert: Getting a record deal at that time was like winning the lottery. It wasn't like now where there are so many social media and music platforms. Back then I was working so hard [at Sylvia Young], really trying to learn and prove myself. The only girl who had a record deal in my class was Billie Piper. She was so beautiful, she really looked and sounded like a pop star. A record company executive was opening up *Music Week* and he saw her and thought, 'She's the pop star we need.'

Laura Snapes: This is definitely the era when pop becomes product. It's funny – the Spice Girls were formed from an ad and they worked so well because of all their vibrant, conflicting personalities. But when labels tried to replicate that, they took all the craziness out and just tried to create something unthreatening that would appeal to kids and not cause their parents any undue worry. If any of the Spice Girls had tried to get into pop just a year or two later, they probably would have been counted out because they weren't necessarily blandly cute and obliging in that way. That said, whoever spotted Billie did a good job as she was obviously hugely talented.

Hugh Goldsmith: Understandably, Sylvia wanted the two of us to meet in advance of me meeting Billie. I remember Sylvia telling me that Billie was one of her most talented students and, in today's terminology, a triple threat, with great expertise in acting, dancing and singing. To my ears, this sounded like a fantastic combination, all of which would be invaluable if Billie was interested in diving into the world of pop. At the second meeting, I met Billie and her dad, Paul. Billie had a wonderful brightness and positive energy about her and Paul was clearly, and understandably, a very protective and straight-talking dad.

Jodi Albert: Billie was so talented. I was delighted for her. She wanted me to be her backing dancer but unfortunately it wasn't possible as I wasn't yet over eighteen.

Hugh Goldsmith: In the first instance, we agreed it would be a good idea for Billie to record a demo track to see how she felt in the studio. At this point, Cheryl and Billie started working together on the music and they bonded brilliantly. In addition to Cheryl, I had other female colleagues at Innocent – Justine Bell, Deborah Lynam and, later, Sara Freeman – who I knew would help Billie feel at home. Because, even though Billie and I got on great, it was important to me that on a day-to-day basis she would always feel a strong sense of female support and care within the label.

Justine Bell, former A&R coordinator, Innocent Records: My first impression of Billie was super positive. I liked her a lot straight away. Billie always had a vibe about her that you wanted to be around. She was never over the top and thirsty for attention. She was just cool and friendly and funny and magnetic. Even before she was famous, when you were with her people looked. She had something that you couldn't quite put your finger on.

MNEK: Billie Piper was Britney before Britney; let's start there. She's the template. I've read a lot about the story of Billie and it's really interesting because there was no intention of her coming in as a pop singer.

Hugh Goldsmith: Cheryl Robson oversaw the A&R on Billie's first album and her focus was on making a pop R&B album, reflecting the mood of the moment and also Billie's personal taste.

MNEK: She started recording these demos and did a cover of Changing Faces' 'G.H.E.T.T.O.U.T.' [on the B-side of 'Because We Want To']. She's an R&B head. But then the *Honey to the B* album is this teen pop record.

Hugh Goldsmith: 'Because We Want To' was a bit of a red herring because it was a much younger-sounding track than the rest of the album.

Laura Snapes: It undersold the other singles from *Honey to the B*, which were more sophisticated – more R&B-influenced,

definitely bridging that gap between Robyn and Britney Spears, who was months off launching.

Hugh Goldsmith: The media frenzy and profile Billie received as a result of being the youngest female to ever enter the UK charts at number one was incredible. However, topping the charts on debut really is a blessing and a curse. It's a blessing because the artist becomes a household name overnight but a curse because, after having reached those dizzy heights, it's not unusual for unnecessary pressure and expectation to kick in on subsequent releases.

Justine Bell: I had no clue what was going to happen [with 'Because We Want To']. I'd been working at a label for five years [before Innocent] where everything had failed so the idea of having a number one with a brand-new label seemed impossible. But I was really hoping it would be successful – Hugh had offered to buy me a new motorbike jacket if it was, so I was buzzing when we got the midweeks!

MNEK: 'Because We Want To' could only have been a first single. It's her 'Wannabe'.

Laura Snapes: Billie definitely slid into a lane that the Spice Girls created. And she was always on kids' TV so you couldn't help but know who she was.

Hugh Goldsmith: Billie's follow-up singles from that first album were a much more accurate reflection of the sound of the album and closer to Billie's preference for R&B.

MNEK: The single edit of [second single and number one] 'Girlfriend' by Cutfather & Joe is one of the best teen pop records ever. Fun fact about Billie: 'Girlfriend', 'Saying I'm Sorry Now' and 'Whatcha Gonna Do' were all covers of songs by a failed R&B girl group from the UK called First Class. Their version of 'Girlfriend' is still on YouTube.

Hugh Goldsmith: After Cheryl left Innocent to go to Warner's, I took over Billie's A&R [for 2000's *Walk of Life*] and, with her being older and the sound of pop having moved on following the arrival of Britney, we focused on making a more mature pop album. Happily, the album's first single, 'Day and Night', was a triumphant comeback for Billie, debuting at number one with 100,000 sales.

Justine Bell: It's really tricky [transitioning to an older audience] and we definitely spent a lot of time trying to figure out how to make it work.

Laura Snapes: You grow up so massively between the ages of fifteen and eighteen. Obviously she's going to want to express herself differently. I think it also reflects the turbo-ing of pop more generally. On the one hand it's the Americanisation, but on the other it's the Scandification – you can trace such a direct line between NSYNC's 'Bye Bye Bye', which came out January 2000, produced by Cheiron, to 'Oops! ... I Did It Again', released that April and also produced by Cheiron, and 'Day and Night', released that May and produced by Stargate. They all sound the same!

Justine Bell: Much of what we did with Billie was successful, but not everything. The 'Walk of Life' single was quite different both in terms of styling and sound because we were trying to find a way to grow her musically. The single didn't connect.

Laura Snapes: She got loads of grief from fans of Ritchie Neville for dating him. Then she got the really nasty tabloid coverage once she turned eighteen and was dating Chris Evans and treated as – gross – 'fair game'. And even though she had that globalised pop sound by her second album, a tinpot British pop star was never going to be able to compete with the Britneys and Christinas of this world, though I imagine she was still worked nearly as hard. It must have been thankless and pretty lonely.

Justine Bell: Was I surprised when she retired from pop? Not really. She had stepped into a new life with Chris [Evans] and that had offered her new opportunities. Plus it meant she could have a rest. The schedule had been full-on for a long time.

Hugh Goldsmith: I didn't foresee some of the challenges that lay ahead for Billie as a young solo female in such a demanding environment and, to this day, I remain relieved and happy she got through the difficult times and went on to become such a brilliant and successful actor. In spite of the tough times, Billie writes in her book [2006's *Growing Pains*] that she would do it all again but knows that I wouldn't, and she's right.

'I actually credit Kraftwerk with inventing Atomic Kitten'

Post-Spice Girls, the hunt was on for a girlband that could replicate their success. Or even just 10 per cent of it. While Girl Thing aimed for pure mimicry, the Sugababes for something cooler, while in Liverpool an unlikely amalgam of the Spice Girls, All Saints and Oasis was being haphazardly constructed by two members of '80s experimental pop practitioners OMD. Originally called Exit, then Honeyheads, then later Automatic Kitten (the change to Atomic Kitten happened after a mishearing that stuck), the three-piece initially included Kerry Katona, Liz McClarnon and soon-to-be-Sugababe Heidi Range.

Andy McCluskey: I continued as OMD through the '90s but I realised I was banging my head against a brick wall. I was conceited enough to still feel like I could write good songs, I just felt like the vehicle was considered beyond its sell-by date. Everyone thinks this is the most bizarre thing, but I actually credit Kraftwerk with inventing Atomic Kitten. I'd become quite friendly with Karl Bartos. I was talking to him about the fact I was going to stop doing my own music and write for other people. He said, 'Don't be a songwriting whore and give your songs to your publisher, just create a vehicle for the songs.' He asked me what the best pop group was and I said a three-piece girlband. Boybands are usually terrible because they sell records largely because love is deaf as well as blind. Girlbands have to have good music. So Karl Bartos said to me, 'Okay, create a three-piece girlband.' So Kraftwerk invented Atomic Kitten.

Stuart Kershaw: We'd actually talked about doing an electronic boyband. Almost like a Kraftwerk thing, but with boys. I know that sounds nuts, but no one had ever done it. We'd write all the music and they'd front it, but it would be us carrying on OMD, basically.

Andy McCluskey: We put an advert in the *Liverpool Echo*, just asking for girls who could sing and dance. It started, however, with an acquaintance of mine called Davy T, who is a DJ. He had a techno band called the Porn Kings. He came in the studio one day and said, 'Are you still trying to do a girlband?' His actual words were, 'There's this girl in my band who is a star and she's wasting her time waving her tits around behind me.' He showed me a video of them playing this techno festival in Cologne and there was Kerry [Katona] in this pink one-piece trouser suit, miming keyboards and clapping along and I just went, 'I've got to meet her.'

Stuart Kershaw: She had this incredible energy. She kind of took your breath away because of how energetic she was, a real presence, and you need someone like that in a band.

Andy McCluskey: She was only seventeen. In she comes to the studio, a bundle of energy, and within sixty seconds she goes, 'Do you want to see me photos?', and she gets out her topless photographs. I thought, 'This is a very interesting interview technique.' She wanted to be a page-three girl, but she'd been in foster care so she couldn't do it until she was eighteen. I said, 'Right, give me a year before you become a model and I'll try to make you a pop star.' She couldn't sing. I was always sat in the corner running the computer and Stuart and our engineer were always at the desk looking at her and whenever she got frustrated she'd just lift her top up and go, 'I'm only in this band for my tits.'

Stuart Kershaw: When she did get it right, [her voice] was a really lovely thing. But it was getting her to focus. She was far more interested in doing other things. People had told her she couldn't sing but it was more a lack of pitching.

Andy McCluskey: It was Marilyn Monroe syndrome – she'd been through a lot of problems, she was unhappy in her own skin, but she had something about her that was infectious. I just thought, 'She's going to be a star'; she will bang her head through a wall to be a star, because she thinks being rich and famous will make her feel better. As it turned out, it didn't. I had no idea what I was letting her in for. In manufactured pop they take these kids and they squeeze them through a bunch of shapes and go, 'You're the square one, you're the round one, you're the pretty one, and we're going to dress you like this.' With Kerry, I just thought, 'You're in and now I'm going to find some singers.' That's when I met Liz and Heidi Range.

Liz McClarnon: I went to a stage school and my singing teacher was like, 'Somebody wants to start a band and I know him and he was really famous in the '80s.' So she introduced us. I'd never done an audition before so I was quite wet behind the ears. It was very on trend to wear really crazy contact lenses at the time. I had these bright blue contact lenses and I walked in and Andy was like, 'I hope you can sing because you really look the part.' I sang 'Right Now' for him and he put me in the band. Kerry was already in the band then.

Stuart Kershaw: Heidi was fourteen or fifteen and she had this amazing voice. We weren't sure in the end if she was going to be old enough to do it and she left before we signed. That meant we had to re-vocal everything she had done and we'd based the whole thing around her, so from a production point of view it was a nightmare.

Andy McCluskey: Heidi Range has got one of the most incredible voices I've ever recorded in my life. This meek little schoolgirl would come in and then you'd put her in front of a microphone and Shirley Bassey would come out. She left and then regretted it for two years, so I was delighted for her when she did get into the Sugababes [in 2001]. So we had to re-audition and met Natasha.

Natasha Hamilton: Andy put an advert in the local Liverpool paper called the *Echo*, looking for girls with attitude.

Liz: And he got one!

Natasha: My mum saw the advert and so she phoned up and booked it. I was doing auditions left, right and centre, because my path was definitely wanting to be a singer. I turned up on the Friday afternoon and there was supposed to be a full day of auditions, but I was the first one in and everyone else got sent home. It was quite a strong audition for me. I ended up singing Atomic Kitten songs and they had me there for hours. Apparently Andy said that some of my vocals from my audition ended up on the actual 'Right Now' single.

Andy McCluskey: Quite by accident we had a blonde, a brunette and a redhead. I realised that effectively myself and Stuart Kershaw were kind of like parents in absence. We felt an obligation to those girls. Liz McClarnon and Natasha Hamilton are smart girls. And we persuaded their parents to let them join a pop group.

Liz: Our mums had to sign our record deals. I do remember the conversation my mum had with my sixth-form teacher, who was just like, 'Wait, she's what? She's leaving school to, what, be a pop star?' I was doing four A levels at the time. My mum was like, 'I'm going to give it a year and that's all she's got.'

Stuart Kershaw: When I wasn't in the studio I was taking them to do PAs up and down the country, so I got to hear whether they were happy or not with things. To be a big brother to them sort of thing and help them with problems. When I was in a band you'd make up and get on with it, but blokes are different to girls. Guys would go, 'Right, I'll hit you in the face and we'll all be fine,' but I don't think it works like that with girls.

Liz: It was very much in the Spice Girls mould because they had opened the door for girlbands. When we were kids it was all boybands, we didn't really have anybody, and then the Spice Girls came along and once you got over the, 'Oh, it's girls and they're being really loud,' you absolutely went, 'That's the same as me.' From a business point of view people were thinking, 'That's going to make money, let's do more of that', but from a young woman's point of view we were like, 'Yes, I want to do this, they look so empowered.' Personally, looking at the Spice Girls, I loved that they weren't polished and I think that worked for us as well. From a fanbase point of view, especially a same-sex fanbase, you can look up at them and aspire to achieve what they have.

Natasha: I think one of the draws with Atomic Kitten was that we were not polished at all. It was literally just go and do what you want to do. We didn't know how to do our hair or our make-up. We didn't have a stylist. I'll never forget Andy taking me, Liz and Kerry shopping around the markets in Liverpool to get our stage clothes. I ended up with a pair of flared jeans with an oriental patterned skirt that went over the top, massive platform shoes and a yellow hi-vis vest. That was my stage outfit. It was so ridiculous, it was brilliant. We were just three normal girls. I'd come from very humble beginnings so for me to be taken shopping around town and not have to pay for it, I was like, 'This is AMAZING!' It was the best day of my life.

Andy McCluskey: We spent a long time recording what would become the bulk of the first album. I went to my publishing company, who I had made millions of pounds for, and I said, 'I've got a new project, can you take it to labels.' They came back and basically said, 'We don't think it's good enough.' But they said they would waive their ownership of it, meaning that if we took it somewhere else and got a deal it would be ours. So we set up some showcases in London via my lawyer.

Natasha: I'd done so many auditions and been in other 'bands', working out of someone's shed recording music, so to then turn up at a recording studio with Andy who had already had the fame, for me it was like, 'This is special.' I knew it wasn't just someone trying to make it. I was like, 'We are going to make it.' I knew from day dot, deep down in my soul, I knew it was for me. This is the golden ticket.

Stuart Kershaw: We knew what we wanted and we targeted Hugh when we were marketing it to the record companies.

Hugh Goldsmith: I first became aware of Atomic Kitten when I received a demo tape from their manager, Martin O'Shea. There were a lot of girlbands around at the time and I wasn't actively looking for one for the label. However, there was an energy in the music on that demo that was totally compelling and the songs were brilliant. It was a breath of fresh air to find a new act that already had great songs in place. So I arranged with Martin for the band to come down from Liverpool to put on a showcase at Nomis Studios in Shepherd's Bush.

Stuart Kershaw: Hugh had done things with Billie and he had this pop sensibility. You knew he'd be able to get the right people in the right jobs to do the right pushing in the right places.

Hugh Goldsmith: I will never forget the immense blast of Girl Power that hit me when meeting Atomic Kitten for the first time. They were like the Spice Girls on steroids! Martin later told me the intention was that Atomic Kitten would channel 'the spirit of Oasis in a girl band'. The girls were down to earth, hilarious and full of energy and I was so impressed by their showcase I stopped them halfway through the second song to tell them I wanted to sign them there and then. Not something I'd done before or have since.

Andy McCluskey: He goes, 'Girls, come here, come here,' and they came down to the front and he said, 'I'm going to sign you.' They were just bouncing off the walls. I was gobsmacked. But I kept saying to them, 'Getting a record deal doesn't mean you're there.' It means someone's going to give you the ladder but you still have to climb it.

Justine Bell: Initially I didn't love everything about them. It was Hugh who saw the potential. In time I came to appreciate their hustle. They were full-on and Kerry was a massive character who always kept things interesting. We had some run-ins but I liked her a lot. It was a wild time. We had lots of girls on the label. All big characters – Martine [McCutcheon], Billie, Atomic Kitten.

Simon Jones, Martine McCutcheon's former PR: I remember with Martine we were going through some requests and it was like, 'Oh, you've been offered the cover of *Cosmopolitan* magazine,' which was a big deal. I can remember her saying, 'I don't know if I want to do that.' Then she said, 'What you need to do, Simon, when a request comes in, you need to think, "Would Barbra do it?"' Now I know you're thinking Windsor, but it was Streisand. So the benchmark that we were supposed to live by was 'Would Barbra Streisand do this?'

Andy McCluskey: The reality was that the first Atomic Kitten album came out after they had three top-ten singles, but only went to number thirty-nine.

Natasha: I remember being absolutely gutted. I really wanted it to be better than that. We knew we had a last chance with 'Whole Again', and from the minute we sang that song we knew it was special, but we steered away from the ballads. It was about the high-intense pop or the middle of the road. I think everyone was nervous to take a punt on such a slow song for a pop band.

Andy McCluskey: Paul Conroy at Virgin said to Hugh, 'You've spent a few millions on this and it's not selling, pull the plug now.'

Hugh Goldsmith: I'm someone who worships at the altar of the song because the game-changing impact of a truly fantastic song can never be underestimated. A game-changing song has the power to rescue a doomed career, sustain a successful career or indeed launch a career that would never have happened without it.

'In my ear was my wife, who had always felt "Whole Again" was the strongest track on the album'

Just as he'd had to do back in 1992, Goldsmith found himself offering up one last roll of the dice to a struggling pop act that had exhausted media goodwill. Originally released in Japan in March 2000, their debut album Right Now *featured the original, spoken-word-heavy version of 'Whole Again'. After Atomic Kitten performed its new, more radio-friendly incarnation night after night during the band's support slot with Steps to an increasingly rapturous reception, it was decided 'Whole Again' would be the song to gamble everything on. It would eventually spend a month at number one in the UK and sell over a million copies. All that, despite the band having to halt promo to quickly find a new member . . .*

Hugh Goldsmith: In A&R terms, Andy McCluskey and I had a difference of opinion as to how 'Whole Again' should be arranged. I want to stress here that I have the utmost respect for Andy as an artist and songwriter. He is brilliant in both fields and, in 'Whole Again', he and Stuart wrote a fantastic song. However, their original version of the song featured spoken vocal verses all the way through in addition to a spoken vocal in the middle eight.

Natasha: It was actually Kerry's song and me and Liz just sang on the chorus. It was a great album track but we needed a top-three hit.

172

Hugh Goldsmith: I was concerned, as were our radio plug-gers, that [the spoken-word verses] might hinder the song's uptake at daytime radio because this aspect made it similar in style to 'Never Ever' by All Saints, which was still receiving significant airplay at that time. So I asked Andy if he would consider adding melody to the verses so they could be sung not spoken. However, understandably, he wasn't too keen on reworking his original composition but he did agree that it would be okay for me to experiment with other writers. As a result, I reached out to a number of other songwriters. Eventually, Bill Padley and Jeremy Godfrey came through with the solution and the million-selling number one, 'Whole Again', as everyone now knows it, was ready to go.

Natasha: When they made the melody to the verses and we heard it, we were like, 'Oh my God, this is mega.' It totally lifted the song up to a level that was like, 'Wow.'

Andy McCluskey: We couldn't understand why they weren't more successful. I think Virgin thought they had the new baby Spice Girls. So myself and Stuart and their manager Martin O'Shea got together and said, 'Right, let's go back to Innocent and Virgin, we still believe in this band.' They hadn't given us the second half of the advance for delivering the album, which was £50,000, so we said, 'You keep that and give us the cata-logue back.'

Hugh Goldsmith: At the point we released 'Whole Again', the project was haemorrhaging money and I came under a lot of pressure from Virgin's financial director to drop the band.

I even told Martin that this was the case. However, he did a brilliant job of persuading me to put pressure back on Virgin's FD to release me enough budget to fund one final throw of the dice with the new 'Whole Again'. Also, in my ear was my wife, Carrie, who had always felt this was the strongest track on the album and that we should somehow try to get it released.

Andy McCluskey: So Hugh is straight off to Paul Conroy going, 'They've obviously got another contract, they want to release "Whole Again" as a single, please don't let them go to another label.' But we didn't have another deal. We were going to waive £50,000 and try to release 'Whole Again' ourselves. What we ended up doing was accidentally bluffing Virgin into giving them one more chance. They went from spending £150,000 on videos to making a video for 'Whole Again' for £25,000. And that was basically just a cheap copy of the Sugababes' video for 'Overload'. And bang it goes straight in at number one.

Hugh Goldsmith: Martin did indeed offer to waive the final £50,000 advance the band were owed if we would consider allowing them to release 'Whole Again' independently. There was no way I wanted to let this happen, especially after all the hard work that had gone into the new version of 'Whole Again', and in a way Martin did me a favour with his request. It gave me the ammunition to go back to my bosses and put them under pressure to let me try one more single release. Thankfully, they agreed, but I was given a massively reduced marketing budget to do the job.

Justine Bell: ['Whole Again'] was a complete game-changer, which I can take absolutely no credit for. By this time I thought we were dropping the band and to be honest I'd moved on. Hugh wouldn't let it go, though. He was obsessed with making the song a hit and giving them one last chance. He pulled in all kinds of favours to make sure the single was properly stocked in-store and that the girls got decent promo. He totally made it happen against the odds.

James Masterson: January in the music industry used to be defined by the exhaustion factor. So music sales would plummet. But that opened the door to acts being able to sneak in and have hits when they wouldn't have normally. The great story from that January period was the resurgence of Atomic Kitten, who had spent 2000 flinging out singles with nobody paying them much attention. So one final throw of the dice was 'Whole Again', which was released in early 2001 when not a lot was going on.

Lee Thompson: Atomic Kitten, number one with 'Whole Again', and Radio 1 wouldn't play that song. They just wouldn't touch it. But it was huge for The Box.

Andy McCluskey: Before that we were approached by our publishers saying, 'Listen, this hasn't been a global hit yet, there are two artists who would like to cover "Whole Again" for America and the rest of the world, would you give it to them?' And we said no. We wrote it for Atomic Kitten and we only write for Atomic Kitten. We saw ourselves as part of the group. The whole thing was the industry – the girls were the shop window and we were creating it.

Stuart Kershaw: We had calls from Clive Calder [at Jive] saying, 'Can Britney have it?' And we said, 'Well, the girls are doing it and so we have to give them a chance to do it really.' It was crazy. We didn't even want to write with other acts because we thought we might dilute what we had.

Andy McCluskey: Not only did we turn down Britney Spears but we turned down Celine Dion.

Natasha: Celine Dion?! I knew Britney [wanted it] but I didn't know Celine did.

Liz: I think it's a little bit simple for Celine. She would have belted it.

'I'm a blagger, basically. I just thought, "Why not? Just go for it." I winged it'

With all the signs pointing to 'Whole Again' being massive, and with the video on heavy rotation, Kerry Katona announced she was leaving the band in the weeks leading up to the single's release. Having ridden the pop roller-coaster through a corkscrew's worth of twists and turns, Liz and Natasha knew they couldn't let the momentum die and so set about finding a replacement. At the same time, Eurovision Song Contest 1999 fifth-place runners-up Precious were splitting up, meaning one member, Jenny Frost, was about to become a free agent.

Stuart Kershaw: It felt like walking into a wall every time you try to open a door. But the reason we were successful was because our mentality was, 'If it's a wall then we'll either knock it down or climb over it or walk around it.' We were so determined.

Andy McCluskey: We had persuaded Kerry to stay on and do ['Whole Again']. So the single was coming out and they were all getting together for the *Pepsi Chart Show* in London. Kerry got in the van and basically had a breakdown and went, 'I can't do it.' Natasha just went, 'Right, fuck her.' She'd already been in touch with Jenny Frost, who was in Precious, but they'd just finished. So Natasha calls up Jenny and says, 'You're in the band from today, get in a taxi and go to the ITV studios, you're on the *Pepsi Chart Show* in two hours, and on the way learn the words to "Whole Again".' It was ruthless. To be honest, Natasha and Kerry always had a fairly fractious relationship.

Natasha: What actually happened was I already knew [Kerry was leaving]. Me and Kerry were really close and she confided in me that she was going to leave but she told me not to tell anyone. I was seventeen and I'm a very loyal person, so I didn't want to ruin our trust. But I knew that we needed to prepare. In the end, I spoke to Martin and said he couldn't tell anyone else. He was like, 'Everyone needs to know!' I'll never forget, we were in a Chrysler Voyager in Edgware and Martin was like, 'Kerry's leaving the band,' and Liz, who was always dead quiet, literally screamed. She opened the door of the Chrysler and ran down the street and I remember running after her, grabbing her and hugging her. I said, 'Listen, Atomic Kitten isn't just about Kerry. It's about three girls. We're going to make this work.' We were both crying and I was like, 'We're going to do this.'

Jenny Frost: I was with the girls from Precious – in a club called Pop – and we were out to be like, 'We had a good run, we all love each other, but let's call it a day,' and we were saying cheers with a bottle of Champagne. Tash was next to us. She was like, 'Babe, I need to talk to you,' and I was like, 'Give me a minute, we're just having a toast because we've split the band up.' Then she went, 'Well, I *really* need to talk to you then.' She dragged me off to the loo.

Natasha: She asked what was going on and I told her Kerry had left and we were due to be on the *Pepsi Chart Show* and we needed someone tomorrow. 'Whole Again' was already being played on the radio with Kerry's vocals. It was right in the middle of our promo trail. One day I spoke to Jenny, the next day she was having a meeting with us and then the following day she was at the *Pepsi Chart Show* singing. She had the words to 'Whole Again' on a piece of paper.

Jenny: It was like, 'Listen, we're releasing this song, if it goes well then great, but if it doesn't we'll be dropped so it's a bit of a risk for you.' I didn't care, I was like, 'Let's go for it!' It worked out very well. Literally fast-forward about sixteen hours and I was performing it live on TV. I'm a blagger, basically. I just thought, 'Why not? Just go for it.' I winged it.

Andy McCluskey: That's why whenever 'Whole Again' was performed on TV it all had to be live because we didn't have a track with Jenny Frost on it because she'd only joined the band on the day of the first TV show.

Stuart Kershaw: We'd gone from the luxury of having weeks with the girls singing and practising and getting things right to getting them for two hours on a Wednesday afternoon.

James Masterson: For the first time ever, they were newsworthy and so you could put on the front page of the newspaper:

178

'Kerry Katona leaves Atomic Kitten and is having Brian from Westlife's baby'. And the record flies to number one and stays there for a month and it made Atomic Kitten.

Andy McCluskey: Kerry started her connection with Brian quite early on and it was like a millennial pop version of Romeo and Juliet. The two of them were followed everywhere they went by security. Westlife and the Kittens were never allowed to turn up at a hotel at the same time, because it was always the boyband fans outside. They had to close the curtains to the bar downstairs so fans couldn't see in. Kerry and Brian used to have to sneak off to either the ladies or the gents to have a fag in a cubicle and talk to each other. The bodyguard used to have to kick the door down and go, 'Get out, you can't be together.'

Hannah Verdier: It was really heartbreaking when Kerry Katona left. She was a good old girl. Her life could have been so different. When she got together with Brian she was so happy. They tried to give them Atomic Kitten names and she was like, 'I'm Sex Kitten.' She'd put herself out there as the sexy one.

Jenny: I think if I hadn't been in Precious before it would have been more difficult [to join an existing band] because everybody did love Kerry. But the fans were happy that the band was continuing, so that made the transition smoother and easier. I've got such a gung-ho attitude that I kind of just went for it. But I think that throughout my time with Atomic Kitten I did always feel like I was blagging it. I felt that. For the other girls, that's all they've ever wanted to do is be performers from when they were young. I never did. I did always feel like maybe somebody else deserved to be there more than I did. There was quite a bit of inner turmoil throughout the band era, but I managed to drink my way through it.

Andy McCluskey: The next thing, the album was re-released and it sold 1.5 million worldwide.

Hugh Goldsmith: People thought we were crazy pulling the album from the shops at the point that 'Whole Again' was a huge hit. There's no doubt we sacrificed a level of album sales in the January to March window, but by re-releasing the repackaged album in August 2001 on the back of a second number-one single [the band's cover of 'Eternal Flame'], it flew to the top of the album charts before going on to sell 600,000 copies. Kerry had left the band and, with Jenny joining just as 'Whole Again' took off, it was a no-brainer to get her involved vocally across the updated album. This process also gave us the chance to add songs to the album in a similar vein to 'Whole Again', thereby giving new fans of the band a better listening experience. The first edition had been primarily quite young-sounding up-tempo pop.

Brian Dowling, *Big Brother 2* winner and co-presenter of *SM:TV*: I got to sing with Atomic Kitten. I did the talking part from 'Whole Again' with Jenny Frost.

Jenny: When Brian was in *Big Brother* he used to sing 'Whole Again', so when he won and he came out we got him to perform it with us at G-A-Y. Everyone went wild.

Jeremy Joseph: There was one time [at G-A-Y] where we got soldiers in and we abseiled Atomic Kitten from the ceiling.

That was quite funny. One of the girls chickened out last minute and ran down the stairs, one managed to do it and the other got stuck halfway. That was during the first track.

Natasha: Oh my God, it was the worst idea we've ever had for a show in our lives. Firstly, the three of us are absolutely terrified of heights. So why we thought abseiling from the rafters of a very high theatre would be a great idea, I don't know. In rehearsals Liz's harness snapped so she was hanging upside down. So Liz said she wasn't going to do it but me and Jenny still had to do it. Then Jenny's rope was twisted so she was still stuck at the top. I was stuck halfway down. The intro music had finished and everyone was looking as if to say, 'This is crap.'

Jenny: That was absolutely ridiculous. You were always trying to outdo other bands at G-A-Y. You used to do it to get your picture in the paper to then try to get the sales up in the week. The outfits couldn't get any smaller so it was like, 'Let's abseil from the ceiling!'

'We did have musical differences . . . We wanted them to do our songs!'

After re-releasing 'Right Now' in August 2001 and watching it sail to the top of the UK charts, Atomic Kitten were one of Europe's biggest pop acts. Finally the good ship Kitten seemed to be on smoother waters. Behind the scenes, however, a messy and protracted divorce centring around money and publishing splits was taking place between Andy and Stuart on one side and the band's management on the other. Despite this, Andy and Stuart would get three songs on the band's second album, 2002's chart-topper Feels So Good, *but their contributions, none of which were selected as singles, would fight for their place alongside some of pop's biggest hitmakers, including Stargate, Ian Masterson and Steve Anderson.*

Andy McCluskey: Because Stuart and I had created the band we saw ourselves as part of it. We created them to be the vehicle for our songs, so we weren't like other songwriting units. We participated in part of the record royalty and obviously we had the publishing royalty, too. This started to cause problems in the band because the manager could only commission what the girls were earning and they weren't earning a lot. This is part of the problem in manufactured pop – all of the record royalty goes to pay off the advances, which include massive amounts of money for production, video, promo costs, clothing, hairdressers, tour support. The publishing money is free to go to whoever wrote the songs. And because the girls didn't write the songs, they had no income stream. They were just on a wage to live on and the manager was commissioning 20 per cent of not very much, so he was unhappy.

Stuart Kershaw: [On the second album] they wanted more publishing or the manager decided he wanted more of the publishing, so he wanted more writers. It was a good opportunity for them to wrestle control away from us. It's a sad thing but that's business. That's how it happens, with people whispering in people's ears. The band are no longer down the road for you to have a chat with; they're off on tour.

Andy McCluskey: 'Whole Again' broke the mould and then of course became the mould. Because the next thing is that Hugh Goldsmith calls me into his office and says, 'Right, we want a new album and I don't like the new direction, in fact we don't want a new direction.' He said, 'I want "Whole Again", "Whole Again" and more "Whole Again" and, if you don't write it, I'll find someone else who will.' And, in the end, he did.

Hugh Goldsmith: Atomic Kitten had found their place in the market with 'Whole Again' and it would have been crazy not to follow through with more songs of a similar nature. However, I certainly didn't want them to be exactly the same! One of our mantras at Innocent was a phrase coined by Justine to sum up the pop market and what fans primarily wanted from their artists: 'More of the same but different.' And that's what we were after in this situation.

Andy McCluskey: We actually had our [production deal] contract torn up [by the band's management]. For the next four years after that we were told we couldn't speak to the girls other than through lawyers. Which was a painful experience.

Hugh Goldsmith: Andy's falling out and parting of the ways with Atomic Kitten was not something I was involved in. I was aware that there was tension between the two parties but I was still quite taken aback when Martin called me one day to say he and the band had terminated their agreement with Engine, Andy's production company.

Stuart Kershaw: We gradually drifted apart. Which is a cliché, like 'musical differences'. But we did have that because we wanted them to do our songs.

Hugh Goldsmith: Also, it's important to mention that the girls had begun to co-write songs themselves and these songs also needed to be considered for inclusion on the records.

Steve Anderson, songwriter and producer, 'Feels So Good': We were writing for Kylie's *Fever* album. It was a really sunny day and we wrote this big pop song. She demoed it and it sounded great, but it was too pop for *Fever* so it got to one of the guys at Innocent and they took it for Atomic Kitten. I remember going in with them and in those days with these bands the music bit was given the least amount of time in any of their schedules. Even to the point where, when I did Jenny's vocals, she was in the middle of guest-editing some magazine and she came in and said, 'I've literally got fifteen minutes to do this.' About 1 per cent of their life was spent on making the records.

Andy McCluskey: The reality is that we wouldn't have had the time to crank out a whole new album that quickly. The subsequent albums were made more like other band's albums were – the whole thing was written, all of the backing vocals were done by session singers because the band didn't have enough time to go in and sing all these harmonies. You go in, you sing your topline and then you get out because you've got to be on *Top of the Pops*. Those girls never stopped.

Natasha: One time our tour manager said we had two days off in one year. It was crazy. It was constant. It was exhausting. We were still kids really and you just wanted to go and hang out with your mates or be with your family, but you couldn't because you were working. You're living an intense adult career still as a child. There were times when it clashed, you'd be exhausted or not well or having a bloody breakdown.

Jenny: The schedule was ridiculous and it was really stressful, but compared to actual real life it's not. You've got somebody booking your flights, somebody carrying your bags, somebody doing your hair and make-up. At the time, you think, 'Oh my God, it's sooo difficult,' but it really wasn't.

Lucie Cave: My very first four-page interview for *Heat* was with Atomic Kitten. It was the Jenny Frost era and Natasha had just had a boob job and Liz was going out with Lee Ryan, who had just crashed his car because he was pissed. There was a lot to talk about. Anyway, it was the most hideous experience I've ever had because Jenny was really moody. I'd ask questions and every time she'd say, 'Next question.' She would stare and make me move on. Jenny wanted me to ask them something about the music. But they couldn't even remember songs that were on their album anyway.

Jenny: I was quite worldly wise and quite protective of the girls, so I often came across like the bitch in interviews. I was in a relationship so there were no scandals to talk about, but they were always digging at Tash and Liz's romantic life. They didn't want to talk about it. If someone had just had their heart broken and I knew that they'd been crying before the interview then the journalist would be pecking, so I'd be like, 'No, we're not talking about that.' So I came across like a bitch, but I was just being protective. There are some people that probably think to this day that I am a bitch but I don't actually give a shiny shite. I was always protecting the girls.

Lucie Cave: I told Mark [Frith, then *Heat* editor] what happened and he said, 'If you don't feel like you got anything, we'll pull the interview.' And they needed us back then. So our features editor phoned their PR, who was like, 'She's really sorry, she knows she was in a bad mood, can we do her bits again?' We said no. Then Mark came up to me later and he said, 'Write it as it happened – how excited you were to go and interview them, just talk to the reader through that whole experience and let them be there with you and keep everything in.' So I did. If someone's going to be moody they shouldn't be able to get away with it.

Jenny: I can remember the exact interview. Liz had just broken up with somebody and she was so upset she was shaking. I was saying, 'She doesn't want to talk about it.' In the end, I said, 'Listen, we're not fucking talking about it.' I remember seeing [Lucie] on *Loose Women* once and she said Atomic Kitten were the worst interview she'd ever had and I was like, 'Well, thank you.'

Hannah Verdier: I remember once with Atomic Kitten we were trying to get a cover shot and they were at each other. Jenny was ill and she was saying, 'This can't happen,' and she kind of had me pinned up against the wall in the studio. I was begging for ten more minutes to get the shot and she was like, 'This is my life; you can't do this.' Obviously then the bosses come in and tell them to get on with it. They were exhausted kids.

'I was a mum, trying to be a pop star'

At the end of 2003, Atomic Kitten released their third album, Ladies Night, *a fairly anodyne collection of soft-focus pop that felt increasingly*

staid in comparison with the DayGlo music being made by the likes of
Girls Aloud and the Sugababes. It peaked at number five, their first album
to miss the top spot. It was also their first album since Natasha Hamilton
had given birth to her first son in October 2002. By early 2004, the band
were falling apart and a 'hiatus' was announced ahead of a greatest hits
album and a farewell tour. Behind the scenes, Innocent was also entering
its final phase, with Hugh Goldsmith leaving at the end of 2003 to start
the Brightside label.

Liz: Now I know why it started because Tash and I have become a lot closer and I understand where she was. But at the time, I was told that Tash just didn't want to do it any more. I was like, 'Really?' I also did want a bit of time off myself. At that time, that's how I saw it. Now, looking back, it wasn't like that at all and I can totally see what Tash was going through.

Jenny: We weren't given a lot of information. I remember being in a hotel room and being told Tash has gone home, she can't do it any more, and then we sat down with her and she just said she needed a break. There was never any drama or anything.

Natasha: It was difficult because I had postnatal depression. I was very sick actually. It wasn't getting dealt with because I wasn't admitting to anyone what I was going through because in my head I was being ungrateful. It was like, 'I've got the world at my feet, I'm in the biggest girlband on the planet, I've got money, I've got a home, I should be happy.' But I wasn't. Back then with postnatal depression there were no young, twenty-year-old women discussing it. No one was discussing it. How it made you feel. That it was normal. I literally thought there was something wrong with me. It went on and by the time I was finally diagnosed, it was too late, I think. A lot of relationships had fractured because of me not saying my truth and people not understanding.

Liz: You can't blame yourself in that way.

Jenny: I think we saw it coming. Tash was struggling. Now as a mother myself I can see why she was struggling. At the time, I totally got it and there wasn't one moment where I was like, 'Ugh.' I just thought, 'It is what it is.' At that point, we were all getting a bit weary anyway.

Natasha: It was very much, 'The show must go on regardless, we don't really care what's wrong with you.' My doctor was saying, 'She needs six months to a year off,' and I was told, 'Well, you've got two [months] to get better and when you come back we want to know whether you're in or you're out.' It was very much like a threat and I couldn't live like that. We didn't have anyone who we could confide in and who could help. Quite often any help was, 'Send them to a doctor and put them on Prozac and everything will be fine.' I was a mum, trying to be a pop star. I was on one side of the world and my baby was at home with my mum. I missed out on those integral moments to bond. I had six weeks' maternity leave. I remember my first gig back after having Josh was the Disney tour. I had an emergency C-section, so I'd had my tummy cut open and I'd been stitched up. When you have a C-section, you have six weeks' downtime and back into light exercise. But with me I was back on stage in heels doing full-on dance routines. That had a psychological effect because I didn't feel glamorous. I didn't feel like a pop star. I felt fat. I just felt like an exhausted mum. Presenting yourself to people as a happy pop star when actually you want to go home and cry and be with your baby. Living that life continuously for months on end breaks you down.

In 2005, the band reunited briefly to release 'Cradle 2005', an updated version of a song from *Right Now*. A year later, they reunited again to record a cover of the Farm's 'All Together Now', which became a charity single associated with the 2006 FIFA World Cup. Years later – after a brief return to the original, Kerry-era line-up for *The Big Reunion* in 2012 – Jenny, Liz and Natasha would have another brush with football after 'Whole Again' was transformed into 'Southgate You're the One (Football's Coming Home Again)' during England's run to the final of the 2020 Euro football tournament. The updated version peaked at number fourteen.

'I had come up with LADS, as in Lee, Ant, Dunc and Si'

By 2001, the traditional boyband bubble was close to bursting. In America, the Backstreet Boys were about to enter a hiatus following 2000's lacklustre Black & Blue, *while NSYNC were essentially laying the foundations for Justin Timberlake's solo stardom. Five, meanwhile, were flying the flag for the UK boybands, but by that point the flag was on fire and the band members were using it as a weapon on each other. Even A1, whose music (and centre partings) skewed closest to the US boyband archetype, were about to regenerate as Travis. In this context, Blue, AKA Lee Ryan, Simon Webbe, Antony Costa and Duncan James, felt like a breath of fresh air. Musically, like Damage and Another Level before them, they skewed closer to R&B, but, via their work with the increasingly ubiquitous Stargate, it always landed with a huge pop thud. While their boyband predecessors favoured slick choreography, Blue's dance moves were slightly more rudimentary, the kind you might see around the bar at a Slug and Lettuce after the fourth shot of sambuca. Their sound, mixed with their propensity to smize in pictures and say what they wanted in interviews, gave them an air of cool that was often missing from their more controlled peers. It wasn't all plain sailing, though, as what started as a five-piece suddenly became a trio . . .*

Hugh Goldsmith: Blue was formed when I offered Daniel Glatman the same deal Simon Cowell and I had given Chris Herbert a few years earlier [with Five]. I thought Daniel was a very smart young guy with lots of drive and ambition so offered him a drawdown fund of £10,000 to seek out talented young singers that might form the basis of a cool new pop act, which he would then manage. Our original intention was that this new act would be mixed gender and that it might include a couple of people playing instruments. However, soon after starting the process, we decided to make our new group a boyband and changed our brief to Daniel.

Antony Costa: Me and Duncan knew each other from my local area of Golders Green. I used to see him with his bandmates when I was with my bandmates and we'd always chat. To cut a long story short, we became really good mates. Later I found a guy, Daniel Glatman, who was looking to put a band together, so me and Duncan went for it. We went to a place called Nomis Studios for the audition. I knew Lee from various boyband auditions and so did Dunc, but me and Dunc didn't know that we both knew Lee. If that makes sense. So I called Lee up and told him about the band and he wanted in. Then that grew to a five-piece with these two guys called Richard and Spencer.

Hugh Goldsmith: The five-guy line-up was finally in place and contracts were about to be signed. However, after Justine saw the band together for the first time and gave us her comments, we agreed that something wasn't right with the line-up. So, literally moments before the signing, we changed our minds. The band was too similar to a lot of boybands already in the market.

Justine Bell: I didn't like two of them. It seems incredibly harsh but it just didn't feel right and I'm glad we went with our gut.

Antony: We were a five-piece for literally two weeks. I've had longer three-course dinners, you know what I mean. It was horrible. When we got the phone call that day, we were in Dunc's Fiat Cinquecento and Daniel rang and said, 'Look, wherever you are, you need to get to the office, we need an emergency meeting.' We were like, 'Fucking hell, it's done, the dream's over.' For the two lads it was devastating. An acting agent friend of mine said to me, 'It's show business and not show friends.' I will take that to the grave. There's a time when you've got to think about yourself. I was eighteen years old and I had one GCSE. My whole life was based on getting in this band and trying to make it work. I spoke to my mum and dad and they said, 'Look, it's great you're a loyal person but you don't want to live with regrets.'

Hugh Goldsmith: It was an incredibly difficult thing to do and, to this day, I feel bad about dashing the hopes of two young guys about to sign a life-changing record deal. However, we knew we had to make the change and Blue would not have come about if we hadn't done so.

Antony: Because I'd seen what had happened to the other two lads who hadn't made it, I was always worried I wasn't good enough. The first year or so I was constantly living life on an edge because I was scared the other three would turn around and go, 'Look, Ant, it's not really working, we're going to look elsewhere.' Even though I was one of the founding members so to speak.

Hugh Goldsmith: This took the band back to a three-piece and created room for Simon to join and for the line-up to finally be complete.

Antony: Lee kept talking about a guy called Simon that he knew who'd come down from Manchester that could write, rap and sing. Simon also knew Duncan from another boyband audition so it all intertwined into one really.

Justine Bell: It just worked. Four great voices, four decent-looking lads. Cool, but not trying too much, and they worked exceptionally hard charming everyone they came into contact with.

Antony: At the time, P!nk was really smashing it and we were just talking about names and I think it was Simon who said, 'What about Blue?' We were all like, 'Yeah, what is that? It doesn't make sense.' But the thing is it doesn't mean anything; it's just a colour. But then you look at bands like Simply Red, Black Sabbath, Deep Purple. I had come up with LADS, as in

Lee, Ant, Dunc and Si. But that never worked because you can't be sixty years old and be called LADS.

Hugh Goldsmith: We definitely wanted to move away from the squeaky clean, overtly good-looking vibe of many other boy groups around at the time. We wanted them to have a bit of edge, humour and attitude.

Antony: I think Another Level were sort of dying down and from what I gather they wanted to put something like that in the market. Like an R&B boyband. One that blokes and girls can like, and dads and mums.

Jordan Paramor: I loved Blue. They were hilarious. They took it seriously but they were also just having a laugh. I really enjoyed hanging out with them. They treated me like one of the lads. All these girls would be screaming at them and completely in love with them and I'd be thinking, 'I just sat in a car with them for three hours farting constantly and sitting on my face.'

MNEK: The music was older, it was cooler, but also it wasn't an all-white band. Simon absolutely helped give the group a bit of a weight and an ability to do the more R&B-leaning records.

Chantelle Fiddy, journalist: If you look at how they were putting the bands together, there was often that consideration. 'Have we got a balance?' Look at S Club 7, Blue – it's like, 'Let's get a good mix so we can cover all bases.' Blue couldn't have sampled half the songs they sampled, like Biggie's 'Hypnotize' on 'Fly By II', without having Simon in the band.

MNEK: Controversially, I think their version of 'Too Close' [released as their second single] is superior to Next's original. I think Lee sings the hell out of it; the production is sleeker. The Blue one is tuned and Y2K polished.

Hugh Goldsmith: Billie's 'Day and Night' was the first record I worked on with Stargate, whose talent I'd previously admired from afar, and I also brought them in to work on Blue.

MNEK: Stargate were doing all the hits then. They were clearly inspired by R&B music but they knew they didn't have the culture in them to do it from a rough point of view. So they were like, 'Right, let's polish it up, let's make it really bright and really intentionally pop. Let's take everything we know from Scandinavia and blend the best of both worlds.' R&B and hip-hop were massive parts of teen pop, but it was more the groove of it or the musicality of it.

Hallgeir Rustan: We realised immediately that there was something special about Blue. Hugh Goldsmith had found these guys who were all really good singers – perhaps not the best dancers – and when they came to Trondheim [to record] all the girls fell head over heels. They were so fun to work with and full of ideas. 'All Rise' was basically written and recorded on a tough hip-hop track. We wanted the vocals to be tough and tight, especially in the chorus. We joked that they should be as tight as a marching band so we made them march while recording.

Antony: For me, when we first recorded 'All Rise', it was never a first single. It was too hard, very military. I was like, 'What is this song?' My first single choice was always 'If You Come Back'. But, when we came back to London, Hugh Goldsmith said, 'Guys, I've got some great news. I've got the mix of your first single.' When we sat down in his office and he said, 'It's "All Rise".' We just looked at each other like, 'Really?' Then he played the finished version and we were like, 'Oh, wow.'

'Lee calls me and says, "I think I might have said something . . ."'

By September 2001, Blue were one of the UK's biggest bands. 'All Rise' had peaked at number four, spending two months in the top twenty, while follow-up 'Too Close' earned them their first number one. Pulling the classic '00s pop trick of following two upbeat bops with a ballad that would lead into the album, their third single was 'If You Come Back', a top-tier emotional wind tunnel powered by Lee Ryan's vocal. With their debut album due for release at the end of November, AKA during the all-important Q4 period, the band travelled to New York to film 'If You Come Back''s video. The first day of filming took place on 11 September 2001.

Hugh Goldsmith: Justine and I were in New York with Blue and Atomic Kitten when the 9/11 atrocity took place. It's important to remember that Blue were actually standing on the Brooklyn shoreline, about to start shooting a video, when they witnessed the second plane hitting the World Trade Center.

Antony: It was traumatic because our families couldn't get in touch with us for twenty-four to forty-eight hours. It was a tragedy and it changed the world to this day, but to be there was just mind-blowing. It was like being in a blockbuster movie where people were running around and there was smog and smoke everywhere. We ended up getting evacuated to Tarry-town with Atomic Kitten for ten days. They were filming the video the day after, so on the 12th, and we were filming on the 11th. So we saw the second plane hit and saw the building collapsing from over near Brooklyn Bridge. From there we got evacuated.

Jenny: It really affected me. When we got back to the UK eventually, I wasn't sleeping at all and I was hospitalised for a few days. Every time I slept, I'd have these screaming nightmares. They just put me in hospital for a few days and knocked me out so I could sleep. I was a wreck. They said I had PTSD and that I needed to sleep. I had therapy after-wards. It was one of those moments I couldn't talk about for a really long time. Some of the things that we saw that day, you know.

Antony: I think we were [suffering from PTSD] in a way that we never really spoke about. We never shared a bedroom but that night when we were evacuated I remember sharing a room with Dunc and sitting up all night. It was a crazy time.

Jenny: Everybody was fucking traumatised. It affected us all for a long time. We used to fly so much. Before that, I never had an issue flying, but still to this day I'm not a good flyer.

Antony: We managed to fly back to the UK and I remember going straight to Southampton to do an outdoor gig.

Hugh Goldsmith: Fast-forward to the end of a long day of interviews back in London, with the same question being asked over and over again, and Lee snapped, saying something he deeply regretted, which resulted in huge levels of hatred being aimed at him for many months. Lee was only eighteen and what he wanted to say came out all wrong.

Simon Jones, Blue's former PR: They'd had a PR and they weren't happy so they brought me in just before that single and the album. We'd started doing press and we'd done a little bit of media training, but not much. I can remember sitting at my desk and for some reason they had gone into *The Sun*. I didn't even know they were doing it. Someone on their digital team had taken them in to do some sort of live thing for *The Sun* and didn't think to tell me or the PR team they were doing this. They walked over to the Bizarre desk and Dominic Mohan and he's like, 'Can I have a quick chat with the boys?' Why they thought it was a good idea to have a chat with *The Sun*, I don't know.

Antony: I think it got to a point where the trauma of it had built up and it felt like no one was really interested in our music. It was about, 'What did you see? How did it happen?' One of the lads, he just said, 'Look, can we just not talk about this any more, it's really hurting us emotionally; if you want to talk about some-thing serious, let's talk about other stuff like whales being killed or dolphins being executed' – I don't know, I can't remember the exact words he said. From that it was the front-page headline you see today. [Lee Ryan is quoted as saying: 'Who gives a fuck about New York when elephants are being killed? Animals need saving and that's more important. This New York thing is being blown out of proportion . . .']

Simon Jones: They got in a car afterwards and Lee calls me and says, 'I think I might have said something.' It's my favourite line ever: 'I think I might have said something.' There are certain individuals that you don't want to hear that from. He told me and the colour drained from my face. I knew instantly it was going to be a disaster. I know Dominic, I know Bizarre, I know *The Sun*; they're going to want to turn this into something. So I rang Dominic and said, 'Oh, I understand that Blue were in,' and he said, 'Yeah, I was going to call you, Lee said some pretty horrific things.' Then it went into overdrive.

Justine Bell: Hugh was away at the time and I recognised this was dangerous and needed to be contained. I went into the office at about 7 a.m. and wrote a statement, which I got Lee to sign off on and post online apologising. It was a difficult time. Hugh pulled in a million favours to dampen down the impact.

Hugh Goldsmith: After having finally finished overseeing the making of the Blue album I was exhausted and decided to take a short break in a remote part of the Scottish Highlands with my wife and three kids. We were so remote I didn't even have a mobile phone signal. What could possibly go wrong?! So there I was, in the local pub, enjoying a whisky, when the phone behind the bar started to ring. It was Steve Morton, Virgin's director of promotions, who had somehow tracked me down to alert me to the interview and the fact that the story would run on the front page of the next day's *Sun* newspaper. We were told there was no way *The Sun* would change their minds even though our press people had done everything they could to persuade them not to run the story.

Simon Jones: There wasn't really anything we could do. I was trying to explain to Dominic that he didn't mean it disrespectfully; he just meant he didn't want to talk about it any more. Obviously Dominic felt he came across as disrespectful to the victims. I can remember it coming out. The label thought it was going to ruin them. You can imagine the ramifications for the online person who took them into *The Sun* without telling the PR.

Hugh Goldsmith: I was completely gutted and my immediate instinct was to call my contacts at media outlets like Radio 1, Capital Radio and breakfast TV to try to stop the story running on all their news bulletins the next morning, thereby limiting the damage somewhat. So I set up a 'war room' in the pub and started making the calls. Thankfully, the radio and TV stations were totally sympathetic and, to this day, I feel so grateful they didn't make matters much worse than they already were by running the story in all their bulletins.

Simon Jones: The next day *The Sun* ran a poll saying, 'Should Lee Ryan be fired from Blue, ring this number'. It was a big story in America: this UK band are saying, 'Fuck New York and fuck what happened'. It was made out to be that he didn't give a shit about the people that died in the Twin Towers, which to be fair to Lee is not what he was saying. He was just not very eloquent at that point in his life and wasn't expressing his thoughts in a clear way. *The Sun* knew what they were doing. Lee was being asked about serious things like 9/11.

Justine Bell: I had to go on tour with them for a week to make sure Lee didn't get cornered by journalists who might encourage him to say something else that could damage the band. Thank God there was no social media.

Antony: I think that was a defining moment. From that point onwards in a weird sort of way it put Blue on the map in terms of being in the bigger picture. All of a sudden people were interested in our relationships. And you just think, 'Wow, we're interested in making music and having a good time and making people happy.'

Justine Bell: It felt awful at the time but it probably helped them in the long run. Everyone knew who they were because of the tabloid stuff so it probably helped them monetise their profiles after the band split.

Simon Jones: There wasn't a day that went by where they weren't in the tabloids. They were just great fodder. They were out shagging girls, they were falling out of nightclubs, they were getting drunk, they were having arguments. They were always saying things that were cheeky. Once the papers realise a band is giving them stories, it almost becomes a self-fulfilling prophecy because every day they go into conference and go, 'Anything on Blue?' It felt relentless. They'd say, 'I heard Lee shagged this girl last night,' and I'd be like, 'How do you know that?' Things were leaking from inside the camp all the time. People on the inside were being paid to give stories. Sometimes I would feel like people were suggesting I had leaked stuff, but why would I? It's much easier to think I was doing it than say someone from their families. Often it is family.

Hugh Goldsmith: By now, there was already a very strong brotherly bond within the group and Lee was given the full support of his fellow band members at an extremely difficult time.

Jordan Paramor: We were at a gig somewhere with them and they were being asked to promote a male cancer charity. There was a 'Balls to Cancer' T-shirt and Lee put it on and said, 'I'm okay to wear this, aren't I?', and everyone shouted, 'No, no, take it off.' Just in case people thought he wasn't coming from a helpful place. Because it was out of context. Management were worried people might think he was taking the piss. Lee was devastated by the 9/11 thing. It haunted him and I think it still does.

Iain James, Triple 8: Artists are so much more switched on now with everything – their finances, their artistry, their marketing. In my day we did not have a clue. It's a blessing that we didn't become successful, because if Lee Ryan said what he said, God knows what *we* would have said.

Peter Robinson: Blue were a very Capital FM band. They made sense in that time where Capital FM was the biggest station in London. You'd see people that looked like Blue out and about in London clubs. They had an incredible vocalist in Lee as well. He was a brilliant pop star and a terrible pop star at the same time.

MNEK: Lee is an OG vocalist. Let's be clear. 'If You Come Back' and 'Fly By II' are proper classic boyband records regardless of region, because they sang the fuck out of those songs.

Antony: Lee also had an obsession with fire extinguishers. I remember being at the Copthorne Hotel in Newcastle and after a gig we went back to the hotel for a drink but it was Newcastle United's Christmas party, so Alan Shearer was there. And my good friend Dale Winton, who is no longer with us any more, he came up to see me and we were all having a laugh. That was the first time I got Dale Winton pissed on tequila. He was loving life, he was dancing and singing. Fabulous man. Miss him terribly. Anyway, Lee got a fire extinguisher out and hosed all the Newcastle team and the people in the bar. Dale was like, 'Oh my God, what's happening? This is fun! This is rock 'n' roll!' They tried to do us for the dry-cleaning bill but Lee ended up paying it all, I think.

Simon Jones: [Getting a 2004 feature in *Observer Music* magazine] was a big deal for the record label. They always loved it when a music broadsheet got on board.

Alexis Petridis, journalist: You were seeing that transference of power in terms of music journalism. Broadsheets didn't really cover pop music in its broadest sense really until the '90s. We were probably to blame to a certain degree for the collapse of things like *NME* and *Q,* because we were doing what they did but with a broader remit. We didn't have to service any particular tribal demographic or anything like that. You could cover anything you wanted.

Simon Jones: We took them to Dubai for the piece. Beforehand with the boys I was like, 'This is really important; don't say anything stupid, don't fuck this up.' We go to the gig and then there's an afterparty at some rich guy's house. I was nervous about it. Then one of the girls that was with us who shall remain nameless thought it would be funny to get sugar out and line it up as if it was lines of coke. I thought it *was* coke so I was panicking. I was trying to clear it up before anyone saw it and it became 'my night of coke with Blue'. I had a massive row with this girl like, 'That's not funny, it could have ruined this piece with *The Observer*.'

'You had two blond guys, an ex-model and a Greek geezer, do you know what I mean?'

A boyband is a delicate ecosystem. Built to be lusted after via cheeky maga-zine articles in everything from Smash Hits *to* Attitude, *it can be tricky for the members who perhaps don't get the full glare of the spotlight. For Blue, whose first two albums had both gone four times platinum in the UK, the tabloid focus was Duncan and Lee, while Simon – a former model and often the band's anchor – rarely struggled to get attention. It meant one member often felt sidelined.*

Simon Jones: I didn't get on with Antony. At the time, I think it might have been based on insecurity, but the problem was all the magazines were interested in Lee, Duncan and Simon. They'd say things like, 'Well, we'll do four covers but we don't want to print the Antony one.' I'd be like, 'Well, you have to – I can't go to him and say that.'

Hannah Verdier: When we were doing the covers on the very left-hand side you'd always put the ugly one. So you'd put, say, Gary Barlow there because you'd have a flap with a free gift covering his face. The boring one goes behind the free gift and the good-looking one goes in the middle.

Jordan Paramor: I was twenty-four when Blue started and I remember my friends saying, 'God, I fancy Lee from Blue.' She'd never said that about anybody from 911 or Five. They weren't dressed in Technicolour boyband outfits; they were the cool face of boybands. I remember another friend having a real crush on Antony because she thought she'd have more of a chance.

Antony: I felt like I was an easy target. I wasn't the blond-haired, blue-eyed boy or the one with the big muscles and the six-pack and the chiselled jaw. You had two blond guys, an ex-model and a Greek geezer, do you know what I mean?

Jordan Paramor: We used to call the ones that always stood in the back behind the main guys the plumbers in pop. No one knew what they were called or what they did. All bands had one that was slightly less popular.

Simon Jones: Often these magazines would take it upon themselves to just stick someone on the cover if something fell through. So it was fine when you were controlling it and saying, 'It's got to be all four boys,' but there were eight or nine of these mags; you couldn't control every cover they did. They'd just email and say, 'We've made a decision, we're putting Duncan on the cover this month.' But it was always Lee, Duncan or Simon. Antony is a lovely bloke, but at the time this tension built up where it was like, 'You're doing a shit job . . . for me.' I couldn't change the game we were in.

Antony: Because you don't feel that you're good enough to be in a band, you don't feel like you're good enough to be on stage and you don't feel like people like you. So you're always worrying. It got to a stage where I didn't feel confident and I used to make excuses. It wasn't me. So I thought, 'You know what, only you can change this,' so I came out of my shell a bit.

Simon Jones: For the last era of Blue, Antony had his own, separate PR. Obviously it was a waste of money and time, but I think it was the manifestation of the insecurity that developed from not resonating in the media as much as the other three boys. Just wanting to blame somebody for that, which I do understand because that was my job. He didn't think I was delivering for him.

'She gave us this weird dirty look as if to say, "Who the fuck are these four boys?"'

A clear reflection of Blue's impact came via the rarified company they kept. Not only did they release singles with both Elton John [2002's 'Sorry Seems to Be the Hardest Word'] and Stevie Wonder [2003's 'Signed, Sealed, Delivered, I'm Yours'], they were also invited to spend time with fashion goddess Donatella Versace. Apparently a huge fan of their oeuvre, in 2001 Donatella extended an invite to her show at Milan Fashion Week. Only, well, there was a breakdown in communication and Donatella actually wanted Blur. Blur not Blue.

Simon Jones: I remember them going to the Donatella Versace thing, but I didn't hear until way after the fact what had happened.

Antony: Her PR company over here phoned up our press people at the time and said, 'Donatella wants Blue to come over.' We thought it was amazing. We got kitted out in Versace in Mayfair.

Simon Jones: The boys were made up, like, 'Donatella has personally invited us.'

Antony: Then we got flown over by private jet. We were lining up after the show and she gave us this weird dirty look as if to

205

say, 'Who the fuck are these four boys? Why are they wearing my gear?' I said to Simon that it was a bit weird. He went, 'Maybe she doesn't smile, who knows?' Anyway, we get home and our PR company phoned back and were like, 'We're so sorry, but she wanted Blur and not Blue.' She Instagrammed a picture of her and Damon [Albarn] the other month and tagged me in it saying, 'I've met my man.' It was great.

Hugh Goldsmith: They were the hottest new act in the UK by early 2002, so when I reached out to Lucian Grainge to see whether Elton would be interested in duetting with the guys on their version of 'Sorry Seems to Be the Hardest Word' I was hoping for a yes and, happily, that is what I got.

Antony: Elton John said that *All Rise* was the best album of 2001. He's quoted as saying that. We'd already finished the *One Love* album and I think it was Lee who said, 'What if we do a cover of Elton John?' We went in and did 'Sorry Seems to Be the Hardest Word', but originally Elton was only going to play the piano on it and not sing it. Then he heard our version and he came down and he said, 'Would you mind if I just laid the vocal down?', and we were all like, 'You crack on, mate.' These are his words: 'If it's fucking shit, I won't be offended, just take it out.' Anyway, he did it and it's what you hear today. One take.

Hallgeir Rustan: We arrived well prepared in the studio in London and Sir Elton John was to arrive at midday. We thought he would probably show up in the evening. But at 12 p.m. he was in the studio ready to work. Before the London session, we had rented the fattest grand piano in Trondheim and recorded the piano track on 'Sorry Seems to Be the Hardest Word' ourselves. After all the vocals on the song were finished, we asked Sir Elton John if he could play on the grand piano that was standing there in the studio. He sat down and played through the song once and, oh my God, it sounded ten times better than what we had worked on in Trondheim. Also, if he didn't have music, he could easily have been a comedian – so funny.

Justine Bell: Blue were perceived as a cool act and Elton John always seems up for that. He seemed to genuinely get on with the boys, too, when they recorded together. Initially he said he couldn't do a video with them. It took Duncan about five minutes to talk him into it. We shot the video the next week.

Hugh Goldsmith: A year later, I made another call to Lucian and this time it was to see whether we could interest Stevie Wonder in duetting with the band. As a result, I was able to enjoy one of the most memorable experiences of my career in the shape of two nights in Dr Dre's recording studio with Stevie Wonder. The surreal experience was topped off at about 3 a.m. on the second night when Stevie, who I was sat next to at the desk while we were mixing his vocals, called his assistant and started singing his version of 'Happy Birthday' down the phone to her!

After the release of their third chart-topping album, *Guilty*, at the end of 2003, Blue were starting to fracture. Tellingly, it was their first album to sell less than a million copies in the UK. A year later, they released the *Best of Blue* compilation, led by the pointedly titled single 'Curtain Falls'. By 2005, the band were on hiatus, with each member dabbling in solo material to varying degrees of success. Somewhat hampering their abilities to properly cash in on a reunion, Blue were one of the few pop acts of the time to treat the hiatus as exactly that, often cropping up in tabloids, on the nostalgia tour circuit and occasionally in the charts every few years. In 2011, they reunited for Eurovision, finishing in eleventh place with the single 'I Can', co-produced by Hallgeir Rustan (that role was almost thrown into doubt after Antony, displaying a deft ability to multi-task, was papped urinating while getting some cash out and texting on his phone). A fourth album, *Roulette*, followed in 2013, with another, *Colours*, arriving two years later. In 2022, they returned for an arena tour and released their sixth album, *Heart & Soul*, which was compromised slightly by Lee being arrested after allegedly becoming abusive on a flight. *Heart & Soul* entered the charts at number twenty-two, their lowest-peaking album so far.

6

Don't stop movin':
How S Club 7 became
pop's hardest-working band

While Chris Herbert healed his wounds after his Spice Girls sacking via Five's relentless drama, Simon Fuller – who had been handed his P45 in November 1997 – immediately started work on what would become S Club 7. In fact, the neat story goes he dreamt it all up the day after he saw the underside of Geri's clomping Buffalo boot. Having witnessed the global dominance of the Spice Girls first-hand, Fuller was keen to make his next move similarly all-encompassing. There were some important tweaks on his mood board, however: where there was five before, let there be seven. Just girls? Come on, let's mix that up too; think Steps but glossier. Sure, we could shlep them around radio, TV and magazines for months upfront of the debut single or we could launch them via their own children's BBC TV show in which the band/brand play (slightly) fictionalised versions of themselves and debut music in every episode? So that's what he did.

Auditions started via *The Stage*, with Jon Lee, Paul Cattermole, Tina Barrett (who was at that point one third of Face2Face, later Mis-Teeq) and Hannah Spearritt all plucked out of 10,000 hopefuls. Rachel Stevens, meanwhile, was separately approached by two producers from Fuller's 19 management and asked to record a demo. Those five only became S Club 7 after three of the original hopefuls were fired. In the end, Jo O'Meara and Bradley McIntosh completed the picture and the UK gained its first fourteen-legged, all-purpose, sugar-pop behemoth.

'At the time, I was working at Pizza Hut in Chessington World of Adventures'

James Masterson: The biggest cultural shift, the tipping point for the revival of the pop music industry, was Princess Diana dying. Elton John performed his new version of 'Candle in the Wind' at the funeral and then rush-released it. In its first full week on sale it became the first song in history to sell a million copies during a week. The majority of those were on a CD single. That cemented the idea of the CD single being a mass-market consumer product. Supermarkets saw this demand and so music went from being a niche interest to something you could get your hands on absolutely everywhere. The CD single became a pester product in the same way a bar of chocolate might be. The record industry realised this by pushing forward acts who had distinct appeal to children. Sales started to shoot through the roof. This was to the benefit of every single pop act that emerged in this period.

Peter Loraine: It was at a time when Polydor's main acts, aside from Boyzone, were Cast, Shed Seven, Gene and a bunch of guitar bands. We were coming out of Britpop, the Spice Girls were ginormous, All Saints were doing really well, and [Polydor] didn't have anything pop. The first real thing we did was we went to Simon Fuller and asked what he was doing next.

Chris Herbert: Simon Fuller had been sacked by the Spice Girls and he was taking refuge down in Portofino in Italy at Sophia Loren's villa. He got a message to Simon Cowell and said, 'Look, you, me and Chris should get together to talk about our war stories.' So we went and spent about three days hanging out. Fuller said to me at one point, 'If you were to do another band, what would it be?' I said I had this idea of doing a mixed group, boys and girls, with more than five members, and it would be multi-cultural. At the time, I had a working title of United Colours because of the United Colors of Benetton adverts. Fuller was like, 'This is a great idea, we can build a TV show around it.' We left it that we were going to explore the idea more but nothing came of it. Then all of a sudden S Club 7 pop up. Make of it what you will.

Colin Barlow, former head of Polydor Records: The TV show for S Club 7 was absolutely revolutionary. What Fuller realised was that if you had a pop band and Radio 1 don't like them then it's not going to work, but if you've got a TV show then you don't have to worry about Radio 1. Everything with S Club 7 was built around the fact that Simon wanted to get an act to an audience, rather than have a gatekeeper at Radio 1 telling him that his act wasn't cool enough to be on the radio.

Peter Loraine: Simon had three ideas; he had 21st Century Girls, who were four rocky girls who played instruments and drove tanks in their videos; then there were three brothers who were like the British Hanson; and we were like, 'We want S Club.' At that point they were just called S Club and there were only five of them, so no Bradley and no Jo.

Jo O'Meara: I was singing in a country-and-western-themed restaurant in Guildford. I'd wait tables and then the music would start and whatever you were doing you'd have to stop, run to the stage, sing the song and carry on waiting the tables. A member of 19 management was in that evening having dinner. They approached me and said I'd be perfect for this new project Simon Fuller was putting together. So I went along to the audition.

Sam Bloom: I actually auditioned for S Club 7 and I got down to the final rounds with Hannah and Jon. I think I got replaced by Bradley at the end, just before they all got together.

Bradley McIntosh: I wasn't sure if they were 100 per cent keen on me. I did the audition and at the time I was working at Pizza Hut in Chessington World of Adventures. I didn't hear anything back for a while.

Jo: I was petrified going into the audition because the queue was so so long. I remember walking into this really horrible little room and I had to sing a couple of songs and then they got me to recite an acting piece. When I was auditioning for the band, I thought it was just a band; I had no clue there'd be a TV show alongside it. I sang Fleetwood Mac's 'Dreams' and then they wanted something up-tempo, which I didn't really do back then, so I just burst into 'I Wanna Dance with Somebody' by Whitney Houston. Then I got recalled to go and meet Simon.

Bradley: Funnily enough I got fired from Pizza Hut about a week after the audition, so I was on my way to get my P45 when I found out they wanted me to go and see them again. I remember going back to Pizza Hut and saying, 'Yeah, I'm going to be in a band,' and them being like, 'Yeah, whatever, mate, sure.'

Jo: The first time we all met was at [PR legend] Nicki Chapman's house and that's when we were told we were officially S Club 7. That was the start of a brand-new pop adventure. I found it tricky because the other five members had already bonded.

Bradley: Because of that [me and Jo] always had a strong bond together. We always ended up being in the studio for the longest as well.

Jo: Back then you all either lived together in a house, like the Spice Girls did, or you would get taken on days out. We would go to the Trocadero in London and we'd play arcade games or go bowling. Go for dinner, go to the cinema. That was all bonding exercises to get us working together as a unit, so it was quite tough because they all knew each other. Me and Bradley felt like the odd ones out at first. We went to Italy and stayed at the most unbelievable villa that Simon had hired out. He took us out on a private boat and we went shopping in Capri. We had a private chef. It was different to what I was used to back home, that was for sure.

Bradley: We had three-course meals and lots of wine. He could see the bond. Then he sat us in this room and started to explain that there would be a TV show. I knew some of the other guys were from stage school and I'm thinking to myself, 'Do they know I have no experience in acting?' I wasn't going to say anything, I didn't want to lose the job.

Jo: The shock was, 'Oh, by the way, you fly to Miami in two weeks to film your own TV show.' I'd never done any acting in my whole life. All of a sudden I had a hundred pages of script to learn in ten days. It was so frightening. That was first mentioned when we were all together in that room for the first time.

Bradley: I didn't know [Jo had never acted before either]. I felt like I was the only one who had come straight out of Pizza Hut. From that moment on it was full speed ahead, but obviously you go through all the legal stuff with contracts and get all the parents together. That process took a few months. There was an advance. I can't remember how much it was – maybe £50,000 or £100,000. I didn't really care about those things back in the day. I was just living the dream. I never once checked my bank account when I was in S Club 7. All I knew was that this card gets money out of the wall. That's it. Whenever I needed money, it just came out. I was sixteen when I first started.

Jo: So many people have asked me, 'What does the "S" stand for?', and I've tried to come up with theories. 'Simon' is the obvious choice. But then I was thinking, 'Is it some sort of a connection with the number nineteen?', because 'S' is the nineteenth letter of the alphabet. It's not even a secret thing we can never disclose because we don't know what it is.

Bradley: We just came to the conclusion that it's Simon's Club. S is the nineteenth letter of the alphabet and that's Simon's company, 19 management. Why wouldn't it be anything other than Simon's Club? If I was Simon, it would have been called B Club 7.

'We were in a villa in Barbados and in between waterskiing we went through all the scripts'

For the first series of the S Club 7 TV show, Miami 7, *the band travelled to, well, Miami, where they shot thirteen episodes in no time at all. The show's scripts were overseen by Simon's brother and* Spiceworld *pensmith Kim Fuller, who created a fairly depressing world around them. Promised fame and fortune by their management, the fictional band move to Miami only to find themselves penniless and performing for scraps. Each episode would feature a new song, while the opening theme tune to* Miami 7 *– launched in April 1999, two months before any music was officially released – was the (real) band's debut single and first number one, 'Bring It All Back'. The format was repeated in subsequent series, with 2000's* L.A. 7 *– in which Linda Blair co-stars as rollerblading landlady Joni, who accidentally runs Bradley over – led by number-two hit, 'Reach'. The show, which also featured various spin-off TV movies, was sold to 100 countries, attracting 90 million viewers worldwide.*

Colin Barlow: Simon wanted it to look like programmes like *Saved by the Bell* and *Sweet Valley High.* He wanted sunshine. They wanted to film it in America so it didn't just look like a parochial,

UK-based programme. It made people think of it as a global proposition.

Peter Loraine: I can remember sitting in a meeting room trying to explain how it was such a fine line between aspirational and too young and baby-ish. I remember saying, 'It can't look like *Grange Hill*.' We knew we had the slot on BBC at 5.10 p.m., which was the *Byker Grove* slot or the *Grange Hill* slot or the *Blue Peter* slot. I knew it couldn't be like those things; that it needed to have a gloss to it. Simon Fuller turned to me and said, 'Okay, we'll film it in Miami, then.' Literally the colour drained from the face of the person from the BBC as the budget for each episode went through the roof.

Andrew Margetson, director, *Miami 7* and *L.A. 7*: I knew that Simon Fuller and [TV producer] Malcolm Gerrie, who were the main players in the S Club project at the time, were struggling to agree on a director, and someone who worked for Simon put me forward. At the time, I was signed up to do another series of [Channel 4 kids' drama] *Renford Rejects*, which was fun, but shooting in Kensal Green compared to going to Miami . . . I was a young guy. Also, Simon was very charming, very persuasive, he sold it very convincingly. He played me the music, which I liked. I said to him, 'Here's the deal, I want to do the TV series but I also want to make the music videos. I wanted to be 360 on it.' Looking back, I think Simon was very shrewd because he wanted his team helming that project – he didn't want the BBC to control it.

Peter Robinson: It was really well put together because not only was this happening in the UK but the show was in dozens of other countries as well. That plan was done by somebody else first. It was done with [boyband] North & South by [manager] Tom Watkins [in 1998 and 1999]. That was the same sort of idea really – let's have a kids' TV show, *No Sweat*, and then let's launch a band off it. But it didn't really work and maybe it's the songs or the band.

Andrew Margetson: I'd grown up on *The Monkees* and it was always Simon's [reference point] because he'd look up to that show. It wasn't a radical idea, but it was smart to do it with a modern pop act. To use TV to sell records.

Jo: We were often compared to the Monkees and Micky Dolenz came on set one day and we all had a video made of us doing the Monkees walk along the beach.

Andrew Margetson: For me, the challenge was that some of them had done some acting but most of them had done nothing. And there was no casting involved; they're there, that's it. I spent a week with them workshopping, just to build their confidence. I got some actor friends involved. From where they came from to where they ended up is something I'm really proud of. We worked so hard. To run a whole show for thirteen episodes was brutal. I had to stick to the punishing schedule, but we were all kids and we did it.

Jo: [In the show] I was always the tomboy that was good at fixing cars and didn't take much nonsense from anyone. That was given to me but then I did kind of create it myself because it's always fun to play that kind of a character. Because I'm more cockney and the Essex one, it was a natural fit for me to become an *EastEnders* character, I suppose.

217

Bradley: I wouldn't say the character version of myself was accurate. I was willing to play that role. Only aspects were right, like I might be more sleepy, but that was because I was a party guy. That was never explained in the TV show. They made me a ladies' man as well, which I was, but not in that cheesy way. It was like I was Pepé Le Pew.

Andrew Margetson: Kim [Fuller, Simon's brother] controlled the scripts and they were written by a number of people, one of whom was Georgia Pritchett, who is now doing *Succession*. Quite the trajectory. There was a great writers' meeting before the shoot, where Simon flew the writers and me out to Barbados. We were in a villa in Barbados and in between waterskiing and whatever we went through all the scripts. I also remember after shooting one summer, I was with Simon in a villa in the south of France and Lucian Grainge was there. I remember showing them the music video for 'Bring It All Back' and them being wowed by it and thinking, 'Right, this is it, this is how showbiz works.'

Bradley: We did get the job done but there were a lot of times where people would say, 'Right, stop the laughing, guys, stop messing around.' It's like with any group of friends, all you need to do is look at them and you start laughing. We messed about a lot. It didn't feel like work.

Andrew Margetson: [Filming] was going to be difficult because the way I wanted to shoot it, partly because there's seven of them, involved a lot of long takes, so they had to remember a lot of lines. I couldn't break it up into small pieces because the nature of the beast meant that if you gave Jo a close-up you had to give everyone a close-up. Everyone was equally weighted. It put a bit of pressure on them because you'd shoot a three-minute take and then Bradley would screw up the last line. They learned very quickly.

Bradley: [The schedule] was constant. It was five or six days a week. Up at 4 a.m. most days because you had to start shooting at sunrise, so at 6 a.m. It was tough.

Jo: It was easier to just move us all as one, which could be really annoying if on the TV show I might not be in a scene until 2 p.m. but I still had to be picked up at 3 a.m. I'd literally sit around the whole day waiting for my scene, which might be one line.

Andrew Margetson: I remember there were some things in the script they didn't like. Simon had this idea, or maybe it was Kim, that they would have their own language. In those early episodes, there was this word 'parp', which was meant to be like 'rubbish' or 'poo', and they hated saying that. They had this idea that it would spread and every kid in the playground across Britain would be saying 'parp'. That was one of the few things they weren't enthusiastic about, to be honest.

Bradley: Eventually I made friends in LA so after work they'd come to my apartment. I made myself right at home – I bought a PlayStation, I got a music system. We stayed in this place called Oakwood Apartments, which was quite big. Stevie Wonder's son was staying in one of the other apartments and I made friends with him. I was just up until late and then I'd say, 'Guys, you've got to go, I've got two hours until I'm being picked up.'

Andrew Margetson: The constant worry was that they would run off and go crazy. We went into Miami at the end of filming series one and we stayed in a nice hotel on South Beach and I remember Jon, who was only sixteen, got a tattoo. Obviously he just lied about his age. Simon always had someone in charge of looking after the band. I remember later in LA we were put up in the Standard and the first night they went out on Sunset and partied and by the second night they were in a different hotel away in the valley somewhere. They were young so of course they wanted to have fun.

Jo: I shared a room with Rachel. We always wanted to share because we didn't like staying on our own, so we'd be together drinking cups of tea and learning scripts for the next day. I didn't drink and I never went out. I was a bit of a geek.

Bradley: Jo and Rachel were boring. Well, not boring – they were professional, that's what it was. They'd go to bed nice and early and be the first ones in the van in the morning. I'd be the last. But it's not because I was unprofessional – I was living the dream. I was having so much fun.

Andrew Margetson: [The TV show] was very valid and I was always proud of it and of the band. Of course we all want to be the Beastie Boys, but they were credible in a different way. Also: great singles. The target age group is younger, but it's still a valid audience. And it still gave a lot of pleasure to a lot of people.

Jo: We found out really late on the Saturday [that 'Bring It All Back' was number one] because the next day we were performing one of our first ever shows in front of 100,000 people at Party at the Park. Then when we were on stage they stopped everything and Dr Fox came on and announced it and 100,000 people just erupted. It was unbelievable. We were all running around the stage like loonies. Our first album was recorded primarily in Sheffield, but then once the TV show hit off and we were in America we had to keep the albums going at the same time as filming. That's why when we would have a day off from filming it wasn't a day off because we'd have to go straight to the studio.

Bradley: I remember we used to count the days off we had per year and it was less than a week's worth. We had days off but we wouldn't class them as proper days off because we'd be in LA, in our apartment. That's not a day off to me. A day off to me would be with my family and friends at home, not just in a cell.

Jo: We once flew to San Francisco to perform a show and we were literally on stage for fifteen minutes. We then flew straight back.

Hannah Verdier: They worked so hard. I saw them so exhausted that some of them were napping while the other ones were doing the interviews.

'In some way, S Club 7 weren't naff enough'

While the TV show pointed the band at the right audience, the music was key. The band had, after all, been put together as a pop act, with the TV show a surprise addition for many. Their debut album, S Club, released in October 1999 featured a classic mix of hi-energy, frictionless bops and syrupy Hallmark card ballads. Follow-up album 7, which was somehow recorded and released just eight months later, became the band's only number-one album (it stayed in the UK top forty for thirty-eight weeks), with classic ballad 'Never Had a Dream Come True' later giving them their second UK chart-topper and only US top-ten single. They also won a BRIT Award for Best British Breakthrough in 2000, beating the likes of Phats & Small and the Wiseguys. The success was, as ever, well-earned, with the band squeezing in celebrations in the back of minivans.

Peter Robinson: It's not as simple as saying, 'If you put something on TV then people will definitely like the record.' There was something else about S Club, which was the members of the band and the fact that the music was really good.

Andrew Margetson: The way it had worked was when I came on board they had already made that first album. So we made that series and then they made the second album. I know Simon found those songs from the top songwriters – [ex-pop star and songwriting legend] Cathy Dennis was involved. I don't know how they fitted recording in because it seemed to me that we were filming constantly.

Hallgeir Rustan: Our managers Tim Blacksmith and Danny D knew Simon Fuller well and they had a couple of meetings where they played some demos including [what became second single] 'S Club Party'. The brief was short – make songs that would work for the TV series and on the radio. This was a brand-new show, with completely unknown artists, so the second verse of 'S Club Party' [which features a description of each member, à la 'Wannabe'] was made so you got to know them in a funny way.

Simon Ellis: Simon called and said, 'I've got this new band called S Club 7, do you fancy writing some songs for them?' I hadn't really written songs professionally before. So I was like, 'Yeah, I'll give it a go.' Then he said, 'Do you fancy writing with Cathy Dennis?' I knew who she was but Cathy was just starting out [as a songwriter for other people]. We were two relative unknowns in the songwriting world. We got together and wrote [third single] 'Two in a Million' on that first day. We played it down the phone to Simon, with me on piano and Cathy singing, and he said, 'That's a hit.' We looked at each other like, 'This is crazy, it can't be this easy.'

Peter Loraine: It sounds really arrogant but there was no consideration that it wouldn't work. The music was so brilliant, the seven of them were so amazing, the backing from having the TV show was so great. When we started talking to people months before we were going to launch, *Smash Hits* would be like, 'Yeah, we'll put them on the cover.' When you work at a record company you have these planning meetings that are bespoke to an act and you go round the table and ask, 'What have we got at press? What's happening at radio?' With them we'd get to the TV person, who was Nicki Chapman at the time, and she'd say, 'I've confirmed fifty television appearances for them for the first single.'

Paul Flynn: S Club 7 came into the office of my first London job at the *Daily Express*. I worked on a very short-lived men's section for a newspaper called XY. It was the first newspaper response to the massive success of lad mags. [S Club 7] did that thing that I imagine everybody did with newspapers post-Spice Girls, which was they would come in, everyone stops working for a minute, they lip synch to the single and that guaranteed them top spot on the celebrity pages. By Sunday they were number one.

Bradley: With a lot of this stuff, it takes a while to sink in. A lot of the accolades I appreciate more now than I did then. There was so much going on and we were so busy back then. We were really proud to be nominated and to win a couple [of BRIT Awards].

Andrew Margetson: Halfway through filming *L.A. 7* they got a BRIT Award [for British Breakthrough Act] and I remember someone arriving on set with the awards and them having to do a little speech remotely. They were so excited and so happy. It was amazing to see that journey for them.

Simon Ellis: 'Never Had a Dream Come True' very nearly didn't happen. Cathy and I had written a bunch of songs for S Club and we were on a bit of a roll. The day we wrote that song, I pitched up at Cathy's house and the way we do it is I would start playing piano and Cathy would 'la, la, la' some melodies. We started about 11 a.m. and by 7 p.m. we had nothing. All I wanted to do was go home. Cathy said, 'Look, let's just give it another ten minutes and see what happens.' So she went downstairs to make a coffee and while she was doing that I started playing the 'Never Had a Dream Come True' melody and Cathy shouted, 'What's that? That sounds great.' By the time she'd made the coffee and walked up the stairs, she had half the lyric for the chorus, the title and all of the melody for the chorus. We finished it in about twenty minutes.

Jo: We didn't get that much time to digest how big a deal that [US top-ten hit] was. We were already on to the next thing. It is an amazing song and I definitely appreciate it more now.

Simon Ellis: Jo's not only the best singer in the band, she's one of the best singers this country has ever produced. Simon thought it was such a massive hit that no one else was going to sing it; it had to be Jo.

Jo: I would have been happy to share the vocals – it would have been a lot easier for me. Those songs were given to me and you can't say, 'No, I'm not doing it.' But yeah, I did feel a little bit like, 'Ooh, I hope they don't get the hump.' I think every single band in the world has a lead singer. It's very rare that you get a completely mixed band.

Malcolm McLean: In some way, S Club 7 weren't naff enough for me. Even if they had slightly matching outfits they would never do the whole flammable, everyone's wearing tur-quoise version like Steps. S Club definitely thought they were a lot cooler than that and they probably were. Relatively.

Bradley: Like best friends do, you have your bickering moments over little things. You're tired. I was definitely the little bro of the band.

Jo: It was very hard to get space because we were always together working. Or travelling to the next thing. Sometimes it would be really hard to just get half an hour sat in a room by yourself. When we were in tour buses – or that famous radio bus, which was horren-dous, because it was really cramped and small, like an old tin bus –

Jon would put his headphones in, I would put mine in, and we'd all make out we couldn't hear if someone was talking to you. We were known for being very loud, our band, and I'm not naturally a loud person, so sometimes I'd think, 'Please, I need a bit of peace.'

Peter Loraine: If you think of the cycle of a band, they record an album, they tour an album, they promote an album – they did all those things but within it [S Club] were always recording a TV series as well. It was really intense.

Jo: If you didn't get number one it was classed as a failure. When you think back at artists who were dropped when they only made top twenty – it's harsh. There was a lot of pressure on us to get number-one singles and number-one albums, which we did get.

Jordan Paramor, author, *S Club 7: 7 Heaven*: I forgot I did that [book] because I wrote it in a weekend. I did all the interviews over the phone, all in one night. It was a Friday night, one after the other, bang bang bang, and I wrote it all over the weekend. They were in LA so I had to stay up until about 3 a.m. because of the time difference and I'd have an hour with each of them. It was no *War and Peace*.

Jo: We used to feel quite hard done by sometimes, but we were young. Jon was only fifteen. When I think about it that's a baby really.

Paul Flynn: I once went to Venice Beach and interviewed Jon, Bradley and Paul for *Attitude*. *FHM*, who were on the same trip, did the girls for their cover. We were supposed to do the boys on the cover but because Jon hadn't talked about his sexuality in the interview we did them inside. It was completely up to him to talk about it. Our thoughts at the magazine with Jon was that if he doesn't want to talk about it that's fine, it's up to him, but we're not going to cover it up or do any fucking beards. No telling stories about made-up girlfriends.

Nigel Dick, director, *Seeing Double*: It took me about five minutes of meeting [Jon] to suspect that he batted for the other team, as they say. He sort of personified a certain character, a certain personality, which I loved. It was never mentioned. It wasn't like, 'Okay, lads, let's go down the strip club, Jon won't be coming.' There was none of that. No whispering behind backs.

Paul Flynn: With S Club, you can't hide that fizzing energy pop music gives you, particularly in your adolescence, because it dovetails so perfectly – here are these people presented for you to fancy, here's this music that's made to react with your nervous system, and in the middle of that, 'Oh my God, am I having weird feelings about Paul Cattermole? Yes I am, but I can talk about everything else pop is giving me and not about having a sly wank about Bradley.' That's pubescence and that's the way pop music works really brilliantly with it.

Nigel Dick: Subsequently I read an article with him discussing being gay [Jon came out in 2010] and I was like, 'Good for him, I'm happy that he's happy.' The whole theory of a pop band when it's crystallised down to its essence is that you want to have thousands of screaming girls running after you. We weren't quite so emancipated all that time ago [to think] that there might have been a few screaming boys as well.

Jo: We used to like being in America because once we did get famous in the UK it was hard to go out and be free and be yourself, because there would constantly be paparazzi around. You didn't get much time to yourself. The only time you could be 100 per cent yourself was when you were indoors. So when we were in America we loved it over there.

Bradley: As someone who always wanted to be in a band and sing, I'd say a small percentage is actually singing. You're promoting. You're on *Top of the Pops* and it's not because you don't want to sing live, you just haven't got the time to do the rehearsals. You've got seven people, so if you haven't got the right sound engineer you could sound awful. We probably would have anyway. But with a tour you have months of rehearsals and vocal coaches, you work out all your harmonies, you're doing stage rehearsals and you get this beautiful blend. Being on tour was the reason I wanted to be in a band.

Jo: All of our favourite parts of the whole experience were being on tour. I always said I was a singer, but singing was only 20 per cent of my job in S Club. Going on tour was when I was at my happiest. I didn't do a lot of singing in the band, even though I did. If that makes sense.

'We were just about to sign a contract with a certain breakfast cereal . . . Sugar Puffs'

S Club 7's second BRIT Award arrived in 2002, winning Best British Single for stone-cold party starter, 'Don't Stop Movin''. It was a song – their third number one, chart fans – that seemed to elevate them in the eyes of critics and more 'discerning' pop fans from perma-smiling brand ambassadors to something approaching the parameters of credible. That trajectory was helped by the fact that on 20 March 2001 the boys in the band were caught smoking weed and cautioned by the police on the way to the Pepsi Chart Show. *Having been ignored by the tabloids, they were suddenly front-page news.*

Bradley: 'Don't Stop Movin'' was the one where we moved beyond the young kid, teenybopper audience. That one made us cool all of a sudden. Even older people were like, 'It's got a good feel to it, a bit disco, a bit "Billie Jean".'

Simon Ellis: Everybody loves that song. It's one of those timeless classics. Obviously it's a bit of a pastiche of disco and of 'Billie Jean'. Very similar drumbeat and bassline, which me and [co-writer] Sheppard Solomon had for a long time.

Hannah Verdier: I don't know how [S Club 7] got through the net of becoming famous because it felt quite late for that sort of [pop act] in a way. I think 'Don't Stop Movin'' buoyed them, obviously. I remember when they did 'Don't Stop Movin'' we were at *CD:UK* and Paul was telling everyone it was behaving like a number-one record. He was going into the mechanics of it.

Jo: That was our breakthrough single in a lot of ways. We were all kids when we started but then we became adults in the band, so we wanted to do cooler music and be a bit more edgy.

Simon Ellis: The 'Don't Stop Movin'' sessions are legendary in the S Club world. I was working in a studio in Farnham in Surrey. Jo had already been down to sing her bits the day before and the other members had done the backing vocals. I got Bradley in and he turned up about 2 p.m. I turned around to the recording desk and pressed play, but heard nothing from Bradley. He'd obviously been out all night and was fast asleep. So I thought, 'Shit, this is really not going to happen.' We got him to start singing but he sounded like he was still asleep. It was awful. I even thought about getting someone else in to sing it and try to impersonate Bradley. Anyway, I sent Bradley home. Then it got to about midnight – this was the last day in the studio – so I called somebody at 19 management and I said, 'Find Bradley and get him down here.'

Bradley: They needed me to vocal the song, but I was at the club. So they sent a team from 19 management to track me down. I remember someone walked in and said, 'Bradley, we need you at the studio.' I jumped into a car, straight out of a nightclub, and went to the studio.

Simon Ellis: He pitches up with this carrier bag full of beer and goes into the vocal booth. He was out of there by 2 a.m. and went back to the club. Great.

Bradley: The first take is what they ended up keeping. It's me after I'd just woken up, half tipsy.

Colin Barlow: They were really good people. Pop music at that time hadn't yet got to our version of the Gallaghers. We did have Brian Harvey in East 17 but that was as mad as it would go. They were always seen as very pure and that show was always very positive. They were really good role models for kids.

Nikki Whelan: I was a bit more sensitive to everything as a teen. Like when the S Club boys were arrested for smoking cannabis. Find me a boyband that doesn't do that. So tame.

Jo: Do you know what, how silly, for one. I think they were literally walking through Leicester Square. They weren't even supposed to be there because we were filming for the *Pepsi Chart Show* at the Roundhouse in Camden and we had to be on stage in forty-five minutes. Then we got a phone call from someone in the office saying the boys have been arrested and they're at the police station. I remember sitting there thinking, 'What is going on here?'

Nikki Whelan: I'd bunked off school – I was about fifteen – and had gone up to see them at the *Pepsi Chart Show*. There was this little paparazzi guy – I hated him – and we were just wondering why they hadn't turned up. He was like, 'I've just seen them. They went down the road in a police car.' I just thought he was trying to wind us up.

Jo: I don't know how they did it but they let them go and they got to the Roundhouse and we got on stage on time.

Andrew Margetson: I remember thinking, 'Smoking a big spliff in public, come on.' That's pretty mad.

Bradley: There's something really funny around that story. Believe it or not we were just about to sign a contract with a certain breakfast cereal . . . Sugar Puffs. That's why I think people started to say it was a publicity stunt because we lost our deal with Sugar Puffs after we got caught smoking puff. We were just young.

Jo: We went straight back to number one with 'Don't Stop Movin'' after that and we developed the new nickname

Spliff Club 7 for a little while. We went from being a really cheesy band to people thinking we were cool and starting to buy our records.

'I took S Club Juniors trick-or-treating once and we went to Sophie Ellis-Bextor's house'

Keen to keep control of his brand and aware perhaps that it's trickier to control exhausted young adults, in September 2001 Fuller launched a TV show, S Club Search, *to basically find the next S Club 7. The resulting band, S Club Juniors (later rebranded S Club 8 after S Club 7, later S Club, split), were all in their early teens or younger. They scored six UK top-ten singles with Polydor and two of their members – Frankie and Rochelle – later went on to make up two-fifths of Polydor's quite good girl-band the Saturdays.*

Jo: To me, we were just filming another TV show. It was all auditions and getting the babies prepped. Not babies, Juniors.

Bradley: There was a competition on BBC for young kids to get the opportunity to sing alongside S Club 7 and perform with us. Then with the last fifty kids we went to meet them and pick the last eight. There were nine in the beginning but then one of them got a scholarship and it became eight. I hope that scholarship turned out well for him, you know.

Jo: It's when you saw [the final line-up] you started thinking, 'Which one is meant to be my little mini me?' That's what we all thought – we're being ousted here. And there was one more member!

Barry Stone, songwriter and producer: With S Club Juniors, the first thing we did was a song, 'Automatic High', we had written for another band. At the time it came out, it was a bit like, 'Is this suitable for children to be singing?', because it had lyrics about being ready any time. It obviously didn't bother Simon Fuller so we were happy to go with it. I don't think we were that bothered about the lyrical content back then. It didn't really occur to us; we just wrote what sounded good.

Hannah Robinson, songwriter: ['Only You,' from 2002's debut album, *Together*] was my first cut as a songwriter. I knew they were after that '60s pastiche-y sound, which I find quite easy to do. You know what you're trying to achieve. I never met them at all. We just sent the song off and then my publisher called to tell me they'd recorded it.

Colin Barlow: It was hilarious because you had a meeting with mum and dad, plus child, and all of 19 management. I don't think there have been many kiddy bands. They were a lot better than people give them credit for. It was great when we later did the Saturdays because Rochelle and Frankie already had the understanding of how it all worked, so they were on a different level when they went into the band.

Barry Stone: At that time, myself and Julian [Gingell] had a studio – well, a programming room – in the corner of a very big rehearsal building called The Depot on Brewery Road in north London. It was used by people like Blur and Oasis, Elastica, to rehearse for their big tours. So all the indie rock people and we were in the corner making this fun pop music. It was really bizarre when S Club Juniors used to come in because you'd have Chrissie Hynde in the café with all these kids running around. And they had their chaperones and their teachers.

Hannah Verdier: It's difficult to interview kids. It felt weird. Also, they were taking it more seriously than the adults were because they wanted to seem more grown-up.

Peter Loraine: It was done completely by the books. They were allowed to work four hours a day, or six if you got special permission from the council. They were chaperoned, looked after properly, did schooling. It was as good as it could have been.

Barry Stone: They'd have their tutors and all the kids would have their lessons in a separate room. Then we'd grab one of them for our allotted time, which we couldn't go over because we'd get a knock at the door. They couldn't sing with us for too long; I think it was twenty-five minutes at a time. Then we'd have to do the next one. It was a different way of working but we'd get into the rhythm of it. A lot of the times they would also come with a film crew so some of your allotted time would be taken up by pretending to record in front of the cameras. Which was slightly annoying because you needed to get on with stuff but you'd have to push faders up and down for a camera shot.

Peter Loraine: I took S Club Juniors trick-or-treating once and we went to Sophie Ellis-Bextor's house. I remember one of them was cheeky to her.

'It was like spending Saturday morning in Claire's Accessories with a migraine'

A month before S Club Junior's debut single, the Cathy Dennis co-penned 'One Step Closer', their S Club mothership lost a member. On 28 March 2002, Paul Cattermole quit to return to his musical roots, AKA nu-metal noise merchants, Skua. Under contract to finish filming the fourth series of the band's TV show, Paul's departure was written into the script for the Barcelona-based Viva S Club. *For the remaining members, now rebranded S Club, the work continued and they went straight into filming their first (and only) film,* Seeing Double. *A £3.4 million global box office 'smash', it centred around an evil Svengali figure who creates a cloned robot version of the band because he's losing his vice-like grip on the real-life originals. Once again, it was co-written by Simon's brother, Kim Fuller.*

Bradley: Paul wasn't quite feeling it and he wanted to go off and do his own music with his rock band. We were prepared for it. I think we made the right decision in calling ourselves S Club and not S Club 6. It was cool; we're still friends now. We did it the right way, so there wasn't any animosity in the band.

Jo: I think it was the beginning of the end when Paul left. We did go on for another year, but it wasn't the same when he went. S Club 7 is S Club 7, innit, so when you've spent that amount of time as a unit and then one flies the nest it just didn't feel the same. People did have relationships in the band. We weren't told to keep them secret, but we were away a lot. It's not my place to talk about [Paul and Hannah's] relationship. I will say that when they were together they were very happy.

Nigel Dick: One Monday afternoon my phone rings and it's Alan Barnette, who had produced the S Club TV series and was very much in bed with Simon Fuller. He said he was making an S Club movie and asked if he could send me the script that afternoon. Then he said, 'If you like it, I want you to get on a plane to Barcelona on Thursday.' Then he added, 'By the way, the script isn't very good but we're going to make it better.' An hour later, a messenger was on the doorstep with the script. I had a word with my agent, who told me not to do it, but I was like, 'Fuck it, if I say yes, I'm going to spend three months in Barcelona and somebody else is paying for it.'

Bradley: [Filming] was really quick. We could have done a lot more with it, to be fair.

Nigel Dick: The interesting thing when you get to meet a bunch of people who have been together for years is that they have their own internal dialogue. Even if they don't like each other, they still have a common experience. Gradually as you start to spend time around them you start to see the friction between certain band members, but the point is you try to become part of their circle so you can enhance the good parts and cover the less fabulous parts. You want to understand them. And you want them to have trust in you because you're going to be working with them in a very intense environment.

Bradley: Nigel didn't make it feel like work. He'd make us say these funny things before every take, like, 'I am wearing no pants.' Just to get us into this character or whatnot.

Nigel Dick: Kim is a very nice guy, lovely chap, but he felt that he really had the essence of S Club running through his veins. It was clear he didn't. There's one scene where Bradley gets out of the car and there are dogs barking in the distance and he says, 'Who let the dogs out?' I remember questioning this line and Kim said, 'Oh, this is total Bradley.' Of course, on the first day of shooting the movie, Bradley comes up to me and goes, 'I would never say that.' If there had been time I would have said we needed someone else to come in and make the script cooler.

Bradley: Yeah, it was a little bit out of touch right there.

Nigel Dick: Gareth Gates was in it. God knows what stage his career was at at that point. It was like, 'Hey, Gareth, how would you like to play Gareth Gates in this movie?' One afternoon at Heathrow [for a scene featuring cloned pop stars] there was an Elton lookalike, a Madonna lookalike, a Michael Jackson lookalike and actual Gareth Gates all climbing on the same plane. For the band, the trickiest thing was the clones. 'Okay, in this scene am I a clone or am I my real movie self?'

Bradley: I didn't know who I was from time to time. At one point in the film, I can see it now, I'm playing it almost robot-like when I'm in the shower and I definitely played that wrong. If it wasn't for the clothes we were wearing, I wouldn't know which character I was.

Nigel Dick: To be fair to them, if you were Robert De Niro or Meryl Streep, you walk on set on the morning and you've got three Meryl Streeps to worry about – there's Meryl, there's

Meryl in the movie and there's Meryl the robot version. You could go to RADA for twenty years and not come up with a good solution for that. If it was confusing for them, I can guarantee it was confusing for me. In some scenes, half of them were the S Clubbers and half were the clones. So you had robotic Jon and real Jon in a scene with himself.

Jo: At that time, I had disintegrating crumbled discs in my lumbar twelve and thirteen. One of them was crumbling and the one underneath was under pressure so it was bulging, which caused it to sit on the sciatic nerve. The last few months of the band I was very highly medicated. I was on a lot of painkillers. I had to stop dancing. I could just about walk. That was a tough time because I was in agony for a lot of that last bit.

Nigel Dick: We had to come up with an endless bunch of gags to explain why Jo wasn't with the rest of them. It was a very strange dynamic because it would be like setting up the opening of 'A Hard Day's Night' and the four guys are running towards the camera, only Ringo's in a wheelchair.

Bradley: It was easier for her because there were scenes she didn't have to film. There's a scene where we're running through the streets of Barcelona and, when we get to the place, Jo's just waiting there on the side of the road. They had to write that in because she couldn't do all the running.

Nigel Dick: Essentially the speed with which I became the director and the movie went ahead was because they'd just finished shooting their last series, so all the machinery was in place – the art department, the art director, the AD, the cameraman. For some reason, the director who had been working on the last series got let go or jumped ship. If we shut it all down and turned it on again later, it would cost a bunch of money that people didn't have. These external forces govern the making of these things.

Jo: I have watched [the film] since. It's a cracker, innit . . . I tried to get my little boy to watch it and the first time he was too young to care and now he's too old to care. He's not one bit interested.

Bradley: Apparently that film is great hangover TV – we're trying to get it on Netflix.

Peter Bradshaw, film critic, *The Guardian*: Watching *Seeing Double* was like spending Saturday morning in Claire's Accessories with a migraine, or like witnessing the origin myth of a tween supervillain combo or pre-adolescent fascist dictatorship.

Pete Whelan: We wanted to go [to the *Seeing Double* premiere]. Not just stand outside, but actually go. The daytime soap *Doctors* was filmed in Birmingham where I lived at the time and so I phoned up S Club's record company and was like, 'I'm Christopher Timothy from *Doctors*' agent and he wants to bring his two kids to the S Club premiere.' They asked how many tickets we wanted and where to send them.

Nigel Dick: It played in Leicester Square. My two goddaughters, who were in their teens, were in the movie, so they came to the premiere with me. We arrived in a limo and there were loads of screaming fans. It was nice to have that moment. Then the next day the band fucking disbanded. Guys, could you not have waited! Could you not have sucked it in for a few more days?

'The level of their popularity is so hard to come by'

On 21 April 2003, almost four years to the day since they launched with Miami 7, *S Club announced they were to split while on stage in London during their S Club United tour (support came from, you guessed it, the newly christened S Club 8). Despite recently signing a contract extension, the warning signs had been there for a while. The previous November's fourth album,* Seeing Double, *had stalled at seventeen, while the album's disco-tinged lead single, 'Alive', had peaked at number five. The pep and infectious enthusiasm of those early singles had been replaced by something more undeniably desperate. In June, the band released a thirteen-track 'best of' called* Best: The Greatest Hits of S Club 7, *which peaked at number two.*

James Masterson: Downloading took off between 2002 and 2004 and you see that in the way the CD single market precipitously dropped. Newer music fans came along and said, 'Why do we need to pay for music? I can just click onto Napster and there's my music collection.' You then saw that with the steady decline of the cheery, chirpy pop acts. What always tends to happen is whenever the younger audience goes missing, the charts start to skew older. That was why acts such as the Killers, Keane and Coldplay were the people who were dominating the charts around that era.

Jo: I think there was a sense of relief because I needed it to be over. I'd had enough. I just wanted to feel normal again. I didn't know what feeling normal was, actually. I didn't really know who I was as Jo O'Meara. I was always Jo from S Club and I was always that character. You do then want peace. I hadn't had that for nearly six years.

Bradley: I think a lot of us were exhausted by that point. We were so tired, we were so overworked, we were ready to see what was next. Some people wanted to go into TV, some wanted to do their own albums, some just wanted to go on holiday for six months.

Simon Ellis: For me personally, after 'Don't Stop Movin'' it felt like things were coming to an end. Simon [Fuller] called me and said, 'We need another "Don't Stop Movin"'.' That's always a mistake, because you'll never better the original. There are so many elements that come together when you're writing a pop song that have to be right and if one element is off then it misses. 'Alive' is a little bit like painting by numbers. It went to number five and everyone was like, 'Meh, it didn't go to number one.' It didn't go to number one because it wasn't as good as 'Don't Stop Movin''.

Peter Loraine: It made me really sad when S Club wanted to break up. I understood why, but I wondered at that time if maybe they couldn't see the wood for the trees. The level of their popularity is so hard to come by. When you step out of the group, whatever group it is, it's very hard to maintain that as a solo artist. Very few people have.

Jeremy Joseph: We always wanted to be part of a band's history. We did the very last thing S Club did together. They split on stage at G-A-Y. When you're no longer making money for a label or management, they don't care about you any more. They were just going to finish it on a low and we said, 'Come on, let's finish it on a high.' And as a band they said, 'Yes please.'

Bradley: We always had a great relationship with the G-A-Y audience and the guys there because it was pretty much the only club gigs we'd ever do. We were so busy we didn't have time to do that stuff, so it was either do a tour or do your TV stuff. It was great and we always got a great response from the crowd.

Jordan Paramor: S Club 7 worked so hard, my God. I think the sad thing is now, they're looking back and going, 'Where's the money?'

Jo: You can look at it in all different ways. All I can say is we probably could have done better [financially], but we could have done a whole lot worse. I've had a career out of it and I still have a career out of it today.

Bradley: It's up for debate really. I did a lot with my money. I invested it and still do today. My dad was the one who put me on to that because he saw I was spending a hell of a lot. I'd fill up two or three taxis with my mates and I'd pay. Then when we got to the club I'd put my card down. My dad was like, 'At the end of all this, what are you going to have to fall back on?' I bought my first property in 2000 and from there it just grew. We earned a lot of money. Maybe in comparison to Simon Fuller it doesn't seem a lot.

Jo: Not knowing what was next, or what I was supposed to be doing, was a huge shock. I'd just come out of something that was so military and then it stopped so quickly. I didn't know how to be without it. We were told what to do, told where to go, told when I'm eating. Literally everything was done for me; the only thing I had to think about was the job I had to do.

Bradley: I always wanted to do music. I always thought I would be in music, which is why I didn't take school too seriously. When you're that young, the world is all a bit of a dreamland. This little south London boy who wasn't sure where he was going, one day ends up in a band and then ends up performing for the Queen at her Golden Jubilee [in June 2002]. I was in disbelief, like, 'How did I get here?' Everyone was in the room – the Queen, the prime minister, Prince Charles, William and Harry. It was so intimidating, all these grand paintings. Who gets the chance to go to the Queen's palace?

Five months after the split was announced, Rachel Stevens released her debut solo single, 'Sweet Dreams My LA Ex', which peaked at number two. Between 2003 and 2005, Rachel scored four more top-ten singles and landed two top-thirty albums (including 2005's cruelly ignored *Come and Get It*). In 2006, Bradley briefly joined Upper Street, a boyband hybrid featuring members of Steps, 911, Another Level and New Kids on the Block, while Tina took a break from music. Hannah and Jon, meanwhile, moved into acting. In the ensuing years, various iterations of S Club would go on to perform at clubs and universities, before S Club 7 reunited for an arena tour in 2015. They reunited again in February 2023 to announce another tour to mark their twenty-fifth anniversary.

7

Re-rewind:
UK garage's pop absorption

Pop absorbs, recontextualises and manipulates the genres around it, hoovering up the best bits and bolting them on. By the late '90s, UK garage, incubated in south London, was starting to move from an underground movement and into the top ten. Inspired by garage house and taking elements from R&B, jungle and dance-pop, UK garage, with its percussive bounce and sun-kissed, chilled Champagne feel, was the perfect playground for pop. It's where Victoria Beckham ventured in 2000 and the genre Liberty X dabbled in for their debut single a year later. But the genre's truly defining mainstream crossover star, Craig David, emerged in late 1999 via 'Re-Rewind (The Crowd Say Bo Selecta)', an effects-laden, catchphrase-heavy garage megabanger that would later come to define him. A number-two smash, it saw him collaborate with fellow Southampton residents Artful Dodger, AKA Mark Hill and Pete Devereux, with the former going on to produce Craig's classic debut album, 2000's *Born to Do It*. Evidence of both UK garage's pop appeal and the influence of Craig's success arrived swiftly, with labels quick to commission chart-friendly garage remixes for the likes of new pop-R&B crossover girlband Mis-Teeq, AKA Alesha Dixon, Sabrina Washington and Su-Elise Nash.

While Craig's first single proper, 'Fill Me In' (a UK number one) carried the fluttering rhythms of two-step garage, the rest of *Born to Do It* cast its creator not as a soundsystem MC, but as an edge-free, pop-leaning, R&B impresario ready to take on his US counterparts.

'The closest thing I can link it to would be riding a surfboard on top of a wave'

Craig David: The first garage record I can remember is a song by Scott Garcia called 'It's a London Thing' in 1997. It came onto my radar in one of the Southampton clubs I was performing at called the Old Oriental. Mark Hill and Pete Devereux were playing upstairs in the house and garage room and I was downstairs in the R&B/hip-hop room with DJ Flash. I was an MC at the time. I was hearing this song and I was like, 'What is this?' Then I started getting into more of the vibe that the Artful Dodger were playing, where it was sampling R&B tracks and putting them over this new rhythm, which was going through a phase of being speed garage or garage or two-step. It was still trying to find its feet.

Chantelle Fiddy: At that time, I lived in Bedfordshire, in a little village, but I used to live in Southampton. So when Craig

David first appeared it was like, 'Oh my God, someone famous from Southampton, who is also good-looking.' I thought he was the shit.

Craig David: I had put out a song with the Artful Dodger called 'What Ya Gonna Do' [in 1998] and that was my first experience of going to London and hearing pirate radio stations as soon as I hit the M25. It was R&B but it was over a garage beat. There were these great R&B sampled vocals that were being used. It was just a euphoric time.

Chantelle Fiddy: The thing you have to remember about garage, and I don't know how to say this in PC terms, but there was a big part of it that was very Essex. Very cheesy. There was this idea that the cheesier you made the vocals, i.e. sped-up R&B vocals, you're going to get the women in the dance and the more women in the dance the more men you'll get. A lot of it was played with that view in mind.

MNEK: Garage was a real home-grown sound and it was able to take all the best things we love about pop music and make it faster. Before then we'd seen house and we'd seen techno and we'd seen disco, but it was usually four to the floor, but garage was more rhythmic and it spoke to Black people. Of course we've seen homogenised versions of it over the years, but everyone knows the real thing when you hear a So Solid record or a Craig record or the Artful Dodger or Mis-Teeq. Anything produced by Sunship, that's the real stuff. Everything else is garage lite.

Ceri Evans, AKA Sunship: The one thing that really attracted me to UK garage was that it was a little bit of everything. The more commercial stuff was obviously less dark. Something like the Artful Dodger stuff that crossed over is quite bubblegum, feel-good. It's got that throwaway, happy-go-lucky feel, like [Sunship's remix of Sweet Female Attitude's] 'Flowers' to a certain extent.

Craig David: I didn't know ['Rewind'] would be as successful on a commercial level. That people would hear it outside of my circle, which was Artful Dodger and my mum, basically. I was living at home at the time.

Chantelle Fiddy: It wasn't like you heard all these stories like, 'Oh, yeah, Craig David's been rolling with drug dealers, he's a bad boy, he's got a long list of offences.' He was a nice guy. You had these two scenes running parallel. You always had this underground. I went to Aya Napa with So Solid and that was my first experience of being in the club with people buying up all the Champagne just to pour it on the floor so you could dance in it. That was the excess of UK garage in that world. So if you don't want to be in that lane you've got the more inno-cent, commercial lane.

Craig David: ['Fill Me In'] was the song that once I played it to the record label I was so proud. That song to me has all the sensibility of my roots in garage but at the same time this infec-tious guitar. I think originally Mark was playing [the guitar riff] as part of a remix for a song by a boyband. I had to say to him, 'Woah, what's this?' I was like you need to give them a different guitar riff because that's mine.

Chantelle Fiddy: If you look at the lyrics it was very of the moment. He was definitely appealing to – and we don't use the word 'urban' any more – what was deemed at the time as this 'urban' audience and I think that was quite a new thing in the UK. In inner cities you'd always have pockets of Black music that wasn't popular elsewhere, but this was taking it outside of that. He's not from London; he's from Southampton. Every teenager could relate to that story [in 'Fill Me In'] of the parents coming home. It was a bit naughty.

Craig David: I adopted this [story-telling lyrical] style while I was listening to the R&B of that time, but also before that it would have been Terence Trent D'Arby and Michael Jackson. Then also a lot of the reggae that my dad would play to me. It was like, 'Take me by the hand and walk me through what you're trying to portray,' but then at the same time having the ability to keep it generic enough so it doesn't feel like my story and no one else could tap in.

Max Giwa, co-director, 'Fill Me In': The one thing [the label] stipulated was that they wanted a narrative-driven music video as opposed to just a normal video where it's him perform-ing with loads of girls. Craig came from the pirate radio scene so [the video's intro] was a homage to that. A nod back to where he started from. It was their moment. The pioneers of a British movement were these kids: Craig, So Solid, Wiley, Dizzee.

Craig David: To have a number one, to be on *Top of the Pops*, to have artists I was a fan of be fans of my music, it was so sur-real. It was like, 'Someone pinch me.' The closest thing I can link it to in terms of a metaphor would be riding a surfboard on top of a wave and never feeling like you were coming off of it. The view was beautiful, the vibe was great. Everything I had felt was being mirrored back to me in the world. It was incredible.

Hannah Verdier: Craig David was the first [UK garage star] we covered [in *Smash Hits*]. We did a double cover with him and Samantha Mumba. We had Luck and Neat on the cover, and Oxide and Neutrino as well. That is the last time, around the early '00s, where music was homogenous. Pretty much it was all one genre and you'd know the words to everything. You couldn't escape it.

Jamelia: I had to do shows with [the pop stars of the time] but I wasn't really a fan. I think I was fighting inner demons because I knew I didn't want to be a pop artist. I did love a couple of songs by All Saints and a couple by Girls Aloud, but they weren't me. I wanted to be like Mary J. Blige.

Su-Elise Nash, Mis-Teeq: The idea was we'd be an R&B girlband. That's where we thought we were going to go. [Late '90s girlband] N-Tyce and Eternal had been pretty big in the UK at least and definitely in my atmosphere and my environment. They would have been groups I would have looked up to. So that girl-group model is kind of what we were looking at at that stage.

Lee Thompson: The Box played everything that was doing well in the chart. We had a very good relationship with Relentless, who were putting out Daniel Bedingfield, DJ Pied Piper, So Solid. They were huge Box crossover records, absolutely.

Chantelle Fiddy: It was at that time in the industry where if you got the right remix – like Mis-Teeq did with [debut single, 2001's]

'Why?' – everything changed overnight. They went top ten with their debut single.

Su-Elise: 'Why?' was a really beautiful R&B song, but that remix [by Matt 'Jam' Lamont and DJ Face] really put us on the map. There weren't any other girl groups doing garage music. It was something we were all listening to in the clubs and party-ing to, but it wasn't something that had been done. It was very male-dominated, garage music, at that time. There weren't a lot of female artists exploring that genre. How it took off was abso-lutely amazing. It was what we all wanted but it wasn't anything we had ever thought would come so quickly as it did.

Chantelle Fiddy: I think the thing that really stood out for them was having Alesha [Dixon] MC-ing. It wasn't always the best, but you could easily get people involved with it, which is half the battle with pop.

Ceri Evans: She sounded like the real deal.

Chantelle Fiddy: The only other female MC around at that time was Ms Dynamite and she was very very authentic. Alesha wasn't that – she was from Welwyn Garden City.

Su-Elise: Alesha had been experimenting with MC-ing from the beginning so we were like, 'Yeah, let's do that, that's a cool touch.' We would all go out, we would party at TwiceasNice, that was the rave to be at back then. That was all garage. Guys like Mikee B and [DJ] Spoony are the ones that championed us at the start. In order to get that first hit we had to do so much graft. We were going to every PA in every club in every corner of the UK. Giving the DJs the track, saying, 'Please can you play this.' Of course we had help from our team, but we were signed to a pretty small independent label at that stage. When we then got to work with Sunship on [UK number two] 'All I Want', it was such an honour.

Ceri Evans: I also did [remixes for Craig David of] 'Rendez-vous', 'Fill Me In', 'Walking Away', '7 Days', too. I very largely contributed to keeping him credible. There was a big divide between the signed pop stuff and the real underground. [Pop stars] were literally queuing up to have the remixes from me. I made the most of it financially: I was getting up to £15k a remix, which in those days wasn't bad. I could turn them over in three or four days. I did Christina Aguilera and Mary J. Blige remixes, too. I think that was more the labels wanting to get some more sales in the UK – it was all about money, money, money.

Chantelle Fiddy: When you look at [Daniel Bedingfield's] 'Gotta Get Thru This', there's a bit of beef around it. The version that was really popular originally said 'DND Edit' and that's Artwork from Magnetic Man. I remember interviewing Daniel and he got very angry about it – he felt like he'd done all the work and they'd added a few touches and they were getting the credit. But I wonder if the idea of putting 'DND Edit' at the end was to give it that co-sign – that this is someone on the garage scene.

Ceri Evans: [Pop absorbing UK garage] probably did upset the purists. I'd been making music since 1980, so the top of my list is survival. If you can say you're a purist then fantastic, good for you, but very few people can afford to be. Why am I going to complain about the way a scene's going if people are putting sustenance my way for myself and my family?

Su-Elise: You've got to remember R&B in the UK, apart from Craig David, hadn't really crossed into the mainstream that much. It was more American artists. So to be doing something really left [with UK garage] felt really good. We had our own niche and we were putting our own stamp on things.

'Craig David is a legend, so no BRIT Award can define him now'

By the time of the 2001 BRIT Awards, Born to Do It *— the fastest-selling debut by a British solo male artist in the UK and a million-seller in America — had spent over five months in the UK top ten. Having side-stepped away from garage thanks to musical sex diary '7 Days' and MOR ballad 'Walking Away', Craig was one of pop's biggest superstars. As a result, he was the most nominated artist at the BRITs, with six nods, including Best Single for '7 Days' and Best Album. In the end, he walked away (apols) with zero awards, losing every category to a white artist. To make matters worse, he'd also been booked to perform, with the leaked results at least allowing him to work a jibe at the snub into his live version of 'Fill Me In'. It felt like the music industry had welcomed Craig to the party — in fact, they'd sold tickets to the party off the back of his success — only to piss in his Champagne. For the BRITs, and their sporadic use of the Best Urban Act award category, it wouldn't be the first time they'd be accused of ignoring the successes and cultural dominance of Black artists.*

Marvin Humes, VS and JLS: One of the biggest music industry scandals of all time was Craig David not winning a

BRIT Award. He's one of the most influential, pioneering artists. He created his own music. Look, it's not the be-all and end-all, but Craig was so original when he came onto the scene. It's not spoken about enough how important and influential Craig David was to the music industry in our country.

Craig David: It was a strange period because firstly I was shocked I'd been nominated for that many. I will say that Bono going up on stage and singing 'One' and then going into 'Walking Away' was a huge moment for me. The original of 'Walking Away' had used a sample of 'One', which we couldn't get cleared, but then for him to show homage performing it to me as an eighteen-year-old kid at the BRITs was incredible. People like Elton John were on stage saying, 'If there's a better singer in the UK than Craig David then I'm Margaret Thatcher.' Dane Bowers had gone up and said a piece about how it was a travesty. It was front page of *The Sun* because it had already leaked that I hadn't won. If I'd have ended up winning just one, it would have been like, 'Okay, cool,' but to be nominated for six and get nothing and for that to happen around it – it was more memorable than actually winning.

Jamelia: Being nominated for a [BRIT] was just as great as a win [Jamelia was nominated eight times with no wins]. It meant that I was being recognised. As you get older and wiser, you do start to recognise things like [being nominated for Best Urban Act in 2005]. I think one of the really interesting things when it comes to Black artists behind the scenes, especially at that time, is we had a shared experience that was not only unique to us but that we had to keep a secret. We didn't want to lose our jobs. There were many conversations about things like that: 'Why is there an urban category? What does "urban" mean?'

Su-Elise: I didn't have a problem with that categorisation. I owned that. R&B music didn't come from pop music; that's not where it originated from, you know. It's its own weapon and I think acknowledging that is not a negative thing. Maybe you don't want to be pigeon-holed into a category and that I can understand, because it can be hard once you're seen as something to branch out.

Jamelia: At the time, 'urban' translated as 'Black'. So anybody doing any type of music that had a Black person singing was thrown into the urban category. But all the other categories were singled out by music.

Su-Elise: As we were taking this journey with Mis-Teeq, everything was starting to open up. Garage music stopped being seen as underground. When we're talking about urban, we're talking about music coming from the streets.

MNEK: The importance of those award shows was much greater then. It felt like that's all that mattered. If you had a BRIT or a Grammy, it could change your life. Craig David is a legend, so no BRIT Award can define him now. He's done wonders for any Black boy doing R&B music from the UK.

Chantelle Fiddy: [Craig] was the first time I'd heard somebody who was Black-British doing something in that R&B world and making it really cool. It was uplifting.

Tisha Martin, the 411: We were touted as the 'hip-hop Supremes' with our first single [2004's 'On My Knees'] and there really wasn't anything like our sound coming out of the UK at that time.

Carolyn Owlett, the 411: I think behind the scenes we were a bit of a risk. Our A&Rs really had to push hard for our deal. The head of Sony at the time didn't believe we would work at all so getting the green light to even make an album was a struggle.

Tisha: For our first single to go in at number four shows there was obviously some acceptance of UK R&B girlbands!

Jamelia: People like Craig and people like the Sugababes, I saw them as doing the same thing I was doing, which is, 'We know we want to do R&B but we can't because we're British and we're in the UK.' So it was kind of like pop/R&B. But I wanted to be an R&B artist. I grew up in inner-city Birmingham. My ambitions included being a forensic scientist first of all, until I realised I'd have to deal with dead people. Then I wanted to be a midwife until I realised I had to deal with the downstairs of every female. Then I went to Notting Hill Carnival for the first time when I was fifteen years old. I used to record tapes of myself singing and pretend they were my album. My London cousins took the tape and put it into the hi-fi system to embarrass me, but they were like, 'This is really good.' The next day at Carnival my cousin spoke to one of the DJs and told him I could sing. I was horrified. I ended up getting on stage and singing 'Right Here' by SWV. Weirdly an A&R man who worked at EMI was in the crowd and he approached my mum and asked if she would be okay with bringing me in for a meeting. That conversation ended with him offering me a record deal that was more than my mum's annual salary.

MNEK: Every Black artist has to ask, 'What do I have to do to get to the next level?' There is a limit with R&B music both sonically and also commercially.

Tanya Boniface, the 411: Americans do R&B really well because it's where true Rhythm and Blues originated. They pump a lot of money into their acts to help break them and it shows. The belief is there. For example, we had to drop two top-five singles before [Sony] would sign off on our album! If we had the same level of investment and nurturing and label support that the US acts get, I am certain we would have had a really long and fruitful career.

Jamelia: There was an element of code switching, like, 'If you want to be here, this is what you have to do.' I was okay with that because I still got to make R&B records, they just weren't the singles. The songs that were chosen as singles were always pop/R&B. 'Superstar' wasn't my favourite choice. People are always surprised when I say I was literally crying in the studio when I was told I had to record that song. I hated it. It was so pop. Also, it had been number one for a Danish *Popstars* contestant [Christine Milton], so for me it felt like I was taking something from someone. That didn't sit well with me.

Carolyn: I think the label struggled with where our sound should sit. Especially after we released 'On My Knees' and then followed up with 'Dumb', which was far more pop. The decision to head back towards a more urban sound with 'Teardrops' felt like they were trying to keep us that little bit cooler. At the end of the day, pop sells far more units than R&B in the UK, so they were brave to do that.

Tisha: 'Teardrops' was a song none of us wanted and then when it didn't land in the top five we lost the label's fire around us as a band.

Carolyn: There were several studio sessions where our A&R visited and announced, 'If it's not top five, you're out.' That says it all really. Everything always had to be done under so much pressure, with such high expectations and within such a short time frame.

Jamelia: My music videos sometimes cost a quarter of a million pounds and people aren't making videos like that any more. I'd had my second daughter in 2005 and so the label basically bought one of the flats near where I lived and all the producers would just come there [to record 2006's 'Walk with Me']. I could go home and breastfeed my daughter and then get back to the studio. I'm sure they're not doing that sort of shit now. That's why I owed the label £11 million after I finished. They wrote it off, so it's cool. But £11 million does not surprise me – I was taking private jets to places.

'In the UK industry, it is not fun to feel like there's this fucking ceiling'

If Born to Do It *had been an R&B album with some of the mannerisms of UK garage, by 2002's second album* Slicker Than Your Average,

Craig had ditched the pretence. In many ways it was a smart move, as garage's success was waning, but for some people Craig was so embedded in the commercial rise of such a quintessentially British genre that a move to a more Americanised sound felt jarring. From the title down to the high-gloss sheen of the video for ludicrous Willy Wonka-tastic lead single, 'What's Your Flava?', people were suspicious of Craig's motives. It felt like the bubble had burst as his success slowly started to morph into caricature.

Chantelle Fiddy: The nail in the coffin for UK garage was Victoria Beckham and Dane Bowers' 'Out of My Mind' [released in August 2000]. Overnight, nobody could fuck with it in the way they used to. I think it was also overkill of Sweet Female Attitude's 'Flowers' as well [released in the same week as 'Fill Me In', it peaked at number two behind it]. That was a very divisive song and a divisive commercial highlight for garage. A lot of the tracks that are synonymous with garage to the mainstream aren't what would be synonymous to the underground.

Ceri Evans: UK garage ruined itself. The music took a darker turn and with that it became more aggressive. It peaked and it was actually quite incredible how quickly it all stopped. For a few years after, it was a dirty word. It was a bit like someone coming out as Tory now – you just don't say it because you'll be vilified. You couldn't say you were anything to do with garage.

Craig David: It was a strange period for me. Everything had been working up to *Born to Do It* and there was also this feeling of how to recreate something that had been my whole life up to this one album. A lot of people were saying, 'Just keep doing what you're doing.' I think me and Mark Hill had done something so special [on that debut] that with everything else we were trying to replicate what we'd done. It felt like we were on the back foot a bit. By that point we knew what worked, whereas before we didn't and that was the fun of it. But I was getting a good rapport with a production team called Ignorants, who were doing a lot of remixes at the time. It was a new energy.

Max Giwa: A lot of the urban artists of that era wanted to have their own identity and the ones that then crossed over felt they had to capture the American market, so when they came back people would say, 'Oh, you've gone American,' but the British sound had moved on. It's about trying to adapt.

Dania Pasquini: Now they're quite proud to sound British. They don't have to Americanise themselves to make money in the States. It's global now.

MNEK: Garage is so British and the British have a weird sense of loyalty when it comes to things like that. They say the same thing about Adele now she's in LA doing her thing and doesn't want to live in Tottenham no more. After a while, especially being a person of colour in the UK industry, it is not fun to feel like there's this fucking ceiling.

Ceri Evans: With Craig, he didn't want to do a weird, quirky dance genre; he wanted to be a global superstar. You don't become that making UK garage. But the attraction of UK garage was its originality; it was ours. At the time, there was some amazing R&B from America, but it was all so clinical and clean. We liked the rough edges over here.

MNEK: When you go to America, where there's ample opportunities for artists of colour, it's appealing. Craig, Jamelia and Mis-Teeq were all acts who were inspired by American R&B because that was the only R&B that was being pushed like that. America is always pegged as the place where things are bigger and better. That is tempting. If they kept doing the British thing it would have been nice for everyone else, but would we still be paying attention now?

Hallgeir Rustan: Mis-Teeq were England's answer to Destiny's Child. It was Girl Power at its best and it shone through in the songs and attitude of the vocals. 'Scandalous' still works on radio and in clubs. When it entered the top forty in the US, we realised it was possible to succeed there as well. It gave us motivation to have more faith in what we were doing.

Su-Elise: In the US, 'Scandalous' was picked to replace Britney Spears' 'Outrageous' in *Catwoman*. Not a big stretch from 'Outrageous' to 'Scandalous', is it? So we got to feature in a Hollywood blockbuster, which really helped.

Chantelle Fiddy: There was this big thing of, 'You have to conquer America.' You get a little bit of success at home and then you start changing your formula to hit the American market. If you look at So Solid's second album [2003's *2nd Verse*], no garage, all rap. It was absolutely awful. I could see exactly what was going to happen, but you got gassed because somebody in the label told you it was a good idea and you're going to crack this market and make all this money.

Max Giwa: We wanted to make glossy, beautiful videos but it would be British and we weren't trying to chase the Americans. If they wanted us, they'd come and get us. We wanted to stand out in the crowd. We wanted to create our own visual stamp so people could identify you and say, 'I want that for my artist.' We made brands out of these people. Craig is still going today and people still talk about 'Walking Away', '7 Days', the hat.

Craig David: I felt like 'What's Your Flava?' was so different that it was going to be a Marmite song for some people. It ended up being one of my biggest synced records in terms of getting various different restaurant chains using it. As you can imagine.

MNEK: Garage is a culture. It's beyond the genre. Craig would have his singles that were R&B but he's known for the garage records because they're quintessentially British and they were distinctive. There was no one doing what he was doing at that time. That's why he got pigeon-holed in that way. To be able to do those records and still maintain your Blackness is a great thing and something he shouldn't let go of, and I think he knows that.

Craig David: The slippery slope you could get into is that if you define yourself by numbers then I could easily look at *Slicker Than Your Average*, an album that sold 3.5 million albums, and compare that to *Born to Do It*, which did 7 million. The record label were projecting [*Slicker Than Your Average*] would be 10 million, so as an artist at the time I was buying into that, like, 'Oh, is it not hitting right?' I look at 3.5 million now and think, 'What the hell are you talking about?' I'd take that all day every day.

Chantelle Fiddy: I was sent to LA to interview Justin Timberlake for *Justified* [in 2002] for *Touch* magazine. I was the only music journalist on the trip. Then *Touch*'s editor at the time, Toussaint Davy – bearing in mind we all knew how big that album was going to be – made a decision to put Craig on the cover instead. For that second album. I remember being in the office going, 'What are you doing?' I think part of Tous's rationale was just wanting someone Black to win, you know. You don't want the white guy in America to win. You want the Black guy in the UK to win. But the music just didn't cut it, sadly.

Jamelia: Eventually, I felt more comfortable being in the indie rock world [than the pop world] because in my head they were real musicians. Coldplay were on the same label as me and our A&R guy told me that Chris Martin wanted to meet me. I was a massive fan so I was like, 'You what, mate?' Chris was in the studio recording and invited me down. I remember at the time Gwyneth Paltrow was banging on about this macrobiotic diet she was on and so the first thing I was astonished by was the fact she was sitting there eating chocolate digestives. I was thinking, 'Well, that's not part of your diet.' Then she said to me, 'I think you're the greatest soul singer alive.' I was like, 'What?' Chris is at the piano and he asks me to sit down next to him and just 'vibe'. I'd never worked like that before, but we built [2004's 'See It in a Boy's Eyes']. To be a Black girl from Birmingham that then goes and picks up a *Q* Award [for Best Single] – are you mad? Looking back now, I was allowed in because I was with Chris Martin. On the wall in my office I've got a picture of Bono kissing my hand at the *Q* Awards. The

Mercury Music Prize nomination [in 2004, for *Thank You*] – what? I know now you have Black artists being nominated, but at the time we weren't in that space.

'I got the feeling he wanted to show off the ways I was failing'

First broadcast in 2002 on Channel 4, comedian Leigh Francis' surrealist sketch show Bo' Selecta! *was an instant hit. Built around celebrity stalker Avid Merrion, it saw Francis don (both white and black) latex masks to appear as everyone from Mel B to Elton John to Kelly Osbourne. Michael Jackson was represented as a foul-mouthed hospital patient. The central character, however, was Craig David, played as an egotistical Yorkshireman with a plastic kestrel called Kes. The show, and its various spin-offs, ran until 2006, before returning for a two-part special in 2009 following Jackson's death. For Craig, no longer a commercial powerhouse, the show quickly turned him into a figure of ridicule. It also represented the public face of how Black artists were being treated behind the scenes, with a long-standing assumption – that Black faces don't sell magazines – now contorted into fact.*

Craig David: There was a relentless onslaught from [Leigh Francis], which I could never quite understand. The show was obviously called *Bo' Selecta!* and it was referring to one of my biggest hits, 'Rewind'. So what had been – well, it still is, because the song has stood the test of time – a cultural reference to when people were getting really hyped in the club and they wanted the DJ to rewind the song – something so entrenched in the culture and garage music that we were celebrating – had this guy continuously poking fun at it. But then also at me.

263

Chantelle Fiddy: I think [*Bo' Selecta!*] really undermined him as a person and him as an artist and him being taken seriously.

Ceri Evans: There's an amazing video online of his manager at the time, Colin Lester, blowing his stack because people were saying that *Bo' Selecta!* ruined his career. We just thought it was a bit funny. We thought it was amazing that mainstream shows were talking about someone we knew.

Craig David: The impact it had on me was I was trying to save face and trying to hold it down and be like the music is the thing. But it wasn't like I didn't feel it every time someone was shouting my name in a northern accent. I got the feeling he wanted to show off the ways I was failing. Like when he went to America it wasn't about success, it was about how it wasn't working. I was thinking, 'Did I do something to you?' I had to just ride the storm and I'm so thankful that the second wave of my music happened and that made it more poignant for me. Not sweeter because I'm not one to hold onto grudges or sip from the poisoned chalice, because I'm done with that. That's so dead in the water now. People recognising the music and who I am as an artist is a blessing.

Chantelle Fiddy: Let's also not forget these were the days where most magazines would be like, 'Well, we've got one Black artist in this month.' Forget the fact you've got twenty white artists in. It was very hard to get people to expand their view of Black music and all the different styles around that.

Craig David: I actually missed [the *Melody Maker*'s controversial 2000 'UK garage, my arse' cover, in which a Black actor dressed as Craig is pictured sitting on a toilet]. Thankfully. I saw the image, but years later. The music was doing such moves that there was nothing that could change that.

Hannah Verdier: I don't think it was [difficult for Black artists to get on the cover of *Smash Hits*] and that pleases me to say because when I've worked on women's magazines you wouldn't have anyone Black on the cover. The publishing director would actually say, 'If in doubt put a blonde on because that sells.' It was out-and-out racism. *Smash Hits* had a history of putting anyone interesting on the cover. I don't think I'm looking back idealistically, because I can see the misogyny, but when it comes to race it wasn't a problem.

Chantelle Fiddy: I used to work for *Smash Hits* on an ad-hoc basis and they were one of the more liberal publications and didn't go, 'Ooh, have we got too many Black or brown faces in?' It was more like, 'Whatever is cool and of the moment then we're putting them in.'

Simon Jones, former Mis-Teeq PR: I can remember an editor of a magazine telling me they wouldn't put a Black person on the cover. Quite openly. Telling me, 'We won't put Mis-Teeq on the cover because they're Black girls and they won't sell.'

Su-Elise: We would be featured inside magazines, but in terms of that coveted magazine cover we did struggle, definitely. Especially in the beginning. The general consensus in that world back then was that three Black girls on the cover of a UK magazine wasn't going to sell the magazine. We had a lot of barriers to break down and a lot of doors to knock on in order to get that changed. We just took everything back to the music. With the music came the sales and with the sales came the fame and the acknowledgement in the industry. Then people were like, 'Okay, maybe we can do this, maybe this will work.' Attitudes did start to change. But in those early days it was a little bit disheartening.

Chantelle Fiddy: It was more the style press and the newspapers that were the issue. If you did put somebody Black on the cover it had to be a woman; it couldn't be a man because that would never sell.

MNEK: I heard this podcast with Celena from the Honeyz and she was talking about how on magazine covers people would purposefully cover her and Heavenli's faces and leave Mariama's because she was lighter. They would cover the Black faces.

Simon Jones: I can remember one magazine saying, 'We'll do an Alesha cover,' which was a big deal because Mis-Teeq hadn't had any covers at that point. So they'd shoot the three girls inside but only Alesha on the cover. Obviously the label wanted to do it because these magazines were so important. That must have been very hard to swallow for Su-Elise and Sabrina [Washington]. It definitely created tension within the band.

MNEK: Because Alesha and even Su-Elise were very much the more palatable options. Sabrina, who was the singer, wasn't even given half the limelight. Those things were happening and no one would be commenting on it but now it's so different. We've come too far for that to happen again.

Simon Jones: The label would be applying pressure like, 'Why are Atomic Kitten on the cover of every magazine?', and I remember sitting in a meeting and someone saying, 'Well, they don't put Black people on the cover of magazines.' It was just talked about like it was normal. We did the shoot but I think it was done begrudgingly.

Su-Elise: Alesha was a female MC, she had something different about her and she is so friendly and outgoing that maybe her personality put her in front of the right people.

Jamelia: I was encouraged to wear my hair like Naomi Campbell's. Obviously I was a fan so I said yes. They didn't want the Jamelia that walked into the label office all those years ago; they wanted a certain version of me. By the time my record deal ended, I was being pushed into being very sexualised and very European-looking. I remember saying to them, 'What's wrong with me as I am?' I was probably a size ten, but sample size was a six. So around that time I was a matchstick because I thought that's what I had to look like to be successful. Not eating? I'm Jamaican. We eat. There's this double existence, especially when you're Black and Jamaican, because I'd go out into the world as a celebrity and then I'd go to Grammie's house and she'd be like, 'What is wrong with you? Let me feed you.' I just got to a point where I was like, 'This is exhausting.'

Su-Elise: We'd actually started recording tracks for a third album. But the label went under, they owed us a lot of money, so financially that was a big strain on us. We lost out. But in business, shit happens. We shopped around trying to look for a third deal with the management we were with at the time, but we were being told that what we were looking for wasn't out there. Now, in hindsight, whether we were being told the right information, I don't know. I wasn't in the room when those meetings were being held but I have an inkling that there was other stuff on the table that didn't get to us. Also, Alesha specifically had said she was quite tired and was having second thoughts at the time. I remember thinking, 'Well, Mis-Teeq is all three of us so if it's not going to be all three of us then maybe this is the end of an era and a journey.' And what a journey.

Craig David: So many of the old systems and things that were 'okay' or 'you just laugh along' have changed now. It's unfortunate that so many people have to suffer before you see change, but we are in a place where the conversation is a lot different to what it was in the '90s and early '00s.

In 2015, after his mash-up of 'Fill Me In' and Diplo and Skrillex's 'Where Are Ü Now' on 1Xtra went viral, Craig experienced a cultural and critical renaissance among a younger generation who had never heard of Leigh Francis. In 2016, his sixth album, *Following My Intuition*, peaked at number one, giving him his first chart-topper since *Born to Do It*. In 2020, *Bo' Selecta!* was removed from Channel 4's All4 streaming service in the wake of the Black Lives Matter protests following the murder of George Floyd.

8

The slow rise of pop outsiders Xenomania

UK pop in the early '00s was split into two strands. On the one side there were songs built around pastiche that gleefully recalled vintage pop hitmakers such as ABBA or Chic and wedding-reception-proof genres like disco or funk. On the other side was a Scandinavian approximation of US R&B spear-headed at first by the likes of Denniz PoP and Max Martin with Five, then later owned by Norwegian trio Stargate, whose work had graced albums by the likes of Hear'Say, Blue and Atomic Kitten. For Brian Higgins, a musician and songwriter who'd followed up a global hit in the shape of Cher's 'Believe' with radio silence, pop was in desperate need of a riotous kick up the backside. Alongside songwriter Miranda Cooper and a host of musicians drawn from every corner of the music world (including an ex member of KLF's touring band), Higgins built hit factory Xenomania and set about re-wiring pop's brain chemistry.

The songs Xenomania would create for Girls Aloud and the Sugababes were often sutured together from a handful of different elements; verses from song one were fused with a chorus from song two, while a bridge from song three was reworked with an element of song four to make song five. Individual lines were often sung by each band member, in various different keys, before finally being pieced together like a brain-frying jigsaw puzzle. Genres were also gleefully spliced together, reflecting Higgins' own disparate music tastes. The roaring return of guitar music via early '00s preeners the Strokes et al. was reflected in Xenomania's ability to make guitars in pop fun rather than purely an exercise in authenticity box-ticking. But their success wasn't overnight. Failed bands, false starts and a huge amount of time spent unpicking and rebuilding pop's constituent parts meant they were close to missing their moment.

'It was ahead of its time in terms of what was going on'

Brian Higgins, songwriter and producer: I hated the pop sound at the time. I couldn't stand it. I detested it. It was just so sugar sweet and so similar to itself. There was also the clean-cut, Swedish R&B sound. I started to really analyse these records just to hone my dislike of them.

Miranda Cooper, Xenomania's chief songwriter: I don't know if there are many people who have come from dancing into songwriting. Dannii Minogue spotted me through the window at Pineapple Dance Studios in London and went, 'You're new, do you want to be my dancer?' I also did loads of stuff for PJ & Duncan and then Gina G. At the time, Peter Loraine was the editor of *Top of the Pops* magazine and he used to do a fun thing like, 'Who snogged who?', and I was always in there somewhere. When I first started writing for Girls Aloud, I remember passing him in the Polydor offices and he was like, 'Miranda, what are you doing here?'

Peter Loraine: She had a name – Miranda the Dancer. When she went to Eurovision [in 1996] to dance with Gina G, she became our Eurovision roving reporter.

Miranda Cooper: Yes, I did. When I was younger I didn't know you could be a songwriter. I loved dancing, but it was just being moving scenery. I did have a nagging feeling that maybe this wasn't going to be what I was going to do forever.

Peter Loraine: That year, Morten Harket from A-ha was the presenter of Eurovision and I remember he was hanging out with them and then, when Gina G didn't win, he didn't want to know.

Miranda Cooper: But it was there that I met Steve Allen from Warners and he said, 'Oi, love, have you ever thought about being in a pop duo?' I think it was Brian [Higgins] and Saint Etienne who had come up with this idea of doing this cool, kitsch, pop duo. They saw me and this other girl Chloé [Treend] on *Top of the Pops* and we became T-Shirt. We covered Hot Chocolate's 'You Sexy Thing' and somehow it became this big hit in Australia. In the UK, we were doing PAs in Romford and *Mizz* magazine roadshows. It was the really fun but not massively elegant world of pop.

Brian Higgins: Xenomania actually started in November 1995. That was when Steve Allen offered me a record deal as an artist, but really it was to cement my creative relationship with him. I would make records for the label, so Dannii Minogue's 'All I Wanna Do' was the first hit for Xenomania. Cher's 'Believe' was the second. I was working in the day in another job through all of that. Although my song had become what it had become I was still in a suit and tie. I didn't leave that job until 'Believe' went to number one in America [in March 1999].

Miranda Cooper: T-Shirt were asked to tour Australia but I had started going down to Brian's studio. Brian had a backing track that he asked me to write on. So I took it home and I don't know how I knew what to do, but I came back with a full song called, 'Hey I'm OK'. I grew up listening to musicals, mainly, but then my brother was into punk and indie. He'd give me lots of the Cure and the Sex Pistols and Blondie. I was massively into Transvision Vamp, as well. This splurge came out, which actually I feel like somewhere in there is where Girls Aloud sits. I also wrote another song with the line 'I've got a cherry red scooter, with a hot pink hooter'. Brian, bless him, was like, 'This is awesome.' So I turned down the chance to tour Australia [with T-Shirt] and they got another blonde in to replace me. No one even noticed.

Brian Higgins: I got into a project with Miranda Cooper at the time 'Believe' was successful called Moonbaby. That was really the sound of Girls Aloud in its newborn state. It was ahead of its time in terms of what was going on.

Miranda Cooper: I'd always been the one on stage so it didn't enter my head that I might not be the best person to be the vehicle for my songs. I thought I should be the artist. We were in Brian's little garden shed; it was me and Matt Gray, Brian, Tim Powell. I would get the 4.20 p.m. train down to Kent from Victoria every day, because Brian had a normal job. There were rumbles of things happening with this song 'Believe', but we were in a bubble. That's all we did for three years from 1997, basically, doing the Moonbaby thing and not realising that actually it was the blueprint for Sugababes and Girls Aloud.

Brian Higgins: Pete Tong signed it [to London Records], so I worked very closely with him. It was an invaluable working experience for me because he taught me an awful lot about how I could make it better. He was a very hard taskmaster. He was also the coolest man on the planet at that time, the number-one tastemaker.

Miranda Cooper: It was a really exciting, big deal. And then it was awful. They said, 'You can either be Natalie Imbruglia or All Saints.' We thought we were making this wonderful art and it was reduced down. Also, I just wasn't good enough. What they had signed was the writing and the chemistry we had together. When I got dropped, I was pretty broken. I wasn't even sure I wanted to do music any more. Pete Tong used to say, 'She won't be there, will she?' when he'd come down because I was a reminder of this great black hole of debt. I'd never met anyone like Brian; he knew exactly what he wanted to do. I was just holding on to his coattails. Obviously 'Believe' had happened and all these people were phoning him saying, 'Can you do this?

Can you do that?', and he'd say, 'No, I've got this amazing girl, Moonbaby, it's going to be a huge hit.' Then when it went tits up, he thought, 'Shit, I better get my house in order.' He brought in this girl, Lisa Cowling, who he'd worked with at Reed, the publishing company. I thought, 'I don't want some fucking girl coming in.' She was there to build me up and make me feel better and it was just a meeting of pure joy. We wrote tonnes and tonnes of songs.

Brian Higgins: I think working on the Moonbaby project moved me away from purely dance-pop. I had made a record in 1992 which was about making multiple versions of the same thing that I'd then piece together again. The first version took about eighteen months to make. So that idea of [crafting songs from various other bits of songs] had been kicking around in my mind for a while.

Miranda Cooper: [The end of Moonbaby] meant that when we did get our first opportunity with the Sugababes, we were ready.

9

Sugababes:
The sweet and the sour

While not as buoyantly in your face as 'Wannabe' four years earlier, 'Overload', the debut single from the teenage Sugababes —
AKA north-Londoners Mutya Buena (aged fifteen), Keisha
Buchanan (fifteen) and Siobhán Donaghy (sixteen) — was equally
revelatory in terms of the evolution of the British girlband. For
a teen audience whose teeth were set on edge by the post-Spice
Girls sugar rush, 'Overload', which nonchalantly fused breakbeat
rhythms, flamenco guitar and a cacophonous middle eight, represented something genuinely cool. The fact that the band themselves eschewed dance routines, matching outfits and smiling,
AKA the era's three pop mainstays, only made them stand out
more, with their diffidence and grunge-y aesthetic a siren call to
equally 'whatever' teenagers unmoved by DayGlo motivational
anthems. Lyrically, 'Overload', like much of 2000's *One Touch*
album, represented a snapshot of teenage life: a time of confused
emotions, heightened hormones and on-the-surface yearning.

More of a critical than commercial success, *One Touch* was the only album to feature that first line-up of friends. From there, new members – Heidi Range (2001–11), Amelle Berrabah (2006–11) and Jade Ewen (2009–11) – were airlifted in almost with each new album. While the top-tier, attitude-heavy hits continued to pile up – the Sugababes' six UK number ones are second only to the Spice Girls' nine when it comes to the most chart-toppers by British girlbands – their personnel troubles eventually started to overshadow the music. Their revolving-door policy when it came to members, mixed with pop's inherent mission statement that the song is king, meant most fans invested in the Sugababes brand as opposed to the individuals.

At the start, however, were three girls gleefully skipping school to hang out in a studio and partake in their favourite hobby. That they were formed almost by accident – initially as the Sugababies – only added to that early sense of alchemy.

'Some days we'd be in the studio until the sun came up'

Siobhán: Ron [Tom, manager] was my best friend at school's brother-in-law and she said to him that I could sing. He had also met Mutya's dad in a supermarket. So he was managing the two of us as solo artists. Me and Mutya had met before and so we wanted to do a duet. Then Mutya brought Keisha to the studio from school.

Keisha: I just really liked singing and so I begged my mum, asking if I could go to the studio so I could be around it. Originally I was just there to support Mutya as a friend.

Siobhán: It was totally not on anyone's mind that we would be a group. Ron just announced it to us; not, 'Would you like to . . .?' or 'How about this?' It was more, 'This is what we're doing.' We were so young that we were like, 'Okay then.'

Mutya: We became the Sugababes on that day. It didn't feel real. We were just three teenage girls trying to sing and do school at the same time.

Siobhán: Ron always said that he thought the three of us individually were amazing but that we were really exceptional together. We were quite shy and from regular working-class families. We weren't media trained, which quickly became obvious to people when we came out.

Keisha: We'd do half a day at school and then go straight to the studio afterwards. Sometimes we'd skip days. We didn't do much by the books. Some days we'd be in the studio until the sun came up and then we'd go home and we would jump in the shower, change uniforms and then go back to school again. And then we'd leave before lunchtime. We were Energizer Bunnies.

Siobhán: I think Mutya and Keisha were actually expelled because of how little they were attending at one point. Ron used to come down [to the studio] with all his mates, which annoyed us because it would be a party and they'd be opening booze. It wouldn't be for us – we were only interested in the music and the singing. The rest of it was just noise going on around us.

Keisha: I'm always going to hold dear the early days of us being berated by our teachers for missing homework, but just not really caring. It was my absolute dream and my absolute joy to sing and create music. It came with a lot of long nights, but when I look back, hats off to us.

Mutya: We had such a fast childhood but I guess back then it didn't seem like that.

Keisha: My mum would always double-check, like, 'Are you sure you're not tired?' I think we were all just really adamant that it was something we wanted to do.

Mutya: My parents were overly supportive. I had already been touring Europe when I was nine, doing Filipino dancing and singing. For me it just felt normal. I also went on [Michael Barrymore's ITV show] *My Kind of People* with a Filipino group doing some dancing. Then they called me back to come and sing. I had already been on the *Royal Variety Show*, doing Hawaiian dancing to 'Under the Sea'. So when we were in the Sugababes I was so comfortable performing and travelling around.

Siobhán: My parents never guided me down a certain path. It was never like, 'Wouldn't it be amazing if you were a doctor?' Ron used to come and visit the house a lot and my parents loved him. They were happy we were in safe hands. It always used to flabbergast me because he'd go out into our garden and spark up a spliff and I'd be looking at my parents like, 'Is this alright?' But I always felt quite disconnected from my friends [at school] and felt so jealous when they were doing their A levels and going off to university. We just went down a different road.

Mutya: We definitely had people who explained [financial] stuff but I feel like it still went over our heads. We were too young to be bothered about a contract and sitting down trying to figure out what was going on. I would like to turn back time and read everything properly.

Siobhán: We had a really good lawyer and our parents always had to be in the room when things like that were being explained to us. It really was explained to us too; how many albums the deal was for and what was expected of us. I remember at one point they said that as an indemnity against me not fulfilling my part of the contract they could come for my parents' house. They'd worked for it their whole lives.

Mutya: We were paid monthly. You couldn't give a fourteen-year-old a card and be like, 'Here you go, do what you want with it.' We were all very disciplined with the money, but also you just want to go out and have fun and forget about it.

Siobhán: I remember we got transferred £3,000 but I think it was a million-pound deal. That's a whole other conversation.

'They hung out like a little girl gang'

The credible space the Sugababes would eventually settle into was one carved out by London Records labelmates All Saints. Billed as the cool alternative to the Spice Girls, they'd arrived in 1997 with 'I Know Where It's At', a swaggering amalgam of R&B and pop that mixed delicious harmonies with untouchable, cool-older-sister attitude. While other pop acts looked like they were trying very hard, All Saints made every element of the pop game look effortless, even revitalising slam poetry via the spoken-word intro to classic second single, 'Never Ever'. As with the Sugababes, however, it had taken a while to find the right sound and for everything to click into place. For both bands, the catalyst was Massive Attack and Neneh Cherry collaborator Cameron McVey and his team of grumpy misfits.

Cameron McVey, songwriter and producer: London Records had All Saints and loads of people had worked on their stuff but they couldn't get anywhere with it. I used to get those kind of projects; they were usually a quarter of a million pounds in the hole and they'd be like, 'Send it to Cameron and he'll sort it out.' Then the same thing happened with the Sugababes. I was like the Red Adair of the music industry, putting out fires. You never get me in when things are going well. It's always when you're in the shit and there's nothing else left to try.

Felix Howard, songwriter: What [Cameron] did with All Saints is nothing like what he did with the Sugababes. On All Saints, they had some really good people. He didn't have to do a rescue job like he had to on Sugababes. All Saints had Shaznay, who is a great songwriter, and they were more of a together unit.

Cameron McVey: As far as I was concerned, like with All Saints, [Sugababes] had people who could really sing and who had a real personality. I can't do anything that's not real. I can't do any of that fake stuff where some rich guy wants his daughter to sing and they can't. I trained at PWL and we worked with a lot of people there that couldn't sing and I had a real problem with that.

Mutya: All Saints opened up the urban side, the cooler side of the girl groups. Obviously we all looked up to the Spice Girls, they opened up doors for everybody, but All Saints as a British group was my ideal. If I wasn't in the Sugababes I would love to be in something like All Saints. Of course I wore combat trousers like them. Of course.

Siobhán: They were probably the only all-female group that showed us we could be alternative and work. I didn't have it in me to do choreographed dance routines. I was just too awkward. I still am. Somebody with a bubbly personality and a gorgeous smile – that just wasn't me.

Keisha: Normally for a lot of bands you'd go in the studio and before you even make a record there will be whispers of, 'You're going to be the next this or that,' but we were three girls from north-west London who were into R&B and indie.

Cameron McVey: We'd all come off a really long pro-ject, so everyone was in a bad mood. We were all working in different rooms and everyone was grumpy because nobody wanted to do pop. My daughters [amazing pop artiste] Mabel and [amazing pop artiste] Tyson were in the studio and they really liked the girls. They were basically A&R-ing it. I didn't know anything about it; I was like, 'What do you think of this one?'

Jony Rockstar, songwriter and producer: I used to work for a producer called Howie B, and then Cameron [McVey] scooped me up. I worked with him on a Neneh Cherry record that never materialised, but I was part of his production team.

The [Sugababes] gig came in to Cameron and he likes to remind me that I didn't want to do it because I hated the name.

Siobhán: The name came from Ron Tom. We hated it. When you're that young, you want to be grown-up. I think we assumed we'd think of something else.

Cameron McVey: Jony was one of the grumpy ones saying, 'I don't want to fucking do this.' We gave him a couple of spliffs, locked him in the room and he came up with the beat for 'Overload'. By the end of the first day, he said, 'I told you I should do this, this is the best project ever.'

Felix Howard: Jony hated everyone. And smoked weed all fucking day. If he didn't want you in the room, he would keep turning the music up really loud.

Jony Rockstar: It was like, 'What? Why are we doing this?' They were also fourteen-year-old girls. Obviously it was a great move in the end. I absolutely loved their vibe and they had phenomenal voices. They had that new-world, multi-cultural identity that was far more authentic back then. It didn't feel staged or contrived. It was organic. They hung out like a little girl gang.

Cameron McVey: The great thing about the 'Babes is they're like the Supremes in that it's three voices that don't clash. They can sing over any noise and just make it work. All three of them have perfect pitch.

Jony Rockstar: Their tones were so different but so complimentary. Like an act of God.

Siobhán: All of us were into the big American R&B scene. The first song I sang to Ron Tom was by En Vogue and we loved Monica and Brandy, Aaliyah, Missy Elliott. Garage was also a massive part of all of our lives. Me and Mutya used to go to the under-18 raves. You'd get your mixtape at school on cassette. You'd learn the songs in the week and then go out on the weekends with probably a quarter bottle of vodka.

Cameron McVey: They were so naughty, the three of them. They were devils.

Keisha: We were adamant we wanted to have a garage sound. Me and Mutya – not many people know this – we started a garage girlband with two other members. Briefly. And we were rapping by the way. I'll take full credit for that because Mutya's going to dive under the table with embarrassment when she finds out I've shared this news.

Mutya: Wow. I was Little Miss Naughty and she was Curvy K. We used to pretend we were garage MCs.

Siobhán: That was kind of behind the scenes. I don't know what I thought of that.

Mutya: My household was full of all different types of music. My dad would play the guitar every night and I would sit with him and sing. So we all had something to add to the mix. As the Sugababes we were able to jump into different types of music while still sounding very soulful. That's the thing about it; we could go pop but there'd still be a bit of soul in there.

Jony Rockstar: It was the Blair years, it was Britpop, it was celebrating British culture, being proud of that. The music was art imitating life in that respect. We were all really having a great time. There was no political upheaval. It was pre-9/11. They were some very golden years, so people wanted to hear uplifting, fun, cool music. They didn't want depressing music.

Siobhán: I think we were cooler [than a lot of other pop acts at the time]. But, funnily enough, Keisha was a massive pop fan. She loved S Club 7, A1 – that was totally her thing. I don't know if she admitted to that.

Keisha: My first ever CD singles I bought were Jay-Z and Foxy Brown's 'I'll Be' and Robson & Jerome's 'Up on the Roof'. I was the person who was listening to both S Club Juniors and 2Pac.

Siobhán: She fancied Bradley from S Club 7. Me and Mutya refer to Keisha as Disney. All that happy pop stuff, she loves it.

Keisha: We knew we were different but it wasn't above me to buy the pop classics either.

Siobhán: The way the *One Touch* album evolved would never have been intentional for us. To a certain extent a lot of it would have gone over our heads. Even some of the lyrics we came out with, I don't think we understood the connotations around some of it. And how grown-up it was.

Mutya: When you're singing or writing when you're so much younger, you never question things. I look at stuff now that I wrote back then and think, 'What was I thinking?' I knew that our lingo and everything was different.

'Everyone said they couldn't write and that they were a bunch of idiots'

The liner notes of a pop album quickly became a battleground in the '00s. If the act's name wasn't featured in the songwriter credits then it became a stick to beat them with. Being a 'manufactured' pop act was the antithesis of authentic guitar music typically made by white men, whose names would often still appear next to a list of seasoned hitmakers and songwriters-for-hire. To the gatekeepers of credible, a lack of input conjured up ideas of conveyor belts, songwriting committees and old men putting words in teenage mouths. While that's not entirely inaccurate, it also ignores the will of the artists and the bigger industry framework they were working in. For the Sugababes, being given the opportunity to write unlocked their sound and allowed them to capture a moment.

Keisha: At first [producer/songwriter] Don-E was writing a lot for us. However, he really set the tone for how we sing – he pretty much taught us where to stack our harmonies. The sound you hear when you call it 'the Sugababes sound' definitely came from him. When it came to writing, Cameron McVey was really encouraging about us sharing our thoughts. I remember saying, 'I don't write songs, I write poetry,' and he was like, 'Well, let me hear it.' We all felt so good having to vent on paper.

Cameron McVey: Everyone said they couldn't write and that they were a bunch of idiots and I was like, 'What are you talking about?' I just said, 'Write about what you want to write about because you're writing tunes for young people.' We were excited to work with kids because we were so jaded by all these people doing this pompous left-field music.

Siobhán: One day Cameron sent us home with a backing track. He wanted it to be from us. I'm a bit of a perfectionist so I took it really seriously, like that was my homework. I actually tortured myself. I wanted to be really good at it, because of imposter syndrome. There are all these musicians out there who are natural songwriters and I've always felt that I wasn't, but that if I tried really hard I can put something good together. In my head I always felt like I had to try harder than everyone else.

Felix Howard: Cameron would have said, 'I don't talk like a fourteen-year-old girl therefore I need this fourteen-year-old girl to tell me how to talk.' Which is hardly ever the case in the music industry.

Mutya: It was just nice to have that creativity on that first album. Writing was the first thing we knew. Then after that with every album people would always know that we wrote our own music, so they allowed us to be open and free with what we wanted to do. We've always been open-minded about taking songs that have already been written for us, but it's quite nice to know that people would be like, 'Okay, cool, we know the girls can write, let them get on with it.'

Cameron McVey: On the first day, Siobhán basically wrote most of 'Overload' and we mixed it that day. The board mix from the end of day one is the version they released.

Jony Rockstar: A lot of my life is quite hazy but I do remember those 'Overload' sessions vividly. Originally on 'Overload' we had the verse melody as the chorus and the chorus melody was the verse. I switched them around. I was using breakbeats and I had this sampled bassline that I'd cut up. It was very organic. We didn't reference other music or say, 'Let's do a song like this.'

Felix Howard: [Jony Rockstar] would sit there in a marijuana cloud and he would work on this tiny piece for hours and hours. In this green smoke and terrifyingly loud music, Siobhán and I fashioned the skeleton of what became 'Overload'.

Siobhán: I loved that day. It was very relaxed. I don't think I really understood where we were going with the lyrics in the room. It just felt like a series of random stuff we were saying, but I remember the first time I sang my bit I did know how special it was.

Felix Howard: At the time, 'Overload' was called 'Ragga Train', which is a Cameron McVey-ism. It was not thought to be a single. [London Records founder] Tracy Bennett, to his credit, picked that one out of the crowd and said it was the single. It sounded nothing like what was being made in pop at that time. And still doesn't. It's a curate's egg – you couldn't ever make it again because it was made in such a weird way.

Cameron McVey: There's a big thump you can hear when the middle eight comes in because there used to be an electric short on the desk in that room, so you can hear this bang where it was me making it come back to life again. I never send anyone into a booth. There's the sound of one of them complaining about their homework in the background. We were more strict about their homework than we were about the recording. Like: 'You've got to do your homework or we're not recording.'

Mutya: I never thought about ['Overload' entering the top ten]. If I could turn back time now, I feel like I would appreciate everything a hundred times more. I probably would have taken things a little more seriously than I did then. But I can't help the fact we were so young and a lot of people forgot about that, too.

Felix Howard: Brian [Higgins] was inspired by 'Overload'. He is a fabulous magpie. He takes tiny bits of tunes and sticks them together and makes songs out of them. He works in an incredibly unique way. 'Sound of the Underground' is pretty close [to sounding like 'Overload']. It wasn't as close as the Christina Aguilera tune 'Make Over' [from 2002's *Stripped*], which we successfully sued them over and now have a piece of.

Jony Rockstar: If you listen to the *One Touch* album it's pretty lo-fi. It was just authentic. We live in such a contrived reality now that when things are authentic they really do shine and that album was made with pure love. You know, we were a bunch of rowdy guys. We were loud party guys, we were going out after and it was kind of rock 'n' roll back then, in the music business. They were just lovely sweet girls, who fucking delivered. So we loved them.

Cameron McVey: We were nuts. I had bought the house behind the studio so I was trying to bang a hole in the wall so I could go straight into my front room. Then one day Madonna turned up and [producer and mixer] Mark 'Spike' Stent said to me, 'You've got to move; M is coming through the room.' I was eating my breakfast at the time. I was like, 'Fucking good luck moving me, mate. I'm having my sausage and egg. Fuck off.'

Siobhán: From the get-go, and especially because of the single choice [with 'Overload'], we felt in a very alternative music world rather than pop.

Cameron McVey: I had [late iconic stylist] Judy Blame involved with them, so that meant it sat in a really good place. The visuals were really good, the videos were really good. I got to choose the singles. We just got total free rein, which you never get out of a record company unless they're in the shit.

Siobhán: Our first showcase was at Ronnie Scott's. Our first tour was with *NME*. And the crowd was so much older than us. If we had expected teenage screaming fans, we were thoroughly disappointed.

Keisha: At our shows we'd be like, 'Why is everyone fifty years older than us?' We knew we were different.

Alexis Petridis, former *Select* magazine editor: They seemed to me to be like a mixture of All Saints and a bit of that Massive Attack sound. They seemed to be a cut above. 'Overload' was a record that got played a lot in the *Select* offices when it came out.

'Doing anything that was like acting was alien to all three of us'

There's a shocking moment, watching now, about forty-five seconds into the minimalist video for 'Overload', shot by fashion photographer Phil Poynter. After a couple of attempts at a smile, Mutya breaks into a full-on, teeth-baring, eyes-twinkling giggle. In fact, all three members smile at various

points, almost despite themselves. Performing the song later on Top of the
Pops, *viewers used to peppy, mimic-in-the-playground jazz hands were met
with the incongruous sight of three teenagers sat on stools looking at their laps
while a propulsive, forward-motion breakbeat rhythm chugged out around
them. In lieu of the standard high-octane arm choreography, Mutya, Keisha
and Siobhán would occasionally turn to look to the left or the right, a shrug
of acknowledgement at industry norms. It meant they were often called moody
or sullen, an accusation that would later underpin conversations around the
various line-up changes.*

Keisha: We had performance training because they said we
were really shy.

Siobhán: There was a guy that did the choreography for 'Overload'. He would also do mock interviews so we could practise
answering questions. That was it. No one ever said, 'You look a
little bit moody.' I almost wish someone had said that to us.

Mutya: I knew how to do interviews but I was too young
and a bit, 'Hmm, okay.' Quite unbothered. But it was weird
because that unbothered look really appealed to people. I
would get a lot of *NME* journalists wanting to do interviews
with me because they thought I had attitude. To be honest,
that wasn't the case, it was just because of how I grew up in my
area. I was a little bit cooler, if you get what I mean. I looked
like I was moody or rude, but, at the same time, people took it
in and people liked it.

Keisha: We weren't moody. Even with our friends, if we were
all laughing and joking, as soon as a camera came on us, everyone

would have straight faces. Now it's seen as a cool thing, whereas we just naturally didn't smile. And we didn't realise how that was coming across.

Siobhán: I remember having to have a glass of wine on the 'Overload' shoot because they had to loosen me up. I think someone in the glam team suggested the wine, so we can't blame Phil. All I had to do was walk in a straight line, pull my sunglasses down and look over my shoulder, but for me it was so big. Doing anything that was like acting was alien to all three of us.

Mutya: We came from an era where there were a lot of pop groups. The *Smash Hits* days. There was indie but you also had your Girls Alouds, your Atomic Kittens, your Blues, your Blazin' Squads. Everything was a bit more upbeat then, so having the Sugababes where people think we're moody and don't know how to take us, I found it funny. We'd be walking in and people wouldn't know whether to say hi or not.

Siobhán: The other girls would go and chat [to other bands] a lot more than I did. I was just really awkward. I think we were somewhere one day and A1 were there, and this is really mean of me, but I ignored them. I just totally didn't think they were cool.

Christian Ingebrigtsen: We had fun with most of the bands but we weren't the most popular. We were a little bit too squeaky clean for a lot of them. We didn't feel like the most popular band on the road.

Siobhán: They had that 'Take on Me' cover out and I thought that was horrendous. I remember *Smash Hits* magazine would

291

try to get us to laugh. All we would do was lift the corner of our mouths for the photos.

Keisha: I wish people had given us a bit more slack because we were kids.

Siobhán: We just didn't want to be fake. We'd have to go back to our friends and we were worried they would laugh at us. Who walks down the street grinning ear to ear? No one. It was more normal what we were doing.

Laura Snapes: They weren't like their really slick pop peers – I don't want to call them bratty, but they were just sixteen-year-olds who sometimes just couldn't be fucking bothered and they didn't hide that.

Siobhán: It's such a complicated time in your life to navigate something like [being thought of as moody]. I realise now how much that has affected me moving forwards in terms of my anxiety. I was super confident before I entered that band and definitely didn't come out of it that way. I don't think anyone is going to come out unscathed when you start your career at such a young age.

'I packed my bag and I went home'

The band's ingrained laissez-faire attitude also meant it was easy for genuine sadness to go unnoticed. Or ignored. On 22 August 2001, while on a promo tour in Australia and Asia, Siobhán quit, less than a year after One Touch's *release. A swirl of false information followed, ranging from the mundane ('management tried to say I had a kidney infection') to the ridiculous (no, she didn't climb out of a toilet window, never to be seen again). Relationships within the band had turned sour, often escalated, they say, by the adults around them.*

Siobhán: There was definitely a disconnect between myself and Keisha and so there was an element of the people working with us that was a bit 'divide and conquer'. I just felt isolated and lonely and so I just focused on doing a good job.

Keisha: We weren't encouraged to have a relationship with each other. I guess there's more power in having the upper hand. Some people prefer discord because then you're the person who always fixes it. Create the mess and then we all come to you to fix it. It's a tricky subject because it's had so much impact on my life. I don't really like to dwell on it. Mainly because I have younger nieces and nephews and whenever there's an issue or a problem I always want to empower them and tell them how special they are. I have a passion for helping young girls and it's a shame that wasn't embraced in our situation.

Siobhán: We initially signed a production deal, which wouldn't have been great for us. We should have been on a standard management contract, so when we communicated successfully and spoke to our lawyer we were able to negotiate it to a better place. We changed our contract. They don't want you doing that. We were so in the dark about a lot of things. I do think they kept us in a way that made us suspicious of each other. That meant we made people in our team our confidants rather than each other, so it wouldn't have even crossed our minds that those decisions were ours to make. And actually we were paying for everybody.

We didn't have that understanding back then so we just behaved ourselves and did pretty much what we were told.

Keisha: At that time, I feel like none of us were happy. Unfortunately towards the end of that era there was so much darkness.

Siobhán: I had been warning the team for a while. I needed more support. I didn't feel like I was being treated very well and I needed the adults to monitor that better. But they didn't; they were too busy off out. Even when we were away, especially on that tour, any minute they could, they were off doing fabulous things while we were working. It just meant that some of the stuff going on went unchecked. So I was like, 'Okay, if this is what we're saying, that I am on my own with this, then I can tell you that I can't deal with it.' So I packed my bag and a flight was arranged for me and I went home.

Mutya: I feel like a lot of adults could have done better. There could have been a lot more communication and there didn't need to be all the dividing. But that's the industry. It's very divide and conquer. It's very snake-y and shark-y; you just have to work out who you can and can't talk to.

Siobhán: Communication had broken down to the point where I didn't even think [sitting down with the band] was going to be helpful. In a sense the decision had been made for me. I was so isolated. And I knew I would be replaced. There had been conversations about replacing another member as well, before I left, which I found unacceptable. It was also a conversation before I left the band that we were going to go to another label. So there was definitely an onward journey and in someone like [lawyer and new manager] Sarah Stennett, it was hardly going to be the end of the road. She is a force of nature. I totally made the right decision for me and I have never looked back. Even when 'Freak Like Me' went to number one I was happy for them, but I was also happy for myself.

'Heidi's a true Liverpool trooper; she just got on with it'

Aged just seventeen, Mutya and Keisha had already experienced a lifetime's worth of music industry highs and lows. As quickly as they were let go by London Records, however, they were snapped up by Island Records, and a new member in the shape of ex-Atomic Kitten member Heidi 'Queen of the middle eight' Range was brought in. It was another period of adjustment, but one that this time felt tinged with hope.

Keisha: I remember thinking, 'Ugh, I just want to be happy.' We wanted to continue and have some fun because everything felt so heavy.

Mutya: We didn't even have enough time to be like, 'Oh, it's over,' because we had an offer for a new deal. It wasn't that long after we got dropped that me and Keisha got re-signed and then Heidi came along.

Keisha: That's when the fun really started. Not in terms of the loss of [Siobhán], but it was a brand-new start; a brand-new label, a brand-new member.

Mutya: I remember not being sure how old [Heidi] was. I was like, 'She doesn't look our age, that's not right.' I thought she was older. I remember asking to see her passport and everything.

Keisha: Originally one of our friends wanted to join but I think she was fifteen at the time. And we'd just got out of the age group where the rule was you could only work a certain amount of days a year, which meant we missed out on touring. We didn't want to take a step back now that we were of age. We were told that we were going to be looking at a girl from Liverpool called Heidi, and she came in, pretty girl, lovely smile, great energy, upbeat. I taught her this horrendous dance routine because by then I'd started developing myself as a choreographer. I taught her this whole routine and she went along with it. Years later she was like, 'That routine was horrendous.' Lots of rolling on the floor.

Mutya: I was very sceptical [about Heidi coming in]. I had been in a group with Siobhán for so many years so to have some new person come into her place felt weird. I felt like me and Keisha had worked so hard to get to where we'd got to, so to let someone just jump in for me felt a bit not right. But obviously it was the best thing to do in that moment and I don't have any regrets. I was happy with how it went.

Jony Rockstar: [Them having a new member] was of no consequence to me. Heidi could really sing, so that's all I cared about. I felt a little protective of Heidi while working on [second album *Angels with Dirty Faces*] because I could tell she was a bit intimidated. I'm sure it was very weird for Keisha and Mutya, but they were lovely to her. We all knew each other, we all had a working relationship, and then here's Heidi. But she's a true Liverpool trooper; she just got on with it. And she wrote the middle eight of 'Stronger', the whole thing. She delivered.

Keisha: In the early days we all had the same resting bitch face and so we all had that same vibe. Under the circumstances Siobhán left in, there were obviously things said. So when Heidi arrived, she was sunshine, biggest smile, she came from a background where she had done all these dance competitions, so that perfect pop picture so to speak. When you put that in the middle of our stone faces it just highlighted it even more.

Mutya: Heidi did bring the pop factor and I can never fault her for it because she did her job within the Sugababes.

Keisha: Sometimes I look back and I'm like, 'Just smile! Please, for the love of God!' So when you pair that with us two and all the controversy that surrounded the breakup of Sugababes 01, people just judged us.

'The band were very suspicious of me because I hadn't done anything other than a trendy single'

While One Touch *had gone gold and eventually peaked at number twenty-six, it was hardly an earth-shattering success. The Sugababes were cool, which carried credibility, but they weren't a household name. If they were written about at all in the tabloids in 2001, it was because of in-fighting and accusations of bullying. So Island knew they needed a Big Song to re-launch them – one that would build on 'Overload''s critical consensus as 'Pop it's Okay to Like', while also blowing the minds of people who don't care about the moronic concept of 'guilty pleasures'. While work started immediately with then relatively unknown songwriters and producers Xenomania, the raw, semi-illegal single that would save them was being played in sweaty nightclubs in east London by a mysterious bootlegger called Girls on Top.*

Darcus Beese, former A&R Director, Island Records: My lawyer at the time, Sarah Stennett, was also representing the Sugababes. Sarah told me the Sugababes were getting out of their London Records deal and when I went to see them with my boss, Nick Gatfield, they were doing rehearsals with Heidi. At that point I think Sarah had them in with Brian [Higgins]. [Future single] 'Round Round' was there as a real rough demo, well before 'Freak Like Me' happened.

Brian Higgins: I really liked them and I thought 'Overload' was a fantastic record. Their voices were incredible. I think they had just been dropped the first day they came down to work with us. I felt like [Sarah] knew what she was doing and that there was a record deal up their sleeve.

Darcus Beese: I loved the *One Touch* album. 'Overload' gave you the template of how to make records in terms of the Sugababes. I'd like to think we extended what they were doing on *One Touch* into what they did with *Angels with Dirty Faces*, then obviously they went stratospheric. But initially 'Freak Like Me' and 'Round Round' were an extension of what I thought was cool coming out of the *One Touch* era.

Keisha: We were recording and trying to get the new single and our A&R said, 'Hey, there's an underground track called "Freak Like Me".'

Darcus Beese: At the time, Ross Allen and I were in the Island A&R department. In a meeting one day, Ross played the 'Freak Like Me' bootleg 7-inch. The samples hadn't been cleared but it was just this fucking amazing piece of music. I think it was [Island President] Nick Gatfield that said, 'This would be great if the Sugababes cut it.'

Richard X, 'Freak Like Me' producer: I don't think anyone thought it was going to be big; it was more like, 'Here's a girl-band who were quite cool, AKA they were in the *NME*, but then they were dropped and could we just do something with this?' It's funny, I don't think anyone thought that would be a very successful record. Even in the industry. It just didn't seem to make any sense.

Darcus Beese: At the time, Richard X was this kind of bootleg kid doing his shit under the radar [as Girls on Top] not wanting to be found out. So Ross either knew him or got hold of him. At first Richard was really cautious because he thought we were coming to bust him.

Richard X: I was buying those odd electronica singles, or IDM as they were called, in the late '90s and that was quite an interesting area for a while, but then it got really up its own backside. I think what I was doing [with 'Girls on Top'] was a reaction to that po-faced-ness – I was reaching back to the pop electronica, so sampling the Human League or Kraftwerk. My stuff fitted into a bit of electroclash, a bit of that [trendy London club night] Trash scene, into indie discos.

Darcus Beese: We ended up meeting him in a café in Brixton and we were like, 'All above board, how do we work together?

299

We'd love the Sugababes to cut it.' Ross and I convinced him. Off the back of that, Richard X went and signed to Virgin but we got 'Freak Like Me'.

Richard X: The reason Virgin signed me is because I was a very cheap deal and it was an interesting scene. The Soulwax record ['As Heard on Radio Soulwax Pt 2'] hadn't come out yet, which is another benchmark of the bootleg era. Also, Virgin thought they could clear my Kraftwerk and Whitney Houston bootleg ['I Wanna Dance with Numbers'], because they had contacts with Kraftwerk. Then I got this report back from Kraftwerk that said they thought it was the worst record they'd ever heard but in the best-looking sleeve. That for me was great.

Keisha: The moment we heard ['Freak Like Me''s] first verse me and Mutya started jumping up and down screaming because we knew the song back to front. We'd been singing the R&B version by Adina Howard since primary school. They printed out lyrics, which we threw to the side. Heidi had never heard it before, but we were old-school R&B heads. We just wanted the mic. We didn't know anything about 'Are "Friends" Electric?', all we cared about was that our friends at school would know we'd finally done an R&B track. We wanted to be accepted by our peers so much.

Mutya: I wasn't sure at first. I loved Gary Numan but I didn't see how it could work until we did it. No one had brought anything out like that so it was quite risky. The label knew, the management knew. Then when we did the video it made more sense.

Cameron McVey: The girls went off to work with Darcus at Island and he called me up to work on [*Angels with Dirty Faces*]. But then I heard the first single and said, 'I can't top that, it's a number one,' and that's what happened. The only place I could go was down.

Felix Howard: When I came back [to work with the Sugababes], there was no Cameron. He'd decided to take Siobhán's side on everything. Jony and I were told, 'Don't work with them, fuck them,' and we were like, 'Shut up.' So we worked with them again. I liked Heidi. I wanted to stay out of all that shit: people have fights; it's showbiz. I didn't think it had anything to do with me.

Richard X: The band were very suspicious of me because I hadn't done anything other than a trendy single. They were in a difficult position, too. Heidi had joined and she was obviously finding her feet, so it was like a new beginning for everyone.

Keisha: I remember us arranging our parts [with Richard X]. We were so excited because there'd been this shift in energy. Lots of optimism. It felt really good.

Richard X: [We recorded] in Shepherd's Bush for one session and then another in Kilburn. It was a vocal recording to a backing track, so it wasn't like we were making the music, so labels would put you in any little studio then. Especially if they didn't have to impress the band.

Mutya: It wasn't hard for us to go into the studio and lay our vocals down.

Richard X: If you've ever been and listened to a singer you know on record and they just open their mouths and it's them, that's what they're like. They're characterful. That's what makes them great.

Darcus Beese: I was always a voices man. The fact that there was a girl group who had those vocals was probably the success of the group in terms of credibility.

Richard X: There's three or four different versions of 'Freak Like Me'. My one was used in the video and for some radio releases, then there was another one that I didn't know had been done. I was in a club and heard it for the first time. They'd changed the drums and I remember being like, 'Why would you do that?' My whole purpose was that they were raw records. You're deliberately making things a bit crushed, which is that annoying low-res sound that's very much the sound of terrible MP3 players. I wanted crunchy and horrible. By the time they got it to the Sugababes, it wasn't my record, ultimately. You do your work on it and then it becomes theirs.

Darcus Beese: Clearing the publishing was a fucking nightmare, but Gary Numan was amazing. He liked the idea that another generation was discovering it. I remember we did an early version that I ended up cutting onto 7-inch and we called it 'Are Freaks Electric?' by Sugababes vs Girls on Top.

Richard X: I don't remember that being a conversation either. I wasn't bothered about it; it's just out of your control.

Darcus Beese: We put the bootlegs in Rough Trade and off the back of that I think Sara Cox played it on Radio 1 and it all exploded from there.

Mutya: Then it went to number one – imagine that!

Alex Needham: In terms of pop music, that was definitely the stuff to focus on. You wouldn't do all the TV talent show stuff. Also, electroclash basically turned into that sort of pop music, with the same sounds and to a certain extent the same aesthetic. The bootleg things Erol [Alkan, DJ and producer] was doing at Trash, that was a cool indie thing, but then Kylie did it at the BRITs [in 2002, with her mash-up of 'Can't Get You Out of My Head' and 'Blue Monday'] and the Sugababes did it with 'Freak Like Me'.

Brian Higgins: I think 'Freak Like Me' was a very important record. It's also a very aggressive pop record, especially at that time. I think it showed the extent to which Radio 1 were prepared to back the Sugababes and were prepared to back an excellent record. I think it informed a lot.

Richard X: The Rough Trade wall was where you had a certain type of pop music before the '00s. It was often indie-infused. Then suddenly those sounds were in the charts or being used by bands. There was a need to freshen things up. Pop's always picked from the underground and the influence of dance music on pop was a big one. Also, the Americans were doing better records. I remember that early part of the '00s you had Timbaland and Missy and all this exciting stuff. They were massively weird, big records and every other month seemed to be them flipping everything on its head. It does make a certain pop mentality that it's just about little boybands or little girlbands just seem a bit . . . square.

Keisha: We had something to prove. We wanted the industry and our peers to embrace us. At first it was really difficult. Even with 'Freak Like Me', I remember we had done the BRITs and I was watching an interview and they were like, 'They've got the number one, but do we honestly think they're going to have another album?' I was quite a stubborn little mule when I was a teenager and I was like, 'You'll see!' To say you've won a BRIT for any girlband is amazing. I was always confused about the category in which we won [Best Dance Act]. Whoever was on the committee that year clearly lost the plot.

Mutya: Oh my God, imagine. I actually forgot we won one! I still don't believe it. I have to pinch myself and say, 'Mutya, these are your achievements.'

Keisha: I remember we did the *NME* but we also did the MOBO Awards, then we also did the Trevor Nelson show and then we were on the *Smash Hits* tour and then we were doing the BRITs. We were covering so many bases, so it was like, 'Are we an R&B band?' No. 'Are we a pop band?' I guess, but it wasn't straight pop. So I can understand why someone was like, 'Just put them in the dance category.'

Darcus Beese: That was so random. We were crossing genres and banging styles together. Later on I got them to cover 'I Bet You Look Good on the Dancefloor' [by the Arctic Monkeys] and all of a sudden they were appearing at the *NME* Awards. They could inhabit loads of different genres.

SUGABABES

Keisha: I think we were seen more as a Black band because I think Mutya's race was ambiguous – people didn't really know where she was from. I think people thought she was mixed race, as in Black and white, whereas she was Asian and white. I think people assumed because of how she was and how she was raised that that helped us be more embraced on the urban side because it looked like there were two Black girls in the band.

Mutya: For most of my life, until people started knowing where the Philippines was, a lot of people used to call me Black-Japanese, Black-Chinese, mixed-race. I was never the race I was. For me, I found it irritating because I've always been very open about what race I was, but people weren't listening. Or they didn't understand. I used to get attacked a lot for being a race that I wasn't. I'd get people coming up to me being quite rude, then when I would correct them they'd be cool. It made no sense. It was so racist. Then Myleene Klass came out, who is the same race as me, and Vanessa from the Saturdays, too. Then people were like, 'Oh, the Philippines, okay, I know where that is.' It was hard back then because everyone looked at me like I was an alien.

Myleene Klass, Hear'Say: Mutya was the only Filipina that I knew of in a band. She has one of the best voices in pop. An outstanding talent and is hugely respected in the Filipino community. It's clear to many that I'm mixed race but no one ever knew where I was from. It shows the importance of visibility. If you can't see it, you can't be it. And music opens that door to everyone.

'You weren't allowed dogs in the hotel, so Heidi would smuggle it in in her handbag'

The success of 'Freak Like Me' in April 2002 helped prove that UK pop acts could hold their own when it came to weird. It solidified the idea it didn't need to all be pastiche or gloriously one-dimensional. By helping push an underground sub-genre into the mainstream, the Sugababes appeared, to the general public at least, to be at the cutting edge of something cool once again. It also gave them a platform to go anywhere next, having proved they could easily handle R&B, pop, indie, soul and, according to the BRITs panel, dance. For Angels with Dirty Faces' *second single, 'Round Round', they collaborated with Brian Higgins and Miranda Cooper, whose careers had yet to be sky-rocketed by Girls Aloud. Equally weird and unexpected, 'Round Round' (just about) fused together an obscure drum-loop sample, two separate verse melodies and a middle section swiped from a different song. It was the start of a creative relationship that saw them collaborate on five more top-ten singles across 2003's* Three *and 2005's* Taller in More Ways *albums.*

Darcus Beese: On first meeting when you went down [to the Xenomania studio in Kent], the energy was off the scale. It was something I hadn't seen before in my young A&R career.

Keisha: They work in a strange way but I actually embraced that. Sometimes you don't want to spend sixteen hours on one song. I would write maybe ten different verses, the other girls the same, and Brian would just pick the ones he felt were the best. Sometimes the beats were completely different because they were different genres – so 'Round Round', there's a whole ballad in the middle eight that was from a completely different song.

Darcus Beese: ['Round Round'] was a brave choice but it was so compelling as a record. And you were coming off the back of a huge record like 'Freak Like Me', so you were starting to own the lane. I think Sugababes dictated rather than followed.

Miranda Cooper: Brian and I used to go to Paris for the day – very extravagant, but he had all the 'Believe' money – and we used to go around the record stores and pick up CDs based on their front covers. Then we'd come back and go through all of it. Most of it would be complete dross, but he found this beat ['Tango Forte' by German production team Dublex Inc.] on a compilation, which was the start of 'Round Round'. We didn't have computers in those days so I would write down every song I wrote. Brian would say, 'Bring out the list,' and I would sing every chorus I'd ever done over this beat and see what went with it. We got the chorus for 'Round Round' and they came in and sung it and it sounded ace.

Darcus Beese: There were these real obscure samples that we had to clear and that was the exciting thing about how Brian put his stuff together. Across a couple of records he made some real compelling, best of breed songs. I think the girls' voices helped as well in terms of keeping it Sugababes. Brian just facilitated this pop landscape for them that was just off the scale.

Jon Shave, former Xenomania producer and songwriter: I remember going down [to the studio] and they had the first, eight-minute version of 'Round Round', which was just a chorus on a loop of the sample. But it immediately jumped out as this vital idea.

Miranda Cooper: I remember being in Amsterdam really stoned and coming up with the first verse. The Sugababes were involved in the writing, so we'd normally start with a chorus idea and then they'd be involved in the verses. The whole thing was quite an abrasive sound, probably because we were quite abrasive people. We wanted it so much. We were really sick of being unsuccessful. After all that time, the first song we put out went to number one.

Mutya: We'd stay down there for a week or so and just have so many songs on the go, it was very confusing, but then when he'd put it together it was like, 'Ah, okay.'

Miranda Cooper: They were so cool. I remember going back to London with them and feeling like they were in the upper sixth form and I was in the fourth form.

Brian Higgins: I knew that with Mutya's voice we could make incredible records.

Jon Shave: She was one of the best singers I've ever been around. As soon as she opens her mouth it just sounds like a record. She manages to communicate endless amounts of charisma and attitude and intrigue in every syllable.

Felix Howard: Mutya has the best voice of all of that girlband generation. She is absolutely the number one. She's wildly ahead of everyone else.

Darcus Beese: It was always the battle over who would start a Sugababes song. You can guess where the issues rose because it was always Mutya. They were great at ballads because of

Mutya. She could emote like nobody's business. She was the one that gave ballads like 'Stronger' and 'Caught in a Moment' the weight in terms of emotion. Heidi was the 'take it to the bridge' person. Keisha could give you the power and the ad-libs and the runs. Mutya would give you the depth and the truth.

Keisha: The only hard thing around that time was staying down where [Brian] was, because it was in the middle of nowhere. I remember we stayed in this little cottage across the street, but for any teenager once you're done for the day you want to go and hang out with your friends. Instead we were in the middle of nowhere.

Mutya: Kent was so far and we were so young so no one was driving. They put us in this creepy hotel. I would sneakily get my friend who drove to come pick me up and get me out of Kent and bring me back the next day. Or I'd get my friends to come over to the hotel and we'd have a party there.

Darcus Beese: Brian tells a brilliant story as to why the album is called *Angels with Dirty Faces*. It's because Mutya would disappear. She once turned up a day later after going missing and Brian said the car rolled up, there was this music playing, all this bass banging out of the car, the door opens and all this smoke comes out and Mutya steps up like butter wouldn't melt. That's where the title came from. Did you ever hear the story where she walked out of the Shepherd's Bush Empire gig? They were just about to do their encore and it's like, 'Why haven't they come back on?' The story was that Mutya had just walked out. She had the hump. Just walked out the stage door and fucking went home.

Miranda Cooper: One time the girls wanted to stay in London and Brian said, 'Well, sometimes we go to hotels.' We used to go to the country for two or three nights and turn our phones off and just write and write and write and make ourselves silly with weed and God knows what. So he said, 'Let's do something in London.' They ended up choosing the Dorchester hotel. We were in this suite and I remember Heidi had a pug, and you weren't allowed dogs in the hotel, so she'd smuggle it in in her handbag.

Jon Shave: And it would poo all over the carpets.

Keisha: Of course we wanted to be in London, because we wanted to see our friends, which is kind of normal for a teenager. As an adult now, I can't think of anything better than a sleepy village.

Mutya: I love the quiet now.

'The Blazin' Squad boys fancied us lot like crazy'

Angels with Dirty Faces *was followed by* Three, *which also went multi-platinum, establishing the Sugababes as a proper Q4 act, i.e. their albums were locked in for the music industry's September–December sales jamboree. It also meant an escalation in their workload, with that checklist of TV shows, magazines and tabloid interviews becoming increasingly important. While in the past they'd always been too young or, in Siobhán's case, too unwilling (poor A1) to hang out with other bands, now they relished being on the same promo loop as acts, including their newly created peers in ludicrous pop bangerdom, Girls Aloud. The increased success, however, also brought with it unwanted attention.*

Keisha: People think that when you're in a band it's just you three, but it wasn't; there were always about ten other people travelling with you but they were all adults. If you ever go on the internet, any events that the Sugababes and Girls Aloud were at together it will be Girls Aloud and then me next to them. I would ditch my bandmates. I loved being in their presence.

Mutya: When we were doing the *Smash Hits* tour, we had so much fun. Blazin' Squad were there, Blue, Big Brovaz; there was Gareth Gates, A1, everyone that you can think of in pop. We all hung out. We used to cause mischief in the hotel, play Knock Down Ginger. The Blazin' Squad boys fancied us lot like crazy. We chilled with and hung around so many amazing people like P!nk, Black Eyed Peas. Once we were on the same stage as Britney Spears.

Keisha: The only band we had a bit of a weird thing with was Atomic Kitten, but I think the press kind of built that up bigger than it needed to be. It was because Heidi used to be in that band and I think a couple of things were said between one of their members and Mutya. But that was the most gangster it got.

Mutya: Back then, all I remember was being flown from one place to another to another. One time we did *CD:UK* and I did an interview alongside Cheryl and Posh Spice, Victoria. [Heidi and Keisha] had left to go to the airport before me, so when it was done I was flung on a motorbike straight to the airport. Another time I had to get a helicopter down to somewhere near the sea to do a festival. It was very 'move, move, move'.

Keisha: I'll let her tell her story but it was also a really diffi-cult time [for Mutya] because [the way the tabloids wrote about her] affected the band. It affected her even wanting to have her picture taken. There should have been more done to protect her at that time. There was a TV show and they were counting down Britain's mingers or something and they billed it as me and Heidi as the soft pop princesses and then there's Mutya. She experimented with her style and she's always been that way. We laugh about it now, but when you're young it's not nice at all. Who wants to go out on stage when you think people are laugh-ing at you?

Mutya: It was depressing. I feel traumatised by these people. I never understood why they had such hate for me. I literally would say boo and they'd make it into a story that got really per-sonal. It was how I looked and things I didn't like talking about in public. I was always in the paper for something and most of the time it was bullshit. I never understood why they wanted to talk my name. Today it's even worse because of the internet and social media. Thank God we didn't have that back then. I don't know how I'm still standing. But I will not let them affect me now.

'We all felt like we wanted to support her whatever her reasons were'

By the time fourth album Taller in More Ways – *which saw the band work with American super-producer Dallas Austin – became the band's first UK number-one album in October 2005, Mutya was already contemplating her future. Now with a nine-month-old daughter and suffering from postnatal depression, her focus had shifted and she officially left the band on 21 December. The contentious Xenomania-created 'Red Dress' was then lined up as the first release to feature new recruit Amelle Berrabah. Taller in More Ways was eventually re released with new artwork and Amelle's vocals replacing Mutya's on three songs.*

Mutya: I didn't like 'Red Dress'. I hated it. But then I had left by the time they released it as a single, thank God.

Jon Shave: Around the time there were other struggles going on and it was bigger than just 'Red Dress'. It was difficult to get [Mutya] to the studio and it was difficult to keep her in the studio.

Miranda Cooper: She sounded amazing even though she sounded absolutely over it.

Brian Higgins: Mutya was very laid-back [in the studio]. We'd teach her the chorus and she'd go into the room to sing it and I was always waiting for the moment she was going to say, 'I'm not singing this.' Literally waiting. I could feel our career in the balance, just waiting for her to sing. Then the music would start and you'd think she was going to sing and she wouldn't. Then the music would come back around again and then she'd start singing and it was like, 'Fuck me, it's incredible.' Horrible getting to that point.

Darcus Beese: It was always a fight as to what the singles were. Apart from 'Freak Like Me' it was always a fight. But Mutya really hated 'Red Dress'. Although by that point I think she was starting to hate the whole scenario.

Mutya: If I'm going to sing a song I have to make sure it makes sense to me and it makes sense to you. I don't want to go up and sing anything. That's not what I'm here for. If I don't like it I won't just go, 'I'm not doing it,' but I will say that I'm not sure. 'Red Dress', for me, was just no. The chorus didn't make sense. Everyone was like, 'It's amazing,' and I'd be, 'What are you even talking about?'

Miranda Cooper: That Sugababes album [*Taller in More Ways*] was difficult to make. It was quite chaotic. I remember once Mutya went out to get lunch and never came back.

Darcus Beese: Listen, the girls were never 100 per cent trusting of the situation in terms of the process. They were very headstrong and when you're dealing with three different people you've got to deal with their different personalities. If X thinks you're talking to Y and Y thinks you're talking to Z, then that creates a dynamic. With the girls, they could have enjoyed it a lot more. There was always in-fighting in the group. Whether it was Siobhán, Heidi, Keisha or Mutya, there was always something going on. It's about how long you can keep them together. There's going to come a time when it's going to implode.

Mutya: There were a lot of things going on. There were deeper things. At the same time, me having my daughter didn't help. Not having any time off, still being in the studio breastfeeding until 5 a.m. That took a lot out of me. Then I got baby blues and depression is a bitch. Having no one understand you during that time can really be hard. Just feeling like I was alone in my head. Don't get it twisted: the label were supportive, but not in the way

314

of 'You can have some time off.' I was seven or eight months pregnant in Atlanta recording the album. Then, two weeks after I gave birth, I was back in the studio finishing the album. Within a few months we did the video for [lead single] 'Push the Button' and it was the skinniest I've ever been in my life because we were just working, working, working. I was only twenty.

Keisha: It was such a heavy load. Extremely hard, both personally and professionally. Personally because I'd been with Mutya every day at that point since I was nine years old. Even though we started to have a lot of distance between us as we got older, it was like my arm wasn't there. But I understood that it was necessary at that time for her to go. We all felt like we wanted to support her, whatever her reasons were. So the actual split was amicable. Then, professionally, I felt like there was a lot on my shoulders. I felt like I had to carry way more, both behind the scenes and publicly. Everything that used to be on Mutya – any name-calling, anything – it just shifted automatically onto me and only me. I felt the weight of that.

Darcus Beese: What management were always really good at was being ready to flip something. Mutya was one person that you couldn't let leave the Sugababes. I had many evenings trying to convince her not to go. We got through the pregnancy, she had her baby, but she just wasn't enjoying it. Her relationship with the other two had gone south. At some point you've got to start thinking [about the future]. We'd released 'Push the Button' and she'd done the video for [second single] 'Ugly' and then she said, 'I'm gone.' As we were trying to convince her we had to go, 'Fuck, what's plan B?', and they had Amelle.

Mutya: To be honest, before I'd even left the band, [Amelle] had recorded six songs of mine. It was weird. She came in forty-eight hours after I left and then they had my album cover up on the shelves for two more weeks and then took it down. She already had six songs on that album that she had covered, so you do the maths. I don't need to tell anyone what happened. That tells you that she'd been doing it from a long time ago, as in before I said I was leaving. It should never have been done that way. No one wants to be a back-up. I found it very sneaky.

Darcus: I remember [management] playing me Amelle's voice and being like, 'This is a bit too spooky.' We were guided by Mutya just going, 'I'm out.' But the narrative on the outside starts to go, 'Oh, she was in the wings waiting,' but it wasn't like that.

Keisha: For any member who's entered the band, we've always been told there's been extensive research and 'we happened to find this person' or 'we didn't know this person'. You can read between the lines for yourselves; I won't say anything else. But later we did a *CD:UK* interview and Mutya was there to support us on our first TV appearance with Amelle.

Mutya: I came and said hello because people were trying to say I was hating. How could I hate? I left the group for her to take my space, so that makes no sense. I walked in and said, 'Hi, pleased to meet you,' like, 'We're cool, we're cool.' Then I got banned and was told I couldn't perform under the same roof as the girls because I made them feel uncomfortable. That was fucking bullshit. I was in the Sugababes my whole entire life; no one's going to tell me anything else. That's my baby regardless. It was pretty deep. For a long time I didn't see Keisha because obviously I was upset with the things I was hearing. Me and Keisha are always going to be close because we grew up together and obviously they did her wrong too later on.

'It felt like the Hello! *magazine end of the Sugababes*'

Now becoming adept at brushing herself down and carrying on, Keisha found herself as the sole original member of the Sugababes. Having lost the edge that Mutya gave them, the band re-grouped via 2006's Overload: The Singles Collection, *which featured twelve UK top-ten hits, and 2007's spectacularly unpleasant Girls Aloud collaboration 'Walk This Way' (it was for charity). That was followed by the shiny* Change *album (another UK number one) and then quickly by 2008's patchy* Catfights and Spotlights. *At some point in September 2009, after work finished on the disastrous* Sweet 7 *album, Amelle briefly quit, before Keisha was ousted instead and hastily replaced by Eurovision Song Contestant 2009 fifth-place runner-up Jade Ewen.*

Keisha: It was the first time for Heidi to have a member leave, but for me I was seasoned in what to do. It was about embracing [Amelle]. I was given the role of teaching her the ropes and making her feel as comfortable as possible with this shitstorm going on around us. Again it was about having to prove ourselves. Every article was, 'That's it, they're done, Mutya has such a prominent voice in the group,' and we had to read those things. Again, I was like, 'Well, you'll see!' ['About You Now'] is the biggest song we've ever had. It was number one for a month.

Darcus Beese: I convinced Dr Luke and Cathy Dennis to come and do a writing session and the girls cut 'About You Now'.

Keisha: [With *Change*] I understood the assignment, let me put it that way. Is it my favourite album? Definitely not. 'My Love Is Pink' was probably my least favourite song of all time. I actually deny my voice is on that to anyone who asks. I don't know that song, I don't know who sang it.

Darcus Beese: I love 'My Love Is Pink'. 'Never Gonna Dance Again' is amazing too and there's a demo of that song somewhere with Mutya's vocals. The original.

Keisha: I feel like the songs [on 2008's *Catfights and Spotlights*] were great but just not for us. I remember conversations where they were trying to recreate *One Touch*. They were trying to go dark and cool because they felt like everyone was saying it was going a bit too pop.

Darcus: I had just been made co-president of Island, which brings a lot of different responsibilities. I knew Klas Åhlund from all the stuff we were doing with [Swedish pop icon] Robyn, so I got him to come in and start working with the Sugababes. He had some Robyn demos that him and Max [Martin] had done, so we used those records as a jump-off. That album probably signals the end of the Sugababes. When we picked the singles it just felt like we were running out of ideas. It was all a bit starting to push water up a hill.

Keisha: Unfortunately someone from management was given the position of the lead and he was making decisions that I can only describe as extremely naff. Never in my life have I been in a creative process where someone had come in and said, 'We've got to do this' or 'Radio wants this'.

Darcus Beese: They were starting to reach the end of their cycle. The artwork for *Change* felt like the *Hello!* magazine end of the Sugababes.

Keisha: Then there was the album *Sweet 7*, which technically I recorded. We had the first single [the Bruno Mars-assisted 'Get Sexy'], which I think had gone to radio, and they had to pull it and re-do my vocals. The one thing I will say is that up until that point I had the most fun with Heidi and Amelle and it's the most horrendous music I've ever recorded in that line-up. I absolutely loved [that time], which is so ironic because that's the line-up I got booted out of. I don't know what happened there.

Mutya: I was shocked. I didn't see it coming. I remember going on GMTV when I found out that she had been kicked out. They were asking me about her being a bully and I was like, 'I didn't leave because she bullied me.' She's definitely not a bully. I know how it feels when people are doing the most and lying and it's not nice. I felt sorry for Keisha. It was crazy. They just thought the name was bigger than the people in the band and unfortunately for them it's the group of people that makes it. It's vocals.

Jony Rockstar: They became a commodity. So many people were relying on their success for their own wage packet and that's when it just goes horrible. Music isn't about that.

Felix Howard: There's an allegory about a boat – if you have a ship made of wood and gradually you substitute each plank out but you keep the structural integrity of the boat, by the time you've removed all the planks is it the same boat?

Siobhán: It was definitely a step too far for me. But then even when Mutya was replaced, sure, they went on to have their biggest hit ever, but it just didn't mean anything to me. The whole point was that it wasn't manufactured and here it was about as manufactured as it could be.

Mutya: Over the years I'd always bump into Siobhán.

Siobhán: We would see each other at random fashion parties and we'd always be really excited to see each other, which was nice. Even when myself and Keisha finally ran into each other, it was just so obvious that being so young and not being supported in the way we needed had been so detrimental to our relationship. It just didn't need to be like that.

Keisha: Me exiting the group will obviously be the lowest point [of the Sugababes journey], but there were so many positive highlights. There's finally seeing Michael Jackson at the World Music Awards [in 2006]. Then to be introduced by Whitney Houston at the Fashion Rocks event, that was amazing. We got to go to the afterparty and she was performing in front of only about thirty people. Then there's always going to be the highlight of me jumping offstage and giving Simon Cowell the most embarrassing lap dance of all time at a corporate Christmas party. I had a Sasha Fierce moment and forgot myself.

'If I touch hands with another fucking icon, I'm going to drop on the floor'

While Keisha remained the Sugababes Recruitment Agency's longest employee, Siobhán and Mutya both released solo material. Continuing with London Records and working with some of the same team as One Touch, *Siobhán released the* Revolution in Me *album in 2003. That was followed in 2007 by the bewitching alt-pop cult classic,* Ghosts. *Mutya, meanwhile, leaned into her love for R&B on 2007's top-ten* Real Girl, *an album that featured two legends. Oh, and she also supported Prince on tour.*

Siobhán: The one takeaway I had was how much I loved making music and being in the studio. London Records reached out to me to see if I wanted to do anything on my own and I did. I just rolled with it.

Cameron McVey: It was so much fun; it was such a laugh. She's just got this killer voice. When you're writing with her you can say 'sing this' and she'll just do it. The only other person I think is like her is Michael Stipe – he is one of those people you can say 'sing me this' to and he'll do it there and then.

Siobhán: It was very therapeutic but so much damage had been done that really until a good few years later I hadn't really bounced back completely. I've been left a bit of a nervous wreck by it all. It's much easier to look back on it now because it is so different. And how nice it is that the three of us have been able to be back together and operate on such a different level with each other. Most people don't get the chance to have that. But with [second album] *Ghosts*, in my naïvety I thought that if you made something

321

that to you sounds great then that is the best thing you can put out. Rather than it having to be a certain BPM or a certain sound. Obviously I've always shot myself in the foot in that sense.

Darcus Beese: Mutya had George Michael [on 'This Is Not (Real Love)'] and Amy Winehouse ['B-Boy Baby'] on one album – who does that? [*Real Girl*] was probably where I really learned how to dig an album out of an artist that doesn't want to come to the studio.

Jony Rockstar: I didn't write [*Real Girl*'s 'Strung Out'], I just produced it. I think I may have been sent the vocal.

Felix Howard: I have a song ['It's Not Easy'] on that record and I'm very grateful for it but I had no creative input in that album really.

Mutya: Basically, with George Michael, he approached the Sugababes' management while I was in the group and said he wanted to record a song with me. And my manager said no. He said I was busy with the girls, which was crazy. It's George Michael! I will make time and drop the girls for five seconds. So I was like, 'Okay, what will be will be,' but I was upset the opportunity had gone. Then when I left the band I got another phone call and it was like, 'I know Mutya's not with the girls now, would she be interested in coming to the studio?' I thought it was a joke. But we set a date and I went into the studio and there he was, swivelling in his chair. I was like, 'Argh!'

Darcus Beese: It was mind-blowing. I don't even know if she realised at the time how off the scale [it was] and how lucky she was.

Mutya: Because I thought it was a joke I didn't tell my mum I was going and she's the biggest Wham! and George Michael fan. He was probably the nicest, most genuine person I've ever met in my life. I'm not just saying that because he's George Michael, you're fucking crazy, but he never did anything to make me feel insecure about how I was singing. I was talking to someone and they were like, 'You know he's only worked with four female artists' – that would be me, Whitney Houston, Mary J. Blige and Aretha Franklin. Only four females and I'm one of them. I cherish that like it's my party trick.

Darcus Beese: I remember I said to Amy about this hook that she never used, which was 'B-Boy Baby', and she only said yes because it was Mutya.

Mutya: We were friends as well as labelmates. She had such a kind soul. Whenever we'd see each other at award shows we'd go for a sneaky cigarette. I feel blessed that I was able to work with two legends.

Darcus Beese: There's a story where Prince invited Mutya to do an afterparty gig to jam and sing some songs and she looked at her watch and was like, 'Nah, I'm going out with my mates to a club.' Sorry, Prince, I'm out.

Mutya: I opened for Prince. I got to meet him and he told me that his favourite song of mine was 'Suffer for Love' and he wanted to sing it with me at the afterparty . . . then my manager said no, I had to go somewhere else. They were ruining my life! The next day I was doing something in Leicester somewhere and they wanted to leave straight after the show. I didn't understand it. Then I heard that I was Prince's screensaver on his laptop, like my album cover. I was also told not to look at him, so I came offstage at the O2 at rehearsals and while I'm walking towards the dressing room I see this smallest little thing ever. I'd heard he was always with his security so I was expecting to get jumped by somebody but it was him talking to me. If I touch hands with another fucking icon and legend, I'm going to drop on the floor. I was so blessed to work alongside any of them.

Tom Findlay, Groove Armada: We had an A&R man called Jonnie Blackburn and I think it was his idea to work with Mutya [on dance behemoth 'Song 4 Mutya (Out of Control)']. I think he got where the record was heading, which was quite pop. I still to this day think Mutya has got one of the great UK female pop voices that there has ever been.

Mutya: Groove Armada are amazing. We wrote that with [songwriter extraordinaire] Karen Poole.

Tom Findlay: Mutya did it all in my funny little basement studio in Stoke Newington. It was really surreal. I always fondly remember Mutya having a battered sausage for lunch. I enjoyed that as a detail. It made her feel very human to me. She bought a really stinky battered sausage to my studio.

Darcus Beese: [Making the album] was like getting blood out of a stone.

Mutya: I was dropped for some of the strangest reasons and it wasn't because I wasn't selling music. I was definitely dropped on a personal reason. I was selling music. I was number two [with lead single 'Real Girl'] behind Rihanna's 'Umbrella', so that's just dumb.

Darcus Beese: Hopefully she's proud of that album because she should be.

'Here we go again'

The enduring legacy of Sugababes' debut, One Touch, *is buffeted by ideas around what could have been. Of potential lost. So rumours in 2012 of a reunion of the original members – or 'Origibabes' as website Popjustice called them – caused mild panic in pop fans of a certain age. A major stumbling block was the right to use the Sugababes name, given an earlier legal attempt by Mutya in 2010 – just before the release of* Sweet 7 *– led to her only being able to use it on stationery, paper gift wrap and paper gift-wrapping ribbons. To that end, their first release after the reunion, the depressingly prophetic 'Flatline', was released as Mutya, Keisha, Siobhán and, annoyingly, sans Sugababes wrapping-paper tie-ins. After parting ways with label Polydor after that one single, the original trio disappeared again, only to return as the Sugababes for 2021's delayed twenty-year celebration of* One Touch. *In 2022, they embarked on a sold-out UK tour following a rapturously received Glastonbury performance and, that Christmas, finally released a range of Sugababes wrapping paper, alongside an album,* The Lost Tapes, *featuring MKS songs that never officially saw the light of day a decade earlier.*

Siobhán: It was exactly because Keisha was no longer in the Sugababes [that we reunited]. Never would I have thought there would be something that would happen to so unite our feelings. How could we not get together and have that conversation? It was just too tempting. Then of course the minute we were together we were like, 'I wonder what it would sound like if we sang together,' and by that point the curiosity is too strong. The minute we got into the studio and did a three-part harmony it was like, 'Ahh.' It was almost annoying that it was so good because how can we not carry on? Then it's, 'Here we go again!'

10

From Boyzone to Busted:
How the boyband evolved

Louis Walsh: You just need a good band and good songs. Why do people like you always try to over-analyse things? It's just a boyband with good songs.

Boyzone, Westlife and the rise of the stool-botherers

Boyzone, AKA Ronan Keating, Stephen Gately, Mikey Graham, Keith Duffy and Shane Lynch, were formed in the shadow of Take That. Or, rather, they were formed by manager Louis Walsh in 1993 as Ireland's answer to their UK counterparts, who, by the time Boyzone released debut album *Said and Done* in the summer of 1995, were already on their way out. Take That's final musical gift, however, had been 'Back for Good', an immaculate ballad that seemed to aim straight at the hearts not just of teenagers but their mums, too. For

Boyzone, this slower tempo was the template for their 'oeuvre', eschewing the usual 'banger, banger, ballad' pop singles strategy and picking instead to chuck in an up-tempo for charity or perhaps as a fourth single. Covers would also be a mainstay, as would chunky-knit rollnecks.

'Boyzone were like a pound-shop version of Take That'

Holly Jade-Johnston: Me and my friend flew to Dublin to search for Boyzone. I was fifteen. All we had was an issue of *Smash Hits* as it had a guide to which part of Dublin they lived in. The first house we tracked down was Stephen Gately's. We knocked on the door and his wee mum was stood in her bathrobe. He wasn't there but she invited us in anyway. His *Smash Hits* awards were on the mantlepiece and she allowed me to have a picture taken with one of them. Mikey was my favourite so we went and met his mum. We met Shane's siblings. Nobody was at Ronan's house.

Colin Barlow: It was a glorious time for pop music when *Smash Hits* was the great influencer. I'd worked on East 17 when I was in publishing and they were the rivals to Take That, so all of a sudden there was a market in pop music. Boyzone came from nowhere – they were signed to the Irish company, had a hit in Ireland and then we picked the record up.

Louis Walsh: I was the driving force of Boyzone. I put them together, I picked the name, I picked every single song they ever had. I was involved in every single thing.

Holly Jade-Johnston: What I liked about Boyzone was they were like a pound-shop version of Take That. Boyzone were attainable. They weren't quite as polished. You felt like you could touch them.

Lee Brennan: The first time I met Boyzone [at a club gig], we didn't have any songs to perform so I had to pretend I had a sore throat and the other two guys just went on and did their crazy dance routines. When Boyzone went on we put our hoods up and walked into the club to see if they were any good at dancing and Spike was like, 'Nah, they haven't got the dancing vibe at all.'

Gregg Masuak, director, 'Baby Can I Hold You': They were pretty boys. Ronan was the Gary Barlow of Boyzone in that he's sensible, he's professional, he's kind. Mikey was just there for the ride, just a nice average bloke. Shane always looked so lovingly at the camera. He was stuck in wanting to be the sexy one so he'd spend a lot of time brooding. He turned up with weird braided hair and it was like, 'Oh, for fuck's sake, why do you do this to yourself?'

Alex Needham: Boyzone were a classic example of people that didn't really want to do it particularly. The three guys who weren't Ronan and Stephen were really grumpy about it. Shane was the grumpiest of the lot. Boyzone were never good, were they? When you went to see them, it was never a good performance.

Holly Jade-Johnston: Boyzone opened up the Ice Blast [a ride in Blackpool Pleasure Beach] and I remember my friend phoned me on the landline to tell me. I just happened to have a banner I had made that said 'Mikey' on it. So I got there and watched them on the ride holding my banner. That's when everyone started calling me 'Mikey Banner'.

Colin Barlow: I think in our lifetimes [Louis Walsh and Simon Cowell] were brilliant strategists for that market. They got what that pop audience wanted and they were brilliant at understanding the marketplace.

Louis Walsh: [Both Boyzone and Westlife were] for girls. Girls and gay guys. They like boybands. There wasn't any plan or plot, it was just 'do a boyband' and that's it.

Holly Jade-Johnston: As well as Boyzone, I also loved OTT with all my heart. I was on MTV Select once with Donna Air, asking her to play OTT. I remember it cost my mum about £50 in calls. But before social media, [the fans] were penpals; you'd write to each other. We used to have Friendship Books that were basically made out of index cards. You'd put down your favourite bands, so OTT, Take That, Boyzone, then underneath you'd brag about all the things you'd done with the band like 'chased through a carpark'. Then you'd pop it in an envelope and pass it on to your friend. It was always lesser bands like Orange Orange, Upside Down, Ultra. We loved them because we could meet them.

Lee Thompson: Somebody once referred to the audience of regional radio pop shows as 'the council estate girls'. Not in a disparaging way. What they meant was they were the most loyal pop fans. You could have an evening show interview with

NSYNC – who I remember coming to Viking radio in 1999 – but a band like Code Red, for example, would have more people waiting outside. They could speak to them directly, whereas the American boybands were more aloof superstars.

'Simon Cowell would always tell me: "Nothing's cooler than selling a lot of records"'

By 1999, with six UK number-one singles under their Burton belts, Boyzone were ready to 'try out new things', AKA Ronan was keen to go solo. For fans of immaculate balladry performed by five Irish men this was clearly devastating news, but thankfully Louis Walsh had a plan. Initially formed as 'pop vocal group' Six as One in 1997, and featuring Kian Egan, Mark Feehily, Shane Filan plus three others, Walsh took them to BMG. After an audition, they were rejected by Simon Cowell, who called them the ugliest band he had ever seen in his life. Three members were dropped and swiftly replaced by Nicky Byrne and Brian McFadden, the latter initially changing the spelling of his first name from Brian to Bryan to help with the look of his autograph. Satisfied with the genetic make-up of the newly named Westside, later Westlife, Cowell signed them to BMG and Walsh cleverly employed Ronan Keating as their 'co-manager'. Cowell and Walsh also put them in the studio with British songwriters Wayne Hector and Steve Mac, as well as flying them to Sweden to work with the likes of Max Martin, Rami, Andreas Carlsson, Per Magnusson and Jörgen Elofsson. Like Boyzone, they favoured ballads, but also leaned into the late '90s surge in post-Cheiron mid-tempos as favoured by the Backstreet Boys and Britney. The formula worked, with Westlife's first seven singles all debuting at number one in the UK. By the time they went on hiatus in 2010, six years after Brian 'Bryan' McFadden's departure, they'd doubled that tally.

Alex Needham: [Westlife] were just Boyzone: the second generation.

Holly Jade-Johnston: They were a lesser Boyzone.

Louis Walsh: [Simon and I] thought about the punters. People. We were never trying to be trendy or be in the *NME*. Or at the *Q* Awards. This was just aimed at people. That's why Westlife are still selling out arenas. We couldn't care less if Radio 1 liked it. We had TV and regional radio. We had all the magazines. The Saturday TV shows were very important for Westlife.

Lauren Cochrane, senior fashion writer, *The Guardian*: There was a bit of a thing about white around the millennium, including white parties, and Westlife definitely plugged into that in their style – as well as bringing a not-very-subtle reference to heaven and angels complete with pray hands long before emojis. Their hair and the nice shirts were also all about making sure they had broad appeal – beyond teenagers to a more grown-up demographic who would like the smartness.

Savan Kotecha, songwriter and producer: [Simon] was so good at putting these projects together – they weren't the cool projects; they were the projects that sold. [Westlife] were smart and they listened to Simon. He just had his finger on what the punters would like. He'd always tell me: 'Nothing's cooler than selling a lot of records.'

Louis Walsh: [Westlife] had these great producers and writers including Steve Mac. He writes ballads and that's his thing – he's really good at them. We didn't get any better than him or the

Swedish people. It was Simon Cowell and me that decided what they were going to do. It just worked.

Savan Kotecha: Everything I was doing at that point was with [Swedish producers] Quiz and Lorossi and they were pitching solely to Simon. We would basically be writing for Simon Cowell rather than the particular artist. He had a very specific pop taste and we just happened to be some of the people able to nail that. He was really good at taking care of songwriters and producers and very loyal.

Steve Anderson: My feeling on Simon Cowell is he is literally one of the best A&R men ever. Simon has what I call punter's ears. He's not technical but he can hear the general public, basically. When I was working on Westlife's 'Where We Are' [in 2009], he would call me up and say, 'There's something that happens at fifty seconds in, I don't know what it is, it just doesn't sound right to me.' I'd go to fifty seconds in and he would be right.

Savan Kotecha: [2001's 'Bad Girls'] was meant for [future 'Despacito' hitmaker] Luis Fonsi. He then decided not to use it, so Quiz and Lorossi played it to Westlife. This was the time when Simon wanted Westlife to be what Westlife was, which was doing ballads, but they were young guys who went out and partied. They were like, 'This is an edgy song for us, we're going to do it,' and it was my first big break. It was a bonus track [on *World of Our Own*], but I was getting royalties off an album that sold 5 million copies. Suddenly I could pay my rent.

Louis Walsh: Absolutely [the songs are more important than the band]. Look at the Backstreet Boys – the songs are better than any of them. There was no solo career there. If you have Max Martin or Brian Higgins or Steve Mac committed to a band then that's all you need. I was lucky with Westlife because I had Simon Cowell. His day job was A&R and he really worked – he picked all the covers with me and I'd be on the phone to him every day. We picked 'Mandy', 'I Have a Dream', 'You Raise Me Up'. We picked all those songs ourselves. That's why it worked. It was just me and him and them.

Savan Kotecha: The pop artists had a lot less control in general than they do now. Back then you had Simon Cowell at the peak of his powers, creatively. There was a lot of record-label influence on the songs and they found great songs. We don't have that as much nowadays.

James Masterson: During this period of colossally high record sales, [songs] didn't necessarily stick around long enough to have a huge cultural impact. Westlife were the poster child for this kind of phenomenon because they managed to get the marketing absolutely down pat. You can say what you like about Louis Walsh, but he certainly knew how to time releases. He could almost guarantee Westlife getting to number one.

Lee Thompson: [The Box] were the most important when it came to Westlife videos. [The label] would always give it to us first to see how it performed over the weekend and then it would go to MTV on the Monday. The reason The Box was so important to the labels was it was the first line of promotion when it came to doing your pre-sale at Woolworths. Bearing in mind Woolworths were huge – if you weren't stacked at

Woolies on a Monday morning then you weren't going to be in the top twenty.

James Masterson: During this whole frantic era there was a great phenomenon of the Woolworths six. The guy who was the chief music buyer at the time instigated this policy that Woolworths, who accounted for a sizeable proportion of CD sales on the high street, were only going to stock six of the new releases each week. If you weren't one of those six, that put a huge dent in your chart position in week one. Shops were the gatekeepers for all of this.

Lee Thompson: Bookers at *CD:UK* would see how songs were performing at The Box and then decide whether to have them for Saturday morning TV. It all worked in tandem. The Box, *CD:UK* and Woolies were the three most important linchpins to all of those big pop hits in the late '90s and early '00s. More so than Radio 1 and commercial radio.

Steve Anderson: There is no frontman [in Westlife]. I think the rule of boybands and girlbands is that there really shouldn't be a singular front person.

Louis Walsh: If you have two or three lead singers then you're fine. With NSYNC they had Justin and with Take That it was Gary and Robbie. You always have one or two better singers, but everyone has to be featured if you want the band to last and you want a happy band. They all have to have a role.

Nigel Dick, director, Westlife's 'Swear It Again' (US version): When you're doing a boyband you're promoting

334

good-looking young men so that girls can scream at them. Just show me more boys, really. If there are five guys in a band then you have to cater to all the fans of each member – this girl loves the blond boy, this one loves the short guy – so if they don't get to see their guy a lot, there will be complaints.

Dania Pasquini: Westlife were the band your mum would listen to and they knew that. They had to work that. They were good lads. We threw rain on them. And a wind machine to get those clothes rippling.

Max Giwa: The thing about Simon was he was open to any idea. It was like, 'If you can do it, make it happen.' He's very in tune with the public outside of London because his thing was, 'If the mother in Leeds is sitting in her kitchen washing the dishes listening to this then we've cracked it.' That was his ethos with the music and the videos.

Brian Dowling: I interviewed Mariah Carey [on *SM:TV*] once. She was singing that song with Westlife, the Phil Collins cover [2000's 'Against All Odds'], and it was almost like she'd never met them before. It was so odd. In my mind I'm going, 'She has met them before, right?' Westlife loved [*SM:TV*'s often rowdy band vs band football match] Eat My Goal. They put a fucking gay Irish man in goal and I was like, 'This will not be happening.' Westlife wanted to fucking batter me every Saturday morning.

Lucie Cave: During the *Smash Hits* tour, we'd be in the bar until 4 a.m. and I remember saying to Brian McFadden, 'I've got to go and wake you up in your room in half an hour' [to film for Trouble TV]. So I'd have to quickly go to bed, they'd have to climb into bed having had no sleep and then I'd knock on the door with the camera crew like, 'Wake up!' I remember at one point they had condoms on the bedside table – not used ones – and we had to pixelate them out because it was kids' TV.

Savan Kotecha: All pop artists want to be cool at some point. They want to be edgier than their music. That's sometimes the downfall.

Simon Jones, former Westlife PR: [Westlife] wanted to be in *i-D* magazine. I was called into a meeting because they weren't happy. They wanted to do fashion and ideally they wanted to do *i-D* magazine or the cover of *GQ*. I was like, 'That's never going to happen.' I was just trying to be realistic. Then they said they wanted to be on the cover of *Cosmopolitan*, but they'd only done one guy on their cover and that was David Beckham. And they were like, 'Yeah, and . . .?' Why would they be bothered about those things when their fanbase was Julie in Norwich, and they don't care about those magazines? You have to hit your fans and let them know there's a record out. They were never going to be in the fashion world.

In 2019, after dabbling in solo careers, the four members of Westlife regrouped for their eleventh album (and eighth UK number one), *Spectrum*, which was followed in 2021 by *Wild Dreams* and another stadium tour. As for Boyzone, they reunited in 2010 with fourth album *Brother*, named in memory of Stephen Gately, who tragically died the year prior from a pulmonary oedema.

In 2018, they released the fairly self-explanatory *Thank You & Goodnight* album.

A numbers game: 911, A1 and Triple 8

'Ben A1 came in for a shoot and had to get his curtains ironed down'

While Boyzone aimed to heal the hearts of broken-hearted Take That fans via soppy ballads, 'Bodyshakin'' hitmakers 911, AKA Lee Brennan, Jimmy Constable and Spike Dawbarn, were keen to move them onto the dancefloor. As with early Take That, 911 battled for attention early on, initially releasing their debut single independently in 1996. For Ben Adams, Paul Marazzi, Christian Ingebrigtsen and Mark Read, AKA A1, who emerged two years later, their focus was also seemingly on defining late '90s boyband traits, be it curtain hairstyles, retina-burning all-white outfits or hi-NRG pop. By 2003, in a post-Justin-Timberlake-goes-solo world, however, that boyband iconography was starting to look as staid as a white sleeveless tee, with major label certainties Triple 8, AKA David Wilcox, Iain James, Jamie Bell, Josh Barnett and Justin Scott, attempting a harder-edged sound to general indifference.

Lee: Spike and Jimmy were on [late-night dance show] *Hitman and Her*, which was presented by Pete Waterman and Michaela Strachan. At the time, I was working in a ten-pin bowling centre in Carlisle. I wrote a letter one night and took it to my local radio station Sea FM basically saying I'm looking to start singing, are there any roadshows I can do? My letter was faxed to the guy looking after Spike and Jimmy. He rang me at Hollywood Bowl and said he was looking to put a boyband together, do I want to come and meet him? A few weeks later I met Spike and Jimmy in a Burger King. I left my full-time job and told my family I was moving to Glasgow to be in a boyband. I just go for it, me. I don't worry about failure. We moved into our manager's house and signed on the dole basically.

Christian Ingebrigtsen: I went to the Liverpool Institute of Performing Arts, and I studied songwriting and vocals. In December of 1997, I got an email from my songwriting teacher saying, 'If you want to be in a boyband, this could be your big break.' I immediately turned to my friend sitting next to me and said, 'What's a boyband?' I had no idea. He explained to me: 'It's like the Backstreet Boys.' I replied and said I could do it. Vicky Blood and Tim Byrne had this vision of creating a boyband where all the members were songwriters and musicians, rather than actors or models or dancers. They auditioned 3,000 people initially but then they realised that songwriters and musicians don't go to auditions for boybands, so they started looking at performing arts schools.

Alex Needham: [A1] had the same management as Steps. I remember doing one of Tom Watkins' bands, North and South, and by the late '90s, early '00s, I think you just had a generation of bands where the record companies and the managers had taken control. You've not got a Bros or Pet Shop Boys situation where you've got a pretty strong creative force saying, 'No, we're not going to do that.' The managers have really taken over completely and these people will put up with being moulded. Then you end up with something like A1, where they're very bland and embarrassingly super gay. It's just a middle-aged gay guy's idea of what a pop band should be and there's something that's inauthentic about it.

338

Iain James, Triple 8: We formed the embryonic part of the band in Bristol between myself and Justin. We were really into music and it was a really good way of getting ourselves out of trouble. We were really dedicated and committed to making it work. We lost a few members along the way and then we came to London and got spotted by some producers. Before we knew it, we were making demos and looking for more members. We felt that having five people just looked better than four. Three doesn't work. Remember 911?

Lee: Straight away when Take That split our manager said, 'There's a huge gap for a new boyband,' which is why he put it together so quickly. That was the angle we approached major labels with at the start, but they weren't interested. Our manager was adamant there would always be an audience wanting boybands doing their pelvic thrusts. He looked at the blueprint of Nigel Martin-Smith and what he did with Take That. And Nigel used to get Take That doing the full circuit of under-18s, over-18s, the gay clubs, all of it. So we did that for the first fifteen months before we got signed. It was crazy.

Christian: I sent a demo I had made and they asked me to come to London to meet the other boys. That was Paul and two other guys from the initial auditions who weren't the songwriters and musicians they were looking for. I met Tim in Steve Mac's studio. This was at the same time as Westlife were being made as well. Initially Tim had organised for Steve to do all the writing with us, but because I didn't really want to do [A1], I immediately said I wanted to write the songs. And if not I wasn't interested. It was a bit of reverse psychology that kind of worked. In the end, when

Steve Mac realised we wanted to write all the songs ourselves, he focused on Westlife, where he could get his songs placed.

Iain: I knew [Chris Herbert] had worked with the Spice Girls and Five and as soon as he sat down with us and gave us his story we were like, 'Okay, I think we're in good hands here.' We were doing everything on our own, for years, and we didn't know what the hell we were doing.

Chris Herbert: I loved Triple 8. That was the culmination of everything I had learned up to that point. They were so hard-working; they were so well-rehearsed. They were great songwriters.

Iain: I remember at the time Polydor really liked this idea of us as a sort of 'lad band'. I think because we hadn't been to performing arts school, we were just some kids from the street with no experience, it was easy to tag us with that. A bit naughty and a bit rough. We liked having arguments and airing our dirty laundry.

Christian: For a while I rented a cupboard in Bow, which was a very scary area back then. It had a single 90cm mattress on the floor, but that had to be lifted up in order to get in and out of the room. I lived there for six months and then I stayed at a mate's house until the management decided we should get a place together. They rented a place for us in east Acton, which I'm sure we paid for.

Lee: Our manager secured an investor called Frank. He invested about £10,000 initially so we set up our own label for our first two singles. After Take That, a lot of bands were put together by labels, but we did it really organically. Our first single went in at number thirty-eight and then we did twenty-one on the second single. Suddenly labels were like, 'Who are these guys getting in the charts without any TV behind them?' Then it was a bidding war and we signed with Virgin and released our third single.

Lauren Cochrane: You could see the remnants of Britpop in 911's look – from the haircuts to the slightly retro T-shirts. They also occasionally played into a rave moment with the dummy around the neck and the baggy silhouettes. They were aiming for a slightly edgier look than a lot of the more polished boybands from this era.

Christian: I wasn't into the pop scene in the way the other guys were. I hadn't heard of Steps until I joined A1 and we went on tour with them. That was really instrumental in creating an audience for us and also the *Smash Hits* tour we did with Westlife. We did quite a lot before we got signed and that was one of the advantages of Tim coming from the world of television. We were on *SM:TV* and *CD:UK* before we were signed by Sony.

Iain: I remember doing gigs with [Westlife] and being like, 'Make the most of it, lads, your time's up soon.' Which obviously it wasn't. I remember having a very strong feeling of confidence slash arrogance. But you needed that. The main aim was to knock Westlife off of those stools. To try to be the anti-that.

Lee: Virgin put us up in a hotel in Maida Vale, so we had little apartments each in there. I remember I wanted to go to the West End so I'd ring my tour manager and he'd get a car and a Merc would turn up. What a lifestyle. You'd have your driver waiting for you outside the club until you were ready to leave.

Holly Jade-Johnston: I remember we went on a rollercoaster with A1 in Blackpool.

Hannah Verdier: Ben A1 came in for a shoot and he was having a fag outside and his curtains were all over the place. He had to get them ironed down. It was like the dream was over; it was shattered.

Lauren Cochrane: The curtains were very much of this era too, the kind of hairstyle seen on David Beckham and Michael Owen.

Hannah Verdier: We had A1 on the *Smash Hits* tour. It was carnage. Always in the middle of the night the hotel alarm would go off because the fans wanted to see Paul A1 in his knickers outside.

Christian: We realised we liked the train much more than cars, so the label would rent us a whole carriage. Once we were going to Nottingham and I'm on the phone to a friend and a person comes in from the car in front of ours. I'm like, 'This guy's the spitting image of the prime minister.' And it actually was Tony Blair. He was joking about how his security detail had told him there were several hundred young people at the platform and he wondered if we might have something to do with that. Then he asked for our autograph for his children. This was at the time when George Bush and Tony Blair were the most important people on the planet. It was a big deal. So we were all calling our family. Later he was waving to us from the platform and we're waving back from the train and then suddenly we see our head of security going, 'Wait, wait, get off.' We were so excited we had forgotten to get off the train. All the fans were watching us leave. Security had to drive and pick us up at the next train station.

Jordan Paramor: I went to LA with B*Witched and I remember getting in the lift with Lindsay and someone else and one of them said, 'Oh, God, what will Lee say?' And that was the moment I realised Lindsay was dating Lee from 911. We all suspected. She quickly said to me, 'You won't put that in [the mag], will you?'

Lee: The last thing a fan wants to see is their favourite boy-band member with a girlfriend. It loses something for fans is what we were told. Towards the end of 911, my now ex-wife Lindsay was in B*Witched and we slowly started coming out as being together. After a while we were like, 'Right, that's it, we're together.' [B*Witched] were very sweet and innocent.

Jordan Paramor: When you're young you genuinely think you're going to marry these people. You think you're in with a shot. Lee was a big heartthrob so for him to be dating someone from B*Witched, not only would they be asked about it in every interview, but it might turn some fans off.

Iain: [The label] spent over £2 million on us and we didn't even release our album. Management should have sat us down, but I think they just wanted us to cause trouble and spend money we didn't have. It's almost like a mad professor behind it with the puppet strings going, 'What can we conjure up here?' Financial ruin? Maybe some fights? Drug and alcohol abuse? Getting a female pop star pregnant? I remember doing *CD:UK* and it was the biggest budgeted debut performance. The buzz around it was huge, you could feel it. All the other bands were whispering.

Peter Loraine: I had this idea with Triple 8, which was kind of a very naïve version of what Twitter would become, where we made tens of thousands of little business cards. Each boy had their picture on it and on the back was their phone number. We gave them mobile phones and you could text them or ring them and they'd speak to you. We'd have these days when it would be marked in their diary 'Triple 8 to spend all afternoon texting people'. They'd be giving out these cards at *CD:UK* like, 'Anyone want my phone number?'

Iain: It was a way of interacting with fans in a new way. We always used to get told off for not answering them or for turning them off. Or just phoning our mates. I didn't really want to speak to Julie from Grimsby at 3 a.m. It was constant.

Peter Loraine: It was a good idea until the mobile provider presented us with a bill for £25,000 for these five phones. One of them had a friend who lived in America and they'd been on the phone with them night after night, just whizzing up the bill.

Christian: When we won the BRIT Award [in 2001], Noel Gallagher was outraged that they'd awarded that to a boy-band like us. Looking back now, I'm immensely proud we beat Coldplay to British Breakthrough Act.

Pete Selby, former music retail buyer: I was working for Our Price and at that point I was still rather dazzled by the sheer pomp of the event. I remember standing at a Portaloo urinal next to one of the A1s just after they had won their award. He was on the phone to his mum. It was rather touching. But I also remember thinking, 'Enjoy this moment – you in the Portaloo with a BRIT on your new tiny Nokia . . . this is the pinnacle.' It seemed very bittersweet.

Lee: We were just about to switch on the Christmas lights in Birkenhead and it was literally about ten minutes before we went on stage. There'd been so many arguments and conversations over the weeks, so we went into the broom cupboard backstage and me and Spike said, 'We think it's time to end it, Jimmy.' He didn't want it to end. Our deal was finished and we weren't getting on well and mentally we were wrecked.

Christian: Sony was really trying to break us in America. NSYNC were the big band over there, so they were the inspiration. We had been in America for three months at that point and had to go back to Asia so we didn't lose those markets that we actually had. That's when the horrible thing happened and four girls died at a stampede at our signing in Indonesia. That just stopped everything. We wanted to honour their custom by observing a period of mourning for five months. Then when we started over again that's when we decided to go in a completely different musical direction [via 2001's immaculate, soft-rock opus 'Caught in the Middle'].

Lee: We just [announced we were breaking up] live on Chris Moyles' radio show. I remember fans crying outside Radio 1. We all got into our separate cars and didn't speak to each other again for about a year.

Iain: Lucian Grainge, the head of Universal, called us into a meeting and pretty much said, 'I expect your first three singles to go in at number one and then we'll release the album.' I was like, 'Okay . . .' He justified it by saying, 'So you guys have got to work really hard.' We *were* working hard. When [first single, 'Knockout'] went in at eight and ['Give Me a Reason'] went in at nine, I don't think Lucian was best pleased.

Chris Herbert: I thought those singles were really representative of that time. They straddled pop and also N.E.R.D and those kinds of bands. It was brilliant. I really put my whole heart into that band but it just didn't connect quick enough. I think if the label had stuck with it we could have grown it.

Iain: We were due to release the album and he just said no. That's when the ground gets pulled from underneath you. It was a killer. We'd worked our bollocks off. I'd written the majority of [the album] myself and it just didn't see the light of day. As quickly as it all blew up, it just disappeared.

Lee: I had to check out of the hotel that I'd been living in. They were happy to get me a car and then the train back home, but after that it was like someone had pulled the rug away. I was completely lost for a long time. I became very low and depressed in 2001, very sad about lots of things. I hated being recognised because I felt like a failure. You're the guy that *was* in that group, you're not the guy that *is* in a group. I'd always be recognised in the supermarket. Kids used to shout stuff and it really affected me mentally.

Christian: We had time in that period [of mourning] and so the studio was our playground. 'Caught in the Middle' would have been number one in any other week that year, but it was beaten by 'Hero' by Enrique Iglesias. But follow-up 'Make It Good' was our lowest-charting single ever and it was number eleven. I think it went over the heads of some of our fans and a lot of people that would enjoy that song wouldn't listen to us because we were a boyband. We fell between two stools. We had a song called '2:59', which is a very rock-pop thing, and the management hated it. We could see that's where things were headed and McFly did that exact sound after us. We were all very exhausted, but it was just going to be a break. But that break lasted for eight years.

Iain: I'm still buddies with a couple of Westlife guys and we laugh about it now. Mark and Shane will say, 'Ah, bless you, guys, you really did try but you just couldn't beat the power of the fans.' Which is true. Blue knew what suited them, Busted knew what suited them and Westlife what suited them. Ultimately that was our downfall – we didn't quite know who we were as a brand and a boyband.

Chris Herbert: There was another band we were launching up against called D-Side. We specifically set ourselves up to be the antithesis of them. They were going to be the new Boyzone and we were going to be the new Five. Their launch didn't quite happen and neither did ours, so they switched [style] and came into our lane. No one won at the end of the day.

Peter Loraine: It was too formulaic by then. What was really sad was that I don't believe they had the songs. Iain is the most phenomenal songwriter and at that time we had people in Sweden writing tunes for them. It was a shame we didn't tap into what we had with him.

Busted, McFly and using guitars for good

'For Kerrang!*, it almost felt like they were spoiling our bands'*

As the new millennium marched onwards, surviving a non-existent 1 January bug and barely surviving a very real existential crisis post-9/11, pop in the UK started to look for something more 'authentic' to rub up against the march of TV talent shows. Taking its cues from the likes of Green Day and Blink-182, pop-punk landed its first superstar in the shape of Canadian grump Avril Lavigne, whose debut single 'Complicated' arrived in March 2002. Six months later the choreography agnostic Busted, AKA teenagers James Bourne, Matt Willis and Charlie Simpson, released their debut single, the very-much-not-okay-in-the-modern-era 'What I Go to School For', a Daily Mail *headline in song form about a school boy being groomed by his teacher. Its follow-up, 'Year 3000', featured lyrics about triple-breasted women, a wank fantasy that put a PG spin on the crude lyrical template of their American heroes. The genesis of 'What I Go to School For' was started by Matt and James years before Busted's creation, with the pair eventually joined by exceptionally eyebrow-ed Charlie, who beat a certain Tom Fletcher to the final place. Later, Busted's management, Prestige, would give Tom his own band, the equally guitar-obsessed McFly, alongside Dougie Poynter, Danny Jones and Harry Judd, who would arrive in Busted's slipstream but eventually outlast them. Prestige also decided to have their cake and eat it via V, AKA Antony Brant, Aaron Buckingham, Mark Harle, Kevin McDaid and Leon Pisani, a very old-school boyband simultaneously being destroyed by their creators.*

Iain: I remember Busted exploding right next to us at the same sort of time. I'd studied pop's cyclical nature. You've only got a few years before the next sub-genre kicks in.

Chris Herbert: There was a switch. You were getting more guitar bands and then you had a boyband come along that played guitars. I could see it happening.

James Bourne: There was a lot of music around I didn't like – I didn't like S Club 7, for example. I liked Westlife's songs but I thought they weren't as cool as the Backstreet Boys. It wasn't exciting.

Ashley Bird, *Kerrang!* magazine editor, 2002–05: I was the editor of *Kerrang!* that had to fight the authenticity battle for a couple of years. The spoiler alert is that I didn't feature Busted in the magazine. Or McFly. Or Avril Lavigne. *Kerrang!* was always about real bands – people who had got together, played in a garage, practised, done a load of gigs and then maybe somewhere down the line a label signed them and said, 'You should get rid of your drummer,' and the band said, 'No, we're a real thing.'

James: I played guitar from a really young age. I would play songs by Green Day, Oasis and Nirvana all the time. I had this understanding of guitar bands.

Jonathan Bown, former assistant editor, *Smash Hits*: We were really used to super-groomed boybands at the time. We were starting to see a lot of groups coming out of shows like *Popstars*. At the same time that was happening there was this super-produced R&B sound coming out of America, then you also had bands like Blink-182 that were providing something different. Something like Busted was a real response to that.

Ashley Bird: Authenticity was always a thing for us until Linkin Park came along in 2000 and made us start to question everything. The rumours were that the label had brought in the singer at least, if not the rest of the band. It was the first time *Kerrang!* had faced this 'Are they a label creation or are they not?' question. The conclusion we came to was they were alright to appear in the magazine. What was happening at the same time was that authentic pop-punk was getting more commercial. So for the first time we had readers and bands who were – not to sound disrespectful to *Kerrang!* readers because I absolutely was one of them – pretty. And looked after their hair. Of course that gets the attention of a major label world for whom that works. We had to ask, 'How much is *Kerrang!* going to accept in terms of this commercial side of things?'

James: Back then the pop music business and the alternative business felt like two separate entities. Everyone wants to be successful, I don't care whether you're indie or pop. People [in the indie world] wanted the success we had and were trying to find reasons to bring us down – they couldn't believe sixteen-year-old kids wrote these songs. I really felt like we had the makings of a real band but we were marketed as a boyband, so there was this weird thing where we were like a boyband but we had this knowledge of real music.

Ashley Bird: For Busted, a band who had grown up listening to Green Day and Blink-182, this new concept came up, which is a label-created pop-punk band. That, for *Kerrang!*, was an existential crisis. I think Matt and James from Busted initially met at another audition for another boyband. I think the whole process came about via auditioning for label creations.

James: [Before we signed to Island] we went to Simon Cowell's office at BMG. The beginning of the meeting with him was really cold. He scanned the room and I was at the end and he went, 'So what's the story?' He didn't say anything. Before you knew it the ball was in your court and you had to respond. Simon wanted us to add a drummer as a permanent member of the band. Which probably was a really good idea, but we didn't want to at the time. Before the Simon Cowell meeting we did have people say, 'Look, we don't know what this is and we don't know where it belongs – you're not a band, you're not a boyband, you're not anything.' But I think Simon Cowell saw the potential, and because he saw it, it meant other people started to as well. Word had gotten around the music industry.

Jenessa Williams, journalist and McFly super-fan: Listening back to Busted now, I can't hear much in it that couldn't have held its own among any of the pop-adjacent artists who do get that kind of rock coverage now. I think McFly in particular definitely fell foul to that long-established sexism that dictates that artists who are broadly loved by girls can't be any good. I was always really enraged by that, wishing that I could read 'proper' interviews that gave insight into them as artists as well as the fluffy 'what's your favourite colour?' pop magazine stuff.

Hannah Verdier: The first time I saw Busted was when their record company asked a few of the *Smash Hits* staff to go to the rehearsal studio to check out their new 'rock boyband'. It was clear the record company had a firm idea of what they wanted. Busted played a couple of songs, including 'What I Go to School For', which had a bit of sauciness, delivered by Mattie, who was like a baby Robbie Williams, with a wink for the mums. I think using us as a focus group was a smart move. As was putting on a showcase with loads of free booze and school dinners.

Pete Selby: Some of the more important media partners were invited to the studio to watch a nascent Busted. Retailers were lower down the pecking order so a colleague and I were invited to Island head office and plonked on a sofa in the tiniest kitchenette, while the three lads – pre-pop-punk makeover and in very sensible knitwear – performed a few energetic numbers acoustically. Only Matt didn't have a bass guitar so he sort of jigged about on the spot and did things with his hands while James and Charlie did all of the musical heavy lifting. Oh and there was no free booze.

James: Matt had an early idea of a song but it wasn't about what 'What I Go to School For' is about now. I made one of the lyrics he had rhyme with 'member of staff' and I was like, 'We have to take this down the school theme.' We started laughing about our experiences at school. We drew on experience but it was done in a way that wasn't completely autobiographical.

Jonathan Bown: It must be tricky for them to perform that song now. You'd have to inject a heavy dose of irony. At the time, they were young enough for it to seem okay. You certainly couldn't have got away with a teacher character going, 'That's what I go to school for.' I think people liked that cartoon-y element. It helped broaden their appeal. They were a much edgier alternative to your Westlifes.

James: I liked Westlife songs but I thought they were boring lyrically. After a while, a lot of the lyrics start to look the same: 'I need you', 'I miss you', 'You make me complete'. Very predictable. I felt like we had a way of keeping our lyrics fresh and you never knew what our next song was going to be about.

Ashley Bird: Singing about triple-breasted women and fancying your science teacher is the kind of thing that goes down quite well in *Kerrang!* world. Blink-182 are the massive bridge between that authentic world and the pop one.

James: We followed up 'What I Go to School For' with another song ['Year 3000'] that was better and bigger. I think that's the reason Busted had the effect it did and why we opened the floodgates for more. That was a trend that no one had really seen.

Jonathan Bown: The acts coming out of the talent shows were so groomed and so micro-managed. They could perform but could also say very little. The good thing about Busted is that you had three very different personality types. Charlie went to [public school] Charterhouse, he was clearly from a privileged background. You had Matt, who was almost the exact opposite, who had had quite a difficult upbringing and at one point was living with James. Then you had James, who was the Gary Barlow type. That was an interesting dynamic.

Ashley Bird: For us, it almost felt like they were spoiling our bands. Every band that is a real band that we cover, every time they do a star jump on stage it was like, 'This has all been spoilt.'

Lauren Cochrane: In a way, you could put Busted in the indie sleaze moment. Their style was meant to signify that they were an alternative boy band from the peroxide hair to the caps and the vacant stares, which were quite Damon Albarn via John Lydon. It was all quite on the nose.

Jonathan Bown: I remember one interview that was quite difficult to do. We hired a location house that had a nice pool outside and I had to interview them while I was sitting on a pool inflatable. As we were talking to each other we'd start floating in opposite directions. I'd have to try to paddle my way back to them. They were much more up for a bit of a laugh.

James: In those days our tour manager had our passports so often I would get in the Addison Lee and genuinely not know where I was going. We had management do our schedule and we'd be told we were being picked up at a certain time, but there would be so much in our day we wouldn't be told about. I would get in the car with nothing and we'd go to the airport and fly to Denmark and then do four Scandinavian countries in one day.

'Nobody seemed keen to give a band like McFly the same degree of praise as Arctic Monkeys'

By the middle of 2003, Busted were firmly rooted as one of pop's biggest acts. Matt and James were living in pop's very own village, AKA Princess Park Manor, alongside members of Girls Aloud, Blue and the Sugababes (Charlie had quickly left to move in with friends). On long lonely nights, James would write songs while Matt slept on a La-Z-Boy sofa post-pizza slump. Idyllic, right? Not quite. Keen to have another songwriter to collaborate with for what would become Busted's second album, A Present for Everyone, *James asked his management to call in Tom Fletcher, who had very briefly been part of Busted. Signed as a songwriter by Busted's management, Tom would later meet Danny at the auditions for V before the pair would audition bassist Dougie and drummer and former Charlie schoolmate Harry. McFly's debut single, '5 Colours in Her Hair', emerged in March 2004.*

Tom Fletcher: I went to the Busted auditions and saw Matt Willis there. I'd known Matt from Sylvia Young and it wasn't that we didn't like each other; we just weren't compatible. He was this cool kid, super popular, and I was a bit more of a teacher's pet. I asked if he was there for the audition and he was like, 'No, I'm in the band already.' I just assumed there was no way I was getting in. But the audition went really well. I was at the same audition as Charlie, so they told us we were both in the band. I remember really clearly my younger sister had a Halloween party and the phone rang and it was Busted's manager and he was like, 'Hey, Tom, so we've decided we're just going to keep it as a three-piece so you're no longer required.' I was heartbroken. But he said he really liked my songwriting and that he really wanted to work with me.

James: I called management and said, 'Can you send Tom round? I wouldn't mind writing songs with someone.'

Tom: We were just inseparable. The first group of songs we started writing included 'Air Hostess' and 'Crashed the Wedding', songs that would become number-one singles for Busted. I left college and went on tour with Busted, too, and shared James's hotel room. Me and James are both super nerds. We'd stay up until 6 a.m. but we weren't doing the rock 'n' roll thing of throwing TVs out of hotel windows; we were ordering vanilla milkshakes and watching movies. I was aware that that kind of stuff was going on, maybe with some other bandmates, but what was genuinely exciting for me was I suddenly had a friend who was as into songwriting as I was. And who also loved *Back to the Future* and *Star Wars*.

James: Tom was definitely down about not making it into Busted, so I said to him, 'You can have your own band, write the songs, and you can basically dress the same [as Busted], but we can make your songs you. We can set your music apart and can add major sevenths and minor chords.'

Tom: We both had this love for the Beach Boys and the Beatles, so we had a few songs that had those influences. Those songs became the basis of what would become McFly.

James: All these songs like 'That Girl', 'Memory Lane' and 'Obviously' started happening quickly.

Lauren Cochrane: Style-wise, McFly felt like they were playing into the Abercrombie bro look that was popular in the '00s. They were British but they have the look of Californian surf and skate kids from the Quicksilver T-shirts to the backwards caps and sun-kissed hair.

Jonathan Bown: I thought some of the songs on [debut album] *Room on the 3rd Floor* were incredibly mature. They'd write songs about adults going through midlife crises. It certainly felt like '5 Colours in Her Hair' was an entry in and then after a few more singles they found their groove. But it also struck me as slightly unfair as a pop fan that you had a band like the Arctic Monkeys, who were in their teens and played their own instruments, but who were heralded as lyricists for a generation and put on this pedestal as amazing songwriters. But nobody seemed particularly keen to give a band like McFly the same degree of praise.

Tom: I remember getting booed at rock events. If we went to see bands like the Used or Green Day we'd have to take security with us because people would want to kick the shit out of us. Just to say, 'I punched a guy from McFly.' One of the first times we were written about in the *NME* and – please excuse the language – they had a picture of us and they captioned it: 'Wanker, Cunt, Dickhead, Twat'. We were sixteen- and seventeen-year-old kids, so seeing a magazine with your idols in put that under a picture of you was heartbreaking.

Jenessa Williams: I really appreciated how off-path they were willing to wander, how non-patronising that kind of experimentation felt to a young listener. Also, MySpace had happened and there were tonnes of bands I discovered both through McFly's networks and just the wider sense of genre-blurring discovery. It was a really, really great time to be a music fan.

Tom: People said that we were the reason they'd moved on to bands like the Arctic Monkeys. People that were looking for the next thing. That also came with its own frustrations because we were growing up and we wanted to be a credible band, too. We didn't just want to play to thirteen-year-old girls for all of our lives.

Jordan Paramor: Busted and McFly's rockier sound and honesty about their lifestyle also set them aside from other boy-bands. While other bands were creating anodyne 'appeal to everyone' personas, they were more open about being flawed and acting like twats. I remember Dougie telling me a particularly horrific story about the time he pooed into a cup on their tour bus and he wasn't in the least bit worried people might fancy him less because of it. They smoked and drank and openly had girlfriends, instead of rolling out the classic 'I'm looking for the right girl' line every time they were interviewed.

Paul Flynn: I went to the McFly house and I've never ever been more depressed in my life. It was like the modern-day equivalent of *Brookside*. A new-build estate on a London ring road so they can get everywhere easily. No delineation of them having personalities.

Tom: Logistically it all made sense to live in London together, but we didn't want to live in that apartment complex that Busted and Girls Aloud lived in. There was a house ten minutes around the corner. That was the best decision I'd ever made because suddenly we were four kids – Dougie was fifteen, he'd just dropped out of school in Year 10 – and we had no one with us. At the time, it was the biggest house I'd ever seen. This huge five-bedroom house in north London. We were all disgusting in terms of hygiene and cleanliness. In terms of the rock 'n' roll lifestyle, Harry was pretty bad. He was a public-school boy from a very different background and he introduced some of the more stereotypical rock 'n' roll elements that I was against bringing into our house. He grew up in dorms where they'd always shower with each other all the time. When we're on tour, even now, if you're in the shower, you can guarantee Harry will get in with you.

Paul Flynn: Harry Judd was absolute kit off at *Attitude*. He was the ultimate paragon of how bands a bit later would have members for the gay press.

Tom: Playing at G-A-Y was amazing. They would fill you with alcohol before you'd go on stage and it's this amazing, electric atmosphere. It was so much fun. Normally, we were playing to young teenage girls wearing bunny ears, so suddenly we'd be in front of nineteen-year-old gay men at 2 a.m. and we could get naked and swear.

'I remember standing outside the venue afterwards and Charlie speeding off in his Porsche'

On Christmas Eve, 2004, Charlie – who by this point had started his hard-rock side project, Fightstar – called the band's management to inform them he was keen to leave Busted. On 14 January 2005, at London's Soho Hotel, the band announced they were eschewing the Sugababes option of switching in a new member and instead were splitting up. As quickly as they'd arrived, all chunky Vans, frayed sweatbands and checkerboard belts, Busted were gone, swallowed whole by a quest for authenticity that had gotten out of hand.

James: Charlie got some shit from a band he went to see live and he had a hard time dealing with the attention he was getting. He's two years younger than me and Matt, so back then he cared very much about what critics said. I personally didn't care. When you're getting number ones that often and you're writing songs for your own band and McFly and you're getting seven number-one records in a year, people can say what they want, it doesn't bother you.

Jonathan Bown: We went to the press conference. I was a fan as much as anything else, so I was really sad when they split. I remember standing outside the venue afterwards and Charlie speeding off in his Porsche. I thought that was a good analogy for the fact that Charlie was going to be alright, but I did feel for the other two. For them it was very much their lifeline.

James: I was sad for it to end but it wasn't like I was this suicidal weirdo. I was partly excited, actually. It was an adjustment because you're losing something that has been an amazing thing in your life but you're also getting back time you didn't think you were going to have.

Tom: Busted didn't have a super tight friendship – they were three very different individuals. The management knew with [McFly] that they had to let it seem like we were organically choosing each other as friends. That was a career-defining decision because the core of our longevity is that we haven't killed each other because we're still mates. You can't just shove three completely separate people in a band together and expect it to last twenty years. They will self-destruct.

Jonathan Bown: It was clear from our engagements with them that Charlie was getting increasingly unhappy. And increasingly unhappy at the thought of holding a silly prop or answering questions about snogging someone or whatever. Plus he had another creative avenue with Fightstar. He felt very compromised by the boyband label. But it did feel like a shock and it did feel like the knives were out for Charlie from the Busted fans after it happened.

James: If someone doesn't feel like they're being represented creatively in their own self, it's like, 'Okay, if you can do both, do both.' He was working around the clock to do both. So, when he just wanted to do Fightstar, that was interesting to me because you're literally in this band that's killing it and you could use that to fund your really amazing other thing. He had it all. But I understand why he wanted to focus on what he wanted to focus on. That wasn't hard for me to understand because Busted was my Fightstar.

Ashley Bird: We [at *Kerrang!*] had to think about it and it was like, 'Okay, so we didn't do Busted but now he's doing this.' The point was he found his guys for [Fightstar]. In the beginning they weren't very good and it took them a year or so to work it out. I said, 'Most of the bands we do cover got together in their late teens, it's just that Charlie's day job wasn't working in McDonald's, it was being in Busted.' Obviously he had a leg up straight away, but you could tell he loved that music. We saw it as a different thing. So we did cover Fightstar.

James: Busted have made so many bad choices in our career. But I do think us splitting up was a good thing. I think it preserved the integrity of what it was. It was the reason we were able to come back with a bang. A lot of people have tried to come back and failed and I credit that to the way we ended it. In the beginning I think people really thought we were these sell-out, manufactured, commercial pop stars and that couldn't be further from the truth. We were turning down these huge Argos offers to make these shitty acoustic guitars with our faces on the boxes. The three of us went, 'Well, fuck that, our fans are going to go and buy a real guitar from a real guitar shop.'

Hugh Goldsmith, founder, Brightside: It definitely felt like pop was moving in the direction of a more guitar-driven sound at that time and both Busted and McFly were highly successful in capitalising on this in a big way. [Pop-rockers with excellent fringes] Rooster were the first artist I signed to Brightside, my new JV label with Sony/BMG, and there's no doubt that the success of Busted and Maroon 5 led my colleagues and I to think that a more rocky-sounding band could be successful in the market at that time. However, it was never our intention for the band to be as mainstream pop as groups like Busted or McFly because the guys in the band would not have felt comfortable in that lane. Their influences were artists like Led Zeppelin, Cream and others from that era.

Tom: Following on from us there were a few bands that tried to do it, like Rooster, but for some reason they just missed the bus by ten seconds.

Jenessa Williams: I think both Busted and McFly have laid incredibly clear foundations for future acts – without Busted, there would be no McFly, but without McFly, there would be no 5 Seconds of Summer or the Vamps. Even One Direction;

a lot of the styling and cheeky presentation in the early days really borrowed from that beachy-Britannia 'everylad' image that McFly did on their first album.

James: We had a bigger impact on this era of pop than any other band. We changed it. One year at Christmas I went to buy a guitar and a guy came up to me and was like, 'We've sold so many guitars and it's because of your band.' McFly were part of the Busted ripple effect. You've got these people that have been in the manufactured bands, the Simon Fuller bands, but Busted was this different thing. Given the time we were together – two years and three months – the impact of that is pretty unrivalled.

'They were creating the devil that was killing us'

While Busted were re-shaping the boyband parameters, their management team were keen to not just make another band in their mould via McFly, but to also get more mileage out of the more traditional boyband setup. Inevitably, it proved tricky, but not for want of trying, with V's only album, 2004's actually-very-good You Stood Up *(a number-86 smash), featuring production from the likes of Stargate, Xenomania and Mark Taylor.*

Peter Robinson: There'd been attempts [by Prestige] at a boyband before Busted called Skandal, with a K. They were a really old-school boyband and it hadn't really worked. Busted ended up being a huge success, McFly ended up being launched off the back of Busted, so that all fitted in. The management had created this weird situation where they could provide a band who were a reaction to their other band. They'd changed the tone of pop music to being about guitars, so they were like, 'Okay, what if we used one of these guitar bands to launch an old-fashioned boyband?'

Kevin McDaid, V: I saw the advert via *The Stage*. I sang really terribly at the audition because I was very nervous. I think I sang 'Flying Without Wings' by Westlife, which is ironic [Kevin would later date Westlife's Mark Feehily from 2005 to 2012]. I also had to do a little dance, which was the cringiest thing you can imagine. They just put a song on and I freestyled in a room with about fifty guys. Mortifying. I just pretended I was in the club. I was only seventeen so I probably shouldn't have been in clubs, but I was.

James: [Our managers at Prestige] Richard and Fletch were doing V. I really wasn't involved in it at all. I just knew they wanted to do a 'real' boyband.

Kevin: Busted were at their peak of their early success. But they were also the band that changed pop music. Danny from McFly was found at the V auditions. So it was bizarre that we were being put together at the same time. Music was massively changing – it was going very indie in terms of the credible side of things and then within pop music fans were seeing their favourites with instruments. So it was terrible timing for V. It did feel like there was a commitment there from [Prestige] to make it work, but they were creating the devil that was killing us.

Tom: What we couldn't see at the time was that Busted and McFly were helping this little shift in the perception of what pop music was. It was right at the back end of bands like Blue, who were having the last stages of their major success. All the boybands that were coming along like D-Side and Triple 8 were just not working. Busted and McFly just killed that type of boyband off.

James: I never understood [the move to create V] at the time. There were songs I'd written with Tom that they'd try to use to break V. There was one issue of *Smash Hits* that only featured Busted, McFly and V.

Jonathan Bown: I've got a reasonable head for remembering songs, but I'd struggle to name a V song.

Kevin: I literally felt like my dream had just come true. I used to watch *Top of the Pops* and think, 'How do I get from being in this living room to that show and doing music like that?' I just thought, 'Wow, this is it.' Then we moved to London. It was a five-bedroom, five-bathroom duplex modern apartment, but you're paying for it. The cost was taken out of our advance, like everything is. But you're not really told how that works.

Steve Anderson: I was signed to Universal back then and there was a writing camp put together and people were pitching songs. It was going to be the next big thing. It was very classy; it was live strings, it was beautiful production, it was Justin Timberlake-sounding.

Kevin: From the start, we were told, 'Look, boys, this is a phenomenon, worldwide smash, or it's nothing.' All or nothing, basically. We had a fantastic band and we had some great songs and we had what it takes to have gone further, but the timing wasn't on our side.

Steve Anderson: That [V writing camp] was very much, 'Let's just make an album really quickly.' If you have to make an album in three months then it's not the time to sit down with the five boys in the band and say, 'What do you want to sing about?'

Miranda Cooper: I think [V's second single] 'Hip to Hip' was a Moonbaby cast-off. That was very much us still learning how to record that many people. We were still in the trenches trying to be heard.

Brian Higgins: [V's management] were putting nice pressure on us. They were on Island, the same label as the Sugababes, so they would be really persistent about it and eventually we got them down [to Westerham]. It was difficult because we never really had the passion for a lot of these other projects. There was no passion like there was for Girls Aloud.

Kevin: We were on the road promoting [third single] 'You Stood Up' and we just knew it was done. We felt a pull back from the label straight away. Then the album came out and it bombed.

Felix Howard, co-writer, 'You Stood Up': I vomited something out in five minutes and it ended up on their album. I was very confused about that. It was a strange song anyway and it was even stranger that they sang it. By that point I was moving into A&R.

Kevin: We were dropped by our label and we literally had a week to move out of our home. It was as harsh as that. Nothing prepares you for when that rug is pulled from underneath you and how you deal with that on every single level. And with zero support. I refused to move back home, so I moved in with our choreographer Kate and stayed with her while I found my feet.

While McFly carried on until 2010, ironically scoring their low-est-charting album with *Above the Noise*'s dance-pop experiment, a career resurgence occurred when they joined forces with Matt and James in 2013 to form unholy pop-punk hybrid, McBusted. The success of their arena tour seemed to catch the attention of Charlie, who returned to Busted in 2015 for the knowingly titled Pigs Can Fly tour. A new album, 2016's *Night Driver*, saw the trio move into soft-focus synthpop. It didn't last long, with 2019's *Half Way There* leaning heavily into pop punk. McFly, meanwhile, reunited in 2019, releasing a new album, *Young Dumb Thrills*, a year later.

'It's kind of like being in school and school is not the place you come out in'

While the boyband evolved across the first half of the decade in terms of sound, style and success, one depressing constant remained. For gay band members like V's Kevin, it was decided it was much easier for them to stay in the closet, with the pressure of their bandmates' livelihoods resting on their shoulders should the 'inevitable' happen and a band's young, female audience turn their backs en masse. Even within the context of reality TV slowly breaking down barriers in terms of showcasing the full gamut of human existence, the pop industry, be it within bands or on music-focused TV, seemed to still be caught up on a decade-old falsehood.

Kevin: I had a conversation with my management and they asked me how I wanted to deal with my sexuality publicly. It was decided that we would almost neither confirm nor deny. But really that means you're denying it. By then, all the people interviewing me, whether it was mags or TV shows, all knew I was gay because I'd have drinks with them in bars afterwards. I wasn't hiding it. If journalists asked me who I fancied [in print], I just used to say Christina Aguilera because I was genuinely obsessed with her.

MNEK: The limited media and the limited knowledge was instrumental in [people staying in the closet]. *Smash Hits* and all the teen mags were appealing to young girls. That's what the research was saying. With that research and those results the label was like, 'Well, we're in a heteronormative world,' and obviously their aim is to sell shit. Some of these pop artists, it wasn't about expressing their soul or saying everything on their spirit, they were just trying to sing and dance and get this bag real quick. They're not trying to ruin a business, which they're constantly being told they will.

Brian Dowling: When I was first asked to present *SM:TV*, I was like '. . . the fucking show? On a Saturday morning? That's live!' I thought, 'Well, I'm a gay guy, this is a kids' television show' – I genuinely thought, 'Am I allowed?' I know that's a stupid thing to say. It hadn't been done before.

Kevin: We had a really interesting moment on *Popworld*. I've had this conversation with Simon [Amstell] since and it's a pretty bizarre moment to be put into because you wouldn't get away with it now. [Two of us from V] were doing an interview and Simon said, 'Oh, it's okay now to have gay members in a band, it's not an issue.' Then he was like, 'Now would be a good time if someone wanted to come out now, on TV.' We froze. He went on to say, 'Not both of you, just one of you.' I didn't get it at the time, it went straight over my head, but it was naughty because he knew I was gay. And they aired it on the show.

Paul Flynn: I always hated that Simon Amstell thing of 'tell me you're gay'. I would suspect that he regrets it now.

Brian Dowling: If you were a guy in a band, teenage girls had to fancy you to buy your records. But gay guys also buy pop music. I think it is so naïve of people. Also, if you have five guys in a band, chances are at least one of them would be bisexual or gay. It was record labels that were run by straight men that didn't think outside the straight box.

Kevin: I didn't know what to fucking do, I was a kid. I also had a responsibility for the boys' lives and careers; it wasn't just me. I didn't want to ruin the dreams of four other guys in my band. At the same time, I was unashamedly gay and I was very confident that I would not be going back into the closet.

Brian Dowling: [The producers] were very mindful of my private life, let's put it that way. They wanted my private life to remain private, even though I was openly gay and hosting a TV show. When I would go on a red carpet I'd be told, 'You can walk a red carpet on your own or if you want to bring a girlfriend.' I was dating my now husband back then and it was never acknowledged that I was in a relationship.

MNEK: I think about Mark Feehily and Stephen Gately and how for both men in those groups there was no safe space. It's kind of like being in school and school is not the safe space where you're ready to tell everyone you are gay because you don't know what's going to come next.

Brian Dowling: Back then it was label board meetings – 'Should they come out?' Sometimes people were forced to come out because newspapers had the story. People should never have done that.

Simon Jones: I was asleep and [Blue's] Duncan [James] called me about 4 a.m. He said he had something to tell me and said, 'I like boys as well as girls.' I was like, 'Okay, that's fine.' He was worried it would be a really big deal. Later a showbiz journalist called and said, 'I have a story that Duncan James is gay.' It was for the *News of the World* and they had a kiss-and-tell from this guy he'd been seeing. They did that age-old trick of, 'We don't want to run this story, in fact we're not going to run it, but we think it would be great if he came out and did it with us.' It is blackmail. Why have you done the interview if you're not going to run it? The reason is because you've got all the facts and you can hold it over us.

Brian Dowling: You had to conform to what gay version they wanted you to be. We'd have to go on CITV to promo *SM:TV Live* but my clothes were carefully picked for me. I'd be told to rein it in or don't be so excitable. And 'excitable' to me meant camp. It doesn't bother me now and I wouldn't hold those people accountable because they didn't know. I once got a chance to interview Britney Spears. Britney fucking Spears. I remember the next day in *The Sun* they removed the page-three girl and they had a huge picture of me and Britney and it said, 'Queen of

Pop meets Queen of TV'. I don't care how offensive that was. I did not fucking care.

Simon Jones: It made Duncan feel very unsettled that they had this interview in their back pockets. He hadn't come out; he hadn't told his family. You've started a chain of events now that can't stop. We didn't want to do it with the *News of the World*, but imagine if we hadn't. They'd have started a hate campaign. That's what these papers do. They rely on a culture of fear where the PR and celeb are too scared to go against them. If we had gone somewhere else their entire mission would have been to bring Duncan James down. We did the coming-out interview and it was fine. But would he have come out at that point? Probably not.

Brian Dowling: It was very much like I was taking on a different character. They were fearful. I remember someone locked myself and [co-host] Tess [Daly] in a room to stop me from shooting *Celebrity Streetmate* for Children in Need. They had said, 'We can't really see you being gay,' etc. and then I'm booked on a show looking for men. Tess and I were howling. But also really panicked. I was banging on the door saying, 'You open this mother-fucking door now.' The door was opened and I went and did it. It was a very odd situation to be in. In a way, I found that I couldn't express myself any more. I wanted to live my best gay life.

11

'Have you ever been hungover on morning TV?'

Drinking isn't big and it isn't clever, obviously, but it can be amusing to think of pop stars utilising a mask of respectability to hide a monstrous hangover on, say, *CD:UK*. While their indie counterparts were almost assumed to be having wild nights out and living the rock 'n' roll lifestyle to the fullest, pop's coterie of early twentysomethings were either shamed for doing the same or assumed to be tucked up in bed learning their songs. For some there simply wasn't time to have a proper night out, while for others an early morning start was the perfect excuse not to go to bed. All rise? More like one (more) for sorrow.

'Someone was trying to give me an injection to make me stop throwing up'

Louise: It's one thing that people don't always know about me, but I love a tequila. Always have, always will. I have been totally hungover on *CD:UK*. People thought that if you were in the world of pop you didn't go out and party, but of course you did. The Met Bar had my name written all over it.

Bradley, S Club 7: I partied enough for two lifetimes. I'd party until 3 or 4 a.m., get home and my driver would be waiting outside my house. I'd literally run in, have a quick shower – or a cat lick as they say – and then get in the car, have a nap, get to the TV studio and crawl under the table with a pillow I'd brought with me. Then I'd do it all again that night. I don't know how I'm still alive, to be honest with you.

Mutya, Sugababes: I was the worst. How I looked at things was, 'Okay, my call time is 4 a.m., I'll do hair and make-up at 5 a.m., so if I want to go out I can go straight from the rave to the *GM:TV* studio, there are showers, and then get ready.' If I'd have gone home I would have just gone to sleep. That was the lifestyle back then. You'd go to the clubs in central London and you'd bump into everybody. I went [to the Met Bar] a couple of times but I was more about Propaganda, Pop, Chinawhite. I was in the in-crowd.

Christian, A1: They worked us so hard that there just wasn't time. It did happen – we had parties and got drunk – but most of the time I would look at the calendar and think, 'If I drink tonight, when is the next day I can sleep in?' It would be in two months.

Nadine Coyle, Girls Aloud: Back then I couldn't hold my drink – it was like two drinks and I was done for. Do you remember [ITV's] *Grease Mania*? I was throwing up on the stage during soundcheck. Oh, God, it was horrendous. Someone from LWT was trying to give me an injection to make me stop throwing up. Something to relax my muscles because I was just vomiting and vomiting. But it made it so that I just threw up really relaxed. I can see the hangover when I watch those clips.

Kelli Young, Liberty X: Most people were hungover on *CD:UK.*

Tony Lundon, Liberty X: I definitely recall being badly hungover on *This Morning*. It was the day after we'd done our number-one celebrations [for 'Just a Little'] and Lorraine Kelly was interviewing us. I vaguely recall Kevin [Simm] closing his eyes on live TV beside me.

H, Steps: We didn't go home. *SM:TV* was like opening a dressing-up box on Saturday morning. It was hangover TV, for the viewers and for us.

Brian Dowling: One time I got drunk and fell down a flight of stairs at a party. I was so shit-faced. I had done a tan and I didn't have time to wash it off. So I had to go to Cat [Deeley]'s dressing room and use her shower – don't think mine had a shower. Tess [Daly] was like, 'You fucking stink of alcohol.' I only did it once in two years because it's just not worth it on live TV.

Una Healy, the Saturdays: We never really went out. We were always fresh and bushy-tailed because we never had time to go out. We weren't a hungover band.

Ritchie, Five: You think about it, you're seventeen. Prior to this you've been raiding coin jars in your mum's house to get a couple of Hoochs or Mad Dog 20/20s. Then all of a sudden you're going to these industry parties where the whole bar is just free wine. You're downing it. I probably should have thought, 'I'm in a band, there's media here, I should probably not have too much to drink,' but it was the '90s, man!

James, Busted: Those 5 a.m. starts meant we hadn't gone to bed. You'd just get in the car and go. I had an Addison Lee driver shout at me once because he thought I was a slob. I was asleep and we got to the studio and he was like, 'WAKE UP! GET OUT OF THE CAR, YOU'RE HERE.' He was telling me off.

Kevin, V: I actually went out with my TV plugger of all people to a party and I had *Blue Peter* the next morning. I went on without a wink of sleep and reeking of booze. I felt like death all day and then we had to walk through this paper thing and smash it. When I watched it back on TV it didn't even show me. I could have just been in bed.

Lee, 911: I wasn't a really big drinker, so I wasn't hungover, but I was just terrible with mornings. So we'd park our tour bus outside *The Big Breakfast* or something at 2 a.m. and then get woken up to go on the show. They used to want you in really early, even if we weren't on for four hours.

Natalie Appleton, All Saints: I had a very embarrassing morning on *CD:UK* once. We were talking to Ant and Dec and we all had sunglasses on because we couldn't see. We went to a commercial break and I had to go because I couldn't breathe, it was really bad, and I got this phone call from my mum being like, 'What's the matter with you!' Then they came back from the break and I wasn't there. Our hairdresser was throwing up in the toilet. I was throwing up before we actually went live. Mortifying.

Daizy Agnew, Girls Can't Catch: We did a Radio 1 interview the day after a night out with JLS. We partied with them, then we went back to the A&R guy's house and got a car home at 5 a.m. Then I slept in until about 2 p.m. and did a Radio 1 interview. We were a bit wild, to be honest. We'd go out loads. We bumped into Dane Bowers quite a bit so we'd go to his after-parties. I was literally living the rock 'n' roll life and I do not regret that.

Liz, Atomic Kitten: It wasn't always because we were leading the party lifestyle; it was more because we had the chance to grab a drink after an insane day. Then you'd only have two hours' sleep. There was one night where we were allotted forty minutes for sleep. That included G-A-Y and a *CD:UK*.

Natasha, Atomic Kitten: Either me or Jenny would be asleep under the make-up table or trying to find a dark corner to sleep in.

Jenny, Atomic Kitten: Oh my God, I used to be unable to speak. I wouldn't have slept. I'd go there absolutely hungover. Honestly, I'm so embarrassed by some of the states I got in. I remember the doorbell went once and we'd all be partying and I'd be like, 'Oh, the neighbours are complaining again,' and it would be, 'No, it's your driver, you're going to work.'

Claire, Steps: I might have been [hungover on TV] a couple of times. One year, I think it was the year we got our award [in 2000], the BRITs were on a Friday and we had to do *SM:TV* the next morning. I'd had an hour's sleep and I was absolutely hanging. I was still drunk. We were performing 'Deeper Shade of Blue' and wearing leather and studs and stuff. I remember feeling really hot and very aware that I must have stank. I have this memory of being there that day and standing next to Geri Halliwell. She looked up at me and went, 'Oh, you're really pretty, aren't you?' I thought that was nice at first, but then I thought it was a bit weird. Did she think I was some kind of monster before?

* Natalie Appleton quotes taken from my interview for *Guardian Guide*, 21 July 2018

12

Popstars, Pop Idol and the explosion of TV talent shows

Originally started in 1999 in New Zealand and eventually sold to fifty countries, the *Popstars* format revolutionised British popular culture when series one launched in January 2001. Suddenly pop music was Saturday-night entertainment, and everyday people – already tabloid catnip thanks to the emerging *Big Brother* – were being transformed into superstars on a weekly basis. Unlike the plethora of other TV talent shows that followed in its wake, from *Pop Idol* to *Fame Academy* to *The X Factor*, *Popstars* was presented as a rudimentary documentary as opposed to a glittering live show that required a voting public. All the decisions in regards to who would make the winning band were to be made by its three judges: TV producer and proto Simon Cowell, 'Nasty' Nigel Lythgoe; Polydor A&R Paul Adam; and the Spice Girls' former PR, Nicki Chapman. While the first six episodes followed the audition process and the eventual creation of Hear'Say, AKA Myleene Klass, Kym Marsh, Noel Sullivan, Danny Foster and Suzanne Shaw, the second half of the series followed the band living together, doing interviews and recording. The final episode, the only one shown live, captured their reaction to debut single 'Pure and Simple' crashing into the charts at number one.

'I still have the odd person telling me they voted for me'

While the show's format dictated there would only be one ultimate winner, its success soon created a splinter group. For Kelli Young, Michelle Heaton, Tony Lundon, Kevin Simm and Jessica Taylor, who would form Liberty (later Liberty X), they represented another soon-to-be-TV-talent-show-staple; the lucky 'loser' who, outside of the full-beam glare, could quietly make success work for them.

Craig McLean, journalist, *The Face*: Obviously the paradigm now is that TV shows make pop stars but back then TV shows had not made pop stars. *Pop Idol* hadn't come, *The X Factor* hadn't come, so *Popstars* was the first one. Suddenly mainstream television was making bands and the show was shining a light on the hitherto secret backroom behaviour of your Svengalis.

Colin Barlow: Lucian Grainge had been approached by Granada television and a guy called Nigel Lithgow who had put *Popstars* together. Lucian agreed to do the deal to be the record label. Then Paul Adam, who worked with me at the time, was asked to be one of the judges. I don't think we realised at the time that it was a life-changing thing. Pop music was big but it had never got to that level of becoming Saturday-night television. It was a phenomenon. The single sold a million copies in two weeks.

Myleene: I had initially seen the auditions in *The Stage*. It later transpired that when I was working at LWT as a backing vocalist on *The Lily Savage Show*, the auditions were happening in the same building. I had to go.

Kelli Young, Liberty X: At the time, I had been auditioning for *Lion King*, the musical. I was down to my final recall for the main part and so I knew when the *Popstars* audition date was but it clashed with my recall. Then on the morning I just woke up and felt that I had to go to the *Popstars* audition. Proper *Sliding Doors* moment.

Myleene: I was told by one of the producers of the show I would definitely have guaranteed work for the next six weeks minimum and over Christmas, which for a jobbing musician was brilliant news. I turned down the role of Mary Magdalene in Andrew Lloyd Webber's *Jesus Christ Superstar* as I had just done a year in the West End in *Miss Saigon*. I wanted a new challenge away from doing the same thing every day.

Tony Lundon, Liberty X: I was living in London and the plan was to learn how to write and produce music. I was running out of funds because it wasn't really working. Before I went back to Ireland to go to university to study law, my mum called and said, 'You should check this *Popstars* thing out, as your last-ditch attempt.' So I did.

Myleene: My family thought I was mad; one job was guaranteed, the other wasn't financially stable. Then the TV company started making dolls of us and it felt like it could go on a bit longer than six weeks.

Peter Robinson: You think about what TV talent shows are like now, and then you look at an old episode of [*Popstars*], it was like it was shot on zero budget. It's also the pacing of it and the colours in it and the personalities. The whole thing is incredibly flat for what was early Saturday-night television. It's just a documentary.

Myleene: People have forgotten how crude and bare the initial shows were. A real reflection of true auditions; makeshift chairs, extendable tables, grotty rehearsal rooms. They've forgotten the original format to the extent I still have the odd person telling me they voted for me and I haven't the heart to break it to them. The shows are so ingrained in how we understand and consume this form of media, these talent shows, that they are endlessly parodied and all get lumped into one.

Colin Barlow: I also did *Fame Academy* [in 2002], which was more like *Big Brother*. The BBC had them filmed in the house so you watched them doing loads of things as it went on. I think *Fame Academy* is one of the most underrated talent shows. Lemar, Alex Parks, David Sneddon – there were some really great people on that show.

Tony: I wasn't experienced with auditions – I'd only done one before. I had no reference point or expectations. I was definitely impressed with the level of production we were dealing with. I got a sense that if a broadcaster is placing that much of a priority on it, it's going to be a big TV show. I obviously had no idea it would help spawn a whole host of other TV shows and a whole generation of pop acts.

Kelli: We all had to sing '. . . Baby One More Time', hence why Darius [Danesh] did that. We all had to sing it but Darius's version obviously became the most famous.

Tony: I remember we all had to sing a track of our choosing and I hadn't done very well in the previous round and so I sang a U2 song that I felt comfortable with. I definitely did not do a rendition of '. . . Baby One More Time', that much I can tell you.

Peter Robinson: I was at *NME* at that point and running the pop part of their website. At the time, we were around the corner from LWT so they'd bike over the VHS tapes and we got a call once saying, 'Darius is around, do you want to interview him?' He'd just been kicked out so we did a video interview with him. I bumped into him a few weeks later on the Underground and he was struggling with a suitcase and he'd broken his arm. It just seemed like the really sad decline of Darius . . . Then the next thing you knew he was back on TV [being amazing on *Pop Idol*].

Lucie Cave: It was all about the underdogs with *Heat*, so we put Darius on the cover. He was one of the biggest talking points. In the same way that later on we'd put the Cheeky Girls on the cover.

'I would say the politics that lie behind that decision can't have been too pretty'

It's easy to argue the near irrelevance of the actual music when it comes to TV talent shows. For decades prior, pop acts had clamoured for attention via magazines and performances on more niche TV shows aired early in the morning or just after tea on a Thursday night. Personalities would have to leap off the pages or emerge instantly during a three-minute performance, but in the world of TV talent shows the fame game was flipped on its head; instant exposure meant you were famous before you'd really done anything. Still, the show's winners would need a song and something that would chime with a pop world shuffling away from the brightly coloured hues of Steps (who were on the verge of splitting) and S Club 7. The answer, as it turned out, lay not in the vault of some super-producer or on the nib of a white-hot songwriter's pen, but as an album track on pop flop Girl Thing's debut album.

Kelli: I remember the second round of auditions they put us into groups and everyone had to sing 'Never Ever' by All Saints. And when you listen to 'Pure and Simple' and 'Never Ever' they're not a million miles apart.

Peter Robinson: 'Pure and Simple' was on Radio 2 recently and I thought, 'This is better than I would expect it to sound now, but also not very good.' Both those things at the same time. In that kind of weird post-Spice Girls, pre-Girls Aloud era of pop music, which in hindsight wasn't always very good, when I first heard 'Pure and Simple' I thought, 'That's good.' It's just not amazing.

James Masterson: The talent shows helped to ensure that the end of the CD single era had one final huge exclamation point. It's interesting that it was timed to climax in the spring, because that was considered a nice easy, fallow time, when there wasn't much competition around.

Craig McLean: There was feverish anticipation for that single, but from *The Face*'s point of view they were still trying to be the place that would tell you first about things. Which was slowly being eroded by the early arrival of the internet. While we couldn't be the first to tell you about *Popstars*, or indeed the band, we could be the first people to tell you the story of what these people were like. That's why I spent a week with them; going to *CD:UK*, on the video set and some dance rehearsals. It felt like a cultural phenomenon and we could be the first people to pick it apart.

Myleene: I remember [first hearing 'Pure and Simple'] really well as it wasn't even our song. It belonged to a band called Girl Thing. I would say the politics that lie behind that decision can't have been too pretty. I also remember a lot of the producers we worked with couldn't read music and thought it was mad I could hear what notes were missing for harmonies or chords. I couldn't believe I'd tortured myself at music school for so long when maybe I hadn't needed to.

Chris Herbert: [As well as managing Girl Thing and, later, Hear'Say] I also managed 'Pure and Simple''s songwriters, so Pete Kirtley and Tim Hawes, who wrote it with Alison Clarkson, AKA Betty Boo. So I put them to work with Girl Thing and they came up with 'Pure and Simple'.

Peter Robinson: I'd brought the Girl Thing album on import on CD – great days – and their original version of 'Pure and Simple' on that sounded like a 'Never Ever' rip-off. I guess that was the point of it. It does strike you as strange that for the most focused-on and most exciting pop band in the country at that point, they just found a song that already existed.

Jodi Albert: 'Pure and Simple' was earmarked as our third single.

Chris Herbert: [Simon Cowell] was in limbo, deciding what the next [Girl Thing] single was going to be or whether there even was going to be a next single. I was lobbying for 'Pure and Simple'. This went on for ages and the writers were getting frustrated because they knew it was a hit and it was going to end up sitting on a shelf somewhere. Meanwhile, I was managing Hear'Say and we were looking for a first single, so we played 'Pure and Simple' to Paul Adam and he was like, 'This is brilliant, this is the first single.' The songwriters were like, 'Yeah, absolutely.'

Colin Barlow: [Girl Thing] were not doing that well and I think the songwriters at the time got the opportunity to put a song on the biggest TV show in the country.

Peter Robinson: The song was already out there, so if a song's been released you can cover it. It's also what happened in America with 'Year 3000' and the Jonas Brothers [who released a cover of the Busted song in 2006].

Chris Herbert: That was the thing. Simon Cowell could have blocked it if it hadn't come out on the Australian album. He held the master. But we just rerecorded it as a cover. I was under massive pressure from Simon Cowell saying, 'You need to take control, this can't happen,' and at that point I was like, 'I'm in complete conflict here: I manage the songwriters,

I manage both bands, I'm going to have to step away and you guys can fight this out yourselves.' Anyway, Simon didn't win; the songwriters did. It went on to be the fastest-selling debut single.

Peter Robinson: Thinking about it from Girl Thing's label's perspective, if you wanted to drop a band and avoid a difficult conversation, saying to them, 'Ooh, yeah, we were going to put a lot of money and effort behind this but, sorry, that song's gone so we can't do that now' would be a nice way of getting out of the conversation.

'We had people pranking us, going through our bins and putting hexes on our lawn!'

Before 'Pure and Simple' could be released, the process of whittling down the brave young souls continued. By episode five, with the final ten chosen, ratings reached 11.35 million. Episode six, shown just a few hours later, was watched by 12.63 million as the final band was unveiled and the members of what was becoming Liberty X were told the bad news. The TV phenomenon was also rapidly becoming a tabloid one, a state heightened even more when Nasty Nigel started earning that moniker via some appalling comments about Kym Marsh's body. As a documentary showing the mechanics of the music industry, Popstars was also succeeding in showing some fairly unsavoury aspects of its treatment of women.

Kelli: For the final section of the auditions, we had to stay in a hotel in London for a few days. I remember forming real friendships with certain people. Tony was one of them. I started putting my dream band together in my head.

Myleene: At the time, we were running alongside *Big Brother* and the formats of getting to know real people on a 24-hour basis felt new, risky, cutting edge. It was a completely alien idea for me. At music college you're drilled that whatever happens, the show must go on, keep up a professional front, smile even if everything is crumbling. Suddenly I was in a world where everyone was crying in the auditions or in the waiting room, revealing their vulnerabilities, their fears, their family's personal predicaments. We were being followed by cameras all the way home as we gave a blow-by-blow account of whether we'd received a callback or not. The anticipation, the cliff hangers, the added adrenaline of our fellow auditionees and our own families was like a pressure cooker. If you messed up the words, you didn't just make them up and carry on. It was dissected and a massive drama was built around it. It went against everything I knew.

Tony: The crew came over to Galway. They were with me for at least a day before they gave me the news. In that twenty-four hours it was pretty evident I wasn't getting in the band. Nasty Nigel came over with a director from the series, who was this heavy-set guy. I remember my mum put a plate of freshly baked scones on the table when they arrived and they couldn't really eat. They were all picking at it. My mum said to me, 'Well, the big lad's not eating, you're not getting in the band.' Nasty Nigel was well versed in hiding his emotions, if he had any, which I'm assuming he did.

Myleene: I got my break in the band when the rehearsal pianist didn't show up one day. People were panicking in front of me that they couldn't run their music, they didn't know the key, they were tail spinning. I went back to my day job and started rehearsing with them. It was then that Nicki Chapman said, 'You never told us you could play the piano.' It had never occurred to me to mention it. Getting into the band was an amazing feeling but I still didn't really know what it actually meant or what was ahead of me.

Kelli: I personally was disappointed [not to be picked for Hear'Say]. However, when they started to put stuff out, I understood why they didn't pick me. They had a vision for what that band was going to be and I didn't fit into that. It was not the kind of music I would have wanted to do.

Myleene: We moved into 'the *Popstar* house' and lived together for months. It was brilliant for us to do as a band but we were vulnerable. Overnight fame and no security at the house meant we had people pranking us, going through our bins and putting hexes on our lawn! It was also a crash back to reality when you turned over a painting or picture hanging on the wall to see a number written in sharpie because it was all from a prop company. We were literally living on a set with microphones hidden in teapots. It was surreal.

Kelli: They didn't know each other and they were thrown together really quickly. Having to gel as housemates as well as professionally. Kym felt she had to lie about having kids throughout the whole process otherwise she would never have been chosen to be in the group, which I think is probably accurate.

Lucie Cave: Now that would be a reason to put her in the band. You'd want that inclusivity. Things have changed so much. Remember Jade in *Big Brother* and people calling her a pig? The newspapers were saying 'burn the pig' and even Graham Norton would dress as a pig on his show talking about Jade. That would never happen now. It was just that sort of cultural landscape at the time and I guess the outcome of everyone being able to be famous meant that everyone could own a piece and say what they wanted about them.

Craig McLean: [Before *Popstars*] we'd never seen ordinary unknown people have their lives suddenly blown apart on stage. Kym Marsh taken to task for being a single mother and being told her bum's too big on television. We'd never cared about quote-unquote ordinary people. Pop artists before the show were extraordinary, but *Popstars* the TV show made the ordinary extraordinary.

Hannah Verdier: Hear'Say were an example of the way women were treated. Nasty Nigel saying, 'Kym, Christmas is coming and the goose is still fat.' It was abuse. The way the girls from Hear'Say were treated was shocking.

Colin Barlow: It was a time when those situations were mass tabloid news. We had this fantastic office in Chiswick and you'd have blacked-out cars driving them in for meetings because you'd have *The Sun*'s photographers outside.

Hallgeir Rustan: [Working with] Hear'Say was madness. Viewers who had followed *Popstars* didn't know the final line-up, so before it was announced the whole band was staying in Trondheim, recording the songs in Stargate Studios. Some British paparazzi had figured out the plan and set themselves up outside the studio. We had to smuggle the band in and out the back doors of the studio and we had to have security guards at the front doors.

Myleene: For a couple of weeks we wore masks as we jumped in and out of our Previa – the car of choice for all bands – going from studios to meetings to shoots. It was like regressing, being a kid again. I get why youngsters in the music industry lose their minds. You get treated like a child and so you start acting like one. We were told we were the fattest band in pop countless times so we made a point of eating numerous bars of chocolate and fast food in defiance. We played Knock Down Ginger on No. 10. It was Tony Blair's time and his son Euan opened the door while we stood there covered in face paint feeling a bit stupid, then slid down his banisters when they let us in. Less rock 'n' roll, more juvenile. We were idiots. We had a tribute band, Near'Say, that would follow us around in their own van. Can you imagine our Previa, a secondary van behind us of 'lookalikes', then paparazzi on bikes and sometimes police outriders, too? Crazy times.

Tony: Going back to normal life [after not making the band] for me was going back to London. I was working part-time, but we were put on a retainer and asked in return not to speak about the results. I suddenly had a few months where there was a wage coming in for doing nothing apart from keeping my trap shut.

Craig McLean: They were waiting in the wings to take the place of anyone who failed.

Tony: We were in a contract with LWT and so there must have been an option to swap us in if something went wrong [with a member of Hear'Say].

Kelli: As [the show] started to get more and more popular we started getting approached a lot by journalists or people in the street asking if we were in the band. We'd signed NDAs so we couldn't say anything. But it was getting harder and harder to keep it a secret. We were starting to become famous, so it was a really weird experience because week by week, the ratings were massive but we were just not protected at all. I was getting paparazzi outside college taking photos of me. I had experiences of paps going through my bins at home. We were just watching it all unfold like the public were, but with all the knowledge.

Craig McLean: Everybody in the country was watching the TV show. This was before social media, barely any internet, so you could only go by TV ratings and this was the dominant thing. It felt like it was a pop culture revolution happening on a Saturday evening.

Tony: It was weird when the show started airing because I definitely didn't realise our faces would be in *The Sun*. I was really uncomfortable at that time about not being in control of how people perceived me.

Kelli: The only people we could speak to about what we were experiencing was [the members of what would become Liberty X]. We started calling each other: 'This just happened to me,' or 'Oh my God, Michelle's just been chased down the street.' Then we were getting interview requests and ITV were sending us out in twos and threes to do little interviews.

Tony: As soon as the [Hear'Say] reveal happened, we were brought out as the 'flopstars' and I remember feeling pretty used. We were essentially promoting the show while Hear'Say were in with stylists.

Peter Robinson: Thinking about it, is *Popstars* not only the first but also the last true exciting pop show like that? Because there was genuine jeopardy; you either win or you can fuck off. Later it would become the narrative that actually you don't want to win *The X Factor*, you want to come second. Because then you don't have to do all this stuff and you can find your own voice. With *Popstars* it genuinely did seem that you'll either win it or you're nobody. I suppose all game shows need to have some sense of jeopardy.

Tony: I remember it being written into the contract that if anybody did go off and sign a record deal that you would be under the umbrella, shall we say, of LWT. I don't know if I'm still under an NDA, but I'm going to presume no one gives a shit and that they won't come after me.

Kelli: Tony and I were the only ones who lived in London, so there were a couple of occasions where I invited everyone to stay at my place. Through that we bonded even more. One time we were booked to go on *Lorraine* and the night before Kevin had a radio interview to do. He happened to say, 'Well, I'm staying at Kelli's, there's a few of us here,' and they asked us to sing something all together. So we did and we just looked at each other like, 'Wow, we actually sound really good.'

Tony: The level of profile we had been afforded gave us an opportunity.

Kelli: They'd done all the hard work for us. They'd picked ten people that included a baritone, an alto, a soprano, like all the pieces of the puzzle were there. We ended up going on *Lorraine* and she asked us what we planned to do next and one of us just blurted out that we were thinking of being a band ourselves. ITV went mad because that was not part of their plan at all. At that time, Hear'Say hadn't even released a single, so the last thing they wanted was competition. What was lovely about forming what became Liberty ourselves was that we were able to steer the ship. We didn't have that manufactured pop bubble situation. We were real rebels because we did it all on ITV's time. It was mortifying for them that we used the platform to announce we were going to be a band ourselves.

Colin Barlow: Hear'Say was a phenomenon. I don't think anyone at Polydor appreciated how big it was.

Chris Herbert: We didn't know what to expect. We knew it had a decent TV audience but none of us knew that would convert into sales. It felt like uncharted territory and so bloody exciting. I remember the morning the single hit radio, I was driving at the time and I flicked through four stations and it was playing simultaneously across all of them.

Colin Barlow: It was that big that Hear'Say performed on the BRITs.

Myleene: I remember the booing from the music industry got pretty loud. We just sang louder. I also remember that someone said our styling was dreadful and that we looked like we'd just left an office party. For me it was next level. I met Beyoncé, got an autograph from Eminem – he signed it 'To Marlene from Marshall Mathers' – and seeing as I was actually booked to have sung backing vocals for Robbie Williams but was now appearing in my own right, I had the time of my life.

Kelli: All of us are northern, bar Tony who is Irish, and I remember we couldn't think of a band name and someone said, 'We're just us five, aren't we?' So we toyed with being called Us Five for a bit but it didn't sit right. I can't remember where Liberty came from. It stuck because we felt free.

'I really like Will Young, but you can't mention him in the same breath as the Jam'

While the members of Liberty X navigated record-deal meetings with some of pop's biggest players, their victors were starting to deal with the first waves of a backlash. While Big Brother *allowed the viewers control,* Popstars *presented its winners fully formed, encouraging a sense of, 'Who do you think you are?' when the inevitable pop-star makeover took place. Meanwhile, Simon Fuller, a keen fan of* Popstars, *was tweaking the format for his own TV talent show,* Pop Idol. *Arriving seven months after the release of 'Pure and Simple', the first season of* Pop Idol *– which, like* Popstars: The Rivals *after it, did include live shows and public votes –*

gave the world Will Young. An auditions-circuit veteran, having previously auditioned for future Pop Idol *judge Simon Cowell on* This Morning *alongside Lee Ryan, Will would later stand out not just for his silky voice but for his ability to stand up to Cowell. Unlike* Popstars, Pop Idol *was keen to not only find one winner, but as many acts as possible. It's where* Popstars *reject Darius Danesh finally came good, finishing third behind Will and Gareth Gates and eventually scoring that coveted number-one single with 'Colourblind' in 2002. Sadly, Darius died in August 2022, aged forty-one.*

Tony: We started being brought [by LWT] to various meetings, the most memorable of which was with Pete Waterman. I remember we were with Pete and he was talking to us at length about his success with Steps. We were played some tunes that as young people we wouldn't really have bought into. We made a point that we didn't want to be another Steps because Pete kept referring to them. Essentially it didn't end well.

Kelli: We had a meeting with a particular, now very famous, A&R. He asked us our vision for the group, what kind of music we wanted to do and how we wanted to look. Tony tended to be more of the spokesman of the group, so he said we wanted to go more down the R&B/pop route. We left the meeting and our representative at the time came out to talk to us and said, 'He's really enamoured with you, he's really interested in signing you, however, he'd rather sign the group without Kelli as he feels like she is steering things down the R&B route and he doesn't think that's where you guys sit in the marketplace.' Then it was, 'But don't worry, we can find opportunities for Kelli, she can do her own R&B thing, but for the rest of you I think it would be better if you went your own way as a pop group without Kelli.'

Tony: The assumption Kelli was behind our sound happened a lot. I don't mind naming names; we went to see Simon Cowell. I very much remember Kelli answering some questions and I answered some. Simon referenced the Spice Girls and that most recent R&B album [2000's *Forever*] that hadn't performed well commercially. I was quite surprised to learn afterwards that Nigel had taken Kelli aside and said there was a solo opportunity for her and that maybe the other four [of us] would have a separate deal. Pete Waterman was mentioned in regards to producing [the band]. I definitely didn't want to do the Pete Waterman thing.

Kelli: I remember saying to the others, 'If that's what you guys want to do, I'm not going to hold the four of you back.' That was a real bonding experience for us. It was a collective vision we had. That was one of the experiences that made us realise we were all on the same page. No one was going to separate us from one another.

Tony: We would have been malleable and open to experienced producers and people we respected. Not that we didn't respect Pete Waterman or Simon Cowell, but they were of an era. The stuff they were playing us didn't feel like we would be more than a one-hit wonder. A quick hit and then consigned to the dustbin. I would rather do something else and fail than a Fast Food Rockers song.

Myleene: The first time I ever appeared on *Top of the Pops* it was as a backing vocalist for Cliff Richard and that blew my mind. To go there in my own right, not standing behind anyone, was next level. Being in *Smash Hits* and all the mags we shot, can you imagine, growing up reading and watching it all and then actually standing in your own dream. It doesn't feel real. We also learned about the snobbery of publications or their readers. The uproar when we were on the cover of *The Face* and *NME*. The biggest band of its time, the dawn of a new era of music, and grown men were complaining and sending letters of complaint and death threats. Mad.

Craig McLean: We did Hear'Say at *The Face* in that sweet spot where anticipation was everything, but it was moving so fast already that you could see the sweetness turning sour. They'd been in the bubble of a TV studio and a TV show and suddenly they were being thrust into the public arena. At that video shoot there was a video crew filming the video and there was a *CD:UK* video crew filming the video crew filming the band. Pop was eating itself very quickly.

Peter Robinson: The *NME* were already doing [Hear'Say on the cover] and they came to me because I'd been covering them a lot on the website. The headline from it was, 'The band that killed pop'. That it would change the way pop worked. And it did. Because it had been made like a documentary and so therefore happened in the past, it was more like a *Masked Singer* thing of it all being this secret. *Pop Idol* built on that by turning it into more of a live thing and doing the battle-bus stuff around the country with Will and Gareth, but what was happening on *Popstars* felt, in the world of pop music, like an incredibly exciting thing. What people didn't realise was that it was going to pretty much put in motion the decimation of pop music A&R in this country and the pop music press.

Pete Waterman, judge on *Pop Idol*: [TV talent shows] were very new then. Very unusual. I guess we really didn't know what we were doing. But once we got the gist of what was going on, we really enjoyed it. It was bloody boring though, Christ. Being there for fourteen hours some days listening to absolute crap was a bit difficult. Some days you'd go in and sit there for six or seven hours without seeing one act that was any good.

Lucie Cave: With Hear'Say, the boys were really boring and the girls were much more interesting and they became celebrities in their own right. The soap opera of their love lives quickly overtook what they'd done music-wise; Kym and Jack Ryder, there was Suzanne and Love Rat Darren Day. We'd always coin names for people and that would stick. Darren Day was always Love Rat Darren Day and whenever we talked about Will Young it was What Ho Will Young because he was so posh.

Paul Flynn: Gareth was so perfect, so no one expected Will to win.

Pete Waterman: [It was always] Will for me. This is the reason *Pop Idol* was such a good show because Simon was fully convinced Gareth was his man and I always knew that Will was going to be the winner because I saw the public's reaction.

Dania Pasquini: We directed Gareth Gates' 'Unchained Melody' video. He ended up being the runner-up. Here's the thing, though: Simon gives us a call and says, 'I want you guys to film either the winner's video or the runner-up's video and you're going to go to Florida and I'm going to let you know who has won while you're flying over there.' So we get the call and we're doing Gareth Gates. Then we're told it's 'Unchained Melody'. So we basically came up with the idea on the plane. We landed and Gareth was flown in.

James Masterson: Will Young's debut single ['Evergreen/ Anything Is Possible'] was released a full week after the final had aired, simply to give the label enough time to manufacture enough CDs. He then became the first person to sell a million copies of a single in the first week. That was the final exclamation point of the CD era pre-downloads.

Chris Cowey: I thought [TV talent shows] were a useful source of manufactured pop music. It replaced stuff that was in the same genre, that was pure pop. We did lock horns once when Will Young had won *Pop Idol* and the record company wanted to have Will on the same [episode of *TOTP*] as Gareth Gates, but they wanted him to do two songs. I just said no. The plugger who was looking after him said, 'But, Chris, this is the first act since Frankie Goes to Hollywood or the Jam that has had this kind of effect.' I really like Will Young, but you can't mention him in the same breath as the Jam. I said no and management withdrew his availability.

Paul Flynn: Will came out the first week *Pop Idol* finished [in March 2002]. But he'd sort of outed himself very cleverly on the show. They asked that classic 'who would you most like to go on a date with?' question and Will said the Queen Mother. The gayest answer ever.

Brian Dowling: He was out to all his family and friends. There was no secret and there was reassurance in that sense. I remember the first time we met we didn't talk. It was odd. I think we were aware we were two gay guys that had come from two huge reality TV shows. I was very mindful of people getting the wrong idea. I remember seeing him and thinking, 'I have felt everything you are going through.'

Paul Flynn: The thing with Will was he was very rare in the pop market at the time. He had a university degree and nobody did. Finding your way in the music industry was university for those kids. So they hadn't had that contemplative time to lose themselves and find themselves. Will knew who he was. And his identity was a gay identity recognisable from that time. He knew the sadness of being gay at that time and he knew the happiness of it. I think at that time he was the first person to have the first release coincide with him being out. Laws were changing around that time for gay people, too [Section 28 was repealed in Scotland in 2000 and three years later in England and Wales]. Equality was on its way to happening in Britain and that has real-world consequences. I remember having a conversation with my mum about Will and thinking, 'Oh my God, you want him to be my boyfriend.' That was the role he had for Marks & Spencer's Britain.

Pete Waterman: By [*Pop Idol* season two], Simon had lost it. He didn't want to do it any more. That's why I walked off [after Michelle McManus was announced as the winner]; it was a joke. The public could see it was nonsense and there's a point where you can't cheat the public. You have to take it seriously. As Bill Shankly said, 'It's more serious than death.' You're asking people to give you their pocket money. If you don't take that seriously then you shouldn't be doing it.

'What started to happen was this pendulum swing and we became the antithesis to Hear'Say'

Hear'Say's fall from their pedestal was vertiginously steep. While their chart-topping debut album Popstars *had shifted 300,000 copies in its first week, second single 'The Way to Your Love''s first week sales of 75,000 were substantially down on 'Pure and Simple''s opening gambit of 500,000. While that sort of decline made sense given they were no longer being beamed into living rooms every week, to the media it was a clear sign their time was over. Nine months after their debut, the band released their second album,* Everybody, *which peaked at number twenty-four. In January 2002, Kym Marsh quit, replaced for one single by Lisa Scott-Lee's husband Johnny Shentall, who won his place via, you guessed it, a televised audition process. It was while promoting that single, 'Lovin' Is Easy', that the band started to receive abuse from the public, with one man arrested after threatening the band at a motorway service station in Leicestershire. As Hear'Say's fortunes started to dip, Liberty X landed a record deal with Richard Branson's V2 label.*

Myleene: Everywhere we went, people would wave their CDs out the windows of cars or cry and scream in our faces like scenes reminiscent of the Beatles or the Spice Girls. It didn't feel real. We had a number one and were the most famous band in the country but we were all pretty broke and I was still paying off my student debt. In fact, my first Hear'Say cheque – and it was a cheque – paid off my student loan and bought my piano. I had to wait for the next pay day for my piano stool.

Peter Loraine: [Polydor] literally couldn't manufacture the CDs quick enough. It was crazy. They must hold some strange record for the quickest jump to success and the most dramatic fall from grace afterwards. They sold a million copies of that album.

Kelli: After Hear'Say released 'Pure and Simple', they were quite unpopular. So from a press perspective it was, 'Well, we don't like them so we're definitely not going to like the rejects.' We were on the back foot. Behind the scenes, wonderful things started to happen, like Richard Branson had seen that *Lorraine* interview and he got in touch trying to sign us. Plus we were getting into the studio and realising we could write our own stuff and engineer our own sound. Behind the scenes things were going beautifully, but to the public everybody just thought we were going to be rubbish.

Malcolm McLean: For bands that weren't created in front of us on telly it was a much slower decline. Even with B*Witched, when most people were saying, 'They haven't done anything for years,' we were like, 'Oh, we saw them at the airport and they do gigs here and there.' But with Hear'Say we went to see them around 'Pure and Simple' and they literally stopped traffic. It was total gridlock outside the *Pepsi Chart Show*. So that gave us the impression that they were the new Spice Girls; they're going to take over the world, look at how many people are here. But that lasted for all of that single.

Jamelia: My real first single was 'Money', which went top five when I was eighteen. This is why I really empathise with artists of today because I still felt, even after having three years of development, like I was propelled into the limelight. Now it's one day nobody knows you and the next day you're famous and you're supposed to be a star.

Myleene: I still have copies of the day diaries and there was one time in three months that we had just two days off. In which I did my laundry. We were often broken. Anyone that thinks pop is a world of bubblegum has no idea how hard these bands actually work. The hours are brutal and schedules are like no others. No rock stars would be able to keep up with what these pop bands do, namely because they probably couldn't or wouldn't. It's hardcore.

Malcolm McLean: We went to see them promoting the second single ['The Way to Your Love'] and we could already tell it was over. Even though they got another number one, we would see the fans on the ground and it was like, 'Well, there's six of us now and there used to be six hundred.'

Myleene: We were hated by most. Booed at the BRITs and constantly heckled and criticised for our weight and looks. The music industry didn't feel we'd earned our right to be there. It wasn't enough that we'd gone to music school – most of the music industry can't read music but I was getting heckled – and other members had done the club/pub circuits, others were trained, incredibly talented performers. To many in the industry it wasn't okay that we hadn't made the journey as a band and worked what in their eyes was the hard, long way up. We hadn't earned our stripes. We hadn't publicly suffered enough to get there. Basically, they were jealous.

Colin Barlow: I think with Hear'Say, because they were the guinea pigs, they took more pressure than anyone. The general public felt like they knew them.

Myleene: It was extremely hard on us and our families. They were equally thrust into the spotlight with no idea of how to deal with any of it. Phones ringing through the night from fans. People sleeping under the windows of our homes or taking pics through the gaps in the curtains. Old friends or exes selling out. The good was great, phenomenal in fact – my mum and dad stayed longer than I did at a famous pop star's party once as I was too tired. But there were very testing, very pressured times. We often found it frustrating that people assumed we had changed and would treat us with that assumption in mind, not realising *they* had changed.

Tony: At the time, it was more, 'You're on your journey, best of luck to you, but we don't really care.' But, in hindsight, [Hear'Say's demise] was horrible. I feel grateful that I wasn't in an entity that got built up only to be torn down as fast as possible. I don't think there's a cabal of media types in sync with each other to spin narratives and then spin the opposite, but I think there's this tendency towards that that's a bit weird to me. There's almost this vacuum where the narrative stalls and you know it's going to reverse. With that kind of band, where they're not in control, it feels inevitable. The speed with which it happened was really harmful.

Chris Herbert: It was driven by the media. This was a mad experiment of how the media can elevate a band. The press had got behind them and it was all really positive, but like any soap opera story there has to be a start, a middle and an end. The media, the papers, the tabloids – they wrote that storyline. They wanted to create the stories about the in-fighting and then they wanted to write a lot of negative press about the demise of the band. It was a rapid rise – record-breaking single, record-breaking tour, record-breaking merchandise sales – and then it just dropped off a cliff. It was a really harsh experience.

Malcolm McLean: There was a backlash because people saw them at their most raw [on the TV show], being called fat or crying, so there was this impression that people thought they owned them. If it was S Club 7, you'd be like, 'Well, I had nothing to do with your creation and I don't own any part of you,' but with Hear'Say, and other acts that followed like Gareth Gates, it was like, 'We created you.' Even though we hadn't with Hear'Say specifically. I saw a girl outside a studio once, she was a Blue fan and she had it in for Noel. She called him every name under the sun, just screaming it at his face like, 'You fat gay cunt.' It was so horrible.

Dean Piper: I got sent to Amsterdam and I was put in the Grand Hotel. I was told that Robbie Williams was going to be there and I had to follow him around. So I had to sit in reception with my photographer and hope that he came out and went on a bender. But he didn't come out. Instead Gareth Gates did. He was like seventeen and I followed him all night, watched him walk past all the strippers and prostitutes. I look back on that and think, 'Hang on, this was a seventeen-year-old kid.' We had no qualms about plastering him on the front page.

Craig McLean: It was a democratising of pop culture. Suddenly it was a gladiatorial arena where normal folk could have a shot at stardom. You risked getting ripped apart by lions or the judges, but there was a way for them to do it. There'd always been star finders, but this was something that was primetime entertainment. That also created a generation who were happy to go on TV and think, 'I don't mind if Nasty Nigel is mean to me or Simon Cowell rips my family and me apart – in fact I'd rather do that than never have a go.'

Tony: There's something really quite horrible about the fact you're given this opportunity to transform but because that transformation is visible it induces jealousy. When you hide that transformation people just receive the finished entity and buy into you as an otherworldly star. Even these successful entertainers who do this transformation behind closed doors, they really believe they are that person too and they never want to go back.

Kelli: What started to happen was this pendulum swing and we became the antithesis to Hear'Say. I think the image we came out with was a little bit edgier, a bit more real. Less bubblegum.

Craig McLean: The legacy of *Popstars* is every other TV talent show. It showed that those kinds of shows could be successful in terms of TV viewers, it proved that in terms of being in pop magazines that these bands were smash hits and it showed that there's a huge appetite for seeing how the ugly duckling becomes a swan. It showed a generation that actually getting on TV could be a way to pop stardom.

'We had to change our name and do it quickly before we released another record'

Released in September 2001, the debut single of the so-called 'flopstars' Liberty, 'Thinking It Over', peaked at number five. Just as they were about to start working on what would become their debut album, however, a legal notice was sent from representatives of another musical act called Liberty. The case went to the High Court and the band had to rethink. Having arrived at this point the hard way, they weren't about to stop now.

Tony: Nobody wanted to give us any tracks. The one decision we did make was to hire a manager, Gary Wiltern, who had managed a band called Worlds Apart. They had created a nice career for themselves in France and Germany. Our thinking was, 'Fuck the UK, if we're flopstars here then that doesn't mean we don't have what it takes.' He got us set up in some writing sessions and Kelli and I were doing them. The very first session we did, we wrote 'Thinking It Over'.

MNEK: If they had been under Syco or the 19 management umbrella, for example, they would have been told to just make teeny-bopper stuff or anything like Hear'Say was making at the time. Here they had 'Thinking It Over,' a garage-lite song. It was current, it was fresh, it wasn't appealing to, you know, Phil and

Jill in Doncaster. It's a great pop record inspired by garage music. They had a longer career than Hear'Say because they had more time to develop and cultivate their sound and their vibe.

Kelli: When we put out 'Thinking It Over' we actually released it anonymously on a white label because we didn't think anyone would play it if they knew who it was by.

Malcolm McLean: The first time I heard 'Thinking It Over' we were on the Hear'Say tour, seeing them everywhere, and I was livid because it was really good. People would laugh and call them 'flopstars', then they did that and everyone loved it.

Kelli: The success of 'Thinking It Over' attracted another band called Liberty, who sued us in the High Court. They filed a case against us for basically trying to harness their fans and popularity, which obviously we did not do.

Tony: It was a pretty ridiculous claim. There was an opportunity for a settlement between them and V2, but it went to the High Court and the version of events I was given was that because we didn't provide much of a defence the case was awarded to that group.

Kelli: They had the smaller outfit and we had these London lawyers, a big law firm, so they didn't want to be seen to be hammering them. But then when the judge made his ruling he said because we hadn't argued our case fully he had no choice but to rule in their favour, so they won.

Tony: They weren't awarded any damages. It was pittance. But we had to change our name. I do remember a poll [in *The Sun*, allowing readers to vote on a new name] and people saying, 'Let the people be involved in it all.' I thought it was a great idea as long as we weren't wedded to the results, like if they wanted to call us Flopstars.

Kelli: They voted on Ex Liberty. But we preferred the X on the end.

'We felt like we never had anybody on our side until that moment'

While 'Thinking It Over' was a hit, it wasn't a career-defining smash. In a period where pop acts would enter high and drop like a stone, it was hard to make a song that would stand the test of time. For the newly named Liberty X, however, their defining moment was waiting for them on a CD-R, ready to turn them from TV talent show runners-up to credible, BRIT Award-winning superstars. That led to a collaboration with producer Richard X on mash-up 'Being Nobody', before the dream started to fizzle out.

Tony: We got lucky with 'Just a Little'. Our first single did well, then the second one, 'Doin' It', got to number fourteen. We knew we were in trouble. Everyone agreed, label included, that we should record a few more tracks. In that period, Michelle went to a writing session and they played her 'Just a Little'. As I understand it, it was intended for Anastasia and she turned it down, which is why they played it to Michelle. She came back and was like, 'They played me this song that was quite cool.'

Kelli: Michelle Escoffery, who wrote it, had done the demo vocal and she's got a really amazing R&B voice. I remember thinking, 'It's a massive song, it's wicked, but we are going to have to really do it justice.'

Tony: I took a photograph of Jess, Kelli and myself holding the track and I think we had our fingers up as in this is a number one.

Kelli: Once we recorded it and added bits I was like, 'Oh my God, this is banging.' Then it just all snowballed. Everyone at the label was so excited and it was just meetings and chats about the video.

Tony: We had an incredible stylist, Michelle Clapton, who went on to become the costume designer for *Game of Thrones*. She had a contact in the fetish fashion world and the girls were like, 'Yeah, fuck it, we can pull this off.'

Kelli: The song is so sexy. We just had to be sexy in the video. It couldn't be us coming out in baggy trousers. We weren't afraid to be risqué. We didn't want to be seen as a bubblegum pop outfit; that's not what we are. We all sat around a table and came up with the *Entrapment* idea for the video. Everything just rolled from there, like, 'What if we danced with canes?'

Tony: Another word for a cane is a crutch, so if you'd taken that cane away from me I felt more exposed. Our poor choreographer saw myself and Kev and thought, 'Fuck, what am I going to do?'

MNEK: We think of Liberty X's records more now than we think of Hear'Say's. 'Just a Little' is a classic. It's not a classic in the way 'Pure and Simple' is, which is ironic. 'Just a Little' is a genuinely great record.

Tony: Winning a BRIT [for Best British Single in 2003] was crazy. We could hold our heads up high – we had a number one and a BRIT Award. It changes the way you feel about yourselves. From that moment onwards you get to say, 'You know what, I don't have to worry about how I'm perceived – it just is what it is.'

Kelli: I remember the whole day. We were rehearsing for our tour and then we had hair and make-up arrive to get us ready and the label had put on a limo. It was probably one of the most pop star-y days of my life. Then to actually win, it was totally mad. That was voted for by the public, so it felt all the more special. We felt like we never had anybody on our side until that moment. We'd really achieved something.

Tony: [The workload] was constant. We had our own limited company because our manager and tour manager had instilled some good practices in us so we voted on things. We knew that our finances were such that we had to go out and gig because that was our money, because back then touring earnings belonged to the band. We knew that whatever happened with the records we wouldn't do very well because of the way the deal was structured. So we did our promo during the day and then we gigged in the evening.

Kelli: We just didn't sleep for seven years. I'm being genuine about that. We used to have two weeks off at the start of January, because that was when the music industry pretty much shut down. We worked non-stop, fifty weeks of the year for seven years. Then we started to get international success around

2003 and it just multiplied. We made time to have fun. Michelle made time. She really didn't sleep.

Tony: 'Freak Like Me' was absolutely banging, so the possibility of working with Richard X made me very excited. We were at the point where we needed a producer who had the chops to take it to the next level. We got the feeling that we needed a superstar producer or someone with designs on becoming one. Finances at the label dictated that we weren't going to go in with a superstar producer for a whole album, but we did get to do a few tracks with Richard. To me he was in line with that 'Just a Little' and 'Thinking It Over' sensibility. Pop stuff that isn't too sweet.

Richard X: I liked that Liberty X were the underdogs who'd done well; that chimed with me. Also with my anti-glamour stance and trying to diffuse everything that Virgin wanted me to do. I was never going to be all 'look at me' or be hip. I was hip for like a week. Even using the word 'hip' tells you a lot. My thing was a reaction to that glamour, so Liberty X suited my mindset. The success of that song was down to them. My friends were very confused seeing me on *CD:UK* just doing a little dance.

Kelli: He used to come and do performances and stand in the back with his grey boiler suit, pretending to press buttons. We'd be there giving it all the moves. We did some of the promo trail with him, which was quite funny. I think he liked seeing all the madness and then going home.

Richard X: They tolerated me. I was always the weakest link in the album campaign. They were really nice and funny and I was really dour and pretentious. They would be happy to play along with any pop star chat.

Steve Anderson: I remember we did a writing camp with Liberty X. You'd work with individual members of the band and so it would depend really on who you got. Obviously from the band's point of view, mainly financially, but also a little bit creatively, they wanted to be part of the songwriting.

Hannah Robinson, songwriter, 'Everybody Cries': I'm sure they won't mind me saying but that single came with the worst video I've ever seen. They're walking down a railway line and there's rubbish coming out of black bin bags falling from the sky. I was gutted because it didn't really do that well, but looking back now, if I had that chart entry today [number fourteen], I'd be over the moon.

Tony: Even my kids rip the piss out of me when they see that video. One of them said it was the worst music video he'd ever seen. It's hard to disagree.

After scoring eight UK top-ten singles and three top-thirty albums, Liberty X called it a day in 2007. In 2012, they joined a number of their '00s peers on ITV's *The Big Reunion*, before disbanding again in 2014. In 2016, Kevin Simm won the fifth series of *The Voice*, before later replacing Marti Pellow in Wet Wet Wet. Tony, meanwhile, moved into TV and film production. Jessica, Kelli and Michelle still perform as Liberty X.

13

What will the neighbours say? How Girls Aloud tore up the rulebook

By the summer of 2002, TV talent show formats were springing up faster than you could say 'singing is my passion'. *Pop Idol*, launched in late 2001, had ditched *Popstars'* documentary-style feel and, looking to chime with the democratisation of everything boom post-*Big Brother*, opened the outcome up to the viewing public via live shows. Keen to expand on this further, *Popstars: The Rivals* drew from one unexpected result of the original *Popstars*: the tabloid-created rivalry between winners Hear'Say and 'losers' Liberty X. This was cleverly built into the show, with a boyband and a girlband created to go head-to-head, with the winner (hopefully) landing the coveted Christmas number-one spot.

Looming over the show was the spectre of Hear'Say, who, despite only releasing their first single in March 2001, had acrimoniously split by the time the first *Popstars: The Rivals* live show aired in October 2002. Of course, the realities of the music industry don't matter when the promise of something life-changing is at stake, and so it was that hundreds and hundreds of hopefuls joined queues in London, Manchester and Glasgow for a chance to be critiqued by judges Louis Walsh (who earlier that year had completed a stint as a judge on the Irish version of *Popstars*, which featured a certain Nadine Coyle), Pete Waterman and 'Heaven and Hell (Being Geri Halliwell)' hitmaker Geri Halliwell. From there, the two bands were whittled down to ten boys and ten girls, with each group chucked in a big house together during the live shows. While both Kimberley Walsh and Nicola Roberts missed out initially on the final ten, fate saw that they would eventually take their rightful place in Girls Aloud, AKA one of the UK's biggest and best girlbands.*

'It was a bit more like panto'

Louis Walsh: I never wanted to be on TV, ever. But the fact I was there with Pete Waterman and Geri, that sounded fun. I was very naïve to television. I'm a lot wiser now. But I think it helped, the fact that I was naïve.

Nicola: I used to do all the local competitions and my mum and dad subscribed to *The Stage*. I remember seeing this advert saying, 'TV auditions to make a group on ITV'. So I recorded myself onto a CD and didn't really think anything of it. It felt

---

* Kimberley replaced Hazel Kaneswaran, who was disqualified for being ten days older than the maximum age limit, while Nicola replaced Nicola Ward, who quit the show over what she considered the 'exploitation' of the contestants.

like such a long shot. The auditions fell while I was on holiday in Devon, so I had to be driven to Manchester and then driven back to Devon to continue my holiday.

Kimberley: My dance teacher at the time handed me the application and was like, 'I've half filled this out, you've got to send it off.' I didn't know if it was for me. It seemed a bit terrifying, the whole thing. But she gently persuaded me.

Nicola: The year before, when I was watching *Popstars* with Hear'Say and Liberty X, it all felt quite far removed. It was just something I'd watch in my very normal living room at home; there was no correlation.

Kimberley: I thought *Popstars: The Rivals* was going to be the same as the previous *Popstars* format, so I did get a sharp shock when I realised what the actual process was going to be. But I was in it way too deep at that point.

Nicola: Even with *Pop Idol*, I was just watching while getting ready to get drunk in the local place that used to let underage people in. That was it. Watching Will Young win, like, 'Oh, yeah, great, he's won, pass the lipstick, how much money have we got? Am I going to be able to afford a WKD or a Smirnoff Ice?' That was where I was at.

Kimberley: I wasn't thrilled at the idea of doing a show that was live on TV to millions of people. It seemed like a higher level of anxiety. I was pretty confident that I would find a way of making singing a big part of my life, but these shows do require a bit of luck and a bit of drama. I didn't bring any drama.

WHAT WILL THE NEIGHBOURS SAY?

Nadine: I had been on Irish *Popstars* [in 2001]. They had an over-18s limit and I'd just turned sixteen at the time. I didn't know they had an age limit when I applied and then when I found out someone there was like, 'Oh, it doesn't matter.' Then I got disqualified.

Louis Walsh: I had kept in touch with Nadine. She was very damaged after the Irish *Popstars* thing because it was front-page news and it made out she was lying. She was never going to sing again.

Una Healy: I actually met Nadine [on Irish *Popstars*]. The night before we auditioned we all sat together in the living room and went around the circle and sang a bit. I just remember Nadine singing and going, 'Oh my God, she's amazing.' Then she was removed from the show because of her age, which was actually a bit of a blessing in disguise for her.

Louis Walsh: I knew I was doing this show [*Popstars: The Rivals*] so I called her up and said, 'You have to go for it.' She didn't want to. I told her she had to and that she was a great singer, so she went for it. That's the truth.

Nadine: That is true. It wasn't that I was close to giving up on singing, I just didn't like that type of show. It was very much about making a TV show rather than singing. A friend of mine was auditioning for the Girls Aloud version and Louis was like, 'You must audition, you must, I will never speak to you again.' So I went to Scotland to audition. You don't think you're going to win these things.

Nicola: Initially it was just about getting myself through the process. It was, 'Do I know my song? Can I sing my song? Am

417

I happy with my song? Will the audience like my song?' It was self-contained in that way. Once we'd made it into the group, you could zoom out and it was about how do we beat the boys and get to number one?

Nadine: You were seeing people's dreams ripped away from them. I was sixteen or seventeen. There were people there older than I was and their dreams were being shattered and I found that hard to deal with on a day-to-day basis. I had loads of random illnesses that I haven't had since being in that process.

Kimberley: [The chart battle element] felt like it made it all a bit more light-hearted. It was a bit more like panto, that side of things.

Nicola: There were definitely some stronger characters in the house. Older girls, more experienced girls, that liked to dominate. I'd never lived away from home – I'd just done my GCSEs. I was quite nervous around new characters.

Kimberley: It wasn't cameras in your face the minute you wake up in the morning, but you were being filmed rehearsing and stuff like that. It was just about to the level I could cope with. I'd done quite a bit of TV acting so I had done jobs that meant living away from home, so that side of it was okay for me.

Nicola: I was late to the house and so I joined just before the live shows. I remember one of the other girls saying, 'If she gets through after we've been in the house for weeks, it's going to be a joke.' This girl wasn't a very good singer. So I was thinking, 'Well, we'll see.' And then she was the first one out.

WHAT WILL THE NEIGHBOURS SAY?

'Let's go and do something so exciting that even if we lose we've got a career'

For the as-yet-unnamed girlband, who were still having their numbers whittled down, second place seemed inevitable. As with the Spice Girls six years earlier, the industry thinking was that there wasn't really an audience for a girlband and that pop fans would always gravitate towards a band of cute dimples and swept fringes if given a choice. It was going to take a very special song to change that fate. Unbeknown to everyone, an undeniable banger – the drum 'n' bass meets surf guitar curio that is 'Sound of the Underground' – was sitting on producer Brian Higgins' computer. The only problem was that while it was always meant for a girlband, it wasn't Girls Aloud.

Brian Higgins: [Xenomania] had a girl group, Orchid, that we'd put together. I'd thought long and hard about what sound we needed to break a girl group in the UK.

Miranda Cooper: I remember being really cross. Moonbaby had gone and then Brian was like, 'We've got this girlband,' so I remember seething about it. When I wrote 'Sound of the Underground' I definitely thought it was for Moonbaby part two.

Brian Higgins: 'Sound of the Underground' was written to a very dark piece of drum 'n' bass. The process of turning it into a pop song started in around April 2002. I made the initial version of the record with the surf guitars and imported that record into the studios of two Tims – Tim Larcombe and Tim Powell. I was walking up the stairs between the three studios and hearing everything that was going on with these three versions – my original, what Tim Larcombe was doing with it and what

419

Tim Powell was doing with it. I heard the record coming out all mashed together. I literally said, 'Bassline from that one, this bit from that one, then add that to that, and that's the record.'

Miranda Cooper: I wrote it with Niara Scarlett in my little flat. I would go round with my notepad and just write words and concepts down. Anytime we would write we'd have lots and lots of backing tracks. We'd have our dictaphones and we'd press play and then we'd just sing over the top. Just a stream of consciousness. Then I would go through all of my lyrics and try different ones and the same lyrics would pop up over loads of different tracks. But with 'Sound of the Underground' I was singing, 'The wheels on the bus go round and round' over and over.

Brian Higgins: Colin Barlow heard the record and said, 'That's the record of the year in my opinion.'

Colin Barlow: As we started to do *Popstars: The Rivals*, I just knew that was the song I wanted to use. I took the mantle of helping scout for the girls.

Peter Loraine: Colin called me into his office and said, 'Here you go, it's your dream, you can go and do the new Bananarama.' There was a video tape with loads of footage of different people that had entered and we sat and watched it together. There were maybe about twenty girls that were in consideration. At that point, they didn't have any members, obviously, or a single, so it was like, 'What is this going to be? What are we going to try to do? Are we going to do something like Eternal? Or Atomic Kitten?' Musically it could have gone in any direction. Visually it could have gone in any direction.

Brian Higgins: Colin phoned me up out of the blue and said, 'You know that song, I think we have a vehicle for it.' He told me what it was. The truth is I never really believed him. I thought, 'There's no way you're going to put that out as the first single [from a TV talent show] because it's always a dreadful song.'

Miranda Cooper: I remember at the time Brian and I thinking that reality TV was over, it was just saturated, and that maybe we shouldn't do this. It was either going to be a cover of 'Stay Another Day' by East 17 or 'Sound of the Underground'. We just thought there was no way they were going to go with our song.

Brian Higgins: Did I watch the show? No. I'm not interested in things like that. I don't understand things like that.

Colin Barlow: Towards the end when Pete [Waterman] had his classic boyband [One True Voice] with the nice mid-tempo ballad, I sat with everyone and played them 'Sound of the Underground'. They thought I was absolutely mad. I said to them, 'The odds are we're never going to win – the boyband should win by a mile, so let's go and do something so exciting that even if we lose we've got a career.' I felt the song was that good.

Miranda Cooper: Later, Brian and I were invited down by ITV to the big house called Horizons, where all the girls were, and we played the song and they totally didn't get it. They were into Mariah Carey and thought they'd have their beautiful moment song.

Nicola: A few weeks before the end of the show, I found a CD in the house and it had all these potential singles on it. Someone had said to me, 'Oh, "Sound of the Underground" is the one they're going with.' I remember putting it on and thinking, 'No one's going to understand this. *I* don't understand this.' I was quite concerned. As a teenager, as a music listener, it was all about those sweet melodies, being able to connect to the song, like, 'Does this reflect my life? Does this remind me of the boy I like?' And it couldn't have been further away from anything I'd been listening to. It felt like a risky move.

Peter Loraine: Colin said, 'We've found the first song,' and he played it and from that moment onwards everything fell into place. Straight away you could picture who would work with them, what it should look like. Never before has there been such a defining song. There was no getting away from the fact they were a manufactured band. What you're getting is five very different people who all potentially would have their own ideas, but no experience whatsoever. No time to learn, no time to grow, no time to experience how anything worked. They were very reliant on a team who would say, 'This is what it's going to be like.'

Colin Barlow: That's when the genius of Peter Loraine came to the fore. Naming the band, coming up with the whole punk ethos [around 'Sound of the Underground'] and then really creating something edgy. It was exactly the right group.

Kimberley: Everything would have led you to believe [the boys would win]. For sure. But then when we heard the songs I did think, 'Ah, maybe not.'

Peter Robinson: I was doing the book [*Popstars: The Rivals: The Official Inside Story*] and it had a split cover, so one with One True Voice on the cover and one with Girls Aloud on the cover. I think

I'm right in saying they printed more copies of the boys' one. *Smash Hits* got me to do a cover story but it was with One True Voice. The whole thing was 'here come the boys', basically.

Louis Walsh: I thought I was going to get the boys. But then they gave me the girls and it was like, 'Oh, God.' But Colin Barlow found 'Sound of the Underground' and Brian Higgins gave them all their hits.

Nadine: As soon as I heard the songs, I didn't worry about [us losing] at all. The boys were super talented, great singers, but I knew from hearing our song that there wouldn't be much competition.

Nicola: I don't know why Colin went with Brian and that song. Why didn't he go with somebody who had done a load of Atomic Kitten records? Or straight to Biff, who had worked with the Spice Girls?

Peter Loraine: There was one member, who didn't make the final band, who when we went to play all ten of them 'Sound of the Underground' she said, 'No, no, no, that's not the song that will be launching my group.' I remember thinking to myself, 'I really, really hope you're not in the final line-up.'

Kimberley: I was so relieved that it wasn't going to be this generic pop ballad. We were coming out of that era so I would have known then that it was probably going to be a short-lived thing. I just remember not really knowing if I loved the song itself but just being glad it was something different. A bit edgier.

Keith Semple, One True Voice: I remember thinking [Sound of the Underground] was a catchy song. I remember liking the mix of the song better than ours and thinking it was more edgy and current. As an already touring rock musician, I was not interested in boybands. However, I thought we had established ourselves on the show as competent musicians and singers and would not be considered a boyband going forward. Of course that turned out to be wrong!

Louis Walsh: I knew it was going to walk all over radio and kill Pete Waterman and his group. I was happy with that. It was a great song.

Alexis Petridis: It keyed into a much wider tradition of brilliant, trashy, balls-out, British pop music. It wasn't watered down R&B. It felt really British for a start, because it had that drum 'n' bass undertow to it. They were making records that were far better than they needed to be. Which is not really the ethos of people who make records for TV talent-show winners. Most of the things that have been huge hits off the back of these TV talent shows have been rubbish. The plan works in the short term and seldom works in an extended sense. It was a record by someone who really understood what makes British pop music good and unique.

Peter Robinson: In the space of a week, backstage at where they made it, which was in the same building they filmed *CD:UK*, I got played the One True Voice song by Pete Waterman and then I went into Polydor to hear the Girls Aloud song. That week I placed a £50 bet on Girls Aloud being the Christmas number one and that paid for my Christmas. The odds were brilliant because everyone thought the boys would win.

'Louis made sure Pete always felt that he'd lost'

As the live shows continued, the bands slowly started to form, with the Louis Walsh-managed Girls Aloud in one corner and One True Voice, stewarded by Pete Waterman, in the other. While Pete Waterman had plumped for a mid-paced, vanilla cover of a Bee Gees album track ('Sacred Trust') for the Burton-suited boys, the strappy top and polyester-trousered girls had started recording the upbeat, decidedly edgier 'Sound of the Underground'. With each passing week, the band gained a member: Cheryl Tweedy, Nicola Roberts, Nadine Coyle and Kimberley Walsh had all made it through, with the final spot a battle between Sarah Harding and judge favourite Javine Hylton. It wasn't the only controversial moment, with Pete Waterman – who let's remember was sending out his boyband with a cover – furious that 'Sound of the Underground' had existed before the show started.

Brian Higgins: I went to see them when there were ten girls. I didn't watch any of [the show] until literally the throwing-out bit, so then I had to find a way to make sure the five people who made it in fitted. We recorded everyone, all ten girls.

Miranda Cooper: We'd have to delete the vocal of the person who got chucked out. I remember Javine sounded great on it and we were gutted when she went.

Peter Loraine: Everyone thought it was a slam dunk that Javine would be in, so depending on what the line-up was it was 'Version A, send that off,' 'Version B, send that off.' When Javine didn't get in, it was like, 'Oh . . .', because she was all over the song. By this point, we'd also done a photoshoot with six members using every different configuration. There was a photo session that had Kimberley, Nicola, Sarah, Nadine and Javine. And then we'd switch out Kimberley and put Cheryl in.

Nadine: I thought Javine was going to make it into the band. I almost took it for a given. But I truly believe that, without those other four girls, it just would not have worked in the way it did. It was a really nice, harmonious thing. We're all very different – very different backgrounds, very different people in general.

Louis Walsh: I thought [Javine] was going to be one of the stars of the group. The public were in charge of Girls Aloud; it wasn't me. At the end of the day, they are in charge because they decide if they're going to like a song.

Colin Barlow: Thank God Sarah Harding got that last place because she became the heartbeat of that group. It's funny now, putting Sarah into that song made it more pop, whereas the way Javine sang it, it had more of a garage, urban feel. The pop-ness Sarah brought to it made it much more mass appeal.

Iain James: I remember [*Popstars: The Rivals*] very clearly because we all fancied [Girls Aloud] and we were picking which one we were trying to chat up basically. They had that boyband as well, One True Voice, and Polydor were very much, 'That's your direct competition.' We used to watch it and very arrogantly just used to laugh, like, 'This isn't a competition.'

Peter Waterman: [Doing that show] was horrible. Everybody was cheating. They'd made the bloody record three months before the show. And I'm believing that you've got to start when the bands were found. How naïve was I? It's a good record, but I was played it before we started, like, 'This is going to be their single.'

Brian Higgins: He's just a bad loser, I think.

Keith: Their song was simply better, whether it already existed or not.

Peter Robinson: If you know you've got to have a song ready by the middle of December, you start looking as early as possible. You don't go, 'Oh, we've won, shall we think about writing a song?'

Colin Barlow: I love Pete but he wanted to win so badly and Louis made sure Pete always felt that he'd lost. There's a bitterness there that the two of them have always played on. If you put them in a room together now, within two minutes they'd bring it up. They were so desperate to win that the rivalry was beyond intense.

Louis Walsh: [Pete] didn't talk to me for years when Girls Aloud won. He thinks he invented pop music. He told me once that he invented pop music and he believed it. We didn't cheat; we just had a better song and a better group. Obviously. Girls Aloud went on to have twenty hits and he had no hits with One True Voice. Listen, he's a nice guy, he's just slightly out of touch with today's market.

Nadine: Our team, I think it was Peter Loraine, came up with the very crafty thing to do, which was to record their song and put it on our B-side.

Peter Loraine: The Bee Gees were signed to us as well and so we got the girls to record a version of 'Sacred Trust'. We were going to put a sticker on the front of the CD saying, 'Includes

"Sacred Trust"'". It was decided by my boss that that was one step too far. Too dirty.

Colin Barlow: I don't know why we didn't do that. We should have done that.

Peter Robinson: I remember Pete Waterman going, 'We've got an unreleased Bee Gees song.' And it's not; it had come out before as an album track. If you're going to cover a Bee Gees song, don't cover a not very good one. I mean the boys weren't great together. Even when I was doing the *Smash Hits* shoot, one of the members was becoming a problem and needed to get a bollocking from the PR. That was before the song was even out.

'That was the moment of one pop era ending and another one beginning'

By the end of November 2002, the pop cosmos had two brand-new stars, but the show's ultimate prize – that coveted Christmas number one, to be announced on a later show – was still up for grabs. Relishing in their underdog status, Girls Aloud, along with their tight-knit marketing team and despite an increasingly absent Louis Walsh, set about electioneering up and down the country, their genius slogan – Buy Girls, Bye Boys – quickly searing its way into the public consciousness. On 22 December, having sold 213,000 to One True Voice's 147,000 (another Popstars: The Rivals *act, the Cheeky Girls, were at number three with searing polemic 'Cheeky Song (Touch My Bum)'), Girls Aloud were crowned the winners.*

Peter Loraine: We had a week to do everything. There wasn't time to be trying things out. It very much needed to be, 'Here's the song, now go.' And off we went.

Nadine: My mum was crying her eyes out that night I got into the band because we had to leave immediately and go to a hotel. No time for them to have a conversation with me to make sure I was okay. It was extreme.

Kimberley: It was pretty full-on. It was literally like go to a hotel, then start the Buy Girls, Bye Boys promo the next day. We just lived out of a Chrysler for the next however many weeks until it charted. I'd never had sleep deprivation like it.

Nicola: I have never, and I will never, work that hard again in my life. Our feet did not touch the ground.

Jeremy Joseph: When *Popstars* happened, we approached the TV company about putting on One True Voice and Girls Aloud at G-A-Y. I remember Louis and Pete being very competitive at G-A-Y with what they did. Louis brought on someone from Westlife just to try to make sure the girls got more press on the Monday. I'll tell you what the interesting thing was: when you looked in the dressing room, the girls were all sat together. They were a group. Whereas the boys were very apart. It didn't feel like a unit.

Nicola: I remember we were about to leave somewhere and our tour manager was like, 'The label have just put this new thing in the schedule,' and we were all crying because we were emotionally and physically and mentally exhausted. But it was like we were athletes running for the finish line. We used to do crazy things like we'd stop at red lights and open the car door and be like, 'Buy our single – don't buy the boys' single.'

Peter Loraine: There were certain areas of the media, like *Smash Hits* and Capital radio, who were on the boys' side. Capital were doing a takeover with the boys, so I bought all the advertising spots around their appearance. It was so exciting. We had things where if you went to Asda there'd be someone there to sticker you with the Buy Girls, Bye Boys badge. When you went to HMV, we glued big Girls Aloud footprints to the floor so you followed it to the CD rack where 'Sound of the Underground' was. I had the budget, so we just ran riot. The brief was to win. When we went back for the episode to reveal who would be number one, I remember in the green room Pete [Waterman] saying to me, 'You nailed it because you had time to do two CD singles and we only had time to do one.' I remember thinking, 'What the hell are you on about?' The line-up of the boys was announced a week before the girls. They had seven days ahead of us to get everything prepped.

Peter Robinson: Girls Aloud winning was the moment of one pop era ending and another one beginning.

Pete Waterman: No. No, no, no. Nothing to do with musical trends, we just had five guys who should never have been together.

Keith: Pete was obviously a genius in his earlier career. Although I disagreed with his choices on our style, single release and the band not being allowed to perform instruments live, I understand that in the '80s and early '90s he was on the top of the industry.

Kimberley: I can't actually remember getting the chance to celebrate. We got the number one just before Christmas and so I think that was the first time any of us went back home after getting in the band. Then it was just more about having time to reflect on the madness of the past six weeks. You're sat there on Christmas Day watching yourself performing the Christmas number one on *Top of the Pops* and it's just a bit of a bizarre moment.

Keith: I still have the gold disc on my wall for a number-two British hit and over 400,000 singles sold. That can in no way be considered anything but an awesome achievement. I will always be proud of that.

Nicola: The word 'whirlwind' doesn't do it justice. You've gone from being nobody to then trying your best to get through a competition to being in a group to then promoting a song and having a number one. You go back home for Christmas to your normal life. It was like being put in a washing machine with loads of fucking red socks and expecting it to all come out white. It was honestly the most crazy, far-fetched few months of our lives.

'Someone said, "Oh, he's at Currys buying Cheryl a Hoover"'

The beautiful thing about early TV talent shows was the genuine rush of seeing a very normal person or group of people stepping, Stars in Their Eyes-*style, through the smoke and coming out the other side as bonafide pop stars. The tricky thing for major labels, however, is that it's hard to then reverse-engineer the years of development most pop acts go through before they're presented to the public. If Nicola Roberts has been voted into a band for her singing but also her feisty attitude, for example, the public don't want her to then reappear months later as someone varnished to a dazzling sheen. For Girls Aloud, a rabble whose debut single and punk-esque marketing had underpinned their zero-fucks-given attitude, it was vital they remained true to themselves. Even after they were dumped in an old asylum in the middle of nowhere (Friern Barnet) with no time to buy a vacuum cleaner.*

Laura Snapes: Even though a band like Steps were just as hothoused as Girls Aloud, with Steps, that took place in private. All the edges of their personality were sanded off, so you had this happy-clappy product that was obviously aimed at kids. The journey – 'The Journey' – of Girls Aloud on a show meant you got to know them as people before they became pop stars. You saw where they all came from in a very literal sense and I think that encourages a stronger sense of bonding.

Alexis Petridis: They seemed like souped-up versions of ordinary young women. That was the thing that seemed exciting about them as people. I once interviewed them over lunch at the OXO Tower and I always remember Nicola Roberts looking at the menu and going, 'No, no, no.' She wouldn't eat anything. Then she proceeded to go into her handbag and pull a bag of Nik Naks out and eat them at the table. It was brilliant.

Paul Flynn: I could dress their story up. I could take those kids who I did go to school with and who did come from nothing and who didn't have nice upbringings and who weren't privileged and who didn't go to university and I could treat them with the same amount of dignity as the people who don't fucking deserve it but who went to the right schools. The respect they get automatically, I could give to those pop stars. They're fulfilling something and that something is an escape.

Nicola: The benefit of us not knowing the situation we were in was that we would go into the label and just talk to them in a way that was a lot less eloquent than we are now. We'd just be like, 'Yeah, we're not fucking doing it.' And that's how we'd speak to them.

Colin Barlow: It was hilarious. I don't think they ever knew what any of us did. They knew there were certain people in their lives that they saw regularly but they didn't know what that person did. Peter [Loraine] was very integral in their lives and I drove all the music, but they'd see me once in a while and I'd be like, 'You did the Disney Awards and you didn't perform very well,' and they didn't know why they were being called in and told off. They had this wonderful naïvety to it all. They weren't street-savvy kids in regards the music industry – they were five girls who had just won a TV show.

Nicola: It was [just] us, we had no manager, and the schedule would just constantly change.

Kimberley: I think it's been quite heavily documented, and I've said plenty on this subject, but Louis was very much a manager on paper. That was as far as it went. Me and him did have a few clashes along the way.

Nicola: He did nothing. He wouldn't pick the phone up. He literally did nothing and we just paid him.

Louis Walsh: I wasn't [a hands-on manager]. I was working with Westlife and doing loads of other things. I wasn't able to help [Girls Aloud] with their hair and their make-up and their styling – I wasn't any good at that. They were great at that. And Polydor were great. And Peter Loraine was very much involved. So they did most of it.

Colin Barlow: Louis was the most hands-off manager you had ever met.

Nadine: There were all these people running around doing jobs – tour managers, A&Rs, marketing people, TV pluggers, all of these words put together that I'd never heard before – so it was hard to figure out what people were supposed to be doing. It was like, 'Who is in charge? Are we just aimlessly running around the UK? Who is deciding what's happening?'

Louis Walsh: I didn't have a great relationship with them because I did say [Nadine] was the best singer. So obviously the other four hated me anyway. I shouldn't have said it but she was the best singer by a mile and she sang the lead on every single track.

Kimberley: I was a little bit older so I could stick up for the rest of the girls and try to take control. Just so it didn't get out of hand.

Nadine: Kimberley did a lot. I had to do it at the beginning because for some random reason they had decided that me and Hazel [Kaneswaran] should be the ones flown over to London to pick the lawyers and the accountants. I was seventeen. To this day, I don't know why I was the one chosen. I was also having to deal with Brian Higgins, too. I remember we were on stage at *Top of the Pops* and my phone was going crazy and I was like, 'I cannot do it any more, someone is going to have to take over.' So I said, 'Kimberley, you went to university, did you not? You seem smart enough, could you not take some of these calls?' So she did. Hilary [Shaw, manager] arrived a few years in, before our first tour [in 2005].

Kimberley: I wouldn't say I was the manager but I think the general day-to-day logistics and looking after our wellbeing and finances and stuff, I took that on in a mother-hen role maybe.

Colin Barlow: Kimberley was the boss. She used to have a clipboard.

Nicola: I'd be like, 'Kim, I really want to go out in Liverpool at the weekend, can you tell the label I've got a wedding please?' And she'd be like, 'Nic, you've had four weddings this month, I'm not sure we can get away with another one.' So I'd say: 'Can you tell them it's a christening? That I've got my friend's kid's communion? Tell them someone's turning seventy.' The guys at the label must have just laughed their heads off. Throughout the week, we'd do all our TV shows and promo, whatever they wanted us to do, but we were teenage girls so I did want to be back home chilling in my friend's car [at the weekend]. And I did really want to get drunk because I wasn't supposed to. But then you'd come back on the Monday and have a lawyers meeting, then an accountants meeting, then a stylist meeting. The two worlds just couldn't have been any further apart.

Colin Barlow: There was a point where Kimberley was head girl and she was somebody I'd call up and she'd say, 'Right, we've got a problem, this has happened, these two aren't talking, what do I do?' Kimberley would always pull it together. Now when I look at bands I'm like, 'Who is the Kimberley?' If you don't have a Kimberley, you don't have a group. I don't think Sugababes had a Kimberley and that's why they changed personnel so much.

Peter Loraine: I was overseeing everything for them at that time. Their diary was kept out of our office. But in addition, where are they going to live? None of them lived in London. How are they going to pay for their food when they haven't made any money yet? All those things needed sorting. One particular day, my boss appeared in my doorway and it was like, 'Where's Peter?', and someone said, 'Oh, he's at Currys buying Cheryl a Hoover.' Because she was having a meltdown like, 'There's no time to do anything, I can't even clean my apartment, I don't even have a Hoover.' So I went and got her a Hoover.

Nicola: We all lived in the same building. It was called Princess Park Manor. It used to be an old mental asylum. It was in Friern Barnet and as soon as you came out of the gates of this complex there was just nothing there. I don't know why they wanted us there.

Kimberley: I was with Nadine. Nicola and Cheryl were together and then Sarah was, by choice, on her own. I didn't blame her, to be honest. I think she was happy to have the one bit of time away from us.

Nadine: I was seventeen! My parents had done everything before that. They decided how late I could stay out. I'd never had a job. I had nothing that made me an adult, at all.

Kimberley: It was quite the place at the time. The Sugababes were there. In fact, Keisha and I were next-door neighbours.

Keisha: We literally shared a wall in our apartment block. She probably heard things she shouldn't have – I was in a weird relationship back then.

Kimberley: It was nice to know you had someone living next door that you could call on if you needed to. We'd all go out for a night out and the afterparty would just be back there because everyone was going back there anyway. I feel grateful we were part of that last surge of pop bands because that was the most fun part of being in a band. In this generation after us, I don't think it was quite the same. There weren't as many pop bands and it was all quite separate because of the nature of not having the likes of *CD:UK* and *Top of the Pops*. It was a different vibe completely.

Nicola: We didn't know how to work our heating. We didn't know you were supposed to answer letters.

Peter Loraine: This actually happened with Nicola. 'Peter, our electricity's gone off.' I was like, 'Right, okay, we'll speak to them, but I'm assuming you've paid the bill?' 'What?' 'You must have had a bill?' 'I don't think so, we never get any bills.' 'What do you mean you don't get any bills?' 'We don't get any post.' 'Have you checked downstairs in your mailbox?' 'No, what's that?' So downstairs in their apartment was about a year's worth of correspondence.

Kimberley: The record company took over so much of our lives, so in her defence maybe she assumed they would take care of every part of it.

Nadine: They teach you algebra [at school], but no one teaches you how to live as an adult or pay bills.

'We made a conscious decision that we could listen to that other music in our own time'

While the commercial success of 'Sound of the Underground' was to some degree a given, its critical acclaim was unusual. No debut single from a TV talent-show winner before (or after) had managed to cross over to the likes of NME and the broadsheet supplements. As work started on what would become the band's debut album, named after that call-to-arms smash, the girls were given a brief taste of working with songwriters and producers who weren't part of the Xenomania stable. In fact, the (slightly patchy, let's be honest) 2003 album wound up featuring input from the likes of Steve Anderson, ex-Westlife member Brian McFadden and 'Pure and Simple' co-writer Alison Clarkson, AKA Betty Boo. Towards the end of recording, with that elusive second single still missing, Polydor returned to Brian and Miranda – who had just returned from working with Britney Spears in LA – who presented the band with 'No Good Advice'. Like 'Sound of the Underground', its core sound – Blondie covering 'My Sharona' – was out of step with pop in 2003. To the point where a brief rebellion was mounted by a band keen to replicate the music they were listening to for pleasure.

Paul Flynn: I really loved the second single, 'No Good Advice'. All the references were so classic; it didn't sound like the references that were around at that time. American music was so future-facing and exciting, but all the British stuff just sounded like watered-down versions of that.

Richard X: It was 'No Good Advice' that I really loved. I felt like they were kindred spirits. They seemed like the sort of band that could fit in my world.

Kimberley: The second single was the main focus while we were working on the album. We were very mindful that it had to be something equally as strong.

Brian Higgins: There was a bit of vengeance in that song. It was the sound of defiance and that was so integral to how we approached that whole decade. We felt we knew better than anyone else about what was a pop record and how great pop could be. 'No Good Advice' in many ways was proof that Xenomania as a creative unit was starting to fire on all cylinders.

Peter Robinson: Anyone who goes on that sort of show isn't quite sure of what to expect when they go into a recording studio for the first time. Then if you add the fact that you're going down to an old vicarage in some ridiculous village in the middle of nowhere and having these really bizarre sounds thrown at you and lyrics, it must have been hard to work out what the song actually was. It's hundreds of interpretations later that there's this magic route through the whole thing. It's extraordinary. I can't imagine it's very enjoyable for an artist unless you submit yourself to the process.

Nicola: Did Brian mention the time we tried to ditch Xenomania? We went back to Brian about February-ish time and he was playing us all these different tracks, little verse and chorus sections. I think there were elements of 'No Good Advice'. But it was all very different to what we were into. We were all listening to Christina Aguilera, Blu Cantrell, more generic female pop-led stuff. With a little bit more of a narrative lyrically. We sat in his backroom as a group and decided we were going to tell him that we didn't like the music. We were like, 'We'll tell him we don't think it's very us and we just don't want to do it.' He comes in and says, 'Girls, is there a problem?' I think it was me that said it. Maybe it was me and Cheryl. We were always the ones – we'd think it as a group but the others would never say it, so we did. And we'd always get into trouble for that.

Jon Shave: They tried to stage a bit of mutiny. He left them in no uncertain terms that it wasn't quite their place to decide that at that point. He insisted they submitted to the process and, to be fair to them, from that moment they absolutely did.

Nadine: I remember several meetings where they tried to get rid of Brian. Several! I liked what Brian was doing. I did think some of the stuff was a bit too whacky. But I always felt like I could say that. He would ask for our perspective on what was happening in our lives, so lyrically it could be more aligned to how we were living rather than from a man in his thirties or Miranda.

Kimberley: He'd play us a song and it was almost like, 'No, you can't have an opinion on this.' Basically, you've got to sing it like robots and we were never going to be okay with that. So it didn't go down very well from his point of view. He wasn't entertaining it, but we said it anyway.

Nicola: Brian literally gave us this twenty-minute rant about how if we don't like it we can go, but we don't have any options and we don't know what we're talking about and we should be so grateful that we're there. He left the room saying, 'So you just think about all those things I've just said.' Early on we made a conscious decision that we could listen to other music in our own time.

Colin Barlow: The fights I had with the girls at the time were just, 'Trust me, you've got to go with these records because you're pushing boundaries – if we play safe and come out with a really lightweight pop record no one will play it.' They didn't get that. People love the edginess of Girls Aloud and records like 'Love Machine' – which they hated at the time – and 'Biology' were so important because they became a guilty pleasure for an *NME* audience that wanted to be cool. Then the penny dropped and Nicola and the others suddenly started to realise that these records are really beneficial to us.

Brian Higgins: [Xenomania] were indie. We infiltrated pop. I was old enough to understand what Roxy Music meant, fusing guitars and electronics. Depeche Mode, New Order, all of these bands. But pop music at that time of Girls Aloud was dreadful because it was being made by cynical guys who were trying to get themselves into the minds of teenagers and write what they think they like. I didn't want anything to do with that. Half the people who worked at Xenomania would never have generally found themselves working on a girl group from a TV show. Never. Not because they were snobby; they just wouldn't have moved in those circles.

Miranda Cooper: I remember people really urging us after they won to get out, that we'd got the best out of it. Then Colin played the album and we just felt like it wasn't our vision for them.

Brian Higgins: Colin sent me the [*Sound of the Underground*] album and I was in LA because we were working with Britney Spears.

Miranda Cooper: We got a phone call from Britney's team saying, 'We want "Sound of the Underground",' and we were like, 'Well, it's already been a hit here, does that matter?' They said they wanted something like it. So we went out to LA and worked with her for a week. We got her to do the same thing as with Girls Aloud – she sang her twenty-eight different choruses or what-ever, and there's a CD I've got of all of her vocals. She recorded 'Graffiti My Soul', which sounded awesome. Brian was like [to Britney's label], 'You can only have it if it's going to be her first single,' and I think they said, 'Fuck off.' So it ended up being a Girls Aloud album track [on 2004's *What Will the Neighbours Say?*].

Brian Higgins: I do look back on that and think I was as bloody-minded about that as I was about everything else, but that's why it sounded the way it did. You can't dilute any of it. You can't suddenly pull off a mask; it has to be real.

Colin Barlow: What became really apparent was that any time we put the girls with anyone else, it just didn't sound like anyone. It just sounded like a bunch of girls singing a song.

Brian Higgins: I was annoyed about [the album]. It was bad. I said, 'The rest of this album isn't worthy of our song,' and I really meant it. So Colin said, 'What can you do?', and so we did six more tracks for about £4,000. Really cheap, just to kill everyone and make the album work. So we got them back in and recorded in a very rough-and-ready way.

Miranda Cooper: I think the thing that turned that album around was 'Jump'. It wasn't a done deal for them at all. The fact that we got the broadsheets and music press was brilliant, and that's what drove a lot of their success until the mainstream came on board.

Peter Loraine: After 'No Good Advice' was number two and 'Life Got Cold' got to number three, it felt like things were going in the wrong direction. Then Richard Curtis called saying they wanted someone to record 'Jump' for *Love Actually*. My boss came to me and said, 'I've told him the girls will do it.' I thought it was the wrong move, that it didn't sit well with what they stood for, and he was like, 'You need to understand that something drastic has to change here financially because we're in the hole hugely.' So begrudgingly off we went to do a cover of 'Jump' and it saved the day, to be honest.

Brian Higgins: I couldn't stand 'Jump'. I hated it. I was trying to find a way to make it more aggressive, because the original [by the Pointer Sisters] annoyed me. I wanted to do something that affected the way you heard that record, because it was too sweet. It gave Polydor a stronger position and the album went platinum. It sort of saved them. I think Lucian Grainge knew that this wave of indie-dom was coming and that pop music was going to die. The official word was, 'Everyone, get out of pop, it's fucked.'

Alexis Petridis: I think Xenomania were able to [own Girls Aloud's sound] because Louis Walsh wasn't interested. Nobody really cared. So somebody had to take the reins that maybe wouldn't have been allowed to do that if the usual dark forces were in motion. Also, Brian had a reason to keep them and for them not to be given the same rubbish as everyone else.

Brian Higgins: Colin phoned me and said, 'You need to make the whole of the second album,' and I remember being a bit unsure. But he was like, 'Nope, you have to do it, that's it.'

Colin Barlow: By the second album [2004's *What Will The Neighbours Say?*], no one could get near Girls Aloud. My view was he'd bought the rights to do everything. He was super tough on the girls. No one makes records like they did.

Brian Higgins: I was just happy to please Colin. He understood that these two entities – Girls Aloud and Xenomania – could not be separated. Some of the covers we did were probably pressure he was being put under to make sure there was some situation where they might get some airplay. Radio 1 wouldn't touch them because of the Guildford nightclub incident [in January 2003, Cheryl was found guilty of assault occasioning actual bodily harm but cleared of the racially aggravated assault of nightclub toilet attendant Sophie Amogbokpa]. The best they ever got at Radio 1 was the B-list until [2006's] 'Something Kinda Ooooh'. But that was good from our perspective because once we realised radio were never going to support them we were able to make more and more strange records and have fun with that.

'Not only did you sing five choruses for one song, you sang all of that in five keys'

Girls Aloud's brief taste of the more straightforward recording studio practices for a pop band soon started to feel like a distant memory. At Xenomania,

444

demos didn't exist. Backing tracks numbered the hundreds, as did Miranda Cooper's bank of lyrical ideas. Songs would often resemble the aural equivalent of magic eye posters, with a chorus from one song morphed into the verse of another or vice versa. It was a process that felt more natural, however, as their run of twenty consecutive UK top-ten singles started to gather momentum.

Brian Higgins: Because the music was constantly being made, there'd be eighty or ninety musical ideas that would have been created from the albums being delivered to them coming round for the next one eight months later. We'd be making music that whole time for Girls Aloud and the Sugababes – we wanted to run the two groups together but keep the sound separate. We'd write about fifteen or sixteen songs and that would be it. And in those songs had to be the singles, had to be everything.

Nicola: We wouldn't have dared ask to hear what they were doing with the Sugababes. Brian controlled his surroundings acutely and I think it was important for him in terms of how he was able to differentiate the two. The Sugababes were very edgy; they were the All Saints to our Spice Girls. We had a blonde, we had a brunette, we had a really leggy one. We were very tabloid-heavy. Also, the Sugababes got to work with other producers as well, whereas for us it was only Brian because our sound was so specific.

Brian Higgins: No one [hears the finished song at the time]. I just can't do that. Nothing sounded like the final version at the start. That's the whole point. The records would be made well after the girls had left. We'd deem an idea a hit and then we'd expand it into a bigger piece of music.

Nicola: I remember being in LA shooting the 'Call the Shots' video and we had *Tangled Up* delivered to us. We were in a room in the Standard, I think, and Hilary played it while we were all sat around the bed. We were just like, 'Yeah . . .', and we started comparing it to *Chemistry*. Like it's not got what that album had. Little did we know that *Tangled Up* was actually our best one.

Nadine: On that album, Brian and Miranda came out to LA [where I was living] and we worked in a studio in Sunset Marquis. We'd just finished the [Chemistry] tour and I think the rest of the girls were off on holiday and I would get a few days and then it would be straight in the studio trying to get the songs together. The songs would then be chosen by Brian and the girls would come in at a later date and sing.

Nicola: Some people reading this will be like, 'What, you just used to have your record handed to you?', but the way in which the songs were formulated, it had to be that way. We didn't know how a song was going to be curated.

Brian Higgins: The band members weren't picked because of the suitability of their voices together; they were picked by the public based on their personalities. The truth of the matter is to get them to sit incredibly comfortably on one record was difficult. But they also had a rock singer in Nadine, which meant she could sing all sorts of stuff very loudly. Which was thrilling from my perspective because the louder it is, the faster it is, the better it is.

Nicola: We were in the studio a long time doing all of these different sections and we had to sing the songs in five different keys. So not only did you sing four verses and five choruses for one song, you sang all of that in five keys. That was just one song idea. People would say, 'Oh, I bet they don't all stand around the same microphone,' and we'd be like, 'Do you want to try doing a song in eighteen parts that's in five different keys around one microphone?' Someone would have been killed.

Miranda Cooper: I remember Shaznay Lewis on a review show on Radio 1 saying ['The Show'] sounds like four songs gelled together and I remember thinking, 'Yes, basically.'

Nicola: One day I took my sister to the studio and when we left she was like, 'Is that what you have to do every time?', and I'd be like, 'Yeah.'

Miranda Cooper: We had five or six different studios set up and, when I say 'studio', we had these screens made and then we'd put a duvet over the top. And sometimes it was in the loo because it would be a better sound in there. We'd have a list in each studio of what needed to be done and the girls would go around each one. Then we'd get everything loaded into Brian's computer and we'd give the individual bits stars out of five and put what key worked. It sounds like it was a special formula but actually it was hugely creative.

Brian Higgins: In the songwriter industry, everyone was like, 'Let us at Girls Aloud, let us in,' and so I thought that if we lose one single slot we'll lose it all. We were motivated every year to make them better and to make us better. It was very creatively greedy. It was a sickness really.

Peter Robinson: You could tell that a lot of the people around the band were really excited by the band. Thinking back, maybe that was one of the big differences compared to a lot of pop music that had come before that. Like, say, with Atomic Kitten – who around that band was excited by it? Were the label excited? They might be excited by the success, but that's not the same. Or management? Or the songwriters and producers? They did some efficient music, but were they really excited by it? The members of the band – did they find it exciting? Girls Aloud showed it could be something people should be excited about.

'It would always be "I really like Xenomania" or "I'm not saying I like Girls Aloud"'

In 2006, Sheffield indie saviours the Arctic Monkeys appeared on BBC Radio 1's Live Lounge where they covered Girls Aloud's 2004 opus 'Love Machine'. At that time – let's call it peak joyless 'guilty pleasure' syndrome – it was par for the course for indie stalwarts to strip back a pop bop to highlight the song's apparently hereto untapped brilliance using their weapon of choice: the acoustic guitar. With the Arctic Monkeys cover, it served to double down on what a bonkers song 'Love Machine' was and also how Girls Aloud's best moments often used guitars in far more interesting ways than most indie bands. (In 2008, they'd poke fun at some of their NME Awards drinking buddies on caustic B-side 'Hoxton Heroes'.) It was also just one of many moments in which Girls Aloud transcended their pop bubble, often appearing in the pages of the NME or reviewed in Q or given space in broadsheet supplements such as the Observer Music Monthly. That Girls Aloud had done it via a TV talent-show route just made the whole thing more surprising.

WHAT WILL THE NEIGHBOURS SAY?

Brian Higgins: Girls Aloud started as the real underdogs and then the Guildford incident happened and they were literally hated. That's why when the *NME* adopted them it was like, 'Yes.' Everyone else thought they were this racist pop group, which was absurd.

Nicola: We were aware that we had cool press. We knew that critically it was working, which Brian must have loved.

Brian Higgins: It felt like we'd found a community. I felt great about that. They understood it, intellectually. Around *Tangled Up* we were still in our creative zenith. Franz Ferdinand were flirting around us, Arctic Monkeys were, Coldplay covered 'Call the Shots'. The whole world seemed to understand what we were doing.

Miranda Cooper: We agreed to do the Franz Ferdinand album [in 2007] but the reality was they were too much of their own entity. They were taking hours EQ-ing one drum sound and Brian was just like, 'Write with us, let's collaborate.'

Brian Higgins: I invariably found getting people to realise the material just isn't very good too painful. I would eventually feel like they were dragging me to the place where the worst ideas existed. I was used to going where I wanted to go, to where the best ideas were, and no one would stop me. I would invariably resign from these projects and say, 'I can't do that.' That was certainly the case with Franz Ferdinand. We were blurring the boundaries between pop and indie so well that it was inevitable those groups would come in to try to work it out. I think we were really our own band and we needed to work with artists that didn't write their own songs. The most undiluted, best version of Xenomania was that. When people came in to break off the bit they wanted, the inspiration they no longer had, I would find that difficult because I would start seeing through them creatively.

Alexis Petridis: The Girls Aloud songs felt futuristic at a time when 'alternative music', or what was being presented as alternative music, was feeling ever more like a re-hash of stuff that had come before. If you look at the history of indie music, it's always had an element of the past to it, but you'd sprinkle your own thing on top of it. And that sprinkling of your own thing had just ceased to happen. [Girls Aloud's music] just seemed more futuristic and exciting than, say, 'She Moves in Her Own Way' by the Kooks. It didn't seem peculiar to me or out of the ordinary to say these records were good. I didn't feel like I was fighting for pop music.

Peter Robinson: That's kind of why I started Popjustice. This idea that you don't have to love the band in order to be able to love the music. Even though I did love a lot of pop bands, at the heart of it I always loved the music and I think that's what happened throughout the 2000s with Girls Aloud and Sugababes – people began to have a grudging respect. But then it would always be 'I really like Xenomania' or 'I'm not saying I like Girls Aloud.'

Laura Snapes: In the '90s, Britpop reached a critical mass where rock stars were being invited to No. 10 and what was underground went totally overground. So in the '00s you see publications like *NME* trying to re-entrench the idea of an underground and a cool alternative to the mainstream that's not just what has come before. But by the end of that decade stuff like Kaiser Chiefs and Arctic Monkeys were the mainstream again, so the alternative look and the whole hipster thing went mainstream, too. I wonder if pop reflexively gains a new sort of appeal because it's like we don't need this dumb separation of mainstream and alternative any more, it just started to seem really false.

Alexis Petridis: People always revere early '80s new pop, but it only works if it's popular with people who aren't going, 'The semiotics of this are very interesting.' It's got to be popular with kids. That's the point. Whatever you see yourself as doing, unless you're actually in the charts and unless the people buying your records are not *NME* readers, they're tweens, then it doesn't work, no matter how clever you're being. I interviewed Girls Aloud for *GQ* magazine and they were gratified by it. But it was not part of the game plan. Like, finally the man we were attempting to reach with our music is here!

Colin Barlow: When we did the Girls Aloud *Greatest Hits* album [in 2006], we did market research and they were such a guilty pleasure that we didn't put their pictures on the sleeve. We created more generic imagery so that anyone could buy a Girls Aloud best of and it sold a million copies. If you were a guy, it was alright to have a Girls Aloud album.

Peter Robinson: There was something quite chaotic about the band. Peter Loraine and Sundraj [Sreenivasan, the band's PR] did a really good job of harnessing that and channelling it in the right direction. It was quite messy and unsanitised. The way Sundraj was choosing the journalists he was taking the band to and the places he was positioning them in. It was about keeping the *Smash Hits* side of things ticking over but also going, 'Okay, this music doesn't sound like a lot of pop, so therefore this band doesn't have to do everything other pop bands always have to do.'

Peter Loraine: It was such a collaborative thing. There was a big debate over what was going to be the third single from *Tangled Up*, then it's decided it's going to be 'Can't Speak French', so we get them to sing it in French [for B-side 'Je Ne Parle Pas Français']. But no one can speak French, so we have to find someone who can teach them.

Peter Robinson: I guess there's something exciting about a big stupid pop band doing something exciting and edgy. Compared with a band like the Sugababes, who as soon as they came out went straight to *NME* and straight to *The Face*. They were cool from the start, so the idea of a big pop band being cool is more exciting than a cool band being cool.

Paul Flynn: The thing is, Girls Aloud weren't amazing. They were sort of ephemerally amazing. People would say, 'Oh, Girls Aloud are the new Spice Girls,' but they're nothing like the Spice Girls. The Spice Girls were driven, ambitious, they had this demonic energy to them. Girls Aloud reminded me of Bananarama. That sort of 'can't be arsed' attitude.

'It was very much stiff upper lip and we just got on with it'

The rise of Girls Aloud chimed not only with the rise of celebrity magazines, but also with the explosion in reality TV. Suddenly a new stratum of celebrity had been created, one that seemed more accessible and attainable.

That in turn made for a blurring of the lines between what is up for grabs and what isn't, with the blunt, critical language used towards celebrities in print often mirroring the chats viewers would have at home. Gobby, opinionated and frank, Girls Aloud were a tabloid dream, with Sarah, Cheryl and Nicola singled out for specific attention as the years went on. For Nicola, this focus soon morphed into personality takedowns following bullying by the likes of Busted's Matt Willis and DJ Chris Moyles (the then Radio 1 breakfast host called Nicola '[the] ropey-looking ginger one', 'horsey chops' and a 'sour-faced old cow' on air).

Nicola: The media were more interested in girls having cat-fights than pillow fights. We definitely weren't wallflowers and if somebody said something nasty we'd say something. Plus we were always being asked about it all in interviews. We didn't have the decorum to go, 'We're not getting involved in that.' Being a little rough and ready, if someone says, 'Oh, Lily Allen's slagged Cheryl off,' your natural reaction is to get your back up as a tough girl.

Kimberley: [The label] never encouraged us, but anything that was in there was natural. I don't think the label minded it because it was all promo at the end of the day. Nothing was fake.

Nicola: Our tour manager used to put newspapers in the car, God only knows why because it was so unhealthy. We'd have *The Sun*, the *Star*, the *Mirror*, the *Sport* – Christ – and then *People, News of the World*. We'd be in every single one. It would be one of us on the cover of the *Sport* coming out of a night-club or someone saying something nasty about me or Cheryl spotted here. It just felt like that was life. It was a time when we didn't really talk about our mental health, we didn't talk about bullying, it was very much stiff upper lip. So no one ever came to me and said, 'I can see you're struggling.' There was none of that. We didn't talk about it. It wasn't a rallying-around situation, it was just, 'That's happening.'

Kimberley: It was difficult to watch [Nicola struggling with negative coverage] but you were never quite sure how much she'd seen and she was so young we just wanted to protect her [from it] as much as possible. Now in retrospect I feel like she was holding it all inside and suffering in silence. I probably should have dealt with it differently. You just wouldn't get away with it now – she was a seventeen-year-old girl.

Nicola: We didn't necessarily have the emotional intelligence to be able to have a perspective on it, whereas if that was happening now I'd be strong enough to say, 'This is a load of shit, why are you doing this?' Back then we just had to take it.

Nadine: I didn't take much nonsense from anybody. People would say, 'Nadine's difficult' or 'Nadine's a diva,' but I'm not. I'm just not going to let somebody talk to me like shit. If that makes me a diva then so be it. I thought everyone in the band should have that 'fuck it' attitude. If someone's being abusive then the floor is open for you to snap back. I remember someone [Matt Willis from Busted] called Nicola a rude ginger bitch and so I told her to paint it on her skirt [for a performance at G-A-Y in 2003]. I was like, 'Fuck them, write it, don't let them intimidate you.' Who are these people? FUCK OFF.

WHAT WILL THE NEIGHBOURS SAY?

Lucie Cave: Girls Aloud represented a cross-section in the same way you had with the Spice Girls. With Cheryl, the stories just didn't stop coming and she was a showbiz journalist's dream really in terms of who she was and where she'd come from. She was stunningly beautiful and she obviously still had that grit about her. Then there was that story in the papers about her and the toilet attendant, which is something she took ages to shake off. Inevitably that makes her even more interesting as a celebrity.

Alexis Petridis: It was at a point where everything was becoming increasingly streamlined and media training had become a bigger thing. I can see why – people kept saying really stupid things. Like Lee Ryan. But as a journalist it's really boring and actually as an audience it's really boring as well. I'm not in any way condoning what Cheryl did, but fights happen in nightclub toilets all the time to ordinary people. People get drunk and do stupid things all the time. Girls Aloud felt a bit uncontrolled. There was always this mad stuff around them.

Dean Piper: Girls were always on the front of the papers. Guys would only get on the front page if they were really doing something bad, like drugs or affairs or an arrest, but girls could get on there if they wore an outfit or if they were thin or if they'd pulled a Posh Spice and got a footballer boyfriend. It was an opportunity to have five bits of fresh meat in the celebrity circuit. Girls Aloud were the first proper TV talent-show pawns for the papers to play with when they came out of a show like that. It felt like a big deal.

Nicola: We felt misogyny from the media in what women are supposed to do and what they're not supposed to do compared to a male artist. But in our own world we felt really powerful in being five women. It's nice that we weren't media-trained because we were able to have a voice and were never silenced.

Kimberley: We did *Blue Peter* and they made us dress as nurses from different eras. We didn't kick off about it at the time – it's *Blue Peter*, it's an institution – but we were in a band trying to be cool. Some things you just knew you had to do. Any of the tabloids you were just like, 'Oh, God, do we really have to?' In one sense they're asking us to do a piece of promo, but you know that the next week they're going to be writing some rubbish about you so you'd feel resentful you had to play the game.

'No, help the Pet Shop Boys out on somebody else's time'

By 2008, Girls Aloud were in a curious position of being a cult pop band with four top-twenty albums under their studded H&M belts. While the top-ten hits had kept coming, it still felt like their music was perhaps a bit too left-of-centre to have properly infiltrated the 'two albums a year from Tesco' portion of the mainstream. That all changed after Cheryl replaced Sharon Osbourne as a judge on the fifth series of The X Factor *in the summer of 2008. Suddenly, the band was being mentioned in front of millions of people each week. Keen to harness this new audience, Xenomania knew the band needed a big first single to launch fifth album* Out of Control. *In the end, they came up with two: 'The Promise' and 'The Loving Kind'. For the girls, however, there was only ever one choice – and they were keen to make their voices heard.*

Nicola: We definitely felt a gear change. The TV shows we were doing were bigger, our outfits were way more expensive, we were selling out more shows. We didn't have social media [to gauge], so it was more, 'How many times do we see ourselves on TV? How many times are we on the radio? How many times are we in the newspapers?' I think Cheryl being on *The X Factor* introduced us to a bigger audience – the show was getting 10 million viewers every weekend. It opened the doors for us as a group.

Brian Higgins: We knew they were ready to be a supergroup, so therefore they needed a supergroup sound. A step up from everything we'd done before. And more commercial really. The minute the piece of music that went on to become 'The Promise' was identified it was ring-fenced as the first single. So me and Miranda sat down and planned strategically how we were going to write the song, where we were going to write it, what time of day we were going to write it. Everything. To have an appointment with a number-one record.

Miranda Cooper: We were so sure of ourselves at that point. We were moving so much into the mainstream – actually, about to be chucked out the other side. One day Brian said, 'Let's write our number-one hit for Girls Aloud.' I said I didn't feel like it – could we do it tomorrow? And we did it. It was weird with that song because it wasn't spiky, it was mainstream, and it wasn't shocking lyrically. We were a bit nervous about it: is this what people want?

Brian Higgins: We couldn't mess it up. We went in at 5 p.m. on a Wednesday, a beautiful sunny day, and we wrote 'The Promise' in about seven minutes. We sat at opposite ends of the room and sang our ideas and threw them all in together. 'The Promise' has an intro, then the chorus, then there's verse one and pre-chorus one. Then there's another chorus. Then there's verse two, which is different from verse one, pre-chorus two, which is different to pre-chorus one, and another chorus and a middle section. So seven different melodic parts. That's their more commercial sound.

Nicola: Because I used to write a little bit I knew how to work the computer in the writing room. I've never told Brian this, but I'd go into the computer and open the folder that said 'Girls Aloud – options' and I'd click through everything. I remember hearing all these parts for 'The Promise' and saying to the other girls, 'There's a song that I like, it feels retro, almost like Motown, it's so cool.'

Miranda Cooper: I remember 'The Loving Kind' was difficult because that was going to be the first single.

Nicola: They were like, '"The Loving Kind" is the single we're going with,' and we all categorically said, 'We will not promote this song, we won't do any press, we basically will not work for you if this is the song you want to put out first.'

Nadine: I said, 'Well, I'm going to fly back to LA, phone me whenever "The Promise" is the single and I'll come back.' It worked. Literally within an hour it was 'The Promise' and we all continued with our days.

Kimberley: We'd got to the point in our careers where we were like, 'We're the ones that have to go and front it and if we don't believe in it then that's crazy.' So we dug our heels in.

Nicola: We were calling each other saying, 'If Colin rings you or Brian rings you, don't you dare buckle, stand strong with the group!' Colin was like, 'This is career suicide if you go with this song as your first single.' But we felt it was right, and it was. It was a huge machine around us but it also felt really close-knit. Because of the foundations that we built early on, we were still able to communicate personally with the label. We never felt like we couldn't have an opinion, because we'd started off with that dynamic between us and them.

Nadine: It was a strategic play as to why they wanted 'The Loving Kind'. They were working with an act that had written it. Was it Duran Duran? No, it was somebody anyway. Pet Shop Boys? And I was like, 'No, help the Pet Shop Boys out on somebody else's time.'

Miranda Cooper: I think probably Colin loved the idea 'The Loving Kind' was [co-written by] the Pet Shop Boys. It was a good story. 'The Promise' was my favourite and it was the right choice.

Colin Barlow: The fact they were so passionate about it was the reason to do it. It was good to see because sometimes I'd have moments with them where I'd be saying, 'You've got to be more passionate about your music, you've got to have ownership.' I think 'The Promise' is a magical moment for that group because it felt like it was their song. Maybe 'The Loving Kind' would have been that classic thing of going safe, while 'The Promise' wasn't safe. The girls had realised that to go with something risky was a bigger look for them. 'The Promise' was them growing up.

Peter Loraine: To win the BRIT [for Best Single for 'The Promise' in 2009] was brilliant for them, because they deserved it. I absolutely can't bear music snobbery. I would find it hard when people who liked indie bands would diminish the achievements of pop acts.

Miranda Cooper: On *Out of Control*, Nadine was living in America and wasn't that reliable about turning up to the studio when she was supposed to, so Sarah really stepped forward. Her moments on 'The Promise' were obviously amazing. She was very much taking over that lead role.

'We understood it was beautiful'

Five months after signing a new record deal, in July 2009, Girls Aloud announced a hiatus, a move eventually delayed slightly so they could support Coldplay at Wembley Stadium. Solo albums followed for Cheryl, Nicola, Nadine and Kimberley, while Sarah dabbled in acting. In 2012, to celebrate their ten-year anniversary, the band reformed, releasing stomping single 'Something New' and another greatest hits album, Ten. On the final date of the accompanying hits tour, the band (minus Nadine) posted a TwitLonger announcing they were to split.

Kimberley: I don't know [what Girls Aloud's legacy is]. I don't really think you can objectively look at yourself in that way. I'd love to know how other people see us and what we are and what we stand for.

Nicola: I think our legacy is how lawless our songs were. How we paved our own way in our own lane. We really did take risks and against the odds we as five very normal girls managed to achieve incredible things with an incredible team around us. We weren't moulded within a Sylvia Young-type situation so we all had different personalities. You can kind of see me awkwardly dancing around to the song, then you've got someone like Cheryl who's a born performer, and then Sarah's quirky personality . . . I just think the different ingredients of the five of us meant you didn't have this static image of the group.

Nadine: A lot of people took a lot of strength from those songs and from our journey. And still do. Also, the songs haven't aged. They still sound as fresh today.

Brian Higgins: We understood it was beautiful. Everything about it was beautiful. There's the tension in the sound, which is us not wanting to cock it up, but it was a beautiful sum of its parts.

Alexis Petridis: It hinged on them as much as it did the producers. If it hadn't, Xenomania would have gone on to launch loads of other amazing artists, and they didn't. They tried to launch people like Mini Viva [in 2009] and it didn't work. There was no one that came out of a TV talent show that was remotely like them. Girls Aloud seemed like a blip, an aberration. Something that happened almost by mistake.

Miranda Cooper: People would ask, 'Do you think the best songs would have worked with anyone else?', and they wouldn't. It's a special alchemy. With Girls Aloud, we got close to finding this magic.

Tragically, in September 2021, the band's heart-on-the-sleeve force, Sarah Harding, died aged just thirty-nine from breast cancer. In the months before her death, the band reunited for sleepovers, re-living a whole lotta history.

Nadine: Whenever we all met up recently with Sarah, she just wanted to watch [2006's documentary series *Girls Aloud: Off the Record*]. Every episode. We sat and watched them all in our PJs.

14

The saga of Rachel Stevens' 'Some Girls'

How did a glam rock-inspired song alluding to blow jobs and dangerous power dynamics in the music industry recorded by an ex-member of S Club 7 become a charity single? And why did it (allegedly) cause a former Spice Girl to lock herself in a car by way of protest? If these are questions you've ever asked yourself, then I don't believe you, but please read on regardless.

The ludicrous 'Some Girls' is one of the more storied singles of the '00s. It also represents the way songs would ping-pong around labels before settling on a home. Having plied her trade as one-seventh of acting/singing/smiling triple threats S Club 7, Rachel Stevens was in a strange position as a solo artiste by the start of 2004. While her debut single 'Sweet Dreams My LA Ex', an intoxicating mix of tabloid-ready drama (albeit someone else's – it was co-written by Cathy Dennis for Britney Spears as a response to Justin Timberlake's

'Cry Me a River') and Swedish experimentalists Bloodshy & Avant's skeletal production, had crashed into the charts at number two in September 2003, the David Bowie-sampling follow-up 'Funky Dory' stalled at a disastrous twenty-six. In an era where you were only as good as your last single, Stevens was seemingly headed towards the dumper. She did, however, still have S Club 7 overlord Simon Fuller in her corner, a man who could sniff out a hit from 100 miles away.

Thankfully for Rachel, in a small studio in London, Richard X and his rebellious songwriting cohort Hannah Robinson had started work on something completely bonkers that would be strangely perfect for her.

'The idea was the casting couch'

Richard X: 'Some Girls' was about making a pop record with my sounds and my ideas and my slightly odd sense of humour. I like that multi-layered thing; I like records about records. That's kind of what 'Some Girls' is. It was the first time I met Hannah and it was a fortuitous meeting.

Hannah Robinson: We hit it off immediately. He liked the melodies I was singing and we were always talking about topics that could work for lyrics.

Richard X: I think it was done with Girls Aloud in mind.

Hannah Robinson: It definitely wasn't 'This is for Rachel.'

Richard X: It had this glam rhythm and there was a lot of German electroclash influences, Goldfrapp was doing that stuff, too. I made the demo of 'Some Girls' pretty much as you hear it but with Hannah singing it. It's quite a dark story.

Hannah Robinson: I don't even know how we got on to what we were talking about. It's one of those things where it could have been more ordinary but we took it somewhere else. When you think about Epstein and Weinstein, the song is probably ahead of the curve in terms of its subject matter.

Richard X: The idea was the casting couch. Hannah was on board with that and she brought a lot of ideas to the table, so we had her lyrics and my lyrics. I would never have done a singalong melody like it does in the chorus, that was Hannah's idea, but it was perfect because it just sounds quite insane.

'I didn't have any other thoughts than, "Geri is going to ruin my song"'

The mythology of 'Some Girls' is a glorious hotchpotch of gossip, mis-understandings and truths stranger than fiction. As is the way with these things, the demo – still featuring Hannah's vocal – had managed to work its way out of Richard's studio and on to the stereos of various A&Rs and managers – including Geri Halliwell's – keen to dabble in a more experimental pop world post-'Freak Like Me' and Girls Aloud. Even after the creators of 'Some Girls' had settled on the perfect vehicle for their song, there were still fights to be had, revenge songs to be written and a few rumours regarding Geri to settle.

Hannah Robinson: 'Some Girls' ended up being a song that people liked and wanted.

Richard X: Actually [underrated Norwegian pop star] Annie wanted to do 'Some Girls', but it had already gone. It wasn't important to me that Rachel Stevens had done the music she'd done in S Club; it was just important that she'd been in a band. It fitted so well with what we were doing.

Hannah Robinson: At that time, I was working on Geri's album with [songwriter and producer] Ian Masterson. She came in and I had no idea she'd had the track sent to her – as far as I knew, Rachel was cutting it – and the first thing she said was, 'I'm so excited about recording this song, I've got a new middle eight.'

Simon Jones: I feel certain that I heard her version. I definitely know it was the plan to release it. And I remember the conversations of, like, 'We don't have that song any more.' It was awful.

Richard X: I've never met Geri Halliwell, but I just thought [her version] was going to be rubbish. You stand and fall by your records and I was saying things about left-field pop, so you can't do something rubbish at that stage. You can't have something so out of your control. My publisher at Warner Chappell had played it to whoever and it was like, 'Geri is doing this.' *Is* doing this. They already had a director for the video. I think it was David LaChapelle. It was like, 'Geri's got some good ideas for it,' and then, 'Has anyone asked Richard about this?' The answer was no.

Hannah Robinson: Then she said she wanted to change part of the song and I rather naïvely said, 'Oh, that song's gone.' It didn't go down very well. –

Richard X: It was dangerous ground for Hannah.

Hannah Robinson: A phone call was made while I was standing there. She called her manager and said she was unhappy and then the next minute my manager was being called. I remember the quote from her manager to mine was, 'Can you let Hannah know she'll never work in this town again.' I then have this relayed to me later and I am absolutely beside myself, I'm in tears. Geri is an icon. I was lucky to be working with her and I'd already upset her by saying she couldn't have the song she wanted. It was snowballing. I thought my career was in the bin. It wasn't Geri who relayed that information, it was her management, which is completely different.

Richard X: I did not give any thought to the commercial value of Geri doing it. I didn't give any consideration to what Hannah thought either. I didn't have any other thoughts than, 'Geri is going to ruin my song.' I didn't want Geri hamming it up.

Hannah Robinson: Time passes and Ian and I are invited to LA by Geri to continue writing. There was this huge element of pressure because they wanted 'Some Girls', but it had already happened. Songs don't happen like that every day.

Richard X: I think because they'd presumed the whole campaign was a cert, they had the song, they'd just forgotten to ask me. But with Rachel it felt perfect. We fit in this world; this is '00s world, this is not patronising pop, and she'd be great for it. Also, the song projects so well onto her. It made so much more sense. Later I was told Geri had locked herself in her car in protest. I would have loved to have seen it, obviously.

Hannah Robinson: In LA there was a situation where Geri was in the car. That did happen. There's been a few stories that have merged, so I just want to set the record straight. It had been a really strange morning that day anyway because I'd been sick in her car. She had to pull over while she was on her phone. We arrived at the studio and there was something in the press that day that had upset her. So she said, 'I'm going to sit in the car for a bit.' This is at 11 a.m. Ian and I were in this amazing studio and there were security cameras everywhere so we could see Geri hop into this SUV. We sat there having a coffee, still watching the CCTV to see when she was coming back. I think the car door opened at 6 p.m. It transpires she'd fallen asleep. So somewhere along the line that's morphed into it being about the 'Some Girls' thing, but that's not the case.

Richard X: She did write a reaction song.

Hannah Robinson: Didn't it say, 'excuse me Mr X' or something? I feel like I did get to hear that but I don't know how.

Richard X: It was a glam song, so it was a bit like 'Some Girls', but it was like, 'Excuse me Mr X / Let me kiss your lips / Unwind my knickers from this twist'. I think I probably turned it off at that point.

'I was trying to evoke this glam era and the idea of post-industrial wastelands'

Rather than focus on the more everyday lyrical motifs of the era, the pair quickly started transposing their passion for black humour into pop songs that didn't rely on comforting relatability. Songs were formed via studio-based

gossip sessions or from tabloid whispers or, in the case of Annie's excellent
'Me Plus One', from a Geri saga that was still unravelling. Remixes, mean-
while, were inspired by the post-industrial 1970s and necessitated Richard
asking Rachel Stevens questions about the Winter of Discontent.

Hannah Robinson: We would take inspiration from all sorts
of silly stuff. For instance, a producer friend of mine once invited
me to a Cathy Dennis party. I idolised Cathy. So I went to
Richard's studio and I said, 'You'll never guess what, I'm going
to Cathy's party.' Then the next day my friend calls and says,
'Oh, Han, you can't come, she's only celebrating having a new
kitchen so it's just a few of us.' The next day I went back in
with Richard and said I was really disappointed, so we wrote
a song called Cathy's Party. The chorus goes something like,
'Everybody's going to Cathy's party, everybody's going but me'.
The songs that have less meaning always felt a bit more meh.
'Me Plus One' by Annie, for example, was loosely based around
Geri [and the 'Some Girls' saga]. It was very jokey and it wasn't
meant to be unpleasant at all.

Richard X: When we did the recording of 'Some Girls', I
took [Rachel] to one side and said, 'Look, I've got this idea for
the remix.' It was just a way of getting some off-the-cuff stuff
and if you've ever met Rachel she's really guarded. So I sat her
down for this Q&A and she went along with it. I was trying to
evoke this glam era and the idea of the 1970s, the post-industrial
wastelands of the north. She was very confused. The idea behind
it was ZTT. They used to have these very long B-sides where
they'd cut up interviews with Frankie [Goes to Hollywood] or
Paul Morley. So I wanted to do that. No one questioned it. It

was only when the Sports Relief thing came along that my plans for it all fell apart. That was quite scary. 'Richard, I've got really exciting news for you . . .' It always starts like that.

'No one ever asked what it was about – they just heard it as a fun thing'

Launched in 2002 as part of the biennial Friday-night charity event Comic Relief, the more energetic Sport Relief came with an accompanying fundraising single. In 2002, this meant Elton John re-working 'Your Song' as a duet with opera singer Alessandro Safina. In later years, acts like McFly, JLS and Little Mix would all release songs tangentially linked to either the charity's get-up-and-go spirit or the event's prevailing mood of offering hope and emotional support to those in need. But in July 2004, for reasons unknown, a song about the dark machinations of the music industry set to a glam rock beat was selected. It peaked at number two.

Hannah Robinson: Half the time you'd deliver a song like that and [the label] would not hear what you were writing about. 'Some Girls' has a really dark subject with a really pop melody. I didn't worry until I heard it was going to be a charity record. That did feel a little bit inappropriate.

Richard X: Maybe the song was just there on the desk and it was like, 'Oh, this will do.' You know that feeling when you've done something a bit naughty at school and you're just laughing hysterically because the naughtiness is continuing.

Hannah Robinson: No one ever asked what it was about. Rachel didn't ask either. The lyrics were there in front of her. The oral sex stuff is implied in regards to the Champagne making it taste so much better, but that could also be about making something more palatable.

Richard X: I think a journalist brought up [the fact the song alludes to blow jobs] with Rachel in an interview and she was horrified. I didn't tell her because she didn't ask. If she'd asked what she was singing about, I would have said about the idea of the casting couch being prevalent in the industry. In the era we're in now, we wouldn't have done that. But at the time it was the up-and-down world of showbiz.

'It's telling a story – it just happens to be a rude one'

While 'Some Girls' took on a life of its own, unwittingly causing problems everywhere it went, another Richard X and Hannah Robinson curio was still waiting for a home. Once again, what had started out as a playful, black-humoured lyric meant to poke and prod at a standard lyrical trope – this time the rubbish boyfriend – had quickly gone down a very different road.

Richard X: One person who had a narrow escape was Paloma Faith, because she was also signed to [Simon Fuller's management company] 19 at that time. She was going to do some electropop with me. But Frankie [Bridge, neé Sandford] cut a couple of songs we'd already done. One was called 'Birthday', which is quite unsavoury. Ask Hannah about that one. Ask her why we would do that to someone like Frankie.

Hannah Robinson: It's really important that you know we did not write this with her in mind. It was just the result of something I said. Basically, Richard and I were talking and I

471

started waffling on about men who insist on having anal sex with women. There was some joke flying around the room like, 'only on your birthday', that kind of thing. This turned into, 'Let's do a song, it will be hilarious.' Some of the lyrics are 'You tried to turn this girl around / You tried to do me over'. When you first hear that, it could just be about a rat bag, but as the song goes on there's lyrics like, 'Something's up and my earth isn't moving'. We had so much fun coming up with all these little double entendres. In the second verse it goes, 'You said it was a compliment underneath the covers / You said that we could make a change and put it all behind us'. Basically someone heard it and wanted Frankie to do it. All of a sudden it felt really wrong. It's telling a story – it just happens to be a rude one. I'm relieved nothing happened with it. I mean she did record it, but it was never released.

15

The X Factor's journey to cultural domination

By the mid-'00s, pop music felt intrinsically linked with Saturday-night television. After two seasons as the pantomime villain on *Pop Idol*, Simon Cowell, resplendent in ludicrously high-waisted stone-washed denim, was itching for something new. In fact, what he wanted most was more control, with the consensus being that 2003's second, and final, season of *Pop Idol* had somehow settled on the 'wrong' winner in Michelle McManus. In conjunction with Sony Music, Cowell successfully pitched a new talent show, *The X Factor*, to ITV in 2004. Scrapping *Pop Idol*'s age limit of twenty-six, *The X Factor* would further differentiate itself from Simon Fuller's creation by splitting its contestants into three categories: 16–24s, Over-25s and Groups. The show's winner would then be awarded a million-pound contract with Cowell's new label, Syco.

By 2007's fourth series, the 16–24s category had been split into Boys and Girls as – surprise surprise – the younger contestants started to dominate. Keeping the added competitive frisson between judges, as initiated years before in *Popstars: The Rivals*, each of *The X Factor*'s industry overlords – Simon, Louis Walsh and Sharon Osbourne, initially, with more added and subtracted throughout the show's fifteen series – were handed a specific category to 'mentor'.

The shiniest of shiny floor Saturday entertainment shows, *The X Factor* launched on 4 September 2004 with 5.25 million viewers. By the time Steve Brookstein was announced as the inaugural winner on 11 December, the show had peaked at over 9 million. While everything was going swimmingly from a TV point of view – and the 6 million votes logged for Brookstein alone in the final must have been music to ITV's ears – 35-year-old Brookstein's win felt like a disappointment. His brand of sensibly suited Pizza Express jazz undermined the brazen confidence of the show's title. While Brookstein's look and sound may have slotted into the post-Bublé boom in nice men doing nice covers of nice songs, Brookstein himself seemed unwilling to play nice. He would be the last winner from the more worldly wise 'Overs' category for nine years.

'We didn't have a band name on the day so we put "the Smiths" down on our application'

Each series of The X Factor *was split into four distinct phases: auditions (thousands of people, lots of 'joke' contestants); bootcamp (fewer people, more tears); judges' houses (swimming pools, yet more tears); and, finally, the live shows (long-winded 'controversies', proper guest pop stars). As the decade wore on,* The X Factor *continued to hunt for stars who could not only prove the show worked in the UK but also on a global stage. Along the way, it found contestants that could easily slot into what was successful at that time (Shayne Ward's mix of Robbie Williams' cheeky sex appeal and Justin Timberlake's sleek sophistication), while also conjuring up ones that felt like old-school throwbacks to an era only half a decade old (step forward, Jedward and the Steps-esque Same Difference). It was at the audition stage, however, that acts got an early taste of what they were letting themselves in for.*

Paul Flynn: Cowell was like Malcom McLaren or Tony Wilson suddenly had a pop iteration. There was something so 'I don't give a fuck' about him. His idea was so simple – let's just put people on television each week doing karaoke and tart it up. He was really canny.

Steve Brookstein, winner, series one: I was on my way to a gig and I saw [*The X Factor*] advertised on TV. I took a note of the number, called it and they said they'd send me a form. The funny thing was I completely forgot about it. Three days before my audition, I found the letter among my other unopened letters that always accompanied me and I was like, 'What's this? It's not brown, it's not threatening.' I opened it and it was ITV talking about an audition date. I was like, 'Oh, when is it? Ah, it's three days away, that's lucky I opened it.' Or not. Depends how you look at it now.

Shayne Ward, winner, series two: I actually missed my first audition. You get a letter sent but I had gone on holiday. So they suggested I go to the open day. You get a lot of scouts now who see you online, but back in my day – during the war! – you just turned up and queued.

Paul Flynn: Shayne reminded me of every working-class lad that went to my comprehensive school. He is much more archetypal Manchester than Liam Gallagher. He worked in a shoe shop in the Arndale. He was that lad that you'd go in and you'd buy your shoes there because he served you. Absolute heartthrob.

Sean Smith, Same Difference, third place, series four: At the time, I was doing a show called *Dancing Queen*, which was touring the UK. I was loving it, but I had been doing that level of show for years and I wanted my big break. The year before we did *X Factor* was Leona [Lewis] and Ray [Quinn], and Leona went on to have a huge multi-platinum album all over the world, so I think we felt like it was at a peak time to give it a try.

Joe McElderry, winner, series six: I was a massive fan of the show. To transition to being part of it and winning it was a surreal process. I auditioned first in 2007 when I was fifteen. It was the first year they lowered the age categories. I got to bootcamp and on the second day I absolutely freaked out. I didn't feel ready for it. I was just overwhelmed. I don't think they'd ever had anyone go, 'Actually, I'm not doing this' before. Everyone said I was an idiot and that I'd made the biggest mistake ever. But I trusted my decision.

Steve: I was at an age where I had been involved in music for a long time. I'd been writing, producing and working with artists, but I'd also had a lot of things that had gone wrong. So I had very low expectations that things would work out; that's how I am. I've always been a pessimist. I suppose that's why things go wrong, because I think they're going to go wrong. Funnily enough I had a Rolodex back in the day and it had all the record labels and A&R men in it. And Simon Cowell was in there. I remember I called his office a couple of times and he never answered.

Sean: I wanted to go for it [as a solo act] and my sister Sarah came along for the day to support me. We kept having to do all the cheering for camera and it was getting a bit monotonous. Sarah was thinking about leaving and all of a sudden a guy appeared with a clipboard and a camera and focused on Sarah. She was all bright and bubbly in the queue so they were like, 'What are you singing today?' She said she was just here for me and brought me in like, 'Hi.' All of a sudden they brought us to the front of the queue. She filled out an application and they asked us to sing together. We did probably the worst rendition of Bryan Adams and Mel C's 'When You're Gone' I've ever heard. We looked at each other like, 'That's game over,' and they said, 'You're through!'

Oritsé Williams, JLS, runners-up, series five: We had been a band for a year before, doing everything we could. People think that JLS was put together on *The X Factor* and that's definitely not the case. Anyone that would hear us sing, we would sing to. It got to the stage where it felt like no one thought a band of Black men had an opportunity in a commercial market coming from the UK. But we believed. After exhausting all these opportunities for a year, I remember we got in Marvin's car and we all just said the same thing, which was '*X Factor*'.

Marvin Humes, JLS: My experience in [2004 mixed-gender also-rans] VS was a large part of the beginning of JLS because we were all so naïve and wet behind the ears, but I'd had a bit of experience. I'd had two top-twenty singles, I'd toured with Blue and had a little taste of the pop industry. So to carry that into JLS and no one knowing that much about VS was a positive thing.

Sean: We didn't have a band name on the day so we put 'the Smiths' down on our application. The producers were like, 'I'm really sorry but you need to change the name.' That's when Sarah came up with Same Genes, which I thought was a bit weird. We loved *Friends* at the time and I remember a joke on there where Ross says, 'Same difference.' So I suggested that and Sarah went, 'Yeah, because we're the same but different, that works.' Of course they filmed us at that moment and it made us look really ridiculous.

Steve: [Sharon and Louis] knew I was a good singer and I was going to go through. They'd filmed me prior to my audition chatting and singing for [host] Kate Thornton. Then I went in and at the time the impression was that Louis and Sharon weren't meant to like me and it was Simon who could say, 'No, I think he's got something.' Then Simon gets me in his group and he takes me and shapes me and turns me from this rough-and-ready not-very-good vocalist into this superstar and Simon wins again. And it went to plan. That's the bit that annoys you – from day one it was all a farce. I knew a lot about the industry and how it worked in terms of the deals people do, but I never knew it was that bad.

Sean: There were people that were clearly not good singers but they were telling them, 'You're fantastic, you're going to go through, they'll love you.' They were setting them up for a fall and it was obvious they weren't there mentally sometimes. With us it was more, 'Come on, guys, you need to ramp it up, you're really excited, hug for the camera!' Of course when you step out there and you look that crazed, the first reaction from the judges is going to be, 'Woah.' One of the big lines Simon said was, 'You are possibly two of the most annoying people I have ever met.'

'There were little things I noticed them doing to get reactions'

Having survived the audition process, the wannabes were then put through their paces via seemingly endless rounds of singing in a line on stage in an empty theatre. For the producers, bootcamp was an early indication of who the real stars of the show were going to be. For the contestants who didn't make it, however, it was a nice excuse to get drunk and perhaps snog someone you'll likely never see again.

Marvin: The difference with us was that we were so ready for this process. This is the problem with a lot of artists that have been on the show that have had problems since: we were so strong as a band. They tried to throw so much at us – they made a band [Priority] in bootcamp to rival us at Judges' Houses because they didn't want us to be so confident we'd make it through. Simon and the team would say the other band were better than us. They would always put us down even when we knew we smashed it.

JB Gill, JLS: Because we'd been together for almost two years by that point, them trying to throw a curveball saying, 'Here's a list of songs to prepare overnight' didn't worry us – we already knew who would sing what and how to break down the parts.

Yvie Burnett, *The X Factor* vocal coach: JLS knew each other. They had this natural brother mentality so they sang well together and they had similar styles so that worked from the start.

Sean: The other contestants at bootcamp were all a lot cooler than us. That gave us a weird niche. But even then people were saying to us, 'Guys, it was really cheesy but it was good entertainment.' They weren't seeing us as any threat. Even in bootcamp when they're filming you can feel that they're focusing quite a lot on you. But I also remember bootcamp being very sexual among everyone else. Everyone was going into each other's bedroom and me and Sarah were like, 'Right, we're here to focus and win this thing.'

Steve: There are a lot more people in bootcamp than you realise. You get to meet a lot of people and so many of them are really nice. There was a bonding thing going on. The problem was that they don't feed you, they give you some water and people start to get a bit agitated, like, 'Why are we waiting around for so long?' It gets some people's emotions up and so then they start filming people getting upset. There were little things I noticed them doing to get reactions.

Joe: I'd made a pact with myself like, 'If you go back in this show you absolutely cannot leave, no matter how traumatic.' Bootcamp was the most exhausting week of my life in terms of learning new songs and the challenges they set us. All I remember is being sat in the bar area and just continuous amounts of Domino's pizzas being delivered.

Sean: Because of my solo application, we were put into the Boys category rather than the Groups. Our room in bootcamp was in the boys' corner so we had all the girls coming into the boys' room. Everyone's walking around with their shirts off, hoping the cameras would come around. Me and Sarah just wanted to sleep because we had the biggest day of our lives coming up. Once they'd done their filming and been kicked out, they didn't care any more. In the end, we just went out and embraced it.

'I'm not being funny, but my sister's got a better house than Simon does'

Once the contestants had been whittled down to the final fifteen (later twenty-one), they'd be paired up with their (apparently unsuspecting) judges and whisked off to sun-soaked places like Barbados, Dubai or, in Louis' case, grey Dublin. Or, in season one, glamorous, er, London. There they'd fight for their place in the final three (later four) and their chance to sing live in front of millions of people every week.

Louis Walsh: I always got the worst category. We never knew what category we were going to get until we opened those fucking doors. Simon would wind me up sometimes and I would be thinking I was getting a really good category and the doors would open and I'd think, 'Oh . . .' One time I was like, 'I don't want this category.' I was just being honest. Who wants the Overs? Simon was making those decisions but denying he was. He was in control of the whole show.

Shayne: [Louis' Judges' Houses round] was in Dublin and there were people going to Miami or LA. We all went to this empty, cold apartment in Dublin. It wasn't Louis' house.

Steve: We stayed local. Simon had a place in Holland Park. Funnily enough it wasn't very far from where I used to work in a recording studio. It was an area I knew really well. I wasn't impressed. I'm not being funny, but my sister's got a better house than he does. It was in an expensive area, it was fancy, but many years ago I was an estate agent in Wimbledon so I've seen big houses. It had no personality. It looked like a show home.

Sean: Our bootcamp was in a stunning house in Marbella. The grass was all perfectly cut. I remember going to the loo and it had fancy black toilet paper. It was an incredible experience. We were led to believe it was Simon's house, but I wasn't convinced.

Joe: We flew to Marrakesh. We had this beautiful house on the outskirts of the city. This huge villa. But we were there for two days. We flew in, did some filming with *Xtra Factor* on the first night. Then we filmed the performances the next day, found out if we were through and then came back on the last flight out that evening.

Sean: I had to honour my contract for *Dancing Queen*, so I was in Scotland doing the show and then I was going to Judges'

Houses. We had to fly over [to Marbella] and I was so ill and sweaty. When you watch back our performance I'm white as a sheet and I've got a cold sore as well because I was so rundown.

Joe: You didn't sign [a contract] when you won the show; you signed it before you won the show. Everybody signs the contract at the Judges' Houses stage. Then within [the contract] are stages of where you get to in the competition. Would I sign that contract again now? No. I understand because it's a business, but I do think things have changed a lot since then. The welfare of contestants on TV shows is a much bigger focus now. But I do think there should have been an independent person who does not financially benefit from inside that dissects those contracts. I wouldn't have signed that and, if I'd had an independent person, they wouldn't have advised me to. Or they would have said, 'Let's make these changes and then sign it.'

Steve: We didn't have an NDA. They have NDAs now because of me. If it wasn't for me they wouldn't have thought about them. They learned a lesson there. I can say what the fuck I like.

'If people broke some of the house rules you'd usually see them go out that week'

Finally, after months of auditions, protracted 'you're in my final three!' announcements dished out in featureless rented homes and saying the word 'journey' ad infinitum, the show's final nine (later twelve) were ready to face the general public via the Live Shows. They were also whisked away from their lives and jobs and housed in a mansion barely able to contain them let alone the paparazzi swarming outside. Once again, the shadow of Big Brother *loomed, with contestants' activities filtered out via both spin-off show* The Xtra Factor *and the tabloids. The increased attention from the latter – helped by the arrival of new judges, Dannii Minogue in 2007 and Cheryl Cole in 2008 – also led to a reliance on so-called sob stories, AKA anything vaguely traumatic in someone's life that could be used to create a narrative arc within the show. Not only that, but contestants had to roll with the punches when it came to being in the shadows of the previous winner. In 2006, Leona Lewis quickly became the ultimate* X Factor *winner of the '00s, riding a narrative arc of Lewisham receptionist turned proper Global Superstar. Fortunes change, however, and, following Leon Jackson's surprising win, the 2008 contestants were told that rather than the top three being offered a contract with Syco, only the winner would be signed.*

Joe: That weekend we moved into the house was the weekend the Judges' Houses episode aired, so we had to sneak around London with bags over our heads trying to get to meetings. In our year the interest in terms of the media had gone stratospheric. It dominated the front pages of every paper like it never had before. It was intense.

Shayne: [The live shows] were just non-stop. A whirlwind. It was interviews, rehearsals, more contracts – just signing everything – just a tidal wave.

Louis Walsh: I really worked hard on [Shayne]. He had everything that Steve didn't have – he was young, he looked good, he could sing, he could get those high notes. He was distinctive.

Yvie Burnett: I had something to prove [with Shayne]. I had done vocal coaching a bit, but I was basically an opera singer who had changed career. My husband, Gordon, used to work with Louis on some of his bands. They were out for lunch and [Louis] said he needed a new vocal coach for *The X Factor*. Gordon said, 'Oh, my wife's a vocal coach.' Louis said, 'Let me see her,' because my husband was quite plump then and Louis just assumed I'd be this little fat woman. It's so Louis, isn't it? Then he saw a picture and said, 'Oh, she'd be good on telly!' From then, Louis and I really hit it off. I had this bit between my teeth and I really wanted to do it for Louis.

Marvin: The year before our show, Leon Jackson, Rhydian and Same Difference were the top three acts. Let's face it, it didn't work out for them in the long run unfortunately, so Simon sat us all down and said in series five he was only going to sign the winner.

Sean: I didn't realise until afterwards, but the producers all lived in the house with us and then they go, 'Right, come on, guys, we're all going to play spin the bottle tonight.' And you're going, 'What?' 'Oh, you guys don't have to play, but let's get some people together so we have some stories to feed to the papers.'

Oritsé: You've got researchers in the house with you and you think they're your chaperones but really they're also spies. If people broke some of the rules, you'd usually see them go out that week. It was crazy. A lot of stories were coming out and people wouldn't know why or how, so they were panicking.

Steve: We were in apartments. I shared with Verity [Keays]. Rowetta [Satchell] didn't want to share with me and I didn't want to share with Rowetta. She was playing the game so much.

So we didn't get on. When people have baggage, they get triggered by certain people and certain types. She was triggered by me. At the time, I was a relatively confident man in my midthirties. I was in a good place.

Joe: The way it worked was if you had a mortgage, or if you had a professional job, they covered all of your expenses and bills for the whole time you were on the show. We used to get a wage of about £60 a week for food and drink. But there was catering everywhere so we didn't even need it, to be honest.

Marvin: What we believed in massively was manifesting our career. Every single night before we did the show we sat down with our list of everything we wanted to achieve – a number-one record, a number-one album, a video shoot in LA. Literally it was 300 things on this list. Out of those 300 entries we probably ticked off 180, which for us was incredible. Aston's mum worked in the sexual health arena and so we'd always discussed being role models for safe sex. We wanted to be ambassadors for guys who looked like us but were younger than us. [So having our own brand of condoms, released in 2010] was a conversation we'd had with Aston's mum from before we did *The X Factor*.

Louis Walsh: I was scared when I first started because I was walking out on a Saturday night with Simon Cowell and Sharon Osbourne. Everyone knows them two, they're household names, so it was, 'Who is that little twat from Ireland in the middle? Who is he? What is he doing there? Why is he there?'

Yvie Burnett: Because Louis can be funny and say silly things I don't think people realise that man's talent. Louis can choose songs for absolutely anyone and he can choose them brilliantly.

Louis Walsh: I do know music and I do pick songs and I'm very good at what I do. That's why Simon had me there because he knew I liked songs and was involved in picking songs.

Yvie Burnett: He used to forget people's names [on the live shows] and he would go, 'Who is that?' during the ad break. I'd have to write their names down and what they were singing and pass it to him.

Marvin: I believe we hit peak *X Factor* because of Leona's success in series three. It just got bigger and bigger because we had Cheryl on the panel, who was probably the biggest celebrity in the UK at that time. It was appointment viewing on a Saturday night. The numbers were incredible.

Louis Walsh: [Leona] was great. She didn't pop for three or four weeks into the show and then she popped. Simon was behind her and we needed an international superstar and later she had the Ryan Tedder song 'Bleeding Love'. That was an international hit.

Lucie Cave: Obviously amazingly talented but quite boring to write about. [It was about] the more personality they had, the more hiccups, the more they went out and got pissed or snogged someone they shouldn't.

Louis Walsh: It doesn't matter about personality – Whitney had no personality. It's all about the voice.

Alexis Petridis: I always remember the series after [Leona] won, people would audition and Simon Cowell would go '. . . but you were doing a Leona Lewis song.' As if it didn't really matter what you were doing to the oeuvre of Frank Sinatra or if you honked your way through 'I Say a Little Prayer' – that was fine. Just don't touch the unimpeachable oeuvre of Leona Lewis, who has now been big for all of six months.

Dean Piper: After [Leona], it did become about who was wearing what, who was bitching. Every week we weren't giving our story to the editor, we were being told, 'This week Cheryl's the splash, so can you find the story.' It worked that way around. That's a really shitty way to do it. That's one of the reasons I stopped doing my *Sunday Mirror* column because I couldn't write about Cheryl Cole every fucking week.

Joe: [Our house] was near Golders Green, on the corner of Hampstead Heath. It was a footballer's house that they were renting out. I went to the Starbucks nearby on the Friday and nobody batted an eyelid. By the Sunday evening, once the Judges' Houses episode had aired, I walked out of the house and the paparazzi were jumping out of cars. When someone says you're famous overnight, it was the exact description of what happened. I thought I was going to be attacked – I'd never experienced paparazzi before. Nobody even said, 'By the way this might happen.'

Steve: [Fame] was funny. It was surreal. I never got excited about it. I'd joke about it. People would ring me up and be like, 'Steve, you're on this bloody show.' The biggest thing I'll take away from it was the *Sliding Doors* moment because I'd just supported Dionne Warwick in Croydon and off the back of that I'd been asked to support Lionel Richie at Wembley. I gave all that up to go on *The X Factor* and now I'm thinking, 'Ah, man, that was a silly move.' A lot of bad things were said about me but I've never been fame-hungry. Never. I wanted success but it wasn't about the fame. It was about singing great songs and doing them well. You want an audience.

Sean: We were different to what everyone else was doing. Amy Winehouse was huge so everyone was trying to emulate that sound or people were trying to be Snow Patrol. It's a Saturday night and people are getting ready to go out, they have *The X Factor* on and we're doing 'Tragedy'.

Louis Walsh: You need [people like Jedward] for the show. Wagner. The chicken man [series one auditionee Robert Unwin, who worked in a chicken factory]. You need everything for a TV show. People just get bored of singers; they want to see and hear something different. *The Voice* has never had a hit artist or a hit record.

Yvie Burnett: It wasn't just about having a Leona Lewis voice. Sometimes Jedward would be what you wanted that night. You wanted the entertaining person. You had to make them as good as you possibly could. Nothing was as fun as *The X Factor* back in the day, when we were allowed to be a little maybe non-PC and laugh at people. Now you'd be like, 'Should I really be laughing?' They did that thing where the bad people would come on during the final and do a medley – it was terrible, but it was so good. Some of them are probably still 'so and so from *The X Factor*' and they can do a little appearance somewhere.

Oritsé: Bands hadn't been successful before us [on *The X Factor*]. People didn't seem interested. Everyone wanted another Leona. Or a solo artist. I say this in the most humble way, but JLS really brought back the era of the pop band. Boybands were pretty much non-existent.

Shayne: I grew up listening to Backstreet Boys and NSYNC and the boyband era, so to be compared to JT [on the show] I was like, 'Yeah, sure.' I had both my ears studded many years before. I think it was cubic zirconia. JT's were likely diamonds.

Steve: Winning it wasn't the issue. As a singer you just want to get through the night. I wanted to just make sure that when I got on that stage, I didn't look like a dick. There was one night where the monitors weren't working and I missed my cue. This is live in front of millions of people! The only reason I got back into the song was because my vocal coach, Annie Skates, started mouthing the words to me. It was that pressure and then on top of that I had Louis Walsh saying I looked like a serial killer. [During an appearance on ITV's *This Morning* ahead of the final, Louis said, 'I think he's just a very average singer. He just stands there and smiles. He's like Fred West.']

Louis Walsh: He was a let-down.

Steve: [Later] I was in a room with Louis on my own and I was fighting back the urge to punch him. It was just me and him and I was going to knock him out. I don't mind saying it – I had history of going to prison. I'd had a night in prison from getting in fights. Maybe that was the reason I didn't knock him out. To go on national TV and start saying that I look like a serial killer . . . He deserved to get knocked out, to be honest.

Louis Walsh: He was a good singer, but he was like a pub singer, cabaret singer, he wasn't going to be international. Ever.

Steve: They've got this thing of undermining hardworking people. And they've damaged our industry. Whereas before people would look at these singers doing these jobs and respect them, now everyone who is singing in a pub is a wannabe, or a failed wannabe, as opposed to people who have a great living and are going out gigging and making people happy. I used to love doing social clubs. Not everyone can spend £60 on an Adele ticket and sit there bored.

Louis Walsh: We were looking for a star.

Steve: Sharon Osbourne called me a cunt in rehearsals. She said, 'You're just a fucking cab driver, you're shit, you're a cunt, you disrespected me.' The reason I disrespected her was because she was a nasty piece of work. There was a duo called 2 To Go and they were a lovely couple. In rehearsal, Sharon's telling them [their performance] was brilliant and they're both smiling and excited and then on the live show Sharon ripped the piss out of them. Later when it came to rehearsals before the final – and she'd been slagging me off all week, every week – Sharon was trying to give me like, 'Steve, that was really good,' and I just ignored her. 'You fucking cunt.' It was really uncomfortable.

Lucie Cave: Steve Brookstein was such a moody shit.

Steve: Simon doesn't want this story to come out about Sharon Osbourne going round calling a contestant a shit. You can't do that. So I go into his dressing room and Sinitta and his ex-girlfriend, Jackie St Clair, are there. Jackie opens her coat up and she had nothing on apart from a thong and high heels. Simon Cowell is sitting there smoking. I'm a bit embarrassed. This was in his dressing room just before the live final. It was absolutely mad. Once it finished, he's sitting there and he says, 'I thought you needed to relax.' He's smiling. And Sinitta and Jackie get embarrassed. I said, 'Simon, what the fuck are you doing?' I lost my temper with him. He didn't like that. Nobody talks to Simon in that way. Our relationship was always a bit edgy afterwards.

Sean: I remember on one of the live shows we did 'Tragedy' and people were like, 'These guys are great,' and we went through. The week after we did a session with Brian [Friedman, the show's choreographer] and we only had ten minutes to learn the choreo. When the cameras came in, we were all over the shop. Then he started doing bits to the camera saying, 'I'm worried about these guys this week.' We were like, 'What just happened? Last week we had two hours for choreo, today we've had ten minutes.' They do it to freak you out and give a bit of drama. I remember going back to the house and saying to Sarah, 'I think they're trying to get us out this week.' Simon was our mentor but the thing with that was you'd barely ever speak to him. Apart from in the semi-final when he was worried we'd go out and he came to us and said, 'Right, what are we going to do with you guys?' We then went into his dressing room and opened a bottle of Cristal and had a conversation. It was so surreal but amazing.

Joe: They didn't try to put a sob story on for me but they did used to try to make me cry. One of the producers, who I really love and who was very supportive of me on and off camera, he used to try to ask me a question and I'd look behind the camera and say, 'I'm not going to cry.' He used to go, 'For God's sake, Joe, we just need a bit of emotion.' I'd say, 'I'm not crying over a singing competition.'

Oritsé: They pulled me aside by myself and started asking about my mum, who has multiple sclerosis. She went through the worst transition when we were on the show. They saw what was going on. They started asking me about my home life situation and they told me I was a young carer and they were looking at me crying. I just kept saying, 'I'm here with my group and I want it to be about us and our talent.' I didn't want my personal life talked about in that way. It was real life, it wasn't something for publicity.

Sean: This is the semi-final now and you're getting to the nitty gritty. Niki [Evans], who came fourth in the end, her big story was that her father had passed away and he left the application form for the *X Factor* in his will for her. They played on it a lot throughout the show. It was a time when stuff on social media was just starting to come in and she was hearing people saying, 'She's only there because of her dad,' which was heartbreaking. The story in the semi-finals was going to be she was going to sing 'Dance with My Father'. But because she was getting trolled she refused. They then needed a sad angle, so they went back to our original application form where you have to write down your best and worst moments in life and at the top of our list was Sarah being bullied at school. They decided to go with that angle instead, which actually really connected with the audience. For that little five-minute VT [they aired] we must have talked to them for about five hours, until they just wore us down. It was like having a therapy session. Our minds were going to really deep, truthful places. It was a one-on-one session with a producer who's going, 'Right, I'm really sorry but today we're going to talk about your bullying, I hope that's okay.' There was a lot of stuff they were coaxing out of Sarah that I didn't know had been happening, so of course we're both trying not to cry. The funny thing was that when it came to the final it was like, 'Simon has a group in the final so he looks great.' All of a sudden they just wanted vox pops of us saying, 'We're having such a great time going back to our home town of Portsmouth!'

Steve: They filmed our dinner [at Simon's house before the final] but there wasn't a moment when I was just sitting down with Simon and Sinitta, his sidekick, and Annie Skates. We didn't have that intimate dinner where we actually had a chat. Simon was off talking to people, then the dinner was laid out. But I saw them dishing it up and it was M&S. I don't mind M&S, but [it was] microwave Chinese just put in fancy bowls and made to look nice. Then it's getting cold and I can't eat because they haven't started filming yet. I'm becoming empty. This food would have been great when it was hot, but because of the situation, I can't complain about it. They start getting into the emotional side, talking to me like, 'You must really want this.' By then I had some negative press about who I was and what I was about, plus there were some other stressful things going on behind the scenes that were getting me down. I got emotional and they did break me for a moment there. It was pretty sad.

Sean: We were getting hammered by Louis Walsh but it would make people vote for us. Then the next year he falls in love with Jedward and signs them – the hypocrisy of that man.

Louis Walsh: I didn't like [Same Difference]; they were too cheesy. It's Butlin's. We're not looking for Butlin's; we're looking for Wembley.

Sean: I remember my nan would always go up to him and say, 'Why are you so horrible to my grandkids?' And he'd say, 'Don't worry, it's getting them more votes.' He'd say to us that he wasn't that nasty. He didn't want us to think it was fake but he also didn't want us to hate him. I got the feeling he was being fed stuff to say by Simon. That whole goodie and baddie thing from a pantomime.

Louis Walsh: I knew Same Difference weren't the reason I was there. I was there to find somebody who was going to have a career.

Shayne: I'm Louis' only win. I know Simon won a couple and then obviously all the judges that came later. We formed such a good bond on the show and then that continued because I was then managed by Simon and Louis afterwards.

Steve: One of the things that was also weird on the *X Factor* final night was my manager came into my room to ask me about my family. My heritage is a bit of a mixed bag. You knew what your family was and you've seen photographs from when you're a baby, so you know what the reality is, but then you'd always have people saying, 'He ain't your dad,' and then my Jewish background meant I'd be called a tight Jew, and then my dad's South African so I'd be called a racist. All these things throughout my life meant I'd always questioned my reality. It was bizarre that my manager would come in and say, 'The *News of the World* are running a story that you're adopted.' I was like, 'Er . . . no.' But I still thought that journalists had done their research and knew what they were doing. They were saying, 'Your real parents are from Birmingham and they're drug dealers.' This is before I'm about to go on stage. I've got my manager telling me I'm adopted and my parents are from fucking Birmingham. *News of the World* are going to run this story. Before my mum and dad turn up for the live final, I call my mum and say, 'This is going to sound really weird, and please be honest with me, but am I adopted?' And she went, 'Of course you're not.' Even twenty years on, it still fucks me up.

Louis Walsh: I wanted to beat Simon and beat Sharon no matter what I did. And, later, I especially wanted to beat Cheryl. That competitiveness is 100 per cent real. But Simon was always helping Cheryl.

Steve: Looking back, I don't think I was meant to win it, ultimately. This was all about [the Louis Walsh-mentored runners-up] G4. You've got Coca-Cola and Pepsi. McDonald's and then Burger King. You've got Greggs, you've got Pret a Manger. Well, you had Il Divo, a male opera group doing pop songs, and then you had G4 doing the same old bollocks. People love it, let them love it, I don't care. There's a certain market for that. But the fact was they had been the bottom two; I was never in the bottom two.

'I had to speak to Beyoncé because Alexandra couldn't'

While Steve Brookstein and Shayne Ward had to convince the public of their respective talent all alone, from series three onwards, the top-three finalists would be supported by some of pop's biggest superstars (and West-life) in order to encourage those all-important votes. As the show's viewing figures increased and the amount of music TV shows shrunk (both Top of the Pops *and* CD:UK *had finished in 2006), artists looking to promote their latest single were drawn to* The X Factor's *live results shows. Knowing the viewing figures would peak for the final, the producers were able to nab some actual proper legends looking to impart some of their wisdom to the contestants – therefore seeming more down to earth, a new character trait for pop superstars the show itself had helped usher in – while also flogging their latest single. It reached its apex in 2008 when Alexandra Burke snotted on Beyoncé's shoulder after an incredible version of 'Listen'.*

Shayne: One thing I did understand from the get-go is that it is a conveyor-belt industry. You always want to aim for longevity but you know that by the time you get to the label the next show is coming. The next year of the show you had the duets, but we didn't have those. I wish we had because George

Michael was on one year with Joe McElderry and I would have loved that.

Joe: On the Monday they'd said to Olly [Murs] and Stacey [Solomon] that they were getting Robbie Williams and Michael Bublé respectively. For me they were like, 'We're still working out a duet partner for you.' I assumed no one wanted to sing with me. But they were in full-blown negotiations to try to get George Michael. It got to the Thursday and I still didn't have a duet partner. It was like, 'Am I going to end up singing "The Climb" with Simon?' Then they rang me at midnight and said, 'George Michael has agreed to come on the show and sing with you.'

Malcolm McLean: When I look back to these years we would be spending all our time watching music channels. You didn't need to see an exclusive video on a TV show like *Top of the Pops* any more. It didn't have the power it used to have and they wouldn't be able to get the biggest stars.

Paul Flynn: I always feel like *Big Brother* took over from *Top of the Pops*. *Big Brother*, especially the Friday-night evictions, were so *Top of the Pops*. They had that energy and rush. The crowd were a cross between the audience on *Top of the Pops* and a quite shit nightclub. It felt like it had that similar energy and ultimately there was that coronation at the end of it; who is number one? It was, 'Where does the public stand this week on the issue of the day?'

Alexis Petridis: The decline of *Top of the Pops* suggested there was a breadth of places you could get information about pop music from. I think the charts were becoming increasingly irrelevant as a straightforward marker of success. *Smash Hits* as a whole idea was predicated on irreverence. You could tie its demise in with the end of Simon Amstell and Miquita Oliver [who left *Popworld* in 2006], who both seemed to be operating in that irreverent way that *Smash Hits* did towards pop stars. It became increasingly difficult to be like that towards pop stars [post-*The X Factor*] because everyone was so on message that you couldn't ask them daft questions and get a revealing answer.

Jonathan Bown: I left a few months before *Smash Hits* closed. To be there for almost three years was incredible, but I did always feel like I'd arrived at the party after all the sausage rolls had gone. It went through quite an identity crisis in its final years. It was clear the landscape was changing. Things were narrower after *The X Factor* started. What appealed to me about *Smash Hits* as a kid was you'd have an interview with A-ha next to an interview with the Cure. I think there was an element of losing that. Everyone we were interviewing was from quite a small stable.

Louis Walsh: JLS would have won but Simon pulled a fast one and got Beyoncé to sing a duet [with Alexandra Burke] in the final. It was changed.

Marvin: Initially we heard we were going to sing 'Umbrella' with Rihanna. Because we did 'Umbrella' in the semi-final and we won the public vote for the first time. We don't know what happened. We were thinking there was going to be this Rihanna versus Beyoncé moment, you know, JLS versus Alexandra. Listen, I'm a big fan of Westlife, I've got mad respect for them, so I was buzzing to sing with them. I wouldn't want Rihanna now; I wouldn't change anything.

Yvie Burnett: We went into Beyoncé's dressing room and Alex was just a mess. Literally couldn't breathe. I had to speak because she couldn't. I remember Beyoncé's people were filming us, which we found a bit ridiculous. I said to Beyoncé, 'Look, Alex wants to do this particular line [in 'Listen'], it's her favourite line,' and Beyoncé said, 'Ooh, I don't know, I love that line, why don't we do it together?' So I said, 'Right, deal.' I'm doing all the talking. Then we went out and rehearsed it and I was coaching Alex through it from the stage and Beyoncé's saying, 'Coach me on that, too.' I thought, 'Yeah, okay, Beyoncé.' She was just being funny but it was such a surreal moment, like I'm standing here coaching Beyoncé doing a duet. I think [the show] finished at the right time because you're never going to emulate that again.

Louis Walsh: Anyway, JLS were great and they've had a great career and if Beyoncé hadn't appeared with Alexandra they would have won. But it's fine.

Dean Piper: If you became a judge on that show, you had to realise you were Simon's bitch. The puppet master had hold of you. You couldn't just have one slice of the pie, you had to eat the whole damn thing. I feel like the female judges were scrutinised, played with and toyed with in the public arena far more than the men were. Cheryl, Dannii and Sharon knew they had their money coming in and it would give them a platform for other things – like would Cheryl have had a solo career as sparkling as it was if it wasn't for that? Probably not. But they really had to give up a shitload.

Louis Walsh: Simon never told us the votes. We never knew who was in the bottom two and we were always trying to find out. He knew, but he was pretending he didn't. It's his show, it's his world. We're all lucky to be breathing the air. They never told us. We were standing there like pricks on the stage waiting. That was absolutely real. Waiting and hoping we were going to get through. We were all very involved and we all wanted to beat each other.

Joe: George made the whole thing about me and not him, which not a lot of stars do. I hadn't rehearsed that famous high harmony line from 'Don't Let the Sun Go Down on Me' because I assumed he would want to do it, but at the end of the first run-through he was like, 'Why are you not singing the harmony?' He said, 'It's not about me, it's about you, you need all of the moments in this song. I am coming to sing with *you*.' So we changed. He was very humble.

Shayne: Everything around you is so fast [after you win]. You essentially become part of the machine then. There was a press conference straight away on stage, then a quick hello to my family. I performed six songs at G-A-Y and then the next morning was *Top of the Pops* to record the Christmas special. It was the first time you could download a winners' single that night so I knew quickly that I was en route to number one with 'That's My Goal'.

James Masterson: *The X Factor* hit on the gimmick of making the single available as quickly as possible – sending Andi Peters to the printing plant and showing him holding up a copy of the single. [In an era of digital downloads] *The X Factor* was still a way of focusing people on buying pop music even if at the time people didn't necessarily do so. Shayne was the first *X Factor* winner to have his single released with the aim of having the number one on the Christmas chart. Steve Brookstein's single didn't come out until early the next year. Although Shayne's single was immediately available as a digital download, it still wasn't a mass-market product. It was, 'Yes, you could download it now but wait until Wednesday when the CD will be ready.'

Joe: I remember standing behind the double doors before they announced the winner and Simon turned to [Olly and I] and said, 'Guys, I have no idea what's going to happen here, but I genuinely wish you both the best of luck in the world.' Then the doors opened and I can't remember anything until the next morning being on *GM:TV*. It was like being drunk.

Steve: For the after-show party, I was only given two tickets. So all my family couldn't come. It's packed with press and all these people – nobody I knew. I don't think they liked that I only stayed for a few minutes and then went to a restaurant across the road with my family and friends.

Sean: It literally flipped the second we finished third. It was like it was over as far as the producers were concerned. I'll never forget it: we were driven around by fancy Addison Lee cars at the time and then the day after the final it all came crashing down. They said, 'Well, can you get your grandad to pick you up?' We were like, 'Okay, yeah, sure.' It was just so painful.

'Can you imagine people listening to "Killing in the Name" on Christmas Day?'

The long slog of a TV talent show can make its culmination feel like the pinnacle. But of course the hard work, as Cowell was always quick to state, actually starts once the show finishes and you're thrust into a music industry that's already gearing up for the next load of contestants. Like with Popstars *and* Hear'Say *back in 2001, it can also give a distorted reading, one in which 'winners' become 'losers' and acts given more time to breathe outside of the full-beam spotlight eventually start to come good. For some, external forces beyond their control can upend careers, be it a recession that closes Woolworths or, in the case of Joe McElderry, an online campaign keen to deal* The X Factor, *and Simon Cowell, its first real blow as the decade came to an end.*

Shayne: The problem is that if you believe when you get somewhere that you are the finished product then you're setting yourself up for the biggest fall. I am a sponge. I am not afraid to ask questions. I want to learn and soak stuff in. They were in control, so for me as a 21-year-old on a million-pound, three-album contract, I was happy to let it be that way.

Savan Kotecha: I would say back then, in general, the artist's point of view was almost irrelevant. They were pop songs that could be released by any artist and they would be the same song. It didn't matter. What I've noticed in the past decade, and that's been a big lesson for me, is that the artist's point of view is very important and you can't deny them that. Back then the artist's opinion didn't really matter to the record label that much.

Steve Anderson: There were lots of writers in lots of big studios just writing songs. There was a massive need for songs back then, especially when it came to the TV talent show. Anyone that was in those shows did ultimately need a record.

Sean: We went on the *X Factor* tour and the reason we got signed [to Syco] is because we sold loads of merchandise. More than anyone else. So they started seeing that the people who liked us really did buy into it. Literally. The other great thing was Steps' manager Tim Byrne was a creative director [on the tour] that year and he knew what to do with us. So Simon was saying to him, 'What did you do with Steps and how can we emulate that here?'

Steve: Given the demographic of who watches the show, every week I was told I was the housewives' favourite. This is what really pissed me off because that was my demographic and yet my album comes out for Father's Day. What the fuck was that about? G4's album came out for Mother's Day. I was thinking, 'But I won and their album comes out before mine?', and it's at the biggest time of the year. The best week for selling records back then was Mother's Day. They were purposefully fucking with me.

James Masterson: In mid-2006, to balance up this demand for digital songs with the demands of the high-street stores, the rule was changed so that a download could count towards the charts a week before the CD single. So in 2007 the high-street stores were consigned to history because all legally downloaded songs could now count towards the chart with or without a physical version. That's when Woolworths and the supermarkets realised the CD single era was very much over. From that point onwards, the digital download became the dominant force. It was the great democratisation of the pop charts because before then there were always gatekeepers.

Joe: They sat us down quite early on in the show [to talk about the Rage Against the Machine campaign], so we were aware of it. They were like, 'When the next set of journalists come in, they might mention this campaign, it's nothing to do with the contestants, it's about Simon and the show and I'm sure by the time the show's over it will be gone.' I've got the attention span of a gnat so I probably wasn't listening anyways. Never got asked about it, but then on *GM:TV* it was mentioned and I'd forgotten. The person interviewing me had said, 'It's tight in the midweeks so far,' and I didn't have a clue. They had to explain that the single was doing really well but we needed to get it higher because of what's happening with this campaign.

James Masterson: Joe very nearly wasn't the first victim. In 2008, Alexandra Burke released her version of 'Hallelujah' to general eyebrow raising. And it did indeed make the Christmas number one that year. But at number two was Jeff Buckley's version and it was the first time two versions of the same song had been numbers one and two that week. His version was behind it by a long way but it's interesting that it was this spontaneous outpouring of support for what is not hard to argue is the superior version of the song.

Peter Robinson: The question is: Do you want to hurt Simon Cowell or do you want to hurt Joe McElderry? I was going to say Simon Cowell probably didn't give a shit, but then it was maybe one of the first times where there was a bit of a wobble for *The X Factor*.

Louis Walsh: It was just publicity for the show. It was fine. It didn't really matter. Both of them had hits. It was like Blur versus Oasis, or Take That versus East 17, or the Spice Girls versus whoever it was [All Saints]. It didn't matter. Joe was good. He's a good singer, a good performer. Not a star, but a good performer.

Joe: Two things. One: I was too exhausted to care. And two: I was so excited by what had happened I was just like, 'I've got a song out and I've just won the biggest show on television.' Everything else was irrelevant to me. Also, there was something quite exciting about it. People were saying, 'There's never been a chart battle like this in about ten years.' It was the first time where people genuinely didn't know what was going to be Christmas number one. *The X Factor* had had it in the bag for the past five years. It was a proper battle.

Peter Robinson: There's something in this kind of idea of going against *The X Factor* and saying, 'It's a popularity contest, it's not about the music,' but then at the same time trying to get a song to number one, which is equally not about the music. It's about making a point. The question there is, what point are you trying to make? Also, you're using music that wasn't intended to be number one.

James Masterson: It was inevitable that this backlash was growing because people were getting tired of Christmas being ruined by *The X Factor* putting out their latest song and it would go to number one regardless of how good it was. You could make good use of Facebook to bring people together for a common cause. You can argue 'til the cows come home about how genuine that was because people were so invested in the idea of getting this Rage Against the Machine song to number one that people were boasting that they brought forty or fifty copies at one time. There wasn't any real barrier to do that. There were rules in place to prevent chart hyping, but it always worked on the basis that it was labels themselves doing it. Nobody had conceived that the general public would try to engineer getting a song to number one.

Joe: They hated the idea of reality television creating number-one singles. The ironic thing is both songs were owned by Sony BMG. By making this point, all you're doing is making everyone more money. It baffles me now. I'd never heard of them. Not really my genre. Can you imagine people listening to that song on Christmas Day? We helped each other sell way more records. There was no loser in the end and I was able to get to number one the week after.

Shayne: Recording the first album happened straight away. This is where the craziness comes in because that's when I found out I had vocal nodules. I came offstage after G-A-Y at 2 a.m., all the adrenaline, and I said to my then tour manager, 'Paul, I've done something to my throat.' We spoke to the label, did *Top of the Pops* and then went to Harley Street and they said I had nodules. I was terrified. When you watch the show as a viewer and someone gets a sore throat, you always get people who say they're doing it for show, but they really have. It's all the interviews, all the talking, it's non-stop work.

Yvie Burnett: Some people have just got a voice that naturally has a lot of stamina. Then there are other people who will literally lose their voice just like that. A lot of it is other things that will make you lose your voice. For example, Alexandra Burke. She would talk really loudly with her mates and so then she'd lose her voice. I had to get her to shut up and look after her actual speaking voice. Her singing voice wasn't the problem.

Shayne: I remember recording my first album on cortisone injections and it was the scariest thing. I guess it was scary for the label too – I'd just won the show and now I had problems with my throat. The first album doesn't feature any of my falsetto because I lost it.

Yvie Burnett: It's something that is a lesson for all of us within these big juggernaut shows. We had worked constantly together every day then suddenly he had to go off on his own without me. He was tired and he was travelling and he was partying a bit, I suppose – he'd just won *The X Factor*. Then he got ill and had to sing on an infection. With hindsight maybe there's a way within these shows that you keep going with them for a little while after.

Steve: ['Against All Odds'] wasn't the song I wanted to release. I appreciate that they had to release it. But there was so much damage done in terms of my perception of reality and what people had tried to do to me and say about me. The lies. It was still fresh in my mind about the Fred West thing. I found it hard to smile.

Sean: There was a mistake early doors with us. Butlin's came in for us and they were paying such good money that our

508

management team agreed to it. I think it made us too accessible, so when we did come back a year later [with 'We R One'] we were holiday camp entertainers rather than massive pop stars. Also, the year after us was so great with JLS and Alexandra Burke, and JLS didn't sign with Syco, so that gave them an extra layer of coolness. We were then doing gigs with artists on the line-up from that year's *X Factor* who had finished tenth, but because people had only just seen them on TV they were bigger stars.

Jamelia: As an artist who felt like they were slogging their guts out, there was an element of jealousy that these people got to have this huge promotion on a show and they weren't even necessarily going to have longevity. People like myself, and other artists around at the time, we practically disappeared because you can't compete with an *X Factor* winner. Doesn't matter if they're good, bad or ugly. It became dispiriting because every song I wrote was a labour of love. It wasn't about just getting the songs from people. As an artist it was dispiriting to see, but not as a person – I'm always happy to see people succeed. But it stopped me feeling confident enough to put out music because I couldn't compete with that. It got to the point where the label would say, 'We can't release around Christmas or January,' but then that little timeframe would keep expanding.

Paul Flynn: I interviewed Shayne for *The Observer* and I went to Manchester to watch the *X Factor* live show. His girlfriend turned to me and said the last time they were in this arena was to watch Justin Timberlake. I did that story with Shayne and wrote it sympathetically, so [Syco] played me his debut album and I hated it. It sounded like a Westlife album and I wrote as much. It didn't sound like the pop star he wanted to be. He wanted to be Justin Timberlake and they'd made him sound like Richard Clayderman.

Savan Kotecha: I was having success in America so when it was time for Shayne's second album [2007's *Breathless*] Simon called me and said, 'Hey, the second album's yours, whoever you want to work with.' Simon wanted to make Shayne the UK's Justin Timberlake and that's what we tried to do. Then at the end [of recording] he said, 'I'm not going to release [the album] without a reggae song.' It was like, 'Oh no!' That's why we had to write 'If That's OK with You'. I love that song but I think it might have hurt the whole campaign. It was such a Marmite song. Simon just had it in his head that if you can crack a reggae song then it's usually a global thing. I want this to be phrased positively towards Simon because we're still close and I love him, but we were so against the reggae thing that we thought that if we made 'If That's OK with You' overly cheesy Simon would understand and be like, 'Oh, okay, never mind, we won't do a reggae song.' But it was the opposite and he was like, 'This is a smash! We're going with this.'

Steve: I did an interview with *Closer* magazine [in 2005] and the female journalist said, 'You're a hit with the ladies, what about with the men?' I said, 'Well, if they like me they like me.' And she said, '. . . but do you like them?' I knew what she was implying. I'm not an idiot. I said, 'Yeah, I've questioned my sexuality.' I was actually quite upfront and said, 'A guy sucked my dick,' and she was like, 'Oh.' It was like, 'This is *X Factor*,

ITV, primetime family viewing, they don't want to know this kind of shit.' I was like, 'All I'm saying is that I tried it and it wasn't for me.' I was in a threesome with a girlfriend who was always having me with other women, and once she said, 'Do it with another guy,' and I said, 'Oh, alright then.' Anyway, there's absolute panic and my manager is having a go at me, saying we have to do an interview with *The Sun* to sort it out. I was a brand and that wasn't my branding. My branding was macho man, likes the women, pals with Simon. So I did an interview with *The Sun* and they basically presented a double-page spread with lots of quotes that weren't from me. They let me look at it [before it ran] and it was all about my shame. It was an apologetic piece about how I regret doing what I did. But I don't regret it. I was a survivor of abuse. This had nothing to do with shame. I got really angry about that and told my manager, 'I can't believe you're fucking doing this. I want this piece pulled.' It never got printed. But soon after I was told my record deal was over and the narrative was I couldn't sell records and that G4 were the real winners.

Sean: We were obviously earning good money and everyone kept asking us, 'So how's the recession affecting you?', and we were saying, 'We'd not really noticed it.' We'd never earned so much money! It was like, 'We're in a recession?' But then it affected us in the biggest way possible because when Woolworths went under they took a lot of our [album] stock with them. We went to our management saying we needed to get the stock back and sent to HMV or whatever. They said that if people wanted it they'd be able to get it. But it's not the same when you're going to be a big cardboard cut-out as you walk in the shop. Even our TV adverts were all geared towards Woolworths.

Shayne: Looking back and being a lot older now, I had a great many years with [Syco] and it was a three-album deal. I never took it for granted. Yes, it's always going to be upsetting and sad when you part ways with a label, but then I'd already come to peace with it when there was a three-year gap between albums two and three. I kind of knew. You part ways on good terms and that's the best way to be because you'll meet these people again. I walked away with the masters for my third album [2010's *Obsession*], which is a rarity.

Louis Walsh: He should have done better. I would still be working with him but Syco dropped him. He had hits in different places and he ticked every single box.

Steve: I wasn't dropped; I asked to leave. I said to them, 'I want to leave the record label, this isn't working, is it? I know what's going on, you're just going to bury my career over time.' We just needed to come to some arrangement. The reason I picked the time that I did to leave was I had to make my stand before the second season of *The X Factor* because they'd want me to come back on the show and say, 'It's so great.' I said to them that I would do that but they had to let me out of the record deal and pay me off. I said, 'You've told everyone it's a million-quid record deal, you've not even spent £300,000 and I've not even released a video.' My second single was pulled. There was no effort being put into my career. They offered me £12,500. So I told them to stick it up their arse. I didn't even ask for much – it was a million-pound deal and I asked for £50,000. Simon then went on TV to say I couldn't sell records and that they might have to let me go. Once he'd done that, I knew they were going to have to bite the bullet and not have me on the show [in 2005] and just ruin me.

Sean: When we got dropped, the management company called and said they'd decided not to take up the option and do the second single. We wanted to call Simon and thank him for the opportunity, but we couldn't even get hold of his PA. That was the saddest thing – we only wanted to say thank you. But of course that would have been awkward for him, building someone up to then drop them. The other bad thing is you're still famous, but you don't want it to come out that you've been dropped. You're waiting for it to be in the papers. That was really tough. I really wish I'd enjoyed it more. I was too serious about it all. Now I'd give a lot to have some of those experiences we had again. I'd lap them up for all it's worth.

Steve: I was going to go to the press and tell people I wanted to leave the label and I got a phone call from Max Clifford. He said, 'Steve, I'd love to see you at this event and doing this and that, but it ain't going to happen if you talk to the press. If you try to tell people what's happened, we will bury you.' They had the power. Every time I would go to the press the journalist would say, 'Don't worry, I'll get the story printed,' and Simon would have the story pulled. I did one with the *News of the World* and I showed the journalist all the evidence of what had been going on and he couldn't run the story. It was replaced with a pro-Simon Cowell story and me getting totally slammed. I had that for over a decade.

Joe: [Splitting with the label] was amicable but I was told about it via email. They were like, 'We're not taking up the second album option but if Joe wants to come in for a cup of tea to chat about it we can.' I remember reading the email and thinking, 'Well, what have we got to chat about? Are you just going to list all the reasons you're not taking up the option?' That is part of the demise of the show – they didn't look after the artists in terms of creating a career, they just stuck with whatever made the most money at the time. In a short term that is always going to work, but for longevity and a long-term brand it won't. The audience start to think, 'What's the point of me paying to vote if you're just going to drop them in six months?' Which is why the viewing figures dropped as the years went on. I love the show and I had a great time on the whole. There are parts of the industry that are wonderful and parts that are dreadful. But that's like any job you do. But do I regret any of it? Absolutely not.

Steve: I go through periods of regretting [doing the show]. But you can't regret because the one thing I have got is my wife and my children and you don't know where you'd be if you made different choices in life. Where it would have led you. I've become more in touch with my faith and I believe the reason I've gone through this is because I had lessons to learn. I'm a better person now than I was when I was younger. Life isn't meant to be easy.

Paul Flynn: What Cowell sold really beautifully was this idea of a better life. They didn't deliver on it but they fulfilled the fantasy of it and we all need to see that fantasy.

Peter Robinson: It's funny looking back on *The X Factor* now because, while it was a really big TV show, how useful was it really? There was a lot of noise and shouting for a handful of decent pop stars.

After Joe McElderry's Facebook-instigated attack left *The X Factor* bloodied and bruised at the decade's end, the show rebounded in 2010 with One Direction, who, despite finishing third in season seven, went on to become a Spice Girls-level global phenomenon for the next half a decade. In 2011, Little Mix, who became the first band to win, went on to release six multi-platinum albums across a decade-long career. From there, despite flashes of brilliance (Misha B, Ella Henderson, Fleur East), the show increasingly became less about the acts and more about changes in hosts and judges. In a music era that had switched from CDs to digital to streaming during the show's lifespan, launching a brand-new act with that all-important number-one single was becoming increasingly tricky. In 2015, winner Louisa Johnson became the first contestant signed to Syco not to release an album, a move replicated in 2017 by Rak-Su and the show's final winner, Dalton Harris, in 2018. In 2021, ITV announced they'd axed the show after seventeen years.

Annoying fade-out

By 2006, every single one of UK pop's cultural markers had disintegrated. *Top of the Pops* aired its final episode – aside from the Christmas specials, natch – on 30 July, five months after *Smash Hits* published its final issue. In March of that year, a recently Ant & Dec-less *CD:UK* aired for the final time, while a month later Simon Amstell and Miquita Oliver quit *Popworld*. The ecosystem that had housed the late-'90s and early-'00s pop boom in the UK had vanished, with the grip of the so-called media gatekeepers loosened by the rise of the www (over 50 per cent of UK households had internet access by 2005).

There were other factors, too. The success of digital downloads had shifted the chart rules, making it all seem unnecessarily complicated (things would get worse when streaming hit in 2014) and therefore less of a direct marker of a song's success. Downloads also meant that songs were starting to be released quicker, with none of the exciting six-week build-up that therefore necessitated pop stars doing the rounds of morning TV shows and magazine photoshoots. Releasing digitally also meant singles could be retroactively switched to 'buzz tracks' if things weren't taking off, with videos downgraded to a lyric video if necessary. Speaking of videos, YouTube arrived in 2005, while music TV channels like The Box started to chime more with the democratisation of culture kickstarted by reality TV. Why wait to see if your favourite song was going to be on *Top of the Pops* when you could just punch it into a keyboard or vote for it from your couch?

The success of *The X Factor* by 2006 meant that new pop stars were being found via an annual conveyor belt, with the idea of off-screen auditions or club tours etc. seeming almost perverse. On the flip side, the rise of social media, and specifically music platform MySpace, gave us a whole new breed of pop star, spearheaded by Lily Allen, who arrived that summer. The internet – which had tried to kill off the music industry altogether via illegal file-sharing sites such as Napster – was opening up a new avenue for beleaguered A&Rs. Positioned in direct opposition to the world of manufactured pop, Allen was the figurehead for its move towards the Very Real, assisted by social media's reliance on solipsism. Gone were broad-stroke generalities or high-gloss emotions and depthless platitudes, replaced by text-speak sentiments and sweary, diaristic tales of complex youth.

Suddenly fans also had a direct relationship with pop stars like Allen, with MySpace and Facebook allowing them to message and chat with their idols. Fans could also watch their faves progress in real time, becoming part of that all-important Journey, far removed from the inauthenticity of a Saturday-night TV show. *The X Factor*'s dominance meant that for a raft of new pop-adjacent artists – La Roux, Little Boots, Florence Welch –

being positioned clearly as the alternative was hugely important. This re-entrenched the idea of a more defined alt-pop strata, which then slowly became all-encompassing in the 2010s as pop the genre moved away from its meaning as 'pop as in popular'.

What *The X Factor* had also done was sanctify vocal prowess. This then cast the manufactured pop that came before it in an even worse light. Acts who harked back to that era, à la Same Difference, were viewed as frivolous relics. Even within the very inauthentic world of *The X Factor*, the idea of credibility was being fostered as this new bastion of pop. Sensible hat-botherer Matt Cardle beating One Direction in 2010 is evidence of that. His win also chimed with the rise of singer-songwriters like Adele, Sam Smith and Ed Sheeran, who, despite being teenagers and early twentysomethings, made music aimed at a much older audience. Pianos and guitars replaced synths and drum machines, and glorious escapism via a so-called 'throwaway' pop song was surpassed by a need to earnestly wallow in reality. Performative sadness had replaced choreography, and 'meaningful' lyrical content was now way more important than being emotionally moved by a top-tier melody.

In 2006, Twitter arrived. Seemingly utilised at first as a nice way to enjoy *The X Factor* in a large group (down a shot for every time Louis Walsh says, 'You're like a young [insert famous Black artist here]'), it quickly became an often negative feedback loop. It also focused on the personalities of pop stars, a part of the pop game that hadn't always been as crucial post-Spice Girls. There were now fewer places to hide as camera phones arrived and pop stars could be spotted in clubs, in supermarkets or, say, weeing up against a cash machine while on their phone. Tweets were also picked up by tabloids and celebrity magazines, with frustrated missives fired off in anger now used as official statements.

This focus on relatability had its positives. Popstars were able to reiterate that actually they were human too, which in turn led to important conversations happening around representation, race and mental health. Initially empowering self-empowerment anthems ruled the roost, as did positivity bangers aimed at undoing decades' worth of one-sided narratives. Over time, however, Twitter became imprisoning for pop stars, with their professional and personal lives entwined in the palm of their hands. If the workload for '00s pop stars was exhausting, they could at least switch off. Nowadays, it's difficult to see when anyone can take a breath.

All that reality can be overwhelming and recently, as the world has literally started to burn, a yearning for the late '90s and early '00s has started to grow. It's piping-hot nostalgia for a time of big, dumb (but not actually dumb) pop, made by disposable (but not actually disposable) pop stars that you could choose to either fully love or keep at arm's length – that seem frozen in amber; happy (but not actually always happy) and dressed in all-white everything.

At the heart of all of this nostalgia, though, for me at least, are the songs. This was, after all, the era where the single was key. While writing *Reach for the Stars* I gorged myself on a playlist of this decade's top-tier bangers, bops and ballads. Immaculately constructed for optimum pop culture dominance, the best songs from this era – 'Say You'll Be There', 'Just a Little', 'Keep on Movin'', 'Don't Stop Movin'', 'Whole Again', 'If You Come Back',

'No Good Advice', 'Fill Me In', 'Overload', 'Day and Night', 'Some Girls', 'One for Sorrow', 'Thank You', 'Colourblind', 'Pure Shores', 'Flying Without Wings', 'Scandalous', 'Caught in the Middle', the list goes on – feel laser-focused to deliver pure, unadulterated serotonin every single time.

Who doesn't need a huge gulp of that in their lives?

Acknowledgements

A huge, chart-topping, platinum-selling thank you first of all to everyone who gave up their time to speak to me for the book. This weighty tome would have been about 400 pages shorter if you hadn't, and I hope I've done your stories justice. To the pop stars, thank you for the music, which sustained me during lockdown and led to this idea bubbling up in the first place. Thank you to Pete Selby at Nine Eight Books, who asked to meet me to see if I had any book ideas and then sat slack-jawed while I ranted at him for about an hour about '90s and '00s pop. I'm sorry for all the emails! Thanks also to Melissa Bond for her eye for detail and unwavering enthusiasm and to Lizzie Dorney-Kingdom for handling the press. Big shoutout to my agent, Matthew Hamilton, and to Steve Leard for the amazing cover.

Special thanks to all the PRs who helped organise the interviews and to the videotelephony software programme Zoom for making my life easier. I also want to give an extra shout out to Peter Loraine, Simon Jones, Gemma Cutting and Jordan

Paramor for going the extra mile when it came to landing some of the interviews.

I also want to thank all the people who helped keep me sane during this whole process: Candice Carty-Williams, Hattie Collins, Harriet Gibsone, Priya Elan (extra special thanks for reading an early, 25,000-word version of the Sugababes chapter), Stephen Churchill, Kasia Churchill, exemplary advice-giver Paul Flynn, Peter Robinson (thanks for the date framework idea), David Goggin, Fiona Goggin, Laura Snapes (extra special thanks for reading an early, 25,000-word version of the Girls Aloud chapter), Alim Kheraj, Owen Myers, David Russell, Holly-Jade Johnston, Duncan Hammond, Holly Hammond, Georgia Fazan-Clarke, Luisa Gibbons, Kate Grinnell, Dave Grinnell, Michael Hann, Hanna Hanra (and for lending me Pam the dog when I needed her) and Gwilym Mumford. If I've forgotten anyone, it's because my brain is now mush.

Thanks to my family: Mum, Ian, Sonya and Lottie-Joy (can't wait to play you Girls Aloud's classic album *Tangled Up* on a loop as you get older). This book is dedicated to the memories of two amazing women: my nan, who unashamedly loved pop; and my auntie Karen, who was a complete icon in every sense of the word.

My biggest source of inspiration throughout this process, more so than 'Some Girls', 'Scandalous' or 'Just a Little', was my love, Ben Gazur, who I first bonded with over Busted. None of this would have been possible without you. It's also important you know that I have finally forgiven you for constantly getting Girls Aloud and the Sugababes mixed up, even while we were attending a gig by the latter. Thank you for always being there for me, and for being you.